Federal Tax Accounting

Frank L. Brunetti

Contributing Author
Marty D. Van Wagoner

Wolters Kluwer

Editorial Staff

Editor .... Barbara L. Post, Esq.
Production .... Jennifer Schencker, Ranjith Rajaram, Prabhu Meenakshisundaram

ISBN 978-0-8080-5456-6

2700 Lake Cook Road
Riverwoods, IL 60015
800 344 3734
CCHCPELink.com

Printed in Canada

About the Author

Frank L. Brunetti, is a full-time professor at Fairleigh Dickinson University in Madison, New Jersey, and is an attorney admitted to the New York and New Jersey State bars. He serves as of Counsel to the Lyndhurst, New Jersey law firm of Scarinci Hollenbeck.

He is the author of many books and articles on accounting methods and periods and other tax-related topics, including the AICPA Tax Accounting course for its national CEA program and Fundamentals of Federal Tax Accounting for the American Bar Association. Frank L. Brunetti frequently conducts seminars on tax accounting topics and other tax-related matters.

A graduate of Rutgers University, Duquesne University School of Law, and New York University's LL.M. in Taxation program, Frank L. Brunetti has been teaching tax accounting and related tax courses for almost 40 years and has been practicing law for over 45 years. He is also a member of a number of professional organizations, including the American Bar Association, the New Jersey Bar Association, the New York Bar Association and others and regularly participates in the taxation sections of each association. He was an observer and contributor to the Committee of Experts on International Cooperation in Taxation of United Nations for 15 years.

About the Author

About the Contributors

Jeffrey R. Pittard, Esq., is a graduate of Boston University's College of Communication, Seton Hall University School of Law, and New York University School of Law's LL.M. in Taxation program. Jeffrey is admitted to practice law in New York, New Jersey, Connecticut and Florida and currently is the Section Chief of the Tax, Trusts and Estates Department at Scarinci Hollenbeck in Lyndhurst, New Jersey, where he focuses on Tax Controversy and Estate Planning and Administration.

Marty D. Van Wagoner, CPA, received his Bachelor of Arts in Accounting, with a minor in Spanish, as well as his Master of Business Administration, at the University of Utah. He is a licensed CPA in Utah and is a member of the AICPA and the Utah Association of Certified Public Accountants (UACPA). Marty served the UACPA as Treasurer, Vice-President, President-Elect, and President, as well as on various committees and as an instructor of continuing professional education (CPE). He was on Council for the AICPA. He was also an adjunct professor at the University of Utah for several years. Marty teaches CPE courses across the country for the AICPA, Surgent McCoy and other CPE providers, with an emphasis on audit and accounting update courses. Marty is the author of Chapter 12 of this text.

Acknowledgments

Frank L. Brunetti wishes to express his thanks to the excellent assistance provided by Jeffrey R. Pittard for generously donating countless hours of research and suggestions over the past year.

Frank would like to acknowledge the contributions of his colleagues, his experience in the Fairleigh Dickinson University MST program and lecturing on various tax matters for the AICPA and other organizations, and his past and present students. Frank would like to acknowledge the contribution of Marty D. Van Wagoner, CPA.

Jeffrey Pittard would like to thank his wife, Amanda, and his daughters, Lilah and Sylvie, for their support and patience in this endeavor.

Preface

This book is a resource for the tax practitioner as well as for students of taxation in graduate MST programs or LL.M. programs. The general rules for methods of accounting can be found in subtitle eight, chapter 1, subchapter E, part 2, subpart A of the Internal Revenue Code (Code). However, the Code is only the beginning of learning tax accounting. Of course, there are the regulations, but many tax accounting rules are found in other IRS-issued guidance, such as revenue rulings and revenue procedures, and case law from numerous Tax Court cases, District Court cases, Appeals Court cases, and Supreme Court cases that supplement the tax accounting rules. Compounding the study of taxation, is the fact that the IRS-issued guidance, and the court at times, seemingly disagree with one another—and sometimes even themselves! This publication is arranged by topic and ties together many of these rules that both the practitioner and student should be familiar with.

As a result of the Tax Cuts and Jobs Act (2017), there have been substantive and procedural changes to the Code, which are reflected in the text. Chapter 1 provides the overall structure and differences between financial accounting and tax accounting.

Chapter 2 introduces the "annual accounting system," which is the basis for tax accounting. Because timing is the main issue for tax accounting, it is important to understand the annual accounting system, how it applies, and the effect of its various doctrines. Chapter 2 covers tax accounting doctrines such as claim of rights, relief for repayment of claim of rights under IRC § 1341, time value of money and tax benefit.

Chapter 3 provides the rules for an entity's tax year, including discussions of the calendar year, fiscal year, and 52–53-week year. It also provides the rules for required years and alternate years. As the selection of a tax year is a critical decision to be made by a new business, Chapter 3 discusses the natural business year, the annual business cycle, the seasonal business cycle, and IRC § 444 as well.

Chapter 4 discusses the rules regarding methods of accounting, timing issue, the selection of an accounting method, book conformity, conversion work-papers and the mechanism of adopting or changing a tax year.

Chapter 5 provides a detailed discussion of the cash receipts and disbursements method of accounting, covering topics such as cash equivalency, constructive receipt, economic benefit, and deferred payment arrangements. It also discusses the rules for prepaid period costs, deduction of interest, the limitation on the cash method under IRC § 448, and when a cash method taxpayer may take a deduction.

Chapter 6 covers the accrual method including the rules for inclusion of income (known as the "all events test"), prepaid income, service warranty, and deposits. It also discusses when a taxpayer using the accrual method may take a deduction under the economic performance requirements.

Chapter 7 provides the rules for changes in accounting methods—those that are automatic, non-automatic and service-initiated—as well as the procedures for applying for a change of accounting.

Chapter 8 explores the heart of tax accounting—inventory and the rules necessary to maintain inventory.

Chapter 9 provides a detailed discussion of the uniform capitalization rules under IRC § 263A focusing on the general rules, producers, resellers, and interest capitalization.

Chapter 10 provides an analysis of the benefits and detriments of the installment method of reporting sales. Chapter 10 also covers the dealer rules, contingent payment sales, non-dealer rules, mortgages and other liabilities and disposition and modification of installing obligations.

Chapter 11 discusses long-term contracts including manufacturing contracts, construction contracts, home construction contracts, the completed contract method and percentage of completion method.

Chapter 12 provides a discussion of the accounting for income taxes.

Chapter 13 focuses on which expenses may be deducted and which must be capitalized. It covers the rules for when a taxpayer may be able to take a deduction for material supplies, capital expenditures, amounts paid to acquire or produce tangible property, amounts paid to prove tangible property, and amounts paid to acquire intangibles and acquire or create intangibles. Additionally, it covers the rules for the small business taxpayer, certain de minimis safe harbor rules, capitalization elections and coordination with IRC § § 162 and 263A. This chapter provides many examples of these rules. It should be noted that the final tangible property regulations are effective tax years 2014 and afterwards. The regulations are very detailed and should be consulted to ensure compliance.

Chapter 14 provides the rules relating to time value of money, unstated interest, original interest discount, investment interest, and qualified residential interest.

There is vast literature on tax accounting issues in the form of articles and journals which can be used as a supplement to this guide. Because tax accounting is ever-changing, the practitioner must keep up with these changes as they occur from time to time.

Frank L. Brunetti

September 2020

Summary of Contents

Table of Contents

7

Change in Accounting Method

8

Inventory

9

Uniform Capitalization Rules

10

Installment Method

11

Long-Term Contracts

12

Accounting for Income Taxes

13

Distinguishing between Capital Expenditures and Repairs

14

The Time Value of Money

1

Introduction

§ 1.01 Overview

Black's Law Dictionary (7th ed. 1999) defines accounting as "The act or a system of establishing or settling financial accounts; the process of recording transactions in the financial records of a business and periodically extracting, sorting, and summarizing the recorded transaction to produce a set of financial records. Also termed *financial accounting*."

The American Institute of Certified Public Accountants (AICPA) has defined accounting as "the art of recording, classifying, and summarizing in a significant manner and in terms of money, transactions and events that are, in part at least, of a financial character and the results therefrom."

Understanding financial accounting is important, but financial accounting is not the same as tax accounting.[1] Tax accounting is a structure of accounting methods focused on computing taxes rather than the appearance of public financial statements. The Internal Revenue Code, which dictates the specific rules that companies and individuals must follow when preparing their tax returns, governs tax accounting. Tax accounting focuses on the preparation, analysis and presentation of tax returns and tax payments. Tax accounting issues often arise in many different circumstances of your daily practice. A tax accountant ensures that companies and individuals comply with tax laws when filing their federal and state income tax returns. Tax accountants also provide tax-planning advice. For this reason, a fundamental understanding of the principles of tax accounting is important to your tax practice.[2]

For example, Daisy Company might use one accounting method for calculating depreciation when it reports financial results to investors, but tax laws may require it

[1] *See* § 1.02, *infra*.
[2] *See* § 1.03, *infra*.

to use a different method for tax accounting purposes. As a result, Daisy Company might have one net income number on the financial statements filed with the SEC and a different net income number filed with the IRS.

The tax accounting section of the Internal Revenue Code (hereafter "Code") is found in Subchapter E. The Service also discusses tax accounting in many IRS pronouncements, rulings, and tax cases. The materials in this book introduce tax practitioners to the tax accounting issues most often faced in daily practice.

The *when* question is the subject of tax accounting and this book. It is all about timing. Of course, a taxpayer should know that she has an item of income, loss, deduction, credit, etc., to report on her federal income tax return, but *when* to report the item is a critical question. Tax accounting rules determine *when* the incidence of tax-recognized events are taken into account for federal income tax purposes. These accounting issues often involve issues of significant tax consequences that are concerned with *when* particular items should be includable in income or deductible or listed as a credit. When businesses are audited, very often the items in dispute depend on the resolution of tax accounting issues. Accordingly, as a practicing accountant one should provide scrutiny to a client's tax accounting issues, as a failure to do so could lead to significant penalties for the taxpayer and the return preparer.

The need for a clear understanding of the critical nature of tax accounting was aptly pointed out and given approval by the Supreme Court in *Burnet v. Sanford and Brooks Co.*,[3] where the Supreme Court had to determine *when* income should be included by the taxpayer. The answer to the question was crucial for the government. Without knowing when income would be collected it would be nearly impossible to maintain a budget, to borrow, to fund programs, etc. Not knowing or having the ability to project the government's revenue stream would cause chaos.

As one might imagine, the government and the taxpayer have competing interests. There are also a variety of interpretations from jurisdiction to jurisdiction that one needs to be aware of in the implementation of tax accounting provisions.

In order to decide *when* a tax event should be taken into account one needs to know the available choices. Without knowing the choices, one cannot make the decision as to the best way to report the item. In *Burnet v. Sanford and Brooks Co.*,[4] the Supreme Court had to decide between a transactional approach to tax accounting versus an annual accounting approach or periodic approach. There are advantages and disadvantages to each method. However, as stated above, the revenue stream and the necessity of running a government requires annual accounting and certainty. In this text, we will explore all of these issues as we study the various tax accounting doctrines.

In addition to accounting doctrines, this book discusses the following topics:

- The Entity's Tax Year;
- Methods of Accounting;
- The Cash Receipts and Disbursements Method;
- The Accrual Method;

---

[3] 282 U.S. 359, 51 S. Ct. 150, 75 L. Ed. 383, 2 USTC ¶636 (1979).

[4] 282 U.S. 359, 51 S. Ct. 150, 75 L. Ed. 383, 2 USTC ¶636 (1979).

- Change in Accounting Method;
- Inventories;
- Uniform Capitalization Rules;
- Installment Sales;
- Long-Term Contracts;
- Accounting for Income Taxes;
- Distinguishing between Capital Expenditures and Repairs; and
- The Time Value of Money.

As important as tax accounting is, one still must understand financial accounting. A corporation's financial statements are prepared in accordance with generally accepted accounting principles (GAAP). The purpose of these statements is quite different from the corporation's income tax return. The ASC 740 approach produces an income tax expense (also known as "income tax provisions") for income currently reported on a corporation's combined financial statement. This approach follows the matching principle, where all expenses related to earning income are reported in the same period as income without regard to when the expenses are actually paid. Chapter 12 discusses ASC 740 in more detail.

§ 1.02 Financial Accounting vs. Tax Accounting

Financial accounting governs financial reporting. Aspects of financial accounting include the preparation of balance sheets, statements of retained earnings, income statements, and other financial statements. The primary function of financial accounting is to provide useful and accurate information to those who need to use it, such as financial companies, advisors, shareholders, etc.

Tax accounting and financial accounting are not functionally equivalent. In *Thor Power Tools Co. v. Commissioner*,[5] Justice Blackmun addressed the distinction between the two methods as follows:

> The primary goal of financial accounting is to provide useful information to management, shareholders, creditors and others properly interested; the major responsibility of the accountant is to protect these parties from being misled. The primary goal of the income tax system, in contrast, is the equitable collection of revenue; the major responsibility of the Internal Revenue Service is to protect the public fisc. Consistently with its goals and responsibilities, financial accounting has as its foundation the principle of conservatism, with its corollary that possible errors in measurement [should] be in the direction of understatement rather than overstatement of net income and net assets. In view of the Treasury's markedly different goals and responsibilities, understatement of income is not destined to be its guiding light. Given this diversity, even contrariety, of objectives, any presumptive equivalency between tax and financial accounting would not be acceptable.

[5] 439 U.S. 522, 99 S. Ct. 773, 58 L. Ed. 2d 785, 79-1 USTC ¶9139 (1979).

Nonetheless, tax accounting draws on financial accounting concepts, such as the "Generally Accepted Accounting Principles" (GAAP). These concepts are often used to augment the distinctly different regime of tax accounting.

§1.03 Why Study Tax Accounting?

Whether you are an attorney, an accountant, or a financial advisor, you *will* face circumstances in your daily practice involving matters of tax accounting. For example:

- When advising a client as to whether his new business should be a "C" corporation, "S" corporation, partnership, or LLC, the selection of a tax year or accounting method is important—especially now with the new partnership audit rules;
- If a client were selling property on an installment basis, it would be important to know if the buyer were a related party or if the installment obligation was contingent on future unknown factors;
- If a client's corporation were going to make an "S" election, it would be important to know if the fiscal year of the corporation could end on a date other than December 31st;
- If your client were to start a service business that has inventory, it would be important to know under what circumstances a taxpayer would be required to "maintain inventories";
- It would be important to know the tax treatment of the receipt of a promissory note by a cash method taxpayer and by an accrual method taxpayer;
- It is necessary to understand whether the receipt of a prepayment by a cash or an accrual method taxpayer is treated the same or differently;
- Whether an accrual method taxpayer can prematurely accrue a liability; and
- If your client were audited would you be concerned if she were reporting an item erroneously and would you like to know whether you could correct the error before, during, or after the audit and what penalties she might face?

These and many more questions are explored in this text.

Tax accounting has become increasingly important, as the government's need for revenue has increased with the general attitude that tax brackets should remain the same or be decreased. Indeed, the Tax Cuts and Jobs Act (TCJA) (P. L. 115-97, Dec. 22, 2017), which decreased both the corporate and individual income tax brackets, came with a projected $1.5 trillion deficit that could very likely result in further changes to tax accounting rules beyond those contained in the legislation.

Tax accounting is largely non-political. As an observation, a change in a tax accounting rule is more likely to go unnoticed by the general public than a tax rate increase.

Tax accounting is ever-evolving. Some of its complex rules are a product of a number of factors including:

- The relationship between tax accounting and financial accounting;
- What choices a taxpayer makes in selecting a tax accounting system;

- The continuously changing tax system which measures income and allows deductions as economic principles change;
- Taxpayers' erroneous efforts to achieve their own goals;
- The ability to administer a tax system in an efficient manner;
- The political atmosphere that may exist from time to time including tax rates, deductions, etc., and the need to raise revenue;
- The constant tension between generally accepted accounting principles (GAAP) and tax accounting; and
- The tension between taxpayers and the Internal Revenue Service and interpretations of tax accounting rules by the courts.

Taxpayers begin with the ability to choose a tax year and a tax accounting method but do they really know how these rules affect their business? That is often important and should be the province of the tax advisor. Moreover, as the tax rules change, the tax brackets change and the tax principles change, so the tax advisor must be aware of how these changes affect her client's tax accounting method and what changes must be implemented to avoid the imposition of penalties not only against the taxpayer but also against the tax preparer. The tax accounting changes brought about by the TCJA illustrate the importance of knowing the rules and principles that have changed and how to implement these changes.

As we shall see, the government has been granted great latitude in its ability to impose an appropriate tax accounting method for a taxpayer,[6] yet, at the same time, if the taxpayer is using a tax accounting method properly and does not abuse the tax accounting method, the government has little ability to impose a change.[7]

Both from the point of view of the cash method and the accrual method, the IRS and the courts often look to see how the accounting method matches revenue with expenses and whether there is a distortion of income. As we shall also see, the "time value of money" plays an important role. During the 1980s, taxpayers took advantage of high interest rates and the "time value of money" to take premature tax deductions. These abuses led to the enactment of IRC § 461(h) that resolved many of these inequities.

The general framework of the tax accounting rules and principles is that the Commissioner will often look to accelerate income and deferred deductions; this is found in many provisions including Code sections, regulations, revenue rulings and other IRS guidance.

Because of the annual accounting principle, as discussed in this text, harsh inequities can be imposed on taxpayers. Over time, Congress has attempted to address these inequities with the enactment of Code sections governing net operating loss provisions, the installment sales method, the tax benefit rule, claim of right, IRC § 1341 and other ameliorative provisions.

---

[6] *Thor Power Tools Co. v. Comm'r*, 439 U.S. 522, 99 S. Ct. 773, 58 L. Ed. 785, 79-1 USTC ¶ 9139 (1979).

[7] Where a taxpayer's method of accounting is an acceptable method, the IRS has not been allowed to arbitrarily require a change. The IRS may not reject, as not providing a clear reflection of income, a method of accounting employed by the taxpayer which is specifically authorized by the Internal Revenue Code or Treasury regulations and which has been applied on a consistent basis. *Prabel v. Comm'r*, 91 T.C. 1101, 1111-1112 (1988); *Hallmark Cards, Inc. v. Comm'r*, 90 T.C. 26, 31 (1988).

§1.04 Tax Records Maintenance

Taxpayers must maintain records, including regular books of account and "such other records and data as may be necessary," to support the entries on the books of account and on the return, such as reconciliation of any differences between the books and the tax return.[8] If such books and records are not properly maintained, a possible challenge to the taxpayer's method of accounting could occur. In addition, before a taxpayer can request a change of its method of accounting, the taxpayer must notify the Commissioner whether the taxpayer's books, records, and financial statements conform to the proposed method of accounting. Before the change can be used, the Commissioner's consent will be needed in order to use the new method.[9]

IRC §6001 requires that taxpayers maintain accounting records so that they can file a correct return. The implementing regulations provide, in pertinent part:

> Except as provided in paragraph (b) of this section, any person subject to tax under subtitle A of the Code . . . or any person required to file a return of information with respect to income, shall keep such permanent books of account or records, including inventories, as are sufficient to establish the amount of gross income, deductions, credits, or other matters required to be shown by such person in any return of such tax or information.[10]
>
> ******
>
> *Notice by district director requiring returns, statements of the keeping of records.* The district director may require any person, by notice served upon him, to make such returns, render such statements, or keep such specific records as will enable the district director to determine whether or not such person is liable for tax under subtitle A of the Code, including qualified State individual income taxes . . . .[11]

Sanctions and penalties may be imposed on taxpayers who fail to comply with these mandated recordkeeping requirements. The absence of records may be evidence of fraud[12] or negligence.

Rev. Proc. 98-25[13] provides basic requirements that the Internal Revenue Service considers to be essential in cases where a taxpayer's records are maintained within an automatic data processing (ADP) system. These records include punch cards, magnetic tapes, disks, and other machine-sensible records that are used for recording,

---

[8] Reg. §1.446-1(a)(4).

[9] IRC §446(e). *See* Rev. Proc. 97-27, 1997-1 CB 680, §8.04(7).

[10] Reg. §1.6001-1(a).

[11] Reg. §1.6001-1(d).

[12] *Stephens v. Comm'r*, 255 F.2d 108, 58-1 USTC ¶9519 (10th Cir. 1958).

[13] 1998-1 CB 689.

consolidating, and summarizing accounting transactions and records within a taxpayer's ADP system. These records must be retained as long as their contents may become material.

A taxpayer with assets of $10 million or more at the end of its taxable year must comply with the record retention requirements of Rev. Proc. 80-52[14] and Rev. Proc. 98-25.[15] A controlled group of corporations is considered to be one corporation and all assets of all members of the group are aggregated.

A taxpayer with assets of less than $10 million at the end of its taxable year must comply with the record retention requirements of Rev. Rul. 80-52 and Rev. Proc. 98-25[16] if any of the following conditions exists:[17]

- All or part of the information required by IRC § 6001 is not in the taxpayer's hardcopy books and records, but is available in machine-sensible records;
- Machine-sensible records were used for computations that cannot be reasonably verified or recomputed without using a computer (*e.g.*, Last-In, First-Out (LIFO) inventories);
- The taxpayer is notified by the District Director that machine-sensible records must be retained to meet the requirements of IRC § 6001;
- A Controlled Foreign Corporation (CFC), a domestic corporation that is 25% foreign-owned, and a foreign corporation engaged in a trade or business within the United States at any time during a taxable year that maintains machine-sensible records within an ADP system must comply with the requirements of Rev. Proc. 98-25[18] to satisfy the recordkeeping requirements of IRC § 964(c), IRC § 982(d), IRC § 6038A(c)(4), and IRC § 6038C (and the regulations thereunder); or
- An insurance company that maintains machine-sensible records within an ADP system to determine losses incurred under IRC § 832(b)(5) must comply with the requirements of Rev. Proc. 98-25. For this purpose, the machine-sensible records for a particular taxable year include the records for that year and the seven preceding years, all of which must be retained so long as they may become material to the examination of an insurance company's federal tax return.

  A taxpayer's use of a third party (such as a service bureau, time-sharing service, value-added network, or other third-party service) to provide services (*e.g.*, custodial or management services) in respect of machine-sensible records does not relieve the taxpayer of its recordkeeping obligations and responsibilities under IRC § 6001 and Rev. Proc. 98-25.

---

[14] 1980-2 CB 828.
[15] 1998-1 CB 689.
[16] 1998-1 CB 689.
[17] 1980-2 CB 828.
[18] 1998-1 CB 689.

A willful failure to keep records is a misdemeanor under IRC §7203[19] and could be considered an attempt to evade or defeat a tax under IRC §7201.[20] Moreover, a taxpayer who fails to maintain records cannot use a fiscal year end.[21]

Under Reg. §31.6001-1(e), records must be kept for at least four years after the due date of the return or for as long as their contents may be material. Yet Rev. Proc. 98-25[22] states, regarding the retention of records, "at a minimum, this materiality continues until the expiration of the period of limitations for assessment, including extensions, for each tax year." Therefore, when determining how long to keep records, a tax practitioner should look at the relevant statute of limitation periods including extensions.

Example 1-1

Taxpayer, a C corporation, has been in existence since 1937. It manufactures metal products. It makes dividend distributions from time to time to its shareholders. How long must it maintain its financial and tax records and supporting entries?

As earning and profits under IRC §312 require an annual computation and because any distribution under IRC §316 is deemed a dividend unless proven otherwise, it would seem that earnings and profits records must be kept indefinitely.[23] Unfortunately, the IRS has issued no binding guidance specifically stating how long the records must be kept. Notwithstanding, should a corporation distribute property to a shareholder, it is required to demonstrate that the distribution is not from earnings and profits.[24]

In Rev. Rul. 58-601,[25] the Service ruled that an accountant's worksheets regularly maintained to reconcile differences between book depreciation and tax depreciation meet the requirement of permanent auxiliary records if:

---

[19] Fraudulent failure to file return penalties were upheld against taxpayer who did not file returns after 1985. Taxpayer's testimony that he was "making a stand" against the IRS showed that his later claims for not filing based upon accountant's advice, belief that filing was voluntary, and Hawaiian sovereignty were designed to mislead IRS. Also, taxpayer had his masonry license deemed inactive, yet continued his business, ceased using a business checking account and dealt in cash only and converted insurance settlement to cash rather than depositing it. *Marsh, John W.*, T.C. Memo. 2000-11.

[20] Fraud conviction upheld for sugar refining corporation willfully engaging in scheme to overstate "LIFO" inventory. *U.S. v Ingredient Technology Corp.*, 698 F.2d 88, 83-1 USTC ¶9140, *cert denied* 462 U.S. 1131 (1983).

[21] IRC §441(g); Reg. §1.441-1(c)(2)(ii).

[22] 1998-1 CB 689.

[23] *See* Form 5452, *Corporate Report of Nondividend Distributions.*

[24] *Id.* All corporations that have made nondividend distributions to their shareholders must file Form 5452.

[25] 1958-2 CB 81. *See also* Rev. Rul. 59-389, 1959-2 CB 89; Rev. Rul. 71-333, 1971-2 CB 244 and Rev. Rul. 74-383, 1974-2 CB 146.

- they provide an accurate, reliable and readily accessible basis for reconciliation; and
- originals of "sheets" are turned over to the taxpayer and are associated with his regular books of account.

Therefore, they should be retained so long as they may be material in the administration of tax law.

However, in Rev. Rul. 68-420[26], an accountant's work papers did not meet the bookkeeping requirements of Reg. § 1.593-7(a) because they were not associated with the taxpayer's regular books of account and entries were not transferred to its reserve accounts.

[26] 1968-2 CB 257.

2

Tax Accounting Doctrines

§ 2.01 Annual Accounting Doctrine

As discussed in Chapter 1, tax accounting statutes and rules can be found in codified form in Subchapter E of the Internal Revenue Code, IRC §§ 441 through 483, and the accompanying regulations. Additionally, tax accounting rules are found in Revenue Procedures, Revenue Rulings, and many IRS pronouncements. It is not only in these source items where we find tax accounting rules, but in judicial decisions that result in "doctrines," which in many instances become codified into Code sections. These include:

- The annual accounting system,[1]
- The claim of right doctrine,[2]
- IRC § 1341, computation of tax where taxpayer restores substantial amount held under claim of right,[3]
- The *Arrowsmith* doctrine,[4] and
- The tax benefit rule.[5]

[A] The Annual Accounting System

IRC § 441(a) has codified the principles of *Burnet v. Sanford and Brooks Co.*,[6] which determined that a taxpayer must compute his income on the basis of a taxable year.[7] The term "taxable year" means:

- The taxpayer's *annual accounting period*, if it is a calendar year or a fiscal year;
- The calendar year;
- The period for which a return is made, if the return is made for a period of less than 12 months;
- The filing of a return for a period of at least 12 months, in the case of an FSC or DISC;[8] or
- If the taxpayer elects, a year consisting of 52–53 weeks.[9]

---

1 *See* § 2.01, *infra*.

2 *See* § 2.02, *infra*.

3 *See* § 2.03, *infra*.

4 *See* § 2.04, *infra*.

5 While technically not tax accounting sections, IRC §§ 172 (net operating losses) 170 (charitable contributions), 165 (losses) and 166 (bad debts) all affect the tax treatment and timing of these items.

6 282 U.S. 359, 51 S. Ct. 150, 75 L. Ed. 383, 2 USTC ¶ 636 (1979). Moreover, other Code sections are affected by the annual accounting system, *e.g.*, IRC § 267 where a deduction is deferred because the other party is related.

7 For a discussion of the entity's tax year, *see* Chapter 3, *infra*.

8 IRC § 441(b).

9 IRC § 441(f).

The term "annual accounting period" means the annual period on the basis of which a taxpayer regularly computes his income in keeping his books.[10] If a taxpayer does not keep books, the Code provides an accounting period for him—the calendar year.[11] Chapter 3 discusses the tax year in greater depth.

The annual accounting system was approved by the Supreme Court in *Burnet v. Sanford and Brooks Co.*[12] In this case, the taxpayer was a government contractor who agreed to dredge the Delaware River from 1913 through 1916. In 1913, 1915, and 1916, the government contractor's books reflected a loss. In 1914, the contractor's books reflected income. However, the contractor did not include the amounts received as income for the tax year 1914 on its 1914 tax return. In 1915, work under the contract was abandoned, and in 1916, suit was brought to recover for breach of warranty of the character of the material to be dredged. The judgment for breach of warranty in favor of the contractor was affirmed in 1920.[13]

The Commissioner assessed a deficiency against the contractor for the year 1920, the year in which the contractor recovered from the government the money it owed him. The contractor argued to the Court that since it had no profits on the contract, it should not have to pay any taxes. The contractor also contended that since the dredging produced an overall loss, it should not have to report any income for tax purposes. The IRS, however, determined that the contractor had income in 1920 and said that the contractor should determine its income on an annual basis.

The issue thus framed by the Supreme Court was whether tax accounting should be computed on an annual basis or on a transactional basis. The Court noted that all prior revenue acts, as well as the statute in effect at the time, referred to an *annual accounting period*. The Court concluded that in 1920 the contractor should have determined whether it had income under the statute and that prior losses had no effect on that year. In reaching its conclusion, the Supreme Court reasoned:

> It is the essence of any system of taxation that it should produce revenue ascertainable and payable to the government at regular intervals and that only by such a system is it practical to produce a regular flow of income and apply methods of accounting assessment and collection capable of a practical operation. Moreover in order for the government to run it has to have a predictable source of income and transactional taxation could not produce such predictability.[14]

The annual accounting doctrine can produce harsh results as it divides up transactions which may span more than one tax year into annual periods, some of

---

[10] IRC § 441(c). Taxpayers who had always kept books on fiscal-year basis were required to file on fiscal-year basis, *Willingham Loan & Trust Co.*, 15 BTA 931 (1929).

[11] IRC § 441(g). This is so whether the taxpayer does not have an accounting period or the taxpayer does not keep books.

[12] 282 U.S. 359, 51 S. Ct. 150, 75 L. Ed. 383, 2 USTC ¶ 636.

[13] *Sanford and Brooks v. Comm'r*, 35 F.2d 312 (4th Cir. 1929).

[14] 9 AFTR at 606. 282 U.S. 359, 365, 2 USTC ¶ 636. It is to be noted that *Sanford and Brooks* was decided before net operating losses were adopted by the Code.

which may produce income and some of which may produce losses. Today, the Internal Revenue Code has a relief provision in IRC § 172 that allows for net operating losses. Under this provision, a taxpayer can spread out losses over multiple tax periods.[15] Other tax accounting provisions that reduce the harshness of the annual accounting doctrine include IRC § 1341,[16] which provides relief from the claim of right doctrine, and IRC § 111,[17] which provides relief under the tax benefit doctrine.

Example 2-1

Nancy is a self-employed consultant and reports her income using the cash method of accounting. In December of Year One she expects to receive $300,000 of income from her consulting. In Year Two, because of changes in the industry, she expects to receive $50,000 of taxable income.

Nancy recently met with a colleague who offered her the opportunity to consult on a new project for a total payment of $100,000. The project would be completed in Year One. Nancy has not yet entered into a contract but her colleague has suggested that she might want to be paid in Year Two even though the services will be rendered in Year One.

What advice would you give to Nancy regarding the timing of the receipt for payment of her consulting services?

Assuming that in Year One Nancy will be in a higher income tax bracket than she would be in Year Two, it might be appropriate to have the income from the new consulting contract paid in Year Two rather than Year One. If she were paid in Year One, her income would be $400,000 and likely taxed at the highest bracket. If she were paid in Year Two, she would likely be in a lower tax bracket. The countervailing issue, however, is that if she renders services in Year One but does not get paid until Year Two, her status vis-a vis the obligor is that of a creditor. She has merely a right to receive income which will not come into fruition until Year Two. This issue will be further explored in Chapter 5 under the cash equivalency doctrine where we will consider whether she still may have income in Year One nevertheless.

The annual accounting system sometimes can be viewed as a barrier which separates income from year-to-year. This barrier can have severe consequences where taxpayers have periodic increases or decreases in income from year-to-year. On the

---

[15] The NOL deduction equals the total of the NOL carryovers and the NOL carrybacks to a specific year. Under the TCJA, it is limited to 80% of taxable income, determined without regard to the deduction. This limit does not apply to losses in years preceding 2018. Under the Coronavirus Aid, Relief, and Economic Security (CARES) Act, there is now a five-year carryback for operating losses of corporate taxpayers. The carryback of losses had been previously eliminated in the Tax Cut and Jobs Act ("TCJA"), but CARES reinstates carrybacks for Net Operating Losses (NOLs) arising in taxable years beginning after December 31, 2017, and ending before January 1, 2021.

[16] *See* § 2.03, *below*.

[17] *See* § 2.05, *below*.

other hand, it could create opportunities for the taxpayer to shift income or deductions from one year to another. In this text we will discuss these issues and the consequences thereof. Indeed, a taxpayer may be severely penalized for manipulating a tax system, as explained in Chapter 7.

[B] Application of the Annual Accounting System

A deduction that is proper in the year taken is unaffected by later events. If these later events have significance, then they will affect such later year.

In *Grace M. Barnett*,[18] a depletion deduction of 27½% was taken on the bonus paid to the taxpayer for granting an oil and gas lease that the taxpayer included in income for that year. In 1935, the lease was terminated without any oil or gas having been extracted from the property covered by the lease. The tax regulations provided that if mining operations were abandoned before removal of the minerals, the deduction previously taken would not be changed. The excess of the deduction over the actual depletion, however, would be treated as income in the year of abandonment. The Board of Tax Appeals held the regulations valid, basing its decision on the annual accounting system. Clearly the deduction was proper at the time and a subsequent change or interpretation of the regulation had no effect on the proper reporting of the item. Thus, the annual accounting system prevents a taxpayer from filing an amended return for the prior year.

Deduction improper in year claimed.

In *Cooperstown Corporation v. Commissioner*,[19] the court stated that no deduction was warranted for a tax payment for which indisputably no liability existed, and that it was within the Commissioner's power to disallow the deduction for a payment for which there was no legal liability resting upon the taxpayer. The Court further observed that there is a necessity that the taxpayer be under actual or apparent obligation for the payment at the time it is made in order for it to be deductible as an ordinary and necessary business expense.[20]

Question: How would an excessive payment of a state income tax estimated payment be dealt with when the taxpayer has good reason to believe that the payment will likely be partially refunded?

Answer: The deduction would not be permitted since there was no legal basis for the payment and was merely voluntary.[21]

---

[18] 39 BTA 864, 865 (1939). These regulations were affirmed in *Douglas v. Comm'r*, 322 U.S. 275, 44-1 USTC ¶9326 (1944), where the court recognized that the annual accounting system prevented an adjustment to the tax year in which the deduction was claimed. *See also* Rev. Rul. 73-537, 1973-2 CB 197.

[19] 144 F.2d 693, 44-2 USTC ¶9453 (3d Cir. 1949). *See also William H. Leonhart*, T.C. Memo. 1968-98.

[20] *Cf. Baltimore Transfer Co.*, 8 T.C. 1 (1947); *Bartlett v. Delaney*, 173 F.2d 535, 49-1 USTC ¶9219 (1st Cir. 1949).

[21] *See* Chapter 6, *infra*, the All-Events Test, where one of the requirements for a deduction is that the taxpayer must have a legal obligation. At best, such a payment would be considered a deposit and not presently deductible.

Deduction not taken in tax year originally available.

The hardship that is demonstrated by the annual accounting system can be seen where a taxpayer is denied a deduction in the year other than in the year in which the deduction should have been taken under its method of accounting. The fact that the taxpayer might otherwise have a proper deduction does not allow the taxpayer to take a deduction if it violates the annual accounting system. In *H.E. Harman Coal Co. v. Commissioner*,[22] an accrual method taxpayer was notified that tax deficiencies were owed for the tax years 1938 and 1939. The taxpayer paid these deficiencies and took a deduction in 1941 when it made the payment. Under of the annual accounting system, the Tax Court held the deduction was not available in 1941, the year the tax was paid, because under the accrual method only the earliest years to which the deficiencies related were the years in which the deduction should have been taken. The fact that the taxpayer failed to amend its tax return for such years resulted in a loss of these deductions.

Under the accrual method of accounting, if a later asserted state tax deficiency is not contested, deduction of the additional amount is permitted for federal tax purposes in the year to which it relates, not the year to which the deficiency is asserted or agreed. In order to obtain a deduction, the taxpayer must file an amended return.[23]

In addition, Reg. § 1.461-1(a)(3) provides:

> *Effect in current taxable year of improperly accounting for a liability in a prior taxable year.* Each year's return should be complete in itself, and taxpayers shall ascertain the facts necessary to make a correct return. The expenses, liabilities, or loss of one year generally cannot be used to reduce the income of a subsequent year. A taxpayer may not take into account in a return for a subsequent taxable year liabilities that, under the taxpayer's method of accounting, should have been taken into account in a prior taxable year. If a taxpayer ascertains that a liability should have been taken into account in a prior taxable year, the taxpayer should, if within the period of limitation, file a claim for credit or refund of any overpayment of tax arising therefrom. Similarly, if a taxpayer ascertains that a liability was improperly taken into account in a prior taxable year, the taxpayer should, if within the period of limitation, file an amended return and pay any additional tax due. However, except as provided in IRC § 905(c) and the regulations thereunder, if a liability is properly taken into account in an amount based on a computation made with reasonable accuracy and the exact amount of the liability is subsequently determined in a later taxable year, the difference, if any, between such amounts shall be taken into account for the later taxable year.

---

[22] 16 T.C. 787 (1951). *See also Keller-Dorian Corp. v. Comm'r*, 153 F.2d 1006, 46-1 USTC ¶ 9200 (2d Cir. 1946).

[23] The rule is well established that for deduction purposes taxes accrue when all events have transpired which determine the amount of the tax and the taxpayer's liability therefor. *E.g., United States v. Anderson*, 269 U.S. 422 (1926); *Standard Paving Co. v. Comm'r*, 13 T.C. 425, 447 (1949); *Oregon Pulp & Paper Co. v. Comm'r*, 47 BTA 772, 780 (1942); *Haverty Furniture Co. v. Comm'r*, 20 BTA 644 (1930).

Example 2-2

A business paid a contested tax deficiency plus interest and deducted the interest payment on its 1986 tax return. After settlement, the IRS computed the actual interest due and issued a refund for the difference between the actual interest and the interest paid. The business wished to amend its 1986 return to deduct the entire interest amount it paid.

Noting that returns must be filed based on the facts known at the time of filing, the Service acknowledged that although the entity was entitled to deduct the entire amount of interest paid when the original return was filed, it chose to deduct a lesser amount. The Service concluded that the entity could not file an amended return to increase the interest deduction once it learned the correct amount of its interest liability.[24]

But an accrual-basis nursing home must report the actual amount of readily calculable year-end adjustments with respect to income earned for services rendered during the taxable year to Medicaid patients in the taxable year the services are performed.[25]

However, not all deductions can be taken in the year in which the expense is incurred. For example, IRC § 460H limits the amount of compensation that is permitted as a deduction by a fiscal-year personal service corporation (PSC) when there is a failure to meet certain minimum payment amounts in the deferral period of the elected tax year.

A PSC which had made an IRC § 444 election applies IRC § 280H and Reg. § 1.280H-1T to limit the amount of deferral available to owners. Since these organizations are generally owned by individuals reporting on a calendar year, a fiscal year corporation might be tempted to defer the payment of compensation until after December 31 so as to defer the receipt of owner compensation by a year. The operation of Reg. § 1.280H-1T prevents this.[26]

Income reported before proper year.

If a taxpayer reports an item of income in a year before the proper year of inclusion and pays the taxes thereon, the taxpayer, if the statute of limitations has not run, can amend his tax return to obtain a refund of the amount so claimed. On the other hand, if the statute of limitations has run, the taxpayer is still required to report the income in the proper year regardless of having reported it in an improper year.[27]

A double inclusion of income occurs when there is income included in one tax year that has also been erroneously included in a previous tax year (where the return can no longer be amended). It also occurs when an item is included in the income of

---

[24] FSA 893, Vaughn #893.

[25] Rev. Rul. 81-176, 1981-2 CB 112.

[26] *See* § 3.14[F], *infra*.

[27] *Chatham & Phenix National Bank*, 1 BTA 460 (1925). *See also Redcay*, 12 T.C. 806 (1949). The mitigation sections of IRC §§ 1311-1314 might provide relief to the taxpayer.

one taxpayer and that same item has been erroneously included in the income of a related taxpayer.[28]

Example 2-3

Nancy White, a cash-basis taxpayer, erroneously included on her Year 1 return an item of $10,000 accrued rent that she actually received in Year 2. White's Year 2 return was filed on April 15 of Year 3, and the time within which the IRS could assess a deficiency did not expire until April 15 of Year 6. If the IRS, on February 3 of Year 6, asserts a deficiency that is sustained by the Tax Court, White would have to pay additional Year 2 tax. She could not, however, file a claim for refund of the Year 1 overpayment, since the statute of limitations would have expired. The mitigation rules may however allow an adjustment.[29]

Income reported in a later year.

The annual accounting system also prevents income from being reported in a later year if it should have been reported in an earlier year.[30]

[C] Event Occurring After the Reported Year

Change in law. One might think that if there were a change in law or a change in the validity or interpretation of a law or regulation subsequent to the year of reporting that one would be able to avoid the annual accounting system and change the result in the earlier year. That is not always the case. In *Freihofer Baking Co. v. Commissioner*,[31] the taxpayer's purchase of flour in 1935 included a processing tax. The taxpayer accrued and deducted this tax in the year of purchase. In 1936, the processing tax was declared unconstitutional retroactively and the tax was refunded. The taxpayer attempted to account for the refund by filing an amended return for 1935. The tax court found that filing an amended return was improper and that the refund should have been reported as income in the year of its receipt in accordance with the annual accounting system.[32]

Suppose, through legislation, a state imposes a retroactive tax on events which occurred during an earlier year. Assume that the tax is held to be constitutional. Assume further that the tax is paid in the current year. Can the taxpayer amend the prior-year tax return to which the tax relates and take a deduction in such year? In

---

[28] See relief afforded under IRC § 1312(1); Reg. § 1.1312-1.

[29] IRC § § 1311-1314.

[30] *Policy Holders Agency, Inc. v. Comm'r*, 41 T.C. 44 (1963). IRC § 481 may provide relief as well.

[31] 45-2 USTC ¶ 9400, 151 F.2d 38 (3d Cir. 1945). *See also Baltimore Transfer Co. v. Comm'r*, 8 T.C. 1 (1947) and *Electric Tachometer Corp. v. Comm'r*, 37 T.C. 158 (1961). *Cf. Gulf Oil Corp. v. Comm'r*, 914 F.2d 396, 90-2 USTC ¶ 50,496 (3d Cir. 1990).

[32] The result can also be reconciled with the tax benefit doctrine under IRC § 111.

Van Norman Co. v. Welch,[33] the taxpayer was a manufacturing corporation. In 1935, Massachusetts had in effect corporation excise taxes that carried a certain rate of tax and which did not include machinery in the base of calculation. In 1936, the Massachusetts legislature provided that the 1935 corporate excise tax should include machinery in its basis of calculation and also increased the rate of tax by 10%. These laws were approved on June 16, 1936, and June 24, 1936, respectively, and became effective on those dates. The taxpayer's federal income tax return for 1935 was due and filed on March 15, 1936. This additional Massachusetts tax assessed for 1935 in the year 1936, based on corporate excess as at December 31, 1935, and on income of the calendar year 1935, amounted to $1,212.91.

The issue was whether the Commissioner was right in disallowing the deduction of this additional amount for the tax year 1936 and requiring that it be accrued in the 1935 return.

In *First National Bank in St. Louis v. Commissioner,*[34] it was held that increased capital stock tax rates were not deductible in the year prior to the tax liability fixed by statute although the taxpayer used the accrual basis. However, the Supreme Court in *Fawcus Machine Co. v. United States,*[35] required accrual in the prior year of a retroactively imposed federal excess profits tax wherein the tax rate change was but one step in a continued and reasonably to be anticipated process of change. The court there said: "The act was passed in ample time to allow the taxpayer to readjust its accounts for that year by including these taxes."[36] The *Van Norman Co* court noted that, in *Dixie Pine Products Co. v. Commissioner,*[37] the Supreme Court held that a tax accrues in the year when all events have occurred which fix the amount of the tax and determine the liability of the taxpayer to pay it. In *Dixie Pine Products Co.*, it was held that a taxpayer on the accrual basis who was contesting his liability for a state tax could not claim a deduction for the tax in the year imposed (and actually paid), but had to await the taxable year in which his liability for the tax was finally adjudicated. In the case at bar, there was neither liability for the additional tax nor could its amount be known in 1935. The event which fixed the amount of the additional tax and made the taxpayer liable to pay that extra sum was the enactment of the two statutes in June of 1936. Because the tax was not fixed until the following year, the deduction was allowed in 1936.

Taxpayer tries to retroactively change the facts that have occurred in a prior year.

If a taxpayer takes action in a current year in an attempt to change the tax consequences of the events that occurred in an earlier year, his actions will not affect the earlier year but they may be taken into account for tax purposes, if at all, in the year taken.[38]

---

[33] 44-1 USTC ¶9231, 141 F.2d 99 (1st Cir. 1944). The court determined that the taxpayer should not be required to keep its books open beyond a reasonable time after the close of the year. The taxpayer was permitted a deduction in 1936 for a tax retroactively imposed for 1935.

[34] 1 T.C. 370 (1942).

[35] 282 U.S. 375 (1931).

[36] *Fawcus Machine Co. v. United States*, 282 U.S. 375 (1931).

[37] 64 S. Ct. 364 (1944).

[38] *Noble v. Comm'r*, 66-2 USTC ¶9743 (9th Cir. 1966).

State court rulings that affect prior years.

It is not uncommon for a state court, especially a matrimonial court, to amend or change a ruling which is made in a prior year. This is often seen in situations where a determination made as to the amount of alimony and child support is initially determined and in a subsequent year the court changes the amounts retroactively (*nunc pro tunc*).[39] From a tax perspective, the question is whether the state law decision changing the facts of an earlier year is significant for federal tax purposes. Generally, the actions of a state court are not binding on the IRS.[40] Only in the case of a state court correcting an error previously made will the change be recognized.[41] Additionally, a federal court in deciding a tax case, must accept as binding a decision of the highest court of the state. Decisions of lower courts are to be given only "proper regard." This decision resolves the very confused law of lower courts attempting to reconcile state law and federal tax law. An adversarial dispute is more likely to be accepted than a non-adversarial dispute. But only the highest state court decision can be binding on federal courts.[42]

[D] Rescission of Agreement

The annual accounting system becomes complicated when a transaction which results initially in gain from the disposition of property, in both character and amount, is later rescinded in the same year. When repayment involves a rescission of the initial sale, there is an additional basis issue.[43]

---

[39] [Latin, Now for then.] When courts take some action *nunc pro tunc*, that action has retroactive legal effect, as though it had been performed at a particular, earlier date. http://legal-dictionary.thefreedictionary.com/nunc+pro+tunc.

[40] *Gordon v. Comm'r*, 70 T.C. 525 (1978) (decree recharacterizing child support as alimony not given retroactive effect; character of payments as child support unchanged despite evidence of oral agreement to make payments as alimony).

[41] *Muss v. Comm'r*, 29 TCM 758, T.C. Memo. 1970-171 (*nunc pro tunc* amendment). *See Graham v. Comm'r*, 79 T.C. 415 (1982) (refusing to recognize *nunc pro tunc* correction of wording of original decree from "family" support to child support; in granting *nunc pro tunc* decree, state trial court violated law as announced by highest court of state, and its decision thus could be disregarded).

[42] *Estate of Bosch*, 67-2 USTC ¶12,472, 387 U.S. 456 (1967). *See also Estate of Draper v. Comm'r.*, 536 F.2d 944 (1st Cir. 1976).

[43] *See* Rev. Rul. 80-58, 1980-1 CB 181 where the Service stated that no gain is recognized under IRC §1001 on the sale of land by a taxpayer who accepts reconveyance of the land and returns the buyer's funds in the taxable year of the sale. If the reconveyance occurs after the taxable year of sale, the seller must report the sale in the taxable year of sale and acquire a new basis in the property when it is reconveyed, such basis being equal to the amount paid for the reconveyance. The ruling defines rescission as "the abrogation, canceling, or voiding of a contract that has the effect of releasing the contracting parties from further obligations to each other and restoring the parties to the relative positions that they would have occupied had no contract been made. A rescission may be effected by mutual agreement of the parties, by one of the parties declaring a rescission of the contract without the consent of the other if sufficient grounds exist, or by applying to the court for a decree of rescission." *Id.* at 181-182.

Situation 1

In February 2020, A, a calendar year taxpayer, sold a tract of land to B and received cash for the entire purchase price. The contract of sale obligated A, at the request of B, to accept reconveyance of the land from B if, at any time within nine months of the date of sale, B was unable to have the land rezoned for B's business purposes. If there was a reconveyance under the contract, A and B would be placed in the same positions they were in prior to the sale.

In October 2020, B determined that it was not possible to have the land rezoned and notified A of its intention to reconvey the land pursuant to the terms of the contract of sale. The reconveyance was consummated during November 2020, and the tract of land was returned to A, and B received back all amounts expended in connection with the transaction.

Situation 2

Same situation as above, except that B had one year to reconvey the property to A. In January 2021, B determined that it was not possible to have the land rezoned and notified A of its intention to reconvey the land pursuant to the terms of the contract of sale. The reconveyance was consummated during February 2021, and the tract of land was returned to A. B received back all amounts expended in connection with the transaction. Because of the annual accounting principle, the reconveyance resulted in a taxable event and the gain (loss) must be recognized.

The legal concept of rescission refers to the abrogation, cancellation, or voiding of a contract that has the effect of releasing the contracting parties from further obligations to each other and restoring the parties to the relative positions that they would have occupied had no contract been made. A rescission may be effected by mutual agreement of the parties, by one of the parties declaring a rescission of the contract without the consent of the other if sufficient grounds exist, or by applying to the court for a decree of rescission. For the rescission to be effective, both buyer and seller must be put back in their original positions.[44]

The annual accounting concept requires that one must look at the transaction on an annual basis using the facts as they exist at the end of the year. That is, each taxable year is a separate unit for tax accounting purposes.[45]

In Situation 1, the rescission of the sale during 2020 placed A and B at the end of the taxable year in the same positions as they were prior to the sale. Thus, the original

---

[44] *Hutcheson v. Comm'r*, T.C. Memo. 1996-127.

[45] *See Security Flour Mills Co. v. Comm'r*, 321 U.S. 281, 44-1 USTC ¶9219 (1944).

sale is to be disregarded for federal income tax purposes because the rescission extinguished any taxable income for that year with regard to that transaction.[46]

In Situation 2, as in Situation 1, there was a completed sale in 2020. However, unlike in Situation 1, because only the sale and not the rescission occurred in 2020, at the end of 2020 A and B were not in the same positions as they were prior to the sale. The rescission in 2021 is disregarded with respect to the taxable events occurring in 2020. The sale stands for 2020.

Regarding adjustment to basis, Rev. Rul. 74-501[47] holds that there is no adjustment to the basis of the old stock where a shareholder exercised stock rights and paid the subscription price for the new stock, which subscription price was later returned to the shareholder in the same taxable year in which the rights were issued because the market price of the stock had depreciated to a price below the subscription offer (akin to Situation 1).

§ 2.02 Claim of Right Doctrine

Under the claim of right doctrine, a taxpayer who receives income under a "claim of right," *i.e.*, free of restrictions, must include that income in gross income in the year of receipt. The claim of right doctrine is based on the annual accounting period for reporting income. Income must be determined at the close of the taxable year without regard to possible subsequent events as required by the annual accounting system.[48] The claim of right doctrine was first clearly articulated by the Supreme Court in *North American Oil Consol. Co. v. Burnet*.[49] The principal function of the claim of right doctrine is to determine the proper taxable year in which the taxpayer must report income.[50]

Issues which raise the claim of right doctrine include:

- Prepaid income;
- Illegal income;
- Mistake;
- Agreement to refund;
- Receipt by trustees or conduits;
- Deposits; and
- Deductions for repaid amounts.

In *North American Oil*, the taxpayer was a drilling company that was drilling for oil on land owned by the United States. The government instituted a suit against the company to regain possession and, in 1916, the government secured the appointment of a receiver to supervise the drilling company's operations and to hold its income

---

[46] *Penn v. Robertson*, 115 F.2d 167, 40-2 USTC ¶ 9707 (4th Cir. 1940).

[47] 1974-2 CB 98.

[48] *Burnet v. Sanford & Brooks Co.*, 282 U.S. 359 (1931).

[49] 286 U.S. 417 (1932). The claim of right doctrine has been reaffirmed by the Supreme Court on several occasions, and thus has become a firmly established principle of federal income taxation.

[50] *Id.*

from its drilling activity. The receiver collected the income but did not make any payments to the company. In 1917, the district court dismissed the government's suit and the receiver paid the collected income to the drilling company. The money paid to the company in 1917 represented the net profits it had earned from its drilling activities on the property in 1916 during the receivership.

The net profits were entered on the company's books as income, and were reported as income on an amended return filed in 1918. In an audit of that return, the IRS determined that the income was realized in 1917, not 1918. On appeal to the Supreme Court, the issue was in which tax year were the net profits considered to be taxable income. After holding that the profits were not income to the taxpayer while the property was operated by the receiver, the Court determined that the net profits were taxable as income in 1917, the year in which they were paid to the taxpayer. This determination was grounded in the now famous quote by Justice Brandeis:

> If a taxpayer receives earnings under a claim of right and without restriction as to its disposition, he has received income which he is required to return, even though it may still be claimed that he is not entitled to retain the money, and even though he may still be adjudged liable to restore its equivalent. [Citations omitted.] If in 1922 the government had prevailed, and the company had been obliged to refund the profits received in 1917, it would have been entitled to a deduction from the profits of 1922, not from those of any earlier year.[51]

The claim of right doctrine has been reaffirmed by the Supreme Court on several occasions since *North American Oil* and has become a firmly established principle of federal income taxation.[52] The claim of right doctrine is based on the concept of the annual accounting system for the reporting of income.[53] Under this concept, income must be determined at the close of the taxable year without regard to possible subsequent events. All revenue acts which have been enacted since the adoption of the 16th amendment, have uniformly assessed taxes on the basis of annual returns showing the net result of all taxpayer transactions during a fixed accounting period, either the calendar year or a fiscal year.

[A] Effect of Doctrine

The claim of right doctrine applies even when the taxpayer is *not entitled to retain* the income and might be *obligated to return it*. Accordingly, the doctrine applies, among other things, to income received under a mistake of fact. Consider the following hypothetical, for example.

---

51 286 U.S. at 424.

52 *See Skelly Oil Co. v. United States*, 394 U.S. 680, 69-1 USTC ¶9343 (1969).

53 *See* §2.01, *supra*.

A taxpayer receives a bonus from his employer in 2020 that the employer later asserts was incorrectly computed. In 2021, the taxpayer repays a portion of the bonus. Under the annual accounting system and the claim of right doctrine, the taxpayer cannot amend his 2020 return to exclude from income the portion of the bonus he repaid in the later year. The annual accounting system and the claim of right doctrine fixes the year in which the taxpayer received income even though the taxpayer was ultimately not entitled to retain the money.[54]

In *Glenn Hightower v. Commissioner*,[55] the Petitioner and Daniel O'Dowd each owned 50% of the stock of an S corporation. O'Dowd exercised his rights under the shareholders' agreement to buy the Petitioner's shares. The Petitioner opposed the buyout in arbitration proceedings to which Petitioner and O'Dowd had agreed to be bound. In 2000, the arbitrator ruled against the Petitioner and Petitioner received $41,585,388 in exchange for his stock. Petitioner deposited the payment in an interest-bearing account. From 2000 to 2003, Petitioner unsuccessfully opposed the buyout in the California state courts. The petitioner received no dividends from the corporation in 2000, but he retained the right to receive dividends and vote his shares of stock. The court ruled that the Petitioner was taxable on the payment he received for his stock and related interest in the years paid.

[B] Circumstances Where Doctrine Applies

The claim of right doctrine relates to *when* income is taxable rather than *whether* it is taxable.[56]

Where the following circumstances exist, the claim of right doctrine applies:

- Receipt by the taxpayer of *income* in whatever form;
- Control by the taxpayer without restriction over the utilization or the disposition of money or property; and
- Assertion by the taxpayer of some claim of right or entitlement to receipt.[57]

The claim of right doctrine does not apply to money or property received under circumstances where the receipt is not income, such as in the case of a loan or an advancement. The doctrine does not create income where no income exists.[58] For example, assume the following:

---

[54] *See United States v. Lewis*, 51-1 USTC ¶9211, 340 U.S. 590 (1951).

[55] T.C. Memo. 2005-274.

[56] *Growers Credit Corp. v. Comm'r*, 33 T.C. 981 (1960).

[57] Actual receipt of the income may not be necessary if the principle of constructive receipt applies. Claim of right applies to both the cash and the accrual method of accounting. However, the Claim of Right Doctrine does not apply unless there is a reasonable expectation that the income which has accrued will be received. *See Brooklyn Union Gas Co. v. Comm'r*, 62 F.2d 505, 3 USTC ¶1033 (2d Cir. 1933).

[58] *Bohn v. Comm'r*, 72-1 USTC ¶9286, 456 F.2d 851 (8th Cir. 1972).

> Sam obtains a $25,000 loan from a bank, secured, in part, by property that he does not own. Although it is likely that Sam will be required to return the money before the end of the loan term and that he has received the money under a claim of right, he has not received income. Because loan proceeds are not gross income, the claim of right doctrine does not apply to Sam's transaction.[59]

In TAM 9735002, the Service ruled that membership deposits received by a country club were nontaxable loans, not income.

Agency also plays a role in claim of right.

For a cash method taxpayer, the claim of right doctrine does not apply unless the income in question has actually or constructively been received. Thus, in *All Americas Trading Corp. v. Commissioner*,[60] the Tax Court held that kickbacks received by a corporation's purchasing agents were not included in the corporation's gross income under the claim of right doctrine in the year that they were received by the agent, even though the corporation sued the agent for them, because the agent had command over the kickbacks and the corporation had not actually or constructively received them.

[C] *Uncertainty of Income Status or Amount*

The claim of right doctrine does not apply to the receipt of money or property if, at the time of receipt, it cannot be determined whether the money or property received constitutes income. Consider, for example, the following:

> In 2020, Dan receives $5,000 from Matt as consideration for an option to purchase real property for $60,000. Dan's adjusted basis in the property is $65,000. The option expires on December 31, 2021. The $5,000 will be ordinary income if the option is permitted to expire without exercise, or will be non-taxed return of capital if the option is exercised. In 2020, it is impossible to determine whether the $5,000 will be income because Matt's decision will not be known with certainty until December 31, 2021. The claim of right doctrine does not apply with respect to the $5,000 received in 2020.[61]

---

[59] One might argue that the "loan" may not be a loan at all but obtained under false information and under fraudulent circumstances. Whether the transaction is a loan is a question of fact. *See James v. United States*, 94-1 USTC ¶50,071, 366 U.S. 21 (1961), where the court said:

Whenever a taxpayer acquires earnings, lawfully or unlawfully, without the consensual recognition, express or implied, of an obligation to repay and without restriction as to their disposition, "he has received income which he is required to return, even though it may still be claimed that he is not entitled to retain the money, and even though he may still be adjudged liable to restore its equivalent." In such case, the taxpayer has "actual command over the property taxed—the actual benefit for which tax is paid. . . . " This standard brings wrongful appropriations within the broad sweep of "gross income"; it excludes loans.

[60] 29 T.C. 908 (1958). *See also Comm'r v. Turney*, 82 F.2d 661 (5th Cir. 1936).

[61] *Cf.* IRC § 1234.

On the other hand, if the money to be received constitutes income but the total amount of income to be received has not yet been determined, the claim of right doctrine *is* applicable. The following hypothetical is illustrative.

> Meg owns land that is condemned by the state. Her adjusted basis in the land is $150,000. The parties cannot agree on the fair market value of the land, but the state concedes that it is worth at least $500,000. The parties agree to litigate the issue, because Meg contends that the land is worth $750,000. In 2020, the state pays Meg $600,000. Litigation is expected to be final in 2021. Under the claim of right doctrine, Meg has $450,000 of gain realized in 2020 even though she may have additional gain in subsequent years.

An interesting case where the nature of the transaction provided uncertainty is Private Letter Ruling 200308046 where a father, concerned with his own medical situation and desiring a simple and orderly accounting of his affairs, deeded his personal residence to his sons but retained a life estate. Prior to the execution of the deed, the father requested and received an oral promise from his two sons to reconvey the property to the father if he wanted the residence returned. The deed was executed on Date 1. Three years later, father wanted to move to another state and asked his sons to return the residence so that he could sell the property. Both sons refused. Shortly thereafter, the father brought a lawsuit seeking to create a constructive trust and a reconveyance of the residence. After opposing the father's lawsuit, the sons, under a stipulation of settlement on Date 2, and ordered by the court, deeded the residence back to the father.

Notably the father continued to use the residence and the sons never had either actual command or actual benefit from residence. The sons did not realize income in any form after they received the residence. The court determined the gift to be invalid. Since the sons had no command over the property, they never owned it under a claim of right.[62]

[D] Claim of Right vs. Prepaid Income

In Chapter 6, we examine the accrual method and prepaid income. Most cases that have examined prepaid income generally do not address claim of right.[63] There is similarity between prepaid income cases and claim of right cases. In both instances, the taxpayer has a right to the income but is subject to a continuing obligation to repay it. In the prepaid income cases, the contingency arises because the taxpayer has

---

[62] The Service distinguished its ruling from *Healy v. Comm'r*, 345 U.S. 278, 53-1 USTC ¶9292 (1953), when a law-abiding taxpayer mistakenly receives income or property in one year, which receipt is assailed and found to be invalid in a subsequent year, the taxpayer must nonetheless report the amount as "gross income."

[63] *See Automobile Club of Michigan v. Comm'r*, 353 U.S. 180, 57-1 USTC ¶9593 (1957) (prepaid income was not addressed); *American Automobile Association v. United States*, 367 U.S. 687, 61-2 USTC ¶9517 (1961) (prepaid income not addressed); *Schlude v. Comm'r*, 372 U.S. 128, 63-1 USTC ¶9284 (1963) (again prepaid income was not addressed).

not yet performed the services for which prepayment has been made and, thus, has not yet earned the income. As a result, the issue is whether prepayment constitutes income when it is received. In the claim of right cases, the receipt is income, but the appropriate year for its inclusion in gross income is in question.

[E] Restrictions on Disposition

The claim of right doctrine is inapplicable if there are restrictions on the taxpayer's disposition of the funds, provided the restrictions arise out of the receipt of the funds and not as a result of independently established restrictions, such as a garnishment of wages. These restrictions may be imposed by law or by contractual arrangement. Examples of restrictions on the disposition of income that render the claim of right doctrine inapplicable include:

- The deposit of funds in a joint bank account pending determination of proper apportionment between the joint tenants;
- The segregation of prepaid legal fees into a restricted account pursuant to a state code of professional responsibility; and
- Restrictions imposed by a state agency upon a regulated utility.[64]

[F] Funds Received by Agent or Trustee

Closely related to restrictions on disposition is a taxpayer's receipt of funds in the capacity of an agent or trustee. In this situation, the taxpayer is described as a "mere collector or conduit through whom or which the income passes" and he is not taxed under the claim of right doctrine, even if the funds are commingled with his general assets.[65] Similarly, if the taxpayer is acting merely as a conduit for funds that constitute income to another person, the claim of right doctrine does not apply.[66]

It is not clear whether agency or trusteeship must be established by a legally enforceable agreement. Some courts have buttressed their findings of a conduit relationship with the existence of legally enforceable agreements, while other courts have held a taxpayer to be a conduit in the absence of such an agreement. If a

---

[64] *Cf. Monroe Abstract Corp. v. Comm'r*, 41 BTA 5, 9 (1940) (arrangement between taxpayer and company insuring its title searches requiring taxpayer to deposit a portion of its income from title searches in a reserve account against future losses was held not to prevent taxation of amounts placed in reserve). *But cf. Preston v. Comm'r*, 35 BTA 312, 321 (1937), *acq.* (two attorneys received a check payable to the order of both for services rendered but could not agree upon their respective shares; funds held in account pending determination of such). *See also Collins v. Comm'r*, 31 TCM 835 (1972) (funds deposited in restricted bank account pending outcome of litigation).

[65] *Lashell's Estate v. Comm'r*, 208 F.2d 430, 435, 54-1 USTC ¶9102 (6th Cir. 1953) (no claim of right income where agreement to pay funds to another actually performed, without regard to whether or not agreement legally enforceable); *Brown v. Comm'r*, 36 TCM 468, 470 (1977) (taxpayer found to be a conduit in third party's tax avoidance scheme).

[66] *See, e.g., Nunez v. Comm'r*, T.C. Memo. 1969-216.

taxpayer retains the funds for himself in contravention of an applicable agreement, his status as a conduit is destroyed, and he can be taxed on the retained amount.[67]

[G] *Bona Fide Nature of Claim*

The claim of right doctrine applies as long as the taxpayer treats the income (including illegal income) as belonging to him.[68] So long as the taxpayer's claim is bona fide and exists at the time of the receipt, the doctrine applies, even though the taxpayer has claimed the income through a mistake, or other event. This situation is consistent with the principle that an embezzler must include embezzled funds in gross income but is not entitled to the relief allowed under IRC § 1341. Congress intended to limit the applicability of IRC § 1341 to cases where the taxpayer received the income under a claim of right.[69] In order to utilize the relief provided by IRC § 1341, the taxpayer must have a bona fide and legitimate claim to the income at the time of receipt.[70] Moreover, if the taxpayer has a bona fide claim to the income, and receives the income "without restriction as to its disposition," the income is still received under a claim of right "even though it may still be claimed that he is not entitled to retain the money, and even though he may still be adjudged to restore its equivalent."[71]

[H] *Repayment of Claim-of-Right Income*

The claim of right doctrine applies regardless of whether the taxpayer acknowledges the possibility he will be required to repay some or all of the money received

---

[67] *Cf. Mathers v. Comm'r*, 57 T.C. 666, 679-80 (1972), *acq.* (taxpayer-retailer who retains sales taxes in contravention of state law taxed under claim of right). *See also Angelus Funeral Home v. Comm'r*, 47 T.C. 391, 398-99 (1967), *acq, aff'd*, 407 F.2d 210, 69-1 USTC ¶9216 (9th Cir.), *cert. denied*, 396 U.S. 824 (1969) (amounts deposited in valid trust includable by trustee where agreement granted trustee wide discretion as to use of funds).

[68] When a taxpayer acquires earnings, lawfully or unlawfully, without the consensual recognition, express or implied, of an obligation to repay and without restriction as to their disposition, "he has received income which he is required to return, even though it may still be claimed that he is not entitled to retain the money, and even though he may still be adjudged liable to restore its equivalent." *James v. United States*, 366 U.S. 213, 219, 61-1 USTC ¶9449 (1961), *citing Rutkin v. United States*, 343 U.S. 130, 137, 52-1 USTC ¶9260 (1952).

[69] *See generally McKinney v. United States*, 574 F.2d 1240 (5th Cir. 1978) (embezzled funds not received under a claim of right; IRC § 1341 treatment denied to taxpayer upon repayment of funds); *see also United States v. Skelly Oil Co.*, 69-1 USTC ¶9343, 394 U.S. 678 (1969); *Van Cleave v. United States*, 83-2 USTC ¶9620, 718 F.2d 193 (6th Cir. 1983); Reg. §§ 1.1341-1(a)(1), (2). *See* ¶2.03, *infra*.

[70] *See Perez v. United States*, 553 F. Supp. 558, 83-1 USTC ¶9106 (M.D. Fl. 1982).

[71] *North American Oil Co. v. Burnet*, 286 U.S. 417, 424 (1932); *see, e.g., Lewis v. Comm'r*, 340 U.S. 590 (1951) (employee received salary bonus under a bona fide claim of right, even though employee was subsequently required to return the bonus when it was discovered that the bonus was based on incorrect salary computations). *See* ¶2.03 *infra*.

and whether the money is set aside as a reserve for repayment, because there is no involuntary restriction on use.[72]

[I] Agreement to Repay—Renouncement

Mere possession of income that a taxpayer admits belongs to another person may put the income beyond the reach of the claim of right doctrine. For example, in *Commissioner v. Turney*,[73] Turney challenged the decision of the Board of Tax Appeals that one-half of the amounts of bonus money paid in 1929 to him by the lessee under two oil and gas leases was not taxable as income. Turney owned the surface rights to the land, but the right to minerals in that land was reserved by the state of Texas. The Board of Tax Appeals said that Turney's receipt of the funds had the effect of obligating him unconditionally to pay that money to another. The fact that at the time of the hearing before the Board of Tax Appeals Turney had not complied with his obligation as agent did not entitle him to receive taxable income. That money being income of the state, in the hands of its agent, was forbidden to be included in Turney's gross income.[74] The claim of right doctrine does not apply if the taxpayer, either before or immediately after receiving the income, renounces any right to it.[75] For a renouncement to be effective, it must occur during the taxable year in which the money is received.

In *U.S. v. Merrill*,[76] the plaintiff, Merrill, received $12,500 of his executor's fee in 1939 and the remaining $7,500 thereof in 1940. Both payments were made out of his deceased wife's segregated one-half share of the community property. At the end of the year 1940, Merrill made entries in the books of the estate and in his personal books to show an indebtedness by him to the estate of $10,000, an amount which had been erroneously paid to him from the deceased wife's share of the property. This amount was repaid in cash by Merrill in 1943 to the trust set up pursuant to his wife's will.

The Service argued that Merrill received the entire $20,000 fee out of his wife's estate under a "claim of right" in the years 1939 and 1940 and was therefore taxable on the full amount of the respective sums actually received by him during those years, despite the fact that $10,000 of that amount was received out of his wife's estate as a result of a mistake and was repaid in a later year. The Court cited *North American Oil Consolidated Co. v. Burnet*,[77] with the most oft-quoted statement of the "claim of right" rule:

---

[72] In *Etoll Estate v. Comm'r*, 79 T.C. 676 (1982), the tax court held that the claim of right doctrine applied to receivables collected by a partner under an agreement allocating all of the partnership assets to the partner upon dissolution, even though the other partner successfully challenged the agreement and even though the partner acknowledged the possibility of the other partner's success, because the partner initially used the amount collected for personal purposes.

[73] 36-1 USTC ¶9167, 82 F.2d 661 (5th Cir. 1936).

[74] 82 F.2d 661, 662, 36-1 USTC ¶9167.

[75] *Bishop v. Comm'r*, 25 T.C. 969 (1956).

[76] 211 F.2d 297, 54-1 USTC ¶9275 (9th Cir. 1954).

[77] 286 U.S. 417, 3 USTC ¶943 (1932).

> If a taxpayer receives earnings under a claim of right and without restriction as to its disposition, he has received income which he is required to return, even though it may still be claimed that he is not entitled to retain the money, and even though he may still be adjudged liable to restore its equivalent.[78]

In *Merrill*, the taxpayer received an overpayment of $2,500 from his deceased wife's estate in 1939. The mistake was not discovered until 1940 and the sum was not repaid until 1943. As executor, he paid the funds to himself, as an individual, under an honest mistake. As an individual, he received the funds under a good faith claim of right. He therefore had to include in income the $2,500 he erroneously received from his wife's share of the community funds in 1939.

A different issue was presented with respect to the $7,500 in executor's fees which were mistakenly paid out of the wife's share of the community property in 1940. As to that part of the fee, the mistake was discovered in the same year as the sum was received (1940) and appropriate adjustments were made in his own books and those of his wife's estate in that year in recognition of the mistake. Accordingly, the court determined the $7,500 receipt in 1940 was outside the operation of the "claim of right" rule.

In so holding, the court said:

> We are not aware that the rule has ever been applied where, as here, in the same year that the funds are mistakenly received, the taxpayer discovers and admits the mistake, renounces his claim to the funds, and recognizes his obligation to repay them. We think there is no warrant for extending the harsh claim of right doctrine to such a situation. In such case the Internal Revenue Bureau is not faced with the problem of deciding the merits of the claim to the funds received, for the question has been resolved by the interested parties. No question is here raised as to the bona fides of Merrill's 1940 bookkeeping entries relative to the mistaken payments. Good faith is indicated by the fact that the taxpayer's $7,500 obligation to the estate was not only recognized by him in 1940 but was paid in cash in 1943.
>
> We conclude that Merrill is not taxable on the $7,500 in executor's fees which he received in 1940, but that he is taxable upon the $2,500 he received in 1939.[79]

Although the *Merrill* exception has been recognized in several circuits,[80] it has been limited, rather than expanded, in the years since its inception. *Merrill* has been interpreted to require that the obligation to repay be unconditional in the year of

---

[78] 286 U.S. 417, 424, 3 USTC ¶943.

[79] 211 F.2d 297, 302, 54-1 USTC ¶9275.

[80] *Hope v. Comm'r*, 471 F.2d 738, 73-1 USTC ¶9168 (3d Cir.), *cert. denied*, 414 U.S. 824 (1973); *Comm'r v. Gaddy*, 344 F.2d 460, 65-1 USTC ¶9342 (5th Cir. 1965); *Frelbro Corp. v. Comm'r*, 315 F.2d 784, 63-1 USTC ¶9388 (2d Cir. 1963).

receipt; contingent liabilities will not suffice.[81] Also, the exception has been applied only to funds received by mistake, and has not been extended to funds received through embezzlement or other illegal means.[82]

Courts that reject *Merrill* point out that it was decided under the 1939 Code, before the existence of IRC § 1341, which eliminates the harsh effect upon which the exception is based.[83] It has also been observed that the exception was established upon stipulated facts without argument by the IRS. The most compelling justification for a rejection of the *Merrill* exception is its inherent inconsistency with the cash method,[84] which recognizes income and deductions upon actual receipt and payment, not upon a mere agreement to repay. Since the Supreme Court has yet to decide this issue, the continuing vitality of the exception is uncertain.[85]

Indeed, in *Nowlin v. Commissioner*,[86] the taxpayer sold stolen computer monitors to a third party for a check for $100,000. In doing so, the taxpayer exercised complete, unrestricted dominion and control over the $100,000 check from the date of the sale (Sept. 18, 1989) until the check was seized by police on October 12, 1989.

The taxpayer argued that because police seized the proceeds of the sale during the same taxable year of the sale, the exception to the claim of right doctrine set out in *United States v. Merrill* relieves the taxpayer from realizing a gain.[87] In the *Merrill* case, the taxpayer was allowed to exclude a sum mistakenly received for his services as executor under a claim of right where, in the same year the funds were received, he "discovers and admits the mistake, renounces his claim to the funds, and recognizes his obligation to repay them."[88]

---

[81] *Hope v. Comm'r*, 471 F.2d 738, 742, 73-1 USTC ¶ 9168 (3d Cir. 1973), *cert. denied*, 414 U.S. 824 (1973) (claim of right doctrine inapplicable where taxpayer's obligation to return funds from sale of stock was subject to a condition precedent, the filing of a suit for rescission of the sale, a condition entirely within the taxpayer's control).

[82] *Buff v. Comm'r*, 496 F.2d 847, 74-1 USTC ¶ 9353 (2d Cir. 1974) (embezzler who signed a confession of judgment in same year as embezzlement); *United States v. Hauff*, 461 F.2d 1061, 1067, 72-1 USTC ¶ 9433 (7th Cir.), *cert. denied*, 409 U.S. 873 (1972) (fraud); *Norman v. Comm'r*, 407 F.2d 1337, 1338, 69-1 USTC ¶ 9245 (3d Cir.), *cert. denied*, 395 U.S. 947 (1969) (no consensual agreement to repay embezzled funds at time of receipt); *Krakowski v. Comm'r*, T.C. Memo. 1993-266, 65 TCM 2969 (repaid embezzled campaign funds were received under claim of right and were taxable to taxpayer in year received; taxpayer received money under mistaken belief that she had legal right to remaining campaign funds, and in year of receipt she did not discover mistake, renounce claim to the funds, and recognize repayment obligation; correctness of her belief was irrelevant to application of claim of right doctrine. Taxpayer had no unequivocal contractual, statutory, or regulatory duty to repay, and she had unrestricted use of funds).

[83] For a discussion of IRC § 1341 relief, *see* § 9.03, *below*.

[84] *See* Chapter 4, *infra*, for a discussion of the cash method of accounting.

[85] *See Don E. Williams Co. v. Comm'r*, 429 U.S. 568, 77-1 USTC ¶ 9221 (1977) (contribution to profit sharing plan not paid by delivery of promissory demand note and therefore no deduction to cash method taxpayer); *Helvering v. Price*, 309 U.S. 409, 40-1 USTC ¶ 9336 (1940) (substitution of one note for another not payment); *Eckert v. Burnet*, 283 U.S. 140, 2 USTC ¶ 714 (1931) (substitution of new note for worthless note on which taxpayer was guarantor insufficient to support worthless debt deduction).

[86] T.C. Memo. 1992-456.

[87] *United States v. Merrill*, 54-1 USTC ¶ 9275, 211 F.2d 297 (9th Cir. 1954).

[88] *Id.* at 304.

The *Nowlin* court noted facts were distinguishable from those in *Merrill*. The taxpayer's acts were criminal in nature, not the result of an honest or good faith mistake. *Merrill* emphasized the "good faith" nature of the taxpayer's mistake. In *Nowlin*, there was no evidence of good faith or honest mistakes. Moreover, the court said the application of *Merrill* is based upon the consensual recognition of an obligation to repay within the same year the funds are obtained.[89] There was no consensual recognition of an obligation to repay in *Nowlin*.

Moreover, the court said "it is of little consequence that [Taxpayer]personally received no money from the transaction, for it is the power to dispose of income and the exercise of that power that determines whether taxable income has been received."[90] Additionaly, the court said that even if it applied *Merrill* the taxpayer's argument would fail.

Example 2-4

In 2020, Bernie sold stock to Gullible. Bernie did not own the stock, but made it appear as though he did. Bernie therefore has no adjusted basis, but the amount received is amount realized, and his gain equals the amount realized. Under the claim of right doctrine, Bernie must include the gain in gross income because he treated the sales proceeds as though they were his own.

The claim of right doctrine applies if the recognition of the other person's right to the income is not bona fide. Thus, a taxpayer's promise to repay embezzled funds, given in the form of an affidavit of confession signed at the employer's insistence, is meaningless if there is no bona fide intent to repay and never any repayment in fact.[91]

[J] Contingent Repayment Obligations

Application of the claim of right doctrine is not precluded merely because the taxpayer is subject to a contingent obligation to repay some or all of the income that the taxpayer has received.[92]

In *Rosenberg v. Commissioner*,[93] the tax court held that an attorney who collected a legal fee, but who agreed to repay a portion of the fee if the litigation was unsuccessful, was required to include the entire fee in gross income under the claim of right doctrine, regardless of whether a portion was repaid in a subsequent year.

---

[89] *Buff v. Comm'r*, 58 T.C. 224 (1972), *rev'd.*, 74-1 USTC ¶9353, 496 F.2d 847 (2d Cir. 1974).

[90] *Hardin v. United States*, 72-1 USTC ¶9464, 461 F.2d 865, 872 (5th Cir. 1972), quoting *Sammons v. United States*, 70-2 USTC ¶9678, 433 F.2d 728, 732 (5th Cir. 1970)).

[91] *Buff v. Comm'r*, 496 F.2d 847 (2d Cir. 1974).

[92] *Phillips v. Comm'r*, 238 F.2d 473, 56-2 USTC ¶10,067 (7th Cir. 1956).

[93] T.C. Memo. 1956-68. *See also Nordberg v. Comm'r*, 79 T.C. 655 (1982), *aff'd by court order*, 720 F.2d 658 (1st Cir. 1983).

[K] *Deduction in Case of Repayment*

In *North American Oil Consolidated v. Burnet*,[94] the Supreme Court ruled that if a taxpayer included a receipt in gross income under the claim of right doctrine and was required to repay it in a subsequent taxable year, the taxpayer is entitled to a deduction in the year of repayment.[95] Typically, the taxpayer's right to a deduction in the year of repayment depends on whether the repayment meets the requirements of the statutory provisions permitting deductions.

Various statutory provisions support deductions for repayment of amounts received under a claim of right. If the repayment is made in connection with a trade or business, an activity engaged in for the production of income, or a transaction entered into for profit, IRC §§162, 212, and 165, respectively, support the deduction. Most repayments of claim-of-right income are authorized under one or more of these provisions. Even deductions for repayments of embezzled funds can be justified under IRC §165(c)(2), as losses incurred in transactions entered into for profit.[96]

[L] *Pending Disputes*

The claim of right doctrine often applies when a taxpayer receives income with respect to which there is a dispute and the taxpayer treats the income as though there is no dispute.[97]

Disputes frequently arise with respect to compensation agreements.[98] They also arise often in connection with construction contracts.[99] An example is *United States v. Lewis*.[100] In *Lewis*, the Court of Claims reviewed a refund suit of an alleged overpayment of a taxpayer's 1944 income. On his 1944 income tax return, the taxpayer reported about $22,000, which he had received that year as an employee bonus. Because of subsequent litigation in a state court, however, it was decided that the taxpayer's bonus had been improperly computed and therefore the taxpayer was

---

[94] 286 U.S. 417, 3 USTC ¶943 (1932).

[95] 286 U.S. 424, 3 USTC ¶944. Subsequently, the Court twice reaffirmed the position barring adjustments to income for the year of receipt. *Healy v. Comm'r*, 345 U.S. 278, 53-1 USTC ¶9292 (1953).

[96] Generally, it is immaterial to the taxpayer which of these provisions is used to support the deduction; however, a difference will result if a net operating loss is involved. *See Yerkie v. Comm'r*, 67 T.C. 388 (1976) (repayment of embezzled funds deductible under IRC §165(c)(2) as loss incurred in transaction entered into for profit cannot support net operating loss deduction under IRC §172 which generally requires operation of trade or business). *See also James v. United States*, 366 U.S. 213, 220, 61-1 USTC ¶9449 (1961) (to extent victim recovers misappropriated funds, there is a reduction of embezzler's income); Rev. Rul. 65-254, 1965-2 CB 50 (deduction allowed embezzler on repayment of embezzled funds). Public policy does not bar deduction of these repayments since these payments are neither illegal payments nor penalties. *See* IRC §§162(c)(2), 162(f); Rev. Rul. 82-74, 1982-1 CB 110 (taxpayer who makes restitution after committing arson sustains a deductible tax loss to extent amounts previously included in income).

[97] *See Topeka Flour Mills, Co. v. Comm'r*, 12 BTA 147 (1928).

[98] *See Downing v. Comm'r*, 43 BTA 1147 (1941).

[99] *See Pederson v. Comm'r*, 14 BTA 1089 (1929).

[100] 51-1 USTC ¶9211, 71 S. Ct. 522 (1951).

required to return approximately $11,000 to his employer. Until payment in 1946, taxpayer had at all times full use of the $22,000 and used it as his own in good faith, although mistaken. The taxpayer attempted to recompute his 1944 taxes but the government said that the taxpayer should treat the repayment in 1946 as a "loss." The position of the government clearly demonstrated the application of the annual accounting concept; that is, once the year is closed, one cannot revisit the tax year and recompute one's taxes. The Supreme Court, relying on *North American Oil*,[101] reiterated what the Court said at that time which was that nothing in the language of the decision provides an exception merely because a taxpayer is mistaken as to the validity of his claim. Again, citing *Burnet v. Sanford and Brooks*,[102] the Supreme Court interpreted the claim of right doctrine to provide finality to the period within which income should be reported. The Court said that the annual accounting concept was deeply rooted in the federal tax system; therefore, the taxpayer was required to report income in 1944, when he had unrestricted control over the funds, rather than recomputing his income. The taxpayer was allowed to obtain a deduction, however, in 1946 when he repaid the income.

[M] Violations of Law; Illegitimate Claims

The claim of right doctrine applies if the taxpayer treats the income as belonging to him even though the taxpayer's claim to the income violates the law.[103] In applying the claim of right doctrine to illegally obtained income, the Supreme Court, in *James v. United States*,[104] restated the claim of right doctrine without using the phrase "claim of right."

> When a taxpayer acquires earnings, lawfully or unlawfully, without the consensual recognition, express or implied, of an obligation to repay and without restriction as to their disposition, "he has received income which he is required to return, even though it may still be claimed that he is not entitled to retain the money, and even though he may still be adjudged liable to restore its equivalent." *North American Oil v. Burnet*, supra, at p. 424. In such case, the taxpayer has "actual command over the property taxed—the actual benefit for which the tax is paid," *Corliss v. Bowers*, supra. This standard brings wrongful appropriations within the broad sweep of "gross income;" it excludes loans.[105]

---

[101] 286 U.S. 417, 3 USTC ¶943 (1932).

[102] 282 U.S. 359, 51 S. Ct. 150, 75 L. Ed. 383, 2 USTC ¶636 (1979).

[103] *James v. United States*, 366 U.S. 213, 61-1 USTC ¶9449 (1961). *See also Ianniello v. Comm'r*, 98 T.C. 165 (1992), which held that convicted racketeers must recognize taxable income for skimming receipts even though the receipts were later forfeited to the government. *James* reversed *Comm'r v. Wilcox*, 41-1 USTC ¶9188, 66 S. Ct. 546 (1946), where the Supreme Court held that embezzled money does not constitute taxable income to the embezzler in the year of the embezzlement under §22(a) of the Internal Revenue Code of 1939.

[104] 366 U.S. 213, 81 S. Ct. 1052, 6 L. Ed. 2d 246, 61-1 USTC ¶9449.

[105] 366 U.S. 213, 215, 61-1 USTC ¶9449.

Embezzled funds are included in the gross income of the embezzler under the claim of right doctrine.[106]

[N] *Additional Basis for Claim of Right*

Breach of Fiduciary Duty

The claim of right doctrine applies to a trustee's misappropriation of loan funds procured by the trust through the trustee's fraudulent behavior.[107] It also applies to income received under compensation contracts procured in a manner that violates the taxpayer's fiduciary duty to another person, even if some or all of the amounts so received must be returned in a subsequent year.[108]

Breach of Contract

The claim of right doctrine applies to income received through breach of contract, even though the amounts received must later be returned.[109]

§2.03 IRC §1341 Relief for Repayment of Claim of Right Receipts

[A] *Generally*

Because of the application of both the claim of right doctrine and the annual accounting system, such as in the *Lewis*[110] case, where the deduction in the year of repayment of an item previously included in gross income under the claim of right doctrine does not provide as much of a reduction in tax liability as the tax generated by the previous income inclusion, Congress enacted IRC §1341. Under IRC §1341, a taxpayer is permitted to forgo the deduction in the year of repayment so that they can reduce their tax liability for that year by the amount of the tax liability generated by the previous inclusion. Without IRC §1341, a taxpayer who has received income under a claim of right would often be unable to achieve tax parity.

There are a number of factors which prevent the taxpayer from receiving enough benefit from the deduction to offset the tax paid on the receipt of the income:

- the taxpayer's income in the year of the deduction may be in a lower tax bracket than in the year the income was received;
- the general rate of taxation may be lower in the later year;

---

106 In contrast, in *Kreimer v. Comm'r*, T.C. Memo. 1983-672, the tax court held that loans obtained through false pretenses were not included in gross income under the claim of right doctrine because there was a consensual recognition that they would be repaid, even though the lenders were unaware that the money had been used for purposes other than for those which the loan was made.

107 *Webb v. United States*, 15 F.3d 203 (1st Cir. 1994).

108 *Griffin v. Smith*, 101 F.2d 348 (7th Cir. 1938), *cert. denied*, 308 U.S. 561 (1939).

109 *Phillips v. Comm'r*, 262 F.2d 668 (9th Cir. 1959).

110 51-1 USTC ¶9211, 71 S. Ct. 522 (1951).

- the deduction may be a capital loss subject to the limitation on the deduction of capital losses, while the receipt of the money may have been ordinary income.

IRC § 1341 provides a statutory framework for relief from the claim of right doctrine. Under IRC § 1341(a), if income is included for a prior taxable year because it "appeared that the taxpayer had an unrestricted right to such income," a deduction is allowable for the tax year subsequent to the year of inclusion. Moreover, the taxpayer is permitted to recompute his taxable income in the year of repayment so as to neutralize the tax payment that was made on the prior year's income.

If the reduction exceeds the tax for the current year, the excess is treated as an overpayment of tax for the current year, made as of the last day for the filing of the return. The taxpayer is entitled to a refund.

Only those repayments that are made because the taxpayer did not have an unrestricted right to the income reported under a claim of right are eligible for IRC § 1341 relief.

[B] Conditions Necessary for IRC §1341 Relief

In order to obtain the benefits of IRC § 1341, certain requirements must be met:

- The item was included in gross income in a previous tax year;[111]
- The inclusion occurred because the taxpayer appeared to have an unrestricted right to the item;[112]
- In a later year, the taxpayer was entitled to a deduction;[113]
- The deduction was allowed because it was established after the close of the year of inclusion that the taxpayer did not have an unrestricted right to the item;[114]
- the amount of the deduction exceeded $3,000;[115] and
- The item has not arisen by reason of the sale of inventory type property, other than by a regulated public utility.[116]

IRC § 1341 applies both to cash and accrual method taxpayers.[117] The regulations say that in the case of a taxpayer on the cash method who constructively received an item of income under a claim of right and included such item of income in gross income in a prior year (or years), the provisions of IRC § 1341 shall be applicable to the taxable year in which the taxpayer is required to relinquish his right to receive such item of income. If the taxpayer is on an accrual method, IRC § 1341 shall apply

---

111 IRC § 1341(a)(1).
112 *Id.*
113 IRC § 1341(a)(2).
114 *Id.*
115 IRC § 1341(a)(3).
116 IRC § 1341(b)(2).
117 Reg. § 1.1341-1(e).

to the year in which the obligation properly accrues for the repayment of the item included under a claim of right.[118]

The phrase "because it appeared that the taxpayer had an unrestricted right to such income" has been examined in a number of Revenue Rulings, notably Rev. Rul. 68-153.[119] In this ruling, the IRS described what it believed Congress meant when it created the relief under IRC § 1341. The IRS said the term "appeared" refers to a *semblance of an unrestricted right* in the year received, as distinguished from an *unchallengeable right* and from *absolutely no right at all*. The former is more than an "apparent right," and the latter, less than an "absolute right." Whether the taxpayer has the "semblance of an unrestricted right" in the year of inclusion depends on all the facts available at the end of such year. Accordingly, a repayment of embezzled funds, even though it may be deductible, is not eligible for IRC § 1341 relief because the funds were not received under a semblance of an unrestricted right.[120] Similarly, funds received by smuggling marijuana were not afforded IRC § 1341 relief.[121]

As to payments which a taxpayer has an unchallengeable right to receive, the statutory restrictions seem designed to ensure a direct connection between the receipt of the payment items and their required repayment. It must be established in the subsequent year that in the year of inclusion the taxpayer did not in fact, or in law, have an unrestricted right to the amount in question.[122] If the right to the payment is absolute, the fact that a subsequent liability arises in a related transaction should not entitle the taxpayer to the special relief of IRC § 1341. Accordingly, bad debt deductions are not entitled to IRC § 1341 treatment because, even though the debt is uncollectible, the taxpayer's right to payment is unrestricted. This principle has also been applied to a seller of stock who commenced litigation to rescind a sale. Moreover, IRC § 1341 relief was held to be unavailable because the taxpayer, who could elect not to rescind, failed to show that his right to the sale proceeds was restricted.[123]

---

[118] *Id.*

[119] 1968-1 CB 371.

[120] Rev. Rul. 65-254, 1965-2 CB 50, 51. Note that the general rule of IRC § 1341(a) also does not apply with respect to restorations pursuant to the terms of a contract of prepaid interest when the note is paid in advance or to payment pursuant to the terms of a contract of liquidated damages and breach thereof because, in both cases, the taxpayer had an absolute right to retain the amounts as of the time of receipt and the ensuing liability to restore such amounts arose due to subsequent events. *See* Rev. Rul. 58-226, 1958-1 CB 318, and Rev. Rul. 67-48, 1967-1 CB 50.

[121] *Wood v. Comm'r*, 863 F.2d 417, 89-1 USTC ¶ 9143 (5th Cir. 1989). *See also Perez v. United States*, 553 F. Supp. 558 (M.D. Fl. 1982), 83-1 USTC ¶ 9106 (conspiracy to commit mail fraud).

[122] IRC § 1341(a)(2).

[123] *Hope v. Comm'r*, 471 F.2d 738, 743, 73-1 USTC ¶ 9168 (2d Cir.), *cert. denied*, 414 U.S. 824 (1973); *see also Wallace v. United States*, 309 F. Supp. 748, 70-1 USTC ¶ 9232 (S.D. Iowa 1970), *aff'd*, 439 F.2d 757, 71-1 USTC ¶ 9281 (8th Cir.), *cert. denied*, 404 U.S. 831 (1971) (IRC § 1341 inapplicable to dividends received by taxpayer on stock owned by him and paid over to former wife pursuant to divorce decree); *Uhlenbrock v. Comm'r*, 67 T.C. 818 (1977) (IRC § 1341 unavailable to executor who, after receiving commissions in one year, was required to pay additions to tax in a later year for failing to file an estate tax return; the addition to tax, although related to duties as executor, did not constitute repayment of commissions).

If the taxpayer's right to the item was unchallengeable in the year of inclusion but was undermined by facts arising subsequently, IRC § 1341 does not apply because the taxpayer's right to the item in the year of inclusion already exists. As examples, consider a repayment of prepaid interest when a debt is paid in advance and a payment of liquidated damages under a contract. In each case, the taxpayer is entitled to a deduction, but not to IRC § 1341 relief.[124]

Example 2-5

In early 2020, T. J Watters signed a contract with the Cardinals agreeing to play linebacker position for compensation of $10,000,000. He also agreed to a bonus of $1,000,000 for each sack that he made during the 2020 season. During the year, T. J Watters made 15 full sacks and two half sacks. For that T. J Watters was paid $16,000,000.

In March of the following year, the league changed the rules so that half sacks were no longer considered to be a statistic worthy of compensation. The football club requested a repayment from T. J Watters and eventually T. J Watters repaid the amount he received for the half sacks ($1,000,000). In 2020, T. J Watters included the half sacks compensation in income because he had an absolute right to the income at that time. The change in the rules in 2021 requiring T. J Watters to repay the half sack income arose in a subsequent year and therefore IRC § 1341 does not apply to the repayment.

In order for IRC § 1341 to apply, there must also be a sufficient connection (nexus) between the receipt and the later repayment (a relationship between deduction and inclusion). For example, in *Albert J. Uhlenbrock v. Commissioner*,[125] the executor of an estate used his own funds to pay a portion of a late filing penalty owed by the estate. The executor sought to deduct this payment under IRC § 1341 as if it were a repayment of a portion of his previously reported executor's commission.

(Footnote Continued)

See also Rev. Rul. 69-115, 1969-1 CB 50 (salary payments disallowed as unreasonable and repaid pursuant to agreement not subject to IRC § 1341); Rev. Rul. 67-437, 1967-2 CB 296 (same for repayments of reimbursed travel and entertainment expenditures). *See also* Rev. Rul. 68-153, 1968-1 CB 371, 372 (IRC § 1341 inapplicable when "[a]ll the facts available to the taxpayer in the year of inclusion indicated that the amount received was correctly computed using a proper freight or passenger rate, but all or part of the amount was restored in [a later year] because of a 'subsequent event,' such as a passenger ticket refund or a transit adjustment arising when goods shipped and billed at a local freight rate became entitled to a lower through rate"); Rev. Rul. 67-48, 1967-1 CB 50 (IRC § 1341 inapplicable to liquidated damages paid by taxpayer upon breach of contract); Rev. Rul. 58-226, 1958-1 CB 318 (IRC § 1341 inapplicable to repayments of prepaid interest when debtor prepaid loan principal).

[124] *See* Rev. Rul. 67-48, 1967-1 CB 50 (liquidated damages for breach of employment contract); Rev. Rul. 58-226, 1958-1 CB 318 (refund of prepaid interest).

[125] 67 T.C. 818 (1977).

The court held that while payment of the late filing penalty related to the taxpayer's general duties as executor, it did not constitute repayment of commissions.

In *Kraft v. United States*,[126] a podiatrist was convicted of mail fraud for filing false claims with an insurance company. The funds were received by his corporation which also employed another doctor. The doctor asserted that as a result of the repayment he was entitled to a claim of right. His claim was based on the fact that he knew at the time of filing the claim that he was not entitled to receive payment from the insurance company because erroneous names were given to the insurance company. The facts clearly demonstrated that the funds were received as a result of wrongful or illegal actions and, thus, do not benefit from IRC § 1341 relief. The recipient knowingly accepted monies under false pretenses by submitting claims under the names of false and fictitious individuals. He should have been aware that he had no "right" to the monies. Moreover, the repayment was not connected to the receipt of money from the insurance company as he never made a claim of right to the money received from the insurance company. Although the insurance company made payments in his name, he immediately deposited the funds directly in the account of his professional corporation. The corporation reported the payments as taxable income. The doctor elected to receive his taxable income from the professional corporation which co-mingled the insurance payments with funds from other sources. The doctor never included the insurance payments in his gross income. In other words, the doctor failed to meet the requirements for a deduction under IRC § 1341 because the doctor's obligation to make restitution to the insurance company did not arise out of the same circumstances, terms and conditions of his receipt of taxable income from the corporation.

In AOD 1992-008, the Service stated it will not follow the decision in *Barrett v. Commissioner*,[127] which allowed the taxpayer to take a credit under IRC § 1341 for the amount paid in settlement of a civil suit.

In 1981, Joseph Barrett, a shareholder in a stock brokerage firm, purchased options to buy stock based on "insider information" given to him by a fellow broker. Barrett sold the options within one week of purchase for $189,230. He reported $187,223 in short-term capital gain on his 1981 income tax return. The Securities and Exchange Commission (SEC) investigated the transaction but did not pursue criminal or administrative proceedings against him. However, third parties sued Barrett in private civil proceedings. Barrett settled the claim by disgorging $54,400 of his profit from the sale of the options. Barrett and his wife claimed a credit of $54,400 on their 1984 income tax return. They initially claimed the settlement payment as a business expense under IRC § 162. The Service disallowed the deduction. The Barretts then argued for a $54,400 credit under IRC § 1341.

The Tax Court held that the Barretts were entitled to the credit. The court reasoned that, because of the reduction in short-term gain of $54,400, the Barretts did

---

[126] 93-1 USTC ¶ 50,278, 991 F.2d 292 (6th Cir. 1993). *See also Culley v. United States*, 99-1 USTC ¶ 50,492 (Fed. Cl. 1999), and *Griffits v. United States*, 54 Fed. Cl. 198 (2002).

[127] 96 T.C. 713 (1991). (For a summary of the Tax Court's opinion, see Tax Notes, May 27, 1991, p. 1018.)

not have an "unrestricted right" to the proceeds from the sale of the options. The court relied on the decision in *United States v. Skelly*[128] for the proposition that when a settlement payment evidences sufficiently the absence of a taxpayer's unrestricted right to an item, IRC § 1341 is triggered. The Service stated that the Tax Court failed to consider whether there was evidence of a nexus between the obligation to repay and the original option profits received by the Barretts. Because no evidence was introduced substantiating the characterization of the payment as a settlement, the Service disagreed with the Tax Court's holding and will try to distinguish it on its facts in future cases. However, the Service will not appeal the decision "because its reasoning is incomplete."

An interesting case with taxpayer-favorable results is *Van Cleave v. United States*.[129] The taxpayer, Eugene Van Cleave, was president and majority stockholder of his closely-held corporation. In 1969, the corporation adopted a by-law requiring corporate officers who received income from the corporation that was determined by the Internal Revenue Service (IRS) to be excessive—and so not deductible by the corporation as a business expense—to pay back the amount determined to be excessive to the corporation. In addition, Mr. Van Cleave entered into a separate agreement requiring him to reimburse the corporation for nondeductible compensation.

Mr. Van Cleave received $332,000 in salary and bonuses in 1974. During 1975, the IRS audited the corporation's return, determined that $57,500 of Mr. Van Cleave's salary was excessive, and disallowed that portion of his salary as a deduction to the corporation. In December 1975, pursuant to the corporation's by-law and the agreement between Mr. Van Cleave and the corporation, Mr. Van Cleave repaid the nondeductible $57,500.

Mr. Van Cleave reported the full compensation on his calendar year 1974 income tax return. On his 1975 return, prepared with the repayment to the corporation in mind, he calculated his tax liability by using IRC § 1341. The IRS audited the return, and allowed a deduction for 1975 but disallowed the use of IRC § 1341, resulting in a tax deficiency of $5,987.34. Mr. Van Cleave paid the deficiency and brought an action for a refund.

The case turned on the interpretation of IRC § 1341.

The district court held that IRC § 1341 treatment was not available to Mr. Van Cleave because it determined that his repayment was voluntary. The district court determined that it was voluntary because Mr. Van Cleave owned a substantial majority of the stock and in that sense controlled the corporation. The district court also seemed to be persuaded by the argument that, if Mr. Van Cleave were allowed IRC § 1341 treatment under these circumstances, this would open the door to tax avoidance in that taxpayers who controlled corporations could "test the waters" in setting their compensation without risk of an adverse tax result.

On appeal, the issue of "voluntary repayment" was not argued by the IRS. Rather they argued that Mr. Van Cleave had more than an *appearance* of an un-

---

[128] 394 U.S. 678, *reh'g denied*, 395 U.S. 941 (1969).

[129] 718 F.2d 193, 83-2 USTC ¶ 9620 (6th Cir. 1975).

restricted right to the excess compensation in the year in which it was received, and that the right to the compensation became restricted only upon the occurrence of the IRS audit and determination in a subsequent year. The government maintained that, since Mr. Van Cleave had an unrestricted right to the compensation in the year of receipt, contingent only upon the happening of an event in a subsequent year, IRC § 1341 was not available to him.

In reversing the District's Court's decision, the Sixth Circuit agreed with the Fifth Circuit's reading of IRC § 1341 and held that a restriction on a taxpayer's right to income that does not arise until a year subsequent to the time of receipt did not affect the availability of an IRC § 1341 tax adjustment.

[C] Tax Calculation under IRC § 1341

IRC § 1341 relief is similar to amending the prior year tax return except that unlike with regard to an amended tax return, no interest for the intervening period is paid by the government and indeed no amended return is filed.

IRC § 1341(a)(4) provides that the tax is determined by deducting the repayment for the year when made.

Under § 1341(a)(5), the taxpayer computes tax liability through a three-step process:

- First, tax liability for the year of repayment is computed without taking into account the deduction for repayment;
- Second, the taxpayer computes the decrease in tax liability for the year of inclusion, including alternative minimum tax, that would result solely from excluding from gross income for that year an amount of income equal to the repayment (subject to limitations described in § 1341(a)(5)(b)); and
- Third, the taxpayer computes tax liability for the year of repayment by subtracting the result computed in the second step from the result computed in the first step.

[1] Recomputation of the Tax

Two methods for computing tax liability under IRC § 1341 are available.

The first method allows a taxpayer to claim a deduction to the extent of the claim of right amount previously included in gross income. This method is simply a restatement of preexisting law; it neither increases nor restricts the rules for deductibility of claim of right restorations that had developed under the common law of taxation. In computing the tax liability under this method, the amount allowable as a capital loss deduction is subject to the restrictions of IRC §§ 1211 and 1212,[130] even though these restrictions are not considered in determining the applicability of IRC § 1341.

---

[130] These include the loss limitation of the lower of $3,000 or the excess of the losses over gains.

The second method for computing tax liability under IRC § 1341 reduces the tax liability for the year of restoration (computed without the deduction) by decreasing the tax in the year of inclusion by the amount that would have resulted had the claim of right amount not been included in gross income in that year. The amount of tax payable for the current year under this method is first computed without taking any deduction for restoration payments. The amount of tax so computed is then reduced by the decrease in tax in the prior year that would have resulted from the exclusion of the item included in gross income under a claim of right in that year. If the decrease in tax in the prior year exceeds the tax otherwise payable in the current year (computed without the deduction), the excess is treated as an overpayment in the current year and can be claimed as a refund.

Which method should be used? IRC § 1341 requires taxpayers to use the method of computing tax liability which results in the lesser tax liability. If the tax liability is the same under both methods, the first method is used. If it is determined that the second method results in the lesser tax liability, the claim of right deduction cannot be taken into account for any purpose in computing taxable income or loss for the current taxable year.

If the amount restored relates to items included in gross income in more than one prior taxable year and the amount attributable to each of those years cannot readily be identified, the regulations[131] provide that the amount attributable to each prior year is determined by allocating the deduction in proportion to the claim of right inclusions in those years.

The tax for the current year is computed in the following way:

(1) Compute the tax in the usual way, as if IRC § 1341 did not exist, taking the repayment as a deduction.
(2) Recompute the tax in the usual way, except that the repayment is not taken as a deduction.
(3) Recompute the tax (including the minimum tax) for the earlier year, excluding the receipt of the income, to the extent to which it has been repaid.
(4) Subtract the tax in 3 from the actual tax for the earlier year.
(5) Reduce the tax in 2 by the savings in 4. The result is the tax for the current year, if it is less than the tax in 1.

In making the above computations, the following must be taken into account:

- If the earlier year is not open for adjustments, it is not opened by virtue of this section.
- If the earlier year is still open, other adjustments by way of carrybacks, carryovers, credits and allowances are made before any computations are made for the purposes of this section.
- In either event, deductions that depend on the amount of adjusted gross income, taxable income, or net income (contributions and medical expense) are recomputed under this section.
- The tax for both years is deemed to include personal holding company taxes and accumulated earnings taxes.

---

131 Reg. § § 1.1341-1(d)(1)(i), 1.1341-1(d)(3).

[2] Amount of Exclusion from Gross Income in Prior Taxable Years

The amount to be excluded from gross income for the prior taxable year (or years) in determining the decrease in tax under IRC § § 1341(a)(5)(B) and 1341(b)(1)(ii) shall be the amount restored in the taxable year, but shall not exceed the amount included in gross income in the prior taxable year (or years) under the claim of right to which the deduction for the restoration is attributable, and shall be adjusted as provided in Reg. § 1.1341-1(d)(2)(ii).

Example 2-6

For the taxable year 1952, an individual taxpayer had long-term capital gains of $50,000 and long-term capital losses of $10,000, a net long-term gain of $40,000. He also had other income of $5,000. In 1956, taxpayer restored the $50,000 of long-term gain. He had no capital gains or losses in 1956 but had other income of $5,000. If his tax liability for 1956, the taxable year of restoration, is computed by taking the deduction into account, the taxpayer would be entitled to a deduction under IRC § 1211 of only $1,000 on account of the capital loss (currently $3,000). However, if the taxpayer computes his tax under IRC § § 1341(a)(5) and 1341(b)(1)(ii), it is necessary to determine the decrease in tax for 1952. In such a determination, $50,000 is to be excluded from gross income for that year, resulting in a net capital loss for that year of $10,000, and a capital loss deduction of $1,000 (currently $3,000) under IRC § 117(d) of the Internal Revenue Code of 1939 (corresponding to IRC § 1211 of the Internal Revenue Code of 1954) with carryover privileges. The difference between the tax previously determined and the tax as recomputed after such exclusion for the years affected will be the amount of the decrease.[132]

[3] Computation of Amount of Decrease in Tax

In computing the amount of decrease in tax for a prior taxable year (or years) resulting from the exclusion from gross income of the income included under a claim of right, there must first be ascertained the amount of tax previously determined for the taxpayer for such prior taxable year (or years). The tax previously determined shall be the sum of the amounts shown by the taxpayer on his return or returns, plus any amounts which have been previously assessed (or collected without assessment)

[132] *See* Reg. § 1.1341-1(d)(2)(iv).

as deficiencies or which appropriately should be assessed or collected, reduced by the amount of any refunds or credits which have previously been made or which appropriately should be made.

No item other than the exclusion of the income previously included under a claim of right shall be considered in computing the amount of decrease in tax if reconsideration of such other item is prevented by the operation of any provision of the internal revenue laws or any other rule of law. However, if the amounts of other items in the return are dependent upon the amount of adjusted gross income, taxable income, or net income (such as charitable contributions, foreign tax credit, deductions for depletion, and net operating loss), appropriate adjustments shall be made as part of the computation of the decrease in tax.

Example 2-7

For the taxable year 1954, a corporation had taxable income of $35,000, on which it paid a tax of $12,700. Included in gross income for the year was $20,000 received under a claim of right as royalties. In 1957, the corporation was required to return $10,000 of the royalties. It otherwise had taxable income in 1957 of $5,000, so that without the application of IRC § 1341 it had a net operating loss of $5,000 in that year. Facts also come to light in 1957 which entitled the corporation to an additional deduction of $5,000 for 1954. When a computation was made under paragraph (b)(1)(i) of IRC § 1341, the corporation had no tax for the taxable year 1957. When a computation was made under paragraph (b)(1)(ii) of IRC § 1341, the tax for 1957, without taking the restoration into account, was $1,500, based on a taxable income of $5,000. The decrease in tax for 1954 was computed as follows:

Tax shown on return for 1954		$12,700
Taxable income for 1954 upon which tax shown on return was based		35,000
Less: Additional deduction (on account of which credit or refund could be made)		5,000
Total		30,000
Tax on $30,000 (adjusted taxable income for 1954)		10,100
Taxable income for 1954, as adjusted	$30,000	
Less exclusion of amount restored	10,000	
Taxable income for 1954 by applying paragraph (b)(1)(ii) of IRC § 1341	20,000	
Tax on $20,000		6,000
Decrease in tax for 1954 by applying paragraph (1)(ii) of IRC § 1341		4,100

Tax for 1957 without taking the restoration into account		1,500
Amount by which decrease exceeds the tax for 1957 computed without taking restoration into account		2,600

(The $2,600 is treated as having been paid on the last day prescribed by law for the payment of the tax for 1957 and is available as a refund. In addition the taxpayer has made an overpayment of $2,600 ($12,700 less $10,100) for 1954 because of the additional deduction of $5,000.)[133]

Example 2-8

Assume the same facts as in Example 2-7, except that, instead of the corporation being entitled to an additional deduction of $5,000 for 1954, it is determined that the corporation failed to include an item of $5,000 in gross income for that year. The decrease in tax for 1954 is computed as follows:

Tax shown on return for 1954		$12,700
Taxable income for 1954 upon which tax shown on return was based		35,000
Plus: Additional income (on account of which deficiency assessment could be made)		5,000
Total		40,000
Tax on $40,000 (adjusted taxable income for 1954)		15,300
Taxable income for 1954 as adjusted	$40,000	
Less exclusion of amount restored	10,000	
Taxable income for 1954 by applying paragraph (b)(1)(ii) of IRC § 1341	30,000	
Tax on $30,000		10,100
Decrease in tax for 1954 by applying paragraph (b)(1)(ii) of IRC § 1341		5,200
Tax for 1957 without taking the restoration into account		1,500
Amount by which decrease exceeds the tax for 1957 computed without taking the restoration into account		3,700

---

[133] *See* Reg. § 1.1341-1(d)(4)(iii).

(The $3,700 is treated as having been paid on the last day prescribed by law for the payment of the tax for 1957 and is available as a refund. In addition, the taxpayer has a deficiency of $2,600 ($15,300 less $12,700) for 1954 because of the additional income of $5,000.)[134]

Example 2-9

For the taxable year 1954, a corporation had taxable income of $25,000, on which it paid a tax of $7,500. Included in gross income for the year was $10,000 received under a claim of right as commissions. In 1956, the corporation was required to return $5,000 of the commissions. The corporation had a net operating loss of $10,000 for 1956, excluding the deduction for the $5,000 restored. When a computation is made under either paragraph (b)(1)(i) or paragraph (b)(1)(ii) of IRC § 1341, the corporation had no tax due for the taxable year 1956. The decrease in tax for 1954 is computed as follows:

Tax shown on return for 1954		$7,500
Taxable income for 1954 upon which tax shown on return was based		25,000
Less: Additional deduction (on account of net operating loss carryback from 1956)		10,000
Net income as adjusted		15,000
Tax on $15,000 (adjusted taxable income for 1954)		4,500
Taxable income for 1954, as adjusted	$15,000	
Less: exclusion of amount restored	5,000	
Taxable income for 1954 by applying paragraph (b)(1)(ii) of IRC § 1341	10,000	
Tax on $10,000		3,000
Decrease in tax for 1954 by applying paragraph (b)(1)(ii) of IRC § 1341		1,500
Tax for 1956 without taking the restoration into account		None
Amount by which decrease exceeds the tax for 1956 computed without taking the restoration into account		1,500

(The $1,500 is treated as having been paid on the last day prescribed by law for the payment of the tax for 1956 and is available as a refund. In addition, the taxpayer has

---

[134] *Id.*

an overpayment of $3,000 ($7,500 less $4,500) for 1954 because of the net operating loss deduction of $10,000.)[135]

Example 2-10

For the taxable year 1959, a corporation reporting income on the calendar year basis had taxable income of $20,000 on which it paid a tax of $6,000. Included in gross income for such year was $100,000 received under a claim of right as royalties. For each of its taxable years 1956, 1957, 1958, 1960, 1961, and 1962, the corporation had taxable income of $10,000 on which it paid tax of $3,000 for each year. In 1963, the corporation returned the entire amount of $100,000 of the royalties. In such taxable year, the corporation had taxable income of $25,000 (without taking the deduction of $100,000 into account), and had a net operating loss of $75,000 (taking the deduction of $100,000 into account). In determining whether IRC §§1341(a)(4) or 1341(a)(5) applies, the corporation computed the lesser amount of tax referred to in IRC §1341(a) by applying the rules provided in IRC §1341(b)(4).[136]

[4] Method of Accounting

The provisions of IRC §1341 and the discussion above is applicable in the case of a taxpayer on the cash receipts and disbursements method of accounting only to the taxable year in which the item of income included in a prior year (or years) under a claim of right is actually repaid. However, in the case of a taxpayer on the cash receipts and disbursements method of accounting who constructively received an item of income under a claim of right and included such item of income in gross income in a prior year (or years), the provisions of IRC §1341 are applicable to the taxable year in which the taxpayer is required to relinquish his right to receive such item of income. IRC §1341 is applicable in the case of other taxpayers only to the taxable year which is the proper taxable year (under the method of accounting used by the taxpayer in computing taxable income) for taking into account the deduction resulting from the restoration of the item of income included in a prior year (or years) under a claim of right. For example, if the taxpayer is on an accrual method of accounting, IRC §1341 applies to the year in which the obligation properly accrues for the repayment of the item included under a claim of right.

---

135 *See* Reg. §1.1341-1(d)(4)(ii).

136 *See* Reg. §1.1341-1(d)(4)(iii).

[D] $3,000 Limitation

IRC § 1341 only applies if the deduction allowable for the restoration exceeds $3,000. This limitation must be met in each year IRC § 1341 is applied.[137] The deductions in any one year, however, can be aggregated if they relate to items of income "of the same class." Thus, the restoration of sales commissions of $501 to each of six customers would probably qualify for IRC § 1341 treatment even if the sales commissions were reported in gross income in more than one prior taxable year. Although the regulations pertaining to IRC § 1341 do not define what items of income are "of the same class," other regulations denote certain items of income as a "specific class of income,"[138] *e.g.*, dividends, interest, business income, and rent.

[E] Transactions That Are Not Available for IRC § 1341 Treatment

Inventory. IRC § 1341 is not applicable to deductions attributable to repayment of items included in gross income in a prior year on account of the sale or disposition of inventory.[139] For example, in 2019, XYZ Corp. sold widgets with a basis of $400,000 for a total amount of $800,000, generating income of $400,000. In 2020, $100,000 was returned to customers who returned items purchased in 2019 because they were defective. Under IRC § 1341, the mitigation rules are not applied to the refund.

Bad debts. IRC § 1341 is not applicable to deductions for bad debts.[140]

Dealer reserve credits. IRC § 1341 is not applicable to dealer reserve credits.[141]

Legal fees and other expenses. IRC § 1341 does not apply to legal fees or other expenses incurred by a taxpayer in contesting the restoration of an item previously included in income.[142]

Example 2-11

A sold his personal residence to B in a prior taxable year and realized a capital gain on the sale. C claimed that under an agreement with A he was entitled to a five-percent share of the purchase price since he brought the parties together and was instrumental in closing the sale. A rejected C's demand and included the entire amount of the capital gain in gross income for the year of sale. C instituted action and, in the taxable year, judgment is rendered against A who pays C the amount involved. In

---

[137] This limitation was imposed for "administrative reasons." S. Rep. No. 1622, 83d Cong., 2d Sess. 118 (1954); H.R. Rep. No. 1337, 83d Cong., 2d Sess. 87 (1954).

[138] *See, e.g.*, Reg. § 1.652(b)-2.

[139] IRC § 1341(b)(2); Reg. § 1.1341-1(f)(1).

[140] Reg. § 1.1341-1(g).

[141] *Brown v. Comm'r*, T.C. Memo. 1961-214. This is because these credits are not amounts previously included in income and hence cannot be the subject of a later determination that the taxpayer did not have an unrestricted right to the amount paid.

[142] Reg. § 1.1341-1(h).

addition, A pays legal fees in the taxable year which were incurred in the defense of the action. IRC § 1341 applies to the payment of the five-percent share of the purchase price to C. However, the payment of the legal fees, whether or not otherwise deductible, does not constitute an item restored for purposes of IRC § 1341(a).

Failure to Report Income in a Prior Year. As discussed in § 2.01, income taxes are assessed annually. If an error is made in the computation of tax for one year, it cannot be corrected by making an erroneous computation of tax for a later year to try to correct this.[143]

§ 2.04 The *Arrowsmith* Doctrine

The "*Arrowsmith* doctrine" is another tax accounting doctrine that mitigates the harsh impact of the annual accounting system. Its name is derived from the Supreme Court decision in *Arrowsmith v. Commissioner.*[144] Pursuant to the *Arrowsmith* doctrine, the *character* (*i.e.*, capital or ordinary) of a gain or loss on a transaction is determined by the character of the gain or loss recognized on a related transaction in a prior taxable year.

In *Arrowsmith,* the Supreme Court was forced to deal with the annual-transactional accounting controversy. The taxpayers in the case had received distributions in 1937, 1938, 1939, and 1940, in connection with the liquidation of their closely held corporation. They properly reported these distributions as capital gains. Subsequently, the corporation was liquidated. In 1944, a judgment was rendered against the liquidated corporation, and the former shareholders were required to satisfy this judgment personally. On their 1944 returns, the taxpayers deducted the full amount of the judgment as an ordinary loss from a business transaction. The amount fully offset an equivalent amount of ordinary income. The Commissioner contended that the 1944 loss should be treated as a capital loss because it arose as a result of the liquidation which gave rise to capital gain. If accorded capital treatment, each loss could offset only a limited amount of ordinary income in 1944.

The Supreme Court decided to hear the case because of a split between the Third Circuit, which had held in *Commissioner v. Switlik*[145] that such losses were ordinary, and the Second Circuit, which had held in *Commissioner v. Arrowsmith*[146] that such losses were capital. The Supreme Court affirmed the Second Circuit's decision in *Arrowsmith.*

---

[143] *Ryan v. Comm'r,* 42 T.C. 386 (1964). Notwithstanding where there is a change in method of accounting under IRC § 481, there shall be taken into account those adjustments which are necessary solely by reason of the change to prevent amounts from being omitted or duplicated. *See* Chapter 7, *infra.*

[144] 344 U.S. 6, 52-2 USTC ¶ 9527, *rehearing denied,* 344 U.S. 900 (1952).

[145] 184 F.2d 299, 50-2 USTC ¶ 9446 (3d Cir. 1950).

[146] 193 F.2d 734, 52-1 USTC ¶ 9152 (2d Cir. 1951), *aff'd,* 344 U.S. 6, 52-2 USTC ¶ 9527 (1952).

In upholding the Second Circuit's decision, the Supreme Court noted that its decision to take into account what occurred in a prior year did not violate the principle of annual accounting because it did not require the reopening of any prior year's returns. The Court observed that the principle of annual accounting is not violated when tax treatment in one year affects tax treatment in another year, so long as the prior year's return is not reopened.

The Supreme Court reasoned that since the payments by the shareholders were so integrally associated with prior capital gains, the payments must be treated as falling within the definition of "capital losses." The Court stated that it was "plain that [the shareholder's] liability as transferees was not based on any ordinary business transaction of theirs apart from the litigation proceedings." If the losses had been incurred in the year of the distributions, they would have reduced the amount of capital gains to the shareholders.

Accordingly, where a sale or exchange in one year is followed by a return of all or some portion of the amounts received in the earlier transaction, the character of the gain or loss on the return transaction will be made on the basis of the character of the gain or loss on the earlier transaction. Therefore, despite the annual accounting concept, events in one year may determine the character of gain or loss in another year where the later gain or loss is attributable to events that are integrally related to the events of the earlier year.

Under the *Arrowsmith* doctrine, two transactions, one occurring subsequent to the other and each integrally related, are treated as parts of the same transaction, so that the subsequent event relates back to and is given the same character as the prior transaction. This relation-back doctrine is premised on the idea that the tax consequences should be the same as if the prior and the subsequent transactions had occurred at the same time.[147]

The *Arrowsmith* doctrine was applied broadly in *United States v. Skelly Oil Co.*,[148] where a natural gas producer made refunds to its customers for excess charges received in prior years. In its returns for the prior years, the taxpayer had included these excess amounts in income and had calculated its oil and gas depletion allowance accordingly. In the year of the refunds, the taxpayer deducted the total amount refunded without an adjustment for the prior effect of the depletion allowance. The Service sought to reduce the amount of the deduction for refunds by the related depletion allowance taken in the prior returns. The Supreme Court held for the Service. Notwithstanding the annual accounting system, the Court agreed to limit the taxpayer's deduction in the subsequent period based on the favorable tax treatment accorded the receipts in the earlier years. The Court stated:

> Nevertheless, the annual accounting concept does not require us to close our eyes to what happened in prior years. For instance, it is well settled that the prior year may be examined to determine whether the repayment

---

[147] *Seagate Technology, Inc. v. Comm'r*, T.C. Memo. 2000-361.

[148] 69-1 USTC ¶9343, 394 U.S. 678 (1969).

> gives rise to a regular loss or a capital loss. *Arrowsmith v. Commissioner*.[149] The rationale for the Arrowsmith rule is easy to see; if money was taxed at a special lower rate when received, the taxpayer would be accorded an unfair tax windfall if repayments were generally deductible from receipts taxable at the higher rate applicable to ordinary income. The Court in *Arrowsmith* was unwilling to infer that Congress intended such a result.[150]

The courts have given broad application to the *Arrowsmith* doctrine. For example, in *Cummings v. Commissioner*,[151] the Court of Appeals was called upon to consider whether a payment made in satisfaction of an apparent liability under § 16(b) of the Securities Exchange Act of 1934 (SEA) fell under the *Arrowsmith* doctrine. Cummings had been the chairman of the board and chief executive officer of Consolidated Foods and was offered a large block of stock in MGM in 1959. He was told that MGM was experiencing management problems, and that if he became a director, three members of the board would resign. Cummings subsequently purchased 51,500 shares of MGM stock for over one million dollars and was elected to the board.

Subsequently, the price of the MGM stock rose, and on April 17, 1961, Cummings sold 3,400 shares of MGM stock for a total of $227,648.88. This profit was reported as a long term capital gain on his 1961 return. Between September 18th and October 2nd of 1961, however, Cummings bought back 3,000 shares of the stock for $146,960.00. This purchase was made within six months of the sale and brought him within the provisions of § 16(b) of the Securities Exchange Act of 1934, making the difference between the sale price and the purchase price, $53,870.00, recoverable by MGM. Apparently, Cummings was unaware of his liability until after MGM, in preparation for its 1962 annual meeting, submitted its proxy material to the SEC. On January 16, 1962, the SEC informed MGM that if Cummings had realized profit from his sale and purchase of its stock, it would have to be noted in its proxy statement. Cummings believed that if any violation of the Securities Act did occur, it was inadvertent; nevertheless, he decided to remit $53,870.00 to MGM.

Cummings treated his repayment as a deduction against ordinary income on his 1962 return. This deduction was disallowed, and a deficiency was assessed. The IRS maintained that long-term capital gain treatment was appropriate. The tax court held that the payment was characterized as ordinary income because it was a necessary business expense incurred to protect Cummings' business reputation. The Court of Appeals for the Second Circuit reviewed the case and applied the *Arrowsmith* doctrine. In applying the doctrine, the court looked at whether there was a "nexus," *i.e.*, a connection, between the SEC § 16(b) repayment and the earlier capital gain. The court said that the nexus was apparent. The repayment had its genesis in the earlier sale. Thus, for tax purposes, Cummings' repayment of the profit from the sale and purchase of MGM stock was appropriately regarded as an adjustment to his capital

---

[149] 344 U.S. 6, 52-2 USTC ¶ 9527 (1952).

[150] 394 U.S. 678, 681, 69-1 USTC ¶ 9343.

[151] 506 F.2d 449, 74-2 USTC ¶ 9799 (2d Cir. 1974).

gain. The court drew analogies to *United States v. Skelly Oil Co.*[152] The court went on to observe that the SEC § 16(b) payment was designed to restore the status quo prior to the offending sale and that if it were not to apply the *Arrowsmith* doctrine, *Cummings* would be awarded a windfall that would contravene the policy of the securities statute.

Arrowsmith is applied not only where there is a gain followed by a loss, but also where there is a loss followed by a gain or where there are both gains and losses.[153]

Arrowsmith, while widely applied, does have limitations. For example, in *Nahey v. Commissioner*,[154] a taxpayer (through two S corporations) purchased the assets of Wehr Corporation, including a pending lawsuit against Xerox Corporation that arose from the conduct of Wehr's trade or business. Because the taxpayer considered the lawsuit speculative as to value, no portion of the assets' purchase price was assigned to the lawsuit. Six years later, after the sale, the lawsuit was settled and the taxpayer received a $6 million settlement. The taxpayer argued that the settlement proceeds were capital gain because the lawsuit was purchased from Wehr in a capital transaction, namely, the purchase of Wehr's assets. The Tax Court disagreed and held that the proceeds were ordinary income to the taxpayer. The court's reasoning was based primarily on the lack of the existence of an underlying sale or exchange. The court specifically rejected the argument by the taxpayer that the *Arrowsmith* doctrine required capital gain treatment because the proceeds related to the prior acquisition of assets. In doing so the court stated that:

> The acquisition of Wehr's assets was not the basis for the lawsuit against Xerox, and the settlement in favor of the S corporations was not related to the leveraged buyout. The origin of the claim in this case was Xerox's breach of contract, as detailed in the complaint filed by Wehr in the District Court. The treatment of the settlement proceeds as ordinary income or capital gain is not dependent on the fact that the S corporations acquired Wehr's assets in a capital transaction. As such, the *Arrowsmith* doctrine is inapplicable.[155]

Citing *Fahey v. Commissioner*,[156] the court noted that in order for *Arrowsmith* to apply there must be more than the mere occurrence of a sale or exchange of the subject asset at some point in time; the sale or exchange must be proximate to the event which gave rise to the gain.

The *Arrowsmith* doctrine applies to both claim of right and tax benefit situations generally converting what would otherwise have been ordinary deductions into capital losses or capital gains into ordinary income. There are very few cases in which the conversion is favorable to the taxpayer. There are, however, some circumstances

---

[152] 394 U.S. 678, 69-1 USTC ¶ 9343 (1969).

[153] *See Smith v. Comm'r*, 48 T.C. 872 (1967); Rev. Rul. 79-278, 1979-2 CB 302; *Lowe v. Comm'r*, 44 T.C. 363 (1965); *Comm'r v. Adam, Meldrum, & Anderson Co.*, 215 F.2d 163, 54-2 USTC ¶ 9538 (2d Cir. 1954).

[154] 111 T.C. 256 (1998).

[155] 111 T.C. 256, 266.

[156] 16 T.C. 105 (1951). *See also* Priv. Ltr. Rul. 200743003.

in which deducted expenditures resulting from the disposition of capital assets have been allowed to retain capital or § 1231 gain status.[157]

§ 2.05 The Tax Benefit Rule

Simply stated, the tax benefit rule provides that if an item is properly deducted from income in one year, but is recovered by the taxpayer in a later year, the item must be reported as income in the later year, but only to the extent that the earlier deduction provided a tax benefit.[158]

A classic application of the rule is illustrated in *Alice Phelan Sullivan Corp. v. United States*.[159] In this case, the taxpayer, in each of two years, donated real estate to a charity on the condition that it be used for religious or educational purposes. The value of the two gifts, which were deducted as charitable contributions, totaled $8,706.93. These deductions reduced the donor-taxpayer's tax liability by $1,877.49. Several years later, the donee decided not to use the real estate for its designated purposes and returned the realty to the donor. The court held that the donor had to include the total amount deducted ($8,706.93) as income in the year of recovery, to be taxed at that later year's tax rates. Because the tax rates in the year of recovery were higher than in the year that the deduction was taken, the tax due in the later year was greater than the amount of tax saved in the earlier year. The taxpayer argued, on the basis of *Perry v. United States*,[160] that it should owe tax only on the amount of tax saved in the earlier years, namely $1,877.49. Overruling *Perry*, the Court of Claims held that the concept of annual accounting required that the amount deducted in the earlier year be included in income and taxed at the rates in effect in the year of recovery.[161] This ruling is known as the inclusionary side of the tax benefit rule because it includes amounts deducted in earlier years.

The Tax Court has stated that the tax benefit rule acts as a counterweight to the annual accounting concept.[162]

It should be noted, however, that the tax benefit rule does not represent a purely annual accounting approach to taxation. If it did, the amount included in income in the year of recovery would have been the *then* fair market value of the realty in *Alice Phelan Sullivan Corp.*, which may have been substantially higher than its fair market value in the year of the gift that was allowed as a deduction. By limiting the amount included in income in the later year to the amount that produced a tax benefit in the earlier year, the tax benefit rule represents a transactional approach to tax accounting in that it looks at the entire transaction over the course of more than one year to

---

[157] Rev. Rul. 79-278, 1979-2 CB 302.

[158] Initially a judicial doctrine, the tax benefit rule is now codified in IRC § 111.

[159] 381 F.2d 399, 67-2 USTC ¶ 9570 (Ct. Cl. 1967).

[160] 160 F. Supp. 270, 58-1 USTC ¶ 9400 (Ct. Cl. 1958).

[161] 381 F.2d at 403.

[162] See *Estate of David B. Munter v. Comm'r*, 63 T.C. 663 (1975).

determine what should be included in income. This is known as the exclusionary aspect of the rule because it excludes the amount that did not produce a tax benefit.[163]

The tax benefit rule is not limited to the recovery of a charitable gift; other types of recoveries are also subject to the tax benefit rule.[164]

An actual recovery of an amount deducted need not be realized in order for the tax benefit rule to apply. In *Hillsboro National Bank v. Commissioner*,[165] the Supreme Court rejected this viewpoint, holding instead that "the tax benefit rule ordinarily applies to require the inclusion of income when events occur that are *fundamentally inconsistent* with an earlier deduction."[166] The Court went on further to characterize a "fundamentally inconsistent" event in the following manner: "if that event had occurred within the same taxable year, it would have foreclosed the deduction."[167] The Court added, if such a fundamentally inconsistent event transpired in the context of a transaction that is granted non-recognition by the Code, then a case-by-case determination must be made as to whether the tax benefit rule overrides the non-recognition provision.[168]

Finally, it should be noted that the tax benefit rule originated as judge-made law.[169] In 1942, however, Congress formally endorsed this judge-made rule by the enactment of the predecessor of IRC § 111. In its original form, IRC § 111 specifically covered only the exclusionary aspect of the rule, but by implication affirmed the inclusionary aspect. Further, the predecessor to IRC § 111 specifically applied its exclusionary aspect only to bad debts, refunded taxes and "delinquency amounts," *i.e.*, interest on past due taxes. In *Dobson v. Commissioner*,[170] however, the Court confirmed that the exclusionary aspect of the rule covered more than just the items enumerated in the predecessor to IRC § 111, and the Treasury amended its regulations to follow the *Dobson* decision. In 1984, Congress broadened the scope of IRC § 111 so that, among other things, the exclusionary aspect of the rule applies to "any amount deducted in any prior taxable year to the extent such amount did not reduce income subject to tax."[171]

Exclusionary aspect to the tax benefit rule. The tax benefit doctrine does not apply to amounts received as income for the first time to which no prior deduction is related. *Dobson v. Commissioner*,[172] a 1943 Supreme Court case is often referred to as

---

[163] *Id.* at 276.

[164] *See, e.g.*, *Putnam National Bank v. Comm'r*, 50 F.2d 158, 2 USTC ¶747 (5th Cir. 1931) (involving the collection of debts that had previously been deducted as uncollectible). Common applications of the rule include prior deductions for taxes, interest, charitable contributions, etc.

[165] 460 U.S. 370, 83-1 USTC ¶9229 (1983).

[166] *Id.* at 372.

[167] *Id.* at 383-84.

[168] *Id.* at 385.

[169] *See, e.g.*, *Alice Phelan Sullivan Corp.*, 67-2 USTC ¶9570, 381 F.2d at 402-03; Note, *The Tax Benefit Rule—A Judicially Broadened Tool for Transactional Tax Equity*, 37 Vand. L. Rev. 1351, 1352-53 (1984).

[170] 320 U.S. 489, 44-1 USTC ¶9108 (1943).

[171] IRC § 111(a) (1982), *as amended by* the Tax Reform Act of 1984, Pub. L. No. 98-369, § 171(a), 98 Stat. 494, 698.

[172] 44-1 USTC ¶9108, 320 U. S. 489 (1943).

the "exclusionary" side of the rule to distinguish it from the line of cases referred to as the "inclusionary" cases, such as *Hillsboro*. In *Dobson*, the taxpayer purchased stock in which the taxpayer suffered a deductible loss of $41,600. He also suffered a subsequent loss of $28,163. He took deductions on his return for each year in which he had these losses. In a subsequent year, the taxpayer learned that the stock had not been registered under state law and filed a suit against the seller alleging fraud. He asked for rescission of the entire transaction and offered to return the proceeds of the stock or an equivalent number of shares plus interest. The suit was settled giving him a net recovery of $45,000. Twenty-three thousand dollars was allocable to the stocks sold in 1930 and the balance was allocable to the stock sold in 1931. In his return for 1933, he did not report as income any part of the recovery. The Commissioner adjusted the taxpayer's 1939 income by adding as ordinary gain the recovery attributable to the shares sold but not the portion of it attributable to the shares unsold. The recovery upon the shares sold was not however sufficient to make good the taxpayer's original investment in them. If the amounts recovered had been added to the proceeds received in 1930 and 1931, they would not have altered the taxpayer's income tax liability for these years because even if the entire deduction claimed on the account of these losses had been disallowed, the returns would still have shown net losses. The government tried to argue the annual accounting concept to compel the taxpayer to report income in the year of recovery. The Court noted that the transaction as a matter of fact produced no economic gain. It did not produce a tax benefit to the taxpayer. It therefore excluded the gain.[173]

The inclusionary component of the tax benefit rule is the mirror image of the claim of right principle. The "fundamental inconsistency" principle, however, appears to have no counterpart in the claim of right area perhaps because it is hard to find any situation where there would be an inconsistency. There is however no statutory or judicial equivalent to the IRC § 1341(a)(5) principle. The statutory exclusionary aspect of the tax benefit rule may be viewed as a rough equivalent since it allows avoiding current inclusion where the proper deduction provide no tax benefit. It does not however adjust for rate or other tax characteristic differences.

Note

The taxpayer has the burden of proof that a deduction in a prior tax year did not produce a tax benefit.[174]

The Tax Benefit Rule can apply to:

- Credits- IRC § 111(b)(1);
- Professional fees;[175]

[173] *See also Clark v. Comm'r*, 40 BTA 333 (1939), *acq*.

[174] *Charleston Nat'l Bank v. Comm'r*, 20 T.C. 253 (1953).

[175] The tax benefit doctrine applies to fees paid to professional advisors and deducted in prior tax years that are recovered in the current tax year because the advisors' errors generated a tax benefit subsequently disallowed by the IRS. *Mittelman v. Comm'r*, 7 T.C. 1162 (1946).

- Insurance premiums;[176]
- Employee benefit contributions;[177]
- Employee benefit expenses;[178]
- Miscellaneous business expenses;[179]
- Taxes,[180] including rebated property taxes, personal property taxes and estate taxes; and
- Losses.[181]

As demonstrated, the tax benefit rule has wide application and tries to ensure that a deduction, credit, or similar such item previously taken when later recovered results in an appropriate tax consequence.

---

[176] *Finance Security Co. v. Comm'r*, 69 F.2d 829 (5th Cir. 1934).

[177] Rev. Rul. 73-528, 1973-2 CB 13.

[178] *Giordano v. Comm'r*, T.C. Memo. 1977-95.

[179] *Buck Glass Co. v. Hofferbert*, 176 F.2d 250, 49-2 USTC ¶9356 (4th Cir. 1949).

[180] *Universal, Inc. v. Comm'r*, 109 F.2d 616, 40-1 USTC ¶9228 (7th Cir. 1940).

[181] Rev. Rul. 71-161, 1971-1 CB 76.

3

The Entity's Tax Year

§3.01 Introduction

Taxable income for every taxpayer is computed on, and a return is made for, a period known as a "taxable year." Except as otherwise provided in the Code and the regulations, a taxable year may not cover a period of time greater than 12 calendar months.[1]

---

[1] Reg. §1.441-1(a)(2).

The term "tax year" means the calendar year or the fiscal year upon which taxable income is computed or, in the case of a "short year," the period for which a return is made, *i.e.*, a period of less than 12 months.[2]

Unless an entity or taxpayer begins its tax year on the first day of January or the first day of the month, in the case of a fiscal year, the first year will be a short tax year.

Example 3-1

Able Corporation is incorporated on February 15, 2020 and adopts the calendar year as its taxable year. The Corporation's first taxable year is a short taxable year beginning February 15, 2020 and ending on December 31, 2020.[3]

Exceptions and special rules are provided for 52-53-week years,[4] personal service corporations,[5] S corporations[6] and partnerships.[7]

§ 3.02 Calendar Year

The term "calendar year" means a period of 12 consecutive months beginning January 1 and ending on December 31st.

A taxpayer must make its return on the calendar year basis if the taxpayer:

- keeps no books and records;[8]
- does not have an annual accounting period;[9] or
- has an accounting period that is not a fiscal year as defined in IRC § 441.[10]

A taxpayer who has not established a fiscal year must make its return based on a calendar year.[11]

---

[2] Reg. § 1.441-1(b).

[3] A short year may be required when a taxpayer changes its tax year.

[4] *See* § 3.04, *infra.*

[5] *See* § 3.12[C], *infra.*

[6] *See* § 3.12[D], *infra.*

[7] *See* § 3.13, *infra.*

[8] IRC § 441(g).

[9] An annual accounting period, as defined in IRC § 441(c), is the basis on which the taxpayer regularly computes income in keeping its books.

[10] A retail business did not establish a fiscal year where it had, over ten years, closed its annual accounting period on dates running from January 22 to January 28. *Parks-Chambers* Inc, 46 BTA 144 (1942). Similarly, an entity's accounting period that ended in the latter part of December, but not on the last day of the month, did not qualify as a fiscal year. *Swift & Co*, 69 Ct. Cl. 171, 38 F.2d 365, 2 USTC ¶ 481 (Cl. Ct. 1930). *See also* Rev. Rul. 85-22, 1985-1 CB 154 and Rev. Proc. 85-15, 1985-1 CB 516.

[11] *Id.*

§ 3.03 Fiscal Year

The term "fiscal year" means a period of 12 consecutive months ending on the last day of any month other than December, or a 52-53-week taxable year, if the taxpayer has elected such period.[12] A fiscal year will be recognized only if the taxpayer's books are kept in accordance with the fiscal year chosen.[13]

Books and records include invoices, receipts, journals, general ledgers, and similar classifying information which support income and expenses.[14] An individual taxpayer who uses journals and ledgers to record receipts and disbursements will have sufficient record to satisfy the requirement for keeping books and records.[15] Informal records such as bank statements, check stubs, dividend statements, and rent receipts do not constitute books and records.[16] Books and records must be closed as of the last day of the tax year and must be conformed to the accounting period used for financial statement purposes and reports to creditors.[17]

---

[12] Reg. § 1.441-2.

[13] IRC § 441(b)(1); Reg. § 1.441-1(b)(3). *See Brown v. United States*, 68-2 USTC ¶ 9657 (M.D. Fla. 1968) (a corporation keeping calendar year basis books could not adopt a fiscal year as its taxable year and, as a result, its S corporation election was untimely); *MacLean v. Comm'r*, 73 T.C. 1045 (1980) (resident alien's failure to maintain books and records precluded adoption of fiscal year for tax purposes).

Where a corporation kept its books on a fiscal year basis, a board's resolution directing the adoption of a calendar year retroactively was ineffective. *Iron Mountain Oil Co. v Alexander*, 37 F.2d 231 (10th Cir.1930). Most individuals have no choice about what taxable year they use since IRC § 441(g) requires the calendar year for taxpayers who either keep no books or who otherwise lack an annual accounting period. Reg. § 1.441-1(b)(7) explains that "books" must be "sufficient to reflect income adequately and clearly." Merely having a checkbook—the extent of most individuals' books—is probably not adequate. *See Stryker v. Comm'r*, 36 BTA 326 (1937).

See generally Reg. § 31.6001-1(d) *Records of employees* which provides:

> "While not mandatory (except in the case of claims), it is advisable for each employee to keep permanent, accurate records showing the name and address of each employer for whom he performs services as an employee, the dates of beginning and termination of such services, the information with respect to himself which is required by the regulations in this subpart to be kept by employers, and the statements furnished in accordance with the provisions of Reg. § 31.6051-1."

[14] Reg. § 1.441-1(b)(7), which provides: Books include the taxpayer's regular books of account and such other records and data as may be necessary to support the entries on the taxpayer's books and on the taxpayer's return, as for example, a reconciliation of any difference between such books and the taxpayer's return. Records that are sufficient to reflect income adequately and clearly on the basis of an annual accounting period will be regarded as the keeping of books. *See* IRC § 6001and the regulations thereunder for rules relating to the keeping of books and records.

[15] *Godson, E.M.*, 5 CCH TCM 648 (1946); *Gill, Robert S. v. United States*, 258 F.2d 553, 58-2 USTC ¶ 9717 (5th Cir. 1958).

[16] *Klempner, Harry W. v. Seldon R. Glenn*, 82 F. Supp. 626, 49-1 ¶ USTC 9150 (W.D. Ky. 1949); *Brooks, Louis M.*, 6 T.C. 504 (1946); *Stryker, Max H.*, 36 BTA 326 (1937), *acq.*, 1937-2 CB 27; Priv. Ltr. Rul. 7844042.

[17] *See* Rev. Proc. 2006-45, 2006-2 CB 851, § 6.02 (exclusive automatic approval procedures for corporations); Rev. Proc. 2006-46, 2006-2 CB 859, § 6.02 (exclusive automatic approval procedures for partnerships, S corporations, and personal service corporations); Rev. Proc. 2002-39, 2002-1 CB 1046, § 5.04(3) (non-automatic approval procedures).

A taxpayer who must use a calendar year under the Code may not adopt a fiscal year without obtaining the approval of the Commissioner.[18]

§3.04 The 52-53-Week Taxable Year

The 52-53-week year is a year that ends on the same day of the week with reference to the end of a specific calendar month instead of on the last day of the calendar month itself.[19] A taxpayer that adopts or changes to a 52-53-week year must keep its books on the same basis.[20] While the adoption of a 52-53-week year generally does not have substantial tax consequences, it can be advantageous for business purposes.

A corporation engaged in a retail business will generally use a 52-53-week year because that business will normally have predictable heavy business days (such as Friday). The use of a 52-53-week year will avoid having inclusion of four Fridays in one period and five in another, as would happen with calendar month business closings.

The adopted 52-53-week year is a fiscal year that always ends on the same day of the week and always ends on whatever date this day last occurs in a calendar month, *or* whatever date this day falls that is nearest to the last day of the calendar month.[21]

Example 3-2

ABC Supermarkets, Inc. has elected a taxable year that always ends on the last Friday in July. For 2020, the fiscal year-end would be July 24, 2020.

If, however, ABC Supermarkets, Inc. had elected a taxable year that always ends on the Friday nearest to the end of July, then for 2020, the fiscal year would end on July 31, 2020.

As the 52-53-week year is not determined on a calendar basis, it would be longer or shorter in any given year.

An election of a 52-53-week taxable year by an existing eligible taxpayer with an established taxable year is treated as a change in annual accounting period that requires the approval of the Commissioner. Thus, a taxpayer must obtain approval to change from its current taxable year to a 52-53-week taxable year, even if such 52-53-week taxable year ends with reference to the same calendar month. Similarly, a

---

[18] IRC §442. A taxpayer that has adopted an annual accounting period (as defined in Reg. §1.441-1(b)(3)) as its taxable year generally must continue to use that annual accounting period in computing its taxable income and for completing its federal income tax returns. If the taxpayer wants to change its annual accounting period and use a new taxable year, it must obtain the approval of the Commissioner, unless it is authorized to change without the approval of the Commissioner under either the Internal Revenue Code or the Regulations thereunder. Reg. §1.442-1(a).

[19] IRC §441(f)(1).

[20] Reg. §1.441-2(d).

[21] Reg. §1.441-2.

taxpayer must obtain approval to change from a 52-53-week taxable year, or to change from one 52-53-week taxable year to another 52-53-week taxable year. However, a taxpayer may obtain automatic approval for 52-53-week taxable year in administrative procedures published by the Commissioner.[22] The change to a 52-53-week tax year will result in a short year. The short period resulting from the change will always be a period of 359 days or more or of six days or less. Annualization is not required because in the case of a period of 359 days or more, the short period is treated as a full taxable year, and in the case of a period of six days or less, the short period is not treated as a separate year, but is added to and deemed part of the following year.[23]

A taxpayer adopting a 52-53-week taxable year must file with its federal income tax return for its first taxable year a statement containing the following information:

- The calendar month with reference to which the 52-53-week taxable year ends;
- The day of the week on which the 52-53-week taxable year always will end; and
- Whether the 52-53-week taxable year will always end on the date on which that day of the week last occurs in the calendar month, or on the date on which that day of the week falls that is nearest to the last day of that calendar month.[24]

§ 3.05 Short Tax Year

[A] *Short Tax Year Defined*

A short tax year is a tax year of less than 12 months. A short period tax return may be required when a taxpayer:

- Is not in existence for the entire year;[25]
- Changes its accounting period; or
- Files its final income tax return.

[B] *Not in Existence Entire Year*

Even if a taxable entity was not in existence for the entire year, a tax return is required for the time it was in existence. Requirements for filing the return and figuring the tax are generally the same as the requirements for return for a full year (12 months) ending on the last day of the short tax year.

---

[22] *See* Reg. § 1.442-1(b) for procedures for obtaining such approval.

[23] Reg. § 1.441-2. *See* Example 3-5, below.

[24] Reg. § 1.441-2(b)(1)(ii)(c).

[25] IRC § 443(a)(2).

For a short year that occurs resulting from an initial or final year of existence, taxable income is computed as though the year were a full 12 months. However, in all cases of short years involving changes in accounting period, income must be annualized.[26] That is, it must be determined with reference to an actual 12-month period that begins or ends with the short period.[27]

Example 3-3

XYZ Corporation was organized on July 1, 2020. It elected the calendar year as a tax year. Therefore, its first return is due in April 2021.[28] This short period tax return will cover the period from July 1, 2020 through December 31, 2021.

Example 3-4

A calendar year corporation dissolved on July 23, 2020. Its final return is due by October 15, 2020. It will cover the short period from January 1, 2020 through July 23, 2020.

Special rules for the short period required effecting the change. If a change to or from a 52-53-week taxable year results in a short period (within the meaning of Reg. § 1.443-1(a)) of 359 days or more, or six days or less, the tax computation under Reg. § 1.443-1(b) does not apply. If the short period is 359 days or more, it is treated as a full taxable year. If the short period is six days or less, such short period is not a separate taxable year but instead is added to and deemed a part of the following taxable year.[29]

Example 3-5

A taxpayer having a fiscal year ending April 30, obtains approval to change to a 52-53-week tax year ending the last Saturday in April for tax years beginning after April 30, Year 1. This change involves a short period of 362 days, from May 1, Year 1, to April 27, Year 2, inclusive. Because the

---

26 Reg. § 1.6012-1(a)(2)(v); Reg. § 1.443-1(a).

27 *Id.*

28 The Surface Transportation and Veterans Health Care Choice Improvement Act of 2015 (P.L. 114-41) applies to the 2017 filing season (2016 tax returns). It changed the due date for C corporation tax returns to the 15th day of the fourth month after the close of the regular tax year.

29 Reg. § 1.443-1(b)(1)(ii).

change results in a short period of 359 days or more, it is not placed on an annual basis and is treated as a full tax year.[30]

Example 3-6

Assume the same facts as in Example 3-5, except that the taxpayer changes for tax years beginning after April 30, Year 2, to a tax year ending on the Thursday nearest to April 30. This change results in a short period of two days, May 1 to May 2, Year 2. Because the short period is less than seven days, tax is not separately computed. This short period is added to and deemed part of the following 52-53-week tax year, which would otherwise begin on May 3, Year 2, and end on May 1, Year 3.[31]

[C] Short Period Tax Calculation

General rule. If a taxable year is a short period, less than 12 calendar months, a separate return is generally necessary for the short period.[32] Because our income tax system is progressive, taxpayers could reap benefits from a short-period return if some adjustments were not required; therefore, income must be annualized; however, self-employment tax is figured on the actual self-employment income for the short period.[33] A short-period return is not necessary, however, if:

- the short period is six days or less, or 359 days or more, and
- the short period results in a change to or from a 52-53-week taxable year.[34] A 52-53-week taxable year is not considered a short period, although it may be a few days short of 12 calendar months.

Thus, the taxpayer is required to do the following to annualize a short-period tax return:

- Annualize the short-period income (12÷Number of Months in the Short Period);
- Compute the tax on the annualized income;
- Convert the tax on the annualized income to a short-period tax (Number of Months in the Short Period÷12).

---

30 Reg. § 1.441-2(b)(3), Example 1.
31 Reg. § 1.441-2(b)(3), Example 2.
32 IRC § 443(a)(2).
33 Reg. § 1.443-1(b).
34 IRC § 441(f)(2)(B); Reg. § 1.443-1(a)(1).

Example 3-7

Finch Corporation, a manufacturer and a C corporation, obtained permission to change from a calendar year to a fiscal year ending September 30, beginning in 2020. For the short period January 1 through September 30, 2020, the corporation's taxable income was $48,000. The tax rates and the resultant short-period tax are as follows:

Taxable Income	Tax Rate
$75,000	21%

Calculation of Short Period Tax
Annualized income
$48,000 × (12 ÷ 9) = $64,000
Tax on annualized income
$64,000 × 21%= $13,440
Short Period Tax =
(13,440 × (9÷ 12) = $10,080
Tax with annualizing: $10,080
Tax without annualizing: 10,080[35]
Difference resulting from annualizing = 0

Individuals. An individual must figure income tax for the short tax year as follows.

(1) Determine adjusted gross income (AGI) for the short tax year and then subtract actual itemized deductions for the short tax year. Deductions must be itemized when filing a short period tax return;[36]
(2) Multiply the dollar amount of exemptions by the number of months in the short tax year and divide the result by 12;
(3) Subtract the amount in (2) from the amount in (1). The result is modified taxable income;
(4) Multiply the modified taxable income in (3) by 12, and then divide the result by the number of months in the short tax year. The result is the annualized income;
(5) Figure the total tax on the annualized income using the appropriate tax rate schedule; and
(6) Multiply the total tax by the number of months in the short tax year and divide the result by 12. The result is the tax for the short tax year.

In computing the taxable income of a taxpayer other than a corporation for a short period, the personal exemptions allowed individuals under IRC § 151 (and any deductions allowed other taxpayers in lieu thereof, such as the deduction under IRC

---

[35] Because the Tax Cuts and Jobs Act eliminated the corporate graduated rates, the tax whether annualized or not is the same.

[36] Reg. § 1.443-1(b)(1)(iv).

§ 642(b)) shall be reduced to an amount which bears the same ratio to the full amount of the exemptions as the number of months in the short period bears to 12.[37]

Example 3-8

A taxpayer filing as a single taxpayer was granted permission under IRC § 442 to change his annual accounting and files a return for the short period of ten months ending October 31, 2020. He has income and deductions as follows:

Income	$60,000
Tax-exempt interest	$500
Dividends	$750
Total Income	**$61,250**
Deductions	
Real estate taxes	($10,000)
Charitable contributions	($17,000)
Itemized deductions	($27,000)
Taxable income for the ten-month period before annualizing	$34,250
Taxable income annualized (34,250 × (12÷10))	$41,100
Taxable income for short period	$34,250
Annualization	12÷10
Taxable income annualized	$41,100
10% × $9,525	$953
12% × $29,175	$3,501
22% × $2,400	$528
Total tax	$4,982
Tax for the ten-month period ($4,982 × (10÷12))	$$4,152

Exception method. The exception method is a refund procedure that corporations can use when the annualized tax under the general method exceeds the tax computed for an actual 12-month period.[38] The corporation must first timely file a short-period return computing its tax based on the general rule (annualized) method. If the corporation later finds that the exception method would result in a lower tax, a claim for refund can be filed. If the corporation is liquidating, it can use a 12-month period ending on the last day of the short period.[39]

---

[37] Reg. § 1.443-1(b)(1)(v). Note the deduction for the personal exemption has been suspended under the TCJA for tax years 2018–2025.

[38] IRC § 443(b)(2).

[39] IRC § 443(b)(2)(B)(ii).

Example 3-9

Cardinal, Inc. has taxable income of $70,000 for the short period beginning January 1 and ending February 29.

Under the general rule method, Cardinal has annualized income of $420,000 and a tax liability of $14,700 for the short period. Cardinal files its tax return for the short period on June 15 and pays the $14,700 tax due with the return.

As it turns out, Cardinal incurred losses during the remainder of the 12-month period that would have been included in its tax year except for the change. As a result, Cardinal has taxable income of $5,000 for the 12-month period. The annualized tax on this amount is $1,050. Cardinal can request a refund in the amount of $13,650.

Note

A net operating loss in a short tax year is not annualized.[40] In the case of a return filed for a period of less than 12 months due to a change in the accounting period of the taxpayer, IRC § 443(b) states that the "net income" shall be annualized. There is no provision by implication or otherwise, that permits a "net loss" sustained during a short taxable period, occasioned by a change of accounting period, to be annualized for carryback and carryover purposes relating to net operating losses.[41]

Returning to the Example 3-7 above, assume that Finch's taxable income for the calendar year 2020 was $60,000. The tax on the full 12 months of income would have been $12,600. The short-period tax would be $9,450. Thus, if Finch utilized this option, the tax for the short period would be $9,450 (rather than $10,080) as calculated above.

[D] Final Taxable Year

When an individual dies, a tax return is required to be filed for the decedent by the 15th day of the fourth month after the close of the individual's regular tax year. The decedent's final return will be a short period tax return that begins on January 1 and ends on the date of death. In the case of the decedent who dies on December 31, the last day of the regular tax year, a full calendar year tax return is required.

---

[40] Rev. Rul. 56-463, 1956-2 CB 297.

[41] *See* IRC § 172(b). There is now a five-year carryback for operating losses of corporate taxpayers. The carryback of losses had been previously eliminated in the Tax Cut and Jobs Act ("TCJA"), but the Coronavirus Aid, Relief, and Economic Security (CARES) Act reinstates carrybacks for Net Operating Losses (NOLs) arising in taxable years beginning after December 31, 2017, and ending before January 1, 2021.

Example 3-10

Agnes Green was a single, calendar year taxpayer. She died on March 6, 2020. Her final income tax return must be filed by April 15, 2020. It will cover the short period from January 1, 2020 to March 6, 2020.

§ 3.06 Required Tax Years

[A] *Required Tax Years of Taxpayers*

The "required taxable year" is the tax year that taxpayers are required to use under the Internal Revenue Code or Regulations thereunder. For example, the "required taxable year" is the taxable year determined under IRC § 706(b) in the case of a partnership, IRC § 1378 in the case of an S corporation or an electing S corporation, and IRC § 441(i) in the case of a Personal Service Corporation (PSC).[42]

In addition, in some cases, "Permitted Years" are allowed. The term "permitted taxable year" means that instead of the required taxable year, a taxpayer may be able to elect a different year-end such as:

- a natural business year;[43]
- an ownership taxable year;[44]
- a taxable year elected under IRC § 444;[45]
- a 52-53-week taxable year;[46] or
- any other taxable year for which the taxpayer establishes a business purpose to the satisfaction of the Commissioner.[47]

Below is a list of some of the permitted years and the authority therefor:

- C corporations other than Personal Service Corporations—any tax year if supported by the company's books and records;[48]

---

[42] Without taking into account any taxable year that is allowable by reason of an IRC § 444 election, Reg. § 1.441-1(c)(2)(i) provides that a newly-formed partnership, S corporation, or PSC that wants to adopt a taxable year other than its required taxable year, a taxable year elected under IRC § 444, or a 52-53-week taxable year that ends with reference to its required taxable year or a taxable year elected under IRC § 444 must establish a business purpose and obtain the approval of the Commissioner under IRC § 442. As described in Rev. Proc. 2006-46, 2006-2 CB 859, the Commissioner's approval can be automatic.

[43] Rev. Proc. 2006-46, 2006-2 CB 859.

[44] *Id.*

[45] *Id.*

[46] IRC § 441(f).

[47] Rev. Proc. 2006-46, 2006-2 CB 859.

[48] Reg. § 1.441-1(b).

- Partnerships—must generally use the taxable year of a majority of its partners unless they can establish a business purpose for a different tax year, or can make an IRC § 444 election;[49]
- S Corporations—must use a calendar year or ownership year, unless they can establish a business purpose for a different tax year, or can make an IRC § 444 election;[50]
- Personal Service Corporations (PSCs)—must use a calendar year unless they can establish a business purpose for a different tax year, or can make an IRC § 444 election;[51]
- Individuals—can use any tax year supported by their books and records;[52]
- Trusts—are required to use a calendar year;[53] and
- Estates—use a calendar or fiscal year.[54]

The Code and Regulations also specify required taxable years for the following entities, funds, and trusts:

- members of an affiliated group that file consolidated returns;[55]
- certain foreign corporations;[56]
- foreign sales or domestic international corporations;[57]
- insurance companies;[58]
- nuclear decommissioning funds;[59]
- designated or qualified settlement funds;[60]
- common trust funds;[61]
- real estate investment trusts;[62] and
- real estate mortgage investment conduits.[63]

[B] First Effective Year

An individual who is considered a new taxpayer may adopt in his or her first return a fiscal year without obtaining prior approval. A new taxpayer adopts a

---

[49] IRC § 706(b)(1); Rev. Proc. 2002-38, 2002-1 CB 1037. *But see* § 3.07[F] and [G], *infra.*
[50] IRC § 1378; Reg. § 1.441-1(b); Rev. Proc. 2002-38, 2002-1 CB 1037.
[51] IRC § 441(i); Reg. § 1.441-3; Rev. Proc. 2002-38, 2002-1 CB 1037.
[52] Reg. § 1.441-1(b).
[53] IRC § 664(a).
[54] *See* Reg. § 1.441-1(b)(2) for a complete list of required tax years.
[55] Reg. § 1.1502-76.
[56] IRC § 898(c)(1)(A).
[57] IRC § 441(h); Temp. Reg. § 1.921-1T(a)(11), (b)(4), and (b)(6).
[58] IRC § 843; Reg. § 1.1502-76(a)(2).
[59] Reg. § 1.468A-4(c)(1).
[60] Reg. § 1.468B-2(j).
[61] IRC § 584(i).
[62] IRC § 859.
[63] IRC § 860D(a)(5); Reg. § 1.860D-1(b)(6).

taxable year by filing its first federal income tax return using that taxable year.[64] The term "new taxpayer" means a taxpayer subject to U.S. taxation for the first time. For example, a U.S. citizen or resident whose taxable income rises above the threshold for filing a return for the first time, or a nonresident alien who becomes engaged in a U.S. business for the first time is considered a new taxpayer.[65]

The first effective year is the first taxable year for which an adoption, change, or retention in annual accounting period is effective. Thus, in the case of a change in tax year, the first effective year is the short period required to effect the change. The first effective year is also the first taxable year for complying with all the terms and conditions set forth in the letter ruling granting permission to effect the adoption, change, or retention of the taxpayer's annual accounting period.

§ 3.07 Adoption, Change or Retention of Taxable Year

[A] *Adoption of Taxable Year*

A new taxpayer may adopt any taxable year that satisfies the requirements listed below, without the approval of the Commissioner.

- The tax year must be the same as the person's or entity's annual accounting period if such period is a calendar year or a fiscal year;
- The tax year must not exceed 12 calendar months, unless it qualifies as a 52-53-week year; or
- The taxpayer must keep and maintain books of account and records based upon its annual accounting period.[66]

A new taxpayer adopts its taxable year by filing its first federal income tax return using that taxable year.[67] A taxpayer is not required to obtain the Commissioner's consent.[68] A taxable year is *not* adopted by the filing of an application for an automatic extension of time to file a federal income tax return,[69] the filing of an

---

[64] Reg. § 1.441-1(c)(1).

[65] A taxpayer's newly formed sole proprietorship is not a new taxpayer. Therefore, the taxpayer may not adopt a taxable year for the proprietorship that differs from the taxpayer's own. *Vance v. Comm'r*, 56 TCM 1408 (1989).

[66] Reg. § 1.441-1(b)(7) defines "books" as follows: "Books include the taxpayer's regular books of account and such other records and data as may be necessary to support the entries on the taxpayer's books and on the taxpayer's return, as for example, a reconciliation of any difference between such books and the taxpayer's return. Records that are sufficient to reflect income adequately and clearly on the basis of an annual accounting period will be regarded as the keeping of books." *See* IRC § 6001 and the regulations thereunder for rules relating to the keeping books and records.

[67] Reg. § 1.441-1(c)(1).

[68] Reg. § 1.441-1(c)(1).

[69] Form 7004, *Application for Automatic Extension of Time To File Certain Business Income Tax, Information, and Other Returns.*

application for an employer identification number,[70] or the payment of estimated taxes.[71]

[B] Change of Taxable Year

Once a taxpayer has adopted a taxable year, the adopted tax year must be used by the taxpayer in computing its taxable income and in making its returns for all subsequent years, unless the taxpayer obtains approval from the Commissioner to make a change[72] or the taxpayer is otherwise authorized to change its taxable year without the approval of the Commissioner.[73]

[C] Retention of Taxable Year

In certain cases, a partnership, S corporation, electing S corporation, or personal service corporation (PSC) will be required to change its taxable year unless it obtains the approval of the Commissioner under IRC § 442 or it makes an election under IRC § 444[74] to retain its current taxable year (if possible). A corporation using a June 30th fiscal year, for example, which subsequently becomes a PSC or elects to be an S corporation and, as a result, is required to use the calendar year under IRC §§ 441(i) or 1378, respectively, must obtain the approval of the Commissioner to retain its current fiscal year. Similarly, a partnership using a taxable year that corresponds to its required taxable year must obtain the approval of the Commissioner to retain its taxable year if its tax year changes as a result of a change in ownership which would dictate a different tax year under the least aggregate deferral test.[75] However, a partnership that has previously established a business purpose to use a taxable year is not required to obtain the approval of the Commissioner if its required taxable year changes as a result of a change in ownership.[76]

[D] Commissioner's Pronouncements

The IRS has prescribed several Revenue Procedures allowing a taxpayer to adopt, change, or retain an annual accounting period. These Revenue Procedures describe the business purpose requirements (including a natural business year[77] and

---

[70] Form SS-4, *Application for Employer Identification Number.*

[71] Reg. § 1.441-1(c)(1); IRS Pub. 538. The adoption of the revised regulations cleared up much confusion in this area.

[72] Reg. § 1.441-1(e). Generally, you must file Form 1128 to request IRS approval to change your tax year. If you qualify for an automatic approval request, a user fee is not required.

[73] Rev. Proc. 2002-38, 2002-1 CB 1037.

[74] *See* § 3.14, below for a discussion of the IRC § 444 election.

[75] *See* § 3.13, below.

[76] Rev. Proc. 2006-46, 2006-2 CB 859.

[77] *See* § 3.07[E], below, for a discussion of "business purpose."

an ownership tax year[78]) and the terms, conditions, and adjustments necessary to obtain the Commissioner's approval.[79] Rev. Proc. 2002-39[80] provides the general rules for establishing business purpose and obtaining the Commissioner's prior approval of an adoption, change, or retention in annual accounting period through application to the IRS national office.

Automatic approval can be found in these Revenue Procedures:

- Rev. Proc. 2006-45[81] (describing automatic approval procedures allowing certain corporations to adopt, change, or retain an annual accounting period);
- Rev. Proc. 2006-46[82] (allowing partnerships, S corporations, electing S corporations, and personal service corporations to establish business purpose and to get automatic approval to adopt, change, or retain an annual accounting period);
- Rev. Proc. 2003-62[83] superseding Rev. Proc. 66-50[84] (providing automatic approval procedures allowing individuals to change from a fiscal to a calendar tax year);[85]
- Rev. Proc. 85-58[86] and Rev. Proc. 85-15[87] provide rules to correct invalid accounting periods;
- Rev. Proc. 87-27[88] provides rules for employee retirement plans and trusts; and
- Rev. Proc. 85-58[89] and Rev. Proc. 76-10[90] provide rules for exempt organizations.

[E] Approval of Commissioner

Where the taxpayer establishes a "business purpose" *and* agrees to the Commissioner's terms, conditions, and adjustments for the adoption, change, or retention, such adoption, change, or retention of a tax year will be approved by the Commissioner.[91] In determining whether a taxpayer has established a business purpose and which terms, conditions, and adjustments are required, consideration will be given to

---

[78] *See* § 3.11, below, for a discussion of an ownership taxable year.
[79] *See* Reg. § 1.442-1(b)(3).
[80] 2002-1 CB 1046.
[81] 2006-2 CB 851.
[82] 2006-2 CB 859.
[83] 2003-2 CB 299.
[84] 1966-2 CB 1260.
[85] Reg. § 1.442-1(b)(3).
[86] 1985-2 CB 740.
[87] 1985-1 CB 516.
[88] 1985-1 CB 580; *modified* by Ann. 88-97, 1988-26 IRB 47.
[89] 1985-2 CB 740.
[90] 1976-1 CB 548; *modified* by Rev. Proc. 79-3, 1979-1 CB 483.
[91] Rev. Proc. 2006-46, 2006-2 CB 859.

all the facts and circumstances relating to the adoption, change, or retention, including the resulting tax consequences.[92] Such terms, conditions, and adjustments may include adjustments necessary to neutralize the tax effects of a substantial distortion of income that would otherwise result from the requested change of the annual accounting period, including:

- a deferral of a substantial portion of the taxpayer's income;
- shifting of a substantial portion of deductions, from one taxable year to another;
- similar deferral or shifting in the case of any other person, such as a beneficiary in an estate;
- the creation of a short period in which there is a substantial net operating loss, capital loss, or credit (including a general business credit); or
- creation of a short period in which there is a substantial amount of income to offset an expiring net operating loss, capital loss, or credit.[93]

[F] Business Purpose

A taxpayer may use a taxable year other than its required taxable year if it satisfies the IRS that it has a business purpose for so doing.[94] An adoption, change, or retention of a taxable year will be approved by the Commissioner where the taxpayer establishes a "business purpose." Generally, the requirement of a business purpose is satisfied, and adjustments to neutralize any tax consequences are not required, if the requested annual accounting period coincides with the taxpayer's natural business year,[95] required tax year,[96] or ownership tax year.[97]

In the case of a partnership, S corporation, electing S corporation, or personal service corporation, a change in tax year in order to defer income to partners, shareholders, or employee-owners will not be treated as a business purpose.[98]

[G] Natural Business Year

A partnership, S corporation, electing S corporation, or personal service corporation can automatically elect a "natural business year"[99] by satisfying the following three-part, "25-percent gross receipts test." The 25% gross receipts test is described here first because it is the most objective and the most mechanical in application.

---

[92] Reg. § 1.442-1(b)(2).

[93] Rev. Proc. 2002-39, 2002-1 CB 1046, § 2.06.

[94] IRC § 441(i)(1); *see also* IRC § § 706(b)(1)(C), 1378(b); and Reg. § 1.442-1(b)(2).

[95] Reg. § 1.441-1(b)(2).

[96] *See* § 3.05 for a discussion of required tax year(s).

[97] *See* § 3.11 for a discussion of an ownership taxable year.

[98] Reg. § 1.442-1(b)(2).

[99] Rev. Proc. 2006-46, 2006-2 CB 859.

Part 1—Prior three years' gross receipts

- Gross receipts from sales and services for the most recent 12-month period that ends with the last month of the requested annual accounting period are totaled and then divided into the amount of gross receipts from sales and services for the last two months of this 12-month period.
- The same computation as above is made for the two preceding 12-month periods ending with the last month of the requested annual accounting period.[100]

Part 2—Natural business year

- Except as provided below, if each of the three results described in Part 1 equals or exceeds 25%, then the requested annual accounting period is deemed to be the taxpayer's natural business year.
- The taxpayer must determine whether any annual accounting period other than the requested annual accounting period also meets the 25-percent test. If one or more other annual accounting periods produce higher averages of the three percentages (rounded to 1/100 of a percent) than the requested annual accounting period, then the requested annual accounting period will not qualify as the taxpayer's natural business year.

Part 3—Special rules

- To apply the 25-percent gross receipts test for any particular year, the taxpayer must compute its gross receipts under the method of accounting used to prepare its federal income tax returns for such taxable year.
- If a taxpayer has a predecessor organization and is continuing the same business as its predecessor, the taxpayer must use the gross receipts of its predecessor for purposes of computing the 25-percent gross receipts test.
- If the taxpayer (including any predecessor organization) does not have a 47-month period of gross receipts (36-month period for requested taxable year plus additional 11-month period for comparing requested taxable year with other potential taxable years), then it cannot establish a natural business year under Rev. Proc. 2006-46.[101]
- If the requested taxable year is a 52-53-week taxable year, the calendar month ending nearest to the last day of the 52-53-week taxable year is treated as the last month of the requested taxable year for purposes of computing the 25-percent gross receipts test.

Example 3-11

An S corporation proposes to adopt a March 31 year-end. Its gross receipts from sales and services for the most recent 12-month period that ends with the last month of the requested annual accounting and the

---

[100] *Id.* § 5.07.

[101] 2006-2 CB 859.

amount of gross receipts from sales and services for the last two months of this 12-month period are as follows:

	Gross Receipts 12 months ending		
	Mar-18	**Mar-19**	**Mar-20**
Feb	75,000	80,000	85,000
Mar	80,000	85,000	90,000
Subtotal	155,000	165,000	175,000
% of total receipts	**28.18%**	**27.50%**	**26.52%**
Apr – Jan	395,000	435,000	485,000
Total	550,000	600,000	660,000

Based on this information, the gross receipts for the last two months of the requested tax year exceed 25% of the 12-month period. Therefore, March 31 will be considered the corporation's natural business year.

[H] Ruling Requests

If the taxpayer is not eligible for an automatic approval, Rev. Proc. 2002-39[102] provides procedures for establishing "business purpose" and for obtaining the Commissioner's approval to adopt, change or retain an annual accounting period for federal income tax purposes. Rev. Proc. 2002-39 is a revision and modification of Rev. Rul. 87-57,[103] in which the IRS issued advice to taxpayers unable to meet the requirements for a natural business year.[104] Unlike Rev. Proc. 2006-45, and Rev. Proc. 2006-46, Rev. Proc. 2002-39 does not grant automatic relief. Instead, a taxpayer who does not otherwise qualify for automatic relief can apply to the Commissioner for a ruling to change its tax year. It should be noted, however, that the Commissioner would grant permission to adopt, change, or retain a tax year only in rare and unusual circumstances.

If the requested tax year coincides with the entity's natural business year, a business purpose is established under Rev. Proc. 2002-39. The "natural business year" of an entity can be determined under any of the following tests:

- the Annual Business Cycle Test;
- the Seasonal Business Test; or
- the 25-percent gross receipts test, (aka) "Natural Business Year";[105] or

---

[102] 2002-1 CB 1046, *modified by* Notice 2002-72, 2002-2 CB 843; Rev. Proc. 2003-34, 2003-1 CB 856; Rev. Proc. 2003-79, 2003-2 CB 1036; Rev. Proc. 2018-17, 2018-9 IRB 384; and USTR 86,065.

[103] 1987-2 CB 117.

[104] Rev. Proc. 2002-39, 2002-1 CB 1046, § 5.03. *See* § 3.07[G] *infra*.

[105] *See* § 3.07[G] *infra*.

- based on all the relevant facts and circumstances the taxpayer can establish a business purpose under the "facts and circumstances test."[106]

[I] Annual Business Cycle Test

The Annual Business Cycle Test applies if the entity's gross receipts from sales and services for the short period and the three immediately preceding tax years indicate that the entity has a peak and a non-peak period of business. The natural business year is considered to end at the end of the highest peak period or "soon after" the close of the highest peak period of business. A business whose income is steady from month to month throughout the year will not meet this test.

A taxpayer that has not been in existence for a sufficient period to provide gross receipts information for the three immediately preceding taxable years may provide information other than gross receipts to demonstrate a peak and non-peak period of business, such as a description of its business and/or reasonable estimates of future gross receipts.[107]

Rev. Proc. 2002-39 provides a "safe harbor" where one month will be deemed to be "soon after" the close of the highest peak period of business.[108]

Example 3-12

A, a corporation, operates a retail business. The highest peak of A's annual business cycle occurs in December each year. In January, a significant amount of the merchandise that was purchased by A's customers in December is either returned or exchanged. A's natural business year is deemed to end on December 31st, or soon after the close of the highest peak period of business in December (January 31st). Accordingly, under the provisions of Rev. Proc. 2002-39, a request by A for a taxable year ending either December 31st or January 31st would be granted, subject to the general terms and conditions of the Revenue Procedure.

[J] Seasonal Business Test

If the taxpayer's gross receipts from sales and services for the short period and the three immediately preceding taxable years indicate that the taxpayer's business is operational for only part of the year (*e.g.*, due to weather conditions) and, as a result, the taxpayer has insignificant gross receipts during the period the business is not

---

[106] Rev. Proc. 2002-39, 2002-1 CB 1046, § 5.03.

[107] Rev. Proc. 2002-39, 2002-1 CB 1046, § 5.03(1).

[108] Rev. Proc. 2002-39, 2002-1 CB 1046, § 5.03(1)(b).

operational, the taxpayer's natural business year is deemed to end at, or soon after, the operations end for the season.[109]

A taxpayer that has not been in existence for a sufficient period to provide gross receipts information for the three immediately preceding taxable years may provide information other than gross receipts to demonstrate that it satisfies the requirements of a seasonal business, such as a description of its business and/or reasonable estimates of future gross receipts.[110]

Rev. Proc. 2002-39 provides a "safe harbor" such that an amount equal to less than 10% of the taxpayer's total gross receipts for the year will be deemed to be "insignificant," and one month will be deemed to be "soon after" the close of operations.

Example 3-13

B, a partnership, operates a ski resort from November through March of each year. During September and October, and during April, employees prepare the resort for the ski season, and close it down for the season, respectively. The resort earns less than 10% of its annual gross receipts during the period of April through October, when it is closed. B's natural business year is deemed to end on March 31st or soon after the close of the resort operations (April 30th). Accordingly, under the provisions of Rev. Proc. 2002-39, a request by B for a taxable year ending on either March 31st or April 30th would be granted, subject to the general terms and conditions of the Revenue Procedure.

[K] Facts and Circumstances Test

A taxpayer may establish a business purpose based on all the relevant facts and circumstances. This method of establishing a business purpose does not apply to automatic approval requests. Reasons like those listed below, which are administrative in nature or based on convenience, are insufficient to establish a business purpose for a particular tax year under the facts and circumstances test.[111]

- Using a particular year for regulatory or financial accounting purposes;
- Using a hiring pattern, such as typically hiring staff during certain times of the year;

---

[109] Rev. Proc. 2002-39, 2002-1 CB 1046, § 5.03(2).

[110] Rev. Proc. 2002-39, 2002-1 CB 1046, § 5.03(2).

[111] For other examples of situations in which a business purpose is not established, as well as examples of situations in which a substantial business purpose has been established, *see* Rev. Rul. 87-57, 1987-2 CB 117. Most of the situations mentioned in the Revenue Ruling are now covered by the annual Business Cycle Test and the Seasonal Business Cycle Test.

- Using a particular year for administrative purposes, such as for the admission or retirement of partners or shareholders, for the promotion of staff or for compensation or retirement arrangements with staff, partners, or shareholders;
- Using a price list, model year, or other item that changes on an annual basis;
- Deferring income to partners or shareholders; or
- Using a particular year used by related entities and competitors.

[L] *Taxpayers Deemed to Have Established a Business Purpose*

A taxpayer (other than a partnership, S corporation, electing S corporation, or PSC) that does not establish a business purpose for the requested annual accounting period under Rev. Proc. 2002-39, generally will be deemed to have established a business purpose if it provides a non-tax reason for the requested annual accounting period and agrees to the additional terms, conditions, and adjustments described Rev. Proc. 2002-39, which are intended to neutralize the tax effects of any resulting substantial distortion of income.[112]

Non-tax reasons for the requested annual accounting period may include administrative and convenience business reasons such as those described in § 5.02(1)(b) of Rev. Proc. 2002-39, and cited above. The Service anticipates that an individual taxpayer that is not a sole proprietor will be able to establish a non-tax reason for a fiscal year only in rare and unusual circumstances.[113]

§ 3.08 General Terms and Conditions

As with many current Revenue Procedures, Rev. Proc. 2002-39 (as well as Rev. Proc. 2006-45,[114] Rev. Proc. 2006-46,[115] Rev. Proc. 2002-39,[116] and Rev. Proc. 2003-62)[117] has a number of general terms and conditions that apply to all taxpayers trying to obtain approval to change a taxable year:

- **Short period tax return**. The taxpayer must file a federal income tax return for the short period required to effect a change in the annual accounting period by the due date of that return, including extensions. The taxpayer's taxable income for the short period generally must be annualized and the tax must be computed in accordance with the provisions of IRC § 443(b) and Reg. § 1.443-1(b).[118]

---

[112] Rev. Proc. 2002-39, 2002-1 CB 1046, § 5.02(2).

[113] *Id.*

[114] 2006-2 CB 851.

[115] 2006-2 CB 859.

[116] 2002-1 CB 1046.

[117] 2003-2 CB 299.

[118] However, for changes to (or from) a 52-53-week taxable year referencing the same month as the current (or requested) taxable year, *see* special rules in Reg. § 1.441-2. *See also*, for example, Reg.

- **Subsequent year tax returns**. Returns for subsequent taxable years generally must be made on the basis of a full 12 months (or on a 52-53-week basis) ending on the last day of the requested taxable year, unless the taxpayer secures the approval of the Commissioner to change its requested taxable year.
- **Record keeping/book conformity**. The books of the taxpayer must be closed as of the last day of the first effective year. Thereafter, the taxpayer must compute its income and keep its books and records (including financial statements and reports to creditors) on the basis of the requested taxable year, except that this requirement shall not apply:
  - — to books and records maintained solely for foreign law purposes (*e.g.*, foreign tax reporting purposes) or
  - — if the requested taxable year is either the taxpayer's required taxable year or ownership taxable year.[119]

§ 3.09 Automatic Approvals

Rev. Proc. 2006-45[120] provides the exclusive procedures to be followed by certain corporations (other than S corporations and personal service corporations) to obtain the automatic approval(s) necessary to change their annual accounting period(s) under IRC § 442 and Reg. § 1.442-1(b).[121] A corporation complying with all the applicable provisions of Rev. Proc. 2006-45 will be deemed to have established a business purpose and will be deemed to have obtained the approval of the Commissioner to change its annual accounting period.

[A] How Do the Automatic Approval Procedures Apply?

The automatic approval procedures apply to a corporation (including a member of a consolidated group) that wants to change to or from a 52-53-week tax year. Notwithstanding that corporations listed in numbers (1), (3), (4), (7), (9), and (12) below are excluded from these procedures, the automatic approval procedures apply to a corporation (including a member of a consolidated group) that wants to change from a 52-53-week tax year that references a particular month to a non-52-53-week tax year that ends on the last day of that month, and vice versa.

(Footnote Continued)

§ § 1.706-1(b)(8)(i)(B), 1.852-3(e), 1.857-2(a)(4), 1.1378-1(c)(2) and 1.1502-76 for exceptions to the annualization rule for a partnership, RIC, REIT, S corporation, and subsidiary corporation ceasing to be a member of a consolidated group, respectively.

[119] Note that this is one of the exceptions to the general rule that a taxpayer can maintain conversion workpapers to convert its GAAP book to cash.

[120] 2006-45 IRB 851. This Revenue Procedure has been modified and clarified by Rev. Proc. 2007-64, 2007-2 CB 818.

[121] This Revenue Procedure modifies, amplifies, and supersedes Rev. Proc. 2000-11, 2000-1 CB 309.

The automatic approval procedures apply to a corporation that wants to change to a natural business year that satisfies the 25-percent gross receipts test,[122] with the caveat that corporations listed in numbers (2) and (3) below are excluded from these procedures. If the taxpayer qualifies for more than one natural business year under the 25-percent gross receipts test, the fiscal year producing the highest average of the three percentages is used.[123]

The automatic approval procedures apply to a controlled foreign corporation (CFC) that wants to revoke its one-month deferral election under IRC § 898(c)(2) and wants to change its tax year to the majority United States shareholder year, notwithstanding that corporations listed in numbers (1) to (12) below are excluded from these procedures.[124]

The automatic procedures *do not* apply to the following corporations:

(1) a corporation that has a prior change in accounting periods within the most recent 48-month period ending with the last month of the requested tax year;
(2) a corporation with an interest in a pass-through entity;
(3) a corporation that is a shareholder of certain foreign sales corporations (FSCs) or interest charge domestic international sales corporations (IC-DISCs);
(4) an FSC or IC-DISC;
(5) an S corporation;
(6) an electing S corporation;
(7) a Personal Service Corporation (PSC);
(8) a Controlled Foreign Corporation (CFC);
(9) a tax-exempt organization;
(10) a possessions corporation;
(11) a cooperative association; and
(12) a corporation with a required tax year.[125]

§ 3.10 Alternative Tax Year(s)

In some instances, entities may adopt a different taxable year or retain their existing taxable year.[126] Taxpayers may also elect to use a 52-53-week taxable year that ends with reference to their required taxable year.[127]

A partnership, S corporation, or personal service corporation may use a taxable year other than its required taxable year if the taxpayer:

---

122 *See* § 3.07[G], *infra*, for a discussion of the "25-percent gross receipts test."
123 Rev. Proc. 2006-45, 2006-2 CB 851, § 5.04.
124 Rev. Proc. 2006-45, 2006-2 CB 851, § 4.01.
125 Rev. Proc. 2006-45, 2006-2 CB 851, § 4.01.
126 *See* § 3.07[C], *infra*, for a discussion of retention of taxable years.
127 *See* § 3.04, *infra*

- elects to use a taxable year other than its required taxable year under IRC § 444;
- elects to use a 52-53-week taxable year that ends with reference to its required taxable year (as provided in paragraph (b)(2)(ii)(A) of IRC § 444);[128]
- elects to use a 52-53-week taxable year that ends with reference to a taxable year elected under IRC § 444;[129] or
- establishes a business purpose to the satisfaction of the Commissioner under IRC § 442,[130] or has a grandfathered fiscal year.

A specified foreign corporation, as defined in IRC § 898(b), may use a taxable year other than its required taxable year if it elects a 52-53-week taxable year that ends with reference to its required taxable year (as provided in paragraph (b)(2)(ii)(A) of IRC § 444) or makes a one-month deferral election under IRC § 898(c)(1)(B).

§ 3.11 Ownership Taxable Year

For an S corporation or an electing S corporation, an "ownership taxable year" is the taxable year (if any) that, as of the first day of the first effective year, constitutes the taxable year of one or more shareholders (including any shareholder that concurrently changes to such taxable year) holding more than 50% of the corporation's issued and outstanding shares of stock. A shareholder that wants to concurrently change its taxable year must follow the instructions generally applicable to taxpayers changing their taxable years contained in Reg. § 1.442-1(b), Rev. Proc. 2006-45, or any other applicable administrative procedure published by the Commissioner.[131]

Shareholders that are tax-exempt under IRC § 501(a) are disregarded if they are not subject to tax on any income attributable to the S corporation. This is similar to the principles for determining the taxable year of a partnership under Reg. § 1.706-1. Tax-exempt shareholders are not disregarded, however, if the S corporation is wholly owned by the tax-exempt entities.

§ 3.12 Corporations

[A] Generally

A C corporation may adopt as its tax year a calendar or fiscal year. In either case, the corporation should maintain books on the basis of the selected year.[132]

---

[128] *See*, for example, Reg. §§ 1.441-3 (PSCs), 1.706-1 (partnerships), 1.1378-1 (S corporations) and 1.1502-76(a)(1) (members of a consolidated group).

[129] *See* § 3.14 *below* for a discussion of the IRC § 444 election.

[130] Rev. Proc. 2006-46, 2006-2 CB 859.

[131] Rev. Proc. 2006-46, 2006-2 CB 859, § 6.06.

[132] IRC § 441(c).

A corporation may use only one tax year for all of its businesses. The same tax year must be used by all of its divisions. If a different tax year is required or needed, then the divisions should be separated into difference businesses.[133]

[B] Initial Tax Year

A corporation in existence during any portion of a tax year must file a federal tax return.[134] If the corporation was in existence only for a portion of the annual accounting period, a fractional or short year return must be filed.

Often newly-formed corporations are dormant for a period before there is business activity. This can happen, for example, when the corporate-taxpayer's attorney files a certificate of incorporation and then the taxpayer does nothing with the corporation until sometime later. Books and records may not be kept during this dormant period. Nonetheless, the corporation must file a tax return for its initial dormant period, unless it is relieved from doing so because it had never perfected its organization. If the corporation has not transacted business, has no income, and has no shareholders, it is not a corporation for federal tax purposes and relief from filing a tax return may be granted by the District Director upon presentation of all of the facts.[135]

Where such relief has not been granted, a dormant corporation that fails to file a return may be subject to penalties for its initial inactive period.[136] Moreover, the corporation could be denied the choice of a fiscal year because it failed to take steps necessary to establish an annual accounting period.[137] The failure to maintain books and records, even during an initial dormant period, may result in the entity's inability to select a fiscal year.[138] Accordingly, a new corporation should be careful to

---

[133] Businesses which file a consolidated return must use the tax year of the parent corporation. Reg. § 1.1501-76.

[134] *See* Instructions for Forms 1120 and 1120-A and Reg. § 1.6012-2(a)(2). A corporation in existence during any portion of a taxable year is required to file a return. If a corporation was not in existence throughout an annual accounting period (either calendar year or fiscal year), the corporation is required to file a return for that fractional part of a year during which it was in existence. A corporation is not in existence after it ceases business and dissolves, retaining no assets, whether or not under state law it may thereafter be treated as continuing as a corporation for certain limited purposes connected with winding up its affairs, such as for the purpose of suing and being sued. If the corporation has valuable claims for which it will bring suit during this period, it has retained assets and therefore continues in existence. A corporation does not go out of existence if it is turned over to receivers or trustees who continue to operate it. If a corporation has received a charter but has never perfected its organization and has transacted no business and has no income from any source, it may, upon presentation of the facts to the district director, be relieved from the necessity of filing a return. In the absence of a proper showing of such facts to the district director, a corporation will be required to file a return. Reg. § 1.6012-2(a)(2).

[135] Rev. Rul. 60-51, 1960-1 CB 169; Reg. § 6012.2(a)(2).

[136] IRC § 6651(a)(1).

[137] *See* IRC § 441(g). *See also* Chapter 2, *infra*.

[138] In *Calhoun v. United States*, 370 F. Supp. 434, 74-1 USTC ¶ 9104 (D. Va. 1973), a corporation was denied the right to adopt a fiscal year and to elect S status because it failed to maintain proper books and records during its dormant period.

maintain books and records on an annual accounting basis, and file its tax return in accordance therewith.[139]

[C] Personal Service Corporations

A personal service corporation may select, as its taxable year, from any of the following options:[140]

- a calendar year, or a "short period" ending on December 31;
- a fiscal year, or "short period" (other than a short period ending on December 31) if the corporation obtains the approval of the Commissioner;
- a taxable year elected under IRC § 444; or
- a 52-53-week taxable year ending with reference to the calendar year.

In effect, personal service corporations are subject to the same rules as partnerships and S corporations.

For an entity to be classified as a personal service corporation the following requirements must be met:

- the taxpayer must be a C corporation as defined in IRC § 1361(a)(2) for the tax year;
- the principal activity for the tax year is the performance of personal services;
- the personal services must be substantially performed by employee/owners; and
- the employee/owners must own, using attribution rules, more than 10% of the fair market value of the outstanding stock on the last day of the tax year.[141]

Only certain enumerated activities are treated as the performance of personal services. The regulations refer to those services described in IRC § 448(d)(2)(A), *i.e.*, activities which involve the performance of services in the fields of health,[142] law, engineering, architecture, accounting, actuarial science, or the performing arts[143] and

---

[139] *See* IRC § 441(g).

[140] Reg. § 1.441-3.

[141] Reg. § 1.441-3(c)(1).

[142] The performance of services in the field of health means the provision of medical services by physicians, nurses, dentists, and other similar healthcare professionals. The performance of services in the field of health does not include the provision of services not directly related to a medical field, even though the services may purportedly relate to the health of the service recipient. For example, the performance of services in the field of health does not include the operation of health clubs or health spas that provide physical exercise or conditioning to their customers. Temp. Reg. § 1.448-1T(e)(4)(ii).

[143] The performance of services in the field of the performing arts means the provision of services by actors, actresses, singers, musicians, entertainers, and similar artists in their capacity as such. The performance of services in the field of the performing arts does not include the provision of services by persons who themselves are not performing artists (*e.g.*, persons who may manage or promote such artists, and other persons in a trade or business that relates to the performing arts). Similarly, the performance of services in the field of the performing arts does not include the provision of services by persons who broadcast or otherwise disseminate the performances of such artists to members of

consulting.[144] If an activity is not specifically described in the statute or regulations, it will not be treated as the performance of personal services.[145]

Consider the following examples of what is or is not considered personal services:

- Veterinarians, even though they may perform boarding and grooming services that are incidental to health care are personal services;[146]
- Physical therapists employed by a corporation engaging solely in the business of providing physical therapy services are personal services;[147]
- Claim staking for mineral rights, similar to, but not considered to be, engineering services, are not personal services;[148]
- Tax return preparation and bookkeeping services provided to clients are accounting services for purposes of defining a qualified personal service corporation, even where providing tax return preparation and bookkeeping services does not constitute "public accounting" and does not require a CPA license under state law; these services were held to be personal services;[149] and
- Persons who broadcast or otherwise disseminate the performances of artists to members of the public (*e.g.*, employees of a radio station that broadcasts the performances of musicians and singers) are not performing personal services.[150]

[D] S Corporations

The tax year of an S corporation shall be a "permitted year."[151] A permitted year is a year that ends on December 31st or any other accounting period for which the corporation establishes a business purpose to the satisfaction of the Secretary.[152] An electing S corporation that wants to adopt, change to, or retain a taxable year other than its required taxable year must request approval of the Commissioner on Form 2553, *Election by a Small Business Corporation*. The election form is filed with the

(Footnote Continued)

the public (*e.g.*, employees of a radio station that broadcasts the performances of musicians and singers). Finally, the performance of services in the field of the performing arts does not include the provision of services by athletes. Temp. Reg. § 1.448-1T(e)(4)(iii).

[144] The performance of services in the field of consulting means the provision of advice and counsel. The performance of services in the field of consulting does not include the performance of services other than advice and counsel, such as sales or brokerage services, or economically similar services. Temp. Reg. § 1.448-1T(e)(4)(iv).

[145] Priv. Ltr. Rul. 8913012.

[146] Rev. Rul. 91-30, 1991-1 CB 61. *modified* by Rev. Rul. 92-65, 1992-2 CB 94.

[147] Priv. Ltr. Rul. 9222004.

[148] Priv. Ltr. Rul. 9232009.

[149] *Rainbow Tax Service, Inc.*, 128 T.C. 42 (2007).

[150] Temp. Reg. § 1.448-1T.

[151] IRC § 1378(a).

[152] IRC § 1378(b).

service center designated in the instructions applicable to Form 2553. The election is not valid unless all shareholders of the corporation at the time of the election consent to the election. However, once a valid election is made, new shareholders need not consent to that election.

§ 3.13 Partnerships

[A] Generally

Under IRC § 706(b), a partnership must adopt a required tax year under one of the following three rules which are applied in successive order:

- the "Majority Interest Rule";
- the "Principal Partner Rule"; or
- the "Least Aggregate Deferral Rule."

The rules which govern the selection and change of a partnership's tax year are designed to ensure that the partnership's tax year conforms to the tax year of its owners unless the partnership has a business purpose for selecting a different tax year or makes an IRC § 444 election.[153]

[B] Rule #1: Majority Interest Rule

A "majority interest tax year" is the tax year that, on the testing day, constituted the tax year of one or more partners having (on the testing day) an aggregate interest in partnership profits and capital of more than 50%.[154]

Example 3-14

Annox Co., a Delaware partnership, has the following members:

Tan Corp. Inc. which owns 75% of Annox and has a year ending on October 31st, and Cal Lang, an individual who has a year ending December 31st and who owns the remaining 25% of Annox. The application of the "majority interest rule" results in the partnership year ending on October 31st.

---

[153] *See* § 3.14, *below*, for a discussion of the IRC § 444 election.

[154] IRC § 706(b)(4)(A)(i). The testing day is the first day of the partnership tax year, or, a representative period as may be prescribed by the Secretary if such period is more representative of the ownership of the partnership. IRC § 706(b)(4)(A)(ii). If a partnership is required to change its tax year to the majority interest tax year, it is not required to change to another tax year for either of the two tax years following the year of change. IRC § 706(b)(4)(B).

[C] Rule #2: Principal Partner Rule

If a tax year cannot be established under the majority interest rule, then the tax year shall be the same tax year as that of all of its "principal partners," *i.e.*, partners with an interest of 5% or more in the partnership's capital or profits.[155]

Example 3-15

Annox Co., a Delaware partnership, has the following members:

Tan Corp. Inc. which owns 49% of Annox and has a year ending on October 31st; Coral Corp. which owns 4% of Annox and has a year ending August 31st; and a variety of individuals, corporations, and other entities who together own the balance of the partnership but each individually owns no more than 2% of the partnership. The application of the "Principal Partner Rule" results in the partnership year ending on October 31st.

[D] Rule #3: Least Aggregate Deferral Rule

If a partnership tax year cannot be established under the "Majority Interest Rule" or the "Principal Partner Rule," IRC § 706(b)(1)(B)(ii) provides that the calendar year will be used unless the Secretary, by Regulations, prescribes another period. The Secretary has prescribed the "Least Aggregate Deferral Rule" for this situation. Under Reg. § 1.706-1(b)(3), the tax year that will result in the least aggregate deferral of income to the partners will be the required tax year.

The aggregate deferral for a particular year is equal to the sum of the products determined by multiplying the month(s) of deferral for each partner that would be generated by that year and each partner's interest in partnership profits for that year.

Note, a partner may have different capital interest for profits and losses. The least aggregate deferral rule is applied by reference to the partner's profit interest. For purposes of IRC § 706(b), a partner's interest in partnership profits is generally the partner's percentage share of partnership profits for the current partnership taxable year. If the partnership does not expect to have net income for the current partnership taxable year, then a partner's interest in partnership profits instead must be the partner's percentage share of partnership net income for the first taxable year in which the partnership expects to have net income.[156]

For purposes of applying the least aggregate deferral rule, tax-exempt partners are disregarded. In determining the taxable year (the current year) of a partnership under IRC § 706(b) and the Regulations thereunder, a partner that is tax-exempt under IRC § 501(a) shall be disregarded if such partner was not subject to tax under Chapter 1 of the Internal Revenue Code on any income attributable to its investment in the partnership during the partnership's taxable year immediately preceding the current year.[157]

---

[155] IRC § 706(b)(1)(B)(ii).

[156] Reg. § 1.706-1(b)(4)(ii).

[157] Reg. § 1.706-1(b)(5).

The partner's tax year that produces the lowest sum when compared to the other partners' tax years is the tax year that results in the least aggregate deferral of income to the partners and will be used as the tax year for the partnership. If the calculation results in more than one tax year qualifying as the tax year with the least aggregate deferral, *i.e.*, a "tie," the partnership may select any one of those tax years as its tax year. However, if one of the qualifying tax years is also the partnership's existing tax year, the partnership must maintain its existing tax year. The determination of the tax year that results in the least aggregate deferral of income is generally made at the beginning of the partnership's current tax year.[158]

Example 3-16

An example of how this rule is applied follows.

Assume Abe and two corporations, Xeon and Yale, form a partnership. The parties are unrelated. Abe's year-end is 12/31, Xeon's year-end is 6/30, and Yale's year-end is 9/30. The ownership interests of Abe, Xeon, and Yale are 20%, 40%, and 40%, respectively. Since no one partner owns a majority interest, the "Majority Interest Rule" does not apply. Likewise, the "Principal Partner Rule" is inapplicable because there is more than one principal partner (Abe, Xeon, and Yale) who do not have the same tax year. Accordingly, the partnership must rely on the "Least Aggregate Deferral Rule" to determine its taxable year. In applying this rule to this hypothetical partnership, the following comparisons should be made.

Partnership Tax Year End	Partner	Year End	Profits Interest	Months of Deferral	Aggregate Deferral
12/31	Abe	12/31	.20	0	0
	Xeon	6/30	.40	6	2.4
	Yale	9/30	.40	9	3.6
				TOTAL	6.0
9/30	Abe	12/31	.20	3	.6
	Xeon	6/30	.40	9	3.6
	Yale	9/30	.40	0	0
				TOTAL	4.2
6/30	Abe	12/31	.20	6	1.2
	Xeon	6/30	.40	0	0
	Yale	9/30	.40	3	1.2
				TOTAL	2.4

[158] Reg. § 1.706-1(b)(3).

Based upon the above comparisons, the partnership required year end is 6/30 because it produces the least aggregate deferral unless, of course, the partnership qualifies for a different tax year under the business purpose doctrine, or makes an IRC § 444 election.

Example 3-17

Tax Exempt Partner. Assume that partnership A has historically used the calendar year as its taxable year. In addition, assume that A is owned by five partners, four calendar year individuals (each owning 10% of A's profits and capital) and a tax-exempt organization (owning 60% of A's profits and capital). The tax-exempt organization has never had unrelated business taxable income with respect to A and has historically used a June 30 fiscal year. Finally, assume that A desires to retain the calendar year for its taxable year beginning January 1, 2018. Under these facts and the least aggregate deferral rule, A would be required under IRC § 706(b)(1)(B)(i) to change to a year ending June 30, for its taxable year beginning January 1, 2018. However, under the special rule provided in IRC § 706(b)(5)(i), the partner that is tax-exempt is disregarded, and A must retain the calendar year, under IRC § 706(b)(1)(B)(i), for its taxable year beginning January 1.[159]

[E] Procedural Requirements

Note the following if a partnership changes its tax year due to the application of the "Least Aggregate Deferral Rule":

- the change in accounting period will be treated as a change initiated by the partnership and it will be deemed to have the consent of the Commissioner;
- a computation of the least aggregate deferral should be attached to the short period return;[160] and
- the partnership must complete and file a Form 1128, *Application to Adopt, Change, or Retain a Tax Year*, and should write at the top of the form "FILED UNDER REV. PROC. 2006-46." The completed form must be mailed to the Director, Internal Revenue Service, Attention: ENTITY CONTROL, where the partnership files its federal income tax return, no earlier than the day following the end of the first effective year and no later than the due date (including extensions) for filing the federal income tax return for the first effective tax year. A general partner who has personal knowledge of the facts must sign

---

[159] The same rule applies in the case of a foreign partner. Reg. § 1.706-1(b)(6).

[160] To effect the change, a partnership must show that the requirements of Reg. § 1.706-1 are satisfied in a statement setting forth the computations required to establish the taxable year that results in the least aggregate deferral of income to the partners.

the Form 1128. A user fee is not required. The partnership also must timely file a tax return for the short period required to effect the change and attach a copy of the Form 1128. The partnership must then file subsequent tax returns for full 12-month periods ending on the last day of the requested tax year.[161]

[F] Special De Minimis *Rule*

If the tax year that results in the least aggregate deferral produces an aggregate deferral that is less than .5% when compared to the aggregate deferral of the current tax year, the partnership's current tax year shall be treated as the tax year with the least aggregate deferral. The partnership will not be permitted to change its taxable year.[162]

§3.14 IRC §444 Election

A partnership, an S corporation, or a personal service corporation that does not wish to use a required tax year may make an IRC §444 election to adopt a fiscal year without first seeking the Commissioner's consent. Three conditions must be met:

(1) the entity must not be a member of a tiered structure;

(2) the entity must not have made an IRC §444 election previously; and

(3) generally, the fiscal year must not be a "deferral period" of more than three months, *i.e.*, the fiscal year end must be a September, October, or November.[163]

[A] Deferral Period

The term "deferral period" means the number of months between the last day of the elected tax year and the last day of the required tax year. For example, if you elected a tax year that ends on September 30 and your required tax year is the calendar year, the deferral period would be three months (the number of months between September 30 and December 31).

---

[161] A change that does not qualify for automatic approval must be made under Rev. Proc. 2002-39, 2002-1 CB 1046.

[162] *See* Reg. §1.706-1(b)(3)(iii).

[163] IRC §444(b).

Example 3-18

ABC, a C corporation, that historically used a tax year ending October 31, elects S status and wants to make an IRC § 444 election for its tax year beginning November 1. ABC's required tax year under IRC § 1378 is a calendar tax year. In this case, the deferral period of the tax year being changed is two months. Thus, ABC may elect to retain its tax year beginning November 1 and ending October 31 or elect a tax year beginning on December 1 (with a deferral period of one month). However, it may not elect a tax year beginning October 1 because the three-month deferral period would be longer than the two-month deferral period of the tax year being changed. If ABC elects a tax year beginning on December 1, it must file a short tax year return beginning November 1 and ending November 30.

[B] Effect of IRC § 444 Election

Partnerships and S corporations. An electing partnership or S corporation must file Form 8752, *Required Payment or Refund under Section 7519*, for each year the election is in effect. Form 8752 is used to determine and make the payment required under IRC § 7519 or to obtain a refund of net prior year payments. Form 8752 must be filed by May 15 following the calendar year in which each applicable election year begins.

The IRC § 444 election will end if the partnership or S corporation willfully fails to comply with the requirements of IRC § 7519.

Personal service corporations (PSC). An electing PSC should not file Form 8752. Instead, it must comply with the minimum distribution requirements (see below) of IRC § 280H for each year the election is in effect. If the PSC does not meet these requirements, the applicable amounts it may deduct for payments made to its employee-owners may be limited.

To determine the required minimum distribution and the maximum deductible amount, use Schedule H (Form 1120), *Section 280H Limitations for a Personal Service Corporation (PSC)*. Attach Schedule H to the income tax return of the PSC for each tax year the PSC does not meet the minimum distribution requirements.

The IRC § 444 election will end if the PSC is penalized for willfully failing to comply with the requirements of IRC § 280H.

[C] When to File

Form 8716 must be signed and filed by the earlier of:

(1) The 15th day of the 5th month following the month that includes the 1st day of the tax year the election will be effective; or
(2) The due date (not including extensions) of the income tax return for the tax year resulting from the IRC § 444 election.

Items 1 and 2 relate to the tax year, or the return for the tax year, for which the ending date is entered on line 5 of Form 8716.

Under Reg. § 301.9100-2, the entity is automatically granted a 12-month extension to make an election on Form 8716. To obtain an extension, type or legibly print "Filed Pursuant To § 301.9100-2" at the top of Form 8716, and file the form within 12 months of the original due date.

Attach a copy of Form 8716 to Form 1065, Form 1120S, or Form 1120 for the first tax year for which the election is made. Below are two examples illustrating the filing requirements for Form 8716.

Example 3-19

AB, a partnership, begins operations on September 13, 2020, and is qualified to make an IRC § 444 election to use a September 30 tax year for its tax year beginning September 13, 2020. AB must file Form 8716 by December 15, 2020,[164] which is the due date of the partnership's tax return for the period from September 13, 2020 to September 30, 2020.

Example 3-20

The facts are the same as in Example 3-19, except that AB begins operations on October 21, 2020. AB must file Form 8716 by February 15, 2021, the 15th day of the fifth month of the tax year for which the election will first be effective.

An S corporation must state on Form 2553 its intention to make an IRC § 444 election or a back-up IRC § 444 election.[165] Form 8716 need not be attached to Form 2553.

There is an automatic extension of 12 months to make the IRC § 444 election.[166]

Members of certain tiered structures may not make election. No election may be made under IRC § 444(a) by an entity that is part of a tiered structure other than a tiered structure that consists entirely of partnerships and/or S corporations all of which have the same tax year. An election previously made will be terminated if an entity later becomes part of a tiered structure that is not allowed to make the election.[167]

---

[164] The December 15th year end represents the change in entity tax return due dates.

[165] The election is made on Part II, Section R.

[166] *See* the Form 8716 instructions for more information.

[167] *See* Temp. Reg. § 1.444-2T for other details.

[D] Required Payments/Distributions

As a result of making an IRC §444 election, the entity must make the "required payments" pursuant to IRC §7519.

[E] Required Payment for Partnership or S Corporation

A partnership or an S corporation must make a "required payment" for any tax year:

- the IRC §444 election is in effect; and
- the required payment for that year (or any preceding tax year) is more than $500.[168]

This payment represents the value of the tax deferral the owners receive by using a tax year different from the required tax year.

Form 8752 must be filed each year the IRC §444 election is in effect, even if no payment is due.[169] If the required payment is more than $500 (or the required payment for any prior year was more than $500), the payment must be made when Form 8752 is filed. If the required payment is $500 or less and no payment was required in a prior year, Form 8752 must be filed showing a zero amount.[170]

Form 8752 must be filed and the required payment made (or zero amount reported) by May 15th of the calendar year following the calendar year in which the applicable election year begins.[171] Any tax year for which an IRC §444 election is in effect, including the first year, is called an "applicable election year." If a partnership's applicable election year begins July 1, 2020, for example, Form 8752 must be filed by May 15, 2021.

Example 3-21

Assume Westcott Corp., an existing corporation, converts from a C corporation to an S corporation and elects under IRC §444 to retain its September 30 year, rather than convert to a calendar year. The election is to be effective October 1, 2020. Westcott Corp. will make its IRC §444 election on a timely filed Form 2553. Because Westcott is an electing S corporation, it need not file Form 8716 separately, nor does it need to attach a copy to Form 2553. Since the election begins October 1, 2020, the first required payment is due May 15, 2021.

---

[168] IRC §7519(a).

[169] Temp. Reg. §1.7519-2T.

[170] Reg. §1.7519-2T(a)(2)(i).

[171] *See* Instruction for Form 8752 and Temp. Reg. §1.444-3T.

Example 3-22

Required payment where no applicable payments are made:

Following the same facts as the prior example:

Westcott Corp. had net income of $1,200,000 for the year ending September 30, 2020 (its last year as a C corporation) and $1,800,000 for the year ending September 30, 2021 (its first year as an S corporation). No salary or other compensation was paid to any of its shareholders. The required payment (where no salary or other applicable payment is made to a shareholder of the corporation) can be determined using the following formula:

Required Payment = (P × R × D × NI) - PP

where

P = The applicable percentage (for tax years commencing in 1990 or thereafter, P is 100%)

R = The highest tax rate charged to individuals pursuant to IRC § 1 + 1% (or 38%).

D = The deferral ratio (total months in deferral period (3) divided by total months (12)).

NI = The net income for the prior taxable year.

PP = The prior required payment balance.

Required Payment due on May 15, 2021 for its first election year ended September 30, 2020:

(100% × 38% × 3/12 × $1,200,000) – 0 = $114,000.

Required Payment due on May 15, 2022 for its second election year ended September 30, 2021:

(100% × 38% × 3/12 × $1,800,000) – $114,000 = $57,000.

Example 3-23

Required payment where applicable payments are made:

Following the same facts as in the prior two examples, Westcott Corp. paid $240,000 in salary to a shareholder in 12 equal installments during its year ending September 30, 2020. During its year ending September 30, 2021, Westcott paid the same salary to the shareholder; in addition, the shareholder received a $100,000 bonus on January 1, 2021. The required payment where applicable payments are made to a shareholder can be determined using the following formula:

Required Payment = ((D × (NI + AP) - A) × P × R) – PP

where

AP = The amount of applicable payments made by the corporation during the prior taxable year.

A = The aggregate amount of applicable payments made during the deferral period.

Note: The deferral period for the year ended September 30, 2020 would be October 1, 2020 through December 31, 2020.

Required Payment due on May 15, 2021 for its first election year ended September 30, 2020:

((3/12 × ($1,200,000 + $240,000)) – ($240,000 × 3/12) × 100% × 38%) – 0 = $114,000.

Required Payment due on May 15, 2022 for its second election year ended September 30, 2021:

((3/12 × ($1,800,000 + $340,000)) – ($240,000 × 3/12) × 100% × 38% – $114,000 = $66,500.

If all of the applicable payments had been made pro-rata, an additional $25,000 would have been included in the shareholders income as of December 31, 2020 ($340,000 × 3/12 = $85,000, $240,000 × 3/12 = $60,000). The additional required payment reflects the tax effect of this deferral ($25,000 × 38% = $9,500).

[F] Minimum Distribution for Personal Service Corporation

In order to negate a deferral of income by employee-owners, a personal service corporation with an IRC § 444 election in effect must distribute minimum amounts to employee-owners by December 31st of each applicable year.[172] If it fails to make these distributions, it may be required to defer certain deductions for amounts paid to employees-owners. The amount deferred is treated as paid or incurred in the following tax year.[173]

Calculation of minimum distribution amount. A personal service corporation (PSC) meets the minimum distribution requirement for an applicable election year if, during the "deferral period" for that tax year, the total applicable amounts[174] for all employee-owners (determined by excluding applicable amounts carried over from the preceding tax year) equal or exceed the lesser of:

---

172 Temp. Reg. § 1.280H-1T(b)(1).

173 Temp. Reg. § 1.280H-1T(b)(2).

174 The "applicable amount" for a tax year is any amount that is otherwise deductible by a personal service corporation in such year and includible at any time, directly or indirectly, in the gross income of a taxpayer that during such year is an employee-owner. Temp. Reg. § 1.280H-1T(b)(4)(i).

(a) the amount determined under the "preceding year test";[175] or
(b) the amount determined under the "three-year average test."[176]

For purpose of the above rule, "deferral period" is defined in IRC § 444(b)(4) and means the number of months between the beginning of the fiscal tax year elected under IRC § 444(a) and the following December 31.[177]

Example 3-24

Q, an accrual-basis personal service corporation, makes an IRC § 444 election to retain a year ending January 31 for its taxable year beginning February 1, 1987. Q has four employee-owners, B, C, D, and E. For Q's applicable election year beginning February 1, 1987 and ending January 31, 1988, B earns $6,000 a month plus a $45,000 bonus on January 15, 1988; C earns $5,000 a month plus a $40,000 bonus on January 15, 1988; D and E each earn $4,500 a month plus a $4,000 bonus on January 15, 1988. Q meets the minimum distribution requirement for such applicable election year if the applicable amounts during the deferral period (*i.e.*, $220,000) equal or exceed the amount determined under the preceding year test or the three-year average test.

Maximum deductible amount. To compute the maximum deductible amount, take the sum of (1) the applicable amount paid during the deferral period of the applicable election year, plus (2) the product of the amount determined under "1" above, divided by the number of months in the deferral period of the applicable election year, multiplied by the number of months in the nondeferral period (*i.e.*, the portion of the applicable election year after the portion of such year constituting the deferral period) of the applicable election year.[178]

Example 3-25

XYZ, Inc. is an accrual method PSC with a taxable year ending January 31. It makes an IRC § 444 election to retain a year ending January 31 for its taxable year beginning February 1, 2021. For its applicable election year

---

[175] The minimum distribution amount under this "preceding year test" is determined by:

(1) dividing: (a) the "applicable amounts" during the taxable year preceding the applicable election year by (b) the number of months (but not less than one) in the preceding tax year, and
(2) multiplying the result from (1) by the number of months in the deferral period of the applicable election. Temp. Reg. § 1.280H-1T(c)(2)(i).

[176] The "three-year average test." In order to pass this test, the "applicable amounts" for the PSC's deferral period of the current applicable election year must equal or exceed the "applicable percentage" of the PSC's "adjusted taxable income" for such deferral period. IRC § 280H(c)(1)(B); Temp. Reg. § 1.280H-1T(c)(3)(i).

[177] IRC § 444(b)(4).

[178] Temp. Reg. § 1.280H-1T(d).

beginning February 1, 2021, XYZ, Inc. does not satisfy the minimum distribution requirement. Furthermore, XYZ, Inc. has three employee-owners, A, B, and C. A and B have been employee-owners of XYZ, Inc. for ten years. Although C has been an employee of XYZ, Inc. for four years, C did not become an employee-owner until December 1, 2020, when C acquired five of the 20 outstanding shares of XYZ, Inc. stock. For XYZ, Inc.'s applicable election year beginning February 1, 2021, A earns $5,000 a month plus a $40,000 bonus on January 15, 2021, and B and C each earn $4,000 a month plus a $32,000 bonus on January 15, 2021. Thus, the total of the applicable amounts during the deferral period of the applicable election year beginning February 1, 2021 is $143,000. Based on these facts, XYZ, Inc.'s deduction for applicable amounts is limited to $156,000, determined as follows—$143,000 (applicable amounts during the deferral period) plus $13,000 (applicable amounts during the deferral period, divided by the number of months in the deferral period, multiplied by the number of months in the nondeferral period).

[G] Failure to Make Required Payments

Required payments are treated as a subchapter C tax for purposes of interest on underpayments, penalties and collection. Accordingly, interest is imposed at the underpayment rate under IRC § 6621 on any required payment that is not paid by the due date. A penalty of 10% is imposed on the underpayment. Fraud and negligence penalties may also apply.[179] If the failure to make the required payment is willful, the IRC § 444 election will terminate.[180]

[H] Ending the Election

The IRC § 444 election remains in effect until it is terminated. If the election is terminated, another IRC § 444 election cannot be made for any tax year.[181]

A termination of an IRC § 444 election is effective:

- in the case of a change to the required year, on the first day of the short year caused by the change;
- in the case of a liquidating entity, on the date the liquidation is completed for tax purposes;
- in the case of willful failure to comply, on the first day of the taxable year (determined as if an IRC § 444 election had never been made) determined in the discretion of the District Director;

---

179 IRC § 7519(f)(4)(a).

180 Priv. Ltr. Rul. 9419002; Reg. § 1.444-1T(a)(5).

181 IRC § 444(d)(2)(B).

- in the case of membership in a tiered structure, on the first day of the taxable year in which the entity is considered to be a member of a tiered structure, or such other taxable year determined in the discretion of the District Director;
- in the case of termination of S status, on the first day of the taxable year for which S status no longer exists; or
- in the case of a personal service corporation that changes status, on the first day of the taxable year for which the entity is no longer a personal service corporation.

The election will also end if either of the following events occurs:

- An S corporation's S election is terminated. However, if the S corporation immediately becomes a PSC, the PSC can continue the IRC §444 election of the S corporation.
- A PSC ceases to be a PSC. If the PSC elects to be an S corporation, the S corporation can continue the election of the PSC.[182]

In the event that an IRC §444 election is terminated by the IRS due to the entity's willful failure to comply with required payments or distributions, and the termination results in a short taxable year, an income tax return is required for the short period. In order to allow the IRS to process the affected income tax return in an efficient manner, a partnership, S corporation, or personal service corporation that files a short period return should type or legibly print at the top of the first page of the income tax return for the short taxable year: "SECTION 444 ELECTION TERMINATED." In addition, a personal service corporation that changes its taxable year to the required taxable year is required to annualize its income for the short period.[183]

§3.15 Back-Up IRC §444 Elections

[A] Generally

A partnership, S corporation, or personal service corporation (PSC) can file a back-up IRC §444 election if it requests (or plans to request) permission to use a business purpose tax year. If the request is denied, the back-up IRC §444 election must be activated (if the partnership, S corporation, or PSC otherwise qualifies).[184]

[B] Making the Election

The general rules for making an IRC §444 election, as discussed earlier,[185] apply to backup IRC §444 elections. When filing Form 8716, type or print "BACK-UP

---

182 Temp. Reg. §1.444-1T(a)(5)(i).
183 Temp. Reg. §1.444-1T(a)(5)(ii).
184 Temp. Reg. §1.444-3T(b)(4).
185 *See* §3.14, *infra*.

ELECTION" at the top of the form. However, if Form 8716 is filed on or after the date Form 1128 or Form 2553 is filed, type or print the following at the top of Form 8716[186]:

- "FORM 1128 (or FORM 2553) is filed, and
- "FORM 1128 (or FORM 2553) BACK-UP ELECTION."

[C] *Activating the Election*

A partnership or S corporation activates its back-up IRC § 444 election by filing the return required and making the required payment with Form 8752. The due date for filing Form 8752 and making the payment is the later of the following dates:

- May 15th of the calendar year following the calendar year in which the applicable election year begins; or
- 60 days after the partnership or S corporation has been notified by the IRS that the business year request has been denied.

A personal service corporation activates its back-up election by filing Form 8716 with its original or amended income tax return for the tax year in which the election is first effective and by printing on the top of the income tax return, "ACTIVATING BACK-UP ELECTION."[187]

§ 3.16 Correction of Erroneous Tax Year

A change in tax year to conform to a change in the annual accounting period used by a taxpayer in keeping its books requires the prior approval of the Commissioner.[188] There are situations, however, where taxpayers with an established annual accounting period have been filing their returns based on a different tax year, without challenge or question by the IRS.

Where a corporation has regularly maintained its books and records using a particular year-end, but erroneously files its federal income tax returns using a different tax year-end, the consent of the Commissioner is not required in order to change its tax year-end to its book year-end. Such a change is a change from a nonconforming to a conforming method.[189]

This type of change does not require a short-period return or an annualization of the short-period income. The first return for the correct tax year and the immediately preceding return for the 12-month erroneous period would overlap, resulting in a double reporting of income for the overlapping months. The part of the tax for the

---

[186] Reg. § 1.444-1T(b)(4)(ii).

[187] Reg. § 1.444-1T(b)(4)(iii).

[188] *See* Rev. Proc. 85-15, 1985-1 CB 516 in which the IRS has provided a procedure for correcting the adoption of an improper tax year.

[189] *See* Rev. Rul. 58-256, 1958-1 CB 215.

erroneous period, applicable to the overlapping income, will be treated as an advance payment on the tax payable on the first return for the correct tax year.[190]

Although returns are mistakenly filed based on an erroneous tax year, they are nonetheless "returns" effective to start the running of the statutory period limiting the time for the IRS's assessment of deficiencies. While the limitation period begins to run only when the returns for the erroneous tax years (which include information for the correct tax year) have been filed, the limitation period technically relates to the correct tax year.[191]

§3.17 Correction of Improper Taxable Year

If a taxpayer has been using a fiscal year, that year is nevertheless improper if:

- the taxpayer keeps no books;
- the taxpayer does not have an annual accounting period; or
- the taxpayer has an annual accounting period but it does not qualify as a fiscal year because it does not end on the last day of a calendar month and is also not a valid 52-53-week year.[192]

A taxpayer using an improper fiscal year may receive automatic approval to change to a calendar year. It obtains automatic approval by completing Form 1128 and attaching it to the amended federal income tax return that is filed on a calendar year basis and corrects the most recently filed federal income tax return that was filed based on an improper annual accounting period. At the top of page 1 of the Form 1128, the taxpayer should type or print "FILED UNDER REV. PROC. 85-15."[193]

Example 3-26

If a taxpayer began business on May 15 and adopted an annual accounting period ending on May 14 (a period of exactly 12 months), it has adopted an improper accounting period and should file an amended return for the period May 15, the day business began, through December 31, the last day of the calendar year. The income and deductions reported on the originally filed federal income tax return would be adjusted to reflect only that income and those deductions attributable to the period of May 15 through December 31. Subsequent federal income tax returns must be filed on the calendar year basis.[194]

---

[190] *American Hide & Leather Co. v. United Sates*, 284 U.S. 343, 3 USTC ¶855 (1931); *Paso Robles Mercantile Co. v. Comm'r*, 33 F.2d 653 (9th Cir. 1929), *cert. denied*, 280 U.S. 595 (1929).

[191] *CEM Securities v. Comm'r*, 72 F.2d 295, §4 USTC ¶6328 (4th Cir. 1934).

[192] IRC §441(g).

[193] Rev. Proc. 85-15, 1985-1 CB 516.

[194] *Id.*

§ 3.18 Final Entity Year

[A] Corporations

When a corporation ceases business, dissolves, and retains no assets, its existence ends, and its final taxable period closes. Regardless of whether the corporation is treated as a continuing corporation under state law to wind up its affairs, the corporation's federal tax existence ends.[195] State law usually requires a corporation to remain in existence until it has satisfied or made provision for all of its liabilities and distributed all of its assets.[196]

A corporation may result in a "de facto dissolution,"[197] thereby terminating its existence for federal income tax purposes, before its formal dissolution under state law. Once a corporation effects a de facto dissolution, the corporation's existence has ceased for federal tax purposes, even if it has never been formally dissolved and its existence is continued indefinitely under the state law.[198] The requirement for filing federal returns does not apply to a corporation not in existence for federal tax purposes, regardless of its status under the law of its state of incorporation.[199]

[B] Partnerships

A partnership is considered as terminated if no part of any business, financial operation, or venture of the partnership continues to be carried on by any of its partners in a partnership.

A partnership's own taxable year does not close as a result of the death of a partner, the entry of a new partner, the liquidation of all or a portion of a partner's interest, or the sale or exchange of partnership interests amounting to less than 50% of the total partnership interests within a 12-month period.[200]

A partnership taxable year does close, however, with respect to a particular partner that liquidates, sells or exchanges its entire interest, or dies.[201]

---

[195] Reg. § 1.6012-2(a)(2). A corporation is not in existence after it ceases business and dissolves, retaining no assets, whether or not under state law it may thereafter be treated as continuing as a corporation for certain limited purposes connected with winding up its affairs, such as for the purpose of suing and being sued.

[196] *See* Rev. Rul. 71-129, 1971-1 CB 397.

[197] De facto is a Latin expression that means "in fact, in reality, in actual existence, force, or possession, as a matter of fact" (literally "from fact"). In law, it often means "in practice but not necessarily ordained by law" or "in practice or actuality, but not officially established."

[198] *A B C Brewing Corporation v. Comm'r.*, 224 F.2d 483, 55-2 USTC ¶ 9538 (9th Cir. 1955).

[199] Rev. Rul. 60-51, 1960-1 CB 169. A newly reactivated corporation, which previously had been inactive for a number of years, is considered to be a new taxpayer for purposes of adopting a taxable year which meets the requirements of IRC § 441. The prior approval of the Commissioner is not required where the facts disclose that the corporation existed for a number of years in name only, even though, during its prior actual operations, the corporation had computed its taxable income on the basis of a different taxable year.

[200] IRC § 706(c)(1).

[201] IRC § 706(c)(2).

§3.19 Case Study

In 2011, "Diamond" Frank Brady, Joe Banke and Nord Stromme, Inc formed Frank's Haberdashery Emporium, LLC ("the Emporium") which, at formation, did not file Form 8832. For 2011 and thereafter, the LLC was taxed as a partnership and filed its return with a 12/31 year-end based on the majority interest rule.

The parties are unrelated.
Frank Brady's tax year ends 12/31.
Joe Banke's tax year ends 12/31.
Nord Stromme, Inc.'s tax year-end is 11/30.

Their ownership interests are as follows:

Frank Brady: 30%
Joe Banke: 50%
Nord Stromme, Inc.: 20%

The Emporium sells men's accessories, including ties, belts, gloves, scarves, etc. Typically, the Emporium has a "busy season" prior to Father's Day and Christmas.

At the time of formation, the Emporium's year-end was 12/31.

On May 15, 2015, Joe Banke formed JB Inc. as a C corporation and transferred all of his interest in the Emporium into JB, Inc. It selected May 31 as its year-end.

The Emporium has the following gross receipts:

	2015	2016	2017	2018	2019
January	$ 150,000	$ 158,000	$ 165,000	$ 174,000	$ 182,000
February	200,000	105,000	110,000	150,000	158,000
March	300,000	90,000	95,000	99,000	104,000
April		120,000	126,000	132,000	139,000
May		**210,000**	**221,000**	**232,000**	**243,000**
June		**315,000**	**331,000**	**347,000**	**365,000**
July		105,000	110,000	116,000	122,000
August		120,000	126,000	132,000	160,000
September		135,000	142,000	149,000	156,000
October		150,000	158,000	165,000	174,000
November		150,000	158,000	165,000	174,000
December		150,000	158,000	165,000	210,000

(A) What year end(s) can the partnership choose for 2020?
(B) What year end must the partnership use for 2020?

Analysis:
Tax year as per IRC § 706(B)

Partnership Tax Year End	Partner	Year End	Profits Interest	Months of Deferral	Aggregate Deferral
December 31	Frank Brady	12/31	30%	0	0.00
	JB, Inc.	5/31	50%	5	2.50
	Nord Stromme, Inc.	11/30	20%	11	2.20
					4.70
May 31	Frank Brady	12/31	30%	7	2.10
	JB, Inc.	5/31	50%	0	0.00
	Nord Stromme, Inc.	11/30	20%	6	1.20
					3.30
November 30	Frank Brady	12/31	30%	1	0.30
	JB, Inc.	5/31	50%	6	3.00
	Nord Stromme, Inc.	11/30	20%	0	0.00
					3.30

[A] Discussion

Application of least aggregate deferral test. Applying the least aggregate deferral test demonstrates that a December 31 year end produces an aggregate deferral of 4.70 months; the May 31 year end produces an aggregate deferral of 3.30 months; the November 30 year end produces an aggregate deferral of 3.30 months. Under the Regulations, the taxpayer, since there is a tie as to the deferral, can choose either May 31 or November 30 as their year-end.

Application of natural business year. If you examine the number of sales, it appears that sales in June are the highest and, therefore, under the business purpose test, if you examine May and June, they are the highest two months, producing 25% of gross receipts, resulting in a natural business year. There are other months which may also meet a 25% test; however, because these two months are the highest, if the taxpayer chooses to select a natural business year ending in July, it must choose July as its year-end.

Application of IRC § 444. Finally, the taxpayer may choose an IRC § 444 election in which case the year end could be September, October, or November.

Recapping, the required year-end would be either May 31 or November 30 under the least aggregate deferral test; the alternate year end under the natural business year would be July 30, and under IRC § 444, the taxpayer can select September, October, or November as its year end.

Appendix 3-1 Filled-in Form 1128 and Attachment

Form **1128** (Rev. October 2014) Department of the Treasury Internal Revenue Service

Application To Adopt, Change, or Retain a Tax Year

▶ Information about Form 1128 and its separate instructions is available at *www.irs.gov/form1128.*

OMB No. 1545-0134

Attachment Sequence No. **148**

Part I General Information

Important: *All filers must complete Part I and sign below. See instructions.*

Type or Print

Name of filer (if a joint return is filed, also enter spouse's name) (see instructions) Frank's Haberdashery Emporium	Filer's identifying number 12-3456789
Number, street, and room or suite no. (If a P.O. box, see instructions) 123 Somewhere St.	Service Center where income tax return will be filed Cincinnati
City or town, state, and ZIP code Anytown, USA	Filer's area code and telephone number/Fax number (201) 345-6789 / ( )
Name of applicant, if different than the filer (see instructions)	**Applicant's identifying number** (see instructions)
Name of person to contact (if not the applicant or filer, attach a power of attorney)	Contact person's area code and telephone number/Fax number ( ) / ( )

1 Check the appropriate box(es) to indicate the type of applicant (see instructions).

☐ Individual
☑ Partnership
☐ Estate
☐ Domestic corporation
☐ S corporation
☐ Personal service corporation (PSC)
☐ Cooperative (sec. 1381(a))
☐ Controlled foreign corporation (CFC) (sec. 957)
☐ Foreign sales corporation (FSC) or Interest-charge domestic international sales corporation (IC-DISC)
☐ Specified foreign corporation (SFC) (sec. 898)
☐ 10/50 corporation (sec. 904(d)(2)(E))
☐ Trust
☐ Passive foreign investment company (PFIC) (sec. 1297)
☐ Other foreign corporation
☐ Tax-exempt organization
☐ Homeowners Association (sec. 528)
☐ Other (Specify entity and applicable Code section)

2a Approval is requested to (check one) (see instructions):

☐ Adopt a tax year ending ▶ (Partnerships and PSCs: Go to Part III after completing Part I.)

☑ Change to a tax year ending ▶ 7/31

☐ Retain a tax year ending ▶

b If changing a tax year, indicate the date the present tax year ends (see instructions). ▶

c If adopting or changing a tax year, the first return or short period return will be filed for the tax year beginning ▶ , 20 , and ending ▶ , 20

3 Is the applicant's present tax year, as stated on line 2b above, also its current financial reporting year? ▶ ☐ **Yes** ☐ **No**

If "No," attach an explanation.

4 Indicate the applicant's present overall method of accounting.

☐ Cash receipts and disbursements method ☑ Accrual method

☐ Other method (specify) ▶

5 State the nature of the applicant's business or principal source of income.

Sale of Men's Clothing Accessories

Signature—All Filers (See **Who Must Sign** in the instructions.)

Sign Here

Under penalties of perjury, I declare that I have examined this application, including accompanying schedules and statements, and to the best of my knowledge and belief, it is true, correct, and complete. Declaration of preparer (other than filer) is based on all information of which preparer has any knowledge.

▶ Signature of filer | Date | ▶ Type or print name and title

Paid Preparer Use Only

Print/Type preparer's name	Preparer's signature	Date	Check ☐ if self-employed	PTIN
Firm's name ▶			Firm's EIN ▶	
Firm's address ▶			Phone no.	

For Privacy Act and Paperwork Reduction Act Notice, see separate instructions. Cat. No. 21115C Form **1128** (Rev. 10-2014)

Form 1128 (Rev. 10-2014) Page **2**

Part II **Automatic Approval Request** (see instructions)

• Identify the revenue procedure under which this automatic approval request is filed ▶

Section A—Corporations (Other Than S Corporations or Personal Service Corporations) (Rev. Proc. 2006-45, or its successor)

		Yes	No
1	Is the applicant a corporation (including a homeowners association (section 528)) that is requesting a change in tax year **and** is allowed to use the automatic approval rules under section 4 of Rev. Proc. 2006-45 (or its successor)? (see instructions) . . . ▶		
2	Does the corporation intend to elect to be an S corporation for the tax year immediately following the short period?		
	If "Yes" and the corporation is electing to change to a permitted tax year, file Form 1128 as an attachment to Form 2553.		
3	Is the applicant a corporation requesting a concurrent change for a CFC, FSC or IC-DISC? (see instructions) . ▶		
	Section B—Partnerships, S Corporations, Personal Service Corporations (PSCs), and Trusts (Rev. Proc. 2006-46, or its successor)		
4	Is the applicant a partnership, S corporation, PSC, or trust that is requesting a tax year **and** is allowed to use the automatic approval rules under section 4 of Rev. Proc. 2006-46 (or its successor)? (see instructions) . . . . . ▶		
5	Is the partnership, S corporation, PSC, or trust requesting to change to its required tax year or a partnership, S corporation, or PSC that wants to change to a 52-53 week tax year ending with reference to such tax year? . ▶		
6	Is the partnership, S corporation, or PSC (other than a member of a tiered structure) requesting a tax year that coincides with its natural business year described in section 4.01(2) of Rev. Proc. 2006-46 (or its successor)? Attach a statement showing gross receipts for the most recent 47 months. (See instructions for information required to be submitted) . . . ▶		
7	Is the S corporation requesting an ownership tax year? (see instructions) . . . ▶		
8	Is the applicant a partnership requesting a concurrent change pursuant to section 6.09 of Rev. Proc. 2006-45 (or its successor) or section 5.04(8) of Rev. Proc. 2002-39 (or its successor)? (see instructions) . . . ▶		
	Section C—Individuals (Rev. Proc. 2003-62, or its successor) (see instructions)		
9	Is the applicant an individual requesting a change from a fiscal year to a calendar year? . . . ▶		
	Section D—Tax-Exempt Organizations (Rev. Proc. 76-10 or 85-58) (see instructions)		
10	Is the applicant a tax-exempt organization requesting a change? . . . ▶		

Part III **Ruling Request** (All applicants requesting a ruling must complete Section A and any other section that applies to the entity. See instructions.) **(Rev. Proc. 2002-39, or its successor)**

Section A—General Information

		Yes	No
1	Is the applicant a partnership, S corporation, personal service corporation, or trust that is under examination by the IRS, before an appeals office, or a Federal court? . . . ▶		✔
	If "Yes," see the instructions for information that must be included on an attached explanation.		
2	Has the applicant changed its annual accounting period at any time within the most recent 48-month period ending with the last month of the requested tax year? . . . ▶		✔
	If "Yes" and a letter ruling was issued granting approval to make the change, attach a copy of the letter ruling, or if not available, an explanation including the date approval was granted. If a letter ruling was not issued, indicate when and explain how the change was implemented.		
3	Within the most recent 48-month period, has any accounting period application been withdrawn, not perfected, denied, or not implemented? . . . ▶		✔
	If "Yes," attach an explanation.		
4a	Is the applicant requesting to establish a business purpose under section 5.02(1) of Rev. Proc. 2002-39 (or its successor)? . . . ▶	✔	
	If "Yes," attach an explanation of the legal basis supporting the requested tax year (see instructions).		
b	If your business purpose is based on one of the natural business year tests under section 5.03, check the applicable box. ☐ Annual business cycle test ☐ Seasonal business test ☐ 25-percent gross receipts test Attach a statement showing gross receipts from sales and services (and inventory cost if applicable) for the test period. (see instructions)		
5	Enter the taxable income or (loss) for the 3 tax years immediately preceding the year of change and for the short period. If necessary, estimate the amount for the short period. Short period $ 101,000 First preceding year $ 243,000 Second preceding year $ 228,000 Third preceding year $ 216,000 **Note:** *Individuals, enter adjusted gross income. Partnerships and S corporations, enter ordinary income. Section 501(c) organizations, enter unrelated business taxable income. Estates, enter adjusted total income. All other applicants, enter taxable income before net operating loss deduction and special deductions.*		

Form **1128** (Rev. 10-2014)

Form 1128 (Rev. 10-2014) Page 3

		Yes	No
6	Corporations only, enter the losses or credits, if any, that were generated or that expired in the short period: Generated / Expiring Net operating loss . . . . $ ______ $ ______ Capital loss . . . . $ ______ $ ______ Unused credits . . . . $ ______ $ ______		
7	Enter the amount of deferral, if any, resulting from the change (see section 5.05(1), (2), (3) and 6.01(7) of Rev. Proc. 2002-39, or its successor) . . . . ▶ $ ______		
8a	Is the applicant a U.S. shareholder in a CFC? . . . . ▶		✔
	If "Yes," attach a statement for each CFC providing the name, address, identifying number, tax year, the percentage of total combined voting power of the applicant, and the amount of income included in the gross income of the applicant under section 951 for the 3 tax years immediately before the short period and for the short period.		
b	Will each CFC concurrently change its tax year? . . . . ▶		✔
	If "Yes" to line 8b, go to Part II, line 3. If "No," attach a statement explaining why the CFC will not be conforming to the tax year requested by the U.S. shareholder.		
9a	Is the applicant a U.S. shareholder in a PFIC as defined in section 1297? . . . . ▶		✔
	If "Yes," attach a statement providing the name, address, identifying number, and tax year of the PFIC, the percentage of interest owned by the applicant, and the amount of distributions or ordinary earnings and net capital gain from the PFIC included in the income of the applicant.		
b	Did the applicant elect under section 1295 to treat the PFIC as a qualified electing fund? . . . . ▶		✔
10a	Is the applicant a member of a partnership, a beneficiary of a trust or estate, a shareholder of an S corporation, a shareholder of an IC-DISC, or a shareholder of an FSC? . . . . ▶		✔
	If "Yes," attach a statement providing the name, address, identifying number, type of entity (partnership, trust, estate, S corporation, IC-DISC, or FSC), tax year, percentage of interest in capital and profits, or percentage of interest of each IC-DISC or FSC and the amount of income received from each entity for the first preceding year and for the short period. Indicate the percentage of gross income of the applicant represented by each amount.		
b	Will any partnership concurrently change its tax year to conform with the tax year requested? . . . . . . ▶		✔
c	If "Yes" to line 10b, has any Form 1128 been filed for such partnership? . . . . ▶		✔
11	Does the applicant or any related entity currently have any accounting method, tax year, ruling, or technical advice request pending with the IRS National Office? . . . . ▶		✔
	If "Yes," attach a statement explaining the type of request (method, tax year, etc.) and the specific issues involved in each request.		
12	Is **Form 2848,** Power of Attorney and Declaration of Representative, attached to this application? . . . . ▶	✔	
13	Does the applicant request a conference of right (in person or by telephone) with the IRS National Office, if the IRS proposes to disapprove the application? . . . . ▶	✔	
14	Enter amount of **user fee** attached to this application (see instructions) . . . . ▶ $		

Section B—Corporations (other than S corporations and controlled foreign corporations) (see instructions)

		Yes	No
15	Enter the date of incorporation. ▶		
16a	Does the corporation intend to elect to be an S corporation for the tax year immediately following the short period? . . . . ▶		
b	If "Yes," will the corporation be going to a permitted S corporation tax year? . . . . ▶		
	If "No" to line 16b, attach an explanation.		
17	Is the corporation a member of an affiliated group filing a consolidated return? . . . . ▶		
	If "Yes," attach a statement providing **(a)** the name, address, identifiying number used on the consolidated return, tax year, and Service Center where the applicant files the return; **(b)** the name, address, and identifying number of each member of the affiliated group; **(c)** the taxable income (loss) of each member for the 3 years immediately before the short period and for the short period; and **(d)** the name of the parent corporation.		
18a	Personal service corporations (PSCs): Attach a statement providing each shareholder's name, type of entity (individual, partnership, corporation, etc.), address, identifying number, tax year, percentage of ownership, and amount of income received from the PSC for the first preceding year and the short period.		
b	If the PSC is using a tax year other than the required tax year, indicate how it obtained its tax year. ☐ Grandfathered (attach copy of letter ruling) ☐ Section 444 election (date of election ______) ☐ Letter ruling (date of letter ruling (attach copy))		

Form **1128** (Rev. 10-2014)

Form 1128 (Rev. 10-2014) Page **4**

Section C—S Corporations (see instructions)

		Yes	No
19	Enter the date of the S corporation election. ▶		
20	Is any shareholder applying for a corresponding change in tax year? . . . . ▶ If "Yes," each shareholder requesting a corresponding change in tax year must file a separate Form 1128 to get advance approval to change its tax year.		
21	If the corporation is using a tax year other than the required tax year, indicate how it obtained its tax year. ☐ Grandfathered (attach copy of letter ruling) ☐ Section 444 election (date of election ________) ☐ Letter ruling (date of letter ruling (attach copy))		
22	Attach a statement providing each shareholder's name, type of shareholder (individual, estate, qualified subchapter S Trust, electing small business trust, other trust, or exempt organization), address, identifying number, tax year, percentage of ownership, and the amount of income each shareholder received from the S corporation for the first preceding year and for the short period.		

Section D—Partnerships (see instructions)

		Yes	No
23	Enter the date the partnership's business began. ▶ 1/1/2011		
24	Is any partner applying for a corresponding change in tax year? . . . . ▶		
25	Attach a statement providing each partner's name, type of partner (individual, partnership, estate, trust, corporation, S corporation, IC-DISC, etc.), address, identifying number, tax year, and the percentage of interest in capital and profits.		
26	Is any partner a shareholder of a PSC as defined in Regulations section 1.441-3(c)? . . . . ▶ If "Yes," attach a statement providing the name, address, identifiying number, tax year, percentage of interest in capital and profits, and the amount of income received from each PSC for the first preceding year and for the short period.		
27	If the partnership is using a tax year other than the required tax year, indicate how it obtained its tax year. ☐ Grandfathered (attach copy of letter ruling) ☐ Section 444 election (date of election ________) ☐ Letter ruling (date of letter ruling (attach copy))		

Section E—Controlled Foreign Corporations (CFC)

28	Attach a statement for each U.S. shareholder (as defined in section 951(b)) providing the name, address, identifying number, tax year, percentage of total value and percentage of total voting power, and the amount of income included in gross income under section 951 for the 3 tax years immediately before the short period and for the short period.		

Section F—Tax-Exempt Organizations

		Yes	No
29	Type of organization: ☐ Corporation ☐ Trust ☐ Other (specify) ▶		
30	Date of organization. ▶		
31	Code section under which the organization is exempt. ▶		
32	Is the organization required to file an annual return on Form 990, 1120-C, 990-PF, 990-T, 1120-H, or 1120-POL? ▶		
33	Enter the date the tax exemption was granted. ▶ ________ . Attach a copy of the letter ruling granting exemption. If a copy of the letter ruling is not available, attach an explanation.		
34	If the organization is a private foundation, is the foundation terminating its status under section 507? . . . . ▶		

Section G—Estates

35 Enter the date the estate was created. ▶

36 a Attach a statement providing the name, identifying number, address, and tax year of each beneficiary and each person who is an interested party of any portion of the estate.

b Based on the adjusted total income of the estate entered in Part III, Section A, line 5, attach a statement showing the distribution deduction and the taxable amounts distributed to each beneficiary for the 2 tax years immediately before the short period and for the short period.

Section H—Passive Foreign Investment Companies

37 If the applicant is a passive foreign investment company, attach a statement providing each U.S. shareholder's name, address, identifying number, and percentage of interest owned.

Form **1128** (Rev. 10-2014)

ATTACHMENT TO FORM 1128
FRANK'S HABERDASHERY EMPORIUM, LLC
12-3456789

In 2011, "Diamond" Frank Brady, Joe Banke and Nord Stromme, Inc. formed Frank's Haberdashery Emporium, LLC ("the Emporium") which at formation did not file Form 8832. The partnership proceeded to file a partnership tax return with a 12/31 year-end based on the majority interest rule.

The parties are unrelated.
Frank Brady's tax year ends 12/31.
Joe Banke's tax year ends 12/31.
Nord Stromme, Inc. tax year-end is 11/30.

Their ownership interests are as follows:

Frank Brady's 30%
Joe Banke 50%
Nord Stromme, Inc. 20%

The Emporium sells men's accessories, including ties, belts, gloves, scarves, etc. Typically, the Emporium has a "busy season" prior to Father's Day and Christmas.

At the time of formation, the LLC's year-end was 12/31.

On May 15, 2015, Joe Banke formed JB Inc. as a C corporation and transferred all of his LLC interest into the Emporium. JB, Inc.

The Emporium has the following gross receipts:

	2015	2016	2017	2018	2019
January	$ 150,000	$ 158,000	$ 165,000	$ 174,000	$ 182,000
February	200,000	105,000	110,000	150,000	158,000
March	300,000	90,000	95,000	99,000	104,000
April		120,000	126,000	132,000	139,000
May		210,000	221,000	232,000	243,000
June		315,000	331,000	347,000	365,000
July		105,000	110,000	116,000	122,000
August		120,000	126,000	132,000	160,000
September		135,000	142,000	149,000	156,000
October		150,000	158,000	165,000	174,000
November		150,000	158,000	165,000	174,000
December		150,000	158,000	165,000	210,000

Analysis:
Tax year as per IRC § 706(B)

Partnership Tax Year End	Partner	Year End	Profits Interest	Months of Deferral	Aggregate Deferral
December 31	Frank Brady	12/31	30%	0	0.00
	JB, Inc.	5/31	50%	5	2.50
	Nord Stromme, Inc.	11/30	20%	11	2.20
					4.70
May 31	Frank Brady	12/31	30%	7	2.10
	JB, Inc.	5/31	50%	0	0.00
	Nord Stromme, Inc.	11/30	20%	6	1.20
					3.30
November 30	Frank Brady	12/31	30%	1	0.30
	JB, Inc.	5/31	50%	6	3.00
	Nord Stromme, Inc.	11/30	20%	0	0.00
					3.30

Application of Natural Business Year
If you examine the number of sales, it appears that sales in June are the highest. Therefore, under the business purpose test, if you examine May and June, they are the highest two months which produces 25% of gross receipts and results in a natural business year. There are other months which may also make a 25% test; however, because these two months are the highest, if the taxpayer chooses to select a natural business year ending in July, it must choose July as its year-end.

Appendix 3-2 Filled-in Form 8716

Form **8716** (Rev. September 2017) Department of the Treasury Internal Revenue Service

Election To Have a Tax Year Other Than a Required Tax Year

▶ Go to *www.irs.gov/Form8716* for the latest information.

OMB No. 1545-0123

Type or Print	Name: FRANK'S HABERDASHERY EMPORIUM, LLC	Employer identification number
	Number, street, and room or suite no. (or P.O. box number if mail is not delivered to street address): 123 SOMEWHERE ST.	
	City or town, state, and ZIP code: ANYTOWN, USA	

1 Check applicable box to indicate type of entity.
☑ Partnership
☐ S corporation (or C corporation electing to be an S corporation)
☐ Personal service corporation (PSC)

2 Name and telephone number (including area code) of person who may be called for information:

	Month	Day	Year
3 Enter ending date of the tax year for the entity's last filed return. A new entity should enter the ending date of the tax year it is adopting	12	31	2020
4 Enter ending date of required tax year determined under section 441(i), 706(b), or 1378			
5 **Section 444(a) Election.** Check the applicable box and enter the ending date of the first tax year for which the election will be effective that the entity is (see instructions): ☑ Adopting ☐ Retaining ☐ Changing to	12	31	2021

(Line 4 has Month and Day columns only.)

Under penalties of perjury, I declare that the entity named above has authorized me to make this election under section 444(a), and that the statements made are, to the best of my knowledge and belief, true, correct, and complete.

▶ Signature and title (see instructions) ▶ Date

General Instructions

Section references are to the Internal Revenue Code unless otherwise noted.

Purpose of Form

Form 8716 is filed by partnerships, S corporations, and personal service corporations (as defined in section 441(i)(2)) to elect under section 444 to have a tax year other than a required tax year.

When To File

Form 8716 must be signed and filed by the earlier of:

1. The 15th day of the 5th month following the month that includes the 1st day of the tax year the election will be effective, or

2. The due date (not including extensions) of the income tax return for the tax year resulting from the section 444 election.

Items **1** and **2** relate to the tax year, or the return for the tax year, for which the ending date is entered on line 5 above.

Under Regulations section 301.9100-2, the entity is automatically granted a 12-month extension to make an election on Form 8716. To obtain an extension, type or legibly print "Filed Pursuant To Section 301.9100-2" at the top of Form 8716, and file the form within 12 months of the original due date.

Where To File

File Form 8716 at the applicable IRS address shown below.

If the entity's principal place of business or principal office or agency is located in ▼	Use the following address ▼
Connecticut, Delaware, District of Columbia, Florida, Georgia, Illinois, Indiana, Kentucky, Maine, Maryland, Massachusetts, Michigan, New Hampshire, New Jersey, New York, North Carolina, Ohio, Pennsylvania, Rhode Island, South Carolina, Tennessee, Vermont, Virginia, West Virginia, Wisconsin	Department of the Treasury Internal Revenue Service Center Cincinnati, OH 45999
Alabama, Alaska, Arizona, Arkansas, California, Colorado, Hawaii, Idaho, Iowa, Kansas, Louisiana, Minnesota, Mississippi, Missouri, Montana, Nebraska, Nevada, New Mexico, North Dakota, Oklahoma, Oregon, South Dakota, Texas, Utah, Washington, Wyoming	Department of the Treasury Internal Revenue Service Center Ogden, UT 84201

An entity without a principal office or agency or principal place of business in the United States must file Form 8716 with the Internal Revenue Service Center, P.O. Box 409101, Ogden, UT 84409.

For Paperwork Reduction Act Notice, see instructions. Cat. No. 64725S Form **8716** (Rev. 9-2017)

Appendix 3-3 Form 2553

Form **2553**
(Rev. December 2017)
Department of the Treasury
Internal Revenue Service

Election by a Small Business Corporation
(Under section 1362 of the Internal Revenue Code)
(Including a late election filed pursuant to Rev. Proc. 2013-30)
▶ You can fax this form to the IRS. See separate instructions.
▶ Go to *www.irs.gov/Form2553* for instructions and the latest information.

OMB No. 1545-0123

Note: This election to be an S corporation can be accepted only if all the tests are met under *Who May Elect* in the instructions, all shareholders have signed the consent statement, an officer has signed below, and the exact name and address of the corporation (entity) and other required form information have been provided.

Part I Election Information

Type or Print	Name (see instructions)	**A Employer identification number**
	Number, street, and room or suite no. If a P.O. box, see instructions.	**B** Date incorporated
	City or town, state or province, country, and ZIP or foreign postal code	**C** State of incorporation

D Check the applicable box(es) if the corporation (entity), after applying for the EIN shown in **A** above, changed its ☐ name or ☐ address

E Election is to be effective for tax year beginning (month, day, year) (see instructions) . . . . ▶ ______

Caution: A corporation (entity) making the election for its first tax year in existence will usually enter the beginning date of a short tax year that begins on a date other than January 1.

F Selected tax year:

(1) ☐ Calendar year
(2) ☐ Fiscal year ending (month and day) ▶ ______
(3) ☐ 52-53-week year ending with reference to the month of December
(4) ☐ 52-53-week year ending with reference to the month of ▶ ______

If box (2) or (4) is checked, complete Part II.

G If more than 100 shareholders are listed for item J (see page 2), check this box if treating members of a family as one shareholder results in no more than 100 shareholders (see test 2 under *Who May Elect* in the instructions) ▶ ☐

H Name and title of officer or legal representative whom the IRS may call for more information	Telephone number of officer or legal representative

I If this S corporation election is being filed late, I declare I had reasonable cause for not filing Form 2553 timely. If this late election is being made by an entity eligible to elect to be treated as a corporation, I declare I also had reasonable cause for not filing an entity classification election timely and the representations listed in Part IV are true. See below for my explanation of the reasons the election or elections were not made on time and a description of my diligent actions to correct the mistake upon its discovery. See instructions.

Sign Here

Under penalties of perjury, I declare that I have examined this election, including accompanying documents, and, to the best of my knowledge and belief, the election contains all the relevant facts relating to the election, and such facts are true, correct, and complete.

▶ ______ **Signature of officer** ______ **Title** ______ **Date**

For Paperwork Reduction Act Notice, see separate instructions. Cat. No. 18629R Form **2553** (Rev. 12-2017)

Form 2553 (Rev. 12-2017) Page **2**

Name	**Employer identification number**

Part I **Election Information** *(continued)* **Note:** If you need more rows, use additional copies of page 2.

J Name and address of each shareholder or former shareholder required to consent to the election. (see instructions)	**K** **Shareholder's Consent Statement** Under penalties of perjury, I declare that I consent to the election of the above-named corporation (entity) to be an S corporation under section 1362(a) and that I have examined this consent statement, including accompanying documents, and, to the best of my knowledge and belief, the election contains all the relevant facts relating to the election, and such facts are true, correct, and complete. I understand my consent is binding and may not be withdrawn after the corporation (entity) has made a valid election. If seeking relief for a late filed election, I also declare under penalties of perjury that I have reported my income on all affected returns consistent with the S corporation election for the year for which the election should have been filed (see beginning date entered on line E) and for all subsequent years.		**L** Stock owned or percentage of ownership (see instructions)		**M** Social security number or employer identification number (see instructions)	**N** Shareholder's tax year ends (month and day)
	Signature	Date	Number of shares or percentage of ownership	Date(s) acquired		

Form **2553** (Rev. 12-2017)

Form 2553 (Rev. 12-2017) Page **3**

Name	Employer identification number

Part II Selection of Fiscal Tax Year (see instructions)

Note: All corporations using this part must complete item O and item P, Q, or R.

O Check the applicable box to indicate whether the corporation is:

1. ☐ A new corporation **adopting** the tax year entered in item F, Part I.

2. ☐ An existing corporation **retaining** the tax year entered in item F, Part I.

3. ☐ An existing corporation **changing** to the tax year entered in item F, Part I.

P Complete item P if the corporation is using the automatic approval provisions of Rev. Proc. 2006-46, 2006-45 I.R.B. 859, to request (1) a natural business year (as defined in section 5.07 of Rev. Proc. 2006-46) or (2) a year that satisfies the ownership tax year test (as defined in section 5.08 of Rev. Proc. 2006-46). Check the applicable box below to indicate the representation statement the corporation is making.

1. Natural Business Year ▶ ☐ I represent that the corporation is adopting, retaining, or changing to a tax year that qualifies as its natural business year (as defined in section 5.07 of Rev. Proc. 2006-46) and has attached a statement showing separately for each month the gross receipts for the most recent 47 months. See instructions. I also represent that the corporation is not precluded by section 4.02 of Rev. Proc. 2006-46 from obtaining automatic approval of such adoption, retention, or change in tax year.

2. Ownership Tax Year ▶ ☐ I represent that shareholders (as described in section 5.08 of Rev. Proc. 2006-46) holding more than half of the shares of the stock (as of the first day of the tax year to which the request relates) of the corporation have the same tax year or are concurrently changing to the tax year that the corporation adopts, retains, or changes to per item F, Part I, and that such tax year satisfies the requirement of section 4.01(3) of Rev. Proc. 2006-46. I also represent that the corporation is not precluded by section 4.02 of Rev. Proc. 2006-46 from obtaining automatic approval of such adoption, retention, or change in tax year.

Note: If you do not use item P and the corporation wants a fiscal tax year, complete either item Q or R below. Item Q is used to request a fiscal tax year based on a business purpose and to make a back-up section 444 election. Item R is used to make a regular section 444 election.

Q Business Purpose—To request a fiscal tax year based on a business purpose, check box Q1. See instructions for details including payment of a user fee. You may also check box Q2 and/or box Q3.

1. Check here ▶ ☐ if the fiscal year entered in item F, Part I, is requested under the prior approval provisions of Rev. Proc. 2002-39, 2002-22 I.R.B. 1046. Attach to Form 2553 a statement describing the relevant facts and circumstances and, if applicable, the gross receipts from sales and services necessary to establish a business purpose. See the instructions for details regarding the gross receipts from sales and services. If the IRS proposes to disapprove the requested fiscal year, do you want a conference with the IRS National Office?

☐ Yes ☐ No

2. Check here ▶ ☐ to show that the corporation intends to make a back-up section 444 election in the event the corporation's business purpose request is not approved by the IRS. See instructions for more information.

3. Check here ▶ ☐ to show that the corporation agrees to adopt or change to a tax year ending December 31 if necessary for the IRS to accept this election for S corporation status in the event (1) the corporation's business purpose request is not approved and the corporation makes a back-up section 444 election, but is ultimately not qualified to make a section 444 election, or (2) the corporation's business purpose request is not approved and the corporation did not make a back-up section 444 election.

R Section 444 Election—To make a section 444 election, check box R1. You may also check box R2.

1. Check here ▶ ☐ to show that the corporation will make, if qualified, a section 444 election to have the fiscal tax year shown in item F, Part I. To make the election, you must complete **Form 8716,** Election To Have a Tax Year Other Than a Required Tax Year, and either attach it to Form 2553 or file it separately.

2. Check here ▶ ☐ to show that the corporation agrees to adopt or change to a tax year ending December 31 if necessary for the IRS to accept this election for S corporation status in the event the corporation is ultimately not qualified to make a section 444 election.

Form **2553** (Rev. 12-2017)

Form 2553 (Rev. 12-2017) Page 4

Name	Employer identification number

Part III **Qualified Subchapter S Trust (QSST) Election Under Section 1361(d)(2)*** **Note:** If you are making more than one QSST election, use additional copies of page 4.

Income beneficiary's name and address	Social security number
Trust's name and address	Employer identification number

Date on which stock of the corporation was transferred to the trust (month, day, year) . . . . ▶

In order for the trust named above to be a QSST and thus a qualifying shareholder of the S corporation for which this Form 2553 is filed, I hereby make the election under section 1361(d)(2). Under penalties of perjury, I certify that the trust meets the definitional requirements of section 1361(d)(3) and that all other information provided in Part III is true, correct, and complete.

Signature of income beneficiary or signature and title of legal representative or other qualified person making the election Date

*Use Part III to make the QSST election only if stock of the corporation has been transferred to the trust on or before the date on which the corporation makes its election to be an S corporation. The QSST election must be made and filed separately if stock of the corporation is transferred to the trust **after** the date on which the corporation makes the S election.

Part IV **Late Corporate Classification Election Representations** (see instructions)

If a late entity classification election was intended to be effective on the same date that the S corporation election was intended to be effective, relief for a late S corporation election must also include the following representations.

1 The requesting entity is an eligible entity as defined in Regulations section 301.7701-3(a);

2 The requesting entity intended to be classified as a corporation as of the effective date of the S corporation status;

3 The requesting entity fails to qualify as a corporation solely because Form 8832, Entity Classification Election, was not timely filed under Regulations section 301.7701-3(c)(1)(i), or Form 8832 was not deemed to have been filed under Regulations section 301.7701-3(c)(1)(v)(C);

4 The requesting entity fails to qualify as an S corporation on the effective date of the S corporation status solely because the S corporation election was not timely filed pursuant to section 1362(b); **and**

5a The requesting entity timely filed all required federal tax returns and information returns consistent with its requested classification as an S corporation for all of the years the entity intended to be an S corporation and no inconsistent tax or information returns have been filed by or with respect to the entity during any of the tax years, **or**

b The requesting entity has not filed a federal tax or information return for the first year in which the election was intended to be effective because the due date has not passed for that year's federal tax or information return.

Form **2553** (Rev. 12-2017)

Appendix 3-4 Form 8752

Form **8752**

Department of the Treasury
Internal Revenue Service

Required Payment or Refund Under Section 7519

▶ **Don't attach this form to Form 1065 or Form 1120-S; file it separately.**

▶ **Go to *www.irs.gov/Form8752* for the latest information.**

For the required payment figured using the net income from the base year ending ____________, 2019

▶ **Due by May 15, 2020.**

OMB No. 1545-0123

2019

Type or print

Name of partnership or S corporation | Employer identification number

Number, street, and room or suite no. If a P.O. box, see instructions.

City or town, state or province, country, and ZIP or foreign postal code

A Check applicable box to show how entity is classified for federal income tax purposes: **(1)** ☐ Partnership **(2)** ☐ S Corporation

B If this is the entity's first tax year, skip lines 1 through 10, enter -0- on line 11, and check this box . . . ▶ ☐

C If this form is being filed to claim a full refund of the net required payment balance because of a terminating event, skip lines 1 through 9a, enter -0- on line 9b, complete lines 10–12, and check this box . . . ▶ ☐

D If the entity had a short base year (a base year of less than 12 months), check this box. See the line 1 instructions for the definition of "base year" . . . ▶ ☐

1	Net income for base year. If the entity had a short base year, increase the net income for the short base year by the applicable payments made during the base year (line 2 below), and multiply the result by the ratio of 12 over the number of months in the short base year. Carry out the ratio to at least 3 decimal places. If zero or less, enter -0- . . .	1	
2	Applicable payments made during base year . . .	2	
3	Deferral ratio. Divide the number of months in the deferral period by 12 and enter the result as a percentage. Carry out your answer to at least the nearest tenth of a percent . . .	3	. %
4	**Line 1 deferred amount.** Multiply line 1 by line 3 . . . **Caution:** If the entity had a short base year, skip lines 5 and 6 and go to line 7.	4	
5	**Line 2 deferred amount.** Multiply line 2 by line 3 . . . **5**		
6	Applicable payments made during the deferral period of the base year . . . **6**		
7	If the entity had a 12-month base year, subtract line 6 from line 5. If zero or less, enter -0-. If the entity had a short base year, enter the applicable payments made during the deferral period of the applicable election year . . .	7	
8	Net base year income. If the entity had a 12-month base year, add lines 4 and 7. If the entity had a short base year, subtract line 7 from line 4. If zero or less, enter -0- . . .	8	
9a	Multiply line 8 by 38% (0.38) . . . ▶ **9a**		
b	If line 9a is more than $500 or the required payment for any prior tax year was more than $500, enter the amount from line 9a here. Otherwise, enter -0- . . . ▶	9b	
10	Net required payment balance. Enter the excess of the required payments made for all prior years over the refunds of any required payments received for all prior years . . .	10	
11	**Required payment due.** If line 9b is larger than line 10, subtract line 10 from line 9b. See the line 11 instructions for payment options . . .	11	
12	**Refund of net prior year payments.** If line 10 is larger than line 9b, subtract line 9b from line 10	12	

Sign Here

Under penalties of perjury, I declare that I have examined this return, including accompanying schedules and statements, and to the best of my knowledge and belief, it is true, correct, and complete. Declaration of preparer (other than taxpayer) is based on all information of which preparer has any knowledge.

Keep a copy of this form for your records.

▶ Signature of officer, partner, or limited liability company member | Date | ▶ Title

Paid Preparer Use Only

Print/Type preparer's name	Preparer's signature	Date	Check ☐ if self-employed	PTIN
Firm's name ▶			Firm's EIN ▶	
Firm's address ▶			Phone no.	

For Paperwork Reduction Act Notice, see the instructions. Cat. No. 64988D Form **8752** (2019)

General Instructions

Section references are to the Internal Revenue Code unless otherwise noted.

Future developments. For the latest information about developments related to Form 8752 and its instructions, such as legislation enacted after they were published, go to *www.irs.gov/Form8752.*

What's New

New filing addresses. The filing address for partnerships and S corporations located in certain states has changed. See *Where to file* below.

Purpose of form. Partnerships and S corporations use Form 8752 to figure and report the payment required under section 7519 or to obtain a refund of net prior year payments.

Section 7519 payments are required of any partnership or S corporation that has elected under section 444 to have a tax year other than a required tax year.

Who must file. A partnership or S corporation must file Form 8752 if it made a section 444 election by filing Form 8716, Election To Have a Tax Year Other Than a Required Tax Year, and its election is in effect for the tax year. A partnership or S corporation that terminates its section 444 election or liquidates must also file Form 8752 to claim a refund of its net required payment balance. Form 8752 must be filed for each year the section 444 election is in effect, even if the required payment for the applicable election year is zero. See section 7519(c) for details.

Don't file Form 8752 for a personal service corporation (as defined in Regulations section 1.441-3). Instead, file Schedule H (Form 1120), Section 280H Limitations for a Personal Service Corporation (PSC), with the corporation's income tax return.

When to file. For applicable election years beginning in 2019, Form 8752 must be filed and the required payment made on or before May 15, 2020.

For your base year ending in 2019, you must use the 2019 Form 8752. You can't use the 2019 Form 8752 for your base year ending in 2020.

However, Temporary Regulations section 1.444-3T(b)(4)(iii) provides a special rule that extends the due date for filing Form 8752 and making the required payment related to certain back-up section 444 elections.

Where to file. File Form 8752 at the applicable IRS address listed below.

If the entity's principal place of business or principal office or agency is located in:	Use the following address:
Connecticut, Delaware, District of Columbia, Georgia, Illinois, Indiana, Kentucky, Maine, Maryland, Massachusetts, Michigan, New Hampshire, New Jersey, New York, North Carolina, Ohio, Pennsylvania, Rhode Island, South Carolina, Tennessee, Vermont, Virginia, West Virginia, Wisconsin	Department of the Treasury Internal Revenue Service Kansas City, MO 64999
Alabama, Alaska, Arizona, Arkansas, California, Colorado, Florida, Hawaii, Idaho, Iowa, Kansas, Louisiana, Minnesota, Mississippi, Missouri, Montana, Nebraska, Nevada, New Mexico, North Dakota, Oklahoma, Oregon, South Dakota, Texas, Utah, Washington, Wyoming	Department of the Treasury Internal Revenue Service Ogden, UT 84201

An entity without a principal office or agency or principal place of business in the United States must file Form 8752 with the Internal Revenue Service Center, P.O. Box 409101, Ogden, UT 84409.

Penalties. If the required payment isn't made by the due date, the entity may have to pay a penalty equal to 10% of the underpayment. For this purpose, "underpayment" means the excess of the required payment over the amount (if any) of such payment made on or before the due date for the applicable election year. The penalty will not be imposed if the entity can show that the failure to pay on time was due to reasonable cause and not willful neglect. If you include this penalty with the entity's payment, identify and enter the penalty amount in the bottom margin of page 1. Don't include the penalty in the *Required payment due* space on line 11. Other penalties may also apply. If the entity receives a notice about a penalty after it files Form 8752, the entity should send us an explanation and we will determine if the entity meets reasonable cause criteria. Do **not** attach an explanation when filing Form 8752.

Amended return. To correct an error in a Form 8752 already filed, file an amended Form 8752 and write "Amended Return" across the top.

Specific Instructions

For the applicable election year beginning in 2019, enter the ending date of the base year ending in 2019. See the definitions of applicable election year and base year under *Line 1. Net income for base year,* later.

Address. Include the suite, room, or other unit number after the street address. If the Post Office doesn't deliver mail to the street address and the entity has a P.O. box, show the box number instead of the street address.

Item B. If an applicable election year is the entity's first year of existence (that is, it is a newly formed entity and therefore doesn't have a base year), the required payment is zero.

Item C. If the entity terminated its section 444 election and the termination took effect for a tax year ending in 2019, or the entity liquidated during a tax year ending in 2019, check this box. The entity should claim a full refund of the net required payment balance shown on line 10. See section 7519(c)(3) to determine when you are eligible for the refund.

A partnership's section 444 election ends if the partnership changes its accounting period to its required tax year or some other permitted year, it is penalized for willfully failing to comply with the requirements of section 7519, or it becomes a member of a tiered structure and the same tax year exception doesn't apply (see Temporary Regulations section 1.444-2T for more about tiered structures).

An S corporation's section 444 election ends if it changes its accounting period to a calendar year or some other permitted year, it is penalized for willfully failing to comply with the requirements of section 7519, it becomes a member of a tiered structure and the same tax year exception doesn't apply (see Temporary Regulations section 1.444-2T), or its S corporation election terminates (unless it immediately becomes a personal service corporation).

See Temporary Regulations section 1.444-1T(a)(5)(ii) for the effective date of the termination of a section 444 election.

Once a section 444 election is terminated, the entity may never make another section 444 election.

Line 1. Net income for base year. The term "base year" means the tax year preceding the applicable election year. Any tax year for which a section 444 election is in effect, including the first tax year the section 444 election is made, is an applicable election year. For example, if you are completing Form 8752 for the applicable election year beginning October 1, 2019, and ending September 30, 2020, the base year is the tax year beginning October 1, 2018, and ending September 30, 2019.

Partnerships. Line 1 net income is the aggregate (not less than zero) of the partnership's items of income and expense, other than tax-exempt income, nondeductible expenses, and guaranteed payments under section 707(c). When figuring this amount, disregard any limitations at the partner level. For base years beginning in 2018, line 1 should equal the amount on the 2018 Form 1065, line 1, of *Analysis of Net Income (Loss)*, plus the aggregate items of income and expense, if any, reported on the attached statement for Schedule K, line 20c (but not less than zero).

S corporations. Line 1 net income is the aggregate (not less than zero) of the corporation's items of income and expense, other than tax-exempt income and nondeductible expenses. When figuring this amount, disregard any limitations at the shareholder level. For base years beginning in 2018, line 1 should equal the amount on the 2018 Form 1120-S, Schedule K, line 18, plus the aggregate items of income and expense, if any, reported on Schedule K, line 17d (but not less than zero). For this purpose, all S corporations must complete Schedule K, line 18.

If an S corporation was a C corporation for its base year, the C corporation's taxable income is treated as the net income of the S corporation for the base year. See Temporary Regulations section 1.7519-1T(b)(5) for other details.

Line 2. Applicable payments. In general, the term "applicable payments" means any amount deductible in the base year that is includible at any time, directly or indirectly, in the gross income of any partner or shareholder who was a partner or shareholder during the base year. However, the term doesn't include guaranteed payments. Examples of applicable payments are officer's compensation, wages, and rent paid to any partner or shareholder.

If the S corporation was a C corporation for its base year, applicable payments of the C corporation are treated as if received from an S corporation.

Line 3. Deferral ratio. The deferral period is the number of months between:

- The beginning of the elected tax year, and
- The close of the first required tax year ending within such a year.

For example, the required tax year for an S corporation is the calendar year, ending on December 31. If an S corporation elects a tax year beginning on November 1, there would be 2 months between the beginning of the elected tax year and the end of the required tax year (December 31). The deferral period for the elected tax year would be 2 months.

Line 9b. If you enter zero on line 9b and you didn't make any prior year required payment for which a refund can be claimed, enter zero on line 10, skip lines 11 and 12, and complete the signature section. You are required to file Form 8752 to show that you have a zero liability for the applicable election year beginning in 2019.

Line 11. Required payment due. If you are enrolled in the Electronic Federal Tax Payment System (EFTPS), you can pay your balance due online or by phone. EFTPS is a free service provided by the U.S. Department of Treasury. If you aren't required to use EFTPS, you may still participate voluntarily. To pay the balance due, get more information, or enroll in EFTPS, visit *www.eftps.gov* or call 1-800-555-4477.

To pay by check or money order. Enclose a check or money order for the amount on line 11 payable to "United States Treasury." Write the entity's employer identification number and "Form 8752" on the check or money order.

Line 12. Refund of net prior year payments. No refund will be made before the later of: **(a)** April 15, 2020, or **(b)** 90 days after Form 8752 is filed per section 7519(c)(3). No interest will be paid on the amount refunded.

Paperwork Reduction Act Notice. We ask for the information on this form to carry out the Internal Revenue laws of the United States. You are required to give us the information. We need it to ensure that you are complying with these laws and to allow us to figure and collect the right amount of required payment.

You are not required to provide the information requested on a form that is subject to the Paperwork Reduction Act unless the form displays a valid OMB control number. Books or records relating to a form or its instructions must be retained as long as their contents may become material in the administration of any Internal Revenue law. Generally, tax returns and return information are confidential, as required by section 6103.

The time needed to complete and file this form will vary depending on individual circumstances. The estimated burden for business taxpayers filing this form is approved under OMB control number 1545-0123 and is included in the estimates shown in the instructions for their business income tax return.

If you have suggestions for making this form simpler, we would be happy to hear from you. You can send us comments from *www.irs.gov/FormComments*. Or you can write to the Internal Revenue Service, Tax Forms and Publications, 1111 Constitution Ave. NW, IR-6526, Washington, DC 20224. Don't send the form to this office. Instead, see *Where to file*, earlier.

4

Methods of Accounting

§4.01 Methods of Accounting

[A] Overview

The tax accounting portion of the Internal Revenue Code (Subchapter E) contains the rules for accounting periods and methods of accounting. These rules can be found in the Code and Regulations and in many IRS pronouncements, rulings, and tax cases. The material in this chapter introduces the tax practitioner to the tax accounting topics one faces. Accounting methods determine the time when an item of income and deduction is recognized. Additionally, a method of accounting does not determine *if* an item is income.

Although no comprehensive definition of "method of accounting" exists in the Code or Regulations, the Regulations do provide that the term "method of accounting" includes not only the overall method of accounting, but also the accounting treatment of any item.[1] Several characteristics of a "method of accounting" are stated in the Regulations, Revenue Rulings, Revenue Procedures and tax court cases.[2] A "method of accounting" has the following characteristics:

- It affects the computation of a material item;[3]
- It is consistently applied and is predictable;[4]
- It conforms to generally accepted accounting principles;[5]
- It clearly reflects income;[6] and
- It has been adopted.[7]

IRC § 446 provides for the following overall methods of accounting:

- the cash receipts and disbursements method;
- the accrual method;
- installment sale;[8]
- any other method permitted by the Code; or
- any combination of the foregoing methods permitted under Regulations prescribed by the Secretary.[9]

The major topics covered in this chapter include the "book conformity rule" and "clear reflection of income."

---

[1] Reg. § 1.446-1(a)(1).

[2] It is recognized that no uniform method of accounting can be prescribed for all taxpayers. Each taxpayer shall adopt such forms and systems as are, in his judgment, best suited to his needs. Reg. § 1.446-1(a)(2).

[3] Reg. § 1.446-1(e)(2)(ii)(a) provides that a material item is any item that concerns the timing of income or deductions. In Revenue Procedures, the IRS has explained that an item concerns timing, and is therefore considered a method of accounting, if "the practice does not permanently affect the taxpayer's *lifetime* income, but does or could change the taxable year in which income is reported. The term "item" is used to indicate any recurring incidence of income or expense. Examples include: real estate taxes, Reg. § 1.446-1(e)(2)(iii), Example 2; corporate officers' bonuses are items, *Connors, Inc. v. Comm'r*, 71 T.C. 913 (1979); and employees' vacation pay, *Oberman Mfg. Co. v. Comm'r*, 47 T.C. 471 (1967), *acq.*, 1967-2 CB 3, *See, e.g.*, TAM 8201015.

[4] Reg. § 1.446-1(e)(2)(ii)(a) states that "in most instances," a method of accounting is not established without a "pattern of consistent treatment" of an item. The "consistency" referred to is consistent treatment of a particular item over time, not consistency between the contemporary treatment of different items.

[5] Reg. § 1.446-1(a)(2).

[6] IRC § 446(b).

[7] As stated in Reg. § 1.446-1(a)(2), "A method of accounting which reflects the consistent application of generally accepted accounting principles in a particular trade or business in accordance with accepted conditions or practices in that trade or business will ordinarily be regarded as clearly reflecting income, provided all items of gross income and expense are treated consistently from year to year."

[8] IRC § 453.

[9] IRC § 446(c).

In general, tax accounting is conceptually a simple topic, however, taxpayers often have difficulty with:

- The complexity of tax laws;
- Laws which are a product of political, fiscal and economic policy;
- Laws which change constantly; and
- Laws which often have no logic.

In tax accounting one can find that:

- Compliance is difficult and in some cases expensive; and
- Enforcement may not be uniform.

[B] Financial Accounting v. Tax Accounting

Financial accounting governs financial reporting. Aspects of financial accounting include the preparation of balance sheets, statements of retained earnings, income statements and financial statement presentations. The primary function of financial accounting is to provide useful and accurate information to users of this information.

Tax accounting and financial accounting are not functionally equivalent. In *Thor Power Tool Co. v. Commissioner*,[10] Justice Blackmun addressed the distinction as follows:

> The primary goal of financial accounting is to provide useful information to management, shareholders, creditors and others properly interested, the major responsibility of the accountant is to protect these parties from being misled. The primary goal of the income tax system, in contrast, is the equitable collection of revenue; the major responsibility of the Internal Revenue Service is to protect the public fisc. Consistently with its goals and responsibilities, financial accounting has as its foundation the principle of conservatism, with its corollary that possible errors in measurement [should] be in the direction of understatement rather than overstatement of net income and net assets. In view of the Treasury's markedly different goals and responsibilities, understatement of income is not destined to be its guiding light. Given this diversity, even contrariety, of objectives, any presumptive equivalency between tax and financial accounting would not be acceptable.[11]

Nonetheless, tax accounting draws on financial accounting concepts, such as the Generally Accepted Accounting Principles (GAAP). These concepts augment the distinctly different regime of tax accounting.

In 2018, the IRS stated it will grant automatic consent to a taxpayer that wants to change its method for income recognition to a method under the FASB "New

---

[10] 439 U.S. 522, 79-1 USTC ¶9139 (1979).

[11] *Id.* at 542.

Standards" for identifying performance obligations, allocating transaction price to performance obligations, and/or considering performance obligations satisfied.[12]

IRC § 446(c) contains the following permissible methods of accounting:

The cash method. Under the cash method,[13] the taxpayer recognizes income upon the actual or constructive receipt of cash, a cash equivalent, property, or services.[14] The taxpayer is generally entitled to a deduction in the year in which an expense is paid. However, if an expenditure results in the creation of an asset having a useful life that extends substantially beyond the close of the tax year, the expenditure may not be deductible (or may be only partly deductible), because it may be a capital expenditure.[15]

The accrual method. Under the accrual method, the taxpayer generally recognizes income upon the earlier of (i) when income is "earned," *i.e.*, when all the events which fix the taxpayer's right to such income have occurred, or (ii) when the income to be received can be estimated with reasonable accuracy.[16]

The taxpayer is entitled to a deduction in the year in which (i) the taxpayer has incurred a legal obligation to pay the item, (ii) the amount to be paid can be determined with reasonable accuracy, and (iii) economic performance has occurred (or is deemed to have occurred).[17] As with the cash method of accounting, there are numerous exceptions and qualifications. For example, in some cases, advance receipts of income may be deferred by an accrual method taxpayer.[18] Under the economic performance rules applicable to the accrual method, some liabilities (*e.g.*, workers' compensation and tort liabilities) are not deductible until paid.[19]

Hybrid method. The Code also allows for a hybrid method of accounting, *i.e.*, a combination of methods of accounting, provided the combined method clearly reflects income and is consistently used.[20] A common example of a permissible hybrid method is the use of the accrual method to account for sales and purchases along with the use of the cash method to account for other items of income and expense.[21]

While the Code does not contain a comprehensive list of accounting methods for specific items, it does prescribe methods of accounting for specific items, *e.g.*, the LIFO, FIFO, Uniform Capitalization rules, and inventory methods. The Code also prescribes methods of accounting for specific types of taxpayers, *e.g.*, the long-term contract methods for construction contractors.

---

[12] Rev. Proc. 2018-29, 2018-22 IRB 634. *See* Chapter 7, *infra.*

[13] Reg. § 1.446-1(c).

[14] Items of gross income and expenditures which are elements in the computation of taxable income need not be in the form of cash. It is sufficient that such items can be valued in terms of money. Reg. § 1.446-1(a)(3).

[15] Reg. § 1.446-1(a)(1).

[16] Reg. § 1.446-1(c)(1)(ii)(A).

[17] IRC § 461(h)(2)(c).

[18] *See* Rev. Proc. 2004-34, 2004-22 IRB 991.

[19] Reg. § 1.446-1(h)(2)(c).

[20] *See also* Reg. § 1.446-1(c)(1)(iv).

[21] *See* Reg. § 1.446-1(c)(1)(iv).

[C] *The Timing Issue*

Tax accounting is concerned primarily with timing, that is, *when* an item should be recognized as income or as an expense. An accounting method usually affects the timing of recording transactions by determining the taxable year in which items of income and deductions will be allocated in a consistent and predictable way.

Example 4-1

Joan Lawless, Esq., received a check for services on December 31, 2020, in the amount of $1,000. The check was drawn on the same bank where Joan maintains her office banking. Rather than depositing the check that day, Joan decides to put the check away and have her office manager deposit the check on the next banking day, January 2, 2021.

In what year should Joan include the $1,000? This will depend on her particular method of accounting.[22]

[D] *Selecting an Accounting Method*

A taxpayer may elect, on his first income tax return, to use any method of accounting that clearly reflects his income and that he regularly uses in keeping his books and records.[23] The latter requirement is satisfied even if the tax accounting method used by the taxpayer differs from the financial accounting method used by the taxpayer in keeping his books and records.[24]

Once an accounting method is selected, it cannot be changed without the permission of the Commissioner.[25]

[E] *Book Conformity Rule*

The book conformity rule requires that a taxpayer compute his taxable income in conformity with the method of accounting he regularly uses in computing his income in keeping his "books."[26] This is necessary to ensure that the Commissioner has

---

[22] For the cash method, *see* Chapter 5, *infra*; for the accrual method, *see* Chapter 6, *infra*.

[23] IRC § 446.

[24] *See* "Conversion Work Paper," § 4.01[F], *infra*.

[25] IRC § 446(e).

[26] IRC § 446(a); Reg. § 1.446-1(a). "Except as provided in paragraph (b) [of Reg. § 1.6001-1], any person subject to tax under subtitle A of the Code . . . or any person required to file a return of information with respect to income, shall keep such permanent books of account or records, including inventories, as are sufficient to establish the amount of gross income, deductions, credits, or other matters required to be shown by such person in any return of such tax or information." Reg. § 1.6001-1(a).

sufficient information to determine a taxpayer's income and expenses during an audit.[27]

The regulations require that each taxpayer make a return of his taxable income for each taxable year and maintain such accounting records as will enable him to file a correct return. Accounting records include the taxpayer's regular books of account and such other records and data as may be necessary to support the entries on his books of account and on his return.[28]

Recordkeeping systems range from simple manual systems to extremely sophisticated computerized ones. Systems can be maintained in-house, or outside service centers can be used. The nature of the business and the volume of transactions will influence the form of system adopted. Regardless of the form the system takes, certain elements are essential. At minimum, there should be:

- A chart of accounts.
- A general ledger.
- Accounting records for:
  - Sales.
  - Receivables.
  - Purchases.
  - Payables.
  - Cash receipts.
  - Cash disbursements.
  - Payroll.
  - Fixed assets.
  - Inventory, if applicable.
- A filing system containing documentation to support the accounting records.

A taxpayer whose sole source of income is wages is not required to keep formal books in order to have an accounting method. Tax returns, copies thereof, or other records may be sufficient to establish the use of the method of accounting used in the preparation of the taxpayer's income tax returns.[29]

Are all taxpayer records "books" for purposes of the book conformity rule? The Court, in *St. Luke's Hospital v. Commissioner*,[30] said books are "complete and full information from which an accountant could determine net income . . . ."[31] It is fair to say, therefore, if a taxpayer's records have an opening and closing balance, and contain enough information to make a tax return, his records are "books." Typically, books consisting of a journal and a general ledger which classify and summarize entries contained in the books of original entry are considered adequate for cash basis taxpayers.

---

[27] Reg. § 1.446-1(a)(4) (providing that a taxpayer's accounting records include "such . . . records and data as may be necessary to support the entries . . . on [the]return"). Notwithstanding, a taxpayer whose sole source of income is wages does not need to keep formal books. Reg. § 1.446-1(b)(2).

[28] Reg. § 1.446-1(a)(4).

[29] IRC § § 263A, 471, and 472.

[30] 35 T.C. 236 (1960).

[31] 35 T.C. at 242.

For purposes of applying this rule, the courts have generally reasoned that a taxpayer's "books" include work papers which reconcile income reported on its financial books with income reported on its income tax return; consequently, different accounting methods can generally be utilized for tax purposes provided that adequate work papers reconciling the two sets of records are maintained.[32]

On the other hand, informal records such as receipts, bank statements, notations on check stubs, etc., are generally not regarded as books of account and do not support the use of a fiscal year. In *Atlas Oil and Refining Corp. v. Commissioner*,[33] the Tax Court said:

> If anything, it is the audit reports assembled annually for the apparent purpose of producing the figures upon which the tax returns could be based that must be cast aside in any examination of the petitioner's actual system of accounting. These reports were not a part of its books and are not adequate for us to conclude that it was either on a fiscal year basis or that, as respondent insists, it maintained a double set of accounts.[34]

Accordingly, records consisting of check stubs, receipts and dividend statements are not "books" because they do not show income kept on an annual basis. A checkbook alone, without an opening balance and a closing balance, is not sufficient.[35] Regulation § 1.441-1(b)(7) provides that books include the taxpayer's regular books of account and those other records and data as may be necessary to support the entries on the taxpayer's books and on the taxpayer's return, as for example, a reconciliation of any difference between these books and the taxpayer's return. Records that are sufficient to reflect income adequately and clearly on the basis of an annual accounting period will be regarded as the keeping of books[36] .

---

[32] Rev. Rul. 68-83, 1968-1 CB 190 and TAM 9103001 and FSA 1999-1086 that reversed TAM 9113003.

[33] 17 T.C. 733 (1951).

[34] *See Maclean v. Comm'r*, 73 T.C. 1045 (1980) (where no books produced at trial except tax returns). *See also Godson v. Comm'r*, 5 TCM 648 and *St. Luke's Hospital v. Comm'r*, 35 T.C. 236 (1960).

[35] Where a taxpayer uses different accounting methods for financial reporting and tax purposes, the IRS and the courts disagree as to the kind of records that the taxpayer must make of the necessary adjustments. The IRS requires that the adjustments be reflected on the taxpayer's permanent books and records, or on permanent auxiliary records. Rev. Rul. 68-35, 1968-1 CB 190; Rev. Rul. 67-147, 1967-1 CB 105. The IRS has stated that, for this purpose, permanent auxiliary records are records that are prepared in the normal course of business; that are sufficiently complete and accurate to provide a reliable and readily accessible basis for reconciling the regularly maintained books of account and the tax returns; that, if originally prepared as accountants' work sheets or work papers, are turned over to the taxpayer and associated with his regular books of account; and that are retained so long as their contents may become material in the administration of any revenue law. Rev. Rul. 58-601, 1958-2 CB 81. In *Max H. Stryker v. Comm'r*, 36 BTA 326 (1937), the court said "We have heretofore held that informal records such as check stubs, rent receipts, and dividend statements are not books." *See also Louis M. Brooks v. Comm'r*, 6 T.C. 504 (1946).

[36] *See* California FTB Informational Publication No. 1158, 01/01/2002 and Regulations: NY: NYCRR 158.1 Permanent books of account or records and contents of New York State income tax returns and other forms. NY Tax Law, § 658(a) and (b).

On the other hand, in *Charles v. Doyle*,[37] a gambler's books were held to accurately reflect income; although the original winning tickets had been discarded, the duplicates and weekly summaries were kept. Deductions were allowed for the gambler for rents and wages, although gambling was illegal, where these deductions were less than his illegal income. The taxpayer did not retain the original gambling tickets known as "safety tickets"; however, he did retain carbon copies of the safety tickets for each day of operation, and the daily sheets made from these carbon copies. Each day he placed these sheets in a large envelope bearing the date with a copy of the safety tickets written that day. The envelope also contained the "wall sheets" for the day and the "scratch sheets" which showed the entries for that day and the results of the previous day. The monthly summary sheets were recapitulated and served as the basis for the preparation of the taxpayer's income tax returns. The Tax Court held that the Commissioner's reconstruction of gross income and arbitrary increase in income by 14% was unwarranted. The records maintained by the bookkeeper were deemed to be adequate.

In limited cases, the Code or the Regulations explicitly require a taxpayer to conform its book and tax accounting methods. Examples of situations in which conformity is required include:

- Use of Last in, First out (LIFO) inventories;[38]
- Treatment of coupons and trading stamps;[39]
- Capitalization of costs into inventory;[40] and
- Time of reporting sales of utility services.[41]

The fact that a taxpayer is required to use or change to a particular accounting method for financial reporting or regulatory purposes does not mean that the taxpayer is required to use or change to the same accounting method in computing its taxable income.[42]

[F] Conversion Work Papers

IRC § 446 states "Taxable income shall be computed under the method of accounting on the basis of which the taxpayer regularly computes his income in keeping his books." Since a taxpayer must compute his tax liability consistent with his books, may he use one method of accounting to maintain his financial records and a different method of accounting for reporting taxable income? Often taxpayers have assumed it is their right to choose one method of tax accounting in keeping books but a different method for reporting taxes, as long as sufficient workpapers reconciling

---

37 13 TCM 1171 (1954).

38 IRC § 472(c).

39 Reg. § 1.451-4(c)(6).

40 Reg. § 1.471-11(c)(2)(iii).

41 Rev. Rul. 72-114, 1972-1 CB 124.

42 *National Airlines v. Comm'r*, 9 T.C. 159 (1947); *Fidelity Assocs. Inc. v. Comm'r*, 63 TCM 1889. *See also The Optimal Relationship Between Taxable Income and Financial Accounting Income: Analysis and a Proposal*, 97 Geo. L. J 423 (2009).

the different methods are available. While this view has apparently been accepted by both the tax-writing committees of Congress and, on occasion, the National Office, examining agents continue to assert a violation of the book conformity requirement when that conformity is based only on conversion workpapers.

The regulations under IRC § 446 provide little guidance as to the scope of this provision. Indeed the regulations state "It is recognized that no uniform method of accounting can be prescribed for all taxpayers. Each taxpayer shall adopt such forms and systems as are, in his judgment, best suited to his needs."[43]

As provided in IRC § 446, the book conformity requirement is straightforward. A taxpayer must compute income for tax purposes on the same basis it computes income for book purposes. Consequently, if a taxpayer wishes to use a particular method or methods for tax purposes, the taxpayer needs only to adopt those methods for book purposes. Unfortunately the decision to adopt a book accounting method is generally made at the beginning of the business. By the time the taxpayer's attention has turned to tax reporting opportunities, its book method has already been established, and much flexibility has been lost. Consequently, tax advisors should encourage taxpayers to consider tax reporting methods at the beginning of business activities. The book method may thereafter be changed to conform to the demands of financial recordkeeping and decision making, but the tax methods will have been properly established. This is important, since a change in book methods generally does not require a change in tax methods.

Consider, for example, a corporation that is required to supply accrual-basis financial information to its lender, yet uses the cash method for tax reporting. In order to facilitate the preparation of its income tax return, the corporation will prepare work papers that provide reconciliation between net income for financial statement purposes and taxable income as reflected on its tax return. The permissibility of this practice under the Code has been addressed by the Tax Court and the Internal Revenue Service in several decisions and rulings.

In *Patchen v. Commissioner*,[44] a professional engineering partnership used the cash method on its books and in its tax returns for the years 1946 and 1947. In 1948, the partnership installed an accrual system for its business needs, but in preparing its federal income tax returns, it continued to use the cash method. The partnership's books were converted to cash basis through the preparation of memorandum journal entries kept in its accountant's work papers and not entered on the books. The Tax Court concluded that the principal aims of conformity (the most important of which is to provide sufficient information for an accurate audit) and consistency were satisfied by memorandum journal entries allowing the accrual system to yield cash basis results.

---

[43] Reg. § 1.446-1(a)(2).

[44] 27 T.C. 592 (1956), *aff'd part and rev'd in part*, 258 F.2d 544, 58-2 USTC ¶ 9733 (5th Cir. 1958).

In *St. Luke's Hospital, Inc. v. Commissioner*,[45] the Tax Court continued the trend established in *Patchen*. In *St. Luke's*, the taxpayer was a hospital that had requested and obtained permission to change from the accrual to the cash method for tax purposes. The consent letter issued to the taxpayer-hospital did not specifically require that the hospital's books be kept on the cash method, so the hospital continued to maintain its books on the accrual method. Adjustments converting the accrual records to the cash method were prepared by the hospital's accountants and were retained with the accountants' work papers. The Commissioner contended that the consent granted by him allowing the hospital to change to the cash method for tax purposes was inoperative because the hospital had not complied with IRC § 446(a). The Court ruled in favor of the taxpayer and pointed out that the hospital had proven that its books and records were sufficient to correctly reflect cash basis income and to clearly reflect income even though adjustments and closing entries had to be made.

In *Hi-Plains Enterprises, Inc. v. Commissioner*,[46] the Tax Court concluded that a feedlot operator was a farmer and, thus, entitled to use the cash method, and cited *St. Luke's* for the proposition that an accountant's adjustments of book entries are properly part of a taxpayer's books in converting a taxpayer's accrual system to a cash basis system.[47]

In *Fidelity Associates Inc. v. Commissioner*,[48] the Tax Court held that the IRS abused its discretion by changing the accounting method of an accrual method S corporation that treated commissions on installment sales as fully deductible current expenses for tax purposes, but treated part of the commissions as deferred expenses for financial accounting purposes. The Tax Court stated that IRC § 446(a) does not require absolute conformity between tax and financial accounting methods, so long as taxable income is accurately reflected.

The Tax Court noted that "it is well recognized that tax accounting requirements may diverge from financial accounting standards and that financial accounting standards are not controlling for tax purposes." However, in allowing a difference between book and tax reporting for commissions on installment sales, the court said that the taxpayer's books and records included sufficient data to readily permit a reconciliation of any differences in the treatment between tax and book reporting.[49]

In addition to Tax Court decisions permitting the use of reconciled entries, the Internal Revenue Service has published two Revenue Rulings addressing the use of reconciled entries.[50]

---

[45] 35 T.C. 236 (1960). In AOD 1991-007, the Service withdrew its 1963 nonacquiescence and substituted its acquiescence in the Tax Court's decision in *St. Luke's Hospital, Inc.*, regarding deviation from strict book-tax conformity.

[46] 60 T.C. 158 (1973).

[47] *See also American Fletcher Corp v. United States*, 86-1 USTC ¶ 9283 (7th Cir.1987), *aff'd*, 832 F.2d 436, 87-2 USTC ¶ 9603; Priv. Ltr. Ruls. 9103001, 9818004.

[48] T.C. Memo. 1992-142.

[49] *Id.*

[50] Rev. Rul. 68-35, 1968-1 CB 190; Rev. Rul. 68-83, 1968-1 CB 190.

In Rev. Rul. 68-35,[51] the IRS held that a corporation engaged in banking that maintained books on the cash method and filed income tax returns on the cash method could continue to use the cash method for federal income tax purposes even though it kept its books, for quarterly statement purposes, on the accrual method of accounting.

In Rev. Rul. 68-83,[52] the taxpayer was a national bank that was subsequently required by banking regulations to prepare financial statements on the accrual method. Prior to this requirement, it used the cash method for book and tax purposes. The IRS ruled that the taxpayer could continue to file its federal income tax returns on the cash method as long as its permanent books and records reflected a proper reconciliation between the accrual and the cash methods. If the taxpayer wanted to change its method of accounting it could do so by filing a Form 3115. If the conformity requirement of IRC §446(a) was given strict application, the taxpayer would have been required to request a change in its overall accounting method. The proper interpretation of Rev. Rul. 68-83, however, is that the IRS allows the reconciliation of entries.[53]

[G] Record Retention Requirements

Generally, cancelled checks, accounts payable and accounts receivable ledgers, customer and vendor invoices, and so forth should be kept for a minimum of seven years. However, other business records, such as year-end financial statements, insurance records, patent records, appraisals, and fixed asset purchases, should be kept permanently. Self-employed individuals owning a small business should seek the advice of their accounting firm or law firm in obtaining specifics regarding records retention requirements. Further information can also be found in IRS Publication 583, *"Starting a Business and Keeping Records."*

§4.02 Material Items

[A] Generally

The accounting treatment of any "material item" is considered to constitute a "method of accounting."[54] The term "item" means any recurring incidence of income or expense. The term "material item" involves the proper time (or in some instances the relative monetary value of the item in absolute terms) for the inclusion of an item

---

[51] 1968-1 CB 190.

[52] 1968-1 CB 190.

[53] *See also* Priv. Ltr. Rul. 9103001. In AOD 1991-007, the Commissioner withdrew its non-acquiescence and substituted its acquiescence in the Tax Court's decision in *St. Luke's Hospital, Inc. See* N. 35, *supra. Cf.* Rev. Rul. 68-420, 1968-2 CB 257, where an accountant's work papers did not meet the bookkeeping requirements of Reg. §1.593-7(a) because they were not associated with the taxpayer's regular books of account and the entries were not transferred to its reserve accounts.

[54] Reg. §1.446-1(e)(2)(ii)(a).

of income or the taking of a deduction.[55] The IRS has explained that an item concerns timing, and is therefore considered a method of accounting, if "the practice does not permanently affect the taxpayer's *lifetime* income, but does or could change the taxable year in which income is reported.[56]

In *Schuster's Express, Inc v. Commissioner*,[57] the Tax Court concluded that if a treatment does not affect a taxpayer's lifetime income, but only affects the assignment of items to taxable periods, then it is an accounting method; if it would affect that taxpayer's lifetime income, e.g., the permanent exclusion of items of income or deduction of nondeductible items, it is an error. If a change leaves a taxpayer's lifetime taxable income constant but affects when it is recognized, the change concerns an "item that involves the proper time for the inclusion of [an] item in income or the taking of a deduction."[58] In TAM 9429001, the National Office prohibited the parent of an affiliated group from changing its treatment of payments to a subsidiary for prior years so that the parent's deductions could be taken into account, rather than being deferred under former Reg. §1.1502-13(b)(2). The parent argued that it was correcting an erroneous application of the regulations as they existed before being amended in 1995, and not changing its accounting method. The National Office rejected this argument and advised that the consistent deferral of deductions for intercompany transactions affected the timing of an item and, therefore, constituted a method of accounting. Current regulations now confirm that the timing rules under Reg. §1.1502-13 are a method of accounting.[59]

[B] Absolute Materiality

Before the 1970 amendment to the Regulation adding "timing" as an element of materiality, the courts used the absolute materiality test based on the amount at issue. In *Dorr-Oliver, Inc., v. Commissioner*,[60] the Tax Court found a $25,000 item to be material in both an absolute and relative sense. The court stated that the issue was whether an unauthorized change in method of accounting for accrued vacation pay amounted to "a substantial change of a material item."[61] The court first noted, "No clear standards exist for determining materiality."[62] Although the taxpayer argued that $25,000 was not material, the court reasoned, "[i]n our view $25,000 is seldom insubstantial."[63]

It should be noted that the IRS's view of materiality deals with the timing issue and not with the absolute or relative magnitude of the item being considered, *i.e.*, "materiality" in an auditing sense. Consequently, even if an item is small, its treatment constitutes a "method of accounting" if timing of the item is affected. In *I.*

---

55 *Id.*

56 *See* Rev. Proc. 2002-18, 2002-1 CB 678, §2.01(1).

57 66 T.C. 588 (1976).

58 Reg. §1.446-1(e)(2)(ii)(a).

59 *Id.*

60 40 T.C. 50 (1963).

61 *Id.* at 54.

62 *Id.* at 54.

63 40 T.C. at 54-55.

Lewis Corporation v. Commissioner,[64] a $5,500 item was material to a corporation with net assets of $4 million. Notwithstanding the IRS's view of materiality, the Claims Court has applied a quantitative test and has ruled that a change in the treatment of an item requires IRS permission only if the magnitude of the change is "substantial."[65]

While some cases appear to adopt the IRS's position, many courts, including the Tax Court on frequent occasions, have applied a quantitative analysis to determine whether an item is material, although the cases exhibit considerable confusion as to exactly what amounts are to be compared.[66] On the other hand, the IRS treats the issue of "timing" as conclusive and does not recognize any quantitative threshold for materiality, relative or absolute.[67]

[C] Immaterial Items

Unlike material items, "immaterial items" do not affect the timing of income or expense recognition. The following are considered to be immaterial:

- A treatment of an item which affects the taxpayer's lifetime income, but not the assignment of items to taxable periods, *e.g.*, treatment of a dividend as deductible salary, which is properly adjusted through the filing of amended returns.[68]
- A change in allocation method which affects the computation of the absolute amount of an expense item, but not the period in which such item is reported, *e.g.*, the method of apportioning deductions between U.S.-source and foreign-source income.[69]

---

[64] 22 TCM 35 (1963).

[65] *See Cincinnati, New Orleans, and Texas Pacific Railway Co. v. United States*, 424 F.2d 563, 70-1 USTC ¶9344 (Cl. Ct. 1970).

[66] *Witte v. Comm'r*, 513 F.2d 391 (D.C. Cir. 1975) (holding that an $88,000 item was "material"); *Broida, Stone & Thomas, Inc. v. United States*, 204 F. Supp. 841, 843 (N.D. W. Va. 1962) (holding that a $6,660 item adding 10% to taxable income was "certainly" material), *aff'd without opin.*, 309 F.2d 486 (4th Cir. 1962); *Southern Pac. Transp. Co. v. Comm'r*, 75 T.C. 497, 672–87 (1980) (holding that items totaling $120,000 over three years were "material" in absolute terms even if relatively insignificant; the table reproduced in the opinion compared rail embankment expenditures at issue to operating revenues, operating expenses, capital expenditures, total investment, net taxable income, and total depreciation); *Coors v. Comm'r*, 60 T.C. 368, 399 (1973).

[67] *See, e.g.*, Rev. Rul. 79-378, 1979-2 CB 201 (ruling that a change in the method of accruing interest on installment obligations is a change in method of accounting); Rev. Rul. 71-248, 1971-1 CB 55 (ruling that a change in the treatment of software expense is a change in a method of accounting). *See also Knight-Ridder Newspapers v. United States*, 743 F.2d 781 (11th Cir. 1984) (discussion centering on timing issue exclusively); *Primo Pants Co. v. Comm'r*, 78 T.C. 705 (1982) (in interpreting parallel provision in Reg. §1.446-1(e)(2)(ii)(c) to effect that a change in an accounting method includes "a change in the treatment of any material item used in the overall plan for identifying or valuing items in inventory," court extensively discussed timing issue without any quantitative analysis); *City Gas Co. of Fla. v. Comm'r*, 47 TCM 971 (1984), on remand from 689 F.2d 943 (11th Cir. 1982) (discussing only timing issue); *Gen. Dynamics Corp. v. United States*, 69 Fed. Cl. 180 (2005) (discussing timing issue without any quantitative analysis under Reg. §1.446-1(e)(2)(ii)).

[68] *Schuster's Express v. Comm'r*, 66 T.C. 588 (1976); Reg. §1.445-1(e)(2)(ii)(b).

[69] *See* Priv. Ltr. Rul. 8545011 and *Occidental Petroleum Corp. v. Comm'r*, 55 T.C. 115 (1970).

[D] "Different" Items

"Items" will be considered "different" items where they differ in some way that is relevant to the tax treatment of the item, *e.g.*, different payment terms for different classes of receivables. "Items" will not be considered different items merely because they occur at different points in time.

§ 4.03 Clear Reflection of Income

The general rules governing methods of accounting require that an accounting method must clearly reflect income.[70] IRC § 446(b) provides that if no method of accounting has been regularly used by the taxpayer, or if the method used does not *clearly reflect income*, the computation of taxable income shall be made under such method as, in the opinion of the Secretary, does clearly reflect income. Neither the Code nor regulations define what clearly reflects income. The concept of " clear reflection of income" is central to tax accounting; clear reflection of income is influenced by many factors but not controlled by any one.[71] If a taxpayer's method of accounting challenged by the Commissioner were to prevail, the taxpayer must demonstrate that the Commissioner's determination is arbitrary, capricious, and without a sound basis in fact or law.[72] A method of accounting which reflects the consistent application of generally accepted accounting principles in a particular trade or business in accordance with accepted conditions or practices in that trade or business will ordinarily be regarded as clearly reflecting income, provided all items of gross income and expense are treated consistently from year to year.[73] However, the fact that an accounting method is consistent with GAAP does not, by itself, satisfy the clear-reflection-of-income standard.[74]

---

[70] IRC § 446(b).

[71] *See* TAM 9603004 (advising that a method of accounting that was permissible by one taxpayer (using a sliding scale method of depreciation for television film contract rights) was not permissible by another taxpayer because it did not clearly reflect income for the other taxpayer).

[72] *Ansley-Sheppard-Burgess Co. v. Comm'r*, 104 T.C. 367 (1995). *See Sierracin Corp. v. Comm'r*, 90 T.C. 341, 368 (1988). That standard was described in *Sierracin* as follows:

> Section 446(b) and sections 1.451-3(e), 1.446-1(a)(2), and 1.446-1(b)(1), Income Tax Regs., vest respondent with broad discretion in determining whether a taxpayer's contracts should be severed so as to clearly reflect income. "Since the Commissioner has "[m]uch latitude for discretion," his interpretation of the statute's clear reflection standard "should not be interfered with unless clearly unlawful." Thor Power Tool Co. v. Comm'r, 439 U.S. 522, 532 (1979).

Similarly, under IRC § 482, the IRS can distribute, apportion or allocate gross income, deductions, credits, or allowances between two or more businesses under common control to prevent tax evasion or for clear reflection of income.

[73] Reg. § 1.446-1(a)(2).

[74] *Thor Power Tool Co v. Comm'r*, 439 U.S. 522, 79-1 USTC ¶ 9139 (1979).

An often cited definition is found in *Caldwell v. Commissioner*,[75] where the Second Circuit said "clear reflection of income" means that income should be reflected with as much *accuracy* as standard methods of accounting practice permit.[76] In *Caldwell*, a taxpayer argued that IRC § 446 requires only that the adopted method of accounting reflect income *clearly*, not accurately. The taxpayer said that "clearly" means merely that a taxpayer's books be kept "fair and honestly." The court disagreed and said "while taxpayers' honesty and good faith have not been in the slightest impugned in the present case, we read 'clearly reflect the income' in IRC § 446 to mean rather that income should be reflected with as much accuracy as standard methods of accounting practice permit."[77] An earlier case, *Osterloh v. Lucas*[78] (which the taxpayer in *Caldwell* cited in support of his position), the court commented that:

> if th[e] requirement [of clear reflection]is absolute, it is safe to say that books kept on the basis of cash received and disbursed will rarely, if ever, reflect the true income . . . . But we do not think that any such literal construction was contemplated. In our opinion, all that is meant is that the books shall be kept fairly and honestly.

The conflict between these two concepts runs through this area of the law.[79] The IRS has also taken the position that *Caldwell* represented a rejection of *Osterloh* and similar cases.[80] However, the *Osterloh* language continues to be cited.[81]

---

[75] 202 F.2d 112, 53-1 USTC ¶ 9218 (2d Cir. 1953). *See also Knight-Ridder Newspapers, Inc. v. United States*, 743 F.2d 781 (11th Cir. 1984), where the court found that the IRS did not abuse its discretion in forcing newspaper corps to change from cash to accrual method. Newspaper was material part of business requiring use of inventories which allowed the IRS to require the newspaper company to use the accrual method. The IRS's consent to use cash method in earlier year did not bar the IRS from changing to accrual method during subsequent year in which it was apparent that cash method did not clearly reflect income.

[76] The problem, however, is that if taken literally, it would, among other things, virtually preclude the use of the cash method.

[77] *See also Veritas Software Corp. & Subsidiaries, et al. v. Comm'r*, 133 T.C. 297 (2009). In *Ford Motor Company and Affiliated Companies v. Comm'r*, 102 T.C. 87 (1994), Ford's deductions for accrual of total future payments made to tort claimants under structured settlements, did not clearly reflect income. The IRS determination limiting deductions to cost of annuity contracts purchased to fund payments the taxpayer was obligated to make under settlement agreements was sustained. Satisfaction of "all events" test for accrual did not preclude the IRS from using IRC § 446(b) to correct gross distortion of the taxpayer's true economic obligation caused by accrual of its obligations over 58 years. And, IRC § 461(h), which puts accrual basis taxpayers on cash method of accounting for tort liabilities, did not limit authority of the IRS under IRC § 446(b) to rectify abusive distortions by limiting deductions under clear reflection of income standard for tax years prior to effective date of IRC § 461(h).

[78] 37 F.2d 277, 278–79 (9th Cir. 1930).

[79] *See, e.g., Wilkinson-Beane, Inc. v. Comm'r*, 420 F.2d 352, 356 n.12 (1st Cir. 1970).

[80] *See, e.g.*, GCM 39589 (Apr. 30, 1986).

[81] *Magnon v. Comm'r*, 73 T.C. 980, 1005 (1980), *acq.*, 1981-2 CB 2.

This does not mean, however, that a taxpayer is required to compute its taxable income on the basis of the Generally Accepted Accounting Principles ("GAAP"), where the Code or Regulations specifically provide for the use of an alternative accounting method.[82] A taxpayer who can show that its accounting method conforms to GAAP or regulatory guidelines will generally (but not always) have established that his method of accounting clearly reflects income.[83] Conversely, a taxpayer will find it difficult to show that its accounting method clearly reflects income if it is not in accordance with GAAP or regulatory accounting principles.[84] In situations like this, the courts will often require the taxpayer to demonstrate that its method of accounting produces a result which is "substantially identical" to the result obtained using the IRS's selected method, *e.g.*, the GAAP method.[85] When the taxpayer attempts to use a method that is otherwise improper because it is contrary to an explicit mandate in the Code or regulations, courts generally have assumed that the result under one method is presumptively correct, and that the ability of any other method to clearly reflect income can be measured by comparing the results under the two systems. If the use of a method is contrary to an explicit mandate in the Code or the regulations, the taxpayer is precluded from arguing that it is in accord with generally accepted accounting principles (GAAP) or otherwise clearly reflects income in an abstract sense.[86]

§4.04 Consistency and Predictability

[A] Generally

Consistent treatment of an item is an element of a method of accounting. A characteristic inherent in "consistent" treatment is predictability, *i.e.*, the method involves a rule that will yield consistent results when applied to different occurrences of items. Accordingly, a "method of accounting" is not established without a pattern

---

[82] *See, e.g., Thor Power Tool Co. v. Comm'r*, N. 10, *supra.*

[83] *See* Reg. §1.446-1(a)(2).

[84] *Coors v. Comm'r*, 60 T.C. 368 (1973).

[85] *See, e.g., Caldwell v. Comm'r*, 202 F.2d 112, 53-1 USTC ¶9218 (2d Cir. 1953); *Ansley Sheppart-Burgess Co. v. Comm'r*, 104 T.C. 367 (1995), *cited with approval. The Travelers Insurance Co. v. United States*, 303 F.3d 1373 (Fed. Cir. 2002) and TAM 9113003. *Contrast Hospital Corporation of America and Subsidiaries v. Comm'r*, T.C. Memo. 1996-105, where a hospital was permitted to utilize a hybrid method of accounting which did not result in a mismatching of income and expense, even though the use of such method did not produce a result substantially identical to that obtained under the pure accrual method.

[86] In *Thor Power Tool Co. v. Comm'r*, 439 U.S. 522 (1979), the taxpayer sought to write down inventory for tax purposes by a method that the Tax Court had found as a fact was in accordance with GAAP. It argued that there was a presumption that a method in accordance with GAAP clearly reflected income. The Supreme Court stated that "the presumption petitioner postulates is insupportable in light of the vastly different objectives that financial and tax accounting have .... Given this diversity, even contrariety, of objectives, any presumptive equivalency between tax and financial accounting would be unacceptable." 439 U.S. 522, 542–43 (1979).

of *consistent treatment* of the item in question.[87] "Consistency" does not, however, require that different "items" be treated in a like manner; consequently, distinguishing between different items and different occurrences of an item is of critical importance.

The treatment of a material item in the same way in determining income or deductions in two or more consecutive tax returns represents a consistent treatment of that item. The consistent but erroneous treatment of a material item for two or more years is the adoption of an accounting method.[88] However, if a taxpayer treats an item properly in the first return that reflects the item, it need not have a consistent treatment in two or more consecutive tax years before the taxpayer is considered to have adopted an accounting method.[89]

In TAM 9847004, the IRS ruled that two thrift institutions had failed to use permissible accounting methods for bad debts when they failed to maintain positive reserve balances at the end of the year before their acquisition by a savings bank because a bad debt reserve cannot have a negative (debit) balance. Thus, the taxpayer's accounting practice regarding its bad debts did not constitute a method of accounting. For an accounting practice to constitute a method of accounting, it must be consistent.[90] Consistency requires that the accounting practice lead to predictable results when applied to a set of facts. An accounting practice is not a method of accounting if it is arbitrary or random.

Example 4-2

Mary Jones has been practicing law for the last five years as a solo practitioner and using the cash method of accounting. At the inception of her practice, she issued bills on the first of the month on an hourly basis to all of her clients for which she had rendered services in the past month. Any receipts received were deposited into the firm checking account on a regular basis. In November and December 2018, Mary generated significant billable hours. To alleviate the impact of receiving large amount of receipts at year-end, Mary skipped her normal billing for November and sent her December bills out at the end of the month.

Question: What implications if any do you see for Mary?

Answer: Upon review of Mary's practice one can that say that she developed a method of accounting for the billing portion of her business. Her consistent monthly billing practice when used repeatedly became a method of accounting. A method of accounting is generally understood to refer to any regularized practice or procedure for determining when to

[87] Reg. § 1.446-1(c)(2)(ii). No method of accounting will be regarded as clearly reflecting income unless all items of gross profit and deductions are treated with consistency from year to year.

[88] Rev. Proc. 2015-13, 2015-5 IRB 419, § 2.01(2); *Diebold Inc. v. United States*, 891 F.2d 1579, 90-1 USTC ¶ 50003 (Fed. Cir. 1989).

[89] Rev. Rul. 90-38, 1990-1 CB 57.

[90] Reg. § 1.446-1(e)(2)(ii)(a).

recognize items of income and expense. Hallmarks of an accounting method are consistency, certainty, and predictability.

Mary's method of accounting fails to clearly reflect income by manipulating her business (billing). By changing her billing practice, she has changed the timing of her income. By changing the timing of the receipt of income, she has made a material change in accounting which could cause the IRS to argue that she has changed her accounting method without its permission in violation of IRC § 446(e).

A taxpayer's method of accounting will not clearly reflect his income if it fails to represent the income "accurately," that is, with as much accuracy as "standard methods of accounting practice permit."[91]

In *National Adjusting Assn's v. Commissioner*,[92] a taxpayer's method of accounting was held to be insufficiently accurate where the taxpayer was an accrual method debt collection agency which earned commissions when debts that clients assigned to it for collection were paid, regardless of whether payment was made to the taxpayer or directly to the client. Because some clients delayed reporting amounts they had received from debtors or from assigned accounts to the taxpayer, there was always some uncertainty at the end of the taxpayer's year as to how much it had earned during that year. The taxpayer included in its taxable income estimates of the income that it expected from unreported amounts, but failed to demonstrate the accuracy of these estimates. Accordingly, the taxpayer's method of accounting failed to reflect its income clearly.

To be accurate, a taxpayer's method of accounting must not distort income; it must be measured against some objective standard. Some examples of where the method of accounting may be problematic are:

- A cash basis limited partnership could not deduct interest it prepaid on nonrecourse notes where the prepayment significantly increased the partnership's losses and caused a distortion.[93]
- Due to the oil embargo of 1974, a cash method taxpayer unexpectedly accumulated a large number of unpaid accounts receivable. The taxpayer's method of accounting resulted in an extreme mismatching of income and expenses and did not clearly reflect the taxpayer's income. The IRS required the taxpayer to use the accrual method temporarily.[94]

---

[91] *Coors v. Comm'r*, 60 T.C. 368 (1973), where the taxpayer failed to capitalize an improvement. The fact that the company has followed its accounting practices for many years without being challenged did not mean that the accounting method clearly reflected income. The court noted that the Commissioner may, in the exercise of his discretion, order such a change; *Comm'r v. Asphalt Prods. Co. Inc.*, 482 U.S. 117, 87-1 USTC ¶ 9341 (1987), where the Commissioner determined that, because of the increases in the taxpayer's inventories and accounts receivable, the company's traditional cash-basis bookkeeping did not "clearly reflect income," for the 1974 tax year, and it was therefore required to compute its 1974 income on an accrual basis.

[92] 32 BTA 314 (1935).

[93] *Pearlstein v. Comm'r*, 58 TCM 699 (1989).

[94] *Comm'r v. Asphalt Prods. Co. Inc.*, 482 U.S. 117, 87-1 USTC ¶ 9341 (1987).

- In *National Builders, Inc.* v. *Commissioner*,[95] the court recognized that there will be some distortion in using the cash method. However, a departure from the cash method system is justified only where there would otherwise be a material distortion of a taxpayer's true income. In a going business there are certain overlapping items, both of income and deduction, and so long as these overlapping items do not materially distort the income that may be included in the year in which the taxpayer, pursuant to a consistent policy, takes them into his accounts such distortion will not present a problem.[96]
- A taxpayer was required to use the accrual method for tax purposes because the cash method resulted in a mismatching of income and expenses. The taxpayer billed its clients before performing services, anticipating that income would be received during the period expenses were incurred. This was an attempt to match income and expenses. The cash method, however, had the effect of allowing deductions of expenses during the period but deferring income.[97]
- A change in the treatment of customer fees received was not an accounting method change when the taxpayer had excluded customer connection fees from income by treating them as nontaxable capital contributions under IRC § 118. The IRS determined that the fees were taxable income. The Tax Court concluded that the change would be a permanent difference, not a timing difference and, thus, was not an accounting method change.[98] Subsequently in Rev. Rul. 2008-30,[99] the IRS found that connection fees charged by a regulated public utility that were treated by the utility as contributions in aid of construction (CIACs) under IRC § 118 and were excluded from gross income as capital contributions should have been included in gross income and had to be capitalized over a proper recovery period. The IRS concluded that this was a change in accounting method under IRC §§ 446 and 481.

[B] Multiple Businesses

Notwithstanding the "consistency" requirement discussed above, the Code and Regulations specifically permit a taxpayer engaged in two or more separate and distinct trades or businesses to adopt different accounting methods for each business, provided that a complete and separable set of books are maintained for each trade or business.[100] Otherwise, the adoption of different accounting methods for different businesses will be disallowed.[101] For example, a taxpayer may account for the

---

[95] 12 T.C. 852 (1949).

[96] *Id.* at 860.

[97] Priv. Ltr. Rul. 9113003.

[98] *Saline Sewer Co. v. Comm'r*, T.C. Memo. 1992-236, 63 CCH TCM 2832, *nonacq*.

[99] 2008-1 CB 1156.

[100] *See* IRC § 446(d); Reg. § 1.446-1(d).

[101] *See* TAM 9408003.

operations of a personal service business on the cash receipts and disbursements method and a manufacturing business on an accrual method, provided such businesses are separate and distinct and the methods used for each clearly reflect income. The method first used in accounting for business income and deductions in connection with each trade or business, as evidenced in the taxpayer's income tax return in which such income or deductions are first reported, must be consistently followed thereafter.

[C] Computational Errors

Computational errors consistently do not constitute a method of accounting.[102] In Priv. Ltr. Rul. 8947004, the IRS ruled that only a change in the taxability of an item (*e.g.*, whether it is deductible or nondeductible) is a correction of an error. A change in the time for taking an item into account is not a correction of an error, rather it is a change in accounting method. This appears to constitute a restriction on what the IRS will accept as an "error" as opposed to an erroneous accounting method.

An accounting procedure, consistently applied, may constitute a method of accounting even if the procedure is erroneous. In *Wayne Bolt and Nut Co. v. Commissioner*,[103] for example, the Court found that the taxpayer's consistent failure to take physical inventory constituted an erroneous method of accounting rather than an "error."

§4.05 Adopting an Accounting Method

[A] Generally

In order for a taxpayer to use a particular method of accounting, the method must have been "adopted" by the taxpayer. Rev. Rul. 90-38[104] provides the following guidelines for determining when a taxpayer has "adopted" a particular method of accounting:

- If the method of accounting is correct, the use of such method on a single tax return will indicate that the taxpayer has adopted the method, once the due date for such return has passed;

---

[102] Reg. §1.446-1(e)(2)(ii)(b); *North Carolina Granite Corp. v. Comm'r*, 43 T.C. 149 (1964).

[103] 93 T.C. 500. *See also* Reg. §1.446-1(e)(1); *Estate of Biewer v. Comm'r*, 41 T.C. 191 (1963). In FSA 892, Vaughn # 892, the IRS's consent was required to change an erroneous inventory accounting method used for four years, where the taxpayer consistently calculated an improper amount for its closing inventory, even when the taxpayer was substituting a correct new accounting method.

[104] 1990-1 CB 57.

- If the method of accounting is erroneous, the filing of two consecutive returns utilizing such erroneous method will indicate that the taxpayer has adopted the erroneous method of accounting.[105]

[B] Mechanics of Adoption

A method of accounting is adopted on the first return in which the item has tax significance.[106] In some cases, a method of accounting is adopted by simply using the method; in other cases, a formal election statement is required. A change of accounting requires the Commissioner's consent.[107]

[C] New Entities

As a general rule, a new entity may adopt its own set of accounting methods. The successor corporation to a partnership is considered a new entity free to adopt its own accounting methods.[108]

§ 4.06 Restrictions on Use of Accounting Methods

The Code and the Regulations contain restrictions on a taxpayer's ability to use the following accounting methods (or combinations of methods) in certain or, in some cases, all circumstances:

- Use of the cash method by certain entities;[109]
- Certain combinations of the cash and accrual methods;[110]
- A method of accounting which fails to maintain inventories where the sale of merchandise is a material income-producing factor;[111] and
- The use of the cash method by taxpayers required to maintain inventories.[112]

---

[105] *See also* TAM 9429001, TAM 9421003, and *Hitachi Sales Corp. of America v. Comm'r*, T.C. Memo. 1994-159, wherein the taxpayer's erroneous accounting procedures were found to constitute methods of accounting since such methods had been consistently utilized by the taxpayers.

[106] 41 T.C. 191 (1963), *aff'd*, 65-1 USTC ¶9245 (6th Cir. 1965).

[107] IRC § 446(b). *See* Chapter 7.

[108] *See Ezo Products Co. v. Comm'r*, 37 T.C. 385 (1961). Prop. Reg. § 1.1502-17 would adopt an anti-abuse rule where there is an IRC § 351 transfer of assets between members of a consolidated group. Under such a rule, the transferee would be required to continue the accounting methods of the predecessor where the purpose for the transfer is to permit the adoption of new accounting methods without obtaining IRS consent. This rule is similar to the rule which requires the successor in a tax-free corporate reorganization to generally continue the accounting methods of the predecessor.

[109] Note that IRC § 447 precludes certain taxpayers engaged in the trade or business of farming from using the cash method; *see* IRC § 448.

[110] *See* Reg. § 1.446-1(c)(1)(iv)(a).

[111] *See* Reg. § 1.446-1(a)(4)(i).

[112] *See* Reg. § 1.446-1(c)(2)(i).

5

The Cash Receipts and Disbursements Method

§ 5.01 Generally

The cash receipts and disbursements method of accounting ("the cash method") is based on the principle of actual receipts, constructive receipt, and actual disbursements (payment). Accordingly, under the cash method, income is recognized generally in the year of actual or constructive receipt. Expenses are deductible generally in the year of actual payment.[1] The cash method encompasses all items of income, including cash, property, and services.[2]

There are many advantages to the cash method of accounting. For one thing, it is simple to use and to audit. It provides for the payment of taxes when the taxpayer has the funds to make payment. Other advantages include:

- The potential for an indefinite deferral of when to report income;
- Control over the timing of deductions including accelerating deductions before year end; and
- The simplification of the accounting process for determining the amount of income taxable.

Issues often raised in connection with the cash method include whether the method is available to the taxpayer; whether the method clearly reflects income; whether an item of income has been actually or constructively received; whether the form of income should be taxed upon receipt; whether and in what form payment has occurred; and whether the payment of an item is currently deductible.[3]

The use of cash method can result in the deferral of income and the acceleration of deductions, such as through the build-up of receivables or pre-paying expenses.

---

[1] Reg. § 1.446-1(c)(1)(i).

[2] *Id.*

[3] At all times in the study of the cash method or in the study of any accounting system for that matter, one must keep in mind the power of the IRS to change a taxpayer's method. IRC § 446(b) allows the IRS to require the taxpayer to change his method of accounting if, in its opinion, the taxpayer's method does not clearly reflect income. *Thor Power Tool Co. v. Comm'r*, 439 U.S. 522 (1979). Moreover, under IRC § 448, the taxpayer is required to use the accrual method and to maintain inventories if the taxpayer is a C corporation or a partnership with a C corporation as a partner, with more than $26 million, on average, of gross receipts. In addition, if the taxpayer's gross receipts exceed $26 million, a taxpayer cannot use the cash method if the purchase, production, or sale of merchandise is an income-producing factor. In that case, the taxpayer must keep inventories and use the accrual method for the inventory items (Reg. §§ 1.446-1(c)(2) and 1.471-1). *See* § 5.07, *infra*, Limitation on Cash Method's Use.

Under the cash method, there is no requirement to maintain inventories.[4] As a result, the IRS views the cash method as not clearly reflecting income whenever its results differ materially from the accrual method.[5] On the other hand courts recognize that it is possible for the cash method of accounting to clearly reflect income, even though, at the end of the tax year, there will almost always be some unpaid accounts due the taxpayer and some unpaid obligations owed by the taxpayer.[6] Hence, the failure of a taxpayer to include year-end accounts receivable in income is not a sufficient reason to require the taxpayer to use the accrual method.[7] In *Galedrige Construction Inc. v. Commissioner*,[8] a paving contractor was paid as late as 30 days after they completed their jobs, and therefore reported income up to 30 days later than they would under the accrual method. In upholding the use of the cash method, the court allowed the taxpayer to continue to use the cash method because the taxpayer "consistently used the cash method of accounting without any evidence that it attempted to prepay expenses unreasonably or purchase supplies in advance, does not have inventories, and is not required to use an inventory method of accounting."[9]

The cash method is predominantly used by service providers who are not engaged in the sale of merchandise. These service providers can be in the form of a sole proprietor, a partnership, a limited liability company or a corporation.[10] These service providers are typically accountants, lawyers, doctors, veterinarians, dentists, engineers, architects, actuaries, performers, and consultants, among others.[11] The TCJA greatly expanded the ability of taxpayers to use the cash method.

Taxpayers who sell merchandise and would otherwise be required to maintain inventories, who have average annual a tax year beginning after December 31, 2017, and who have average annual gross receipts for the preceding three years under $26 million can use the cash method.[12] Accordingly, these taxpayers can use a method of accounting for inventory that either (1) treats inventories as non-incidental materials and supplies, or (2) conforms to the taxpayer's financial accounting treatment of inventory either as an "applicable financial statement" as defined in IRC § 451(b)(3) or conforms to the taxpayer's books and records. Any change in method of accounting that a taxpayer makes pursuant to this new rule is treated under IRC § 471(c)(4) as made with the consent of the Secretary.

---

[4] Except for supply inventories under Reg. § 1.162-3, Materials and Supplies. *See* § 13.01, *et seq.*

[5] *Thompson Electric, Inc. v. Comm'r*, T.C. Memo. 1995-292, 69 TCM 3045.

[6] *Osterloh, A.F. v. Lucas*, 37 F.2d 277 (9th Cir. 1930); *see also Zaninovich v. Comm'r*, 616 F.2d 429, 437 (9th Cir. 1980).

[7] *Jim Turin & Sons Inc v. Comm'r*, 219 F.3d 1103, 2000-2 USTC ¶ 50,610 (9th Cir. 2000).

[8] T.C. Memo. 1997-240, 73 TCM 238.

[9] *Id.* at 1491.

[10] Subject to IRC § 448.

[11] Service providers also include: plumbers, electricians, banks, hospitals, and contractors.

[12] IRC § 448(b)(3).

§ 5.02 Income Recognition

An item of gross income is recognized in the year in which it is *actually* or *constructively* received, regardless of when it has been earned.[13]

[A] Actual Receipt

Actual receipt occurs in the following situations:

- A transfer of money, property, or services to the taxpayer;[14]
- A transfer of property (or money) to a third party at the taxpayer's direction or for the taxpayer's benefit;[15]
- An obligation of the taxpayer is cancelled or offset;[16] or
- Receipt by the taxpayer's agent of money or property on the taxpayer's behalf.[17]

In TAM 9519002, the taxpayer sold life insurance policies as an agent of an insurance company. The taxpayer reported income using the cash method of accounting. Under the agency agreement with the insurance company, once an agent sold a policy, the policyholder makes the premium payment(s) directly to the company. Thereafter, the policyholder deals directly with the company on all matters pertaining to the policy. Consequently, the services performed by the company's agents, including the taxpayer, with respect to a policyholder or an insured were fully completed once the policy was sold and issued.

Under the Agency Agreement the company compensated the taxpayer as each policy was sold. The company considered the commission to be "earned" ratably when the first year's premium payment(s) was made by the policyholder.

The Agency Agreements were an "Advance Commission System" under which the company agreed to make cash "advances" to its "advanceable" agents upon their sales of its insurance policies. Under this system, once an agent submits an insured's application to buy a policy and agreement to pay the premiums monthly by preauthorized bank draft, the company made a cash advance to the agent in an amount equal to the percentage of the maximum commission payable from the sale of the policy. The company made this cash advance before the policyholder actually made all of the monthly premium payments to the company. Thus, the agent received a percentage of the full commission due from the sale of the policy prior to the time the commission was deemed "earned" and payable to that agent. The taxpayer and the company referred to the cash advances as "loans."

---

[13] IRC §§ 446, 451.

[14] For example, receipt of a car, use of an employer's vacation home, or barter transaction. *See* Rev. Rul. 80-52, 1980-1 CB 100.

[15] *See, e.g., Henritze v. Comm'r*, 41 BTA 505 (1940).

[16] *See, e.g., Shuster v. Helvering*, 121 F.2d 643, 41-2 USTC ¶ 9601 (2d Cir. 1941).

[17] *See, e.g., Diescher v. Comm'r*, 36 BTA 732 (1937).

The company reported as compensation income to the taxpayer on Forms 1099 only in the amount of commissions earned and paid to the taxpayer during each of the taxable years by way of cash payments, offsets against the taxpayer's debit balance or other debts owed by the taxpayer to the company. Consequently, the company did not include on Forms 1099 the full amounts of the cash advances made to the taxpayer during each of the taxable years. The IRS, however, argued that the cash advances were not loans, but instead advance commissions includible in gross income as compensation in the taxable year received by the taxpayer.

The IRS determined that advances of commissions to a taxpayer under an agreement that places no personal liability of repayment on him constitute income to the recipient when the advances are received.[18] These advances were nothing more than advance salary or other payment for services which are includible in income by the taxpayer when received.[19] Further, commissions received in advance for the services of a cash-basis salesman are income when received and any portion of the commission later paid back should be deducted as a loss when returned.[20] If, however, the taxpayer has an unconditional personal obligation to repay an amount advanced to him, the advance may be a loan, which would not be includible in income, since the concept of income excludes loans which must unconditionally be repaid.[21]

Similarly, in Rev. Rul. 81-147,[22] A, a self-employed commissioned salesperson, receives commissions from Y company. A used the cash receipts and disbursements method. It was the practice of Y to pay the entire commission earned at the time a sale is completed. A was required to repay the commissions, in whole or in part, if the customers fail to pay their obligations to Y. In 1979, Y paid A commissions of $19,000, of which $9,000 was subject to possible repayment. In the same year, A repaid $2,000 of the commissions received in 1979. In 1980, Y paid A commissions of $26,000, of which $6,000 was subject to possible repayment. In 1980, A paid $1,000 of the commissions received in 1979 and $4,000 of the commissions received in 1980.

Reg. § 1.6041-1(c) provides that income is fixed when it is to be paid in amounts definitely predetermined. Income is determinable whenever there is a basis of calculation by which the amount to be paid may be ascertained. The fact that the payments may be increased or decreased in accordance with the happening of an event does not make the payments any the less determinable. A salesman working by the month for a commission on sales that is paid or credited monthly receives determinable income.

In 1979, the gross amount paid by Y to A was $19,000, all of which was fixed and determinable. Because the $2,000 repayment represented a return of part of the $19,000 paid in that year, the actual payment from Y to A in 1979 was $17,000, and this amount was reportable under IRC § 6041. Similarly, in 1980 Y made gross

---

[18] *Moorman v. Comm'r*, 26 T.C. 666, 674 (1956).

[19] *Beaver v. Comm'r*, 55 T.C. 85, 90 (1970).

[20] Rev. Rul. 72-78, 1972-1 CB 45.

[21] *James v. United States*, 366 U.S. 213, 219 (1961). *See also Shuster v. Helvering*, 121 F.2d 643 (2d Cir. 1941), where the taxpayer recognized income when loans representing advances made to him under his contract were offset against amounts due to him under the contract.

[22] 1981-1 CB 573.

payments to *A* of $26,000. Because of the $4,000 repayment, however, the payments in that taxable year aggregated $22,000. The $1,000 repayment related to a previous year and, therefore, was not taken into account in determining the aggregate of the payments during the current year for purposes of IRC § 6041. It is, however, deductible by A in the year it is repaid.

On the other hand, income is not recognized where the taxpayer loans another party money, which loan, in turn, is utilized to pay the taxpayer or, alternatively, when a taxpayer receives a check returned for insufficient funds.[23]

Income recognition under the cash method involves the application of several important tax accounting doctrines. The first of these doctrines is the "cash equivalency" doctrine;[24] the second, the "constructive receipt" doctrine;[25] and the third, the "economic benefit" doctrine.[26]

Example 5-1

Arnold owns an acre of rental property. Sheila rents the property for one year giving Arnold readily tradable stock worth $5,000 in lieu of the first year's rent. How much income does Arnold recognize?

Answer: Arnold will report the value of the stock upon its receipt. Even though the stock is not cash, it is readily tradable into cash, has a value that can be readily tradable into cash, and is a cash equivalent.[27]

---

[23] *See, e.g., Helvering v. Martin-Stubblefield*, 71 F.2d 944 (8th Cir. 1934), where the taxpayer approved a loan and the borrower as security offered as collateral his promissory note in favor of the taxpayer for the amount of the loan and a mortgage on certain real estate to secure it. The borrower received the amount of the loan less 2% that was retained by the taxpayer as a commission for its services, which is credited to the "Unearned Commissions" account on its books. When the loan was repaid or the notes were sold by the taxpayer at a discount, the commission was treated as earned, at which time the net amount was determinable. The taxpayer made a charge against the "Unearned Commissions" account and a corresponding credit was entered on the "Earned Commissions" account. Citing *Blair Comm'r v. First Trust & Savings Bank*, 39 F.2d 462 (5th Cir. 1930), the court said that the commission was not actually received until the taxpayer received what it had previously paid out plus the commission. The deduction of the commission from the face of the loan brings nothing back into the coffers of the taxpayer.

[24] *See* § 5.03, *infra*.

[25] *See* § 5.04, *infra*.

[26] The "economic benefit" doctrine taxes a cash basis taxpayer on the receipt of "property" conferring a present economic benefit, regardless of whether the taxpayer is immediately capable of realizing upon it. *See Pulsifer v. Comm'r*, 64 T.C. 245 (1975).

[27] *See* IRC § 1001(b).

§ 5.03 The Cash Equivalency Doctrine[28]

[A] Generally

Often a question will arise as to whether the receipt of an intangible item such as a promissory note should be treated as the receipt of cash or property and includable in income under the cash-basis method of accounting. The term "cash equivalent" can be applied to any intangible right to future performance if it is transferable for value. Intangibles also include:

- receipt of a contract right,[29]
- an executory contract,[30] or
- a chose in action.[31]

The cash equivalency doctrine is an important feature of the cash method of accounting. It applies to many transactions, including unfunded second-party promises to pay that are received for services, rent, royalties, bonuses on leases or licenses of property, judgments and lottery winnings.[32] Notwithstanding, whether an obligation is a cash equivalent is generally determined based on common law standards developed by the courts with some assistance from the Service. As a consequence, the current approach to cash equivalency suffers from the lack of a uniform standard. There is also uncertainty in applying the particular tests, given the fact-intensive, imprecise inquiry that is required.[33]

IRC § 451 provides that the amount of any item shall be included in gross income for the taxable year in which received by the taxpayer, unless, under the method of accounting used in computing taxable income, such amount is to be properly accounted for as of a different period. Similarly, Reg. § 1.61-2(d)(4) provides:

> *Stock and notes transferred to employee or independent contractor.* Except as otherwise provided by IRC § 421 and the regulations thereunder and 1.61-15 (relating to stock options), . . . if a corporation transfers its own stock to an employee or independent contractor as compensation for services, the fair market value of the stock at the time of transfer shall be

---

[28] The term is ordinarily used to refer to certain obligations of the other party in an income-generating transaction. The theory is that the taxpayer is capable of realizing income upon such obligations before maturity.

[29] Priv. Ltr. Rul. 8504004.

[30] An executory contract is where some contractual expectations are yet to be done by one or more parties. *See* Rev. Rul. 69-89, 1969-1 CB 59.

[31] A right to personal things of which the owner has not the possession, but merely a *right of action* for their possession. A right to receive or recover a debt, demand, or damages on a cause of, or for a tort connected with contract, but which cannot be made available without recourse to au action. Personalty to which the owner has a right of possession in future, or a right of immediate possession, wrongfully withheld, is termed by the law a chose in action.

[32] *See* Brown, *Proposing a Single, Simpler Test for the Cash Equivalent,* Tax Lawyer, Vol. 71, No. 3 (2018).

[33] *Id.*

> included in the gross income of the employee or independent contractor. Notes or other evidences of indebtedness received in payment for services constitute income in the amount of their fair market value at the time of the transfer. A taxpayer receiving as compensation a note regarded as good for its face value at maturity, but not bearing interest, shall treat as income as of the time of receipt its fair discounted value computed at the prevailing rate. As payments are received on such a note, there shall be included in income that portion of each payment which represents the proportionate part of the discount originally taken on the entire note.[34]

An example of the application of this regulation is in Rev. Rul. 73-173.[35] In Rev. Rul. 73-173, a cash basis taxpayer received breeding rights in thoroughbred stallions as compensation for services. The IRS had to determine whether under certain circumstances the receipt of breeding rights constituted compensation income that would be reportable by the taxpayer. These rights were nontransferable on a lifetime basis but annual rights could be transferred. Some of the contracts gave the taxpayers the right to breeding services for the lifetime of the stallion. These rights were freely transferable and were not conditioned on the continued performance of services.

Citing Reg. § 1.451-1, the IRS determined that the taxpayer was in receipt of income. Relying on *Cowden v. Commissioner*[36] (discussed later), the IRS determined that the current contractual rights that were received were unconditional, freely transferable, readily salable, and therefore, income was realized at the time of their receipt to the extent of the present value of the breeding rights. The IRS also said that if the breeding rights were not transferable, and therefore not marketable, the taxpayer would only have received a contractual right which would be fulfilled in the future, and that the income from these breeding rights would only be included in income in the taxable year in which they were earned or made available.

In Rev. Rul. 68-606,[37] a cash method taxpayer received an installment bonus contract as consideration for an oil and gas lease. The lease provided for an unconditional fixed bonus to the taxpayer payable in cash in the year of execution as well as two equal cash installments in the following two years. The IRS noted certain items of indebtedness are properly deemed to be equivalent to cash, but not all evidences of indebtedness are property the fair market value of which is includable in the income

---

[34] The principle of the regulation requires an item received by a taxpayer include income even if the item is of little or no value so the item can be recorded in the books and records and would be auditable. *But see Cambria Dev. Co. v. Comm'r*, 34 BTA 1155 (1936) (fair market value of buyers' obligations under land sales contracts nil when they could not be discounted), *acq.*, 1937-1 CB 4, *nonacq.* on another issue, 1937-1 CB 31; *Board v. Comm'r*, 18 BTA 650 (1930) (promissory notes issued for salary includible at fair market value, but because of issuer's ruinous financial condition notes had no fair market value), *acq.*, IX-2 CB 6; *Essex v. Comm'r*, 21 BTA 270 (1930) (notes given to contractor could not be sold or used as collateral and issuer became insolvent shortly thereafter; held, they had no ascertainable market value although they were not conclusively worthless so as to allow loss), *acq.*, X-2 CB 21.

[35] 1973-1 CB 40.

[36] 289 F.2d 20, 61-1 USTC ¶ 9382 (5th Cir. 1961).

[37] 1968-2 CB 42.

of a taxpayer on the cash receipts and disbursements method of accounting. Citing *Helvering v. Brunn*,[38] the IRS said a deferred cash payment obligation which is readily marketable and immediately convertible to cash is property the fair market value of which is income to a cash-method taxpayer in the year of receipt to the extent of that obligation's fair market value. It noted that it is well settled that taxable income is not limited to cash income, but may also include the fair market value of property received by the taxpayer. The IRS thus concluded that the taxpayer must include the contract rights in income in the year for which the lease was executed since the obligation was transferrable and readily saleable.

On the other hand, non-negotiable notes are generally not considered to be income.[39] Reg. § 1.61-2(d)(4) however, requires an inclusion of a note that does not bear interest at "its fair discounted value computed at the prevailing rate." Does this mean that if the note cannot be discounted at "the prevailing rate" that it not be treated as income? One might think so except for Reg. § 1.61-2(d)(1) which in part provides:

> Except as otherwise provided . . . if services are paid for in property, the fair market value of the property taken in payment must be included in income as compensation. If services are paid for in exchange for other services, the fair market value of such other services taken in payment must be included in income as compensation.

This portion of the regulations would suggest no matter the "fair market value" of the note or other intangible, its value, even if it were worthless and therefore zero, must be included in income. The reason behind the regulation is for audit purposes. If the item is not reported it cannot be audited. However, if it is reported, no matter the value, it can be audited. One argument raised is that the failure to report the item might be a change of accounting without the Commissioner's consent[40] or the failure to report the item does not clearly reflect income.[41] Some argue that the standards of "property with ascertainable fair market value" and "cash equivalent" are the same. In some circumstances, an obligation has no ascertainable fair market value or zero value. If an obligation is sufficiently speculative, it will not trigger income recognition, whether the test is cash equivalence or ascertainable fair market value.[42]

---

[38] 309 U.S. 461 (1940).

[39] *See* Reg. § 15A.453-1(b)(3)(iii) and *Gunderson Bros Engineering Corp. v Comm'r*, 42 T.C. 419 (1964). *See also Crosby v. Comm'r*, 14 BTA 980 (1929) (contingent non-negotiable notes, received by cash basis taxpayer for purchase of interest in law partnership, held not equivalent of cash and not income in year issued). Contracts received from purchasers of duplex homes in partial payment had ascertainable market value when received. Includible by cash-basis taxpayer in year of sale to extent of 50% of the face value. *Joan E. Heller Trust, et al. v. Comm'r.*, 382 F.2d 675, 67-2 USTC ¶ 9626 (9th Cir. 1967). *See also Max Kronenberg v. Comm'r*, 64 T.C. 428 (1975), where obligation was worth less than face value and where note was non-negotiable, unsecured and payable from inventory sales only.

[40] *See Schiners v. Comm'r*, 69 T.C. 511 (1977).

[41] IRC § 446(b).

[42] *See* Mertens, *Law of Federal Income Taxation* § 11.05 at 11–13 ("property or evidences of indebtedness are treated alike so far as the doctrine of equivalent of cash is concerned, whether they are

A counterweight to Reg. § 1.61-2(d)(4) is the "cash equivalency doctrine." The concept of "cash equivalency" was considered in *Cowden v. Commissioner*.[43] In *Cowden*, the taxpayer received a bonus payment under an oil, gas, and mineral lease in the amount of $511,192.50. Upon the receipt of the "initial bonus payment" in 1951, the taxpayer had "in hand" a small amount of cash and a contractual obligation requiring the payor to make future deferred payments of cash over a two-year period. The taxpayer sought to delay reporting the entire bonus as income until the contractual obligation was paid. The IRS assessed a deficiency against the taxpayer claiming that he had received income in the initial year of the contract. To illustrate the transaction, consider the following:

Example 5-2

Receipt of $10,223.85 plus a contractual right to receive $250,484.31 "no earlier than January 5" and "no later than January 10" 1952; and a contractual right to receive $250,484.31 "no earlier than January 5" and "no later than January 10" 1953. In reality, the taxpayer had in hand $10,223.85 and a contractual promise to receive in the following year and $250,484.31 in the year after that another $250,484.31.

On appeal to the Fifth Circuit, in *Cowden v. Commissioner*,[44] the Court made it clear that the *substance* and *not the form* of the transaction should control. The Court flatly rejected any notion that a cash equivalent had to be a negotiable instrument, stating that the income tax law deals in economic realities, and that such a requirement would be "mere formalism." The Court considered the following factors in determining the cash equivalency status of the bonus:

- Whether the instrument itself was a negotiable promissory note;
- Whether the debtor was solvent;
- Whether the agreement was unconditional and transferable and not subject to set-off;
- Whether there was a market for the obligation;
- Whether the obligation could be sold; and
- Whether the obligation could be sold at a small or reasonable discount.

The Court's primary focus was whether the contractual obligation received by the taxpayer was readily convertible into cash. Important in its analysis, the Court stated that negotiability is not the sole test of taxability. The fact that an obligation is

(Footnote Continued)

received as compensation for services, as consideration for the sale of property, or in any other way"). *E.g., Edelman v. United States*, 329 F.2d 950 (Ct. Cl. 1964) (attorneys' rights to contingency fees remained "entirely too speculative to permit ready salability," despite settlement of will contest, because of uncertainties affecting value of estate).

[43] 289 F.2d 20 (5th Cir. 1961).

[44] *Id.*

not a promissory note in negotiable form[45] does not make it or prevent it necessarily from being a cash equivalent. Moreover, the Court concluded that the mere fact that the bonus had a fair market value[46] did not necessarily mean that it was the equivalent of cash.[47]

In its analysis, the court said:

> A promissory note, negotiable in form, is not necessarily the equivalent of cash. Such an instrument may have been issued by a maker of doubtful solvency or for other reasons such paper might be denied a ready acceptance in the market place. We think the converse of this principle ought to be applicable. We are convinced that if a promise to pay of a solvent obligor is unconditional and assignable, not subject to set-offs, and is of a kind that is frequently transferred to lenders or investors at a discount not substantially greater than the generally prevailing premium for the use of money, such promise is the equivalent of cash and taxable in like manner as cash would have been taxable had it been received by the taxpayer rather than the obligation. The principle that negotiability is not the test of taxability in an equivalent of cash case such as is before us, is consistent with the rule that men may, if they can, so order their affairs as to minimize taxes, and points up the doctrine that substance and not form should control in the application of income tax laws.[48]

The cash equivalency doctrine provides that a taxpayer is in receipt of income for tax purposes when he is in receipt of a cash equivalent. Not all items of income under the cash method are recognized as a cash equivalent on receipt. Uncertainty and confusion in the case law and rulings stem from a lack of clarity and uniformity in their application.[49]

A review of rulings and cases produces varying tests. In Rev. Rul. 68-606,[50] the IRS stated that a deferred payment application which is readily marketable and immediately convertible to cash is a cash equivalent. The facts were very similar to *Cowden*.

---

45 A promissory note is an unconditional promise made in writing by one person to another to pay on demand to the payee, or at a fixed or ascertainable future time, sum certain in money, to order or bearer. These notes are governed by the Uniform Commercial Code, https://definitions.uslegal.com/n/negotiable-promissory-note/.

46 *See* § 5.04, *infra*, for a discussion of fair market value.

47 Stating it another way, if the obligation had a face amount of $100 but could only be sold for $20, the obligation would likely not be a cash equivalent.

48 289 F.2d 20, 23 (5th Cir. 1961). The Fifth Circuit remanded the case to the Tax Court. The Tax Court, applying the criteria set by the Fifth Circuit, determined that the taxpayer was treated as receiving a cash equivalent. T.C. Memo. 1961-229. *See also* CCA 201334037.

49 Richard L. Mieves, *Revenue Ruling 79-292 and Deferred Reporting*, 36 U. Miami L. Rev. 175, 201 (1982).

50 1968-2 CB 42.

In Rev. Rul. 73-173,[51] the IRS ruled that a cash method taxpayer was required to include upon receipt the fair market value of breeding rights in thoroughbred stallions which were received as compensation for services as the rights were "readily transferable, readily marketable, and immediately convertible to cash."

The treasury regulations, on the other hand, rest on "received in payment" as a test for a cash equivalency if provided as compensation for services. "Ascertainable fair market value" has also been suggested as a cash equivalent test regardless of whether the obligation has a deep discount.

In *Felt v. Commissioner*,[52] the taxpayer did not include income resulting from the sale of stock of Reliance Savings Association at $10 per share in return for notes from Specialty Finance, doing business as David Felt, which note was secured by Reliance stock.

The Tax Court agreed with the Commissioner and treated the notes as cash equivalents and valued the notes at face value. The character of the gain was capital. The taxpayer challenged the treatment of the notes being valued at face value. The Fifth Circuit, citing *Cowden*, found that the requirements necessary for a promissory note not to be treated as a cash equivalent did not exist. The taxpayer argued that the value of the notes should be limited to the value of the collateral securing them, *i.e.*, the Reliance saving stock. The court declined to consider the arguments as it was not raised at trial. The taxpayer had also argued that because the transaction was rescinded two years later in 1988, he did not have to report the sale in 1986. Relying on *North American Oil v. Burnett*,[53] the Fifth Circuit said the later rescission did not affect the taxpayer's obligation to recognize the sale when it occurred in 1986 under the principle of the annual accounting doctrine.[54]

Juxtapose *Cowden* with *J.A. Williams*.[55] In *Williams*, a taxpayer received an unsecured, non-interest bearing promissory note in 1951 for services rendered. At the time of the transaction, the taxpayer understood that the maker of the note was unable to pay anything on the note, until the maker acquired and sold at least part of some timber property. The taxpayer attempted on ten to fifteen occasions to sell the note without success. Finally, in 1954, he collected some money from the maker and discharged the note. He did not receive full payment. The Tax Court held that the note had no fair market value in 1951 and could not be the equivalent of cash in the year of receipt.[56]

---

[51] 1973-1 CB 40.

[52] 433 Fed. Appx. 293 (5th Cir. 2011).

[53] 286 U.S. 417 (1932).

[54] *See* Chapter 4 *infra*.

[55] 28 T.C. 1000 (1958).

[56] *See also Barnsley v. Comm'r*, 31 T.C. 1260 (1959); *Andrews v. Comm'r*, 135 F.2d 314 (2d Cir. 1943), and *Ennis v. Comm'r*, 17 T.C. 465 (1951). *See also Weeden's Estate v. Comm'r*, 685 F.2d 1160 (9th Cir. 1982), where the court said: "If a promise to pay in the future is contingent on unknown facts or circumstances, or if the right to receive payment is speculative, then the obligation may have no ascertainable fair market value. In this situation, a cash basis taxpayer realizes no income as a result of the contract until payment is made." Whether property has an ascertainable fair market value and the amount of such value present questions of fact to be resolved on the basis of all of the facts and circumstances in the case, *Riss v. Comm'r*, 368 F.2d 965 (10th Cir. 1966); *Campagna v. United States*, 290

A hypothetical application of the cash equivalency doctrine is illustrated in the following examples.

Example 5-3

Woodrow Call is a cash basis individual taxpayer who is a shareholder in a C corporation that manufactures bicycles. In 2020, Mr. Call received a dividend distribution from the corporation in the form of a promissory note which was payable either (1) upon receipt in exchange for a bicycle at any of its stores up to the retail value of $175 or (2) on June 1, 2021 for $200 in cash.

If the note were transferable, and if there was a market for the note for a reasonable discount, Woodrow Call will recognize income in 2020 in the amount of $175 under the cash equivalency doctrine, even if he waits until 2021 to receive $200 in cash. If Mr. Call waits until June 1, 2021 to receive cash, he will recognize an additional $25 in income in 2021.

Example 5-4

Mary, a cash method taxpayer, in 2020, agrees to settle her defamation claim against her former employer for four payments of $200,000 each, payable annually beginning on December 1, 2020 in equal annual installments on the anniversary date. At the time of the settlement her employer is solvent. The risk of default is negligible. Mary could easily assign her rights to the note for about $500,000. What are the tax consequences of the settlement Mary?

This question raises the issue as described in *Cowden*. Is the note a cash equivalent?

In Mary's case the instrument is not a negotiable promissory note but a contract right which appears to be assignable. It appears the debtor is solvent and the agreement is unconditional. There also appears to be a market for the obligation and it could be sold. It appears that the discount is about 38%.[57] The question is whether the discount is reasonable. One would have to consider the time frame, four years, the discount rate, and compute the present value of the installment payment and compare it with what a normal discount rate would be to conclude as to whether the discount is reasonable. If the discount is unreasonable, then the taxpayer may not be in possession of a cash equivalent and may be able to forego

(Footnote Continued)

F.2d 682 (2d Cir. 1961); but it is also true that in only rare and extraordinary circumstances will property be considered not to have an ascertainable fair market value. Reg. § 1.1001-1(a).

[57] The discount of $300,000 is determined as follows: 300.000/800,000=37.5%

reporting. Notwithstanding, relying on Reg. § 1.61-2(d)(4), the IRS would argue that the fair market value of the note must be reported. Clearly this example underscores the uncertainty of the application of the cash equivalency doctrine, especially in light of its varied interpretations.

Example 5-5

James works for Dewey, Cheatem, and Howe, LLP, which provides financial services. James's employer is financially embarrassed and is unable to pay their employees. On December 24, his employer gives James a promissory note for his unpaid salary with a due date of June 30 of the following year with no interest accruing. What are the tax consequences to James of receiving the note?

The same analysis would have to be performed as in Example 5-4. Notwithstanding, relying on Reg. § 1.61-2(d)(4) the IRS would argue that the fair market value of the note would need to be reported. On the other hand, under *Williams*, it would appear a court might find that James has no income in the year of the receipt of the note.

The cash equivalency doctrine, as framed by the *Cowden* court, has not been accepted by the IRS although it is often cited. The difficulty with the doctrine is that even though an obligation has a value, it still may not rise to the level of being a cash equivalent if it has not met the requirements of the *Cowden* case. If it has not, then the item need not be reported as income until it is paid or later becomes a cash equivalent. This doctrine is one that injects uncertainty and ambiguity into a tax accounting system where certainty is the guiding principle. The cash equivalency doctrine has been rejected in several circuits where the transaction was subject to IRC § 1001.[58] In the article entitled *Proposing a Single, Simpler Test for the Cash Equivalent*,[59] the author recommends that there be a single test for determining whether an obligation calling for future payments is a cash equivalent. The proposed test would generally define a cash equivalent as an obligation that is readily tradable in an established securities market. By avoiding the aforementioned problems, the proposed test would promote the simplicity and liquidity policies that underlie the cash method of accounting. The proposed test would also create consistency with the results under the installment method of reporting when a taxpayer receives a

---

[58] *See Heller Trust v. Comm'r*, 382 F.2d 675 (9th Cir. 1967), where deferred payment contracts with a fair market value of 50% of face value were taxable although not negotiable. *See also Barnsley v. Comm'r*, 31 T.C. 1260 (1959); *Andrews v. Comm'r*, 135 F.2d 314 (2d Cir. 1943). In TAM 8952061, the IRS ruled that receipt of a mortgage as payment was income on receipt. In *Bright v. United States*, 926 F.2d 383 (5th Cir. 1991), the taxpayer received a large check prior to year-end and argued that it was not a cash equivalent because it was not readily marketable and convertible into cash. The Court noted that cash was available to the taxpayer the same day. The Court added that the large amount of the check did not affect its marketability. *But see* CCA 201334037.

[59] Brown, *Proposing a Single, Simpler Test for the Cash Equivalent*, Tax Lawyer, Vol. 71, No. 3 (2018).

deferred payment obligation on the sale of property. To prevent possible abuses, the article also considers the adoption of certain measures that apply in connection with the installment method.

§ 5.04 Receipt of Property

[A] *Generally*

While cash can be recognized easily as an item of income, the receipt of property is not as clear. Items that are generally regarded as a cash equivalent include:

- Automobile usage;
- Bargain purchases;
- Barter transactions;
- Insurance;
- Interest-free loans;
- Lodging;
- Meals; and
- Vacation.

These items are tangible and provide a recognizable benefit upon receipt. Though they are not cash, they are the equivalent of cash because they have an ascertainable value, and the receipt is therefore, income to the recipient.[60]

[B] *Fair Market Value*

How is value measured? The Code does not provide a general definition of "fair market value" for income tax purposes. The regulations, however, adopt the following definition in connection with specific income tax issues:

> The fair market value is the price at which the property would change hands between a willing buyer and a willing seller, neither being under any compulsion to buy or sell and both having reasonable knowledge of relevant facts.[61]

---

[60] *See* IRC § 6867, *Presumptions where owner of large amount of cash is not identified.* Cash is described as (1) foreign currency, (2) any bearer obligation and (3) any medium of exchange of a type that has been frequently used in illegal activities and is specified as a cash equivalent in regulations. These mediums of exchange include coins, precious metals, jewelry, precious stones, postage stamps, traveler's checks in any form, negotiable instruments (including personal checks, business, official bank, cashier's notes, and money orders) that are either in bearer form, endorsed without restriction, made out to a fictitious payee, or otherwise in a form where title to that instrument passes on delivery, incomplete instruments (including personal checks, business checks, official bank checks, cashier's checks, notes, and money orders) signed but with the payee's name omitted, and securities or stock in bearer form or otherwise in a form where title passes on delivery. Presumably, Bitcoins are considered cash.

[61] Reg. § 1.170-1(c)(1).

This definition was adopted for purposes of valuing charitable contributions of property, assets of pension plans, and real property interests disposed of by nonresident aliens and foreign corporations for purposes of the special tax on estate and gift dispositions, and adopted by the courts for general income tax purposes.[62]

When a taxpayer receives an intangible from a property transaction it calls into consideration whether the cash equivalency doctrine or some other rule might apply.

In *Warren Jones Co. v. Commissioner*,[63] a cash basis taxpayer sold an apartment building and received, in return, cash and the buyer's promise (in the form of an executory contract) to pay the balance of the purchase price, *i.e.*, a contract right. The promise was not in the form of a note but was part of a standard real estate contract. In the state of Washington, where the sale took place, there was a market for such contracts at a price that reflected a substantial discount from the price at which contracts of this nature were normally sold. Following the *Cowden* case, the Tax Court held that the contract was not income because it was not the equivalent of cash. In overruling the Tax Court, the Ninth Circuit Court of Appeals applied IRC § 1001(b), holding that, except in "no market" cases, such as in *Burnet v. Logan*,[64] the fair market value of the property received in the exchange must be included in the amount realized.[65] The distinguishing point made was that where income is derived from the *sale or disposition of property* the amount received must be reported as income in the year of receipt regardless of the value of the note.[66]

The court's analysis rested on a review of the history of IRC § 1001(b). In the court's view, the issue presented was whether IRC § 1001(b) required the taxpayer to include the fair market value of its real estate contract in determining the "amount realized" during the taxable year of the sale. In citing the Revenue Act of 1924, the court noted "Under the 1924 statute, where income is realized in the form of property, the measure of the income is the fair market value of the property at the date of its receipt."

Comparing IRC § 453 as persuasive evidence in support of the interpretation of IRC § 1001(b) for which the Commissioner contended, the court noted the installment basis of reporting deferred income was Congress's method of providing relief from the rigors of IRC § 1001(b). In its report on the Revenue Act of 1926, the Senate

---

[62] *United States v. Campbell*, 897 F.2d 1317 (5th Cir. 1990); *Peck v. Comm'r*, 752 F.2d 469 (9th Cir 1985); *Andrews v. Comm'r*, 135 F.2d 314 (2d Cir. 1943), *cert. denied*, 320 U.S. 748 (1943).

[63] 524 F.2d 788 (9th Cir. 1975), *rev'g* 60 T.C. 663 (1973).

[64] 283 U.S. 404 (1931) (which is of questionable value as discussed later in Chapter 10).

[65] Subsequent cases have delineated a separation of the two doctrines. In *Watson v. Comm'r*, 613 F.2d 594 (5th Cir. 1980), the Court of Appeals for the 5th Circuit applied the *Cowden* standard. In *Campbell v. United States*, 661 F.2d 209 (Ct. Cl. 1981), the Court cited *Warren Jones* for the proposition that where the fair market value of an obligation can be ascertained, that amount must be included in the amount realized under IRC § 1001(b).

For the distinction between notes taken as payment for services and notes taken as evidence of the underlying claim, *see Dial v. Comm'r*, 24 T.C. 117, 122-123 (1955) (cash method taxpayers not taxed on the value of mortgage bonds evidencing claim for unpaid salaries), Reg. § 1.61-2(d)(2); and Rev. Rul. 76-135, 1976-1 CB 114 (cash method lawyer received and discounted client's note in 1973, when accepted as payment for services).

[66] *See* IRC § 1001(b).

Finance Committee expressly noted that in sales or exchanges not qualifying for the installment basis, deferred-payment contracts

> . . . are to be regarded as the equivalent of cash if such obligations have a fair market value. In consequence, that portion of the initial payment and of the fair market value of such obligations which represents profit is to be returned as income as of the taxable year of the sale.

Notably in footnote 9 the *Warren Jones* court noted "the Tax Court adopted as its definition of 'cash equivalency' certain language from the opinion in *Cowden v. Commissioner* . . . . In our view, the holding in *Cowden* does not conflict with the prior decisions of our court or with our present decision."

The *Warren Jones* decision was a victory for the Internal Revenue Service. By requiring the taxpayer to report the value of an intangible (in this case a contract right) when a sale or exchange transaction occurs regardless of its value, the IRS successfully blocked the taxpayer's attempt to defer the recognition of income based on the cash equivalency doctrine.[67] A factor which differentiates *Warren Jones* from *Cowden* is that *Warren Jones* involved the sale of property while *Cowden* was not a sale or exchange but one involving "services."[68]

Under *Warren Jones*, if an obligation has an ascertainable fair market value, the year of actual or constructive receipt determines income recognition. Consider the following hypothetical, for example.

Example 5-6

> Alan sells an acre of land (with potential environmental issues) to Bill for $100,000. Alan receives a demand promissory note with a face amount of $100,000 bearing adequate interest. However, due to Bill's questionable creditworthiness and the condition of the land the note cannot be sold at face value and has a value at the time of receipt of only $60,000. When must Alan recognize income and at what value?
>
> Following the *Warren Jones* decision, the fair market value of the property received in the exchange must be reported as the amount realized in the year of receipt. In this case $60,000. The difficulty which Alan faces is that when he collects any amount in excess of $60,000, the excess will be ordinary income as the initial receipt of the note is a capital transaction, but the receipt of the balance is not.

---

[67] With respect to sales of real property and casual sales of personal property, the IRS has taken the position that the doctrine of cash equivalence is neither applicable nor relevant. It would seem that IRC § 1001(b) provides substantial support.

[68] Indeed, in Footnote 9 of the *Warren Jones* opinion, the Court said its decision did not conflict with the *Cowden* decision. As noted above, the cash equivalency doctrine could also apply to rents, royalties, bonuses on leases or licenses of property, judgments and lottery winnings.

In *Campbell v. United States*,[69] the Court of Claims, citing *Warren Jones*, followed suit. The notes received by the taxpayer of restricted corporate securities in connection with the sale of business were unsecured, non-negotiable (i.e., subject to personal defenses), unregistered (and the taxpayer did not have the right to compel registration in the future), and subordinated to the issuer's liabilities to various banks. The court held that, in order for a security to have no ascertainable fair market value, there must be no "reasonable factual basis from which to determine the probable sum that fair negotiations between a hypothetical buyer and seller would produce,"[70] and held the notes includible at discounts of 40% to 42%.

The comparison of the *Warren Jones* case and the *Cowden* case indicates that there are now at least two different definitions of the term "cash equivalents," starting with the *Warren Jones* definition for contract rights received in a deferred payment sale of a capital asset and the *Cowden* definition for the receipt of a deferred payment sale where the income realized is ordinary income.

In 2003, the IRS ruled privately that the cash equivalency doctrine does not apply to tax cash basis lottery winners on the fair market value "determined at the discounted present value" of assignable lottery winnings in the year won on the theory that there was no prevailing market discount applied to lottery prize payments and that it had therefore not been established that prizes are frequently transferred to lenders or investors at a discount not substantially greater than the prevailing premium for the use of money.[71]

[C] The Constructive Receipt Doctrine

In order to trigger taxation, the taxpayer's right must be fully mature, i.e., the taxpayer must have a right to present payment. In order to establish constructive receipt, something more is needed than the taxpayer's possession of a simple matured right. Constructive receipt is described in Reg. § 1.451-2(a):

> Income although not actually reduced to a taxpayer's possession is constructively received by him in the taxable year during which it is credited to his account, set apart for him, or otherwise made available so that he may draw upon it at any time, or so that he could have drawn upon it during the taxable year if notice of intention to withdraw had been given. However, income is not constructively received if the taxpayer's control of its receipt is subject to substantial limitations or restrictions.[72]

---

[69] 661 F.2d 209 (Ct. Cl. 1981).

[70] *Id.* at 215.

[71] Priv. Ltr. Rul. 200031031; *see also* Priv. Ltr. Rul. 9639016 and TAM 9808002. *See* § 5.04[K] for a discussion of qualified prize options under IRC § 451(J).

[72] *See, e.g.*, FSA 200038002 (advising that taxpayer possessing "unfettered" control over subscription money that publishing company maintains for his benefit is in constructive receipt of funds, whether he draws on it or not, and therefore receives income in the year the company receives those amounts). *But see* IRC § 451(j) (tax effect of options to choose between cash payment or annuity for prizes and awards); Priv. Ltr. Rul. 9639016, Priv. Ltr. Rul. 9624009 (ruling that lottery winners do not

Example 5-7

Dave Slyme, a salesman for Chaos Corporation, is in arrears in his alimony payments to his former wife, Mildred. Mildred has subpoenaed his 2020 income tax returns for their court date scheduled on May 31, 2021. Slyme is scheduled to receive a substantial bonus from Chaos on December 31, 2020 because he has already met all of his sales goals for 2020, but has requested Chaos to defer payment of both the bonus and his November - December salary until 2021, so that his 2020 tax return will show that he cannot afford the alimony payments. He does so on November 30, 2020.

How much, if any of Slyme's salary or bonus can be deferred?[73] Only his December salary can be deferred. At the time Slyme make his request for a deferral, he has already earned his salary except for December which he can defer. Slyme cannot "turn his back" on income already earned. Slyme has already earned the bonus and the November salary, he has a legal right to receive payment in 2020 and will have constructive receipt of the income in 2020, even if he delays actual receipt until 2021. Slyme can, however, effectively defer his December 2020 salary because it is income neither earned nor due.

The constructive receipt doctrine requires a taxpayer to include in taxable income money or property that is subject to his will or control. The purpose of the constructive receipt doctrine is to preclude a taxpayer from deferring income by "turning his back on income" controlled by the taxpayer. Both the IRS and the taxpayer may invoke the doctrine.[74] It should be noted that it may be to a taxpayer's advantage to show that income was received in a year prior to actual receipt, *i.e.*, in a year where the taxpayer would be in a lower income tax bracket or can be offset with losses.[75]

The economic benefit conferred upon the receipt of an item as well as the power to collect or reject an item are important factors in determining whether a taxpayer is in constructive receipt of an income item for tax purposes. Conversely, substantial limitations or restrictions on receipt will help to defeat the application of the doctrine. Items which often raise the issue whether a taxpayer is in constructive receipt of income include checks, interest income, dividend income, rental income, lottery prize proceeds, escrow agreements, deferred payment agreements, etc.

(Footnote Continued)

have current income from annuitized prizes merely due to unexercised right to assign future annuity payments in exchange for a discounted cash payment). *See* § 5.04[E] *infra.*

[73] Rev. Rul. 71-419, 1971-2 CB 220.

[74] *Hyland v. Comm'r*, 175 F.2d 422 (2d Cir. 1949); *Vander Poel v. Comm'r*, 8 T.C. 407 (1947).

[75] *See* discussion of *Hornung v. Comm'r*, at § 5.04[E], *infra.*

[D] *Substantial Limitations or Restrictions*

A key element in the application of the constructive receipt doctrine is the determination of whether there is an imposition of a substantial limitation or restriction. Cash or property that can only be obtained by satisfying a condition *is not* constructively received unless the condition is inconsequential.[76] Constructive receipt requires the receipt of a matured, vested right.

To prevent constructive receipt, a substantial restriction must exist prior to the time when the right to receive the income arises. A "substantial limitation" can arise by agreement, if it is made before the "receipt" occurs.[77] There are a number of factors that are relevant in determining whether a substantial restriction exists, including

- Whether consent of another party is required in order to obtain funds;[78]
- The understanding of the parties;[79]
- Whether the taxpayer has a legal right to receive the item in question or must give up valuable existing rights;[80]
- The income is subject to a legal dispute;[81]
- The financial ability to pay the item;[82] and
- Whether a party has control over the item to affect the timing of its receipt.[83]

---

[76] *H. Blum v. Higgins*, 150 F.2d 471, 45-2 ¶USTC 9343 (2d Cir. 1945).

[77] *Estate of Williamson v. Comm'r*, 29 T.C. 51 (1957) (no constructive receipt of stock sale proceeds when taxpayer was required under agreement with buyer to "loan" proceeds to the corporation), *acq.*, 1958-2 CB 8.

[78] *See, e.g., Duffy v. Comm'r*, T.C. Memo. 1996-556, where an employee whose employer withheld from his paycheck an amount claimed by the employer was due him on a debt from the employee to the employer for reimbursement of excess travel allowance did not constructively receive the amounts withheld because the employee disputed the fact of the liability. Similarly, in Priv. Ltr. Rul. 8151114, two law firms were engaged in a dispute over the division of a fee. The fee was paid in the form of a check that required the consent of both to negotiate. They agreed to deposit the check with a broker for investment of the proceeds without any commitment as to the ultimate percentage of ownership. The agreement required the consent of both firms before any action was taken with respect to the account. The IRS ruled that the requirement of securing the other firm's consent was a substantial limitation, such that the amount of the fee was not includible in income.

[79] *E.g., Fischer v. Comm'r*, 14 T.C. 792 (1950), *acq.*, 1950-2 CB 2. *See also Johnson v. Comm'r* 25 T.C. 499 (1955) (vice president not in constructive receipt of salary paid by check when officers agreed among themselves not to cash them until president authorized them to do so; evidence existed that corporation did not have available funds to cover check). *But see Frank v. Comm'r*, 22 T.C. 945 (1954), *aff'd per curiam*, 226 F.2d 600 (6th Cir. 1955) (lump sum settlement deferred at the request of taxpayer was constructively received).

[80] *Patterson v. Comm'r*, 510 F.2d 48 (9th Cir. 1975) (a farmer's agreement with a purchaser of his potato crop provided for three fourths of its proceeds on demand subject to a repayment if the crops deteriorated between the date of payment and the delivery date. The amount available on demand was not constructively received, because substantial restrictions existed despite insurance coverage). *But see Blum v. Higgins*, 150 F.2d 471 (2d Cir. 1945), where the court said that the doctrine of constructive receipt is applied, however, if the rights which the taxpayer is required to surrender in order to receive the money are not "sufficiently substantial."

[81] *Parr v. Scofield*, 89 F. Supp. 98 (W.D. Tex. 1950).

[82] *See Charles Goodman, et al. v. Comm'r*, 6 TCM 1031 (1946) (receipt of check on an overdrawn account of a solvent corporation not constructive receipt).

[83] *See* FSA 200151003 where the obligor issued a note but was financially unable to pay.

In *Bones v. Commissioner*,[84] a taxpayer disputed the amount due under an employment agreement. His employer tendered a check to him for what purportedly was full payment. The taxpayer protested the tendered amount and attempted to settle the dispute with his former employer. The following year, the taxpayer was informed that the employer would be willing to settle with him on a fair basis so he negotiated the check he had received in the previous year. The former employee received additional money as part of the settlement as well.

In the year the check was tendered, the IRS sought to include in the employee-taxpayer's income the amount of the check under the constructive receipt doctrine. The Court, however, held that a bona fide dispute existed between the petitioner and the employer, and this dispute was not settled until the following year. The Court correctly noted that if the taxpayer had negotiated the check when tendered, it would have resulted in an accord and satisfaction[85] of the disputed claim. Under the circumstances of the case, however, the Court held that the taxpayer had a legal right to refuse to accept the check when offered to him. Thus, the taxpayer was not in constructive receipt of income when the initial check was tendered.[86]

A similar result was reached in *Patterson v. Commissioner*.[87] In this case, a farmer entered into a "potato growing agreement" under which he was required to grow, harvest and store his potato crop. His compensation was based on the quality and quantity of the potatoes grown and stored. The potatoes were harvested and stored in the fall; delivery took place in February. The taxpayer was paid for his crop in January. The contract provided that the farmer was entitled to receive payment on December 31st, or January 5th, at his option. However, upon payment the farmer was required under the contract to purchase insurance on the stored crop. The Court held that the requirement to purchase insurance constituted a substantial limitation preventing constructive receipt.[88]

---

[84] 4 T.C. 415 (1944).

[85] An agreement (*accord*) between two contracting parties to accept alternate performance to discharge a preexisting duty between them and the subsequent performance (*satisfaction*) of that agreement. An accord and satisfaction differs from a *modification* in that a modification immediately discharges a preexisting duty, whereas an accord and satisfaction does not discharge a preexisting duty until the agreed upon alternate performance occurs. *See, e.g., Rose Inn of Ithica, Inc. v. Great American Ins. Co.*, 75 AD 3d 737 (N.Y. App. Div. 2010).

[86] *But see Stoller v. Comm'r*, 46 TCM 345 (1983), where taxpayer refused to accept check in payment of services, because he thought the amount tendered was insufficient. The court held the taxpayer was in constructive receipt since an endorsement "without prejudice and under protest" would have preserved his right to demand the additional amount due.

[87] 510 F.2d 48 (9th Cir. 1975). In contrast, in *Shelton v. Comm'r*, 612 F.2d 1276 (10th Cir. 1980), the court held that the requirement of posting "a normal fiduciary bond in a probate proceeding" before receiving income was not a substantial limitation, distinguishing *Patterson* on the grounds that "[t]he fees for such bonds are standard and modest, and would not be different in amount whenever obtained."

[88] *See also Griffith v. Comm'r*, 35 T.C. 882 (1961), where the cash surrender value of an insurance policy was not constructively received by a taxpayer who would have to surrender his interest in the policy.

In *Ames v. Commissioner*,[89] the court considered whether the taxpayer constructively received income from illegal espionage activities during 1985, when it was allegedly promised and/or set aside for him, or when the funds were received and/or deposited in his bank accounts during the taxable years 1989, 1990, 1991, and 1992 in the amounts of $745,000, $65,000, $91,000, and $187,000, respectively. In the fall of 1985, Ames received a communication from a Soviet agent that $2 million had been set aside for him in an account that he would be able to draw upon. Ames was told that the money was being held by the Soviet Union, rather than in an independent or third-party bank or institution, on Ames's behalf. During the years 1989, 1990, 1991, and 1992, Ames and his wife made deposits of cash received in connection with his unlawful espionage activities in the amounts of $745,000, $65,000, $91,000, and $187,000, respectively. Ames contended that he constructively received most of the unlawful espionage income in 1985, and, accordingly, he was not required to report the income received and deposited during the taxable years 1989, 1990, 1991, and 1992. The IRS contended that the income was reportable in 1989 through 1992, the years petitioner actually received and deposited cash in his bank accounts. Ames conceded that the funds deposited during the years at issue represent cash received from the Soviet Union during the years of the deposits. Ames argued, however, that most of the amounts he received during the taxable years under consideration were constructively received in 1985. The court noted the Ames's argument was to "foil . . . respondent's determination that the unlawful income was reportable during the years before the Court. In any event, the essence of constructive receipt is the unfettered control over the date of actual receipt."[90] Citing *Paul v. Commissioner*,[91] the court noted that Ames did not have ready access to the money because certain conditions had to be met or had to occur before he could gain physical access to any funds. Ames had to contact the Soviets, using a complex arrangement of signal sites, to determine whether a "withdrawal" could be made. Next, the Soviets had to arrange to have the cash transferred into the United States and have it secretly left in a prearranged location for petitioner. There was no certainty that these conditions and steps could be accomplished under the existing circumstances, and the conditions represented substantial risks, limitations, and restrictions on petitioner's control of the funds, assuming they were even in existence and segregated for his exclusive benefit.

---

[89] 112 T.C. 304 (1992).

[90] 112 T.C. at 313.

[91] *Paul v. Comm'r*, T.C. Memo. 1992-582. No constructive receipt where taxpayer would have had to travel 68 miles in order to turn in winning lottery ticket. Constructive receipt of income has been found where a corporation offers payment or pays by check in one year, but the recipient refuses delivery or fails to cash the check until the following year. *See, e.g., Frank v. Comm'r*, 22 T.C. 945 (1954). *See also Thomas v. United States*, 213 F.3d 927 (6th Cir. 2000), where the taxpayer won the Ohio lottery in December, Year 1, but was not paid until January, Year 2. The only action required of the taxpayer was to submit a claim form and the winning ticket to the lottery commission, which he did on December 14, Year 1. Because of various validation and verification procedures, the prize money was not paid until more than a month later. The taxpayer's right to the prize had not vested or become irrevocable until Year 2. The court found no constructive receipt.

The court determined that so long as the Soviets retained control over any funds or promised set-asides, there was no practical or legal way in which petitioner could compel payment. Assuming that some type of account was created and funds were segregated for Ames, he did not have ready access to it, and certain conditions had to be met or had to occur before he could gain physical access to any funds, hence Ames did not constructively receive the income before it was made physically and/or practically available to him. If the KGB had questioned petitioner's loyalty at any time before payment, there is no assurance that Ames would have continued to receive cash deliveries or payments. So long as the Soviet Union retained the ability to withhold or control the funds, there was no constructive receipt. Accordingly, the court held that Ames received and failed to report income in the amounts of $745,000, $65,000, $91,000, and $187,000 for the years 1989, 1990, 1991, and 1992, respectively.

The sometimes blurry distinction drawn by the courts and the IRS can be seen in Rev. Rul. 69-92,[92] where a cash basis taxpayer was required to include as income in the year received that portion of the contract price withheld pending completion of the contract, even though the taxpayer was required to deposit other property to secure release of the withheld amount. However, in *Bizzack Bros. Construction Corp. v. Commissioner*,[93] the fact that the taxpayer released the retainage held in escrow under similar conditions[94] did not affect the Tax Court's finding that the funds were never subject to the taxpayer's "dominion and control."

[E] *Power to Collect*

Sometimes, the possession of a simple matured right is not sufficient to establish constructive receipt if the taxpayer cannot collect. The regulations state that constructive receipt occurs when income is "credited to the account, set apart, or otherwise made available . . . ." Thus, in addition to the right to receive, constructive receipt requires *the power to collect*. This issue arises often in check cases,[95] as well as other circumstances.

In *Hornung v. Commissioner*,[96] for example, the taxpayer, a football player, was notified on the afternoon of December 31st that he had won a Corvette automobile for being selected as the most valuable player in a championship football game.[97] Hornung treated the award as income in the same year that he was announced as the winner. The Tax Court held that the fair market value of the Corvette was not includable in Hornung's income for that year because he was not given the title or the keys to the car or anything else to "evidence his ownership or right to possession." Moreover, as a practical matter, it was impossible for Hornung to obtain possession

---

[92] 1969-1 CB 138.

[93] 41 TCM 173 (1980).

[94] 41 TCM at 175.

[95] *See Loose v. United States*, 74 F.2d 147 (8th Cir. 1934), and § 5.04[E], *infra*.

[96] 47 T.C. 428 (1967), *acq*. 1967-2 CB 2.

[97] The game was played on December 31st in Green Bay, WI, and the car was located at NFL headquarters in New York City, NY.

of the car before the end of the year. He was in Green Bay Wisconsin and the automobile was at National League headquarters in New York City. The car simply had not been "set aside" for him and delivery was not dependent solely on his own actions. The Court held that the taxpayer was not in constructive receipt of the Corvette until the next year when he obtained possession and title.

In *Richard A. Childes,*[98] an attorney who entered into a contingent fee arrangement agreed to a deferred payment of his fee before any amounts due were required to be paid. Before the case was settled, annuity contracts were purchased to provide for payment of the fee. The Tax Court held that the attorney neither constructively received the fair market value of the annuity contract nor the amounts paid for them in the year they were purchased.

In *Hooper v. Commissioner,*[99] the "power to collect" as an application of the constructive receipt doctrine was once again considered. In this case, a cash basis landlord and tenant were entities owned by the same individuals. The tenant who had been paying rent to the landlord decided not to pay rent even though sufficient funds were available. The unpaid rent accumulated until, several months later, the landlord contributed the property to his corporation in an IRC § 351 transaction. The IRS ruled, and the Tax Court agreed, that the unpaid rent was income to the landlord. The Tax Court said that the exercise of absolute control over the funds by the common owners warranted the application of the constructive receipt doctrine.

In Rev. Rul. 72-317,[100] the IRS restated its position and its interpretation of the regulations. The issue presented was whether an authorized but undrawn salary was includable in gross income in 1970 when the taxpayer was the president of the corporation and had actual and constructive control of the corporation's vote and books. The corporation in 1970 resolved to pay a salary to the taxpayer and accrued the expense on its books. The salary could have been paid during the year without financial embarrassment to the corporation. The taxpayer merely had to make the necessary monthly book entries. Accordingly, the authorized but undrawn salary was includable in his income in 1970.

In *Robinson v. Commissioner,*[101] the taxpayer, a boxer, contracted to defer the proceeds of his championship fight. Before the fight, Robinson entered into a contract with the promoter that deferred some of the fight purse until some months after the fight. Because the due date for payment had been fixed before the fight took place, the taxpayer could not be in constructive receipt of income after winning the fight. The IRS argued that the entire fight proceeds were taxable in the year of the fight and imposed a lien on the funds in the hands of the promoter. On petition to the Tax Court, the Court held that the original deferral was effective and the amount of the proceeds includable as income in the year of the fight was limited to the amount actually paid to the taxpayer or on his behalf.[102]

---

[98] 103 T.C. 634 (1964).

[99] T.C. Memo. 1995-108.

[100] 1972-1 CB 128.

[101] 44 T.C. 20 (1965), *acq. and acq. in result,* 1976-2 CB 2.

[102] *See also Single v. Comm'r,* T.C. Memo. 1988-549 (taxpayer not in constructive receipt of state tax refund checks wrongfully withheld by his wife without his knowledge); Priv. Ltr. Rul. 200945005

[F] Economic Benefit Doctrine

Separate from the doctrine of cash equivalency and constructive receipt is the "economic benefit" doctrine,[103] under which a cash basis taxpayer must recognize income upon the receipt of property conferring a present economic benefit, regardless of whether the taxpayer is capable of immediately recognizing it through assignment or otherwise. Accordingly, it is not necessary for the taxpayer's interest to be assignable, or for the taxpayer to be entitled to immediate possession, to constitute an "economic benefit." However it is necessary for there to be identifiable "property" and for the taxpayer's rights to that property to have vested, even if the taxpayer is not entitled to immediate possession. The income is immediately taxable under the economic benefit doctrine on the fair market value of the property conferring the present economic benefit, if the following conditions are present:[104]

- There is an identifiable "property," such as a trust, an escrow account, or a similar arrangement, where the transferred assets are protected from the transferor's creditors; and
- The taxpayer's rights to the property have "vested" (even though the taxpayer may not be entitled to immediate possession), *i.e.*, the taxpayer has a present, indefeasible right to the future receipt of the property.[105]

For example, in Priv. Ltr. Rul. 9336001, an attorney's fees were paid by the purchase of an annuity. As part of a settlement, the defendant's liability insurers paid the plaintiff's attorney's fees by purchasing single-premium annuities and naming the attorney as beneficiary of the annuity. The liability insurers remained owners of the policies and reserved the right to change the beneficiaries. The insurers also remained obligated to make periodic payments to the attorney if the annuity payments were not made from the contract.

Under Texas law, the annuity policies were not subject to the claims of the attorney's creditors. The attorney could not assign his interest in the policies. Additionally, his right to future payments was not readily transferable or marketable.

The Service ruled that the fair market value of the right to receive the annuity payments was includable in the attorney's income in the year the annuities were purchased. The Service concluded that the attorney's right to receive payments under

(Footnote Continued)

(taxpayer was not in constructive receipt of disbursement check where he was informed on December 31 of Year 1 that the check from his former employer's deferred compensation plan was available for pickup, but office where it was held was closed on that day; taxpayer allowed to report check as income in Year 2, when he actually received payment).

[103] Under the economic benefit doctrine, an obligor's promise to make a payment to an obligee in the future constitutes a taxable benefit if the promise has an ascertainable value. *Minor v. United States*, 772 F.2d 1472 (9th Cir. 1985).

[104] *See Sproull v. Comm'r*, 16 T.C. 244 (1951) and TAMs 9420009, 9326019, and 9241006.

[105] *See Thomas v. United States*, 213 F.3d 927 (6th Cir.2000) (district court properly held that cash basis taxpayers had to include Ohio lottery winnings in income in year money was received, not prior year when he won lottery; economic benefit doctrine did not apply because taxpayer did not have an irrevocable right to money contained in a separate Ohio lottery fund).

the annuity polices constituted nonforfeitable property transferred in connection with the performance of services for purposes of IRC § 83. The Service reasoned that the attorney's compensation for service became funded and secured and thus became property.

In *Sproull v. Commissioner*,[106] a corporation paid a trustee the sum of $10,500 in 1945 as compensation for past services rendered by petitioner. The trustee was directed to hold, invest and pay over this sum to petitioner or his estate in two installments in 1946 and 1947. The trustee, pursuant to the agreement, paid to petitioner by check the sum of $5,250 on December 26, 1946, and a like sum on December 26, 1947.

The petitioner in his 1946 calendar year return included as income the first $5,250 received from the trustee and in his 1947 calendar year return included as income the $5,250 received from the trustee in 1947.

In arguing that the constructive receipt doctrine did not apply, Sproull made the following arguments:

- that although the sum was fixed and paid by his employer as compensation for services, he actually received no part of the money in 1945;
- that he could not have reduced any part of the money to possession in that year because of the time limitations on payment to him set in the trust instrument; and
- that he had no control of the corporate action in establishing the trust, nor was such action taken at his suggestion or pursuant to his direction.

Notwithstanding the court framed the question as follows:

> was "any economic or financial benefit conferred on the employee as compensation" in the taxable year. If so, it was taxable to him in that year. This question we must answer in the affirmative. The employer's part of the transaction terminated in 1945. It was then that the amount of the compensation was fixed at $10,500 and irrevocably paid out for petitioner's sole benefit.[107]

Important was the fact that the fund had a value equivalent to the amount paid over for his benefit, and that this beneficial interest could have been assigned or otherwise alienated.

Consider the following, for example.

Example 5-8

> T, a cash basis taxpayer, is employed by Zeon Corporation, which provides insurance to its employee's spouse and heirs should the employee die. The cost of the insurance per employee is $1,000 per year. John

---

[106] 16 T.C. 244 (1951).
[107] *Id.*

Goldsmith is one of the employees covered by the insurance program. As the insurance program provides a direct economic benefit to Goldsmith he has income in the amount of the benefit provided, *i.e.*, $1,000.[108]

Employer-purchased life insurance is a common example of an economic benefit.[109]

[G] Check Income

It is well-settled law that the receipt of a check is tantamount to the receipt of cash, even if the check is not deposited or otherwise negotiated,[110] provided that its receipt is not subject to "substantial limitations"[111] and there is no reason to suppose it will be dishonored. The year in which a check is received determines when it must be recognized as income, even when the check is received after banking hours.[112] A good example is the *Bright v. United States*[113] case. In *Bright*, a check was received on December 27, 1985 by cash-basis taxpayer's agent and deposited on same day. The Fifth Circuit determined the check was income on receipt 1985 even though funds were not available to taxpayer until January 3, 1986, the date when the depositary bank collected it. Receipt of the check was receipt of a cash equivalent; the funds would have been available immediately if the check had been cashed at payor bank. Neither the maker nor the payor bank restricted the check's negotiability. The fact that the amount of the check was large was immaterial.

Checks are regarded generally as a cash equivalent even though not immediately cashed or negotiated. The receipt of a check will result in the receipt of income to a cash basis taxpayer so long as there is no substantial limitation and there is no reason

---

[108] *Goldsmith v. United States*, 586 F.2d 810 (Cl. Ct. 1978). Taxable on the value of the promises in the year that the promises were made. These promises, however, were not represented by a note or other written document that would be assignable. Importantly, the court did not discuss at all whether the promises were intended as payment, were readily marketable or whether the insurance owner (presumably the employer) was subject to claims of creditors.

[109] *But see Centre v. Comm'r*, 55 T.C. 16, 20 (1970) (where insurance policies "remain[ed] an asset of the employer to which all creditors have rights and the employee acquire[d] no immediate rights thereto"; no economic benefit); Rev. Rul. 72-25, 1972-1 CB 127 (no economic benefit where employer purchases annuity policy as to which it is both owner and beneficiary); Rev. Rul. 68-99, 1968-1 CB 193 (same when employer purchases life insurance policy). *See also* GCM 37019 (Feb. 25, 1977) (no economic benefit when transfer not irrevocable).

[110] *Bright v. United States*, 926 F.2d 383 (5th Cir. 1991). *See Fong v. Comm'r* 48 TCM 689, 722–23 (1984) (date of actual or constructive receipt controlled, not date of deposit), *aff'd without opin.*, 816 F.2d 684 (9th Cir. 1987).

[111] *Fischer v. Comm'r* 14 T.C. 792 (1950) (agreement to defer deposit of check as matter of accommodation was "substantial limitation") *acq.*, 1950-2 CB 2.

[112] *Kahler v. Comm'r*, 18 T.C. 31 (1952). The receipt of a check is sufficient even if not immediately cashed. *Margaret G. Harrison*, T.C. Memo. 1992-172; *Lavery v. Comm'r*, 5 T.C. 1283 (1945).

[113] *Bright v. United States*, 926 F.2d 383 (5th Cir. 1991). Interestingly, IRS Publication 538, *Accounting Periods and Methods*, reminds taxpayers that "[y]ou cannot hold checks or postpone taking possession of similar property from one tax year to another to postpone paying tax on the income. You must report the income in the year the property is received or made available to you without restriction."

to believe the check will not be honored.[114] A check received subject to a restriction, such as an understanding that it would not be cashed until the following year, may not be income.[115]

An interesting (and often cited case) case is *Davis v. Commissioner*.[116] The taxpayer in *Davis* had been terminated by her employer and was told not to expect a severance pay check until the following year. However, in late December of the same year, a severance check was sent by the employer to the taxpayer by certified mail, return receipt requested, and a postal employee attempted to deliver the certified letter on December 31, 1974. The taxpayer was not at home, so the postal employee left a notice that stated the letter could be picked up at the branch post office after 3:00 p.m. that day. When the petitioner returned home, the branch post office was closed. She did not pick-up the certified letter containing the check until January 2, 1975.

The employer took the severance payment as a deduction in 1974. The taxpayer excluded it as income on her 1974 return and attached an explanatory note. The Tax Court was compelled to determine whether the taxpayer was in constructive receipt of the severance income in 1974. The IRS contended that since the severance payment was unqualifiedly committed on December 31, 1974, and the check was made available to the petitioner at the post office after 3:00 p.m. of the same day, the taxpayer was in constructive receipt of the income. The taxpayer argued that there was no constructive receipt of income since the check was mailed in the ordinary course of business, was not actually received until 1975, and was not intentionally delayed in transit by the taxpayer.

---

[114] *Kahler v. Comm'r*, 18 T.C. 31 (1952). *But See David P. Morgan*, TC Summary Opinion 2010-29. Analogous cases include those where a check was drawn and delivered in one year and cashed in a subsequent year. Under the negotiable instruments law, payment by check is a conditional payment subject to the condition that it will be honored upon presentation, and once such presentation is made and the check is honored, the date of payment relates back to the time of delivery. *See Broussard v. Comm'r*, 16 T.C. 23 (1951); *Spiegel v. Comm'r*, 12 T.C. 524 (1949) and cases cited therein. In *Estate of Kamm v. Comm'r*, 349 F.2d 953 (3d Cir. 1965), the court concluded that "the rule which treats [receipt of a check that is subsequently honored in due course]like the receipt of money for determining the time of income realization is reasonable and should be followed." 349 F.2d at 955–56.

In the *Spiegel* case the court said, at page 529:

> It would seem to us unfortunate for the Tax Court to fail to recognize what has so frequently been suggested, that as a practical matter, in everyday personal and commercial usage, the transfer of funds by check is an accepted procedure. The parties almost without exception think and deal in terms of payment except in the unusual circumstance, not involved here, that the check is dishonored upon presentation, or that it was delivered in the first place subject to some condition or infirmity that intervenes between delivery and presentation.

But see Goodman, et al. v. Comm'r, 6 TCM 1031 (1946), where receipt of check on an overdrawn account of a solvent corporation was *not* constructive receipt.

[115] *E.P. Madigan*, 43 BTA 549 (1941); *Fischer v. Comm'r*, 14 T.C. 792 (1950).

[116] T.C. Memo. 1978-12.

The Tax Court agreed with the taxpayer and held that there was no constructive receipt, since the taxpayer had not "turned her back" on the severance pay nor took any steps to prevent actual receipt.[117]

Davis can be compared with *Visco v. Commissioner*.[118] In *Visco*, the taxpayer was a reading specialist who was suspended from her position with the district school board for willfully violating school laws when she failed to follow directives of superiors. Visco appealed the board's decision to dismiss her. The secretary of education reversed the board's decision and ordered the district to reinstate the taxpayer to the position that she had held or a comparable position, with backpay plus interest at 6% per annum. The district employed the taxpayer from September of 1991 until June of 1992. The school district issued two checks to the taxpayer, each dated December 21, 1992, totaling $59,079.78. These checks represented backpay and interest on backpay of $108,509.02 after payroll deductions. The school district also issued a check to the taxpayer dated December 21, 1992, in the amount of $3,195.84 as reimbursement for benefits the taxpayer had not received. A courier presented the checks to the taxpayer on December 28, 1992. The taxpayer took the checks and called the district's attorney and told him she was refusing the checks. The taxpayer then returned the checks to the courier.

The taxpayer characterized the district's attempt to deliver the checks as a settlement offer, which she rejected. The court disagreed. Before delivering the checks, the Commonwealth Court established the exact amount due the taxpayer for backpay, interest on backpay, and benefits. The court noted that the school district was not negotiating; it was complying with the Commonwealth Court's order. Consequently, when the courier delivered the checks to Visco on December 28, 1992, she had the right to a specific amount of money and the power to receive that money. In her refusal to accept the checks, she turned her back on the income. The court held that the taxpayer was in constructive receipt of her backpay in 1992.

In *Kahler v. Commissioner*,[119] the Tax Court held that it was irrelevant that the taxpayer received a check after banking hours on December 31, so that he could not present it for payment until the next year. The court's opinion appeared to be based

---

[117] Receipt of checks or other items of income at year end are particularly troublesome. For example, where a taxpayer requested a check be mailed in 1943, but was not actually received until 1944, the Court held that the taxpayer was nevertheless in constructive receipt since he could have picked up the check personally. *McEuen v. Comm'r*, 196 F.2d 127 (5th Cir. 1952). In *Loose v. United States*, 74 F.2d 147 (8th Cir. 1934), a taxpayer suffered a stroke, and consequently was unable to personally avail himself of actual receipt. Since the taxpayer had actual notice of the availability of the income and since his wife had power of attorney, constructive receipt was found using the agency theory, *i.e.*, receipt by the agent is receipt by the principal. In *Evans*, T.C. Memo. 1988-228, no constructive receipt was found even though the taxpayer controlled the corporation that was to pay a bonus. The Court held that bonuses were to be paid if working capital was available and the taxpayer had a fiduciary responsibility to determine the adequacy of working capital. This determination could have been made prior to year end.

[118] T.C. Memo. 2000-77.

[119] 18 T.C. 31 (1952).

both on a cash equivalence analysis and the commercial law treatment of a check as conditional payment that if honored, relates back to the date of delivery.[120]

In some instances, the inability to obtain possession of the check may result in a substantial limitation and prevent constructive receipt. In *Baxter v. Commissioner*,[121] the Ninth Circuit reversed the Tax Court regarding a check that was received at year end. The taxpayer received a check in early January that he could have picked up on December 30th if he had driven 40 miles. The Court of Appeals said it would have been futile for the taxpayer to have made an 80-mile round-trip to collect the check for which he could not have received credit at a bank before January 2. Under these facts, he did not receive the income until January.[122]

Example 5-9

In each case below, determine if the taxpayer has received income:

- Al receives his paycheck on December 30, but he does not cash it until January 5.[123]
- Al was ill from December 28 to January 5. He went back to work on January 6, and received his check at that time.[124]
- Al received his paycheck after the bank that it was issued on closed.[125]
- Al's employment was terminated and Al's employer sent his last check to him by certified mail. On December 31 when the mail carrier came to deliver the check, Al was not home, and he received a notice to come to the post office to pick up his certified

---

[120] 18 T.C. at 34. *Cf. Estate of Spiegel v. Comm'r*, 12 T.C. 524 (1949). *See also Lavery v. Comm'r*, 158 F.2d 859 (7th Cir. 1946), *aff'g* 5 T.C. 1283 (1945), in which, although the Seventh Circuit states that a check transferred on December 30 was "the equivalent of cash," both opinions emphasize that the taxpayers had the opportunity to cash the check on December 30 or 31, both of which were business days, and the circuit court opinion suggests that the result might be different if the check arrived after business hours on the last day of the year.

[121] 816 F.2d 493 (9th Cir. 1987).

[122] Note the important distinction regarding the treatment of earned income under the cash and accrual method. While income may be earned by a cash method taxpayer she does not have income until actual or constructive receipt thereof.

[123] The general rule with respect to checks is that the year of receipt controls even if the check is received after banking hours. Checks are generally regarded as a cash equivalent and even if not immediately cashed or negotiated will still result in the receipt of income to a cash basis taxpayer, so long as there is no substantial limitation and there is no reason to believe the check will not be honored. *Bright v. United States*, 926 F.2d 383 (5th Cir. 1991).

[124] The general rule will apply so long as there is no substantial limitation and there is no reason to believe the check will not be honored. In this case Al's illness does not rise to a level of a substantial restriction or limitation. *See Loose v. United States*, 74 F.2d 147 (8th Cir. 1934), where a taxpayer suffered a stroke and was unable to personally avail himself of actual receipt. Since the taxpayer had actual notice of the availability of the income and since his wife had her husband's power of attorney, constructive receipt was found.

[125] *See* note 79, *supra*.

mail letter. Because the post Office had closed, he could not obtain his termination check until January 2.[126]

- Al was sent on assignment to work at a temporary location. Al received a check in early January which he could have picked-up on December 31th if he had driven 40 miles to the company's home office.[127]
- Al sent his brother down to receive his check on December 30, and his brother was mistakenly arrested on the way home with the check and put in jail. Al was not permitted to see him until January 2.[128]

On the other hand, where the payor lacked funds to make the payment, there can be no constructive receipt.[129]

Once a taxpayer has constructive receipt of the payment, it does not matter if he actually receives the payment and, if he does, when. In *Millard v. Commissioner*,[130] the taxpayer received a check as a distribution from an IRA account in 2001 which he never cashed. In 2003, he presented the check to the issuing bank. The bank cancelled the check and then issued a second check reflecting current date. The tax court held that the amount of the original check was constructively received in 2001.

[H] *Interest Income*

Interest income is recognized generally by a cash basis taxpayer in the year of actual or constructive receipt. Reg. § 1.451-2(a) provides that income is constructively received when it is credited to the recipient's account, set apart for him, or otherwise made available. Amounts payable on interest coupons that have matured and are payable, but which have not been cashed, are constructively received in the tax year in which the coupons mature, unless it can be shown that there are no funds available to pay interest during that year.[131]

---

[126] This is similar to *Davis v. Comm'r*, T.C. Memo. 1978-12, *supra*, except the taxpayer in *Davis* was told not to expect a check until the following year.

[127] In *Baxter v. Comm'r*, 816 F.2d 493 (9th Cir. 1987), the Ninth Circuit reversed the Tax Court regarding a check that was received at year end. The taxpayer received in early January a check that he could have picked-up on December 30th if he had driven 40 miles. The Court of Appeals said it would have been futile for the taxpayer to have made an 80 mile round-trip to collect the check that he could not have received credit for at a bank before January 2. Under these facts, he did not receive the income until January.

[128] Receipt by an agent is receipt by the principal. Income in year 1.

[129] *Noel v. Comm'r*, 50 T.C. 702, 706-707 (1968), *citing Jacobs v. Comm'r*, 22 BTA 1166, 1169 (1931), and *Gullett v. Comm'r*, 31 BTA 1067, 1069 (1935).

[130] T.C. Memo. 2005-1992.

[131] Reg. § 1.451-2(b).

If there is a substantial limitation or restriction, however, no constructive receipt exists. Pursuant to the regulations,[132] the following conditions are *not* substantial restrictions:

- A requirement that an account or earnings thereon be withdrawn in multiples of even amounts;[133]
- The fact that the taxpayer would receive earnings that are not substantially less by an early withdrawal;[134]
- A requirement that the earnings may be withdrawn only upon a withdrawal of all or part of a deposit or account;[135] or
- A requirement that notice of intent to withdraw be given in advance of the withdrawal.[136]

But the following are:

- An amount equal to three months' interest must be forfeited upon withdrawal or redemption before maturity of a one year or less certificate of deposit, time deposit, bonus plan, or other deposit arrangement;[137] and
- Interest on a six-month certificate is not credited or made available before maturity without penalty.[138]

Interest credited by a bank to a customer's account prior to year end is income in the year in which the interest is credited. Accordingly, interest on a passbook account is includable in income in the year earned. Certificates of deposit (CDs) that mature after more than a year, while not resulting in constructive receipt,[139] will nonetheless create original issue discount income (OID) under IRC §§1272 and 1275.[140]

---

[132] Reg. §1.451-2(a).

[133] Reg. §1.451-2(a)(1).

[134] Reg. §1.451-2(a)(2).

[135] Reg. §1.451-2(a)(3).

[136] Reg. §1.451-2(a)(4).

[137] Reg. §1.451-2(a)(2).

[138] Rev. Rul. 80-157, 1980-1 CB 186. *See also* Rev. Rul. 73-487, 1973-2 CB 153, interest credited by a bank on a two-year certificate of deposit purchased prior to January 1, 1971, under the terms of which interest is payable at the conclusion of the term and principal and interest may be withdrawn only in an emergency with bank approval, is not includible in the gross income of a cash-method taxpayer until the taxable year in which the original term of the certificate is concluded, unless received in an earlier taxable year under the emergency withdrawal provisions.

[139] If the CD provides for a substantial penalty for withdrawal of interest prior to maturity, no constructive receipt occurs until maturity.

[140] In the case of certain deposits made after December 31, 1970, in banks, domestic building and loan associations, and similar financial institutions, the ratable inclusion rules of IRC §1232(a)(3) apply. *See* Reg. §1.1232-3A. Accrued interest on unwithdrawn insurance policy dividends is gross income to the taxpayer for the first taxable year during which such interest may be withdrawn by him. Reg. §1.451-2(b).

[I] Dividend Income

Dividend income is treated similarly to interest income. Income is recognized when the dividend is made available to the shareholder. However, an exception exists for year-end dividends.[141]

> Dividends on corporate stock are constructively received when unqualifiedly made subject to the demand of the shareholder. However, if a dividend is declared payable on December 31 and the corporation followed its usual practice of paying the dividends by checks mailed so that the shareholders would not receive them until January of the following year, such dividends are not considered to have been constructively received in December.[142]

[J] Rental Income

Rental income (including prepayment) is included as income in the year of receipt regardless of the time period to which it relates. The "claim of right doctrine" provides the basis for this rule of inclusion.[143] In *W. W. Millsaps*,[144] the Tax Court did not find constructive receipt of rent where payment of the rent in advance was offered but rejected in the year before it was due under a rental agreement. A retired farmer rented land to three brothers who offered payment of rent earlier than required in the rental agreement to avoid a landlord's lien attaching to their crops. The brothers put the rent money in escrow with a bank with instructions to pay the landlord on a definite date. No constructive receipt was found because the landlord did not have an unlimited right to the money and the bank would not have paid him earlier than instructed.

---

[141] Reg. § 1.451-2(b). Note the same regulation provides accrued interest on unwithdrawn insurance policy dividends is gross income to the taxpayer for the first taxable year during which such interest may be withdrawn by him.

[142] However, if the dividends are credited to the taxpayer's brokerage account on December 31, the taxpayer is in constructive receipt of the income. *See Baker v. Comm'r*, 81 F.2d 741 (3d Cir. 1936) and Reg. § 1.451-2(b) (second sentence).

[143] *See, e.g., Morris-Poston Coal Co. v. Comm'r*, 42 F.2d 620 (6th Cir. 1930). If a taxpayer receives income under a "claim of right" and without restriction as to its disposition, the taxpayer must report the income in the year regardless of its method of accounting. *North Am. Oil Consol. v. Burnet*, 286 U.S. 417, 427 (1932). Notwithstanding generally, if a deposit is held by the landlord to secure the tenant's performance under the lease and must be repaid to the tenant upon lease termination (assuming tenant compliance with the lease), the deposit is neither taxable income to the landlord nor a deductible expense. *See* Chapter 2 for a discussion of claim of right.

[144] T.C. Memo. 1973-146.

[K] Prizes and Awards

While state lotteries sometimes pay out their prizes in the form of an annuity for a term of years, prize winners often are given the option of receiving their prizes as lump sum payments. If the option is given after the lottery has been won under the normal application of the constructive receipt doctrine, this choice would require the winner to include income in the year the proceeds are won. The surrender of the right to the annuity in order to receive a cash payment is not considered a substantial restriction that would prevent the application of the constructive receipt doctrine. If the lottery winner is given the option of receiving the annuity or a lump sum, prior to purchasing his ticket, the constructive receipt doctrine will not apply, since he never had an unrestricted right to receive the income.

In order to avoid conflicting results like these, Congress enacted IRC § 451(h) (now IRC § 451(j) after amendment by the TCJA). Under this section, a cash basis prize winner who is granted the option to choose a single cash payment in lieu of a qualified prize (or portion thereof), i.e., an annuity, within 60 days after becoming entitled to the prize is not required to include amounts in gross income immediately if the annuity is exercised merely by reason of having the option.[145] The term "qualified prize" means any prize or award that: (1) is awarded as part of a lottery, jackpot, game or similar arrangement; (2) does not relate to past services performed or require performance of substantial future services; and (3) is payable over a period of at least ten years.[146] Consider, for example, the following:

Example 5-10

> X, a cash-basis individual, wins a $1,000,000 lottery prize and becomes entitled to the prize on July 15th. X has until September 5th to choose either 20 annual payments of $50,000 each or a lump-sum payment of $ 623,111 (the present value of the annuity, assuming a 5% interest factor). Because X's option to choose the lump sum is a qualified prize option, it is disregarded in determining the tax year for including the prize in income. Therefore, if X chooses the annuity, he includes each annuity payment in income in the year in which he becomes entitled to it.

Without this rule, a prize winner choosing an annuity after winning the lottery would be taxed under constructive receipt principles on income not actually received and might not have enough cash to pay the tax on that income.

---

[145] IRC § 451(j).

[146] IRC § 451(j)(2)(B). *See also* IRC § 74.

Example 5-11

Luke plays the weekly "lotto" just about every week. On December 31, 2019, Luke held a ticket for that evening's lottery drawing. The drawing was held at 9:00 PM. Luke, not one to miss a good time, left for his New Year's Eve parties at 8:00 PM. Luke thoroughly enjoyed the evening and returned home at 4:00 AM the next day. When Luke arose in time for the evening news, he found that he was the only person with the winning ticket worth $14,000,000.

- When should Luke report his winnings?
- Is the ticket a cash equivalent?
- Does Constructive Receipt apply?
- Does Luke have income under any other theory?

In some states, a prize winner can assign future award payments. In Priv. Ltr. Rul. 200031031, the applicability of IRC § 451(j) (pre-2018 IRC § 451(h)) is not affected by the mere presence of a state law permitting assignment. The IRS explained that the constructive receipt doctrine requires that the amount credited to the winner's account be subject to unqualified demand. A state law allowing assignment does not accelerate or otherwise alter the winner's rights to receive award payments, and, therefore, does not subject the award to unqualified demand. Furthermore, the IRS stated the cash equivalency doctrine (because of the lack of prevailing market rate discounts) and the economic benefit doctrine do not apply to require current inclusion of the award's value in the winner's gross income.

Lottery winners generally are cash basis taxpayers. Taxation of the value of an annuitized lottery prize in the year the prize is won requires application of one of three tax doctrines: constructive receipt, economic benefit, or cash equivalence.[147]

---

[147] *Constructive Receipt*—The value of an annuitized lottery prize under a state lottery would not be taxable by reason of the constructive receipt doctrine. The winner has no current right to receive the prize. Constructive receipt requires that an amount credited to an individual's account be subject to unqualified demand. *Robinson v. Comm'r*, 44 T.C. 20 (1965). *See also* Priv. Ltr. Rul. 200031031.

Economic Benefit—The doctrine of economic benefit requires a determination that the actual receipt of property or the right to receive property in the future confers a current economic benefit on the recipient. Economic benefit applies when assets are unconditionally and irrevocably paid into a fund or trust to be used for a taxpayer's sole benefit. *Sproull v. Comm'r*, 16 T.C. 244 (1951), *aff'd per curiam*, 195 F.2d 541 (6th Cir. 1952); Rev. Rul. 60-31, 1960-1 CB 174 (Situation 4). If the Lottery purchased an annuity and irrevocably named a lottery winner as the beneficiary of the annuity, the lottery winner could be taxed in the current taxable year on the value of the annuity under the economic benefit doctrine. Lotteries that purchase annuity contracts to fund prize payments avoid application of the economic benefit doctrine by naming the lottery rather than the winner as the owner and beneficiary of the annuity. Accordingly, the present value of annuitized prizes would not be taxable by reason of economic benefit.

Cash Equivalency—Amounts that are not taxable under constructive receipt or economic benefit may satisfy the requirements for inclusion in income under the doctrine of cash equivalency. Under this doctrine, a taxpayer is treated as having income when he or she receives property that is the "equivalent of cash." Decisions in cases involving cash equivalency have been based on the facts and circumstances of the particular cases; neither the Code nor the regulations define cash equivalency. In situations where a contract provided for deferred payments and no notes or other evidences of

[L] Escrow Agreements

Cash basis taxpayers are often faced with the choice of deferring income or receiving cash or a cash equivalent. Many taxpayers try to have it both ways; they try to defer income and replace its receipt with an intangible, with an escrow, or another security arrangement. There is a problem in that the greater the financial security, the closer the arrangement becomes to either the receipt of a cash equivalent or constructive receipt. Escrows are often used to provide financial security yet defer income. In the common case of a trust or an escrow account, the key to determining whether a "transfer" of "property" has occurred is whether the transferred assets are protected against the possibility of invasion by the transferor's creditors, because economic benefit requires a present indefeasible right to the future receipt of the property.

In *Reed v. Commissioner*,[148] a taxpayer was obligated under a shareholder option agreement to sell his corporate stock. While the closing was to take place in November 1973, it did not actually occur until December 27, 1973. In an attempt to delay income for tax purposes, Reed entered into a contract whereby the payment at closing was made to an escrow agent who disbursed the funds on January 3, 1974. Reed received no interest or investment income during the term of the deposit. Reed indicated that he would not have executed the sale if the purchaser had not agreed to this modification. The transaction was completed, and Reed was paid on January 3, 1974.

Upon audit, the Commissioner determined that the sale should have been reported in 1973 and Reed received a Notice of Deficiency. Reed appealed to the Tax Court. The Tax Court found in favor of the IRS. The Court held that Reed received an economic benefit when the funds were irrevocably deposited with the escrow agent. The short period of deposit and disbursement made the account fully taxable.

Reed appealed the Tax Court's determination to the First Circuit. The Court entertained the issues expressed in the following three questions.

(1) Did Reed constructively receive the proceeds on December 27, 1973?

(2) Did Reed receive an economic benefit on December 27, 1973?

(3) Was payment to the escrow agent payment to Reed?

As to the first issue, *i.e.*, constructive receipt, the Court examined whether the escrow arrangement was self-imposed. The Court decided that a unilateral condition (one imposed by one party to the transaction) could not prevent constructive receipt.

(Footnote Continued)

indebtedness were given, the contract rights, which were not of a type commonly sold or given as part of the purchase price, were held not to be property and, therefore, not a cash equivalent. Priv. Ltr. Rul. 200031031. *See also* Priv. Ltr. Rul. 9639016 and TAM 9808002. The receipt of future lottery payments by a Lotto Jackpot winner pursuant to the procedures established by the State statute, as amended by the TCJA, will not cause such payments to be treated as income for federal income tax purposes in advance of the receipt of such payments from the Fund.

[148] 45 TCM 398, 400 (1982), *rev'd on other grounds*, 723 F.2d 138 (1st Cir. 1983). *See also, e.g.*, *Bassett v. Comm'r*, 33 BTA 182 (1935), *aff'd per curiam on another issue*, 90 F.2d 1004 (2d Cir. 1937); *Depew v. Comm'r*, 27 BTA 515 (1933), *nonacq.*, XII-2 CB 16.

Nonetheless, the Court, in following *Busby v. United States*,[149] concluded that the escrow agreement was bilateral and was a valid modification of the original agreement. Moreover, the restriction on the time of payment was determined by the Court to be a substantial limitation sufficient to prevent the constructive receipt doctrine from mandating that the income be included in the prior year.[150]

As to the other two issues, *i.e.*, economic benefit and constructive receipt by the taxpayer's agent, the Court concluded that Reed did not receive an economic benefit since Reed did not receive any benefit by way of interest or income under time value of money. Moreover, the Court reasoned that since the escrow agent acted on behalf of both Reed and the purchaser, the agent was not under the control of Reed and, therefore, was not his agent.

Transfers of property in trust or to an escrow account have been the subject of numerous cases and rulings. The key to determining whether a transfer of property results in the receipt of income is whether the transferred assets are protected against the possibility of invasion by creditors. If the funds can be reached by creditors, then the transferee does not have an indefeasible right to the future receipt of the property and he will not be deemed to have income in the year the trust or escrow was established.[151]

An escrow agreement would seem to prevent actual payment or constructive receipt; however, where the escrow contains cash or a cash equivalent, such as bank certificates of deposit or treasury notes, the escrow (or the obligation that it secures) will be considered payment under the installment payment rules.[152]

The economic benefit doctrine was applied to cause current taxation in the following cases and rulings, notwithstanding the presence of an escrow:

---

[149] 679 F.2d 48 (5th Cir. 1982).

[150] The case law does not seem to draw a distinction between the deferral of earned and unearned income provided the amounts are not yet due. *See Oates v. Comm'r*, 207 F.2d 711 (7th Cir. 1953) and *Veit v. Comm'r*, 8 T.C. 809 (1947), *acq.* 1947-2 CB 4, *Veit v. Comm'r*, 8 TCM 919 (1949), sometimes known as *Veit I* and *Veit II*, respectively.

[151] In Priv. Ltr. Rul. 9420009, the IRS ruled that there was no constructive receipt of directors' fees deferred in an unfunded plan. In accordance with Rev. Proc. 92-65, 1992-2 CB 428, the plan allowed a participant to elect to defer a portion of his director's fees if the election was made before the start of the calendar year when the fees were earned. Because the participants had only the company's unsecured promise to pay the deferred compensation, the taxpayer did not recognize income under the constructive receipt or economic benefit doctrines. The modern day "secular trust," on the other hand, has the opposite result in that, at the inception of the trust, the taxpayer recognizes taxable income because the taxpayer's rights are secured. In such cases, it is not uncommon to fund the obligation with a commercial insurance contract. *See* Priv. Ltr. Rul. 8841023.

Cases which have ruled constructive receipt despite the use of escrows include *Harris v. Comm'r*, 477 F.2d 812 (4th 1973) (sales proceeds due incompetent placed in escrow at direction of the court were constructively received); *Bell's Estate v. Comm'r*, 60 T.C. 469 (1973) (gain on sale of property for annuity taxed to seller because annuity promise was secured by escrow of property and cognovit judgment—a judgment entered after a written confession by the debtor without the expense of ordinary legal proceedings); and *Watson v. Comm'r*, 613 F.2d 594 (5th Cir. 1980) (cotton farmer constructively received sale proceeds when cotton gin arranged for irrevocable letter of credit ensuring compliance with deferred payment arrangement). *Cf. Busby v. United States*, 679 F.2d 138 (5th Cir. 1982).

[152] *See* Reg. § 15a.453-1(b)(3), Example 8.

- A contest award payable in more than 12 monthly installments, but irrevocably set aside in an escrow account.[153]
- A fixed amount in settlement of an alimony obligation due a wife, deposited with an attorney under a binding arrangement that prevented the husband from backing out of the proposed settlement.
- New York Lottery winnings of a minor, when the funds were held by his parents in a custodial account until majority.[154]
- The present value of a minor's Irish Sweepstakes winnings, at the time the funds were paid over to a court, even though the funds were to be held by the court until the minor reached majority.[155]
- A personal injury damage award transferred to a trust for a minor's benefit.[156]

On the other hand, the economic benefit doctrine *did not* apply, and income was not accelerated, when the controlling state statute required a 20-year payout of the state lottery prize because there was no irrevocable set-aside of funds for the benefit of any particular lottery winner and, in any tax year within the payout period, winners had no right to obtain a sum greater than 1/20th of the total amount of their prize.[157]

[M] Deferred Payment Agreements

Deferred payment agreements (also known as non-qualified deferred compensation) are a popular method for rewarding employees and delaying the receipt of future income. Deferred payment agreements pose another aspect of the constructive receipt doctrine and the economic benefit doctrine and are often the subject of litigation.

A typical plan provides for employees to receive a lump sum or installment payments on retirement or termination of service. Avoiding lump sum taxation will depend on an analysis of the following factors:

- Whether the plan was funded (an unfunded plan usually involves some risk of nonpayment, which constitutes a substantial limitation).
- Whether the participant's interest in the plan was secured.
- Whether the payment election could be made only before the payments were due or ascertainable.
- Whether there were substantial limitations on the participant's right to receive the income.

---

153 Rev. Rul. 62-74, 1962-1 CB 68.

154 *Joseph Anastasio*, 67 T.C. 814 (1977). The Tax Court pointed out that the doctrine of constructive receipt and the doctrine of economic benefit are significantly different in concept, "although admittedly the decided cases have not always been a model of clarity in respect of the distinction."

155 *Stephen W. Pulsifer*, 64 T.C. 245 (1975).

156 *E.T. Sproull*, 16 T.C. 244 (1951).

157 TAM 9808002.

- Whether interest is payable in installments and when interest thereon accrues (interest that accrues after the first installment goes against constructive receipt).

For example, "rabbi trusts" established to secure employer's promises under contracts for deferred compensation are typically vulnerable to the employer/grantor's creditors under certain circumstances, such that they do not create an economic benefit, despite the fact that the taxpayer typically has a vested right to future receipt when the transfer occurs.[158]

If the employer chooses to fund a deferred compensation arrangement by purchasing a life insurance or annuity policy, the employer may want to arrange that the policy be the sole property of the employer and subject to the claims of its creditors to avoid constructive receipt of premium payments by employee-participants.

Where a rabbi trust (an unfunded plan) is used, under which an employer transfers funds to an irrevocable trust held for the benefit of employees, the independent issuance to an employee of an insurance policy that guarantees payment under the trust will not cause the future benefits to be presently included in the employee's income. The employee must, however, include any increase in salary intended as reimbursement of policy premiums, in gross income.

The IRS has provided guidelines for avoiding the pitfalls of the cash equivalence and the economic benefit doctrines in Rev. Rul. 72-25,[159] which approved a deferred compensation plan under which the employee, upon attaining age 65, obtained the right to the proceeds of an "investment account" maintained on the employer's internal books. Under the plan in the ruling, "neither the taxpayer nor his beneficiary has any interest in the account nor in any other assets of the employer . . . [and the plan] does not create an escrow account or trust fund or any other form of asset segregation by the employer for the benefit of the employee"; thus, there is no economic benefit. Furthermore, "[t]he benefits . . . are not subject in any manner to anticipation, alienation, sale, transfer, assignment, pledge, encumbrance, or liable for the debts, contracts, liabilities, engagements, or torts of the taxpayer or his beneficiary"; therefore, the taxpayer's rights are not the equivalent of cash.

In Rev. Rul. 60-31,[160] the IRS issued advice with respect to a variety of fact patterns involving compensation for services and the deferment of payment of that compensation. The IRS stated that any contributions made by an employer on behalf of an employee to a trust was to be included in the income of the employee for the taxable year during which the contribution was made if the employee's interest in the

---

[158] For examples of these kinds of arrangements, *see* Priv. Ltr. Rul. 8740044 and Priv. Ltr. Rul. 8737091

[159] 1972-1 CB 127.

[160] 1960-1 CB 174. In the first three fact patterns, the IRS concluded that the taxpayer was not in constructive receipt as the taxpayer had merely an unfunded contractual right. These arrangements are known as Rabbi Trusts. In the fourth fact pattern, based on *Sproull v. Comm'r*, 16 T.C. 244 (1951), the IRS ruled that the taxpayer was in constructive receipt. In fact, in pattern five, the IRS initially ruled in favor of constructive receipt under a joint ventureship theory but later reversed itself in Rev. Rul. 70-435, 1970-2 CB 100.

contribution was non-forfeitable at the time the contribution was made. Likewise, where an unconditional payment was made to an escrow agent on behalf of a taxpayer, the IRS concluded that income was received in the year of payment.[161]

A nonqualified deferred compensation (NQDC) plan is an elective or non-elective arrangement between an employer and an employee to pay the employee compensation at some time in the future. NQDC plans differ from qualified plans in that they do not meet all of the requirements of IRC § 401(a). The terms of these arrangements differ widely, but their common objective is to provide tax deferral for a specified period. NQDC plans may provide for payment upon retirement, death, disability, or termination of employment. Others may permit payment after a specified number of years.

The most commonly used types of NQDC plans are salary reduction arrangements, bonus deferral plans, top-hat plans, and excess benefit plans.

- **Salary reduction arrangements:** This type of plan simply defers the receipt of otherwise currently taxable compensation by allowing the executive to select a percentage or dollar amount to be taken out of current salary and have the employer pay the deferred amount at a future date.
- **Bonus deferral plans:** This is similar to a salary reduction arrangement, except that it defers receipt of an employee's bonus.
- **Top-hat plans:** Also known as Supplemental Executive Retirement Plan (SERP). These are NQDC plans primarily for a select group of management or highly compensated employees to supplement qualified retirement plans.
- **Excess benefit plans:** Also known as benefit equalization plans or benefit replacement plans. These are NQDC plans that provide benefits to employees whose benefits under the employer's qualified plan are limited by IRC § 415.

All NQDC plans are either unfunded or funded. Most NQDC plans are intended to be unfunded arrangements because of the tax advantages. With an unfunded arrangement, the employee has only the employer's "mere promise to pay" the deferred compensation in the future and the promise to pay is not secured in any way. The employer may simply keep track of the benefit in a bookkeeping account or may invest the funds in annuities, securities, or insurance arrangements. In order to help fulfill its mere promise to pay the employee, the employer may transfer funds to a trust that remains a part of the employer's general assets, subject to the claims of the employer's creditors upon insolvency.

Generally, a funded arrangement exists if assets are set aside from the claims of the employer's creditors, for example, in a trust, escrow, or annuity.[162]

If a deferred compensation plan does not comply with IRC § 409A, all amounts deferred under the plan for all taxable years are currently includible in gross income to the extent not subject to a substantial risk of forfeiture and not previously included in gross income.

---

[161] These arrangements are known as secular trusts and result in immediate taxation to the beneficiary. *See* Priv. Ltr. Rul. 8841023.

[162] *See* Internal Revenue Manual § 4.23.5 Technical Guidelines for Employment Tax Issues.

§ 5.05 Expenses—Deductions

[A] Generally

Under IRC § 461(a), "the amount of any deduction or credit allowed . . . shall be taken for the taxable year which is the proper taxable year under the method of accounting used in computing taxable income." Under this statute, deductions are permitted for current expenditures when they are paid by a cash basis taxpayer or by the taxpayer's agent.[163] Under the cash method, a taxpayer claims deductions in the year in which cash or property is actually paid or transferred.[164] It does not matter when the expense was incurred, and, unlike with income, there is no constructive payment doctrine. If an expenditure results in the creation of an asset having a useful life that extends beyond the close of the tax year, the expenditure may not be deductible, or may be only partly deductible, for the tax year in which made. A "payment" can be made in various ways (*e.g.*, by check or debit card, credit card, third-party note, etc.). This is known as "actual payment." A payment can be made:

- with borrowed funds;[165]
- by a third party as a loan that the taxpayer repaid in a later year;[166] or
- for an expense incurred in an earlier year.[167]

There must be evidence that the taxpayer paid the expense for a deduction to be allowable.[168] IRC § 461(a) is amplified by Reg. § 1.461-1(a)(1) which provides, in pertinent part:

> Under the cash receipts and disbursements method of accounting, amounts representing allowable deductions shall, as a general rule, be taken into account for the taxable year in which paid . . . . If an expenditure results in the creation of an asset having a useful life that extends substantially beyond the close of the taxable year, such an expenditure may not be deductible, or may be deductible only in part, for the taxable year in which made.[169]

---

[163] Reg. § 1.461-1(a)(1).

[164] In CCA 201935011, the IRS determined that a contribution by an employer to a trust of a qualified retirement plan maintained by that employer must be payment of cash or its equivalent or property to the trust in order to be deductible under for the employer's taxable year in which the contribution is made under the objective outlay-of-assets test set forth in *Don E. Williams Co. v. Comm'r*, 429 U.S. 569 (1977).

[165] *Crain v. Comm'r*, 75 F.2d 962, 35-1 USTC ¶9217 (8th Cir. 1935).

[166] *McAdams v. Comm'r*, 15 T.C. 231 (1950).

[167] *Rosenthal v. Comm'r*, T.C. Memo. 1982-369, 44 CCH TCM 316.

[168] *Zand v. Comm'r*, T.C. Memo. 1996-19, 71 CCH TCM 1758.

[169] Reg. § 1.461-1(a)(1).

Under this regulation, an expense payment may not be deductible if it creates an asset life longer than one year that is properly amortizable or depreciable. Consider the following hypothetical:

Example 5-12

T makes monthly deposits of property taxes into an escrow account. T's payments total $3,000 during 2019. The escrow agent makes no payments to taxing authorities during 2020. In January 2021, the escrow agent pays $2,500 to the taxing authority. T is not entitled to a deduction in 2020, since no payments were made during 2020 to the taxing authority. T is entitled to a $2,500 deduction in 2021, since payment is made by her agent in such year.

On the other hand, cash basis taxpayers are entitled to "certain deductions in the computation of taxable income which do not involve cash disbursements during the taxable year, such as deductions for depreciation, depletion, and losses, under IRC §§167, 611, and 165 of the Code, respectively."[170] Likewise, a cash basis taxpayer is allowed a deduction for amounts paid as offsets against a debt owed the taxpayer or by the application of property in a creditor's possession against the debt.[171]

Taxpayers should be well alerted to avoid paying expenses or debts with property that has "built-in gain." A depreciated asset may give the taxpayer a deduction but may also trigger income.

[B] Alternative Timing Rules

The regulations provide for alternative timing rules. If the liability of a taxpayer is subject to IRC §170 (charitable contributions), IRC §192 (black lung benefit trusts), IRC §194A (employer liability trusts), IRC §468 (mining and solid waste disposal reclamation and closing costs), or IRC §468A (certain nuclear decommissioning costs), the liability is taken into account as determined under that section and not under IRC §461 or the regulations thereunder.[172]

---

[170] Reg. §1.461-1(a)(1).

[171] In general, cash basis taxpayers deduct an expense when "paid" by the taxpayer or by the taxpayer's agent. *See* Reg. §1.461-1(a)(1) and *Comm'r. v. Bradley*, 56 F.2d 728 (6th Cir. 1932). There is, however, no concept of "constructive payment." *See Massachusetts Mutual Life Insurance Co. v. United States*, 288 U.S. 269 (1933).

[172] For special rules relating to certain loss deductions, *see* IRC §§165(e), 165(i), and 165(l), relating to theft losses, disaster losses, and losses from certain deposits in qualified financial institutions.

[C] Constructive Payment

While the doctrine of constructive receipt is applicable to income items, there is *no* such doctrine with respect to expense items, *i.e.*, constructive payment.[173] Consequently, despite the fact that a taxpayer must recognize income under principles of constructive receipt where, for example, his corporate employer credits an unpaid salary to his account, the corporation (if the employer is using the cash method) is not entitled to a deduction under a doctrine of constructive payment.

In *Vander Poel, Francis & Co. v. Commissioner*,[174] a corporate taxpayer kept its books on the cash basis. In 1942, it voted certain salaries to its two principal officers and stockholders which it duly credited to their accounts, unconditionally. During the year, the two officers drew certain portions of these salaries and the balance was left to their credit with petitioner. They could have drawn the balance of these salaries if they had elected to do so. The Commissioner allowed as a deduction for petitioner the portions of the salaries paid during the taxable year and disallowed the balance because petitioner was on the cash basis and is entitled to deduct only the amounts of the salaries that were actually paid. On the other hand, the officers were in constructive receipt of income as they had the ability, if they wished, to draw the balance of their salaries.[175]

[D] Note and Check Payments

There is an important distinction between a promissory note and a check. A cash basis taxpayer cannot obtain a deduction by tendering a promissory note for payment even if the note is a cash equivalent to a recipient.[176] Payment by check, on the other hand, *does* constitute payment.[177] Checks do not represent final payment relieving a debtor of liability, but rather constitute only conditional payment which becomes absolute when the creditor presents the check to the bank, which then honors it.[178]

---

[173] *See Vander Poel, Francis & Co.*, 8 T.C. 407 (1947).

[174] 8 T.C. 407 (1947).

[175] *See also Unico Sales & Marketing Inc.*, T.C. Memo. 1999-242, 78 TCM 150, in which a solely owned, cash method family corporation could not deduct unpaid accrued wages owed to cash method directors and officers: constructive payment claim was meritless where such payment was not a necessary corollary of constructive receipt; and IRC § 267 case law involving income/expense mismatching as to taxpayers using different accounting methods did not apply.

[176] *Helvering v. Price*, 309 U.S. 409 (1940). *See also* Rev. Rul. 77-257, 1977-2 CB 174 (note given for services does not create deduction for cash basis taxpayer); Rev. Rul. 70-647, 1970-2 CB 38 (interest on prior loan not paid by new note covering old principal and accrued interest). It is interesting to note that there is no symmetry here. While a taxpayer will not get a deduction upon the issuance of a note as "payment," the recipient may very well have income under the cash equivalency doctrine.

[177] *Estate of Spiegel v. Comm'r*, 12 T.C. 524 (1949), *acq.* 1949-2 CB 3.

[178] *Edward E. Thorpe, et ux. et al.*, T.C. Memo. 1998-115.

In *Don E. Williams Co. v. Commissioner*,[179] the Supreme Court observed that the line between a promissory note and a check is thin but distinct. A promissory note (even if secured) is still only a promise to pay and does not represent the paying out or reduction of assets. A check, on the other hand, is a direction to a bank for immediate payment and is treated as conditional payment of cash.[180] A cash basis taxpayer's check constitutes payment when issued to the payee if honored on presentation, even if the presentment does not occur until the following year and despite the taxpayer's ability to issue a stop payment order.[181] In *Estate of Spiegel v. Commissioner*,[182] the Tax Court held that a check represented conditional payment of a charitable contribution which related back to the date of delivery of the check, provided it was honored in due course.[183]

In check cases, the issue often becomes whether delivery of a check has occurred. In *Witt's Estate v. Fahs*,[184] the District Court held that mailing a check to a charity constitutes delivery, under the theory that the post office is both the transmitting agent of the sender and the receiving agent of the recipient. In *Estate of Spiegel v. Commissioner*,[185] the Tax Court held that a check represented "conditional payment" of a charitable contribution that related back to the date of delivery of the check, provided it was honored in due course, stating that a check "was necessarily placed in a different category from a mere promise to pay; or even from such a promise reduced to formal terms and issued in the form of a negotiable promissory note."

If a check is not accepted or not honored, the issue becomes murkier. In *Weber v. Commissioner*,[186] the Tax Court held that a check did not constitute payment when the payee returned it rather than presenting it for payment.[187] On the other hand, in *Reedy v. Commissioner*,[188] a charitable deduction was allowed notwithstanding the check was returned because of an IRS levy when "they had every good reason to believe

---

[179] 429 U.S. 569 (1977).

[180] 429 U.S. at 582-583. Under Article 4 of the UCC, if a check is presented to a payor bank, the bank must make payment if there is a sufficient amount in the account to make the payment.

[181] *See Estate of Spiegel v. Comm'r*, 12 T.C. 524 (1949), *acq.* 1949-2 CB 3, and Rev. Rul. 54-465, 1954-2 CB 93.

[182] *Id. See also Williams v. Comm'r*, 429 U.S. 569 (1977).

[183] Similarly, in Rev. Rul. 76-135, 1976-1 CB 114, the IRS ruled that while a cash basis taxpayer's negotiable promissory note issued for legal services was income to the lawyer at its fair market value, "payment" only occurred as the taxpayer made payments on the note. *Accord Guren v. Comm'r*, 66 T.C. 118 (1976) (negotiable demand note of solvent maker was not "payment" of a charitable contribution).

[184] 56-1 USTC ¶9534 (S.D. FL. 1956).

[185] 12 T.C. 524 (1949), *acq.*, 1949-2 CB 3. *See also Comm'r v. Bradley*, 56 F.2d 728 (6th Cir. 1932) (holding that a deduction was proper on the decedent's final return when his check, delivered and accepted before his death, was honored after his death).

[186] 70 T.C. 52 (1978).

[187] Similarly, in *Estate of Hubbell v. Comm'r*, 10 T.C. 1207 (1948), the Court held that state taxes were not paid on the decedent's final tax return when the bank refused payment, even though refusal was because the bank was informed of the death of the maker and there were sufficient funds in the account.

[188] T.C. Memo. 1981-590, 42 TCM 1401 (1980).

that it would be paid when presented to the bank for payment," and promptly took steps to make good on it afterwards.

On the other hand, when checks are mailed on December 31 of one year, but are dated January 1 of the following year, the deduction is not allowable until the later year. The restriction on the face of the checks imposed at the time they are mailed limits the time when the proceeds might be collected.[189]

[E] *Payment with Borrowed Funds*

A cash basis taxpayer can pay an obligation with borrowed funds and obtain a deduction so long as payment occurs. A simple example is paying a bill by credit card.[190] Problems arise, however, where a taxpayer makes a payment to the party from whom he has borrowed funds to make the payment. In situations like these, the taxpayer may not be entitled to a deduction.[191] Consider the following:

Example 5-13

> A taxpayer owes a bank money. Not having the ready funds to pay the interest due on the loan, the taxpayer borrows additional money from the bank and pays the bank the interest due. No deduction is allowed because payment has not been made in the form of cash but rather by note.[192] The theory is that while in form there has been a cash payment, in substance, the taxpayer merely substituted one obligation for another larger obligation.

In *Davison v. Commissioner*, a cash basis partnership entered into an agreement to borrow up to $29 million. The lender made an initial disbursement of $19,645,000. Pursuant to the loan agreement, the lender applied $227,647.22 of the initial disbursement as a credit for interest owed on a previous loan. Pursuant to a subsequent

---

[189] *Brooks v. Comm'r*, 49 T.C. 253 (1967).

[190] Rev. Rul. 78-39, 1978-1 CB 73.

[191] The general rule is that when a deductible payment is made with borrowed money, the deduction is not postponed until the years in which the borrowed money is repaid. The rationale for the rule is that taxpayers should not be able to elect the year in which expenses can be deducted from income. *See Irving Segall*, 30 T.C. 734, 739-740 (1958); *Hazel McAdams*, 15 T.C. 231, 235 (1950), *aff'd*, 198 F.2d 54 (5th Cir. 1952); *E. Gordon Perry*, 28 BTA 497, 500 (1933); *Robert B. Keenan*, 20 BTA 498, 499 (1930); *Edwin R. Crawford*, 11 BTA 1299, 1302 (1928); *Patrick v. United States*, 186 F. Supp. 48, 52 (W.D. S.C. 1960), *aff'd*, 288 F.2d 292 (4th Cir. 1961), *rev'd on other grounds*, 372 U.S. 53 (1963).

[192] *Granan v. Comm'r*, 55 T.C. 753 (1971). For a cash basis taxpayer, payment must be made in cash or its equivalent. *Don E. Williams Co. v. Comm'r*, 429 U.S. 569, 577-578 (1977); *Eckert v. Burnet*, 283 U.S. 140, 141; *Menz v. Comm'r*, 80 T.C. 1174, 1185 (1983). The delivery of a promissory note is not a cash equivalent but merely a promise to pay. *Helvering v. Price*, 309 U.S. 409, 413 (1940); *Nat Harrison Associates, Inc. v. Comm'r*, 42 T.C. 601, 624 (1964). Where a lender withholds a borrower's interest payment from the loan proceeds, the borrower is considered to have paid interest with a note rather than with cash or its equivalent and, therefore, is not entitled to a deduction until the loan is repaid. *Menz v. Comm'r*, *supra*, at 1186.

modification, the lender agreed to advance $1,587,310.46 to enable the borrower to satisfy its current interest obligation to the lender. The lender made a wire transfer of $1,587,310.46 to the borrower's bank account on December 30, 1980. On December 31, 1980, the borrower made a wire transfer to the lender to satisfy the borrower's current interest obligation. The net effect of the December 30-31 transaction was to increase the principal amount of the borrower's loan from the lender by $1,587,310.46. The borrower claimed interest deductions of $227,647.22 and $1,587,310.46 and reported an ordinary loss on its partnership return.

The Tax Court held the borrower was not entitled to interest deductions under IRC § 163(a), ruling that a cash basis borrower is not entitled to an interest deduction where the funds used to satisfy the interest obligation were borrowed for that purpose from the same lender to whom the interest obligation was owed. In those circumstances, there has been no "payment" of interest; rather, "payment" has merely been postponed.[193]

Similarly, simultaneous credit card transactions have been held not to constitute payment[194] and, therefore, cash basis taxpayers will not receive a deduction in this situation. The critical issue in these cases is whether the funds are subject to the borrower's "unrestricted control."[195]

On the other hand, payment by credit card has been held to be payment by a cash basis taxpayer if the IRS deems the payment has been made with borrowed funds.[196] As for "pay by phone" arrangements, the date to be used in determining when allowable deductions may be taken by a cash method taxpayer using a "pay by phone" account is the date the financial institution paid the amount, as reported on a monthly statement sent to the taxpayer.[197]

Rev. Rul. 80-248[198] addressed the tax aspects of reverse mortgage loans to individuals who own their own homes and occupy them as their principal residence. The ruling held that a cash basis borrower has not paid the interest for federal income tax purposes. The payment occurs when the taxpayer pays the interest in cash or by transferring the property.

[F] Prepaid Expenses

As a general rule, a deduction is allowable under the cash method when payment is made. However, as Reg. § 1.461-1(a)(1) provides:

> If an expenditure results in the creation of an asset having a useful life that extends substantially beyond the close of the taxable year, such an

---

[193] *Davison v. Comm'r*, 107 T.C. 35 (1996).

[194] *Blitzer v. United States*, 684 F.2d 874 (Ct. Cl. 1982).

[195] *See, e.g., Blitzer v. United States*, 684 F.2d 874, 885–87 (Ct. Cl. 1982).

[196] Rev. Rul. 78-39, 1978-1 CB 73. The use of a bank credit card to pay an expense for medical care qualifies as the payment of a medical expense in the year the credit card charge is made regardless of when the bank is repaid.

[197] Rev. Rul. 80-335, 1980-2 CB 170.

[198] 1980-2 CB 164.

expenditure may not be deductible, or may be deductible only in part, for the taxable year in which made.[199]

This regulation applies to prepaid rent, compensation, insurance premiums, and supplies.

Obviously, the cash method provides considerable "planning opportunities" for a taxpayer paying a debt at year's end and delaying the receipt of income. Often, this results in the potential for abuse, which the IRS has attempted to combat. The IRS will argue generally against the deductibility of a prepayment on two grounds: first, there is no business purpose; and second, the payment fails to clearly reflect income.[200] When the issue concerns prepaid expenses, which are not otherwise capital expenditures, the timing of the transaction and whether the item should be capitalized become blurred. There is a significant number of decisions regarding prepayment, many of which were decided as tax shelter cases that proliferated during the 1970s and 1980s. Since then, the IRS and Congress have responded with a host of cases, rulings and statutory changes.[201]

One such case is *Keller v. Commissioner*,[202] involving prepaid intangible drilling costs. In *Keller*, the Tax Court held that the prepayments were, in essence, deposits. A deposit is not a payment and therefore cannot support a deduction. The Court applied the following three-part test for determining whether a "true" prepayment exists:[203]

(1) The prepayment must represent a real payment and not a deposit;
(2) The prepayment must be made for a business purpose and not merely for the purpose of tax avoidance; and
(3) The prepayment must not result in a material distortion of income.

In Rev. Rul. 79-229,[204] the IRS re-examined Rev. Rul. 75-152[205] in the context of a prepayment for livestock feed. The IRS noted that generally, amounts paid by persons engaged in the business of raising or feeding livestock, or on the cash method for feed to be consumed by their livestock in the taxable year of payment or in a subsequent taxable year are ordinary and necessary business expenses under IRC §162.

---

199 Reg. §1.461-1(a)(1).

200 IRC §446(b).

201 With revisions to the regulations under IRC §263 there is some overlapping. *See* Reg. §§1.263(a)-1, 1.263(a)-2, 1.263(a)-3; T.D. 9636, 78 Fed. Reg. 57,685 (Sept. 3, 2013) (providing rules relating to capitalization of expenses incurred to produce or improve tangible property) (generally effective for tax years beginning on or after January 1, 2014).

202 725 F.2d 1173 (8th Cir. 1984).

203 The decision followed Rev. Rul. 75-152, 1975-1 CB 144, later superseded by Rev. Rul. 79-229, 1979-2 CB 210. In Rev. Rul. 79-229, the IRS identified the following as indicative of a deposit:

- A contract for an indefinite quantity,
- A right to a refund, and
- A right to substitute other products.

204 1979-2 CB 210.

205 1975-1 CB 144.

Citing Reg. § 1.162-12, the IRS said, however, before a deduction can be made in the year of payment, the cost of feed to be consumed by the livestock must occur in the current year or the following year. Second, the prepayments must be a payment for the purchase of food rather than a deposit. Next, the prepayment must be made for business purposes and not for tax avoidance. Finally, the deduction of such costs and the taxable year prepayment must not result in a material distortion of income.[206]

The IRS examined circumstances under which prepayments had occurred and discussed various court decisions. The IRS noted that the court decisions allowing a deduction for prepaid feed from those disallowing the deduction is the acquisition of, or the reasonable expectation by the taxpayers of receiving, some business benefits as a result of the pre-prepayment.[207] The IRS gave several examples of business benefits including the fixed minute maximum pricing scheme and securing a supply of feed when there is a feed shortage. Additionally, whether the prepayment was a condition normally imposed by the seller in an arm's length transaction.

On the other hand, the IRS takes the position that under IRC § 461, transactions involving prepayments which were conducted by investor groups or hedge funds is not a "clear reflection of income."[208] The IRS also went into a lengthy discussion of material distortion of income in various cases; this was juxtaposed with the legitimate business practice of the taxpayer. The Service, in Rev. Rul. 79-229,[209] superseding Rev. Rul. 75-152, reiterated that unless the taxpayer meets all three tests described in Rev. Rul. 75-152, amounts paid for feed to be consumed by livestock in a subsequent year will not be deductible in the tax year paid.

It is therefore clear that cash basis taxpayers can be denied a current deduction for prepayment in abusive situations even if the expenditures are otherwise current expenses and the payments are not deposits.[210]

In applying the three-part test, the focus is on whether the prepayment is reasonable in the context of the agreement between the parties and the practice in the industry. A voluntary payment made before it is due presumably lacks business purpose. Moreover, where the parties are related, payments may not be in accordance with customary business practices. Each situation must be examined closely. Consider the following hypothetical, for example:

Example 5-14

On December 1, 2020, Farmer Grey orders 800 pounds of chicken feed for his chicken farm. The feed is delivered on December 15, 2020, and Farmer Grey makes full payment. It is anticipated that the feed will last up to six months.

---

[206] Rev. Rul. 79-229, 1979-2 CB 210.

[207] *See Ernst v. Comm'r*, 32 T.C. 181 (1959) *acq.*, 1959-2 CB 4.

[208] *See Burke v. Comm'r*, 533 F.2d 768 (2d Cir. 1976).

[209] 1979-2 CB 210.

[210] *See e.g., Bonaire Dev. Co. v. Comm'r*, 679 F.2d 159, 162 (9th Cir. 1982).

Applying the three-part test, it is reasonable to draw the following conclusions.

- The expenditure is a payment and not a deposit or refundable.[211]
- There is a valid business purpose, *i.e.*, the fee is cheaper in bulk and it will last the winter when it is needed.
- While the feed will have a useful life beyond the close of the tax year, the distortion to income will be minimal.[212]

[G] Prepaid Period Costs

[1] 12-Month Rule

Prepaid period costs, such as insurance, rent, and taxes, raise additional tax accounting issues. While the regulations would require capitalization if the useful life of the prepayment extends beyond the close of the taxable year, this rule has been relaxed in some cases.[213] In *Zaninovich v. Commissioner*,[214] for example, the Ninth Circuit allowed a calendar year, cash basis taxpayer a deduction for the prepayment of rent of 11 months for the period of December 1st to November 30th of the following year, stating that it is permissible to deduct an expenditure that is not allocable to a period extending more than 12 months beyond the end of the year of the expenditure.[215]

---

[211] Refundability is not always clear. In *Schenck v. Comm'r*, 686 F.2d 315 (5th Cir. 1982), a taxpayer made a prepayment of $20,000 on December 30 to a cooperative for fertilizer for the following year. While the payment was not refundable, if the taxpayer failed to take delivery of the fertilizer, then the payment could be applied to any other goods at the cooperative or even carried over for use in another year. In addition, apparently there was no business purpose for the payment. The deduction was disallowed.

[212] *See, e.g., Agro-Jal Farming Enterprises, Inc., et al. v. Comm'r*, 145 T.C. 145 (2015), *Schenk v. Comm'r*, 686 F.2d 315 (5th Cir. 1982) (nonrefundable advance payment for fertilizer not deductible; payment was deposit; payer could apply payment to other items); *Grynberg v. Comm'r*, 83 T.C. 255 (1984) (cash method taxpayer denied deductions for oil and gas "delay rentals"; rentals paid in December but not due until February and March of following year); *Gragg v. United States*, 74 AFTR 2d 94-5073 (5th Cir. 1994) (pattern of annually escalating "enormous" feed purchases near end of year followed by annually escalating resales of feed early in the next year negated any claim of business purpose for prepaid feed purchases). IRC §464 serves as a statutory buttress for the relevant cases and rulings, which explicitly allows farming syndicates (as defined) to deduct amounts paid for farm supplies only when the materials are used or consumed, unless a later date is otherwise applicable.

[213] Reg. §1.461-1(a). If an expenditure results in the creation of an asset having a useful life which extends substantially beyond the close of the taxable year such an expenditure may not be deductible, or may be deductible only in part, for the taxable year in which made. Prepaid interest, however, must be deducted in the year to which previously allowable, with the exception of "points" paid with respect to a principal residence. IRC §461(g). *See* §5.06[A], *infra*.

[214] 616 F.2d 429 (9th Cir. 1980) and *Commission v. Boylston Market Ass'n*, 131 F.2d 966 (1st Cir. 1942).

[215] On the other hand, in *Sorrell v. Comm'r*, T.C. Memo. 1987-351, 53 TCM 1362 (1987), the Tax Court rejected the *Zaninovich* approach and insisted that an expense that covers a one-year period is not fully deductible in the year of payment if the covered payment extends beyond the taxable year. In

In *U.S. Freightways Corp. v. Commissioner*,[216] the government litigated the issue of whether the then existing regulations required the capitalization of prepaid expenses that did not provide more than a 12-month benefit after year end. The government won the case in the Tax Court but the decision was reversed on appeal. The Seventh Circuit held that the existing regulations contained a 12-month rule as an exception to capitalization and that the government was barred from requiring the capitalization of expenses meeting that rule. The case was remanded to the Tax Court to provide it the opportunity to determine whether the expenses could be disallowed under the clear-reflection-of-income test of IRC § 446(b), but the IRS did not pursue this issue.

In Rev. Rul. 68-643,[217] the IRS gave tacit approval to the one-year rule as set forth in Rev. Rul. 68-643, in which the IRS stated that it would consider prepaid interest covering a period extending more than 12 months beyond the end of the year of the prepayment as distorting income, but that it would evaluate prepayments for shorter periods on a case-by-case basis.

The judicially created 12-month rule was codified and adopted in Reg. § 1.263(a)-4(f).[218] Although the Seventh Circuit in *U.S. Freightways* focused on how long the period of benefit extended solely in relation to the end of the taxpayer's tax year, the current regulation modifies the rule so that the test is not made solely with reference to the end of the tax year. Under this regulation, a taxpayer is generally not required to capitalize amounts paid to create any right or benefit for the taxpayer that does not extend beyond the earlier of the following two "reference points":

(1) Twelve months after the first date on which the taxpayer realizes the right or benefit, or
(2) The end of the tax year following the tax year in which the payment is made.

In applying the 12-month rule, it is important to recognize that the reference points are applied with respect to an amount only when the amount has either been paid or incurred. The reference point(s) is not the execution date of the contract. Thus, the date a taxpayer first realizes benefits from the entire contract may not be the same date the taxpayer first realizes any benefits from an incurred expenditure

---

(Footnote Continued)

INDOPCO, Inc. v. Comm'r, 503 U.S. 79 (1992), the Supreme Court made it clear that prepayments that cover more than one year must be capitalized under Reg. § 1.461-1(a)(1).

[216] 270 F.3d 1137 (7th Cir, 2001), *rev'g* 113 T.C. 329 (1999).

[217] 1968-2 CB 76. In Rev. Rul. 69-582, the IRS modified Rev. Rul. 68-643 to provide that prepayment of "points" equal to 6% of the face amount of a residential mortgage did not produce a material distortion of income.

[218] Reg. § 1.263(a)-4(f), which provides, in pertinent part:

> *In general.* Except as otherwise provided in this paragraph (f), a taxpayer is not required to capitalize under this section amounts paid to create (or to facilitate the creation of) any right or benefit for the taxpayer that does not extend beyond the earlier of—
>
> (i) 12 months after the first date on which the taxpayer realizes the right or benefit; or
> (ii) The end of the taxable year following the taxable year in which the payment is made.

under the contract. Even where the benefit period of an entire contract extends beyond 12 months, the 12-month rule may still apply. Reg. § 1.263(a)-4(f), Example 2, illustrates this important point:

Example 5-15

On December 1, 2005, N corporation pays a $10,000 insurance premium to obtain a property insurance policy (with no cash value) with a 1-year term that begins on February 1, 2006. The amount paid by N is a prepaid expense described in paragraph (d)(3) of this section and not paragraph (d)(2) of this section. Because the right or benefit attributable to the $10,000 payment extends beyond the end of the taxable year following the taxable year in which the payment is made, the 12-month rule provided by this paragraph (f) does not apply. N must capitalize the $10,000 payment.[219]

Example 5-16

Assume the same facts as in Example 5-15, except that the policy has a term beginning on December 15, 2005. The 12-month rule of this paragraph (f) applies to the $10,000 payment because the right or benefit attributable to the payment neither extends more than 12 months beyond December 15, 2005 (the first date the benefit is realized by the taxpayer) nor beyond the end of the taxable year following the taxable year in which the payment is made. Accordingly, N is not required to capitalize the $10,000 payment.[220]

A common misconception is that a taxpayer who enters into a multi-year contract for services (whether or not all or a portion of the services are prepaid up front) is ineligible to apply the 12-month rule to the contract because the benefit under the contract extends beyond 12 months. This is not so. Where no prepayment is made, or where a taxpayer prepays a liability that is not considered a "payment liability,"[221] the benefit period under the contract may extend beyond 12 months even though the benefit period related to the amount "incurred" may not. Moreover, a payment liability may also fit under the 12-month rule where a multi-year contract exists but the taxpayer prepays only the amount related to the next year.[222]

---

[219] Reg. § 1.263(a)-4(f)(8), Example 1.

[220] Reg. § 1.263(a)-4(f)(8), Example 2.

[221] A payment liability generally is a liability for which economic performance is satisfied only on making a payment on such liability.

[222] Reg. § 1.263(a)-4(f)(5).

For purposes of the 12-month rule, amounts paid to terminate a contract otherwise subject to capitalization creates a benefit that lasts for the unexpired term of the agreement immediately before the date of the termination. If the contract provides for termination after a notice period, a benefit lasts for the amount of time by which the notice period is shortened by a payment.

[2] Exceptions to 12-Month Rule

The 12-month rule is inapplicable under the regulations to several categories of intangibles, including, acquired intangibles, created financial interests, amounts paid to create an amortizable IRC § 197(c) intangible, and amounts paid to create an intangible of indefinite duration.[223]

The exclusion of financial interests from the 12-month rule creates an incongruity for taxpayers who enter into supply or customer contracts. If the subject matter of the contract is services, or rent of property, or the license of an intangible, the 12-month rule may apply to the contract. If, however, the subject matter of the contract is the sale of goods, the regulations treat the contract, even though it is the same overall type of contract, as a financial instrument (if it meets the definition of either a forward contract or option contract) and it is ineligible for the 12-month rule.

[3] Elective Capitalization

Although employee compensation, overhead, and certain *de minimis* costs are not required to be capitalized, the regulations allow taxpayers to annually elect to capitalize such costs. The annual election is made separately for each transaction and applies to any combination of the categories of intangibles listed in the previous section.[224] Accordingly, a taxpayer may elect to capitalize employee compensation, but not overhead, related to a particular transaction.

The election is made by treating the costs as facilitating the transaction on the taxpayer's timely filed original return for the tax year during which the costs are paid. No election statement is required because an annual election is revocable without the IRS's consent. A taxpayer making the election inadvertently might be able to unwind the inadvertent capitalization of costs.[225]

Taxpayers may likewise elect to not use the 12-month rule on an annual basis.[226] This election, however, applies to all similar transactions during the tax year on a category-by-category basis. For example, at a taxpayer's discretion, the election may be made to apply to all nonrenewable 12-month service contracts but not to all prepaid insurance contracts for 12 months.

---

[223] Reg. § 1.263(a)-4(f).

[224] *See* § 5.16.

[225] Reg. § 1.263(a)-4(f)(7).

[226] Reg. § 1.263(a)-4(f)(7).

§ 5.06 Interest Expense

[A] Prepaid Interest

Under IRC § 461(g), a cash basis taxpayer is required to capitalize and amortize any interest expense paid that relates to a period extending beyond the close of the taxable year. In essence, the cash basis taxpayer is placed on the accrual method for purposes of deducting interest.[227] The amount "allocable" to a given period is determined under the "economic accrual" method, under which a constant interest rate is applied periodically to the outstanding balance, including interest previously accrued but unpaid.[228]

"Prepaid points" are treated differently. The prepayment of points in respect of indebtedness incurred in connection with the purchase or improvement of the taxpayer's principal residence and secured by a mortgage on that residence is deductible, provided that the prepayment is an established business practice in the area and the amount does not exceed what is generally charged.[229] Such points are immediately deductible and are not considered to create original issue discount on the obligation.[230] In order to be eligible for this treatment, the points must be actually paid, not discounted.[231]

In the case of refinancing, however, the IRS has held in Rev. Rul. 87-22[232] that points paid upon refinancing are ineligible for immediate deduction except to the extent that the proceeds are used for improvements rather than to pay off the prior loan. The Tax Court has agreed with the IRS;[233] however, the Eighth Circuit has disagreed, reasoning that IRC § 461(g) merely requires that the indebtedness be incurred "in connection" with the purchase.[234]

---

[227] Accordingly, a cash basis taxpayer achieves nothing by prepaying interest that will be earned during the year. It can, however, defer until the succeeding year the deduction for such interest by postponing payment until that year. It might be worth incurring some cost to do so.

[228] *See* Rev. Rul. 83-84, 1983-1 CB 97 (economic accrual for both cash and accrual basis taxpayers).

[229] IRC § 461(g)(2).

[230] Rev. Proc. 87-15, 1987-1 CB 624.

[231] *See* Rev. Proc. 87-15, 1987-1 CB 624, § 3.02.

[232] 1987-1 CB 146.

[233] *Beek v. Comm'r*, 80 T.C. 1024 (1983).

[234] *Huntsman v. Comm'r*, 91 T.C. 917 (1988), *rev'd*, 905 F.2d 1182 (8th Cir. 1990) (part of loan settlement charges treated as points in connection with refinancing a taxpayer's home loan was not currently deductible, since the transaction was not to buy the principal residence, but to pay off the first loan, so the exception did not apply). Although the IRS disagrees with *Huntsman*, it decided not to appeal because the issue lacked administrative importance. The IRS will not follow *Huntsman* outside of the Eighth Circuit. AOD 1991-002. Points paid to refinance a short-term balloon mortgage on a taxpayer's residence should be amortized over the life of the loan.

The IRS has ruled that the Rule of 78's is not allowable for computing an interest expense. Rev. Rul. 83-84, 1983-1 CB 97. Moreover, the IRS has ruled that the Rule of 78's is a method of allocating interest on a loan and represents a purely mechanical formula that has no economic substance.

[B] *Rule of 78's*

[1] Generally

The Rule of 78's is a method of allocating interest on a loan among time periods or installments during the term of the loan. The amount of interest allocable to each period is determined by multiplying the total interest payable over the life of the loan by a fraction. The numerator of the fraction is the number of installment periods remaining on the loan at the time the calculation is made, and the denominator is the sum of the number of installments for the term of the loan.

Even where a loan agreement provides that interest is earned in accordance with the Rule of 78's, no deduction is allowed for interest in excess of the economic accrual of interest.[235]

Economic accrual of interest is determined in accordance with the method used for determining accrual of interest under the original issue discount rules by applying the effective rate of interest to the unpaid balance of the loan for a given period. The effective rate of interest is a uniform rate over the term of the loan and is based on the amount of the loan and the repayment schedule provided in the loan agreement. Accordingly, a debtor (regardless of whether the cash method or accrual method of accounting is used) may deduct in each year only the interest that economically accrues, and may not deduct any additional interest attributable to the Rule of 78's computation. Consider, for example, the following:

Example 5-17

A taxpayer that uses the accrual method of accounting borrows $100,000, payable in 30 annual installments of $12,414 each. The total interest on the loan will be $272,420 (30 × $12,414 = $372,420; $372,420 – $100,000 = $272,420). The terms of the loan state that interest is earned in accordance with the Rule of 78's computation, and the taxpayer computes its annual interest deduction using the Rule of 78's. The effective rate of interest on this loan is 12%. The table below shows the overall transaction.

	Years of Period	Payments	Principal	Interest	Fraction	Interest
1	$100,000	$12,414	$ 414	$12,000	30/465	$17,575
2	99,586	12,414	464	11,950	29/465	16,990
3	99,122	12,414	519	11,895	28/465	16,404
4	98,603	12,414	582	11,832	27/465	15,818
5	98,021	12,414	651	11,763	26/465	15,232

[235] Rev. Rul. 75-541, 1975-2 CB 195.

Years of Period		Payments	Principal	Interest	Fraction	Interest
6	97,370	12,414	730	11,684	25/465	14,646
7	96,640	12,414	817	11,597	24/465	14,061
8	95,823	12,414	915	11,499	23/465	13,474
9	94,908	12,414	1,025	11,389	22/465	12,889
10	93,883	12,414	1,148	11,266	21/465	12,303
11	92,735	12,414	1,286	11,128	20/465	11,717
12	91,449	12,414	1,440	10,974	19/465	11,131
13	90,009	12,414	1,613	10,801	18/465	10,545
14	88,396	12,414	1,806	10,608	17/465	9,959
15	86,590	12,414	2,023	10,391	16/465	9,374
16	84,567	12,414	2,266	10,144	15/465	8,788
17	82,301	12,414	2,538	9,876	14/465	8,202
18	79,763	12,414	2,842	9,572	13/465	7,616
19	76,921	12,414	3,183	9,231	12/465	7,030
20	73,738	12,414	3,565	8,849	11/465	6,444
21	70,173	12,414	3,993	8,421	10/465	5,859
22	66,180	12,414	4,472	7,942	9/465	5,272
23	61,708	12,414	5,009	7,405	8/465	4,687
24	56,699	12,414	5,610	6,804	7/465	4,101
25	51,089	12,414	6,283	6,131	6/465	3,515
26	44,806	12,414	7,037	5,377	5/465	2,930
27	37,769	12,414	7,882	4,532	4/465	2,343
28	29,887	12,414	8,828	3,586	3/465	1,757
29	21,059	12,414	9,887	2,527	2/465	1,172
30	11,172	12,414	11,172	1,242	1/465	586
Totals		372,420	100,000	272,420		272,420

[C] Prepayment of Principal

If an agreement provides that interest is earned under the Rule of 78's, and the borrower amortizes the loan by using the effective rate of interest and the borrower prepays the principal balance (as computed under the Rule of 78's computation), then the excess of the principal balance (as computed under the Rule of 78's computation over the principal balance as shown under the effective rate of interest computation) is deductible as additional interest in the year the prepayment is made. The excess is treated as an additional fee for the use of money.[236] For example, consider the following hypothetical:

Example 5-18

On November 26th, Year 1, an individual, A, borrows $10,000 from a bank to use for home improvements. The terms of the financing agreement provide for a self-amortizing loan with level monthly payments of $222.44 for five years. The amortization schedule implies an effective rate of interest of 12%. The agreement further states that interest is to be earned and principal is to be amortized in accordance with the Rule of 78's method.

On May 26th, Year 4, A prepays the loan in full. In accordance with the loan agreement, the last payment totaled $6,045.53. This amount included the monthly payment of $222.44 and the loan balance of $5,823.09, which was determined by the application of the Rule of 78's.

If the loan had been amortized using the effective interest rate of 12% instead of the Rule of 78's, the last payment would have totaled $5,963.38. This amount includes the monthly payment of $222.44 and the loan balance of $5,740.94, determined using an amortization schedule based upon the effective interest rate for the loan. Using the Rule of 78's, A's total payment to the lender is $82.15 greater ($6,045.53 – $5,963.38).

During the time the loan was outstanding, A did use the effective rate of interest for purposes of determining his deduction for interest expense. Accordingly, A may deduct the $82.15 excess as interest expense in Year 4.[237]

---

[236] Rev. Rul. 68-643, 1968-2 CB 76.

[237] Rev. Rul. 86-42, 1986-1 CB 82.

§ 5.07 Limitation on Cash Method's Use

[A] Generally

As previously described, the cash method has a history of abuse. Consequently, there have been a number of congressional responses to deal with these abuses.

[B] IRC § 467 Rental Agreements

IRC § 467 requires a lessor and lessee of tangible property to treat rents consistently and to use the accrual method of accounting (and time value of money principles) regardless of their overall method of accounting. In addition, in certain cases involving tax avoidance, the lessor and lessee must take rent and stated or imputed interest into account under a constant rental accrual method, pursuant to which the rent is treated as accruing ratably over the entire lease term.

IRC § 467 applies only to leases (or other similar arrangements) that constitute § 467 rental agreements. The term § 467 rental agreement means a rental agreement that has increasing or decreasing rents or deferred or prepaid rents.[238]

Example 5-19

A and B enter into a rental agreement that provides for a ten-year lease of personal property, beginning on January 1, 2020, and ending on December 31, 2029. The rental agreement provides for accruals of rent of $10,000 during each month of the lease term. Under the regulations, $120,000 is allocated to each calendar year. The rental agreement provides for a $1,200,000 payment on December 31, 2020.

The rental agreement does not have increasing or decreasing rent as described in the regulations. The rental agreement, however, provides for prepaid rent under the regulations because the cumulative amount of rent payable as of the close of a calendar year exceeds the cumulative amount of rent allocated as of the close of the succeeding calendar year. For example, the cumulative amount of rent payable as of the close of 2020 ($1,200,000 is payable on December 31, 2020) exceeds the cumulative amount of rent allocated as of the close of 2021, the succeeding calendar year ($240,000). Accordingly, the rental agreement is an IRC § 467 rental agreement.

IRC § 467 lease rules do not apply to any amount to be paid for the use of property if the sum of the following amounts does not exceed $250,000:[239]

---

[238] Reg. § 1.467-1(c).
[239] IRC § 467(d)(2).

- the aggregate amount of payments received as consideration for the use of the property, and
- the aggregate value of any other consideration to be received for the use of the property.

Thus, under the regulations, a rental agreement is not an IRC § 467 rental agreement if, as of the "agreement date" it is not reasonable to expect that the sum of the aggregate amount of rental payments under the rental agreement and the aggregate value of all other consideration to be received for the use of property will exceed $250,000, taking into account payments of contingent rent, and other contingent consideration.

Additionally, IRC § 467 imposes recapture rules on the lessor upon the disposition of the property, which are in addition to other recapture rules imposed by the Code.[240]

[C] IRC § 448 Entity Limitations

IRC § 448 provides that the following "entities" cannot use the cash method of accounting:

- C corporations,
- Partnerships that have C corporations as partners, and
- Tax shelters.

The cash method may be used, however, by individuals, S corporations (regardless of their gross receipts), and qualifying partnerships, as well as by qualified personal service corporations.[241]

The Tax Cuts and Jobs Act (TCJA) expanded the general limit on the use of the cash method for tax years beginning after December 31, 2017. Under revised IRC § 448, a C corporation or a partnership with a C corporation partner that meets a gross receipts test can qualify to use the cash method of accounting.[242] A C corporation or a partnership with a C corporation partner meets the gross receipts test for a tax year if its average annual gross receipts for the three-tax-year period that ends with the tax year preceding such tax year do not exceed $26 million.[243] The average

---

[240] An IRC § 467 rental agreement is a rental agreement

(1) for the use of tangible property,
(2) to which the no-more-than $250,000 exception, doesn't apply, and
(3) under which there are either:

(a) one or more amounts allocable to the use of property during a calendar year that are to be paid after the close of the calendar year following the calendar year of the use of the property
(b) increases in the amount to be paid as rent
(c) prepaid rents or
(d) decreasing rents.

[241] *See* § 5.07[D], *infra*.

[242] IRC § 448(b)(3), *as amended by* the TCJA.

[243] IRC § 448(c)(1), *as amended by* the TCJA.

annual gross receipts amount of $26 million is adjusted for inflation for tax years beginning after December 31, 2018, using the Chained Consumer Price Index for All Urban Consumers (C-CPIU) in the cost-of-living adjustment.[244]

Notwithstanding, as with the prior law, tax shelters are not allowed to use the cash method even if they meet the gross receipts test.[245] Taxpayers subject to IRC § 448 that (1) are engaged in service businesses and provide qualified services or (2) meet the IRC § 448(c) gross receipts test, may adopt a special "nonaccrual experience method" to account for receivables, under which they may defer the accrual of a portion of their receivables that, based on their experience, will not be collected, in effect providing such taxpayers with an indirect reserve for bad debts.[246]

Steps for the Gross Receipts Test.

- determine gross receipts for each year in the three-tax-year period;
- compute the average annual gross receipts for the three-tax-year period; and
- determine if the average annual gross receipts for the three-tax-year period are $26 million or less (to be adjusted for inflation for tax years beginning after 2018).

PRACTICE NOTE

Many additional C corporations and partnerships with a corporate partner will be able to use the cash method under the $26 million gross receipts test since the prior test capped the amount of qualifying annual gross receipts at only $5 million.

PRACTICE NOTE

The other exceptions to the general limitation on the use of the cash method continue to apply for qualified personal service corporations and taxpayers other than C corporations. Thus, qualified personal service corporations, partnerships without C corporation partners, S corporations, and other passthrough entities are allowed to use the cash method without regard to whether they meet the $26 million gross receipts test if the cash method clearly reflects income and the entity is not a tax shelter.[247]

---

244 IRC § 448(c)(4), *as added by* the TCJA.

245 IRC § 448(a)(3).

246 For a futher discussion of the non-accrual experience method, *see* § 6.02[L], *infra.*

247 Conference Report on H.R. 1, Tax Cuts and Jobs Act (H. Rept. 115-466).

PRACTICE NOTE

The three-year testing ends with the tax year *before* the tax year for which the taxpayers are being tested and not, as under the prior law, with the tax year for which the taxpayers are being tested.

Example 5-20

Assume that in 2018, X has gross receipts of $23 million. In 2019, its gross receipts were $24 million and in 2020, its gross receipts were $30 million. The gross receipts test is applied for the period during which X has average annual gross receipts for the three-taxable-year period ending with 2020 of $25.6667 million (($23 million + $24 million + $30 million) ÷ 3). Thus, for taxable year 2021, this section applies and X must change from the cash method for such year. For the tax years preceding 2020, the average annual gross receipts did not exceed $26 million.

Accounting method changes. The TCJA amends IRC § 448(d)(7) by providing that the accounting method change rules in IRC § 448(d)(7) apply to *any* change made under IRC § 448(d)(7). The TCJA also removes the IRC § 481(a) adjustment rules that were provided by IRC § 448(d)(7) under the prior law for changes to which accounting method changes rules in IRC § 448(d)(7) apply.

The special IRC § 481 adjustment periods for IRC § 448 accounting method changes of up to four years and up to ten years for a hospital have been eliminated for tax years beginning after December 31, 2017.

The accounting method changes to which IRC § 448(d)(7) applies continue to be treated is made with IRS consent.[248]

Large farming corporations.

Prior Law: Large C corporations and partnerships with a C corporation partner that are engaged in the trade or business of farming were generally required to use the accrual method.[249] Farming C corporations and farming partnerships with a C corporation partner that meet a $1 million gross receipts test and family farming C corporations that meet a $26 million gross receipts test were not required to use the accrual method and could use the cash method instead.[250] Exceptions to the required use of the accrual method also applied for certain types of farming businesses.

The TCJA expanded the ability of farming C corporations (and farming partnerships with C corporation partners) that can use the cash method. Under the expanded rule, for tax years beginning after December 31, 2017, a farming C

---

248 *See* DCN #34 and 122 in the instructions to Form 3115.

249 IRC § 447(a).

250 IRC § 447(d).

corporation or a farming partnership in which a C corporation is a partner can use the cash method if it meets the $26 million gross receipts test.[251]

Example 5-21

F corporation is engaged in farming and is not a family corporation. After taking into account aggregation rules (IRC § 448(c)), F has gross income of $20 million in 2017, $25 million in 2018, and $30 million in 2019. Because F's gross receipts for 2017, 2018, and 2019 do not exceed 25 million, IRC § 447 does not require F to use the accrual method in 2020.

Accounting method changes. The TCJA replaces the prior law accounting method change rules in IRC § 447 with a rule that states that the accounting method change rules apply to any change made under IRC § 447 and is treated as initiated by the taxpayer with the Commissioner's consent.[252]

Proposed reliance regulations on small business tax accounting rules.[253] In July 2020, the IRS issued proposed reliance regulations that: (a) implement legislative changes to IRC § § 263A, 448, 460, and 471 that simplify the application of those tax accounting provisions for certain businesses having average annual gross receipts that do not exceed $25,000,000 ($26,000,000 in 2020), adjusted for inflation and (b) contain special accounting rules for long-term contracts under IRC § 460 to implement legislative changes applicable to corporate taxpayers.

The Tax Cuts and Jobs Act (P.L. 115-97) made changes to small taxpayer exceptions from the IRC § 448 cash method of accounting restriction, the IRC § 263A uniform capitalization (UNICAP) rules, the IRC § 460(e) restrictions on the completed contract method of accounting, and the IRC § 471 inventory accounting rules. One of the changes was to make a uniform threshold for qualifying as a small taxpayer under these provisions, *i.e.*, average annual gross receipts that do not exceed $25,000,000, adjusted for inflation.[254]

The TCJA made additional amendments to the IRC § 460 rules for long-term contracts to reflect the fact that the TCJA repealed the corporate alternative minimum tax (AMT) imposed by IRC § 55 and added the base erosion anti-abuse tax.[255]

The proposed regulations make numerous changes to existing regulations to implement the above changes made by the TCJA.

IRC § 448 proposed regulations. IRC § 448(a) generally prohibits C corporations, partnerships with a C corporation as a partner, and tax shelters from using the cash receipts and disbursements method of accounting (cash method). However, IRC § 448(b)(3) provides that IRC § 448(a) does not apply to C corporations, and partner-

---

[251] IRC § 447(c), *as amended by* the TCJA.

[252] IRC § 447(d), *as amended by* the TCJA.

[253] Preamble to Prop Reg. REG-132766-18; Prop Reg. § § 1.448-1, 1.448-2, 1.448-3, 1.471-1.

[254] TCJA Sec. 13102.

[255] IRC § 59A. TCJA Sec. 12001 and TCJA Sec. 14401.

ships with a C corporation as a partner, that meet the IRC § 448(c) gross receipts test. This gross receipts test also requires the aggregation of gross receipts for all persons treated as a single employer under IRC § § 52(a), 52(b), 414(m) or 414(o) (aggregation rule).[256]

Section 13102(a) of the TCJA amended the IRC § 448(c) gross receipts test to permit a taxpayer (other than a tax shelter) to meet the test if the taxpayer's average annual gross receipts for the three-taxable-year period ending with the year preceding the current tax year does not exceed $25 million and indexed the $25 million threshold for inflation (IRC§ 448 small business taxpayer exemption).

Aggregation rule. The proposed regulations clarify that the gross receipts of a C corporation partner are included in the gross receipts of a partnership if the aggregation rules apply to the C corporation partner and the partnership.[257]

Changing to and from the cash method. Prior to its amendment by the TCJA, a taxpayer met the gross receipts test of IRC § 448(c) if its average annual gross receipts did not exceed $5 million for all prior three-taxable-year periods. Once a taxpayer's average annual gross receipts had exceeded $5 million, a taxpayer was prohibited under IRC § 448 from using the cash method for all subsequent tax years.

The TCJA removed the requirement under IRC § 448(c) that all prior tax years of a taxpayer must satisfy the IRC 448(c) gross receipts test for the taxpayer to qualify for the cash method for tax years beginning after December 31, 2017.

A taxpayer that meets the IRC § 448(c) gross receipts test in the current tax year must obtain the written consent from IRS before changing to the cash method if the taxpayer had previously changed its overall method from the cash method during any of the five tax years ending with the current tax year.[258] The IRS reasons that a taxpayer that makes multiple changes in its overall method of accounting within a short period of time may not be treating items of income and expense consistently from year to year, and a change back to the cash method within the five-year period may not clearly reflect income, as required by Reg. § 1.446-1(a)(2), even if IRC § 448 otherwise does not prohibit the use of the cash method.[259]

The proposed Regulations also do not contain specific procedures to make a method change from the cash method to a permissible method. The IRS has determined that providing a single procedure in administrative guidance, such as Rev. Proc. 2015-13 (or any successor) will reduce confusion for taxpayers wishing to make voluntary changes in a method of accounting, ensuring compliance with IRC § 448.[260]

[D] Qualified Personal Service Corporations

Even if a corporation is a "C" corporation and its average annual gross receipts exceed $26 million, it may be permitted to use the cash method if it is a qualified

---

[256] IRC § 448(c)(2).

[257] Preamble to Prop Reg. REG.-132766-18.

[258] Prop. Reg. § 1.448-2(g)(3).

[259] Preamble to Prop Reg. REG.-132766-18.

[260] Preamble to Prop Reg. REG.-132766-18.

personal service corporation.[261] A corporation is treated as a qualified personal service corporation if it meets both a functional and an ownership test.

Functional test. The functional test is met if substantially all of the corporation's activities involve the performance of services in certain fields,[262] including the fields of accounting, actuarial services, architecture, consulting, engineering, health, law, or the "performing arts."

If substantially all of a corporation's activities involve the performance of "consulting" services, the functional test is satisfied. Consider the following two examples.

Example 5-22

A taxpayer is in the business of providing economic analyses and forecasts of business prospects for its clients. Based on these analyses and forecasts, the taxpayer advises its clients on their business activities. The taxpayer may analyze, for example, the economic conditions and outlook for a particular industry that a client is considering entering. The taxpayer will then make recommendations and advise the client on the prospects of entering the industry, as well as on other matters regarding the client's activities in the industry. The taxpayer provides similar services to other clients, involving, for example, economic analyses and evaluations of business prospects in different areas of the United States or in other countries, or economic analyses of overall economic trends and the provision of advice based on these analyses and evaluations.

The taxpayer is engaged in the performance of services in the field of consulting.

---

[261] IRC § 448(b)(2).

[262] IRC § 448(d)(2); Temp. Reg. § 1.448-1T(e)(4). Substantially all of the activities of a corporation are involved in the performance of services in [a qualifying field], only if 95% or more of the time spent by employees of the corporation, serving in their capacity as such, is devoted to the performance of services in a qualifying field. For purposes of determining whether this 95-percent test is satisfied, the performance of any activity incident to the actual performance of services in a qualifying field is considered the performance of services in that field. Activities incident to the performance of services in a qualifying field include the supervision of employees engaged in directly providing services to clients, and the performance of administrative and support services incident to such activities. Pursuant to IRC § 11(b)(2), a qualified personal services corporation is subject to a flat rate 21% corporate income tax. *See Alron Engineering & Testing Corp. v Comm'r*, T.C. Memo. 2000-335 (corporation was not a qualified personal services corporation because engineering services did not constitute "substantially all" of the services it provided). *But see Grutman-Mazler Engineering, Inc. v. Comm'r*, T.C. Memo. 2008-140.

Example 5-23

A taxpayer is in the business of providing services that consist of determining a client's electronic data processing needs. The taxpayer studies and examines the client's business, focusing on the types of data and information relevant to the client and the needs of the client's employees for accessing this information. The taxpayer then makes recommendations regarding the design and implementation of data processing systems intended to meet the needs of the client. The taxpayer does not, however, provide the client with additional computer programming services distinct from the recommendations made by the taxpayer with respect to the design and implementation of the client's data processing systems.

The taxpayer is engaged in the performance of services in the field of consulting.

The IRS has stated that the term "performing arts" is defined generally as arts, such as, drama, dance and music, which involve performance before an audience. Persons who perform services related to the performing arts but who do not perform before an audience will not be considered to perform services in the field of performing arts.[263]

Ownership test. The ownership test generally limits stock ownership to certain types of persons. The "ownership test" requires that 95% of the entity's stock be owned directly or indirectly by:

- Current or retired employees,
- The estate of a current (for two years from his or her death) or retired employee, or
- Persons who acquire the stock by reason of death of such employees.[264]

"Indirect" ownership interests may be held through a partnership, an S corporation, another qualified personal service corporation, or a grantor trust. No other form of attribution applies; however, community property laws are disregarded.[265] Stock held in a qualified plan is treated as held by the employee.[266]

---

[263] *See* TAM 9416006, holding that a corporation that employed the services of a motion picture director could not use the cash method. Note that the performance of services in the field of the performing arts does not include the provision of services by persons who broadcast or otherwise disseminate the performances of such artists to members of the public (*e.g.*, employees of a radio station that broadcasts the performances of musicians and singers).

[264] Temp. Reg. § 1.448-1T(e)(5).

[265] Temp. Reg. § 1.448-1T(e)(5)(iii), § 1.448-1T(e)(5)(iv).

[266] Temp. Reg. § 1.448-1T(e)(5)(v).

6

The Accrual Method

§6.01 Generally

The accrual method is authorized as a permissible method of accounting in IRC §446(c). It was authorized by Congress "to enable taxpayers to keep their books and make their returns according to scientific accounting principles by charging against income earned during the taxable period, the expenses incurred in and properly attributable to the process of earning income during the period."[1] Unlike the cash method of accounting, the accrual method of accounting generally does not concern itself with when taxpayers actually receive payment for goods or services. Most

---

[1] *United States v. Anderson*, 269 U.S. 422, 440 (1926).

businesses use the accrual method for tax purposes. Some are required to do so because they are C corporations, partnerships with a C corporation as a partner, or tax shelters[2] or because they are required to maintain inventories.[3] While the accrual method bears resemblance to GAAP (Generally Accepted Accounting Principles), there are many differences. The IRS views the accrual method as the most accurate method of tax accounting. It is often used by the IRS to challenge a taxpayer's use of the cash method. The accrual method usually requires more record keeping than the cash method and is more complex than the cash method.

The TCJA greatly expanded the ability of taxpayers to use the cash method. Taxpayers who sell merchandise and would otherwise be required to maintain inventories, who have a tax year beginning after December 31, 2017, and who have average annual gross receipts under $26 million for 2019 and 2020 can use the cash method.[4] Accordingly, these taxpayers can use a method of accounting for inventory that either (1) treats inventories as non-incidental materials and supplies, or (2) conforms to the taxpayer's financial accounting treatment of inventory either as an "applicable financial statement" as defined in IRC § 451(b)(3) or conforms to the taxpayer's books and records. Any change in method of accounting that a taxpayer makes pursuant to this new rule is treated under IRC § 471(c)(4) as made with the consent of the Secretary.[5]

In 2018, the IRS stated it will grant automatic consent to a taxpayer to change its accounting method situation for income recognition to a method under the new FASB "New Standards" for identifying performance obligations, allocating transaction price to performance obligations, and/or considering performance obligations satisfied.[6]

While not identical to financial accounting, it shares some of the rules and often works in conjunction with financial accounting and GAAP. Under the TCJA, there is even more similarity between GAAP and tax accounting.

[A] How Do Accrual Tax Accounting and Accrual Financial Accounting Differ?

Financial accounting and accrual tax accounting are not the same. Accrual tax accounting usually results in earlier reporting of income and later reporting of expenses than accrual financial accounting.

The TCJA requires a taxpayer to recognize income no later than the tax year in which the income is taken into account as income on (1) an applicable financial statement (AFS) or (2) such other financial statement under rules specified by the IRS.[7] This rule is referred to as "the AFS conformity rule."

---

[2] IRC § 448.

[3] Reg. § 1.446-1(c)(2)(i). *See* § 5.07, *supra.*

[4] IRC § 448(b)(3).

[5] *See* § 6.02[N], *infra.*

[6] Rev. Proc. 2018-29, 2018-22 IRB 634. *See* Chapter 7, *infra.*

[7] IRC § 451(b) *as amended by* 2017 Tax Cuts and Jobs Act § 13221(a).

Specifically, the TCJA provides that, for an accrual basis taxpayer, the all-events test with respect to any item of gross income (or portion thereof) will not be treated as met any later than when that item (or portion thereof) is taken into account as revenue in:[8]

- an applicable financial statement (AFS, defined below) of the taxpayer,[9] or
- such other financial statement as the IRS may specify for purposes of IRC § 451(b).[10]

Thus, the TCJA requires a taxpayer to recognize income no later than the tax year in which that income is taken into account as income on an applicable financial statement (AFS) or another financial statement under rules specified by IRS. For example, under the TCJA, any unbilled receivables for partially performed services must be recognized to the extent the amounts are taken into income for financial statement purposes.[11]

This rule does not apply to:

- a taxpayer which does not have a financial statement described above for a tax year,[12] or
- any item of gross income in connection with a mortgage servicing contract.[13]

Thus, the TCJA requires a taxpayer to recognize income no later than the tax year in which that income is taken into account as income on an applicable financial statement or another financial statement under rules specified by the IRS but provides an exception for long-term contract income to which IRC § 460 applies.

Under the accrual method, income is recognized generally in the year in which:

- The taxpayer has a fixed right to receive income;[14] and
- The amount of income can be determined with reasonable accuracy.

This is referred to as the "All-Events Test." These events need not occur at the same time or in the same year. The determination of whether income is accruable is based on information available to the taxpayer at the end of the tax year.[15]

---

[8] IRC § 451(b)(1)(A).

[9] IRC § 451(b)(1)(A)(i).

[10] IRC § 451(b)(1)(A)(ii).

[11] Com Rep, *see* ¶ 5043.

[12] IRC § 451(b)(1)(B)(i).

[13] IRC § 451(b)(1)(B)(ii).

[14] Reg. § 1.446-1(c)(1)(ii) and 1.451-1(a). This rule differs from the financial accounting rule that provides that income is recognized at the time of performance giving rise to income, *e.g.*, when services are performed or goods shipped.

[15] *H.L.S. Excavating v. Comm'r*, T.C. Memo. 1982-454. Subsequent events have no effect on recognition of income. A taxpayer, using an accrual method of accounting, must accrue an item in the year in which the taxpayer acquires a fixed and unconditional right to receive the amount, even though actual payment is to be deferred. There must be no contingency or unreasonable uncertainty qualifying the payment or receipt. Income does not accrue to a taxpayer using an accrual method until there arises in him a fixed or unconditional right to receive it. The time when an item accrues is largely a question of fact, to be determined in each case. *San Francisco Stevedoring Co.*, 8 T.C. 222 (1947). *See also United States v. Anderson*, 269 U.S. 422 (1926); *Continental Tie & Lumber Co. v. United States*, 286 U.S. 290 (1932).

Expenses are deductible generally in the year in which:

- All events have occurred that establish the fact of liability;
- The amount of the liability can be determined with reasonable accuracy;[16] and
- Economic performance has occurred.[17]

These general rules are subject to modification by a number of specific provisions of the Code, regulations and other pronouncements.

The TCJA amended IRC § 451 by redesignating IRC § 451(b) through (i) as IRC § 451(c) through (j) and adding a new IRC § 451(b) that provides:

> (b) Inclusion not later than for financial accounting purposes.
> (1) Income taken into account in financial statement.
> (A) In general. In the case of a taxpayer the taxable income of which is computed under an accrual method of accounting, the all-events test with respect to any item of gross income (or portion thereof) shall not be treated as met any later than when such item (or portion thereof) is taken into account as revenue in—
> (i) an applicable financial statement of the taxpayer, or
> (ii) such other financial statement as the Secretary may specify for purposes of this subsection.

In other words, income inclusion for tax purposes has to match inclusion for certain financial reporting purposes. Thus, taxpayers subject to this rule must include an item in income for tax purposes, upon the earlier satisfaction of the all-events test or recognition of revenue in the applicable financial statements (or other specified financial statement).[18] According to the Conference Report that accompanied the legislation, this means, for example, that any unbilled receivable for partially performed services must be recognized to the extent the amounts are taken into income for financial statement purposes. Income from mortgage servicing contracts is not subject to the new rule. The new rule also does not apply to a taxpayer that does not have either an applicable financial statement or another specified financial statement.[19]

[B] *Treatment of Debt Instruments*

For tax years beginning after 2017[20] (and for tax years beginning after 2018 for income from a debt instrument having original issue discount (OID)), an accrual basis taxpayer has to recognize income no later than the tax year in which the income is taken into account as revenue in:

---

[16] *United States v. Anderson*, 269 U.S. 422 (1926); *Koehring v. United States*, 421 F.2d 715 (Cl. Ct. 1970).

[17] Reg. §§ 1.446-1(c)(1)(ii) and 1.461-1(a)(2); IRC § 461(h).

[18] *See* § 6.02[N], *infra*.

[19] *Id.*

[20] Pub. L. No. 115-97, § 13221(c).

- an applicable financial statement (AFS); or
- another financial statement, as specified by the IRS (AFS income inclusion rule). The all-events test as to any item of gross income (or portion thereof) would not be treated as met any later than when that item (or portion thereof) is taken into account as revenue.[21]

The AFS income inclusion rule generally does not change the treatment of a transaction for federal income tax purposes.[22] For example, a rental agreement that is treated as a lease for federal income tax purposes may be treated as a sale or financing for AFS purposes, or *vice versa*.[23] Similarly, any unbilled receivables for partially performed services have to be recognized to the extent the amounts are taken into income for financial statement purposes because the taxpayer is not changing the treatment of the transaction when it includes in income amounts included in its AFS.[24]

The IRS has issued proposed reliance regulations that provide additional guidance on the application of the AFS income inclusion rule to accrual method taxpayers.[25] The proposed regulations confirm that the AFS income inclusion rule applies on an item-by-item basis.[26] Thus, for any taxpayer with an AFS, the all-events test with respect to *any item* of gross income, or portion thereof, is met no later than when that item, or portion thereof, is taken into account as revenue in the taxpayer's AFS.[27] The proposed regulations also provide that the AFS income inclusion rule applies on a year-by-year basis and, thus, an accrual method taxpayer with an AFS in one tax year that does not have an AFS in another tax year has to apply the AFS income inclusion rule in the tax year that it has an AFS, but does not apply the rule in the tax year in which it does not have an AFS.[28]

The AFS income inclusion rule does not apply to (a) a taxpayer that does not have a financial statement described above for a tax year[29] or (b) any item of gross

---

[21] IRC § 451(b)(1)(A).

[22] Prop. Reg. § 1.451-3(e).

[23] Prop. Reg. § 1.451-3(e)(1).

[24] Notice of Proposed Rulemaking, REG-104870-18, Taxable Year of Income Inclusion under an Accrual Method of Accounting, Fed. Reg. Vol. 84, No. 174, p. 47191, Sept. 9, 2019, Explanation of Provisions, Sec. 1.C.

[25] Prop. Reg. § 1.451-3. These regulations are proposed to apply to tax years beginning on or after the date the final regulations are published in the Federal Register. Prop. Reg. § 1.451-3(n)(1). However, in the case of a specified fee, Prop. Reg. § 1.451-3(i)(2) is proposed to apply for a taxpayer's first tax year beginning one year after the date the Treasury decision adopting the regulations as final is published in the Federal Register. Prop. Reg. § 1.451-3(n)(2). Until the final regulations are published, a taxpayer generally may rely on the proposed regulations for tax years beginning after 2017 (or, in the case of the specified credit card fees defined in Prop. Reg. § 1.451-3(i)(2), for tax years beginning after 2018), provided the taxpayer consistently applies all the applicable rules contained in the proposed regulations to all items of income during the tax year. Prop. Reg. § 1.451-3(n)(3)(i).

[26] *See* Notice of Proposed Rulemaking, REG-104870-18, Taxable Year of Income Inclusion under an Accrual Method of Accounting, Fed. Reg. Vol. 84, No. 174, p. 47191, Sept. 9, 2019, Explanation of Provisions, Sec. 1.A.

[27] Prop. Reg. § 1.451-3(b).

[28] Prop. Reg. § 1.451-3(d).

[29] IRC § 451(b)(1)(B)(i).

income in connection with a mortgaging servicing contract;[30] the all-events test rules apply instead. Thus, "normal" mortgage servicing rights are included in income on the earlier of when they are earned or received under the rules below (*i.e.*, not averaged over the life of the mortgage), and "excess" mortgage servicing rights are treated as stripped coupons under IRC § 1286 (and, thus, subject to the OID rules).[31]

[C] Coordination with Special Methods of Accounting

The AFS income inclusion rule also does not apply to any item of gross income for which the taxpayer uses a special method of accounting provided under any provision of Chapter 1 of the IRC governing normal income taxes and surtaxes, other than any provision of part V of subchapter P (capital gains and losses).[32]

§ 6.02 Income Recognition

[A] Fixed Right to Receive Income

The origin and operation of the accrual method of accounting of income was set forth in *Spring City Foundry Co. v. Commissioner*,[33] in which the Supreme Court stated:

> . . . keeping accounts and making returns on the accrual basis, as distinguished from the cash basis, import that it is the right to receive and not the actual receipt that determines the inclusion of the amount in gross income. When the right to receive an amount becomes fixed, the right accrues.[34]

In *Spring City*, the taxpayer kept its books on the accrual method. From March 1920 to September 1920, the taxpayer sold goods to a customer who became indebted to the taxpayer in the amount of $39,983.27, represented by an open account and unsecured notes. In the latter part of 1920, the customer found itself in financial straits. Efforts at settlement failed. The customer filed for bankruptcy and a receiver was appointed. In the spring of 1922, the receiver paid to the customer's creditors, including the taxpayer, a dividend of 15% and, in 1923, a second and final dividend of 12$^1/_2$%. The taxpayer argued before the Supreme Court that, in 1920, the customer's debt was worthless and, therefore, was not recognizable as gross income in that year. The Supreme Court disagreed, holding that the taxpayer's right to the amount due was a

---

[30] IRC § 451(b)(1)(B)(ii).

[31] *Id.*

[32] IRC § 451(b)(2). *See* IRC § 1271 through IRC § 1288, covering special capital gain and loss rules for bonds and other debt instruments, except as provided in IRC § 451(b)(1)(B)(ii).

[33] 292 U.S. 182 (1934).

[34] *Id.* at 184-85.

fixed right in 1920 and, therefore, should have been included in the taxpayer's gross income for that year.[35]

As a practical matter, the IRS will take the position that the right to receive income for an accrual method taxpayer becomes fixed at the earlier of:

- The date required performance occurs,
- The date payment becomes due,[36] or
- The date payment is made.[37]

In determining whether a right to receive income has become fixed, a number of factors should be considered, including:

- Any agreement of the parties;
- The substance of the transaction;
- The time when services are to be rendered or when property is to be delivered;
- Whether contingencies or conditions exist;
- Whether the contingencies are a condition precedent or condition subsequent; and
- Whether a disputed or acknowledged liability exists.

Note, however, that state or local tax refunds are includible in an accrual method taxpayer's income at the *earlier* of either when the taxpayer receives payment or a notice that state authorities have approved the refund claim.[38]

[B] Inclusion on Date of Payment

Under the "claim of right" doctrine, if a taxpayer receives income under a claim of rights and without restriction as to its disposition, it must be reported for federal income tax purposes in the taxable year of receipt even though the taxpayer may claim that it is not entitled to retain income and may in fact, be liable to restore it.[39] In

---

[35] *See also* Rev. Rul. 84-31, 1984-1 CB 127.

[36] Although it could be argued that in particular circumstances income should be recognized at the time payment is due, this would not be appropriate in all cases, such as where accounts receivable are purchased at less than their face amount, and such accounts are already due. *See Rhodes Jennings Furniture Co. v. Comm'r*, 9 TCM 1019 (1950), *aff'd*, 192 F.2d 1022 (6th Cir. 1951).

[37] Rev. Rul. 74-607, 1974-2 CB 149. Rev. Rul. 74-607 has been clarified by Rev. Rul. 83-84, 1983-1 CB 97 and obsoleted by Rev. Proc. 94-29, 1994-1 CB 616. *See also Johnson v. Comm'r*, 184 F.3d 786 (8th Cir. 1999). The objective is to determine at what point in time the seller acquired an unconditional right to receive payment under the contract. *Lucas v. North Texas Lumber Co.*, 281 U.S. 11 (1930).

[38] Rev. Rul. 2003-3, 2003-1 CB 252. Earlier guidance, which was revoked, was predicated on the conclusion that approval by state authorities was ministerial in nature. The IRS now considers state review to be substantive, and not merely procedural. Rev. Rul. 65-190, 1965-2 CB 150, and Rev. Rul. 69-372, 1969-2 CB 104, are revoked. Rev. Proc. 2002-9, 2002-1 CB 327, is modified and amplified. The IRS noted that based on this ruling, it has elsewhere withdrawn its 1988 nonacquiescence in *Doyle, Dane, Bernbach, Inc., v. Comm'r*. 79 T.C. 101 (1982).

[39] *See North American Oil Consolidated v. Burnet*, 286 U.S. 417 (1932). *But see* §6.03 for the treatment of prepaid income.

which case, a deduction will be typically available in the year of repayment.[40] In order for an amount to be includable in the taxpayer's income under the claim of right doctrine, the following requirements must be satisfied:

- the property received is, in fact, income subject to tax (as opposed to nontaxable receipt);
- income must be actually or constructively received;
- the taxpayer treats the funds received as belonging to him and there is no consensual recognition by the taxpayer of an obligation to repay; and
- there is no restriction on disposition of the income by the taxpayer, with such restrictions being substantial enough to deprive the taxpayer of economic benefit of possessing the amounts.[41]

[C] *Inclusion on Date of Payment—Prepaid Income*[42]

A common application of the claim of right doctrine to accrual method taxpayers occurs when the taxpayer receives prepaid income, *i.e.*, amounts that would have been received by the taxpayer during the taxable year on account of services, sale of goods, or other income producing activities, which will be performed in future taxable years (*i.e.*, the income will be "earned" in such later years). In general, the effect of the claim of right doctrine in the case of prepaid income (*i.e.*, service income, advance payment (whether or not refundable) for goods, rents, interest, etc.) is to cause the inclusion of the amount received in taxable income currently even though the income has not yet been earned.[43]

Three major exceptions to this rule apply to advance payments received by an accrual basis taxpayer for tax years beginning after 2017:[44]

- Payments for future goods and services;[45]
- Payments as prepaid subscription income;[46] and
- Payments as prepaid membership income.[47]

These exceptions allow an accrual method taxpayer to defer the accrual of prepaid income.

---

[40] *Id.*

[41] *See Houston Industries Inc. and Subsidiaries v. Comm'r*, 32 Fed. Cl. 202 (Cl. Ct. 1994), *aff'd*, 125 F.3d 1442 (Fed. Cir. 1997) (Cl. Ct. 1994).

[42] *See* § 6.03, *infra*.

[43] *See, e.g., Automobile Club of Michigan v. Comm'r*, 353 U.S. 180 (1957); *American Automobile Association v. United States*, 367 U.S. 687 (1961); Reg. § 1.61-8(b).

[44] Pub. L. No. 115-97, § 13221(c).

[45] IRC § 451(c); Prop. Reg. § 1.451-8; *see* § 6.03[F], *infra*.

[46] *See* § 6.03[J], *infra*.

[47] IRC § 456.

[D] Inclusion on the Date the Amount Is Due

For an amount to be includable on the date that it is due, the following requirements must be satisfied:

- Payment is contemplated on such date under the terms of the arrangement between the taxpayer and the other party;
- Any material contingencies on the taxpayer's eventual receipt of income have been removed, and the other party does not contest the claim;[48] and
- The amount is considered collectible on the date that is due.[49]

The fact that the taxpayer may not be able to legally enforce payment does not preclude inclusion on the date payment was due.[50]

[E] Effect of Signing a Contract

Income is not accruable upon the signing of a contract, but on the date that payment is contemplated under such contract.

In TAM 9533002, the Service ruled that a cemetery company recognizes income from the sale of burial rights in the year the sales contract was executed. The contract provided that no interest in the burial rights vested in the purchaser until the purchase price and finance charges were paid in full. Upon receipt of the entire purchase price, the cemetery issues a "Certificate of Burial Rights" which was equivalent to title. After issuance of a Certificate of Burial Rights, the purchaser could sell those rights to a third party.

The purchaser could pay the remaining balance of the purchase price and the accrued finance charges at any time and obtain the Certificate of Burial Rights. Additionally, where the contract was for burial rights in more than one space, in the event of the death of a member of the purchaser's immediate family, the purchaser was entitled to burial rights with respect to a single space upon payment of the purchase price and finance charge applicable to the single space.

In the event of default by the purchaser, the cemetery had the option to declare the entire balance immediately due and payable and to enforce collection by any legal means, or to cancel the contract and to retain the payments received.

The Service ruled the contract imposed on the seller an absolute and enforceable obligation to convey title and full payment; the contract gave the seller an absolute right to receive the contract price; and the contract gave the seller an absolute right to interest on unpaid portions of the purchase price.

---

[48] *See* Priv. Ltr. Rul. 9434013 where the final payment under a settlement agreement was not accruable in income until received because the suit involving the claim was not concluded at that time.

[49] FSA 199904031, FSA 74, Vaughn #74.

[50] *See* Rev. Rul. 83-106, 1983-2 CB 77.

[F] Inclusion on the Date the Amount Is Earned

In order for an amount to be includable on the date on which it is earned, the following requirements must be satisfied:

(1) Performance has taken place on the part of the taxpayer, which is determined as follows:
- Income from services accrues when performance is completed (rather than as a taxpayer engaged in the activity);[51]
- Income from the sale of goods is earned when the sale takes place;[52]
- At the taxpayer's option, either shipment, delivery, acceptance, or when title passes to the customer; and
- Interest and rents are earned with the passage of time.

(2) Any material contingencies on the taxpayer's eventual receipt of income have been removed; and the claim is not being contested by the other party (for example, retainage or situations where the ultimate receipt of income is contingent upon future earnings or future events).

(3) The amount is considered collectible on the data that is due.

Income recognition cannot be deferred where ministerial acts affect only the timing of payment.[53] An exception is in the case of magazines and books.[54]

In CCA 200721016, the Service ruled that an accrual method taxpayer had income from the sale of permanent seat licenses (PSLs) when each installment payment became due and payable or each installment payment was received, whichever happened first. The taxpayer had limited recourse rights if a payment was not made by the purchaser. The Service said that a taxpayer's performance under the contract occurred when all payments are made. As the performance requirement was not met until payment of the final installment, the Service concluded that the taxpayer must properly accrue income as each installment is due and payable, or payment is made, whichever occurred first.

---

[51] However, if services are "severable," a portion of the income is properly allocated to each service provided under the contract *See Decisions, Inc.*, 47 T.C. 58 (1966), *acq.*, 1967-2 CB 2, where there was no severability. *But see* Rev. Rul. 79-195, 1979-1 CB 177, where severability was found to exist.

[52] Unless there is an advance payment treated differently under Prop. Reg. § 1.451-8. *See* § 6.03[H], *infra.*

[53] Even if the terms of the sales agreement made acceptance of the system a condition precedent to the right to receive the income, formal acceptance would generally not be required for the right to the income to attach. *See Dally v. Comm'r*, 227 F.2d 724 (9th Cir. 1955) (contractor's right to income was in the year it delivered a house, not in a later year when a properly certified invoice was submitted, even though the contract specifically provided for payment upon the submission of a properly certified invoice); Rev. Rul. 98-39, 1998-2 CB 198 (accrual method manufacturer's liability to pay a retailer for cooperative advertising services is incurred in the year the services are performed, not when the required claim form is submitted). The return of an acceptance form by the customer is merely a ministerial act, and is not required to establish taxpayer's right to the income under the all-events test.

[54] *See* TAM 9143083.

In FSA 74, Vaughn #74, the Service advised that initiation fees charged by a health club, payable in monthly increments, are accruable when a member contract is signed, rather than as paid each month.

The club gave new members the option of paying their initiation fees and annual dues in a lump sum at the beginning of the contractual term or in monthly installments. The initiation fees were larger than annual dues and, as stated in each new member contract, were generally nonrefundable because the club incurs most of its cost of enrolling and servicing new members in the first 30 days.[55] Because the contracts required that the initiation fees relate to services provided during the first month of the contracts, and because performance with respect to initiation fees occur during the first month, the fees accrue at that time even if payment was made later.[56]

In *Commercial Solvents Corporation v. Commissioner*,[57] the taxpayer was using the accrual method and entered into an agreement with a Canadian corporation (Northwest) to manage Northwest's business for an annual fee. The fee was to commence when commercial production of Northwest began. The latter occurred on December 1, 1956. On December 31, 1956, petitioner had a fixed and unconditional right to receive its fee. Beginning in 1957, Northwest was in financial difficulties. During 1957, it borrowed approximately $4,500,000 from a bank. The bank, as a condition for granting the loans, required petitioner to agree not to collect its fee as long as Northwest was indebted to the bank. On December 31, 1957, Northwest still owed the bank over $2,300,000. The Tax Court held:

- the fee for December 1956 was accruable as income taxable to petitioner in 1956, and
- the fee for the calendar year 1957 was not accruable as income taxable to petitioner in 1957.

In *United States v. Harmon*,[58] a contractor did construction work for the United States. All of the contracts were cost plus fixed fee contracts. The contracts provided for a fixed fee and for the advancement from time to time of the construction costs and periodical payments on the fixed fee. The contracts also provided that the government should retain 30% of the fixed fee and pay it to the Contractor upon a final acceptance of the work by the government. The construction work on all three projects was completed in the latter part of 1943 subject to the approval of several governmental agencies.

---

[55] The contract terms were: (1) The initiation fee was generally nonrefundable since the club incurs most of its costs of enrolling and servicing the new member in the first thirty days; (2) "Buyer agreed that the initiation fee is due and owing to Seller upon signing the agreement in consideration of the fact that Seller will expend substantially all the costs of enrolling and servicing the new member within thirty days"; and (3) "Buyer agreed that the initiation fee covered Seller's cost of enrolling Member and providing initial services, was non-refundable, and, if financed must be paid in cash or on the following terms set out below regardless of the duration of membership."

[56] FSA 74, Vaughn # 74. In FSA 1816, Vaughn #1816, the IRS held that the recreational facility membership initiation deposits are not includible in income in the year of receipt or should be treated as nontaxable deposits or loans as they were refundable and the taxpayer had no guarantee that it could keep the membership fees.

[57] 42 T.C. 455 (1964).

[58] 205 F.2d 919 (10th Cir. 1953).

The taxpayer kept his books on an accrual basis. The court determined that during 1943 the taxpayer did not have the right to receive a definite, certain amount of the retained fee. At the end of 1943, the taxpayer's interest in the retained portion of the fixed fee was subject to set-offs and deductions, if any, which might be revealed by the final audits. A number of things remained to be done upon which the determination of that amount depended. The audits had not been completed. The outstanding claims had not been paid. The taxpayer's right to be credited with all these claims had not been finally determined. These matters were not determined until in 1944 and until that was done the taxpayer's interest in the amount of the fixed fee remaining in the government's hands was not established with finality and certainty.

Accordingly, an unconditional liability on the part of the government to pay the taxpayer a fixed and definite sum did not arise in 1943. It could not arise until all audits had been completed and an adjustment with respect to claims had been made. This did not occur until 1944 and as a result, no income tax liability arose with respect to the amount in question until in 1944.

Note

The fact that a liability may never be paid does not prevent its accrual, if there is a reasonable expectation at the time of the accrual that it will be paid.[59]

On the other hand, if there is no reasonable expectation a liability will be paid, then a taxpayer may not accrue the liability. Thus, a taxpayer was not allowed to accrue a deduction for his share of rental expenses of a partnership in which he was a general partner, where the rental expenses became due under an "acceleration clause" as a result of the partnerships' default under the relevant leases, but the partners themselves had ceased operating and were insolvent and the taxpayer himself was bankrupt.[60]

[G] Conditions Precedent

A condition precedent is a condition in a contract that must take place before a party to a contract must perform. Conditions precedent can prevent the accrual of income.[61]

---

[59] *Helvering v. Russian Finance & Construction Corp.*, 77 F.2d 324 (2d Cir. 1935).

[60] *In re J.C. Investments Inc.*, 15 BR 392, 81-2 USTC ¶ 9775 (Bankr. M.D. Fla. 1981).

[61] Ballantine's Law Dictionary (1969). *See also* http://dictionary.law.com/Default.aspx?typed=condition%20precedent&type=1.

Conditions precedent preventing the accrual of income in the following:

- Goods sold on approval;[62]
- Goods rejected under the UCC or goods sold on a C.O.D. basis;[63] and
- Disputes that remain unresolved.[64]

In *Ringmaster, Inc.*,[65] the taxpayer contracted for the sale of ring binders to the United States. The contract in question provided that all supplies shall be subject to inspection and testing by the government prior to final acceptance. The government also expressly reserved the right to terminate the contract. The court held that these provisions operated to create a condition precedent, which prevented a completed sales transaction from arising until inspection and tests had been made. In contrast, the taxpayer's sales agreements pass title, risk of loss, and the benefits and burdens of ownership when the goods were shipped, not when the customer accepted the goods, and the customer's right to terminate the agreement or reject the goods was limited.

Likewise, where a taxpayer's right to income is conditioned on the approval of a third party and that approval is not yet obtained, the income will not be considered to have accrued.[66]

Example 6-1

Mary is in the business of manufacturing Faberge Egg replicas. Tom ordered one each of the Imperial Easter Egg, the Mozart Egg, and the Elephant Egg. All three eggs were shipped to Tom on December 31, 2020 on condition that payment would not be required if the eggs did not meet with Tom's satisfaction. Each egg sold for a price of $2,500. How much should Mary record as income from the sale in the year 2020?

Mary will not have to record the sale if her right to the income has not been fixed before year-end. In determining whether a right to receive income has become fixed, a number of factors must be examined including whether contingencies or conditions exist.

As the goods are "shipped on approval" *i.e.*, Tom's approval, if Tom disapproves the shipment, then Mary will not have to record income in 2020.[67]

---

[62] *Ringmaster, Inc. v. Comm'r*, T.C. Memo. 1962-187, 21 TCM 1024 (1962), where income did not accrue since the buyer had not committed to purchase goods until he approved them as meeting specifications.

[63] Rev. Rul. 70-68, 1970-1 CB 122.

[64] Rev. Rul. 2003-10, 2003-1 CB 288.

[65] *Ringmaster, Inc. v. Comm'r*, T.C. Memo. 1962-187, 21 TCM 1024 (1962).

[66] *United States v. Safety Car Heating and Lighting Co.*, 297 U.S. 88 (1936); *Mutual Tel. Co. v. United States*, 204 F.2d 160 (9th Cir. 1953).

[67] *Ringmaster, Inc. v. Comm'r*, T.C. Memo. 1962-187, 21 TCM 1024 (1962), *dismissed per curiam*, 319 F.2d 860 (8th Cir. 1963); *Webb Press Co. Ltd. v. Comm'r*, 3 BTA 247 (1925), *acq.* 1927-1 CB 6.

The voluntary payment of dues and whether such was a condition precedent was discussed in *Billings v. Campbell, Jr.*,[68] where the plaintiff brought an action to recover $56.00 which was 20% of $280.00 paid by the plaintiff as an allegedly voluntary contribution to the Brookhaven Country Club. He was assessed and paid such amount and brought suit to recover the payment. A like assessment was made against the other members of the Brookhaven Country Club.

In organizing the club, it was necessary for the members to raise the necessary funds to acquire the property for the club and to make the improvements thereon. Each person intending to be a member did this, or was willing to do so, by "contributing" $280.00. At the time they were organized, it was a less sum, but at the time that Billings paid his excise tax it was $280.00. Although it was supposed to have been a voluntary contribution, all contributors who contributed uniformly used the same figure, namely, $280.00.

The issue was whether the payment of these contributions was a condition precedent to becoming members of the club. In other words, was the initiation fee supposedly due by every incoming member really a condition precedent to being a member and for some convenience or other reason called a contribution? The court noted that these contributions became assets and were used for purchasing their building.

The court ruled:

> . . . that these voluntary contributions performed every function of an initiation fee regularly charged and called as such and that designating it under a different title in no way lessens its importance or diminishes its value or function. To use an old vernacular, the rose smells just as sweet by some other name. This excise tax it appears is paid by other similar country clubs and organizations of that type, and calling it by a different name doesn't excuse the membership of paying the excise tax imposed by law.

Hence, there did not exist a condition precedent which would prevent accrual of income.[69]

On the other hand, some conditions precedent will not prevent the accrual of income. For example, the need to perform a mathematical calculation will not prevent accrual.[70] Similarly, in *Charles Schwab Corp. v. Commissioner*,[71] the Supreme

---

[68] 188 F. Supp. 261 (N.D. Tex. 1960).

[69] *Id.*

[70] *Resale Mobile Homes, Inc. v. Comm'r*, 965 F.2d 818 (10th Cir. 1992), *cert. denied*, 506 U.S. 874 (1992). *See also Perry Funeral Home, Inc. v. Comm'r*, T.C. Memo. 2003-340, 86 TCM 713 (2003), where the taxpayer entered into preneed funeral contracts and received payments in advance of death for goods and services to be provided later at the contract beneficiary's death. These payments were refundable at the contract purchaser's request, pursuant to state law, at any time until the goods and services were furnished. Perry, an accrual basis taxpayer, included these payments in income not in the year of receipt but in the year in which the goods and services were provided.

[71] 107 T.C. 282 (1996), *aff'd*, 161 F.3d 1231 (9th Cir. 1998), *cert denied*, 528 U.S. 822 (1999). *See also* Rev. Rul. 98-39, 1998-33 IRB 4.

Court held that a brokerage house must accrue commission income on the securities trade date and not the settlement date. The Court said executing a customer's order on the trade date was a condition precedent that fixed the taxpayer's right to receive a commission. The fact that there had to be ministerial functions performed between trade and settlement dates was not sufficient to prevent the accrual of income. The fact that an executed trade could be canceled before settlement did not make the taxpayer's right to the commission indefinite or contingent.

Moreover, once the services were performed, the establishment of the fact of liability under the all-events test was not delayed by an additional requirement in the agreement that a claim or documentation be submitted to obtain payment if such act is ministerial. See *Dally v. Commissioner*,[72] where a contractor's right to income was fixed in the year it delivered houses, not in later year when a properly certified invoice was submitted, even though the contract specifically provided for payment upon the submission of a properly certified invoice.[73]

[H] Conditions Subsequent

A condition subsequent is a condition in a contract which fulfills liability upon the contract and operates to defeat or annul the liability upon subsequent failure of the other party to comply with its terms.[74] Unlike a condition precedent, a condition subsequent does not prevent a taxpayer from accruing income.[75]

A condition subsequent occurs where:

- The taxpayer is required to return any amount that has been received; or
- The taxpayer loses the right to receive income.[76]

Restrictions placed on a fund after a transaction has taken place constitute a condition subsequent, which does not affect the rights of a taxpayer at the point of sale. Income will accrue regardless.[77]

In *Bigler v. Commissioner*,[78] gross income could not be reduced by the value of credits that the taxpayer/corporation might have to give customers if they returned items originally purchased with remanufactured auto parts. The taxpayer did not retain title to the items and had no way of forcing customers to return them, so any liability to eventually supply the credit was contingent on a future event and was not accruable at the point of the original sale.

---

[72] 227 F.2d 724 (9th Cir. 1955), *cert. denied*, 351 U.S. 908 (1956).

[73] *See also Frank's Casing Crew & Rental Tools, Inc. v. Comm'r*, T.C. Memo. 1996-413. where the contractor's preparation and sending of the invoices were ministerial acts that did not postpone accrual of income otherwise earned.

[74] Ballantine's Law Dictionary (1969).

[75] *J.J. Little & Ives Co. v. Comm'r*, T.C. Memo. 1966-68, 25 TCM 372 (1966); Ballantine's Law Dictionary (1969).

[76] *See, e.g., Western Oaks Building Corp. v. Comm'r*, 49 T.C. 365 (1968).

[77] *Id.*

[78] T.C. Memo. 2008-133, 95 TCM 1525.

In *Colonial Wholesale Beverage Corp. v. Commissioner*,[79] a deduction for projected refunds of bottle deposits was not allowed, because the liability to make the refund was contingent upon the customer actually returning the bottle. Moreover, escrows with conditions subsequent do not affect the determination of a closed or open transaction.[80]

Example 6-2

> Slick Steve's is a discount appliance chain. All of his merchandise is sold with a "30 day money back guarantee." On December 31, 2019, Bill Wall purchased a washer for his new home. On January 5, 2020, Bill returned the appliance and received his money back. How should Slick Steve account for the sale?

The condition, *i.e.*, the 30-day money back guarantee is a condition subsequent. Unlike a condition precedent that can prevent accrual of income, a condition subsequent will require that income in the first instance be recognized. These conditions might be:

- That the taxpayer is required to return any amount that might be received, or
- The taxpayer loses a right to receive income that had previously become fixed.

In such event, the return of that item is an expense item, not as unrecorded income.

[I] Passage of Title and Business Practice

The passage of title to goods and the business practice of the taxpayer play an important role in determining when an item of income should accrue. Reg. § 1.446-1(c)(1)(ii)(C) provides, in part:

> No method of accounting is acceptable unless, in the opinion of the Commissioner, it clearly reflects income. The method used by the taxpayer in determining when income is to be accounted for will generally be acceptable if it accords with generally accepted accounting principles, is consistently used by the taxpayer from year to year, and is consistent with the Income Tax Regulations. For example, a taxpayer engaged in a manufacturing business may account for sales of the taxpayer's product

---

[79] T.C. Memo. 1988-405.

[80] *See Consolidated Gas & Equipment Co of America v. Comm'r*, 35 T.C. 675 (1961), where seven-eighths of the price was paid by the buyer and all incidents of ownership in land were transferred to the buyer, but one-eighth of the price was placed in escrow and was to be returned to the buyer if title defects developed that the seller was unable to clear up within one year. The sale was completed when the initial payment was made and the incidents of ownership were transferred. *See also Fletcher, Samuel v. United States*, 71-1 USTC ¶ 9155 (7th Cir. 1971).

> when the goods are shipped, when the product is delivered or accepted, or *when title to the goods passes to the customers* [italics added], whether or not billed, depending on the method regularly employed in keeping the taxpayer's books.

While no single factor is controlling, the passage of title is the most significant factor to be considered in determining whether income has accrued to the taxpayer.[81]

The retail industry. The Internal Revenue Manual provides an analysis of the retail industry and timing of income. A common practice in tax planning is a taxpayer's effort to defer the recognition of income items. Deferring items of income provides an economic benefit to retailers from time value of money. The longer the period between the date an item is received and the date the item is included in gross income, the greater the economic benefit. Indeed in the high inflation years of the 1980's, Congress enacted IRC §461(h) to combat abuses by taxpayers who tried to take advantage of deferring income.

Under accrual basis accounting, the right to receive, not actual receipt, triggers the inclusion of an item in income. Rev. Rul. 74-607[82] provides the right to receive becomes fixed at the earlier of any of the following three events:

- Required performance happens.
- Payment is due.
- Payment is received.

The determination of when a sale occurs (and the right to receive income is fixed) requires consideration of all the facts and circumstances of a particular transaction or arrangement. The terms of a retailer's sales agreement represent the legal rights and obligations of the parties and are relevant in determining when the all-events test is met. Several factors are considered, but no single factor is controlling.

- Passage of title is perhaps the most conclusive circumstance.
- Transfer of possession is also significant.
- Other factors include the existence of conditions precedent or subsequent and whether the right to receive is contested.
- Certainty of receipt, however, has never been a requirement for the accrual of income. Otherwise, an accrual method taxpayer could shift at will the reporting of income from one year to another.

Example 6-3

Songbird, LLC, an accrual method taxpayer, builds and sells homes. Songbird has an arrangement with the Midwestern National Bank that

---

[81] *See, e.g., Hallmark Cards, Inc. v. Comm'r,* 90 T.C. 26 (1988). Also, in *Pacific Grape Products Co. v. Comm'r,* 219 F.2d 862 (9th Cir. 1955), *rev'g* 17 T.C. 1097 (1952), the Court held a fruit canner may accrue income on undelivered orders received and deduct estimated costs where income from the annual pack could be accurately ascertained and the practice had been used by the industry for years.

[82] 1974-2 CB 149.

they will make mortgages covering 80% of the purchase price. Under the loan commitment, Songbird must retain 20% of the purchase price in "reserve" in the event a purchaser defaults. This "reserve" is held by the bank and is released periodically to Songbird as the debt is reduced. How should this "reserve" be handled for tax purposes?

The tax treatment of the reserve has been discussed in a number of "Dealer Reserve" cases. In *Western Oaks Building Corporation v. Commissioner*,[83] the taxpayer-seller received cash from the sale of a house from the purchasers, cash from a savings and loan association on a mortgage loan to the purchaser, and a savings account or savings and loan shares set up in seller's name, restricted so that seller could only withdraw $100 from the account for every $200 paid by the purchaser on the principal of the mortgage loan. In the event that the purchaser defaulted and the seller did not take over the property and the mortgage, the amount in the restricted account would be forfeited. The petitioners were not otherwise liable in case of a default.

The Tax Court held that an accrual method taxpayer was required to include in gross income the face amounts of the savings accounts or savings and loan shares when received, *i.e.*, the full sales price. The restriction, which had nothing to do with the sale, did not prevent accrual of income to the taxpayer. The requirement of a "Reserve" is at best a condition subsequent.

Incorrect amount or quality. In Rev. Rul. 2003-10, discussing disputed liabilities,[84] the Service considered circumstances where a retailer shipped an incorrect amount or quality of goods. It concluded that:

- Under the all-events test of IRC § 451, if a taxpayer using an accrual method of accounting overbills a customer due to a clerical mistake in an invoice and the customer discovers the error and, in the following taxable year, disputes its liability for the overbilled amount, then the taxpayer accrues gross income in the taxable year of sale for the correct amount.

- Under the all-events test of IRC § 451, a taxpayer using an accrual method of accounting does not accrue gross income in the taxable year of sale if, during the taxable year of sale, the customer disputes its liability to the taxpayer because the taxpayer shipped incorrect goods.

- Under the all-events test of IRC § 451, a taxpayer using an accrual method of accounting accrues gross income in the taxable year of sale if the taxpayer ships excess quantities of goods and the customer agrees to pay for the excess quantities of goods.

---

[83] 49 T.C. 365 (1968).

[84] 2003-1 CB 288.

Example 6-4

The Art Mart (a retailer) sells art supplies at retail. On December 31, 2019, the Art Mart receives a check for $1,000 for a quantity of supplies that it has in inventory. The goods are shipped on January 3, 2020. When must the Art Mart recognize gross income?

The passage of title to goods and the business practice of the taxpayer play an important role in determining when an item of income should accrue. Reg. § 1.446-1(c)(1)(ii)(C) provides in part:

> The method used by the taxpayer in determining when income is to be accounted for will generally be acceptable if it accords with generally accepted accounting principles, is consistently used by the taxpayer from year to year, and is consistent with the Income Tax Regulations. For example, a taxpayer engaged in a manufacturing business may account for sales of the taxpayer's product when the goods are shipped, when the product is delivered or accepted, or when *title* to the goods passes to the customers, whether or not billed, depending on the method regularly employed in keeping the taxpayer's books.

While no single factor is controlling, *passage of title is the most significant factor* to be considered.[85] In the case of merchandise, income is generally earned when the sale occurs; consequently, Art Mart must include $1,000 in its 2020 taxable income when the goods are shipped. But under Rev. Rul. 74-607, payment was received in 2019.[86] However, the obvious question is: when does title pass in a commercial transaction? If you follow the ruling, since payment was received in 2019, income must be reported in that year. However, if the payment is an advance payment, Prop. Reg. § 1.451-8 may determine when the item should be included in income.[87]

Article 2-401 of the Uniform Commercial Code, which has been adopted by all states,[88] provides:

> (1) Title to goods cannot pass under a contract for sale prior to their identification to the contract (Article 2-501), and unless otherwise explicitly agreed the buyer acquires by their identification a special property as limited by this Act. Any retention or reservation by the seller of the title (property) in goods shipped or delivered to the buyer is limited in effect to a reservation of a security interest. Subject to these provisions and to the provisions of the Article on Secured Transactions (Article 9), title to goods passes from the seller to the buyer in any manner and on any conditions explicitly agreed on by the parties.

---

[85] *Hallmark Cards, Inc.* 90 T.C. 26 (1988).

[86] 1974-2 CB 149.

[87] *See* § 6.03[F] *infra*.

[88] While the UCC has been adopted in all the states there are some variations.

(2) Unless otherwise explicitly agreed, title passes to the buyer at the time and place at which the seller completes his performance with reference to the physical delivery of the goods, despite any reservation of a security interest and even though a document of title is to be delivered at a different time or place; and in particular and despite any reservation of a security interest by the bill of lading

(a) if the contract requires or authorizes the seller to send the goods to the buyer but does not require him to deliver them at destination, title passes to the buyer at the time and place of shipment; but

(b) if the contract requires delivery at destination, title passes on tender there.

(3) Unless otherwise explicitly agreed where delivery is to be made without moving the goods,

(a) if the seller is to deliver a document of title, title passes at the time when and the place where he delivers such documents; or

(b) if the goods are at the time of contracting already identified and no documents are to be delivered, title passes at the time and place of contracting.

(4) A rejection or other refusal by the buyer to receive or retain the goods, whether or not justified, or a justified revocation of acceptance revests title to the goods in the seller. Such revesting occurs by operation of law and is not a "sale."

One might ask why the UCC is important to tax accounting. An example of its relevance is found in *Epic Metals Corp. & Subs. v. Commissioner*.[89] Epic Metals Corp. ("Sales") was an S corporation which sold products manufactured by its parent EMC ("Manufacturing"). Sales reported its income on the cash method of accounting. Manufacturing reported its income on the accrual method. Manufacturing was engaged in the manufacture and sale of metal products, primarily metal decking, typically custom ordered. It did not sell its fabricated metal decking directly to the ultimate user. Sales, which was a sales company, was a separate corporation. The two corporations filed a consolidated tax return.

Sales derived most of its product of custom fabric metal decking from Manufacturing, which it sold without installation. Sales maintained its orders for metal decking through its own sales department. It did not solicit orders that required installation. In carrying out its business, Sales never had physical possession of the metal decking (or any other inventory). When an order was placed with Manufacturing the order was always shipped FOB[90] fabricator's place of business. The customers always had the right to select the mode of transportation and the specific carrier to transport the goods.

---

[89] T.C. Memo. 1984-322.

[90] Free on board (FOB) is a trade term that indicates whether the seller or the buyer has liability for goods that are damaged or destroyed during shipment between the two parties. "FOB shipping point" (or origin) means that the buyer is at risk while the goods are shipped, and "FOB destination" states that the seller retains the risk of loss until the goods reach the buyer. http://www.investopedia.com/terms/f/fob.asp#ixzz4VJHiRlZh.

A typical transaction between Sales and Manufacturing was where Sales would solicit orders from customers. It would deliver the sales order to Manufacturing that had its own personnel that manufactured the custom fabrication metal decking. Once Manufacturing completed the custom fabrication pursuant to the Sales order, Manufacturing, as directed by Sales, loaded the metal decking onto transportation requested by the customer for shipment to Sales customers' job site. The customer bore the freight charges and had the right to select the method of shipping. Manufacturing then sent an invoice for the metal decking to Sales and Sales paid the invoice. Sales bore the credit risk should the customer default on the contract. Sales declared itself a vendor and received a sales tax exemption from the Pennsylvania tax department.

In its notice of deficiency, the Service determined that the accrual method of accounting should have been used by Sales to properly reflect income. The use of the accrual method of accounting resulted in an increase in Sales' taxable income for the taxable year 1974 of $1,386,605. It also increased for 1976 by $238,037.

Invoking IRC § 471 regarding the requirement to maintain inventories to clearly reflect income, the Commissioner determined that Sales' method of accounting was erroneous.

The court looked to the Pennsylvania Uniform Commercial Code to determine when title passed to the buyer. The commissioner argued that Sales' arrangement whereby it never had physical possession of the metal decking was insufficient to avoid the requirements to maintain inventories for tax accounting purposes. The commissioner stated that momentary title was sufficient to require the use of inventories. Citing the Uniform Commercial Code, which provides that if the seller is authorized to send the goods to the buyer but did not require him to deliver them at that at the destination, title passes to the buyer at the time and place of shipment. Because Sales' bill of lading and shipping papers were was used by Manufacturing to ship the goods, this bills of lading created momentary ownership by Sales of the goods and fulfilled the requirements of the Uniform Commercial Code; hence Sales had title, if only for a moment.

As Sales had momentary title to the metal decking, the court held that Sales must maintain inventories and was required to use the accrual method of accounting.

This is one of many instances where the tax consequences of a transaction will be influenced by the Uniform Commercial Code as title and ownership are a matter of state law. Only after the state law issue is resolved can an interpretation be made under federal tax law.

Example 6-5

An optometrist sells custom ordered eyeglasses. Assume the optometrist maintains no stock of lenses or frames (except for some sample frames to show customers), but custom orders glasses from a third party manufacturer. Must the optometrist use the accrual method of accounting for purchases and sales of eyeglasses and lenses?

Notwithstanding having no inventory, *Epic Metal* would require the optometrist to use of the accrual method.[91]

If the optometrist operated through a personal service corporation and was not required to use the accrual method would the corporation nevertheless be required to use accrual method?[92]

This issue is explored further in Chapter 8.

[J] Amount Realized

The amount realized by a cash basis taxpayer is significantly different from the amount realized by an accrual method taxpayer. When a cash basis taxpayer receives a promissory note, for example, the cash basis taxpayer either reports the fair market value of the instrument under IRC §1001(c),[93] or nothing at all (if the cash equivalency doctrine is applicable and its application dictates that income should not be recognized). In contrast, the fair market value of a note received by an accrual method taxpayer from a solvent maker is irrelevant in determining the amount realized under the accrual method. The IRS has held that when an accrual method taxpayer receives a long-term obligation for property he must realize the face amount of the obligation, and any money received.[94]

[K] Doubts About Collectability

An accrual method taxpayer does not accrue income on an item where there is a reasonable doubt as to its collectability, as stated in a number of cases and rulings.[95] The doubt may be established because of financial condition, insolvency, or other circumstances affecting the obligation.

---

[91] Rev. Rul. 74-279, 1974-1 CB 110. An optometrist who maintains a supply of eyeglasses and frames for sale and display purposes and who includes in their sale price an amount for services must use inventories pursuant to the provisions of IRC §471 and therefore the proper method of accounting is the accrual rather than the cash method. *See also Fame Tool & Mfg. Co. v. Comm'r*, 334 F. Supp. 23 (S.D. Ohio 1971) (custom tool and die maker had to use inventories for work in process although it maintained no finished goods inventories); Rev. Rul. 73-485, 1973-2 CB 150 (taxpayer provided artificial limbs and orthopedic braces to handicapped charging one un-itemized price for the prosthetic devices, instruction in their use, and custom fitting).

[92] *See* IRC §448.

[93] *See also* Reg. §1.61-2(d)(4).

[94] Rev. Rul. 79-292, 1979-2 CB 287. *Campbell v. Unites States*, 661 F.2d 209, 81-2 USTC ¶9676 (Cl. Ct. 1981).

[95] *See Clifton Mfg. Co. v. Comm'r*, 137 F.2d 290 (4th Cir. 1943), and *Commercial Solvents Corp. v. Comm'r*, 42 T.C. 455 (1964), *acq.* 1965-1 CB 4. In *Corn Exchange Bank v. United States*, 37 F.2d 34 (2d Cir. 1930), the Court said "[a] taxpayer, even though keeping his books upon an accrual basis, should not be required to pay a tax on accrued income unless it is good and collectible, and where it is of doubtful collectability or it is reasonably certain it will not be collected, it would be an injustice to the taxpayer to insist on taxation." *See also Jones Lumber Co. v. Comm'r*, 404 F.2d 764 (6th Cir. 1968).

Note

This exception appears to be inconsistent with the *Spring City Foundry* decision, and it is infrequently applied.[96]

An illustration of the "reasonable expectancy doctrine" is discussed in Priv. Ltr. Rul. 9434013. In the ruling, an accrual method corporation settled a breach of contract claim against a customer who defaulted. The settlement amount was for an agreed amount. A portion was paid at the time of the settlement and the balance was to be paid at a specified future date in the following year. If the defendant did not pay, the taxpayer could either file an agreed-upon judgment or proceed with legal action to enforce the award.

The taxpayer had no ability to enforce the settlement agreement before the due date for the second payment, and had no legal right to the second payment before the date set for the second payment. The date for the second payment was determined at arms-length by the parties. The second payment was made on the due date.

In the ruling, the service determined that as long as the taxpayer's entitlement to income was disputed by the obligor, all the events had not occurred to fix the right to the income in question or its amounts.

The IRS noted that a dispute is resolved when either the obligor acknowledges the liability, or a court or other forum that has finality determines the liability. Citing *Snyder Air Products Inc. v. Commissioner*,[97] where an award from the condemnation of property accrued in the first fiscal year ending May 31, 1970, the year in which the litigation on the matter was concluded, the Service found in taxpayer's favor. The key point the Service was making was that a judgment does not accrue until the time to appeal has expired even when no appeal has been filed.

In *H. Liebes & Co. v. Commissioner*,[98] the court noted the right to income is not fixed until a judgment is no longer appealable or the time for appeal has expired.

---

[96] *But see Procacci v. Comm'r*, 94 T.C. 397, 416, n.10 (1990), where the Court stated:

> The "reasonable expectancy" doctrine relates to the accrual method of accounting, under which a taxpayer includes an income item in gross income when all the events have occurred which fix the right to receive the income and its amount can be determined with reasonable accuracy [...] However, if it is reasonably certain that the income will not be collected in the tax year or within a reasonable time thereafter, the taxpayer is justified in not accruing the item.

It is important to note that the implication of this statement is that an amount may not have to be accrued where the collection of the item is anticipated and the time of collection only will be delayed.

[97] 71 T.C. 709 (1979). In *Lamm v. Comm'r*, 873 F.2d 194 (8th Cir. 1989), a partnership unsuccessfully claim the mortgage note was userious in a foreclosure proceeding. Because it failed to file a required bond for the sheriff sale was not stayed pending the outcome of the appeal. The mortgagee purchased the property at a sale in 1977. In 1978, the Minnesota Supreme Court rejected the claim that the mortgage note was usurious and declined to exercise its power to invalidate the foreclosure sale.

In applying the all-events test, the court upheld the Service's position that the sale did not occur until 1978 on the ground that the appeal on the usury grounds effectively contested the validity of the debt discharged and the disposal of the mortgage property so that the year of the state Supreme Court decision (1978) was the proper year for in conclusion.

[98] 90 F.2d 932, 938 (9th Cir. 1937).

Where an obligation is judicially contested, it is well recognized that liability is not fixed until "the last bell [is] rung in the last court."[99]

[L] *Non-accrual Experience Method for Services Receivable (NAE)*

Taxpayers eligible to use the NAE method may use one of the following safe harbor methods of accounting or an alternative method that meets certain requirements. The non-accrual experience method applies to amounts received for "qualified services" or by certain "small businesses." "Qualified services" are services in the fields of:

- health,
- law,
- engineering,
- architecture,
- accounting,
- actuarial science,
- performing arts, or
- consulting.

Other service businesses may use the non-accrual experience method only if the average annual gross receipts of the business do not exceed the gross receipts test of IRC § 448(c).[100] For example, if a service provider using the non-accrual method experience indicates that only $96,000 out of every $100,000 of his invoices receivable are collected, the service provider will accrue only $96 of income when he sends out a bill for $100. If the full $100 is paid, however, the service provider must include the additional $4 when received. The application of the non-accrual experience method involves several steps.

(1) A ratio of bad debts (net of recoveries) to gross receivables is computed for the six-year period ending with the current year (or for the period of the taxpayer and/or predecessor's existence, if shorter). A taxpayer may petition the IRS to utilize a shorter computation period where the make-up of its receivables has changed dramatically.

(2) If the taxpayer elects to apply the non-accrual experience method utilizing a separate receivable system, the taxpayer applies the calculated bad debt percentage to each receivable outstanding at year-end and that portion is neither recognized as income nor added to basis. Any difference between the basis of the receivable and the amount ultimately collected is recognized as income or as a bad debt in the year of collection.

---

[99] *Thompson v. Comm'r*, 761 F.2d 259, 265 (6th Cir. 1985). *Schlumberger Technology Corp. v. United States*, 99-1 USTC ¶ 50,128 (S.D. Tex. 1998), and *Gillis*, 402 F.2d at 506 (liability does not accrue and cannot be deducted as long as it is judicially contested by one of the parties).

[100] A corporation or partnership meets the gross receipts test of this subsection for any taxable year if the average annual gross receipts of such entity for the three-taxable-year period ending with the taxable year which precedes such taxable year do not exceed $25,000,000 adjusted for inflation after 2017.

(3) If the taxpayer elects to apply the non-accrual experience method utilizing a periodic system, the taxpayer maintains a reserve balance equal to the calculated bad debt percentage multiplied by the outstanding year-end receivable balance. Bad debts and recoveries are charged or credited to the reserve.

[M] Safe Harbors

The safe harbor and alternative methods are as follows:[101]

- *Six-year Moving Average Method.* The income amount not accrued is determined by a formula based on the taxpayer's experience over the current and preceding five tax years. When the receivable is collected, any amount that was not expected to be collected (*i.e.*, the amount not accrued) must be taken into income.
- *Actual Experience Method.* The two options under this method are (a) three-year moving average, and (b) up to three-year moving average. Under both of these methods, the accounts receivable at the beginning of a year are tracked to determine what percentage of those accounts was actually never collected.
- *Modified Black Motor Co. Method.* The uncollectible amount is computed by first determining the ratio of bad debts charged off (adjusted for recoveries) for the current tax year and the five preceding tax years relative to the total accounts receivable at the end of those years. This ratio is applied to the outstanding receivables at the end of the current tax year. The resulting amount is then reduced by the receivables generated and written off during the current tax year to arrive at the current-year uncollectible amount.
- *Modified Six-year Moving Average Method.* The taxpayer determines the uncollectible amount by multiplying its ending accounts receivable by the modified six-year moving average percentage. That percentage is computed by dividing the sum of net bad debts for the current and five preceding years (except that bad debts charged off in the same year the receivable was generated are not counted) by the sum of the receivables at the end of the current and five preceding years.[102]
- *Alternative Non-accrual-experience Method.* A taxpayer may use an alternative non-accrual-experience method that clearly reflects the taxpayer's actual non-accrual experience, provided the taxpayer's alternative non-accrual-experience method meets the self-test requirements.
- *Book Safe Harbor Method.* A taxpayer computes its uncollectible amount by multiplying the portion of the year-end allowance for doubtful accounts attributable to NAE-eligible accounts receivable on its financial statements by

---

[101] Reg. § 1.448-2(f).

[102] Reg. 1.448-2(e)(5).

95%. This method appears in a Revenue Procedure, not in the regulations, and is not subject to the self-testing requirements.[103]

[N] Certain Special Rules for Taxable Year of Inclusion

The Tax Cuts and Jobs Act (TCJA) requires a taxpayer to recognize income no later than the tax year in which the income is taken into account in an (i) applicable financial statement (AFS) or (ii) such other financial statement specified by the IRS.[104] Hence, any unbilled receivable for partially performed services must be recognized to the extent taken into income for financial statement purposes.

The special rule does not apply to:

- a taxpayer that does not have an AFS or such other financial statement specified by the IRS for a taxable year,[105] or
- any item of gross income in connection with a mortgage servicing contract.[106]

For purposes of IRC § 451, the all-events test is met with respect to any item of gross income if all the events have occurred which fix the right to receive such income and the amount of such income can be determined with reasonable accuracy.

Coordination with special methods of accounting. IRC § 451(b)(1) does not apply with respect to any item of gross income for which the taxpayer uses a special method of accounting provided under any other provision of Chapter 1 of the Internal Revenue Code, other than IRC § § 1271 through 1288 (except as provided in IRC § 451(b)(1) (1)(B)(ii)).

Applicable financial statement. For purposes of IRC § 451(b), the term "applicable financial statement" means:

(A) a financial statement which is certified as being prepared in accordance with generally accepted accounting principles and which is:

   (i) a 10-K (or successor form), or annual statement to shareholders, required to be filed by the taxpayer with the United States Securities and Exchange Commission;[107]

   (ii) an audited financial statement of the taxpayer which is used for:[108]

      (I) credit purposes,[109]

      (II) reporting to shareholders, partners, or other proprietors, or to beneficiaries,[110] or

---

103 Rev. Proc. 2011-46, 2011-42 IRB 518.

104 IRC § 451(b), as amended by TCJA § 13221(a).

105 IRC § 451(b)(1)(B)(i).

106 IRC § 451(b)(1)(B)(ii).

107 IRC § 451(b)(3)(A).

108 IRC § 451(b)(3)(A)(i).

109 IRC § 451(b)(3)(A)(ii)(I).

110 IRC § 451(b)(3)(A)(ii)(II).

(III) any other substantial nontax purpose, but only if there is no statement of the taxpayer described in (i), above;[111] or

(iii) filed by the taxpayer with any other Federal agency for purposes other than Federal tax purposes, but only if there is no statement of the taxpayer described in clause (i) or (ii);[112]

(B) a financial statement which is made on the basis of international financial reporting standards and is filed by the taxpayer with an agency of a foreign government which is equivalent to the United States Securities and Exchange Commission and which has reporting standards not less stringent than the standards required by such Commission, but only if there is no statement of the taxpayer described in (A), above;[113] or

(C) a financial statement filed by the taxpayer with any other regulatory or governmental body specified by the Secretary, but only if there is no statement of the taxpayer described in (A) or (B) above.[114]

Allocation of transaction price. For purposes of these rules, in the case of a contract which contains multiple performance obligations, the allocation of the transaction price to each performance obligation shall be equal to the amount allocated to each performance obligation for purposes of including such item in revenue in the AFS of the taxpayer.[115]

Group of entities. For purposes of IRC § 451(b)(1), if the financial results of a taxpayer are reported in the AFS as described in IRC § 451(b)(3) for a group of entities, such statement shall be treated as the AFS of the taxpayer.[116]

The IRS has issued proposed reliance regulations that provide additional guidance on the application of the AFS income inclusion rule to accrual method taxpayers.[117] The proposed regulations confirm that the AFS income inclusion rule applies on an item-by-item basis.[118] Thus, for any taxpayer with an AFS, the all-events test with respect to *any item* of gross income, or portion thereof, is met no later than when that item, or portion thereof, is taken into account as revenue in the

---

[111] IRC § 451(b)(3)(A)(ii)(III).

[112] IRC § 451(b)(3)(A)(ii)(III).

[113] IRC § 451(b)(3)(B).

[114] IRC § 451(b)(3)(C).

[115] IRC § 451(b)(4).

[116] IRC § 451(b)(5).

[117] Prop. Reg. § 1.451-3. These regulations are proposed to apply to tax years beginning on or after the date the final regulations are published in the Federal Register. Prop. Reg. § 1.451-3(n)(1). However, in the case of a specified fee, Prop. Reg. § 1.451-3(i)(2) is proposed to apply for a taxpayer's first tax year beginning one year after the date the Treasury decision adopting the regulations as final is published in the Federal Register. Prop. Reg. § 1.451-3(n)(2). Until the final regulations are published, a taxpayer generally may rely on the proposed regulations for tax years beginning after 2017 (or, in the case of the specified credit card fees defined in Prop. Reg. § 1.451-3(i)(2), for tax years beginning after 2018), provided the taxpayer consistently applies all the applicable rules contained in the proposed regulations to all items of income during the tax year. Prop. Reg. § 1.451-3(n)(3)(i).

[118] *See* Notice of Proposed Rulemaking, REG-104870-18, Taxable Year of Income Inclusion under an Accrual Method of Accounting, Fed. Reg. Vol. 84, No. 174, p. 47191, Sept. 9, 2019, Explanation of Provisions, Sec. 1.A.

taxpayer's AFS.[119] The proposed regulations also provide that the AFS income inclusion rule applies on a year-by-year basis and, thus, an accrual method taxpayer with an AFS in one tax year that does not have an AFS in another tax year has to apply the AFS income inclusion rule in the tax year that it has an AFS, but does not apply the rule in the tax year in which it does not have an AFS.[120]

The AFS income inclusion rule does not apply to (a) a taxpayer that does not have a financial statement described above for a tax year[121] or (b) any item of gross income in connection with a mortgaging servicing contract;[122] the all-events test rules apply instead. Thus, "normal" mortgage servicing rights are included in income on the earlier of when they are earned or received under the rules below (*i.e.*, not averaged over the life of the mortgage), and "excess" mortgage servicing rights are treated as stripped coupons under IRC § 1286 (and, thus, subject to the OID rules).[123]

Special methods of accounting to which the AFS income inclusion rules generally do not apply:

1. The crop method of accounting under IRC § 61 and IRC § 162;
2. Methods of accounting provided in IRC § 453 through IRC § 460;
3. Methods of accounting for hedging transactions under Reg. § 1.446-4;
4. Methods of accounting for REMIC inducement fees under Reg. § 1.446-6;
5. Methods of accounting for gain on shares in a money market fund under Reg. § 1.446-7;
6. Methods of accounting for certain rental payments under IRC § 467;
7. The mark-to-market method of accounting under IRC § 475;
8. Timing rules for income and gain associated with a transaction that is integrated under Reg. § 1.988-5, and income and gain under the nonfunctional currency contingent payment debt instrument rules in Reg. § 1.988-6;
9. Except as otherwise provided in Prop. Reg. § 1.451-3(i), timing rules for original issue discount (OID) under IRC § 811(b)(3) or IRC § 1272 (and the regulations under IRC § 1272), income under the contingent payment debt instrument rules in Reg. § 1.1275-4, income under the variable rate debt instrument rules in Reg. § 1.1275-5, income and gain associated with a transaction that is integrated under Reg. § 1.1275-6, and income under the inflation-indexed debt instrument rules in Reg. § 1.1275-7;
10. Timing rules for *de minimis* OID under Reg. § 1.1273-1(d) and for *de minimis* market discount (as defined in IRC § 1278(a)(2)(C));
11. Timing rules for accrued market discount under IRC § 1276 and IRC § 1278(b); and

---

[119] Prop. Reg. § 1.451-3(b).
[120] Prop. Reg. § 1.451-3(d).
[121] IRC § 451(b)(1)(B)(i).
[122] IRC § 451(b)(1)(B)(ii).
[123] *Id.*

12. Methods of accounting provided in IRC § 1502 and IRC § 1503 and the regulations thereunder, including the method of accounting relating to intercompany transactions under Reg. § 1.1502-13.[124]

Exceptions to the AFS income inclusion rule. The AFS income inclusion rule does not apply unless all of the taxpayer's taxable year is covered by an AFS. In addition, the AFS income inclusion rule does not apply to any item of income in connection with a mortgage servicing contract.[125]

No change in the treatment of a transaction. Except as provided in Prop. Reg. § 1.451-3(i)(2), the AFS income inclusion rule does not change the treatment of a transaction for federal income tax purposes. The following are examples of transactions where the treatment for AFS purposes does not change the treatment of the transaction for federal income tax purposes:

(1) A transaction treated as a lease, license, or similar transaction for federal income tax purposes that is treated as a sale or financing for AFS purposes, and vice versa;
(2) A transaction that is not required to be marked-to-market for federal income tax purposes but that is marked-to-market for AFS purposes;
(3) Asset sale and liquidation treatment under IRC § 336(e) or IRC § 338(h)(10);
(4) A distribution of a corporation or the allocable share of partnership items or an income inclusion under IRC § 951, IRC § 951A, or IRC § 1293(a) for federal income tax purposes that is accounted for under the equity method for AFS purposes;
(5) A distribution of previously taxed earnings and profits of a foreign corporation; and
(6) A deposit or conduit payment for federal income tax purposes that is treated as revenue for AFS purposes.[126]

No change to exclusion provisions and the treatment of non-recognition transactions. The AFS income inclusion rule does not change the applicability of any exclusion provision, or the treatment of non-recognition transactions, in the Code, the Income Tax Regulations, or other guidance published in the Internal Revenue Bulletin. The following are examples of exclusion provisions and non-recognition transactions that are not affected by the AFS income inclusion rule:

(1) Any non-recognition transaction, within the meaning of IRC § 7701(a)(45) (for example, a liquidation described in IRC § 332 and IRC § 337, an exchange described in IRC § 351, a distribution described in IRC § 355, a reorganization described in IRC § 368, a contribution described in IRC § 721, or transactions described in IRC § 1031 through IRC § 1045); and
(2) Items specifically excluded from income under IRC § 101 through IRC § 140.[127]

---

[124] Prop. Reg. § 1.451-3(c)(5).
[125] Prop. Reg. § 1.451-3(d).
[126] Prop. Reg. § 1.451-3(e).
[127] Prop. Reg. § 1.451-3(f).

Methods of Accounting. A change in the method of recognizing revenue in an AFS that changes or could change the timing of the recognition of income for federal income tax purposes is a change in method of accounting under IRC §446. A taxpayer may change its method of accounting only with the consent of the Commissioner as required under IRC §446(e) and the corresponding regulations. Accordingly, a taxpayer that changes the method of accounting used to recognize revenue in its AFS is required to secure consent of the Commissioner before computing income using this new method for federal income tax purposes.[128]

§6.03 Prepaid Income

[A] Generally

Prepaid income issues arise in connection with:

- Certain advance payments for goods;[129]
- Certain advance payments for services;[130]
- Certain service warranty contracts;[131]
- Prepaid dues income;[132]
- Prepaid subscription income;[133]
- Rents received pursuant to an IRC §467 rental agreement;[134] and
- Trading stamps and premium coupons.[135]

The all-events test[136] for income recognition for an accrual method taxpayer does not take into consideration what occurs when the taxpayer receives a prepaid item of income.[137] When payment precedes satisfaction of the all-events test, several issues arise, including:

- Whether it is appropriate to require taxation on receipt, especially where the revenue of the government may be adversely affected; and
- Whether the basic characteristics of accrual accounting are distorted by the receipt of prepaid income.

---

128 Prop. Reg. §1.451-3(l).

129 *See* Reg. §1.451-5.

130 *See* Rev. Proc. 71-21, 1971-2 CB 549, *modified by* Rev. Proc. 2004-34, 2004-1 CB 991.

131 *See* Rev. Proc. 92-98, 1992-2 CB 512.

132 *See* IRC §456.

133 *See* IRC §455.

134 An agreement which calls for increasing rents or deferred payments (occurring beyond the close of the calendar year following the year of use), which are generally allocated to the period to which they are attributable under the rental agreement (unless the agreement is a long-term agreement and a tax avoidance motive is present, in which case accrual rental is required).

135 *See* Reg. §1.451-4.

136 *See* §6.01.

137 It is imperative that the item received be income and not a deposit or a loan.

While the deferral of an advanced payment conforms to generally accepted accounting principles (GAAP), unless the advanced payment meets the criteria established in current case law and the rulings, deferral will be not be permitted.

[B] The Trilogy Cases

The treatment of prepaid income was examined in a series of three cases decided by the United States Supreme Court from 1957 through 1963: *Automobile Club of Michigan v. Commissioner,*[138] *American Automobile Association v. United States,*[139] and *Schlude v. Commissioner.*[140] These cases are referred to as the "trilogy cases." In the trilogy cases, the IRS required advance payments to be included in income in the year of receipt without regard to the satisfaction of the all-events test. In all of these cases, the pre-payments were non-refundable and were available to the taxpayer for its use.

In *Automobile Club of Michigan*, the petitioner kept its books and filed its returns on the accrual basis. During the taxable years under review, the taxpayer received advance payment of annual membership dues without restrictions as to their use and disposition. The taxpayer used a pro rata method to include income. The IRS sought to include the advance payments in income in the year of receipt. The Supreme Court agreed with the IRS, finding that the inclusion of the prepayment on a pro rata basis was purely artificial and bore no relationship to the services that the taxpayer may in fact be called upon to render. Because of this artificial structure, the Court ordered that the advance payments be reported as income.

American Automobile Association, the second case of the trilogy, involved the American Automobile Association (AAA), a national automobile club, which provides services to its members on demand, from dues received from its members paid in advance. AAA used the accrual method of accounting. As dues were received, they were deposited in AAA's bank account, without restriction. On its books, AAA treated the dues as unearned income and then recognized income ratably as earned over the 12-month membership period. Any amounts for which no services were rendered were reflected as unearned income at the close of the year. The IRS, exercising its discretion under IRC §446(b), determined that AAA's accounting method did not clearly reflect income. The Court of Claims agreed. The Supreme Court affirmed, rejecting statistical evidence presented by the taxpayer as support for the manner in which it accounted for the prepayment. The Supreme Court stated that AAA's accounting method was artificial and suffered from the same infirmity as the method used by the Automobile Club of Michigan.

Schlude, the final case in the "trilogy," involved prepaid dance lessons. The dance contracts guaranteed students a certain number of hours for lessons and dance parties. The contracts covered the period over which the lessons were to be taken but there was no fixed schedule or specific dates. Lessons could be taken on demand. Income was reported based on the number of hours that lessons were taught within

---

138 353 U.S. 180 (1957).

139 367 U.S. 687 (1961).

140 372 U.S. 128 (1963).

the year multiplied by a designated rate per hour. If there was no activity on a contract, the number of lessons was reduced. The IRS sought to include the prepaid dance lessons in income in the year of receipt. The Supreme Court agreed with the IRS, holding that the taxpayer's method of accounting did not clearly reflect income. The Court focused on the fact that the services were rendered solely on demand as in the other two cases of the trilogy. The Court also pointed out that there were no fixed dates for rendering the services. From a tax policy point of view, the taxpayer's method was arbitrary and created uncertainty.[141]

There have been a number of "post trilogy" cases in which the deferral of prepaid income has been allowed where the method of accounting was *not* artificial. *Artnell Co. v. Commissioner*[142] involved advanced ticket sales for baseball games. The taxpayer deferred the inclusion of ticket sales in income until the year in which the games were played. The Court of Appeals upheld the deferral because the time for performance was fixed, and the related items of income and expenses would be matched.

The Service argued that the baseball schedule nevertheless provided the uncertainty extolled in the Trilogy cases. The court met the objection:

> The uncertainty stressed in those decisions is not present here. The deferred income was allocable to games which were to be played on a fixed schedule. Except for rain dates, there was certainty. We would have no difficulty distinguishing the instant case in this respect.[143]

Similarly, in *Boise Cascade Corp. v. United States*,[144] the deferral of prepaid income was upheld. This case involved a fixed schedule of engineering services that matched income and expenses properly.[145]

In *Tampa Bay Devil Rays, Inc. v. Commissioner*,[146] the issue was whether deposits a partnership received in 1995 and 1996 as payments for advance season tickets and for private suite reservations for Devil Rays baseball games, which were expected to be played in 1998, were to be included in the income of the partnership when received in 1995 and 1996, or in 1998. The court held that the deposits received for the baseball games were governed by the application of the decision in *Artnell Co.* The partnership was permitted to defer reporting the deposits in income until 1998, the first year in which the Devil Rays played major league baseball games. Reporting the income in 1998 more clearly matched the partnership's related expenses that were incurred and deducted in 1998.

---

[141] In *RCA Corp v. United States*, 664 F.2d 881 (2d Cir. 1981) an accrual basis television manufacturer could not defer a portion of prepaid income on service contracts even though the deferral was based on adequately supported statistical projections designed to take into account as revenue each month that portion of prepaid service contract receipts attributable to the services performed that month.

[142] 400 F.2d 981 (7th Cir. 1968).

[143] 664 F.2d at 984.

[144] 530 F.2d 1367 (Ct. Cl. 1976), *cert. denied*, 429 U.S. 867 (1976).

[145] *See also Collegiate Cap & Gown Co. v. Comm'r*, T.C. Memo. 1978-226, 37 TCM 960 (1978); and Rev. Rul. 79-195, 1979-1 CB 177.

[146] T.C. Memo. 2002-248, 84 TCM 394 (2002).

In *Westpac Pacific Food v. Commissioner*,[147] the Ninth Circuit reversed the Tax Court's determination that upfront cash payments that the accrual method grocery partnership received as advance trade discounts on commitment to make future volume purchases had to be included in income in years of receipt. The Ninth Circuit held that the discounts were akin to security deposits or loans/liabilities rather than "accession to wealth"/income at time received because of concomitant purchase requirement and taxpayer's obligation to re-pay to the extent purchase obligations were not met. The fact that taxpayer might have had unfettered use of or complete dominion over funds when received did not in itself make them income or override fact that there was no accession to wealth at receipt date.

[C] Deferral of Income under Rev. Proc. 71-21

In 1971, the IRS declared in Rev. Proc. 71-21[148] that under certain circumstances, a one-year deferral of prepaid income will be permitted. In general, the revenue procedure applies to the prepayment of services received in one year to be rendered by the end of the next succeeding year. It is important to note Rev. Proc. 71-21 does not apply to amounts received under guaranty or warranty contracts or to prepaid rent or prepaid interest.[149]

On the other hand, where an agreement requires a taxpayer to perform contingent services (including the replacement of parts or materials where the obligation to replace is incidental to an agreement providing for the performance of personal services) with respect to property which is sold, leased, built, installed, or constructed by that taxpayer (or a related person), advance payments received with respect to such an agreement may be deferred until the next succeeding tax year only if, in the normal course of business, the taxpayer offers to sell, lease, build, install, or construct the property without such a contingent service agreement.

Rev. Proc. 71-21 was superseded by Rev. Proc. 2004-34.[150]

[D] Advance Payments under Rev. Proc. 2004-34

Rev. Proc. 2004-34,[151] which updated and expanded Rev. Proc. 71-21. By adding IRC § 451(c), the TCJA codified the deferral method of accounting for advance payments for goods and services previously provided by the IRS under Rev. Proc. 2004-34 by providing that a taxpayer which computes taxable income under the accrual method of accounting and receives any advance payment during the tax year, must:

---

147 451 F.3d 970 (9th Cir. 2006).

148 1971-2 CB 549.

149 However, for purposes of Rev. Proc. 71-21 and Reg. § 1.61-8(b) (requiring "advance rentals" to be included in income in the year of receipt), the term "rent" does not include payments for the use or occupancy of rooms or other space where significant services are also rendered to the occupant, such as for rooms or other quarters in hotels, boarding houses, or apartment houses furnishing hotel services, or in tourist homes, motor courts, or motels. *See* Reg. § 1.1362-2(c)(5)(ii)(B)(2).

150 2004-22 IRB 991.

151 2004-22 IRB 991.

(A) Except, include the advance payment in gross income for Inclusion not later than for financial accounting purposes for that tax year. (IRC § 451(c)(1)(A)) or

(B) If the taxpayer elects[152] the application of subparagraph IRC § 451(c)(1)(B) with respect to the category of advance payments to which the advance payment belongs, the taxpayer must (IRC § 451(c)(1)(B))

    (i) to the extent that any portion of the advance payment is required under IRC § 451(b) to be included in gross income in the tax year in which that payment is received, so include that portion (IRC § 451(c)(1)(B)(i)); and

    (ii) include the remaining portion of the advance payment in gross income in the tax year following the tax year in which the payment is received. (IRC § 451(c)(1)(B)(ii)).

In other words, accrual method taxpayers include advance payments as income in the year received unless they elect to defer recognition to the following tax year under IRC § 451(c)(1)(B). However, the one-year deferral is not available for any portion of an advance payment that is recognized in the year as received under the AFS conformity rule. The remaining portion is included in income in the tax year following the tax year received.

The TCJA requires an accrual taxpayer to recognize income no later than the tax year in which that income is taken into account as income in an applicable financial statement (AFS) or another financial statement under rules specified by the IRS, but provides an exception for long-term contract income to which IRC § 460 applies. For example, under the TCJA, any unbilled receivables for partially performed services must be recognized to the extent the amounts are taken into income for financial statement purposes.[153] This rule does not apply to:

- a taxpayer which does not have a financial statement for a tax year;[154] or
- any item of gross income in connection with a mortgage servicing contract.[155]

[E] *"Advance Payment" Defined Under IRC § 451(c)(4)*

Under IRC § 451(c)(4), an "advance payment" is any payment:

- The full inclusion of which in the taxpayer's gross income for the tax year of receipt is a permissible method of accounting under IRC § 451 (determined without regard to IRC § 451);
- Any portion of which is included in revenue by the taxpayer in a financial statement described in IRC § 451(b)(1)(A)(i) or IRC § 451(b)(1)(A)(ii) for a later tax year; and

[152] Under IRC § 451(c)(2)(B), if the election is made, it is effective for all subsequent tax years unless the IRS consents to a revocation. The election is treated as a method of accounting.

[153] Pub. L. No. 115-97, § 13221.

[154] IRC § 451(b)(1)(B)(i).

[155] IRC § 451(b)(1)(B)(ii).

- Which is for goods, services, or other items as the IRS may identify for these purposes.

  Except as otherwise provided by the IRS, an advance payment does not include:

  - Rent;
  - Insurance premiums governed by Subchapter L (IRC § 848);
  - Payments as to financial instruments;
  - Payments as to warranty or guarantee contracts under which a third party is the primary obligor;
  - Payments subject to:
    - — IRC § 871(a) (*i.e.*, the tax on income of non-resident alien individuals not connected with a U.S. business);
    - — IRC § 881 (*i.e.*, the tax on income of foreign corporations not connected with a U.S. business);
    - — IRC § 1441 (*i.e.*, the tax withheld on certain amounts paid to foreign persons); or
    - — IRC § 1442 (i.e., the tax withheld from income of foreign corporations);
- Payments in property to which IRC § 83 applies (taxation of property transferred in connection with the performance of services); and
- Any other payment identified by the IRS for purposes of IRC § 451(c)(4)(B).

An item of gross income is received by the taxpayer if it is actually or constructively received, or if it is due and payable to the taxpayer.

[F] Prop. Reg. §1.451-8

On July 15, 2019, the Treasury removed the receipt of advance payments final regulation[156] and replaced it with Prop. Reg. § 1.451-8, which provides that an accrual method taxpayer shall include an advance payment in gross income no later than in the taxable year in which the taxpayer receives the advance payment as provided under Reg. § 1.451-1(a).

The proposed regulation provides that payment for the following qualify for treatment as an advance payment:

(1) Services;

(2) The sale of goods;

---

[156] T.D 9870 (July 15, 2019) removing Reg. § 1.451-5.

(3) The use, including by license or lease, of intellectual property, including copyrights, patents, trademarks, service marks, trade names, and similar intangible property rights, such as franchise rights and arena naming rights;
(4) The occupancy or use of property if the occupancy or use is ancillary to the provision of services. For example, advance payments for the use of rooms or other quarters in a hotel, booth space at a trade show, campsite space at a mobile home park, and recreational or banquet facilities, or other uses of property, so long as the use is ancillary to the provision of services to the property user;
(5) The sale, lease, or license of computer software;
(6) Guaranty or warranty contracts ancillary to an item or items described in items (1), (2), (3), (4), or (5) above;
(7) Subscriptions in tangible or intangible format. Subscriptions for which an election under IRC § 455 is in effect and is not included in this item;
(8) Memberships in an organization. Memberships for which an election under IRC § 456 is in effect are not included in this item;
(9) An eligible gift card sale;
(10) Any other payment specified by the Secretary in other guidance published in the Internal Revenue Bulletin (see Reg. § 601.601(d)(2)); or
(11) Any combination of items described in the above items.

Items that do not qualify under the proposed regulations as advance payments include:

(A) Rent, except for amounts paid with respect to an item or items described in (3), (4) or (5) above;
(B) Insurance premiums, to the extent the inclusion of those premiums is governed by subchapter L;
(C) Payments with respect to financial instruments (for example, debt instruments, deposits, letters of credit, notional principal contracts, options, forward contracts, futures contracts, foreign currency contracts, credit card agreements (including rewards or loyalty points under such agreements), financial derivatives, or similar items), including purported prepayments of interest;
(D) Payments with respect to service warranty contracts for which the taxpayer uses the accounting method provided in Rev. Proc. 97-38;[157]
(E) Payments with respect to warranty and guaranty contracts under which a third party is the primary obligor;
(F) Payments subject to IRC § 871(a), § 881, § 1441, or § 1442;
(G) Payments in property to which IRC § 83 applies; and
(H) Payments received in a taxable year earlier than the taxable year immediately preceding the taxable year of the contractual delivery date for a specified good.

---

[157] 1997-2 CB 479.

[G] Definitions and Operating Rules

Applicable financial statement. Applicable financial statement has the same meaning as provided in Prop. Reg. § 1.451-3(c)(1).

Eligible gift card sale. Eligible gift card sale means the sale of a gift card or gift certificate if:

- The taxpayer is primarily liable to the customer, or holder of the gift card, for the value of the card until redemption or expiration; and
- The gift card is redeemable by the taxpayer or by any other entity that is legally obligated to the taxpayer to accept the gift card from a customer as payment for items listed in Prop. Reg. § 1.451-8(b)(1)(i)(C)(1) through (11).

Performance obligation. Performance obligation has the same meaning as provided in Prop. Reg. § 1.451-3(c)(3).

Received. An item of gross income is received by the taxpayer if it is actually or constructively received, or if it is due and payable to the taxpayer.

Revenue. Revenue has the same meaning as provided in Prop. Reg. § 1.451-3(c)(4) and is determined under the rules provided in Prop. Reg. § 1.451-3.

Transaction price. Transaction price has the same meaning as provided in Prop. Reg. § 1.451-3(c)(6).

Contractual delivery date. Contractual delivery date means the month and year of delivery listed in the written contract to the transaction.

Specified good. A specified good means a good for which:

- During the taxable year a payment is received, the taxpayer does not have on hand (or available to it in such year through its normal source of supply) goods of a substantially similar kind and in a sufficient quantity to satisfy the contract to transfer the good to the customer; and
- All the revenue from the sale of the good is recognized in the taxpayer's AFS in the year of delivery.

Deferral method for taxpayers with an applicable financial statement (AFS).

An accrual method taxpayer with an AFS that receives an advance payment may elect the deferral method if the taxpayer is able to determine the extent to which advance payments are included in revenue in its AFS in the taxable year received, including a short taxable year (if applicable). A taxpayer that uses the deferral method must:

- Include the advance payment, or any portion thereof, in gross income in the taxable year of receipt to the extent included in revenue in its AFS; and
- Include the remaining portion of such advance payment in gross income in the taxable year following the taxable year in which such payment is received.

Acceleration of advance payments.

A taxpayer that uses the deferral method must include in gross income for the taxable year of receipt or, if applicable, for a short taxable year, all advance payments not previously included in gross income:

- If, in that taxable year, the taxpayer either dies or ceases to exist in a transaction other than a transaction to which IRC § 381(a) applies; or
- If, and to the extent that, in that taxable year, the taxpayer's obligation with respect to the advance payments is satisfied or otherwise ends other than in:

- A transaction to which IRC § 381(a) applies; or
- An IRC § 351(a) transfer that is part of an IRC § 351 transaction in which:
    - Substantially all assets of the trade or business (including advance payments) are transferred;
    - The transferee adopts or uses the deferral method in the year of transfer; and
    - The transferee and the transferor are members of the same consolidated group, as defined in Reg. § 1.1502-1(h).

Example 6-6

Ceasing to exist. A is a calendar year taxpayer and is in the business of selling and licensing computer software (off the shelf, fully customized, and semi-customized) and providing customer support. On July 1, 2018, A enters into a two-year software maintenance contract and receives an advance payment. Under the contract, A will provide software updates if it develops an update within the contract period, as well as online and telephone customer support. A ceases to exist on December 1, 2018, in a transaction that does not involve a Section 351(a) transfer described in Prop. Reg. § 1.451-8(c)(2)(i)(B)(2) and is not a transaction to which Section 381(a) applies. For federal income tax purposes, A must include the entire advance payment in gross income in its 2018 taxable year.

Financial statement adjustments.

Notwithstanding IRC § 451(c)(4)(A)(ii), if a taxpayer treats an advance payment as an item of deferred revenue in its AFS and writes down or adjusts that item, or portion thereof, to an equity account (for example, retained earnings) or otherwise writes down or adjusts that item of deferred revenue in a subsequent taxable year, revenue for that subsequent taxable year includes that item, or portion thereof, that is written down or adjusted.

The proposed regulations provide the following examples:

Example 6-7

On May 1, 2018, A, a corporation that files its federal income tax return on a calendar year basis, received $100 as an advance payment for a two-year contract to provide services. For financial accounting purposes, A recorded $100 as a deferred revenue liability in its AFS, expecting to report 1/4 of the advance payment in revenue in its AFS for 2018, 1/2 for 2019, and 1/4 for 2020. On August 31, 2018, C, an unrelated corporation that files its federal income tax return on a calendar year basis, acquired all of the stock of A, and A joined C's consolidated group. A's short taxable year ended on August 31, 2018, and, as of that date, A had included only 1/4 ($25) of the advance payment in revenue in its AFS. On September 1, 2018, after the stock acquisition, and in accordance with purchase accounting rules, C wrote down A's deferred revenue liability to its fair value of $10 as of the date of the acquisition. The $10 will be included in revenue in A's AFS in accordance with the method of accounting A uses for financial accounting purposes. For federal income tax purposes, A uses the deferral method. For federal income tax purposes, A must take 1/4 ($25) of the advance payment into income for its short taxable year ending August 31, 2018, and the remainder of the advance payment ($75) ($65 write-down + $10 future financial statement revenue) must be included in income for A's next succeeding taxable year.

Example 6-8

On May 1, 2018, B, a corporation that files its federal income tax return on a calendar year basis, received $100 advance payment for a contract to be performed in 2018, 2019, and 2020. On August 31, 2018, D, a corporation that is not consolidated for federal income tax purposes, acquired all of the stock of B. Before the stock acquisition, in its AFS for 2018, B included $40 of the advance payment in revenue, and $60 as a deferred revenue liability. On September 1, 2018, after the stock acquisition and in accordance with purchase accounting rules, D wrote down its $60 deferred revenue liability to $10 (its fair value) as of the date of the acquisition. After the acquisition, B does not include in revenue any of the $10 deferred revenue liability in its 2018 AFS. B does include $5 in revenue in 2019, and $5 in revenue in 2020. For federal income tax purposes, B uses the deferral method. For federal income tax purposes, B must take $40 of the advance payment into income in 2018, and the remainder of the advance payment ($60) ($50 write-down + $10 future financial statement revenue) must be included in income for B's next succeeding taxable year, 2019.

Short taxable year rule

If the taxpayer's next succeeding taxable year is a short taxable year, other than a taxable year in which the taxpayer dies or ceases to exist in a transaction other than a transaction to which IRC § 381(a) applies, and the short taxable year consists of 92 days or less, a taxpayer using the deferral method must include the portion of the advance payment not included in the taxable year of receipt in gross income for the short taxable year to the extent included in revenue in an AFS. Any amount of the advance payment not included in the taxable year of receipt and the short taxable year must be included in gross income for the taxable year immediately following the short taxable year.

Example 6-9

A is a calendar year taxpayer and is in the business of selling and licensing computer software (off the shelf, fully customized, and semi-customized) and providing customer support. On July 1, 2018, A receives an advance payment for a two-year software maintenance contract. Under the contract, A will provide software updates if it develops an update within the contract period, as well as online and telephone customer support. A changes its taxable period to a fiscal year ending March 31 so that A has a short taxable year beginning January 1, 2019, and ending March 31, 2019. In its AFS, A includes 1/4 of the payment in revenue for the taxable year ending December 31, 2018; 1/6 in revenue for the short taxable year ending March 31, 2019; 1/4 in revenue for the taxable year ending March 31, 2020; and 1/4 in revenue for the taxable year ending March 31, 2021. Because the taxable year ending March 31, 2019, is 92 days or less, A must include 1/4 of the payment in gross income for the taxable year ending December 31, 2018, 1/6 in gross income for the short taxable year ending March 31, 2019, and the remaining amount in gross income for the taxable year ending March 31, 2020.

Financial statement conformity requirement.

A taxpayer that uses the deferral method under Prop. Reg. § 1.451-8(c) must use the same financial statement that is used to apply the rules in IRC § 451(b) and the accompanying regulations when applying the deferral method provided in IRC § 451(c) and these regulations.

Allocation of transaction price. A taxpayer using the deferral method under this Prop. Reg. § 1.451-8(c) must use the allocation rules provided in Prop. Reg. § 1.451-3(g).

Rules relating to eligible gift card sales. For purposes of Prop. Reg. § 1.451-8(b)(1)(i)(B) and (c)(1), if an eligible gift card is redeemable by an entity described in Prop. Reg. § 1.451-8(b)(3)(ii) whose financial results are not included in the taxpayer's AFS, a payment will be treated as included by the taxpayer in revenue in its AFS to the extent the gift card is redeemed by the entity during the taxable year.

Examples. The following examples illustrate the rules of the Deferral method for taxpayers with an applicable financial statement (AFS). In each example the taxpayer uses an accrual method of accounting for federal income tax purposes and files its returns on a calendar year basis. Except as stated otherwise, the taxpayer in each example has an AFS.

Example 6-10

Services. On November 1, 2018, A, in the business of giving dancing lessons, receives an advance payment for a one-year contract commencing on that date and providing for up to 48 individual, one-hour lessons. A provides eight lessons in 2018 and another 35 lessons in 2019. In its AFS, A includes 1/6 of the payment in revenue for 2018, and 5/6 of the payment in revenue for 2019. A uses the deferral method. For federal income tax purposes, A must include 1/6 of the payment in gross income for 2018, and the remaining 5/6 of the payment in gross income for 2019.

Example 6-11

Services. Assume the same facts as in Example 6-10, except that the advance payment is received for a three-year contract under which up to 96 lessons are provided. A provides eight lessons in 2018, 48 lessons in 2019, and 40 lessons in 2020. In its AFS, A includes $^{1}/_{12}$ of the payment in revenue for 2018, $^{1}/_{2}$ of the payment in revenue for 2019, and $^{5}/_{12}$ of the payment in gross revenue for 2020. For federal income tax purposes, A must include $^{1}/_{12}$ of the payment in gross income for 2018, and the remaining $^{11}/_{12}$ of the payment in gross income for 2019.

Example 6-12

Goods and Services. On June 1, 2018, B, a landscape architecture firm, receives an advance payment for goods and services that, under the terms of the agreement, must be provided by December 2019. On December 31, 2018, B estimates that $^{3}/_{4}$ of the work under the agreement has been completed. In its AFS, B includes $^{3}/_{4}$ of the payment in revenue for 2018 and $^{1}/_{4}$ of the payment in revenue for 2019. B uses the deferral method. For federal income tax purposes, B must include $^{3}/_{4}$ of the payment in gross income for 2018, and the remaining $^{1}/_{4}$ of the payment in gross income for 2019, regardless of whether B completes the job in 2019.

Example 6-13

Repair Contracts. On July 1, 2018, C, in the business of selling and repairing television sets, receives an advance payment for a two-year contract under which C agrees to repair or replace, or authorizes a representative to repair or replace, certain parts in the customer's television set if those parts fail to function properly. In its AFS, C includes $^{1}/_{4}$ of the payment in revenue for 2018, $^{1}/_{2}$ of the payment in revenue for 2019, and $^{1}/_{4}$ of the payment in revenue for 2020. C uses the deferral method. For federal income tax purposes, C must include $^{1}/_{4}$ of the payment in gross income for 2018 and the remaining $^{3}/_{4}$ of the payment in gross income for 2019.

Example 6-14

Online website Design. D, in the business of building and designing websites, receives advance payments that oblige D to build and design various websites. D tracks each request for a website with unique identifying numbers. On July 20, 2018, D receives online payments for two websites. One of the website requests is submitted and processed on

September 1, 2018, and the other is submitted and processed on February 1, 2020. In its AFS, D includes the payment for the September 1, 2018, website in revenue for 2018 and the payment for the February 1, 2020, website in revenue for 2020. D uses the deferral method. For federal income tax purposes, D must include the payment for the September 1, 2018, website in gross income for 2018 and the payment for the February 1, 2020, website in gross income for 2019.

Example 6-15

Gift Cards. E, a hair styling salon, receives advance payments for gift cards that may later be redeemed at the salon for hair styling services or hair care products at the face value of the gift card. The gift cards look like standard credit cards, and each gift card has a magnetic strip that, in connection with E's computer system, identifies the available balance. The gift cards may not be redeemed for cash and have no expiration date. In its AFS, E includes advance payments for gift cards in revenue when redeemed. E is not able to determine the extent to which advance payments are included in revenue in its AFS for the taxable year of receipt and, therefore, does not meet this requirement of Prop. Reg. §1.451- (c)(1). Therefore, E may not use the deferral method for these advance payments.

Example 6-16

Gift Cards. Assume the same facts as in Example 6-15, except that the gift cards have an expiration date 12 months from the date of sale, E does not accept expired gift cards, and E includes unredeemed gift cards in revenue in its AFS for the taxable year in which the cards expire. Because E tracks the sale date and the expiration date of the gift cards for purposes of its AFS, E is able to determine the extent to which advance payments are included in revenue for the taxable year of receipt. Therefore, E meets this requirement of Prop. Reg. §1.451-8(c)(1) and may use the deferral method for these advance payments.

Example 6-17

Online Subscriptions. G is in the business of compiling and providing business information for a particular industry in an online format accessible over the internet. On September 1, 2018, G receives an advance payment from a subscriber for one year of access to its online database, beginning on that date. In its AFS, G includes 1/3 of the payment in revenue for 2018 and the remaining 2/3 in revenue for 2019. G uses the deferral method. For federal income tax purposes, G must include $^{1}/_{3}$ of the payment in gross income for 2018 and the remaining $^{2}/_{3}$ of the payment in gross income for 2019.

Example 6-18

Membership Fees. On December 1, 2018, H, in the business of operating a chain of "shopping club" retail stores, receives advance payments for membership fees. Upon payment of the fee, a member is allowed access for a one-year period to H's stores, which offer discounted merchandise and services. In its AFS, H includes $^{1}/_{12}$ of the payment in revenue for 2018 and $^{11}/_{12}$ of the payment in revenue for 2019. H uses the deferral method. For federal income tax purposes, H must include $^{1}/_{12}$ of the payment in gross income for 2018, and the remaining $^{11}/_{12}$ of the payment in gross income for 2019.

Example 6-19

Cruise. In 2018, I, in the business of operating tours, receives payments from customers for a ten-day cruise that will take place in April 2019. Under the agreement, I charters a cruise ship, hires a crew and a tour guide, and arranges for entertainment and shore trips for the customers. In its AFS, I includes the payments in revenue for 2019. I uses the deferral method. For federal income tax purposes, I must include the payments in gross income for 2019.

Example 6-20

Travel agent services. On November 1, 2018, J, a travel agent, receives payment from a customer for an airline flight that will take place in April 2019. J purchases and delivers the airline ticket to the customer on November 14, 2018. J retains a portion of the customer's payment (the excess of the customer's payment over the cost of the airline ticket) as its commission. Because J is not required to provide any services after the ticket is delivered to the customer, J earns its commission when the airline ticket is delivered. The customer may cancel the flight and receive a refund from J only to the extent the airline itself provides refunds. In its AFS, J includes its commission in revenue for 2019. The commission is not an advance payment because the payment is not earned by J, in whole or in part, in a subsequent taxable year. Thus, J may not use the deferral method for this payment.

Example 6-21

Broadcasting Rights. K, a professional sports franchise, is a member of a sports league that enters into contracts with television networks for the right to broadcast games to be played between teams in the league. The money received by the sports league under the contracts is divided equally among the member teams. The league entered into a three-year broadcasting contract beginning October 1, 2018. K receives three equal installment payments on October 1 of each contract year, beginning in 2018. In its AFS, K includes 1/4 of the first installment payment in revenue for 2018 and 3/4 in revenue for 2019; K includes 1/4 of the second installment in revenue for 2019 and 3/4 in revenue for 2020; K includes 1/4 of the third installment in revenue for 2020 and 3/4 in revenue for 2021. K uses the deferral method. Each installment payment constitutes an advance payment under Prop. Reg. § 1.451-8(b)(1). For federal income tax purposes, K must include 1/4 of the first installment payment in gross income for 2018 and 3/4 in gross income for 2019; 1/4 of the second installment in gross income for 2019 and 3/4 in gross income for 2020; and 1/4 of the third installment in gross income for 2020 and 3/4 in gross income for 2021.

Example 6-22

Insurance Claims Administration. L is in the business of negotiating, placing, and servicing insurance coverage and administering claims for insurance companies. On December 1, 2018, L enters into a contract with an insurance company to provide property and casualty claims administration services for a four-year period beginning January 1, 2019. Pursuant to the contract, the insurance company makes four equal annual payments to L; each payment relates to a year of service and is made during the month prior to the service year (for example, L is paid on December 1, 2018, for the service year beginning January 1, 2019). In its AFS, L includes the first payment in revenue for 2019; the second payment in revenue for 2020; the third payment in revenue for 2021; and the fourth payment in revenue for 2022. L uses the deferral method. Each annual payment constitutes an advance payment under Prop. Reg. § 1.451-8(b)(1). For federal income tax purposes, L must include the first payment in gross income for 2019; the second payment in gross income for 2020; the third payment in gross income for 2021; and the fourth payment in gross income for 2022.

Example 6-23

Internet Services. M is a cable internet service provider that enters into contracts with subscribers to provide internet services for a monthly fee (paid prior to the service month). For those subscribers who do not own a compatible modem, M provides a rental cable modem for an additional monthly charge (also paid prior to the service month). Pursuant to the contract, M will replace or repair the cable modem if it proves defective during the contract period. In December 2018, M receives payments from subscribers for January 2019 internet service and cable modem use. In its AFS, M includes the entire amount of these payments in revenue for 2019. M uses the deferral method. Because a subscriber's use of a cable modem is ancillary to the provision of internet services by M, and because the cable modem warranty is ancillary to the use of the cable modem, the payments are advance payments. For federal income tax purposes, M must include the advance payments in gross income for 2019.

Example 6-24

License Agreement. On January 1, 2019, N enters into, and receives advance payments pursuant to, a five-year license agreement for the use of N's trademark. Under the contract, the licensee pays N both the first-year (2019) license fee and the fifth-year (2023) license fee upon commencement of the agreement. The fees for the second, third, and fourth years are payable on January 1 of each license year. The contract provides the customer with access to N's trademark throughout the term of the agreement. In its AFS, N includes the fees in revenue for the respective license year. N uses the deferral method. For federal income tax purposes, N must include the first-year license fee in gross income for 2019, the second-year and the fifth-year license fees in gross income for 2020, the third-year license fee in gross income for 2021, and the fourth-year license fee in gross income for 2022.

Example 6-25

Computer Software Subscription. On July 1, 2018, O, in the business of licensing computer software (off the shelf, fully customized, and semi-customized) and providing customer support, receives an advance payment for a two-year "software subscription contract" under which O will provide software updates if it develops an update within the contract period, as well as online and telephone customer support. In its AFS, O includes $^1/_4$ of the payment in revenue for 2018, $^1/_2$ in revenue for 2019, and the remaining $^1/_4$ in revenue for 2020, regardless of when O provides updates or customer support. O uses the deferral method. For federal income tax purposes, O must include $^1/_4$ of the payment in gross income for 2018 and $^3/_4$ in gross income for 2019.

Example 6-26

Performance Obligation. P is in the business of licensing computer software (off the shelf, fully customized, and semi-customized) and providing customer support. On July 1, 2018, P receives an advance payment of $100 for a two-year software subscription that includes a one-year "software maintenance contract" under which P will provide integral software updates within the contract period, as well as a "customer support agreement" for online and telephone customer support. In its AFS, P allocates $80 of the payment to the subscription agreement and $20 to the customer support agreement. With respect to the $80 allocable to the subscription agreement, P includes 1/4 ($20) in revenue for 2018, 1/2 ($40) in revenue for 2019, and the remaining 1/4 ($20) in revenue for 2020. With respect to the $20 allocable to the customer support agreement, P includes 1/2 ($10) in revenue for 2018, and the remaining 1/2 ($10) in revenue for 2019 regardless of when P provides the customer support. For federal income tax purposes, P must include $30 in gross income for 2018 ($20 allocable to the subscription agreement and $10 allocable to the customer support agreement) and the remaining $70 in gross income for 2019.

Example 6-27

Gift Cards Administered by Another. Q corporation operates department stores. U corporation, V corporation, and W corporation are wholly owned domestic subsidiaries of Q that file a consolidated federal income tax return with Q. X corporation is a controlled foreign subsidiary of Q that is prohibited from filing a consolidated return with Q. U sells Brand A goods, V sells Brand B goods, X sells Brand C goods, and Z is an unrelated entity that sells Brand D goods. W administers a gift card program for the Q consolidated group, X, and Z. Pursuant to the underlying agreements, W issues gift cards that are redeemable for goods or services offered by U, V, X, and Z. In addition, U, V, X, and Z sell gift cards to customers on behalf of W and remit amounts received to W. The agreements provide that W is primarily liable to the customer for the value of the gift card until redemption, and U, V, X, and Z are obligated to accept the gift card as payment for goods or services. When a customer purchases goods or services with a gift card at U, V, X, or Z, W reimburses that entity for the sales price of the goods or services purchased with the gift card, up to the total gift card value. In 2018, W sells gift cards with a total value of $900,000, and, at the end of 2018, the unredeemed balance of the gift cards is $100,000. In the consolidated group's AFS, the group includes revenue from the sale of a gift card when the gift card is redeemed. W tracks sales and redemptions of gift cards electronically, is able to determine the extent to which advance payments are included in revenue in its consolidated AFS for the taxable year of receipt, and meets the requirements of Prop. Reg. § 1.451-8(c)(1). The payments W receives from the sale of gift cards are advance payments because they are payments for eligible gift cards. Thus, W is eligible to use the deferral method. At the end of 2018, W includes $800,000 in income in its consolidated AFS. Under the deferral method, W must include $800,000 of the payments from gift card sales in gross income in 2018 and the remaining $100,000 of the payments in gross income in 2019.

Example 6-28

Gift Cards of Affiliates. R is a Subchapter S corporation that operates an affiliated restaurant corporation and manages other affiliated restaurants. These other restaurants are owned by other Subchapter S corporations, partnerships, and limited liability companies. R has a partnership interest or an equity interest in some of the restaurants. R administers a gift card program for participating restaurants. Each participating restaurant operates under a different trade name. Under the gift card program, R and each of the participating restaurants sell gift cards, which are issued with R's brand name and are redeemable at all participating restaurants. Participating restaurants sell the gift cards to customers and remit the proceeds to R, R is primarily liable to the customer for the value of the gift card until redemption, and the participating restaurants are obligated under an agreement with R to accept the gift card as payment for food, beverages, taxes, and gratuities. When a customer uses a gift card to make a purchase at a participating restaurant, R is obligated to reimburse that restaurant for the amount of the purchase, up to the total gift card value. In R's AFS, R includes revenue from the sale of a gift card when a gift card is redeemed at a participating restaurant. R tracks sales and redemptions of gift cards electronically, is able to determine the extent to which advance payments are included in revenue in its AFS for the taxable year of receipt, and meets the requirements of Prop. Reg. § 1.451-8(c)(1). The payments R receives from the sale of gift cards are advance payments because they are payments for eligible gift card sales. Thus, for federal income tax purposes, R is eligible to use the deferral method. In the taxable year of receipt, R must include the advance payment in income to the extent included in its AFS, and must include any remaining amount in income in the taxable year following the taxable year of receipt.

Example 6-29

Gift Cards for Domestic and International Hotels. S is a corporation that operates for the benefit of its franchisee members, who own and operate domestic and international individual member hotels. S collects membership fees from the member hotels in exchange for providing a wide variety of management support services, which include making reservations for customers at the various member hotels. S also administers a gift card program for its members by selling gift cards that may be redeemed for hotel rooms and food or beverages provided by any member hotel. The agreements underlying the gift card program provide that S is entitled to the proceeds from the sale of the gift cards, must reimburse the member hotel for the value of a gift card redeemed, and until redemption remains primarily liable to the customer for the value of the card. In S's AFS, S includes payments from the sale of a gift card when the card is redeemed. S tracks sales and redemptions of gift cards electronically, is able to determine the extent to which advance payments are included in revenue in its AFS for the taxable year of receipt, and meets the requirements of Prop. Reg. § 1.451-8(c)(1). The payments S receives from the sale of gift cards are advance payments because they are payments for eligible gift card sales. Thus, for federal income tax purposes, S is eligible to use the deferral method. In the taxable year of receipt, S must include in income the advance payment to the extent included in its AFS, and must include any remaining amount in income in the taxable year following the taxable year of receipt.

Example 6-30

Discount Voucher. On December 10, 2018, T, in the business of selling home appliances, sells a washing machine for $500. As part of the sale, T gives the customer a 40% discount voucher for any future purchases of T's goods up to $100 in the next 60 days. In its AFS, T treats the discount voucher as a separate performance obligation and allocates $30 of the $500 sales price to the discount voucher. T includes $12 of the amount allocated to the discount voucher in revenue for 2018 and includes $18 of the discount voucher in revenue for 2019. T uses the deferral method. For federal income tax purposes, T must include the $12 allocable to the discount voucher in gross income in 2018 and the remaining $18 allocated to the discount voucher in gross income in 2019.

Example 6-31

Rewards. On December 31, 2018, U, in the business of selling consumer electronics, sells a new TV for $1,000 and gives the customer 50 reward points. Each reward point is redeemable for a $1 discount on any future purchase of U's products. The reward points are not redeemable for cash and have a two-year expiration date. U tracks each customer's reward points and does not sell reward points separately. In its AFS, U treats the rewards points as a separate performance obligation and allocates $45 of the $1,000 sales price to the rewards points. U does not include any of the amount allocated to the reward points in revenue for 2018. U includes $25 of the reward points in revenue for 2019 and $20 of the reward points in revenue for 2020. U uses the deferral method. For federal income tax purposes, U does not include any amount of the reward points in gross income in 2018, and includes the entire $45 allocated to the reward points in gross income in 2019.

Example 6-32

Credit Card Rewards. V, a wholly owned credit card company, issues credit cards. V also has a loyalty program in which cardholders earn reward points for the use of its credit card to make purchases. Each reward point is redeemable for $1 on any future purchases. V may not use the deferral method because payments under credit card agreements including rewards for credit card purchases are excluded from the definition of an advance payment under Prop. Reg. § 1.451-8(b)(1)(ii)(C).

Example 6-33

Airline Reward Miles. On January 1, 2018, W, in the business of transporting passengers on airplanes, sells a customer a $700 airline ticket to fly roundtrip in 2018. As part of the purchase, the customer also receives 7,000 points (air miles) from W to be used for future air travel. In its AFS, W allocates $665 to the roundtrip airfare and $35 to the air miles. In its AFS, the $665 allocated to the airfare is included in Year 1 when the customer takes the roundtrip flight. The $35 allocated to the air miles is deferred and included in Year 3 when the customer redeems the air miles. W uses the deferral method described in Prop. Reg. § 1.451-8(c). For federal income tax purposes, the $665 is included in gross income in Year 1 and the $35 allocated to the air miles is included in gross income in Year 2.

Example 6-34

Chargebacks. Taxpayer X, a manufacturer of pharmaceuticals, is a calendar-year accrual method taxpayer with an AFS. In addition to billing the wholesaler for the sale of the pharmaceuticals at the wholesale acquisition cost under the contract, X generally credits or pays wholesalers a chargeback of 40% of the wholesale acquisition cost for sales made by those wholesalers to qualifying customers. In 2018, X enters into a contract to sell 1,000 units to W, a wholesaler, for $10 per unit, totaling $10,000 (1,000 x $10 = $10,000). The contract also provides that X will issue a 40% chargeback for sales by W to certain qualifying customers. X delivers 600 units to W on December 31, 2018, and bills W $6,000 under the contract. For AFS purposes, X adjusts its revenue by 40% for all sales to W for anticipated chargebacks. As such, in its 2018 AFS, X reports $3,600 ($6,000-$2,400 = $3,600) of revenue from the contract with W, decreasing revenue by $2,400 (40% x $6,000 = $2,400) for anticipated chargeback claims. For federal income tax purposes, under Prop. Reg. § 1.451-3(c)(4), X's 2018 revenue is $6,000 because revenue is not reduced for anticipated chargebacks. Because no portion of the $6,000 is included in revenue in an AFS in a subsequent taxable year (that is, on an AFS after 2018), none of the $6,000 is an advance payment under Prop. Reg. § 1.451-8(b)(1)(i).

Audit protection for taxpayers currently using the deferral method. If a taxpayer uses the Deferral Method for advance payments, the taxpayer's method of accounting for such advance payments under the Deferral Method will not be raised as an issue by the IRS.[158]

[H] *Advance Payments for Goods, Services, and Certain Other Items*

Prior to the TCJA, Reg. § 1.451-5 provided special rules for advanced payment for goods and long-term contracts. These rules were superseded by revised IRC § 451 and by Prop. Reg. § 1.451-8.[159] Effective for tax years ending on or after July 15, 2019, the IRS issued proposed regulations that replace Reg. § 1.451-5, which generally allowed accrual method taxpayers to defer the inclusion of income for certain advance payments, because a provision of the Tax Cuts and Jobs Act (TCJA) overrode the original provision.

Deferral method for taxpayers without an AFS (non-AFS deferral method).

Only a taxpayer described in Prop. Reg. § 1.451-8(d)(2) may elect to use the non-AFS deferral method described in Prop. Reg. § 1.451-8(d)(4).

Taxpayers eligible to use the non-AFS deferral method. A taxpayer is eligible to use the non-AFS deferral method if the taxpayer does not have an applicable financial statement as defined in Prop. Reg. § 1.451-3(c)(1) and is able to determine the extent to which advance payments are earned in the taxable year of receipt, or a short taxable year, if applicable.

Advance payment. For purposes of the non-AFS deferral method, in applying Prop. Reg. § 1.451-8(b)(1)(i)(B), an advance payment is any portion of the payment received that is earned by the taxpayer, in whole or in part, in a subsequent taxable year.

Deferral of advance payments based on when payment is earned.

The non-AFS deferral method described in Prop. Reg. § 1.451-8(d) is a permissible method of accounting that may be used only by a taxpayer described in Prop. Reg. § 1.451-8(d)(2). Under the non-AFS deferral method of accounting, a taxpayer includes the advance payment in gross income for the taxable year of receipt,

---

[158] Rev. Proc. 2011-18, 2011-5 IRB 443, § 5.

[159] *See* T.D. 9870 (July 15, 2019).

including, if applicable, a short taxable year described in Prop. Reg. § 1.451-8(d)(8), to the extent that it is earned in that taxable year and includes the remaining portion of the advance payment in gross income in the next succeeding taxable year.

A payment is earned when the all-events test described in Reg. § 1.451-1(a) is met, without regard to when the amount is received, as defined under Prop. Reg. § 1.451-8(b)(5), by the taxpayer. If a taxpayer is unable to determine the extent to which a payment is earned in the taxable year of receipt, the taxpayer may determine that amount:

- On a statistical basis if adequate data are available to the taxpayer;
- On a straight-line ratable basis over the term of the agreement if the taxpayer receives advance payments under a fixed-term agreement and if it is not unreasonable to anticipate at the end of the taxable year of receipt that the advance payment will be earned ratably over the term of the agreement; or
- By the use of any other basis that in the opinion of the Commissioner results in a clear reflection of income.

Contracts with multiple obligations.

If a taxpayer receives a payment that is attributable to more than one item described in Prop. Reg. § 1.451-8(b)(1)(i)(C), the taxpayer must allocate the payment to such items in a manner that is based on objective criteria.

Objective criteria. A taxpayer's allocation method with respect to a payment described in Prop. Reg. § 1.451-8(d)(5)(i) is based on objective criteria if the allocation method is based on payments the taxpayer regularly receives for an item or items it regularly sells or provides separately or any method that may be provided in guidance published in the Internal Revenue Bulletin.

Acceleration of advance payments. For purposes of paragraph Prop. Reg. § 1.451-8(d), the acceleration rules provided in Prop. Reg. § 1.451-8(c)(2) apply to a taxpayer that uses the non-AFS deferral method.

Advance payments in certain acquisitions and other financial statement adjustments. For purposes of Prop. Reg. § 1.451-8(d), the rules provided in paragraph Prop. Reg. § 1.451-8(c)(3) apply to a taxpayer that uses the non-AFS deferral method.

Short taxable year rule. For purposes of Prop. Reg. § 1.451-8(d), the short taxable year rule provided in Prop. Reg. § 1.451-8(c)(4) applies to a taxpayer that uses the non-AFS deferral method.

Eligible gift card sale. For purposes of Prop. Reg. § 1.451-8(b)(1)(i)(B) and Prop. Reg. § 1.451-8(d)(4), if an eligible gift card is redeemable by an entity described in Prop. Reg. § 1.451-8(b)(3)(ii), including an entity whose financial results are not included in the taxpayer's financial statement, a payment will be treated as earned by the taxpayer to the extent the gift card is redeemed by the entity during the taxable year.

Examples. The rules of Prop. Reg. § 1.451-8(d) are illustrated as follows. In each of these examples, the taxpayer uses the non-AFS deferral method described in Prop. Reg. § 1.451-8(d).

Example 6-35

A, a video arcade operator, receives payments in 2018 for game tokens that are used by customers to play the video games offered by A. The tokens cannot be redeemed for cash. The tokens are imprinted with the name of the video arcade, but they are not individually marked for identification. A completed a study on a statistical basis, based on adequate data available to A, and concluded that for payments received in the current year, x percent of tokens are expected to be used in the current year, y percent of tokens are expected to be used in the next year, and the remaining z percent of tokens are expected to never be used. Based on the study, A treats as earned for 2018 x percent (for tokens expected to be used in that year) as well as z percent (for tokens that are expected to never be used). Using the study, A determines the extent to which advance payments are earned in the taxable year of receipt. A may determine the extent to which a payment is earned in the taxable year of receipt on a statistical basis provided that any portion that is not included in the taxable year of receipt is included in the next succeeding taxable year. Thus, for federal income tax purposes, A must include x percent and z percent of the advance payments in gross income for 2018 and y percent of the advance payments in gross income for 2019.

Example 6-36

B is in the business of providing internet services. On September 1, 2018, B receives an advance payment from a customer for a two-year term for access to its internet services, beginning on that date. B does not have an AFS. B is unable to determine the extent to which the payment is earned in the taxable year of receipt. For federal income tax purposes, B may determine the extent to which the payment is earned in the year of receipt on a straight-line ratable basis over the term of the agreement if it is not unreasonable to anticipate at the end of the taxable year of receipt that the advance payment will be earned ratably over the term of the agreement.

Method of accounting. The use of the deferral method under Prop. Reg. § 1.451-8(c) or the non-AFS deferral method under Prop. Reg. § 1.451-8(d) is the adoption of, or a change in, a method of accounting under IRC § 446 or the accompanying regulations. In addition, a change in the manner of recognizing advance payments in revenue in an AFS that changes or could change the timing of the inclusion of income for federal income tax purposes is a change in method of accounting under IRC § 446 and the accompanying regulations. A taxpayer may change its method of accounting to use the methods described in Prop. Reg. § 1.451-8(c) or Prop. Reg. § 1.451-8(d), or change its manner of recognizing advance payments in revenue in an AFS only with the consent of the Commissioner as required under IRC § 446(e) and the corresponding regulations.

[I] Prepaid Dues Income

Membership organizations employing an accrual or hybrid method of accounting may elect to defer prepaid dues income.[160] If the election is made, prepaid dues income is deferred and included in income ratably over the term of the membership, which cannot exceed 36 months, except to the extent that the taxpayer elects to include current advance payments with respect to membership with a term of 12 months or less. If the taxpayer's liability ceases to exist, any remaining deferred income is immediately taxable.

Example 6-37

Corporation X, a membership organization that files its income tax returns on a calendar year basis, customarily sells three-year memberships, payable in advance. In 2019, it received $160,000 of prepaid dues income for three-year memberships beginning during 2019, and in 2020, it received $185,000 of prepaid dues income for three-year memberships beginning on January 1, 2020. In March 2020, it elected, with the consent of the Commissioner, to report its prepaid dues income under the provisions of IRC § 456 for the year 2020 and subsequent taxable years. The $160,000 received in 2019 from prepaid dues must be included in gross income in full in that year, and except as provided in IRC § 456(d) and § 1.456-7, no part of such income shall be allocated to the taxable years 2019, 2020, and 2021 during which X was under a liability to make available its membership privileges. The $185,000 received in 2020 from prepaid dues income shall be allocated to the years 2020, 2021, and 2022.

[J] Prepaid Subscription Income

Accrual method taxpayers may elect to defer advance payments on subscriptions to newspapers, magazines, or other periodicals.[161] If the election is made, advance payments are deferred and included generally in income ratably over the period of the subscription, except to the extent that the taxpayer elects to include current advance payments with respect to the subscriptions with a term of 12 months or less. If the taxpayer's liability ceases to exist, any remaining deferred income is immediately taxable.

---

160 IRC § 456.
161 IRC § 455.

[K] *Trading Stamps and Coupons*

Accrual method merchants issuing trading stamps or premium (but not discount) coupons together with sales of merchandise, and trading stamp companies in the business of selling trading stamps to these merchants, may establish a reserve for the future redemption of outstanding stamps and coupons.[162] The reserve represents an estimate of the cost of acquiring the merchandise necessary to redeem the number of outstanding stamps and coupons projected to be redeemed, with the amount of the reserve limited to the amount reported for financial reporting purposes. Actual expenses related to merchandise acquisition are charged to the reserve.

[L] *Prepaid Dues Income of Certain Membership Organization*

Under IRC § 456, membership organizations, such as automobile clubs, may elect to spread ratably the reporting of prepaid dues income over the period during which the liability to render services or make available membership privileges exists. The liability must extend beyond the tax year in which prepayment is received, but must not exceed 36 months.[163] Thus, if during the tax year the taxpayer sells memberships for more than 36 months and also memberships for 36 months or less, IRC § 456 does not apply to the income from the sale of memberships for more than 36 months. For purposes of determining the duration of liability, a bona fide renewal of a membership is not considered to be a part of an existing membership.[164]

§ 6.04 Service Warranty Income

The IRS issued a ruling for deferring service warranty income in Rev. Proc. 92-98.[165] It allows for the deferral of income in specified circumstances.

The following requirements must be met in order for a taxpayer to be eligible to elect to use the service warranty income method:

(1) the service warranty contract must be a fixed-term service arrangement for a motor vehicle or other durable good;
(2) the service warranty contract must be purchased at the customer's option;
(3) the service warranty contract must be for a service period which begins in the taxable year the advance payment is received or after the expiration of a fixed-term manufacturer's warranty that begins in the taxable year the advance payment is received; and
(4) the service warranty contract must be related to an insurance contract the taxpayer purchases from an unrelated third party for which the taxpayer makes the entire payment within 60 days after the receipt of the advance payment.

---

162 Reg. § 1.451-4.
163 IRC § 456(e)(2); Reg. § 1.456-1.
164 Reg. § § 1.456-5(a), 1.456-5(b).
165 1992-2 CB 512. This Revenue Procedure was modified by Rev. Proc. 97-38, 1997-2 CB 479.

When these requirements are satisfied, the taxpayer may elect to include a qualified advance payment amount,[166] increased by an imputed interest amount, in gross income over the shorter of

- the period beginning in the taxable year in which the advance payment is received and ending when the service warranty contract terminated; or
- a six-taxable-year period beginning in the taxable year in which the payment is received.

Any excess of the advance payment over the qualified advance payment amount is includable in income in the year of receipt. The following two examples are illustrative.

Example 6-38

A, a calendar year accrual basis taxpayer, elects under Rev. Proc. 97-38 to use the service warranty income method of accounting for its qualified advance payment amounts on service warranty contracts. A sold five service warranty contracts on January 1, 1997, for $800 each. A also sold five service warranty contracts on December 31, 1997, for $800 each. All the service warranty contracts sold by A in 1997 carry a term of five years and run concurrently with the manufacturer's warranties. Further, A pays, within 60 days of the receipt of each advance payment, $600 per contract to an unrelated third party to insure (in an arrangement that constitutes insurance) its obligations under the service warranty contracts. The applicable interest rate, determined in accordance with § 5.04 of Rev. Proc. 97-38, is 10%.

A aggregates all its qualified advance payment amounts on its five-year service warranty contracts, thus determining that $6,000 of qualified advance payment amounts were received in 1997 with respect to the class of five-year service warranty contracts. Applying the "10% and 5-year" factor of .2398 found in the table in the APPENDIX of Rev. Proc. 97-38, A determines that it must report gross income of $1,439 ($6,000 × .2398) in 1997 through 2001 under the election provided in Rev. Proc. 97-38. In addition, A must include in gross income in 1997 the $2,000 payment received for services that is not deferred under this Rev. Proc. 97-38.[167]

---

[166] The qualified advanced payment amount is the portion of an advance payment received by the taxpayer for a service warranty contract that the taxpayer pays to an unrelated third party within 60 days after receipt for an insurance policy insuring the taxpayer's obligations under the service warranty contract.

[167] Rev. Proc. 97-38, 1997-2 CB 479, § 5, Example 1.

§ 6.05 Deposits as Income

Deposits may, in some cases, constitute income. In general, deposits, loans or trust funds are not income so long as the payee segregates the funds, holds them in escrow, or is prevented from using them. When there are no restrictions and the funds are available the question is more difficult to resolve.[168]

An unsegregated deposit can be:

- Prepaid income subject to Rev. Proc. 2004-34;
- Payments to protect a property interest, *e.g.*, damage deposits (usually non-taxable until forfeited by the customer); or
- Amounts received to secure payments for future goods and services (generally non-taxable until applied to receivables for such goods or services).

In *Commissioner v. Indianapolis Power & Light Co.*,[169] the Supreme Court clarified the requirements necessary for a payment to be considered a deposit. The Court looked at whether the taxpayer had:

- A fixed obligation to repay the amount(s) in question; and
- Complete dominion over the amount(s) received by it.

The Court held that as long as the holder of a security deposit has an obligation to repay the amount on the demand of the depositor once the contractual terms have been satisfied, the deposit would not be income.[170] Consider the following example.

Example 6-39

InterFlix provides local cable access to its customers for a monthly fee. At the inception of its service, a new customer must deposit three months of expected service fees as security. At any time after the first six months, if the customer has made timely payments on its bills, the customer may demand repayment of the security, apply the security toward his bill, or buy additional equipment. How should InterFlix treat the security deposit? The security deposit meets the criteria established by the Supreme Court in *Indianapolis Power*. If the only option available would be to apply the security toward services or equipment, the deposit would look more like a prepayment.

---

[168] *Michaelis Nursery, Inc. v. Comm'r*, T.C. Memo. 1995-143, 69 TCM 2300 (1995).

[169] 493 U.S. 203 (1990).

[170] In *Highland Farms v. Comm'r*, 106 T.C. 237 (1996), the Tax Court held that partially refundable entry fees paid to live in a retirement community did not constitute prepaid rent that had to be reported in the year of receipt. The rental contracts signed by community residents provided a schedule based on which they could move out and obtain refunds for a portion of their entry fees. The court placed emphasis on the circumstances that refunds were within the control of the residents and that the operator of the retirement community had no unfettered dominion over the money at the time of receipt. Ultimately, the court held that the taxpayer is reporting of the nonrefundable portions of the entry fees each year clearly reflected income.

In *Burley Tobacco Growers Cooperative Association Inc. v. United States*,[171] the court held that contributions (in the nature of deposits) by members to a farmer's cooperative were income only in the year in which the right of the member to demand a refund either lapsed or was waived.

R.A. Johnson v. Commissioner[172] involved motor vehicle dealers who received a one-time fee in advance for multiyear service contracts. The fees were refundable if a customer canceled the contract, the amount of the refund depended on the time elapsed and the mileage driven. The cost of repairs was irrelevant. The tax court distinguished *Indianapolis Power and Light* and said that the dealer's right to retain the funds was not contingent upon the contract holders' actual future claims for repair services. Rather, it was contingent upon the time elapsed and the mileage driven while the contract remains in force, variables that are entirely independent of the amounts applied to repair services. The court therefore held that the payments were taxable advanced payments rather than excludable deposits.

In *City Gas Co of Florida v. Commissioner*,[173] the circuit court held that if a payment is treated as a security deposit, it is not included in gross income unless and until the payee converts the security deposit monies so that they function other than as a security deposit. The *City Gas* case and others that made contrary decisions on what constituted a deposit led to the Supreme Court's decision in *Indianapolis Power*.

§ 6.06 Expenses—Deductions

[A] Generally

Under the accrual method of accounting, expenses are deductible in the first year in which

(1) All events have occurred that establish the fact of liability;

(2) The amount of the liability can be determined with reasonable accuracy;[174] and

(3) Economic performance has occurred.[175]

This is referred to as the "all-events test." The first two parts of the test are found in Reg. § 1.461-1(a)(2). The third part is the result of the addition of IRC § 461(h).

The term "liability" includes any item allowable as a deduction, cost, or expense for federal income tax purposes. In addition to allowable deductions, the term includes any amount otherwise allowable as a capitalized cost, as a cost taken into

---

[171] 68-2 USTC ¶ 9458 (E.D. Ky. 1968).

[172] 108 T.C. 448 (1997).

[173] 89 F.2d 943 (11th Cir.1982).

[174] *United States v. Anderson*, 269 U.S. 422 (1926); *Koehring v. United States*, 421 F.2d 715, 70-1 USTC ¶ 9242 (Cl. Ct. 1970).

[175] Reg. §§ 1.446-1(c)(1)(ii) and 1.461-1(a)(2); IRC § 461(h), discussed in detail in § 6.07, below.

account in computing cost of goods sold, as a cost allocable to a long-term contract, or as any other cost or expense.[176]

[B] *Fixed Liability Requirement*

In a number of early cases, the courts held that expenditures are deductible only when the activities that a taxpayer is obligated to perform are in fact performed, not when the "fact" of the obligation to perform is determined.[177] A liability is considered to be fixed "when payment is unconditionally due or when the required performance occurs on the part of the other party."[178] A liability is fixed if payment is due under the terms of a contract; however, an optional prepayment by an accrual method taxpayer cannot accelerate the establishment of a liability that is otherwise not fixed until a later year.[179] A liability may be fixed under the terms of a contract,[180] by a statutory or regulatory obligation to perform certain activities,[181] on completion of services or submission of a bill,[182] or by filing a claim.[183] Until 1984, the courts often reached different conclusions. Generally, courts held that a taxpayer may deduct the amount of a liability if all the events that fix the liability have occurred and the amounts can be determined with reasonable accuracy, even though the activities the taxpayer is obligated to perform were not actually performed until a later year. For example, in 1952, the Fourth Circuit held that surface mining reclamation costs that could be estimated with reasonable accuracy were properly accrued when the land was stripped, although the land was not reclaimed until a subsequent year.[184] The position of the Fourth Circuit was extended in 1975 by the Ninth Circuit's decision in *Crescent Wharf and Warehouse Co. v. Commissioner*.[185]

At present, the following principles are applicable in determining whether a fixed liability exists.

---

[176] Reg. § 1.446-1(c)(1)(ii)(B).

[177] *See Spencer, White & Prentis, Inc. v. Comm'r*, 144 F.2d 45 (2d. Cir. 1944), *cert denied*, 323 U.S. 780 (1944). In *Spencer*, a contractor who was engaged in the construction of a subway system and who was required under contract to restore certain property damaged or otherwise affected by the construction was denied deductions for the accrued estimated cost of restoration. The Court held that the liability for work done after the end of the taxable year had not been incurred because the work had not been performed. The Court also held that the deductions were allowable only when the taxpayer's liability to pay became definite and certain. *See, e.g.*, Rev. Rul. 98-39, 1998-2 CB 198.

[178] Rev. Rul. 80-230, 1980-2 CB 169; Rev. Rul. 79-410. 1979-2 CB 213.

[179] Reg. § 1.446-1(c)(1)(ii)(B); Priv. Ltr. Rul. 200619022.

[180] *Decision Inc. v. Comm'r*, 47 T.C. 58 (1966), *acq.*, 1967-2 CB 2.

[181] *United States. v. Hughes Props. Inc.*, 476 U.S. 593, 86-1 USTC ¶ 9440 (1986); *Gold Coast Hotel & Casino v. United States*, 158 F.3d 484, 98-2 USTC ¶ 50,800 (9th Cir. 1998).

[182] *Canton Cotton Mills v. United States*, 94 F. Supp. 561 (Ct. Cl. 1951), 51-1 USTC ¶ 9131.

[183] *United States v. General Dynamics Corp*, 481 U.S. 239 (1987), 87-1 USTC ¶ 9280.

[184] *Harrold v. Comm'r*, 192 F.2d 1002 (4th Cir. 1951).

[185] 518 F.2d 772 (9th Cir.1975).

- No deduction is allowed for reserves (other than those specifically authorized by the Code) or other amounts that are contingent, *i.e.*, with respect to which there is a condition precedent.[186]
- If the taxpayer's obligation is fixed, the possibility that the liability might be reduced or eliminated by later events or that amounts paid might be returned (*i.e.*, by conditions subsequent) are ignored.[187]
- When the fact or amount of liability depends upon the events, which occur during a measurement period, the liability does not accrue until the measurement period ends.[188]
- Where a taxpayer contests the existence of a liability prior to the close of the current taxable year, the liability (to the extent contested) is not considered fixed in the current period.[189]
- A liability is not considered to be fixed in the current period where, by its terms, it does not accrue until the taxpayer is able to make payment.[190] However, a taxpayer's inability to make current payment of an otherwise absolute liability will not prevent generally such liability from becoming fixed for tax purposes.[191]
- A taxpayer's ability to treat a liability as being fixed in the current period is not generally affected by the fact that it will not be paid for some time, or that the time of payment (but not the liability to make payment) is uncertain, or by the fact that it will be paid in installments.[192]
- There is no requirement that the ultimate beneficiary of the liability remain the same, or even be known.[193]
- Where actions, such as filing of a claim, are required on the part of the other party in order to receive payment from the taxpayer, the all-events test is generally not considered satisfied until such actions are taken.[194]

---

[186] *See, e.g., United States v. General Dynamics Corp.*, 481 U.S. 239 (1987).

[187] *See, e.g., United States v. Hughes Properties*, 476 U.S. 593 (1986). A similar result was reached in *Gold Coast Hotel & Casino v. United States*, 158 F.3d 484 (9th Cir. 1997), where like the guaranteed prize on the jackpot in Hughes, Gold Coast's liability to redeem accumulated slot club points was fixed and unconditional under state law once a slot club member accumulated 1,200 points. Moreover, the fact that a club member may choose not to redeem his/her points immediately did not render Gold Coast's otherwise fixed liability conditional.

[188] *See, e.g., ABKCO Industries v. Comm'r*, 482 F.2d 150 (3d Cir. 1973).

[189] *See, e.g.*, Reg. § 1.461-2.

[190] *See Putoma Corp. v. Comm'r*, 66 T.C. 652 (1976), *aff'd*, 601 F.2d 734 (5th Cir. 1979).

[191] *See* Rev. Rul. 70-367, 1970-2 CB 37.

[192] *See, e.g., United States v. Hughes Properties*, 476 U.S. 593 (1986).

[193] *Id.; see also Exxon Mobil Corp. v. Comm'r*, 114 T.C. 293 (2000), where the court said: "The first prong of the all-events test looks only to whether the taxpayer's fact of liability for the costs in question has been established. This test may be satisfied even if it is not known when or to whom costs will be paid."

[194] *See* TAM 9416004 and 9343006.

In addition, a liability can be fixed by a statutory or regulatory obligation to perform certain activities.[195]

Special rules for accruing deductions/credits apply for:

- contested liabilities;[196]
- an accrual method taxpayer's death;[197]
- the ratable accrual of real estate taxes;[198]
- the acceleration of tax accrual;[199] and
- certain dividends and interest.[200]

[C] *Contingent Liabilities*

A deduction for a contingent liability is not allowed. This is so even though the courts have held generally that the length of time between accrual and performance does not affect whether an amount is properly accruable. However, in *Mooney Aircraft, Inc. v. United States*,[201] a taxpayer was not allowed a deduction where the taxpayer gave purchasers of its airplanes bonds redeemable when the planes were permanently retired from service, because the possible interval between accrual and payment was "too long." The court in this case concluded that the likelihood of repayment decreases as the time between accrual and payment increases. Therefore, in its view, there was no reasonable connection between the accrual of the deduction and the payment of the liability.[202]

The IRS takes the position that, for an amount to be deductible, there must be a current liability to pay the amount, and there must not be a contingency as to payment (other than ability of the obligor to pay).[203]

Judicial decisions have made it clear that the all-events test is not satisfied, and a liability is not established, by a statistical probability—however high—that the taxpayer will ultimately pay the expense. The test requires that nothing further be needed to create a fixed liability. If the taxpayer's obligation remains in some way contingent (*i.e.*, dependent on some discrete event that has not yet occurred), the

---

[195] *United States. v. Hughes Props Inc.*, 476 U.S. 593, 86-1 USTC ¶9440 (1986); *Gold Coast Hotel & Casino v. United States*, 158 F.3d 484, 98-2 USTC ¶50,800 (9th Cir. 1998).

[196] *See* §6.09, *infra.*

[197] IRC §461(b); Reg. §1.461-1(b).

[198] *See* §6.08, *infra.*

[199] IRC §461(d).

[200] IRC §461(e); Reg. §1.461-1(e)(1).

[201] 420 F.2d 400 (5th Cir. 1969). For a similar attempt to recognize a current deduction regarding the exercise of warrants issued to induce a purchaser to purchase a company's product, *see Convergent Technologies, Inc.* 70 TCM 87, T.C. Memo. 1995-320 (1995).

[202] In *Malone & Hyde, Inc. v. Comm'r*, T.C. Memo. 1989-604, 58 TCM 631, 639 (1989), *opinion supplemented by*, 66 TCM 1551 (1993), *rev'd*, 62 F.3d 835 (6th Cir. 1995), the court said "The purpose of the first prong of the 'all events' test is to prevent taxpayers from deducting expenditures that may never occur."

[203] Rev. Rul. 72-34, 1972-1 CB 132. *See also Putoma Corp. v. Comm'r*, 601 F. 2d 734 (5th Cir. 1979) and *Restore, Inc. v. Comm'r*, T.C. Memo. 1997-571, 74 TCM 1475 (1997).

deduction will not satisfy the all-events test and may be disallowed. Thus, there can be no accrual if the liability has not actually been incurred and is contingent on an uncertain future event.[204]

[D] *Amount of Liability*

In order for an amount to be deductible under the all-events test, it must be determinable with reasonable accuracy. This rule is satisfied if the amount of the liability, although not definitely ascertained, can be estimated with reasonable accuracy; certainty is not required.

Courts have adopted a rule of reason; they have held that the propriety of an accrual must be judged by the facts that the taxpayer knew or could reasonably be expected to know at the closing of its books for the taxable year.[205] Estimates based on industry-wide experience and the experience of the taxpayer have been accepted. To require a more stringent test would postpone the accrual of an expense to a point where matching it with income would be difficult. In *Kaiser Steel Corp. v. United States*,[206] the court allowed the reasonable accuracy of the amount reserved for anticipated liabilities to be determined by estimating the amount of the liability on an aggregate claim rather than an individual claim basis. However, if a contingency exists, income is deferred until the contingency is resolved.[207]

In general, the IRS takes a more restrictive position. Under its view, the exact amount of the liability must be determinable by a computation based on presently known or knowable factors. For example, the IRS has held that a taxpayer who was in the business of strip-mining did not know, nor was it possible to know, the amount of its expenditures since the reclamation work was not rendered by the taxpayer and the taxpayer did not contract with a third party to perform the services.[208]

§ 6.07 Economic Performance and Accrual of Expenses

[A] *Generally*

In 1984, Congress enacted IRC § 461(h) (the "Act"). In a number of cases prior to the Act, the courts held that expenditures were deductible only when the activities that the taxpayer was obligated to perform *were in fact performed*, not when the "fact" of the obligation to perform was determined.[209] In *Spencer*, a contractor who was

---

[204] *See New York Life Insurance Co. v. United States*, 724 F.3d 256 (2d Cir. 2013); *United States v. Anderson*, 46 S.Ct. 131 (1926).

[205] *Baltimore Transfer Co. v. Comm'r*, 8 T.C. 1 (1947). *See also General Dynamics Corp. v. United States*, 773 F.2d 1224 (Fed. Cir. 1985), *rev'd*, 481 U.S. 239 (1987).

[206] 717 F.2d 1304 (9th Cir. 1983). *See also* TAM 200037004.

[207] Rev. Rul. 80-308, 1980-2 CB 162.

[208] Priv. Ltr. Rul. 7831003.

[209] *Spencer, White and Printis, Inc. v. Comm'r*, 144 F.2d 45 (2d Cir. 1944).

engaged in the construction of a subway system and who was required under contract to restore certain damaged property was denied deductions for the accrual estimated cost of restoration. The court held that the liability for work done after the end of the taxable year had not been incurred because the work had not been performed.

Before enactment of the Act, courts reached different conclusions allowing taxpayers to deduct the amount of a liability if all the events that fix the liability had occurred and the amount could be determined with reasonable accuracy even though the activities the taxpayer was obligated to perform were not actually performed until a later year.[210]

The Blue Book explanation of the changes enacted by Congress in 1984 point toward the significant revenue loss to the government by taxpayers who took premature accrual deductions; *i.e.*, deductions for expenses not yet paid or performed. Noting that a deduction for a contingent liability was not generally allowed because all of the events necessary to fix the liability had not yet occurred, the Blue Book pointed out however that in *Lukens Steel Co. v. Commissioner*,[211] the court allowed the taxpayer to deduct an amount paid to a trust fund benefit under a negotiated supplemental unemployment benefit plan, including amounts accrued in a "contingent liability account" until a targeted fund amount was reached.

The Service however took the position for an amount to be deductible, there must be a current liability to pay that amount, and there must not be a contingency as to payment (other than the ability of the obligor to pay).[212]

The Blue Book noted that the 1984 Congress believed that the prior accounting rules relating to the *time* for a deduction by a taxpayer using the accrual method of accounting should be changed to take into account time value of money and the time a deduction was economically incurred. Congress was concerned about the revenue loss from taxpayers taking overstated deductions. It noted that in many everyday business transactions, taxpayers had incurred (deducted) liabilities to pay expenses in the future. Congress believed that because of the large number of transactions in which deductions might be overstated and because of the high interest rate that existed, the magnitude of the revenue loss was significant.

Congress noted that the prior law *i.e.*, the "all-events test" failed to take into account time value of money and had become the cornerstone for a variety of tax abuses and shelters. In order to correct and limit the abuses, Congress added the "economic performance" requirement to the statute so no deduction would be permitted by an accrual method taxpayer even if the all-events test was satisfied until the taxpayer economically performed.

The principal provided by the Act describes the two most common categories of liabilities: first, cases where the liability arose as a result of another person providing goods and services to the taxpayer and, second, cases where the liability requires the

---

[210] *Harold v. Comm'r*, 192 F.2d 1002 (4th Cir. 1951).

[211] 442 F.2d 1131 (3d Cir. 1971).

[212] Rev. Rul. 72-34, 1972-1 CB 132.

taxpayer to provide goods and services to another person or undertake some activity as a result of its income producing activities.

With respect to the second category, a taxpayer was required to provide property or perform services. Economic performance occurred since the taxpayer provided the property or performance of the services. Citing *Spencer*, the Blue Book said that economic performance occurred as repairs were made by the contractor, *i.e.*, economically performed. Allowing a taxpayer to take a deduction currently for an amount to be paid in the future overstated the true cost of the expense since the time value of money was not taken into account. The deduction is overstated to the extent the face value exceeds the present value of the expense. The longer the period of time involved, the greater the overstatement.

An example of this overstatement of cost can be found in a pre-§ 461(h) case of *Burnham Corp. v. Commissioner,*[213] In *Burmham,* the corporation engaged in manufacturing used the accrual method of accounting. In 1980, Burnham was a defendant in a lawsuit for patent infringement. Pursuant to an agreement settling the suit, Burnham agreed to pay the plaintiff $1,250 per month for the rest of her life, with the first payment to be made in December 1980. The agreement required Burnham to make 48 monthly payments, totaling $60,000, whether or not the plaintiff survived until the end of the 48-month period. In case of her death before the end of this period, Burnham was obligated to make the monthly payments to the plaintiff's estate, until the $60,000 obligation was satisfied. After making payments totaling $60,000, Burnham's obligation to make more monthly payments to the plaintiff was conditioned on the plaintiff's survival, which, as of September 28, 1987, had continued.

Using life expectancy tables, Burnham estimated that the plaintiff would live 16 years beyond 1980. Because 16 years of monthly payments would total $240,000, Burnham claimed a deduction of $240,000 on its 1980 federal income tax return for its obligation to the plaintiff. The Commissioner took the position that Burnham was entitled to deduct no more than $60,000, which represented the sum of payments required for the initial 48-month period.

Holding that Burnham's liability to the plaintiff satisfied the all-events test, the Tax Court[214] concluded that Burnham was entitled to deduct $240,000. In his opinion, Judge Williams reasoned that Burnham's liability to the plaintiff was fixed in 1980, when the settlement agreement was reached, and that the plaintiff's death would merely act to terminate the already established liability.[215]

At the time of the *Burnham* decision, an expense could be deducted under the all-events test when:

- all the events must have occurred which establish the fact of the liability, and
- the amount of the liability must be capable of being determined with reasonable accuracy.[216]

---

213 878 F.2d 86 (2d 1989).

214 90 T.C. 953, 959 (1988).

215 *Id.* at 958.

216 Reg. § 1.461-1(a)(2).

The Commissioner did not dispute that Burnham's liability to the plaintiff satisfied the second prong of the all-events test. The Commissioner argued that since Burnham was not obligated to continue payments to the plaintiff beyond the first 48 months unless the plaintiff continued to live, all the events needed to fix the fact of Burnham's liability had not occurred in 1980. "[T]axpayer has claimed a deduction of an estimated expense," the Commissioner's brief states, "based on an event that had not occurred by the close of the taxable year, i.e., the plaintiff's continued survival each month for a period of 16 years."

The Second Circuit disagreed. The Court did not believe that the plaintiff's continued survival should be viewed as an "event" for purposes of the all-events test. An "event," as the Court views it, was ordinarily something that marks a change in the status quo. The Court said because the plaintiff's survival is merely a continuation of the status quo, it was not an "event." Since nothing but a continuation of the status quo was necessary to obligate Burnham to keep making payments to the plaintiff the Second Circuit viewed Burnham's liability as fixed.

To resolve this concern of premature accruals, Congress enacted IRC § 461(h), which added a third requirement to the "all-events test" for determining the taxable year in which an item may be treated as incurred by an accrual method taxpayer. This requirement provides that the all-events test shall not be treated as satisfied any earlier than the taxable year in which "economic performance" occurs with respect to a liability. This "economic performance" requirement applies to any item allowable as a cost, expense, or deduction, except for certain items for which the Code provides alternative timing rules.

[B] *When Economic Performance Occurs*

When does "economic performance" occur? The following general principles are applicable in making this determination:

- If the liability of a taxpayer arises out of the provision of property or services to the taxpayer by another person, *economic performance occurs* as the property or services are provided;[217]
- If the liability of a taxpayer arises out of the use of property by the taxpayer, *economic performance occurs* as the taxpayer uses such property;[218]
- If the liability of a taxpayer requires the taxpayer to provide property or services, *economic performance occurs* as the taxpayer provides the property or services;[219]
- If the liability of a taxpayer requires payment to another person and arises under a workers' compensation act or arises out of any tort, *economic performance occurs* as the payments to such person are made;[220] and

[217] Reg. § 1.461-4(d)(2)(i).

[218] Reg. § 1.461-4(d)(3)(i).

[219] Reg. § 1.461-4(d)(4)(i).

[220] Reg. § 1.461-4(g)(2)(i). The Regulations identify six types of liabilities, in addition to liabilities arising under a workers' compensation act or out of a tort, for which payment must be made in order

- In the case of any other liability of a taxpayer, *economic performance occurs* at the time determined under the regulations prescribed by the Secretary.

The examples provided below explain when economic performance occurs.

Example 6-40

Services or Property Provided by the Taxpayer. X Corporation, a calendar year, accrual method taxpayer, is an oil company. During March year 1, X enters into an oil and gas lease with Y. In November year 6, X installs a platform and commences drilling. The lease obligates X to remove its offshore platform and well fixtures upon abandonment of the well or termination of the lease. During year 8, X removes the platform and well fixtures at a cost of $200,000.

Economic performance with respect to X's liability to remove the offshore platform and well fixtures occurs as X incurs costs in connection with that liability. X incurs these costs in year 8 when X's employees provide X with removal services. Consequently, X incurs $200,000 for the year 8 taxable year.

Alternatively, assume that during year 1 X pays Z $130,000 to remove the platform and fixtures, and that Z performs these removal services in year 9. X does not incur this cost until Z performs the services. Thus, economic performance with respect to the $130,000 that X pays Z occurs in year 9.

Example 6-41

Services or Property Provided by the Taxpayer. W Corporation, a calendar year, accrual method taxpayer, sells tractors under a ten-year warranty that obligates W to make any reasonable repairs to each tractor it sells. During year 1, W sells ten tractors. In year 8, W repairs, at a cost of $5,000, two tractors sold during year 1.

Economic performance with respect to W's liability to perform services under the warranty occurs as W incurs costs in connection with that

(Footnote Continued)

for economic performance to occur. These liabilities are: (1) liabilities arising out of a breach of contract; (2) liabilities arising out of a violation of law; (3) rebates and refunds; (4) awards, prizes, and jackpots; (5) amounts paid for insurance, warranty, and service contracts; and (6) taxes other than creditable foreign taxes. The regulations provide that creditable foreign taxes are incurred under the rules in effect before the enactment of IRC §461(h). This rule is provided in order to preserve the matching principles underlying the foreign tax credit provisions. The regulations also provide that if IRC §461(h) or the regulations thereunder do not otherwise provide economic performance rules for a liability, economic performance occurs as payment is made to the person to which the liability is owed. The vast majority of liabilities either involves the provision of property or services by or to a taxpayer, or are specifically designated in the statute or the regulations as payment liabilities.

liability. W incurs costs in year 8 when replacement parts are provided to W. Consequently, $5,000 is incurred by W for the taxable year 1.

Example 6-42

Services or Property Provided by the Taxpayer; Long-Term Contracts. W corporation, a calendar year, accrual method taxpayer, manufactures machine tool equipment. In November year 6, W contracts to provide X corporation with certain equipment. The contract is not a long-term contract under IRC § 460 or Reg. § 1.451-3. In year 6, W pays Z corporation $50,000 to lease from Z, for a one-year period beginning on January 1, year 7, testing equipment to perform quality control tests required by the agreement with X. In year 6, pursuant to the terms of a contract, W pays Y corporation $100,000 for certain parts necessary to manufacture the equipment. The parts are provided to W in year 7. W's employees provide W with services necessary to manufacture the equipment during year 7, for which W pays $150,000 in year 7.

Economic performance with respect to W's liability to provide the equipment to X occurs as W incurs costs in connection with that liability. W incurs these costs during year 7, as services, property, and the use of property necessary to manufacture the equipment are provided to W. Accordingly; $300,000 is incurred by W for the year 7.[221]

Alternatively, assume that the agreement with X is a long-term contract as defined in IRC § 460(f), and that W takes into account all items with respect to such contracts under the percentage of completion method as described in IRC § 460(b)(1). The $100,000 W pays in year 6 for parts is incurred in year 6 for purposes of determining the percentage of completion under IRC § 460(b)(1)(A). W's other costs under the agreement are incurred for the year 7 taxable year.

Example 6-43

Services or Property Provided to the Taxpayers. LP1, a calendar year, accrual method limited partnership, owns the working interest in a parcel of property containing oil and gas. During December year 6, LP1 enters into a turnkey contract with Z corporation pursuant to which LP1 pays Z $200,000 and Z is required to provide a completed well by the close of year 8. In May year 8, Z commences drilling the well, and in December year 8, the well is completed.

---

[221] *See* IRC § 263A and the regulations thereunder for rules relating to the capitalization and inclusion in inventory of these incurred costs.

Economic performance with respect to LP1's liability for drilling and development services provided to LP1 by Z occurs as the services are provided. Consequently, $200,000 is incurred by LP1 for the year 8.

Example 6-44

Services or Property Provided to the Taxpayer. X corporation, a calendar year, accrual method taxpayer, is an automobile dealer. On January 15, year 6, X agrees to pay an additional $10 to Y, a manufacturer of automobiles, for each automobile purchased by X from Y. Y agrees to provide advertising and promotional activities to X.

During year 6, X purchases from Y 1,000 new automobiles and pays to Y an additional $10,000 as provided in the agreement. Y, in turn, uses this $10,000 to provide advertising and promotional activities during year 6.

Economic performance with respect to X's liability for advertising and promotional services provided to X by Y occurs as the services are provided. Consequently, $10,000 is incurred by X for the year 6 taxable year.

Example 6-45

Use of Property Provided to the Taxpayer; Services or Property Provided to the Taxpayer. V corporation, a calendar year, accrual method taxpayer, charters aircrafts. On December 20, year 6, V leases a jet aircraft from L for a four-year period that begins on January 1, year 7. The lease obligates V to pay L a base rental of $500,000 per year. In addition, the lease requires V to pay $25 to an escrow account for each hour that the aircraft is flown. The escrow account funds are held by V and are to be used by L to make necessary repairs to the aircraft. Any amount remaining in the escrow account upon the termination of the lease is payable to V. During year 7, the aircraft is flown 1,000 hours and V pays $25,000 to the escrow account. The aircraft is repaired by L in year 8. In year 9, $20,000 is released from the escrow account to pay L for the repairs.

Economic performance with respect to V's base rental liability occurs ratably over the period of time V is entitled to use the jet aircraft. Consequently, the $500,000 rent is incurred by V for the taxable year 7 and for each of the next three taxable years. Economic performance with respect to the liability to place amounts in escrow occurs as the aircraft is repaired. Consequently, V incurs $20,000 for the year 8 taxable year.

Example 6-46

Use of Property Provided to the Taxpayer. X corporation, a calendar year, accrual method taxpayer, manufactures and sells electronic circuitry. On November 15, year 6, X enters into a contract with Y that entitles X to the exclusive use of a product owned by Y for a five-year period beginning on January 1, year 7. Pursuant to the contract, X pays Y $100,000 on December 30, year 6.

Economic performance with respect to X's liability for the use of property occurs ratably over the period of time X is entitled to use the product. Consequently, $20,000 is incurred by X for year 7 and for each of the succeeding four taxable years.

Example 6-47

Use of Property Provided to the Taxpayer. Y corporation, a calendar year, accrual method taxpayer, enters into a five-year lease with Z for the use of a copy machine beginning on July 1, year 7. Y receives delivery of the copy machine on July 1, year 7. The lease obligates Y to pay Z a base rental payment of $6,000 per year at the beginning of each lease year and an additional charge of 5 cents per copy 30 days after the end of each lease year. The machine is used to make 50,000 copies during the first lease year; 20,000 copies in year 8, and 30,000 copies from January 1, year 9, to July 1, year 9. Y pays the $6,000 base rental payment to Z on July 1, year 7, and the $2,500 variable use payment on July 30, year 9.

Economic performance with respect to Y's base rental liability occurs ratably over the period of time Y is entitled to use the copy machine. Consequently, the $3,000 rent is incurred by Y for the year 7 taxable year. Economic performance with respect to Y's variable use portion of the liability occurs as Y uses the machine. Thus, the $1,000 of the $2,500 variable-use liability that relates to the 20,000 copies made in year 7 is incurred by Y for the year 7 taxable year.

Example 6-48

Use of Property Provided to the Taxpayer. X corporation, a calendar year, accrual method taxpayer, enters into a five-year product distribution agreement with Y, on January 1, year 6. The agreement provides for a payment of $100,000 on January 1, year 6, plus 10% of the gross profits earned by X from distribution of the product. The variable income portion of X's liability is payable on April 1st of each subsequent year. On January 1, year 6, X pays Y $100,000. On April 1, year 7, X pays Y $3 million representing 10% of X's gross profits from January 1, year 7, through December 31, year 7.

Economic performance with respect to X's $100,000 payment occurs ratably over the period of time X is entitled to use the product. Consequently, $20,000 is incurred by X for each year of the agreement beginning with the year 6. Economic performance with respect to X's variable income portion of the liability occurs as the income is earned by X. Thus, the $3 million variable-income liability is incurred by X for the year 7 taxable year.

[C] Exception

Volume, frequency of use, or income. If the liability of a taxpayer arises out of the use of property by the taxpayer and all or a portion of the liability is determined by reference to the frequency or volume of use of the property or the income from the property, economic performance occurs for the portion of the liability determined by reference to the frequency or volume of use of the property or the income from the property as the taxpayer uses the property or includes income from the property. If the IRS determines that, based on the substance of the transaction, the taxpayer's liability for use of the property is more appropriately measured ratably over the period the taxpayer is entitled to the use of the property, then the volume or frequency test does not apply.

Example 6-49

X corporation, a calendar year, accrual method taxpayer, enters into a five-year product distribution agreement with Y, on January 1, year 1. The agreement provides for a payment of $100,000 on January 1, year 1, plus 10% of the gross profits earned by X from distribution of the product. The variable income portion of X's liability is payable on April 1 of each subsequent year. On January 1, year 1, X pays Y $100,000. On April 1, year 2, X pays Y $3 million representing 10% of X's gross profits from January 1 through December 31, year 1.

Under this exception, economic performance with respect to X's $100,000 payment occurs ratably over the period of time X is entitled to use the product. Consequently, $20,000 is incurred by X for each year of the agreement beginning with year 1. Under this exception, economic performance with respect to X's variable income portion of the liability occurs as the income is earned by X. Thus, the $3 million variable-income liability is incurred by X for the year 1 taxable year.

[D] *Misapplication of Economic Performance*

In *Giant Eagle v. Commissioner*,[222] the Third Circuit held that a large supermarket chain could currently deduct the costs of loyalty discounts even if its customers had not yet claimed their rewards. The taxpayer offered customers a loyalty "fuelperks! program" that awarded gas discounts, which if unused, expired in three months. In 2006 and 2007, Giant Eagle currently deducted the estimated costs of redeeming a certain portion of the issued but unexpired and unredeemed fuelperks.

The IRS denied the deduction claiming that the obligation to make payment was not fixed. The Tax Court upheld the IRS's denial of the deduction, finding that the discounts became fixed when the discounts were redeemed, not when they were earned.

The Tax Court in a memorandum decision found for the government. The decision was based on the conclusion that the taxpayer did not meet the all-events test. The taxpayer argued that it did meet the all-events test because it compared its transaction to issuing trading stamps or premium coupons with its sales. The taxpayer argued Reg. § 1.451-4(a)(1) provided an exception to the all-events test. Under this exception the taxpayer could deduct an amount equal to the cost of merchandise, cash or other property used for redemption in the taxable year plus the net addition to the provision for future redemptions during the current taxable year (or less the net subtraction from the provision for future redemptions during the taxable year).

The taxpayer argued that these regulations were designed to match revenue with expenses and, as such, the taxpayers were entitled to a current deduction for the portion of coupons that will eventually be redeemed. The taxpayer said that Reg. § 1.451-4(a)(1) applied and therefore it could offset its sales revenue by the estimated future cost of redeeming the outstanding fuelperks!.

The Tax Court cited Rev. Rul. 78-212,[223] where a taxpayer using the accrual method issued coupons with the sale of products that could be redeemed for a discount on the sale price of products purchased in the future. The Commissioners determined that those coupons were "not redeemable in merchandise, cash, or property" because the redemption of coupons was conditioned on an additional purchase of the retailer's product by the consumer. The Commissioners reasoning was that applying this regulation to the taxpayer's fuelperks! program would be inconsistent with the purpose of the IRC § 451, that is to match sales and revenue incurred to generate those revenues. Under the fuelperks! Program, a taxpayer was not obligated to make a redemption but could combine the discounts to offset purchases of gas in the future; therefore, the coupons issued with the sales and the redemption of fuelperks! were conditioned on subsequent purchases making them not redeemable for "merchandise, cash or other property." Accordingly, the Tax Court determined that the taxpayer was not entitled to offset the estimated future costs of redeeming fuelperks against sales revenues under the exception in Reg. § 1.451-4(a)(1).

---

[222] 822 F.3d 666 (3d Cir. 2016).
[223] 1978-1 CB 139.

The court of appeals did not opine on this finding of the Tax Court having decided the case on the application of the all-events test.

The Third Circuit disagreed with the IRS and the Tax Court, reasoning that Reg. § 1.451-4(a)(1) allowed accrual method taxpayers to deduct expenses before they were paid as long as the all-events test has occurred to determine the existence of the liability and the amount of the liability could be "reasonably determined." The Third Circuit said that the Tax Court misapplied the "all events" test as it applied to "recurring expenses."[224] The Third Circuit did not cite or refer to the recurring item exception, nor did the Commissioner bring into question whether the taxpayer made a recurring item election.

Since the recurring item exception must be adopted for the first taxable year in which that type of item is incurred, one might consider if a taxpayer that has failed to adopt the recurring item exception could do so later as a change of accounting. That issue was addressed in Rev. Proc. 2015-14.[225] Section 19 of the ruling provides for changes of accounting. Subsection [G] describes the changes that taxpayers may make including rebates and allowances in order to change to the recurring item exception made under IRC § 461(h)(3) and Reg. § 1.451-5.

However, the change of accounting ruling does not apply to taxpayers' liability to pay a refund. Hence, in *Giant Eagle,* if the taxpayer failed to initially adopt the recurring item exception it would be prohibited from changing its method of accounting for the fuelperks! program.

Citing *United States v. Hughes Properties, Inc.*[226] and *Lukens Steel Co. v. Commissioner,*[227] the Third Circuit determined the taxpayer's anticipated liability was fixed at year's end under contract law principles. Specifically, Giant Eagle characterizes its issuance of fuelperks! rewards as a unilateral contract formed at checkout, which conferred "instant liability" on the supermarket chain to its customers for the rewards they accrued.

Relying on a Pennsylvania state court decision which held that a car dealership, advertising a discount on a future car purchase if a hole-in-one was made on the ninth hole of a local golf course, was obligated to honor its "offer" when a golfer aced the hole despite the dealership's stated intention to end the promotion two days earlier. The court reasoned, "[i]t is the manifested intent of the offeror and not his subjective intent which determines the persons having the power to accept the offer." Because "the offeror's manifested intent, as it appeared from signs posted at the ninth tee, was that a hole-in-one would win the car," the dealer was liable in accordance with such reasonable expectations.[228]

---

224 822 F.3d 666 (3d Cir. 2016).

225 2015-5 IRB 450.

226 476 U.S. 593 (1986).

227 442 F.2d 1131 (3d Cir. 1971).

228 *Cobaugh v. Klick-Lewis, Inc.*, 385 Pa. Super. 587, 561 A.2d 1248 (1989).

The dissent, citing *Gold Coast Hotel & Casino v. United States*[229] for purposes of the all-events test, stated the requirement of an *absolute liability* was critical. The dissent found that after three months there was no liability to the cardholder and furthermore there was no certainty that the point would in fact be redeemed. The dissent would have denied the deduction.

If one discounts the three-month expiration of the reward points and considers it as a condition subsequent, the Third Circuit decision could be rationalized as being consistent with prior case law.

Clearly, the IRS has maintained a different view of gift cards and loyalty discounts. In FAA 200882801F, the IRS ruled a subsidiary of a parent corporation had income from the sale of the parent's gift cards at the time the cards were purchased in or reloaded by stores, but could only take a deduction when the card was ultimately redeemed by a customer.

The Service's analysis was divided into three parts: whether there was gross income; the timing of any income; and the timing of deductions. With respect to the last issue the Service said IRC §461(h)(1) requires economic performance to occur before the all-events test can be satisfied. Under IRC §461(h)(1), if the liability of the taxpayer arises out of another person's providing services to the taxpayer, economic performance occurs as such person provides services.

In other words, a deduction by an accrual method taxpayer may be taken when:

(1) all events that fix the liability have occurred,
(2) the amount of the liability can be determined with reasonable accuracy, and
(3) economic performance has taken place.

Here, explained the IRS, the Sub's liability is to provide gift card holders with the Parent's products. The liability is satisfied by the stores at Sub's direction when customers redeem the cards.

The Service said the Sub's liability is subject to the contingency that gift cardholders must first redeem the card. Once the customer redeems the gift card, but no sooner, Sub's liability is fixed.

In Action on Decision 2016-003,[230] the Service issued a nonacquiesence in the *Giant Eagle's* Third Circuit decision. Stating that the corporation that operated supermarkets and gas stations was entitled under the all-events test to current year deductions for fuelperks/discounts, which customers had accumulated but not yet applied as of tax year's end to fuel purchases. The Service contended that taxpayer's liability for its unredeemed discount coupons was not fixed before a customer purchases fuel. The Service's position was based on controlling Supreme Court decision and belief that the Third Circuit misconstrued cases permitting deduction of liability that was unconditionally fixed at point prior to payment.

In Legal Advice Issued by Field Attorneys (LAFA) 20180101F, the IRS, in applying Reg. §1.451-4, determined that earned rewards issued by a grocery store redeemable for fuel distinguished the Tax Court's decision in *Giant Eagle*.

---

[229] 158 F.3d 484 (9th Cir. 1998).

[230] 2016 AOD LEXIS 3.

A premium coupon, as explained by the Joint Committee on Taxation, is one that is issued in connection with the sale of some item and entitles the holder to tender it (or a number of premium coupons) in exchange for a product, often selected from a catalog, of the customer's choosing, in order to promote the sale of the product with which the coupon is issued.

In Rev. Rul. 78-212,[231] the IRS ruled that Reg. § 1.451-4 did not apply to "discount coupon" expenses (*i.e.*, expenses associated with coupons that provide discounts on the sales price of certain products purchased in the future), reasoning that the right of redemption must be unconditional, with nothing further required from the consumer. The IRS indicated in that ruling that the intent of Reg. § 1.451-4 is to match, in the same tax year, revenues with the expenses incurred in producing those revenues. Implicit to this "matching concept" is that the issuance of a coupon with the sale of a product creates an incidental obligation in an accrual method taxpayer that requires the taxpayer to incur additional expenses at some future time, which is the case for premium coupons but not for discount coupons.

In LAFA 2018101F, the grocery store offered a fuel reward program to its customers. Under the fuel reward program, the customer signed up for a free fuel reward card at a participating grocery store. Each week, the store would have products throughout the store with fuel money linked to them. Fuel rewards varied depending on the actual item purchased. The money earned (fuel reward) was electronically loaded to an enrolled customer's fuel card and could be redeemed for gas at any participating gas station unrelated to the grocery store.

Unlike at some grocery stores, the customers did not earn money off a gallon of gas. Rather, the grocery store customers were entitled to free fuel up to the amount of money loaded on the card. The customer inserted the fuel card just like any credit card, and the pump went off when the total amount of money loaded on the card was reached, or sooner if the customer stopped pumping gas. If the customer desired to purchase more gas than the amount loaded on the fuel reward card, the process of purchasing gas started over, *i.e.*, either with cash or a credit card. Participating gas stations honored the fuel card without condition.

Participating gas stations prepared and provided to the grocery store a weekly report that included the fuel reward redemptions at each participating gas station; the aggregate amount of rewards redeemed by enrolled customers during the reporting period; the total number of fuel card gallons to which rewards applied; and the fuel purchase rebate. Within a specified number of business days after receiving the report, the grocery store remitted payment to the gas station in the amount billed for redeemed rewards less the fuel purchase rebate.

Customers kept the same fuel card indefinitely and rewards were continually added to that card as they were earned. If the card was inactive for a certain period of time, it was deactivated. If the program was terminated by the gas station or the grocery store, the fuel rewards would continue being honored for a certain number of months. The gas station and the grocery store used an average retail price of a gallon

---

231 1978-1 CB 139.

of gas at each respective store. The grocery store's treatment for both book and tax purposes was to immediately expense the fuel rewards at the time of issuance.

The LAFA also considered the Tax Court's decision in *Giant Eagle* and Rev. Rul. 78-212 in applying Reg. § 1.451-4 and concluded that its analysis was consistent with the purpose of the regulations which was to match revenue with expenses and yet did not conflict with the *Giant Eagle* case or Rev. Rul. 78-212.

[E] 3½ Month Exception

While not in IRC § 461(h) itself, under Reg. § 1.461-4(d)(6), a taxpayer may deduct the expenses it has paid for the services or property provided by another party, if the taxpayer can reasonably expect the other party to provide the services or property within three months after the date of payment. Consider the following, for example.

Example 6-50

Taxpayer X is a calendar year taxpayer. On December 1st of year 1, X pays Y $10,000 to paint its offices and X believes the offices will be painted before the end of three months. Due to circumstances beyond X's control, the painting does not take place until the month of May of Year 2. Under the general rule of economic performance, X would not be permitted to take a deduction until Year 2. However, because at the time X made payment, X believed that the services would be performed within $3^1/_2$ months, the economic performance requirement is deemed to have been met in Year 1.

[F] Recurring Items Exception

The more frequently used exception is the recurring item exception. An expense item may be treated as incurred in the taxable year before economic performance occurs, if and only if the following four conditions are satisfied:[232]

(1) The all-events test, without regard to economic performance, must be satisfied with respect to the item during the taxable year.
(2) Economic performance must occur with respect to the item within a reasonable period (but in no event more than $8^1/_2$ months) after the close of the taxable year.

---

[232] IRC § 461(h)(3). The recurring item exception does not apply to interest, workers compensation, tort, breach of contract, and violation of law, or other liabilities of Reg. § 1.461-4 and Reg. § 1.461-5(c). Moreover, the recurring item exception does not apply to any liability incurred by a tax shelter, as defined in IRC § 461(i) and Temp. Reg. § 1.448-1T(b).

(3) The item must be recurring in nature, and the taxpayer must, from year to year, consistently treat items of this type as incurred in the taxable year in which the all-events test (without regard to economic performance) is satisfied.

(4) Either (a) the item must not be a material item, or (b) the accrual of the item in the taxable year in which the all-events test (without regard to economic performance) is satisfied must result in a better matching of the item with the income to which it relates than would result from accruing the item in the taxable year in which economic performance occurs.[233]

[G] Safe Harbor Method of Accounting for Payroll Tax Liabilities

The IRS provides a procedure for an accrual method taxpayer that uses the recurring item exception to the economic performance test under Reg. § 1.461-5 for accruing its payroll tax liabilities and chooses to account for its payroll tax liabilities using the safe harbor method of accounting. The safe harbor does not apply to an employee's portion of FICA tax imposed under IRC § 3101 and deducted by the employer from wages paid to the employee.[234]

Under the safe harbor method of accounting, and solely for purposes of the recurring item exception, a taxpayer is treated as satisfying the requirement in Reg. § 1.461-5(b)(1)(i) for its payroll tax liability in the same year in which all events have occurred that establish the fact of the related compensation liability, and the amount of the related compensation liability can be determined with reasonable accuracy.[235]

[H] Time and Manner of Adopting the Recurring Item Exception

The recurring item exception is a method of accounting that must be consistently applied with respect to a type of item, or for all items, from one taxable year to the next in order to clearly reflect income. A taxpayer is permitted to adopt the recurring item exception as part of its method of accounting for any type of item for the first taxable year in which that type of item is incurred. Except as otherwise provided, the rules of IRC § 446(e) and Reg. § 1.446-1(e) apply to changes to or from the recurring item exception as a method of accounting.

---

[233] IRC § 461(h)(3). Reg. § 1.461-5(b)(4) provides:

i. In determining whether a liability is material, consideration shall be given to the amount of the liability in absolute terms and in relation to the amount of other items of income and expense.

ii. A liability is material if it is material for financial statement purposes under generally accepted accounting principles.

iii. A liability that is immaterial for financial statement purposes under generally accepted accounting principles may be material for purposes of this paragraph (b).

[234] Rev. Proc. 2008-25, Sec. 3, 2008-13 IRB 686.

[235] Rev. Proc. 2008-25, Sec. 3, 2008-13 IRB 686.

A taxpayer may change to the recurring item exception method by accounting for the item on its timely filed original return for such taxable year (including extensions).[236]

[I] Payment

What constitutes payment to another person for purposes of IRC § 461(h)? The regulations[237] provide:

> The term *payment* has the same meaning as is used when determining whether a taxpayer using the cash receipts and disbursements method of accounting has made a payment. Thus, for example, payment includes the furnishing of cash or cash equivalents and the netting of offsetting accounts. Payment does not include the furnishing of a note or other evidence of indebtedness of the taxpayer, whether or not the evidence is guaranteed by any other instrument (including a standby letter of credit) or by any third party (including a government agency). As a further example, payment does not include a promise of the taxpayer to provide services or property in the future (whether or not the promise is evidenced by a contract or other written agreement). In addition, payment does not include an amount transferred as a loan, refundable deposit, or contingent payment.

Whether payment has occurred is determined under the principles applicable to a taxpayer using the cash method of accounting. The regulations provide that payment has not been made to another person unless a cash basis taxpayer in the position of that person would be treated as having actually or constructively received the amount of the payment under the principles of IRC § 451.[238]

Accordingly, the purchase of an annuity contract or other asset does not constitute payment to another person unless the ownership of the annuity contract or other asset is transferred to that person.[239] Moreover, the furnishing of a note or other evidence of indebtedness by a taxpayer, or a promise by a taxpayer to provide property or services in the future, is not payment for purposes of IRC § 461(h). In addition, a payment is not an amount transferred as a loan, deposit, or contingent payment with respect to which the taxpayer may receive a refund or credit.[240]

---

[236] Reg. § 1.461-5(d)(2)(ii).
[237] Reg. § 1.461-4(g)(1)(ii)(A).
[238] Reg. § 1.461-4(g)(1).
[239] Reg. § 1.461-4(g)(1)(ii)(B).
[240] Reg. § 1.461-4(g)(1)(ii)(A).

[J] Person to Whom Payment Is Made

In general, economic performance occurs when payment is made to the person to whom the liability is owed.[241] For example, in the case of a liability arising under a workers' compensation act, economic performance occurs when payment is made to the person entitled to payment under the appropriate act.

On the other hand, a payment to a trust, escrow account, fund, or any person other than the person to whom a liability is owed does not constitute performance. However, payments to certain third persons constitute economic performance. For example, under IRC § 468B, payment to a designated settlement fund constitutes economic performance in the case of certain tort liabilities. The regulations extend the availability of IRC § 468B treatment to a payment to a "qualified fund."

In addition, the regulations provide, in connection with the sale of a trade or business by a taxpayer, if the purchaser agrees to assume a liability of the taxpayer arising out of the trade or business, the taxpayer is deemed to be making payments on that liability for purposes of IRC § 461(h), since the amount of the liability is included in the amount realized by the taxpayer on the transaction. The regulations define "trade or business" using principles drawn from IRC § 355(b) and the regulations thereunder.[242]

The regulations also provide that qualified assignments under IRC § 130, relating to certain personal injury liability assignments, constitute economic performance.

The regulations detail certain liabilities for which payment is economic performance:

- Liabilities arising under a workers compensation act or out of any tort, breach of contract, or violation of law;[243]
- Rebates and refunds;[244]
- Awards, prizes, and jackpots;[245]
- Insurance, warranty, and service contracts;[246] and
- Taxes.[247]

[K] Exceptions to the Economic Performance Test

If a liability of a taxpayer is subject to IRC §§ 170 (charitable contributions), 192 (black lung benefit trusts), 194A (employer liability trusts), 468 (mining and solid waste disposal reclamation and closing costs), or 468A (certain nuclear decommissioning costs), the liability is taken into account as determined under these sections

---

[241] Reg. § 1.461-4(g)(1).
[242] Reg. § 1.461-4(g)(1)(ii)(C).
[243] Reg. § 1.461-4(g)(2).
[244] Reg. § 1.461-4(g)(3).
[245] Reg. § 1.461-4(g)(4).
[246] Reg. § 1.461-4(g)(5).
[247] Reg. § 1.461-4(g)(6).

and not under IRC § 461 or the regulations.[248] Moreover, the "economic performance" requirement is deemed satisfied to the extent that any amount is otherwise deductible under IRC § § 404 (employer contributions to a plan of deferred compensation), 404A (certain foreign deferred compensation plans), or 419 (welfare benefit funds).[249] Rev. Proc. 92-29[250] provides rules for a real estate developer to obtain IRS consent to use an alternative to the economic performance rules in IRC § 461(h) including reclamation closing cost reserves of mining or solid waste per IRC § 468 and transfers to designated settlement funds/qualified settlement funds per IRC § 468B(a).

[L] Ratable Service Contract Safe Harbor Method of Accounting

A taxpayer may treat economic performance as occurring on a ratable basis over the term of the service contract.[251]

A contract is a Ratable Service Contract if:

- the contract provides for similar services to be provided on a regular basis, such as daily, weekly, or monthly;
- each occurrence of the service provides independent value, such that the benefits of receiving each occurrence of the service is not dependent on the receipt of any previous or subsequent occurrence of the service, and;
- the term of the contract does not exceed 12 months (contract renewal provisions will not be considered in determining whether a contract exceeds 12 months). If a single contract includes services that satisfy the requirements of this section and services (or other items) that do not satisfy the requirements of this section, the services (or other items) that do not satisfy the requirements of this section must be separately priced in the contract for the contract to qualify as a Ratable Service Contract.

The following examples illustrate the application of the safe harbor method of accounting for Ratable Service Contracts. In each example, the taxpayer uses an accrual method of accounting for federal income tax purposes, including the use of the 3½-month rule and the recurring item exception, and files its returns on a calendar year basis.

Example 6-51

On December 31, 2019, Taxpayer enters into a one-year service contract with X. Under the contract, X will provide janitorial services on a daily basis to Taxpayer until the end of 2020. Under the contract, Taxpayer pays

---

[248] Reg. § 1.461-1(a)(2)(iii)(B). For special rules relating to certain loss deductions, *see* IRC § § 165(e), 165(i), and 165(l), relating to theft losses, disaster losses, and losses from certain deposits in qualified financial institutions.

[249] *See* Reg. § 1.461-4(d)(2)(iii).

[250] 1992-1 CB 748.

[251] Rev. Proc. 2015-39, 2015-33 IRB 195.

X $3,000 a month to clean Taxpayer's offices. The contract requires Taxpayer to pay for each month's service by the end of the prior month. On December 31, 2019, Taxpayer makes a $3,000 payment to X for the services to be provided in January 2020. Taxpayer reasonably expects X to provide the janitorial services in January. As of December 31, 2019, all events have occurred to establish the fact of Taxpayer's $3,000 contractually required payment and the amount of the liability is determinable with reasonable accuracy.

The contract meets the requirements of a Ratable Service Contract because the janitorial services are to be provided on a regular basis (daily); each daily occurrence of the janitorial service provides independent value, such that the benefits from each occurrence of the service are not dependent on the receipt of previous or subsequent janitorial services; and the contract term does not exceed 12 months. Under the provisions of Rev. Proc. 2015-39, Taxpayer may treat economic performance as occurring ratably under the contract. Thus, under the $3^1/_2$-month rule Taxpayer is allowed to incur a liability in 2019 for the $3,000 paid in 2019. For the services provided from February through December 2020, economic performance occurs ratably as the services are provided to Taxpayer each day, and a liability of $33,000 for these services is incurred in 2020.

Example 6-52

On December 31, 2019, Taxpayer enters into a one-year service contract with X. Under the contract, X will provide landscape maintenance services to Taxpayer from January through December 2020 on a monthly basis. Under the contract, Taxpayer pays X $4,000 a month to maintain Taxpayer's grounds. The contract requires Taxpayer to prepay for the 12 months of services with the full payment of $48,000 due on December 31, 2019. On December 31, 2019, Taxpayer makes the $48,000 payment to X for services to be provided from January 1, 2020, through December 31, 2020. As of December 31, 2019, all events have occurred to establish the fact of Taxpayer's $48,000 contractually required payment and the amount of the liability is determinable with reasonable accuracy.

The contract meets the requirements of a Ratable Service Contract because the maintenance services are to be provided on a regular basis (monthly); each occurrence of the maintenance service provides independent value, such that the benefits from each occurrence of the service are not dependent on the receipt of prior or subsequent maintenance services; and the contract term does not exceed 12 months. Under the provisions Rev. Proc. 2015-39, Taxpayer may treat economic performance as occurring ratably under the contract. Assuming that Taxpayer satisfies the requirements of the recurring item exception, and files its return on September 15, 2020, Taxpayer is allowed to incur a liability in 2019 of $34,000 (8.5 months/12 months × $48,000) for the services provided from January 1 through September 15, 2020. For the services provided from

September 16 through December 31, 2020, the period outside of the recurring item exception, economic performance occurs ratably as the services are provided to Taxpayer during that time and a liability for these services of $14,000 (3.5 months/12 months × $48,000) is incurred in 2020.

Example 6-53

On November 30, 2019, Taxpayer enters into a one-year contract for an environmental impact study with Y. Under the contract, Y must complete and deliver the study by November 30, 2020. In exchange, Taxpayer will pay Y $100,000 when the contract is signed and $400,000 when the study is delivered on November 30, 2020. Taxpayer makes the payments on the specified dates. Y performs work on the study during 2019 and 2020 and delivers the completed study to Taxpayer on November 30, 2020. On November 30, 2019, all the events have occurred that establish the fact of Taxpayer's contractually required payment of $100,000 and the amount of Taxpayer's liability under the contract can be determined with reasonable accuracy.

The contract does not satisfy the definition of a Ratable Service Contract because the contract does not provide for services to be provided on a regular basis. Rather, the contract specifies that Y will provide to Taxpayer only one service, namely a completed and delivered impact study. Each instance of Y's work on the study during the contract period does not provide independent value to Taxpayer. Instead, each instance of work on the study is dependent on the previous and subsequent work on the study to achieve its completion. Thus, Taxpayer may not treat economic performance as occurring ratably over the term of the service contract pursuant to the safe harbor in Rev. Proc. 2015-39 and may not rely on the safe harbor to incur a liability for any portion of the $100,000 in 2019. Instead, economic performance occurs when the study is completed and a liability of $500,000 for this service is incurred upon its completion.

Example 6-54

On December 31, 2019, Taxpayer enters into a one-year service contract with X. Under the contract, X will provide various IT support and maintenance services to Taxpayer, such as providing help desk support to Taxpayer's employees and maintaining Taxpayer's existing software and web pages (IT services). The IT services will be provided on a daily basis through December 31, 2020. In addition, under the contract, X will create an updated human resources software application for Taxpayer (HR software development service). Under the contract, Taxpayer will pay X a flat fee of $3,000 a month for the IT services and the HR software development service. The contract requires Taxpayer to pay for each month's services by the end of the prior month. On December 31, 2019, Taxpayer makes a $3,000 payment to X for the IT services and HR software development to be provided in January 2020. Taxpayer reasonably expects X to provide the IT services in January. As of December 31, 2019, all events have occurred to establish the fact of Taxpayer's $3,000 contractually required payment and the amount of the liability is determinable with reasonable accuracy.

The contract does not meet the requirements of Rev. Proc. 2015-39 because the contract includes the HR software development service that is not provided on a regular basis. Under the terms of the contract, the HR software development service consists of only one service, an update to Taxpayer's human resources software application. Each instance of X's work on updating the software application during the contract period is dependent on the previous and subsequent work to complete the update and does not provide independent value to Taxpayer. Because the contract does not separately price the HR software development service, which does not meet the requirements for a Ratable Service Contract in Rev. Proc. 2015-39, Taxpayer may not treat economic performance as occurring on a ratable basis over the term of the service contract pursuant to the safe harbor in Rev. Proc. 2015-39.

Example 6-55

Same facts as in Example 6-54, except that under the service contract, the HR software development service is separately priced at $12,000, with $1,000 of the $3,000 monthly payment allocated to the software development service. The IT services described in the contract meet the requirements for a Ratable Service Contract because the IT services are provided on a regular basis (daily); each daily occurrence of IT service provides independent value, such that the benefits from each occurrence of the service are not dependent on the receipt of prior or subsequent IT services; and the contract term does not exceed 12 months. Under the provisions of Rev. Proc. 2015-39, Taxpayer may treat economic performance for the IT services as occurring ratably under the contract. Taxpayer incurs a liability in 2019 for $2,000 of the $3,000 payment for IT services under the $3^1/_2$-month rule. For the IT services provided from February through December 2020, economic performance occurs ratably as the services are provided to Taxpayer each day and a liability of $22,000 for these services is incurred in 2020. For the HR software development service liability, economic performance occurs when the service is completed and a liability of $12,000 for this service is incurred upon completion.

[M] *Long-Term Contracts*

For costs incurred under a long-term contract accounted for under the percentage-of-completion method of IRC § 460, economic performance occurs at the earlier of payment or performance.[252]

[N] *Examples—IRC § 461(h)*

Economic Performance as Payment

Example 6-56

During the period of Year 1 through Year 6, Z corporation, a calendar year, accrual method taxpayer, manufactured and distributed industrial products that contained carcinogenic substances. In Year 21, a number of lawsuits were filed against Z alleging damages for injuries from exposure to its products. In settlement of a lawsuit maintained by A, Z agreed to purchase an annuity contract that would provide annual payments to A of $50,000 for a period of 25 years. On December 15th of Year 21, Z pays W, an unrelated life insurance company, $491,129 for the annuity contract. Z retains ownership of the annuity contract.

Economic performance with respect to Z's liability to A occurs as each payment is made to A. Consequently, $50,000 is incurred as an expense by Z for each taxable year that a payment is made to A under the annuity contract. (Z must also include in income a portion of amounts paid under the annuity, pursuant to IRC § 72.) The result is the same if, in Year 21, Z secures its obligation with a standby letter of credit. If, however, Z transfers ownership of the annuity contract to A, an amount equal to the fair market value of the annuity on the date of transfer is incurred by Z in the taxable year of the transfer.

Example 6-57

Assume the same facts as in Example 6-56, above, except that Z is required by court order to pay $15,000,000 to a fund that will assume sole liability for a specified class of tort claims arising out of the manufacture and distribution of its products containing carcinogenic substances. If Z does not (or cannot) elect the application of IRC § 468B (designated settlement fund), then economic performance with respect to the $15,000,000 liability occurs only as payments are made to the underlying

---

[252] Reg. § 1.461-4(k)(2).

tort claimants from the fund. Consequently, Z incurs only those amounts actually paid to the claimants from the fund during the taxable year.

If Z properly elects the application of IRC § 468B, economic performance with respect to the $15,000,000 liability occurs as Z makes payments to the fund.

Recurring Item Exception

Example 6-58

Y Corporation, a calendar year, accrual method taxpayer, manufactures and distributes DVD players. Y offers to refund the price of the DVD player to any purchaser not satisfied with it. During taxable Year 1, 100 purchasers request a refund of the $500 purchase price. Y refunds $30,000 on or before September 15th of Year 2, and the remaining $20,000 after this date but before the end of taxable Year 2.

Economic performance with respect to the $30,000 of refund liability occurs on or before September 15th of Year 2.

Alternately, assume the refund is deductible (or allowable as an adjustment to gross receipts or cost of goods sold) when incurred. If Y does not or is not entitled to adopt the recurring item exception with respect to rebates and refunds, $30,000 is incurred by Y for taxable Year 2. However, if Y has made a proper election under Reg. § 1.461-5 and, as of December 31st of Year 1, all events have occurred that determine the fact of the liability for the $30,000, Y incurs that amount for taxable Year 1.

Because economic performance (payment) with respect to the remaining $20,000 occurs after September 15th of Year 2 (more than 8-1/2 months after the end of Year 1), the amount is not eligible for recurring item treatment under Reg. § 1.461-5. Thus, the $20,000 amount is not incurred by Y until taxable Year 2.

Example 6-59

X Corporation, a calendar year, accrual method taxpayer, is a manufacturer of printing presses. Under its method of accounting, X recognizes sales income upon execution of the sales contract, rather than upon shipment. In December of Year 1, X contracts to pay common carrier, C, $10,000 in June of Year 2, upon delivery of ten presses sold by X in November of Year 1. X generally incurs such shipping costs from one taxable year to the next.

Economic performance with respect to the amount paid to C for shipping services occurs in June of Year 2, as C provides the shipping services.[253]

Alternately, assume that all the events that fix and determine X's $10,000 liability occur in Year 1. If X adopts the recurring item exception, X may deduct $10,000 for its Year 1 taxable year, even though economic performance does not occur until June of Year 2. The $10,000 expense relates to the Year 1 income from the sale, better matching the results from its accrual in the taxable year preceding the year during which economic performance occurs.

Example 6-60

Assume the same facts as in Example 6-59, above, and assume that X files its income tax return for Year 1 on March 15th of Year 2. The costs are ineligible for recurring item exception treatment because economic performance with respect to the costs does not occur before X files a return for the taxable year for which the item would have been deducted under the exception. However, since economic performance occurs within 82 months after Year 1, X may file an amended return claiming the deduction for its Year 1 taxable year.

Example 6-61

Each year, David hires Robert to come in and thoroughly clean the factory when it is closed between December 20th and January 10th. The cost of Robert's service is $10,000. When does David accrue this liability?

For recurring items, the economic performance requirement does not have to be met in the tax year.[254] Under the recurring item exception, an item may be treated as incurred in the taxable year before economic performance occurs.

---

[253] *See* Reg. § 1.461-4(d)(2).

[254] *See* IRC § 461(h)(3).

§ 6.08 Real Property Taxes

[A] Accrual of Real Property Taxes

Real property taxes that relate to a definite period may be accrued ratably over the period, at the taxpayer's election.[255] The election may be made without the IRS's consent for the first taxable year in which the taxpayer incurs real property taxes. The election may be made for each separate trade or business and for non-business activities if accounted for separately. If the election is not made, the expense of real property taxes is incurred under the accrual method provided the following three requirements are satisfied:

- The obligation to pay is fixed;
- The amount determined is reasonably estimated; and
- The economic performance requirement is satisfied.

Economic performance occurs as the tax is paid to the governmental authority that imposes it. Since payment to the governmental authority occurs after the liability to pay the tax becomes fixed and its amount becomes ascertainable, the taxpayer is allowed to deduct the taxes as they are paid to the governmental authority, in the absence of the election.

Assuming the real property tax period straddles two tax years, the taxpayer would have an acceleration of the deduction in the first tax year under the election if the taxes were payable in their entirety at the end of the real property tax period. On the other hand, if the taxes were payable entirely at the beginning of the real property tax period, the taxpayer would come out with an earlier deduction if it did not make the election. If the taxes are payable ratably during the period, the taxpayer would come out even whether or not he made the election.

Example 6-62

A taxpayer on an accrual method reports his taxable income for the taxable year ending March 31. He elects to accrue real property taxes ratably for the taxable year ending March 31, 1955. In the absence of an election under IRC § 461(c), such taxes are accruable on June 1 of the calendar year to which they relate. The real property taxes are $1,200 for 1954; $1,600 for 1955; and $1,800 for 1956. Deductions for such taxes for the taxable years ending March 31, 1955, and March 31, 1956, are computed as follows:[256] :

Fiscal year ending March 31, 1955

April through December 1954 (9/12 of $1,200)	$900
January through March 1955 (3/12 of $1,600)	400
Taxes accrued ratably in fiscal year ending March 31, 1955	1,300

[255] IRC § 461(c); Reg. § 1.461-1(c)(3).
[256] Reg. § 1.461-1(c)(6), Example 4.

Tax relating to period January through March 1954, paid in June 1954, and not deductible in prior taxable years (3/12 of $1,200)	300
Deduction for fiscal year ending March 31, 1955	1,600
Fiscal year ending March 31, 1956	
April through December 1955 (9/12 of $1,600)	$1,200
January through March 1956 (3/12 of $1,800)	450
Deduction for fiscal year ending March 31, 1956	1,650

Example 6-63

The facts are the same as in Example 6-62 except that in June 1955, when the taxpayer pays his $1,600 real property taxes for 1955, he pays $400 of such amount under protest. Deductions for taxes for the taxable years ending March 31, 1955, and March 31, 1956, are computed as follows[257] :

Fiscal year ending March 31, 1955	
April through December 1954 (9/12 of $1,200)	$900
January through March 1955 (3/12 of $1,200, that is, $1,600 minus $400 (the contested portion which is not properly accruable))	300
Taxes accrued ratably in fiscal year ending March 31, 1955	1,200
Tax relating to period January through March 1954, paid in June 1954, and not deductible in prior taxable years (3/12 of $1,200)	300
Deduction for fiscal year ending March 31, 1955	1,500
Fiscal year ending March 31, 1956	
April through December 1955 (9/12 of $1,200)	$900
January through March 1956 (3/12 of $1,800)	450
Taxes accrued ratably in fiscal year ending March 31, 1956	1,350
Contested portion of tax relating to period January through December 1955, paid in June 1955, and deductible, under IRC § 461(f), for taxpayer's fiscal year ending March 31, 1956	400
Deduction for fiscal year ending March 31, 1956	1,750

[257] Reg. § 1.461-1(c)(6), Example 5.

[B] Limitation on Double Accrual

To the extent that the accrual of a tax is accelerated by the action of a taxing jurisdiction, the tax shall be treated as accruing at the time it would have accrued but for the action of the taxing jurisdiction.[258] This rule serves to prevent a deduction in one year of two years' taxes at the time when a state tax liability accrued for federal tax purposes on the assessment or lien date of the state tax.

Accordingly, if the assessment and lien date for a state tax on property used in business was originally July of each year and the state accelerated the lien date of tax Year 2 year to December 31st of Year 1, a calendar year taxpayer is prevented by the rule from deducting in Year 1 both the Year 1 tax and the Year 2 tax. The original July 1, Year 2 accrual date determines the deduction of Year 2 taxes. The July 1 original accrual date also must be used for all subsequent years. Further, the original accrual date must be used by any subsequent owner of the property on the accrual method. The actual accrual date could be used only if the state moved the date back to July 1st or a later date.[259] Consider the following:

Example 6-64

The laws of State A provide that every person owning property located in State A on the first day of January shall be liable for a tax thereon and that a lien for such tax shall attach as of such date. In addition, the laws of State A provide that 60% of the tax is due on the first day of December following the lien date and the remaining 40% is due on the first day of July of the succeeding year.

On January 1, Year 1, X corporation, a calendar year, accrual method taxpayer, owns property located in State A. State A imposes a $10,000 tax on X with respect to that property on January 1, Year 1. X pays State A $6,000 of the tax on December 1, Year 1, and the remaining $4,000 on July 1, Year 2.

Economic performance with respect to the $6,000 of tax liability occurs on December 1, Year 1. Consequently, $6,000 is incurred by X for the Year 1 taxable year. Economic performance with respect to the remaining $4,000 of the tax liability occurs on July 1, Year 2.

If X has adopted the recurring item exception described in Reg. § 1.461-5 as a method of accounting for taxes, and as of December 31, Year 1, all events have occurred that determine the liability of X for the remaining $4,000, X also incurs $4,000 for the Year 1 taxable year.

If X does not adopt the recurring item exception, the $4,000 is not incurred by X until the Year 2 taxable year.

---

258 IRC § 461(d).

259 Reg. § 1.461-1(d).

§ 6.09 Disputed Liabilities

When an accrual method taxpayer disputes a liability, a deduction for the liability is generally disallowed until the dispute is settled by the parties or is finally adjudicated in the courts.

A deduction will be allowed under IRC § 461(f) when a taxpayer, contesting an asserted liability, transfers money or other property beyond its control to provide for the satisfaction of the asserted liability. Under the regulations,[260] a taxpayer may provide for the satisfaction of an asserted liability by transferring money or other property beyond its control to:

- the person who is asserting the liability;
- an escrowee or trustee pursuant to a written agreement (among the escrowee or trustee, the taxpayer, and the person who is asserting the liability) that the money or other property be delivered in accordance with the settlement of the contest; or
- an escrowee or trustee pursuant to an order of the United States, any state or political subdivision thereof.

A taxpayer may also provide for the satisfaction of an asserted liability by transferring money or other property beyond its control to a court with jurisdiction over the contest. Despite the strictness of the regulations, there is judicial authority for less strict enforcement of IRC § 461(f). In *Edison Brothers Stores, Inc. v. Commissioner*,[261] the Tax Court allowed an accrual of a disputed liability. The taxpayer had a dispute with the United States government and placed the disputed amount in trust with a Missouri bank. The U.S. government was not a signatory to the trust and did not learn of its existence until a year later. The Tax Court allowed an accrual of the disputed liability and said that where funds are placed irrevocably beyond the taxpayer's control a deduction will be allowed under IRC § 461(f). The Court based its decision on the trustee's duty to administer the fund for the benefit of the U.S. government and on lack of abuse.

It should be noted that purchasing a bond to guarantee payment of an asserted liability, an entry on the taxpayer's book of account, and a transfer to an account which is within the control of the taxpayer, are not transfers to provide for the satisfaction of an asserted liability. In order for the money or the property to be beyond the control of a taxpayer, the taxpayer must relinquish all authority over such money or other property.[262]

---

260 Reg. § 1.461-2(c).

261 T.C. Memo. 1995-262, 69 TCM 2897 (1995).

262 *See* Reg. § 1.461-2(c)(1). In *Ford Motor Co. v. Comm'r*, 102 T.C. 87 (1994), *aff'd*, 71 F.3d 209 (6th Cir. 1995), the taxpayer entered into structured settlements for various tort claims. The settlements required payments over periods of time as long as 58 years. The taxpayer purchased single premium annuity contracts to fund the structured settlements. The present value of the annuity payments did not exceed the cost of the annuity contracts. The taxpayer accrued a deduction for all the future payments that it was obligated to make to the tort claimants. The IRS said that the taxpayer's method of accounting did not clearly reflect income under IRC § 446(b).

In *Chernin v. United States*,[263] the taxpayer, as general manager of a corporation, paid himself bonuses from 1978-1982 under an alleged oral agreement and deposited most of the funds in bank accounts in Texas. The employer, claiming that the payments were unauthorized, fired the taxpayer, sued him for embezzlement, and obtained temporary restraining orders against withdrawal from the Texas bank accounts and orders of garnishment against them in 1982. In 1983, pursuant to a settlement, the funds were placed in escrow in a Minnesota bank account to be held pending resolution of the embezzlement litigation. Ultimately, the taxpayer won that litigation and substantial damages for breach of his employment contract, and received the funds from escrow.

The taxpayer did not pay his taxes for the years of the bonuses until the litigation was resolved in 1991. Nevertheless, the taxpayer pursued a refund claim in which he claimed a deduction for the 1982 repayment. The Eighth Circuit held that the garnishment entitled the taxpayer to a deduction under IRC § 461(f) as a business loss under IRC § 165(c)(1). The IRS had conceded that the 1983 escrow met the requirements of IRC § 461(f). Relying on a Ninth Circuit opinion in *Chem Aero*[264] that an appeal bond met the transfer requirement, the court concluded that events other than those specified in Reg. § 1.461-2(c)(1) can qualify as a transfer and that the writ of garnishment satisfied the requirement, because it shifted control of the funds from the taxpayer to the bank.

§ 6.10 Reportable Transactions

Reg. § 1.6011-4(a) provides that every taxpayer that has participated (as described in Reg. § 1.6011-4(c)(3)) in a reportable transaction and that is required to file a tax return must attach a disclosure statement to its return. A "reportable transaction" includes any transaction that is the same as or substantially similar to one of the types of transactions that the IRS has determined to be a tax avoidance transaction and identified by published guidance as a listed transaction.[265]

(Footnote Continued)

The Tax Court agreed with the IRS saying that under *Thor Power Tool Co. v. Comm'r*, 439 U.S. 522 (1979), IRC § 446(c) and Reg. § 1.446-1(a)(2), the taxpayer's ability to select a method of accounting is conditioned on said method clearly reflecting income under IRC § 446(b). The Court concluded that the method of accounting selected by the taxpayer did not clearly reflect income because the payouts caused a gross distortion of the taxpayer's true economic obligation to the tort claimants. The Court noted that the introduction of IRC § 461(h) (the economic performance test) was not intended to limit the IRS's authority under IRC § 446(b).

The Court concluded that the taxpayer's treatment of the annuity payments for financial accounting purposes—expensing only the costs of the contracts—resulted in the proper matching of income and expenses and clearly reflected income for tax purposes. It further noted that the true economic cost to the taxpayer was the amount paid for the annuities.

[263] 149 F.3d 805 (8th Cir. 1998).

[264] 694 F.2d 196, 82-2 USTC ¶ 9712 (9th Cir. 1982).

[265] Reg. § 1.6011-4(b)(2). Generally, a listed transaction is not treated as a reportable transaction if the transaction affected the taxpayer's federal income tax liability as reported on any tax return filed after January 1, 2003. Temp. Reg. § 1.6011-4T was removed as published in T.D. 8877 in 65 Fed. Reg. 11205. *See also* Reg. § 1.6011-4(h).

In Notice 2003-77,[266] the IRS included as "listed transactions"[267] transactions in which taxpayers established trusts purporting to qualify under IRC § 461(f) that are the same as or substantially similar to the following transactions:

- Transactions in which a taxpayer transfers money or other property in taxable years beginning after December 31, 1953, and ending after August 16, 1954, and retains certain powers over the money or other property transferred;
- Transactions in which a taxpayer transfers any indebtedness of the taxpayer or any promise by the taxpayer to provide services or property in the future in taxable years beginning after December 31, 1953, and ending after August 16, 1954;
- Transactions in which a taxpayer using an accrual method of accounting transfers money or other property after July 18, 1984, to provide for the satisfaction of a workers' compensation liability or a tort liability (unless the trust is the person to which the liability is owed, or payment to the trust discharges the taxpayer's liability to the claimant);
- Transactions in which a taxpayer using an accrual method of accounting transfers money or other property in taxable years beginning after December 31, 1991, to provide for the satisfaction of a liability for which payment is economic performance under Reg. § 1.461-4(g) (unless the trust is the person to which the liability is owed, or payment to the trust discharges the taxpayer's liability to the claimant), other than a liability for workers compensation or tort; or
- Transactions in which a taxpayer transfers stock issued by the taxpayer, or indebtedness or stock issued by a party related to the taxpayer (as defined in IRC § 267(b)), on or after November 19, 2003.

In Rev. Proc. 2004-31,[268] the IRS provided exclusive procedures for changing the method of accounting for transactions involving the deduction of amounts transferred to trusts under IRC § 461(f), in satisfaction of contested liabilities. In light of Notice 2003-77, 2003-49 IRB 1182, that identified as "listed transactions" specified arrangements in which taxpayers established trusts purportedly qualified under IRC § 461(f), taxpayers are required to disclose these transactions and file amended returns to change method of accounting. Taxpayers who are not required to disclose may either file amended returns or request a change in accounting method.

---

[266] 2003-2 CB 1182.

[267] For purposes of Reg. § 1.6011-4(b)(2) and Reg. § § 301.6111-2(b)(2) and 301.6112-1(b)(2) of the Procedure and Administration Regulations.

[268] 2004-22 IRB 986.

§6.11 Deferred Compensation

[A] Generally

The economic performance rules do not override other provisions of the Code dealing with the timing of deductions. In particular, IRC §§404 and 267 continue to govern the timing of deductions for deferred compensation and compensation paid to related parties, respectively.

[B] IRC §404 Deductions

Under IRC §§404(a)(5) and 404(a)(6), an otherwise deductible contribution paid or incurred with respect to a nonqualified plan, method or arrangement providing for deferred benefits is deductible in the taxable year of the employer in which or with which ends the taxable year of the employee in which the amount attributable to the contribution is includable in the employee's gross income.

Pursuant to Temp. Reg. §1.404(b)-1T, Q&A 2, a plan, method, or arrangement will be treated generally as deferring the receipt of compensation or benefits if the actual payment of such benefits occurs after the 15th day of the third calendar month after the end of the employer's year in which the related services are rendered.

Pursuant to Temp. Reg. §1.404(d)-1T, these rules apply to payments to both employees and independent contractors.

[C] IRC §267 Deduction

IRC §267(a)(2) provides that an accrual method taxpayer can deduct an accrued expense (such as compensation) payable to a related cash basis taxpayer only in the period in which the payment is included in the recipient's gross income.

Among the relationships falling within the scope of this provision are:

- An individual and a corporation having more than 50% in value of the outstanding stock which is owned, directly or indirectly, by or for such individual;
- A personal service corporation and an employee-owner; and
- A partnership, an S corporation, or an individual who is considered to own stock because it is owned by certain family members and related entities.

The following examples are illustrative of the IRC §267 deduction.

Example 6-65

In December year 1, Zeta Corp., a calendar year, accrual method taxpayer, declares a bonus payable to employee C, a calendar year, cash basis taxpayer. C does not actually or constructively own any stock in Zeta. The bonus is actually paid to C on March 1, year 2. Since payment occurred within two and one-half months after year end, Zeta is allowed to deduct the bonus on its year 2 income tax return.

Example 6-66

Assume the same facts as in Example 6-65, above, except that the bonus is not paid until April 1, year 2. In this case, Zeta's deduction is deferred until year 1, since payment did not occur within two and one-half months of year-end.

Example 6-67

Assume the same facts as in Example 6-65, above, except that C owns 80% of the outstanding stock of Zeta. Since Zeta and C are related parties, Zeta's compensation deduction is deferred until year 2 when payment is actually made.

7

Change in Accounting Method

§7.01 Change in Accounting Method

[A] Generally

Once a method of accounting has been adopted a taxpayer cannot change the method without the consent of the Commissioner.[1] A change in a method of accounting includes a change in the overall plan of accounting for gross income or deductions, or a change in the treatment of any "material item" used in that overall plan.[2] A material item is any item that involves the proper timing for the inclusion of the item in income or the taking of the item as a deduction, or both.[3] In determining whether a taxpayer's accounting practice for an item involves timing, the relevant question is whether the practice permanently changes the amount of the taxpayer's lifetime taxable income. If the practice does not permanently affect the taxpayer's lifetime taxable income, but does or could change the taxable year(s) in which the item is reported, it involves timing and is therefore a method of accounting.[4]

Example 7-1

On December 31, Year 1, X corporation, a calendar year taxpayer, had $1,000,000 of income it had earned during the year but had not yet received. If X uses the accrual method, the income is reported in Year 1, when the income is earned. If X uses the cash method, the income is reported in the year in which the receivable is collected. No matter how long X remains in existence, its lifetime taxable income from this transaction is identical, whether it uses the cash method or the accrual method.

A change in characterization (*e.g.*, taxable to nontaxable, or deductible to nondeductible) generally is not considered to be a change in the method of accounting because the recharacterization affects a taxpayer's lifetime taxable income.[5]

---

[1] §446(e). The term "method of accounting" is not defined in the Code or the Regulations. The term implies, however, a set of rules under which a taxpayer ascertains when to include items of income and when to take deductions into account in determining taxable income. *See* Chapter 4.

[2] Reg. §1.446-1(c)(2)(ii). *e.g.*, the method of deducting vacation pay or the treatment of inventory.

[3] *See* Reg. §1.446-1(e)(2)(ii)(a).

[4] *See* Rev. Proc. 91-31, 1991-1 CB 566. *See also Primo Paints Co. v. Comm'r*, 78 T.C. 705 (1982), and *Humphrey, Farrington & McClain v. Comm'r*, T.C. Memo. 2013-23. *See, e.g., Piccadilly Cafeterias, Inc. v. United States*, 36 Fed. Cl. 330 (1996) (change from deducting rent when paid to deducting rent on straight-line basis pursuant to IRC §467(b) was change in accounting method that required IRS consent, because it involved change in treatment of material item).

[5] *Underhill v. Comm'r*, 45 T.C. 489 (1966), where a change to cost recovery method from pro rata method of determining income from certain promissory notes was not considered change in method of accounting because issue involved extent to which payments received were taxable or nontaxable, *i.e.*, character of payment, not proper method or time of reporting payments.

Example 7-2

Company Y receives $10,000 of income in Year 1. Y's later determination that the $1,000 is taxable, rather than exempt, income produces a permanent difference in income. Therefore, Y's method of determining whether income is taxable or tax-exempt is not an accounting method.

Although a method of accounting may exist under this definition without a pattern of consistent treatment of an item, a method of accounting is not adopted in most instances without consistent treatment.[6] Similar treatment of a material item in determining gross income or deductions in two or more consecutively filed federal income tax returns, without regard to any change in characterization of the method as permissible or impermissible, represents consistent treatment of that item.[7] If a taxpayer treats an item properly in the first federal income tax return that reflects the item, however, it is not necessary for the taxpayer to treat the item consistently in two or more consecutive returns to have adopted a method of accounting.[8] Once a taxpayer has adopted a method of accounting, the taxpayer has established a method of accounting. An established method of accounting includes a finalized Internal Revenue Service (IRS) imposed method of accounting under Rev. Proc. 2002-18.[9]

A change in method of accounting occurs when the method of accounting used by the taxpayer for an item (or that would be used if the taxpayer had the item in the year of change) in computing its taxable income for the year of change is different than the taxpayer's established method of accounting used (or that would have been used if the taxpayer had the item in the immediately preceding year) to compute the taxpayer's taxable income for the immediately preceding taxable year.[10]

A change in method of accounting does not include corrections of mathematical or posting errors, or errors in the computation of tax liability (such as errors in computation of the foreign tax credit, net operating loss, percentage depletion, or investment credit).[11]

---

[6] Reg. § 1.446-1(a)(2) provides that "[a] method of accounting which reflects the consistent application of generally accepted accounting principles . . . will ordinarily be regarded as clearly reflecting income, provided all items of gross income and expense are treated consistently from year to year." The courts have given the IRS broad authority in determining when an accounting method clearly reflects income. *See Thor Power Tool Co. v. Comm'r*, 439 U.S. 522 (1979).

[7] *See* Reg. § 1.446-1(e)(2)(ii)(a) and Rev. Rul. 90-38, 1990-1 CB 57, where the taxpayer attempted to change from an erroneous method of accounting retroactively by amending prior returns *See also Diebold, Inc. v. United States*, 891 F.2d 1579 (Fed. Cir. 1989).

[8] The Supreme Court has held that once a permissible election as to a method of accounting for an item has been made on a return, it may not be changed after the time for filing the return has expired. *See Pacific National Co. v. Welch*, 304 U.S. 191 (1938), *see also Lord v. United States*, 296 F.2d 333 (9th Cir. 1961); *National Western Life Insurance Co. v. Comm'r*, 54 T.C. 33 (1970); Rev. Rul. 74-154, 1974-1 CB 59.

[9] 2002-1 CB 678.

[10] Rev. Proc. 2015-13, 2015-5 IRB 419, *modified by* Rev. Proc. 2015-33, 2015-24 IRB 1067, and Rev. Proc. 2017-59, 2017-48 IRB 543.

[11] *See* Reg. § 1.446-1(e)(2)(ii)(b).

Unless specifically authorized by the Commissioner or by statute, a taxpayer may not change its method of accounting without first obtaining the permission of the Commissioner.[12] In many cases, however, the commissioner provides advanced approval, such as in the case of automatic changes of accounting.[13] Along with completing the application to change a method of accounting (Form 3115)[14] a taxpayer must calculate the adjustments to income (positive or negative) as described in IRC § 481.[15]

Rev. Proc. 2019-43[16] provides the general procedures to obtain advance consent of the Commissioner to change a method of accounting that are specifically identified by the IRS. The practitioner should consult this list and other relevant pronouncements to determine whether a contemplated accounting method change is automatic. It is critical to carefully read the defining criteria for each automatic accounting method change to ensure the accounting method change falls within the scope of the Revenue Procedure. In general, the defining criteria are interpreted literally. If a contemplated method change does not meet the literal criteria of a particular automatic method change, the method change must be filed as a non-automatic accounting method change under Rev. Proc. 2015-13.[17] In addition to consulting Rev. Proc. 2019-43,[18] a review of the instructions to Form 3115 provides a list of DCNs (Designated automatic accounting method change number) at the end of the instructions, which denotes 239 accounting method changes. The list is presented for informational purposes only and subject to the most recently issued Revenue Procedures. Adherence to Rev. Proc. 2019-43[19] is important, and often can prevent significant adverse adjustments and penalties to a taxpayer's timing of a deduction or item of income. Rev. Proc. 2019-43[20] makes it clear that there are different rules for taxpayers who voluntarily change their method of accounting[21] and for taxpayers who are under examination. Notwithstanding the strict rules regarding changes in methods of

---

[12] IRC § 446(e) and Reg. § 1.446-1(e)(3). A taxpayer must secure the consent of the Commissioner regardless of whether the taxpayer's established or proposed method is a permissible method or clearly reflects the taxpayer's income and regardless of the administrative guidance used to request consent or to change the established method of accounting. If a taxpayer changes a method of accounting without complying with all the applicable procedures, the taxpayer has initiated a change in method of accounting without obtaining the consent of the Commissioner as required by IRC § 446(e). *See* Rev. Rul. 90-38, 1990-1 CB 57; Reg. § 1.446-1(c)(2).

[13] *See* Rev. Proc. 2019-43, 2019-48 IRB 1107, or its successor.

[14] *See* appendix at the end of this chapter for a completed Form 3115.

[15] Reg. §§ 1.446-1(e)(3)(i) and 1.481-1. Reg. § 1.446-1(e)(3)(ii) provides that the Commissioner may prescribe the administrative procedures under which a taxpayer will be permitted to change its method of accounting. Many Forms 3115 filed under the non-automatic change procedures require additional information and development. Therefore, the IRS recommends that taxpayers file a Form 3115 under the non-automatic change procedures as early as possible during the requested year of change.

[16] 2019-48 IRB 1107.

[17] 2015-5 IRB 419.

[18] 2019-48 IRB 1107.

[19] *Id.*

[20] *Id.*

[21] *Id.*

accounting, a taxpayer may avoid the application of these rules if the change is not a change in accounting but instead is a correction of mathematical or posting errors or the computation of tax liability. Further, a change in the method of accounting also does not include a change in treatment resulting from a change in underlying facts. If the taxpayer has a change in underlying facts, this change may not be a change in method of accounting.[22]

Rev. Proc. 2019-43[23] has been modified by Rev. Proc. 2020-13[24] which provides procedures for a taxpayer that qualifies for the IRC § 263A(i) small business exemption to revoke its prior IRC § 263A(d)(3) election and apply the IRC § 263A(i) exemption in same taxable year. In addition, Rev. Proc. 2020-13 offers procedures for taxpayers that use the IRC § 263A(i) exemption and no longer qualify as small business taxpayers eligible for the exemption and wish to make the IRC § 263A(d)(3) election in the same taxable year that they no longer qualify for the IRC § 263A(i) exemption.

Additionally Rev. Proc. 2019-43 has been modified by Rev. Proc. 2020-25[25] to reflect changes made to depreciation of qualified improvement property placed in service by the taxpayer after December 31, 2017 by the CARES Act '20.[26] The IRS has provided procedures for changing a depreciation method as well as for making a late election for tax years 2018, 2019, or 2020.[27]

[B] *What Constitutes a Change in Accounting Method*

Once a taxpayer has adopted a method of accounting, a "change in method of accounting" occurs when a taxpayer changes its determination of *when* an item of income or expense is recognized. The IRS must consent to the change and can attach conditions.[28]

Unfortunately, the Internal Revenue Code does not define the phrase "change in method of accounting" however the regulations provide guidance.[29] Under the regulations, a change in method of accounting includes:

- A change in an overall plan or system of identifying or valuing items in inventory;[30]
- A change in the treatment of any *material item* used in the overall plan for identifying or valuing items in inventory;[31]

---

[22] Reg. § 1.446-1(e)(2)(ii)(b).
[23] 2019-48 IRB 1107.
[24] 2020-11 IRB 515.
[25] 2020-19 IRB 785.
[26] P.L. 116-136, § 2307 (March 27, 2020).
[27] Rev. Proc. 2015-56, 2015-49 IRB 827 Sec. 5.02(3)(b)(ii) and Rev. Proc. 2019-43, 2019-48 IRB 1107.
[28] IRC § 446(e); Rev. Proc. 2015-13, 2015-5 IRB 419, § 1.04.
[29] Reg. § 1.446-1(e)(2)(ii)(a).
[30] *Id.*
[31] *Id.*

- A change from the cash receipts and disbursement method to the accrual method, or vice versa;[32]
- A change involving the method or basis used in the valuation of inventories;[33]
- A change from the cash or accrual method to a long-term contract method, or vice versa;[34]
- Certain changes in computing depreciation or amortization;[35]
- A change involving the adoption, use or discontinuance of any other specialized method of computing taxable income, such as the crop method;[36] and
- A change where the Internal Revenue Code and regulations specifically require that the consent of the Commissioner must be obtained before adopting such a change.[37]

IRS rulings and cases provide additional guidance. Under these rulings and cases, a change in method of accounting includes:

- A change in computing the cost of LIFO inventory by including the cost of freight-in;[38]
- A change from the use of estimates to the use of actual expenditures in accounting for insurance expenses;[39]
- A change where deductions were based on contributions made to pension plans on account of hours of service performed after the end of the taxable year, but prior to the due date for tax return;[40]
- A change in the method of handling deposits;[41]
- A change in the accrual of commission income on securities from the "settlement date" to the "trade date";[42]
- A change by a utility company from a bimonthly meter reading and billing cycle to a bimonthly reading and interim monthly billing cycle;[43]
- A change in the valuation of used parts recovered and rebuilt on retirement or repair of railroad's equipment;[44]
- The switch from including advance insurance sales commissions in taxable income in the taxable year received to including such commissions in the taxable year;[45] and

---

[32] Id.

[33] *See* IRC § § 471 and 472, and the regulations thereunder.

[34] Reg. § § 1.446-1(e)(2)(ii)(a) and 1.460-4.

[35] Reg § 1.446-1(e)(2)(ii)(a).

[36] *Id.*

[37] *Id.*

[38] Rev. Rul. 80-190, 1980-2 CB 161.

[39] Rev. Rul. 81-93, 1981-1 CB 322.

[40] TAM 200110031.

[41] Rev. Rul. 60-243, 1960-2 CB 160.

[42] Rev. Rul. 74-372, 1974-2 CB 147.

[43] Rev. Rul. 71-429, 1971-2 CB 217; *see also Bay State Gas Co. v Comm'r*, 689 F.2d 1 (1st Cir. 1982).

[44] Rev. Rul. 69-370, 1969-2 CB 35.

[45] *Security Associates Agency Insurance Corp. v. Comm'r*, T.C. Memo. 1987-317, 53 TCM 1239 (1987).

- Switching the time for recognizing escrowed customer payments as gross income from when the escrow agent released funds to the taxpayer to when the customer gave the sale price to the taxpayer.[46]

These are just some examples that the IRS views as a change of accounting. Notwithstanding, the adoption of a new method of accounting is to be distinguished from changing a method of accounting. For example, the owner of a cemetery business, who had generally accounted for plot sales on a cash basis, accounted for mausoleum crypt sales by treating customer payments as deposits until the mausoleum was completed. At that time, all earlier payments were recognized as income and the pro rata share of construction costs was expensed. Because sales of plots were significantly different from the sales of crypts, the method of accounting for crypt sales was a new method of accounting for a different item and not a change in accounting method.[47]

[C] The IRC §481(a) Adjustment

The IRC §481(a) adjustment is a positive or negative adjustment in the amount which is necessary to prevent amounts from being duplicated or omitted as a result of the taxpayer computing its taxable income for the year of change and thereafter using a different method of accounting from the prior method used.[48] The IRC §481(a) adjustment is computed as of the beginning of the year of change. For a change in method of accounting that affects multiple accounts, the taxpayer's IRC §481(a) adjustment for that change is a net IRC §481(a) adjustment. In computing the net IRC §481(a) adjustment for a change, the taxpayer must take into account all relevant accounts. For example, the net IRC §481(a) adjustment for a change in the proper time for deducting salary bonuses under IRC §461 reflects any necessary adjustments for amounts of salary bonuses capitalized to inventory under IRC §263A. The term "IRC §481(a) adjustment" includes a net IRC §481(a) adjustment. Without the IRC §481 adjustment, the following would happen:

Example 7-3

Omission: In Year 2, X, a calendar year taxpayer, changed from the cash to the accrual method. In its cash method Year 1 tax return, X did not recognize its ending accounts receivable of $50,000 (amounts that were not collected as of December 31, Year 1) or deduct its ending accounts payable of $20,000 (amounts that were not paid as of December 31, Year 1). Because X changed to the accrual method of accounting for Year 2, the company will not recognize the December 31, Year 1, accounts receivable when they are collected in Year 2, and will not deduct the December 31,

---

[46] *Johnson v. Comm'r*, 108 T.C. 448 (1997).

[47] *Berger v. Comm'r*, T.C. Memo. 1996-76, 71 CCH TCM 2160.

[48] IRC §481 was added to the Code in 1954.

Year 1, accounts payable when they are paid in Year 2. Therefore, the change to the accrual method will result in an omission of $50,000 of revenue related to the December 31, Year 1, accounts receivable and $20,000 of expense related to the December 31, Year 1, accounts payable.

Example 7-4

Duplication: Prior to Year 2, Y, a calendar year manufacturer, deducted certain expenses prior to the time they were incurred (*e.g.*, prior to the time the all events and economic performance tests are met under IRC §461). In Year 2, Y changed its method of accounting for these expenses to deduct such costs as they are incurred. As of December 31, Year 1, Y had deducted $10,000 of expenses prior to the time they were incurred. Under its new method, Y will deduct the $10,000 of previously deducted expenses again in Year 2, the year the liabilities are incurred under the accrual method of accounting. Thus, the change in method of accounting will result in a double deduction of these expenses.

Without the IRC §481 adjustment in both situations, the taxpayer will either overstate or understate its income as a result of its change in method of accounting.

With an IRC §481 adjustment, the following would result:

Example 7-5

A taxpayer that is not required to use inventories uses the overall cash receipts and disbursements method of accounting and changes to an overall accrual method of accounting. The taxpayer has $120,000 of income earned but not yet received (accounts receivable) and $100,000 of expenses incurred but not yet paid (accounts payable) as of the end of the taxable year preceding the year of change in method of accounting. A positive net IRC §481(a) adjustment of $20,000 ($120,000 accounts receivable less $100,000 accounts payable) is required as a result of the change in method of accounting.

Example 7-6

X Corporation, a calendar year taxpayer, is a producer and capitalizes costs that are required to be capitalized into inventory under IRC §263A. Each February, X Corporation pays a salary bonus to each production employee who remains in its employment as of January 31 for the employee's services provided in the prior calendar year. Under its present method, X Corporation treats these salary bonuses as incurred in the taxable year the employee provides the related services. $40,000 of these salary bonuses were treated as incurred in 2019, $8,000 of which were capitalized into 2020 ending inventory, and $32,000 of which were included in cost of goods sold. For 2020, X Corporation proposes to change its method of accounting to treat salary bonuses as incurred in the taxable year in which all events have occurred that establish the fact of the liability to pay the salary bonuses and the amount of the liability can be determined with reasonable accuracy. The computation of X Corporation's net IRC § 481(a) adjustment for the change in method of accounting for salary bonuses, which reflects the impact of the change in method of accounting on the amount of salary bonuses capitalized into beginning inventory for the year of change, is demonstrated as follows:

Salary bonuses treated as incurred before and after January 1, 2019, under the present method of accounting, but not incurred until on or after January 1, 2019, under the proposed method—$40,000.

Beginning inventory as of January 1, 2019, with capitalized salary bonuses computed under the present method—$100,000.

Beginning inventory as of January 1, 2019, with capitalized salary bonuses computed under the proposed method—$92,000.

Decrease in beginning inventory as of January 1, 2019—($8,000)
Net positive § 481(a) adjustment—$32,000.

When there is a change in method of accounting to which IRC § 481(a) applies, taxable income for the taxable year preceding the year of change must be determined under the method of accounting that was then employed, and taxable income for the year of change and the following taxable years must be determined under the method of accounting for which consent is granted as if that method of accounting had always been used. The IRC § 481(a) adjustment is computed notwithstanding that the period of limitations on assessment and collection of tax may have closed on the taxable years (closed years) in which the events giving rise to the need for an adjustment occurred.[49]

One may ask what is the incentive to make an IRC § 481 adjustment that would result in a positive adjustment where the taxpayer would owe additional taxes?

When an involuntary change is made (usually as a result of an IRS audit), the taxpayer must take the entire IRC § 481(a) adjustment into income in the year of change (usually the earliest open year under examination) regardless of whether the adjustment is positive or negative.[50] However, when a voluntary change (taxpayer-initiated change) is made, the period over which the adjustment is taken into account is dependent primarily upon whether the adjustment is positive or negative. With

---

[49] *See, e.g., Korn Industries, Inc. v. United States*, 532 F.2d 1352 (Ct. Cl. 1976).

[50] Rev. Proc. 2002-18, 2002-1 CB 678, § 5.04(3)

respect to positive IRC § 481(a) adjustments (increases to income), the IRS provides an incentive to taxpayers to voluntarily change from an improper accounting method that understates income; that is, generally, the IRC § 481(a) adjustment is spread over a period of four tax years. For voluntary accounting method changes that result in negative IRC § 481(a) adjustments, taxpayers are generally permitted to recognize the entire § 481(a) adjustment in the year of change.[51]

[D] What Is Not a Change of Accounting

Under the regulations, the following are not a change of accounting:

- An adjustment of any item of income or deduction that does not involve the proper time for including the item in income or the taking of a deduction;[52]
- An adjustment with respect to the addition to a reserve for bad debts or an adjustment in the useful life of a depreciable asset;[53]
- Correction of mathematical or posting errors;[54]
- Errors in the computation of tax liability;[55]
- The recharacterization of an item of income or expense, such as from deductible to non-deductible;[56] and
- Occasions resulting from the continued application of a method of accounting to new or changed facts.[57]

A good example distinguishing a change of accounting with a change in underlying fact is *Decision, Inc. v. Commissioner*.[58] In *Decision*, an accrual method company recognized income when it billed its customers. Decision sold advertising space and billed its customers prior to the time an advertisement was published. Decision then changed its billing policy, and started sending out bills when advertisements were published. As a result of the change in billing policy, Decision delayed the reporting of its taxable income. The Tax Court held that the change in billing practice was not an accounting method change, because both before and after the change, Decision

---

[51] *See* Rev. Proc. 2015-13, 2015-5 IRB 419, § 7.03 *modified by* Rev. Proc. 2015-33, 2015-24 IRB 1067 and Rev. Proc. 2017-59, 2017-48 IRB 543. *See* ¶ 7.04[J] *infra*.

[52] Reg. § 1.446-1(e)(2)(ii)(b).

[53] Reg. § 1.446-1(e)(2)(ii)(b). *See* Priv. Ltr. Rul. 9222017, where the use of a different estimation method to determine the fair market value of foreclosure property did not rise to the level of an accounting method because the estimation method only went to the amount rather than the timing in which an item of income or deduction is taken into account.

[54] Reg. § 1.446-1(e)(2)(ii)(b). *See* TAM 9421003, where the National Office advised that the taxpayer did not merely make a posting error when it switched from deducting all of its software development costs to capitalizing at least two-thirds of them; rather, the taxpayer's consistent treatment of such costs for five years resulted in an accounting method change.

[55] Reg § 1.446-1(e)(2)(ii)(b).

[56] *Id.* (Such as errors in computation of the foreign tax credit, net operating loss, percentage depletion, or investment credit.)

[57] Reg. § 1.446-1(e)(2)(ii)(b).

[58] 47 T.C. 58 (1966).

reported its income when it billed its customers. The change in the income recognition point was caused by a change in the contract with the customers, which was a change in underlying facts (*i.e.*, the date the bills were sent to customers).

The following examples illustrate changes which do not involve a change of accounting method:

- A taxpayer in the wholesale dry goods business computes its income and expenses on the accrual method of accounting and files its federal income tax returns on such basis. Vacation pay has been deducted in the year in which paid because the taxpayer did not have a completely vested vacation pay plan, and, therefore, the liability for payment did not accrue until that year. Subsequently, the taxpayer adopts a completely vested vacation pay plan, which changes its year for accruing the deduction from the year in which payment is made to the year in which the liability to make the payment now arises. The change for the year of deduction of the vacation pay plan is not a change in method of accounting but results, instead, because the underlying facts (*i.e.*, the type of vacation pay plan) have changed.[59]
- A taxpayer did not materially participate in a nursing home activity and failed to treat it as a passive activity under IRC § 469. The correction to recharacterize the activity as a passive activity was not a change of accounting method because the issue was not a matter of the period in which an item of income or deduction was placed.[60]
- A proposal by an IRS examiner to change the amount of the taxpayer's gain or loss on the disposition of preferred stock was not a change of accounting method because it did not involve the timing of the gain or loss.[61]
- A change in the treatment of customer fees received was not a change of accounting method when the taxpayer had excluded customer connection fees from income by treating them as nontaxable capital contributions under IRC § 118. The IRS determined that the fees were taxable income. The Tax Court concluded that the change would be a permanent difference, not a timing difference and, thus, was not a change of accounting.[62]

Courts have been liberal in finding that a taxpayer change in the treatment of an item of income or deduction was caused by an "error" as opposed to a change of accounting. In *Evans v. Commissioner*,[63] the Tax Court found the prior reporting of bonuses by a cash basis taxpayer, in the year authorized rather than in the year

---

[59] Reg. § 1.446-1(e)(2)(iii), Example 3.

[60] Priv. Ltr. Rul. 201035016.

[61] Priv. Ltr. Rul. 200023003.

[62] *Saline Sewer Co.*, T.C. Memo. 1992-236. However, the IRS later nonacquiesed, noting that changing to or from an exclusion under IRC § 118 requires an offsetting decrease or increase in basis and, hence, an offsetting decrease or increase in future depreciation deductions. The result is that the taxpayer's lifetime income does not change only timing. Thus, the change is a change of accounting method. Rev. Rul. 2008-30, 2008-1 CB 1156.

[63] T.C. Memo. 1988-228.

received, even though the treatment occurred for several years did not establish an accrual method of accounting but was only the "misapplication of the cash method."[64]

[E] Material Items

A change in the treatment of any material item used in the overall plan for identifying or valuing items in inventory is a "change in method of accounting."

What is a "material item?" The regulations provide that a material item is any item that involves the proper timing for the inclusion of the item in income or the taking of a deduction.[65]

In determining whether timing is involved, the relevant inquiry is whether the accounting practice permanently affects the taxpayer's lifetime taxable income or merely changes the taxable year in which taxable income is reported.[66] An accounting practice that involves the timing of when an item is included in income or when it is deducted is considered a method of accounting.[67]

Before 1970, the courts determined materiality in "absolute" or "relative" terms. Absolute materiality refers to the size of the adjustment. In *Dorr-Oliver, Inc., v. Commissioner,*[68] an adjustment of $25,000 was held to be material. The Court considered whether a change in accounting for accrued vacation time was a "substantial change of a material item." The Court observed, ". . . $25,000 is seldom insubstantial."

After 1970, the regulations were amended to include "a material item is any item that involves the proper timing for the inclusion of the item in income or the taking of a deduction."[69]

---

[64] *See also North Carolina Granite Corp. v. Comm'r,* 43 T.C. 149 (1964), where the taxpayer used an erroneous method for its depletion deduction in arriving at taxable income. The Tax Court said that the fact that the taxpayer may have repeated its mistake for a number of years does not transform the mistake into a method of accounting. In *United States v. Wardlaw,* 344 F.2d 225 (5th Cir. 1965), the taxpayers changed their method of reporting breeding cattle. They expensed them rather than including them in inventory as they had previously had done, for the reason that the regulation was invalid. The Court of Appeals agreed and further stated: "[W]e think the taxpayers are justified in correcting the error which the regulation imposed. . . . [and] we do not deem this a change in accounting method . . . ." *Id.*

[65] Reg. § 1.446-1(e)(2)(ii)(a). *See, e.g., Wayne Bolt & Nut Co. v. Comm'r,* 93 T.C. 500 (1989), where the Court concluded that a change from an erroneous perpetual inventory system to a physical inventory system amounted to a change in method of accounting because there would be a change in the time when items of income and expense were reported. On the other hand in *Korn Industries, Inc. v. United States,* 532 F.2d 1352 (Ct. Cl. 1976), the Court found no change in accounting method where the taxpayer re-included in its beginning inventories three "cost elements" that for a period of four years had been inadvertently excluded and therefore expensed. The Court in siding with the taxpayer called this a correction of a mathematical or posting error rather than a change of accounting. In Rev. Rul. 77-134, 1977-1 CB 132, the IRS said it would not follow *Korn Industries, Inc.*

[66] Rev. Proc. 91-31, 1991-1 CB 566; *Primo Pants Co. v. Comm'r,* 78 T.C. 705, 723 (1982); *Knight Ridder v. United States,* 743 F.2d 781, 799 (11th Cir. 1984).

[67] *General Motors Corp. v. Comm'r,* 112 T.C. 270, 296 (1999); *Color Arts, Inc. v. Comm'r,* T.C. Memo. 2003-95.

[68] 40 T.C. 50 (1963).

[69] Reg. § 1.446-1(e)(2)(ii)(a).

Absolute materiality has its obvious flaws, and therefore, many courts turned instead to "relative materiality" to decide the issue. Unfortunately, some courts look at the adjustment relative to the gross amount of the item, some look at taxable income, and some look at gross income. Where the amount of the deduction is compared to the total deductions for the items, materiality is generally found. When the amounts are compared to taxable or gross income, the amounts at issue have been held to be material.[70]

The Tax Court has held that "material item" as used in Reg. § 1.446-1(e)(2)(ii)(a) should be read in context as a "material item of gross income or deductions" and not as meaning "a material item of net income."[71]

Where a taxpayer computes its income and expenses, and files its returns, on the accrual method, except for its real estate tax liabilities, which it reports on the cash method, a change to reporting the real estate tax liabilities on the accrual method is a change of accounting method. The change is a change in the treatment of a material item within the taxpayer's overall accounting practice.[72]

When a taxpayer purchased all of the common stock of a real estate investment trust (REIT) owned by a failed bank via a standard FDIC purchase and assumption agreement, erroneously treated the REIT's assets as its own assets and, as a result, erroneously recognized income, its correction of that recognition was not an accounting method change. Since the reported income was an error, not a material item, a IRC § 481 adjustment was not appropriate.[73]

When the Commissioner grants consent to a taxpayer to change its method of accounting the taxpayer may take the adjustment into account in determining taxable income only in the manner and subject to the conditions agreed to by the Commissioner and the taxpayer.[74]

[F] *Change in Character of an Item*

Certain cases, such as *Underhill v. Commissioner*,[75] are sometimes read to stand for the proposition that changes involving a change in the "characterization" of an item (capital or ordinary) is not accounting method changes under IRC § 446. However, Reg. § 1.446-1(e)(2)(ii)(*b*) enumerates numerous adjustments that do not constitute changes in method of accounting but contains no exception for changes that alter the characterization of an item. In fact, the regulations include corrections of erroneous

---

[70] *See, e.g., Leonhart v. Comm'r*, T.C. Memo. 1968-98, *aff'd*, 414 F.2d 749 (4th Cir. 1969).

[71] Id.

[72] Reg. § 1.446-1(e)(2)(iii), Example 2.

[73] LFA 2018060F.

[74] IRC § 481(c); Reg. §§ 1.446-1(e)(3)(ii) and 1.481-4. Effect on earnings and profits. A corporation takes any IRC § 481(a) adjustment resulting from a change in method of accounting into account in computing its earnings and profits. *See* Reg. § 1.312-6 and Rev. Proc. 79-47, 1979-2 CB 528.

[75] 45 T.C. 489 (1966).

characterizations among changes in methods of accounting.[76] Moreover, numerous cases have held that a change in characterization can be a change in method of accounting.[77] A change in method of accounting reflecting a change in the characterization of revenue or expense can also involve a change in the character of taxable income from capital gain (loss) to ordinary income (loss), or vice versa. For example, in *Witte v. Commissioner*,[78] the taxpayer's shift from the cost recovery method of accounting for gain derived from the sale of real estate properties to completed transaction treatment constituted a "change in the method of accounting" within the meaning of the treasury regulations. While the Court found that the change involved the proper timing of a material item, the deficiency determination at issue was based on the finding that the amounts reported as long-term capital gain should be taxed as ordinary income since such amounts were in part interest income and in part income from the sale of properly held primarily for sale.[79]

[G] Adoption of a Method of Accounting

Rev. Rul. 90-38[80] states that a taxpayer has not adopted a method of accounting by virtue of having applied an improper treatment once. However, if the taxpayer applies an improper treatment twice,[81] then he has adopted a method of accounting. Moreover, if a taxpayer adopts a proper method of accounting, then the taxpayer is considered to have adopted that method of accounting the first year that it uses the method. In making this ruling, the IRS relied on two propositions:

---

[76] *See* Example 11 of Reg. §1.446-1(e)(2)(iii) (inventory to depreciable asset). *See also Cargill Inc. v. United States*, 91 F. Supp. 2d 1293, 1297-1298 (D. Minn. 2000) ("Like the petitioner in Witte, Cargill has not directed the Court to any provision of the Code that sets forth such a "characterization" exception. Accordingly, the Court concludes that no such exception exists." *Citing Witte v. Comm'r*, 513 F.2d 391 (D.C. Cir. 1975)).

[77] *See Diebold v. Comm'r*, 891 F.2d 1579, 1583 (Fed. Cir. 1989) (held that a change in treatment from inventory to capital asset constituted an accounting method change); *Cargill*, 91 F. Supp. 2d at 1293 (recharacterization of interest from leasehold to ownership); *Pacific Enterprises v. Comm'r*, 101 T.C. 1 (1993) (recharacterizing "working gas" (inventory) to "cushion gas" (capital asset)); *Standard Oil Co. v. Comm'r*, 77 T.C. 349, 410-411 (1981) (IRC §1250 property to §1245 property); *Capital One v. Comm'r*, 130 T.C. 147 (2008), *aff'd*, 659 F.3d 316 (4th Cir. 2011) (late fees from fee income to OID); *Humphrey, Farrington & McClain, P.C. v. Comm'r*, T.C. Memo. 2013-23 (advanced litigation expenses as deductible business expenses or loans). *See also* Rev. Proc. 2015-14, 2015-5 IRB 450, Section 2 (changing treatment of amounts received from Commodity Credit Corporation from gross income to loan is method change), 3.01 (changing treatment of advanced litigation costs from business expenses to loans), 6.03 (changes from sale to lease, or vice versa, are method changes).

[78] 513 F.2d 391 (D.C. Cir. 1975).

[79] *Witte*, 513 F.2d at 391; *Pacific Enterprises v. Comm'r*, 101 T.C. 1 (1993) (also involved changes between capital and ordinary taxable income). *See also Mingo v. Comm'r*, T.C. Memo. 2013-149 (change in accounting method for partnership interest sale proceeds attributable to unrealized receivables from installment method resulting in capital gain to cash receipts and disbursements method yielding ordinary income).

[80] 1990-1 CB 57.

[81] In Rev. Rul. 72-491, 1972-2 CB 104, the IRS ruled that a taxpayer erroneously using an accelerated method of depreciation for "used" property may file an amended return using a proper method, provided that the taxpayer has not filed the tax return for the succeeding tax year.

(1) the holding in *Diebold, Inc. v. U.S.*,[82] where the court held that the treatment of a material item in the same way in determining the gross income or deductions on two or more consecutively filed tax returns represents consistent treatment of that item for purposes of Reg. § 1.446-1(e)(2)(ii)(a);[83] and

(2) Reg. § 1.446-1(e)(2)(i), which indicates that the consistent, but erroneous, treatment of material items constitutes a method of accounting.

The IRS further explained that Rev. Rul. 90-38[84] is intended to prevent a taxpayer from retroactively changing from an erroneous to a permissible method of accounting without IRS consent by filing amended returns, even if the period for amending the return for the first year in which the erroneous method was used has not expired. This principle was also applied in TAM 9421003, in which the National Office advised that the taxpayer changed its method of accounting when it capitalized most of its software development costs consistently for five years after properly and consistently deducting those costs for 16 years. This change was improper, the National Office stated, because the taxpayer did not obtain the IRS's consent.[85] Citing Rev. 90-38[86] and *Diebold*,[87] the National Office explained that the taxpayer could not use amended returns to retroactively change its accounting method of capitalizing the software development costs to deducting such costs without the IRS's consent.[88]

An established method of accounting includes an IRS-imposed method of accounting under. Rev. Proc. 2002-18.[89]

[H] Change in Underlying Facts

In general, a change in tax reporting is found to be a change in underlying facts, and *not* a change in method of accounting, where the taxpayer continues to apply its existing method of accounting to a change in business practice, a change in economic or legal relationships, or an otherwise after-the-fact situation.

Often a problem arises in distinguishing a change in method of accounting from a change in underlying facts. The issue is whether the changed facts justify different treatment under a single, consistent method of accounting, or whether the change in treatment represented a decision to treat the same "item" in a different way, *i.e.*, a change in method of accounting.

---

[82] 891 F.2d 1579 (Fed. Cir. 1989), *cert. denied*, 498 U.S. 823 (1990).

[83] The regulation provides "in most instances a method of accounting is not established for an item without . . . consistent treatment."

[84] 1990-1 CB 57.

[85] *See also* Priv. Ltr. Rul. 9439002.

[86] 1990-1 CB 57.

[87] *Diebold and Pacific Enterprises v. Comm'r*, 891 F.2d 1579, 1583 (Fed. Cir. 1989).

[88] In TAM 9439002, the IRS ruled that a retroactive change in an erroneous accounting method required the consent of the Commissioner, even if the period for amending the return for the first year in which the erroneous method was used had not expired.

[89] 2002-1 CB 678. Generally, taxpayer required to make involuntary change receives less favorable terms that if it had filed application to make voluntary change.

A change in a method of accounting involves changing a reporting result by the application of a different rule to the same facts, rather than the application of the same rule to different facts. The Service explained:

> Fundamentally, the item itself must be the same as an item previously accounted for with the present method of accounting differing from the prior treatment. Unless the transactions are basically the same, the accounting treatment would not be a "change" of accounting but only a "new" accounting method for a different transaction."[90]

Reg. § 1.446-1(e)(2)(iii) provides two examples of the proper application of the principle regarding a change in underlying facts.

Example 7-7

A taxpayer in the wholesale dry goods business computes its income and expenses on the accrual method of accounting and files its federal income tax returns on such basis. Vacation pay has been deducted in the year in which paid because the taxpayer did not have a completely vested vacation pay plan, and, therefore, the liability for payment did not accrue until that year. Subsequently, the taxpayer adopts a completely vested vacation pay plan that changes its year for accruing the deduction from the year in which payment is made to the year in which the liability to make the payment now arises. The change of the year of deduction of the vacation pay plan is not a change in method of accounting because the underlying facts (that is, the type of vacation pay plan) have changed.

Example 7-8

From 1968 through 1970, a taxpayer had fairly allocated indirect overhead costs to the value of inventories on a fixed percentage of direct costs. If the ratio of indirect overhead costs to direct costs increases in 1971, a change in the underlying facts has occurred. Accordingly, an increase in the percentage in 1971 to fairly reflect the increase in the relative level of indirect overhead costs is not a change in method of accounting but is a change in treatment resulting from a change in the underlying facts.

---

[90] *Federated Department Stores v. Comm'r*, 51 T.C. 500, 513-14 (1968), *nonacq*, 1971-2 CB 4, *aff'd*, 426 F.2d 417 (6th Cir. 1970). *See also Alabama Coca-Cola Bottling Co. v. Comm'r*, T.C. Memo. 1969-123, where the taxpayer switched from expensing to capitalizing the costs of certain signs. The court noted that the taxpayer had previously used a different, less durable type of sign, and stated in *dicta* that if the earlier signs had a useful life of less than one year, capitalizing the new signs would not be a change in method of accounting; on the other hand, if the earlier signs had a useful life in excess of one year, then there would be a change in method.

In each example above, it is clear that the taxpayer has applied its existing method of reporting to a changed fact situation. The different tax consequences arose from a different legal obligation and economic condition, respectively, not from a change in method of reporting.

Similarly, a change in method of accounting does not include adjustments of any item of income or deduction that does not involve the proper time for inclusion of an item or the taking of a deduction. For example, corrections of items that are deducted as interest or salary but which, in fact, are payments of dividends, and of items that are deducted as business expenses but which are in fact personal expenses, are not changes in methods of accounting.[91] Where the character of an item in a particular year is at issue rather than the year in which the item is to be reported, a change in character does not amount to a change in method of accounting and is not subject to the requirement governing such changes.[92]

On the other hand, the IRS occasionally argues that a purported change in underlying facts is actually illusory and does not justify a change in treatment. For example, in Rev. Rul. 60-243,[93] a soft drink manufacturer proposed to remove from its invoices the clause in which it retained title to the bottles, and change its accounting to reflect a sale of the bottles together with the soft drink. The IRS ruled that, as a practical matter, the taxpayer was relying on the "practical certainty" that it would continue to reacquire most of the bottles it sold, and therefore there was no real change in business practice. The IRS's position was based upon the reasoning that there was in substance no sale, and that the change had no practical effect. It did not help the taxpayer's case that the price at which it sold the bottles was far below cost.

Courts are inhospitable to this approach when there is evidence that the terms have been manipulated for no business purpose other than the deferral of income.[94]

Notwithstanding, there are cases where the taxpayer has been successful in changing their business practices without these changes being a change of accounting. In *Hallmark Cards, Inc. v. Commissioner*,[95] the taxpayer had difficulty with its sale of Valentine's Day cards. The taxpayer attempted to utilize a warehouse method whereby Valentine's Day cards would not be shipped to the retailer until the end of

---

91 Reg. § 1.446-1(e)(2)(ii)(b).

92 In *Saline Sewer Co. v. Comm'r*, T.C. Memo. 1992-236, the Court held that a recharacterization in which amounts that should have been treated as income were treated as non-taxable contributions to capital did not result in a change of accounting method. Therefore, the IRS could not use IRC § 481 for a tax adjustment in a closed year. As a result, some of the proposed adjustments were barred by the statute of limitations. In Priv. Ltr. Rul. 9222017, the use of *a different estimation method to determine fair market value of foreclosure property did not rise to a method of accounting* because an estimation method only went to the amount rather than the *timing* in which an item of income or deduction is taken into account.

93 1960-2 CB 160.

94 *See, e.g., Hallmark Cards v. Comm'r*, 90 T.C. 26, 36 n.6 (1988) (taxpayer shipped seasonal material before the end of the year but title did not pass until January 1; court noted that taxpayer's business purpose was unquestioned, distinguishing the case where "a taxpayer has deliberately manipulated the terms of sale so as to prevent income from accruing that it would otherwise become entitled to prior to the end of the taxable year").

95 90 T.C. 26 (1988).

the year so that the retailer would not have the Valentine's Day cards in inventory at year-end. This proved to be unsuccessful. The taxpayer then changed its contract for the sale of Valentine's Day cards with its retailers under its "Valentine's Day Program" where title to the cards passed to the retailer on January 1 of the next year regardless of where the cards were located. The Tax Court held that, under the all-events test, the contract did not provide for transfer of title until after the new year. Therefore, Hallmark was not entitled to payment because the all-events test was not met until the beginning of the next year. As a result, the Valentine's Day contract was held not to be a change of accounting. In footnote number six, the court noted that the taxpayer and the IRS agreed that the adoption of the Valentine's Day Program was the only way to solve the problem of getting the cards to the retailers in time without adversely affecting their income. The court noted that the taxpayer did not deliberately manipulate the terms of its agreement for tax purposes. The court cautioned that it would express no opinion to the tax consequences of any other situation.[96]

Planning Suggestions

- Because of the difference between a change in the underlying facts and a change in method of accounting, a taxpayer should examine its business operations, *e.g.*, billing practices, to delay recognition of income.[97]
- A taxpayer should carefully review the impact of an IRC §481 adjustment before changing its method of accounting. It might be beneficial to continue to use the current method of accounting.
- If the taxpayer is employing an incorrect method of accounting, file Form 3115 early to avoid being disqualified from seeking a voluntary change in accounting before being contacted by the IRS.
- Take advantage of a change in underlying facts.[98]

---

[96] The court said: The business reasons for petitioner's adoption of the Jan. 1 passage of title and risk of loss are sound and have not been disputed. Thus, this is not a case where a taxpayer has deliberately manipulated the terms of sale so as to prevent income from accruing that it would otherwise become entitled to prior to the end of its taxable year. We express no opinion as to the tax consequences of such a situation. *See also Avon Products Inc. v. United States*, 97 F.3d 1435, 96-2 USTC ¶50,525. Accrual-based taxpayer did not impermissibly change its accounting method when it reported Mexican sub's employee profit participation payments in year after they were earned: taxpayer's structuring of payment for tax purposes was not impermissible; and decision to claim deduction in payment year was consistent with IRS's previous treatment.

[97] In *Decision, Inc. v. Comm'r*, 47 T.C. 58 (1966), a delay in year-end billing was held not to be a change in accounting method.

[98] If the taxpayer is going to make a change in underlying facts (*see Hallmar Cards*, 90 T.C. 26 (1988)), he should be aware that after two years if he does not fit within the exception, it will be a change of accounting without the commissioner's consent.

Unless specifically authorized by the IRS or by statute, a taxpayer may not request, or otherwise make, a retroactive change in a method of accounting.[99]

§7.02 Taxpayer Initiated Changes/Voluntary Changes of Accounting

[A] *Generally*

If a taxpayer proposes to change its method of accounting, three conditions apply:

First, the taxpayer must obtain the prior consent of the Commissioner.

Second, the change is subject to the requirements of IRC §481, which requires adjustments to be made to ensure that changes do not result in the double inclusion of items of income or expense or an omission of such items.

Third, the change and any subsequent review are not subject to the applicable statutory periods of limitation; the IRC §481 adjustment would include amounts attributable to years on which the applicable statutory period has otherwise expired.[100]

[B] *Two or More Trades or Businesses*

Different methods of accounting are permitted for each of taxpayer's trades or business.[101] However, no trade or business will be considered separate and distinct unless the taxpayer keeps a complete and separable set of books and records for that trade or business.[102] In considering whether to permit an accounting method change for one of the trades or businesses of a taxpayer, the IRS will consider whether the change will result in the creation or shifting of profits or losses between the trades or businesses, and whether the proposed method will clearly reflect the taxpayer's income as required by IRC §446 and the regulations thereunder.

A taxpayer requesting a change in method of accounting for one of its trades or businesses must identify all other trades or businesses by name and the method of accounting used by each trade or business for the particular item that is the subject of the requested change in accounting method.[103]

If a taxpayer operates two or more separate and distinct trades or businesses and has kept separate books and records (and employed different methods of accounting for the businesses),a separate Form 3115 and a separate user fee is required for each

---

99 *See generally* Rev. Rul. 90-38, 1990-1 CB 57.

100 *See* IRC §§481 and 1311-1314, and *Graff Chevrolet Co. v. Campbell*, 343 F.2d 568 (5th Cir. 1965).

101 Reg. §§1.446-1(d)(1) and 1.446-1(d)(2).

102 *See* Reg. §1.446-1(d)(2).

103 Rev. Proc. 2015-13, 2015-5 IRB 419, §6.02(4).

separate trade or business if the taxpayer desires to change the methods of accounting of the separate trades or businesses.[104]

[C] Consolidated Groups

Separate methods of accounting may be used by each member of a consolidated group, subject to the provisions of IRC § 446 and the regulations thereunder.[105] In considering whether to grant accounting method changes to group members, the IRS will consider the effects of the changes on the income of the group. A common parent requesting a change in method of accounting on behalf of a member of the consolidated group must explain the method of accounting used by each member of the consolidated group for the particular item that is the subject of the Form 3115. Except as provided in Rev. Proc. 2020-1[106] (or its successor), the common parent must submit a separate Form 3115 and, in the case of a non-automatic change, user fee for each member of the consolidated group (and for each trade or business of each member) for which consent for a change in method of accounting is requested.[107]

A common parent may request an identical accounting method change on a single Form 3115 on behalf of more than one member of a consolidated group at a reduced user fee.[108] To qualify, the taxpayers in the consolidated group must be members of the same affiliated group under IRC § 1504(a) who join in the filing of a consolidated tax return, and they must be requesting to change from the identical present method of accounting to the identical proposed method of accounting. All aspects of the requested accounting method change, including the present and proposed methods, the underlying facts, and the authority for the request, must be identical, except for the IRC § 481(a) adjustment. Except for non-automatic Forms 3115, the application must include the following typed or printed language at the top of the letter ruling request "REQUEST FOR USER FEE UNDER § 15.07 OF REV. PROC. 2020-1."

[D] Audit Protection for Taxable Years Prior to Year of Change

One of the most important changes made by Rev. Proc. 97-27 and its successor, Rev. Proc 2015-13, was to provide audit protection. This means that if a taxpayer timely files Form 3115, the IRS will *not* require the taxpayer to change its method of accounting for the same item for a taxable year prior to the year of change.[109]

---

[104] *Id.*

[105] Reg. § 1.1502-17(a).

[106] 2020-1 IRB 1.

[107] *See* Rev. Proc. 2020-1, 2020-1 IRB 1, § 15, for user fees.

[108] *See* § 15.07 of Rev. Proc. 2020-1, 2020-1 IRB 1 (or any successor) for the information required to be submitted with Form 3115.

[109] Rev. Proc. 2015-13, 2015-5 IRB 419, § 8. The IRS has updated procedure for taxpayers to follow to obtain both advance (non-automatic) and automatic consent of IRS to change accounting method

The IRS may, however, make a method change for a prior year in any of the following circumstances:

- The change is not made or is made improperly;[110]
- The requested change is to a sub-method and the IRS's change is to the method itself;[111]
- The IRS's change is a prior-year IRS-initiated change;[112] or
- There is a pending or future criminal investigation or proceeding concerning the taxpayer's tax liability, or the possibility of false or fraudulent statements by the taxpayer relating to its tax liability, for the prior year.[113]

Moreover, there is no audit protection for taxpayers under examination *except* if the taxpayer:

- Has filed for a change of accounting under the three-month window;[114]
- Has filed for a change of accounting under the 120-day window;[115]
- Has filed for a change of accounting under the present method which is not before the district director;[116]
- Is a new member of a consolidated group in CAP (Compliance Assurance Process);[117]
- Has changes Resulting in a Negative § 481(a) Adjustment;[118] or
- Has no Examination-Imposed Change and Item Not Under Consideration.[119]

(Footnote Continued)

described in Rev. Proc. 2015-14, 2015-5 IRB 450 for specified items. Rev. Proc. 2011-14, 2011-1 CB 330, *as amplified, clarified, and modified,* is superseded in part.

[110] Rev. Proc. 2015-13, 2015-5 IRB 419, § 8.02(3).

[111] Rev. Proc. 2015-13, 2015-5 IRB 419, § 8.02(4).

[112] Rev. Proc. 2015-13, 2015-5 IRB 419, § 8.02(9).

[113] Rev. Proc. 2015-13, 2015-5 IRB 419, § 8.02(6).

[114] *See* § 7.06[B], *infra.* The three-month window is the period beginning on the 15th day of the seventh month of the taxpayer's tax year and ending on the 15th day of the tenth month of the taxpayer's tax year. Rev. Proc. 2015-13, 2015-5 IRB 419, § 8.02(1)(a)(ii).

[115] *See* § 7.06[C], *infra.* The 120-day window period begins on the date that the examination ends regardless of whether a subsequent examination has commenced.

[116] *See* § 7.06[D], *infra.* The current method is not before the director when it is: (1) a change from a clearly permissible method of accounting; or (2) a change from an impermissible method of accounting and the impermissible method was adopted subsequent to the tax years under IRS examination on the date the taxpayer files the Form 3115. Rev. Proc. 2015-13, 2015-5 IRB 419, § 8.02(1)(c)(i)(A)–§ 8.02(1)(c)(i)(B).

[117] Rev. Proc. 2015-13, 2015-5 IRB 419, § 8.02. Provided certain requirements are met, audit protection will be provided for a change in method of accounting for an item requested by the common parent of a consolidated group in CAP on behalf of a new member of the consolidated group for the tax year in which the new member became a member of the consolidated group.

[118] Rev. Proc. 2015-13, 2015-5 IRB 419, § 8.02(1)(e)(i)(A)–§ 8.02(1)(e)(i)(B). A taxpayer under IRS examination will receive audit protection if a change in method of accounting for an item results in a negative IRC § 481(a) adjustment for that item for the year of change and would have resulted in a negative IRC § 481(a) adjustment in each tax year under IRS examination if the change in method of accounting for that item had been made in the tax years under examination.

[119] Rev. Proc. 2015-13, 2015-5 IRB 419, § 8.02(1)(f)(i)(A)–§ 8.02(1)(f)(i)(B). Except as provided in § 8.02(1)(f)(ii), of Rev. Proc. 2015-13, for a taxpayer that is under examination for one or more taxable

If a taxpayer currently under examination does not fit into one of the exceptions above, the taxpayer may still change its method of accounting under the procedures of Rev. Proc. 2015-13, but may not obtain audit protection.[120]

[E] *National Office Review*

The national office will deny any Form 3115 requesting consent to make a change in method of accounting in any situation in which the national office determines that permitting the requested change in method of accounting would not clearly reflect income or would otherwise not be in the interest of sound tax administration. As part of this determination, the national office will consider whether the change in method of accounting would clearly and directly frustrate compliance efforts of the IRS in administering the income tax laws. The national office will consider all the facts and circumstances and exercise discretion under IRC §§446(e) and 481(c) in a manner that generally minimizes distortions of income across taxable years, as well as on an annual basis.[121]

[F] *Director Review*

The director may determine whether the taxpayer complied with all the applicable provisions for the change in method of accounting, including, but not limited to, whether:

- The representations on which the ruling was based reflect an accurate statement of the material facts;
- The amount of the IRC §481(a) adjustment was properly determined;
- The change in method of accounting was implemented as proposed in accordance with the terms and conditions of the Consent Agreement and Rev. Proc. 2015-13;
- There has been any change in the material facts on which the ruling was based during the period the method of accounting was used; and

---

(Footnote Continued)

years on the date the taxpayer files a Form 3115, §8.02(1) (no audit protection for taxpayers under examination) ceases to apply to the change in method of accounting for that item as of the date immediately following the earliest date that any of those examinations ends for the taxable year(s) subsequent to that taxable year and prior to the year of change to which the Form 3115 applies, if by the earliest date that any of those examinations ends:

(A) the examining agent(s) does not propose an adjustment for the same item that is the subject of the Form 3115 for the taxable year(s) under examination; and
(B) the method of accounting for that same item is not an issue under consideration within the meaning of §3.08.

[120] Rev. Proc. 2015-13, 2015-5 IRB 419, §8.02(2).
[121] Rev. Proc. 2015-13, 2015-5 IRB 419, §11.02.

- There has been any change in the applicable law during the period the method of accounting was used.[122]

Improperly determined IRC §481(a) adjustment. The director may make any necessary correction to the amount of any IRC §481(a) adjustment and may make any other adjustment(s) that are necessary to properly implement the change in method of accounting for which consent is granted. If the director makes such a necessary correction to the amount of the IRC §481(a) adjustment, the director may take the entire amount necessary to correct the IRC §481(a) adjustment into account in computing the taxpayer's taxable income for the earliest taxable year in the IRC §481(a) adjustment period that is under examination, regardless of whether the statute of limitations under IRC §6501 has expired for one or more taxable years in the IRC §481(a) adjustment period.

Example 7-9

A taxpayer obtained consent to change its method of accounting under Rev. Proc. 2015-13 with a Year 1 year of change. The taxpayer determined that the IRC §481(a) adjustment for this change in method of accounting is a positive adjustment of $75,000, to be taken into account ratably over four taxable years. The taxpayer is under examination for Year 2. The statute of limitations under IRC §6501 has expired for Year 1. As part of the examination of Year 2, the examining agent determines that the correct IRC §481(a) adjustment for this change in method of accounting is a positive adjustment of $100,000. The examining agent may take the entire amount of the $25,000 correction to the IRC §481(a) adjustment into account in the taxpayer's taxable income for Year 2.

Penalties and additions to tax. If the director denies the change in method of accounting or corrects the IRC §481(a) adjustment the director may impose any otherwise applicable penalty, addition to tax, or additional amount on the understatement of tax attributable to the denial of the change in method of accounting or the net amount of any necessary correction(s) to the IRC §481(a) adjustment.

Referral to the national office. If the director recommends that a change made in compliance with all the applicable provisions should be modified or revoked, the director will forward the matter to the national office for consideration before taking any further action, unless the modification relates solely to the amount of the IRC §481(a) adjustment. The referral to the national office is a request for technical advice and the provisions of Rev. Proc. 2020-2[123] (or successor) apply.

---

[122] Rev. Proc. 2015-13, 2015-5 IRB 419, §12.
[123] 2020-1 IRB 107.

[G] *Permission Revoked or Modified if Found to Be in Error*

The national office may revoke or modify a letter ruling issued under the non-automatic change procedures or the grant of consent for an automatic change by letter to the taxpayer giving notice of revocation or modification, if the national office determines, as a result of the director's review or otherwise, that the letter ruling or grant of consent was issued in error or is not in accord with the current views of the IRS.

Except in rare or unusual circumstances, if a taxpayer that changes its method of accounting is subsequently required to change (in the case of a revocation) or modify that method of accounting, the required change or modification will not be applied retroactively, provided that:

- the taxpayer complied with all the applicable provisions;
- the taxpayer neither misstated nor omitted any material facts;
- the material facts on which the consent was based have not changed;
- the applicable law has not changed;
- the taxpayer to whom consent was granted acted in good faith in relying on the consent; and
- applying the change in method of accounting or modification retroactively would be to the taxpayer's detriment.[124]

§7.03 Commissioner's Consent

[A] *Generally*

In general, a taxpayer may not change its method of accounting for tax purposes without the prior consent of the Commissioner.[125] If a taxpayer changes its method without first obtaining the Commissioner's approval, the Commissioner may require the taxpayer to change back to the original method of accounting, or if the year is closed because the statutory period of limitation has run, to the earliest year still open. The Commissioner may also require that an IRC §481 adjustment be made to ensure that all items of income and expense are properly reflected.[126]

There are, however, a number of circumstances where the Commissioner's consent is either not required or is deemed to have been received if the taxpayer meets certain conditions. Over the years, the IRS issued many rulings dealing with isolated issues involving change of accounting methods.

The requirement for advanced IRS consent applies to proper and improper methods of accounting currently in use. If the taxpayer is using an improper accounting method, prior permission must be received before the taxpayer can change to a new method. Some courts, however, have taken issue with this position of the

---

[124] Rev. Proc. 2015-13, 2015-5 IRB 419, §10.03.

[125] IRC §446(e) and Reg. §1.446-1(e)(2)(i).

[126] Rev. Proc. 2015-13, 2015-5 IRB 419, §3.

Commissioner and have argued that prior IRS approval is not required from a change to a correct method from an incorrect method.[127]

§7.04 Procedures for Obtaining Commissioner's Consent for Automatic Changes

[A] Generally

The IRS has published procedures under IRC §446(e) and Reg. §1.446-1(e) for obtaining the Commissioner's consent to change a method of accounting. In 1997, the IRS, concerned about the confusion created by having separate Revenue Procedures for each automatic change, combined virtually all automatic method changes into one overall accounting method change procedure.[128] The IRS again combined virtually all automatic method changes into two accounting method change procedures to be used in tandem when requesting an automatic consent accounting method change.[129] Rev. Proc. 2015-13 contains the procedures used to obtain consent for automatic changes. Rev. Proc. 2019-43[130] contains the current list of automatic consent accounting method changes.

[B] Automatic Changes

Under Rev. Proc. 2015-13,[131] a taxpayer is eligible to request the Commissioner's consent to make a change in method of accounting under the automatic change procedures only if:

- on the date the taxpayer files a Form 3115, the change is described in the List of Automatic Changes;[132]
- on the date the taxpayer files a Form 3115, the taxpayer meets all requirements for the change provided in the applicable section of the List of Automatic Changes;

---

[127] For example, in *Douthit v. United States*, 299 F. Supp. 397 (W.D. Tenn., 1969), *rev'd per curiam*, 432 F.2d 83 (6th Cir. 1970) the Court held that the requirement of prior approval is not applicable to a change in accounting method that is required by applicable law. Since, in this case, the taxpayer was required by a change in law to change its method of accounting, prior consent was not required. *See also Woodward Iron Co. v. United States*, 254 F. Supp. 835 (N.D. Ala. 1966), *aff'd*, 396 F.2d 552 (5th Cir. 1968).

[128] Rev. Proc. 97-37, 1997-2 CB 455.

[129] Rev. Proc. 2015-13, 2015-5 IRB 419, and Rev. Proc. 2015-14, 2015-5 IRB 450, which was superseded by later rulings.

[130] 2019-48 IRB 1107.

[131] 2015-5 IRB 419, §5.

[132] Rev. Proc. 2017-30, 2017-18 IRB 1131 (or its successor), *See also* Instructions to Form 3115.

- within the requested year of change, the taxpayer does not engage in a liquidation or reorganization transaction to which IRC § 381(a) applies;[133]
- the requested year of change is not the final year of the trade or business;[134]
- the taxpayer has not made or requested an overall method change during any of the five taxable years ending with the year of change; and
- the taxpayer has not made or requested a change for the same item during any of the five taxable years ending with the year of change.[135]

Example 7-10

A, an attorney, began business in 2003 and adopted the overall cash method of accounting. For 2010, A changed to an overall accrual method of accounting using the appropriate administrative guidance. A may not use the automatic change procedures for 2014 to change to the overall cash method because of the five-year change limitation in this SECTION 5.04. However, A may still be able to use the automatic change procedures to change the method of accounting the taxpayer will use to treat advances made on behalf of clients for 2014. See section 3.01 of the List of Automatic Changes.[136]

Example 7-11

B, an attorney, began business in 2003 and adopted the overall cash method of accounting. B is a calendar year taxpayer. For the 2011 taxable year, B filed the national office copy of the Form 3115 on January 31, 2011, requesting to change its method of accounting to an overall accrual method under section 14.01 of the APPENDIX of Rev. Proc. 2011-14. B did not implement the requested change to an overall accrual method of accounting on its 2011 federal income tax return. Rather, B timely filed its 2011 federal income tax return using the overall cash method of accounting, and did not attach the original Form 3115 to its return. B may not use the automatic change procedures for 2014 to change to an overall accrual method because of the five-year change limitation in this SECTION 5.04. However, B may still be able to use the automatic change procedures to change the method of accounting the taxpayer will use to treat advances

---

[133] *See* Reg. § 1.381(c)(4)-1(d)(1) and Reg. § 1.381(c)(5)-1(d)(1). However there are exceptions described in Reg. § 1.381(c)(4)-1(a)(4), Reg. § 1.381(c)(4)-1(a)(5).

[134] Rev. Proc. 2015-13, 2015-5 IRB 419, § 5.01(1)(d), § 5.03.

[135] Rev. Proc. 2015-13, 2015-5 IRB 419, § 5.04.

[136] Rev. Proc. 2015-13, 2015-5 IRB 419, § 5.04, Example 1.

made on behalf of clients for 2014. See section 3.01 of the List of Automatic Changes.[137]

Example 7-12

A uses the LIFO inventory method. For 2010, A changed a LIFO inventory sub-method. Specifically, A changed from the average-cost method of determining the current-year cost of inventories to the earliest-acquisitions cost method. For 2014, A seeks to change to the IPIC method of computing the index and value of its dollar-value pools, a method that A has never used. As part of this change, A seeks to change its method of determining the current-year cost of inventories from the earliest-acquisitions cost method to the most-recent acquisitions cost method. A is eligible to change its method of computing the index and value of its dollar-value pools to the IPIC method under this Revenue Procedure. However, A is not eligible to change its method of determining the current-year costs of inventories under the automatic change procedures because A changed its method of accounting with respect to the same LIFO inventory sub-method within the proscribed five-year period.[138]

If, within the five tax years ending with the requested year of change the taxpayer changed its method of accounting for the same item, the IRS National Office will consider the taxpayer's explanation for requesting consent to again change its method of accounting for that same item in determining whether to grant consent for the current request to change the taxpayer's method of accounting.[139]

[C] Procedural Rules for Requesting Consent

Consent to change a method of accounting is made by completing and filing a Form 3115. Ordinarily, a taxpayer may request only one change in method of accounting on a Form 3115. If the taxpayer wants to request a change in method of accounting for more than one unrelated item or sub-method of accounting, the taxpayer must submit a separate Form 3115 for each unrelated item or sub-method, except in certain situations in which the IRS specifically permits certain unrelated changes to be included on a single Form 3115.[140]

---

[137] Rev. Proc. 2015-13, 2015-5 IRB 419, § 5.04, Example 2.

[138] Rev. Proc. 2015-13, 2015-5 IRB 419, § 5.05, Example 1.

[139] Rev. Proc. 2015-13, 2015-5 IRB 419, § 11.02(2)(a)(i).

[140] *See, e.g.*, Rev. Proc. 2015-13, 2015-5 IRB 419, § 14.03, for the List of Automatic Changes. *See also* § 9.02 of Rev. Proc. 2020-1, 2020-1 IRB 1 (or its successor).

The taxpayer must submit a Form 3115 that is accurate and, except as specifically permitted in the applicable section of the List of Automatic Changes, complete. The Form 3115 must include all relevant facts, including all information and representations required by Rev. Proc. 2015-13,[141] the applicable provisions of Rev. Proc. 2020-1[142] (or its successor), the current instructions for Form 3115, and the applicable section of the List of Automatic Changes (in the case of an automatic change).

[D] Designated Automatic Accounting Method Change Number

In the case of a Form 3115 filed under the automatic change procedures, the taxpayer must include the designated automatic accounting method change number found in Rev. Proc. 2019-43 for the specific method change that is being filed in the applicable section of the List of Automatic Changes on the applicable line of Form 3115. For example, the designated automatic accounting method change number for the change in the overall accrual method other than for the first IRC § 448 year (IRC § 446) under section 15.01 of Rev. Proc. 2018-31, as modified by Rev. Proc. 2018-44 and Rev. Proc. 2018-60, in the List of Automatic Changes is 122. Therefore, a taxpayer requesting consent for the change in method of accounting other than for the first IRC § 448 year (IRC § 446) for its taxable year ending December 31, 2020, must enter the number "122" on Line 1(a) of Form 3115.[143] The application must be signed by an individual with authority to bind the taxpayer.

In general, a taxpayer may enter only one designated automatic accounting method change number on a Form 3115. However, where the List of Automatic Changes or other guidance published in the IRB specifically permits or requires a taxpayer to request two or more particular changes in method of accounting on a single Form 3115, the taxpayer must enter the designated automatic accounting method change number for each such particular change being requested on the applicable line of the Form 3115.

Rev. Proc. 2015-13,[144] as modified by subsequent Revenue Procedures, provides the general procedures by which a taxpayer may obtain automatic consent of the IRS to a change in method of accounting described in the List of Automatic Changes.

Rev. Proc. 2019-43[145] contains the current List of Automatic Changes.

Section 15.01 of Rev. Proc. 2018-31 provides automatic changes for certain taxpayers that want to change their overall method of accounting from the cash method to an accrual method, including taxpayers required to make this change by IRC § 448.

---

141 *Id.*

142 2020-1 IRB 1.

143 Currently there are 239 separate automatic changes available.

144 2015-5 IRB 419.

145 2019-48 IRB 1107.

Rev. Proc. 2018-44[146] adds a section to Rev. Proc. 2018-31 that:

1. provides that an eligible terminated S corporation that is required to change from the cash method to an accrual method as a result of a revocation of its S corporation election, and that makes this change to a method of accounting under section 15.01 of Rev. Proc. 2018-31 for the first tax year that it is a C corporation, must take the resulting positive or negative adjustment required by IRC § 481(a)(2) into account ratably during the six-year period beginning with the year of change; and
2. allows an eligible terminated S corporation that is permitted to continue to use the cash method after the revocation of its S corporation election, and that changes to an accrual method under section 15.01 of Rev. Proc. 2018-31 for the first tax year that it is a C corporation, to take the resulting positive or negative adjustment required by IRC § 481(a)(2) into account ratably during the six-year period beginning with the year of change.

Rev. Proc. 2018-44 also notes that, in addition to the change to an accrual method described in section 15.01 of Rev. Proc. 2018-31, an eligible terminated S corporation may have other changes in method of accounting that result in adjustments required by IRC § 481(a) that are attributable to such corporation's revocation of its S corporation election as described in IRC § 481(d)(2). Any such change is not within the scope of Rev. Proc. 2018-44.

Rev. Proc. 2018-31 was modified by Rev. Proc. 2018-60[147] to provide procedures under IRC § 446 and Reg. § 1.446-1(e) to obtain automatic consent of the Commissioner to change methods of accounting to comply with IRC § 451(b), as amended by TCJA. In addition, for the first taxable year that begins after December 31, 2017, certain taxpayers are permitted to make a method change to comply with IRC § 451(b) without filing a Form 3115.

[E] Automatic Changes Added by the TCJA

The automatic changes added by IRC § 448(c)(1) and Rev. Proc. 2019-43[148] include the following:

- Small business taxpayer changing to overrule cash method;[149]
- Small business taxpayer exception from requirements to capitalize costs under IRC § 263;[150]
- Small business taxpayer exception from requirement to account for inventory under IRC § 471;[151] and

---

146 2018-37 IRB.

147 2018-51 IRB 1045. *See also* CCA 201852019.

148 2019-48 IRB 1107.

149 Rev. Proc. 2018-43, 2019-48 IRB 1107, § 15.18.

150 Rev. Proc. 2018-43, 2019-48 IRB 1107, § 12.16.

151 Rev. Proc. 2018-43, 2019-48 IRB 1107, § 22.19.

- Small business taxpayer exceptions from requirements to account for certain long-term contracts under IRC § 460(e) or to capitalize costs under IRC § 263A for certain home construction contracts.[152]

As the IRS continues to issue Revenue Procedures implementing changes made by the TCJA, we expect more rulings to be released. The practitioner should verify that the ruling he or she is relying on is the latest pronouncement made.

Rev. Proc. 2019-43[153] has been modified by Rev. Proc. 2020-13[154] which provides procedures for a taxpayer that qualifies for the IRC § 263A(i) small business exemption to revoke its prior IRC § 263A(d)(3) election and apply the IRC § 263A(i) exemption in same taxable year. In addition, Rev. Proc. 2020-13 offers procedures for taxpayers that use the IRC § 263A(i) exemption and no longer qualify as small business taxpayers eligible for the exemption and wish to make the IRC § 263A(d)(3) election in the same taxable year that they no longer qualify for the IRC § 263A(i) exemption.

Additionally Rev. Proc. 2019-43 has been modified by Rev. Proc. 2020-25[155] to reflect changes made to depreciation of qualified improvement property placed in service by the taxpayer after December 31, 2017 by the CARES Act '20.[156] The IRS has provided procedures for changing a depreciation method as well as for making a late election for tax years 2018, 2019, or 2020.[157]

[F] Year of Change

The tax year of change is that year which is indicated by the taxpayer on the application, and for which the application is timely filed.[158] If the application to file an automatic accounting method change is filed after year-end and before the filing date for the federal income tax return, the taxpayer may choose to implement the accounting method change effective for the year that just ended, or for the year in which the application is filed. The taxpayer, in filing its automatic accounting method change, must designate the year of change on the Form 3115.

[G] Where and When to File

Under Reg. § 1.446-1(e)(3)(i), a Form 3115 must be filed within the requested year of change; however, if the request is for an automatic change of accounting, this filing rule is waived for any Form 3115 filed under the automatic change procedures.[159]

---

152 Rev. Proc. 2018-43, 2019-48 IRB 1107, § 19.01.
153 2019-48 IRB 1107.
154 2020-11 IRB 515.
155 2020-19 IRB 785.
156 P.L. 116-136, § 2307 (March 27, 2020).
157 Rev. Proc. 2015-56, 2015-49 IRB 827 Sec. 5.02(3)(b)(ii) and Rev. Proc. 2019-43, 2019-48 IRB 1107.
158 Rev. Proc. 2015-13, 2015-5 IRB 419, § 3.19.
159 *See* Reg. § 1.446-1(e)(3)(ii). *See* § 7.04[G], *supra*.

A taxpayer requesting to change a method of accounting under the automatic change procedures must complete a Form 3115 and file that Form 3115 in duplicate, as follows:

- Original Form 3115—The original completed Form 3115 (or an electronic version of the Form 3115) must be attached to the taxpayer's timely filed (including any extension) original federal income tax return implementing the requested automatic change for the requested year of change;[160] and
- Ogden copy of Form 3115—A signed copy of the original Form 3115 must be filed with the IRS in Ogden, UT (Ogden copy) at the applicable address in Section 9.05 of Rev. Proc. 2018-1 (or its successor) no earlier than the first day of the requested year of change and no later than the date the taxpayer files the original Form 3115 with the federal income tax return for the requested year of change.[161]

As with prior Revenue Procedures for automatic changes, the taxpayer is not required to pay a user fee.[162] Because the IRS does not send an acknowledgement of receipt for a Form 3115 (original or copy) filed under the automatic change procedures, all submissions should be sent certified mail or by an express service recognized to deliver documents to the IRS.

[H] *Automatic Extension for Form 3115*

An automatic extension of six months from the due date (excluding any extension) of the federal income tax return for the year of change requested on the Form 3115 is granted to file a Form 3115 under the automatic change procedures provided the taxpayer:

- timely filed (including any extension) its original federal income tax return for the year of change;
- files an amended return within the six-month extension period implementing the requested change in method of accounting for the year of change;
- attaches the original Form 3115 to the amended return;
- files a signed copy of the original Form 3115 with the IRS in Ogden, UT at the applicable address set forth in Section 9.05 of Rev. Proc. 2020-1 (or its successor) no later than the date the original is filed with the amended return;
- provides a signed copy of the original Form 3115 to the examining agent, Appeals officer(s) or all counsel to the government, as applicable, as required by Rev. Proc 2015-13, Section 6.03(3); and

---

160 For taxpayers that are required to e-file their federal income tax returns, the copy attached to the federal income tax return may be included as a PDF attachment to the XML portion of the electronic return so long as the duplicate copy was previously filed with the appropriate IRS office. However, if the duplicate copy is being filed with the appropriate IRS office concurrently with the filing of the federal income tax return, the Form 3115 must be submitted in XML.

161 There are similar rules for foreign corporations and partnerships. *See* § 6.03 (ii) and (iii) of Rev. Proc. 2015-13, 2015-5 IRB 419.

162 Rev. Proc. 2015-13, 2015-5 IRB 419, § 6.03(1)(c).

- attaches a statement to the Form 3115 (original, Ogden, and any other copy required by Rev. Proc 2015-13, Section 6.03(3)) that the Form 3115 is being filed pursuant to Reg. § 301.9100-2(b) of the Procedure and Administration Regulations.[163]

[I] Other Extensions of Time

Except in unusual and compelling circumstances or as provided, a taxpayer is not eligible for an extension of time to file a Form 3115 and is not eligible to make a late election.[164]

[J] Terms and Conditions

A change in method of accounting requested must be implemented pursuant to both the terms and conditions provided in Rev. Proc. 2015-13[165] and either the List of Automatic Changes (in the case of an automatic change) or the letter ruling for the change (in the case of a non-automatic change). Notwithstanding the terms and conditions in Rev. Proc. 2015-13,[166] based on the unique facts of a particular case and in the interest of sound tax administration, the national office may prescribe in the letter ruling for a non-automatic change terms and conditions for the requested change in method of accounting that differ from and override those provided in Rev. Proc. 2015-13.[167]

[K] Section 481(a) Adjustment Period

Generally, under Rev. Proc. 2015-13,[168] the IRC § 481(a) adjustment period is one taxable year (year of change) for a negative § 481(a) adjustment, i.e. the taxpayer is receiving a refund, and four taxable years (year of change and next three taxable years) for a positive IRC § 481(a) adjustment, i.e. the taxpayer owes taxes. Generally a taxpayer must take a positive IRC § 481(a) adjustment into account ratably over four years (the year of change and the following three years).[169] Where multiple eligible taxpayers or trades or businesses request an identical change in method of accounting for the same item on a single Form 3115, each taxpayer or trade or business has its own IRC § 481(a) adjustment period.

---

163 Rev. Proc. 2015-13, 2015-5 IRB 419, § 6.03(4).

164 *See* Reg. § 301.9100-3(c)(2) and Rev. Proc. 2018-1 (or its successor).

165 2015-5 IRB 419 and those described in Rev. Proc. 2018-40, 2018-34 IRB 320.

166 *Id.*

167 2015-5 IRB 419.

168 *Id.*

169 Rev. Proc. 2015-13, 2015-5 IRB 419, § 7.03.

[L] *Short Period as a Separate Taxable Year*

If the year of change or any other taxable year during the IRC § 481(a) adjustment period for a positive IRC § 481(a) adjustment is a short taxable year, the taxpayer must take the IRC § 481(a) adjustment into account as if that short taxable year were a full 12-month taxable year.[170]

Example 7-13

A calendar year taxpayer receives permission to change its method of accounting beginning with the 2019 calendar year. The IRC § 481(a) adjustment for this change in method of accounting is a positive adjustment of $60,000 and the adjustment period is four taxable years. The taxpayer subsequently receives permission to change its annual accounting period to September 30, effective for the taxable year ending September 30, 2020. The taxpayer must include $15,000 of the IRC § 481(a) adjustment in gross income for the short period from January 1, 2020, through September 30, 2020.

Example 7-14

Corporation X, a calendar year taxpayer, received permission to change its method of accounting beginning with the 2019 calendar year. The IRC § 481(a) adjustment for this method of accounting change is a positive adjustment of $60,000 and the adjustment period is four taxable years. On July 1, 2020, Corporation Z acquires Corporation X in a transaction to which IRC § 381(a) applies. Corporation Z is a calendar year taxpayer that uses the same method of accounting to which Corporation X changed in 2019. Corporation X must include $15,000 of the IRC § 481(a) adjustment in gross income for its short period for January 1, 2020, through June 30, 2020. In addition, Corporation Z must include $15,000 of the IRC § 481(a) adjustment in gross income for calendar year 2020.

[M] *Shortened Adjustment Periods*

The four-year IRC § 481(a) adjustment period for a positive IRC § 481(a) adjustment does not apply in the following situations:

- Cooperatives-the adjustment generally is one taxable year (year of change);[171]

---

[170] *See* Rev. Rul. 78-165, 1978-1 CB 276.

[171] *See* Rev. Rul. 79-45, 1979-1 CB 284.

- Taxpayers under examination with positive IRC § 481(a) adjustments. The IRC § 481(a) adjustment period is two taxable years (year of change and next taxable year) for a positive IRC § 481(a) adjustment for a change in method of accounting requested when a taxpayer is under examination, unless the change is filed in a three-month window, the change is filed in a 120-day window, the present method is not before the director, or is a new member of a consolidated group in CAP.[172]

[N] De Minimis Election

A taxpayer may elect a one-year IRC § 481(a) adjustment period (year of change) for a positive IRC § 481(a) adjustment that is less than $50,000. To make this election, the taxpayer must complete the appropriate line on the Form 3115 and take the entire IRC § 481(a) adjustment into account in the year of change when it implements the change in method of accounting. To make the election, the taxpayer must affirmatively state that it desires to elect this *de minimis* rule.[173]

[O] Eligible Acquisition Transaction Election

A taxpayer may elect a one-year IRC § 481(a) adjustment period (year of change) for all (but not some) positive IRC § 481(a) adjustments for the year of change if there was an eligible acquisition transaction. An eligible acquisition transaction means:

- For a CFC or a corporation that is not an S corporation, (1) an acquisition of stock ownership interest in the taxpayer by another party that either results in the acquisition of control of the taxpayer or causes the taxpayer's taxable year to end, or (2) an acquisition of assets in a transaction to which IRC § 381(a) applies, and
- For all other taxpayers, an acquisition of an ownership interest in the taxpayer by another party that does not cause the taxpayer to cease to exist for federal income tax purposes (for example, the sale or exchange of a partnership interest that does not cause a technical termination of the partner under IRC § 708(b)(1)(B)).

To make this election, a taxpayer must file, in duplicate, the election statement that contains the required information. The taxpayer must attach the original election statement to the taxpayer's timely filed (including any extension) original federal income tax return for the year of change (even if a non-automatic change is pending with the national office) and file the copy, which must be signed by the Form(s) 3115 filer, with the IRS, no later than the date the taxpayer files the original election statement with its original federal income tax return for the year of change.

---

[172] Rev. Rul. 2015-13, § 7.03(3)(b).

[173] Rev. Proc. 2015-13, 2015-5 IRB 419, § 7.03(3)(c). The election is made by checking the appropriate box on the Form 3115.

The eligible acquisition transaction election statement must include:

- the name and taxpayer identification number of the Form(s) 3115 filer;
- the name of the applicant (taxpayer making the change in method of accounting) on the Form(s) 3115;
- the year of change (including the beginning and ending dates);
- the date of the eligible acquisition transaction;
- the Form(s) 3115 filer's signature and date;
- the following statement: "The Form(s) 3115 filer elects a one-year adjustment period pursuant to Section 7.03(3)(d) of Rev. Proc. 2015-13 for all changes in method of accounting made by the applicant (the taxpayer) pursuant to Rev. Proc. 2015-13[174] for the year of change. The filer agrees that the limitation on tax in IRC § 481(b) and Reg. § 1.481-2 will not be applied for any IRC § 481(a) adjustment for all changes in method of accounting made by the taxpayer"; and
- if the taxpayer is a pass-through entity, such as a partnership, S corporation, or trust, the following representation: "The taxpayer represents that it has obtained (either directly or by delegation) from each owner or beneficiary, as applicable, who was an owner or beneficiary during the year of change, a written agreement that the owner or beneficiary agrees to not apply the limitation on tax in IRC § 481(b) and Reg. § 1.481-2 for any IRC § 481(a) adjustment for all changes in method of accounting made by the taxpayer pursuant to Rev. Proc. 2015-13[175] for the year of change."

Example 7-15

X Corporation enters into an agreement to sell all of X Corporation's stock ownership interest in T Corporation, a wholly owned subsidiary of X, to Z Corporation. T Corporation is a calendar year taxpayer. In the course of Z Corporation's due diligence review of T Corporation, Z Corporation discovers that T Corporation improperly defers advance payments for services. Z Corporation requests that prior to its acquisition of T Corporation's stock, T Corporation change its method of accounting for advance payments for services to a proper deferral method for 2019. On February 28, 2020, Z Corporation acquires X Corporation's stock ownership interest in T Corporation. On March 14, 2020, T Corporation files for an extension of time to file its 2018 federal income tax return. On September 15, 2020, T Corporation files the original and Ogden copy of a Form 3115 under the automatic change procedures to change its method of accounting for advance payments for services for 2019 (year of change), which results in a positive IRC § 481(a) adjustment of $1,000,000. T Corporation follows the procedures in § 7.03(3)(d) of Rev. Proc. 2015-13[176] to elect a one-year

[174] 2015-5 IRB 419.

[175] *Id.*

[176] *Id.*

adjustment period for all changes in method of accounting that it makes pursuant to this Revenue Procedure for 2019 (year of change). Pursuant to this election, T Corporation must take into account the entire $1,000,000 IRC § 481(a) adjustment for its change in method of accounting for advance payments for services in determining its taxable income for 2019 (year of change).

§ 7.05 Procedures for Obtaining Commissioner's Consent for Non-Automatic Changes

[A] Generally

Many Forms 3115 filed under the non-automatic change procedures require additional information and development. Therefore, the IRS recommends that taxpayers file a Form 3115 under the non-automatic change procedures as early as possible during the requested year of change. Moreover, if the taxpayer becomes ineligible to file a Form 3115, the taxpayer will lose the ability to use the four-year IRC § 481 adjustment period, unless the three-month window, 120-day window, or the present method not before the District Director applies.

[B] Eligibility

A taxpayer is eligible to request the Commissioner's consent to make a change in a method of accounting under the non-automatic change procedures only if:

- on the date the taxpayer files a Form 3115 with the national office, the taxpayer is not eligible to use the automatic change procedures to make the change; and
- the requested year of change is not the final year of the trade or business.

[C] When to File Form 3115

A taxpayer requesting to change a method of accounting under the non-automatic change procedures must complete Form 3115 and, except as specifically provided in Rev. Proc. 2015-13[177] or other guidance published in the IRB, file Form 3115 during the requested year of change.[178]

---

[177] *Id.*

[178] *See* Reg. § 1.446-1(e)(3)(i). However, *see, for example,* Rev. Proc. 2015-13, §§ 6.03(2)(a)(ii), 6.03(2)(a)(iii), and 6.03(4)(b), which allow a taxpayer in certain limited circumstances additional time to file a Form 3115 after the year of change.

A taxpayer requesting a change in method of accounting to which Rev. Proc. 2015-13[179] § 8.02(1)(d) (new member of a consolidated group in CAP) applies must file the Form 3115 on behalf of a new member by the earlier of:

- 90 calendar days after the date the new member becomes a member of the consolidated group, or
- 30 calendar days after the end of the taxable year in which the new member becomes a member of the consolidated group.

[D] Certain Transactions to which IRC §381(a) Applies

A party to a transaction to which IRC § 381(a) applies requesting consent to make a non-automatic change described in Reg. § 1.381(c)(4)-1(a)(4) or (5), or in Reg. § 1.381(c)(5)-1(a)(4) or (5) must file the Form 3115 on or before the later of:

(A) the due date for filling a Form 3115 as specified in Reg. § 1.446-1(e), or

(B) the earlier of:

- the day that is 180 calendar days after the date of distribution or transfer, or
- the day on which the acquiring corporation files its federal income tax return for the taxable year in which the distribution or transfer occurred.[180]

[E] Where to File Form 3115

A taxpayer requesting consent to change a method of accounting under the non-automatic change procedures must file its completed Form 3115, together with the appropriate user fee, with the national office at the following addresses:

If a private delivery service is not used, requests for letter rulings should be sent to the following address:

Internal Revenue Service
Attn: CC:PA:LPD:DRU
P.O. Box 7604
Benjamin Franklin Station
Washington, DC 20044

If a private delivery service is used, the address is:

Internal Revenue Service
Attn: CC:PA:LPD:DRU, Room 5336
1111 Constitution Ave., NW
Washington, DC 20224

---

179 *Id.*

180 *See* Reg. § § 1.381(c)(4)-1(d)(2)(iii) and 1.381(c)(5)-1(d)(2)(iii).

Requests for letter rulings may also be hand delivered between the hours of 8:00 a.m. and 4:00 p.m. to the courier's desk at the loading dock of 1111 Constitution Avenue, NW, Washington, DC. A receipt will be given at the courier's desk. The package should be addressed to:

Courier's Desk

Internal Revenue Service

Attn: CC:PA:LPD:DRU, Room 5336

1111 Constitution Ave., NW

Washington, DC 20224

Requests for letter rulings may not be submitted by fax.

[F] User Fee

A taxpayer requesting to change a method of accounting under the non-automatic change procedures must submit the required user fee(s) for its Form 3115. Rev. Proc. 2020-1 (or its successor) contains the schedule of user fees and provides guidance regarding the user fee requirements.[181]

Here are some of the 2020 user fees required for filing for a request for a letter ruling or closing agreement.

- Form 1128, *Application to Adopt, Change, or Retain a Tax Year* –$6,200;
- Non-automatic Form 3115, *Application for Change in Accounting Method* – $10,800; and
- Letter ruling requests for extensions of time to file Form 3115, *Application for Change in Accounting Method* – $11,800.

[G] Taxpayer Under Examination Before an Appeals Office or Before a Federal Court

If the taxpayer is under examination, before an Appeals office, or before a federal court with respect to any income tax issue, the taxpayer must provide an additional signed copy of the original Form 3115 to the examining agent(s), Appeals officer(s), and all counsel to the government, as applicable, no later than the date the taxpayer timely files the Form 3115 (original or Ogden copy, whichever is filed earlier, in the case of an automatic change).[182]

---

[181] Under Rev. Proc. 2019-1, 2019-1 IRB 1, the user fee for a non-automatic change is currently $10,800.

[182] The same requirement exists for partnerships and foreign corporation.

[H] *Extensions of Time to File—Automatic Extension for Form 3115*

An automatic extension of six months from the due date (excluding any extension) of the federal income tax return for the year of change requested on the Form 3115 is granted to file a Form 3115 under the automatic change procedures, provided the taxpayer:

- timely filed (including any extension) its original federal income tax return for the year of change;
- files an amended return within the six-month extension period implementing the requested change in method of accounting for the year of change;
- attaches the original Form 3115 to the amended return;
- files a signed copy of the original Form 3115 with the IRS in Ogden, no later than the date the original is filed with the amended return;
- provides a signed copy of the original Form 3115 to the examining agent, Appeals officer(s) or all counsel to the government, as applicable; and
- attaches a statement to the Form 3115 that the Form 3115 is being filed pursuant to Reg. §301.9100-2(b) of the Procedure and Administration Regulations.

[I] *Other Extensions of Time*

Except in unusual and compelling circumstances a taxpayer is not eligible for an extension of time to file a Form 3115 and is not eligible to make a late election.[183]

[J] *Terms and Conditions of Change*

A change in method of accounting requested must be implemented pursuant to both the terms and conditions provided in Rev. Proc. 2015-13[184] and either the List of Automatic Changes (in the case of an automatic change) or the letter ruling for the change (in the case of a non-automatic change). Notwithstanding the terms and conditions in Rev. Proc. 2015-13,[185] based on the unique facts of a particular case and in the interest of sound tax administration, the national office may prescribe in the letter ruling for a non-automatic change terms and conditions for the requested change in method of accounting that differ from and override those provided in Rev. Proc. 2015-13.[186]

---

[183] *See* Rev. Proc. 2015-13, 2015-5 IRB 419; Reg. §§301.9100-1 and 301.9100-3. *See* Reg. §301.9100-3(c)(2).

[184] 2015-5 IRB 419.

[185] *Id.*

[186] *Id.*

[K] Section 481(a) Adjustment Period

Generally, under Rev. Proc 2015-13,[187] the IRC § 481(a) adjustment period for a non-automatic change is one taxable year (year of change) for a negative § 481(a) adjustment, *i.e.*, the taxpayer is receiving a refund, and four taxable years (year of change and next three taxable years) for a positive IRC § 481(a) adjustment, i.e. the taxpayer owes taxes. Generally a taxpayer must take a positive IRC § 481(a) adjustment into account ratably over the IRC § 481(a) adjustment period. Where multiple eligible taxpayers or trades or businesses request an identical change in method of accounting for the same item on a single Form 3115 each taxpayer or trade or business has its own IRC § 481(a) adjustment period, applied to its own IRC § 481(a) adjustment.

[L] Short Period as a Separate Taxable Year

If the year of change or any other taxable year during the IRC § 481(a) adjustment period for a positive IRC § 481(a) adjustment is a short taxable year, the taxpayer must take the IRC § 481(a) adjustment into account as if that short taxable year were a full 12-month taxable year.[188]

Example 7-16

A calendar year taxpayer receives permission to change its method of accounting beginning with the 2019 calendar year in a situation not described in Rev. Proc. 2015-13[189] § 7.03(3) or 7.03(4). The IRC § 481(a) adjustment for this change in method of accounting is a positive adjustment of $60,000 and the adjustment period is four taxable years. The taxpayer subsequently receives permission to change its annual accounting period to September 30, effective for the taxable year ending September 30, 2020. The taxpayer must include $15,000 of the IRC § 481(a) adjustment in gross income for the short period from January 1, 2020, through September 30, 2020.

Example 7-17

Corporation X, a calendar year taxpayer, received permission to change its method of accounting beginning with the 2019 calendar year. The IRC § 481(a) adjustment for this method of accounting change is a positive

---

[187] *Id.*

[188] *See* Rev. Rul. 78-165, 1978-1 CB 276.

[189] 2015-5 IRB 419.

adjustment of $60,000 and the adjustment period is four taxable years. On July 1, 2020, Corporation Z acquires Corporation X in a transaction to which IRC § 381(a) applies. Corporation Z is a calendar year taxpayer that uses the same method of accounting to which Corporation X changed in 2019. Corporation X must include $15,000 of the IRC § 481(a) adjustment in gross income for its short period for January 1, 2020, through June 30, 2020. In addition, Corporation Z must include $15,000 of the IRC § 481(a) adjustment in gross income for calendar year 2020.

[M] Accelerated Adjustment Periods

The four-year IRC § 481(a) adjustment period for a positive IRC § 481(a) adjustment provided is accelerated on the following situations:

- Ceasing to engage in the trade or business;
- S election effective for year of LIFO discontinuance;
- S election effective for a year after LIFO discontinuance; and
- Certain transfers pursuant to a IRC § 351 transaction within a consolidated group.[190]

[N] Taxpayers under Examination with Positive IRC § 481(a) Adjustments

The IRC § 481(a) adjustment period is two taxable years (year of change and next taxable year) for a positive IRC § 481(a) adjustment for a change in method of accounting requested when a taxpayer is under examination, unless the change is filed in a three-month window, a 120-day window, or if the present method not before the director or a new member of a consolidated group in CAP applies.[191]

[O] De Minimis Election

A taxpayer may elect a one-year IRC § 481(a) adjustment period (year of change) for a positive IRC § 481(a) adjustment that is less than $50,000. To make this election, the taxpayer must complete the appropriate line on the Form 3115 and take the entire IRC § 481(a) adjustment into account in the year of change when it implements the change in method of accounting.

---

[190] *See* Rev. Proc. 2015-13, 2015-5 IRB 419, § 7.03(4).

[191] Rev. Proc. 2015-13, 2015-5 IRB 419, § 8.02(1)(a), § 8.02(1)(b), § 8.02(1)(c), § 8.02(1)(d).

[P] Maintenance of Adequate Records

The taxpayer must maintain accounting records for the year of change and subsequent taxable years to support the method of accounting for which consent is granted to the taxpayer. Accounting records include the taxpayer's regular books of account and such other records and data as may be necessary to support the entries on its books of account and on its return, including for example, a reconciliation of any differences between the method of accounting used in its accounting records and the method of accounting used for federal income tax purposes.

§7.06 Audit Protection for Taxable Years Prior to Year of Change

When a taxpayer timely files a Form 3115, the IRS will not require the taxpayer to change its method of accounting for the same item for a taxable year prior to the requested year of change.

[A] Exceptions

There is no audit protection for taxpayers who are under examination.[192] The IRS may require the taxpayer to change its method of accounting for the same item that is the subject of a Form 3115 filed for taxable years prior to the requested year of change if the taxpayer is under examination as of the date the taxpayer files the Form 3115.

[B] Change Filed within a Three-Month Window

Except in certain circumstances the no audit protection for taxpayers under examination rule does not apply to a request for a change in method of accounting for an item filed in a three-month window if:

- the taxpayer has been under examination for at least 12 consecutive months as of the first day of the three-month window; and
- the method of accounting for the same item the taxpayer is requesting to change is not an issue under consideration as of the date the taxpayer files the Form 3115.

A "three-month window" is the period beginning on the fifteenth day of the seventh month of the taxpayer's taxable year and ending on the fifteenth day of the tenth month of the taxpayer's taxable year. However, if the taxable year is a short taxable year that ends before the fifteenth day of the tenth month after the short taxable year begins, the "three-month window" is the period beginning on the first

---

[192] Unless an application for an accounting change is filed within the three-month window, filed within a 120-day window, made for a method change that is not before the director, or filed a change in method for a new member of a consolidated group in the Compliance Assurance Process (CAP). *See* §7.02[D].

day of the second month preceding the month in which the short taxable year ends and ending on the last day of the short taxable year.[193]

[C] Change Filed within a 120-Day Window

Except as otherwise provided the no audit protection for taxpayers under examination rule does not apply to a request for a change in method of accounting for an item filed in a 120-day window if the method of accounting for the same item the taxpayer is requesting to change is not an issue under consideration as of the date the taxpayer files the Form 3115. However, the 120-day window ends on the date the IRS notifies the taxpayer that jurisdiction for the case has been transferred from Appeals to the examining agent(s) for reconsideration.[194]

A "120-day window" is the 120-day period following the date an examination of the taxpayer ends, regardless of whether a subsequent examination has commenced.[195]

[D] Present Method not Before the Director

The no audit protection for taxpayers under examination rule does not apply to a change in method of accounting for an item when the present method is not before the director. The present method is not before the director when it is:

- a change from a clearly permissible method of accounting; or
- a change from an impermissible method of accounting and the impermissible method was adopted subsequent to the taxable year(s) under examination on the date the taxpayer files the Form 3115.

The question of whether the present method of accounting is a clearly permissible method of accounting or was adopted subsequent to the taxable year(s) under examination may be referred to the national office as a request for technical advice under the provisions of Rev. Proc. 2019-2[196] (or its successor).

The Form 3115 must include a statement that the Form 3115 is filed under §8.02(1)(c) of Rev. Proc. 2015-13.[197]

[E] Change Resulting in a Negative IRC §481(a) Adjustment

The no audit protection for taxpayers under examination rule does not apply to a change in method of accounting for an item that:

---

[193] Rev. Proc. 2015-13, 2015-5 IRB 419, §8.02(a)(iii) has special rules for CFCs.

[194] *See* Rev. Proc. 2015-13, 2015-5 IRB 419, §3.18(1)(c).

[195] The 120-day window provisions in Rev. Proc. 2015-13, 2015-5 IRB 419, §8.02(1)(b)(i) are not available for a CFC or 10/50 corporation.

[196] 2019-1 IRB 106.

[197] 2015-5 IRB 419.

- results in a negative IRC §481(a) adjustment for that item for the year of change; and
- would have resulted in a negative IRC §481(a) adjustment in each taxable year under examination if the change in method of accounting for that item had been made in the taxable year(s) under examination.

Example 7-18

A taxpayer placed Properties A and B in service in its 2010 taxable year. In its 2010 through 2013 taxable years, the taxpayer depreciated Property A using a 7-year recovery period instead of its correct five-year recovery period and depreciated Property B using a five-year recovery period instead of its correct seven-year recovery period. The taxpayer is under examination for its 2012 taxable year. The taxpayer filed a Form 3115 under this Revenue Procedure to request a change in method of accounting for its 2014 taxable year to change its methods of accounting for depreciation for Properties A and B. Under §8.02(1), the taxpayer generally does not receive audit protection for a change in method of accounting filed for its 2014 taxable year. However, under this §8.02(1)(e), the taxpayer may receive audit protection for the change in method of accounting for depreciation for Property A because the IRC §481(a) adjustment for that item required in its 2014 taxable year, and that would have been required in its 2012 taxable year, is negative. However, the taxpayer does not receive audit protection for the change in method of accounting for depreciation for Property B because the IRC §481(a) adjustment for that item required in its 2014 taxable year, and that would have been required in its 2012 taxable year, is positive.

[F] Statement Required

The Form 3115 must include a statement that the Form 3115 is filed under the provisions of §8.02(1)(e) of Rev. Proc. 2015-13.[198]

[G] No Examination-Imposed Change and Item not under Consideration

Except as otherwise provided in Rev. Proc. 2015-13,[199] §8.02(1)(f)(ii), for a taxpayer that is under examination for one or more taxable years on the date the taxpayer files a Form 3115, §8.02(1) (no audit protection for taxpayers under examination) ceases to apply to the change in method of accounting for that item as of the

---

[198] *Id.*

[199] 2015-5 IRB 419.

date immediately following the earliest date that any of those examinations ends for the taxable year(s) subsequent to that taxable year and prior to the year of change to which the Form 3115 applies, if by the earliest date that any of those examinations ends:

- the examining agent(s) does not propose an adjustment for the same item that is the subject of the Form 3115 for the taxable year(s) under examination; and
- the method of accounting for that same item is not an issue under consideration.

Example 7-19

A taxpayer is under examination for 2014 and 2015 as of December 19, 2016, the date the taxpayer files a Form 3115 to request a change in method of accounting for 2016 to change its method of accounting for costs subject to IRC § 263A. Under § 8.02(1), the taxpayer generally does not receive audit protection for a change in method of accounting for which consent is requested while under examination. The 2014 examination ends July 1, 2017, while the 2015 examination is still ongoing. Under § 8.02(1)(f), the taxpayer receives audit protection for the change in method of accounting for costs subject to IRC § 263A as of July 2, 2017, the day immediately following the date the 2014 examination ends, if by that date the examining agents do not propose an adjustment for costs subject to IRC § 263A and the method of accounting for costs subject to IRC § 263A is not an issue under consideration as described in Rev. Proc. 2015-13[200] § 3.08, as long as no other provision of Rev. Proc. 2015-13[201] § § 8.02(2) through 8.02(7) applies to the taxpayer.

[H] *Change Lacking Audit Protection*

The IRS may change a taxpayer's method of accounting for the same item that is the subject of a Form 3115 for taxable years prior to the requested year of change if the description of the change in the List of Automatic Changes, or other guidance published in the IRB, provides that the change is not subject to the audit protection provisions of Rev. Proc. 2015-13[202] § 8.01.

---

200 2015-5 IRB 419.
201 2015-5 IRB 419.
202 2015-5 IRB 419.

[I] Change Not Made or Made Improperly

The IRS may change a taxpayer's method of accounting for the same item that is the subject of a Form 3115 filed for taxable years prior to the requested year of change if:

- the taxpayer withdraws or does not perfect its request (for example, by not providing requested supplemental information);
- the national office denies the taxpayer's request for consent to make a change in method of accounting;
- the taxpayer does not timely implement the change in method of accounting consistent with all the applicable provisions;
- the taxpayer timely implements the change but does not otherwise comply with all the applicable provisions; or
- the national office modifies or revokes the Commissioner's consent for the change in method of accounting retroactively because the taxpayer misstated or omitted material facts.[203]

[J] Change in Sub-method of Accounting

The IRS may change a taxpayer's method of accounting for the same item that is the subject of a Form 3115 filed for taxable years prior to the requested year of change if the taxpayer is changing a sub-method of accounting within the method of accounting. For example, an examining agent may propose to terminate the taxpayer's use of the LIFO inventory method of accounting during a prior taxable year even though the taxpayer changes its method of valuing increments in the current year. In addition, a taxpayer that changes a LIFO inventory sub-method within five years of adopting or changing to the LIFO inventory method does not receive audit protection under Rev. Proc. 2015-13[204] § 8.01.

§ 7.07 National Office Determination

[A] Conference in the National Office

If the national office tentatively determines that the taxpayer's request for change in method of accounting filed under the automatic change procedure does not comply with all the applicable provisions for an automatic change (for example, the taxpayer changed to a method of accounting that varies from the applicable accounting method described in the List of Automatic Changes or the taxpayer is not eligible to use the automatic change procedures for the requested change) or that a request to change a method of accounting filed under the non-automatic change procedures

---

[203] *See* Rev. Proc. 2015-13, 2015-5 IRB 419, § 10.03.

[204] 2015-5 IRB 419.

may be denied, the national office will notify the taxpayer of its tentative adverse determination and will offer the taxpayer a conference if the taxpayer requested one.[205]

[B] Letter Ruling and Consent Agreement

Unless otherwise specifically provided, for a Form 3115 filed under the non-automatic change procedures, the national office will set forth the Commissioner's grant or denial of the taxpayer's request for the Commissioner's consent in a letter ruling. If the letter ruling grants the Commissioner's consent, it will identify the item or items being changed, the terms and conditions under which the taxpayer must implement the change, and the IRC § 481(a) adjustment (if any).[206]

If the taxpayer agrees to the terms and conditions in the letter ruling, the taxpayer must sign and date a copy of the letter ruling (Consent Agreement copy).[207] The taxpayer must return the Consent Agreement to the address provided in the letter ruling within 45 calendar days of the date of the letter ruling. In addition, the taxpayer must attach a copy of the Consent Agreement to the taxpayer's federal income tax return for the year of change, unless § 11.03(2)(e) (letter ruling received after implementing change) applies. If § 11.03(2)(e) applies, the taxpayer must comply with § 7.04(2) of Rev. Proc. 2019-1[208] (or its successor) and attach a copy of the pending Form 3115 or permitted statement to the taxpayer's federal income tax return for the year of change.[209]

[C] Signature Requirements

The Consent Agreement must be signed by, or on behalf of, the taxpayer making the request. The individual(s) signing the Consent Agreement must have the authority to bind the taxpayer in such matters and the Consent Agreement may not be signed by the taxpayer's representative.

---

205 For conference procedures for a taxpayer other than an exempt organization, *see* § 10 of Rev. Proc. 2019-1 (or its successor). It is good policy to always request a conference.

206 *See* Reg. § § 1.446-1(e)(3) and 1.481-4.

207 The signed Consent Agreement copy is an agreement (Consent Agreement) within the meaning of Reg. § 1.481-4(b).

208 2018-1 IRB 1.

209 *See also* Rev. Proc. 2015-13, 2015-5 IRB 419, § 6.03(3)(b) and 6.03(3)(c) for certain foreign corporations and foreign partnerships. *See generally* § 9.17 of Rev. Proc. 2018-1, 2017-1 IRB 1 (or its successor).

[D] *Consent Agreement Copy Not Signed or Change Not Timely or Properly Implemented*

The letter ruling granting consent to the taxpayer for a change in method of accounting is null and void without IRS notification to the taxpayer, except where notification is specifically provided if:

- The taxpayer does not sign and return the Consent Agreement copy within 45 calendar days of the date of the letter ruling (or other date as extended by the national office). In this situation, the national office will notify the taxpayer that the letter ruling granting consent to the taxpayer to change its method of accounting is null and void; or
- The taxpayer timely returns the Consent Agreement but does not implement the change in method of accounting for which consent is granted in the letter ruling for the year of change specified in the letter ruling on the taxpayer's timely filed (including any extension) original federal income tax return for the year of change specified in the letter ruling, or on the taxpayer's amended federal income tax return for the year of change specified in the letter ruling by the later of:
  - — the due date of the taxpayer's timely filed (including any extension) original federal income tax return for the taxable year succeeding the year of change specified in the letter ruling; or
  - — one year from the date of the letter ruling granting consent for the change. However, when the period of limitations on the assessment of tax under IRC § 6501 for the year of change specified in the letter ruling will expire within one year of the date of issuance of the letter ruling, the applicable date is the date that the statute of limitations under IRC § 6501 for the specified year of change expires.

The national office will grant additional time to implement the change in method of accounting for the year of change only if, and to the extent, the taxpayer demonstrates, in writing, that additional time is necessary, as long as the national office does not determine that granting additional time would be contrary to the interest of sound tax administration.

[E] *Disagreement with Terms and Conditions*

If the taxpayer disagrees with the terms and conditions in the letter ruling, within 45 calendar days from the date of the letter ruling, the taxpayer must notify the national office, in writing to the address in the letter ruling, of the disagreement and include an explanation of the reason(s). The national office will consider the reason(s) for the disagreement and notify the taxpayer whether the original letter ruling will be modified. If the national office does not modify the letter ruling, it will so notify the taxpayer and give the taxpayer 15 calendar days from the date of the notification to accept the original letter ruling by signing and returning the Consent Agreement copy.

[F] *Letter Ruling Received After Implementing Change*

A taxpayer that timely files a Form 3115 under the non-automatic change procedures and takes the requested change in method of accounting into account in its federal income tax return for the year of change (and any subsequent taxable year) prior to receiving a letter ruling granting consent for that change has made a change in method of accounting without obtaining the consent of the Commissioner as required by IRC § 446(e) (an "unauthorized change"). Accordingly, the Director may determine when a change is not made in compliance with all the applicable provisions and may deny the unauthorized change. However, the Commissioner's consent, issued subsequent to the requested year of change, applies back to the year of change (and any subsequent taxable year) as of the date of a letter ruling granting consent for that change if the taxpayer timely signs and returns the Consent Agreement copy and implements the change in accordance with all the applicable provisions and § 11 of Rev. Proc. 2020-1[210] (or its successor). If the Commissioner does not grant consent for the change in method of accounting taken into account by the taxpayer, the taxpayer is subject to any interest, penalties, or other adjustments resulting from improper implementation of the change.[211]

[G] *Consent Not Granted for an Automatic Change*

Except as otherwise provided in Rev. Proc. 2015-13[212] § § 11.03(1) and 11.03(3)(b), if the national office determines that a taxpayer filed a Form 3115 requesting consent to make an automatic change without complying with all the applicable provisions for an automatic change, the national office will notify the taxpayer that consent to make the change in method of accounting is not granted. In no event will a Form 3115 filed under the automatic change procedures be treated as a Form 3115 filed under the non-automatic change procedures.

If the national office determines that a taxpayer filed a Form 3115 requesting consent to make an automatic change without complying with all the applicable provisions for an automatic change, the national office, in its discretion, may allow the taxpayer to:

- make appropriate adjustments to conform its Form 3115 to comply with all the applicable provisions; and

- make conforming amendments to any federal income tax returns filed for the year of change and subsequent taxable years.

---

210 2020-1 IRB 1.

211 *See* IRC § 446(f).

212 2015-5 IRB 419.

§7.08 Review by Director

The director may determine whether the taxpayer complied with all of the applicable provisions for the change in method of accounting, including, but not limited to, whether:

- the facts and representations provided by the taxpayer on which the consent for the change in method of accounting is based reflect a complete and accurate statement of the material facts;
- the taxpayer properly determined the amount of the IRC §481(a) adjustment;
- the taxpayer implemented the change in method of accounting in compliance with all the applicable provisions;
- during the period the taxpayer used the method of accounting for which consent was granted, there has been any change in the material facts on which consent for the change was based; and
- during the period the taxpayer used the method of accounting for which consent was granted, there has been any change in the applicable law affecting the propriety of the taxpayer's use of the method of accounting for which consent was granted.

[A] Change Not Made in Compliance with All Applicable Provisions

If the director determines that the taxpayer did not comply with all the applicable provisions for the change in method of accounting, including the requirement to timely return the Consent Agreement, or did not implement the change in method of accounting in compliance with all the applicable provisions, the director may:

- make any adjustments (including the amount of any IRC §481(a) adjustment) that are necessary to bring the change in method of accounting into compliance with all the applicable provisions;
- deny the change in method of accounting and place the taxpayer on a proper method of accounting;[213] or
- deny the change in method of accounting and require the taxpayer to continue to use the prior method of accounting.

[B] Improperly Determined IRC §481(a) Adjustment

The director may make any necessary correction to the amount of any IRC §481(a) adjustment and make any other adjustment(s) necessary to properly implement the change in method of accounting for which consent is granted. If the director makes such a necessary correction to the amount of the IRC §481(a) adjustment, the director may take the entire amount necessary to correct the IRC §481(a) adjustment into account in computing the taxpayer's taxable income for the earliest taxable year

---

[213] *See* Rev. Proc. 2002-18, 2002-1 CB 678 (or any successor).

in the IRC §481(a) adjustment period that is under examination, regardless of whether the statute of limitations under IRC §6501 has expired for one or more taxable years in the IRC §481(a) adjustment period.

Example 7-20

A taxpayer obtained consent to change its method of accounting under this Revenue Procedure with a Year 1 year of change. The taxpayer determined that the IRC §481(a) adjustment for this change in method of accounting is a positive adjustment of $75,000, to be taken into account ratably over four taxable years. The taxpayer is under examination for Year 2. The statute of limitations under IRC §6501 has expired for Year 1. As part of the examination of Year 2, the examining agent determines that the correct IRC §481(a) adjustment for this change in method of accounting is a positive adjustment of $100,000. The examining agent may take the entire amount of the $25,000 correction to the IRC §481(a) adjustment into account in the taxpayer's taxable income for Year 2.

[C] Penalties and Additions to Tax

If the director denies the change in method of accounting pursuant or corrects the IRC §481(a) adjustment, the director may impose any otherwise applicable penalty, addition to tax, or additional amount on the understatement of tax attributable to the denial of the change in method of accounting or the net amount of any necessary correction(s) to the IRC §481(a) adjustment.[214]

[D] Referral to the National Office

If the director recommends that a change made in compliance with all the applicable provisions should be modified or revoked, the director will forward the matter to the national office for consideration before taking any further action, unless the modification relates solely to the amount of the IRC §481(a) adjustment. The referral to the national office is a request for technical advice and the provisions of Rev. Proc. 2020-2[215] (or its successor) apply.

---

[214] Rev. Proc. 2015-13, 2015-5 IRB 419, §12.02(3).

[215] 2020-1 IRB 107.

§7.09 Request to Revise the Year of Change for a Non-Automatic Change

The taxpayer may request, and the national office ordinarily will allow, the taxpayer to revise the year of change for a Form 3115 for a non-automatic change to a subsequent taxable year, but no later than the taxpayer's current taxable year (with no additional user fee), in lieu of submitting a new Form 3115 for the subsequent taxable year, under the conditions discussed below.[216]

[A] Timely Written Request

The taxpayer must submit a written request to revise the year of change for a Form 3115 on or after, but not before, the first day of the fourth month following the month in which the taxpayer's federal income tax return is due (excluding any extension) for the original year of change requested on the Form 3115. For example, a calendar year corporation that files a Form 3115 on December 16, 2019, for a 2020 year of change may submit a written request to revise the year of change to 2020 on or after, but not before, July 1, 2020.[217]

[B] Form 3115 Filed on or Before the Last Day of the Sixth Month of the Year of Change

If the taxpayer filed its Form 3115 on or before the last day of the sixth month of the year of change, the taxpayer may submit a written request to revise the year of change on or after, but not before, the first day of the taxable year following the original year of change requested on the Form 3115. For example, a calendar year taxpayer that files a Form 3115 on June 28, 2019, for a 2019 year of change may submit a written request to revise the year of change to 2020 on or after, but not before, January 1, 2020.[218]

[C] Pending Form 3115

The Form 3115 is pending in the national office (for example, the national office has not issued a letter ruling) on the date of the request.[219]

---

[216] Rev. Proc. 2015-13, 2015-5 IRB 419, § 13.

[217] *Id.*

[218] *Id.* § 13.01(1)(b).

[219] *Id.* § 13.01(2).

[D] *Acceleration and Revision of IRC §481(a) Adjustment*

Unless the Commissioner has determined that the requested change in method of accounting will be made using a cut-off method or a modified cut-off method:

- The taxpayer must agree, in writing, to accelerate into the revised year of change the percentage of any positive IRC §481(a) adjustment the taxpayer would have taken into account for each prior taxable year had the taxpayer not revised the year of change, in an amount limited to seventy-five percent of the IRC §481(a) adjustment. However, the seventy-five percent limitation for the revised year of change will not apply if the taxpayer requests to revise the year of change to a taxable year for which a provision of this Revenue Procedure, the Code, or other guidance published in the IRB, requires a IRC §481(a) adjustment period of two years or less; and
- The taxpayer must agree to provide, in a submission of additional information, the IRC §481(a) adjustment (positive or negative) for the revised year of change within 21 calendar days (or a longer period if agreed to by the national office) after the national office first notifies the taxpayer that its request to revise the year of change is approved.[220]

Example 7-21

A taxpayer requested to revise the year of change for a Form 3115 for a non-automatic change that is pending in the national office to the first succeeding taxable year. The taxpayer must agree to take into account one-half of any positive IRC §481(a) adjustment in the revised year of change and one-fourth in each of its next two taxable years.

Example 7-22

A taxpayer requested to revise the year of change for a Form 3115 for a non-automatic change that is pending in the national office to the third succeeding taxable year. The taxpayer must agree to take into account three-fourths of any positive IRC §481(a) adjustment in the revised year of change and the remaining one-fourth in the next taxable year.

---

[220] *Id.* §13.01(3).

[E] Multiple Applicants on One Form 3115

If the Form 3115 is for an identical change in method of accounting for more than one applicant, the taxpayer must request to revise the year of change for all applicants to which the Form 3115 relates.[221]

[F] Compelling Circumstances

In the case of a taxpayer that does not meet the requirement to revise the year of change for a Form 3115 for a non-automatic change to a subsequent taxable year, a taxpayer with compelling circumstances may request to revise the year of change for the Form 3115, in lieu of submitting a new Form 3115 for the proposed revised year of change. The taxpayer must demonstrate those compelling circumstances in its written request.[222]

Example 7-23

On October 31, 2019, a calendar year partnership with 50 individual partners timely files a Form 3115 for a non-automatic change for its 2019 taxable year. The partnership's Form 1065, *U.S. Return of Partnership Income*, and Schedules K-1, Partner's Share of Income, Deductions, Credits etc., and the partners' Forms 1040, U.S. Individual Income Tax Return, for the requested year of change are all due March 15, 2020. The partnership is not extending this due date. On March 17, 2020, the partnership submits a request to revise the year of change for its pending Form 3115 to its 2020 taxable year. Because the Form 3115 is pending in the national office 30 calendar days prior to the due date of the partners' Forms 1040, the partnership will be unable to provide timely Schedules K-1 that take into account the proposed accounting method change before the partners prepare and file their 2019 Forms 1040 to take into account the partnership's requested change in method of accounting for the 2019 taxable year. Under these compelling circumstances, the national office will ordinarily allow the partnership to revise the year of change for its Form 3115 to its 2020 taxable year. If the accounting method change is approved for the partnership's 2020 taxable year, in lieu of taking into account any positive IRC § 481(a) adjustment over four taxable years, the partnership must take into account one-half of any positive IRC § 481(a) adjustment in its 2020 taxable year and one-fourth in each of its next two taxable years.

---

221 *Id.* § 13.01(5).
222 *Id.* § 13.02.

[G] *Submitting a Request for a Revised Year of Change*

A request to revise the year of change for a Form 3115 pending in the national office must include:

- The name of the Form 3115 filer and, if applicable, each applicant, on the Form 3115;
- The national office reference number (for example, CAM-123456-14);
- The name of the national office contact person for the Form 3115 (if known);
- The due date (excluding any extension) for the Form 3115 filer's federal income tax return for the year of change;
- Whether, in the proposed revised year of change, the taxpayer will cease to engage in the trade or business to which the change in method of accounting relates;
- A statement agreeing to the applicable conditions in § 13.01(3);
- If the request is being submitted pursuant to § 13.02, the compelling circumstances on which the request is based;
- The information required in § 9.09 of Rev. Proc. 2020-1 (or its successor), as applicable;
- The penalties of perjury statement in § 9.08(3) of Rev. Proc. 2020-1 (or its successor); and
- If applicable, a completed Form 2848, *Power of Attorney and Declaration of Representative*, for the revised year of change.[223]

[H] *Notification of Approval or Denial*

The national office will notify the taxpayer of the approval or denial of the taxpayer's request to revise the year of change for a pending Form 3115. The national office may deny a taxpayer's request for a revised year of change for a pending Form 3115 if the national office determines it would not be in the interest of sound tax administration to allow the taxpayer to revise the year of change. A taxpayer is not entitled to a conference with the national office if the request to revise the year of change for a pending Form 3115 is denied.[224]

§ 7.10 Change in Accounting Method—Involuntary Change

[A] *Method Changes Imposed by the Service*

IRC § 446(b) provides that when a taxpayer employs an erroneous accounting method, the IRS may change the taxpayer's method to a method that, in the opinion of the IRS, clearly reflects income. When it discovers an erroneous accounting method

---

[223] *Id.* § 13.03.

[224] *Id.* § 13.04.

that understates income, the IRS normally makes the change in the earliest year under audit and requires that the taxpayer take the IRC § 481(a) adjustment, computed as of the beginning of the year of change, into account entirely in the year of change. Rev. Proc. 2002-18[225] provides terms and conditions for Service-imposed changes in method of accounting that are intended to encourage taxpayers to voluntarily request a change from an impermissible method of accounting before being contacted for examination. Under this approach, a taxpayer that is contacted for examination and required to change its method of accounting by the Service ("involuntary change") generally receives less favorable terms and conditions when the change results in a positive IRC § 481(a) adjustment than the taxpayer would have received if it had filed an application to change its method of accounting ("voluntary change") before the taxpayer was contacted for examination. For example, an involuntary change generally is made with an earlier year of change and a shorter IRC § 481(a) adjustment period for a positive adjustment, and a voluntary change generally is made with a current year of change and a longer IRC § 481(a) adjustment period for a positive adjustment

The Commissioner has broad discretion in determining whether a taxpayer's method of accounting clearly reflects income, and the Commissioner's determination must be upheld unless it is clearly unlawful.[226]

The Commissioner has the discretion to change a taxpayer's method of accounting even though the Commissioner previously changed the taxpayer to that method if the Commissioner determines that the method of accounting does not clearly reflect the taxpayer's income. The Commissioner is not precluded from correcting mistakes of law in determining a taxpayer's tax liability, including the power to retroactively correct rulings or other determinations on which the taxpayer may have relied.[227]

The Commissioner does not have discretion, however, to require a taxpayer to change from a method of accounting that clearly reflects income to a method that, in the Commissioner's view, more clearly reflects income.[228]

The Commissioner may change the accounting method of a taxpayer that is under examination, before an appeals office, or before a federal court.[229]

[B] Method Change Using a Cut-off Method

The Commissioner may determine that certain changes in method of accounting will be made without an IRC § 481(a) adjustment, using a "cut-off method." Under a cut-off method, only the items arising on or after the beginning of the year of change

---

[225] 2002-1 CB 678.

[226] *See Thor Power Tool Co. v. Comm'r*, 439 U.S. 522 (1979); *RCA Corp. v. United States*, 664 F.2d 881 (2d Cir. 1981), *cert. denied*, 457 U.S. 1133 (1982).

[227] *See Dixon v. United States*, 381 U.S. 68 (1965); *Automobile Club of Michigan v. Comm'r*, 353 U.S. 180 (1957); *Massaglia v. Comm'r*, 286 F.2d 258 (10th Cir. 1961).

[228] *See Capitol Federal Savings & Loan v. Comm'r*, 96 T.C. 204 (1991); *W.P. Garth v. Comm'r*, 56 T.C. 610 (1971), *acq*, 1975-1 CB 1.

[229] Rev. Proc. 2015-13, 2015-5 IRB 419.

are accounted for under the new method of accounting. Any items arising before the year of change continue to be accounted for under the taxpayer's former method of accounting. Because no items are duplicated or omitted from income when a cut-off method is used to affect a change in accounting method, no IRC § 481(a) adjustment is necessary.[230]

[C] Previous Method Change Without Consent

The Commissioner may require a taxpayer that has changed a method of accounting without the Commissioner's consent to change back to its former method. The Commissioner may do so even when the taxpayer changed from an impermissible to a permissible method. The change back to the former method may be made in the taxable year the taxpayer changed without consent, or if that year is closed by the running of the period of limitations, in the earliest open year.[231] For example, the Service may change a taxpayer back to its former impermissible method of accounting if the taxpayer changed to a permissible method of accounting without the Commissioner's consent and miscalculated the IRC § 481(a) adjustment, even where the statute of limitations has expired for the year of change.

[D] Penalties

Any otherwise applicable penalty for the failure of a taxpayer to change its method of accounting (for example, the accuracy-related penalty under IRC § 6662 or the fraud penalty under IRC § 6663) may be imposed if the Service imposes an accounting method change.[232] Additionally, the taxpayer's return preparer may also be subject to the preparer penalty under IRC § 6694.

[E] Examination Discretion to Resolve Accounting Method Issues

Under Rev. Proc. 2002-18,[233] an examining agent, using professional judgment in accordance with auditing standards, will make findings of fact and apply Service position on issues of law to determine whether an issue is an accounting method issue and whether the taxpayer's method of accounting is permissible.

---

[230] *See* Examples 7-26 and 7-27, *infra*. *See also* IRC § 263A (which generally applies to costs incurred after December 31, 1986, for non-inventory property), and IRC § 461(h) (which generally applies to amounts incurred on or after July 18, 1984).

[231] *See Comm'r v. O. Liquidating Corp.*, 292 F.2d 225 (3d Cir.), *cert. denied*, 368 U.S. 898 (1961); *Wright Contracting Co. v. Comm'r*, 316 F.2d 249 (5th Cir. 1963), *cert. denied*, 375 U.S. 879 (1963), *reh'g denied*, 375 U.S. 981 (1964), *acq*. 1966-2 CB 7; *Daktronics, Inc. v. Comm'r*, T.C. Memo. 1991-60; *Handy Andy T.V. and Appliances, Inc. v. Comm'r*, T.C. Memo. 1983-713.

[232] *See* IRC § 446(f).

[233] 2002-1 CB 678.

Under Rev. Proc. 2002-18,[234] an examining agent who determines that a taxpayer's method of accounting is impermissible, or that a taxpayer changed its method of accounting without obtaining the consent of the Commissioner, may propose an adjustment with respect to that method only by changing the taxpayer's method of accounting. An examining agent changing a taxpayer's method of accounting will select a new method of accounting by properly applying the law to the facts determined by the agent. The method selected must be a proper method of accounting and will not be a method contrived to reflect the hazards of litigation.

Example 7-24

A taxpayer held long-term zero coupon bonds during the taxable year under examination but did not include any original issue discount (OID) in income for that year. The examining agent determines that the taxpayer should have included OID in income for that year under IRC § 1272. Accordingly, the examining agent will change the taxpayer's method of accounting to include the OID in income in accordance with IRC § 1272 and the regulations thereunder. The examining agent will not impose a method of accounting that is designed to take into account litigation hazards (for example, a method that only requires the accrual of an arbitrary percentage of the OID that would otherwise accrue during the year under IRC § 1272 and the regulations thereunder).

[F] Terms and Conditions of Change

An examining agent changing a taxpayer's method of accounting will make the change in a year under examination. Ordinarily, the change will be made in the earliest taxable year under examination, or, if later, the first taxable year the method is considered to be impermissible. However, in appropriate circumstances, an examining agent may defer the year of change to a later taxable year. For example, an examining agent may defer the year of change if the examining agent determines that:

- the taxpayer's books and records do not contain sufficient information to compute a IRC § 481(a) adjustment for the taxable year in which the change would otherwise be imposed and the adjustment cannot be reasonably estimated;
- the taxpayer's existing method of accounting does not have a material effect for the taxable year in which the change would otherwise be imposed; or
- there are taxable years for which the statute of limitations has expired following the taxable year in which the change would otherwise be imposed.

---

[234] *Id.*

An examining agent will not defer the year of change in order to reflect the hazards of litigation. Moreover, an examining agent will not defer the year of change to later than the most recent year under examination on the date of the agreement finalizing the change.[235]

[G] *Section 481(a) Adjustment*

An examining agent changing a taxpayer's method of accounting ordinarily will impose an IRC §481(a) adjustment, subject to a computation of tax under IRC §481(b) (if applicable). In addition, an examining agent may use a cut-off method to make a change in appropriate circumstances. For example, the examining agent may use a cut-off method to make a change if the agent determines that the taxpayer's books and records do not contain sufficient information to compute an IRC §481(a) adjustment and the adjustment cannot be reasonably estimated. Finally, an examining agent will not make a change on a cut-off method in order to reflect the hazards of litigation.[236]

[H] *Spread of IRC §481(a) Adjustment*

The IRC §481(a) adjustment, whether positive or negative, will be taken into account entirely in the year of change.[237]

[I] *IRC §481(b) Limitation*

IRC §481(b) limits the increase in tax when an IRC §481(a) adjustment is taken into account entirely in the year of change and results in an increase of more than $3,000 in taxable income. The tax increase is limited to the smallest of three amounts:

- the additional tax on the IRC §481(a) adjustment computed by using the tax rates for the year of the change;
- using the three-year spread-back rule under IRC §481(b)(1), or
- using the specific allocation rule under IRC §481(b)(2).

The three-year spread-back rule under IRC §481(b)(1) can be used if the increase in taxable income is more than $3,000 and the old method was used for the two tax years preceding the year of change.

The regulations provide the following examples.[238]

Example (1). An unmarried individual taxpayer using the cash receipts and disbursements method of accounting for the calendar year is required by the Commissioner to change to an accrual method effective with the year 1958. As of January 1, 1958, he had an opening inventory of $11,000. On December 31, 1958, he had a closing inventory of $12,500. Merchandise purchases during the year amounted to

---

[235] Rev. Proc. 2002-18, 2002-1 CB 678 §5.04.

[236] Rev. Proc. 2002-18, 2002-1 CB 678, §5.04(2).

[237] *Id.* §5.04(3).

[238] Reg. §1.481-2(d)(1).

$22,500, and net sales were $32,000. Total deductible business expenses were $5,000. There were no receivables or payables at January 1, 1958. The computation of taxable income for 1958, assuming no other adjustments, using the new method of accounting is as follows:

Net sales		$32,000
Opening inventory	$11,000	
Purchases	22,500	
Total	33,500	
Less closing inventory	12,500	
Cost of goods sold		21,000
Gross profit		11,000
Business expenses		5,000
Business income		6,000
Personal exemption and itemized deductions		1,600
Taxable income		4,400

Under the cash receipts and disbursements method of accounting, only $9,000 of the $11,000 opening inventory had been included in the cost of goods sold and claimed as a deduction for the taxable years 1954 through 1957; the remaining $2,000 had been so accounted for in pre-1954 years. In order to prevent the same item from reducing taxable income twice, an adjustment of $9,000 must be made to the taxable income of 1958 under the provisions of IRC § 481(a) and Reg. § 1.481-1. Since the change in the method of accounting was not initiated by the taxpayer, the $2,000 of opening inventory which had been included in cost of goods sold in pre-1954 years is not taken into account. Taxable income for 1958 is accordingly increased by $9,000 under IRC § 481(a) to $13,400. Assuming that the tax on $13,400 is $4,002 and that the tax on $4,400 (income without the adjustment) is $944, the increase in tax attributable to the adjustment, if taken into account for the taxable year of the change, would be the difference between the two, or $3,058. Since the adjustment required by IRC § 481(a) and Reg. § 1.481-1 ($9,000) increases taxable income by more than $3,000, the increase in tax for the taxable year 1958 attributable to the adjustment of $9,000 (*i.e.*, $3,058) may be limited under the provisions of IRC § 481(b)(1) or (2). See examples (2) and (3).

Example (2). Assume that the taxpayer in example (1) used the cash receipts and disbursements method of accounting in computing taxable income for the years 1956 and 1957 and that the taxable income for these years determined under such method was $4,000 and $6,000, respectively. The IRC § 481(b)(1) limitation on tax with a pro rata three-year allocation of the $9,000 adjustment is computed as follows:

Taxable Year	Taxable Income Before Adjustment	Taxable Income With Adjustment	Assumed Total Tax	Assumed Tax Before Adjustment	Increase In Tax Attributable To Adjustment
1956	$4,000	$7,000	$1,660	$840	$820
1957	6,000	9,000	2,300	1,360	940
1958	4,400	7,400	1,780	944	836
Total					2,596

Since this increase in tax of $2,596 is less than the increase in tax attributable to the inclusion of the entire adjustment in the income for the taxable year of the change ($3,058), the limitation provided by IRC § 481(b)(1) applies, and the total tax for 1958, the taxable year of the change, if IRC § 481(b)(2) does not apply, is determined as follows:

Tax without any portion of adjustment	$944
Increase in tax attributable to adjustment computed under IRC § 481(b)(1)	2,596
Total tax for taxable year of the change	3,540

Example (3).

(i) Assume the same facts as in example (1) and, in addition, assume that the taxpayer used the cash receipts and disbursements method of accounting in computing taxable income for the years 1953 through 1957; that he established his taxable income under the new method for the taxable year 1953, 1954, and 1957, but did not have sufficient records to establish his taxable income under such method for the taxable years 1955 and 1956. The original taxable income and taxable income as redetermined are as follows:

	Taxable income		
Taxable Year	Determined Under Cash Receipts And Disbursements Method	Established Under New Method	Increase Or (Decrease) In Taxable Income
1953	$5,000	$7,000	$2,000
1954	6,000	7,000	1,000
1955	5,500		
1956	4,000		
1957	6,000	10,000	4,000

(1) Undetermined.

(1) Undetermined.

As in examples (1) and (2), the total adjustment under IRC § 481(a) is $9,000. Of the $9,000 adjustment, $4,000 may be allocated to 1957, which is the only year consecutively preceding the taxable year of the change for which the taxpayer was able to establish his income under the new method. Since the income cannot be established under the new method for 1956 and 1955, no allocation may be made to 1954 or 1953, even though the taxpayer has established his income for those years under the new method of accounting. The balance of $5,000 ($9,000 minus $4,000) must be allocated to 1958.

(ii) The limitation provided by IRC § 481(b)(2) is computed as follows: The tax for 1957, based on taxable income of $6,000, is assumed to be $1,360. Under the new method, based on taxable income of $10,000, the tax for 1957 is assumed to be $2,640, the increase attributable to $4,000 of the $9,000 IRC § 481(a) adjustment being $1,280 ($2,640 minus $1,360). The tax for 1958, computed on the basis of taxable income of $4,400 (determined under the new method), is assumed to be $944. The tax computed for 1958 on taxable income of $9,400 ($4,400 plus the $5,000 adjustment allocated to 1958) is assumed to be $2,436, leaving a difference of $1,492 ($2,436 minus $944) attributable to the inclusion in 1958 of the portion of the total adjustment to be taken into account which could not be properly allocated to the taxable year or years consecutively preceding 1958.

(iii) The tax attributable to the adjustment is determined by selecting the smallest of the three following amounts:

Increase in tax attributable to adjustment computed under IRC § 481(b)(2) ($1,280 + $1,492)	$2,772
Increase in tax attributable to adjustment computed under IRC § 481(b)(1) (example (2))	2,596
Increase in tax if the entire adjustment is taken into account in the taxable year of the change (example (1))	3,058

The final tax for 1958 is then $3,540 computed as follows:

Tax before inclusion of any adjustment	$944
Increase in tax attributable to adjustments (smallest of $2,772, $2,596 or $3,058)	2,596
Total tax for 1958 (limited in accordance with IRC § 481(b)(1))	3,540

[J] Appeals and Counsel for the Government Discretion to Resolve Accounting Method Issues

An appeals officer or counsel for the government may resolve an accounting method issue when it is in the interest of the government to do so.[239]

[K] Types of Resolutions

An appeals officer or counsel for the government may resolve an accounting method issue by using any of the means deemed appropriate under the circumstances to reflect the hazards of litigation.[240]

[L] Accounting Method Changes by Appeals or Counsel

An appeals officer or counsel for the government resolving an accounting method issue may treat the issue as a change in method of accounting.

An appeals officer or counsel for the government changing a taxpayer's method of accounting will select a new method of accounting by properly applying the law to the facts. The appeals officer or counsel for the government will not put the taxpayer on an improper method of accounting in order to reflect the hazards of litigation.

An appeals officer or counsel for the government changing a taxpayer's method of accounting may agree to terms and conditions that differ from those ordinarily

---

[239] *Id.* § 6.01.

[240] *Id.* § 6.02(1).

applicable to an examination-imposed accounting method change, including the following (or any combination thereof).

An appeals officer or counsel for the government may compromise the year of change (for example, by agreeing to a later year of change). However, an appeals officer or counsel for the government changing a taxpayer's method of accounting ordinarily will not defer the year of change to later than the most recent taxable year under examination on the date of the agreement finalizing the change, and, in no event, will defer the year of change to later than the taxable year that includes the date of the agreement finalizing the change. Note the following:

- If an IRC § 481(a) adjustment is used, the appeals officer or counsel for the government may compromise the amount of the IRC § 481(a) adjustment (for example, by agreeing to a reduced IRC § 481(a) adjustment). If the appeals officer or counsel for the government agrees to compromise the amount of the IRC § 481(a) adjustment, the agreement must be in writing; and
- An appeals officer or counsel for the government may compromise the IRC § 481(a) adjustment period (for example, by agreeing to a longer IRC § 481(a) adjustment period).[241]

[M] Alternative-Timing Resolution

In lieu of changing a taxpayer's method of accounting, an appeals officer or counsel for the government may resolve an accounting method issue by agreeing to alternative timing for all or some of the items arising during or prior to and during, the taxable years before Appeals or a federal court. The resolution of an accounting method issue on an alternative-timing basis for certain items will not affect the taxpayer's method of accounting for any items not covered by the resolution.[242]

Example 7-25

The Service and the taxpayer agree that the taxpayer will capitalize the inventoriable costs incurred during 2020 that were deducted under the taxpayer's method of accounting. The taxpayer's inventoriable costs covered by the agreement must be capitalized and accounted for under the taxpayer's inventory method. The inventoriable costs that are not covered by the agreement (that is, those costs incurred in taxable years prior and subsequent to 2020) are not affected by the resolution and thus, consistent with the taxpayer's method of accounting, must continue to be deducted.

---

[241] *Id.* § 6.02(2).

[242] *Id.* § 6.02(3).

[N] Time-Value of Money Resolution

In lieu of changing a taxpayer's method of accounting, an appeals officer or counsel for the government may resolve an accounting method issue by agreeing that the taxpayer will pay the government a "specified amount" that approximates the time-value-of-money benefit the taxpayer has derived from using its method of accounting for the taxable years before appeals or a federal court (instead of the method of accounting determined by the appeals officer or counsel for the government to be the proper method of accounting), reduced by an appropriate factor to reflect the hazards of litigation. If the sum of the time-value-of-money benefit (detriment) computed with respect to each taxable year is negative, the specified amount will be zero and no refund will be made to the taxpayer. The specified amount is not interest under IRC § 163(a), and may not be deducted or capitalized. In appropriate circumstances, however, the computation of the specified amount may be tax affected to reflect the approximate effect of a hypothetical tax deduction.[243]

[O] Procedures for a Service-Imposed Accounting Method Change

An examining agent, appeals officer, or counsel for the government changing a taxpayer's method of accounting will provide notice that an accounting method issue is being treated as an accounting method change. However, an appeals officer or counsel for the government resolving an accounting method issue as an accounting method change is not required to provide notice that the accounting method issue is being treated as an accounting method change if such notice has been provided by the examining agent. In addition, if the examining agent has provided notice that an accounting method issue is being treated as an accounting method change and an appeals officer or counsel for the government subsequently resolves such accounting method issue on a nonaccounting-method-change basis, the appeals officer or counsel for the government should provide notice that the accounting method issue has not been treated as an accounting method change.[244]

[P] Form of Notice

The notice must be in writing. If the taxpayer and the Service execute a closing agreement finalizing the change, the notice will be provided in the closing agreement. If the taxpayer and the Service do not execute a closing agreement, the notice ordinarily will be provided in the examiner's report or the Form 870AD (Offer of Waiver of Restriction on Assessment and Collection of Deficiency in Tax and of Acceptance of Overpayment). However, the Service may also provide the notice in a preliminary notice of deficiency, a statutory notice of deficiency, a notice of claim disallowance, a notice of final administrative adjustment, a pleading (for example, a

---

[243] *See* sample computation in Rev. Proc. 2002-18, 2002-1 CB 678, § 6.02(4)(a).
[244] Rev. Proc. 2002-18, 2002-1 CB 678, § 7.01(1).

petition, complaint, or answer) or amendment thereto, or in any other similar writing provided to the taxpayer.[245]

[Q] Content of Notice

The notice must include

- a statement that the accounting method issue is being treated as an accounting method change or a clearly labeled IRC § 481(a) adjustment; and
- a description of the new method of accounting.

The resolution of an accounting method issue will not establish a new method of accounting if the Service does not provide notice.[246]

[R] Finalizing a Service-Imposed Method Change

To implement a Service-imposed change in method of accounting, the taxpayer and the Service should execute a closing agreement under IRC § 7121 in which the taxpayer agrees to the change and the terms and conditions of the change. The Service should make the adjustments necessary to effect a Service-imposed accounting method change to the taxpayer's returns for the taxable years under examination, before Appeals, or before a federal court. These adjustments include the adjustments to taxable income necessary to reflect the new method (including the IRC § 481(a) adjustment required because of the change), and any collateral adjustments to taxable income or tax liability resulting from the change.

If a Service-imposed accounting method change is finalized by a closing agreement, the Service may require that the taxpayer file amended returns to reflect the change for any affected succeeding taxable years for which a federal income tax return has been filed as of the date of the agreement. The amended returns must include the adjustments to taxable income and any collateral adjustments to taxable income or tax liability resulting from the change necessary to reflect the new method. The Service may require that the amended returns be filed prior to execution of the closing agreement finalizing the change. If the Service does not require the amended returns, the taxpayer should file such amended returns. If the Service does not require the amended returns and the taxpayer does not file the amended returns, the Service should make the adjustments necessary to reflect the change for affected succeeding taxable years if and when it examines the returns for those years.[247]

---

[245] *Id.* § 7.01(2).
[246] *Id.* § 7.01(3).
[247] *Id.* §§ 7.02 and 7.03.

[S] *Future Years*

The taxpayer must use the new method of accounting on all returns filed after the date that a Service-imposed accounting method change becomes final unless the taxpayer obtains the consent of the Commissioner to change from the new method or the Service changes the taxpayer from the new method on a subsequent examination.[248]

[T] *Audit Protection*

A taxpayer that executes a closing agreement finalizing a Service-imposed accounting method change will not be required to change or modify the new method for any taxable year for which a federal income tax return has been filed as of the date of the closing agreement, provided that:

- the taxpayer has complied with all the applicable provisions of the closing agreement;
- there has been no taxpayer fraud, malfeasance, or misrepresentation of a material fact;
- there has been no change in the material facts on which the closing agreement was based; and
- there has been no change in the applicable law on which the closing agreement was based.[249]

[U] *Procedures for Resolving Accounting Method Issues on a Nonaccounting-Method-Change Basis*

Under Rev. Proc. 2002-18,[250] an accounting method issue raised by the Service can be resolved on a nonaccounting-method-change basis. In such case the Service and the taxpayer will execute a closing agreement under IRC § 7121. If the accounting method issue is being resolved on an alternative-timing basis the taxpayer must agree to pay the government any taxes and interest due as a result of the resolution. If the accounting method issue is being resolved on a time-value-of-money basis, the taxpayer must agree to pay the government the specified amount because of the resolution.

A closing agreement finalizing the resolution of an accounting method issue on a nonaccounting-method-change basis must comply with the requirements of Rev. Proc. 68-16,[251] and should include the information outlined in the "Model Closing Agreement for Settlement on a Nonaccounting-method-change Basis."[252]

---

248 *Id.* § 7.03(3).

249 *Id.* § 7.04(3).

250 2002-1 CB 678.

251 1968-1 CB 770.

252 *See* APPENDIX B of Rev. Proc. 2002-18, 2002-1 CB 678.

Example 7-26

Examination-imposed Change

Facts. A taxpayer that is a corporation deducted costs that the Service determines should have been capitalized to real property that was placed in service in 2000. The taxpayer incurred and deducted $1,000,000 of the costs in 1996, $2,000,000 in each of 1997 and 1998, and $5,000,000 in each of 1999 and 2000. The taxpayer is examined for the 1997 and 1998 taxable years (1997 is the earliest open year). The examining agent determines that the treatment of the costs is an accounting method issue, and that the taxpayer's deduction of the costs is an impermissible method of accounting. The examining agent therefore proposes an adjustment.

Effect. Under §5 of Rev. Proc. 2002-18,[253] the examining agent is required to properly apply the law to the facts and change the taxpayer to the capitalization method of accounting for the costs. The examining agent imposes the change in 1997, the earliest open taxable year. The examining agent will provide the notice required by §7.01 of Rev. Proc. 2002-18.[254] The examining agent imposes an IRC §481(a) adjustment of $1,000,000 (representing the $1,000,000 of the costs deducted in 1996), the entire amount of which will be taken into account in computing taxable income in 1997. The examining agent also disallows the deductions of $2,000,000 in each of 1997 and 1998. The taxpayer's basis in the property as of the beginning of 1998 is increased by $5,000,000 (representing the $1,000,000 IRC §481(a) adjustment and the disallowance of the $2,000,000 of deductions in each of 1997 and 1998). The method change (once final) is effective for 1997. Thus, the taxpayer is required to capitalize the costs in 1997 and subsequent taxable years; unless the taxpayer obtains the consent of the Commissioner to change the method or the Service changes the taxpayer from the method on subsequent examination.

[V] *Appeals Resolution of Accounting Method Issue as a Method Change with Compromise Terms and Conditions*

Example 7-27

The facts are the same as in Example 7-26 except that the issue of whether the costs should be capitalized is referred to Appeals. The appeals officer believes that hazards of litigation exist with respect to the Service's position. The appeals officer and the taxpayer agree to resolve the accounting method issue by changing the taxpayer's method of accounting

---

[253] 2002-1 CB 678.

[254] *Id.*

for the costs, but with compromise terms and conditions to reflect the hazards of litigation.

Effect. Under Rev. Proc. 2002-18,[255] when the appeals officer changes the taxpayer's method of accounting, the appeals officer is required to properly apply the law to the facts and change the taxpayer to the capitalization method of accounting for the costs.

The appeals officer may make the change using the cut-off method. If the appeals officer makes the change in 1997 using the cut-off method, the appeals officer will disallow the deductions of $2,000,000 in each of 1997 and 1998. The taxpayer's basis in the property as of the beginning of 1998 will be increased by $4,000,000 (representing the disallowance of the $2,000,000 of deductions in each of 1997 and 1998). The method change (once final) is effective for 1997. Thus, the taxpayer is required to capitalize the costs in 1997 and subsequent taxable years; unless the taxpayer obtains the consent of the Commissioner to change the method or the Service changes the taxpayer from the method on subsequent examination.

Alternatively, the appeals officer may compromise the amount of the IRC §481(a) adjustment. If the appeals officer makes the change in 1997 and agrees to reduce the IRC §481(a) adjustment by 25%, the appeals officer will impose a IRC §481(a) adjustment of $750,000 (representing 75% of the amount of the costs deducted in 1996), the entire amount of which will be taken into account in computing taxable income in 1997. The appeals officer will disallow the deductions of $2,000,000 in each of 1997 and 1998. The taxpayer and the appeals officer agree in a closing agreement that basis in the property as of the beginning of 1998 will be increased by $4,750,000 (representing the reduced IRC §481(a) adjustment of $750,000 and the disallowance of the $2,000,000 of deductions in each of 1997 and 1998). The method change (once final) is effective for 1997. Thus, the taxpayer is required to capitalize the costs in 1997 and subsequent taxable years, unless the taxpayer obtains the consent of the Commissioner to change the method or the Service changes the taxpayer from the method on subsequent examination.[256]

§7.11 *Hat Creek* Case Study

The purpose of this problem is to recognize the tax accounting issues created by the fact pattern and to elicit responses based on the materials discusses in this chapter

---

[255] *Id.*

[256] Rev. Proc. 2002-18, 2002-1 CB 678, contains other examples of resolution in Appeals of Accounting Method Issue on an Alternative-timing Basis and Time-value-of-money Basis.

as well as the other chapters in this text. Issues, which might relate to other federal tax issues, should be ignored for purposes of your analysis.

Hat Creek Corp. is owned by 12 individuals and managed by two of the shareholders (Gus McCrae and Woodrow Call). It has been in the sale and repair of computers and printers business for ten years. Its business has been rapidly expanding over the last few years; the owners have concentrated all their efforts on marketing and on technical training for Hat Creek's growing number of employees.

Clara Allen, Gus McCrae's girlfriend, has handled all financial matters including the bookkeeping and filing of all tax returns. Hat Creek is a calendar year C Corporation for tax purposes. Clara has taken tax depreciation on Hat Creek's office building (purchased in January 2011 for $500,000) on a straight-line basis over 20 years. Clair has treated numerous personal expense amounting to over $50,000 per year for the last four years paid by Hat Creek on behalf of its shareholders as business expenses because she does not want to pester the shareholders for expense reports. In doing so, she has estimated what expenses the shareholders incur and established a reserve account to which she added or subtracted what she believed the annual personal expenses to be.

The corporation has had severe cash flow problems for the past year, even though its sales throughout the country have been rapidly increasing. Because of the cash flow crunch, Hat Creek in 2019 decided to change the way it financed its accounts receivables. For sales made on credit, Hat Creek charged a service fee to its customers, which was included in income as the payments were received. For years prior to 2019, Hat Creek was considered the owner of its receivables, assuming the risk for its bad debts. In 2019, Hat Creek changed the nature of its financing arrangements and began to sell its receivables.

The most recent annual gross income reported by Hat Creek is as follows:

- $25,000,000 in 2018
- $27,000,000 in 2019
- $28,000,000 in 2020

Gross receipts are expected to be $30,000,000 in 2021.

In 2017 and 2018, Clara included a $100,000 advance payment for repair services in income, but, in 2019, Clara considered a $150,000 advance payment as a deposit, and included it in income in 2020 when the services were performed. In 2020, Hat Creek also received a $250,000 advance payment for services to be performed in 2021, which Clara also treated as a deposit when received.

Hat Creek maintains its books and records on the cash method of accounting, and tracks its receivables, payables, parts and refurbished printer inventories and miscellaneous accrued items in separate ledgers because an unaudited accrual basis financial statement must be given annually to the bank under the terms of the loan agreement.

Because Hat Creek needs to increase substantially its bank line of credit, the bank now insists on an audited financial statement, and has recommended your accounting firm. It is now January 2, 2021.

[A] Identify the Tax Accounting Issues

Which of Hat Creek's tax accounting practices are methods of accounting, and which are not? Why?

(1) Issue—Has Hat Creek adopted a proper or improper method of accounting? Reg. § 1.446-1(c)(2) provides that in any case in which it is necessary to use an inventory, the accrual method of accounting must be used with regard to purchases and sales. Since Hat Creek has been in the business of selling personal computers and printers, it must use the accrual method.

> **Note:** The TCJA expanded the exception for small taxpayers from the UNICAP rules by providing that, for any taxpayer (other than a tax shelter prohibited from using the cash receipts and disbursements method of accounting under IRC § 448(a)(3)) which meets the gross receipts test of IRC § 448(c) for any tax year, the UNICAP rules would not apply with respect to the taxpayer for that tax year.[257] IRC § 448(c) provides that corporations and partnerships with a corporate partner are permitted to use the cash method only if they have average annual gross receipts of $25 million or less during the preceding three years. This ceiling amount is inflation adjusted and is $26,000,000 for 2019 and 2020. The modification not only increases the dollar limitation but it is also expanded to apply to both producers and resellers of both real and personal property.

As Hat Creek's 2018-2020 gross receipts average exceed $26 million, it cannot use the cash method of accounting.

IRC § 448(c)[258] provides that a business that meets the $25 million gross receipts test can use the cash method of accounting for inventory if it:

- treats inventory as non-incidental materials and supplies; or
- conforms to the business's financial accounting treatment of inventories.[259]

A single $25 million gross receipts test has been put in place for determining whether certain taxpayers qualify as small taxpayers that can use the cash method of accounting, are not required to use inventories, are not required to apply the UNICAP rules, and are not required to use the percentage of completion method for a small construction contract.[260]

Unfortunately, Hat Creek exceeded the $26 million threshold and will be required to capitalize costs under IRC § 263A. They will need to file a request for change of accounting (Form 3115) under DCN #22 and make the IRC § 481 adjustment.

(2) Issue—Is the depreciation taken properly? The *tax depreciation on the office building, on a straight-line basis for over 20 years, is a method of accounting*, because it is

---

[257] IRC § 263A(i)(1).

[258] IRC § 471(c)(1) as added by the TCJA.

[259] IRC § 471(c)(1)(B) as added by the TCJA.

[260] Act Sec. 13102 of the TCJA.

the treatment of a material item that has been consistently used, and it involves the proper time for the taking of a deduction.[261]

(3) Issue—Is the deduction of the personal expenses a method of accounting? Is the reserve for personal expenses a method of accounting? *The deduction of personal expense items is not a method of accounting* even though it is an accounting treatment of a material item that has been consistently used, because it does not involve the timing of a deduction. Under Reg. § 1.446-1(e)(2)(ii)(b), corrections of items that are deducted but which, in fact, are payments of dividends, are not changes in methods of accounting. A changes in characterization (e.g., taxable to nontaxable, or deductible to nondeductible) generally is not considered changes in methods of accounting because the recharacterization affects a taxpayer's lifetime taxable income.[262]

(4) Issue—Was the change in the financing arrangement regarding the collection of Hat Creek's accounts receivable a change of accounting? No. In *Federated Department Stores, Inc. v. Commissioner*,[263] the Tax Court considered the taxpayer's change in the way in which it financed its accounts receivables. Specifically, the issue was whether such fees could continue to be deferred or whether they needed to be included in income at the time the receivables were sold. The Tax Court concluded that, as a result of the new financing arrangement, the service fee income was properly includible in income at the time the receivables were sold, and further held that there was no change in the method of accounting. The Sixth Circuit upheld the Tax Court's decision, noting that "[f]undamentally, the item itself must be basically the same as an item previously accounted for with the present method of accounting differing from the prior treatment. Unless the transactions are basically the same, the accounting treatment would not be a 'change' of accounting but only a 'new' accounting method for a different transaction." Both the Tax Court and the Sixth Circuit found that the transactions in this case were so materially different that no change in accounting method had occurred. Consequently, the taxpayer was not entitled to the provisions of IRC § 481 as a result of the change in the treatment of the service fee income.

(5) Issue—Is the treatment of the advance payment in 2017 and 2018 a method of accounting? *The accounting for the advance payment received in 2017 and 2018 is a method of accounting* under Reg. § 1.446-1(e) because it involves *a material item* (any item that concerns the timing of income or deductions) which has been *consistently used* (over the two tax years of 2017 and 2018). The treatment of the advance payment in 2019 as a deposit is a change of accounting for prepaid items. On July 15, 2019, the Treasury removed the receipt of advance payments final regulation[264] and replaced them with Prop. Reg. § 1.451-8, which provides that an accrual method taxpayer shall include an advance payment in gross income no later than in the taxable year in which the

---

[261] Instructions to Form 3115, DCN #7.

[262] *Underhill v. Comm'r*, 45 T.C. 489 (1966), where a change to cost recovery method from pro rata method of determining income from certain promissory notes was not considered change in method of accounting because issue involved extent to which payments received were taxable or nontaxable, *i.e.*, character of payment, not proper method or time of reporting payments.

[263] 51 T.C. 500 (1968), *aff'd*, 426 F.2d 417 (6th Cir. 1970).

[264] T.D 9870 (July 15, 2019) removing Reg. § 1.451-5.

taxpayer receives the advance payment as provided under Reg. § 1.451-1(a). Notwithstanding, under the same proposed regulation an accrual taxpayer can defer recognition if it has an applicable financial statement (AFS). If the taxpayer does not have an AFS, then under Prop. Reg. § 1.451-8(d) a taxpayer includes the advance payment in gross income for the taxable year of receipt, including, if applicable, a short taxable year described in Prop. Reg. § 1.451-8(d)(8), to the extent that it is earned in that taxable year and includes the remaining portion of the advance payment in gross income in the next succeeding taxable year.

(6) Is there a "book conformity" issue? Because Hat Creek maintains its books and records on the cash basis and files its tax returns on the cash basis, there is *no* book conformity issue. The fact that financial statements are prepared on an accrual basis has no bearing on the basis of accounting allowable for tax purposes. Maintenance of "memorandum" records to facilitate the preparation of financial statements or for internal reference purposes does not create a book conformity issue.[265]

(7) Which of Hat Creek's methods of accounting are impermissible? Why? Hat Creek's overall accounting method is not a permissible method for the following reasons.

(i) Hat Creek was using an impermissible method of accounting prior to 2018 as its average annual gross receipts exceeded $5,000,000 and it was required to maintain inventories; it should therefore apply for a change of accounting. If the change is voluntary,[266] the IRC § 481(a) adjustment period is one taxable year (year of change) for a negative IRC § 481(a) adjustment, that is, the taxpayer is receiving a refund, and four taxable years (year of change and next three taxable years) for a positive IRC § 481(a) adjustment, that is, the taxpayer owes taxes. Generally a taxpayer must take a positive IRC § 481(a) adjustment into account ratably over four years (the year of change and the following three years).[267] Hat Creek should follow the IRS procedures for accounting method changes. Rev. Proc. 2015-13 and Rev. Proc. 2017-30.[268]

(ii) Hat Creek's *method of accounting for tax depreciation on its office building is not a permissible method of accounting*. The permitted class life for a commercial building placed in service in 2011 is 39 years.[269]

(iii) Hat Creek's method of *accounting for advance payments for services in 2019 is a change of accounting*. By recording the 2017 and 2018 prepayments as income, under Rev. Rul. 90-38[270] Hat Creek established a method of accounting. The change in 2019 is a change of accounting.

What will you recommend to Hat Creek, and why?

(1) Hat Creek could must file for a change of accounting from a cash method taxpayer to an accrual method taxpayer under DCN# 122.

---

[265] *Daily Record Co. v. Comm'r*, 13 BTA 458 (1928). *See* discussion in Chapter 4.

[266] *See* § 7.04[I] under Rev. Proc. 2015-13,

[267] Rev. Proc. 2015-13, 2015-5 IRB 419, § 7.03.

[268] Hat Creek may be eligible to apply Rev. Proc. 2015-14, #33.

[269] Hat Creek can apply for an automatic change for depreciation under Rev. Proc. 2015-14, 2015-5 IRB 450.

[270] 1990-1 CB 57.

(2) Hat Creek must adopt the accrual method of accounting and make the IRC § 481 adjustment.
(3) Hat Creek has been using an impermissible method of accounting for tax depreciation on its office building. It has been taking straight-line depreciation over 20 years. The permitted class life for a commercial building placed in service in 2011 is 39 years. *See attached Exhibit 7-1 IRS Form 3115 and attachment.*
(4) Hat Creek must capitalize cost under IRC § 263A and file a Form 3115 using DCN # 22.
(5) Hat Creek should file for a change of accounting from an impermissible method of accounting to a permissible method of accounting before the IRS discovers its noncompliance during an examination, in order to take advantage of the IRC § 481 adjustment.

Hat Creek Corp. comparative, accrual method balance sheet

	2019	2018
Cash	100,000.00	$100,000.00
Prepaid Service Income	250,000.00	100,000.00
Accounts Receivable	3,000,000.00	2,500,000.00
Allowance for Bad Debts	-70,000.00	-70,000.00
Inventory	2,000,000.00	1,500,000.00
Office Building	500,000.00	500,000.00
Accumulated Depreciation	-200,000.00	-175,000.00
Other Fixed Assets	1,550,000.00	1,550,000.00
Accumulated Depreciation other	-300,000.00	-250,000.00
Prepaid Expenses	100,000.00	250,000.00
Total Assets	6,930,000.00	6,005,000.00
LIABILITIES & STOCKHOLDERS EQUITY		
Accounts Payable	500,000.00	750,000.00
Accrued Expenses	100,000.00	100,000.00
Bonuses Payable	250,000.00	100,000.00
Prepaid Service Income	250,000.00	100,000.00
Long-Term Debt	900,000.00	750,000.00
Total Liabilities	2,000,000.00	$1,800,000
Common Stock	30,000.00	30,000.00
Retained Earnings	4,900,000.00	4,175,000.00
Total Stockholders Equity	4,930,000.00	4,205,000.00
Total Liabilities & Stockholders Equity	6,930,000.00	6,005,000.00

Appendix 7-1 Filled-in Form 3115 and Worksheet

Form **3115** (Rev. December 2018) Department of the Treasury Internal Revenue Service

Application for Change in Accounting Method

► Go to *www.irs.gov/Form3115* for instructions and the latest information.

OMB No. 1545-2070

Name of filer (name of parent corporation if a consolidated group) (see instructions) HAT CREEK CORPORATION	**Identification number** (see instructions) 45-1234567 Principal business activity code number (see instructions) 541519
Number, street, and room or suite no. If a P.O. box, see the instructions. 125 MAIN STREET	Tax year of change begins (MM/DD/YYYY) 01/01/2020 Tax year of change ends (MM/DD/YYYY) 12/31/2020
City or town, state, and ZIP code ANYTOWN, USA	Name of contact person (see instructions) LEO ACCOUNTANT
Name of applicant(s) (if different than filer) and identification number(s) (see instructions)	Contact person's telephone number

If the applicant is a member of a consolidated group, check this box . . . ► ☐

If **Form 2848,** Power of Attorney and Declaration of Representative, is attached (see instructions for when Form 2848 is required), check this box . . . ► ☐

Check the box to indicate the type of applicant.

- ☐ Individual
- ☑ Corporation
- ☐ Controlled foreign corporation (Sec. 957)
- ☐ 10/50 corporation (Sec. 904(d)(2)(E))
- ☐ Qualified personal service corporation (Sec. 448(d)(2))
- ☐ Exempt organization. Enter Code section ►
- ☐ Cooperative (Sec. 1381)
- ☐ Partnership
- ☐ S corporation
- ☐ Insurance co. (Sec. 816(a))
- ☐ Insurance co. (Sec. 831)
- ☐ Other (specify) ►

Check the appropriate box to indicate the type of accounting method change being requested. See instructions.

- ☐ Depreciation or Amortization
- ☐ Financial Products and/or Financial Activities of Financial Institutions
- ☐ Other (specify) ►

Caution: To be eligible for approval of the requested change in method of accounting, the taxpayer must provide all information that is relevant to the taxpayer or to the taxpayer's requested change in method of accounting. This includes **(1)** all relevant information requested on this Form 3115 (including its instructions), and **(2)** any other relevant information, even if not specifically requested on Form 3115.
The taxpayer must attach all applicable statements requested throughout this form.

Part I Information for Automatic Change Request

		Yes	No
1	Enter the applicable designated automatic accounting method change number ("DCN") for the requested automatic change. Enter only one DCN, except as provided for in guidance published by the IRS. If the requested change has no DCN, check "Other," and provide both a description of the change and a citation of the IRS guidance providing the automatic change. See instructions.		
a	(1) DCN: 122 (2) DCN: 7 (3) DCN: ____ (4) DCN: ____ (5) DCN: ____ (6) DCN: ____ (7) DCN: ____ (8) DCN: ____ (9) DCN: ____ (10) DCN: ____ (11) DCN: ____ (12) DCN: ____		
b	Other ☐ Description ►		
2	Do any of the eligibility rules restrict the applicant from filing the requested change using the automatic change procedures (see instructions)? If "Yes," attach an explanation.		✓
3	Has the filer provided all the information and statements required **(a)** on this form and **(b)** by the List of Automatic Changes under which the applicant is requesting a change? See instructions.	✓	
	Note: Complete Part II and Part IV of this form, and, Schedules A through E, if applicable.		

Part II Information for All Requests

		Yes	No
4	During the tax year of change, did or will the applicant **(a)** cease to engage in the trade or business to which the requested change relates, or **(b)** terminate its existence? See instructions.		✓
5	Is the applicant requesting to change to the principal method in the tax year of change under Regulations section 1.381(c)(4)-1(d)(1) or 1.381(c)(5)-1(d)(1)? If "No," go to line 6a. If "Yes," the applicant cannot file a Form 3115 for this change. See instructions.		

Sign Here Under penalties of perjury, I declare that I have examined this application, including accompanying schedules and statements, and to the best of my knowledge and belief, the application contains all the relevant facts relating to the application, and it is true, correct, and complete. Declaration of preparer (other than applicant) is based on all information of which preparer has any knowledge.

Signature of filer (and spouse, if joint return)	Date	Name and title (print or type)

Preparer (other than filer/applicant)	Print/Type preparer's name LEO ACCOUNTANT, CPA	Preparer's signature	Date
	Firm's name ►		

For Privacy Act and Paperwork Reduction Act Notice, see the instructions. Cat. No. 19280E Form **3115** (Rev. 12-2018)

Form 3115 (Rev. 12-2018) Page **2**

	Part II Information for All Requests *(continued)*	**Yes**	**No**
6a	Does the applicant (or any present or former consolidated group in which the applicant was a member during the applicable tax year(s)) have any federal income tax return(s) under examination (see instructions)? . . . . . . If "No," go to line 7a.		✓
b	Is the method of accounting the applicant is requesting to change an issue under consideration (with respect to either the applicant or any present or former consolidated group in which the applicant was a member during the applicable tax year(s))? See instructions.		✓
c	Enter the name and telephone number of the examining agent and the tax year(s) under examination. Name ▶ ______ Telephone number ▶ ______ Tax year(s) ▶ ______		
d	Has a copy of this Form 3115 been provided to the examining agent identified on line 6c?		
7a	Does audit protection apply to the applicant's requested change in method of accounting? See instructions. . . . If "No," attach an explanation.	✓	
b	If "Yes," check the applicable box and attach the required statement. ☐ Not under exam ☐ 3-month window ☐ 120 day: Date examination ended ▶______ ☐ Method not before director ☐ Negative adjustment ☐ CAP: Date member joined group ▶______ ☐ Audit protection at end of exam ☐ Other		
8a	Does the applicant (or any present or former consolidated group in which the applicant was a member during the applicable tax year(s)) have any federal income tax return(s) before Appeals and/or a federal court? . . . . . If "No," go to line 9.		✓
b	Is the method of accounting the applicant is requesting to change an issue under consideration by Appeals and/or a federal court (for either the applicant or any present or former consolidated group in which the applicant was a member for the tax year(s) the applicant was a member)? See instructions. . . . . If "Yes," attach an explanation.		✓
c	If "Yes," enter the name of the (check the box) ☐ Appeals officer and/or ☐ counsel for the government, telephone number, and the tax year(s) before Appeals and/or a federal court. Name ▶ ______ Telephone number ▶ ______ Tax year(s) ▶ ______		
d	Has a copy of this Form 3115 been provided to the Appeals officer and/or counsel for the government identified on line 8c?		
9	If the applicant answered "Yes" to line 6a and/or 8a with respect to any present or former consolidated group, attach a statement that provides each parent corporation's **(a)** name, **(b)** identification number, **(c)** address, and **(d)** tax year(s) during which the applicant was a member that is under examination, before an Appeals office, and/or before a federal court.		
10	If for federal income tax purposes, the applicant is either an entity (including a limited liability company) treated as a partnership or an S corporation, is it requesting a change from a method of accounting that is an issue under consideration in an examination, before Appeals, or before a federal court, with respect to a federal income tax return of a partner, member, or shareholder of that entity?		✓
11a	Has the applicant, its predecessor, or a related party requested or made (under either an automatic or non-automatic change procedure) a change in method of accounting within any of the five tax years ending with the tax year of change? . . . . . If "No," go to line 12.		✓
b	If "Yes," for each trade or business, attach a description of each requested change in method of accounting (including the tax year of change) and state whether the applicant received consent.		
c	If any application was withdrawn, not perfected, or denied, or if a Consent Agreement granting a change was not signed and returned to the IRS, or the change was not made or not made in the requested year of change, attach an explanation.		
12	Does the applicant, its predecessor, or a related party currently have pending any request (including any concurrently filed request) for a private letter ruling, change in method of accounting, or technical advice? . . .		✓
	If "Yes," for each request attach a statement providing **(a)** the name(s) of the taxpayer, **(b)** identification number(s), **(c)** the type of request (private letter ruling, change in method of accounting, or technical advice), and **(d)** the specific issue(s) in the request(s).		
13	Is the applicant requesting to change its **overall** method of accounting? . . . . . If "Yes," complete Schedule A on page 4 of the form.	✓	

Form **3115** (Rev. 12-2018)

Form 3115 (Rev. 12-2018) Page **3**

Part II Information for All Requests *(continued)*

		Yes	No
14	If the applicant is either **(i) not** changing its overall method of accounting, or **(ii)** changing its overall method of accounting **and** changing to a special method of accounting for one or more items, attach a detailed and complete description for each of the following (see instructions):		
a	The item(s) being changed.		
b	The applicant's present method for the item(s) being changed.		
c	The applicant's proposed method for the item(s) being changed.		
d	The applicant's present overall method of accounting (cash, accrual, or hybrid).		
15a	Attach a detailed and complete description of the applicant's trade(s) or business(es). See section 446(d).		
b	If the applicant has more than one trade or business, as defined in Regulations section 1.446-1(d), describe **(i)** whether each trade or business is accounted for separately; **(ii)** the goods and services provided by each trade or business and any other types of activities engaged in that generate gross income; **(iii)** the overall method of accounting for each trade or business; and **(iv)** which trade or business is requesting to change its accounting method as part of this application or a separate application.		
	Note: If you are requesting an automatic method change, see the instructions to see if you are required to complete lines 16a–16c.		
16a	Attach a full explanation of the legal basis supporting the proposed method for the item being changed. Include a detailed and complete description of the facts that explains how the law specifically applies to the applicant's situation and that demonstrates that the applicant is authorized to use the proposed method.		
b	Include all authority (statutes, regulations, published rulings, court cases, etc.) supporting the proposed method.		
c	Include either a discussion of the contrary authorities or a statement that no contrary authority exists.		
17	Will the proposed method of accounting be used for the applicant's books and records and financial statements? For insurance companies, see the instructions . . . . If "No," attach an explanation.	✓	
18	Does the applicant request a conference with the IRS National Office if the IRS National Office proposes an adverse response?	✓	
19a	If the applicant is changing to either the overall cash method, an overall accrual method, or is changing its method of accounting for any property subject to section 263A, any long-term contract subject to section 460 (see 19b), or inventories subject to section 474, enter the applicant's gross receipts for the 3 tax years preceding the tax year of change.		

1st preceding year ended: mo. 12 yr. 2019	2nd preceding year ended: mo. 12 yr. 2018	3rd preceding year ended: mo. 12 yr. 2017
$ 28,00,000	$ 27,000,000	$ 25,000,000

b If the applicant is changing its method of accounting for any long-term contract subject to section 460, in addition to completing 19a, enter the applicant's gross receipts for the 4th tax year preceding the tax year of change:
4th preceding year ended: mo. ________ yr. ____ $ ________________

Part III Information for Non-Automatic Change Request

		Yes	No
20	Is the applicant's requested change described in any revenue procedure, revenue ruling, notice, regulation, or other published guidance as an automatic change request? . . . . If "Yes," attach an explanation describing why the applicant is submitting its request under the non-automatic change procedures.		
21	Attach a copy of all documents related to the proposed change (see instructions).		
22	Attach a statement of the applicant's reasons for the proposed change.		
23	If the applicant is a member of a consolidated group for the year of change, do all other members of the consolidated group use the proposed method of accounting for the item being changed? . . . . If "No," attach an explanation.		
24a	Enter the amount of **user fee** attached to this application (see instructions). ▶ $ ________		
b	If the applicant qualifies for a reduced user fee, attach the required information or certification (see instructions).		

Form **3115** (Rev. 12-2018)

Form 3115 (Rev. 12-2018) Page 4

Part IV	**Section 481(a) Adjustment**	**Yes**	**No**
25	Does published guidance require the applicant (or permit the applicant and the applicant is electing) to implement the requested change in method of accounting on a cut-off basis? If "Yes," attach an explanation and do not complete lines 26, 27, and 28 below.		
26	Enter the section 481(a) adjustment. Indicate whether the adjustment is an increase (+) or a decrease (-) in income. ▶ $ 4,947,955 Attach a summary of the computation and an explanation of the methodology used to determine the section 481(a) adjustment. If it is based on more than one component, show the computation for each component. If more than one applicant is applying for the method change on the application, attach a list of the **(a)** name, **(b)** identification number, and **(c)** the amount of the section 481(a) adjustment attributable to each applicant.		
27	Is the applicant making an election to take the entire amount of the adjustment into account in the tax year of change? If "Yes," check the box for the applicable elective provision used to make the election (see instructions). ☐ $50,000 de minimis election ☐ Eligible acquisition transaction election		✓
28	Is any part of the section 481(a) adjustment attributable to transactions between members of an affiliated group, a consolidated group, a controlled group, or other related parties? If "Yes," attach an explanation.		✓

Schedule A—Change in Overall Method of Accounting (If Schedule A applies, Part I below must be completed.)

Part I Change in Overall Method (see instructions)

1 Check the appropriate boxes below to indicate the applicant's present and proposed methods of accounting.

Present method: ☑ Cash ☐ Accrual ☐ Hybrid (attach description)

Proposed method: ☐ Cash ☑ Accrual ☐ Hybrid (attach description)

2 Enter the following amounts as of the close of the tax year preceding the year of change. If none, state "None." Also, attach a statement providing a breakdown of the amounts entered on lines 2a through 2g.

		Amount
a	Income accrued but not received (such as accounts receivable)	$ 3,000,000
b	Income received or reported before it was earned (such as advanced payments). Attach a description of the income and the legal basis for the proposed method.	250,000
c	Expenses accrued but not paid (such as accounts payable)	-500,000
d	Prepaid expenses previously deducted	100,000
e	Supplies on hand previously deducted and/or not previously reported	
f	Inventory on hand previously deducted and/or not previously reported. Complete Schedule D, Part II.	2,000,000
g	Other amounts (specify). Attach a description of the item and the legal basis for its inclusion in the calculation of the section 481(a) adjustment. ▶	
h	**Net section 481(a) adjustment** (Combine lines 2a–2g.) Indicate whether the adjustment is an increase (+) or decrease (-) in income. Also enter the net amount of this section 481(a) adjustment amount on Part IV, line 26.	$ 4,850,000

3 Is the applicant also requesting the recurring item exception under section 461(h)(3)? ☐ **Yes** ☑ **No**

4 Attach copies of the profit and loss statement (Schedule F (Form 1040) for farmers) and the balance sheet, if applicable, as of the close of the tax year preceding the year of change. Also attach a statement specifying the accounting method used when preparing the balance sheet. If books of account are not kept, attach a copy of the business schedules submitted with the federal income tax return or other return (such as, tax-exempt organization returns) for that period. If the amounts in Part I, lines 2a through 2g, do not agree with the amounts shown on both the profit and loss statement and the balance sheet, attach a statement explaining the differences.

5 Is the applicant making a change to the overall cash method as a small business taxpayer (see instructions)? ☐ **Yes** ☑ **No**

Part II Change to the Cash Method for Non-Automatic Change Request (see instructions)

Applicants requesting a change to the cash method must attach the following information:

1 A description of inventory items (items whose production, purchase, or sale is an income-producing factor) and materials and supplies used in carrying out the business.

2 An explanation as to whether the applicant is required to use the accrual method under any section of the Code or regulations.

Form **3115** (Rev. 12-2018)

Schedule B—Change to the Deferral Method for Advance Payments (see instructions)

1 If the applicant is requesting to change to the deferral method for advance payments, as described in the instructions, attach the following information:

a Explain how the advance payments meet the definition of advance payment, as described in the instructions.

b Does the taxpayer use an applicable financial statement as described in the instructions and, if so, identify it.

c Describe the taxpayer's allocation method, if there is more than one performance obligation, as defined in the instructions.

d Describe the taxpayer's legal basis for deferral. See instructions.

e If the applicant is filing under the non-automatic change procedures, see the instructions for the information required.

Schedule C—Changes Within the LIFO Inventory Method (see instructions)

Part I General LIFO Information

Complete this section if the requested change involves changes within the LIFO inventory method. Also, attach a copy of all **Forms 970,** Application To Use LIFO Inventory Method, filed to adopt or expand the use of the LIFO method.

1 Attach a description of the applicant's present and proposed LIFO methods and submethods for each of the following items:

a Valuing inventory (for example, unit method or dollar-value method).

b Pooling (for example, by line or type or class of goods, natural business unit, multiple pools, raw material content, simplified dollar-value method, inventory price index computation (IPIC) pools, vehicle-pool method, etc.).

c Pricing dollar-value pools (for example, double-extension, index, link-chain, link-chain index, IPIC method, etc.).

d Determining the current-year cost of goods in the ending inventory (such as, most recent acquisitions, earliest acquisitions during the current year, average cost of current-year acquisitions, rolling-average cost, or other permitted method).

2 If any present method or submethod used by the applicant is not the same as indicated on Form(s) 970 filed to adopt or expand the use of the method, attach an explanation.

3 If the proposed change is not requested for all the LIFO inventory, attach a statement specifying the inventory to which the change is and is not applicable.

4 If the proposed change is not requested for all of the LIFO pools, attach a statement specifying the LIFO pool(s) to which the change is applicable.

5 Attach a statement addressing whether the applicant values any of its LIFO inventory on a method other than cost. For example, if the applicant values some of its LIFO inventory at retail and the remainder at cost, identify which inventory items are valued under each method.

6 If changing to the IPIC method, attach a completed Form 970.

Part II Change in Pooling Inventories

1 If the applicant is proposing to change its pooling method or the number of pools, attach a description of the contents of, and state the base year for, each dollar-value pool the applicant presently uses and proposes to use.

2 If the applicant is proposing to use natural business unit (NBU) pools or requesting to change the number of NBU pools, attach the following information (to the extent not already provided) in sufficient detail to show that each proposed NBU was determined under Regulations sections 1.472-8(b)(1) and (2):

a A description of the types of products produced by the applicant. If possible, attach a brochure.

b A description of the types of processes and raw materials used to produce the products in each proposed pool.

c If all of the products to be included in the proposed NBU pool(s) are not produced at one facility, state the reasons for the separate facilities, the location of each facility, and a description of the products each facility produces.

d A description of the natural business divisions adopted by the taxpayer. State whether separate cost centers are maintained and if separate profit and loss statements are prepared.

e A statement addressing whether the applicant has inventories of items purchased and held for resale that are not further processed by the applicant, including whether such items, if any, will be included in any proposed NBU pool.

f A statement addressing whether all items including raw materials, goods-in-process, and finished goods entering into the entire inventory investment for each proposed NBU pool are presently valued under the LIFO method. Describe any items that are not presently valued under the LIFO method that are to be included in each proposed pool.

g A statement addressing whether, within the proposed NBU pool(s), there are items both sold to unrelated parties and transferred to a different unit of the applicant to be used as a component part of another product prior to final processing.

3 If the applicant is engaged in manufacturing and is proposing to use the multiple pooling method or raw material content pools, attach information to show that each proposed pool will consist of a group of items that are substantially similar. See Regulations section 1.472-8(b)(3).

4 If the applicant is engaged in the wholesaling or retailing of goods and is requesting to change the number of pools used, attach information to show that each of the proposed pools is based on customary business classifications of the applicant's trade or business. See Regulations section 1.472-8(c).

Form 3115 (Rev. 12-2018) Page 6

Schedule D—Change in the Treatment of Long-Term Contracts Under Section 460, Inventories, or Other Section 263A Assets (see instructions)

Part I Change in Reporting Income From Long-Term Contracts (Also complete Part III on pages 7 and 8.)

1 To the extent not already provided, attach a description of the applicant's present and proposed methods for reporting income and expenses from long-term contracts. Also, attach a representative actual contract (without any deletion) for the requested change. If the applicant is a construction contractor, attach a detailed description of its construction activities.

2a Are the applicant's contracts long-term contracts as defined in section 460(f)(1) (see instructions)? ☐ Yes ☐ No

b If "Yes," do all the contracts qualify for the exception under section 460(e) (see instructions)? ☐ Yes ☐ No
If line 2b is "No," attach an explanation.

c Is the applicant requesting to use the percentage-of-completion method using cost-to-cost under Regulations section 1.460-4(b)? ☐ Yes ☐ No

d If line 2c is "Yes," in computing the completion factor of a contract, will the applicant use the simplified cost-to-cost method described in Regulations section 1.460-5(c)? ☐ Yes ☐ No

e If line 2c is "No," is the applicant requesting to use the exempt-contract percentage-of-completion method under Regulations section 1.460-4(c)(2)? ☐ Yes ☐ No
If line 2e is "Yes," attach an explanation of what method the applicant will use to determine a contract's completion factor.
If line 2e is "No," attach an explanation of what method the applicant is using and the authority for its use.

3a Does the applicant have long-term manufacturing contracts as defined in section 460(f)(2)? ☐ Yes ☐ No

b If "Yes," attach a description of the applicant's manufacturing activities, including any required installation of manufactured goods.

4a Does the applicant enter into cost-plus long-term contracts? ☐ Yes ☐ No

b Does the applicant enter into federal long-term contracts? ☐ Yes ☐ No

Part II Change in Valuing Inventories Including Cost Allocation Changes (Also complete Part III on pages 7 and 8.)

1 Attach a description of the inventory goods being changed.

2 Attach a description of the inventory goods (if any) NOT being changed.

3a Is the applicant subject to section 263A? If "No," go to line 4a. ☐ Yes ☐ No

b Is the applicant's present inventory valuation method in compliance with section 263A (see instructions)? If "No," attach a detailed explanation. ☐ Yes ☐ No

4a Check the appropriate boxes in the chart.

	Inventory Method Being Changed		Inventory Method Not Being Changed
	Present method	Proposed method	Present method
Identification methods:			
Specific identification			
FIFO			
LIFO			
Other (attach explanation)			
Valuation methods:			
Cost			
Cost or market, whichever is lower			
Retail cost			
Retail, lower of cost or market			
Other (attach explanation)			
b Enter the value at the end of the tax year preceding the year of change.	$	$	

5 If the applicant is changing from the LIFO inventory method to a non-LIFO method, attach the following information (see instructions).

a Copies of Form(s) 970 filed to adopt or expand the use of the method.

b **Only for applicants requesting a non-automatic change.** A statement describing whether the applicant is changing to the method required by Regulations section 1.472-6(a) or (b), or whether the applicant is proposing a different method.

c **Only for applicants requesting an automatic change.** The statement required by section 23.01(5) of Rev. Proc. 2018-31 (or its successor).

Form **3115** (Rev. 12-2018)

Part III **Method of Cost Allocation** (Complete this part if the requested change involves either property subject to section 263A or long-term contracts as described in section 460.) See instructions.

Section A—Allocation and Capitalization Methods

Attach a description (including sample computations) of the present and proposed method(s) the applicant uses to capitalize direct and indirect costs properly allocable to real or tangible personal property produced and property acquired for resale, or to allocate direct and indirect costs required to be allocated to long-term contracts. Include a description of the method(s) used for allocating indirect costs to intermediate cost objectives such as departments or activities prior to the allocation of such costs to long-term contracts, real or tangible personal property produced, and property acquired for resale. The description must include the following:

1 The method of allocating direct and indirect costs (for example, specific identification, burden rate, standard cost, or other reasonable allocation method).

2 The method of allocating mixed service costs (for example, direct reallocation, step-allocation, simplified service cost using the labor-based allocation ratio, simplified service cost using the production cost allocation ratio, or other reasonable allocation method).

3 Except for long-term contract accounting methods, the method of capitalizing additional section 263A costs (for example, simplified production with or without the historic absorption ratio election, simplified resale with or without the historic absorption ratio election including permissible variations, the U.S. ratio, or other reasonable allocation method).

Section B—Direct and Indirect Costs Required to be Allocated

Check the appropriate boxes showing the costs that are or will be fully included, to the extent required, in the cost of real or tangible personal property produced or property acquired for resale under section 263A or allocated to long-term contracts under section 460. Mark "N/A" in a box if those costs are not incurred by the applicant. If a box is not checked, it is assumed that those costs are not fully included to the extent required. Attach an explanation for boxes that are not checked.

		Present method	Proposed method
1	Direct material		
2	Direct labor		
3	Indirect labor		
4	Officers' compensation (not including selling activities)		
5	Pension and other related costs		
6	Employee benefits		
7	Indirect materials and supplies		
8	Purchasing costs		
9	Handling, processing, assembly, and repackaging costs		
10	Offsite storage and warehousing costs		
11	Depreciation, amortization, and cost recovery allowance for equipment and facilities placed in service and not temporarily idle		
12	Depletion		
13	Rent		
14	Taxes other than state, local, and foreign income taxes		
15	Insurance		
16	Utilities		
17	Maintenance and repairs that relate to a production, resale, or long-term contract activity		
18	Engineering and design costs (not including section 174 research and experimental expenses)		
19	Rework labor, scrap, and spoilage		
20	Tools and equipment		
21	Quality control and inspection		
22	Bidding expenses incurred in the solicitation of contracts awarded to the applicant		
23	Licensing and franchise costs		
24	Capitalizable service costs (including mixed service costs)		
25	Administrative costs (not including any costs of selling or any return on capital)		
26	Research and experimental expenses attributable to long-term contracts		
27	Interest		
28	Other costs (Attach a list of these costs.)		

Form 3115 (Rev. 12-2018) Page **8**

Part III Method of Cost Allocation *(continued)* See instructions.

Section C—Other Costs Not Required To Be Allocated (Complete Section C only if the applicant is requesting to change its method for these costs.)

		Present method	Proposed method
1	Marketing, selling, advertising, and distribution expenses		
2	Research and experimental expenses not included in Section B, line 26		
3	Bidding expenses not included in Section B, line 22		
4	General and administrative costs not included in Section B		
5	Income taxes		
6	Cost of strikes		
7	Warranty and product liability costs		
8	Section 179 costs		
9	On-site storage		
10	Depreciation, amortization, and cost recovery allowance not included in Section B, line 11		
11	Other costs (Attach a list of these costs.)		

Schedule E—Change in Depreciation or Amortization. See instructions.

Applicants requesting approval to change their method of accounting for depreciation or amortization complete this section. Applicants ***must*** provide this information for each item or class of property for which a change is requested.

Note: See the ***Summary of the List of Automatic Accounting Method Changes*** in the instructions for information regarding automatic changes under sections 56, 167, 168, 197, 1400I, 1400L, or former section 168. **Do not** file Form 3115 with respect to certain late elections and election revocations. See instructions.

1 Is depreciation for the property determined under Regulations section 1.167(a)-11 (CLADR)? ☐ **Yes** ☐ **No**
If "Yes," the only changes permitted are under Regulations section 1.167(a)-11(c)(1)(iii).

2 Is any of the depreciation or amortization required to be capitalized under any Code section, such as section 263A? ☐ **Yes** ☐ **No**
If "Yes," enter the applicable section ▶ ____________

3 Has a depreciation, amortization, expense, or disposition election been made for the property, such as the election under sections 168(f)(1), 168(i)(4), 179, 179C, or Regulations section 1.168(i)-8(d)? ☐ **Yes** ☐ **No**
If "Yes," state the election made ▶ ____________

4a To the extent not already provided, attach a statement describing the property subject to the change. Include in the description the type of property, the year the property was placed in service, and the property's use in the applicant's trade or business or income-producing activity.

b If the property is residential rental property, did the applicant live in the property before renting it? ☐ **Yes** ☐ **No**

c Is the property public utility property? ☐ **Yes** ☐ **No**

5 To the extent not already provided in the applicant's description of its present method, attach a statement explaining how the property is treated under the applicant's present method (for example, depreciable property, inventory property, supplies under Regulations section 1.162-3, nondepreciable section 263(a) property, property deductible as a current expense, etc.).

6 If the property is not currently treated as depreciable or amortizable property, attach a statement of the facts supporting the proposed change to depreciate or amortize the property.

7 If the property is currently treated and/or will be treated as depreciable or amortizable property, provide the following information for both the present (if applicable) and proposed methods:

a The Code section under which the property is or will be depreciated or amortized (for example, section 168(g)).

b The applicable asset class from Rev. Proc. 87-56, 1987-2 C.B. 674, for each asset depreciated under section 168 (MACRS) or under section 1400L; the applicable asset class from Rev. Proc. 83-35, 1983-1 C.B. 745, for each asset depreciated under former section 168 (ACRS); an explanation why no asset class is identified for each asset for which an asset class has not been identified by the applicant.

c The facts to support the asset class for the proposed method.

d The depreciation or amortization method of the property, including the applicable Code section (for example, 200% declining balance method under section 168(b)(1)).

e The useful life, recovery period, or amortization period of the property.

f The applicable convention of the property.

g Whether the additional first-year special depreciation allowance (for example, as provided by section 168(k), 168(l), 168(m), 168(n), 1400L(b), or 1400N(d)) was or will be claimed for the property. If not, also provide an explanation as to why no special depreciation allowance was or will be claimed.

h Whether the property was or will be in a single asset account, a multiple asset account, or a general asset account.

Form **3115** (Rev. 12-2018)

This Form 3115 is being filed pursuant to Reg. § 301.9100-2(b) of the Procedure and Administration Regulations.

Fact pattern: The applicant is a cash method calendar-year stand-alone C corporation.

There is no Form 2848 power of attorney being filed for a paid preparer. The contact person is listed on page 1 of Form 3115.

The applicant is not under examination as of the date the Form 3115 is filed.

The applicant has not made any method changes or requested any other rulings with the prior five tax years, and does not have any current pending ruling requests. The applicant did not engage in an IRC § 381(a) transaction during 2018.

The applicant presently uses the cash method of accounting and wishes to change to the accrual method of accounting because the taxpayer is selling merchandise.

The applicant maintains inventories, the sale of which is a material income-producing factor under Reg. § 1.471-1.

User Fee—each change is an automatic change under Rev. Proc. 2015-13. No user fee is required.

Calculation of the IRC § 481(a) adjustments.

IRC § 481(a) adjustment for a change in accounting method from cash to accrual:	
Accounts Receivable (Gross)	3,000,000
Inventory	2,000,000
Prepaid income	250,000
Accounts payable	(250,000)
Prepaid expenses	100,000
IRC § 481(a) positive adjustment	5,100,000

The adjustment would be reported in income ratably in 2020, 2021, 2022, and 2023 (a four-year spread). See Appendix 7-1 Form 3115.

The adjustment is the gross amount of accounts receivable (not net) because the allowance for bad debts would not be deducted for tax purposes under the accrual method. The gross amount may be reduced, however, by worthless receivables that would have been written off under IRC § 166.

An IRC § 263A adjustment will be required in this case because Hat Creek has gross receipts over $26 million. This change of accounting is not illustrated.

Bonuses Payable: No adjustment is required because this amount would not have been deducted under the accrual method.[271]

[271] IRC § 267(a)(2).

Depreciation

The applicant has been using an impermissible method of accounting for tax depreciation on its office building. It has been taking straight-line depreciation over 20 years. The permitted class life for a commercial building placed in service in 2010 is 39 years.

IRC § 481(a) adjustment for change in depreciation method:	
depreciation taken under old method	200,000
depreciation allowable under new method	(102,045)
IRC § 481(a) positive adjustment	$ 97,955

The adjustment would be reported in income ratably in 2020, 2021, 2022, and 2023 (a four-year spread). See Appendix 7-1 Form 3115.

Appendix 7-2 Instructions for Form 3115

Instructions for Form 3115

(Rev. December 2018)

Department of the Treasury
Internal Revenue Service

Application for Change in Accounting Method

Section references are to the Internal Revenue Code unless otherwise noted.

All references to Rev. Proc. 2015-13 are to Rev. Proc. 2015-13, 2015-5 I.R.B. 419 (as clarified and modified by Rev. Proc. 2015-33, 2015-24 I.R.B. 1067, and as modified by Rev. Proc. 2017-59, 2017-48 I.R.B. 543, and by section 17.02 of Rev. Proc. 2016-1, 2016-1 I.R.B. 1), or any successor.

All references to Rev. Proc. 2018-31 and the List of Automatic Changes are to Rev. Proc. 2018-31, 2018-22 I.R.B. 637 (as modified by Rev. Proc. 2018-60, 2018-51 I.R.B. 1045, Rev. Proc. 2018-56, 2018-50 I.R.B. 985, Rev. Proc. 2018-49, 2018-41 I.R.B. 548, Rev. Proc. 2018-44, 2018-37 I.R.B. 426, Rev. Proc. 2018-40, 2018–34 I.R.B. 320, Rev. Proc. 2018-35, 2018-28 I.R.B. 204, and Rev. Proc. 2018-29, 2018-22 I.R.B. 634), or any successor.

All references to Rev. Proc. 2019-1 are to Rev. Proc. 2019-1, 2019-1 I.R.B. 1, or any successor (updated annually).

Future Developments

For the latest information about developments related to Form 3115 and its instructions, such as legislation enacted after they were published, go to *IRS.gov/Form3115*.

What's New

Small business taxpayers. Effective for tax years beginning after 2017, the Tax Cuts and Jobs Act (P.L. 115-97) expanded the eligibility of small business taxpayers to use the cash method of accounting. The cash method is available for taxpayers that had average annual gross receipts for the 3 preceding tax years of $25 million or less. See the instructions for Schedule A, later. Qualifying small business taxpayers are also exempt from the following accounting rules.

- The requirement to keep inventories. See section 471(c) and the instructions for Schedule A.
- The uniform capitalization rules. See section 263A(i) and the instructions for Schedule D.
- The requirement to use the percentage-of-completion method for construction contracts, expected to be completed within two years. See section 460(e) and the instructions for Schedule D.

Advance payments. See the instructions for Schedule B for changes to the election to defer advance payments.

Terminating S corporations. Special rules apply for eligible terminated S corporations (as defined in section 481(d)(2)) that change their method of accounting from cash to accrual. See the instructions for Part IV.

General Instructions

Purpose of Form

File Form 3115 to request a change in either an overall method of accounting or the accounting treatment of any item.

Method Change Procedures

When filing Form 3115, you must determine if the IRS has issued any new published guidance which includes revenue procedures, revenue rulings, notices, regulations, or other relevant guidance in the Internal Revenue Bulletin. For the latest information, visit IRS.gov.

For general application procedures on requesting accounting method changes, see Rev. Proc. 2015-13. Rev. Proc. 2015-13 provides procedures for both automatic and non-automatic changes in method of accounting.

Automatic change procedures. Unless otherwise provided in published guidance, you **must** file under the automatic change procedures if you are eligible to request consent to make a change in your method of accounting under the automatic change procedures for the requested year of change. See the instructions for Part I later, and the List of Automatic Changes in Rev. Proc. 2018-31.

A Form 3115 filed under these procedures may be reviewed by the IRS. If it is, you will be notified if information in addition to that requested on Form 3115 is required or if your request is denied. No user fee is required. An applicant that timely files and complies with the automatic change procedures is granted consent to change its accounting method, subject to review by the IRS National Office and operating division director.

Ordinarily, you are required to file a separate Form 3115 for each change in method of accounting. However, in some cases you are required or permitted to file a single Form 3115 for particular concurrent changes in method of accounting. See section 6.03(1)(b) of Rev. Proc. 2015-13 for more information.

Note. The List of DCNs (Designated automatic accounting method change number) at the end of these instructions is a list of many accounting method changes and is presented for informational purposes only and subject to the most recently issued Revenue Procedures.

Reduced Form 3115 filing requirement. A qualified small taxpayer qualifies for a reduced Form 3115 filing requirement for the following DCNs: 7, 8, 21, 87, 88, 89, 107, 121, 145, 157, 184–193, 198, 199, 200, 205, 206, 207, and 222. A qualified small taxpayer is a taxpayer with average annual gross receipts of less than or equal to $10 million for the 3 tax years preceding the year of change. See *Year of Change*, later. A reduced Form 3115 filing requirement involves completing only certain lines and schedules of the Form 3115. For qualifying changes and filing requirements, see the List of Automatic Changes.

Non-automatic change procedures. If you do not qualify to file under the automatic change procedures for the requested change in method of accounting for the requested year of change, you may be able to file under the non-automatic change procedures. See *Non-automatic change—scope and eligibility rules*, in Part III, later. If the requested change is approved by the IRS National Office, the filer will receive a letter ruling on the requested change. File a separate Form 3115 for each unrelated item or submethod. A user fee is required. See the instructions for Part III, later, for more information.

Jan 18, 2019 Cat. No. 63215H

Who Must File

The **filer** is the entity or person required to file Form 3115, whether on its own behalf or on behalf of another entity. An **applicant** is an entity, a person, or a separate and distinct trade or business of an entity or a person (for purposes of Regulations section 1.446-1(d)), whose method of accounting is being changed.

For a consolidated group of corporations, the common parent corporation must file Form 3115 for a change in method of accounting for itself and for any member of the consolidated group. For example, the common parent corporation of a consolidated group is the filer when requesting a change in method of accounting for another member of that consolidated group (or a separate and distinct trade or business of that member), and the other member (or trade or business) on whose behalf Form 3115 is filed is the applicant.

For information on the difference between a filer and an applicant, see the *Name(s) and Signature(s)* section, later.

For a controlled foreign corporation (CFC) or 10/50 corporation without a U.S. trade or business, see section 6.02(6) of Rev. Proc. 2015-13.

Generally, a filer must file a separate Form 3115 for each applicant seeking consent to change a method of accounting. A separate Form 3115 and user fee (for non-automatic change requests) must be submitted for each applicant and each separate trade or business of an applicant, including a qualified subchapter S subsidiary (QSub) or a single-member limited liability company (LLC), requesting a change in method of accounting. See section 9.02 of Rev. Proc. 2019-1.

However, identical changes in methods of accounting for two or more of the following in any combination may be included in a single Form 3115.

1. Members of a consolidated group;

2. Separate and distinct trades or businesses (for purposes of Regulations section 1.446-1(d)) of that entity or member(s) of a consolidated group. Separate and distinct trades or businesses include QSubs and single-member LLCs;

3. Partnerships that are wholly owned within a consolidated group; and

4. CFCs and 10/50 corporations that do not engage in a trade or business within the United States where (i) all controlling domestic shareholders (as provided in Regulations section 1.964-1(c)(5)) of the CFCs and of the 10/50 corporations, as applicable, are members of the consolidated group; or (ii) the taxpayer is the sole controlling domestic shareholder of the CFCs or of the 10/50 corporations.

For information on what is an identical change in method of accounting, see section 15.07(4) of Rev. Proc. 2019-1.

When and Where To File

Automatic change requests. Except if instructed differently, you must file Form 3115 under the automatic change procedures in duplicate as follows.

- Attach the **original** Form 3115 to the filer's timely filed (including extensions) federal income tax return for the year of change. The original Form 3115 attachment does not need to be signed.
- File a **copy** of the **signed** Form 3115 to the address provided in the address chart on this page, no earlier than the first day of the year of change and no later than the date the original is filed with the federal income tax return for the year of change. This signed Form 3115 may be a photocopy. For more on the signature requirement, see the *Name(s) and Signature(s)* section, later.

The IRS does not send acknowledgements of receipt for automatic change requests.

For filing procedures relating to automatic change requests for certain foreign corporations and foreign partnerships, see section 6.03(1)(a)(ii) and (iii) of Rev. Proc. 2015-13.

Non-automatic change requests. You must file Form 3115 under the non-automatic change procedures during the tax year for which the change is requested, unless otherwise provided by published guidance. See section 6.03(2) of Rev. Proc. 2015-13. File Form 3115 with the IRS National Office at the address listed in the Address Chart. File Form 3115 as early as possible during the year of change to provide adequate time for the IRS to respond prior to the due date of the filer's return for the year of change.

The IRS normally sends an acknowledgment of receipt within 60 days after receiving a Form 3115 filed under the non-automatic change procedures. If the filer does not receive an acknowledgment of receipt for a non-automatic change request within 60 days, the filer can inquire to:

Internal Revenue Service
Control Clerk
CC:IT&A, Room 4512
1111 Constitution Ave. NW
Washington, DC 20224

*In specified circumstances, you are required to send **additional copies** of Form 3115 to another IRS address. For example, another copy of Form 3115 would be sent, when an applicant is under examination, before an Appeals office, before a federal court, or is a certain foreign corporation or certain foreign partnership. See section 6.03(3) of Rev. Proc. 2015-13 for more information. Also see Part II, lines 6 and 8, later.*

Address Chart for Form 3115

File Form 3115 at the applicable IRS address listed below.

	A non-automatic change request	An automatic change request (Form 3115 copy)
Delivery by mail	Internal Revenue Service Attn: CC:PA:LPD:DRU P.O. Box 7604 Benjamin Franklin Station Washington, DC 20044	Internal Revenue Service Ogden, UT 84201 M/S 6111
Delivery by private delivery service	Internal Revenue Service Attn: CC:PA:LPD:DRU Room 5336 1111 Constitution Ave. NW Washington, DC 20224	Internal Revenue Service 1973 N. Rulon White Blvd. Ogden, UT 84201 Attn: M/S 6111

Late Application

In general, a filer that fails to timely file a Form 3115 will not be granted an extension of time to file except in unusual and compelling circumstances. See section 6.03(4)(b) of Rev. Proc. 2015-13 and Regulations section 301.9100-3 for the standards that must be met. For information on the period of limitations, see section 5.03(2) of Rev. Proc. 2019-1.

However, an automatic 6-month extension from the due date (excluding any extension) of the federal income tax return to file Form 3115 may be available for automatic change requests. For details, see section 6.03(4)(a) of Rev. Proc. 2015-13 and Regulations section 301.9100-2.

An applicant submitting a ruling request for an extension of time to file Form 3115 must pay a user fee for its extension request and, in the case of a non-automatic change request, a separate user fee for its accounting method change request. For the schedule of user fees, see (A)(3)(b), (A)(4), and (A)(5)(d) in Appendix A of Rev. Proc. 2019-1.

Useful Items

You can refer to these items for more informationn changing a method of accounting.

Revenue Procedures (Rev. Proc.)

Rev. Proc. 2019-1. See *Rev. Proc. 2019-1*. This Rev. Proc. provides specific and additional procedures for requesting a change in method of accounting.

Rev. Proc. 2015-13. See *Rev. Proc. 2015-13*. This Rev. Proc. provides the automatic and non-automatic method change procedures to obtain consent of the Commissioner to change a method of accounting.

Rev. Proc. 2018-31. See *Rev. Proc. 2018-31*. This Rev. Proc. contains a list of accounting method changes that may be eligible to file under the automatic method change procedures.

Other Item

Pub. 538, Accounting Periods and Methods. This publication provides general information on accounting methods.

Specific Instructions

Name(s) and Signature(s)

Enter the name of the filer on the first line of page 1 of Form 3115.

In general, the filer of Form 3115 is the applicant. However, in circumstances where Form 3115 is filed on behalf of the applicant, enter the filer's name and identification number on the first line of Form 3115 and enter the applicant's name and identification number on the fourth line. Receivers, trustees, or assignees must sign any Form 3115 they are required to file.

If Form 3115 is filed for multiple (i) applicants in a consolidated group of corporations, (ii) CFCs, (iii) wholly owned partnerships within a consolidated group, and/or (iv) separate and distinct trades or businesses (including QSubs or single-member LLCs), attach a schedule listing each applicant and its identification number (where applicable). This schedule may be combined with the information requested for Part III, line 24a (regarding the user fee), and Part IV (section 481(a) adjustment). If multiple names and signatures are required (for example, in the case of CFCs—see instructions below), attach a schedule labeled "SIGNATURE ATTACHMENT" to Form 3115, signed under penalties of perjury using the same language as in the declaration on page 1 of Form 3115.

Individuals. If Form 3115 is filed for a couple who file a joint income tax return, enter the names of both spouses on the first line and the signatures of both spouses on the signature line.

Partnerships. Enter the name of the partnership on the first line of Form 3115. In the signature section, include the signature of one of the general partners or limited liability company members who has personal knowledge of the facts and who is authorized to sign. Enter that person's name and official title in the space provided. If the authorized partner is a member of a consolidated group, then an authorized officer of the common parent corporation with personal knowledge of the facts must sign.

Non-consolidated corporations, personal service corporations, S corporations, cooperatives, and insurance companies. Enter the name of the filer on the first line of Form 3115. In the signature section, enter the signature of the officer who has personal knowledge of the facts and authority to bind the filer in the matter. Enter that officer's name and official title in the space provided.

Consolidated group of corporations. Enter the name of the common parent corporation on the first line of Form 3115. Also enter the name(s) of the applicant(s) on the fourth line if a member of the consolidated group other than, or in addition to, the parent corporation is requesting a change in method of accounting. In the signature section, enter the signature of the officer of the common parent corporation who has personal knowledge of the facts and authority to bind the common parent corporation in the matter, and that officer's name and official title in the space provided.

Separate and distinct trade or business of an entity. Enter the name of the entity (or common parent corporation if the entity is a member of a consolidated group) on the first line of Form 3115. Also enter the name of the separate and distinct trade or business requesting a change in method of accounting on the fourth line. In the signature section, enter the signature of the individual who has personal knowledge of the facts and authority to bind the separate and distinct trade or business of the entity in the matter, and that person's name and official title in the space provided.

CFC or 10/50 corporation. For a CFC or 10/50 corporation with a U.S. trade or business, follow the same rules as for other corporations. For a CFC or 10/50 corporation that does not have a U.S. trade or business, Form 3115 filed on behalf of its controlling domestic shareholder(s) (or common parent) must be signed by an authorized officer of the designated (controlling domestic) shareholder that retains the jointly executed consent as provided for in Regulations section 1.964-1(c)(3)(ii). If there is more than one shareholder, the statement described in Regulations section 1.964-1(c)(3)(ii) must be attached to the application. Also, the controlling domestic shareholder(s) must provide the written notice required by Regulations section 1.964-1(c)(3)(iii). If the designated (controlling domestic) shareholder is a member of a consolidated group, then an authorized officer of the common parent corporation must sign.

Estates or trusts. Enter the name of the estate or trust on the first line of Form 3115. In the signature section, enter the signature of the fiduciary, personal representative, executor, administrator, etc., who has personal knowledge of the facts and legal authority to bind the estate or trust in the matter, and that person's official title in the space provided.

Exempt organizations. Enter the name of the organization on the first line of Form 3115. In the signature section, enter the signature of a principal officer or other person who has personal knowledge of the facts and authority to bind the exempt organization in the matter, and that person's name and official title in the space provided.

Preparer (other than filer/applicant). If the individual preparing Form 3115 is not the filer or applicant, the preparer also must sign, and include the firm's name, where applicable. Generally, for both automatic and non-automatic changes, the preparer (if not the filer or applicant) must sign the original and copies of Form 3115. If Form 3115 is *e-filed*, the preparer need not sign the original *e-filed* Form 3115 but must still complete the preparer information and, if applicable, must sign the duplicate automatic Form 3115 copy.

Identification Number

Enter the filer's taxpayer identification number on the first line of Form 3115 as follows.

• Individuals enter their social security number (SSN). For a resident or non-resident alien, enter an individual taxpayer identification number (ITIN). If Form 3115 is for a couple who file a joint return, enter the identification numbers of both spouses.

- All others, enter the employer identification number (EIN).
- If the filer is the common parent corporation of a consolidated group of corporations, enter the EIN of the common parent on the first line of Form 3115. Enter the EIN of the applicant on the fourth line if a member of the consolidated group other than, or in addition to, the common parent is requesting the change in method of accounting.
- If the common parent is filing Form 3115 on behalf of multiple applicants in a consolidated group of corporations, multiple CFCs or 10/50 corporations, or multiple and distinct trades or businesses of a member (including QSubs or single-member LLCs), attach a schedule listing each applicant and its identification number (if applicable).
- If the applicant is a foreign entity that is not otherwise required to have or obtain an EIN, enter "Not applicable" in the space provided for the identifying number.

Principal Business Activity Code

If the filer is a business, enter the 6-digit principal business activity (PBA) code of the filer. The principal business activity of the filer is the activity generating the largest percentage of its total receipts. See the instructions for the filer's income tax return for the filer's PBA code and definition of total receipts.

Note. An applicant requesting to change its accounting method under DCN 33 (change to overall cash method for a qualifying small business taxpayer for a tax year beginning before January 1, 2018) and/or DCN 51 (small taxpayer exception from requirement to account for inventories under section 471 for a tax year beginning before January 1, 2018) in the List of DCNs must also attach to Form 3115 the North American Industry Classification System (NAICS) code for the applicant's principal business activity. See Rev. Proc. 2002-28, 2002-1 C.B. 815, for further guidance. This paragraph does not apply to tax years beginning after December 31, 2017.

Address

Include the suite, room, or other unit number after the street address. If the post office does not deliver mail to the street address and the filer has a P.O. box, show the box number instead of the street address.

Year of Change

The year of change is the first tax year the applicant uses the proposed method of accounting, even if no affected items are taken into account for that year.

Example. A calendar year taxpayer that has consistently capitalized certain building repair costs from 2012 to 2017 files a Form 3115 in 2018 to deduct these repair costs. The year of change is calendar year 2018.

Contact Person

The contact person must be an individual authorized to sign Form 3115, or the filer's authorized representative. If this person is someone other than an individual authorized to sign Form 3115, you must attach Form 2848, Power of Attorney and Declaration of Representative.

Form 2848, Power of Attorney and Declaration of Representative

Authorization to (1) represent the filer before the IRS, (2) receive a copy of the requested letter ruling, or (3) perform any other act(s) must be properly reflected on Form 2848. For further details for an authorized representative and a power of attorney, see sections 9.03(8) and (9) of Rev. Proc. 2019-1.

A Form 2848 must be attached to Form 3115 in order for the IRS to discuss a Form 3115 with the filer's representative, even if the filer's representative prepared and/or signed the Form 3115.

If the filer intends to have the authorized representative receive copies of correspondences regarding its Form 3115, it must check the appropriate box on Form 2848.

Option To Receive Correspondence by Fax

A filer that wants to receive, or wants its authorized representative to receive, correspondence regarding its Form 3115 (for example, additional information letters or the letter ruling) by fax must attach to Form 3115 a statement requesting this service. The attachment also must list the authorized name(s) and fax number(s) of the person(s) who is to receive the fax. The listed person(s) must be either authorized to sign Form 3115 or an authorized representative of the filer that is included on Form 2848. For further details on the fax procedures, see section 9.04(3) of Rev. Proc. 2019-1.

Type of Accounting Method Change Requested

Check the appropriate box on Form 3115 to indicate the type of change being requested.

- **Depreciation or amortization.** Check this box for a change in (1) depreciation or amortization (for example, the depreciation method or recovery period), (2) the treatment of salvage proceeds or costs of removal, (3) the method of accounting for dispositions of depreciable property, or (4) the treatment of depreciable property from a single asset account to a multiple asset account (pooling), or vice versa.
- **Financial products and/or financial activities of financial institutions.** Check this box for a change in the treatment of a financial product (for example, accounting for debt instruments, derivatives, mark-to-market accounting), or in the financial activities of a financial institution (for example, a lending institution, a regulated investment company, a real estate investment trust, or a real estate mortgage investment conduit).
- **Other.** For non-automatic change requests, check this box if neither of the above boxes applies to the requested change. In the space provided, enter a short description of the change and the most specific applicable Code section(s) for the requested change (for example, change within section 263A costs; deduction of warranty expenses, section 461; or change to the completed contract method for long-term contracts, section 460).

For automatic change requests, this informational requirement is satisfied by properly completing Part I, line 1, of Form 3115.

As noted on Form 3115, the filer must provide all information relevant to the requested change in method of accounting. All relevant information includes all information requested on Form 3115, these instructions, and any other relevant information, even if not specifically identified on Form 3115 or in these instructions. Table A illustrates, for automatic and non-automatic changes, the Parts of Form 3115 that must be completed. Table B illustrates the Schedule(s) to be completed for common method changes.

Table A: Parts To Complete on Form 3115 for Accounting Method Changes

Information to be completed for automatic and non-automatic change requests

	Part I	Part II	Part III	Part IV
Automatic Change	X	X		X
Non-Automatic Change		X	X	X

Part I—Information for Automatic Change Request

Automatic Changes—Scope and Eligibility Rules

Line 1a. Enter the DCN on line 1(a). These numbers may be found in the List of DCNs at the end of the instructions, the List of Automatic Changes, or in subsequently published guidance. In general, enter a number for only one change. However, the numbers for two or more changes may be entered on line 1(a) if specifically permitted in applicable published guidance to file a single Form 3115 for particular concurrent changes in method of accounting. See section 6.03(1)(b) of Rev. Proc. 2015-13. For example, an applicant requesting both a change to deduct repair and maintenance costs for tangible property (DCN 184) and a change to capitalize acquisition or production costs (DCN 192) may file a single Form 3115 for both changes by including both DCNs 184 and 192 on line 1(a) of Form 3115.

Line 1b. If the accounting method change is not included in the List of Automatic Changes or assigned a number in the published guidance providing the automatic accounting method change, check the box for "Other" on line 1(b) and identify the revenue procedure or other published guidance under which the automatic accounting method change is being requested.

Line 2. If "Yes," provide an explanation as to why the applicant(s) qualifies to file under the automatic change procedures. If other published guidance provides for an automatic change in method of accounting not listed in the List of Automatic Changes, attach a statement citing the guidance. An example of this would be a change from the cash method under Regulations section 1.448-1(h)(2).

Generally, an applicant is only eligible to use the automatic change procedures of Rev. Proc. 2015-13 if it satisfies the following requirements (see section 5.01(1) of Rev. Proc. 2015-13).

1. On the date the applicant files a Form 3115, the change is described in the List of Automatic Changes;

2. On the date the applicant files a Form 3115, the applicant meets all requirements for the change provided in the applicable section of the List of Automatic Changes;

3. The requested change is not to the principal method under Regulations sections 1.381(c)(4)-1(d)(1) or

Table B: Schedules To Complete on Form 3115 for Common Accounting Method Changes

Information to be completed for common method change requests

Common Method Changes	Schedule A		Schedule B	Schedule C		Schedule D			Schedule E
	Part I	Part II		Part I	Part II	Part I	Part II	Part III	
Accrual to Cash	X	X							
Cash to Accrual	X								
Capitalize to Expense									
Expense to Capitalize								X*	X*
Depreciation									X
Long-Term Contracts						X		X	
Inventory Valuation Change							X	X*	
LIFO Change–Including Pooling				X	X				
Change to Deferral Method for Advanced Payments			X						

X Must fully complete section

[shaded] Section need not be completed

X* To be completed if applicable—See instructions regarding Schedules D and E, later

-5-

1.381(c)(5)-1(d)(1);

4. The requested year of change is not the final year of the trade or business (but see the instructions for line 4);

5. For an overall method of accounting change, the applicant has not made or requested an overall method change during any of the 5 tax years ending with the year of change; and

6. The applicant has not made or requested a change for the same item during any of the 5 tax years ending with the year of change.

Note. Some automatic changes in methods of accounting waive some of the above requirements. These changes may be found in the List of Automatic Changes or the published guidance providing the automatic accounting method change.

Line 3. The filer must complete Form 3115, including any required statements or attachments. See *Table A* for the Form 3115 Part(s) required to be completed for all automatic and non-automatic change requests. See *Table B* for a sample of common method changes and the Form 3115 Schedule(s) to be completed for each. Additionally, see published guidance for any additional required information or statements. For example, a method change to use the mark-to-market method of accounting under section 475(e) or (f) (DCN 64) requires an applicant to file an additional statement to satisfy the requirement in section 5.04 of Rev. Proc. 99-17.

Part II—Information for All Requests

Line 4. If no, check "No." If yes, check "Yes" and attach a statement explaining why the applicant is eligible to change its method of accounting. For example, specific guidance may permit an applicant to change its method of accounting in its final tax year. See section 5.03(2) of Rev. Proc. 2015-13 and sections 6.01 (DCN 7) and 6.07 (DCN 107) of Rev. Proc. 2018-31.

Ordinarily, the IRS will not consent to a request for a change in method of accounting when an applicant ceases to engage in the trade or business or terminates its existence. Generally, an applicant is considered to cease to engage in a trade or business if the applicant terminates its existence for federal income tax purposes, ceases operation of the trade or business, or transfers substantially all the assets of the trade to another taxpayer. For example, a cessation of a trade or business occurs when a trade or business is incorporated or the assets of the trade or business are contributed to a partnership. See sections 3.04, 5.01, and 5.03 of Rev. Proc. 2015-13.

Line 5. When an acquiring corporation operates the trades or businesses of the parties as separate and distinct trades or businesses after the date of distribution or transfer, the acquiring corporation must use a carryover method. See Regulations sections 1.381(c)(4)-1(a)(2) and 1.381(c)(5)-1(a)(2). On the other hand, when the acquiring corporation does not operate the trades or businesses of the parties as separate and distinct trades or businesses after the date of distribution or transfer, the acquiring corporation generally will use the principal method. The applicant does not need to secure the Commissioner's consent to use the principal method. See Regulations sections 1.381(c)(4)-1(d)(1) and 1.381(c)(5)-1(d)(1).

Line 6a. Generally, the applicant is under examination with respect to a federal income tax return as of the date the applicant (or filer) is contacted in any manner by a representative of the IRS for the purpose of scheduling or conducting any type of examination of the return. See section 3.18 of Rev. Proc. 2015-13.

Line 6b. Generally, the applicant's method of accounting is an issue under consideration if the examining agent has given the applicant (or filer) written notification specifically citing the treatment of the item as an issue under consideration. If an examining agent does not propose an adjustment for the item that is an issue under consideration during the examination, the item continues to be an issue under consideration after the examination ends only if the issue is placed in suspense. The applicant's method of accounting is an issue placed in suspense if the examining agent has given the applicant (or filer) written notification of the IRS's intent to examine the issue during the examination of the subsequent tax year(s) to be examined. See section 3.08 of Rev. Proc. 2015-13. A partnership or an S corporation has an issue under consideration before examination if the same item is an issue under consideration in an examination of a partner, member, or shareholder's federal income tax return. For consolidated groups, see section 3.08 of Rev. Proc. 2015-13 for issue under consideration rules.

For CFCs and 10/50 corporations, the issue under consideration rules are different. See section 3.08(4) of Rev. Proc. 2015-13.

Lines 6c and 6d. If you answered "Yes" for line 6a, include the name and telephone number of the examining agent, and the tax year(s) under examination in the designated places on line 6c. For any present or former consolidated groups, if there is a tax year under examination, complete the information on line 6c. Provide a copy of Form 3115 to the examining agent, no later than the date the filer timely files Form 3115. See section 6.03(3)(a) of Rev. Proc. 2015-13.

Line 7a. In general, audit protection applies when an application for change in accounting method is granted. See section 8.01 of Rev. Proc. 2015-13. For exceptions where audit protection is not provided, see section 8.02 of Rev. Proc. 2015-13. For example, a change made under DCN 10 in the List of Automatic Changes for an applicant's sale, lease, or financing transactions does not receive audit protection. See the List of Automatic Changes for additional method changes not subject to audit protection.

If no audit protection is given for the requested change, check "No" and attach an explanation. For example, if you are making a change under DCN 10, your explanation is DCN 10. If you are making a change under DCN 7, your explanation could be that none of the items on line 7b applies. If multiple items are being changed on one Form 3115 and at least one item has audit protection and another item does not have audit protection, check both "Yes" and "No."

Line 7b. Generally, the applicant receives audit protection for tax years prior to the year of change if they fall into one of the following categories listed below. If Form 3115 is being filed on behalf of multiple applicants or if multiple items are being changed on one Form 3115, check all that apply and attach a statement identifying which category applies to which applicant or item. Except for "Not under exam" and "Other," the following only apply to applicants under examination.

- **Not under exam.** Check this box if: (A) the applicant is not under exam, and (B) audit protection applies to the item(s) being changed.
- **3-month window.** The 3-month window is the period beginning on the 15th day of the 7th month following the close of the applicant's tax year and ending on the 15th day of the 10th month following the close of the applicant's tax year. For 52-53 week applicants, the tax year begins on the 1st day of the calendar month nearest to the 1st day of the 52-53 week tax year. See Rev. Proc. 2015-33. For applicants with a short tax year ending before the 15th day of the 10th month after the short tax year begins, the 3-month window is the period beginning on the 1st day of the 2nd month preceding the month in which the short tax year ends and ending on the last day of the short tax year. An applicant qualifies under the 3-month window period when (A) it has been under examination for at least 12 consecutive months as of the 1st day of the 3-month window,

and (B) the method of accounting for the same item the applicant is requesting to change is not an issue under consideration. See section 8.02(1)(a) of Rev. Proc. 2015-13. Checking this box satisfies the statement requirement of section 8.02(1)(a)(iv) of Rev. Proc. 2015-13.

• **120-day window period.** The 120-day window is the 120-day period following the date an examination of the applicant ends, regardless of whether a subsequent examination has commenced. An applicant qualifies under the 120-day window period if Form 3115 is filed in a 120-day window and the method of accounting for the same item the applicant is requesting to change is not an issue under consideration. See section 8.02(1)(b) of Rev. Proc. 2015-13. If the applicant checks this box, also include the date the examination ended in the designated space on line 7b.

• **Method not before director.** The present method is not before the director when it is (A) a change from a clearly permissible method of accounting or (B) a change from an impermissible method of accounting and the impermissible method was adopted subsequent to the tax year(s) under examination on the date the applicant files Form 3115. Checking this box satisfies the statement requirement of section 8.02(1)(c)(ii) of Rev. Proc. 2015-13.

• **Change resulting in a negative adjustment.** Check this box if the change results in a negative adjustment. A negative adjustment occurs where an item (A) results in a negative section 481(a) adjustment for that item for the year of change, and (B) would have resulted in a negative section 481(a) adjustment in each tax year under examination if the change in method of accounting for that item had been made in the tax year(s) under examination. Checking this box satisfies the statement requirement in section 8.02(1)(e)(iii) of Rev. Proc. 2015-13.

• **CAP.** This box applies only to consolidated group members participating in the compliance assurance process (CAP). In general, audit protection applies to a new member if the new member is under audit solely by joining a consolidated group that participates in CAP. See section 8.02(1)(d) of Rev. Proc. 2015-13. Checking this box satisfies the statement requirement of section 8.02(1)(d)(ii) of Rev. Proc. 2015-13. If the applicant checks this box, include the date the member joined the consolidated group in the designated space on line 7b.

• **Other.** The List of Automatic Changes or other guidance published in the I.R.B. may provide applicants with audit protection. For example, specific guidance may provide a filer under exam with audit protection. If this box is checked, attach a statement citing the guidance providing audit protection.

• **Audit protection at end of exam.** If the applicant does not fall into one of the categories listed above for line 7b, this box generally should be checked. The applicant may receive audit protection at the end of the examination, provided the examining agent does not propose an adjustment for the same item and the method of accounting for that same item is not an issue under consideration. For certain foreign corporations, the applicant must satisfy additional requirements in order to receive audit protection at the end of the examination. See section 8.02(1)(f) of Rev. Proc. 2015-13.

CAUTION *For CFCs and 10/50 corporations, the rules for audit protection are different. See section 8.02 of Rev. Proc. 2015-13 (different rules for the 3-month window, 120-day window, and audit protection at end of exam).*

Line 8a. If you answered "Yes," complete lines 8b–d.

Line 8b. To determine if the applicant's method of accounting is an issue under consideration by Appeals and/or a federal court, see sections 3.08(2) and 3.08(3) of Rev. Proc. 2015-13.

Line 8c. If you answered "Yes" for line 8a, include the name and telephone number of the Appeals officer(s) and/or counsel to the government, as well as the tax year(s) before Appeals and/or federal court in the designated places.

Line 8d. If you answered "Yes" for line 8a, provide a copy of the signed Form 3115 to the Appeals officer(s) and/or all counsel to the government, as applicable, no later than the date the filer timely files Form 3115. See section 6.03(3)(a) of Rev. Proc. 2015-13.

Line 9. If you answered "Yes" to line 6a or 8a, complete line 9. The information requested on line 9 should be included on a separate attachment.

Line 10. If you answered "Yes," attach an explanation. Unless otherwise provided, the applicant does not receive audit protection for the requested change if it is an issue under consideration. See sections 3.08 and 8.02(7) of Rev. Proc. 2015-13.

Line 11a–c. Unless otherwise provided, an applicant is not eligible to file under the automatic change procedures if the applicant made or requested a prior overall method change or a prior item change (for the same item) within the 5 tax years ending with the requested year of change. For additional details, see section 9.03(6)(a) of Rev. Proc. 2019-1 and section 11.02(2) of Rev. Proc. 2015-13.

Line 12. For further details, see section 9.03(6)(b) of Rev. Proc. 2019-1.

Line 13. If you answered "Yes," complete Schedule A of Form 3115. For example, an overall method of accounting change includes a change from an accrual method to the cash receipts and disbursements method or vice versa. See section 446(c).

Line 14. Provide the information requested on lines 14a–d if the applicant answered "No" to question 13 or if the applicant answered "Yes" to question 13 and also is changing to a special method of accounting for one or more items. With the information requested on line 14b, the applicant also is required to provide a statement of whether or not the applicant has claimed any federal tax credit relating to the item(s) being changed. A special method of accounting for an item is a method of accounting (other than the cash method or an accrual method) expressly permitted by the Code, regulations, or guidance published in the I.R.B. that deviates from the rules of sections 446, 451, and 461 (and the related regulations) that is applicable to the applicant's overall method of accounting (proposed overall method if being changed). For example, the installment method of accounting under section 453, the mark-to-market method under section 475, and the long-term contract method under section 460 are special methods of accounting. See section 15.01(3)(d) of Rev. Proc. 2018-31. If the applicant prepared a Schedule M-3 with its last filed tax return or expects to file a Schedule M-3 with its next tax return, please state whether the applicant's proposed change in method of accounting for federal income tax purposes is related to the applicant's adoption of the International Financial Reporting Standards (IFRS) for financial statement purposes.

Lines 15a and 15b. Provide the requested information for each applicant. For guidance on using different methods of accounting for each trade or business, see section 446(d).

An applicant may include each member of a consolidated group, each wholly owned partnership within a consolidated group, each separate and distinct trade or business of each member of a consolidated group or other entity (even if the change is for all of a member's or other entity's trades or businesses), and each eligible CFC or 10/50 corporation filing a single Form 3115 requesting the identical accounting method change. Also see *Who Must File*, earlier.

Lines 16a–c. For non-automatic changes, the applicant is required to provide a full explanation of the legal basis to support

-7-

the proposed method, including all authorities supporting the proposed method, and a discussion of all contrary authorities. For further details on what is to be included, see Rev. Proc. 2019-1, sections 7.01(9) (statement of supporting authorities), 9.03(1) (facts and other information), 9.03(2) (statement of contrary authorities), 9.03(4) (analysis of material facts), and 9.03(7) (statement identifying pending legislation).

For the following automatic method changes, the applicant is only required to complete lines 16a–b, unless the information on lines 16a–b is otherwise provided in the applicable Form 3115 Schedules A–E: DCNs 6, 7, 28, 51, 54, 55, 64, 65, 82, 94, 108, 111, 114, 127, 194, 200 (only for changes listed in sections 6.12(3)(a)(ix), 6.12(3)(a)(x), and 6.12(3)(b)(viii) in the List of Automatic Changes), 205 (only for changes listed in sections 6.13(3)(h) and 6.13(3)(j) in the List of Automatic Changes), 206 (only for changes listed in sections 6.14(3)(a), 6.14(3)(h), and 6.14(3)(j) in the List of Automatic Changes), 207 (only for changes listed in sections 6.15(3)(a) and 6.15(3)(d) in the List of Automatic Changes), 211, and 218. Line 16c does not need to be completed for applicants filing automatic method changes. For further details on what is to be included, see Rev. Proc. 2019-1, sections 7.01(9) (statement of supporting authorities), 9.03(1) (facts and other information), and 9.03(4) (analysis of material facts).

If the automatic DCN is not specifically listed in the paragraph above, skip lines 16a–c.

Line 17. Insurance companies also must attach a statement indicating whether the proposed method of accounting will be used for annual statement accounting purposes.

Line 18. For details on requesting and scheduling a conference, see sections 9.04(4) and 10 of Rev. Proc. 2019-1.

Lines 19a and 19b. For the calculation of gross receipts for an overall accounting method change request, whether an applicant qualifies as a small business taxpayer for purposes of applying sections 263A and 471, or whether an applicant qualifies as an eligible small business under section 474(c), see section 448(c) and Regulations section 1.448-1T(f)(2)(iv). For tax years beginning before January 1, 2018, the section 448(c) gross receipts test is $5 million or less, and the calculation of gross receipts in determining whether the applicant is a small reseller for purposes of section 263A is described in Regulations section 1.263A-3(b).

For the calculation of gross receipts for determining whether the applicant has an exempt construction contract under Regulations section 1.460-3(b), for contracts entered into after December 31, 2017, in tax years ending after December 31, 2017, see section 448(c) and Temporary Regulations section 1.448-1T(f)(2)(iv). For the calculation of gross receipts in determining whether the applicant has an exempt construction contract, for contracts entered into before January 1, 2018, see Regulations section 1.460-3(b)(3).

Part III—Information for Non-Automatic Change Request

Non-automatic change—scope and eligibility rules. An applicant may not use the non-automatic change procedures if any of the following eligibility limitations apply at the time Form 3115 is filed with the IRS National Office.

1. The change in accounting method is required to be made according to a published automatic change procedure, such as Rev. Proc. 2018-31.

2. The requested year of change is the final year of the trade or business, unless (A) the change is a result of a transaction to which section 381(a) applies, or (B) the applicant demonstrates to the satisfaction of the IRS National Office compelling circumstances, or that it is in the interest of sound tax administration for the applicant to change in its final year.

Line 20. If you answered "Yes," attach an explanation describing why the applicant is not eligible to file a request under the automatic change procedures.

Line 21. Attach true copies of all contracts, agreements, and other documents directly related to the proposed change in method of accounting. See section 9.03(3) of Rev. Proc. 2019-1.

Line 22. Include a statement explaining the reason for the proposed change. See section 7.01(1)(d) and 9.03(1) of Rev. Proc. 2019-1.

Line 23. If you answered "No" to line 23, a common parent requesting a change in method of accounting on behalf of a member of the consolidated group must attach a statement explaining the method of accounting used by each member of the consolidated group for the particular item that is the subject of the method change request. See section 6.02(5) of Rev. Proc. 2015-13.

Lines 24a and 24b. For non-automatic change requests, you must pay a user fee for each applicant. Where the filer is not an applicant, a fee is not required for the filer. See section 15 and Appendix A of Rev. Proc. 2019-1 for information regarding user fees, including reduced user fees and user fees for additional applicants filing identical changes in methods of accounting.

Pay the user fees through www.pay.gov.

Note. Filers filing under the automatic change procedures do not pay a user fee.

Example 1. Filer is the common parent of a consolidated group of corporations. Filer files a single Form 3115 on behalf of itself and two other members of the consolidated group for an identical change in method of accounting. There are three applicants (Filer and the two other members of the consolidated group). Therefore, for a non-automatic change request, all three applicants are required to pay a user fee. The filer applicant must submit the regular user fee under section (A)(3)(b)(i) of Appendix A of Rev. Proc. 2019-1 (or a reduced fee per section (A)(4) of Appendix A of Rev. Proc. 2019-1, if applicable), and the two other applicants qualify for the reduced user fee under section (A)(5)(b) of Appendix A of Rev. Proc. 2019-1.

Example 2. Filer is the common parent of a consolidated group of corporations. Filer is filing a single Form 3115 on behalf of two other members of the consolidated group for an identical change in method of accounting. There are two applicants on Form 3115 (the two members of the consolidated group). Filer is not changing its method of accounting and, therefore, does not pay a fee on account of itself. For a non-automatic change request, both applicants are required to pay a user fee. One applicant must submit the regular user fee under section (A)(3)(b)(i) of Appendix A of Rev. Proc. 2019-1 (or a reduced fee per section (A)(4) of Appendix A of Rev. Proc. 2019-1, if applicable), and the other applicant qualifies for the reduced user fee under section (A)(5)(b) of Appendix A of Rev. Proc. 2019-1.

Example 3. Filer, a single taxpayer, files Form 3115 on behalf of its three separate and distinct trades or businesses. The request is for an identical change in method of accounting. Notwithstanding that Filer is a single taxpayer, there are three applicants on Form 3115. For a non-automatic change request, all three applicants are required to pay a user fee. One applicant must submit the regular user fee under section (A)(3)(b)(i) of Appendix A of Rev. Proc. 2019-1 (or a reduced fee per section (A)(4) of Appendix A of Rev. Proc. 2019-1, if applicable), and the other two applicants qualify for the reduced user fee under section (A)(5)(b) of Appendix A of Rev. Proc. 2019-1.

Part IV—Section 481(a) Adjustment

Line 25. Ordinarily, an adjustment under section 481(a) is required for changes in method of accounting. The section 481(a) adjustment period generally is 1 tax year (year of change) for a negative section 481(a) adjustment and 4 tax years (year of change and next 3 tax years) for a positive section 481(a) adjustment. However, when an applicant is under examination, the section 481(a) adjustment period is 2 tax years (year of change and next tax year) for a positive section 481(a) adjustment for a change in method of accounting requested unless one of the following categories described in line 7b applies: 3-month window, 120-day window period, method not before the director, or CAP.

Also, for certain changes in method of accounting, the applicant must make the change on a cut-off basis or modified cut-off basis. See, for example, Regulations section 1.446-1(e)(2)(ii)*(d)(5)(iii)*. In those cases, there is no section 481(a) adjustment. Under a cut-off basis, only the items arising on or after the beginning of the year of change are accounted for under the new method of accounting. Any items arising before the year of change continue to be accounted for under the applicant's former method of accounting.

If multiple items are being changed on one Form 3115 and at least one item is changed on a cut-off basis or modified cut-off basis and another item is changed with a section 481(a) adjustment, check both "Yes" and "No" and attach a statement identifying which item(s) are being made on a cut-off basis or modified cut-off basis.

An eligible terminated S corporation (as defined in section 481(d)(2)) that is required to change an accounting method as a result of a revocation of its S corporation election must take into account the resulting positive or negative section 481(a) adjustment ratably during the 6-year period beginning with the year of change. In addition, an eligible terminated S corporation that is permitted to continue to use the cash method after the revocation of its S corporation election and that changes to an overall accrual method for the C corporation's first tax year after such revocation may take into account the resulting positive or negative adjustment required by section 481(a)(2) ratably during the 6-year period beginning with the year of change. See Rev. Proc. 2018-44, 2018-37 I.R.B. 426. Section 481(d)(2) defines an eligible terminated S corporation as any C corporation that: (1) was an S corporation on December 21, 2017; (2) revokes its S corporation election after December 21, 2017, but before December 22, 2019; and (3) has the same owners of stock in identical proportions on December 22, 2017, and the revocation date.

If the accounting method change is an automatic change in functional currency under section 985 (see section 29.01 of Rev. Proc. 2018-31), the adjustments required under Regulations section 1.985-5 must be made on the last day of the tax year ending before the year of change. Any gain or loss that must be recognized under Regulations section 1.985-5 is included in income or earning and profits on the last day of the tax year ending before the year of change, and is not subject to section 481. Attach a statement showing the adjustment required under Regulations section 1.985-5. The statement should include the amount of the adjustment required pursuant to Regulations section 1.985-5, a summary of the computation of such adjustment, and an explanation of any other adjustments required by Regulations section 1.985-5.

Line 26. In computing the net section 481(a) adjustment, an applicant must take into account all relevant accounts. For some changes (for example, a change that affects multiple accounts), the section 481(a) adjustment is a net section 481(a) adjustment. See *Example 2*, below, and the example in Schedule A, Part I, line 2h, later.

Attach a statement showing the (net) section 481(a) adjustment for each change in method of accounting for each applicant included in Form 3115. Include a summary of how the (net) section 481(a) adjustment was computed and an explanation of the methodology used to determine it. The summary of computation and explanation must be sufficient to demonstrate that the (net) section 481(a) adjustment is computed correctly. If the applicant is a CFC or 10/50 corporation, or a trade or business of a CFC or 10/50 corporation, and if its functional currency is not the U.S. dollar, state the (net) section 481(a) adjustment in that functional currency. This statement may be combined with the information requested on the fourth line on page 1 (list of applicants and their identification numbers) and on line 24 (user fee).

Example 1. Under its present method, XYZ Corporation is deducting certain costs that are required to be capitalized into inventory under section 263A. XYZ Corporation is proposing to change its method of accounting to properly capitalize such costs. The computation of the section 481(a) adjustment with respect to the change in method of accounting is demonstrated as follows.

Beginning inventory for year of change under proposed method	$120,000
Beginning inventory for year of change under present method	$100,000
Section 481(a) adjustment	**+$20,000**

Example 2. WXY Corporation, a calendar year taxpayer, is a producer and capitalizes costs that are required to be capitalized into inventory under section 263A. Each February, WXY Corporation pays a salary bonus to each employee who remains in its employment as of January 31 for the employee's services provided in the prior calendar year. Under its present method, WXY Corporation treats these salary bonuses as incurred in the tax year the employee provides the related services. For 2019, WXY Corporation proposes to change its method of accounting to treat salary bonuses as incurred in the tax year in which all events have occurred that establish the fact of the liability to pay the salary bonuses and the amount of the liability can be determined with reasonable accuracy, pursuant to section 20.01(2) of Rev. Proc. 2018-31. The computation of WXY Corporation's net section 481(a) adjustment for the change in method of accounting for salary bonuses is demonstrated as follows.

Salary bonuses treated as incurred under the present method, but not incurred under the proposed method		$40,000
Beginning inventory as of Jan. 1, 2019, with capitalized salary bonuses computed under the present method	$100,000	
Beginning inventory as of Jan. 1, 2019, with capitalized salary bonuses, computed under the proposed method	$92,000	
Decrease in beginning inventory as of Jan. 1, 2019		($8,000)
Net section 481(a) adjustment		**+$32,000**

Line 27. An applicant may elect a 1-year section 481(a) adjustment period for a positive section 481(a) adjustment that is less than $50,000. See section 7.03(3)(c) of Rev. Proc. 2015-13. An applicant also may elect a 1-year section 481(a) adjustment period for all positive section 481(a) adjustments for the year of

change if an eligible acquisition transaction occurs during the year of change or in the subsequent tax year on or before the due date for filing the applicant's federal tax return for the year of change. For more details about the eligible acquisition transaction election, see section 7.03(3)(d) of Rev. Proc. 2015-13.

Line 28. If "Yes," explain the nature and amount of the section 481 adjustment attributable to the intercompany transaction(s).

Schedule A—Change in Overall Method of Accounting

Part I—Change in Overall Method

All applicants filing to change their overall method of accounting must complete Schedule A, Part I, including applicants filing under DCNs 32, 33, 34, 122, 123, 126, 127, 128 and 233 in the List of Automatic Changes.

Lines 2a–g. Enter the amounts requested on lines 2a through 2g, even though the calculation of some amounts may not have been required in determining taxable income due to the applicant's present method of accounting.

Note. Do not include amounts that are not attributable to the change in method of accounting, such as amounts that correct a math or posting error or errors in calculating tax liability. In addition, for a bank changing to an overall cash/hybrid method of accounting, do not include any amounts attributable to a special method of accounting. See DCN 127.

Line 2b. Enter amounts received or reported as income in a prior year that were not earned as of the beginning of the year of change. For example, an advance payment received in a prior year for goods that were not delivered by the beginning of the year of change may be reported in the subsequent year if the applicant qualifies under Rev. Proc. 2004-34, 2004-1 C.B. 991. If any amounts entered on line 2b are for advance payments, complete Schedule B. See Notice 2018-35, 2018-18 I.R.B. 520.

Line 2h. Enter the net amount, which is the net section 481(a) adjustment, on line 2h. Also, enter the net section 481(a) adjustment on Part IV, line 26. See the instructions for Part IV, line 26, earlier.

The following example illustrates how an applicant calculates the section 481(a) adjustment when changing to an accrual method, a nonaccrual-experience method, and the recurring item exception.

Example. ABC Corporation, a calendar year taxpayer using the cash method of accounting, has the following items of unreported income and expense on December 31, 2018.

Accrued income	$250,000
Uncollectible amounts based on the nonaccrual-experience method	50,000
Accrued amounts properly deductible (economic performance has occurred)	75,000
Expenses eligible for recurring item exception	5,000

ABC Corporation changes to an overall accrual method, a nonaccrual-experience method, and the recurring item exception for calendar year 2019. The section 481(a) adjustment is calculated as of January 1, 2019, as follows.

Accrued income (line 2a)	$250,000	
Less:		
Uncollectible amount	(50,000)	
Net income accrued but not received		$200,000
Less:		
Accrued expenses (line 2c)	(75,000)	
Expenses deducted as recurring item (line 2g)	(5,000)	
Total expenses accrued but not paid		(80,000)
Section 481(a) adjustment		**+$120,000**

Line 3. Check "Yes" if the applicant is requesting to use the recurring item exception (section 461(h)(3)). The section 481(a) adjustment must include the amount of the additional deduction that results from using the recurring item exception.

Line 5. This question applies to an applicant requesting a change to the overall cash method under section 15.18 of Rev. Proc. 2018-31 (DCN 233) for a tax year beginning after December 31, 2017. See section 15.18(5)(a) of Rev. Proc. 2018-31 to determine whether an applicant qualifies as a small business taxpayer. See also Rev. Proc. 2018-40, 2018-34 I.R.B. 320.

Part II—Change to the Cash Method For Non-Automatic Request

Limits on cash method use. Except as provided below, C corporations and partnerships with a C corporation as a partner may not use the cash method of accounting. Tax shelters, also, are precluded from using the cash method. For this purpose, a trust subject to tax on unrelated business income under section 511(b) is treated as a C corporation with respect to its unrelated trade or business activities.

The limit on the use of the cash method under section 448 does not apply to:

1. Farming businesses as defined in section 448(d)(1).
2. Qualified personal service corporations as defined in section 448(d)(2).
3. For tax years beginning before January 1, 2018, C corporations and partnerships with a C corporation as a partner when the corporation or the partnership has gross receipts of $5 million or less. For tax years beginning after December 31, 2017, C corporations and partnerships with a C corporation as a partner when the corporation or the partnership has gross receipts of $25 million or less (adjusted for inflation). See section 448(c) to determine if the applicant qualifies for this exception.

For farming corporations and partnerships with a C corporation as a partner, see section 447 for limits on the use of the cash method.

Use of the cash method is also limited for a taxpayer that is required to maintain an inventory because the production, purchase, or sale of merchandise is an income-producing factor. However, for tax years beginning after December 31, 2017, see sections 448(c) and 471(c) and sections 15.18 (DCN 233) and 22.19 of Rev. Proc. 2018-31 (DCN 235) for an exception to this requirement for small business taxpayers with average annual gross receipts of $25 million or less (adjusted for inflation).

-10-

Schedule B—Change to the Deferral Method for Advance Payments

In general, advance payments must be included in gross income in the tax year of receipt for federal income tax purposes. However, an applicant may defer the inclusion in income of certain advance payments, as defined in section 4.01 of Rev. Proc. 2004-34, 2004-1 C.B. 991, as modified and clarified by Rev. Proc. 2011-18, 2011-5 I.R.B. 443, and Rev. Proc. 2013-29, 2013-33 I.R.B. 141.

Line 1. Rev. Proc. 2004-34 allows applicants using an accrual method to defer the inclusion in income of certain advance payments to the next tax year. See Notice 2018-35, 2018-18 I.R.B. 520. Applicants requesting to change to the Deferral Method for allocable payments described in section 5.02(4)(a) of Rev. Proc. 2004-34 (other than allocable payments described in section 5.02(4)(c) of Rev. Proc. 2004-34) or for payments for which a method under section 5.02(3)(b)(i) or (iii) of Rev. Proc. 2004-34 applies, must file under the non-automatic change procedures of Rev. Proc. 2015-13. All other applicants generally must file under the automatic change procedures of Rev. Proc. 2015-13.

Schedule C—Changes Within the LIFO Inventory Method

Use this schedule to request a change from one LIFO inventory method or submethod to another LIFO inventory method or submethod. All applicants changing within the LIFO inventory method or submethods must complete Part I. Complete Part II only if applicable.

Part I—General LIFO Information

Line 6. Applicants changing to the IPIC method must use this method for all LIFO inventories. This requirement includes applicants requesting designated automatic accounting method change numbers 61 or 62 in the List of DCNs.

Schedule D—Change in the Treatment of Long-Term Contracts Under Section 460, Inventories, or Other Section 263A Assets

Part I—Change in Reporting Income From Long-Term Contracts

Line 2a. Under section 460(f), the term "long-term contract" means any contract for the manufacture, building, installation, or construction of property that is not completed in the tax year in which it is entered into. However, a manufacturing contract will not qualify as long-term unless the contract involves the manufacture of (a) a unique item not normally included in finished goods inventory or (b) any item that normally requires more than 12 calendar months to complete.

Long-term contracts that do not meet the exceptions under section 460(e) must be accounted for using the percentage of completion method. See section 460 and the related regulations.

Line 2b. To qualify for the contract exceptions under section 460(e), the contract must be:

1. A home construction contract as defined in section 460(e)(5)(A), or

2. Any other construction contract entered into by the applicant if, at the time the contract is entered into, it is expected to be completed within 2 years and the applicant's average annual gross receipts for the 3-year period preceding the tax year the contract was entered into do not exceed the $25 million threshold, adjusted for inflation, set forth in section 448(c).

In the case of contracts entered into before January 1, 2018, a $10 million threshold applies.

Line 2d. Under the simplified cost-to-cost method, only certain costs are used in determining both (a) costs allocated to the contract and incurred before the close of the tax year and (b) estimated contract costs. These costs are: (1) direct material costs; (2) direct labor costs; and (3) allowable deductions for depreciation, amortization, and cost recovery allowances on equipment and facilities directly used to construct or produce the subject matter of the long-term contract. See Regulations section 1.460-5(c).

Part II—Change in Valuing Inventories Including Cost Allocation Changes

If the applicant is currently using a LIFO inventory method or submethod and is changing to another LIFO inventory method or submethod, Schedule D, Part II, is not applicable. Use Schedule C, Changes Within the LIFO Inventory Method.

Line 3. If an applicant is subject to, but not in compliance with, section 263A, generally on the same Form 3115 the applicant must first comply with section 263A before changing an inventory valuation method. The applicant must complete Schedule D, Part III, Method of Cost Allocation. For exceptions, see Regulations section 1.263A-7(b)(2).

Line 5a. If the applicant properly elected the LIFO inventory method but is unable to furnish a copy of Form(s) 970, Application to Use a LIFO Inventory Method, attach the following statement to Form 3115.

"I certify that to the best of my knowledge and belief [name of applicant] properly elected the LIFO inventory method by filing Form 970 with its return for the tax year(s) ended [insert date(s)] and otherwise complied with the provisions of section 472(d) and Regulations section 1.472-3."

Line 5c. Attach the two statements required by section 23.01(5) of Rev. Proc. 2018-31.

Part III—Method of Cost Allocation

Applicants requesting to change their method of accounting for any property (produced or acquired for resale) subject to section 263A or any long-term contracts as described in section 460 must complete this schedule.

If the change is for noninventory property that is subject to section 263A, attach a detailed description of the types of property involved.

There are several methods available for allocating and capitalizing costs under section 263A, and for allocating costs to long-term contracts. A change to or from any of these methods is a change in accounting method that requires IRS consent. Using the applicable regulations and notice listed below, the applicant should verify which methods are presently being used and the proposed methods that will be used before completing Schedule D, Part III. These methods are as follows.

1. Allocating Direct and Indirect Costs

- Specific identification method—Regulations sections 1.263A-1(f)(2) and 1.460-5.
- Burden rate method—Regulations sections 1.263A-1(f)(3)(i) and 1.460-5.
- Standard cost method—Regulations sections 1.263A-1(f)(3)(ii) and 1.460-5.
- Any other reasonable allocation method—Regulations sections 1.263A-1(f)(4) and 1.460-5.

2. Allocating Mixed Service Costs

- Direct reallocation method—Regulations section 1.263A-1(g)(4)(iii)(A).
- Step-allocation method—Regulations section 1.263A-1(g)(4)(iii)(B).
- Simplified service cost method:

  —Using the labor-based allocation ratio—Regulations section 1.263A-1(h)(4).
  —Using the production cost allocation ratio—Regulations section 1.263A-1(h)(5).
- Any other reasonable allocation method—Regulations section 1.263A-1(f)(4).

3. Capitalizing Additional Section 263A Costs

- Simplified production method:

  —Without historic absorption ratio election—Regulations section 1.263A-2(b)(3).
  —With historic absorption ratio election—Regulations section 1.263A-2(b)(4).
- Simplified resale method:

  —Without historic absorption ratio election—Regulations section 1.263A-3(d)(3).
  —With historic absorption ratio election—Regulations section 1.263A-3(d)(4).
- U.S. ratio method—Notice 88-104, 1988-2 C.B. 443.
- Any other reasonable allocation method—Regulations section 1.263A-1(f)(4) (including the methods listed above under *Allocating Direct and Indirect Costs*).

Schedule E—Change in Depreciation or Amortization

All applicants requesting to change their method of accounting for depreciation or amortization must complete Schedule E of Form 3115. Applicants changing their method of accounting for depreciation or amortization under the automatic change procedures should see the depreciation changes in the List of DCNs below.

Do not file Form 3115:

1. To make an election under section 167, 168, 179, 197, or 1400I;
2. To revoke an election made under one of those sections;
3. To make or revoke an election under section 13261(g)(2) or (3) of the Revenue Reconciliation Act of 1993 (relating to section 197 intangibles);
4. To change the placed-in-service date;
5. To change the salvage value (except for a change in salvage value to zero when the salvage value is expressly treated as zero by the Code, the regulations, or other published guidance); or
6. To change a useful life under section 167 (except for a change to or from a useful life, recovery period, or amortization period that is specifically assigned by the Code, the regulations, or other published guidance).

List of DCNs

Summary of Automatic Accounting Method Changes

This list includes regulatory automatic changes, changes provided for in Rev. Proc. 2018-31, and automatic changes provided for in other guidance. These automatic changes may be modified or supplemented with additional automatic changes by subsequently published guidance.

The list provides a brief description of the automatic changes in method of accounting made using Form 3115. A filer/applicant may not rely on the list or the descriptions of accounting method changes in the list as authority for making an accounting method change. A filer/applicant that is within the scope of, and complies with, all the applicable provisions of the published guidance that authorizes each listed change may rely on the applicable published guidance as authority for its automatic accounting method change. If any information in the list conflicts with published guidance, the published guidance applies. Each automatic method change described in Rev. Proc. 2018-31, as modified, contains a contact person you may call if you need additional information concerning the change (not a toll-free number).

Each item in the list below:
- Designates an automatic accounting method change number for each change for entry on line 1a of Form 3115.
- Briefly describes the accounting method change and its primary Code section(s).
- Indicates in some cases which schedules of Form 3115 to complete.
- Provides a reference to the basic published guidance (for example, revenue procedure) that provides for the automatic change, which filers should review prior to completing Part I, Information for Automatic Change Request, on page 1 of Form 3115.

Note. Certain retired or obsolete numbers in the List of DCNs have not been replaced in order to maintain continuity for the active DCNs.

In the event the underlying authority for any of the DCNs becomes obsolete or is superseded, then a change can no longer be made under such DCN.

List of DCNs	
No.	**Change**
1	**Commodity Credit Corporation loans (section 77)**—for loans received from the Commodity Credit Corporation, **from** including the loan amount in gross income for the tax year in which the loan is received **to** treating the loan amount as a loan. See section 2.01 of Rev. Proc. 2018-31. **Note.** This change is implemented on a cut-off basis.
2	**Advances made by a lawyer on behalf of clients (section 162)—from** treating advances of money to or on behalf of their clients for litigation or other client expenses as deductible expenses **to** treating those advances as a loan. See section 3.01 of Rev. Proc. 2018-31.
3	**ISO 9000 costs (section 162)—to** treating the costs as deductible, except to the extent they result in the creation or acquisition of an asset having a useful life substantially beyond the tax year. See section 3.02 of Rev. Proc. 2018-31.
4	**Restaurant smallwares costs (section 162)—to** the smallwares method described in Rev. Proc. 2002-12, 2002-1 C.B. 374 (that is, as materials and supplies that are not incidental under Regulations section 1.162-3). See section 3.03 of Rev. Proc. 2018-31.
5	**Bad debts (section 166)**—for an applicant other than a bank, **from** accounting for bad debts using a reserve or other improper method **to** a specific charge-off method that complies with section 166. See section 4.01 of Rev. Proc. 2018-31.
6	**Bad debt conformity for banks (section 166)**—for banks other than new banks, **to** the method that conforms to Regulations section 1.166-2(d)(3) for the first time the bank makes this change, or **to** involuntarily revoke this method. This change does not fall under the procedures of Rev. Proc. 2018-31. Instead, see Regulations section 1.166-2(d)(3). **Note.** This change is implemented on a cut-off basis and generally with audit protection, but with some conditions or limitations.
7	**Depreciation or amortization (impermissible to permissible) (sections 56, 167, 168, 197, 280F, 1400I, 1400L, 1400N, and former section 168)—from** an impermissible method **to** a permissible method for changes allowed under Regulations section 1.446-1(e)(2)(ii)*(d)*, and for depreciable property owned at the beginning of the year of change. Complete Schedule E of Form 3115. An applicant changing its method of accounting for depreciation because of a change described in designated automatic accounting method change number 10 (sale or lease transactions) must file Form 3115 according to the designated change number 10. Additionally, a qualified small taxpayer qualifies for a reduced Form 3115 filing requirement. See section 6.01 of Rev. Proc. 2018-31.
8	**Depreciation (permissible to permissible) (sections 56 and 167)—from** a permissible method **to** another permissible method listed in section 6.02 of Rev. Proc. 2018-31. Complete Schedule E of Form 3115. Change is implemented on a modified cut-off basis. An applicant making a change from a permissible to another permissible method of depreciating MACRS property must file Form 3115 according to designated change number 200. Additionally, a qualified small taxpayer qualifies for a reduced Form 3115 filing requirement. See section 6.02 of Rev. Proc. 2018-31.
10	**Sale, lease, or financing transactions (sections 61, 162, 167, 168, and 1012)—from** improperly treating property as sold, leased, or financed **to** a permissible method as described in section 6.03 of Rev. Proc. 2018-31. See section 6.03 of Rev. Proc. 2018-31. **Note.** This change is implemented on a cut-off basis and does not receive audit protection.
11	**Obsolete**. See change number 7.
12	**Obsolete**. See change number 7.
13	**Obsolete**. See change number 7.
14	**Obsolete**. See change number 7.
15	**Obsolete**. See change number 210.
16	**Amortizable bond premium (section 171)—from** amortizing bond premium **to** not amortizing the premium (revoking the section 171(c) election). See section 5.01 of Rev. Proc. 2018-31. **Note.** This change is implemented on a cut-off basis and generally also is made with audit protection, but with conditions or limitations.
17	**Research and experimental expenditures (section 174)—from** the capitalization method **to** another permissible method, **from** the expense method **to** another permissible method, **from** the deferred expense method **to** another permissible method, **from** the current period of amortization **to** a different period of amortization under the deferred expense method, or **from** treating research and experimental expenditures under any provision of the Internal Revenue Code other than section 174 **to** treating such expenditures under section 174. See section 7.01 of Rev. Proc. 2018-31. **Note.** This change is implemented on a cut-off basis and does not receive audit protection.
18	**Computer software expenditures (sections 162 and 167)**—for costs of developed, acquired, leased, or licensed computer software, **to** deductible expenses or capital expenditures and amortization (for developed software), **to** capital expenditures and depreciation or amortization (for acquired computer software), or **to** deductible expenses under Regulations section 1.162-11 (for leased or licensed computer software). Complete Schedule E of Form 3115 for changes relating to acquired computer software or developed computer software if the change is to capital expenditures and amortization. See section 9.01 of Rev. Proc. 2018-31.

List of DCNs	
No.	**Change**
19	**Package design costs (section 263)—to** the capitalization method, **to** the design-by-design capitalization and 60-month amortization method, or **to** the pool-of-cost capitalization and 48-month amortization method. See section 11.01 of Rev. Proc. 2018-31.
20	**Line pack gas or cushion gas costs (section 263)—to** treating the costs as capital expenditures, the costs of recoverable amounts as not depreciable, and the costs of unrecoverable amounts as depreciable. A taxpayer that changes its method for the costs of unrecoverable amounts also must change to a permissible method of depreciation for those costs. Complete Schedule E of Form 3115 for changes relating to the costs of unrecoverable amounts. See section 11.02 of Rev. Proc. 2018-31.
21	**Removal costs (section 263)**—for certain costs incurred in the retirement and removal of depreciable assets, **to** a method that conforms with Rev. Rul. 2000-7, 2000-1 C.B. 712 or for removal costs in disposal of a depreciable asset, including a partial disposition, as described under Regulations section 1.263(a)-3(g)(2)(i). Additionally, a qualified small taxpayer qualifies for a reduced Form 3115 filing requirement. See section 11.03 of Rev. Proc. 2018-31.
22	**Certain uniform capitalization methods used by resellers and reseller-producers (section 263A)**—for qualifying applicants, **to** a qualifying method or methods. Complete Schedule D, Parts II and III, of Form 3115. See section 12.01 of Rev. Proc. 2018-31, as modified by Rev. Proc. 2018-40 and Rev. Proc. 2018-56.
23	**Certain uniform capitalization methods used by producers and reseller-producers (section 263A)**—for qualifying applicants, **to** a qualifying method or methods. Complete Schedule D, Parts II and III, of Form 3115. See section 12.02 of Rev. Proc. 2018-31, as modified by Rev. Proc. 2018-56.
24	**Obsolete**. See change number 17.
25	**Impact fees (section 263A)**—for impact fees incurred in connection with the new construction or expansion of a residential building, **to** treating the costs as capital expenditures allocable to the building. Complete Schedule E of Form 3115 if the building is depreciable. See section 12.03 of Rev. Proc. 2018-31.
26	**Related party transactions (section 267)**—for losses, expenses, and qualified stated interest incurred in transactions between related parties, **to** disallowing or deferring certain deductions attributable to such transactions in accordance with section 267. See section 13.01 of Rev. Proc. 2018-31.
28	**Bonus or vacation pay deferred compensation (section 404)**—for bonuses that are deferred compensation, **from** treating as deductible or capitalizable when accrued, **to** treating as deductible or capitalizable in the year in which includible in the employee's income, and for vacation pay that is deferred compensation, **from** treating as deductible or capitalizable when accrued **to** treating as deductible or capitalizable in the year in which paid to the employee. See section 14.01 of Rev. Proc. 2018-31.
29	**Grace period contributions (section 404)**—for contributions made to a section 401(k) qualified cash or deferred arrangement or matching contributions under section 401(m), **from** treating contributions made after the end of the tax year but before the due date of the tax return as being on account of the tax year without regard to when the underlying compensation is earned **to** treating such contributions as not being on account of the tax year if they are attributable to compensation earned after the end of that tax year. See section 14.02 of Rev. Proc. 2018-31.
31	**Multi-year insurance policies for multi-year service warranty contracts (section 446)**—for a manufacturer, wholesaler, or retailer of motor vehicles or other durable consumer goods accounting for multi-year insurance policies for multi-year service warranty contracts, **to** capitalizing and amortizing the costs. See section 15.02 of Rev. Proc. 2018-31.
32	**Overall cash method ($1 million) (section 446)**—for qualifying applicants changing **to** the overall cash method. Complete Schedule A, Part I, of Form 3115. Also, complete Schedule D, Parts II and III, as applicable. See section 15.03 of Rev. Proc. 2018-31. **Note.** This change does not apply for any tax year beginning after December 31, 2017.
33	**Overall cash method ($10 million) (section 446)**—for qualifying applicants changing to the overall cash method. Complete Schedule A, Part I, of Form 3115. Also, complete Schedule D, Parts II and III, as applicable. See section 15.03 of Rev. Proc. 2018-31. **Note.** This change does not apply for any tax year beginning after December 31, 2017.
34	**First section 448 year (section 448)**—for an applicant changing **from** the cash method for its first section 448 year that makes the change using the regulation provision in lieu of Rev. Proc. 2015-13. Complete Schedule A, Part I, of Form 3115. Also, complete Schedule D, Parts II and III, as applicable, of Form 3115. This change does not fall under the procedures of Rev. Proc. 2015-13. Instead, see Regulations section 1.448-1. (See automatic method change 123 for taxpayers making the change under Rev. Proc. 2015-13).

-14-

List of DCNs	
No.	**Change**
35	**Nonaccrual-experience method (section 448)**—for an applicant changing: **to** a safe harbor method provided in Regulations section 1.448-2(f)(1) (the revenue-based moving average method), (f)(2) (the actual experience method), (f)(3) (the modified Black Motor method), (f)(4) (the modified moving average method), or (f)(5) (the alternative nonaccrual-experience method); **to** a periodic system; **from** an NAE method to a specific charge-off method; **from** a sub-method of its current NAE method provided in Regulations section 1.448-2 regarding applicable periods to another sub-method regarding applicable periods that is permitted under Regulations section 1.448-2, other than a change to exclude tax years from an applicable period under Regulations section 1.448-2(d)(6); **from** a sub-method of its current NAE method provided in Regulations section 1.448-2 regarding tracing of recoveries **to** another sub-method regarding tracing of recoveries permitted under Regulations section 1.448-2(f)(2)(iii); or, **to** the NAE book safe harbor method described in section 5.01 of Rev. Proc. 2011-46, 2011-42 I.R.B. 518. **Note**. An applicant using the NAE book safe harbor method that wants to make certain changes within the NAE book safe harbor method (as described in sections 5.02 and 5.03 of Rev. Proc. 2011-46) must attach a statement to its federal income tax return in lieu of filing a Form 3115. See Rev. Proc. 2011-46, section 15.04 of Rev. Proc. 2018-31, and Rev. Proc. 2006-56, 2006-2 C.B. 1169. **Note**. Certain changes are made on a cut-off basis.
36	**Interest accrual on non-performing loans (section 451)**—for an accrual method bank accounting for qualified stated interest on non-performing loans, **to** the method whereby interest is accrued until either the loan is worthless under section 166 and is charged off as a bad debt or the interest is determined to be uncollectible. See section 16.01 of Rev. Proc. 2018-31.
37	**Advance rentals (section 451)**—for advance rentals other than advance rentals subject to section 467, **to** inclusion in gross income in the tax year received. See section 16.02 of Rev. Proc. 2018-31.
38	**State or local income or franchise tax refunds (section 451)**—for an accrual method applicant with state or local income or franchise tax refunds, **to** accrue these items in the tax year the applicant receives payments or notice of approval of its refund claim (whichever is earlier), according to Rev. Rul. 2003-3, 2003-1 C.B. 252. See section 16.03 of Rev. Proc. 2018-31.
39	**Capital cost reduction (CCR) payments (section 451)**—for CCR payments (as defined in Rev. Proc. 2002-36, 2002-1 C.B. 993) made by vehicle lessees, **to** the method that excludes these payments from the applicant's gross income and from the applicant's bases in the purchased vehicles. See section 16.04 of Rev. Proc. 2018-31.
41	**Obsolete.**
42	**Timing of incurring employee medical benefits liabilities (section 461)**—for an applicant with an obligation to pay an employee's medical expenses (including medical expenses for retirees and employees who filed claims under a workers' compensation act) that is neither insured nor paid from a welfare benefit fund, **to** treatment as a liability incurred in the tax year in which the applicant's employee files the claim with the applicant; or, if the applicant has a liability to pay a third party for medical services to its employees, **to** treatment as a liability as incurred in the tax year in which the services are provided. See section 20.01(1) of Rev. Proc. 2018-31.
43	**Timing of incurring real property taxes, personal property taxes, state income taxes, and state franchise taxes (section 461)**—for a qualifying applicant, **to** treating these taxes as incurred in the tax year in which the taxes are paid, or **to** account for these taxes under the recurring item exception to the economic performance rules, or **to** revoke the ratable accrual election under section 461(c). See section 20.02 of Rev. Proc. 2018-31.
44	**Timing of incurring workers' compensation act, tort, breach of contract, or violation of law liabilities (section 461)**—for a qualifying applicant accounting for self-insured liabilities arising under any workers' compensation act or out of any tort, breach of contract, or violation of law, **to** treating the liability as incurred in the tax year in which (a) all the events have occurred establishing the fact of the liability, (b) the amount of the liability can be determined with reasonable accuracy, and (c) payment is made to the person to which the liability is owed. See section 20.03 of Rev. Proc. 2018-31.
45	**Timing of incurring certain payroll tax liabilities (section 461)**—for FICA and FUTA taxes, state unemployment taxes, and railroad retirement taxes, to the method under which the applicant may deduct in Year 1 its otherwise deductible FICA and FUTA taxes, state unemployment taxes, and railroad retirement taxes imposed with respect to year-end wages properly accrued in Year 1, but paid in Year 2, if the requirements of the recurring item exception are met; or, for state unemployment taxes and railroad retirement taxes, **to** the method stated above where the applicant already uses that method of accounting for FICA and FUTA taxes. See section 20.04 of Rev. Proc. 2018-31.
46	**Cooperative advertising (section 461)—to** incurring a liability in the tax year in which these services are performed, provided the manufacturer is able to reasonably estimate this liability even though the retailer does not submit the required claim form until the following year. See section 20.05 of Rev. Proc. 2018-31.
47	**Distributor commissions (section 263)—from** deducting distributor commissions **to** capitalizing and amortizing distributor commissions using the distribution fee period method, the 5-year method, or the useful life method. This change is implemented on a cut-off basis and applies only to distributor commissions paid or incurred on or after the beginning of the year of change. See section 11.04 of Rev. Proc. 2018-31. Complete Schedule E of Form 3115.

List of DCNs	
No.	**Change**
48	**Cash discounts (section 471)**—for cash discounts granted for timely payment, when such discounts approximate a fair interest rate, **from** a method of consistently including the price of the goods before discount in the cost of the goods and including in gross income any discounts taken **to** a method of reducing the cost of the goods by the cash discounts and deducting as an expense any discounts not taken, or vice versa. Complete Schedule D, Parts II and III, of Form 3115, as applicable. See section 22.01 of Rev. Proc. 2018-31.
49	**Estimating inventory shrinkage (section 471)**—**from** the present method of estimating inventory shrinkage in computing ending inventory **to** the retail safe harbor method in section 4 of Rev. Proc. 98-29, 1998-1 C.B. 857, or **to** a method other than the retail safe harbor method, provided (a) the applicant's present method of accounting does not estimate inventory shrinkage and (b) the applicant's new method of accounting (that estimates inventory shrinkage) clearly reflects income under section 446(b). Complete Schedule D, Parts II and III, of Form 3115, as applicable. See section 22.02 of Rev. Proc. 2018-31.
50	**Small taxpayer ($1 million) inventory exception (section 471)**—for a qualifying applicant with average annual gross receipts of $1,000,000 or less (see Rev. Proc. 2001-10, 2001-1 C.B. 272), **from** the present method of accounting for inventoriable items (including, if applicable, the method of capitalizing costs under section 263A) **to** treating inventoriable items in the same manner as materials and supplies that are not incidental under Regulations section 1.162-3. Complete Schedule A, Part I, and Schedule D, Parts II and III, of Form 3115, as applicable. See section 22.03 of Rev. Proc. 2018-31. **Note.** This change does not apply for any tax year beginning after December 31, 2017.
51	**Small taxpayer ($10 million) inventory exception (section 471)**—for a qualifying applicant with average annual gross receipts of $10,000,000 or less (see Rev. Proc. 2002-28, 2002-1 C.B. 815), **from** the present method of accounting for inventoriable items (including, if applicable, the method of capitalizing costs under section 263A) **to** treating inventoriable items in the same manner as materials and supplies that are not incidental under Regulations section 1.162-3. Complete Schedule D, Parts II and III, of Form 3115, as applicable. See section 22.03 of Rev. Proc. 2018-31. **Note**. This change does not apply for any tax year beginning after December 31, 2017.
53	**Qualifying volume-related trade discounts (section 471)**—**to** treating qualifying volume-related trade discounts as a reduction in the cost of merchandise purchased at the time the discount is recognized in accordance with Regulations section 1.471-3(b). Complete Schedule D, Parts II and III, of Form 3115, as applicable. See section 22.04 of Rev. Proc. 2018-31.
54	**Impermissible methods of identification and valuation of inventories (section 471)**—for an applicant changing **from** an impermissible method of identifying or valuing inventories **to** a permissible method of identifying or valuing inventories. Complete Schedule D, Parts II and III, of Form 3115, as applicable. See section 22.05 of Rev. Proc. 2018-31.
55	**Core alternative valuation method for remanufactured and rebuilt motor vehicle parts (section 471)**—for remanufacturers and rebuilders of motor vehicle parts and resellers of remanufactured and rebuilt motor vehicle parts that use the lower of cost or market method to value their inventory of cores, **to** the safe harbor method of accounting (the Core alternative valuation method) to value inventories of cores as provided for in Rev. Proc. 2003-20, 2003-1 C.B. 445. Complete Schedule D, Parts II and III, of Form 3115, as applicable. See section 22.06 of Rev. Proc. 2018-31.
56	**Change from LIFO inventory method (section 472)**—for an applicant changing from the LIFO inventory method for its entire LIFO inventory, or for one or more dollar-value pools within its LIFO inventory, **to** the permitted method as described in section 23.01(1)(b) of Rev. Proc. 2018-31. Complete Schedule D, Parts II and III, of Form 3115, as applicable. See section 23.01 of Rev. Proc. 2018-31.
57	**Determining current-year cost under the LIFO inventory method (section 472)**—for an applicant changing its method of determining current-year cost **to**: (a) the actual cost of the goods most recently purchased or produced (most-recent acquisitions method); (b) the actual cost of the goods purchased or produced during the tax year in the order of acquisition (earliest-acquisitions method); (c) the average unit cost equal to the aggregate actual cost of all the goods purchased or produced throughout the tax year divided by the total number of units so purchased or produced; (d) the specific identification method; or (e) a rolling-average method if the applicant uses that rolling-average method in accordance with Rev. Proc. 2008-43, 2008-30 I.R.B. 186, as modified by Rev. Proc. 2008-52, 2008-2 C.B. 587. Complete Schedule C, Part I, of Form 3115. See section 23.02 of Rev. Proc. 2018-31. **Note**. This change is implemented on a cut-off basis.
58	**Alternative LIFO inventory method (section 472)**—for a qualifying applicant that sells new automobiles or new light-duty trucks, **to** the Alternative LIFO method described in Rev. Proc. 97-36, 1997-2 C.B. 450, as modified by Rev. Proc. 2008-23, 2008-1 C.B. 664. Complete Schedule C of Form 3115, as applicable. See section 23.03 of Rev. Proc. 2018-31. **Note**. This change is implemented on a cut-off basis.

List of DCNs	
No.	**Change**
59	**Used vehicle alternative LIFO method (section 472)**—for a qualifying applicant that sells used automobiles and used light-duty trucks, **to** the Used vehicle alternative LIFO method, as described in Rev. Proc. 2001-23, 2001-1 C.B. 784, as modified by Announcement 2004-16, 2004-1 C.B. 668 and Rev. Proc. 2008-23, 2008-1 C.B. 664. Complete Schedule C, Part I, of Form 3115. See section 23.04 of Rev. Proc. 2018-31. **Note.** This change is implemented on a cut-off basis.
60	**Determining the cost of used vehicles purchased or taken as a trade-in (section 472)**—for a qualifying applicant, **to** a method of (a) determining the cost of used vehicles acquired by trade-in using the average wholesale price listed by a consistently used official used car guide on the date of the trade-in; (b) using a different official used vehicle guide for determining the cost of used vehicles acquired by trade-in; (c) determining the cost of used vehicles purchased for cash using the actual purchase price of the vehicle; or (d) reconstructing the beginning-of-the-year cost of used vehicles purchased for cash using values computed by national auto auction companies based on vehicles purchased for cash, where the national auto auction company selected is consistently used. Complete Schedule C, Part I, of Form 3115. See section 23.05 of Rev. Proc. 2018-31. **Note.** This change is implemented on a cut-off basis.
61	**Change to IPIC inventory method (section 472)**—for a qualifying applicant, **from** a non-inventory price index computation (IPIC) LIFO inventory method **to** the IPIC method in accordance with all relevant provisions of Regulations section 1.472-8(e)(3); or, **from** the IPIC method as described in T.D. 7814, 1982-1 C.B. 84 (the old IPIC method) **to** the IPIC method as described in T.D. 8976, 2002-1 C.B. 421 (the new IPIC method), which includes the following required changes (if applicable): **from** using 80% of the inventory price index (IPI) **to** using 100% of the IPI to determine the base-year cost and dollar-value of a LIFO pool(s); **from** using a weighted arithmetic mean **to** using a weighted harmonic mean to compute an IPI for a dollar-value pool(s); and **from** using a components-of-cost method to define inventory items **to** using a total-product-cost method to define inventory items. Complete Schedule C of Form 3115, as applicable. See section 23.06 of Rev. Proc. 2018-31. **Note.** This change is implemented on a cut-off basis.
62	**Changes within IPIC inventory method (section 472)**—for one or more of the following changes within IPIC: (a) **from** the double-extension IPIC method **to** the link-chain IPIC method, or vice versa; (b) **to** or **from** the 10% method; (c) **to** a pooling method described in Regulations section 1.472-8(b)(4) or Regulations section 1.472-8(c)(2), including a change to begin or discontinue applying one or both of the 5% pooling rules; (d) combine or separate pools as a result of the application of a 5% pooling rule described in Regulations section 1.472-8(b)(4) or Regulations section 1.472-8(c)(2); (e) change the selection of BLS tables **from** Table 3 (Consumer Price Index for All Urban Consumers (CPI-U): U.S. city average, detailed expenditure categories) of the monthly CPI Detailed Report **to** Table 9 (Producer price indexes and percent changes for commodity groupings and individual items, not seasonally adjusted) of the monthly PPI Detailed Report, or vice versa; (f) change the assignment of one or more inventory items to BLS categories under either Table 3 of the monthly CPI Detailed Report or Table 9 of the monthly PPI Detailed Report; (g) change the representative month when necessitated because of a change in tax year or a change in method of determining current-year cost made pursuant to section 23.02 of Rev. Proc. 2018-31; or (h) change from using preliminary BLS price indexes to using final BLS price indexes to compute an inventory price index, or vice versa. Complete Schedule C of Form 3115, as applicable. See section 23.07 of Rev. Proc. 2018-31. **Note.** This change is implemented on a cut-off basis.
63	**Replacement cost method for automobile dealers' parts inventory (sections 471 and 472)—to** the replacement cost method for automobile dealers' parts inventory described in Rev. Proc. 2002-17, 2002-1 C.B. 676. Complete Schedule D, Parts II and III, of Form 3115, as applicable. See section 22.07 of Rev. Proc. 2018-31. **Note.** This change is implemented on a cut-off basis.
64	**Mark-to-market (section 475)**—for accounting for securities or commodities by commodities dealers, securities traders, and commodities traders, **to** the mark-to-market method under section 475(e) or (f). An election statement must be filed earlier than the due date of Form 3115. See Rev. Proc. 99-17, 1999-1 C.B. 503, for rules relating to this statement. See section 24.01 of Rev. Proc. 2018-31.
65	**Dealer status changes (section 475)**—for an applicant electing out of certain exemptions from securities dealer status, **to** the mark-to-market method. This change does not fall under the automatic change procedures of Rev. Proc. 2015-13. Instead, see Rev. Proc. 97-43, 1997-2 C.B. 494. **Note.** This change is implemented on a cut-off basis.
66	**Bank reserves for bad debts (section 585)**—for a bank (as defined in section 581, including a bank for which a qualified subchapter S subsidiary (QSub) election is filed) to change **from** the section 585 reserve method **to** the section 166 specific charge-off method. See section 25.01 of Rev. Proc. 2018-31.
67	**Insurance company premium acquisition expenses (section 832)**—for certain insurance companies, **to** a safe harbor method of accounting for premium acquisition expenses set forth in Rev. Proc. 2002-46, 2002-2 C.B. 105. See section 26.01 of Rev. Proc. 2018-31.
68	**Discounted unpaid losses (section 846)**—for insurance companies other than life insurance companies computing discounted unpaid losses, **to** the composite method or **to** alternative methods set forth in Notice 88-100, 1988-2 C.B. 439, and Rev. Proc. 2002-74, 2002-2 C.B. 980. See section 27.01 of Rev. Proc. 2018-31.
70	**Functional currency (section 985)—to** the use of another functional currency for the applicant or its qualified business unit (QBU), other than a QBU described in Regulations section 1.985-1(b)(1)(iii). See section 29.01 of Rev. Proc. 2018-31.

-17-

List of DCNs	
No.	**Change**
71	**Rule of 78s (section 1272)**—for stated interest on certain short-term consumer loans, **from** the Rule of 78s method **to** the constant yield method. See section 15.05 of Rev. Proc. 2018-31.
72	**Original issue discount (sections 1272 and 1273)—to** the principal-reduction method for de minimis original issue discount (OID). See section 30.01 of Rev. Proc. 2018-31. **Note**. This change is implemented on a cut-off basis and does not receive audit protection.
73	**Market discount bonds (section 1278)—from** including market discount currently in income for the tax year to which the discount is attributable **to** including market discount in income for the tax year of disposition or partial principal payment (revoking the section 1278(b) election). **Note**. This change is implemented on a cut-off basis and also generally is made with audit protection, but with conditions or limitations. See section 31.01 of Rev. Proc. 2018-31.
74	**Interest income on short-term obligations (section 1281)—to** currently including accrued interest and discount in income (to comply with section 1281). See section 32.01 of Rev. Proc. 2018-31.
75	**Stated interest on short-term loans (section 1281)**—for a bank using the cash method of accounting, **from** accruing stated interest on short-term loans made in the ordinary course of business **to** using the cash method to report such interest. See section 32.02 of Rev. Proc. 2018-31.
76	**Sales of mortgage loans (section 1286)**—for accounting for certain sales of mortgage loans in which the seller also enters into a contract to service the mortgages in consideration for amounts received from interest payments, **from** a method that is inconsistent with Rev. Rul. 91-46, 1991-2 C.B. 358, **to** a method that is consistent with Rev. Rul. 91-46. However, the change is only an automatic accounting method change for certain taxpayers who are under examination. This change does not fall under the automatic change procedures of Rev. Proc. 2015-13. Instead, see Rev. Proc. 91-51, 1991-2 C.B. 779.
77	**Environmental remediation costs (section 263A)**—for costs incurred to clean up land that a taxpayer contaminated with hazardous waste from the taxpayer's manufacturing operations, **to** capitalizing such costs in inventory costs under section 263A. See section 12.04 of Rev. Proc. 2018-31.
78	**Costs of intangibles and certain transactions (section 263(a))**—for amounts paid or incurred to acquire or create intangibles, or to facilitate an acquisition of a trade or business, a change in the capital structure of a business entity, and certain other transactions, **to** a method of accounting provided in Regulations sections 1.263(a)-4, 1.263(a)-5, and 1.167(a)-3(b). Complete Schedule E of Form 3115 for changes to a method of accounting provided in Regulations section 1.167(a)-3(b). See section 11.05 of Rev. Proc. 2018-31.
79	**REMIC inducement fees (sections 860A–860G)**—for an inducement fee received in connection with becoming the holder of a noneconomic residual interest in a REMIC, **to** a safe harbor method provided under Regulations section 1.446-6(e)(1) or (e)(2). See Rev. Proc. 2004-30, 2004-1 C.B. 950, and section 28.01 of Rev. Proc. 2018-31.
80	**All events test method for credit card annual fees (section 451)—to** a method that satisfies the all events test in accordance with Rev. Rul. 2004-52, 2004-1 C.B. 973. See section 16.05 of Rev. Proc. 2018-31.
81	**Ratable inclusion method for credit card annual fees (section 446)—to** the ratable inclusion method for credit card annual fees. See section 16.05 of Rev. Proc. 2018-31.
82	**Credit card late fees (section 451)—to** a method that treats credit card late fees as interest income that creates or increases OID on the pool of credit card loans to which the fees relate. **Note**. This change is generally made with audit protection, but has conditions or limitations. See section 16.06 of Rev. Proc. 2018-31.
83	**Full inclusion method for certain advance payments (section 451)—to** the full inclusion method as described in section 5.01 of Rev. Proc. 2004-34, 2004-1 C.B. 991. The applicant must be using, or changing to, an overall accrual method of accounting. See section 16.07 of Rev. Proc. 2018-31.
84	**Deferral method for certain advance payments (section 451)—to** the deferral method as described in section 5.02 of Rev. Proc. 2004-34, 2004-1 C.B. 991 (except as provided in section 8.03 and 8.04(2) of Rev. Proc. 2004-34). The applicant must be using, or changing to, an overall accrual method of accounting. See section 16.07 of Rev. Proc. 2018-31 and Notice 2018-35.
85	**Film producer's treatment of certain creative property costs (section 446)—to** account for creative property costs under the safe harbor method provided in Rev. Proc. 2004-36, 2004-1 C.B. 1063. See section 15.06 of Rev. Proc. 2018-31.
86	**Timber fertilization costs (section 162)**—for costs incurred by a timber grower for the post-establishment fertilization of an established timber stand, **to** treat such costs as ordinary and necessary business expenses deductible under section 162. See section 3.04 of Rev. Proc. 2018-31.
87	**Change in general asset account treatment due to a change in the use of MACRS property (section 168)—to** the method of accounting provided in Regulations sections 1.168(i)-1(c)(2)(ii)(E) and 1.168(i)-1(h)(2) (as in effect before January 1, 2012). Complete Schedule E of Form 3115. Change is implemented on a modified cut-off basis. Additionally, a qualified small taxpayer qualifies for a reduced Form 3115 filing requirement. See Regulations section 1.168(i)-1(l)(2)(ii) and section 6.04 of Rev. Proc. 2018-31.

List of DCNs	
No.	**Change**
88	**Change in method of accounting for depreciation due to a change in the use of MACRS property (section 168)—to** the method of accounting provided in Regulations section 1.168(i)-4 or to revoke the election provided in Regulations section 1.168(i)-4(d)(3)(ii) to disregard a change in use of MACRS property. Complete Schedule E of Form 3115. Additionally, a qualified small taxpayer qualifies for a reduced Form 3115 filing requirement. See Regulations section 1.168(i)-4(g)(2) and section 6.05 of Rev. Proc. 2018-31.
89	**Depreciation of qualified non-personal use vans and light trucks (section 280F)**—for certain vehicles placed in service before July 7, 2003, **to** a method of accounting in accordance with Regulations section 1.280F-6(f)(2)(iv). Complete Schedule E of Form 3115. Additionally, a qualified small taxpayer qualifies for a reduced Form 3115 filing requirement. See Regulations section 1.280F-6(f)(2)(iv) and section 6.06 of Rev. Proc. 2018-31.
90	**Insurance companies' incentive payments to health care providers (section 446)**—for deducting provider incentive payments, **to** the method of including those payments in discounted unpaid losses without regard to section 404. See section 15.07 of Rev. Proc. 2018-31.
91	**Up-front network upgrade payments received by utilities (section 61)—to** a safe harbor method provided in Rev. Proc. 2005-35, 2005-2 C.B. 76. See section 1.01 of Rev. Proc. 2018-31.
92	**Allocation of environmental remediation costs to production (section 263A)—to** a method that allocates under section 263A environmental remediation costs to the inventory produced during the tax year such costs are incurred. See Rev. Rul. 2005-42, 2005-2 C.B. 67, and section 12.05 of Rev. Proc. 2018-31.
94	**Credit card cash advance fees (section 451)—to** a method that treats credit card cash advance fees as creating or increasing original issue discount (OID) on a pool of credit card loans that includes the cash advances that give rise to the fees. **Note.** This change is generally made with audit protection, but has conditions or limitations. See section 16.08 of Rev. Proc. 2018-31.
96	**Replacement cost method for heavy equipment dealers' parts inventory (sections 471 and 472)—to** the replacement cost method for heavy equipment dealers' parts inventory described in Rev. Proc. 2006-14, 2006-1 C.B. 350. Complete Schedule D, Parts II and III, of Form 3115, as applicable. See section 22.08 of Rev. Proc. 2018-31. **Note.** This change is implemented on a cut-off basis.
106	**Timing of incurring certain liabilities for services or insurance (section 461)**—for an applicant that is currently treating the mere execution of a contract for services or insurance as establishing the fact of the liability under section 461 and wants to change **from** that method for liabilities for services or insurance to comply with Rev. Rul. 2007-3, 2007-1 C.B. 350. See section 20.06 of Rev. Proc. 2018-31.
107	**Impermissible to permissible method of accounting for depreciation or amortization for disposed depreciable or amortizable property (sections 167, 168, 197, 1400I, 1400L(b), 1400L(c), or 1400N(d), or former 168)**—for an item of certain depreciable or amortizable property that has been disposed of by the applicant and for which the applicant did not take into account any depreciation allowance or did take into account some depreciation but less than the depreciation allowable, **from** using an impermissible method of accounting for depreciation **to** using a permissible method of accounting for depreciation. Complete Schedule E of Form 3115. Additionally, a qualified small taxpayer qualifies for a reduced Form 3115 filing requirement. See section 6.07 of Rev. Proc. 2018-31.
108	**Change by bank for uncollected interest (section 446)**—for a bank (as defined in Regulations section 1.166-2(d)(4)(i)) that uses an accrual method of accounting; is subject to supervision by federal authorities, or by state authorities maintaining substantially equivalent standards; and has 6 or more years of collection experience to change **to** the safe harbor method of accounting for uncollected interest (other than interest described in Regulations section 1.446-2(a)(2)) set forth in section 4 of Rev. Proc. 2007-33, 2007-1 C.B. 1289. See section 15.08 of Rev. Proc. 2018-31.
109	**Rotable spare parts (section 263(a))**—for an applicant that maintains a pool or pools of rotable spare parts that are primarily used to repair customer-owned (or customer-leased) equipment under warranty or maintenance agreements **to** the safe harbor method provided in Rev. Proc. 2007-48, 2007-2 C.B. 110. Complete Schedule E of Form 3115. See section 11.06 of Rev. Proc. 2018-31.
110	**Rotable spare parts (section 471)—from** the safe harbor method (or a similar method) of treating rotable spare parts as depreciable assets, in accordance with Rev. Proc. 2007-48, 2007-2 C.B. 110, **to** treating rotable spare parts as inventoriable items. See section 22.09 of Rev. Proc. 2018-31.
111	**Advance trade discount method (section 471)**—for an accrual method applicant required to use an inventory method of accounting and maintaining inventories, as provided in section 471, that receives advance trade discounts **to** the Advance trade discount method described in Rev. Proc. 2007-53, 2007-2 C.B. 233. See section 22.10 of Rev. Proc. 2018-31.

List of DCNs	
No.	**Change**
112	**Changes to the Vehicle-Pool Method (section 472)**—for a retail dealer or wholesaler distributor (reseller) of cars and light-duty trucks to the Vehicle-Pool Method as described in Rev. Proc. 2008-23, 2008-1 C.B. 664. See section 23.08 of Rev. Proc. 2018-31. **Note.** This change is implemented on a cut-off basis.
113	**Payroll tax liabilities (section 461)**—for an accrual method applicant that wants to change its method for FICA and FUTA taxes **to** the safe harbor method provided in Rev. Proc. 2008-25, 2008-1 C.B. 686, which provides that, solely for the purposes of the recurring item exception, an applicant will be treated as satisfying the requirement in Regulations section 1.461-5(b)(1)(i) for its payroll tax liability in the same tax year in which all events have occurred that establish the fact of the related compensation liability and the amount of the related compensation liability can be determined with reasonable accuracy. See section 20.04 of Rev. Proc. 2018-31.
114	**Rolling-average method of accounting for inventories (sections 471 and 472)**—for an applicant required to account for inventories under section 471 and that uses a rolling-average method to value inventories for financial accounting purposes **to** the same rolling-average method to value inventories for federal income tax purposes, in accordance with Rev. Proc. 2008-43, 2008-30 I.R.B.186. See section 22.14 of Rev. Proc. 2018-31. **Note.** This change must be implemented on a cut-off basis unless the applicant's books and records contain sufficient information to compute a section 481(a) adjustment, in which case the applicant may choose to implement the change with a section 481(a) adjustment.
116	**Obsolete.** See change number 7.
117	**Obsolete.** See change number 205 or 206, as applicable.
119	**Obsolete.** See change number 7.
121	**Repairable and reusable spare parts (section 263(a))**—**to** treat certain repairable and reusable spare parts as depreciable property in accordance with the holding in Rev. Rul. 69-200, 1969-1 C.B. 60, or Rev. Rul. 69-201, 1969-1 C.B. 60. Complete Schedule E of Form 3115. Additionally, a qualified small taxpayer qualifies for a reduced Form 3115 filing requirement. See section 11.07 of Rev. Proc. 2018-31.
122	**Overall accrual method other than for the first section 448 year (section 446)**—for a qualifying applicant for other than its first section 448 year, **from** the overall cash method **to** an overall accrual method. Complete Schedule A, Part I, of Form 3115. Also complete Schedule D, Parts II and III, as applicable. See section 15.01 of Rev. Proc. 2018-31, as modified by Rev. Proc. 2018-44 and Rev. Proc. 2018-60.
123	**Change in overall method from the cash method to an accrual method for the first section 448 year (section 446)**—for an applicant that is required by section 448 to change **from** the overall cash method **to** an overall accrual method and the applicant qualifies to make the change under the automatic consent procedures of Regulations sections 1.448-1(g) and (h)(2) as well as Rev. Proc. 2015-13 for a year of change that is the applicant's first section 448 year. See Regulations sections 1.448-1(g) and (h)(2), and section 15.01 of Rev. Proc. 2018-31, as modified by Rev. Proc. 2018-44 and Rev. 2018-60.
124	**Change from the cash method to an accrual method for specific items (section 446)**—for a qualifying applicant using an overall accrual method and accounting for one or more identified specific items of income and expense on the cash method **to** an accrual method of accounting for the identified specific item or items. See section 15.09 of Rev. Proc. 2018-31.
125	**Multi-year service warranty contracts (section 446)**—for an eligible accrual method manufacturer, wholesaler, or retailer of motor vehicles or other durable consumer goods that wants to change **to** the service warranty income method described in section 5 of Rev. Proc. 97-38, 1997-2 C.B. 479. See Rev. Proc. 97-38 and section 15.10 of Rev. Proc. 2018-31. **Note.** This change is implemented on a cut-off basis and also has a reduced Form 3115 filing requirement.
126	**Overall cash method for specified transportation industry taxpayers (section 446)**—for "specified transportation industry taxpayers," as defined in section 15.11(2) of Rev. Proc. 2018-31, with average annual gross receipts of more than $10,000,000 and not in excess of $50,000,000 **to** the overall cash method. See section 15.11 of Rev. Proc. 2018-31.
127	**Change to overall cash/hybrid method for certain banks (section 446)**—for an eligible bank, as defined in section 15.12(2)(a) of Rev. Proc. 2018-31, **to** an overall cash/hybrid method described in section 15.12(2)(b) of Rev. Proc. 2018-31. See section 15.12 of Rev. Proc. 2018-31.
128	**Change to overall cash method for farmers (section 446)**—for a qualifying applicant engaged in the trade or business of farming to the overall cash method. See section 15.13 of Rev. Proc. 2018-31, as modified by Rev. Proc. 2018-40. **Note.** For applicants changing from the crop method, that portion of the change is implemented using a cut-off method.

List of DCNs	
No.	**Change**
129	**Nonshareholder contributions to capital under section 118 (section 446)—from** excluding from gross income under section 61 certain payments or the fair market value of property received (including customer connection fees received by a regulated public utility described in section 118(c)), by characterizing the payments or the fair market value of property as nontaxable contributions to capital under section 118(a), **to** including the payments or the fair market value of property in gross income under section 61. This change also applies to a regulated public utility described in section 118(c) that changes **from** including in gross income under section 61 payments or fair market value of property received that are contributions in aid of construction under section 118(c) and Regulations section 1.118-2 and that meet the requirements of sections 118(c)(1)(B) and 118(c)(1)(C) **to** excluding from income the payments or the fair market value of the property as nontaxable contributions to capital under section 118(a). See section 15.14 of Rev. Proc. 2018-31. **Note**. The change described in section 15.14(1)(a)(ii) of Rev. Proc. 2018-31 does not apply to contributions made after December 22, 2017.
130	**Retainages not received under long-term contracts (section 451)**—for an accrual method applicant's retainages under section 451 **to** a method consistent with the holding in Rev. Rul. 69-314, 1969-1 C.B. 139. This change does not apply to retainages under long-term contracts as defined in section 460(f). An applicant changing its method of accounting under this section must treat all retainages (receivables and payables) in the same manner. See section 16.09 of Rev. Proc. 2018-31.
131	**Series E, EE, or I U.S. savings bonds (section 454)**—for a cash method taxpayer changing the taxpayer's method of accounting for interest income on Series E, EE, or I U.S. savings bonds **from** reporting as interest income the increase in redemption price on a bond occurring in a tax year **to** reporting this income in the tax year in which the bond is redeemed, disposed of, or finally matures, whichever is earliest. A statement in lieu of a Form 3115 is authorized for this change. See section 17.01 of Rev. Proc. 2018-31. **Note**. This change is implemented on a cut-off basis.
132	**Prepaid subscription income (section 455)**—for an accrual method applicant changing its method of accounting for prepaid subscription income **to** the method described in section 455 and the related regulations, including an eligible applicant that wants to make the "within 12 months" election under Regulations section 1.455-2. A statement in lieu of a Form 3115 is authorized for this change. See section 18.01 of Rev. Proc. 2018-31. **Note**. This change is implemented on a cut-off basis.
133	**Timing of incurring liabilities for bonuses (section 461)—to** treat bonuses as incurred in the tax year in which all events have occurred that establish the fact of the liability to pay a bonus and the amount of the liability can be determined with reasonable accuracy. See section 20.01(2) of Rev. Proc. 2018-31.
134	**Timing of incurring liabilities for vacation pay, sick pay, and severance pay (section 461)—to** treat vacation pay, sick pay, and severance pay as incurred in the tax year in which all events have occurred that establish the fact of the liability to pay vacation pay, sick pay, and severance pay, and the amount of the liability can be determined with reasonable accuracy. The applicant may make this change if the vacation pay, sick pay, and severance pay vests in that tax year and the vacation pay, sick pay, and severance pay is received by the employee by the 15th day of the 3rd calendar month after the end of that tax year. See section 20.01(3) of Rev. Proc. 2018-31.
135	**Rebates and allowances (section 461)**—for an accrual method applicant's liability for rebates and allowances **to** the recurring item exception method under section 461(h)(3) and Regulations section 1.461-5. See section 20.07 of Rev. Proc. 2018-31.
136	**Change from an improper method of inclusion of rental income or expense to inclusion in accordance with the rent allocation (section 467)**—for an applicant that is a party to a section 467 rental agreement and is changing its method for its fixed rent **to** the rent allocation method provided in Regulations section 1.467-1(d)(2)(iii). See section 21.01 of Rev. Proc. 2018-31. **Note**. This change only receives limited audit protection.
137	**Permissible methods of identification and valuation of inventories (section 471)**—for an applicant changing from one permissible method of identifying and valuing inventories **to** another permissible method of identifying and valuing inventories. Complete Schedule D, Parts II and III, of Form 3115, as applicable. See section 22.11 of Rev. Proc. 2018-31.
138	**Change in the official used vehicle guide utilized in valuing used vehicles (section 471)**—for a used vehicle dealer **from** not using an official used vehicle guide for valuing used vehicles **to** using an official used vehicle guide for valuing used vehicles; or **from** using an official used vehicle guide for valuing used vehicles **to** using a different official used vehicle guide for valuing used vehicles. See section 22.12 of Rev. Proc. 2018-31.
139	**Invoiced advertising association costs for new vehicle retail dealerships (section 471)**—for an applicant engaged in the trade or business of retail sales of new automobiles or new light-duty trucks (dealership) **from** capitalizing certain advertising costs as acquisition costs under Regulations section 1.471-3(b) **to** deducting the advertising costs under section 162 as the advertising services are provided to the dealership. See Regulations section 1.461-4(d)(2)(i), and section 22.13 of Rev. Proc. 2018-31.

List of DCNs	
No.	**Change**
140	**Changes within the Used Vehicle Alternative LIFO Method (section 472)**—for a taxpayer using the Used Vehicle Alternative LIFO Method, as described in Rev. Proc. 2001-23, 2001-1 C.B. 784, as modified by Announcement 2004-16, 2004-1 C.B. 668, and Rev. Proc. 2008-23, 2008-1 C.B. 664, **to** use a different "official used vehicle guide" in conjunction with the Used Vehicle Alternative LIFO Method, or **to** a different precise manner of using an official used vehicle guide (for example, a change in the specific guide category that an applicant uses to represent vehicles of average condition for purposes of section 4.02(5)(a) of Rev. Proc. 2001-23). See section 23.09 of Rev. Proc. 2018-31. **Note.** This change is implemented on a cut-off basis.
141	**Changes to dollar-value pools of manufacturers (section 472)**—for a manufacturer that purchases goods for resale (resale goods) and thus must reassign resale goods from the pool(s) it maintains for the goods it manufactures to one or more resale pools, and the manufacturer wants to change **from** using multiple pools described in Regulations section 1.472-8(b)(3) **to** using natural business unit (NBU) pools described in Regulations section1.472-8(b)(1), or vice versa; or wants to reassign items in NBU pools described in Regulations section 1.472-8(b)(1) into the same number or a greater number of NBU pools. See section 23.10 of Rev. Proc. 2018-31. **Note.** This change is implemented on a cut-off basis.
145	**Tenant construction allowances (section 168)**—for an applicant changing from improperly treating the applicant as having a depreciable interest in the property subject to the tenant construction allowances for federal income tax purposes **to** properly treating the applicant as not having a depreciable interest in such property for federal income tax purposes; or **from** improperly treating the applicant as not having a depreciable interest in the property subject to the tenant construction allowances for federal income tax purposes **to** properly treating the applicant as having a depreciable interest in such property for federal income tax purposes. This change is implemented on a cut-off basis and does not receive audit protection. Additionally, a qualified small taxpayer qualifies for a reduced Form 3115 filing requirement. See section 6.08 of Rev. Proc. 2018-31.
146	**Obsolete**. See change number 205.
147	**Obsolete**. See change number 206.
148	**Debt issuance costs (section 446)**—for an applicant changing its method of accounting **to** comply with Regulations section 1.446-5, which provides rules for allocating the costs over the term of the debt. See section 15.15 of Rev. Proc. 2018-31.
149	**Ratable accrual of real property taxes (section 461)**—for an accrual method applicant for real property taxes that relate to a definite period of time **to** the method described in section 461(c) and section 1.461-1(c)(1) (ratable accrual election) for a tax year other than the applicant's first tax year in which real property taxes are incurred. See section 20.08 of Rev. Proc. 2018-31. **Note**. This change has a reduced Form 3115 filing requirement.
150	**Retail sales facility safe harbor for a motor vehicle dealership (section 263A)**—for a motor vehicle dealership **to** treat its sales facility as a retail sales facility as described in section 5.01 of Rev. Proc. 2010-44, 2010-49 I.R.B. 811. See section 12.06 of Rev. Proc. 2018-31.
151	**Reseller without production activities safe harbor for a motor vehicle dealership (section 263A)**—for a motor vehicle dealership **to** be treated as a reseller without production activities as described in section 5.02 of Rev. Proc. 2010-44, 2010-49 I.R.B. 811. See section 12.06 of Rev. Proc. 2018-31.
152	**Deduction for energy efficient commercial buildings (section 179D)**—for an applicant to change its method of accounting to deduct under section 179D amounts paid or incurred for the installation of energy efficient commercial building property, subject to the limits of section 179D(b), in the year the property is placed in service. See Rev. Proc. 2012-39, 2012-2 C.B. 470, and section 8.01 of Rev. Proc. 2018-31. **Note**. This change does not receive audit protection.
153	**Advance payments—change in applicable financial statements (Rev. Proc. 2004-34)**—for an applicant using the deferral method for including advance payments in gross income in accordance with its applicable financial statement (AFS) to change its method **to** recognize advance payments in gross income under Rev. Proc. 2004-34 consistent with a changed manner for recognizing advance payments for its AFS. The requirement in section 6.03(3)(a) of Rev. Proc. 2015-13 to provide an additional copy of the application to the examining agent(s), appeals officer(s), and counsel to the government, if applicable, applies to this application. A statement in lieu of a Form 3115 is authorized for this change. See section 16.10 of Rev. Proc. 2018-31. **Note**. This change is implemented on a cut-off basis and does not receive audit protection.
154	**California franchise taxes (Rev. Rul. 2003-90)**—for an accrual method applicant changing **to** recognizing its California franchise tax liability in the tax year following the tax year in which the tax is incurred under the Cal. Rev. & Tax Code. See section 20.09 of Rev. Proc. 2018-31.
155	**Unearned premiums (section 833)**—for a Blue Cross or Blue Shield organization within the meaning of section 833(c)(2) or an organization described in section 833(c)(3) required to change its method of accounting for unearned premiums because it fails to meet the MLR requirements of section 833(c)(5). See section 26.02 of Rev. Proc. 2018-31.
156	**Gift cards issued as a refund (Rev. Proc. 2011-17)**—for an accrual method applicant who issues gift cards as a refund for returned goods changing **to** treat the transaction as the payment of a cash refund and sale of a gift card in the amount of the gift card, as provided in Rev. Proc. 2011-17, 2011-5 I.R.B. 441. See section 20.10 of Rev. Proc. 2018-31.

-22-

List of DCNs	
No.	**Change**
157	**Classification of wireless telecommunications assets used by wireless telecommunications carriers (sections 167 and 168)**—for applicants that have a depreciable interest in wireless telecommunication assets (as defined in Rev. Proc. 2011-22, 2011-8 I.R.B. 737) used primarily to provide wireless telecommunications or broadband services by mobile phones that are changing **to** the method described in Rev. Proc. 2011-22 to determine the recovery periods for depreciation of certain tangible assets used by wireless telecommunications carriers. Additionally, a qualified small taxpayer qualifies for a reduced Form 3115 filing requirement. See Rev. Proc. 2011-22 and section 6.09 of Rev. Proc. 2018-31.
158	**Wireline network property (section 263(a))**—for certain applicants that have a depreciable interest in wireline network assets (as described in section 4 of Rev. Proc. 2011-27, 2011-8 I.R.B. 740) used primarily to provide wireline telecommunication or broadband services that are changing **to** (a) the wireline network assets maintenance allowance method described in section 5 of Rev. Proc. 2011-27, or (b) the adoption of all, or some, of the units of property described in section 6 of Rev. Proc. 2011-27, to determine whether expenditures to maintain, replace, or improve wireline network assets must be capitalized under section 263(a). See section 3.07 of Rev. Proc. 2018-31.
159	**Wireless network property (section 263(a))**—for certain applicants that have a depreciable interest in wireless network assets (as described in section 4 of Rev. Proc. 2011-28, 2011-8 I.R.B. 743) used primarily to provide wireless telecommunications or broadband services by mobile phones that are changing **to** (a) the wireless network asset maintenance allowance method described in section 5 of Rev. Proc. 2011-28, or (b) the adoption of all, or some, of the units of property described in section 6 of Rev. Proc. 2011-28, to determine whether expenditures to maintain, replace, or improve wireless network assets must be capitalized under section 263(a). See section 3.08 of Rev. Proc. 2018-31.
160	**Electric transmission and distribution property (section 263(a))**—for certain applicants that have a depreciable interest in electric transmission or distribution property (as described in section 4 of Rev. Proc. 2011-43, 2011-37 I.R.B. 326) used primarily to transport, deliver, or sell electricity that are changing **to** the method described in Rev. Proc. 2011-43, to determine whether expenditures incurred to maintain, replace, or improve transmission and distribution property are deductible repairs under section 162 or capitalizable improvements under section 263(a). See section 3.09 of Rev. Proc. 2018-31.
161	**Timing of incurring liabilities under the recurring item exception to the economic performance rules (section 461(h)(3))**—for an applicant changing **to** a method of accounting to conform to any of the holdings in Rev. Rul. 2012-1, 2012-2 I.R.B. 255, which addresses the "not material" and "better matching" requirements of the recurring item exception and distinguishes contracts for the provision of services from insurance and warranty contracts. See section 20.11 of Rev. Proc. 2018-31.
175	**Obsolete**. See change number 199.
176	**Obsolete**. See change number 200.
177	**Obsolete**. See change number 205.
178	**Obsolete**. See change number 206.
179	**Obsolete**. See change number 207.
181	**Plants removed from the list of plants that have a preproductive period in excess of 2 years (section 263A)**—for an applicant that is not a corporation, partnership, or tax shelter required to use an accrual method of accounting and either is changing **to** not applying section 263A to the production of a plant or plants that have been removed from the list of plants with a nationwide weighted average preproductive period in excess of 2 years, **or** is revoking its section 263A(d)(3) election **to** not apply section 263A to the production of a plant or plants that have been removed from the list of plants with a nationwide weighted average preproductive period in excess of 2 years. See Rev. Proc. 2013-20 and section 12.07 of Rev. Proc. 2018-31.
182	**Steam or electric power generation property (section 263(a))**—for an applicant changing its method of accounting for its treatment of expenditures on generation property (as defined in section 4.01 of Rev. Proc. 2013-24, 2013-22 I.R.B. 1142) **to** use all or some of the unit of property definitions and the corresponding major component definitions described in Appendix A of Rev. Proc. 2013-24, to determine whether expenditures to maintain, replace, or improve generation property must be capitalized under section 263(a). See section 3.10 of Rev. Proc. 2018-31.
183	**Change to proportional method of accounting for OID on a pool of credit card receivables (section 1272(a)(6))**—for an eligible taxpayer that wants to change **to** the proportional method of accounting for original issue discount (OID) on a pool of credit card receivables as described in Rev. Proc. 2013-26, 2013-22 I.R.B. 1160. See section 30.02 of Rev. Proc. 2018-31. **Note**. This change is implemented on a cut-off basis.

-23-

List of DCNs	
No.	**Change**
184	**Deducting repair and maintenance costs or capitalizing improvement costs (sections 162 and 263(a))**—for an applicant changing **to** deducting amounts paid or incurred for repair and maintenance costs under section 162 and Regulations section 1.162-4 or changing **to** capitalizing amounts paid or incurred for improvements to tangible property and, if depreciable, to depreciating such property under section 168. Includes a change by an applicant in the method of identifying units of property under Regulations section 1.263(a)-3(e) for purposes of determining whether amounts paid or incurred improve a unit of property under Regulations section 1.263(a)-3. Additionally, a qualified small taxpayer qualifies for a reduced Form 3115 filing requirement. See section 11.08 of Rev. Proc. 2018-31.
185	**Change to the regulatory accounting method (section 162)**—for a regulated applicant changing its method of accounting for amounts paid or incurred to repair or maintain tangible property to follow its method of accounting for regulatory accounting purposes to determine whether an amount paid or incurred improves property under Regulations section 1.263(a)-3, consistent with Regulations section 1.263(a)-3(m). Additionally, a qualified small taxpayer qualifies for a reduced Form 3115 filing requirement. See section 11.08 of Rev. Proc. 2018-31.
186	**Deducting non-incidental materials and supplies when used or consumed (section 162)**—for an applicant changing its method of accounting for non-incidental materials and supplies **to** the method of deducting such amounts in the tax year in which they are actually used or consumed, consistent with Regulations section 1.162-3. Additionally, a qualified small taxpayer qualifies for a reduced Form 3115 filing requirement. See section 11.08 of Rev. Proc. 2018-31.
187	**Deducting incidental materials and supplies when paid or incurred (section 162)**—for an applicant that wants to change its method of accounting for incidental materials and supplies **to** the method of deducting such amounts in the tax year in which they are paid or incurred, consistent with Regulations section 1.162-3. Additionally, a qualified small taxpayer qualifies for a reduced Form 3115 filing requirement. See section 11.08 of Rev. Proc. 2018-31.
188	**Deducting non-incidental rotable and temporary spare parts when disposed (section 162)**—for an applicant changing its method of accounting for costs to acquire or produce non-incidental rotable and temporary spare parts **to** the method of deducting such costs in the tax year in which the taxpayer disposes of the parts, consistent with Regulations section 1.162-3. Additionally, a qualified small taxpayer qualifies for a reduced Form 3115 filing requirement. See section 11.08 of Rev. Proc. 2018-31.
189	**Change to the optional method for rotable and temporary spare parts (section 162)**—for an applicant changing its method of accounting for rotable and temporary spare parts **to** the optional method of accounting for rotable and temporary spare parts (described in Regulations section 1.162-3(e)), consistent with Regulations section 1.162-3. Additionally, a qualified small taxpayer qualifies for a reduced Form 3115 filing requirement. See section 11.08 of Rev. Proc. 2018-31.
190	**Deducting dealer expenses that facilitate the sale of property (section 162)**—for an applicant that is a dealer in property changing its method of accounting for commissions and other costs paid or incurred to facilitate the sale of tangible property **to** the method of treating such costs as ordinary and necessary business expenses, consistent with Regulations section 1.263(a)-1(e)(2). Additionally, a qualified small taxpayer qualifies for a reduced Form 3115 filing requirement. See section 11.08 of Rev. Proc. 2018-31.
191	**Non-dealer expense to facilitate the sale of property (section 263(a))**—for an applicant that is not a dealer in property changing its method of accounting for commissions and other costs paid or incurred to facilitate the sale of property **to** the method of capitalizing such costs, consistent with Regulations section 1.263(a)-1(e)(1). Additionally, a qualified small taxpayer qualifies for a reduced Form 3115 filing requirement. See section 11.08 of Rev. Proc. 2018-31.
192	**Capitalizing acquisition or production costs (section 263(a))**—for an applicant changing its method of accounting **to** capitalizing amounts paid or incurred to acquire or produce property under Regulations section 1.263(a)-2 and, if depreciable, to depreciating such property under section 168. Additionally, a qualified small taxpayer qualifies for a reduced Form 3115 filing requirement. See section 11.08 of Rev. Proc. 2018-31.
193	**Deducting certain costs for investigating or pursuing the acquisition of property (section 162)**—for an applicant changing its method of accounting **from** capitalizing **to** deducting amounts paid or incurred in the process of investigating or otherwise pursuing (a) the acquisition of real property if the amounts meet the requirements of Regulations section 1.263(a)-2(f)(2)(iii), or (b) the acquisition of real or personal property if the amounts are for employee compensation or overhead costs under Regulations section 1.263(a)-2(f)(2)(iv), consistent with Regulations section 1.263(a)-2. Additionally, a qualified small taxpayer qualifies for a reduced Form 3115 filing requirement. See section 11.08 of Rev. Proc. 2018-31.
194	**Change to a reasonable allocation method for self-constructed assets (section 263A)**—for a producer or a reseller-producer **to** a reasonable allocation method under Regulations section 1.263A-1(f)(4) for self-constructed assets or **from** not capitalizing a cost subject to section 263A **to** capitalizing that cost under a reasonable allocation method under Regulations section 1.263A-1(f)(4) that the producer or reseller-producer is already using for self-constructed assets. See section 12.08 of Rev. Proc. 2018-31.

-24-

List of DCNs	
No.	**Change**
195	**Real property acquired through foreclosure (section 263A)**—for an applicant that capitalizes costs under section 263A(b)(2) and Regulations section 1.263A-3(a)(1) to real property acquired through foreclosure, or similar transaction, **to** an otherwise permissible method of accounting under which the acquisition and holding costs for real property acquired through foreclosure, or similar transaction, are not capitalized under section 263A(b)(2) and Regulations section 1.263A-3(a)(1). See section 12.09 of Rev. Proc. 2018-31.
196	**Obsolete.**
197	**Obsolete.**
198	**Partial dispositions of tangible depreciable asset to which the IRS's adjustment pertains (section 168)**—for MACRS property for which the applicant is making a partial disposition election under Regulations section 1.168(i)-8(d)(2)(iii) to the disposition of a portion of the asset to which the IRS's adjustment pertains (as described in Regulations section 1.168(i)-8(d)(2)(iii)). Complete Schedule E of Form 3115. Additionally, a qualified small taxpayer qualifies for a reduced Form 3115 filing requirement. See section 6.10 of Rev. Proc. 2018-31.
199	**Depreciation of leasehold improvements (sections 167, 168, and 197)**—for leasehold improvements in which the applicant has a depreciable interest at the beginning of the year of change, **from** improperly depreciating or amortizing these leasehold improvements over the term of the lease (including renewals, if applicable) **to** properly depreciating or amortizing these leasehold improvements under section 167(f)(1), 168, or 197, as applicable. Complete Schedule E of Form 3115. Additionally, a qualified small taxpayer qualifies for a reduced Form 3115 filing requirement. See section 6.11 of Rev. Proc. 2018-31.
200	**Depreciation of MACRS property (permissible to permissible) (section 168)**—for MACRS property, **from** a permissible method **to** another permissible method listed in section 6.12(3) of Rev. Proc. 2018-31. Certain changes are made on a modified cut-off basis or a cut-off basis. Complete Schedule E of Form 3115. Additionally, a qualified small taxpayer qualifies for a reduced Form 3115 filing requirement. See section 6.12 of Rev. Proc. 2018-31.
201	**Sales-based royalties (section 263A)**—for sales-based royalties (as described in Regulations section 1.263A-1(e)(3)(ii)(U)(2)) properly allocable to inventory property for which the applicant is making a change listed in section 12.10(1) of Rev. Proc. 2018-31. See Rev. Proc. 2014-33 and section 12.10 of Rev. Proc. 2018-31.
202	**Sales-based vendor chargebacks under a simplified method (section 263A)**—for an applicant changing its method of accounting to no longer include cost adjustments for sales-based vendor chargebacks (as described in Regulations section 1.471-3(e)(1)) in the formulas used to allocate additional section 263A costs to ending inventory under a simplified method. See Rev. Proc. 2014-33 and section 12.11 of Rev. Proc. 2018-31.
203	**Sales-based vendor chargebacks (section 471)**—for an applicant changing its method of accounting to treat sales-based vendor chargebacks as a reduction in cost of goods sold in accordance with Regulations section 1.471-3(e)(1). See Rev. Proc. 2014-33 and section 22.15 of Rev. Proc. 2018-31.
204	**Retail inventory method (section 471)**—for an applicant using the retail inventory method, a change **to**: (a) not adjusting the numerator of the cost complement for an allowance, discount, or price rebate required by Regulations section 1.471-3(e) to reduce only cost of goods sold; (b) not adjusting the denominator of the cost complement for temporary markups and markdowns; (c) computing the cost complement using a method described in Regulations section 1.471-8(b)(3) (including changes from a method described in section 1.471-8(b)(3) to another method described in that section) for a retail LCM applicant; or (d) adjusting the denominator of the cost complement for permanent markups and markdowns for a retail cost applicant. See section 22.16 of Rev. Proc. 2018-31. **Note.** A taxpayer making any of these changes for its first or second tax year after December 31, 2014, may use either a section 481(a) adjustment or a cut-off basis to implement the change.
205	**Dispositions of a building or structural component (section 168)**—for MACRS property for which the applicant is making a change listed in section 6.13(3) of Rev. Proc. 2018-31 for disposing of a building or a structural component or disposing of a portion of a building (including its structural components) to which the partial disposition rule in Regulations section 1.168(i)-8(d)(1) applies. Complete Schedule E of Form 3115. Additionally, a qualified small taxpayer qualifies for a reduced Form 3115 filing requirement. See section 6.13 of Rev. Proc. 2018-31.
206	**Dispositions of tangible depreciable assets (other than a building or its structural components) (section 168)**—for MACRS property for which the applicant is making a change listed in section 6.14(3) of Rev. Proc. 2018-31 for disposing of section 1245 property or a depreciable land improvement **or** disposing of a portion of section 1245 property or a depreciable land improvement to which the partial disposition rule in Regulations section 1.168(i)-8(d)(1) applies. Complete Schedule E of Form 3115. Additionally, a qualified small taxpayer qualifies for a reduced Form 3115 filing requirement. See section 6.14 of Rev. Proc. 2018-31.
207	**Dispositions of tangible depreciable assets in a general asset account (section 168)**—for MACRS property for which the applicant is making a change listed in section 6.15(3) of Rev. Proc. 2018-31 for disposing of an asset subject to a general asset account election. Complete Schedule E of Form 3115. Additionally, a qualified small taxpayer qualifies for a reduced Form 3115 filing requirement. See section 6.15 of Rev. Proc. 2018-31.

List of DCNs	
No.	**Change**
208	**Cable network asset maintenance allowance or unit of property method of accounting (section 263(a))**—for certain applicants that operate and have a depreciable interest in cable network assets used in a cable system that provides video, high speed internet, and VOIP phone services that are changing to (a) the network maintenance allowance method for cable network assets described in section 5 of Rev. Proc. 2015-12, 2015-2 I.R.B. 265, or (b) the adoption of all, or some, of the units of property described in section 6 of Rev. Proc. 2015-12, to determine whether expenditures to maintain, replace, or improve cable network assets must be capitalized under section 263(a). See section 3.11 of Rev. Proc. 2018-31.
209	**Cable network customer drops and labor costs associated with installing customer premise equipment (section 263(a))**—for certain applicants that operate cable systems and (a) are changing to the specific identification method described in section 7.01(1) of Rev. Proc. 2015-12, or the safe harbor allocation method described in section 7.01(2) of Rev. Proc. 2015-12 for determining whether customer drop costs (including installations) may be deducted under section 162 or must be capitalized under section 263(a), or (b) are changing to deducting labor costs associated with installing customer premise equipment under section 7.02 of Rev. Proc. 2015-12. See section 3.11 of Rev. Proc. 2018-31.
210	**Depreciation of fiber optic transfer node and fiber optic cable used by a cable system operator (section 168)**—for a cable system operator within the scope of Rev. Proc. 2015-12 that is changing to the safe harbor method of accounting in section 8.03 of Rev. Proc. 2015-12 for determining depreciation of a fiber optic transfer node and trunk line consisting of fiber optic cable used in a cable distribution network providing one-way and two-way communication services. See Rev. Proc. 2015-12 and section 6.17 of Rev. Proc. 2018-31.
211	**Bad debt conformity election by bank after previous election automatically revoked (section 166)**—for an eligible bank changing its method of accounting for bad debts by making the conformity election under Regulations section 1.166-2(d)(3)(iii)(C)*(3)*. See section 4.02 of Rev. Proc. 2018-31.
212	**Change to comply with section 163(e)(3)**—for a taxpayer changing its method or methods of accounting to comply with the requirements of section 163(e)(3), which defers certain deductions attributable to original issue discount debt instruments held by related foreign persons. Any portion of the original issue discount will not be allowable as a deduction to the U.S. person issuer until paid. See section 5.02 of Rev. Proc. 2018-31.
213	**Railroad track structure expenditures (section 263(a))**—for a taxpayer changing its method of accounting for track structures **to**: (a) the safe harbor method provided in Rev. Proc. 2002-65, 2002-2 C.B. 700; or (b) the safe harbor method provided in Rev. Proc. 2001-46, 2001-2 C.B. 263. See section 11.09 of Rev. Proc. 2018-31.
214	**U.S. ratio method (section 263A)**—for a foreign person (as defined in Notice 88-104, as modified by Notice 89-67) required to capitalize costs under section 263A that is changing its method of accounting to the U.S. ratio method (as described in Notice 88-104) or that currently uses the U.S. ratio method and is changing to the U.S. ratio method of a different applicable U.S. trade or business for applying the U.S. ratio method. See section 12.12 of Rev. Proc. 2018-31.
215	**Depletion (section 263A)**—for an applicant changing its method of accounting for depletion to treat these amounts as an indirect cost that is only properly allocable to property that has been sold under Regulations section 1.263A-1(e)(3)(ii)(J). See section 12.13 of Rev. Proc. 2018-31.
216	**An accrual method taxpayer receiving advance payments (section 451)**—that wants to change **to** a method of accounting of including advance payments in income in the tax year of receipt. See section 16.07 of Rev. Proc. 2018-31. **Note**. This change does not apply to any tax year beginning after December 31, 2017.
217	**Retainages received under long-term contracts (section 451)**—for an accrual method applicant's retainages under section 451 **to** a method consistent with the holding in Rev. Rul. 69-314, 1969-1 C.B. 139. This change only applies to retainages under long-term contracts as defined in section 460(f) that are exempt construction contracts (as defined in Regulations section 1.460-3(b)(1)). An applicant changing its method of accounting under this section must treat all retainages (receivables and payables) in the same manner. See section 16.09 of Rev. Proc. 2018-31. **Note**. This change is implemented on a cut-off basis.
218	**Change from the mark-to-market method of accounting to a realization method (section 475)**—for a taxpayer changing its method of accounting for securities or commodities **from** the mark-to-market method described in section 475 **to** a realization method of accounting (for example, by revoking an election under section 475(e), section 475(f)(1), or section 475(f)(2)). A notification statement must be filed earlier than the due date of the Form 3115. See section 24.02 of Rev. Proc. 2018-31. **Note**. This change is generally made with audit protection, but has conditions or limitations. This change also is implemented on a cut-off basis.
219	**Change in qualification as life/non-life insurance company (section 816)**—for a taxpayer changing its qualification under section 816(a) to move **from** a life insurance company taxable under Part I of subchapter L **to** a non-life insurance company taxable under Part II of subchapter L, or vice versa. See section 26.03 of Rev. Proc. 2018-31. **Note**. This change does not receive audit protection.
220	**Economic performance safe harbor for Ratable Service Contracts (section 461)**—for an accrual method taxpayer that wants to change its treatment of Ratable Service Contracts to conform **to** the safe harbor method provided by Rev. Proc. 2015-39, 2015-33 I.R.B. 197. See section 20.12 of Rev. Proc. 2018-31, as modified by Rev. Proc. 2015-39.
221	**Obsolete**.

List of DCNs	
No.	**Change**
222	**Remodel–refresh safe harbor method (section 263)**—for a qualified taxpayer changing **to** the remodel–refresh safe harbor method of accounting provided in section 5.02 of Rev. Proc. 2015-56 for its qualified costs, including the making of a late general asset account election as provided under section 5.02(6)(d) of Rev. Proc. 2015-56. Additionally, a qualified small taxpayer qualifies for a reduced Form 3115 filing requirement. See section 11.10 of Rev. Proc. 2018-31. **Note.** This change is generally made with audit protection, but has conditions or limitations. Certain changes also are implemented on a cut-off basis.
223	**Start-up expenditures (section 195)**— for an applicant changing its method of accounting under section 195 **to** change the characterization of an item as a start-up expenditure, the determination of the tax year in which the taxpayer begins the active trade or business to which the start-up expenditures relate, or the amortization period of a start-up expenditure to 180 months. See section 10.01 of Rev. Proc. 2018-31.
224	**Interest capitalization (section 263A)**—for an applicant changing its method of accounting for interest **from** not capitalizing any interest, capitalizing interest in accordance with its method of accounting for financial reporting purposes, or applying an improper method of capitalizing interest under Regulations sections 1.263A-8 through -14, with respect to the production of designated property, **to** capitalizing interest with respect to the production of designated property in accordance with Regulations sections 1.263A-8 through -14. See section 12.14 of Rev. Proc. 2018-31.
225	**Certain changes within the retail inventory method (section 471)**—for an applicant using the retail inventory method that wants to change **from** including **to** not including temporary markups and markdowns in determining the retail selling prices of goods on hand at the end of the tax year. See section 22.17 of Rev. Proc. 2018-31.
226	**Transfer of interties under the safe harbor described in Notice 2016-36 (section 118)**—for a utility changing **to** the safe harbor method of accounting provided in section III.C of Notice 2016-36 for the treatment under section 118 of a transfer of an intertie, including a dual-use intertie, by a generator to a utility, or for a utility using the safe harbor method of accounting provided in section III.C of Notice 2016-36 and is required to terminate that safe harbor method of accounting. See section 15.16 of Rev. Proc. 2018-31. **Note.** The change from using the safe harbor method of accounting provided in section III.C of Notice 2016-36 to terminating that safe harbor method of accounting is implemented on a cut-off basis.
227	**Change to or from the net asset value (NAV) method (section 446)**—for an applicant that holds shares in a money market fund (MMF) and that wants to change its method of accounting for gain or loss on the shares from a realization method to the NAV method described in Regulations section 1.446-7 or from the NAV method to a realization method. See section 15.17 of Rev. Proc. 2018-31. **Note.** This change is implemented on a cut-off basis and also has a reduced Form 3115 filing requirement.
228	**Organizational expenditures under section 248 (section 248)**— for a corporation changing its method of accounting under section 248 **to** change the characterization of an item as an organizational expenditure, the determination of the tax year in which the corporation begins business to which the organizational expenditures relate, or the amortization period of an organizational expenditure to 180 months. See section 10.02 of Rev. Proc. 2018-31.
229	**Organization fees under section 709 (section 709)**—for a partnership changing its method of accounting under section 709 **to** change the characterization of an item as an organizational expense, the determination of the tax year in which the partnership begins business to which the organizational expenses relate, or the amortization period of an organizational expense to 180 months. See section 10.03 of Rev. Proc. 2018-31.
230	**Change from currently deducting inventories to permissible methods of identification and valuation of inventories (section 471)**—for an applicant changing **from** currently deducting inventories **to** a permissible method of identifying and valuing inventories. See section 22.18 of Rev. Proc. 2018-31.
231	**Changes in the timing of recognition of income due to the New Standards (section 451)**—for an applicant that wants to change its method of accounting for the recognition of income **to** a method under the new financial accounting standards jointly announced by the Financial Accounting Standards Board and the International Accounting Standards Board for: (i) identifying performance obligations, (ii) allocating transaction price to performance obligations, and/or (iii) considering performance obligations satisfied. See Rev. Proc. 2018-29, 2018-22 I.R.B. 634, and section 16.11 of Rev. Proc. 2018-31, as modified by Rev. Proc. 2018-49. **Note.** A taxpayer making this change may implement the change with either a section 481(a) adjustment or on a cut-off basis.
232	**Change to not apply section 263A to replanting costs for lost or damaged citrus plants pursuant to section 263A(d)(2)(C)**—for certain applicants that currently capitalize costs of replanting citrus plants under section 263A(d)(2), **to** not applying section 263A to those costs under section 263A(d)(2)(C). Costs must be paid or incurred after December 22, 2017, and on or before December 22, 2027. See Rev. Proc. 2018-35, 2018-28 I.R.B. 204, and section 12.15 of Rev. Proc. 2018-31. **Note.** The section 481(a) adjustment is calculated by taking into account only amounts paid or incurred after December 22, 2017, and on or before December 22, 2027.
233	**Overall cash method for a small business taxpayer (section 446)**—for a qualifying applicant with average annual gross receipts of $25 million or less (adjusted for inflation) changing **to** the overall cash method. Complete certain lines of Schedule A, Part I, of Form 3115. See Rev. Proc. 2018-40 and section 15.18 of Rev. Proc. 2018-31.

List of DCNs	
No.	**Change**
234	**Uniform capitalization exception for a small business taxpayer (section 263A)**—for a qualifying applicant with average annual gross receipts of $25 million or less (adjusted for inflation) changing **from** capitalizing costs under section 263A **to** no longer capitalizing costs under section 263A, including for self-constructed assets. See Rev. Proc. 2018-40 and section 12.16 of Rev. Proc. 2018-31.
235	**Inventory exception for a small business taxpayer (section 471)**—for a qualifying applicant with average annual gross receipts of $25 million or less (adjusted for inflation) changing its accounting method for inventory items under section 471 **to** one of the following methods: (a) treating inventory as non-incidental materials and supplies under Regulations section 1.162-3; or (b) conforming to the taxpayer's accounting method reflected in its applicable financial statements, as defined in section 451(b)(3) with respect to the taxable year, or if the taxpayer does not have an applicable financial statement for the taxable year, the books and records of the taxpayer prepared in accordance with the taxpayer's accounting procedures. See Rev. Proc. 2018-40 and section 22.19 of Rev. Proc. 2018-31.
236	**Long-term contract exception for small business taxpayer (section 460)**— for a qualifying applicant with average annual gross receipts of $25 million or less (adjusted for inflation) (a) changing **from** the percentage-of-completion accounting method described in Regulation section 1.460-4(b) for exempt long-term constructions contracts described in section 460(e)(1)(B) **to** an exempt contract accounting method described in section 1.460-4(c), or (b) with long-term home construction contracts defined in section 460(e)(1)(A) changing its accounting method **to** stop capitalizing costs under 263A. Complete Schedule D, Part I. See Rev. Proc. 2018-40 and section 19.01 of Rev. Proc. 2018-31.
237	**Recharacterizing costs under the simplified resale method, simplified production method, or the modified simplified production method**—for an applicant that uses or is changing **to** the simplified resale method, simplified production method, or the modified simplified production method and wants to recharacterize a section 471 cost, as defined section 1.263A-1(d)(2), as an additional section 263A cost, as defined in section 1.263A-1(d)(3), or vice versa. See Rev. Proc. 2018–56 and section 12.17 of Rev. Proc. 2018-31.
238	**Revocation of a historic absorption ratio election**—for an applicant that either: (a) uses the simplified resale method with historic absorption ratio election that wants to revoke its historic absorption ratio election and change to the simplified resale method without historic absorption ratio election, or (b) uses the simplified production method with historic absorption ratio election that wants to revoke its historic absorption ratio election and change to the simplified production method without historic absorption ratio election. This change applies to a taxpayer's first, second, or third taxable year ending on or after November 20, 2018. See Rev. Proc. 2018-56 and section 12.18 of Rev. Proc. 2018-31.
239	**Changes in the timing of the recognition of income under section 451(b) (section 451)**—for an applicant with an applicable financial statement that uses an accrual method of accounting and wants to change its method of accounting for the recognition of income to a method that complies with section 451(b), as amended by section 13221 of the Tax Cuts and Jobs Act (P.L. 115-97). This change applies to taxable years beginning after December 31, 2017. See Rev. Proc. 2018-60 and section 16.12 of Rev. Proc. 2018-31.

-28-

Paperwork Reduction Act Notice. We ask for the information on this form to carry out the Internal Revenue laws of the United States. You are required to give us the information. We need it to ensure that you are complying with these laws and to allow us to figure and collect the right amount of tax.

You are not required to provide the information requested on a form that is subject to the Paperwork Reduction Act unless the form displays a valid OMB control number. Books or records relating to a form or its instructions must be retained as long as their contents may become material in the administration of any Internal Revenue law. Generally, tax returns and return information are confidential, as required by section 6103.

The time needed to complete and file this form will vary depending on individual circumstances. The estimated burden for business taxpayers filing this form is approved under OMB control number 1545-0123 and is included in the estimates shown in the instructions for their business income tax return. The estimated burden for individual taxpayers filing this form is approved under OMB control number 1545-0074 and is included in the estimates shown in the instructions for their individual income tax return. The estimated burden for all other taxpayers who file this form is shown below.

Time Per Response

Recordkeeping	60 hours, 1 minute
Learning	16 hours, 25 minutes
Preparing	20 hours
Sending	32 minutes

If you have comments concerning the accuracy of these time estimates or suggestions for making this form simpler, we would be happy to hear from you. You can send us comments from IRS.gov/FormComments. Or you can send your comments to: Internal Revenue Service, Tax Forms and Publications Division, 1111 Constitution Ave. NW, IR-6526, Washington, DC 20224. Do not send Form 3115 to this address. Instead, see *When and Where to File*, earlier.

-29-

8

Inventory

§ 8.01 Inventory

[A] Overview

Inventory accounting is vital to the determination of income for taxpayers in the manufacturing, merchandising, or mining business. Because financial, managerial, and tax accounting are based on a periodic measurement of income, the use of inventories is necessary to properly match costs against revenues to clearly reflect income for a given period. The failure to use inventories can result in (1) improperly matching sales revenue and cost of goods sold in many cases and (2) deferring payment of income taxes. IRC § 471 and the regulations contain the general rule for inventories.

IRC § 471 authorizes the IRS to determine when inventories are necessary to clearly reflect income and to determine what methods of valuation of inventories will be acceptable for tax purposes. The IRS has been given broad regulatory authority by Congress and the courts in the area of inventories.[1]

Inventory accounting is critical in order to determine gross income. In this regard, IRC § 61(a)(2) and § 61(a)(3) provide, in part, that gross income means all income including gross income derived from business and gains derived from dealings in property.[2] Reg. § 1.61-3(a) provides that, in a manufacturing, merchandising, or mining business, "gross income" means the total sales, less the cost of goods sold, plus any income from investments and from other sources. The cost of goods sold should be determined in accordance with the method of accounting consistently used by the taxpayer. Thus, for example, an amount cannot be taken into account in the computation of cost of goods sold any earlier than the taxable year in which economic performance occurs with respect to the amount.[3] Determing gross income is important as IRC § 63 defines the term "taxable income" as gross income minus the deductions allowed by this chapter.[4]

What is cost of goods? The cost of goods sold is the net acquisition cost of merchandise obtained and sold to customers during an operating period and can be calculated by adding the value of the beginning inventory, the cost of new inventory items, the transportation cost, and then subtracting ending inventory amounts.[5]

How is cost of goods sold (COGS) determined? The following items need to be taken into consideration when computing COGS:

- Inventory at the beginning of the year;[6]
- Purchases less cost of items withdrawn for personal use;

---

[1] *Thor Power Tool Co. v Comm'r*, 439 U.S. 522 (1979).

[2] Reg. § 1.61-3(a). If you produce or sell merchandise, you must keep inventory and use the accrual method. Reg. § 1.446-2(i).

[3] *See* Reg. § 1.446-1(c)(1)(ii).

[4] Chapter 1 includes sections 1 to 1400Z-2.

[5] *See, e.g.*, Form 1125-A, *Cost of Goods sold.*

[6] Reg. § 1.471-1.

- Labor costs (generally applies to manufacturing and mining operations);
- Materials and supplies (generally a manufacturing cost);
- Other costs (generally applies to manufacturing and mining operations); and
- Inventory at the end of the year.[7]

Example 8-1

Beginning Inventory		$20,000
Add:		
Net Cost of Purchases	$62,000	
Add:		
Transportation	$1,000	
		$63,000
Less:		
Ending Inventory		$10,000
Cost of Goods Sold		$73,000

When measuring inventories, there are two variables—quality and price—which are converted into their dollar value (quality multiplied by price). While the principle of taking inventory is simple, counting all items available for sale, pricing them, and calculating their value can be complicated and time-consuming. The complications occur because even medium-size companies have numerous items of sizes, types, and qualities they purchase at different unit prices and store at different locations. In addition, measuring inventory may involve including items that not yet have been delivered, which are called "goods in transit."

[B] Inventory at the Beginning of the Year

Beginning inventory is the cost of merchandise[8] on hand at the beginning of the year that is available for sale to customers. A manufacturer or producer should include the total cost of raw materials, work in process, finished goods and materials and supplies used in manufacturing the goods as part of the beginning inventory amount. Containers such as kegs, bottles, and cases, regardless of whether they are on hand or returnable should be included in inventory if title has not passed to the buyer of the contents. If title has passed to the buyer, the containers should be excluded from inventory.[9]

---

[7] IRS Publication 334, § 6; IRS Form 1125-A, *Cost of Goods Sold.*

[8] In *Wilkinson-Beane, Inc. v. Comm'r*, 420 F.2d 353, 356 (1st Cir. 1970), the court defined merchandise as "goods awaiting sale," "article of commerce held for sale," and "all classes of commodities held for sale."

[9] Reg. § 1.471-1.

Generally, beginning inventory amount will be identical to the closing inventory of the prior year. If there is a difference between the ending inventory and beginning inventory, a statement explaining the difference must be included with the filed tax return.

Include the following merchandise in inventory:

- Purchased merchandise if title has passed to you, even if the merchandise is in transit or you do not have physical possession for another reason;
- Goods under contract for sale that you have not yet segregated and applied to the contract;
- Goods out on consignment; and
- Goods held for sale in display rooms, merchandise mart rooms, or booths located away from your place of business.

Do not include the following merchandise in inventory:

- Goods you have sold, but only if title has passed to the buyer;
- Goods consigned to you; and
- Goods ordered for future delivery if you do not yet have title.

Assets—Do not include in inventory assets such as:

- Land, buildings, and equipment used in your business;
- Notes, accounts receivable, and similar assets; and
- Supplies that do not physically become part of the item intended for sale.

[C] Purchases Less Cost of Items Withdrawn for Personal Use

Businesses use the cost of all merchandise bought for sale to calculate purchases. For manufacturers or producers, this includes the cost of all raw materials or parts purchased for merchandise on hand at the beginning of the year manufactured into a finished product.

Trade discounts are the differences between the stated prices of articles and the actual prices paid.[10] Businesses must use the prices paid (not the stated prices) in figuring cost of purchases. Do not show the discount amount separately as an item in gross income.

Cash discounts are amounts suppliers let businesses deduct from their purchase invoices for prompt payments. There are two methods of accounting for cash discounts. Businesses can either include them in a separate income account (added in as part of income) or deduct them from total purchases for the year. Whichever method is used, consistency is required.[11] A change in method is treated as a change of accounting. If you credit cash discounts to a separate account, you must include this credit balance in your business income at the end of the year. Do not reduce your cost of goods sold by the cash discount.

---

[10] Reg. § 1.471-3(b).

[11] Rev. Rul. 73-65, 1973-1 CB 216.

Returns and allowances are amounts for items that are returned by customers to the business. These amounts should be deducted from total purchases during the year.

Merchandise withdrawn from sale for personal or family[12] use or given to charity[13] should be deducted from the total amount of merchandise bought for sale. Deductions are not allowed for items used personally. Personal use items should be included under an account such as "withdrawal," "drawing" or "personal."

Cost of Goods sold will be increased by:

- Pilferage;
- Casualty;[14]
- Physical shrinkage;[15]
- Damages;
- Subnormal goods;[16]
- Goods out of style;[17] and
- Goods used for advertisement.[18]

[D] Labor Costs

For merchandise purchased for resale, cost includes purchasing, handling, storage, and a portion of general administrative costs. Small merchandisers (wholesalers, retailers, etc.) usually do not have labor costs that can properly be charged to cost of goods sold.[19] Labor costs are usually an element of cost of goods sold only in a manufacturing or mining business. For tax years beginning after 2017, the TCJA exempts taxpayers (other than a tax shelter prohibited from using the cash receipts and disbursements method of accounting under IRC § 448(a)(3)) with average annual gross receipts of $25 million or less (indexed for inflation)[20] for the prior three tax years from both UNICAP and inventories rules, regardless of whether merchandise is manufactured or purchased for resale.

In the case of merchandise produced by the taxpayer since the beginning of the tax year, cost means:

(i) the cost of raw materials and supplies entering into or consumed in connection with the product;

(ii) expenditures for direct labor; and

---

12 *John Calamaras*, T.C. Memo. 1960-201.

13 Reg. § 1.170A-1(c)(4).

14 IRS Publication 538, *Accounting Periods and Methods*.

15 IRC § 471(b).

16 Reg. § 1.471-2.

17 Reg. § 1.471-2(c).

18 *Diurovic v. Comm'r*, 487 F.2d 36, 73-2 USTC ¶ 9728 (7th Cir. 1973).

19 If the taxpayer had adopted IRC § 263A these expenses must be capitalized. *See* Reg. § 1.263A-1(e)(3)(ii)(E).

20 Currently $26 million.

(iii) indirect production costs incidental to and necessary for the production of the particular article, including in such indirect production costs an appropriate portion of management expenses, but not including any cost of selling or return on capital, whether by way of interest or profit.[21]

Labor costs properly allocable to the cost of goods sold include both the direct and indirect labor used in fabricating the raw material into a finished, saleable product. Examples of indirect costs include:

- Rent paid for a building used in a manufacturing operation;
- Depreciation of a building/equipment;
- Salaries for a production supervisor and others indirectly involved;
- Warehousing costs; and
- Bottling and packaging labor.[22]

[E] Materials and Supplies

Include the cost of materials and supplies, such as hardware and chemicals, used directly or indirectly in manufacturing goods as part of cost of goods sold. Treat those materials and supplies not used in the manufacturing process as business expenses and deduct them as business expenses at the time of consumption.[23]

[F] Other Costs

Some examples of other costs incurred in a manufacturing or mining process charged to cost of goods sold are:

- Containers;
- Freight-in;[24] and
- Overhead expenses, such as utilities, insurance, etc.[25]

[G] Inventory at the End of the Year

Inventory at the end of the year is also known as closing or ending inventory. The ending inventory will usually become the beginning inventory for the next tax year.

---

[21] Reg. §1.471-3(c). *See* Reg. §1.263A-1 and §1.263A-2 for more specific rules regarding the treatment of production costs for property produced by a taxpayer. The allocation of indirect production costs by producers is covered in Chapter 9, *infra.*

[22] *Id.*

[23] If the taxpayer had adopted IRC §263A these expenses must be capitalized. *See* Reg. §1.263A-1(e)(3)(ii)(E).

[24] *See Gus Blass Co. v. Comm'r*, 18 T.C. 261 (1952), *aff'd*, 204 F.2d 327 (8th Cir. 1953).

[25] *TAM 7914006.*

Once ending inventory has been determined, cost of goods sold are calculated as follows[26]:

- Inventory at the beginning of the year
- Plus net purchases
- Plus cost of labor
- Plus materials and supplies
- Plus other costs
- Minus inventory at the end of the year

Cost of goods sold can be a complex calculation for any business. A formalized recordkeeping system, and tax/accounting software programs will assist in properly calculating cost of goods sold.

The IRS encourages businesses to establish reliable record keeping systems, to accurately report all income, and to properly compute cost of goods sold and other expenses. According to IRS research, the largest component of the tax gap comes from understated business income, including underreported receipts and overstated expenses.

Example 8-2

The cost of goods sold is determined as follows:

Inventory at beginning of year[a]		$37,845
Plus: Purchases	$285,900	
Minus: Items withdrawn for personal use[b]	2,650	283,250
Goods available for sale		$321,095
Minus: Inventory at end of year[c]		32,955
Cost of goods sold		$288,140

[a] Compare this figure with last year's ending inventory. The two amounts should usually be the same.

[b] If you take any inventory items for your personal use (use them yourself, provide them to your family, or give them as personal gifts, etc.) be sure to remove them from the cost of goods sold.

[c] Check to make sure your procedures for taking inventory are adequate. These procedures should ensure all items have been included in inventory and proper pricing techniques have been used.

Hence, cost of goods sold is a residual number necessary to determine gross income.

---

[26] *See* Form 1125-A, *Cost of Goods Sold.*

Example 8-3

Gross receipts	$400,000
Minus: returns and allowances	$14,940
Net receipts	$385,060
Minus: Cost of goods sold	$288,140
Gross profit	$96,920

[H] Periodic Physical Inventory Counts

Inventory records should be adjusted to correspond with actual quantities of goods on hand, as determined by periodic physical inventories.[27] Inventory losses (shrinkage) should be deducted in the year in which such losses are discovered.

Where physical inventory counts are not conducted at year end, the taxpayer makes proper adjustments to those inventories and to its estimating methods to the extent those estimates are greater than or less than the actual shrinkage.[28] Rev. Proc. 98-29[29] applies to a taxpayer requesting the Commissioner's consent to change to a method of accounting for estimating inventory shrinkage in computing ending inventory, using:

(1) the retail safe harbor method, regardless of whether the taxpayer's present method of accounting estimates inventory shrinkage; or

(2) a method other than the retail safe harbor method, provided:

   (a) the taxpayer's present method of accounting does not estimate inventory shrinkage; and

   (b) the taxpayer's new method of accounting (that estimates inventory shrinkage) clearly reflects income under IRC § 446(b).[30]

[I] Inventory Accounting is Governed by IRC §§446 and 471

IRC § 446(a) provides the general rule for determining the proper method of accounting:

---

[27] IRC § 471(b)(1).

[28] IRC § 471(b)(2).

[29] 1998-1 CB 857.

[30] The retail safe harbor method of estimating inventory shrinkage, as described in 4.02 through 4.07 of Rev. Proc. 98-29, may be used in computing ending store inventory by taxpayers that are primarily engaged in retail trade (the resale of personal property to the general public), where physical inventories are normally taken at each location at least annually.

> Taxable income shall be computed under the method of accounting on the basis of which the taxpayer regularly computes his income in keeping his books.

IRC § 471(a) prescribes the general rule for inventories. It states:

> Whenever in the opinion of the [Commissioner] the use of inventories is necessary in order clearly to determine the income of any taxpayer, inventories shall be taken by such taxpayer on such basis as the [Commissioner] may prescribe as conforming as nearly as may be to the *best accounting practice* in the trade or business and as most *clearly reflecting the income*. [Emphasis added.]

Reg. § 1.471-1 provides that inventories must be maintained at the beginning and end of each taxable year in which the production purchase or sale of merchandise is an income producing factor. For example, inventories would be required with respect to merchandise held for sale by a retail store; whereas, no inventories would be required in the case of an accounting firm holding paper, binders, or other supplies. Similarly, the IRS has held that the production, purchase, or sale of merchandise is a material income producing factor in the case of an undertaker selling caskets,[31] a manufacturer of orthopedic braces,[32] an optometrist selling glasses,[33] and a producer of electricity.[34]

In general, a taxpayer must own the work product in order for inventories to be required, *e.g.*, the maintenance of inventory is generally not required where a taxpayer modifies or repairs property owned by another party.[35] The determination of whether a taxpayer owns goods is based on an analysis of all relevant facts and circumstances including:

- Does the taxpayer have a property interest in the cost?
- Does the taxpayer bear the risk of loss if the product is unsuccessful?
- What are the relative amounts of the taxpayers labor cost and material cost included in the product?

Note: Notwithstanding the general requirement that a taxpayer own property in order to be required to maintain inventories, IRC § 263A subjects taxpayers producing property for others to the UNICAP rules.[36]

The regulations establish two tests for inventory to conform. First, it must conform "as nearly as may be" to the "best accounting practice,"[37] a phrase that is

---

31 Rev. Rul. 69-37, 1969-1 CB 130.

32 Rev. Rul. 73-485, 1973-2 CB 150.

33 Rev. Rul. 74-279, 1974-1 CB 110.

34 TAM 9523001.

35 Rev. Rul. 81-272, 1981-2 CB 116.

36 *See* § 9.01, *below*.

37 *See* § 8.02, *below*.

synonymous with "generally accepted accounting principles."[38] Second, it "must clearly reflect the income."[39]

Moreover, the method used to account for inventory must be applied on a consistent basis, *i.e.*, opening inventory must correspond to the prior year's closing inventory, and opening and closing inventories for the same taxable year must be computed on a consistent basis.

Adequate records must be maintained and physical inventories must be taken on a periodic basis.[40]

§ 8.02 Best Accounting Practice

Inventory accounting must conform to the "best accounting practice." Inventory rules cannot be uniform but must give effect to trade customs which come within the scope of the best accounting practice in a particular trade or business.[41]

In *E.W. Bliss Co. v United States*,[42] the court stated that an inventory valued in accordance with generally accepted accounting principles (GAAP) may be considered as one that conforms "as nearly as may be to the best accounting practice in the trade or business."

§ 8.03 Clear Reflection of Income

The method used to account for inventory must "clearly reflect income,"[43] *i.e.*, the inventory practice should be consistent from year to year, with greater weight given to consistency than to the use of any particular method.[44] Yet mere consistency, although persuasive, is not controlling. For example, in *All-Steel Equipment, Inc. v. Commissioner*, the Tax Court noted that consistently using an impermissible method (even with favorable consideration by the IRS on prior audits) does not justify its use.[45]

As IRC § 446(b) provides, if the method of accounting used by the taxpayer "does not clearly reflect income, the computation of taxable income shall be made under such method as, in the opinion of the [Commissioner], does clearly reflect

---

[38] *See Caldwell v. Comm'r*, 202 F.2d 112 (2d Cir. 1953).

[39] Reg. § 1.471-2(a)(2). *See* § 8.03, *below*.

[40] Reg. § 1.471-2(e).

[41] Reg. § 1.471-2(b).

[42] 224 F. Supp. 374, 382 (N.D. Ohio 1963), *aff'd*, 351 F.2d 449 (6th Cir. 1965). This theme can be found in many court decisions, *see, e.g.*, *Van Pickerill and Sons, Inc. v. United States*, 445 F.2d 918 (7th Cir. 1971); *Westpac Pacific Food v. Comm'r*, 451 F.3d 970 (9th Cir. 2006).

[43] IRC § 471.

[44] Reg. § 1.471-2(b).

[45] 54 T.C. 1749 (1970), *acq.* in result, 1978-2 CB 1, *nonacq.*, 1978-2 CB 3, *aff'd in part and rev'd and rem'd in part*, 467 F.2d 1184 (7th Cir. 1972).

income." Similarly, the regulations state that "no method of accounting is acceptable unless, in the opinion of the Commissioner, it clearly reflects income."[46]

While a method of keeping inventory in accordance with generally accepted accounting principles (GAAP) will be presumed ordinarily to meet the "clear reflection of income" test, this presumption will not always be sustained. A good example of this requirement is found in the Supreme Court's *Thor Power Tool Co. v Commissioner*[47] decision.

Thor Power Tool Co. valued its inventory using the "lower-of-cost-or-market value" method.[48] To avoid the expense of subsequent production runs, Thor kept a stock of parts in inventory for tools that it no longer produced. In 1964, Thor instituted a new procedure by which the cost of these parts would be amortized over a ten-year period; moreover, new management wrote off or wrote down, with the approval of the IRS, $3.1 million in obsolete or unnecessary parts, damaged tools, sales samples, and other items that were scrapped or sold at reduced prices. Thor also sought to write down to scrap value inventory (mostly spare parts) held in excess of any reasonably foreseeable future demand. The items were not scrapped but continued to be held for sale at their original prices. Thor offset the write-down against its 1964 sales, resulting in a net operating loss. The IRS disallowed this write-down.

The Supreme Court ruled that the IRS's disallowance of Thor's write-down was acceptable. Writing for the Court, Justice Blackmun explained that although, as the Tax Court found, the write-downs complied with generally accepted accounting principles, inventory must also "clearly reflect income" under IRC § 471. The regulations provide that inventory must be valued at cost unless the market price, which is the bid price or replacement cost, is lower. The Supreme Court found that Thor failed to provide any hard evidence for its determination of "market value" other than management's business experience. The regulations allow market value to be reduced only by showing that the merchandise has been sold for below-replacement cost or as defective inventory.[49]

The *Thor Power* Court agreed with the Commissioner's determination and observed that IRC §§ 446 and 471, with their accompanying regulations, vest the Commissioner with wide discretion in determining whether a particular method of inventory accounting should be disallowed as not clearly reflective of income. This is consistent with prior Supreme Court decisions, which have held that "[t]he Commissioner has broad powers in determining whether accounting methods used by a taxpayer clearly reflect income."[50]

The Court concluded that the taxpayer bears a "heavy burden of [proof]," and that the Commissioner's disallowance of an inventory accounting method is not to be set aside unless shown to be "plainly arbitrary."[51]

---

[46] Reg. § 1.446-1(a)(2).

[47] 439 U.S. 522 (1979).

[48] *See* § 8.09, *below*.

[49] Reg. § 1.471-2(c).

[50] *Comm'r v. Hansen*, 360 U.S. 446, 467 (1959).

[51] *See also Dayton Hudson Corp. v. Comm'r*, T.C. Memo. 1997-260, *rev'd*, 153 F.3d 660 (8th Cir. 1998).

The *Thor Power* decision has come to signify the extensive power of the Commissioner to determine whether a taxpayer's accounting method is proper under IRC § 446.[52]

§ 8.04 Election of Accounting Method

A taxpayer elects an inventory method by utilizing it on his initial return. No special form or formal election statement is required, except in the case of the adoption of LIFO.[53] In general, the LIFO method must continue to be utilized until IRS permission is obtained to utilize a different method.[54]

§ 8.05 Unacceptable Accounting Methods

Taxpayers are prohibited from using the following methods of accounting for inventories:[55]

- The "base stock" method, under which a minimum quantity of inventory that is necessary at all times for normal operations is fixed as to quantity and price, with increases above the base stock being priced using FIFO, LIFO, or average cost;[56]
- The "prime costing" method, under which only direct material costs and direct labor costs are treated as product costs;[57]
- The "variable or direct costing" method, under which only direct material costs, direct labor costs, and variable overhead are treated as product costs;[58] and
- The "practical capacity" concept, under which fixed overhead costs related to a plant's excess capacity (capacity in excess of current requirements) are expensed currently.[59]

The following practices are also prohibited:

- Deducting a reserve for price changes, estimated decline in value, or excess inventory;[60]

---

[52] *United States v. Hughes Properties, Inc.*, 476 U.S. 593 (1986); *Max Sobel Wholesale Liquors v. Comm'r*, 630 F.2d 670 (9th Cir. 1980); *Dayton Hudson Corp. & Subsidiaries v. Comm'r*, 153 F.3d 660 (8th Cir. 1998); *JP Morgan Chase & Co. v. Comm'r*, 458 F.3d 564 (7th Cir. 2006).

[53] IRC § 472. *See* Form 970, *Application to Use LIFO Inventory Method.*

[54] Reg. § 1.472-2. (Note, however, that a taxpayer may generally adopt LIFO at any time.)

[55] Note, however, that a taxpayer may not generally change from one of these methods to another method without IRS consent. *See* Chapter 7, *supra.*

[56] Reg. § 1.471-2(f)(4).

[57] Reg. § 1.471-2(f)(7).

[58] Reg. § 1.471-2(f)(6).

[59] Reg. § 1.263A-2(a)(4).

[60] Reg. § 1.471-2(f)(1); *Thor Power Tool Co. v. Comm'r*, 439 U.S. 522 (1979).

- Stating any part of the inventory at a nominal value;[61]
- Omitting portions of the inventory;[62] and
- Including items in inventory the title to which has not yet vested in the taxpayer.[63]

§ 8.06 Cost Flow Assumptions/Methods

[A] Generally

A taxpayer may determine the costs to be included in ending inventory under any of the following cost flow assumptions/methods:

- Specific identification method;
- First-in, first-out ("FIFO") method;
- Last-in, first-out ("LIFO") method; and
- Average costing (rolling average) method.[64]

The first three of these methods are specifically deemed to be acceptable.[65]

[B] Specific Identification Method

The basic principle of inventory pricing is uncomplicated: a retailer should determine the value of its inventory by determining what it costs to acquire that inventory. When an inventory item is sold, the inventory account should be reduced (credited) and cost of goods sold should be increased (debited) for the amount paid for each inventory item. This method works if a company is using the Specific Identification Method. That is, a company knows the cost of every individual item that is sold. This method works well when the amount of a company's inventory is limited, the value of its inventory items is high, and each inventory item is relatively unique. Companies that use this method include car dealerships, jewelers, and art galleries. The regulations authorize the use of the specific identification method for tax purposes.[66]

The specific identification method involves pricing each individual unit in ending inventory at its actual purchase price. Consider the following, for example.

Assume that a calendar-year taxpayer commences the purchase and sale of widgets on January 1, 2020. The taxpayer purchases widgets in the following quantities and prices during 2020:

---

[61] Reg. § 1.471-2(f)(2).

[62] Reg. § 1.471-2(f)(3).

[63] Reg. § 1.471-2(f)(5).

[64] As indicated in Rev. Proc. 2008-43, 2008-2 CB 186, the IRS will allow the use of rolling and final inventory as an accurate and clear reflection of income for financial statement purposes.

[65] Reg. § 1.471-2(d).

[66] Reg. § 1.471-2(d).

- March 10, 2020: ten widgets at $10 per widget.
- April 15, 2020: 20 widgets at $11 per widget.
- May 19, 2020: 20 widgets at $12 per widget.
- During 2020, the taxpayer sells 30 widgets. On December 31, 2020, the taxpayer has 20 widgets remaining on hand. The 20 widgets on hand can be specifically identified as the 20 widgets purchased on May 19, 2020.
- The taxpayer's December 31, 2020, inventory of widgets would be valued at $240, *i.e.*, 20 widgets at $12 = $240.

A taxpayer muy use the specific identification method in valuing its inventories, if this method is feasible under the taxpayer's accounting system and if it is based on the nature of the goods. Implicit in the decision to use the specific identification method is the fact that the goods are sufficiently different from each other, which allows them to be tracked separately. Even if specific identification is practicable, one may still choose to use one of the cost flow assumptions for accounting purposes rather than specific identification. If a taxpayer is unable to specifically identify the cost of the goods which it sells, as in the case of fungible goods, the cost of the earliest goods purchased or produced during the taxable year and from year to year must be treated as the cost of the first goods sold.[67]

Because of the amount of recordkeeping inherent in the specific identification method, its use is generally practical where the taxpayer has only a relatively small number of items in its inventory.

[C] FIFO Method

The FIFO ("first in, first out") method assumes that the first goods purchased or produced are the first goods sold. It is a widely accepted cost flow assumption for both accounting and tax purposes.[68] FIFO assumes that the first goods purchased or produced are the first goods sold. As a consequence, ending inventories are valued at most recent purchase or production costs.[69]

Consider the following, for example.

Finch Corporation's latest purchases of boxes of widgets are listed below.

July 4	75 boxes for $ 6,536
October 12	100 boxes for $10,000
November 23	35 boxes for $ 3,300
December 31	75 boxes for $ 7,000

---

[67] Reg. § 1.471-2(d). *See Ozark Mills, Inc. v. Comm'r*, 6 BTA 1179 (1927), for a challenge to the taxpayer using the specific identification method. *See also* GCM 38362 (1980).

[68] *See* Reg. § 1.471-2(d).

[69] Reg. § 1.471-2. Goods taken in an inventory which have been so intermingled that they cannot be identified with specific invoices will be deemed to be the goods most recently purchased or produced, and the cost thereof will be the actual cost of the goods purchased or produced during the period in which the quantity of goods in the inventory has been acquired.

Its physical inventory at the end of the year reveals 200 boxes on hand. Its inventory value (at FIFO cost) is computed as follows:

December 31	75 boxes for $ 7,000
November 23	35 boxes for $ 3,300
October 12	90 boxes for $ 9,000
Ending Inventory	200 boxes $19,300

Companies selling perishable goods such as food and drugs tend to use the FIFO method, because cash flow closely resembles the way good flow.

[D] LIFO Method

The LIFO ("last in, first out") method assumes that the most recently purchased or produced goods are sold first. Accordingly, ending inventories are valued at the oldest historical costs. Therefore, the ending inventory value may be determined by starting with the beginning inventory quantities and then the earliest purchases and working forward through the year until all units in inventory have been costed.

Consider the following, for example.

Falcon Company has sales in 2020 of 5,000 boxes of widgets at a sale price of $5.00. Its opening inventory was valued at $3,000 (3,000 boxes at a value of $1.00). During 2020, it purchased 5,000 widgets at a cost of $3.00. It determines gross profit as follows:

Sales, 5,000 units at $5.00			$25,000
Cost of sales			
	Opening inventory		
		3,000 units @ $1.00	$ 3,000
	Purchases		
		5,000 units @ $3.00	$15,000
	Total		$18,000
Less			
Closing inventory:			
		3,000 units @ $1.00	$ 3,000
Cost of goods sold:			$15,000
Gross profit on sales:			**$10,000**

[E] Average Cost Method[70]

Average costing may be computed in different ways, but normally involves the use of a weighted average of beginning inventory and purchases during the year. Weighted average measures the total cost of items in inventory that are available for sale divided by the total number of units that were in inventory at the beginning of the accounting period and that were purchased during the accounting period. Typically, this average is computed at the end of an accounting period.

For example, suppose you purchase five widgets at $20 apiece and five widgets at $40 apiece. You sell five units of product. The weighted average method is calculated as follows:

Weighted Average Inventory Accounting Formula

Total Cost of Goods for Sale at Cost / Total Number of Units Available for Sale = Weighted

Average Cost per Widget

Five widgets at $20 each = $100

Five widgets at $40 each = $200

Total number of widgets = 10

Weighted Average—$300 / 10 = $30

$30 is the average cost of the ten widgets

§ 8.07 Valuation Methods

[A] Generally

In general, a taxpayer required to maintain inventories could value its inventories based on either (i) cost or (ii) lower-of-cost-or-market.[71]

The one exception to this rule is that a taxpayer utilizing the LIFO cost flow assumption may not use the lower-of-cost-or-market method to value inventories.[72]

[B] At Cost Valuations

What is "Cost?" In general, the meaning of "cost" is related to specific merchandise.

In the case of *merchandise on hand at the beginning of the taxable year*, "cost" is the inventory price of the goods.[73]

In the case of *merchandise purchased since the beginning of the taxable year*, "cost" is the invoice price less trade or other discounts (except strictly cash discounts approxi-

---

[70] The IRS now recognizes the weighted-average cost method as an inventory valuation method that clearly reflects income. Rev. Proc. 2008-43, 2008-30 IRB 186.

[71] Reg. § 1.471-2(c). *See* § 8.09, *Infra*.

[72] IRC § 472(b)(2).

[73] Reg. § 1.471-3(a).

mating a fair rate of interest) which may be deducted or not, at the option of the taxpayer, provided a consistent course of action is followed. To this net invoice price is added transportation or other necessary charges incurred in the acquisition of the goods, *e.g.*, import duties. In addition, taxpayers subject to the UNICAP rules must include additional amounts in inventory cost pursuant to IRC § 263A.[74]

In the case of *merchandise produced by the taxpayer since the beginning of the taxable year*, "cost" is (i) the cost of raw materials and supplies entering into or consumed in connection with the product, (ii) expenditures for direct labor, and (iii) indirect production costs incident to and necessary for the production of the particular article, including an appropriate portion of management expenses in such indirect production costs, but not including any cost of selling or return on capital, whether by way of interest or profit.[75]

[C] Discounts

Cost always reflects a reduction for any trade discounts allowed to the taxpayer (provided the economic performance rules have been satisfied).

Cash discounts may be handled in either of the following ways:

(1) Cost may reflect the gross invoice price, with any discounts claimed being treated as an item of miscellaneous income; or

(2) Cost may reflect the invoice price, net of the cash discount, with any unclaimed discounts being treated as an item of miscellaneous expense.[76]

Under Rev. Proc. 2007-53,[77] an accrual method taxpayer that is required to use an inventory method, maintains inventories, and receives advance trade discounts is eligible to adopt the "advance trade discount method." Under the method, an advance trade discount is not recognized as gross income under IRC § 61 upon receipt, and is taken into account in the amount of, in the manner of, and for the tax year in which the taxpayer accounts for the discount in its financial statements. The taxpayer, however, must reduce the cost of the inventory to which the discount relates as the taxpayer purchases the inventory if that treatment results in recognition of the discount for federal tax purposes earlier than the time at which the taxpayer accounts for the discount in its financial statements.

A payment generally is an advance trade discount for Rev. Proc. 2007-53 purposes if:

(1) the payment is received from a seller of merchandise in exchange for a commitment by the taxpayer to purchase a minimum amount of merchandise from the seller within a period that does not exceed five years from the date of the agreement;

---

[74] Reg. § 1.471-3(b).

[75] Reg. § 1.471-3(c). *See also* IRC § 263A.

[76] *See* Rev. Rul. 73-65, 1973-1 CB 216. The definition of "trade discounts" does not include slotting fees, cooperative advertising, non-compete fees, and other amounts that represent compensation for specific services. Note that the method utilized to account for discounts is a "method of accounting."

[77] 2007-30 IRB 233.

(2) the taxpayer is obligated in writing or under industry custom to repay an allocable portion (or all) of the payment if the purchase commitment is not met; and
(3) the taxpayer does not treat the payment as payment for services in its applicable financial statements.

Rev. Proc. 2019-43,[78] § 22.10, provides automatic consent for taxpayers requesting to change their method of accounting to the advance trade discount method described in Rev. Proc. 2007-53. Automatic consent for this change is only available for accrual method taxpayers maintaining inventories.

[D] Advance Rebates

Gross income is not realized upon the receipt of an amount characterized as a deposit or as a rebate of the purchase price. However, gross income is realized upon the receipt of an inducement to purchase merchandise.[79]

[E] Acquisition Costs

Any costs incurred in the acquisition of goods, such as freight-in, must be added to the invoice price.[80] In addition, under the UNICAP rules, "cost" must generally reflect a ratable portion of storage, purchasing, and handling costs (and related overhead) incurred by the taxpayer.[81]

§ 8.08 Lower-of-Cost-or-Market Valuation

[A] Generally

Under the lower-of-cost-or-market valuation method, the "cost" and "market value" of each individual item in the taxpayer's inventory are compared, and the lesser of the figures in each case is selected and utilized to value the particular inventory item.[82] Write-downs, while acceptable for financial reporting purposes, are not permitted for tax purposes.[83]

---

[78] 2019-48 IRB 1107, modified by Rev. Proc. 2020-13, 2020-11 IRB 515.
[79] *See* Rev. Proc. 2007-53, 2007-2 CB 233.
[80] *Gus Blass Co. v. Comm'r*, 204 F.2d 327 (8th Cir. 1953).
[81] *See* § 9.07, § 9.08 and § 9.09.
[82] Reg. § 1.471-4(c).
[83] *Thor Power Tool Co. v. Comm'r*, 439 U.S. 522 (1979).

[B] Market Value Determination

For accounting purposes, the residual usefulness of the inventory is determined by its market value. The term "market" means current replacement cost (whether by purchase or reproduction). With respect to goods purchased and on hand, the term "market" means the current bid price prevailing at the date of the inventory for the merchandise in the usual volume purchased by the taxpayer.[84] The regulations recognize two exceptions to the determination of market value by using replacement or reproduction cost. First, if it is impossible to obtain a bid price (*i.e.*, no open market exists) or quotations are nominal, the best available evidence of fair market value must be used. Such evidence may be specific purchases or sales by the taxpayer or others in reasonable volume, or compensation paid for the cancellation of contracts for purchase commitments.[85]

The determination of the "market value" of a good requires that the following questions be answered:

- Is the good a "normal" good?
- Is the good a "subnormal" good?

[C] "Normal" Goods

Under ordinary circumstances, "market value" for normal goods in inventory means the aggregate of the *current bid prices* (prevailing at the date of the inventory) of the *basic elements of cost* reflected in inventories of goods purchased and on hand; goods in the process of manufacture; and finished manufactured goods on hand.

The determination of the "current bid price" of the basic elements of costs reflected in goods on hand at the inventory date must be based on the usual volume of particular cost elements purchased (or incurred) by the taxpayer.[86]

The "basic elements of cost" include direct materials, direct labor, and indirect costs required to be included in inventories by the taxpayer. For taxpayers to which IRC § 263A applies, the basic elements of cost must reflect all direct costs and all indirect costs properly allocable to goods on hand at the inventory date at the current bid price of those costs, including but not limited to the cost of purchasing, handling, and storage activities conducted by the taxpayer, both prior to and subsequent to the acquisition or production of the goods.

The following are excepted from the general rules for determining market value in the case of "normal" goods:

- Fixed price contracts;[87]
- Obligation to sell goods at a loss;[88]

---

[84] Reg. § 1.471-4(a)(1).

[85] Reg. § 1.471-4(b).

[86] Reg. § 1.471-4(a).

[87] Reg. § 1.471-4(a)(2). *See Ellstrom v. Comm'r*, T.C. Memo. 1955-91, *aff'd*, 235 F.2d 181 (6th Cir. 1956).

[88] *See, e.g.*, Reg. § 1.471-4(b).

- No open market;[89] and
- Offers for sale at a reduced price.[90]

[D] *Excess Inventory*

Excess inventory is inventory that has been purchased or produced in an amount in excess of the reasonable foreseeable needs of the taxpayer. Generally, such inventory bears no physical characteristics distinguishing it from normal goods and usually carries the same offering price as normal goods.

A taxpayer may not generally claim a write-down with respect to excess inventory.[91] The excess goods have to be valued in inventory at replacement costs.[92]

A taxpayer may be able to claim a deduction with respect to excess inventory where

- The taxpayer actually scraps the inventory prior to year-end;
- The taxpayer sells the inventory in a bona fide, arm's-length transaction;[93]
- The taxpayer offers the goods for sale at a reduced price; or
- The goods become obsolete and totally worthless.[94]

[E] *Subnormal Goods*

"Subnormal" goods are goods which are unsalable at normal prices or unusable in the normal way because of damage, imperfections, shop wear, changes in style, odd or broken lots, etc., including second-hand goods taken in exchange.[95] Subnormal goods do not include excess inventory which is indistinguishable from normal inventory. They should be valued at *bona fide* selling price less the direct cost of disposition.[96] Bona fide selling price means actual offering of goods during a period ending not later than 30 days after inventory date. Reg. § 1.471-2(c) provides for the valuation of subnormal goods. LIFO taxpayers may not value subnormal goods below their original cost.[97]

Taxpayers have the burden of proving that goods which are reduced in value are subnormal and are, in fact, valued on the basis of actual offering prices.

---

[89] Reg. § 1.471-4(b).
[90] Reg. § 1.471-3(b).
[91] *See Thor Power Tool Co. v. Comm'r*, 439 U.S. 522 (1979).
[92] *Id.*
[93] Rev. Rul. 83-59, 1983-1 CB 103; *Paccar, Inc. v. Comm'r*, 849 F.2d 393 (9th Cir. 1988).
[94] Reg. § 1.471-2(c).
[95] Reg. § 1.471-2(c).
[96] *See* TAM 9729001.
[97] Rev. Rul. 76-282, 1976-2 CB 137.

[F] *Tax Treatment: Net Realizable Value*

Regardless of whether a taxpayer employs the cost or the lower-of-cost-or-market value method of inventory valuation, subnormal goods should be valued at net realizable value, *i.e.*, the *bona fide selling price* less *direct costs of disposition* (but in no case less than scrap value).[98] "Bona fide selling price" is determined generally on the basis of the 30-day rule offering price. "Direct costs of disposition" include selling expenses (advertising, freight out, commissions, salesmen's salaries, etc.) and costs of renovating or repairing subnormal goods in order to make them saleable, but not general and administrative costs.

In general, net realizable value must be determined based on an actual offering of the goods for sale within 30 days after the inventory date. Several exceptions with respect to certain goods apply to the 30-day rule, including

- Goods that are sufficiently damaged[99] or obsolete to be considered completely worthless, except as scrap;[100]
- Second-hand goods taken in exchange;[101] and
- Raw materials and work-in-process (which should be valued on a reasonable basis, considering the condition and usefulness of the goods).

Sales of goods more than 30 days after the inventory date are not necessarily determinative of the value of such goods at the inventory date if there is evidence of changed circumstances.

A taxpayer utilizing the LIFO valuation method cannot value subnormal goods at net realizable value.[102]

[G] *Year of Worthlessness*

The deduction for the decline in the value of subnormal goods is allowable in the taxable year in which the decline in value occurs. If a decline in value occurred in a prior taxable year and was not claimed by the taxpayer, the IRS may contend that an attempt to claim a current year deduction is an improper change of accounting method.

If a taxpayer is unaware of the worthlessness in his inventory until a subsequent year when its lack of salability is determined, the taxpayer may generally carry goods at cost until the year of determination.

---

98 Reg. § 1.471-2(c); TAM 9729001.

99 Reg. § 1.471-3(c).

100 *Queen City Woodworks & Lumber Co. v. Crooks*, 7 F. Supp. 684 (S.D. Mo. 1934).

101 Rev. Rul. 67-107, 1967-1 CB 115.

102 *See* Rev. Rul. 76-282, 1976-2 CB 137.

[H] Recordkeeping Requirements

Taxpayers must maintain records of dispositions of subnormal goods so the IRS can verify that any write-downs claimed are reasonable.[103]

[I] Illustration of Method

The following hypothetical illustrates the application of the lower-of-cost-or-market method.

Example 8-4

Taxpayer A manufactures tractors. A values its inventory using cost or market, whichever is lower. At the end of 2020, the cost of one of A's tractors on hand is determined as follows:

Direct materials	$3,000
Direct labor	4,000
Indirect costs under IRC § 263A	3,000
Total IRC § 263A costs (cost)	$ 10,000

A determines that the aggregate of the current bid prices of the materials, labor, and overhead required to reproduce the tractor at the end of 2020 are as follows:

Direct materials	$ 3,100
Direct labor	4,100
Indirect costs under IRC § 263A	3,100
Total IRC § 263A costs (market)	$ 10,300

In determining the lower of cost or market value of the tractor, A compares the cost of the tractor, $10,000, with the market value of the tractor, $10,300 thus, under lower of cost or market, A values the tractor at $10,000.

Example 8-5

Taxpayer B purchases and resells several lines of shoes and is subject to IRC § 263A. B values its inventory using cost or market, whichever is lower. At the end of 2020, the cost of one pair of shoes on hand is determined as follows:

---

[103] Reg. § 1.471-2(e).

Acquisition cost	$ 200
Indirect costs under IRC § 263A	10
Total IRC § 263A costs (cost)	$ 210

B determines the aggregate current bid prices prevailing at the end of 2020 for the elements of cost (both direct costs and indirect costs incurred prior and subsequent to acquisition of the shoes) based on the volume of the elements usually purchased (or incurred) by B as follows:

Acquisition cost	$178
Indirect costs under IRC § 263A	12
Total IRC § 263A costs (market)	$190

In determining the lower of cost or market value of the shoes, B compares the cost of the pair of shoes, $210, with the market value of the shoes, $190 thus, B values the shoes at $190.[104]

Example 8-6

XYZ Corp. holds the following three items and its ending inventory:

Item	Cost	Replacement Cost	NRV	Market	LCM
X	50	60	70	60	50
Y	100	80	90	80	80
Z	150	130	100	100	100
					$230

Item X's cost is less than market therefore it is valued at cost. Item Y is normal goods and, consequently, it is valued at the lower of cost or replacement cost. Item Z is a subnormal good and therefore it is valued at the lower of cost or net realizable value.

§ 8.09 Inventoriable Items

The IRS and the courts have determined that a taxpayer is required (or allowed) to account for the costs of the following types of items using inventory accounting[105]:

---

104 *See* Examples in Reg. § 1.471-4.

105 For an illustration where inventories have not been required, see *Seigle v. Comm'r*, 281 F.2d 372 (4th Cir. 1960), where a dealer who bought surplus parts bought up to 1,000,000 items belonging to 1,500 to 2,000 different classifications. In that case, the taxpayer was allowed a fixed percentage of sale price based on an industry experience. *See also Bryan v. Comm'r*, 44 BTA 141 (1941).

- Raw materials, *e.g.*, steel purchased by an automobile producer;
- Supplies held for sale, *e.g.*, replacement parts sold by an appliance manufacturer;
- Scrap produced during the production process which has not yet been physically disposed of; and
- Custom-ordered merchandise, including job order overruns.[106]

Reg. §1.471-1 provides that inventory should contain all finished or partly finished goods, and in the case of raw materials and supplies, only those which have been acquired for sale or which will physically become part of the merchandise intended for sale, such as containers, kegs, bottles, and cases, whether returnable or not, if title thereto will pass to the purchaser of the product to be sold there in.[107]

Strategically, a taxpayer may wish to argue that goods are inventory in order to:

- Qualify for use of a favorable inventory accounting method (*e.g.*, LIFO);
- Qualify for the use of favorable inventory costing procedures (*e.g.*, lower-of-cost-or-market); or
- Qualify for the deferral of income related to the sale of inventory.

On the other hand, a taxpayer might find it advantageous to argue that goods are not inventory in order to:

- Obtain a current deduction for the cost of the goods;
- Qualify for the cash method of accounting; or
- Qualify for capital gain upon sale of the goods.

§8.10 Noninventoriable Items

The IRS and the courts have determined that a taxpayer is *not* required (or allowed) to account for the costs of the following types of items using inventory accounting:

- Items purchased for sale at (or below) cost as a form of advertising, *i.e.*, promotional items, except where the promotional goods are as of the same nature as goods regularly sold by the taxpayer;[108]
- Catalogs which are not sold, but rather utilized to elicit sales;[109]
- Items held for rental, where the primary purpose for holding the property is rental, as opposed to sale;[110]

---

[106] *See* Rev. Rul. 77-228, 1977-2 CB 182 and TAM 9233003.

[107] *See B.A. Ballou & Co. Inc. v. United States*, 7 Cl Ct 658, 85-1 USTC ¶9290 (Cl Ct 1985), where jeweler purchased gold not intended for sale but to preserve his LIFO layers to avoid phantom income; *Epic Metal Corp.*, T.C. Memo. 1984-322.

[108] *See Francisco Sugar Co. v. Comm'r*, 47 F.2d 555 (2d Cir. 1931).

[109] *See Spiegel, May, Stern Go. v. United States*, 37 F.2d 988 (Ct. Cl. 1930).

[110] *See Recordak Corp. v. Unites States*, 325 F.2d 460 (Ct. Cl. 1963); *Pierce-Arrow Motor Car Co. v. United States*, 9 F. Supp. 577 (Ct. Cl. 1935); *Honeywell Inc. v. Comm'r*, 87 T.C. 624 (1986); and *Grant Oil Tool Co. v. United States*, 381 F.2d 389 (Ct. Cl. 1967).

- Rotatable spare parts;[111]
- Supplies which are not held for sale and will not become part of merchandise held for sale;[112]
- Containers with respect to which title does not pass to the purchaser, which are properly treated as a fixed asset;[113]
- Real estate held for sale to customers;[114] and
- Goods the title to which is not vested in the taxpayer notwithstanding the fact that the taxpayer may have physical possession of the goods.[115]

§ 8.11 Periodic Physical Counts

Physical inventories must be taken on a periodic basis.[116] Inventory records should be adjusted to correspond with actual quantities of goods on hand, as determined by periodic physical inventories.

§ 8.12 Spare Parts

[A] Inventory Treatment

Spare parts are treated as inventory where:

- They are held for sale to customers;
- They are held to service customer-owned equipment, in which case, the installation of the spare part in the customer's equipment is, in essence, a sales transaction; or
- They are held to service either customer-owned equipment or leased equipment.[117]

---

[111] *See Honeywell, Inc. v. Comm'r*, T.C. Memo. 1992-453, *aff'd without opinion*, 27 F.3d 571 (8th Cir. 1994).

Rotable and temporary spare parts can be handled in one of four ways:

- Deduct the costs when the parts are disposed of. Reg. § 1.162-3(a)(1), Reg. § 1.162-3(a)(3);
- Adopt an optional method for such costs. Reg. § 1.162-3(a)(3), Reg. § 1.162-3(e);
- Deduct the costs under the elective *de minimis* rule. Reg. § 1.162-3(a)(3), Reg. § 1.162-3(f);
- Elect to capitalize and depreciate the costs. Reg. § 1.162-3(a)(3), Reg. § 1.162-3(d). *See* Chapter 13, *infra.*

[112] *Smith Leasing Co. v. Comm'r*, 43 T.C. 37 (1964).

[113] Rev. Rul. 58-77, 1958-1 CB 118.

[114] *See W.C. and A.N. Miller Development Co. v. Comm'r*, 81 T.C. 619 (1983), and Rev. Rul. 86-149, 1986-2 CB 67.

[115] *See Finance and Guarantee Company v. Comm'r*, 50 F. 2d 1061 (4th Cir. 1931).

[116] Reg. § 1.471-2(e).

[117] However, in *Hewlett Packard Co. v. United States*, 71 F.3d 398 (Fed Cir. 1995), the appellate court reversed the trial court and held that a pool of rotatable spare parts used by the taxpayer to repair computers that it sold was properly treated as a depreciable capital asset rather than as inventory, and that the exchange of parts from the pool for the original parts in the customers' computers did not constitute a sale of merchandise, since the taxpayer's business was a service business. *See* DCN No. 109, 110, 121, 188, 189 in Instructions for Form 3115.

[B] Non-Inventory Treatment

Spare parts are *not* treated as inventory where:

- They are held to service internally-used equipment; or
- They are held to service leased equipment.

Non-inventoriable spare parts are treated as a deferred expense, if short-lived, or as a depreciable capital asset if they represent capital expenditures.

The regulations differentiate between rotable and temporary spare parts. Rotable spare parts are materials and supplies that are acquired for installation on a unit of property, removable from that unit of property, generally repaired or improved, and either reinstalled on the same or other property or stored for later installation.[118]

Temporary spare parts are materials and supplies that are used temporarily until a new or repaired part can be installed and then are removed and stored for later installation.

Standby emergency spare parts are materials and supplies that are:

- Acquired when particular machinery or equipment is acquired (or later acquired and set aside for use in particular machinery or equipment);
- Set aside for use as replacements to avoid substantial operational time loss caused by emergencies due to particular machinery or equipment failure;
- Located at or near the site of the installed related machinery or equipment so as to be readily available when needed;
- Directly related to the particular machinery or piece of equipment they serve;
- Normally expensive;
- Only available on special order and not readily available from a vendor or manufacturer;
- Not subject to normal periodic replacement;
- Not interchangeable in other machines or equipment;
- Not acquired in quantity (generally only one is on hand for each piece of machinery or equipment); and
- Not repaired and reused.[119]

Under the repair regulations,[120] a taxpayer may elect to capitalize and depreciate the cost of any rotable spare part, temporary spare part, or standby emergency spare parts. This election applies to amounts paid during the tax year to acquire or produce any rotable, temporary, or standby emergency spare parts that would otherwise be deductible. Any property for which this election is made is not treated as a material or a supply.

---

[118] *See* Chapter 13, *infra.*

[119] For prior law, *see* Rev. Rul. 81-185, 1981-2 CB 59.

[120] *See* § 13.03. *See also* Reg. § 1.263(a)-3(b). *See, e.g.*, Reg. § 1.263(a)-3, which requires taxpayers to capitalize amounts paid to improve tangible property and IRC § 263A and the regulations under IRC § 263A, which require taxpayers to capitalize the direct and allocable indirect costs, including the cost of materials and supplies, of property produced by the taxpayer and property acquired for resale. *See also* Reg. § 1.471-1, which requires taxpayers to include in inventory certain materials and supplies.

§ 8.13 Containers

The proper treatment of containers used in industry, *e.g.*, beverage containers, cylinder gas containers, etc., depends on the passage of their title.

If title does not pass to the purchaser, the taxpayer should account for the container at cost and be allowed to depreciate the item. In this case, the container should not be inventoried since it is not for sale to customers.[121]

If title does pass to the purchaser, the container is inventoried in the same manner as the merchandise.[122]

§ 8.14 Materials and Supplies

Materials and supplies are properly accounted for as inventory if they are acquired for sale or will physically become part of a product being produced for sale.[123]

Items purchased for customers incidental to services might be either incidental or nonincidental materials or supplies depending on the facts or circumstances.[124] The significance of the classification lies in the fact that, under Reg. § 1.162-3, materials and supplies that are not incidental are deductible only in the year in which they are consumed and used in the business. In effect, the regulation requires that those items be inventoried.[125] Incidental supplies may be deducted immediately when paid for.[126]

Section 4.03 of Notice 2001-76[127] explains that cash-basis taxpayers "must treat all inventoriable items (*e.g.*, items purchased for resale to customers and raw materials purchased for use in producing finished goods) . . . in the same manner as materials and supplies that are not incidental under [Reg. §]1.162-3."

Supplies that are not held for sale and will not become part of merchandise held for sale are not inventoriable.[128] To the extent that supplies are not accounted for as inventory, they are treated as deferred expenses. As such, they are included generally in expenses only when they are actually consumed and used. An exception to this rule applies where the supplies are incidental and no record of consumption is made.

---

[121] Rev. Rul. 75-34, 1975-1 CB 271; *cf. Nehi Beverage Co. v. Comm'r*, 16 T.C. 1114 (1951).

[122] *Dewey Portland Cement Co. v. Crooks*, 57 F.2d 499 (8th Cir. 1932); *U.S. Industrial Alcohol Co.*, 42 BTA 1323 (1940). *See also* Rev. Proc. 79-44, 1979-2 CB 508.

[123] Reg. § § 1.162-3, 1.471-1.

[124] *See* § 13.01; Reg. § 1.162-3(a)(1).

[125] Reg. § 1.162-3(a)(1) provides amounts paid to acquire or produce materials and supplies are deductible in the taxable year in which the materials and supplies are first used in the taxpayer's operations or are consumed in the taxpayer's operations.

[126] Reg. § 1.162-3(a)(2) provides amounts paid to acquire or produce incidental materials and supplies that are carried on hand and for which no record of consumption is kept or of which physical inventories at the beginning and end of the taxable year are not taken, are deductible in the taxable year in which these amounts are paid, provided taxable income is clearly reflected.

[127] 2001-2 CB 613, 615.

[128] *Smith Leasing Co. v. Comm'r*, 43 T.C. 37 (1964).

In such a case, the supplies may be expensed when purchased if taxable income is clearly reflected.[129]

While Reg. § 1.162-3 provides for treatment of materials and supplies, nevertheless these provisions must be coordinated with other Code sections.[130]

In Priv. Ltr. Rul. 9209007, the IRS stated its position that incidental supplies are items of minor importance and not those that are essential or necessary for the taxpayer's business.[131] In this regard, the IRS will assert generally that materials are of nonincidental importance if they are identified for financial reporting purposes, such as

- Supplies consumed in production, *e.g.*, fuel to run production equipment;
- Supplies held for sale in a business where inventories are not required, *e.g.*, gold fillings owned by a dentist;
- Nonmanufacturing supplies, *e.g.*, stationery in a manufacturing business; and
- Short-lived capital assets, *e.g.*, uniforms in a service business.

The current regulations provide a more detailed explanation of materials and supplies:

Materials and supplies are tangible property that are used or consumed in the taxpayer's operations that are not inventory and that—

- Are a component acquired to maintain, repair, or improve a unit of tangible property (as determined under Reg. § 1.263(a)-3(e)) owned, leased, or serviced by the taxpayer and that is not acquired as part of any single unit of tangible property;
- Consist of fuel, lubricants, water, and similar items, reasonably expected to be consumed in 12 months or less, beginning when used in the taxpayer's operations;
- Are a unit of property as determined under Reg. § 1.263(a)-3(e) that has an economic useful life of 12 months or less, beginning when the property is used or consumed in the taxpayer's operations;
- Are a unit of property as determined under Reg. § 1.263(a)-3(e) that has an acquisition cost or production cost (as determined under IRC § 263A) of $200 or less (or other amount as identified in published guidance in the Federal Register or in the Internal Revenue Bulletin) (see Reg. § 601.601(d)(2)(ii)(b))); or

---

[129] Reg. § 1.162-3.

[130] *See, e.g.*, Reg. § 1.263(a)-3, which requires taxpayers to capitalize amounts paid to improve tangible property and IRC § 263A and the regulations under IRC § 263A, which require taxpayers to capitalize the direct and allocable indirect costs, including the cost of materials and supplies, of property produced by the taxpayer and property acquired for resale. *See also* Reg. § 1.471-1, which requires taxpayers to include in inventory certain materials and supplies.

[131] *See also* § 13.01.

- Are identified in published guidance in the Federal Register or in the Internal Revenue Bulletin (see Reg. § 601.601(d)(2)(ii)(b)) as materials and supplies for which treatment is permitted under this section.[132]

§ 8.15 Shrinkage

[A] *Deduction in Year of Loss*

Inventory losses (shrinkage) should be deducted in the year in which such losses are discovered.[133]

[B] *Shrinkage Estimates*

The use of estimates to determine inventories is allowed if:

- The estimates are confirmed by a physical count only after the last day of the taxable year,[134]
- The taxpayer normally does a physical count of inventories at each location on a regular and consistent basis, and
- The taxpayer makes proper adjustments to such inventories and to its estimating methods to the extent such estimates are greater than or less than the actual shrinkage.[135]

§ 8.16 Passage of Title to Goods

[A] *Generally*

It is important to determine when title to goods passes from the purchaser to the seller.[136]

From the seller's standpoint, passage of title may mark the time for recognizing income and excluding an item from income. Alternatively, a taxpayer may recognize

---

[132] Reg. § 1.162-3(c).

[133] Where physical inventory counts are not conducted at year-end in the past, the IRS has argued that the taxpayer should not be allowed to accrue estimated shrinkage losses at year-end (contrast *Altec Corp. v. Comm'r*, 36 TCM 1795 (1977), where no deduction for estimated shrinkage was allowed, with *Dayton Hudson Corp. v. Comm'r*, 101 T.C. 462 (1993), where the court held that a deduction for shrinkage is allowable if the method of determination clearly reflects income). In Rev. Proc. 98-29, 1998-1 CB 857, the IRS issued procedures for taxpayers to change to an accounting method for estimating inventory shrinkage in computing ending inventory, *modified by*, Rev. Proc. 2015-14, 2015-5 IRB 450. *See also* IRC § 471(b). *See* DCN No. 49 in Instructions for Form 3115.

[134] IRC § 471(b).

[135] *See Wal-Mart Stores v. Comm'r*, 153 F.3d 650, 658 (8th Cir. 1998); and Rev. Proc. 2019-43, 2019-48 IRB 1107.

[136] Reg. § 1.471-1.

income generally when the item is shipped, or when the item is delivered and accepted, if the taxpayer utilizes such method on a consistent basis in keeping its books.[137]

From the purchaser's standpoint, passage of title determines whether or not the item is properly included in the taxpayer's inventory, and thus, may influence the taxpayer's income, *e.g.*, through the determination of whether a "LIFO liquidation" has occurred.[138]

[B] Inclusion Rules

Merchandise should be included in inventory only if title to it is vested in the taxpayer.[139] Accordingly, a seller should include in his inventory goods under contract for sale but not yet segregated and applied to the contract, and goods out upon consignment,[140] but should exclude from inventory goods sold (including containers), title to which has passed to the purchaser.[141]

A purchaser should include in inventory merchandise purchased (including containers), title to which has passed to him, even though such merchandise is in transit or for other reasons has not been reduced to physical possession,[142] but should exclude goods ordered for future delivery, the transfer of title to which has not yet been effected. The moment when title passes will depend usually on state law.[143]

[C] Judicial Decisions

The intent of the parties generally controls when title passes under state law.[144] Important judicial decisions addressing the question of when title to good passes include the following:

- *Brown Lumber Company v. Commissioner*,[145] which held that the determination of when title passes involves an inquiry into the intent of the parties to the transaction;
- *Pacific Grape Products Company v. Commissioner*,[146] which held that the title to fungible goods passed when the goods were billed;

---

137 Reg. § 1.446-1(c)(1)(ii)(C).

138 A LIFO liquidation takes place when there is a decrease in a taxpayer's LIFO inventories. In such event, the taxpayer risks having low-basis beginning inventory thereby producing a higher profit than there would have been if the taxpayer had been able to replace its inventory and avoid the liquidation.

139 Reg. § 1.471-1.

140 Reg. § 1.471-1; *Modesto Dry Yard, Inc. v. Comm'r.*, 14 T.C. 374 (1950).

141 *Id.*

142 *Pacific Grape Products Company v. Comm'r.*, 219 F.2d 862 (9th Cir. 1955).

143 *See* Reg. § 1.471-1; *Epic Metals Corporation and Subsidiaries*, T.C. Memo. 1984-322.

144 *See Shasta Industries, Inc. v. Comm'r.*, T.C. Memo. 1986-377.

145 35 F.2d 880 (D.C. Cir. 1929).

146 219 F.2d 862 (9th Cir. 1955).

- *Hallmark Cards, Inc. v. Commissioner,*[147] where the court found that passage of title (per contract) had not occurred even though the items in question had been shipped prior to year-end; and
- *Liggett Group, Inc. v. Commissioner,*[148] where the court found that title did not pass until goods reached a foreign country (per contract), even though the goods were delivered to customers in the United States.

[D] C.O.D. Sales

In Rev. Rul. 70-68,[149] the IRS ruled that a C.O.D. sale is not consummated and title to the goods does not pass until delivery and payment are made. A shipment for which the purchaser has not paid at the close of the year should not be included in gross sales and the merchandise should be included in the seller's year-end inventory.

[E] Consignments

Goods out on consignment should be included in the inventory of the seller, not the purchaser.[150]

[F] Sale or Return Contracts

Goods sold under a contract of sale or return are not includable in inventory where title passes upon the delivery of the goods to a common carrier.[151]

[G] Shipments on Approval

Prior to acceptance by a consignee, gross sales should not include merchandise shipped on approval; rather, such property is properly included in the ending inventory of the seller.[152]

[H] Free on Board

Goods that are shipped FOB are placed "free on board" by the seller. Title to the goods normally passes to the purchaser when the goods are placed in transit. Therefore, the goods are excluded from the seller's inventory when placed in transit.[153]

---

[147] 90 T.C. 26 (1988).

[148] T.C. Memo. 1990-18.

[149] 1970-1 CB 122.

[150] Committee Reports for JCS-2-14, 113th Congress.

[151] Rev. Rul. 71-451, 1971-2 CB 217.

[152] *Cleveland Woolen Mill v. Comm'r,* 8 BTA 49 (1927), *acq.* 1928-1 CB 7.

[153] *Brown Lumber Co., Inc. v. Comm'r,* 35 F.2d 880 (D.C. Cir. 1929).

[I] *Where Title is Not Controlling*

Although the regulations stress that goods are not to be included in inventory unless title is possessed by the taxpayer, title may not always be controlling. In *Honeywell Inc. v. Commissioner*,[154] the court stated that:

> The passing of legal title is among the factors to be considered in determining whether a sale has occurred for Federal income tax purposes.[155] Because it is only one factor, however, it is not determinative. Rather, the determination of whether a sale has occurred is to be governed by the substance of the transaction and not its form. In our view, respondent's focus on title in this case elevates form over substance.[156]

§8.17 Cash Basis Taxpayers

[A] *Historical Position of the IRS*

Conflict between the IRS and taxpayers over the use of the cash method has manifested itself over the years. The source of the conflict involves the sale of merchandise versus the performance of services. Historically, in the view of the IRS, once it was established that merchandise was an income producing factor, inventories had to be maintained,[157] and the use of the accrual method was compulsory.[158]

An illustrative case is *Wilkinson-Beane, Inc. v. Commissioner*.[159] In *Wilkinson*, a cash method undertaker provided complete funeral services which included the supply of caskets. Caskets could not be purchased separately. A single unitemized price was charged. The "magnificence" of the funeral was directly related to the quality of the casket. The undertaker-taxpayer derived approximately 15% of its gross receipts from the caskets.

The IRS required the taxpayer to maintain inventories though the application of Reg. §§1.471-1 and 1.446-1(c)(2)(i). Reg. §1.471-1 provided, in pertinent part,

> In order to reflect taxable income correctly, inventories at the beginning and end of each taxable year are necessary in every case in which the production, purchase, or sale of merchandise is an income-producing factor.

---

[154] 64 TCM 437 (1992).

[155] *Grodt & McKay Realty, Inc. v. Comm'r*, 77 T.C. 1221, 1237 (1981).

[156] *Honeywell*, 64 TCM 437 at 446 (1992).

[157] Reg. §1.471-1.

[158] Reg. §1.446-1(c)(1)(iv).

[159] 420 F.2d 352 (1st Cir. 1970).

Reg. § 1.446-1(c)(2)(i) stated:

> In any case in which it is necessary to use an inventory the accrual method of accounting must be used with regard to purchases and sales unless otherwise authorized under subdivision (ii) of this subparagraph.

Through the interaction of these two provisions the IRS compelled the taxpayer to use the accrual method of accounting.

Agreeing with the IRS, the Tax Court and the Court of Appeals observed that the caskets were "substantial income-producing factors in the taxpayer's business." Since the taxpayer's caskets were "plainly both merchandise and substantial income-producing factors," the accrual method was required.

The IRS's position was reaffirmed in subsequent cases, such as in the case of *J.P. Sheahan Associates, Inc. v. Commissioner*.[160] Sheahan, the taxpayer, was a roofing contractor who did roof repairs and constructed replacement roofs. The taxpayer, who used the cash method since the inception of its business, did not physically maintain inventories because materials were ordered only on an "as needed" basis, and leftover materials were either returned to the supplier for credit or earmarked for another job. Consequently, Sheahan argued that it had no year-end inventory and did not hold merchandise for sale within the meaning of the regulations and should not be required to use the accrual method of accounting.

In its analysis of the case, the Tax Court observed that the mere fact the taxpayer did not have year-end inventory was irrelevant; moreover, the record clearly showed that the materials were held for sale to customers and produced income. The customer was separately billed for the merchandise and the taxpayer added a 25-percent mark up to the billed price. Clearly, merchandise was an income producing factor, and therefore, the taxpayer was required to maintain inventories and hence use the accrual method of tax accounting.[161]

---

160 T.C. Memo. 1992-239.

161 Similar rulings include: Priv. Ltr. Rul. 9524001 (taxpayer, general contractor, billed his client for the job and, in turn, paid his suppliers and subcontractors who provided the materials and labor); *Fred H. McGrath & Son, Inc., v. United States*, 549 F. Supp. 491 (S.D. N.Y. 1982) (undertaker's caskets; facts similar to Wilkinson-Beane); Rev. Rul. 74-279, 1974-1 CB 110 (optometrist's eyeglasses and frames; optometrist charged single sales price for glasses, frames, and "the various services provided," (grinding to prescription, etc.)); Rev. Rul. 73-485, 1973-2 CB 150 (taxpayer provided artificial limbs and orthopedic braces to the disabled, charging one un-itemized price for the prosthetic devices, instruction in their use, and custom fitting); Rev. Rul. 69-537, 1969-2 CB 109 (ruling on Wilkinson-Beane issue); GCM 37699 (Sept. 29, 1978) (reconsidering and reaffirming Rev. Rul. 74-279); TAM 8744005 (taxpayer providing maintenance services for building lighting fixtures at a flat fee which included replacement of light bulbs as necessary). *Knight-Ridder Newspapers v. United States*, 743 F.2d 781 (11th Cir. 1984) (newspaper required to maintain inventories of paper and ink); *Fame Tool & Mfg. Co. v. Comm'r*, 334 F. Supp. 23 (S.D. Ohio 1971) (custom tool and die maker had to use inventories for work in process although it maintained no finished goods inventories); *Middlebrooks v. Comm'r*, T.C. Memo. 1975-275 (advance printing costs for trade magazine inventoriable although when magazines were printed taxpayer immediately sold them to a distributor). *See also Herbert C. Haynes, Inc. v. Comm'r*, T.C. Memo. 2004-185.

[B] Substantial Identity of Result Doctrine

A cash basis taxpayer when faced with the argument that his method of accounting does not clearly reflect income because he does not maintain inventories, may be able to defeat an attempt by the IRS to change his accounting method. To do so, the taxpayer must show that his method of accounting produced a result substantially identical to the result he would have obtained if he used the accrual method of accounting.

In *Wilkinson-Beane*, the taxpayer's accountant prepared a five-year schedule[162] comparing the accrual and cash methods, which showed a variance of less than two-tenths of one percent, which purported to show that the disparity in gross income resulting from the use of the different methods was inconsequential and testified that in this case it was immaterial whether the cash or accrual method was used. The court said "even if we accept taxpayer's reconstruction of accrual method income for the years in question, we cannot agree that the disparities between the accounting methods are negligible." In analyzing this difference, the Court said that the standard to apply is whether the taxpayer's method of accounting reflects his income with as much accuracy as standard methods of accounting permit. To avoid the application of the accrual method, a taxpayer must demonstrate substantial identity of results between his method and the method selected by the Commissioner. The fact that the difference was as small as it was, the Court said, was fortuitous. Furthermore, there was no guarantee that the stability of sales, costs, collections, etc., would continue in the future. Therefore, the Court rejected the taxpayer's use of the cash method.

In *Ansley-Sheppard Burgess Company v. Commissioner*,[163] the application of the substantial identity of result doctrine was again at issue. Like *Sheahan*, the taxpayer was a contractor, who used the cash method, and did not maintain an inventory. The Commissioner wanted the taxpayer to use the percentage-of-completion method except that the taxpayer qualified as a small contractor and was not subject to IRC § 460(a). The taxpayer's average annual gross receipts for the three years preceding the intended change was $2,394.60. If the taxpayer used the percentage-of-completion method it would have included an additional amount of $6,117.00 per year. Nevertheless, the Commissioner said that the taxpayer's method of accounting did not clearly reflect income.

162

Year	Accrual	Cash
1961	$120,284.66	$121,102.12
1962	117,413.78	113,506.86
1963	127,803.92	129,898.72
1964	115,994.42	120,209.64
1965	125,584.68	121,574.92

163 104 T.C. 367 (1995).

The *Ansley-Sheppard* Court said whether a method of accounting clearly reflects income is a question of fact to be determined on a case by case basis. To prevail against the Commissioner, a taxpayer must prove the Commissioner's determination is arbitrary and capricious and without sound basis in fact or law. After noting that the cash method will usually result in some distortion of income, the Court said if the cash method is consistently used and no attempt is made to unreasonably prepay expenses or to purchase supplies, the distortion is not material and over a period of years the distortions tend to cancel out each other.

The Court noted that neither IRC §448 nor §460 was applicable. It concluded, therefore, that the Commissioner abused its discretion in attempting to compel the taxpayer to change its method of accounting. In reaching its conclusion, the Court said that the application of the substantial identity of results test was unwarranted. By refusing to apply the test, the Court did not have to determine if the taxpayer's method of accounting reflected income with as much accuracy as standard methods of accounting practice permit. The Court noted that the application of this standard would, if carried to its logical conclusion, prohibit the cash method of accounting for tax purposes.[164]

[C] Retreat from Historical Positions

Through the early 1990s, the IRS took the position that notwithstanding the fact that a taxpayer was largely providing a service, if he nevertheless also "sold" merchandise he was required to use the accrual method and he had to maintain inventories. Subsequently, the IRS was handed several defeats. An example of the court's reasoning was expressed in *Osteopathic Medical Oncology and Hematology, P.C. v. Commissioner*.[165]

On a tax return reporting just under $3 million of gross receipts, Osteopathic Medical deducted $772,522 as the cost of the chemotherapy drugs it used in treating its cancer patients. In the view of the IRS, the drugs were merchandise and "income producing." Consequently, the IRS insisted that the merchandise be inventoried and that receivables be reflected in the calculation of income. On the corporation's 1995 return, this meant that $31,887 of year-end inventory and $148,557 of year-end receivables were required to be added to taxable income. Writing for the Tax Court majority, Judge David Laro disagreed. "Petitioner's chemotherapy treatment business," he concluded, "is a pure service business and not, as respondent asserts, a mixed service and merchandising business." As such, Osteopathic Medical was entitled to continue with its cash method of accounting.

About the same time, the IRS began to retreat from its assault on the cash basis method of accounting. In Rev. Proc. 2000-22,[166] updated in Rev. Proc. 2001-10,[167] the

---

[164] *See RLC Indus. Co. v. Comm'r*, 98 T.C. 457 (1992), *aff'd*, 58 F.3d 413 (9th Cir. 1995).

[165] 113 T.C. 376 (1999). In an Action on Decision 2000-05 (Apr. 28, 2000), the IRS acquiesced in the decision "in result only." *See also Jim Turin & Sons, Inc. v. Comm'r*, 219 F.3d1103 (9th Cir. 2000).

[166] 2000-1 CB 1008.

[167] 2001-1 CB 272.

IRS decided that any taxpayer with $1 million or less in gross receipts could use the cash basis method of accounting regardless of whether the business held inventory.[168]

Early in 2001, the IRS took a second step in retreat from its assault on cash basis taxpayers. It stopped raising the cash basis issue on its audit of taxpayers with gross receipts exceeding $1 million and placed a moratorium on pending litigation.[169]

Toward the end of 2001, the IRS issued Notice 2001-76.[170] In the notice, the IRS accepted the cash basis method of accounting for some taxpayers with gross receipts of up to $10 million. While announced as merely a proposed revenue procedure in the notice, the IRS also stated that taxpayers could rely on the proposed procedure in filing 2001 returns, and could use its automatic consent procedure to change from the accrual to the cash method under the new rules for 2001.

Accordingly, a taxpayer with average annual gross receipts of up to $10 million can use the cash method of accounting if:

- Its principal business activity is not farming, retailing, wholesaling, manufacturing (except custom manufacturing), mining, publishing, or sound recording; or
- Its principal business activity is the provision of services, even if, as in *Osteopathic Medical*, the taxpayer is providing property incident to the services; or
- A separate and distinct trade or business for which the taxpayer wants to use the cash basis satisfies either of the foregoing requirements, regardless of the taxpayer's primary business activity; or
- In any of those cases, it is not a C corporation or a partnership with C corporation partners, which would be required by IRC § 448 to use the accrual basis because of average gross receipts exceeding $10 million.[171]

§ 8.18 Small Business Taxpayer

[A] *Small Business Taxpayer Defined*

For tax years starting after December 31, 2017, a small business taxpayer, other than a tax shelter, is a taxpayer which meets the gross receipts test under IRC § 448(c) (a taxpayer with "average annual gross receipts" of $25,000,000 or less)[172] that is not prohibited from using the cash method under IRC § 448.

---

[168] *See* DCN No. 50 in Instructions for Form 3115.

[169] *See* IR 2001-114.

[170] 2001-2 CB 613.

[171] *See* DCN No. 51 in Instructions for Form 3115.

[172] Currently $26,000,000 adjusted for inflation.

[B] Small Business Taxpayer Exception

As a result of the Tax Cuts and Jobs Act (TCJA), the statutory changes replace a number of different gross receipts tests for determining what is a small taxpayer with a single gross receipts test with a $26,000,000 threshold. In nearly all cases, the $26,000,000 threshold is a significant increase from the prior thresholds which ranged from $1,000,000 to $10,000,000. The changes not only increase the number of businesses that will qualify as a small taxpayer but also greatly simplify the gross receipts determinations.[173]

A taxpayer who satisfies the small business exception and chooses not to use an overall accrual method with inventories being accounted for under IRC § 471 has the following three options for an eligible trade or business under the Revenue Procedure:

Option 1. The taxpayer can use the overall cash method and account for inventories under IRC § 471;

Option 2. The taxpayer can use an overall accrual method and account for inventoriable items in the same manner as materials and supplies that are not incidental under Reg. § 1.162-3; or

Option 3. The taxpayer can use the overall cash method and account for inventoriable items in the same manner as materials and supplies that are not incidental under Reg. § 1.162-3.

Notwithstanding IRC § 1001 and the regulations thereunder, small business taxpayers that use the cash method for an eligible trade or business shall include amounts attributable to "open accounts receivable" (described below) in income as such amounts are actually or constructively received. However, IRC § 1001 may be applicable to other transactions.

Small business taxpayers that are permitted to use the cash method for an eligible trade or business and that do not want to account for inventories under IRC § 471 must treat all inventoriable items in such trade or business in the same manner as materials and supplies that are not incidental under Reg. § 1.162-3.[174] Notwithstanding, taxpayers are not required to apply IRC § 263A to inventoriable items that are treated as materials and supplies that are not incidental. Items that would be accounted for as incidental materials and supplies for purposes of Reg. § 1.162-3 may still be accounted for in that manner. Whether an item is purchased for resale or use (and thus accounted for as a non-incidental material and supply) or is purchased to provide to customers incident to services (and thus may be accounted for as either an

---

[173] Following the expansion, resulting from changes made by the TCJA, of the universe of certain taxpayers who are permitted to use the cash method of accounting, the IRS modified earlier guidance to broaden areas in which automatic consent procedures to change accounting methods apply. Rev. Proc. 2002-28, 2002-18 IRB 815 and Rev. Proc. 2001-10, 2001-2 IRB 272 are obsoleted for years beginning after 2017. Rev. Proc. 2018-31, 2018-22 IRB 637 is amplified and modified.

[174] New IRC § 471(c)(1)(b)(i).

incidental or a non-incidental material and supply depending on the facts and circumstances) must be determined under general tax principles.

Under Reg. § 1.162-3, materials and supplies that are not incidental are deductible only in the year in which they are actually consumed and used in the taxpayer's business. As described in the Revenue Procedure, inventoriable items that are treated as materials and supplies that are not incidental are consumed and used in the year the small business taxpayer provides the items to a customer. Thus, the cost of such inventoriable items are deductible only in that year, or in the year in which the taxpayer actually pays for the goods, whichever is later. A small business taxpayer may determine the amount of the allowable deduction for non-incidental materials and supplies by using either a specific identification method, a first in, first out (FIFO) method, or an average cost method, provided that method is used consistently.[175] A taxpayer may not use the last in, first out (LIFO) method described in IRC § 472 and the regulations thereunder to determine the amount of the allowable deduction for non-incidental materials and supplies.

In addition, the taxpayer's method of accounting for inventory will not be treated as failing to clearly reflect income if the method conforms to the taxpayer's method of accounting reflected in an "applicable financial statement"[176] (AFS) of the taxpayer for that tax year or, if the taxpayer does not have an AFS for the tax year, the taxpayer's books and records are prepared in accordance with the taxpayer's accounting procedures.[177]

Accounting method changes. Any change in method of accounting made under IRC § 471(c) will be treated as initiated by the taxpayer and made with the IRS's consent.[178]

Proposed reliance regulations on small business tax accounting rules. In July 2020, the Treasury issued new proposed regulations[179] that implement legislative changes made by the TCJA in IRC § 471. The proposed regulations simplify the application of those tax accounting provisions for certain businesses having average annual gross receipts that do not exceed $25,000,000, adjusted for inflation.

Section 13102(c) of the TCJA added new IRC § 471(c) to remove the statutory requirement to take an inventory when the production, purchase, or sale of merchandise is an income-producing factor for a taxpayer (other than a tax shelter) meeting the IRC § 448(c) gross receipts test (Section 471 small business taxpayer exemption). The Section 471 small business taxpayer exemption also requires that the taxpayer meet certain criteria, one of which is that the taxpayer conform its inventory method

---

[175] *See* Reg. § 1.471-2(d).

[176] The term "applicable financial statement" has the same meaning of that term in IRC § 451(b)(3).

[177] IRC § 471(c)(1)(b)(ii).

[178] IRC § 471(c)(4). A taxpayer that wants to change to one or more of the methods of accounting described in Rev. Proc. 2018-40, 2018-34 IRB 320 must, if eligible, use the automatic change procedures in Rev. Proc. 2015-13, 2015-5 IRB 419 and Rev. Proc. 2018-31, 2018-22 IRB 637 (or any successors) as modified.

[179] Preamble to Prop. Reg. REG-132766-18 and Prop. Reg. § 1.471-1.

to the its method of accounting for inventory reflected on an applicable financial statement as defined in IRC § 451(b)(3) (AFS).[180]

Prop. Reg. § 1.471-1(b)(5) uses the term "AFS section 471(c) method" to describe the permissible IRC § 471(c)(1)(B)(ii) method for a taxpayer with an AFS (AFS taxpayer).

Definition of AFS. IRC § 471(c)(2) defines an AFS by cross-reference to IRC § 451(b)(3). Consistent with the statute, Prop. Reg. § 1.471-1(b)(5)(ii) defines the term AFS in accordance with IRC § 451(b)(3), and incorporates the definition provided in Prop. Reg. § 1.451-3(c)(1). That proposed regulation also provides that a taxpayer has an AFS for the tax year if all of the taxpayer's tax year is covered by an AFS.

If a taxpayer's AFS is prepared on the basis of a financial accounting year that differs from the taxpayer's tax year, Prop. Reg. § 1.471-1(b)(5)(ii) provides that a taxpayer determine its inventory for the mismatched reportable period by using a method of accounting described in Prop. Reg. § 1.451-3(h)(4).[181]

Types and amounts of costs reflected in an AFS. The IRS is aware that some taxpayers may interpret IRC § 471(c)(1)(B)(ii) as permitting a taxpayer to capitalize a cost to inventory for federal income tax purposes when that cost is included in the taxpayer's AFS inventory method irrespective of: (1) whether the amount is deductible or otherwise recoverable for federal income tax purposes; or (2) when the amount is capitalizable under the taxpayer's overall method of accounting used for federal income tax purposes. The IRS does not agree with this interpretation because IRC § 471 is a timing provision. IRC § 471 is in subchapter E of chapter 1 of the Code—*Accounting Periods and Methods of Accounting.* It is not in subchapter B of chapter 1, *Computation of Taxable Income.* A method of accounting determines when an item of income or expense is recognized, not whether it is deductible or recoverable through cost of goods sold or basis.[182]

Accordingly, the IRS views IRC § 471(c)(1)(B)(ii) as an exemption from taking an inventory under IRC § 471(a) for certain taxpayers that meet the IRC § 448(c) gross receipts test and not as an exemption from the application of Code provisions other than IRC § 471(a). Accordingly, the proposed regulation requires an AFS taxpayer that uses the AFS § 471(c) method to make book-tax adjustments for costs capitalized in its AFS that are not deductible or otherwise recoverable, in whole or in part, for federal income tax purposes or that are taken into account in a tax year that is different from the year capitalized under the AFS as a result of another Code provision.[183]

The regulations are proposed to be applicable for tax years beginning on or after the date the Treasury Decision adopts them as final and they are published in the Federal Register.[184] However, for tax years beginning after December 31, 2017, and before the date the Treasury Decision adopts the proposed regulations as final

---

180 IRC § 471(c)(1)(B)(ii).

181 Preamble to Prop. Reg. REG-132766-18.

182 Preamble to Prop. Reg. REG-132766-18.

183 Preamble to Prop. Reg. REG-132766-18; Prop. Reg. § 1.471-1(b)(5)(iii).

184 Preamble to Prop. Reg. REG-132766-18; *see also,* for example, Prop. Reg. § 1.460-6(k)).

regulations and publishes them in the Federal Register, a taxpayer may rely on the proposed regulations, provided that the taxpayer follows all the applicable rules contained in the proposed regulations for each Code provision that the taxpayer chooses to apply. For example, a taxpayer using an accrual method with inventory subject to the capitalization rules of IRC § 263A, may rely on Prop. Reg. § 1.448-2 to determine whether it must continue its use of its accrual method and Prop. Reg. § 1.263A-1 to determine its cost capitalizing rules, but may maintain its current inventory method rather than follow the proposed regulations under IRC § 471.[185]

[C] Average Annual Gross Receipts

The gross receipts test is satisfied if, during the three-year testing period, average gross receipts do not exceed $26,000,000 subject to an adjustment for inflation.[186] If a taxpayer has not been in existence for three prior taxable years, the taxpayer must determine its average annual gross receipts for the number of years (including short taxable years) that the taxpayer has been in existence.[187] Under the TCJA, the gross receipts test is satisfied for the tax year if the average annual gross receipts are under the prescribed dollar limit for the three-year tax period ending with the tax year that *precedes* the tax year for which the taxpayer is being tested.

Observation

The three-year testing period ends with the tax year *before* the tax year for which the taxpayer is being tested and not, as under prior law, with the tax year for which the taxpayers is being tested.

Example 8-7

Finch, Inc. has the following gross receipts:

- 2017—$20,000,000
- 2018—$25,000,000
- 2019—$30,000,000

Because Finch's average gross receipts for 2017, 2018, and 2019 do not exceed $26,000,000, IRC § 448 does not bar Finch from using the cash method.

---

185 Preamble to Prop. Reg. REG-132766-18.
186 IRC § 448(c)(4). Currently $26,000,000.
187 *See* IRC § 448(c)(3)(A).

[D] *Aggregation of Gross Receipts*

For purposes of computing gross receipts, all taxpayers treated as a single employer under subsection (a) or (b) of § 52 or subsection (m) or (o) of § 414 (or that would be treated as a single employer under these sections if the taxpayers had employees) will be treated as a single taxpayer.

[E] *Inventoriable Item Defined*

An inventoriable item is any item either purchased for resale to customers or used as a raw material in producing finished goods.

[F] *Open Accounts Receivable Defined*

Under Rev. Proc. 2018-40,[188] open accounts receivable are defined as any receivable due in full in 120 days or less.

[G] *Automatic Change for Taxpayers*

For any taxpayer that is not a corporation or a partnership, the gross receipts test of IRC § 448(c) must be applied in the same manner as if each trade or business of that taxpayer was a corporation or partnership.[189]

A small business taxpayer that wants to use the cash method must follow the automatic change in accounting method provisions of Rev. Proc. 2018-40.[190]

A small business taxpayer that does not want to account for inventories under IRC § 471 must make any necessary change from the taxpayer's inventory method (and, if applicable, from the method of capitalizing costs under IRC § 263A) to treat inventoriable items in the same manner as materials and supplies that are not incidental under Reg. § 1.162-3.

[H] *Single Form 3115 and Reduced Filing Requirement*

A taxpayer is required to complete only the following information on Form 3115 (Rev. December 2018) to make this change:

(a) The identification section of page 1 (above Part I);
(b) The signature section at the bottom of page 1;
(c) Part I;
(d) Part II, all lines except line 16;
(e) Part IV, all lines except line 25; and
(f) Schedule A, Part I, all lines except lines 3, 4 and 5.

---

[188] 2018-34 IRB 320.
[189] IRC § 471(c)(2).
[190] 2018-34 IRB 320.

[I] Concurrent Automatic Changes

A taxpayer making a change to the overall cash method under section 15.18 and a change under sections 12.16 and/or 22.19 of Rev. Proc. 2018-40 for the same year of change may file a single Form 3115 for all changes, provided the taxpayer enters the designated automatic accounting number change number for the changes on the appropriate line of Form 3115.[191] These reduced filing requirements also apply to small taxpayers changing from the accrual method to the cash method under IRC §§263A, 471 and 460.

[J] Existing IRC §481(a) Adjustment

If a taxpayer is taking into account a §481(a) adjustment resulting from a prior, but related, change in method of accounting, at the time it changes its method of accounting, described in section 3 of Rev. Proc. 2018-40, the taxpayer may account for the prior §481(a) adjustment separately from the §481(a) adjustment required by a change in method of accounting described in section 3 of Rev. Proc. 2018-40. For example, a taxpayer that changed from the cash method to an overall accrual method in a prior year and was required to take the relevant §481(a) adjustment into account over four years could continue to take into account any remaining adjustment over the appropriate number of years even if the taxpayer changes to the cash method in the current year under section 3 of Rev. Proc. 2018-40. However, the taxpayer may also choose to combine or net the remaining portion of the prior §481(a) adjustment with the §481(a) adjustment required by the change in method of accounting made under section 3 of Rev. Proc. 2018-40. Any taxpayer choosing to combine or net the §481(a) adjustments indicates this choice in the statement required on Line 26 of Form 3115, *Application for Change in Accounting Method* (Rev. December 2018), required to be filed to make the change(s) in method of accounting under section 3 of Rev. Proc. 2018-40.

---

[191] *See* §6.03(1)(b) of Rev. Proc. 2015-13 for information on making concurrent changes.

9

Uniform Capitalization Rules

§9.01 Uniform Capitalization Rules

[A] Overview

The uniform capitalization rules (UNICAP) set forth in IRC §263A, affect those subsections of IRC §471 which relate to costing. Other subsections remain unchanged. In some cases, such as resellers with gross receipts less than $26,000,000,[1] the "old" costing rules are still applicable for tax years before December 31, 2017.[2] The TCJA expands the exception from the UNICAP rules to include any taxpayer (other than a tax shelter prohibited from using the cash receipts and disbursements method of accounting under IRC §448(a)(3)) that meets the gross receipts test of IRC §448(c).[3] IRC §448(c) provides that corporations and partnerships with a corporate partner are permitted to use the cash method only if they have average annual gross receipts of $25,000,000 or less during the preceding three years. This ceiling amount is inflation adjusted and is $26,000,000 for 2019 and 2020.

The modification not only increases the dollar limitation but also expands the exception to include both producers and resellers of both real and personal property.

Note: The TCJA clarified that tax shelters prohibited from using the cash method of accounting cannot take advantage of the small business exception.

---

[1] Inflation adjusted for 2019. Rev. Proc. 2019-44, 2019-47 IRB 1093.

[2] *See* Reg. §1.471-11. The cash method of accounting and other simpler accounting methods have been made available to more taxpayers. Most taxpayers who meet a $26 million average annual gross receipts test will be able to use the cash method and will not be required to apply the inventory or uniform capitalization (UNICAP) rules, and will not be required to use the percentage of completion method for small construction contracts. For the financial reporting treatment of the uniform capitalization rules, *see* FASB ASC 740-10-25-2, FASB ASC 740-10-25-4, FASB ASC 740-10-25-18, FASB ASC 740-10-25-19, FASB ASC 740-10-25-20, FASB ASC 740-10-30-2, FASB Statement 109, ¶8, ¶10, ¶11.

[3] IRC §263A(i)(1).

For any taxpayer which is not a corporation or a partnership, the gross receipts test of IRC § 448(c) will be applied in the same manner as if each trade or business of the taxpayer is a corporation or partnership.[4]

All businesses under common control must be aggregated for purposes of meeting the gross receipts test. All taxpayers treated as a single employer under IRC § 52(a) or (b) or IRC § 414(m) or (o) are treated as a single employer. Transactions between commonly controlled taxpayers are excluded from determining the gross receipts of the taxpayer.

Prior to the introduction of UNICAP in 1986, manufacturers were required to capitalize all indirect manufacturing costs, while resellers (retailers and wholesalers) were limited to capitalizing only the direct cost of materials and the cost of acquiring the goods.[5]

Furthermore, neither manufacturers nor resellers were required to capitalize any indirect costs such as purchasing, handling and storage, or G&A support or service costs, which directly benefited the manufacturing or resale activities.

Before 1986 and the enactment of IRC § 263A, the costing rules for resellers/retailers were found in Reg. § 1.471-8. The direct costing rules for producers/manufactures were found in Reg. § 1.471-11. These latter rules are the "Full Absorption Rules."

Under the full absorption rules, in addition to manufacturing cost, there are three categories of indirect costs:

- Those costs which are capitalized (Category 1 costs);[6]
- Those costs which are not included in inventoriable costs (Category 2 costs);[7] and
- Those costs, which are either included or not included in inventoriable costs depending upon the taxpayer's treatment on its financial reports (Category 3 costs).[8]

The enactment of IRC § 263A did not repeal the IRC § 471 costing rules but, where appropriate, act as an additional set of rules to be applied along with the existing IRC § 471 costing rules.

These combined set of rules can be illustrated as follows:

IRC § 263A capitalizable interest; *plus*
Additional IRC § 263A costs; *plus*
IRC § 471 costs;
Equals the allocable costs under IRC § 263A.

Depending on the facts, some or all of these rules may apply.

---

[4] IRC § 263A(i)(2).
[5] *See* Reg. § § 1.471-8 and 1.471-11.
[6] Reg. § 1.471-11(c)(2)(i).
[7] Reg. § 1.471-11(c)(2)(ii).
[8] Reg. § 1.471-11(c)(2)(iii).

Proposed reliance regulations on small business tax accounting rules. The IRS has issued proposed reliance regulations[9] that implement legislative changes to IRC § 263A which simplify the application of tax accounting provisions for certain businesses having average annual gross receipts that do not exceed $25,000,000, adjusted for inflation.

The UNICAP rules of IRC § 263A provide that, in general, the direct costs and the properly allocable share of the indirect costs of real or tangible personal property produced, or real or personal property described in IRC § 1221(a)(1) acquired for resale, cannot be deducted but must either be capitalized into the basis of the property or included in inventory costs, as applicable.

Under the TCJA, Section 263A,*Small Business Taxpayer Exemption*, small businesses are exempt from the IRC § 263A rules. For this purpose, a small business is any taxpayer (other than a tax shelter under IRC § 448(a)(3)) meeting the gross receipts test of IRC § 448(c).

Application of gross receipts test to taxpayers that are not corporations or partnerships. Prop. Reg. § 1.263A-1(j)(2)(ii) provides that, in the case of a taxpayer other than a corporation or partnership, the IRC § 448(c) gross receipts test is applied by taking into account the amount of gross receipts derived from all trades or businesses of that taxpayer. Under the proposed regulations amounts not related to a trade or business of that taxpayer, such as inherently personal amounts of an individual taxpayer, are generally excluded from gross receipts. Such excluded amounts include, in the case of an individual, items such as Social Security benefits, personal injury awards and settlements, disability benefits, and wages received as an employee that are reported on Form W-2. The exclusion for wages does not extend to guaranteed payments, which are not generally equivalent to salaries and wages.

Prop. Reg. § 1.263A-1(j)(2)(iii) provides that, when determining whether a taxpayer qualifies for the Section 263A small business taxpayer exemption, each partner in a partnership includes a share of partnership gross receipts in proportion to such partner's distributive share of items of gross income that were taken into account by the partnership under IRC § 703; similarly, each shareholder in an S corporation includes a pro rata share of the S corporation's gross receipts taken into account by the S corporation under IRC § 1363(b).

Uniform interest capitalization rules. Prior to enactment of the TCJA, IRC § 263A(f)(1) required the capitalization of interest if the taxpayer produced certain types of property. The Section 263A small business taxpayer exception applies for all purposes of IRC § 263A, including the requirement to capitalize interest under IRC § 263A(f). Accordingly, the proposed regulations modify Reg. § 1.263A-8 to implement the Section 263A small business taxpayer exemption for purposes of the requirement to capitalize interest.[10]

---

[9] Preamble to Prop. Reg. REG-132766-18; Prop. Reg. §§ 1.263A-1, 1.263A-2, 1.263A-3, 1.263A-4, 1.263A-7, 1.263A-8, 1.263A-9, 1.263A-15, 1.381(c)(5)-1.

[10] Prop. Reg. § 1.263-8(a)(1).

Farming trades and businesses. Prior to enactment of the TCJA, IRC § 263A(d)(3) permitted certain taxpayers to elect not to have the rules of IRC § 263A apply to certain plants that were part of a farming business conducted by the taxpayer.

Taxpayers that made an election under IRC § 263A(d)(3) may also qualify for the Section 263A small business taxpayer exemption and may prefer to apply that exemption rather than the election under IRC § 263A(d)(3). Prop Reg. § 1.263A-4(d)(5) permits a taxpayer to revoke its IRC § 263A(d)(3) election for any tax year in which the taxpayer is eligible for and wants to apply the Section 263A small business taxpayer exemption by following applicable administrative guidance, such as that found in Rev. Proc. 2020-13.[11]

In addition, some taxpayers may be eligible to apply the election under IRC § 263A(d)(3) in a tax year in which they cease to qualify for the Section 263A small business taxpayer exemption. Therefore, Prop. Reg. § 1.263A-4(d)(6) permits such a taxpayer to change its method of accounting from the exemption under IRC § 263A(i) by making an IRC § 263A(d)(3) election in the same tax year by following applicable administrative guidance, such as that found in Rev. Proc. 2020-13.

Prop. Reg. § 1.263A-4(d)(3)(i) removes the requirement that the election under IRC § 263A(d)(3) by a partnership or S corporation be made by a partner, shareholder or member. The IRS believes that the inclusion of this requirement was a drafting error, as IRC § 703(b) and IRC § 1363(c) require the election to be made at the entity level.[12]

IRC § 448(a) generally prohibits C corporations, partnerships with a C corporation as a partner, and tax shelters from using the cash receipts and disbursements method of accounting (cash method). However, IRC § 448(b)(3) provides that IRC § 448(a) does not apply to C corporations, and partnerships with a C corporation as a partner, that meet the IRC § 448(c) gross receipts test. This gross receipts test also requires the aggregation of gross receipts for all persons treated as a single employer under IRC § § 52(a), 52(b), 414(m) or 414(o) (aggregation rule).

[B] General Inventory Rules

Under an inventory method of accounting, costs related to producing, acquiring, storing and handling the inventory are not recovered, *i.e.*, deductible, until the inventory is sold. The result is that most of the costs are not recoverable until the inventory is sold.

Example 9-1

Yellow corp., a calendar taxpayer, begins business on Jan 1, 2019. X uses the specific identification method to identify goods in ending inventory and produces 20 items in 2019. During the current year, 16 items were

---

[11] 2020-11 IRB 515.

[12] Preamble to Prop. Reg. REG-132766-18.

sold. Costs related to production were $25 each. In 2019, Yellow corp. recovers $800 of the costs of producing the items as follows:

Opening inventory	$0
Cost of production	500
Cost of goods available	500
Less ending inventory	(100)
Cost of goods sold	$400

Inventory costs are "above the line" deductions and are recovered as part of the cost of goods sold rather than as deductions in reaching taxable income. The costs relating to inventory are known as "inventoriable costs" or "inventory costs." Currently, deductible costs are referred to as "period costs."

[C] Materials and Supplies

Materials and supplies that do not become part of the finished product are not inventory for tax purposes.[13] Supplies are valued at cost and are normally deducted when consumed.[14] Incidental supplies, however, can be deducted in the year they are purchased.[15] The UNICAP rules do not change the treatment of materials and supplies, which are subject to Reg. § 1.162-3.[16]

The TCJA exempts certain taxpayers from the requirement to keep inventories. Specifically, taxpayers that meet the $26 million gross receipts test are not required to account for inventories under IRC § 471 but rather may use a method of accounting for inventories that either:

- treats inventories as non-incidental materials and supplies; or
- conforms to the taxpayer's financial accounting treatment of inventories.[17]

For non-incidental materials and supplies, a deduction is generally permitted for their cost in the taxable year in which they are first used or are consumed in the taxpayer's operations.[18] The taxpayer's financial accounting treatment of inventories is determined by reference to the method of accounting used in the taxpayer's applicable financial statement or, if the taxpayer does not have an applicable financial

---

[13] Reg. § 1.471-1.

[14] Reg. § 1.162-3(a)(1).

[15] Incidental materials and supplies are those that are kept on hand for which no record of consumption is kept and no physical inventories are taken at the beginning and end of the tax year. They are items of minor importance, such as pens, paper, staplers, toner, and trash baskets. Reg. § 1.162-3(a)(2). *See also* Chapter 13.

[16] Reg. § 1.162-3(b).

[17] IRC § § 263A(i) and 471(c)(1)(B). Rev. Proc. 2018-40, 2018-34 IRB 320, provides guidance for small taxpayers who want to change to a method of accounting that no longer capitalizes costs under IRC § 263A in accordance with changes made by the TCJA.

[18] *See* Reg. § 1.162-3(a)(1).

statement, the method of accounting used in the taxpayer's book and records prepared in accordance with the taxpayer's accounting procedures. In the case of a sole proprietorship, the $26 million gross receipts test is applied as if the sole proprietorship is a corporation or partnership.[19]

[D] Services

Where a tangible product is furnished in conjunction with services, the product is inventory if it is significant in relation to the services provided. Examples of items included in inventory would be eyeglasses furnished in conjunction with eye exams or caskets provided with funeral services.[20] If the value of the product is *de minimis* in relation to the services, for example an injection given by a physician, then the item is not inventory.[21] The IRS frequently asked questions describes incidental and non-incidental supplies.[22]

- **Incidental materials and supplies**—If the materials and supplies are incidental, *i.e.*, of minor or secondary importance, carried on hand without keeping a record of consumption, and no beginning and ending inventories are recorded, *e.g.*, pens, paper, staplers, toner, trash baskets, then you deduct the materials and supplies costs in the taxable year in which the amounts are paid or incurred, provided taxable income is clearly reflected.
- **Non-incidental materials and supplies**—If the materials and supplies are not incidental, then you deduct the materials and supplies costs in the taxable year in which the materials and supplies are first used or consumed in your operations. For example, deduct certain expendable spare parts in a trucking business for which records of consumption are kept and inventories are recorded in the taxable year the part is removed from your storage area and installed in one of your trucks. However, an otherwise deductible material or supply cost could be subject to capitalization under IRC § 263(a) if you use the material or supply to improve property or under IRC § 263A if you incorporate the material or supply into property you produce or acquire for resale.
- **Application with *de minimis* safe harbor**—If you elect to use the *de minimis* safe harbor and any materials and supplies also qualify for the safe harbor, you must deduct amounts paid for these materials or supplies under the safe harbor in the taxable year the amounts are paid or incurred. Such amounts are not treated as amounts paid for materials and supplies and may be deducted as business expenses in the taxable year they are paid or incurred.

The allowable deduction for inventory items treated as non-incidental materials and supplies may be determined by using either a specific identification method, a first-in, first-out (FIFO) method, or an average cost method, provided that method is

---

[19] IRC § § 263A(i) and 471(c)(1).

[20] *See* Rev. Rul. 69-537, 1969-2 CB 109.

[21] *See* § 9.05[G], *infra.*

[22] IRS Frequently Asked Questions 20171227.

used consistently. Items that would be treated as incidental items under Reg. § 1.162-3 (*i.e.*, all such items purchased during the year are deductible) may still be accounted for as incidental items.

Thus, the taxpayer must capitalize these non-incidental costs and deduct them by adjusting the inventory balance through a perpetual inventory record or by taking a year-end physical inventory to determine the amount of supplies and materials.

§ 9.02 Overview of IRC § 263A UNICAP Rules

[A] Introduction

IRC § 263A established a uniform set of cost capitalization rules for most production and resale activities.[23] It is important to note that the regulations promulgated by Treasury are legislative rather than interpretive. This means that unlike most regulations, which are regarded as an interpretation of the statute (and have a presumption of being correct), the IRC § 263A regulations are legislative and are law.[24]

Not only did the IRC § 263A rules redefine the categories of costs to be capitalized, but, by replacing the word "manufacturer" with the broader term "producer," the list of activities to which these rules apply were expanded.[25]

IRC § 263A prescribes a single set of rules (the "Uniform Capitalization" or "UNICAP" rules) for determining the types and amount of costs that must be capitalized and added to ending inventory rather than expensed during the current tax year. Under IRC § 263A, taxpayers must capitalize their *direct costs* and a properly

---

[23] Reg. § 1.263A-1(a)(3) provides the general scope of the statute.

(i) Property to which IRC § 263A applies. Taxpayers subject to IRC § 263A *must capitalize* all direct costs and certain indirect costs properly allocable to—

- Real property and tangible personal property produced by the taxpayer; and
- Real property and personal property described in IRC § 1221(1), which is acquired by the taxpayer for resale.

[24] *See* IRC § 263A(i).

[25] The Senate Committee report of the Tax Reform Act of 1986 provide a background for the change: The uniform capitalization rules will be patterned after the rules applicable to extended period long-term contracts, set forth in the final regulations issued under IRC § 451. Accordingly, taxpayers subject to the rules will be required to capitalize not only direct costs but also an allocable portion of most indirect costs that benefit the assets produced or acquired for resale, including general and administrative and overhead costs and other costs described in Reg. § 1.451-3. The committee recognizes that modifications of the rules set forth in the long-term contract regulations may be necessary or appropriate in order to adapt such rules to production not involving a contract, and intends that the Treasury Department will have the authority to make such modifications. The existing long-term contract regulations provide a large measure of flexibility to taxpayers in allocating indirect costs to contracts inasmuch as they permit any reasonable method of allocation authorized by cost accounting principles. The committee expects that the regulations under this provision will adopt a similarly liberal approach and permit allocations of costs among numerous items produced or held for resale by a taxpayer to be made on the basis of burden rates or other appropriate methods similar to those provided under present law. The regulations may adopt other simplifying methods and assumptions where, in the judgment of the Secretary of the Treasury, the costs and other burdens of literal compliance may outweigh the benefits. P.L. 99-514 (10/22/86).

allocable share of their *indirect costs* to property produced or property acquired for resale.[26]

To determine these capitalizable costs, taxpayers must allocate or apportion their costs to various activities, including production or resale activities. After the enactment of IRC §263A, costs are allocated to the appropriate production or resale activities and the costs are allocated to the items of property produced or property acquired for resale during the taxable year and capitalized to the items (typically inventory) that remain on hand at the end of the taxable year.[27]

§9.03 Application of Rules

[A] Generally

The application of the UNICAP rules involves the following steps:[28]

- Step 1—Determine whether the taxpayer and its activities are subject to the rules.[29]
- Step 2—Determine whether the property is subject to the rules.[30]
- Step 3—Determine whether the costs at issue are subject to the rules.[31]

---

[26] Reg. §1.263A-1(a).

[27] With some exceptions, taxpayers subject to the Uniform Capitalization Rules must capitalize direct costs and an allocable portion of most indirect costs associated with production or resale activities. IRC §§263A(b), (c), (g).

Costs attributable to producing or acquiring property must be capitalized by charging the costs to capital accounts or basis. Costs attributable to property that is inventory in the hands of the taxpayer generally must be capitalized by including the costs in inventory.

[28] The IRS has provided the following steps:

Steps to Approaching Uniform Capitalization Rules
Identify the entities production or resale activities. (Note, a business may be regarded as the producer of property if it contracts with another to produce such property.)

- Did you produce any self-constructed assets?
- Did you produce property for sale to customers?
- Did you resell property to customers?
  - Determine the application of any special rules or exemptions.
  - Identify the costs subject to capitalization.
  - Allocate the mixed service costs to production or resale activities.
  - Allocate all the direct and indirect costs that directly benefit or were incurred by reason of production or resale activities to the property produced or acquired for resale. See steps in computing Uniform Capitalization Allocation.
  - Determine whether you produced "designated property," and, if so, the amount of interest.

[29] *See* §9.04, *below.*

[30] *See* §9.05, *below.*

[31] *See* §9.06, *below.*

- Step 4—For mixed service costs, allocate between production/resale activities and other activities of the taxpayer.[32]
- Step 5—Allocate direct and indirect costs must to inventory.[33]

[B] Exceptions

Not all activities or taxpayers are subject to the UNICAP rules. There are 13 exceptions. These include:[34]

- Small resellers;[35]
- Long-term contracts;[36]
- Costs incurred in certain farming businesses;
- Costs incurred in raising, harvesting, or growing timber;
- Qualified creative expenses;
- Certain not-for-profit activities;
- Intangible drilling and development costs;
- Natural gas acquired for resale;
- Research and experimental expenditures;
- Certain property that is substantially constructed;
- Certain property provided incident to services;
- Certain producers with total indirect costs of $200,000 or less;[37] and
- Loan originations.

Moreover, inventories that are valued at market (under either the market method or the lower of cost or market method) are not subject to IRC § 263A capitalization if the market valuation used by the taxpayer equals the property's fair market value.[38]

§ 9.04 Taxpayers/Activities Applicable under IRC § 263A

[A] Generally

The UNICAP rules apply to:

- Retailers/wholesalers who hold merchandise for resale;

---

[32] *See* § 9.12, *below*.

[33] *See* § 9.13, *below*.

[34] Reg. § 1.263A-1(b).

[35] The small resellers exception found in Reg. § 1.263A-1(b)(1), which provides an exception for $10 million gross receipts, is presumably overridden by the TCJA expansion for small business taxpayers after 2017.

[36] The *long-term contracts exception found in Reg. § 1.263A-1(b)(2)* for certain home construction contracts described in IRC § 460(e)(1), is presumably overridden by the TCJA expansion for small business taxpayers after 2017.

[37] The *de minimis rule* for certain producers with total indirect costs of $200,000 or less exception found in Reg. § 1.263A-1(b)(12) is presumably overridden by the TCJA expansion for small business taxpayers after 2017.

[38] Reg. § 1.263A-1(a)(3)(iv).

- Manufacturers who produce property for sale; and
- Taxpayers who construct assets for their own trade or business.[39]

[B] Trade or Business Application

The UNICAP rules are applied separately to each trade or business of the taxpayer.[40] A taxpayer with several trades or businesses may elect to use a different method (including a simplified method authorized under IRC § 263A) for each trade or business. In general, the more trades or businesses within a particular centralized operation, the greater the flexibility in manipulating methods and costs within each business to minimize the effect of the IRC § 263A rules.

Although the regulations do not define a trade or business, several factors are considered in determining what is a "trade" or "business" for the purpose of applying a method of accounting. Reg. § 1.446-1(d) sets forth the following factors:

- Whether a separate and complete set of books and records exists;
- Whether shifting of profits or losses between trades or businesses exists, so that income is not clearly reflected; and
- Whether each trade or business should be independent and self-sustaining.[41]

[C] Tax Planning Considerations

For taxpayers with a significant mix of products with various inventory turnovers, the UNICAP costs allocated to inventory can be minimized by shifting a larger portion of the costs (primarily general and administrative (G&A) costs) to the business with higher inventory turnovers (lower inventory levels). This is particularly beneficial in an affiliated group situation in which centralized overhead can be reallocated to each trade or business to minimize the capitalization of costs.

A company with several business segments may benefit from treating each segment as a trade or business. Careful tax planning should be done to qualify each segment as a separate business. Note however, that once a trade or business has been established for applying the UNICAP rules, any change in that business constitutes a change in accounting method.

---

[39] Reg. § 1.263A-1(a)(1). Notwithstanding activities or costs which are excepted from the application of UNICAP rules may still be subject to capitalization rules under other provisions of the Internal Revenue Code.

[40] Reg. § 1.263A-1(j)(3).

[41] *Peterson Produce Co. v. United States*, 313 F.2d 609 (8th Cir. 1963). *See* Chapter 4, Methods of Accounting.

[D] *Production Activities*

To apply the UNICAP rules properly, it is necessary to know whether a taxpayer is engaged in a "production activity" (as opposed to a resale activity). The regulations shed some light on the meaning of the root term "produce."[42] The regulations make it clear that "produce" means:

- construct;
- build;
- install;
- manufacture;
- develop;
- improve;
- create;
- raise; or
- grow.

In determining whether an activity is a "production activity," several factors are considered including whether the process:

- Adds utility to the product;
- Makes the product more suitable for use or consumption; or
- Transforms materials into more readily marketable materials.

In Rev. Rul. 81-272,[43] the IRS described several situations in which it determined that the processes engaged in by hypothetical companies constituted "production activities."

Situation 1

> Taxpayer sells printed towels. Taxpayer purchases white towels and contracts with an unrelated party to furnish the dye work and design work. Taxpayer has title to the towels at all times. When the dye work and design work are completed, taxpayer stores, packages, and markets the towels.

Situation 2

> The facts are the same as in Situation (1), except that the unrelated contractor, in addition to dyeing and designing the towels, also stores, packages, and distributes the finished product to the taxpayer's customers.

---

[42] Reg. § 1.263A-2(a)(1)(ii)(A).

[43] Rev. Rul. 81-272, 1981-2 CB 116.

Situation 3

Taxpayer is the unrelated party in Situation 1 that furnishes the dye work and design work for the white towels. Taxpayer does not have title to the towels.

Situation 4

Taxpayer purchases individual parts of dolls, assembles them, and markets the finished product.

Situation 5

Taxpayer is a printer and engraver. Taxpayer purchases raw paper and, when a customer orders paper, prints or engraves the paper in accordance with the customer's specifications.

Situation 6

Taxpayer operates a machine shop and provides stampings in accordance with customers' specifications on goods provided by customers. Taxpayer does not manufacture or sell any items over the counter, nor does it furnish any additional materials. Taxpayer does not have title to the goods on which it works.

In discussing production costs, the Service noted that production costs include costs that are incurred in the processes intended to add utility to a product, making it more suitable for use and consumption. For example, production costs include costs that apply to goods produced naturally, such as the aging of whiskey, as well as costs that apply to goods produced as a result of effort, such as the manufacturing of shoes. Production costs also include the costs incurred to transform already manufactured materials, such as surplus vessels and wrecked automobiles, into more readily marketable scrap materials.[44]

---

[44] *See* Rev. Rul. 79-339, 1979-2 CB 218.

The underlying rationale for the IRS ruling was that the processes added utility to the product and/or made it more suitable for consumption.[45] This ruling (although it preceded the statute) formed a basis for the expansive interpretation of the term "produce" under the IRC § 263A regulations.

[E] Taxpayers Engaged in Production Activities

In general, a taxpayer is not a producer unless the taxpayer is the owner of the property being produced. An exception to this rule provides that property produced for a taxpayer under a contract with another party is treated as property produced by the taxpayer to the extent the taxpayer makes payments or otherwise incurs costs with respect to the property.[46]

In *Von-Lusk v. Commissioner*,[47] a taxpayer incurred costs related to commercial real estate development. At issue was whether Von-Lusk's activities fell within the description of production, *i.e.*, "construct, build, install, manufacture, develop, improve, create, raise or grow." If the activities did, Von-Lusk would be considered a producer under IRC § 263A and would have to capitalize all of its preproduction costs.[48] In making its determination, the Tax Court considered the legislative intent behind the tax statute. The court stated:

> Two purposes behind the enactment of IRC § 263A can be gathered from this legislative history. First, Congress expected that a single set of comprehensive rules would be applied to determine whether to capitalize costs. Second, Congress expected those rules to be applied from the acquisition of property, through the time of production, until the time of disposition. To give full effect to this Congressional purpose a broad definition of "produce" is necessary.

The court concluded that Von-Lusk's activities represented the first steps in the development of the property and, therefore, Von-Lusk "produced" the property, as contemplated by Congress. Accordingly, IRC § 263A applied to the property, and

---

[45] The ruling explained that IRC § 471 applies to taxpayers such as those in Situations 1, 2, 4, and 5 who have title to the goods. In Situations 1, 2, 4, and 5 the taxpayers incurred production costs because costs were incurred as a result of processes that added utility to the products. The fact that a critical part of the processing (Situation 1) or a majority of the processing (Situation 2) is not performed by the taxpayer is not determinative as to whether the taxpayer has incurred production costs. Situations 4 and 5 illustrate that processes that add utility to a product include processes not necessarily associated with the term "manufacturing," such as the assembling of finished parts and the printing or engraving of paper.

[46] IRC § 263A(g)(2). For this purpose, a "contract" is defined as any agreement providing for the production of property if the agreement is entered into before the production of the property to be delivered under the contract is completed. Whether an agreement exists depends on all the surrounding facts and circumstances. Reg. § 1.263A-2(a)T(ii)(B)(2). Notwithstanding Reg. § 1.263A-2(a)T(ii)(A) provides a taxpayer may be considered an owner of property produced, even though the taxpayer does not have legal title to the property.

[47] 104 T.C. 207 (1995). *See also Issachar Ohana, et ux.*, T.C. Memo. 2014-83.

[48] Reg. § 1.263A-2(a)(3)(ii).

Von-Lusk was required to capitalize the direct costs and a proper share of the indirect costs of the property.[49]

Because the application of the reseller rules is different from the producer rules, it is important to understand the difference. Consider *Suzy's Zoo's v. Commissioner*,[50] for example. In this case, the Tax Court held that the taxpayer was a producer rather than a reseller, and therefore, it did not qualify for the [then] "small reseller" exception under the UNICAP rules. In *Suzy's Zoo*, the taxpayer sold greeting cards and other paper products bearing an image of one or more of its licensed cartoon characters. The taxpayer's employees developed and drew the originals of all of the characters, and the taxpayer transferred the original drawings to independent printing companies to reproduce the images of the drawings onto its paper products, which were made by third-party printers on the taxpayer's behalf. The printers were required to reproduce the drawings and to make the products in accordance with the taxpayer's specifications, and they were prohibited from selling the taxpayer's original drawings, reproductions, or paper products to third parties.

The taxpayer argued that it engaged in no manufacturing or production activity with respect to its paper products and that it resold those products after buying them from the producers thereof, namely the printers. Second, the taxpayer argued that it was an artistic business that is exempt from the UNICAP rules by virtue of IRC § 263A(h). The taxpayer asserted that its owner was a qualified employee-owner and that she owns substantially all of the petitioner's stock. Taxpayer also asserted that its cartoon characters were original and unique and that her artwork was reproduced and disseminated through the paper products primarily for the character's aesthetic value.

The IRS responded that the taxpayer did not meet the reseller exception because it produced rather than resold its paper products. It also argued that the taxpayer did not qualify under IRC § 263A(h) because the owner did not own substantially all of the taxpayer's stock and because its paper products were utilitarian rather than unique.

In concluding that Suzy's Zoo was a producer, the court focused on the fact that the printer's reproduction of petitioner's characters onto ordinary paper was merely one small step in petitioner's process of exploiting its characters as sellable images, and the reproduction process was mechanical in nature because it involved little independence on the printers' part and was subject to petitioner's control, close

---

[49] *See also Reichel v. Comm'r*, 112 T.C. 14 (1993), in which a real estate developer had to capitalize real estate taxes on properties he intended to, but never actually, developed. The taxes were indirect expenses to produce/develop property under IRC § 263A. The statute's broad language required capitalization of costs incurred both before and during property's production. The legislative history behind the statute reflected an intent to cover capitalization of property acquisition, production, and holding costs under a single set of rules. In Priv. Ltr. Rul. 9602002, the IRS held that delay rents paid by oil and gas producers were preproduction costs subject to IRC § 263A. A delay rent was for any period that the oil company failed to drill on the property; the taxpayer had to pay rent to the property or mineral owner. The ruling held that the delay rents may not be deducted. The IRS indicated that in light of the regulations, the delay rents were preproduction costs.

[50] 114 T.C. 1 (2000). *See also Oliver W. Wilson, et ux.*, T.C. Memo. 2002-61.

scrutiny, and approval. Based on these facts, the court concluded that the taxpayer was a producer and denied the taxpayer the "small reseller" exemption.

[F] Special Rules for Producers of Creative Properties

In order to alleviate the administrative burden placed on producers of creative properties, IRC § 263A(h) provides an exemption for "qualified creative expenses." Qualified creative expenses are expenses incurred by individuals in the trade or business (excluding employees) of being a writer, artist and photographer. The exemption does not apply to printing, photographic plates, motion picture films, video tapes and similar items.[51]

Further, in determining whether an individual is in the business of being an artist factors to consider include:

- the originality and uniqueness of the item
- its aesthetic value over utilitarian value

A taxpayer is not considered an artist solely by producing jewelry, silverware, pottery, furniture or other similar household items. In order to qualify for this exemption, the individual must be either:

- self-employed, or
- must own directly or indirectly (through attribution rules) substantially all of the stock of a personal service corporation (as defined in IRC § 269A(b)(2)), whose principal activity is the performance of personal services substantially performed by employee owners.[52]

In TAM 9643003, the IRS has held that production and engineering costs incurred to produce sound recording were not exempt from UNICAP rules as IRC § 263A(h) "qualified creative expenses." In TAM 9643003, a demo tape made by a cash-basis freelance musician made was a sound recording that was considered tangible personal property under UNICAP rules. The qualified creative expenses exemption was limited to written creations and a demo tape was "similar item" to excluded film or videotape. Pursuant to Notice 89-67,[53] the exemption under the Technical Corrections and Miscellaneous Revenue Act of 1988 did not apply to "sound recordings . . . or similar items."

§ 9.05 Property Subject to UNICAP

[A] Generally

Property subject to IRC § 263A capitalization includes:[54]

---

[51] IRC § 263A(h)(2).

[52] IRC § 263A(h)(3)(D)(i).

[53] 1989-1 CB 723.

[54] Reg. § 1.263A-1(a)(3).

- Real property and tangible personal property produced by the taxpayer;
- Real property and personal property described in IRC § 1221(1) that is acquired by the taxpayer for resale;
- Property produced in a farming business;
- Costs incurred in the production and resale of creative property; and
- Property produced or acquired for resale by foreign persons.

[B] The Small Business Exception

The TCJA expanded the exception for small business taxpayers from meeting the uniform capitalization rules. Under the TCJA, any business that meets the $26 million gross receipts test, *i.e.*, has gross receipts that do not exceed $26 million, is exempted from the application of IRC § 263A (other than a tax shelter prohibited from using the cash receipts and disbursements method of accounting under IRC § 448(a)(3)).

[C] Average Annual Gross Receipts

Gross receipts are the total amount derived from all of the taxpayer's trades or businesses, excluding the following amounts: (1) returns and allowances; (2) interest, dividends, rents, royalties, or annuities not derived in the ordinary course of a trade or business; (3) receipts from the sale or exchange of capital assets; (4) repayments of loans or similar instruments; (5) receipts from a sale or exchange not in the ordinary course of business; and (6) receipts from any activity other than a trade or business or an activity engaged in for profit.[55]

Gross receipts for a short taxable year must be annualized.[56]

Gross receipts (other than those arising from transactions between group members) are aggregated for purposes of determining whether the $26,000,000 threshold is exceeded.[57]

If a taxpayer has been in existence for less than three years, the taxpayer determines its average annual gross receipts for the number of taxable years that it has been in existence.[58]

The average annual gross receipts test was modified by the TCJA. The gross receipts test is satisfied if, during the three-year testing period, average gross receipts do not exceed $26,000,000 subject to an adjustment for inflation for tax years beginning after December 31, 2018. Under the TCJA, the gross receipts test is satisfied for

---

[55] Reg. § 1.263A-3(b)(2).

[56] Reg. § 1.263A-3(b)(1)(ii).

[57] Reg. § 1.263A-3(b)(3). In determining gross receipts, all persons treated as a single employer under IRC § 52(a) or (b), IRC § 414(m), or any regulation prescribed under IRC § 414 (or persons that would be treated as a single employer under any of these provisions if they had employees) shall be treated as one taxpayer. The gross receipts of a single employer (or the group) are determined by aggregating the gross receipts of all persons (or the members) of the group, excluding any gross receipts attributable to transactions occurring between group members.

[58] Reg. § 1.263A-3(b)(1)(i).

the tax year if the average annual gross receipts are under the prescribed dollar limit for the three-tax-year period ending with the tax year that *precedes* the tax year for which the taxpayer is being tested.

The steps for the application of the gross receipts test are:

- determine gross receipts for each year in the three-tax-year period;
- compute the average annual gross receipts for the three-tax-year period; and
- determine if the average annual gross receipts for the three-tax-year period are $26 million or less (to be adjusted for inflation for tax years beginning after 2018).

[D] *Exception to Required Use of Inventories Expanded for Small Businesses*

The exception to the required use of inventories for taxpayers that qualify as a small business has been expanded. For tax years beginning after December 31, 2017, a business is not required to use inventories if it meets the $26 million gross receipts test of IRC § 448(c).[59] A taxpayer that is not a corporation or partnership should apply the gross receipts test as if each trade or business of the taxpayer were a corporation or a partnership.[60] Thus, in the case of a sole proprietorship, the $26 million gross receipts test is applied as if the sole proprietorship were a corporation or partnership.

Observation

The three-year testing period ends with the tax year *before* the tax year for which the taxpayer is being tested and not, as under prior law, with the tax year for which the taxpayer is being tested.

Example 9-2

Finch, Inc. has the following gross receipts:

2017—$20,000,000
2018—$25,000,000
2019—$30,000,000

Because Finch's average gross receipts for 2017, 2018, and 2019 do not exceed $26,000,000, IRC § 448 does not bar Finch from using the cash method.

---

[59] IRC § 471(c)(1).
[60] IRC § 471(c)(3).

Example 9-3

Assume that, in 2017, X has gross receipts of $24 million. In 2018, its gross receipts were $25 million and in 2019 its gross receipts were 30 million. The gross receipts test is applied for the period during which X has average annual gross receipts for the three-taxable-year period ending with 2019 of $26.333 million (($24 million + $25 million + $30 million) ÷ 3). Thus, for taxable year 2020, IRC § 448 applies and X must change from the cash method for such year.

Example 9-4

Blue Bird, Inc., a calendar-year taxpayer, is in the business of editing films and other media. Blue Bird is not a tax shelter. Blue Bird has gross receipts of $20 million in 2017, $25 million in Year 2018 and $30 million in 2019. Blue Bird is neither a personal services corporation nor a farming business and does not qualify for the exemptions under IRC § 448. Because Blue Bird's average gross receipts, for 2017, 2018 and 2019 do not exceed $26 million, IRC § 448 does not bar Blue Bird's use of the cash method in 2020.[61]

Example 9-5

A Corporation is a reseller. A is related to B and C as controlled group corporations. A is determining whether the $26,000,000 exception is available for calendar year 2020.

Facts:

Annual Gross Receipts: (in millions)	A	B	C
2019	16	14	13
2018	9	17	16
2017	8	21	4

B was sold on December 31, 2017.
C was purchased on January 1, 2017.
C's 2017 gross receipts relate to a six-month short year.

---

[61] The other exceptions to the general limitation on the use of the cash method continue to apply for qualified personal service corporations and taxpayers other than C corporations. Thus, qualified personal service corporations, partnerships without C corporation partners, S corporations, and other pass-through entities are allowed to use the cash method without regard to whether they meet the $25 million gross receipts test if the cash method clearly reflects income and the entity is not a tax shelter.

Is the $26 million exception available to A?

B is excluded since B was sold on December 31, 2018. A and C are affiliated as of the first of the year.

C's gross receipts are included in the test for all three years regardless whether A and C were affiliated for all three years.

Gross Receipts Used for Test

	A	B	C	TOTAL
Tax year				
2019	16	n/a	13	29
2018	9	n/a	16	25
2017	8	n/a	8*	16
				70

(Average (70 ÷ 3 years) $2333 million
* annualized (4 × 12 / 6 = 8)

Conclusion: A is not subject to the IRC § 263A rules since average annual gross receipts are less than $26 million.

Example 9-6

Same facts as Example 9-5, except A has been in existence for only two years.

The average is determined using the lesser of three years or the number of years A has been in existence, two years.

	A	C	Total
2019	16	13	29
2018	9	16	25
			54
Average (54 ÷ 2)			$27 million

Conclusion: Average annual gross receipts exceed $26 million in 2019. A must comply with the IRC § 263A rules for 2020.

[E] Resellers with Production Activities

Prior to the enactment of the small business exception, property produced by a small reseller, *i.e.*, a reseller who satisfies the $10,000,000 exception, was exempt from the UNICAP rules if the taxpayer's production activities were de minimis.[62] Due to the increase in the dollar limitation for the gross receipts test from $10 million to $26 million for both real and personal property and to small producers and small resellers, the regulations, to the extent they are contradictory to the either of those changes, are no longer applicable. Presumably the regulations will be amended to reflect the changes made by the TCJA.

[F] Property Produced Under Contract

In general, property produced for a taxpayer under a contract is considered property produced by the taxpayer.[63]

[G] Long-Term Contract Exemption

Taxpayers must generally use the percentage of completion method to determine income from long-term construction contracts. Two types of long-term construction contracts—home construction contracts and construction contracts by relatively small businesses requiring not more than two years to complete—are excepted from the requirement to use the percentage of completion method and most other requirements of IRC § 460. A taxpayer may account for exempt contracts by any permissible method of accounting, including the completed contract method.[64]

For contracts entered into after December 31, 2017, in taxable years ending after such date, the small business exemption does not apply to tax shelters prohibited from using the cash receipts and disbursements method of accounting under § 448(a)(3). As under prior law, to come within the exemption, the taxpayer must expect it will complete the contract within two years. The annual gross receipts requirements is expanded from the $10 million limit to $26 million (adjusted for inflation) for the taxable year in which the contract is entered into. In applying the gross receipts test to a taxpayer that is neither a corporation nor a partnership, the test is applied as if each trade or business were a corporation or partnership.[65]

[H] Home Construction Contracts

Under IRC § 460(e), neither the percentage of completion method, nor the requirement to allocate cost to contract applies to certain construction contracts including a home construction contract. If the taxpayer meets the gross receipts test of section 448(c) for the taxable year in which such contract is entered into, the taxpayer can use the cash method.

---

[62] Reg. § 1.263A-3(a)(2)(ii).

[63] Within the meaning of Reg. § 1.263A-2(a)(1)(ii)(B)(2). *See* Reg. § 1.263A-2(a)(1)(ii)(B).

[64] *See* Chapter 11, *infra*.

[65] *See* § 9.01 above, *Proposed reliance regulations on small business tax accounting rules.*

The term "home construction contract" means any construction contract if 80% or more of the estimated total contract costs (as of the close of the taxable year in which the contract was entered into) are reasonably expected to be attributable to with respect to—

(i) dwelling units (as defined in IRC § 168(e)(2)(A)(ii)) contained in buildings containing 4 or fewer dwelling units (as so defined), and

(ii) improvements to real property directly related to such dwelling units and located on the site of such dwelling units. For purposes of clause (i), each townhouse or rowhouse shall be treated as a separate building.[66]

[I] *Property Provided Incident to Services Exemption*

Property provided to a client or customer incident to services is exempt from the UNICAP rules if the property:

- Is *de minimis* in amount; and
- Is *not* inventory in the hands of the service provider, *i.e.*, it constitutes "supplies" in the provider's hands.

The determination of whether property is *de minimis* in amount is determined on all of the relevant facts and circumstances. Nonetheless, there is a safe harbor rule. Property will be considered *de minimis* in amount if the acquisition or direct materials cost of the property provided to a client incident to services is less than or equal to 5% of the price charged to the client for services and property.[67] If the acquisition or direct materials cost of the property exceeds (5%) of the price charged for the services and property, the property may be *de minimis* if additional facts and circumstances so indicate. A significant factor in making this determination is the relationship between the acquisition or direct materials costs of the property that is provided to clients and the price that the taxpayer charges its clients for its services and the property.[68]

"Services" is defined with reference to its ordinary and accepted meaning under federal income tax principles. In determining whether a taxpayer is a bona-fide service provider, the nature of the taxpayer's trade or business and the facts and circumstances surrounding the taxpayer's trade or business activities must be considered. Examples of taxpayers qualifying as service providers include taxpayers performing services in the fields of health, law, engineering, architecture, accounting, actuarial science, performing arts, or consulting.[69]

---

[66] *See* § 11.02[C], *infra*.

[67] Reg. § 1.263A-1(b)(11)(iii).

[68] *See, e.g., Wilkinson-Beane, Inc. v. Comm'r*, 420 F.2d 352 (1st Cir. 1970).

[69] Reg. § 1.263A-1(b)(11)(ii).

[J] Small Producers Exemption

Prior to the enactment of the TCJA, the $10 million exception was not available to small business taxpayers who produced personal property that was subject to IRC § 263A. Hence, if a producer using the simplified production method incurred $200,000 or less of total indirect costs in a taxable year, then "additional IRC § 263A costs" allocable to eligible property remaining on hand at the close of the taxable year were deemed to be zero. In determining total indirect costs, a taxpayer excluded any category of indirect costs listed in Reg. § 1.263A-1(e)(3)(iii) that was not required to be capitalized, *e.g.*, selling and distribution costs.[70]

The TCJA expands the exception for small business taxpayers from the UNICAP rules by providing that, for any taxpayer (other than a tax shelter prohibited from using the cash receipts and disbursements method of accounting under IRC § 448(a)(3)) which meets the gross receipts test of IRC § 448(c) for any tax year, IRC § 263A will not apply with respect to the taxpayer for that tax year.[71] It would seem, therefore, that the $26 million exception would apply to producers as well and the "small producer exception" is superseded.

[K] Real Property

Real estate is not inventory;[72] therefore, certain provisions of the Code which relate to inventory (*e.g.*, lower of cost or market and LIFO) are *not* available for real property.[73] However, real property is subject to the uniform capitalization rules if it is:

- produced (constructed) for resale;
- purchased for resale;
- self-constructed for use in a trade or business, or an activity for profit.

Note: The sub-division of land is a production activity. Thus, interest incurred during the production (sub-division) period must be capitalized.

Many real estate developers must follow the long-term contract rules, rather than the UNICAP rules. Generally, any contract, which extends into the next tax year, is a long-term contract.[74]

As under prior law, to come within the exemption, the taxpayer must expect it will complete the contract within two years. The annual gross receipts requirements

---

[70] Reg. § 1.263A-1(e)(3)(iii)(A).

[71] IRC § 263A(i)(1).

[72] Rev. Rul. 69-536, 1969 2 CB 109.

[73] Rev. Rul. 86-149, 1986-2 CB 67. *See* Reg. § 1.263A-1(a)(3).

[74] *See* Chapter 11, Long-Term Contracts.

was expanded from the $10 million limit to $26 million (adjusted for inflation) for the taxable year in which the contract is entered into.[75]

[L] *Separate Implementation for Each Trade or Business*

The regulations stipulate that the UNICAP rules are applied separately for each trade or business of the taxpayer.[76] For example, a taxpayer with several trades or businesses may elect to use a different method (including a simplified method authorized under IRC § 263A) for each trade or business. Generally, the more trades or businesses within a particular centralized operation the greater the flexibility in manipulating methods and costs within each business to minimize the effect of the IRC § 263A rules.

The regulations do not define a trade or business; however, factors which are considered in determining a trade or business to determine a method of accounting in Reg. § 1.446-1(d) include:

- whether there are separate and complete set of books and records;
- whether there are shifting of profits or losses between trades or businesses so that income is not clearly reflected; and
- whether each trade or business is independent and self-sustaining.[77]

[M] *Tax Planning*

For taxpayers with a significant mix of products with various inventory turnovers, the UNICAP costs allocated to inventory can be minimized by shifting a larger portion of the costs (primarily G&A costs) to the business with higher inventory turnovers (lower inventory levels). This is particularly beneficial in an affiliated group situation whereby centralized overhead can be reallocated to each trade or business to minimize the capitalization of costs.

A Company with several business segments may benefit from treating each segment as a trade or business. Careful tax planning is necessary to qualify each segment as a separate business. However, once a trade or business has been established for applying the UNICAP rules, any change in that business constitutes a change in accounting method.

---

[75] IRC § 460(e)(1)(B)(ii) The statute refers to "the gross receipts test of IRC § 448(c)." This amount was $25 million in 2018, which was increased from $5 million effective for taxable years beginning after December 31, 2017.

[76] Reg. § 1.263A-1(j)(3).

[77] *Peterson Produce Co. v. United States*, 313 F.2d 609 (8th Cir. 1963).

§9.06 Methods Available for Production Activities

[A] Introduction

Taxpayers engaged in production activities must comply with the uniform capitalization rules. Production activities include the production of:

- inventory (tangible and intangible);
- real property; and
- self-constructed assets for use in a trade or business or activity for profit.[78]

[B] Producer

Under UNICAP, the term "produce" is an expansive term, which is not simply limited to manufacturing.

Reg. §1.263A-2(a)(1) defines produce to include the following activities: "construct, build, install, manufacture, develop, improve, create, raise or grow."

Consistent with Congress's intent to include a broader base of activities under the UNICAP rules, the definition of a producer extends well beyond manufacturing. As a result, many taxpayers who were not subject to the full absorption rules for manufacturers now must follow the costing rules for producers under UNICAP.

For example, taxpayers involved in installation services are considered producers, while under prior law, installation of a product was generally not a manufacturing activity since it did not change the character of the merchandise.[79]

[C] Producer vs. Reseller

It is important to differentiate between whether an activity is production or resale because the rules for capitalizing costs are different for producers than for resellers.

[D] Property Produced for a Taxpayer under Contract

IRC §263A(g)(2) treats property produced for a taxpayer under a contract (*e.g.*, private label goods), as if the property is produced by the taxpayer. This prevents a taxpayer from having property produced by another party and then selling the product as a means of avoiding the application of the uniform capitalization rules or treating itself as a reseller.[80]

---

[78] Reg. §1.263A-1(a)(3).

[79] As an example, a plumber who not only makes repairs but installs plumbing fixtures such as bathtubs and sinks.

[80] *See, e.g., Suzy's Zoo v. Comm'r*, 114 T.C. 1 (2000).

[E] Full Absorption vs. Super Full Absorption Method

Prior to the UNICAP rules, under Reg. § 1.471-11 manufacturers were required to comply with the full absorption rules under which direct production costs and indirect production costs were capitalized.

[F] The IRC § 263A Super Full Absorption Rules

For resellers and producers, prior to the enactment of the TCJA, IRC § 263A replaced the full absorption method with a super full absorption method. Under UNICAP, all costs that directly benefit production activities must be capitalized, including direct costs (labor and materials) and a larger category of indirect costs. UNICAP expanded upon the cost to be capitalized and reduce the costs which could be expensed.

Under UNICAP, capitalizable costs include:[81]

- Repairs of equipment and facilities;
- Maintenance of equipment and facilities;
- Utilities;
- Rent on equipment and facilities;
- Indirect labor;
- Indirect materials and supplies;
- Tools and equipment the costs of which are not otherwise capitalized;
- Quality control and inspection;
- Taxes deductible under IRC § § 162 and 212 (other than State, local and foreign income taxes);
- Depreciation and amortization (including any § 179 deduction);
- Depletion;
- General and administrative (G&A) costs;
- Service and support costs which directly benefit the production activities;
- Insurance related to production;
- Pension and retirement plan contributions;
- Past service costs;
- Employee benefits;
- Rework labor, scrap and spoilage;
- Engineering and design;
- Purchasing, handling and storage costs;
- Interest incurred during the construction period;
- Bidding costs (if the contract is awarded);
- Licensing and franchising; and
- Capitalizable service costs.

---

[81] Reg. § 1.263A-1(e)(3)(ii).

[G] Limitation on Non-Deductible Costs

The Technical Corrections and Miscellaneous Revenue Act of 1988 (TAMRA) amended IRC § 263A by limiting costs which may be capitalized to only those costs which are otherwise deductible in determining taxable income. The intent of this change was to restrict taxpayers from capitalizing non-deductible costs (*e.g.*, sales tax or personal interest) and deducting them through cost of goods sold or depreciation.

[H] Deductible Costs under the UNICAP Rules

The following costs, sometimes referred to as "period costs", are not required to be capitalized:[82]

- Marketing, selling, advertising and distribution costs;
- Bidding costs on unawarded contracts;
- General and Administrative (G&A) expenses that do not relate to production;
- Research and experimental costs (as defined in IRC § 174);
- Losses deductible under IRC § 165;
- Depreciation and amortization on idle property;
- Income taxes;
- Past service costs;
- Strike costs;
- Repairs not related to production;
- Warranty costs;
- On site storage costs;
- Product liability insurance;
- Package design costs;
- IRC § 179 costs;
- State and local income and franchise taxes; and
- Deductible service cost.

[I] Election to Capitalize Certain Period Costs

Although period costs are not capitalized, a taxpayer may elect to capitalize any period costs provided:

- such costs are capitalized consistently from period to period; and
- by capitalizing such costs, there is not a material distortion of income.[83]

---

[82] Reg. § 1.263A-1(e)(3)(iii).
[83] Reg. § 1.263A-1(j)(2)(i).

[J] Definitions

Because UNICAP, as discussed below, contains several simplified formulas that contain defined terms, it is important to be familiar with these definitions.

[K] IRC §471 Costs

"IRC §471 costs"[84] are costs, other than interest, capitalized by the taxpayer under its method of accounting immediately prior to the effective date of enactment of IRC §263A.[85] They include any non-inventory costs, other than interest, capitalized or included in acquisition or production costs under the taxpayer's method of accounting immediately prior to the effective date of IRC §263A.

In the case of a new taxpayer, IRC §471 costs are acquisition or production costs, other than interest, that would have been required to be capitalized by the taxpayer if the taxpayer had been in existence immediately prior to the effective date of IRC §263A.[86]

[L] IRC §263A Costs

IRC §263A costs[87] are *the sum* of a taxpayer's IRC §471 costs, its additional IRC §263A costs, and interest capitalizable under IRC §263A(f).[88]

Hence the composition of these costs is illustrated as follows:

IRC §263A capitalizable interest, plus
Additional IRC §263A costs, plus
IRC §471 costs,
Equals IRC §263A costs.

[M] Additional IRC §263A Costs

Additional IRC §263A costs[89] are the costs, other than interest, that were not capitalized under the taxpayer's method of accounting immediately prior to the effective date of IRC §263A but that are required to be capitalized under IRC §263A.

[N] Producers

Producers must capitalize:

- direct material costs; and
- direct labor costs.[90]

---

[84] Reg. §1.263A-1(d)(2).
[85] Reg. §1.263A-1(d)(2).
[86] Reg. §1.263A-1(d)(2)(ii).
[87] Reg. §1.263A-1(d)(4).
[88] *See* §9.17, *infra.*
[89] Reg. §1.263A-1(d)(3).
[90] Reg. §1.263A-1(e)(2)(i).

Direct material costs are the costs of materials that become an integral part of specific property produced and materials that are consumed in the ordinary course of production and that can be identified or associated with units or groups of units of property produced.[91]

Direct labor costs include costs of labor that can be identified or associated with particular units or groups of units of specific property produced,[92] including basic compensation, overtime pay, vacation pay, and holiday pay.[93]

[O] Resellers

Resellers must capitalize the costs of property acquired for resale. These acquisition costs include:

- the invoice price of the merchandise;
- transportation costs; and
- other necessary costs incurred in acquiring possession of the goods.[94]

[P] Indirect Labor Costs

Indirect labor costs are labor costs that cannot be directly identified or associated with particular units or groups of units of specific property produced or property acquired for resale. These costs must be capitalized.

[Q] Indirect Material Costs

Indirect material costs are costs that are not an integral part of specific property produced. In addition, the cost of materials that are consumed in the ordinary course of performing production or resale activities that cannot be identified or associated with particular units or groups of units of property are subject to capitalization.

---

[91] Reg. § 1.263A-1(e)(2)(i)(A).

[92] Reg. § 1.263A-1(e)(2)(i)(B).

[93] In Priv. Ltr. Rul. 9426004, the IRS held that a company must capitalize cost of the unclassified time of production employees. In its analysis, the IRS noted that the "direct benefit or incurred by reason of" language of the regulations recognize that an indirect cost does not need to directly benefit a production activity in order to be capitalized. An indirect cost is also capitalized if it is incurred "by reason of" the performance of the production activity. In the case under review, the district director determined that the unclassified time is included in the regular working hours of the full-time employees. Although unclassified time by definition was not directly spent on production, the cost of unclassified time was incurred to pay employees whose primary responsibility was to perform production activities.

[94] Reg. § 1.263A-1(e)(2)(ii). Labor costs that cannot be identified directly with a unit/units or group of specific property produced or property acquired for resale must be capitalized. *See* TAM 9426004.

In Priv. Ltr. Rul. 9609005, the IRS ruled that a company that manufactures hardwood flooring must capitalize the cost of degraded lumber as an indirect production cost and may not write down the cost basis of its inventory. As a result of the degrading of the lumber, there was a combined shrinkage and degraded loss of 12.4%. The company argued that the degraded lumber was subnormal raw material which could be written off under IRC § 1.471-2(c). The IRS said that the cost of raw material that is lost, evaporates, or shrinks during the production process is similar to examples of scrap and spoilage described in Reg. § 1.263A-1(e)(3)(ii)(Q).

§ 9.07 Purchasing Costs

Capitalizable costs include purchasing costs. Purchasing costs are costs associated with operating a purchasing department or office within a trade or business relating to:

- The selection of merchandise;
- The maintenance of stock assortment and volume;
- The placement of purchase orders;
- The establishment and maintenance of vendor contacts; or
- The comparison and testing of merchandise.[95]

Capitalizable purchasing costs include direct and indirect labor costs and related employee benefits, occupancy expenses, material and supplies, vehicle and equipment expenses, tools, telephone, travel, and related general and administrative expenses.

If a person performs both purchasing and non-purchasing activities, the taxpayer must reasonably allocate the person's labor cost between these activities based on the amount of time spent on each activity.

Under Reg. § 1.263A-3(c)(3), a taxpayer may elect to allocate labor costs of all persons using the following 1/3-2/3 rule:

- If less than one-third of a person's activities are related to purchasing, none of that person's labor cost is allocated to purchasing;
- If more than two thirds of a person's activities are related to purchasing, all of that person's labor costs are allocated to purchasing;
- In all other cases, the taxpayer must reasonably allocate labor costs between purchasing and non-purchasing activities.

Example 9-7

Taxpayer O is a reseller that employs three persons, A, B, and C, who perform both purchasing and non-purchasing activities. These persons spend the following time performing purchasing activities: A-25%; B-70%; and C-50%. Under the 1/3-2/3 rule, Taxpayer O treats none of A's labor

[95] Reg. § 1.263A-3(c)(3).

costs as purchasing costs, all of B's labor costs as purchasing costs, and Taxpayer O allocates 50% of C's labor costs as purchasing costs.[96]

Example 9-8

A general manager of a company spends approximately 20% of his time overseeing the purchasing department. The actual purchasing function is performed by several other employees of the company. Can the general manager's salary be excluded as a purchasing cost under the 1/3 de minimis rule?

No, the purchasing labor de minimis rule is not available for G&A service and support for the purchasing department.

§ 9.08 Handling Costs

[A] Generally

In general, handling costs are required to be capitalized under IRC § 263A.[97]

Handling costs include costs attributable to processing, assembling, repackaging, transporting, and other similar activities, with respect to property acquired for resale, provided that the activities do not come within the meaning of the term "produce" as defined in Reg. § 1.263A-2(a)(1).

[B] Processing Costs

Processing costs are the costs a reseller incurs in making minor changes or alterations to the nature or form of a product acquired for resale. Minor changes to a product include, for example, monogramming a sweater or altering a pair of pants.[98]

[C] Assembling Costs

Assembling costs are costs associated with incidental activities that are necessary in readying property for resale, *e.g.*, attaching wheels and handlebars to a bicycle acquired for resale, or assembling toys, such as dolls.[99]

---

[96] Reg. § 1.263A-3(c)(3)(ii)(B).

[97] Reg. § 1.263A-3(c)(4).

[98] Reg. § 1.263A-3(c)(4)(ii).

[99] Reg. § 1.263A-3(c)(4)(iii).

[D] Repackaging Costs

Repackaging costs are the costs a taxpayer incurs to package property for sale to its customers.[100]

Pick and pack costs, on the other hand, are not subject to capitalization under the UNICAP rules. Pick and pack costs are costs incurred inside a storage facility in preparing specific goods for imminent shipment to a particular customer after the customer has ordered those goods.[101]

Pick and pack activities do not include:[102]

- Unloading goods that are received for storage;
- Checking the quantity and quality of goods received;
- Comparing the quantity of goods received to the amounts ordered and preparing the receiving documents;
- Moving the goods to their storage location, *e.g.*, bins, racks, containers, etc.; and
- Storing the goods.[103]

[E] Transportation Costs

Transportation costs are the costs a taxpayer incurs in moving or shipping property acquired for resale. Capitalizable transportation costs include costs incurred in transporting property:

- From the vendor to the taxpayer;
- From one of the taxpayer's storage facilities to another of its storage facilities;
- From the taxpayer's storage facility to its retail sales facility;
- From the taxpayer's retail sales facility to its storage facility; and
- From one of the taxpayer's retail sales facilities to another of its retail sales facilities.[104]

Costs incurred in transporting property include the cost of dispatching trucks, loading and unloading shipments, and sorting, tagging, and marking property. They also include the costs of fuel, insurance and labor costs, and depreciation on trucks and equipment.

Transportation costs that are not subject to capitalization under the UNICAP rules include:[105]

---

[100] Reg. § 1.263A-3(c)(4)(iv).

[101] Reg. § 1.263A-3(c)(4)(vi)(C).

[102] Reg. § 1.263A-3(c)(4)(vi)(C)(2).

[103] *Id.*

[104] Reg. § 1.263A-3(c)(4)(v).

[105] *See* Reg. § 1.263A-3(c)(4)(vi).

- Transportation costs incurred outside a storage facility (including on a loading dock) in delivering goods to an unrelated customer, *i.e.*, distribution costs; and
- Transportation costs incurred outside a storage facility (including on a loading dock) in delivering custom ordered goods from a storage facility to a retail sales facility.

[F] Costs Not Capitalized

The following types of handling are not subject to capitalization under the UNICAP rules:[106]

- Handling costs incurred at a retail sales facility with respect to property sold to retail customers at the facility, *i.e.*, a facility where a taxpayer sells merchandise exclusively to retail customers in on-site sales; and
- Handling costs incurred at a dual function facility (*i.e.*, a facility that serves both as an on-site storage facility (a storage or warehousing facility that is physically attached to, and an integral part of, a retail sales facility) and as an off-site storage facility (a storage facility that is not an on-site storage facility)) to the extent attributable to property sold in on-site sales, with such allocation being based on a ratio of gross on-site sales of the facility to total gross sales of the facility, including the value of items shipped to other facilities of the taxpayer.[107]

Example 9-9

During the year, Redbird Corp. incurs the following handling costs:

Handling goods received from vendors	$100,000
Transporting goods between storage facilities	75,000
Transporting unsold goods from storage facilities to retail locations	60,000
Transporting goods between retail locations	30,000
Handling goods at retail store locations	20,000
Costs of handling at dual function facility (retail sales = $500,000 and cost of merchandise shipped to other locations = $1,000,000)	60,000

All of the first four items are treated as capitalizable handling costs. None of the costs at the retail stores or of shipping goods to customers are capitalizable. Sixty-six and two-thirds percent ($66^{2}/_{3}$%) [*i.e.*,

106 *See* Reg. § 1.263A-3(c)(4), (5).
107 Reg. § 1.263A-3(c)(5)(iii)(B).

$1,000,000/($1,000,000 + $500,000)] of the handling costs incurred at the dual function facility are capitalizable. Consequently, total capitalizable handling costs equal $305,000 [$100,000 + $75,000 + $60,000 + $30,000 + ($60,000 x 2/3)].

§ 9.09 Storage Costs

[A] *Generally*

Storage costs are the costs of carrying, storing, or warehousing property. Storage costs are capitalizable[108] to the extent that they are incurred at an off-site storage or warehousing facility.

[B] *On-Site Storage Facilities*

Storage costs attributable to the operation of an on-site storage facility are not required to be capitalized.[109]

An "on-site storage facility" is a storage or warehousing facility that is physically attached to, and an integral part of, a retail sales facility.[110]

Example 9-10

"Shoes Are Us" operates a shoe store in Anytown, USA. As is typical the front of the store contains sample shoes, benches to try on the shoes and a station for payment. The back of the store is where the shoes are stored which are ultimately sold. As the storage portion and the selling portion are integrated, the entire structure is an on-site facility and therefore none of the costs need be capitalized.

[C] *De Minimis Rule*

- If 90% or more of the cost of a facility is attributable to the on-site storage function, the entire storage facility is deemed to be an on-site storage facility.
- If 10% or less of the cost of a facility is attributable to the on-site storage function, the entire storage facility is deemed to be an off-site storage facility.[111]

---

108 Reg. § 1.263A-3(c)(5).

109 Reg. § 1.263A-3(c)(5)(iii)(C).

110 *Id.*

111 *See* Reg. § 1.263A-3(c)(5).

[D] *Off-Site Storage Facilities*

An "off-site storage facility" is defined as a storage facility that is not an on-site storage facility.[112]

[E] *Dual-Function Storage Facilities*

A "dual-function storage facility" is a storage facility that serves as both an off-site storage facility and an on-site storage facility.[113]

Example 9-11

For the current taxable year, Blue Corp. incurs storage costs as follows:

On-site storage at retail store locations	$150,000
Off-site storage	$300,000
Costs of operating dual function facility (retail sales = $100,000 and cost of merchandise shipped to other locations = $2,000,000)	$100,000

None of the storage costs relative to the on-site storage facilities are subject to capitalization. All of the costs of the off-site storage facilities are capitalizable. Since only 4.76% [$100,000/($100,000 + $2,000,000)] of the costs of the dual function facility are attributable to on-site storage, the entire cost of the dual function facility is treated as an off-site storage facility. Therefore, Blue has total capitalizable storage costs of $400,000 ($300,000 + $100,000).

Example 9-12

Cardinal Corporation is a high-volume retail music, CD, and DVD store chain. Cardinal maintains a warehouse, which is physically attached to its largest store. The warehouse also stores inventory for the company's five other smaller retail stores. Inventory is shipped from the warehouse to each of the retail stores weekly.

The warehouse is considered a dual-function facility. A portion is on-site (physically attached to, and an integral part of, the retail store), and

---

[112] Reg. § 1.263A-3(c)(5)(ii)(F).

[113] Reg. § 1.263A-3(c)(5)(ii)(G).

the other portion is considered off-site storage, despite the fact that it services other retail stores. In order for a facility to be on-site, it must be (a) physically attached to, and (b) an integral part of a retail facility.

Example 9-13

How should the costs of the warehouse be treated for purposes of IRC § 263A?

The taxpayer must allocate the total cost of operating the facility (*e.g.*, all direct and indirect costs) between on-site and off-site functions based on the ratio of gross sales at the facility. The portion of the cost, which relates to on-site storage, is a selling cost. The portion, which relates to off-site storage, must be capitalized.

[F] Service Costs

Service costs are defined as a type of indirect cost (*e.g.*, general and administrative costs) that can be identified specifically with a service department or function or that directly benefit or are incurred because of a service department or function.

Reg. § 1.263A-1(e)(4) refers to support and service costs on a departmental or *function basis*, rather than an *expense* approach. Therefore, all *direct* and *indirect* costs within a service or support department[114] must be considered. If a particular department or function benefits production and non-production (*e.g.*, selling and marketing) activities, the costs are considered *mixed service costs* and must be allocated to production activities or resale activities by using any one of several methods available.

[G] Service and Support Costs

Reg. § 1.263A-1(e)(4)(iii) provides examples of service and support departments which relate to production or resale activities which must be capitalized. These include:

- Administration and coordination of production and resale activities;
- Personnel operations relating to inventory operations;
- Purchasing operations, including purchasing materials and equipment, scheduling and coordinating delivery of materials and equipment to or from factories or job sites, and expediting and follow-up;

---

[114] Under Reg. § 1.263A-1(e)(4)(i)(B), service departments are defined as administrative, service, or support departments that incur service costs. The facts and circumstances of the taxpayer's activities and business organization control whether a department is a service department. For example, service departments include personnel, accounting, data processing, security, legal, and other similar departments.

- Materials handling and warehousing and storage operations;
- Accounting and data services related to inventory operations;
- Data processing;
- Security services related to inventory operations; and
- Legal services.

[H] *Preproduction Costs*

Costs which are potentially subject to capitalization include not only costs incurred during the production process, but also pre-production costs, *i.e.*:

- direct and indirect costs (such as purchasing, storage, handling, and other costs) allocable to property held for future production; and
- indirect costs incurred prior to the beginning of the production period where it is reasonably likely that production will occur in the future.[115]

[I] *Service Costs Not Capitalized*

General and administrative costs which do not directly benefit production activities are not capitalized. Reg. § 1.263-1(e)(4)(iv) provides the following examples of service costs that are not capitalized:

- Functions or departments responsible for overall management, or for setting overall policy, provided that no substantial part of the costs directly benefits an inventory activity;
- General business planning;
- Financial accounting;
- General financial planning;
- General economic analysis and forecasting;
- Internal audit;
- Shareholder, public and industrial relations;
- Tax department;
- Marketing, selling and advertising;
- Personnel policy;
- Quality control policy;
- Safety engineering policy;
- Insurance risk management policy; and
- Environmental management policy.

---

[115] *See* Reg. § 1.263A-2(a)(3).

§ 9.10 Mixed Service Costs

[A] Generally

Mixed service costs (MSCs) are service costs that are partially allocable to production or resale activities (capitalizable mixed service costs) and costs that are partially allocable to non-production or non-resale activities (deductible mixed service costs).[116] A personnel department, for example, may incur costs to recruit factory workers, which are allocable to production activities, and it may incur costs to develop wage, salary, and benefit policies, which are allocable to non-production activities. These costs must be allocated between capitalizable service costs and deductible service costs.

[B] Allocation of Costs

An allocation of mixed service costs between resale or production activities and non-resale or non-production activities must be performed in order to apply the UNICAP rules.

Any one of the following methods may be used to allocate mixed service costs:

- The "facts and circumstances" method (applicable to both producers and resellers);[117]
- The simplified service cost methods for producers;[118] and
- The simplified service cost method for resellers.[119]

[C] De Minimis Rule

A taxpayer may elect[120] to apply the *de minimis* rule in determining the portion of the costs of a mixed service department that are properly allocable to production or resale activities. The rule provides:

- If 90% or more of a mixed service department's costs are deductible service costs, a taxpayer may elect not to allocate any portion of the service department's costs to property produced or acquired for resale.
- If 90% or more of a mixed service department's costs are capitalizable service costs, a taxpayer may elect to allocate 100% of the department's costs to the production or resale activity benefited.

---

116 Reg. § 1.263A-1(e)(4)(ii)(C).

117 Reg. § 1.263A-1(f).

118 Reg. § 1.263A-1(h).

119 *Id.*

120 Reg. § 1.263A-1(g)(4)(ii). Such election constitutes a method of accounting and must be made with respect to all of a taxpayer's mixed service departments.

[D] Taxpayers with Both Production and Resale Activities

A taxpayer engaged in both production and resale activities is considered a producer with respect to both the production and resale activities, and is subject to the UNICAP rules applicable to producers. The taxpayer may elect to apply the simplified production method to *both* its production and resale activities (but not one or the other); in doing so, the taxpayer is precluded from applying the simplified resale method to either its production or resale activities.[121]

[E] Entire Cost of Department

If one of the simplified methods of allocating mixed service costs is selected, the entire cost of a department, including costs within the department that relate entirely to non-production/resale activities, must be allocated between production/resale and nonproduction/resale activities in accordance with the chosen simplified method.

[F] Facts and Circumstances Method

Under the fact-and-circumstances approach to allocating mixed service costs, mixed service costs are allocated among resale or production activities and other activities based on a reasonable factor, such as the service department's total output or the relative amount of resale or production activities compared to other activities.[122] Once a reasonable allocation factor has been determined, an acceptable allocation methodology is used to apportion the mixed service costs of a particular department among production or resale and other activities.

An allocation method is reasonable if, with respect to the taxpayer's production or resale activities taken as a whole—

- The total costs actually capitalized during the taxable year do not differ significantly from the aggregate costs that would be properly capitalized using another permissible method described in Reg. §§1.263A-2 and 1.263A-3, with appropriate consideration given to the volume and value of the taxpayer's production or resale activities, the availability of costing information, the time and cost of using various allocation methods, and the accuracy of the allocation method chosen as compared with other allocation methods;
- The allocation method is applied consistently by the taxpayer; and
- The allocation method is not used to circumvent the requirements of the simplified methods in this section or in Reg. §§1.263A-2, 1.263A-3, or the principles of section IRC §263A.[123]

---

[121] Reg. §1.263A-2(a)(5).

[122] Reg. §1.263A-1(g).

[123] Reg. §1.263A-1(f)(4).

[G] Acceptable Allocation Methods

One acceptable allocation method is the direct reallocation method, under which the total costs of all service departments are allocated to production departments, *i.e.*, no portion of the costs of one service department is allocated to another service department.

Example 9-14

Direct reallocation method.[124]

(i) Taxpayer E has the following five departments: the Assembling Department, the Painting Department, the Finishing Department (production departments), the Personnel Department and the Data Processing Department (mixed service departments). E allocates the Personnel Department's costs on the basis of total payroll costs and the Data Processing Department's costs on the basis of data processing hours.

(ii) Under a direct reallocation method, E allocates the Personnel Department's costs directly to its Assembling, Painting, and Finishing Department, and not to its Data Processing department.

Department	Total dept. costs	Amount of payroll costs	Allocation ratio	Amount allocated
Personnel	$500,000	$50,000	—	<$500,000>
Data Proc'g	250,000	15,000	—	—
Assembling	250,000	15,000	15,000/285,000	26,315
Painting	1,000,000	90,000	90,000/285,000	157,895
Finishing	2,000,000	180,000	180,000/285,000	315,790
Total	$4,000,000	$350,000	—	—

(iii) After E allocates the Personnel Department's costs, E then allocates the costs of its Data Processing Department in the same manner.

Department	Total dept. cost after initial allocation	Total data proc. hours	Allocation ratio	Amount allocated	Total dept. cost after final allocation
Personnel	$0	2,000	—	—	0
Data Proc'g	250,000	—	—	<$250,000>	—
Assembling	276,315	2,000	2,000/10,000	50,000	$326,315
Painting	1,157,895	0	0/10,000	0	1,157,895
Finishing	2,315,790	8,000	8,000/10,000	200,000	2,515,790
Total	$4,000,000	12,000	—	—	$4,000,000

[124] Reg. § 1.263A-1(g)(4)(iii)(A).

Another acceptable allocation method is the step-allocation method, under which mixed service costs are allocated in a sequential fashion (based on the number of other departments benefited) to (1) production departments, (2) non-production departments, and (3) mixed service departments, with costs allocated to non-production or non-resale activities *not* reallocated to production or resale activities (however, costs allocated to another mixed service department are reallocated to other departments).

Example 9-15

The step-allocation method.[125]

(i) Taxpayer F has the following five departments: the Manufacturing Department (a production department), the Marketing Department, the Finance Department (departments that incur only deductible service costs), the Personnel Department and the Data Processing Department (mixed service departments). F uses a step-allocation method and allocates the Personnel Department's costs on the basis of total payroll costs and the Data Processing Department's costs on the basis of data processing hours. F's Personnel Department benefits all four of F's other departments, while its Data Processing Department benefits only three departments. Because F's Personnel Department benefits the greatest number of other departments, F first allocates its Personnel Department's costs to its Manufacturing, Marketing, Finance and Data processing departments, as follows:

Department	Total cost of dept.	Total payroll costs	Allocation ratio	Amount allocated
Personnel	$500,000	$50,000	—	<$500,000>
Data Proc'g	250,000	15,000	15,000/300,000	25,000
Finance	250,000	15,000	15,000/300,000	25,000
Marketing	1,000,000	90,000	90,000/300,000	150,000
Manufac'g	2,000,000	180,000	180,000/300,000	300,000
	4,000,000	350,000	—	—

(ii) Under a step-allocation method, the denominator of F's allocation ratio includes the payroll costs of its Manufacturing, Marketing, Finance, and Data Processing departments.

(iii) Next, F allocates the costs of its Data Processing Department on the basis of data processing hours. Because the costs incurred by F's Personnel Department have already been allocated, no allocation is made to the Personnel Department.

---

[125] Reg. § 1.263A-1(g)(4)(iii)(B).

Department	Total dept. cost after initial allocation	Total data proc. hours	Allocation ratio	Amount allocated	Total dept. cost after final allocation
Personnel	$0	2,000	—	—	$0
Data Proc'g	275,000	—	—	<$275,000>	0
Finance	275,000	2,000	2,000/10,000	55,000	330,000
Marketing	1,150,000	0	0/10,000	0	1,150,000
Manufac'g	2,300,000	8,000	8,000/10,000	220,000	2,520,000
	4,000,000	12,000	—	—	4,000,000

(iv) Under the second step of F's step-allocation method, the denominator of F's allocation ratio includes the data processing hours of its Manufacturing, Marketing, and Finance Departments, but does not include the data processing hours of its Personnel Department (the other mixed service department) because the costs of that department have previously been allocated.

Any other reasonable allocation method, such as the modified direct reallocation method or the linear algebra method, is an acceptable allocation method.

The IRS regulations[126] provide examples illustrating various reasonable factors and relationships that may be used in allocating different types of mixed service costs. The examples are not limiting since taxpayers are permitted to use other reasonable factors and relationships to allocate mixed service costs. The factors or relationships illustrated below may be used to allocate other types of service costs as well.

Security Services. The costs of security or protection services must be allocated to each physical area that receives the services using any reasonable method applied consistently (*e.g.*, the size of the physical area, the number of employees in the area, or the relative fair market value of assets located in the area).

Legal Services. The costs of legal services are allocable generally to a particular production or resale activity on the basis of the approximate number of hours of legal services performed in connection with the activity, including research, bidding, negotiating, drafting, reviewing contracts, obtaining necessary licenses and permits, and resolving disputes. Different hourly rates may be appropriate for different services. In determining the number of hours allocable to any activity, estimates are appropriate, detailed time records are not required to be kept, and insubstantial amounts of services provided to an activity by senior legal staff (such as administrators or reviewers) may be ignored. Legal costs may also be allocated to a particular production or resale activity based on the ratio of the total direct costs incurred for the activity to the total direct costs incurred with respect to all production or resale activities. The taxpayer must also allocate directly to an activity the cost incurred for

---

[126] Reg. § 1.263A-1(g)(4)(iv).

any outside legal services. Legal costs relating to general corporate functions are not required to be allocated to a particular production or resale activity.

Centralized Payroll Services. The costs of a centralized payroll department or activity are allocated generally to the departments or activities benefited on the basis of the gross dollar amount of payroll processed.

Centralized Data Processing Services. The costs of a centralized data processing department are allocated generally to all departments or activities benefited using any reasonable basis, such as total direct data processing costs or the number of data processing hours supplied. The costs of data processing systems or applications developed for a particular activity are directly allocated to that activity.

Engineering and Design Services. The costs of an engineering or a design department are, in general, directly allocable to the departments or activities benefited based on the ratio of the approximate number of hours of work performed with respect to the particular activity to the total number of hours of engineering or design work performed for all activities. Different services may be allocated at different hourly rates.

Safety Engineering Services. The costs of safety engineering departments or activities generally benefit all of the taxpayer's activities and, thus, should be allocated using a reasonable basis, such as the approximate number of safety inspections made in connection with a particular activity as a fraction of total inspections, the number of employees assigned to an activity as a fraction of total employees, or the total labor hours worked in connection with an activity as a fraction of total hours. However, in determining the allocable costs of a safety engineering department, costs attributable to providing a safety program relating only to a particular activity must be directly assigned to that activity. Additionally, the cost of a safety engineering department responsible only for setting safety policy and establishing safety procedures to be used in all of the taxpayer's activities is not required to be allocated.

§9.11 Simplified Service Cost Methods for Allocating Mixed Service Costs

[A] Producers

There are two simplified methods of allocating mixed service costs:

- The production cost-based simplified service cost method; and
- The labor cost-based simplified service cost method.[127]

[127] Reg. §1.263A-1(h).

[B] General Allocation Formula

Under the simplified service cost method, a taxpayer computes its capitalizable mixed service costs using the following formula:[128]

Allocation ratio × Total mixed service costs.

A producer may elect to apply one of these simplified methods with respect to a particular trade or business in the case of the following types of property:[129]

- Inventory property;
- Non-inventory property held for sale in the ordinary course of business;
- Self-constructed assets substantially identical in nature to, and produced in the same manner as, inventory property produced by the taxpayer; and
- Self-constructed assets produced by the taxpayer on a routine and repetitive basis in the ordinary course of the taxpayer's trade or business.

[C] Operational Rules

In general, once the simplified service cost method is elected, it must be used with respect to all qualifying property within the particular trade or business, with necessary allocations between trades or businesses being made on a reasonable basis. A taxpayer may elect, however, to exclude qualifying self-constructed property from its application. This election may be made independently of an election to use the simplified production method.[130]

[D] Production Cost-Based Method

Under the production cost-based simplified service cost method, the amount of inventoriable mixed service costs (MSCs) is determined using the formula below.

Total MSCs × (total production costs* / total costs of operations**)
* Excluding MSCs and interest.[131]
** Excluding MSCs, interest, and taxes based on income.[132]

---

[128] Reg. § 1.263A-1(h)(3).

[129] Reg. § 1.263A-1(h)(3)(ii).

[130] Reg. § 1.263A-1(h)(9).

[131] Reg. § 1.263A-1(h)(5)(ii). Production costs are defined as the total costs (*excluding mixed service costs and interest*) allocable to property produced (and property acquired for resale if the producer is also engaged in resale activities) under IRC § 263A that are incurred in the taxpayer's trade or business during the taxable year.

[132] *Id.* Total costs are defined as all costs (excluding mixed service costs and interest) incurred in the taxpayer's trade or business during the taxable year. Total costs include all direct and indirect costs allocable to property produced (and property acquired for resale if the producer is also engaged in resale activities) as well as all other costs of the taxpayer's trade or business, including, but not limited to: salaries and other labor costs of all personnel; all depreciation taken for federal income tax

Example 9-16

For the taxable year, Yellowbird Corp., incurs the total cost as follows:

Total production costs (excluding MSCs)	$ 5,000,000
Total cost of operations	19,000,000
Total MSCs	2,000,000
Total interest expense	1,500,000
Total income taxes	500,000

Yellowbird uses the production cost-base simplified service cost method to allocate mixed service costs to production. Under such method, the mixed service costs allocable to production are calculated as follows:

$$\$2,000,000 \times \frac{\$5,000,000 - \$1,500,000}{\$19,000,000 - \$2,000,000 - \$1,500,000 - \$500,000} = \$466,6666$$

[E] *Labor Cost-Based Method*

Under the labor cost-based, simplified service cost method, the amount of inventoriable MSCs is determined using the formula below.[133]

Total MSCs × (total IRC § 263A labor costs* / total labor costs*)
* Excluding MSC labor costs.

Example 9-17

Cardinal Corp. for the taxable year incurs costs as follows:

Total production labor costs (excluding MSC labor)	$2,000,000
Total labor costs	10,000,000
Total MSC labor	1,000,000
Total MSCs	3,000,000

Cardinal Corp. uses the labor-based, simplified service cost method to allocate mixed service costs to production. Under this method, the MSCs allocable to production are calculated as follows:

(Footnote Continued)

purposes; research and experimental expenditures; and selling, marketing, and distribution costs. *Such costs do not include, however, taxes described in paragraph (e)(3)(iii)(F) of Reg. § 1.263A-1.*

[133] Reg. § 1.263A-1(h)(4)(i).

$$\$3{,}000{,}000 \times \frac{\$2{,}000{,}000}{\$10{,}000{,}000 - \$1{,}000{,}000} = \$666{,}667$$

[F] Resellers

A reseller may elect to apply the simplified service cost method of allocating mixed service costs with respect to a particular trade or business in the case of the following types of property:[134]

- Inventory property;
- Non-inventory property held for sale in the ordinary course of business;
- Self-constructed assets substantially identical in nature to, and produced in the same manner as, inventory property produced by the taxpayer; and
- Self-constructed assets produced by the taxpayer on a routine and repetitive basis in the ordinary course of the taxpayer's trade or business.

[G] Operational Rules

In general, once the simplified service cost method is elected, it must be used with respect to all qualifying property within the particular trade or business, with necessary allocations between trades or businesses being made on a reasonable basis. A taxpayer may elect, however, to exclude qualifying self-constructed property from its application. This election may be made independently of an election to use the simplified resale method.[135]

§9.12 Allocation of Direct and Indirect Costs

A taxpayer may allocate direct and indirect costs to property subject to IRC §263A with one of the following methods:[136]

- The specific identification method (both producers and resellers);
- The burden rate method (both producers and resellers);
- The standard cost method (both producers and resellers);
- Any other reasonable "facts and circumstances" method;
- The simplified production method (with or without a historical absorption ratio election); or
- The simplified resale method (with or without a historical absorption ratio election).

---

[134] Reg. §1.263A-1(h)(3)(ii).

[135] Reg. §1.263A-1(h)(2)(i).

[136] Reg. §1.263A-1(f), (g).

[A] Restrictions

The allocation methods available for each category of costs are listed below.

Direct material costs. These costs must be allocated using either:

- the taxpayer's inventory method used in accounting for materials, *e.g.*, specific identification;
- the first-in, first-out (FIFO) method;
- the last-in, first-out (LIFO) method; or
- any other reasonable allocation method.[137]

Direct labor costs. These costs may be allocated using:

- the specific identification method;
- the standard cost method; or
- any other reasonable allocation method.[138]

All elements of compensation, other than basic compensation, may be grouped together and then allocated in proportion to the charge for basic compensation.

Indirect costs. These costs may be allocated using:

- the specific identification method;
- the standard cost method;
- a burden rate method;
- one of the simplified allocation methods; or
- any other reasonable allocation method.[139]

[B] Disallowed Methods

Certain methods for allocating direct and indirect costs are disallowed.[140]

In performing allocations of costs under the UNICAP rules, a taxpayer may *not* apply the "practical capacity concept" under which fixed costs are not capitalized because of the relationship between the actual production at the taxpayer's production facility and the practical or theoretical capacity of the facility.[141]

[C] Multiple Trades or Businesses

A taxpayer engaged in multiple trades or businesses will need to allocate the costs that benefit the multiple businesses among the businesses before applying the allocation rules.

---

[137] Reg. § 1.263A-1(g)(1).

[138] Reg. § 1.263A-1(g)(1).

[139] Reg. § 1.263A-1(g)(1).

[140] Reg. § 1.263A-2(a)(4) and (5).

[141] Reg. § 1.263A-2(a)(4).

[D] Taxpayers with Both Production and Resale Activities

In general, a taxpayer engaged in both production and resale activities is considered a producer with respect to both the production and resale activities, and therefore is subject to the special UNICAP rules applicable to producers. Accordingly, the taxpayer may elect to apply the simplified production method to both its production and resale activities (but not one or the other), and is precluded from applying the simplified resale method to either its production or resale activities.

[E] Entire Cost of Department

If one of the simplified methods of allocating direct and indirect costs is selected, the entire cost of a department, including costs within the department that relate entirely to non-production/resale activities, must be allocated between production/resale and non-production/resale activities in accordance with the chosen simplified method.[142]

§ 9.13 Simplified Production Method without Historic Absorption Ratio Election

Under the simplified production method, a taxpayer initially computes its inventory without regard to additional IRC § 263A costs and then adds the additional amount of IRC § 263A costs to its ending inventory. In the case of a taxpayer employing the LIFO method, these costs are added to the current year LIFO layer, as determined before the consideration of IRC § 263A.[143]

[A] Application of Method

The application of the simplified production method involves the steps listed below.[144]

Step 1

An "absorption ratio" is computed as shown below.[145]

---

[142] Reg. § 1.263A-1(h)(6).
[143] Reg. § 1.263A-2(b)(3)(ii)(B).
[144] Reg. § 1.263A-2(b)(3).
[145] Reg. § 1.263A-2(b)(3)(ii)(A).

$$\text{Absorption ratio} = \frac{\text{total additional IRC § 263A costs (excluding interest)}}{\text{total IRC § 471 costs* incurred during the year}}$$

---

* For purposes of the formula, "total IRC § 471 costs" are total production costs incurred during the year under the taxpayer's full absorption costing system.[146]

Step 2

The absorption ratio is used to allocate additional costs to ending inventory, as indicated below.[147]

$$\text{Total additional costs in ending inventory} = \text{absorption ratio} \times \text{total IRC § 471 costs in ending inventory*}$$

---

* For purposes of the formula, "total IRC § 471 costs" in ending inventory are:

- In the case of a FIFO taxpayer, the taxpayer's ending inventory (excluding additional IRC § 263A costs and costs with respect to goods manufactured in prior years); and
- In the case of a LIFO taxpayer, the value of the current LIFO increment (excluding IRC § 263A costs).[148]

Example 9-18

FIFO Inventory Method. Taxpayer J uses the FIFO method of accounting for inventories. J's beginning inventory for 1994 (all of which is sold during 1994) is $2,500,000 (consisting of $2,000,000 of IRC § 471 costs and $500,000 of additional IRC § 263A costs). During 1994, J incurs $10,000,000 of IRC § 471 costs and $1,000,000 of additional IRC § 263A costs. J's additional IRC § 263A costs include capitalizable mixed service costs computed under the simplified service cost method as well as other allocable costs. J's IRC § 471 costs remaining in ending inventory at the end of 1994 are $3,000,000. J computes its absorption ratio for 1994 as follows:

---

146 Reg. § 1.263A-2(b)(3)(ii)(A)(2).

147 Reg. § 1.263A-2(b)(3)(i)(A).

148 Reg. § 1.263A-2(b)(3)(ii)(B). If a LIFO taxpayer sustains an inventory decrement for the year, there are no additional capitalized costs for the current year and the taxpayer is allowed to reduce prior capitalized IRC § 263A costs in reverse chronological order based on the ratio of the reduction in the LIFO layer (pre-IRC § 263A) to the total LIFO layer (IRC § 263A).

$$\frac{\text{Additional IRC § 263A costs incurred}}{\text{IRC § 471 costs}} = \frac{\$1{,}000{,}000}{\$10{,}000{,}000} = 10\%$$

Under the simplified production method, J determines the additional IRC § 263A costs allocable to its ending inventory by multiplying the absorption ratio by the IRC § 471 costs remaining in its ending inventory, as follows:

Additional IRC § 263A costs = 10% × $3,000,000 = $300,000

J adds this $300,000 to the $3,000,000 of IRC § 471 costs remaining in its ending inventory to calculate its total ending inventory of $3,300,000. The balance of J's additional IRC § 263A costs incurred during 1994, $700,000 ($1,000,000 less $300,000) is taken into account in 1994 as part of J's cost of goods sold.

Example 9-19

LIFO Inventory Method. Taxpayer K uses a dollar-value LIFO inventory method. K's beginning inventory for 1994 is $2,500,000 (consisting of $2,000,000 of IRC § 471 costs and $500,000 of additional IRC § 263A costs). During 1994, K incurs $10,000,000 of IRC § 471 costs and $1,000,000 of additional IRC § 263A costs. K's 1994 LIFO increment is $1,000,000 ($3,000,000 of IRC § 471 costs in ending inventory less $2,000,000 of IRC § 471 costs in beginning inventory).

To determine the additional IRC § 263A costs allocable to its ending inventory, K multiplies the 10% absorption ratio ($1,000,000 of additional IRC § 263A costs divided by $10,000,000 of IRC § 471 costs) by the $1,000,000 LIFO increment. Thus, K's additional IRC § 263A costs allocable to its ending inventory are $100,000 ($1,000,000 multiplied by 10%). This $100,000 is added to the $1,000,000 to determine a total 1994 LIFO increment of $1,100,000. K's ending inventory is $3,600,000 (its beginning inventory of $2,500,000 plus the $1,100,000 increment). The balance of K's additional IRC § 263A costs incurred during 1994, $900,000 ($1,000,000 less $100,000), is taken into account in 1994 as part of K's cost of goods sold.

In 1995, K sells one-half of the inventory in its 1994 LIFO increment. K must include in its cost of goods sold for 1995 the amount of additional IRC § 263A costs relating to this inventory, *i.e.*, $50,000 (one-half of the additional IRC § 263A costs capitalized in 1994 ending inventory, or $100,000).

§ 9.14 The Modified Simplified Production Method (MSPM)

For tax years beginning on or after November 20, 2018, the IRS issued final regulations providing several rules regarding allocating costs under IRC § 263A's simplified method uniform capitalization rules for property produced or held for resale (UNICAP rules).[149] The final regulations cover, among other things, a new simplified method of accounting for determining the additional costs allocable to property produced or acquired for resale. The new regulations also redefine how certain types of costs are categorized for purposes of the simplified methods.

Under the previous rules there was an issue regarding the inclusion of negative amounts in additional IRC § 263A costs and whether aggregate additional IRC § 263A costs could be a negative number. A negative amount occurs when a taxpayer capitalizes a cost as an IRC § 263A cost in an amount that is greater than the amount required to be capitalized for tax purposes. For example, if a taxpayer included book depreciation in IRC § 263A costs and the book depreciation was greater than tax depreciation for the year, the taxpayer would have capitalized more depreciation than was required to be capitalized under IRC § 263A for that year. A negative amount might result if the taxpayer did not remove this excess depreciation amount by adjusting IRC § 471 costs but instead made an adjustment to its additional IRC § 263A costs.

The IRS said that including negative amounts in the numerator of the simplified production method formula could result in significant distortions of the amount of additional IRC § 263A costs allocated to ending inventory. Distortions could also occur when the method used to capitalize a cost under IRC § 471 is different than the method used under the simplified production method to remove the cost from ending inventory. The extent of the distortion, and whether it is favorable or unfavorable to the taxpayer, generally depends on when the cost is incurred in the production process and how the cost is allocated to raw materials, work-in-process, or finished goods inventories for purposes of IRC § 471.[150]

[A] The MSPM Method

The regulations provided a new simplified production method called the Modified Simplified Production Method ("MSPM"), to reduce distortions that may result from the simplified production method (SPM). If elected for any trade or business of a producer it must be used for all production and resale activities associated with any of the categories of property to which IRC § 263A applies[151] . A taxpayer using the

---

[149] Reg. § 1.263A-2(c).

[150] *See* Proposed Changes to the Simplified Production Method of Allocating Costs to Inventories, *Eugene Seago*, Journal of Taxation, June 2013.

[151] Reg. § 1.263A-2(c)(2)(i).

MSPM may elect to exclude self-constructed assets from application of the MSPM by following the same rules applicable to a taxpayer using the SPM.[152]

The MSPM in the regulations reduced distortions by more precisely allocating additional IRC § 263A costs, including negative adjustments, among raw materials, work-in-process, and finished goods inventories on hand at year-end. Generally, taxpayers would have determined the allocable portion of pre-production additional IRC § 263A costs using a pre-production absorption ratio of pre-production additional IRC § 263A costs incurred during the tax year over raw materials costs incurred during the tax year.[153] Similarly, under the MSPM in the regulations, taxpayers would have determined the allocable portion of all other additional IRC § 263A costs using a production absorption ratio of production additional IRC § 263A costs incurred during the tax year over production IRC § 471 costs incurred during the tax year.[154]

The regulations provide various formulas to calculate additions to ending inventory under the MSPM.

The General Allocation Formula described in the regulations is:

$$\left(\text{Pre-production absorption ratio} \times \text{Pre-production section 471 costs remaining on hand at year-end}\right) + \left(\text{Production absorption ratio} \times \text{Production section 471 costs remaining on hand at year-end}\right)$$

[B] Effect of the Allocation

The pre-production and production absorption ratios generally are multiplied by the pre-production and production IRC § 471 costs, respectively, remaining in ending inventory or otherwise on hand at the end of each taxable year in which the MSPM is applied. The sum of the resulting products is the additional IRC § 263A costs that are added to a taxpayer's ending IRC § 471 costs to determine the IRC § 263A costs that are capitalized.[155] Except as otherwise provided in Reg. § 1.263A-1 or Reg. § 1.263A-3, additional IRC § 263A costs that are allocated to inventories on hand at the close of the taxable year under the MSPM are treated as inventory costs for all purposes of the Internal Revenue Code.

[C] Definitions

Direct material costs. Direct material costs has the same meaning as described in Reg. § 1.263A-1(e)(2)(i)(A). For purposes of the MSPM, direct material costs include property produced for a taxpayer under a contract with another party that are direct

---

152 Reg. § 1.263A-2(c)(2)(ii).

153 Reg. § 1.263A-2(c)(3)(ii)(B).

154 Reg. § 1.263A-2(c).

155 *See*, however, Reg. § 1.263A-2(c)(3)(iv) for special rules applicable to LIFO taxpayers.

material costs for the taxpayer to be used in an additional production process of the taxpayer.

Pre-production absorption ratio. Under the MSPM, the pre-production absorption ratio is determined as follows:

Pre-production additional IRC § 263A costs ÷ Pre-production IRC § 471 costs

Pre-production additional IRC § 263A costs. Pre-production additional IRC § 263A costs are defined as the additional IRC § 263A costs described in Reg. § 1.263A-1(d)(3) that are pre-production costs that a taxpayer incurs during its current taxable year, including capitalizable mixed service costs allocable to pre-production additional IRC § 263A costs, as described in Reg. § 1.263A-1(c)(3)(iii), that the taxpayer incurs during its current taxable year:

- Plus additional IRC § 263A costs properly allocable to property acquired for resale that a taxpayer incurs during its current taxable year; and
- Plus additional IRC § 263A costs properly allocable to property produced for the taxpayer under a contract with another party that is treated as property produced by the taxpayer that a taxpayer incurs during its current taxable year.

Pre-production IRC § 471 costs. Pre-production IRC § 471 costs are defined as the IRC § 471 costs described in Reg. § 1.263A-1(d)(2) that are direct material costs that a taxpayer incurs during its current taxable year plus the IRC § 471 costs for property acquired for resale (see Reg. § 1.263A-1(e)(2)(ii)) that the taxpayer incurs during its current taxable year, including property produced for the taxpayer under a contract with another party that is acquired for resale.

Pre-production IRC § 471 costs remaining on hand at year-end. Pre-production IRC § 471 costs remaining on hand at year-end that a taxpayer incurs during its current taxable year which remain in its ending inventory or are otherwise on hand at year-end, excluding the IRC § 471 costs that are direct material costs that have entered or completed production at year-end (for example, direct material costs in ending work-in-process inventory and ending finished goods inventory).

[D] Production Absorption Ratio

Under the MSPM, the production absorption ratio is determined as follows:

(Production additional IRC § 263A costs + Residual pre-production additional IRC § 263A costs)

÷

(Production IRC § 471 costs + Direct materials adjustment)

Production additional IRC § 263A costs. Production additional IRC § 263A costs are defined as the additional IRC § 263A costs described in Reg. § 1.263A-1(d)(3) that are not pre-production additional IRC § 263A costs, that a taxpayer incurs during its current taxable year, including capitalizable mixed service costs not allocable to pre-production additional IRC § 263A costs that the taxpayer incurs during its current taxable year. For example, production additional IRC §263A costs include post-production costs, other than post-production costs included in IRC §471 costs.

Residual pre-production additional IRC §263A costs. Residual pre-production additional IRC §263A costs are defined as the pre-production additional IRC §263A costs that a taxpayer incurs during its current taxable year less the product of the pre-production absorption ratio, and the pre-production IRC §471 costs remaining on hand at year-end.

Production IRC §471 costs. Production IRC §471 costs are defined as the IRC §471 costs described in Reg. §1.263A-1(d)(2) that a taxpayer incurs during its current taxable year less pre-production IRC §471 costs that the taxpayer incurs during its current taxable year.

Direct Material Adjustment. The direct materials adjustment is defined as the IRC §471 costs that are direct material costs, including property produced for a taxpayer under a contract with another party to be used in an additional production process of the taxpayer, that had not entered production at the beginning of the current taxable year:

- Plus the IRC §471 costs that are direct material costs incurred during the current taxable year (that is, direct material purchases); and
- Less the IRC §471 costs that are direct material costs that have not entered production at the end of the current taxable year.

Production IRC §471 costs remaining on hand at year-end. Production IRC §471 costs remaining on hand at year-end means the IRC §471 costs, as defined in Reg. §1.263A-1(d)(2), that a taxpayer incurs during its current taxable year which remain in its ending inventory or are otherwise on hand at year-end, less the pre-production IRC §471 costs remaining on hand at year-end.

Costs allocated to property sold. The terms defined in Reg. §1.263A-2(c)(3)(ii) do not include costs described in Reg. §1.263A-1(e)(3)(ii) or cost reductions described in Reg. §1.471-3(e) that a taxpayer properly allocates entirely to property that has been sold.

[E] Allocable Mixed Service Costs

In general. If a taxpayer using the MSPM determines its capitalizable mixed service costs using a method described in Reg. §1.263A-1(g)(4), the taxpayer must use a reasonable method to allocate the costs (*e.g.*, department or activity costs) between production and pre-production additional IRC §263A costs. If the taxpayer's Reg. §1.263A-1(g)(4) method allocates costs to a department or activity that is exclusively identified as production or pre-production, those costs must be allocated to production or pre-production additional IRC §263A costs, respectively.

Taxpayer using the simplified service cost method. If a taxpayer using the MSPM determines its capitalizable mixed service costs using the simplified service cost method described in Reg. §1.263A-1(h), the amount of capitalizable mixed service costs, as computed using the general allocation formula in Reg. §1.263A-1(h)(3)(i), allocated to and included in pre-production additional IRC §263A costs in the absorption ratio described in Reg. §1.263A-2(c)(3)(ii)(B) is determined based on either of the following: The proportion of direct material costs to total IRC §471 costs that the taxpayer incurs during its current taxable year or the proportion of pre-production labor costs to total labor costs that the taxpayer incurs during its current taxable year. The taxpayer must include the capitalizable mixed service costs that are not allocated to pre-production additional IRC § 263A costs in production additional IRC § 263A costs in the absorption ratio described in Reg. § 1.263A-2(c)(3)(ii)(D). A taxpayer that allocates capitalizable mixed service costs based on labor under Reg. § 1.263A-2 (c)(3)(iii)(B) must exclude mixed service labor costs from both pre-production labor costs and total labor costs.

***De minimis* rule.** Notwithstanding Reg. § 1.263A-2(c)(3)(iii)(A) and (B), if 90% or more of a taxpayer's capitalizable mixed service costs determined under Reg. § 1.263A-2(c)(3)(iii)(A) or (B) are allocated to pre-production additional IRC § 263A costs or production additional IRC § 263A costs, the taxpayer may elect to allocate 100% of its capitalizable mixed service costs to that amount. For example, if 90% of capitalizable mixed service costs are allocated to production additional IRC § 263A costs based on the labor costs that are pre-production costs in total labor costs incurred in the taxpayer's trade or business during the taxable year, then 100% of capitalizable mixed service costs may be allocated to production additional IRC § 263A costs. An election to allocate capitalizable mixed service costs under this Reg. § 1.263A-2(c)(3)(iii)(C) is the adoption of, or a change in, a method of accounting under IRC § 446.

[F] LIFO Taxpayers Electing the Modified Simplified Production Method

In general. Under the MSPM, a taxpayer using a LIFO method must calculate a particular year's index (for example, under Reg. § 1.472-8(e)) without regard to its additional IRC § 263A costs. Similarly, a taxpayer that adjusts current-year costs by applicable indexes to determine whether there has been an inventory increment or decrement in the current year for a particular LIFO pool must disregard the additional IRC § 263A costs in making that determination.

LIFO Increment

In general. If the taxpayer determines there has been an inventory increment, the taxpayer must state the amount of the increment in terms of IRC § 471 costs in current-year dollars. The taxpayer then multiplies this amount by the combined absorption ratio, as defined in Reg. § 1.263A-2(c)(3)(iv)(B)(2). The resulting product is the additional IRC § 263A costs that must be added to the taxpayer's increment in terms of IRC § 471 costs in current-year dollars for the taxable year.

Combined absorption ratio defined. For purposes of Reg. § 1.263A-2(c)(3)(iv)(B)(1), the combined absorption ratio is the additional IRC § 263A costs allocable to eligible property remaining on hand at the close of the taxable year, as described in Reg. § 1.263A-2(c)(3)(i)(A), determined on a non-LIFO basis, divided by the pre-production and production IRC § 471 costs remaining on hand at year-end, determined on a non-LIFO basis.

LIFO Decrement

If the taxpayer determines there has been an inventory decrement, the taxpayer must state the amount of the decrement in dollars applicable to the particular year for which the LIFO layer has been invaded. The additional IRC § 263A costs incurred in prior years that are applicable to the decrement are charged to cost of goods sold. The additional IRC § 263A costs that are applicable to the decrement are determined by multiplying the additional IRC § 263A costs allocated to the layer of the pool in which the decrement occurred by the ratio of the decrement, excluding additional IRC § 263A costs, to the IRC § 471 costs in the layer of that pool.

***De minimis* rule for producers with total indirect costs of $200,000 or less.** Reg. § 1.263A-2(b)(3)(iv), which provides that the additional IRC § 263A costs allocable to eligible property remaining on hand at the close of the taxable year are deemed to be zero for producers with total indirect costs of $200,000 or less, applies to the MSPM.

The final regulations modify the MSPM so that taxpayers using the MSPM are not required to separately track direct material costs that are integrated into work-in-process and finished goods inventories. Specifically, the final regulations modify the MSPM by:

- applying the pre-production absorption ratio to only unprocessed direct material IRC § 471 costs incurred during the tax year and remaining on hand at year-end;
- applying the production absorption ratio to all production IRC § 471 costs incurred during the tax year and remaining on hand at year-end, which includes direct material costs that have entered or completed production;
- including the pre-production additional IRC § 263A costs that are not allocated by the pre-production absorption ratio in the numerator of the production absorption ratio; and
- including the direct material costs that have entered or completed production in the denominator of the production absorption ratio.

[G] *Allocation of Mixed Service Costs Under the MSPM*

Mixed service costs are defined as service costs that are partially allocable to production or resale activities (capitalizable mixed service costs) and partially allocable to non-production or non-resale activities (deductible mixed service costs).[156]

The regulations provide that taxpayers must allocate capitalizable mixed service costs to pre-production additional IRC § 263A costs in proportion to the raw material costs in total IRC § 471 costs, with the remaining amount of capitalizable mixed service costs allocated to production additional IRC § 263A costs.[157]

The regulations provide that a taxpayer using the MSPM that capitalizes mixed service costs using the simplified service cost method under Reg. § 1.263A-1(h) may allocate capitalizable mixed service costs to pre-production additional IRC § 263A costs based on unprocessed direct material costs in IRC § 471 costs or, alternatively, based on pre-production labor costs in total labor costs. Additionally, if a taxpayer using the MSPM determines its capitalizable mixed service costs using a method described in Reg. § 1.263A-1(g)(4) (a direct reallocation method, a step-allocation method, or any other reasonable allocation method), the taxpayer must use a reasonable method to allocate the costs (for example, department or activity costs) between

---

[156] Reg. § 1.263A-1(e)(4).
[157] Reg. § 1.263A-2(c)(3)(iii)(A).

pre-production and production additional IRC § 263A costs, unless the taxpayer's departments or activities are identified as exclusively pre-production or production. For example, it may be reasonable for a taxpayer using a method described in Reg. § 1.263A-1(g)(4) to allocate a department's mixed service costs between pre-production and production additional IRC § 263A costs based on labor associated with the department when the department is not exclusively identified as pre-production or production.[158]

In order to reduce compliance costs and burden, the final regulations include a *de minimis* rule that allows taxpayers using the MSPM to allocate 100% of capitalizable mixed service costs to pre-production or production additional IRC § 263A costs if 90% or more of the mixed service costs would otherwise be allocated to that amount.[159]

[H] Property Produced Under a Contract and Property Acquired for Resale Under the MSPM

The final regulations provide that additional IRC § 263A costs properly allocable to property produced under a contract and property acquired for resale are generally included in pre-production additional IRC § 263A costs under the MSPM. Similarly, IRC § 471 costs for property produced under a contract and property acquired for resale are generally included in pre-production IRC § 471 costs under the MSPM.

The regulations clarify that, for purposes of the MSPM, direct material costs include property produced under a contract that are direct material costs for a taxpayer to be used in an additional production process of the taxpayer. These costs are included in pre-production IRC § 471 costs.

[I] Categorization of Costs

The final regulations provide that IRC § 471 costs, additional IRC § 263A costs, and any adjustments to IRC § 471 costs or additional IRC § 263A costs are classified using the narrower of:

- the classifications of costs used by the taxpayer in its financial statement; or
- the classifications of costs in Reg. § 1.263A-1(e)(2), Reg. § 1.263A-1(e)(3), and Reg. § 1.263A-1(e)(4). If a cost is not described within Reg. § 1.263A-1(e)(2), Reg. § 1.263A-1(e)(3), or Reg. § 1.263A-1(e)(4), the cost is classified using the classification of costs used in the taxpayer's financial statement.[160]

---

[158] Reg. § 1.263A-2(c)(3)(iii)(B).
[159] Reg. § 1.263A-2(c)(3)(iii)(C).
[160] Reg. § 1.263A-1(d)(5).

[J] Definition of IRC §471 Costs

The regulations proposed to change existing rules by providing one definition of IRC §471 costs that applied to taxpayers using the simplified resale method (SRM), simplified production method (SPM), or modified simplified production method (MSPM), regardless of whether those taxpayers were in existence before the effective date of IRC §263A. The regulations generally provided that a taxpayer's IRC §471 costs were the costs, other than interest, that the taxpayer capitalized to its inventory or other eligible property in its financial statements. The regulations also provided, consistent with IRS's established administrative practice, that taxpayers must include all direct costs in IRC §471 costs regardless of the treatment of the costs in their financial statements.[161]

The final regulations clarify that a taxpayer's IRC §471 costs are the types of costs capitalized to property produced or property acquired for resale in the taxpayer's financial statement. They also clarify that a taxpayer determines the amounts of its IRC §471 costs by using the amounts of those costs that are incurred in the tax year for federal income tax purposes. They also generally retain the regulations' requirement that IRC §471 costs must include all direct costs of property produced and property acquired for resale.[162]

In order to reduce compliance burdens, the final regulations provide an alternative method that certain taxpayers may use to determine the amounts of their IRC §471 costs. This alternative method is available to a taxpayer that is permitted to include negative adjustments in additional IRC §263A costs to remove IRC §471 costs if that taxpayer's financial statement is described in Reg. §1.263A-1(d)(6)(i), Reg. §1.263A-1(d)(6)(ii), or Reg. §1.263A-1(d)(6)(iii) (for example, a financial statement required to be filed with the Securities and Exchange Commission (SEC) or a certified audited financial statement used for a substantial nontax purpose). This method is not available to a taxpayer if the taxpayer's financial statement is described only in Reg. §1.263A-1(d)(6)(iv) (for example, an unaudited financial statement used for a substantial nontax purpose).

A taxpayer that uses the alternative method determines the amounts of all of its IRC §471 costs by using the amounts of costs capitalized to property produced or property acquired for resale in the taxpayer's financial statement using the taxpayer's financial statement methods of accounting. A taxpayer using the alternative method may not include any financial statement write-downs, reserves, or other financial statement valuation adjustments when determining the amounts of its IRC §471 costs.

In order to limit potential distortions in the simplified methods' absorption ratios, the final regulations require a taxpayer that uses the alternative method to consistently apply the method to all of its IRC §471 costs, including any direct costs required to be included in IRC §471 costs, any costs used for purposes of applying the *de minimis* direct costs rules, any costs included in additional IRC §263A costs

---

[161] Prop. Reg. §1.263A-1(d)(2).

[162] Reg. §1.263A-1(d)(2)(i).

after applying the *de minimis* direct costs rules and the safe harbor rule for certain variances and under- or over-applied burdens, and any costs removed from IRC § 471 costs because such costs are not required to be, or are not permitted to be, capitalized under IRC § 263A. In addition, a taxpayer using the alternative method includes in additional IRC § 263A costs all negative adjustments to remove IRC § 471 costs and all permitted positive and negative book-to-tax adjustments. A taxpayer using the alternative method, and the burden rate or standard cost methods described in Reg. § 1.263A-1(f)(3), determines the book-to-tax adjustments required to be made as a result of differences in financial statement and tax amounts by comparing the actual amount of the cost incurred in the tax year for federal income tax purposes to the actual amount of the cost incurred in the tax year in its financial statement using the taxpayer's financial statement methods of accounting, regardless of how the taxpayer treats its variances or under- or over-applied burdens.[163]

[K] MSPM Example-FIFO

Taxpayer P uses the FIFO method of accounting for inventories valued at cost. P's beginning inventory for 2018 (all of which is sold during 2018) is $2,500,000, consisting of $500,000 of pre-production IRC § 471 costs (including $400,000 of direct material costs and $100,000 of property acquired for resale), $1,500,000 of production IRC § 471 costs, and $500,000 of additional IRC § 263A costs. During 2018, P incurs $2,500,000 of pre-production IRC § 471 costs (including $1,900,000 of direct material costs and $600,000 of property acquired for resale), $7,500,000 of production IRC § 471 costs, $200,000 of pre-production additional IRC § 263A costs, and $800,000 of production additional IRC § 263A costs. P's additional IRC § 263A costs include capitalizable mixed service costs under the simplified service cost method. P's pre-production and production IRC § 471 costs remaining in ending inventory at the end of 2018 are $1,000,000 (including $800,000 of direct material costs and $200,000 of property acquired for resale) and $2,000,000, respectively. P computes its pre-production absorption ratio for 2018 under paragraph (c)(3)(ii)(B) of this IRC, as follows:

Pre-production additional IRC § 263A costs ÷ Pre-production IRC § 471 costs	=	**$200,000 ÷ $2,500,000**	=	**8.00%**

Under Reg. § 1.263A-2(c)(3)(ii)(D)(2), P's residual pre-production additional IRC § 263A costs for 2018 are $120,000 ($200,000 of pre-production additional IRC § 263A costs less $80,000 (the product of the 8% pre-production absorption ratio and the $1,000,000 of pre-production IRC § 471 costs remaining on hand at year-end)).

Under Reg. § 1.263A-2(c)(3)(ii)(D)(4) of this IRC, P's direct materials adjustment for 2018 is $1,500,000 ($400,000 of direct material costs in beginning raw materials inventory, plus $1,900,000 of direct material costs incurred to acquire raw materials during the taxable year, less $800,000 direct material costs in ending raw materials inventory).

[163] Reg. § 1.263A-1(d)(2)(iii); Preamble to T.D. 9843 (Nov. 19, 2018).

P computes its production absorption ratio for 2018 under Reg. § 1.263A-2(c)(3)(ii)(D), as follows:

(Production additional IRC § 263A costs + Residual pre-production additional IRC § 263A costs) (Production IRC § 471 costs + Direct materials adjustment)	=	($800,000 + 120,000) / ($7,500,000 + 1,500,000)	=	10.22%

Under the MSPM, P determines the additional IRC § 263A costs allocable to its ending inventory under Reg. § 1.263A-2(c)(3)(i)(A) by multiplying the pre-production absorption ratio by the pre-production IRC § 471 costs remaining on hand at year-end and the production absorption ratio by the production IRC § 471 costs remaining on hand at year-end, as follows:

Additional IRC § 263A costs = (8% x $1,000,000) + (10.22% x $2,000,000) = $284,400

P adds this $284,400 to the $3,000,000 of IRC § 471 costs remaining on hand at year-end to calculate its total ending inventory of $3,284,400. The balance of P's additional IRC § 263A costs incurred during 2018, $715,600 ($1,000,000 less $284,400), is taken into account in 2018 as part of P's cost of goods sold.

P's computation is summarized in the following table:

	Reference	Amount
Beginning Inventory:		
Direct material costs	a	$400,000
Property acquired for resale	b	100,000
Pre-production IRC § 471 costs	c = a + b	500,000
Production IRC § 471 costs	d	1,500,000
Additional IRC § 263A costs	e	500,000
Total	f = c + d + e	2,500,000
Incurred During 2018:		
Direct material costs	g	1,900,000
Property acquired for resale	h	600,000
Pre-production IRC § 471 costs	i = g + h	2,500,000
Production IRC § 471 costs	j	7,500,000
Pre-production additional IRC § 263A costs	k	200,000
Production additional IRC § 263A costs	l	800,000
Total	m = i + j + k + l	11,000,000
Ending Inventory:		
Direct material costs	n	800,000
Property acquired for resale	o	200,000
Pre-production IRC § 471 costs	p = n + o	1,000,000
Production IRC § 471 costs	q	2,000,000
IRC § 471 costs	r = p + q	3,000,000
Additional IRC § 263A costs allocable to ending inventory	s = v + z	284,400
Total	t = r + s	3,284,400

	Reference	Amount
Modified Simplified Production Method:		
Pre-production additional IRC § 263A costs	k	200,000
Pre-production IRC § 471 costs	i	2,500,000
Pre-production absorption ratio	u = k / i	8.00%
Pre-production IRC § 471 costs remaining on hand at year end	p	1,000,000
Pre-production additional IRC § 263A costs allocable to ending inventory	v = u * p	80,000
Production additional IRC § 263A costs	l	800,000
Residual pre-production additional IRC § 263A costs	w = k-(u * p)	120,000
Production IRC § 471 costs	j	7,500,000
Direct materials adjustment	x = a + g-n	1,500,000
Production absorption ratio	y = (l + w) / (j + x)	10.22%
Production IRC § 471 costs remaining on hand at year-end	q	2,000,000
Production additional IRC § 263A costs allocable to ending inventory	z = y * q	204,400
Summary:		
Pre-production additional IRC § 263A costs allocable to ending inventory	v	80,000
Production additional IRC § 263A costs allocable to ending inventory	z	204,400
Additional IRC § 263A costs allocable to ending inventory	s	284,400
IRC § 471 costs	r	3,000,000
Total Ending Inventory	t	3,284,400

The regulations include additional examples including:

- FIFO inventory method with alternative message to determine amounts of IRC § 471 costs;
- LIFO inventory method;
- Direct materials–based allocation of mixed service costs;
- Labor-based allocation of mixed service costs; and
- *De minimus* rule for allocation of mixed service costs.
- The regulations also provide a detailed discussion of the MSPM with Historic Absorption Ratio Election.

§ 9.15 Simplified Resale Method without Historic Absorption Ratio Election

The simplified resale method is available only to resellers of real or personal property.

Under this method, a reseller may elect to determine the amount of additional IRC § 263A costs that must be capitalized into ending inventory, using the formula shown below.[164]

Combined absorption ratio[165] × IRC § 471 costs remaining on hand at year-end.[166]

[A] Combined Absorption Ratio

The "combined absorption ratio" is equal to the sum of

- The storage and handling costs absorption ratio;[167] and
- The purchasing costs absorption ratio.[168]

[B] Storage and Handling Absorption Ratio

The storage and handling costs absorption ratio is computed using the following formula:

$$\frac{\text{Current year's storage and handling costs}}{\text{Beginning inventory + current year's purchases}}$$

Current year's storage and handling costs are total storage costs and total handling costs incurred during the year that relate to property acquired for resale and other eligible property. These costs include an allocable portion of mixed service costs (MSCs). When the taxpayer uses both the simplified resale method and the simplified service cost method, the amount of MSCs treated as allocable to storage and handling costs is computed using the following formula (which is a variation on the general labor-based simplified service cost formula):

$$\frac{\text{Labor costs attributable to storage and handling (excluding MSC labor)}}{\text{Total labor costs (excluding MSC labor)}} \times \text{ total MSCs}$$

Beginning inventory refers to the IRC § 471 costs (LIFO carrying value in the case of a taxpayer employing LIFO) of any property acquired for resale or other eligible property as of the beginning of the current taxable year.

---

164 Reg. § 1.263A-3(d)(3).
165 Reg. § 1.263A-3(d)(3)(i)(C)(1).
166 Reg. § 1.263A-3(d)(3)(i)(C)(2).
167 Reg. § 1.263A-3(d)(3)(i)(D).
168 Reg. § 1.263A-3(d)(3)(i)(E); Reg. § 1.263A-3(d)(3)(i)(F).

Current year's purchases means generally the IRC § 471 costs incurred with respect to purchases of property acquired for resale during the current taxable year.

[C] Purchasing Costs Absorption Ratio

The purchasing costs absorption ratio[169] is computed using the following formula:[170]

$$\frac{\text{Current year's purchasing costs}}{\text{Current year's purchases}}$$

Current year's purchasing costs are the total purchasing costs incurred during the year that relate to property acquired for resale and other eligible property. These costs include an allocable portion of mixed service costs (MSCs). When the taxpayer uses both the simplified resale method and the simplified service cost method, the amount of MSCs treated as allocable to purchasing costs is computed using the following formula (which is a variation on the general labor-based simplified service cost formula):

$$\frac{\text{Labor costs attributable to purchasing (excluding MSC labor)}}{\text{Total labor costs (excluding MSC labor)}} \times \text{total MSCs}$$

Current year's purchases mean generally the IRC § 471 costs incurred with respect to purchases of property acquired for resale during the current taxable year.

[D] IRC § 471 Costs Remaining on Hand at Year-End

IRC § 471 costs remaining on hand at year-end are:[171]

- In the case of a FIFO taxpayer, the taxpayer's ending inventory (excluding additional IRC § 263 costs and costs with respect to goods purchased in prior years); and

---

169 Reg. § 1.263A-3(d)(3)(i)(E). Reg. § 1.263A-3(d)(3)(iii) provides that the following variations on the simplified resale method are permissible: the exclusion of beginning inventories from the denominator of the storage and handling cost absorption ratio; or multiplication of the storage and handling cost absorption ratio by the total of IRC § 471 costs included in a LIFO taxpayer's ending inventory (rather than by just the LIFO increment) for purposes of determining capitalizable storage and handling costs.

170 Reg. § 1.263A-3(d)(3)(i)(F)(1).

171 Reg. § 1.263A-3(d)(3)(i)(C)(3).

- In the case of a LIFO taxpayer, the value of the current LIFO increment (stated in current year dollars and excluding IRC § 263A costs).[172]

Example 9-20

FIFO inventory method. Taxpayer S uses the FIFO method of accounting for inventories. S's beginning inventory for 1994 (all of which was sold during 1994) was $2,100,000 (consisting of $2,000,000 of IRC § 471 costs and $100,000 of additional IRC § 263A costs). During 1994, S makes purchases of $10,000,000. In addition, S incurs purchasing costs of $460,000, storage costs of $110,000, and handling costs of $90,000. S's purchases (IRC § 471 costs) remaining in ending inventory at the end of 1994 are $3,000,000.

In 1994, S incurs $400,000 of total mixed service costs and $1,000,000 of total labor costs (excluding labor costs included in mixed service costs). In addition, S incurs the following labor costs (excluding labor costs included in mixed service costs): purchasing—$100,000, storage—$200,000, and handling—$ 200,000. Accordingly, the following mixed service costs must be included in purchasing costs, storage costs, and handling costs as capitalizable mixed service costs: purchasing—$40,000 [($100,000 divided by $1,000,000) multiplied by $400,000]; storage—$80,000 [($200,000 divided by $1,000,000) multiplied by $400,000]; and handling—$80,000 [($200,000 divided by $1,000,000) multiplied by $400,000].

S computes its purchasing costs absorption ratio for 1994 as follows:

$$\frac{\text{1994 purchasing costs}}{\text{1994 purchases}} = \frac{\$460{,}000 + \$40{,}000}{\$10{,}000{,}000} = \frac{\$500{,}000}{\$10{,}000{,}000} = 5.0\%$$

S computes its storage and handling costs absorption ratio for 1994 as follows:

$$\frac{\text{Storage and handling costs}}{\text{Beginning inventory plus 1994 purchases}} = \frac{(\$110{,}000 + \$80{,}000) + (\$90{,}000 + \$80{,}000)}{\$2{,}000{,}000 + \$10{,}000{,}000}$$

[172] Note that if a LIFO taxpayer sustains an inventory decrement for the year, there are no additional capitalized costs for the current year and the taxpayer is allowed to reduce prior capitalized IRC § 263A costs in reverse chronological order based on the ratio of the reduction in the LIFO layer (pre-IRC § 263A) to the total LIFO layer (pre-IRC § 263A).

$$= \frac{\$190{,}000 + \$170{,}000}{\$12{,}000{,}000}$$

$$= \frac{\$360{,}000}{\$12{,}000{,}000}$$

$$= 3.0\%$$

S's combined absorption ratio is 8.0%, or the sum of the purchasing costs absorption ratio (5.0%) and the storage and handling costs absorption ratio (3.0%). Under the simplified resale method, S determines the additional IRC § 263A costs allocable to its ending inventory by multiplying the combined absorption ratio by its IRC § 471 costs with respect to current year's purchases remaining in ending inventory:

Additional IRC § 263A costs = 8.0% × $3,000,000 = $240,000

S adds this $240,000 to the $3,000,000 of purchases remaining in its ending inventory to determine its total ending FIFO inventory of $3,240,000.

Example 9-21

LIFO inventory method. Taxpayer T uses a dollar-value LIFO inventory method. T's beginning inventory for 1994 is $2,100,000 (consisting of $2,000,000 of IRC § 471 costs and $100,000 of additional IRC § 263A costs). During 1994, T makes purchases of $10,000,000. In addition, T incurs purchasing costs of $460,000, storage costs of $110,000, and handling costs of $90,000. T's 1994 LIFO increment is $1,000,000 ($3,000,000 of IRC § 471 costs in ending inventory less $2,000,000 of IRC § 471 costs in beginning inventory).

In 1994, T incurs $400,000 of total mixed service costs and $1,000,000 of total labor costs (excluding labor costs included in mixed service costs). In addition, T incurs the following labor costs (excluding labor costs included in mixed service costs): purchasing—$100,000, storage—$200,000, and handling—$200,000. Accordingly, the following mixed service costs must be included in purchasing costs, storage costs, and handling costs as capitalizable mixed service costs: purchasing—$40,000 ([$100,000 divided by $1,000,000] multiplied by $400,000); storage—$80,000 ([$200,000 divided by $1,000,000] multiplied by $400,000); and handling—$80,000 ([$200,000 divided by $1,000,000] multiplied by $400,000).

Based on these facts, T determines that it has a combined absorption ratio of 8.0%. To determine the additional IRC § 263A costs allocable to its ending inventory, T multiplies its combined absorption ratio (8.0%) by the $1,000,000 LIFO increment. Thus, T's additional IRC § 263A costs allocable to its ending inventory are $80,000 ($1,000,000 multiplied by 8.0%). This $80,000 is added to the $1,000,000 to determine a total 1994 LIFO increment of $1,080,000. T's ending inventory is $3,180,000 (its beginning inventory of $2,100,000 plus the $1,080,000 increment).

In 1995, T sells one-half of the inventory in its 1994 LIFO increment. T must include in its cost of goods sold for 1995 the amount of additional IRC § 263A costs relating to this inventory, *i.e.*, one-half of the $80,000 additional IRC § 263A costs capitalized in 1994 ending inventory, or $40,000.

§ 9.16 Interest Capitalization Rules

[A] Generally

The avoided cost method must be used to calculate the amount of interest required to be capitalized under IRC § 263A(f). Generally, any interest that the taxpayer theoretically would have avoided if accumulated production expenditures had been used to repay or reduce the taxpayer's outstanding debt must be capitalized under the avoided cost method. The application of the avoided cost method does not depend on whether the taxpayer actually would have used the amounts expended for production to repay or reduce debt. Instead, the avoided cost method is based on the assumption that debt of the taxpayer would have been repaid or reduced without regard to the taxpayer's subjective intentions or to restrictions (including legal, regulatory, contractual, or other restrictions) against repayment or use of the debt proceeds.[173]

Under the avoided cost method, the taxpayer's debt is subject to capitalization to the extent that the property being produced (either directly or by a third-party pursuant to contract) is:

- Real property;[174]
- Unsevered natural products of land;[175]

---

[173] Reg. § 1.263A-9(a)(1).

[174] Reg. § 1.263A-8(c)(1). Real property includes land, unsevered natural products of land, buildings, and inherently permanent structures; fee ownership, co-ownership, a leasehold, an option, or a similar interest is real property. Expenditures treated as repairs are not treated as the production of designated property.

[175] Reg. § 1.263A-8(c)(2). Unsevered natural products of land include growing crops and plants, mines, wells, and other natural deposits. Growing crops and plants, however, are real property only if the preproductive period of the crop or plant exceeds two years.

- Inherently permanent structures;[176]
- Personal property produced for self-use with the class life of 20 years or more;[177]
- Personal property with an estimated production period exceeding two years;[178] or
- Personal property with an estimated production exceeding one year and an estimated cost exceeding $1 million.[179]

In the case of a building or inherently permanent structure that includes property in the nature of machinery as a structural component, the property in the nature of machinery is real property.[180]

[B] De Minimis Exception for Beer, Wine and Distilled Spirits (for 2018 and 2019)

The IRS regulations contain a *de minimis* rule. Under it, interest capitalization is not required with respect to any property (or improvement to existing property) that has a production period of not more than 90 days and a total production cost (excluding land, the adjusted basis of property used to produce property, and capitalized interest) that does not exceed $1,000,000 divided by the number of days in the production period.[181]

Under the TCJA, the aging period for beer, wine, and distilled spirits (other than spirits that are unfit for use for beverage purposes) are excluded from the production period for purposes of the UNICAP interest capitalization rules.[182] Thus, producers of beer, wine and distilled spirits are able to deduct interest expenses (subject to any other applicable limitation) attributable to a shorter production period. The provision only applies in calendar years 2018 and 2019.

For purposes of the application of the UNICAP interest capitalization rules, the TCJA provides that the production period does not include the aging period for:

(i) beer (as defined in IRC § 5052(a))[183]
(ii) wine (as defined in IRC § 5041(a)), or[184]
(iii) distilled spirits (as defined in IRC § 5002(a)(8)), except those spirits that are unfit for use for beverage purposes.[185]

---

176 Reg. § 1.263A-8(c)(3). Inherently permanent structures include property that is affixed to real property and that will ordinarily remain affixed for an indefinite period of time.

177 Reg. § 1.263A-8(b)T(ii)(A).

178 Reg. § 1.263A-8(b)T(ii)(B).

179 Reg. § 1.263A-8(b)T(ii)(C).

180 Reg. § 1.263A-8(c)(3).

181 Reg. § 1.263A-8(b)(4).

182 IRC § 263A(f)(4).

183 IRC § 263A(f)(4)(A)(i).

184 IRC § 263A(f)(4)(A)(ii).

185 IRC § 263A(f)(4)(A)(iii).

In other words, the provision excludes the aging period for beer, wine and distilled spirits from the production period for purposes of the UNICAP interest capitalization rules. Thus, producers of beer, wine and distilled spirits are able to deduct interest expenses (subject to any other applicable limitation) attributable to a shorter production period.

This exclusion will not apply to interest costs paid or accrued after December 31, 2019.[186] In other words, the exemption expires for tax years beginning after December 31, 2019.

[C] Interest Capitalization Steps

- Identify the appropriate units of property;
- Determine the production period for the unit of property;
- Determine the appropriate periods for which interest computations are required;
- Determine the accumulated production expenditures attributable to the unit of property;
- Determine the debt with respect to which interest capitalization is required and the amounts of interest incurred with respect to such debt; and
- Allocate the interest on subject debt to the property based on accumulated production expenditures.

[D] Identification of Unit of Property

The interest capitalization rules are applied on a property-by-property basis; consequently, it is necessary to properly define the "unit of property" with respect to which the interest capitalization rules are applied.

For purpose of the interest capitalization rules, a "unit of property" includes:

- The property itself;
- Components of property owned by the taxpayer (or a related taxpayer) that are "functionally interdependent"; and
- In the case of real property, a pro rata portion of the cost of any "common features."[187]

[E] Functionally Interdependent Components

Components of property are functionally interdependent if placing one component in service is dependent on placing another component in service. Alternatively, if property is produced for sale, components are interdependent if they are customarily sold as a single unit. Accordingly, dwelling units in a multi-unit building may be treated as separate units of property.

---

186 IRC § 263A(f)(4)(B).

187 Reg. § 1.263A-10(b)(1).

Under the concept of functional interdependence, the underlying land is treated generally as a component of the unit of property.[188]

[F] *Installation Activity*

Production activity and installation activity are not generally aggregated. However, aggregation is required when:

- The taxpayer produces and installs the property for its own use (or for the use of a related party); or
- The taxpayer is treated as the producer of the property and enters into a contract to install the property for use by a customer.[189]

[G] *Common Features*

In general, a common feature includes any real property owned by the taxpayer that benefits real property produced by, or for, the taxpayer (or a related party) and that is not separately held for the production of income.[190]

Example 9-22

X, a real estate developer, begins a project to construct a condominium building and a convenience store for the benefit of the condominium.

X must decide to sell or lease the convenience store.

Because the convenience store is separately held for the production of income from the condominium, the convenience store is not a common feature with respect to the condominium building.

Instead, the condominium is a separate unit of property with a separate production period; therefore, a separate determination of accumulated production expenditures must be made.

[H] *Beginning of Production Period*

With respect to real property, the production period begins on the first date that any physical production activity is first performed with respect to a unit of real property. The production period of a unit of real property produced under a contract begins for the contractor on the date the contractor begins physical production activity on the property. The production period of a unit of real property produced

---

[188] Reg. § 1.263A-10(b)(2).
[189] Reg. § 1.263A-10(d).
[190] Reg. § 1.263A-10(b)(3).

under a contract begins for the customer on the date either the customer or the contractor begins physical production activity on the property.[191]

In the case of personal property, the production period of a unit begins on the first date by which the taxpayer's accumulated production expenditures, including planning and design expenditures, are at least 5% of the taxpayer's total estimated accumulated production expenditures for the property unit. Thus, the beginning of the production period is determined without regard to whether physical production activity has commenced. The production period of a unit of tangible personal property produced under a contract begins for the contractor when the contractor's accumulated production expenditures, without any reduction for payments from the customer, are at least 5% of the contractor's total estimated accumulated production expenditures. The production period for a unit of tangible personal property produced under a contract begins for the customer when the customer's accumulated production expenditures are at least 5% of the customer's total estimated accumulated production expenditures.[192]

[I] *End of Production Period*

The production period for a unit of property ends on the later of (1) the date the unit is placed in service or ready for sale or (2) the date when all production activities cease. In the case of separate apartments in a multi-unit building, each of which is a separate unit of property, the production period ends for each separate apartment when it is ready to be held for sale or placed in service. In the case of a single unit of property that merely undergoes separate and distinct stages of production, the production period ends at the same time (*i.e.*, when all separate stages of production are completed with respect to the entire amount of accumulated production expenditures for the property).

Example 9-23

E is engaged in the original construction of a high-rise office building with two wings. At the end of 2019, Wing #1, but not Wing #2, is placed in service. Moreover, at the end of 2019, all production activities reasonably expected to be undertaken on Wing #1 are completed. Wing #1 and Wing #2 are separate units of designated property. E may stop capitalizing interest on Wing #1 but not on Wing #2.

---

[191] Reg. § 1.263A-12(c)(2).
[192] Reg. § 1.263A-12(c)(3).

Example 9-24

F is in the business of constructing finished houses. F generally paints and finishes the interior of the house, although this does not occur until a potential buyer is located. Because F reasonably expects to undertake production activity (painting and finishing), the production period of each house does not end until these activities are completed.

[J] Suspension of Production Period

If production activities related to the production of a unit of designated property cease for at least 120 consecutive days (cessation period), a taxpayer may suspend the capitalization of interest with respect to the unit of designated property starting with the first measurement period that begins after the first day in which production ceases. The taxpayer must resume the capitalization of interest with respect to a unit beginning with the measurement period during which production activities resume.[193]

[K] Computation Periods

The computation period is the period for applying the avoided cost method. The computation period must occur at least annually, and the period selected must be consistently applied to all units. The use of an annual computation period minimizes the compounding of capitalized interest.[194]

The choice of a computation period is a method of accounting. Any change in the computation period is a change in method of accounting requiring the consent of the Commissioner.[195]

[L] Measurement Dates

Measurement dates are dates for measuring accumulated production expenditures, outstanding traced and nontraced debt, and interest incurred. Measurement dates must occur at equal intervals during the computation period. In the case of an annual computation period, measurement dates must occur at least quarterly. For shorter computation periods, measurement dates must occur at least twice during the computation period and at least four times during the taxable year.[196]

---

[193] Reg. § 1.263A-12(g).

[194] Reg. § 1.263A-9(f).

[195] Reg. § 1.263A-9(f)(1)(ii).

[196] Reg. § 1.263A-9(f)(2).

§ 9.17 Accumulated Production Expenditures

Accumulated production expenditures consist of the cumulative amount of costs required to be capitalized under the UNICAP rules, including amounts required to be capitalized before the start of the production period. The following items are included in accumulated production expenditures:

- Costs related to planning and design activities;
- Interest capitalized in prior periods;
- An allocable share of the cost of common features, including land costs of the common feature;[197]
- The basis of property received in a like-kind exchange;
- The cost of raw land on which the improvement is being constructed, not including demolition costs capitalized under IRC § 380B (with interest attributable to that amount being capitalized into the basis of the improvement, rather than the basis of the land itself);
- General and administrative costs capitalized under the UNICAP rules; and
- The cost or adjusted basis of assets utilized (in a reasonably proximate manner) to produce the property (with allocation being made using a reasonable criteria corresponding to use of the asset, and excluding nonworking hours).[198]

Example 9-25

Delta Corp. constructs an office building. Production begins on Jan. 1, 2020, and ends on December 31, 2020. Delta owns the equipment used in the construction. Delta's cost basis was $50,000. For 2020, the MACRS depreciation was $8,925.

Since the equipment was used for the entire year, all depreciation for 2020 is a production expense and is therefore capitalized.

Example 9-26

In 2020, X uses a bulldozer exclusively to clear the land on several adjacent real estate development projects, A, B, and C. A, B, and C are treated as separate units of property. X decides to allocate the basis of the bulldozer among the three projects on the basis of time. At the end of the first quarter of 2020, the production period has commenced for all three projects. The bulldozer was operated for 30 hours on project A, 80 hours

---

[197] Any reasonable method may be used to perform the allocation, such as relative costs, relative fair market values, or square footage.

[198] Reg. § 1.263A-11.

on project B, and ten hours on project C, for a total of 120 hours for the entire period. For purposes of determining accumulated production expenditures as of the end of the first quarter, 1/4 of the adjusted basis of the bulldozer is allocated to project A, 2/3 to project B, and 1/12 to project C. Nonworking hours, regularly scheduled nonworking days, or other periods in which the bulldozer is temporarily idle[199] during the measurement period are not taken into account in allocating the basis of the bulldozer.

§ 9.18 Interest Subject to Capitalization

[A] Interest Defined

Interest includes all forms of interest, including original issue discount, below market loans, and certain expenses which are treated as substitutes for interest.[200]

[B] Eligible Debt

Eligible debt includes all outstanding debt considered as such for federal income tax purposes, other than:

- Debt with respect to which interest is permanently nondeductible;
- Debt incurred by an exempt IRC § 501 organization, except to the extent that the organization has unrelated business income;
- Reserved, contingent liabilities and deferred taxes;
- Debt with respect to which the interest is personal interest or qualified residence interest;
- Debt between related parties if the interest rate is less than an adequate rate; and
- Non-interest-bearing debt (*i.e.*, payables), unless the payables constitute "traced debt."[201]

[C] Categories of Debt

For purposes of the interest capitalization rules, eligible debt is classified generally into one of two categories:

---

[199] Reg. § 1.263A-1(e)(3)(ii)(V).

[200] Reg. § 1.263A-9(a)(3). Reg. § 1.263A-15(c) contains anti-abuse provisions. Taxpayers may not use loans in lieu of advance payments, tax-exempt parties, loan restructurings at measurement dates, or obligations bearing an unreasonably low rate of interest (even if the rate equals or exceeds the applicable federal rate under IRC § 1274(d)) to avoid the purposes of IRC § 263A(f).

[201] Reg. § 1.263A-9(a)(4).

- Traced debt, *i.e.*, debt for which the proceeds are traced to the unit of property in question; or
- Indirect debt, *i.e.*, all debt of the taxpayer other than traced debt (even if the proceeds of the debt can be traced to a specific unrelated activity).[202]

In the case of indirect debt:

- If a taxpayer is producing more than one property, excess indirect debt (debt not traced to any property) is allocated pro rata to the production expenditures of such properties.
- If a taxpayer has more than one outstanding indirect debt, a pro rata portion of each debt is allocated to excess production expenditures (*i.e.*, production expenditures in excess of traced debt).

Example 9-27

Corporation X, a calendar year taxpayer, is engaged in the production of a single unit of designated property during 2020 (unit A). Corporation X adopts a taxable year computation period and quarterly measurement dates. Production of unit A starts on January 14, 2020, and ends on June 16, 2020. On March 31, 2020 and on June 30, 2020, Corporation X has outstanding a $1,000,000 loan that is allocated to production expenditures with respect to unit A. During the period January 1, 2020, through June 30, 2020, Corporation X incurs $50,000 of interest related to the loan. Under the traced debt rule, the $50,000 of interest Corporation X incurs on the loan during the period January 1, 2020, through June 30, 2020, must be capitalized with respect to unit A.

[D] Interest Required to be Capitalized

With respect to an excess expenditure amount, interest incurred during the computation period is capitalized from the following sources and in the following sequence but not in excess of the excess expenditure amount for all units of designated property:

- Interest incurred on nontraced debt;[203]
- Interest incurred on borrowings described in Reg. § 1.263A-9(a)(4)(iii) (relating to certain borrowings from related persons); and

---

[202] Reg. § 1.263A-9(b). In lieu of distinguishing between traced and indirect debt, a taxpayer may elect to treat all of its debt as indirect debt. If this election (which is irrevocable without IRS consent) is made, (1) all expenditures are treated as excess production expenditures, and (2) eligible debt includes noninterest-bearing liabilities that would be traced debt in the absence of an election not to trace. Reg. § 1.263A-9(d).

[203] Reg. § 1.263A-9(c)(5)(i).

- In the case of a partnership, guaranteed payments for the use of capital (within the meaning of IRC § 707(c)) that would be deductible by the partnership if IRC § 263A(f) did not apply.[204]

Example 9-28

P, a partnership owned equally by Corporation A and Individual B, is engaged in the construction of an office building during 2020. Average excess expenditures for the office building for 2020 are $2,000,000. When P was formed, A and B agreed that A would be entitled to an annual guaranteed payment of $70,000 in exchange for A's capital contribution. The only borrowing of P, A, and B for 2020 is a loan to P from an unrelated lender of $1,000,000 (loan #1). The loan is nontraced debt and bears interest at an annual rate of 10%. Thus, P's weighted average interest rate[205] is 10% and interest incurred during 2020 is $100,000.

Accordingly, the excess expenditure amount is $200,000 ($2,000,000 × 10%). The interest capitalized is $170,000 ($100,000 of interest plus $70,000 of guaranteed payments).

During the production period, interest on outstanding debt is capitalized into asset basis to the extent that it is attributable to production expenditures.

The required amount of interest that must be capitalized is the total amount of interest expense paid or incurred by the taxpayer. The amount of capitalized interest (subject to this limitation) is equal to the sum of:

- Interest on traced debt (to the extent of production expenditures); and
- Interest on indirect debt (to the extent that production expenditures exceed traced debt).[206]

The amount of interest that must be capitalized with respect to nontraced debt is determined generally by multiplying the accumulated production expenditures in excess of traced debt (*i.e.*, the "excess production expenditures") by the weighted average interest rate on all eligible nontraced debt.[207]

The rules below apply in determining the weighted average interest rate on nontraced debt:

- Deferral provisions affecting the deductibility of interest are not taken into account in determining the interest rate;
- If the taxpayer has no nontraced debt outstanding during the computation period, the taxpayer must use the highest Applicable Federal Rate (AFR) under IRC § 1274(d) in effect during the computation period; and

---

[204] Reg. § 1.263A-9(c)(2)(iii).

[205] Determined under Reg. § 1.263A-9(c)(5)(iii).

[206] Reg. § 1.263A-9(a)(2)(i).

[207] Reg. § 1.263A-9(c)(5)(iii).

- If the taxpayer has nontraced debt outstanding, but the rate on the nontraced debt is contingent at the time the tax return is filed, the taxpayer must use the higher of the fixed rate (if any) or the AFR in effect under IRC § 1274(d) on the date of issuance.[208]

Interest capitalized on the excess expenditure amount is limited to the sum of interest incurred on:

- nontraced debt;
- below-AFR borrowings from related parties; and
- guaranteed payments by partnerships for the use of capital. In lieu of using the weighted average interest rate, taxpayers whose average annual gross receipts (including those of related parties under common control and predecessors) for the preceding three, post-1994 years do not exceed $10 million may elect to use the highest AFR in effect during the computation period, plus three percentage points.

A taxpayer electing to use this interest ratio may not trace debt. Election to use the AFR-based rate may be made initially without the IRS's consent. Consent is required to revoke the election or to make an election after revocation.[209]

§ 9.19 Uniform Capitalization Case Study

Assume the following data for a manufacturing company:

Inventory, January 1, 2020:		
IRC § 471 Costs		500,000
Additional IRC § 263 Costs		100,000
Beginning Inventory		550,000
Year 2020 IRC § 471 Costs:		
Direct Labor	3,000,000	
Direct Materials	2,000,000	
Indirect Production Costs	500,000	
Current IRC § 471 Costs		5,500,000
Year 2020 Additional IRC § 263A Costs:		
Indirect Production Costs Not Already Capitalized		
Pension	100,000	
Depreciation	150,000	
Rent	60,000	
Insurance	150,000	
Repairs and maintenance	40,000	
Current Indirect Production Costs Not Already Capitalized		500,000

[208] Reg. § 1.263A-9(c).

[209] Reg. § 1.263A-9(c)(5)(iii).

Mixed Service Costs		
Accounting	105,000	
Office salaries	350,000	
Legal	30,000	
Warehousing	150,000	
Security	85,000	
Current Mixed Service Costs		720,000
Indirect/Mixed Service Costs Exempt from IRC § 263:		
Marketing	150,000	
Selling	175,000	
Advertising	200,000	
Income taxes	150,000	
Distribution	180,000	
Warranty	75,000	
Total Exempt Costs		930,000
Inventory, December 31, 2020:		
IRC § 471 Costs		500,000

The first step is to calculate the portion of the mixed service costs that are allocable to production. Note that the **Total Production Costs for the Year, excluding Mixed Service Costs and Interest**, includes not only 2020 IRC § 471 costs but also 2020 Additional IRC § 263A's indirect production costs.

$$\textbf{Production Mixed Service Costs} = \frac{5{,}500{,}000 + 500{,}000}{5{,}500{,}000 + 500{,}000 + 930{,}000} \times 720{,}000 = 623{,}377$$

The second step is to calculate the **Absorption Ratio** in order to allocate the unapplied indirect production costs and production related mixed service costs to ending inventory. Observe that the **Absorption Ratio's** 2019 Additional IRC § 263A Costs includes not only the mixed service costs allocable to production but also the indirect production costs not already capitalized.

$$\textbf{Absorption Ratio} = \frac{500{,}000 + 623{,}377}{5{,}500{,}000} = 20.42\%$$

The third step is to compute the applicable amount of IRC § 263A costs to allocate to ending inventory.

$$\textbf{IRC § 263A Costs to Add in Ending Inventory} = 20.42\% \times 750{,}000 = 153{,}150$$

Finally, add this additional amount to the IRC § 471 costs already capitalized in ending inventory.

$$\textbf{Ending Inventory} = 750{,}000 + 153{,}150 = \textbf{903,150.}$$

Appendix 9-1 Steps for Applying the UNICAP Rules

STEPS FOR DETERMINING AND APPLYING THE UNIFORM CAPITALIZATION RULES

STEP 1. Does UNICAP apply to property — Reg. § 1.263A-1(a)(3)

See Exempt property — Reg. § 1.263A-1(b)

STEP 2. Which Costs are subject to UNICAP — Reg. § 1.263A-1(e) — See list of costs subject to capitalization

Purchasing — Reg. § 1.263A-3(c)(3)

Handling — Reg. § 1.263A-3(c)(4)

Storage — Reg. § 1.263A-3(c)(5)

Capitalizable Service Cost — Reg. § 1.263A-1(e)(4)

NB Contra Deductible Service Costs — Reg. § 1.263A-1(e)(4)(iv)

Pre-Production Cost — Reg. § 1.263A-2(a)(3)

STEP 3. Allocation of Mixed Service Costs between production/resale activities and other activities of the taxpayer

Facts and Circumstances Method — Reg. § 1.263A-1(g)(4)(iv)

Simplified Service Cost Method for Producers — Reg. § 1.263A-1(h)

Simplified Service Cost Method for Resellers — Reg. § 1.263A-1(h)

STEP 4. Allocation of Direct and Indirect Cost to Inventory — Reg. § 1.263A-1(f) and (g)

Specific Identification Method (both producers and resellers)

Burden Rate Method

Standard Cost Method

Any other "Fact and Circumstance Method"

Simplified Production Method — Reg. § 1.263A-2(b)

Simplified Resale Method — Reg. § 1.263A-3(d)

10

Installment Method

§ 10.01 Installment Method

[A] Generally

Under IRC § 1001(c), the entire amount of gain or loss on the sale or exchange of property must be recognized. If the transaction is an installment sale, gain may be deferred. The installment method does not apply to losses. The installment method is a method of accounting. An "installment sale" is a sale in which at least one or more payments are received after the year of sale.[1] The installment sales rules do not apply if an election is made not to use the installment method or the transaction is one in which the installment method is not applicable. In a typical installment sale, the seller finances all or part of the sale price by receiving payment in the form of a promissory note. The installment sale is reported on Form 6252.

Unless the taxpayer elects out of installment reporting, the installment method is mandatory where the taxpayer has recognized gain.[2]

Example 10-1

On April 1, 2020, Bob sells his motorboat and trailer to Alan. The sale price is $3,000. Bob's basis is $2,500. Al agrees to pay Bob on February 1, 2021.

Since at least one payment is in the taxable year following the sale, the installment method applies. Bob will report gain of $500 when he receives payment in February 2021.

Under the installment method, every installment payment received by a seller under an installment sale has three parts:

- A partial return of the seller's basis in the property sold;
- A portion of the gain on the sale; and
- Interest.[3]

In most instances, taxpayers are required to recognize gain or loss at the time they sell property.[4] In the case of an installment sale, a seller recognizes gain in proportion to the installment payments received. However, interest received must be reported under the taxpayer's regular method of accounting.

---

[1] IRC § 453(b).

[2] IRC § 453(a).

[3] Interest must be reported as ordinary income. Interest is generally not included in a down payment. However, a taxpayer may have to treat part of the payment or a later payment as interest, even if it is not called interest in the agreement. Interest provided in the agreement is called stated interest. If the agreement does not provide for enough stated interest, there may be unstated interest or original issue discount under IRC § 453 or IRC § 1274.

[4] IRC § 1001(a).

Since 1980, there have been a number of changes to installment sales reporting. In addition to the installment sale rules, IRC § 453A contains special rules for non-dealer sales of property,[5] IRC § 453B provides rules for dispositions of installment obligations, and IRC § 453(i) provides for depreciation recapture in the year of sale.[6] IRC § 453C, enacted in 1986, dealt with the proportional disallowance rule and was repealed in 1987. Because of the many changes, exceptions, and special rules made to installment sales reporting, installment sale rules can be a "trap for the unwary." Not having a good working knowledge of these rules can cause a transaction to be taxable in full at the time of the sale even when the taxpayer has received little or no cash.

For example, in *Rose Champy v. Commissioner*,[7] the taxpayer entered into a sale agreement for a total price of $3,200,000. The agreement stated that, at the signing of the agreement, the purchaser had deposited $50,000 with the realty company, and that the balance due, $3,150,000, was payable in cash or cash equivalents upon delivery of the deed. By way of an amendment the deposit was changed to $250,000 and the balance due was changed to $2,950,000.

The closing occurred as planned. The purchaser delivered to the seller a promissory note for $2,950,000 and a mortgage secured by the property was executed. The promissory note stated, in pertinent parts, as follows:

> FOR VALUE RECEIVED, I, STEPHEN J. DE CROSTA, promise to pay to CHAMPY CONSTRUCTION, INC., a Massachusetts Corporation having its principal office at 11 Champy Lane, Methuen, Essex County, Massachusetts, or order, the sum of TWO MILLION NINE HUNDRED FIFTY THOUSAND AND No/100 ($2,950,000.00) Dollars, on *demand from this date*, with interest to be paid monthly at the rate of one percentage point above the prime rate of The First National Bank of Boston, but in any event, no less than ten percent (10%) per annum during said term, and for such further time as the said principal sum or any part thereof shall remain unpaid. Both principal and interest to be payable in legal tender money of the United States of America. Payment shall be first applied to interest then due and the balance thereof remaining applied to principal. [Emphasis added.][8]

The seller never received any money from the buyer other than the $250,000 deposit. As a result, the seller owed a federal income tax liability of nearly $300,000 and had insufficient funds for which to pay the income tax. Looking to Massachusetts law, the court determined the note was payable on demand because no time for payment was stated.

---

[5] *See* § 10.09 below.

[6] *See* § 10.12 below.

[7] T.C. Memo. 1994-355

[8] *Id.*

IRC § 453(f)(4) provides that the receipt of evidence of indebtedness that is payable on demand shall be considered the receipt of payment. Therefore, an obligation received by the taxpayer that is payable on demand shall be considered payment in the year the obligation is received, and shall not be considered an installment obligation payable in future years.[9] The court, citing the regulations, held that the sellers were not entitled to installment reporting.[10]

[B] Election Not to Report on the Installment Method

An installment sale is to be reported on the installment method unless the taxpayer elects not to report on the installment method. An election out of the installment method for any sale must generally be made on or before the due date (including extensions) for filing the seller's income tax return for the year in which the sale occurs.[11] An election out does not apply to all dispositions during the taxable year. Thus, a seller must make a separate election out for each transaction. The seller may not make a conditional election out of the installment method.[12] A taxpayer who elects not to report an installment sale on the installment method must recognize gain on the sale in accordance with the taxpayer's method of accounting.[13]

Treatment of an installment sale when a taxpayer elects not to report on the installment method.

In general. A taxpayer who elects not to report a sale on the installment method must recognize gain on the sale in accordance with the taxpayer's method of accounting. The fair market value of an installment obligation shall be determined in accordance with Temp. Reg. § 15a.453-1(d)(2)(ii) and (iii). In making such determination, any provision of contract or local law restricting the transferability of the installment obligation shall be disregarded. Receipt of an installment obligation shall be treated as a receipt of property in an amount equal to the fair market value of the installment obligation, whether or not such obligation is the equivalent of cash. An installment obligation is considered to be property and is subject to valuation, without regard to whether the obligation is embodied in a note, an executory contract, or any other instrument, or is an oral promise enforceable under local law.

In TAM 8838002, X sold a laundromat on July 30, 1982, for $90,000, which was received in the form of $2,500 in cash at the closing and a deferred payment

---

[9] Temp. Reg. § 15A.453-1(e)(1).

[10] *But cf. Applegate v. Comm'r*, 980 F.2d 1125 (7th Cir. 1992), where farmers' "price later" grain contracts qualified for installment sale reporting treatment because they were distinguishable from typical demand obligations, which would have been considered full payment. Contracts did not specify purchase price and allowed taxpayers/sellers up to one year to demand payment, with price to be determined with reference to buyer's bid price on date selected. Taxpayers' right to wait for favorable bid price was more valuable than right to demand payment of amount specified or computable from terms of typical demand obligation.

[11] IRC § 453(d)(2). A taxpayer may qualify for an automatic six-month extension to make this election. *See* Reg. § 301.9100-1 through § 301.9100-3.

[12] Temp. Reg. § 15a.453-1(d)(3)(ii).

[13] Temp. Reg. § 15a.453-1(d)(2)(i).

promissory note of $87,500. On June 30, 1982, X also sold a laundromat in exchange for a cash down payment of $5,000 at closing and a deferred payment promissory note of $70,000.

The third laundromat that X sold in 1982 was severely damaged by fire earlier in the year. X carried no insurance on the equipment, but received an insurance reimbursement for the building. X sold the remaining assets for $36,000, receiving $2,500 in cash at closing and a deferred promissory note of $33,500.

X prepared his own 1982 tax return, but he has no background in the preparation of tax returns and no knowledge of the rules governing installment sales. X underreported the gain from the sale of two of the laundromats because of his lack of knowledge of how to properly compute tax basis. X reported no gain from the sale of the fire-damaged laundromat's assets.

Notwithstanding the lack of an affirmative election out of the installment method, the National Office indicated that a taxpayer is considered to have elected out of the installment method if the taxpayer fails to report on his or her return any gain from the sale.

However, in *Bolton v. Commissioner*,[14] the Tax Court held that a taxpayer who did not correctly elect out of the installment method in the year of the sale was able to use the installment method to report his gain. In *Bolton*, the taxpayers, who had changed their minds and wanted to report their gain from a 1982 installment sale on the installment method, were permitted to do so because they had reported the sale as a completed transaction on their 1983 return (rather than on their 1982 return). The IRS argued that the taxpayers made a binding election out of the installment method by reporting the sale as a completed transaction, but the court stated that the 1983 election could not override IRC § 453(d), which requires a valid election to be made on or before the due date of the return for the year of the sale. Because no election was made on or before the due date of the 1982 return, a timely election out of the installment method was not made.

Elections after the due date will be permitted only in those rare circumstances when the IRS concludes that a taxpayer had good cause for failing to make a timely election. A recharacterization of a transaction as a sale in a taxable year subsequent to the taxable year in which the transaction occurred (*e.g.*, a transaction initially reported as a lease later is determined to have been an installment sale) will not justify a late election.[15] Generally, an election out of installment sale reporting is irrevocable. An election may be revoked only with the consent of the IRS. A revocation will not be permitted when one of its purposes is the avoidance of federal income taxes or when the taxable year in which any payment was received has closed.[16]

---

14 92 T.C. 303 (1989).

15 Temp. Reg. § 15a.453-1(d)(3)(ii).

16 Temp. Reg. § 15a.453-1(d)(4).

§ 10.02 Benefits/Detriments

The benefits and detriments of the installment method include:

- The deferral of gain recognition;
- An increase in cash flow;
- The gain may be used to absorb NOL's or expiring capital loss carryovers;
- Flexibility in determining the year of recognition of gain;
- Lower or higher taxes if the tax rate is reduced or the taxpayer is in a higher marginal rate at the time of recognition;
- Acceleration of recognition on pledge or disposition;
- Interest charge on certain sales;
- The risk of loss if the buyer defaults;
- Possible adverse tax consequences on repossession; and
- The purchase or sale of property with little or no cash.

§ 10.03 Application of the Installment Method

[A] Generally

The installment method allows for deferral of gain (but not losses) on qualifying sales of property, and allocating the gain over the principal payments on the deferred payment obligation. As an accounting method, the installment method is not limited to cash-method taxpayers, but is available to accrual method taxpayers as well. Nonrecognition transactions, including like kind exchanges, may involve receipt of additional consideration (boot) which may involve deferred payments. When there are deferred payments, there is a need to coordinate the nonrecognition provisions with the installment method.

Because the installment method defers gain recognition to years after the realization event, deferred gain may be accelerated on disposition of installment obligations. Furthermore, when a sale by a corporation of qualifying property is followed by a distribution of the installment obligation to its shareholders, there may be additional complications.[17]

In general, the installment method applies to:

- Sales of real property not held for sale to customers in the ordinary course of trade or business (non-inventory property), and
- Non-dealer sales of personal property not required to be kept in inventory.

Although the installment method is ordinarily used for sales, it is also available for like-kind exchanges when the cash equivalent could be paid on the installment method.[18] The installment method can also be used for a dealer's disposition of non-inventory personal property of a type the dealer does not regularly sell on the

[17] *See* § 10.02 and § 10.03.

[18] IRC § 453(f)(6).

installment plan. On the other hand, dealers are forbidden from using the installment method for sales to customers in the ordinary course of business.[19]

The installment method applies to sales at a gain; it does not apply to loss transactions.[20] Any realized loss must be recognized in the year of sale.

[B] Exceptions

Not all gains or transactions are available for reporting on the installment method. Exclusions from installment sales reporting include:

- Sales of inventory;[21]
- The sale of personal property under a revolving credit plan;[22]
- Sales by dealers of real or personal property;[23]
- Sales resulting in losses;
- Certain sales of depreciable property to a related party;[24]
- Income which is recapturable under IRC § 1245 or § 1250;[25]
- Sales of publicly traded property, such as stocks or securities;[26]
- The portion of any gain attributable to depreciation recapture;[27]
- The gain on the sale of depreciable property to a controlled entity.[28] and
- Dispositions of interests representing income from services.[29]

There are two exceptions to the disallowance of installment reporting:

- Sales of property used or produced in the trade or business of farming;[30] and
- Sale of timeshares for not more than six weeks per year and unimproved residential lots to individuals when the dealer elects to pay interest on the taxes deferred as a result of the use of installment method.[31]

---

19 IRC § 453(b)(2).

20 Rev. Rul. 70-430, 1970-2 CB 51.

21 IRC § 453(b)(2)(B).

22 IRC § 453(k)(1).

23 IRC § 453(b)(2)(a).

24 IRC § 453(g)(1)(A).

25 IRC § 453(i)(1)(A).

26 IRC § 453(k)(2), as discussed in TAM 9306001 and TAM 9603003 stock that is convertible into stock that is traded on an established securities market where the value of the convertible stock is equal to at least 80% of the convertible stock's value.

27 IRC § 453(i).

28 IRC § 453(g).

29 *See Sorensen v. Comm'r*, 22 T.C. 321 (1954), where the taxpayer entered into an employment arrangement whereby he received transferable options exercisable at a future date to purchase stock at a price that was 25% of the then existing market price. The taxpayer sold the options prior to exercise for cash and notes payable over a number of years. The Tax Court denied use of the installment method, holding that the installment sale provisions apply to the reporting of the sale of property on the installment basis, not to the reporting of income from compensation for services.

30 IRC § 453(l)(2)(A).

31 IRC § 453(l)(2)(B) and IRC § 453(l)(3).

The IRS is given regulatory authority to prevent attempts by taxpayers who circumvent these rules with related parties, pass-through entities, or intermediaries.[32]

In Rev. Rul. 93-84,[33] the IRS ruled that a cash basis taxpayer must report gain or loss realized from the year-end sale of stock, traded on an established securities market, in the year in which the trade date falls rather than the year in which the settlement date occurs.

If a sale is ineligible for installment reporting, or if the taxpayer elects not to use installment method reporting, gain will be recognized under the taxpayer's regular method of accounting.

[C] *Cash Basis Taxpayers*

Under general tax accounting rules, a cash basis taxpayer reports gain upon actual or constructive receipt.[34] Absent installment reporting, the amount reported is the sum of money and the fair market value of the property received in excess of the taxpayer's basis in the property. When a cash basis taxpayer receives an installment obligation, the installment obligation is treated as the receipt of property in an amount equal to its fair market value, whether or not the obligation is the equivalent of cash.[35] Reporting on the installment method changes the general rule so that reporting of gain is matched with receipt of payment. In such event, reporting of gain when payment has not been received is deferred.

[D] *Accrual Basis Taxpayers*

Under the accrual method, income is recognized when all events have occurred to establish the right to receive income and the amount of income can be determined with reasonable accuracy. In the case of an installment sale when an accrual basis taxpayer receives a promissory note as payment of a purchase price, the accrual method taxpayer, like the cash method taxpayer, may defer the recognition of gain on the sale or exchange of property until payments are actually received.[36]

§10.04 Computation of Gain

[A] *Generally*

The seller includes in taxable income all interest received on plus the amount of the payments received that represents gain. The portion that represents the return of basis is excluded from income.

---

[32] IRC §453(j).

[33] 1993-2 CB 225.

[34] Reg. §1.446-1(c)(1)(i).

[35] Temp. Reg. §15A.453-1(d)(2)(ii).

[36] Temp. Reg. §15A.453-1(e)(2). *See also* Conf. Rept. No. 106-1004, P.L. 106-573, p. 219.

Gain on the sale is computed by multiplying the *gross profit percentage* times the total installment payments received during the year.[37] The gross profit percentage is a fraction in which the numerator is the gross profit and the denominator is the *contract price*.[38] The use of contract price, rather than the selling price, to determine the gross profit percentage is a rule of administrative convenience. It was designed to deal with the problem of recognizing gain when some payments might be made to a mortgage holder rather than to the seller.[39]

The formula can be expressed as follows:

Gain on sale = gross profit percentage × installment payment

To apply the installment sales gains rules correctly, one needs to have a working knowledge of the terms used in the Temporary Regulations. The current definitions found in Temp. Reg. § 15A.453-1(b) are provided in the subsections below.

The steps to be followed in computing recognized gain on an installment for each taxable year are as follows:

- Determine the selling price;[40]
- Determine the gross profit by subtracting the seller's adjusted basis in the property from the selling price;[41]
- Determine the contract price;[42]
- Determine the gross profit percentage by dividing the gross profit by the contract price;[43] and
- Multiply the gross profit percentage by the total installment payments received by the seller in the taxable year.[44]

[B] Selling Price

Selling price means the gross selling price without reduction to reflect any existing mortgage or other encumbrance on the property (whether assumed or taken "subject to" by the buyer) and, for installment sales after October 19, 1980, the gross selling price is without reduction to reflect any selling expenses. Interest, whether stated or unstated, is not considered part of the selling price.[45]

---

[37] IRC § 453(c).

[38] Temp. Reg. § 15A.453-1(b)(2).

[39] *See Burnet v. S.& L. Building Corp.*, 288 U.S. 406 (1933).

[40] Temp. Reg. § 15A.453-1(b)(2)(ii).

[41] Temp. Reg. § 15A.453-1(b)(2)(v).

[42] Temp. Reg. § 15A.453-1(b)(2)(iii).

[43] Temp. Reg. § 15a.453-1(b)(2)(i).

[44] *See* Example 10-2, *infra*.

[45] Temp. Reg. § 15A.453-1(b)(2)(ii). *See Frizzelle Farms, Inc. v. Comm'r*, 61 T.C. 737 (1974). Neither stated or unstated interest is included in the selling price. Temp. Reg. § 15A.453-1(b)(2)(ii).

[C] Gross Profit

Gross profit means the selling price less the adjusted basis of the property. For sales of real property after October 19, 1980, other than sales by a dealer or casual sales of personal property, commissions and other selling expenses are added to the basis for determining the proportion of payments that is gross profit attributable to the disposition.[46]
Hence, the gross profit can be expressed as follows:

Selling Price
– Adjusted Basis*[47]

Gross Profit

* In the case of sales of real property by a person other than a dealer and casual sales of personal property, commissions and other selling expenses shall be added to basis for purposes of determining the proportion of payments, which is gross profit attributable to the disposition. Such additions to basis will not be deemed to affect the taxpayer's holding period in the transferred property.

[D] Contract Price

Contract price means the selling price reduced by that portion of any "qualifying indebtedness" assumed or taken subject to by the buyer that does not exceed the seller's basis in the property (adjusted for installment sales after October 19, 1980, to reflect commissions and other selling expenses).[48]
Hence, the contract price can be expressed as follows:
Selling Price
– Qualifying Indebtedness that does not exceed the seller's basis in the property

Contract Price

[E] Gross Profit Percentage (Ratio)

Under the installment method, the amount of any payment which is income to a taxpayer is that portion of the installment payment received in that year which the

[46] Temp. Reg. § 15A.453-1(b)(2)(v). *See* Example 10-4, *infra*.

[47] The seller's adjusted basis in the property sold is determined by applying the rules applicable to the computation of basis. If the seller purchased the property, the seller's initial basis is generally equal to the cost of the property. If the seller inherited the property, received it as a gift, built it himself, or received it in a tax-free exchange, the basis must be figured differently.

[48] Temp. Reg. § 15A.453-1(b)(2)(iii).

gross profit realized or to be realized bears to the total contract price (the gross profit percentage or ratio).[49]

[F] Qualifying Indebtedness

Qualifying indebtedness means a mortgage or other indebtedness encumbering the property and indebtedness that is not secured by the property but incurred or assumed by the purchaser incident to the acquisition, holding, or operation of the property in the ordinary course of business or investment.[50]

Qualifying indebtedness does *not* include an obligation that has been incurred incident to the disposition of the property (*e.g.*, legal fees relating to the sale of the property), or an obligation functionally unrelated to the acquisition, etc., of the property (*e.g.*, taxpayer's medical bills). Any obligation or debt that seller incurs, assumes, or places as an encumbrance on the property in contemplation of disposing of the property results in accelerating recovery of seller's basis in the installment sale. Moreover, any obligation created after the acquisition of the property is not qualifying indebtedness if the arrangement results in accelerating the recovery of the taxpayer's basis in the installment sale.[51]

[G] Payment

Payment means principal (but not interest) actually or constructively received during the year on the purchaser's obligation. In addition, payment received in the year of sale includes:[52]

- Contingent deposits received from buyer before the year of sale, or other forfeitable deposits;[53]
- Evidence of indebtedness of the purchaser if the note is secured, directly or indirectly by cash or cash equivalents such as a certificate of deposit or a treasury note;[54]
- In addition, amounts paid in an escrow account solely to secure the purchaser's obligation are considered an amount secured by cash or credit cash equivalent;[55]
- Evidence of indebtedness of the purchaser which is payable on demand;[56]
- Evidence of indebtedness of the purchaser if such obligations are issued by a corporation, a government, or a political subdivision and are readily tradeable

---

[49] Temp. Reg. § 15a.453-1(b)(2)(i).
[50] Temp. Reg. § 15A.453-1(b)(2)(iv).
[51] *Id. See* Examples 10-5 and 10-10, *infra.*
[52] IRC § 453(c) and Temp. Reg. § 15A.453-1(b)(3)(i). *See* Examples 10-6, 10-8, 10-9 and 10-14, *infra.*
[53] Rev. Rul. 73-369, 1973-2 CB 155.
[54] Temp. Reg. § 15A.453-1(b)(3)(i).
[55] *Id.*
[56] IRC § 453(f)(4)(A).

for this purpose, a bond, rather than evidence of indebtedness issued by a corporation or government, is considered to be readily tradable under certain circumstances;[57]

- Evidence of indebtedness from a person other than the person acquiring the property from the taxpayer;
- Cash or other property (valued at its fair market value) received by the taxpayer as a down payment;
- The amount of any indebtedness of the seller to the purchaser which is cancelled in connection with the sale of the property;[58]
- The amount of any nonqualifying indebtedness which is paid or assumed by the purchaser, or to which the property is sold subject to;[59] and
- the amount of any qualifying indebtedness to the extent that the amount of such indebtedness exceeds the seller's adjusted basis for the property (including selling expenses).[60]

[H] *Amounts Not Constituting Payment*

The following amounts do not constitute payment:

- Qualifying indebtedness;[61]
- A *bona fide* wraparound mortgage;[62]
- Evidence of indebtedness of purchaser other than those that are (i) payable on demand, (ii) readily tradeable, (iii) secured by cash or a cash equivalent; and
- A third-party guarantee (including a guarantee by a government agent) of a purchaser's installment obligation, or a qualifying standby letter of credit.[63]

[I] *Selling Expenses*

Selling expenses, such as commissions, are added to basis for the purposes of determining gross profit and the extent to which qualifying indebtedness exceeds basis. The addition of selling expenses does not affect the holding period.[64]

---

[57] IRC § 453(f)(5) and Temp. Reg. § 15A.453-1(e)(1)(i).

[58] Temp. Reg. § 15A.453-1(b)(3)(i).

[59] *Id.*

[60] *Id. See* examples in Temp. Reg. § 15A.453-1(b)(5) and Publication 537, Installment Sales.

[61] Temp. Reg. § 15A.453-1(b)(3)(i).

[62] *See Professional Equities, Inc. v. Comm'r*, 89 T.C. 165 (1987). *See* § 10.11[D].

[63] IRC § 453(f)(3) and Temp. Reg. § 15A.453-1(b)(3)(i).

[64] Temp. Reg. § § 15A.453-1(b)(2)(v), 15A.453-1(b)(3)(i).

Example 10-2

Able, a calendar year taxpayer sells Blackacre in 2018 to Ben for $100,000; $10,000 down and the remainder payable in nine equal annual installments along with stated interest. Able's basis in Blackacre is $38,000. Selling expenses paid by Able are $2,000. The gross profit is $60,000 ($100,000 selling price less $40,000 basis inclusive of selling expenses). The gross profit ratio is 3/5ths (gross profit of $60,000) of the $100,000 contract price. Accordingly, $6,000 (3/5ths of each $10,000 annual payment received) is gain attributable to the sale. $4,000 is return of basis. The interest received is ordinary income to Able.

§ 10.05 Recapture Income

Pursuant to IRC § 453(i), a seller selling depreciable property on the installment method must report the entire amount of IRC § 1245 or IRC § 1250 recapture in the year of sale, which will be treated as ordinary income.[65] The installment method applies only to the gain in excess of the recapture income.[66]

There are several consequences of reporting recapture income. The basis of the property sold will increase by the income recaptured in the year of the sale. The gross profit is reduced by this increased basis to determine the gain on the sale. The portion of each payment that will be treated as gain from the sale will be less because of the recognition of recapture income in the year of sale.[67]

Example 10-3

Sam sells depreciated property with an adjusted basis of $40,000 to Bill for $200,000, payable in ten annual installments of $20,000 per year, starting the year after the sale. Sam has taken depreciation of $60,000 in prior years. All of the $60,000 constitutes recapture income that must be recognized in the year of sale even though no payments are made. Sam's gross profit percentage for each $10,000 payment received is 50% of the total contract price of $200,000 ($40,000 Basis + $60,000 recapture = $100,000).

---

[65] A partner who sells the partner's partnership interest must include as income the share of the partnership's recapture income from depreciated partnership property. IRC §§ 453(i)(2), 751(c).

[66] IRC § 453(i).

[67] IRC § 453(i).

§ 10.06 Examples of Installment Sales

Example 10-4

In 1980, A, a calendar year taxpayer, sells Blackacre, an unencumbered capital asset in A's hands, to B for $100,000: $10,000 down and the remainder payable in equal annual installments over the next nine years, together with adequate stated interest. A's basis in Blackacre, exclusive of selling expenses, is $38,000. Selling expenses paid by A are $2,000. Therefore, the gross profit is $60,000 ($100,000 selling price – $40,000 basis inclusive of selling expenses). The gross profit ratio is 3/5 (gross profit of $60,000 divided by $100,000 contract price). Accordingly, $6,000 (3/5 of $10,000) of each $10,000 payment received is gain attributable to the sale and $4,000 ($10,000 – $6,000) is recovery of basis. The interest received in addition to principal is ordinary income to A.[68]

Example 10-5

C sells Whiteacre to D for a selling price of $160,000. Whiteacre is encumbered by a longstanding mortgage in the principal amount of $60,000. D will assume or take subject to the $60,000 mortgage and pay the remaining $100,000 in ten equal annual installments together with adequate stated interest. C's basis in Whiteacre is $90,000. There are no selling expenses. The contract price is $100,000, the $160,000 selling price reduced by the mortgage of $60,000 assumed or taken subject to. Gross profit is $70,000 ($160,000 selling price less C's basis of $90,000). The mortgage being qualified indebtedness, C's gross profit ratio is 7/10 (gross profit of $70,000 divided by $100,000 contract price). Thus, $7,000 (7/10 of $10,000) of each $10,000 annual payment is gain attributable to the sale, and $3,000 ($10,000 – $7,000) is recovery of basis.[69]

Example 10-6

The facts are the same as in Example 10-5, except that C's basis in the land is $40,000. In the year of the sale, C is deemed to have received payment of $20,000 ($60,000 – $40,000, the amount by which the mortgage D assumed or took subject to exceeds C's basis). Since basis is fully recovered in the year of sale, the gross profit ratio is 1 ($120,000/$120,000) and

[68] Temp. Reg. § 15A.453-1(b)(5), Example 1.
[69] *Id.*, Example 2.

C will report 100% of the $20,000 deemed payment in the year of sale and each $10,000 annual payment as gain attributable to the sale.[70]

Example 10-7

E sells Blackacre, an unencumbered capital gain property in E's hands, to F on January 2, 1981. F makes a cash down payment of $500,000 and issues a note to E obliging F to pay an additional $500,000 on the fifth anniversary date. The note does not require a payment of interest. In determining selling price, IRC § 483 will apply to recharacterize as interest a portion of the $500,000 future payment. Assume that under IRC § 483 and the applicable regulations, $193,045 is treated as total unstated interest, and the selling price is $806,955 ($1 million less unstated interest). Assuming E's basis (including selling expenses) in Blackacre is $200,000, gross profit is $606,955 ($806,955 – $200,000) and the gross profit ratio is 75.21547%. Accordingly, of the $500,000 cash down payment received by E in 1981, $376,077 (75.21547% of $500,000) is gain attributable to the sale and $123,923 is recovery of basis ($500,000 – $376,077).[71]

Example 10-8

A sells the stock of X corporation to B for a $1 million installment obligation payable in equal annual installments over the next ten years with adequate stated interest. The installment obligation is secured by a standby letter of credit (within the meaning of paragraph (b)(3)(iii) of Reg. § 15A.453-1) issued by M bank. Under the agreement between B and M bank, B is required to maintain a compensating balance in an account B maintains with M bank and is required by the M bank to post additional collateral, which may include cash or a cash equivalent, with M bank. Under neither the standby letter of credit nor any other agreement or arrangement is A granted a direct lien upon or other security interest in such cash or cash equivalent collateral. Receipt of B's installment obligation secured by the standby letter of credit will not be treated as the receipt of payment by A.[72]

---

70 *Id.*, Example 3.
71 *Id.*, Example 4.
72 *Id.*, Example 7.

Example 10-9

The facts are the same as in Example 10-8 except that the standby letter of credit is in the drawable sum of $600,000. To secure fully its $1 million note issued to A, B deposits in escrow $400,000 in cash and Treasury bills. Under the escrow agreement, upon default in payment of the note A may look directly to the escrowed collateral. Receipt of B's installment obligation will be treated as the receipt payment by A in the sum of $400,000.[73]

Example 10-10

T sells land with an adjusted basis of $300,000 for cash of $50,000 and a promissory note of $350,000 payable over five years with adequate interest and purchaser assumes a $100,000 mortgage on the property. The mortgage proceeds were used by T to purchase a personal automobile. In this case, the mortgage constitutes nonqualifying indebtedness; consequently, the assumption by the purchaser constitutes a year-of-sale payment, rather than an adjustment to the contract price. T computes the gross profit ratio with respect to the sale as follows:

($500,000 – $300,000) / $500,000 = 40%

As a result of the receipt of cash, the cash down payment, and the debt assumption, T must report gain of $60,000 ($150,000 × 40%) in the year of sale and in addition, team will report a gain of $28,000 (70,000 × 40%) as a result of the collection of each installment on the note.

Example 10-11

T sells land with an adjusted basis of $75,000 for cash of $50,000 and a promissory note of $350,000 payable over five years with adequate interest and purchaser assumes a $100,000 mortgage on the property. In this case, the mortgage exceeds the basis of the property; consequently, the adjustment to the contract price is limited to the portion of the mortgage, which does not exceed basis, and the excess is treated as year of sale payment. T computes the gross profit ratio with respect to the sale as follows:

($500,000 – $75,000) / ($500,000 – $75,000) = 100%

As a result of the receipt of the cash down payment and the relief of debt in excess of basis, T reports a gain of $75,000 ($75,000 × 100%) in the year

[73] *Id.*, Example 8.

of sale. In addition, he will report a gain of $70,000 ($70,000 × 100%) as a result of the collection of each installment on the note.

Example 10-12

Same facts as in Example 10-11 except that the purchaser does not assume the underlying mortgage on the property, but instead, gives T a "wrap-around" mortgage in the amount of $450,000 (payable over five years). In this case, there is no assumption of indebtedness or taking of property subject to indebtedness; consequently, there is no adjustment to the contract price and no portion of the mortgage is deemed to constitute a year-of-sale payment. T computes the gross profit with respect to the sale as follows:

($500,000 – $75,000) / $500,000 = 85%

As a result of the cash down payment, T must report a gain of $42,500 ($50,000 × 85%) in the year of sale. Also, T will report a gain of $76,500 ($90,000 × 85%) from the collection of each installment on the note.[74]

Example 10-13

N sells equipment with an adjusted basis of $50,000 (original cost $60,000, less accumulated depreciation of $10,000) for $10,000 cash and an installment note in the amount of $70,000. The installment note bears interest at an adequate rate and calls for principal payments of $10,000 per year beginning in the year subsequent to the year of sale. Under IRC § 453(i), N must report the $10,000 of IRC § 1245 recapture as ordinary income in the year of sale. N is also allowed to increase its basis in the property by this amount in computing the gross profit:

($80,000 – $60,000) / $80,000 = 25%

Because of the receipt of the cash down payment, N must report an IRC § 1231 gain of $2,500 ($10,000 times 25%) in the in the year of sale (note that the gain is in addition to the $10,000 of IRC § 1245 recapture which must be reported in the initial year). In addition, N will report a gain of $2,500 ($10,000 times 25%) as a result of the collection of each installment on the note.

---

[74] The "wrap-around" mortgage regulations, Reg. § 15A.453-1(b)(3)(ii) were found invalid by *Professional Equities, Inc. v. Comm'r*, 89 T.C. 165 (1987), *acq.*, 1998-2 CB 1.

Example 10-14

T sells Land with an adjusted basis of $300,000 for cash of $150,000 and an installment note in the amount of $350,000. The installment note bears interest at an adequate rate and calls for principal payments of $70,000 per year beginning in the year subsequent to the year of sale. Instead of providing a mortgage, the purchaser is required to deposit $350,000 in an escrow account to secure payment of the note. The amount deposited in the escrow account is treated as payment in the year of sale; consequently, T must report the entire $200,000 ($500,000-$300,000) gain realized on the disposition in the year of sale.

§ 10.07 Contingent Payment Sales

[A] Generally

IRC § 453(j)(2) expressly allows contingent payment sales to qualify for the installment method and instructs the IRS to promulgate rule-making regulations to deal with the uncertainties. The legislative history indicates that, in view of the extension of the installment method to contingent payment sales, the open transaction method of *Burnett v. Logan*[75] should no longer apply.

A "contingent payment sale" is a sale or other disposition of property in which the aggregate selling price cannot be determined by the close of the taxable year in which the sale or disposition occurs.[76] An installment sale in which payment is due in a foreign currency is specifically included within this definition, since the value of foreign currency varies over time in relation to the dollar.[77] Notwithstanding the fact that the selling price is contingent, the installment method of reporting gain applies to these types of transactions. Contingent payment sales must be reported using the installment method unless the seller specifically elects not to have the installment method apply to the sale.[78]

Contingent payment sales do not include transactions in which the installment obligation represents:

---

[75] 283 U.S. 404, 2 USTC ¶ 736 (1931). In *Burnett v. Logan*, the Supreme Court held the Taxpayer, selling stock in consideration of annual payments contingent on iron ore received, was entitled to return of capital investment before paying income tax based on conjectural market value of annual payments.

[76] Temp. Reg. § 15A.453-1(c)(1).

[77] Temp. Reg. § 15A.453-1(c)(5). *But see* IRC § 988, which requires conversion of the foreign currency denominated payments required pursuant to the terms of the installment sale into their dollar values as of the date of sale. The installment sale gain will be determined, and reported as payments are received, based on these dollar values. Any gains and losses attributable to fluctuations in the value of the foreign currency from the date of sale to the date payments are received in the foreign currency will be separately accounted for under the rules of IRC § 988 (generally as ordinary gain or loss).

[78] *See* IRC § 453(d); Temp. Reg. § 15a.453-1(c)(1).

- A retained interest in the property that is the subject of the transaction;
- An interest in a joint venture or other partnership;
- An equity interest in a corporation; or
- Similar transactions regardless of the existence of a stated maximum selling price or a fixed payment term.[79]

Example 10-15

Doris owns 100 acres of land in Wyoming. Edward enters into an agreement to purchase the land and agrees to pay Doris $100 for each ton of bauxite removed from the land. Doris has a basis of $850,000. Edward expects to remove 60,000 tons of bauxite from the land, after which he will convert the property to a fishing and hunting club.

In the first year, Doris receives a payment of $250,000. How does Doris report the sale? Without the contingent payment sales rules, Doris might rely on *Burnet v. Logan*[80] to defer reporting gain until all of her basis recovered. However, because of the changes made to installment reporting in 1981, Doris will report her gain under the contingent payment sales rules.[81]

Contingent payment sales must be reported on the installment method unless the seller specifically elects not to apply the installment method.

The Temporary Regulations provide special rules for determining gain in contingent payment sales and for allocating the seller's basis to payments received and to be received. These regulations apply to:

- Sales for which a maximum selling price is determinable;[82]
- Sales for which a maximum selling price is not determinable but the time over which payments will be received is determinable;[83] and
- Sales for which neither a maximum selling price nor a definite payment term is determinable.[84]

---

[79] Temp. Reg. § 15A.453-1(c).

[80] 283 U.S. 404, 2 USTC ¶736 (1931).

[81] Temp. Reg. § 15A.453-1(d)(2)(iii) says—"Only in those rare and extraordinary cases involving sales for a contingent payment obligation in which the fair market value of the obligation (determinable under the preceding sentences) cannot reasonably be ascertained will the taxpayer be entitled to assert that the transaction is 'open' Any such transaction will be carefully scrutinized to determine whether a sale in fact has taken place." This is an example of an installment sale where there is no maximum selling price or fixed payment period. *See* § 10.07[F].

[82] *See* § 10.07[B].

[83] *See* § 10.07[E].

[84] *See* § 10.07[F].

[B] Stated Maximum Selling Price

A contingent payment sale will be treated as having a stated maximum selling price if, under the terms of the agreement, the maximum amount of sale proceeds that may be received by the taxpayer can be determined by the end of the taxable year in which the sale occurs. The stated maximum selling price is determined by assuming that all contingencies contemplated by the agreement are met, or otherwise resolved, in a manner that will maximize the selling price and accelerate payments to the earliest date permitted under the agreement.[85]

The seller's gain on the sale is determined by treating the stated maximum selling price[86] as *the* selling price. Basis is recoverable ratably as each payment is received.[87] If application of the sales with fixed payment period would substantially and inappropriately defer or accelerate recovery of the taxpayer's basis, a special rule will apply.[88]

Example 10-16

Anne sells all of her stock of Gamma Corporation to Ben for $100,000, payable at the closing, plus an amount equal to 5% of the net profits of X for each of the next nine years. The agreement further provides that the maximum amount that Ann may receive is $2,000,000, inclusive of the $100,000 payment. Anne's basis in the stock is $200,000. Gross profit is $1,800,000; therefore, the gross profit percentage is 90%, *i.e.*, $1,800,000 of $2,000,000. Accordingly, of the $100,000 received by Anne in the year of sale, $90,000 is reportable as gain and $10,000 is treated as a return of basis.[89]

Assume Ann only collects $1,000,000; how is the unrecovered basis treated? Any unrecovered basis will be reported under the rules generally applicable to worthless debt.[90]

---

[85] Temp. Reg. § 15A.453-1(c)(2).

[86] The stated maximum selling price, as initially determined, shall thereafter be treated as the selling price unless and until that maximum amount is reduced, whether pursuant to the terms of the original agreement, by subsequent amendment, by application of the payment recharacterization rule, or by a subsequent supervening event such as bankruptcy of the obligor. When the maximum amount is subsequently reduced, the gross profit ratio will be recomputed with respect to payments received in or after the taxable year in which an event requiring reduction occurs. Temp. Reg. § 15a.453-1(c)(2)(i).

[87] Temp. Reg. § 15A.453-1(c)(2)(i)(A).

[88] *See* Temp. Reg. § 15A.453-1(c)(7).

[89] Temp. Reg. § 15A.453-1(c)(2)(i)(B), Example (1).

[90] Temp. Reg. § 15A.453-1(c)(3)(i), Example (5).

Example 10-17

C owns Blackacre which is encumbered by a long-standing mortgage of $100,000. On January 15, 1981, C sells Blackacre to D under the following payment arrangement: $100,000 in cash on closing; nine equal annual installment payments of $100,000 commencing January 15, 1982; and nine annual payments (the first to be made on March 30, 1982) equal to 5% of the gross annual rental receipts from Blackacre generated during the preceding calendar year. The agreement provides that each deferred payment shall be accompanied by a payment of interest calculated at the rate of 12% per annum and that the maximum amount payable to C under the agreement (exclusive of interest) shall be $2,100,000. The agreement also specifies that D will assume the long-standing mortgage. C's basis (inclusive of selling expenses) in Blackacre is $300,000. Accordingly, selling price is $2,100,000 and contract price is $2,000,000 (selling price of $2,100,000 less the $100,000 mortgage). The gross profit ratio is 9/10 (gross profit of $1,800,000 divided by $2,000,000 contract price). Of the $100,000 cash payment received by C in 1981, $90,000 is gain attributable to the sale of Blackacre and $10,000 is recovery of basis.

Assume C only collects $1,500,000; how is the unrecovered basis treated? Any unrecovered basis will be reported under the rules generally applicable to worthless debt.[91]

[C] Certain Interest Recomputations

When interest is stated in the contingent price sale agreement at a rate equal to or greater than the applicable prescribed test rate referred to in Reg. § 1.483-1(d)(1)(ii) and such stated interest is payable in addition to the amounts otherwise payable under the agreement, such stated interest is not considered a part of the selling price. In other circumstances (*i.e.*, IRC § 483 is applicable because no interest is stated or interest is stated below the applicable test rate, or interest is stated under a payment recharacterization provision of the sale agreement), a special rule is applied in the initial computation and subsequent recomputations of selling price, contract price, and gross profit ratio. The special rule is referred to as the "price-interest recomputation rule." The term "payment recharacterization" refers to a contractual arrangement under which a computed amount otherwise payable as part of the selling price is denominated an interest payment. The amount of unstated interest determined under IRC § 483 or, if IRC § 483 is inapplicable in the particular case, the amount of interest determined under a payment recharacterization arrangement is collectively referred to in this section as "internal interest" amounts. The price-interest recomputation rule is applicable to any stated maximum selling price agreement, which contemplates receipt of internal interest by the taxpayer. Under the rule, stated maximum selling

---

[91] Temp. Reg. § 15A.453-1(c)(2)(iii), Example (5).

price will be determined as of the end of the taxpayer's taxable year in which the sale or other disposition occurs, taking into account all events which have occurred and are subject to prompt subsequent calculation and verification and assuming that all amounts that may become payable under the agreement will be paid on the earliest date or dates permitted under the agreement. With respect to the year of sale, the amount (if any) of internal interest then shall be determined taking account of the respective components of that calculation. The maximum amount initially calculated, minus the internal interest so determined, is the initial stated maximum selling price under the price-interest recomputation rule. For each subsequent taxable year, stated maximum selling price (and thus selling price, contract price, and gross profit ratio) shall be recomputed, taking into account all events which have occurred and are subject to prompt subsequent calculation and verification and assuming that all amounts that may become payable under the agreement will be paid on the earliest date or dates permitted under the agreement. The redetermined gross profit ratio, adjusted to reflect payments received and gain recognized in prior taxable years, shall be applied to payments received in that taxable year.

Example 10-18

A owns all of the stock of X corporation with a basis to A of $20 million. On July 1, 1981, A sells the stock of X to B under an agreement calling for 15 annual payments respectively equal to 5% of the net profits of X earned in the immediately preceding fiscal year beginning with the fiscal year ending March 31, 1982. Each payment is to be made on the following June 15th, commencing June 15, 1982, together with adequate stated interest. The agreement specifies that the maximum amount (exclusive of interest) payable to A shall not exceed $60 million. Since stated interest is payable as an addition to the selling price and the specified rate is not below the IRC § 483 test rate, there is no internal interest under the agreement. The stated maximum selling price is $60 million. The gross profit ratio is 2/3 (gross profit of $40 million divided by $60 million contract price). Thus, if on June 15, 1982, A receives a payment of $3 million (exclusive of interest) under the agreement, in that year A will report $2 million ($3 million × 2/3) as gain attributable to the sale, and $1 million as recovery of basis.[92]

Example 10-19

(i) The facts are the same as in Example 10-18 except that the agreement does not call for the payment of any stated interest but does provide for an initial cash payment of $3 million on July 1, 1981. The maximum

[92] Temp. Reg. § 15A.453-1(c)(2)(iii), Example 1.

amount payable, including the $3 million initial payment, remains $60 million. Because IRC § 483 will apply to each payment received by A more than one year following the date of sale (IRC § 483 is inapplicable to the contingent payment that will be received on June 15, 1982 since that date is within one year following the July 1, 1981 sale date), the agreement contemplates internal interest and the price-interest recomputation rule is applicable. Under the rule, an initial determination must be made for A's taxable year 1981. On December 31, 1981, the last day of the taxable year, no events with regard to the first fiscal year have occurred which are subject to prompt subsequent calculation and verification because that fiscal year will end March 31, 1982. Under the price-interest recomputation rule, on December 31, 1981, A is required to assume that the maximum amount subsequently payable under the agreement ($57 million, equal to $60 million less the $3 million initial cash payment received by A in 1981) will be paid on the earliest date permissible under the agreement, *i.e.*, on June 15, 1982. Since no part of a payment received on that date would be treated as interest under IRC § 483, the initial stated maximum selling price, applicable to A's 1981 tax calculations, is deemed to be $60 million. Thus, the 1981 gross profit ratio is 2/3 and, for the taxable year 1981, A will report $2 million as gain attributable to the sale.

(ii) The net profits of X for its fiscal year ending March 31, 1982 are $120 million. On June 15, 1982, A receives a payment from B equal to 5% of that amount, or $6 million. On December 31, 1982, A knows that the maximum amount he may subsequently receive under the agreement is $51 million, and A is required to assume that this amount will be paid to him on the earliest permissible date, June 15, 1983. IRC § 483 does not treat as interest any part of the $6 million received by A on June 15, 1982, but IRC § 483 will treat as unstated interest a computed part of the $51 million it is assumed A will receive on June 15, 1983. Assuming that under the tables in the regulations under IRC § 483, it is determined that the principal component of a payment received more than 21 months but less than 27 months after the date of sale is considered to be .82270, $41,957,700 of the presumed $51 million payment will be treated as principal. The balance of $9,042,300 is interest. Accordingly, in A's 1982 tax calculations stated maximum selling price will be $50,957,700, which amount is equal to the stated maximum selling price that was determined in the 1981 tax calculations ($60 million) reduced by the IRC § 483 interest component of the $6 million payment received by A in 1982 ($0) and further reduced by the IRC § 483 interest component of the $51 million presumed payment to be received by A on June 15, 1983 ($9,042,300). Similarly, in determining gross profit for 1982 tax calculations, the gross profit of $40 million determined in the 1981 tax calculations must be reduced by the same IRC § 483 interest amounts, yielding a recomputed gross profit of $30,957,700 ($40,000,000 – $9,042,300). Further, since prior to 1982 A received payment under the agreement (1981 payment of $3 million of which $2 million was profit), the appropriate amounts must be subtracted in the 1982 tax calculation. The total previously received selling price payment of $3 million is subtracted from the recomputed maximum selling price of $50,957,700, yielding an adjusted selling price of $47,957,700. The total previously recognized gain of $2 million is subtracted from the recomputed maximum gross profit of $30,957,700, yielding an adjusted gross profit of $28,957,700. The gross profit percentage applicable to 1982 tax calculations thus is determined to be 60.38175%, equal to the quotient of dividing the adjusted gross profit of $28,957,700 by the adjusted selling price of $47,957,700. Accordingly, of the $6 million received by A in 1982, no part of which is unstated interest under IRC § 483, A will report $3,622,905 (60.38175% of $6 million) as gain attributable to the sale and $2,377,095 ($6,000,000 – $3,622,905) as recovery of basis.

(iii) The net profits of X for its fiscal year ending March 31, 1983 are $200 million. On June 15, 1983, A receives a payment from B equal to $10 million. On December 31, 1983, A knows that the maximum amount he may subsequently receive under the agreement is $41 million, and A is required to assume that this amount will be paid to him on the earliest permissible date, June 15, 1984. Assuming that under the tables in the regulations under IRC § 483 it is determined that the principal component of a payment received more than 33 months but less than 39 months after the date of sale is .74622, $30,595,020 of the presumed $41 million ($51 million – $10 million) payment will be treated as principal and $10,404,980 is interest. Based upon the assumed factor for 21 months but less than 27 months (.82270) $8,227,000 of the $10 million payment is principal and $1,773,000 is interest. Accordingly, in A's 1983 tax calculations stated maximum selling price will be $47,822,020, which amount is equal to the stated maximum selling price determined in the 1981 calculation ($60 million) reduced by the IRC § 483 interest component of the $6 million 1982 payment ($0), the IRC § 483 interest component of the 1983 payment ($1,773,000) and by the IRC § 483 interest component of the presumed $41 million payment to be received in 1984 ($10,404,980). The recomputed gross profit is $27,822,020 ($40 million – $10,404,980 – $1,773,000). The previously reported payments must be deducted for the 1983 calculation. Selling price is reduced to $38,822,020 by subtracting the $3 million 1981 payment and the $6 million 1982 payment ($47,822,020 – $9 million) and gross profit is reduced to $22,199,115 by subtracting the 1981 profit of $2 million and the 1982 profit of $3,622,905 ($27,822,020 – $5,622,905), yielding a gross profit percentage of 57.18176% ($22,199,115 / $38,822,020). Accordingly, of the $10 million received in 1983, A will report $1,773,000 as interest under IRC § 483, and of the remaining principal component of $8,227,000, $4,704,343 as gain attributable to the sale ($8,227,000 × 57.18176%) and $3,522,657 ($8,227,000 – $4,704,343) as recovery of basis.[93]

[93] Temp. Reg. § 15A.453-1(c)(2)(ii), Example 2.

Example 10-20

The facts are the same as in Example 10-19 (maximum amount payable under the agreement $60 million) except that the agreement between A and B contains the following "payment recharacterization" provision:

"Any payment made more than one year after the (July 1, 1981) date of sale shall be composed of an interest element and a principal element, the interest element being computed on the principal element at an interest rate of 9% per annum computed from the date of sale to the date of payment." The results reached in Example 10-19, with respect to the $3 million initial cash payment received by A in 1981 remain the same because, under the payment recharacterization formula, no amount received or assumed to be received prior to July 1, 1982 is treated as interest. The 1982 tax computation method described in Example 10-19 is equally applicable to the $6 million payment received in 1982. However, the adjusted gross profit ratio determined in this example will differ from the ratio determined in Example 10-19. The difference is attributable to the difference between a 9% stated interest rate calculation (in this example) and the compound rate of unstated interest required under IRC § 483 and used in calculating the results in Example 10-19.[94]

[D] Reduction/Recomputation of Price

After a contingent payment sale is reported, circumstances may change so that continued reporting on the original method would substantially and inappropriately defer or accelerate recovery of the unrecovered balance of the taxpayer's basis. In this event, the rule to avoid substantial distortion applies.[95]

The stated maximum selling price may be reduced:

- Pursuant to the terms of the original agreement;
- By subsequent amendment;
- By application of the payment recharacterization rule; or
- By a subsequent supervening event, such as the bankruptcy of the obligor.[96]

When the maximum amount is subsequently reduced, the gross profit ratio will be recomputed with respect to payments received in or after the taxable year in which an event requiring reduction occurs. If, as a result of the re-computation, the maximum selling price is less than the unrecovered basis, the seller may take a bad debt deduction.[97]

---

94 Temp. Reg. § 15A.453-1(c)(2)(iii), Example 5.

95 Temp. Reg. § 15a.453-1(c)(7)(iv).

96 Temp. Reg. § 15A.453-1(c)(2).

97 Temp. Reg. § 15A.453-1(c)(2)(iii), Example 5.

Since the basis of the property is spread over the maximum expected selling price, one might be inclined to attempt to avoid this consequence by including provisions (such as contingencies) that would make determining the selling price difficult. This effort, however, will be futile since incidental and remote contingencies are ignored. Moreover, the maximum selling price is viewed as the largest price that can be paid to the taxpayer assuming that all contingencies operate in the taxpayer's favor.[98]

Example 10-21

A owns all of the stock of X corporation with a basis to A of $20 million. On July 1, 1981, A sells the stock of X to B under an agreement calling for 15 annual payments, respectively, equal to 5% of the net profits of X earned in the immediately preceding fiscal year beginning with the fiscal year ending March 31, 1982. Each payment is to be made on the following June 15th, commencing June 15, 1982, together with adequate stated interest. The agreement specifies that the maximum amount (exclusive of interest) payable to A shall not exceed $60 million. Since stated interest is payable as an addition to the selling price and the specified rate is not below the IRC § 483 test rate, there is no internal interest under the agreement. The stated maximum selling price is $60 million. The gross profit ratio is 2/3 (gross profit of $40 million divided by $60 million contract price). Thus, if on June 15, 1982, A receives a payment of $3 million (exclusive of interest) under the agreement, in that year A will report $2 million ($3 million × 2/3) as gain attributable to the sale, and $1 million as recovery of basis.

In 1992, X is adjudged a bankrupt and it is determined that, in and after 1992, B will not be required to make any further payments under the agreement, *i.e.*, B's contingent payment obligation held by A now has become worthless. Assume that A previously received aggregate payments (exclusive of interest) of $45 million and out of those payments recovered $15 million of A's total $20 million basis. For 1992, A will report a loss of $5 million attributable to the sale, taken at the time determined to be appropriate under the rules generally applicable to worthless debts.[99]

[E] Sales with Fixed Payment Period

When a stated maximum selling price cannot be determined, and a maximum period over which payments may be received under the agreement is fixed, the taxpayer's basis (inclusive of selling expenses) is allocated in equal annual increments

---

[98] Temp. Reg. § 15A.453-1(d)(1)(A).

[99] Reg. § 15a.453-1(c)(2)(iii), Example 5.

to the tax years in which payments may be received under the agreement. In making the allocation, it is not relevant whether the buyer is required to pay adequate interest. If the terms of the agreement incorporate an arithmetic computation that is not identical for all taxable years, basis is allocated among the taxable years in accordance with that variable arithmetic component unless, in taking into account all of the payment terms of the agreement, it is inappropriate to presume that payments under the contract are likely to be in accord with the variable component.[100]

Example 10-22

A sells Blackacre to B for 10% of Blackacre's gross yield for five years. A's basis in Blackacre is $5,000,000. Since the sales price is indefinite and the maximum sales price cannot be determined from the term of the contract, basis is recovered ratably over the five-year period. Assuming the taxpayer receives over the five-year period the payments listed below, the taxpayer will report as follows:

Year	Payment	Basis Recovery	Gain Attributable to Sale
1	$1,300,000	$1,000,000	$ 300,000
2	$1,500,000	$1,000,000	$ 500,000
3	$1,400,000	$1,000,000	$ 400,000
4	$1,800,000	$1,000,000	$ 800,000
5	$2,100,000	$1,000,000	$1,100,000*

* Temp. Reg. § 15A.453-1(c)(3)(ii), Example 1.

If in a particular year no payment is received or if the payment is less than the basis allocated to that year, the unrecovered portion of basis is carried forward to the next year. No loss is allowed until it is determined that the debt is worthless or unless the taxable year is in the final payment year.[101] If application of the sales with fixed payment period would substantially and inappropriately defer or accelerate recovery of the taxpayer's basis, a special rule will apply.[102]

Example 10-23

The facts are the same as in Example 10-22, except that the payment in year 1 is only $900,000. Since the installment payment is less than the

[100] Temp. Reg. § 15A.453-1(c)(3)(i).
[101] *Id.*
[102] *See* Temp. Reg. § 15A.453-1(c)(7).

amount of basis allocated to that year, the unrecovered basis, $100,000, is carried forward to year 2.[103]

Year	Payment	Basis Recovery	Gain Attributable to Sale
1	$900,000	$900,000	
2	1,500,000	1,100,000	$400,000
3	1,400,000	1,000,000	400,000
4	1,800,000	1,000,000	800,000
5	2,100,000	1,000,000	1,100,000

Example 10-24

C owns all of the stock of X corporation with a basis of $100,000 (inclusive of selling expenses). D purchases the X stock from C and agrees to make four payments computed in accordance with the following formula: 40% of the net profits of X in year 1, 30% in year 2, 20% in year 3, and 10% in year 4. Accordingly, C's basis is allocated as follows: $40,000 to year 1, $30,000 to year 2, $20,000 to year 3, and $10,000 to year 4.[104]

Example 10-25

The facts are the same as in Example 10-24, but the agreement also requires that D make fixed installment payments in accordance with the following schedule: no payment in year 1, $100,000 in year 2, $200,000 in year 3, $300,000 in year 4, and $400,000 in year 5. Thus, while it is reasonable to project that the contingent component of the payments will decrease each year, the fixed component of the payments will increase each year. Accordingly, C is required to allocate $20,000 of basis to each of the taxable years 1 through 5.[105]

If in any taxable year no payment is received or the amount of payment received (exclusive of interest) is less than the basis allocated to that taxable year, no loss shall be allowed unless the taxable year is the final payment year under the agreement or unless it is otherwise determined in accordance with the rules generally applicable to worthless debts that the future payment obligation under the agreement has become

[103] Temp. Reg. § 15A.453-1(c)(3)(ii), Example 2.
[104] Temp. Reg. § 15A.453-1(c)(3)(ii), Example 3.
[105] Temp. Reg. § 15A.453-1(c)(3)(ii), Example 4.

worthless. When no loss is allowed, the unrecovered portion of basis allocated to the taxable year shall be carried forward to the next succeeding taxable year. If application of the foregoing rules to a particular case would substantially and inappropriately defer or accelerate recovery of the taxpayer's basis, a special rule will apply. See *Special rule to avoid substantial distortion*.[106]

[F] Sales with No Maximum Selling Price or Fixed Payment Period

If a sales agreement neither specifies a maximum selling price nor limits payments to a fixed period, there is a question as to whether a sale has actually occurred or whether, in economic effect, payments received under the agreement are in the nature of rent or royalty income, in which case there will not be a recovery of basis and all amounts received will be ordinary income.[107] Transactions such as these will be examined closely by the IRS.

If a sale has occurred, as a rule, the taxpayer's basis (including selling expenses) is recovered in equal annual increments over a 15-year period, commencing with the date of the sale. If no payment is received or the payment is less than the basis allocated to the year, no loss is allowed unless it can be determined that any future payments have become worthless and it is more appropriate to take a worthless debt deduction. Barring such an event, the excess basis is reallocated in level amounts over the balance of the 15-year term. Any basis not recovered at the end of the 15th year is carried forward to the next year, and thereafter, until all of the basis has been recovered or the obligation is determined to be worthless.

The general rule requiring an initial level allocation of the basis over 15 years will not apply if the taxpayer can establish to the satisfaction of the IRS that the application of the general rule would substantially and inappropriately defer recovery of the taxpayer's basis. If the IRS determines that the initial 15-year period will substantially and inappropriately accelerate recovery of a seller's basis in the early years of the 15-year term, the IRS may require that the basis be reallocated within the 15-year term, but may not require that the basis be allocated over more than 15 years.[108]

Example 10-26

S sells property with the basis of $3 million for 10% of the properties future gross yield. The transaction is properly characterized as a sale, as opposed to a rental or royalty agreement. In year 4, it is determined that no additional payments will be received under the contract.

The payment received in each year and gain recognized are as follows:

---

[106] Reg. § 15a.453-1(c)(7).
[107] Temp. Reg. § 15A.453-1(c)(4).
[108] *Id.*

Year	Payment	Basis Recovery	Gain Recognized
1	$2,000,000	$200,000	$1,800,000
2	$70,000	$70,000.00	0
3	$500,000	$210,000*	$290,000
4	$800,000	$2,520,000**	($1,720,000)

* ($3,000,000 / 15 years) + (130,000 unrecovered basis from year 2/13 years).
** 3,000,000 – 200,000 – 70,000 – 210,000.

However, if in any taxable year, no payment is received or the amount of payment received (exclusive of interest) is less than basis allocated to the year, no loss shall be allowed unless it is otherwise determined in accordance with the timing rules generally applicable to worthless debts that the future payment obligation under the agreement has become worthless; instead, the excess basis shall be reallocated in level amounts over the balance of the 15-year term. Any basis not recovered at the end of the 15th year shall be carried forward to the next succeeding year, and, to the extent unrecovered thereafter, shall be carried forward from year to year until all basis has been recovered or the future payment obligation is determined to be worthless.[109]

[G] Income Forecast Method

The Temporary Regulations allow a taxpayer in an appropriate case to elect to recover basis using the income forecast method. No special form of election is required.[110]

Currently, this method may be used if the property sold is mineral property, a motion picture film, a television film, or a taped television show.[111] The IRS may from time to time prescribe additional property for which the income forecast method may be used. The taxpayer itself may seek a specific ruling from the IRS.

---

[109] Reg. § 15a.453-1(c)(4).

[110] Temp. Reg. § 15A.453-1(c)(6).

[111] *Bizub v. Comm'r*, T.C. Memo. 1983-280. Depreciation deduction based on income forecast method denied. Taxpayers did not show reliable method to compute potential income from film that they had purchased and exhibited. Film industry is of speculative character and total income to be derived from film over its useful life could not be estimated. In a series of later revenue rulings, the IRS permitted use of the income forecast method to depreciate motion picture films, Rev. Rul. 64-273, 1964-2 CB 62, book manuscripts, patents, and master recordings, Rev. Rul. 79-285, 1979-2 CB 91. These rulings also predated the 1981 enactment of section 168 and were based entirely on section 167, which was then the only provision governing depreciation methods. After enactment of section 168, the IRS continued to follow its initial revenue ruling and extended the income forecast method to videocassettes, Rev. Rul. 89-62, 1989-1 CB 78, and video games, Priv. Ltr. Rul. 9323007 (June 11, 1993), on the ground that they are similar to television films. Taxpayers could elect under section 168(f)(1) to use the income forecast method rather than the ACRS.

Calculations. The income forecast method requires an application of a fraction, the numerator of which is the payment received in the taxable year under a contingent payment agreement, and the denominator of which is the forecasted or estimated total payments to be received under the agreement.

To determine the basis recovery in the year of payment, this fraction is multiplied by the taxpayer's basis in the property sold. If, in a subsequent year, it is found that the income forecast was substantially overestimated or underestimated, an adjustment to the formula is required.[112]

The total forecast of estimated payments to be received must be based on conditions known to exist at the end of the taxable year for which the return is filed. No loss is allowed unless the taxable year is the final payment year or unless the payment obligation becomes worthless under the worthless debt rules. Examples of the application of the income forecast method are shown below.

Example 10-27

S sells a television film with a basis of $1,000,000 to B for 5% of the annual gross receipts from the exploitation of the film. S forecasts that the total payments to be received will be $12,000,000 and that $5,000,000 will be received in Year 1; $3,000,000 in Year 2; $2,000,000 in Year 3; $1,500,000 in Year 4; and $500,000 in Year 5. S expects to receive only insignificant receipts after Year 5.

S's basis is initially allocated as follows:

Year	Percentage	Basis
1	50.00	$500,000
2	12.50	$125,000
3	25.00	$ 25,000
4	8.33	$ 8,333
5	4.17	$ 4,167

S reports the sale under the installment method as follows:

Year	Payment Received	Basis Recovered	Gain on Sale
1	$600,000	$500,000	$100,000
2	$150,000	$125,000	$25,000
3	$300,000	$25,000	$275,000
4	$100,000	$ 8,333	$ 91,667
5	$ 50,000	$ 4,167	$ 45,833

112 Temp. Reg. § 15A.453-1(c)(6)(iii).

Example 10-28

Assume the same facts as in Example 10-27, except that S receives no payment in Year 2; $300,000 in Year 3; and additional payments of only $100,000 are estimated. In Year 2, S is not allowed a loss. At the beginning of the Year 3, S's unrecovered basis is $50,000. In Year 3, S must recompute the basis recovery fraction based on the facts known at the end of Year 3: $300,000 (Year 3 payment) divided by $400,000 (estimated current and future payments) = 75%. Accordingly, in Year 3, S recovers $37,500 of the previously unrecovered basis (75% of $50,000).[113]

Video Gaming. In Priv. Ltr. Rul. 9323007, the IRS extended the application of the income forecast method of depreciation to the depreciation of video games. According to the IRS, the application of time-based methods of depreciation to video games would cause a distortion of income because of the uneven flow of income produced by video games. In the letter ruling, the IRS observed that the assets with respect to which the use of the income forecast method has been approved have several attributes in common, notably:

- The physical life of the asset is largely irrelevant to its income-producing ability;
- Each asset has a unique income-producing ability; and
- The useful life of the asset is measured in terms of its income-producing ability.

The IRS concluded that video games shared the same uneven flow of income characteristics as assets described in earlier revenue rulings. Accordingly, the IRS advised that, for the taxpayer to use the income forecast method of depreciation, the taxpayer had to elect to exclude the video games from the modified accelerated cost recovery system in the year they were placed in service.

[H] *Substantial Distortion of Income*

The Temporary Regulations contain rules to prevent the substantial distortion of income. A taxpayer may request a ruling from the IRS to use an alternative method of basis recovery if it is able to show, before the due date of the return, that the application of the normal basis recovery rules will substantially and inappropriately defer recovery of basis.[114] To do this, the seller must show that:

- The alternative method is a reasonable method, and
- Over time, the seller will likely recover basis twice as fast as the rate at which basis would have been recovered under the otherwise applicable normal basis recovery rule.

---

[113] Temp. Reg. § 15A.453-1(c)(6)(iv), Examples 1 and 2.

[114] Temp. Reg. § 15A.453-1(c)(7)(ii). *See, e.g.*, Priv. Ltr. Rul. 9811039 and Priv. Ltr. Rul. 200603017.

Under some circumstances, the IRS may find that the normal basis of recovery rules will substantially and inappropriately accelerate the recovery of basis. In cases like these, the IRS may require an alternative basis recovery unless the seller can demonstrate that:

- The method of basis recovery required by the IRS is not a reasonable method of rateable recovery, or
- It is not reasonable to conclude that the seller, over time, is likely to recover basis twice as fast under the normal applicable rules than it would under the method proposed by the IRS.

§ 10.08 Dealer Rules

[A] *Generally*

In general, dealers in real or personal property are not permitted to use the installment method for reporting sales or other dispositions of property and must report all taxable gain in the year of sale. There are limited exceptions to this rule, however, including:

- Installment sales of farm property,[115] and
- Installment sales of residential lots and timeshares.[116]

Under the installment sales rules, an installment sale does not include a *dealer disposition*.[117] A "dealer disposition" is defined as any disposition of real property that is held by the taxpayer for sale to customers in the ordinary course of the taxpayer's trade or business, or any disposition of personal property by a person who regularly sells or otherwise disposes of personal property of the same type on the installment plan.[118]

[B] *Dealers in Real Property*

Whether a person is a dealer in real property depends on:

- The frequency and number of sales;
- The extent to which the person engages in sales activities;
- The length of time the property has been held;
- The ratio of income from sales to total income;
- The extent of advertising undertaken;

---

115 IRC § 453(l)(2)(A).
116 IRC § 453(l)(2)(B).
117 IRC § 453(b)(2)(A).
118 IRC § 453(l)(1).

- The person's purpose in acquiring the property; and
- Whether the property was listed through a broker.[119]

[C] Dealers in Personal Property

Whether a person is a dealer in personal property depends on:

- The number of installment sales;
- The frequency of installment sales;
- The ratio of installment sales to total sales; and
- Whether the person (seller) holds the seller out to the public as promoting the availability of installment sales.[120]

[D] Farm Property

A dealer may use the installment method to report gain from the sale of property used or produced in the trade or business of farming. Included in the term "farming business" are the activities listed below.

- Cultivating the soil;
- Raising or harvesting any agricultural or horticultural commodity;
- Handling, drying, packaging, grading, or storing on a farm any agricultural or horticultural commodity in its non-manufactured state, but only if the farmer regularly produces more than half of the commodity so treated; and
- Planting, cultivating, caring for, or cutting trees or preparing (other than milling) trees for market.[121]

However, this exception applies only to farmers (*i.e.*, those in the business of farming), and not to merchants. The courts and the IRS have held that the farming exception is not available to non-farming dealers in farm property for sales of property to a farmer, even though the property is to be used by the farmer in the trade or business of farming.[122]

[E] Residential Lots and Timeshares

If an election is made under IRC § 453(l)(2)(B)(i),[123] dealers selling residential lots and timeshares to individuals in the ordinary course of business can continue to use the installment method of reporting gain from the sales. Notwithstanding this election, the dealer is required to pay interest on the deferred tax resulting from the use of

---

[119] *See Gault v. Comm'r*, 332 F.2d 94 (2d Cir. 1964).

[120] *See* Priv. Ltr. Rul. 9337027.

[121] IRC § 2032A(e)(5).

[122] *See, e.g., Thom v. United States*, 134 F. Supp. 2d 1093 (D. Neb. 2001), and TAM 199908040.

[123] An election under IRC § 453(l)(2) is not available for an installment obligation that is guaranteed by any person other than the taxpayer.

the installment method.[124] The dealer must elect, with respect to installment obligations arising from those dispositions, to increase the income tax for any tax year for which payment is received on the obligations by the amount of interest.[125]

Interest is charged with respect to all payments received during any year after the year of the sale. The amount of interest is based on the amount of tax attributable to the payments received during any subsequent year from prior installment sales of timeshares and residential lots.[126] Interest is computed on the tax for the year in which payments are received and attributable to such payments for the period beginning on the date of sale and ending on the date the installment payment is received.[127] The interest is computed at the applicable federal rate (AFR) under IRC § 1274 in effect on the date of the sale (compounded semiannually),[128] and is added to the tax owed for that year.

A dealer may use the installment method to report gain from the sale or disposition of:

- Any residential lot if neither the seller nor any person related to the seller can make any improvements on the lot; and
- A timeshare right to use, or a timeshare ownership interest in, residential real property for not more than six weeks per year, or the right to use specified campgrounds for recreational purposes.

Property held by related parties are treated as held by the individual who financed the purchase.[129]

[F] Interest Charges

A dealer who uses the installment method to report sales of residential lots and timeshares must pay interest on the deferred tax arising from the installment obligation. The amount of interest is based on the amount of tax allocable to the installment gain on the payments received during the year from the installment sales.

Interest is computed on the tax allocable to the installment gain for the period beginning on the date of the sale and ending on the date an installment payment is received. The interest rate is at the applicable federal rate (AFR) in effect on the date of the sale (compounded semi-annually), and is added to the tax owed for that year.

Example 10-29

On March 31, Year 1, Z, a real estate developer (C corporation), sells an unimproved residential lot to B for $500,000. The developer's adjusted

---

[124] IRC § 453(l)(3).
[125] IRC § 453(l)(3)(A).
[126] IRC § 453(l)(3)(B)(i).
[127] IRC § 453(l)(3)(B)(ii).
[128] IRC § 453(l)(3)(B)(i)(III)
[129] S Rept No. 96-1000, 96th Cong., 2d Sess. (1980), p. 17.

basis in the lot is $200,000. B gives Z an installment note calling for principal payments of $50,000 (and market rate interest) each March 31thereafter for a period of ten years. Z makes the election to use the installment method. Z's gain on the sale is $300,000 ($500,000 contract price – $200,000 basis). Of the $50,000 received from B each year, the developer must report $30,000 as gain ([$300,000 gross profit ÷ $500,000 contract price] × $50,000 payment).

Z must begin paying interest on the deferred tax attributable to the Year 2 payment of $30,000 (no interest is charged in Year 1, the year in which the obligation arose). If the increase in the developer's Year 2 tax attributable to the $30,000 gain is $6,300 ($30,000 × 21%),[130] the developer must add to its Year 2 tax an interest payment equal to $6,300 multiplied by the applicable semiannual AFR.

Any interest paid is taken into account in computing the amount of the deduction allowable under IRC § 163 for interest paid or accrued during the year. Note, however, that interest is not charged for any payment received in the taxable year of sale in which the installment obligation arose.[131]

To elect the exception, the taxpayer has to increase the income tax for any tax year in which a payment is received by interest. Interest is determined:

- on the amount of tax for the tax year that is attributable to the payments received during the tax year on the installment obligation;
- for the period beginning on the date of sale and ending on the date the payment is received;
- using the applicable federal rate (AFR) under IRC § 1274 in effect at the time of the sale, compounded semi-annually.

If the interest charges included in the total contract price and payments are subsequently received, payments are first applied against carrying charges or interest.

The AFR used under IRC § 453(l)(3)(B)(i)(III) to calculate the amount of interest for a taxable year is determined under IRC § 1274(d)(1) by treating such weighted average maturity as the term of the installment obligation.[132]

[G] Carrying Charges

Any carrying charges or interest added to the cash selling price must be included in the total contract price of the property. If the interest charges included in the total contract price and payments are subsequently received, payments are first applied against carrying charges or interest.[133]

---

130 Using corporate tax rates.

131 IRC § 453(l)(3)(B)(iii).

132 Priv. Ltr. Rul. 201622007.

133 IRC § 453(l)(2)(C).

§ 10.09 Controlled Entity Sales

[A] Generally

If a taxpayer disposes of depreciable property to a controlled entity, the installment method of accounting cannot be used.[134] Instead, all payments received are treated as received in the year of the sale and taxed as ordinary income.[135] The purchaser cannot increase the basis of the property acquired in the sale until that amount is includible in the seller's gross income.[136] For purposes of this rule, depreciable property means property that, in the hands of the transferee, is subject to the allowance for depreciation under IRC § 167.[137] The rule applies unless the taxpayer establishes that the disposition did not have as one of its principal purposes the avoidance of federal income tax.[138]

The term "controlled entity" includes:[139]

- A seller and any corporation in which the seller owns directly or indirectly more than 50% of the value of the outstanding stock;[140]
- A seller and any partnership in which the seller owns directly or indirectly more than a 50% interest in the capital or profits;[141]
- Two or more partnerships when the same person owns directly or indirectly more than 50% of the interest in the capital or profits in each partnership;[142]
- Two corporations that are members of the same controlled group;[143]
- A corporation and a partnership if the same person owns more than 50% in value of the outstanding shares of the corporation and more than 50% of the interest in capital or profits in the partnership;[144]
- Two S corporations if the same person owns more than 50% in value of the outstanding stock of each corporation;[145]
- An S corporation and a C corporation if the same person owns more than 50% in value of the outstanding stock of each corporation;[146] and
- A seller and any trust in which the seller or the seller's spouse is a beneficiary unless the interest in the trust is a remote contingent interest.[147]

---

134 IRC § 453(g).
135 IRC § 453(g)(1)(B)(i); IRC § 1239(a).
136 IRC § 453(g)(1)(C).
137 IRC § 453(f)(7).
138 IRC § 453(g)(2).
139 IRC § 1239(b).
140 IRC § 453(g)(3), IRC § 707(b)(1)(B).
141 IRC § 1239(b)(1), IRC § 1239(c)(1)(B).
142 IRC § 453(g)(3), IRC § 707(b)(1)(B).
143 IRC § 1239(c)(1)(C), IRC § 267(b)(3).
144 IRC § 1239(c)(1)(C), IRC § 267(b)(10).
145 IRC § 1239(c)(1)(C), IRC § 267(b)(11).
146 IRC § 1239(c)(1)(C), IRC § 267(b)(12).
147 IRC § 1239(b)(2). *See, generally,* IRC §§ 267, 453(g), and 1239.

The controlled entity rule is designed to discourage transactions structured to give the related buyer depreciation deductions on a stepped-up basis before the seller is required to include gain on the sale in income. If the parties can prove that one of the principal purposes of the transaction is *not* the avoidance of federal income tax, the related party rule will not apply. The controlled entity rule will not apply, for example, if at the time of the installment sale a husband and wife are divorced or are legally separated, or if the sale occurs pursuant to a settlement agreement in a proceeding that results in a divorce or separate maintenance decree.[148]

A good example of the application of the rule was applied in *Ralph J. Guenther, et ux., v. Commissioner*,[149] where the taxpayer, who was a realtor with multiple properties, sold depreciable real property to a closely held company, Metropolitan, that was owned 25% by the taxpayer and the balance of 75% equally distributed amongst his four daughters.

The taxpayer had two mortgages on the property when he sold the property. Metropolitan assumed the second mortgage on the property. The mortgage company would have accepted Metropolitan's assumption of liability or alternatively cosignature by the taxpayer on the mortgage in lieu of the transfer primarily because they were concerned that the mortgage would be paid. The taxpayer had taken deductions for depreciation prior to the sale.

On the sale, the property's adjusted basis was increased by virtue of the purchase. The court noted that IRC § 453(g)(1) did not allow an installment sale of depreciable property between related parties. The exception is where the taxpayer could show that the transfer does not have tax avoidance as one of its principal purposes.[150] The taxpayer contended that tax avoidance was not a principal purpose as he testified that the transfer was to avoid foreclosure by the lender. It turned out that the lender would have taken a cosignature rather than having the property transferred and therefore there was no need for the transfer at all. The Tax Court did not accept the taxpayer's reason for making the transfer. As the sale was between controlled entities, IRC § 453(g)(1) applied and the installment sale was denied. The court noted further that there was a significant tax benefit because the depreciation available to Metropolitan was more than doubled what was still available when the taxpayer transferred properties. The transfer started the "depreciation clock" running again with the stepped-up basis.[151]

The related party rule applies only to sales of depreciable property, and therefore does not apply to sales of non-depreciable property. In a case before the IRS, for

---

[148] S. Rep. No. 1000, 96th Cong., 2d Sess. 17 (1980).

[149] 69 TCM 2980 (1995), T.C. Memo. 1995-280.

[150] IRC § 453(g)(2).

[151] *Vest v. Comm'r*, T.C. Memo. 2016-187 (2016) (The fact that taxpayer through installment reporting aimed to defer for ten years all tax on prior gain while giving transferees stepped-up bases in and ability to claim correspondingly large depreciation or amortization deductions on assets transferred, showed that in substance, tax avoidance was one of transaction's principal purposes. The taxpayer's arguments that taxpayer had valid business purpose, or that fact he had large net operating losses precluded finding of tax avoidance, were held unpersuasive.), *aff'd*, 2017-1 USTC ¶ 50,240 (5th Cir. 2017).

example, in which the bulk of a transaction involved unimproved land, the IRS ruled that the portion of the sale price attributable to the non-depreciable land was eligible for installment reporting.[152]

The constructive ownership rules of IRC § 267(c) are applied to determine whether an individual constructively owns stock of a corporation. These rules provide that:

- stock owned, directly or indirectly, by or for a corporation, partnership, estate or trust is considered as being owned proportionately by or for its shareholders, partners, or beneficiaries;[153]
- stock owned by an individual's family, directly or indirectly, is considered owned by the individual;[154] and
- the family of an individual includes his or her brothers and sisters (whether whole- or half-blood), spouse, ancestors and lineal descendants.[155]

[B] Sale to Related Person Followed by Second Disposition

If a taxpayer makes an installment sale (first disposition) to a "related person," a resale (second disposition) by the buyer can trigger the recognition of gain by the initial seller at the time of the second sale.

A "related person" is defined by IRC § 453(f)(1) as one whose stock would be attributable to the first seller under the attribution rules of IRC § 318(a) or under IRC § 267(b). These include:

- The spouse (unless legally separated under a divorce decree or separate maintenance decree), children (including legally adopted children), grandchildren (and other lineal descendants), brothers and sisters (whether whole- or half-blood), parents, and grandparents (and other ancestors);[156]
- a partnership in which the original seller is a partner;[157]
- an estate of which the original seller is a beneficiary;[158]
- a trust of which the original seller is a beneficiary or treated as an owner;[159] and
- a corporation in which the first seller owns, directly or indirectly, 50% or more of the value of the stock.[160]

Additional constructive ownership rules can be found in IRC § 267(b)(3) through (b)(13).

---

152 Priv. Ltr. Rul. 9001013; *see also* Rev. Rul. 68-13, 1968-1 CB 195.

153 IRC § 267(c)(1).

154 IRC § 267(c)(2).

155 IRC § 267(c)(4).

156 IRC § 453(f)(1)(A), IRC § 318(a)(1), IRC § 267(b)(1), IRC § 267(c)(4).

157 IRC § 318(a)(2)(A).

158 *Id.*

159 IRC § 318(a)(2)(B).

160 IRC § 318(a)(2)(C), IRC § 267(b)(2).

Note: The term "related person" includes many more relationships than it does for purposes of the depreciable property rules.[161]

In an installment sale (first disposition) to a related person, the amount realized is limited by the excess of the amount realized on the second disposition over the actual payments that had been received on the first disposition. Since amounts received from the second sale are treated as received by the first seller, payments that the first seller receives later from the first sale up to the amounts treated as received from the second sale are tax-free.[162]

Example 10-30

Sam sells his boat to his daughter Betty on June 1, 2020, for $30,000. Under the terms of the agreement, Betty pays $3,000 at the time of the sale and gives Sam a promissory note payable at the rate of $9,000 per year, due on June 1 of 2021, 2022, and 2023 (along with adequate interest). Betty sells the boat to a third party on July 1, 2021 for $40,000. Sam reports in 2021 $18,000 of income from the second disposition ($30,000 from the original sale less the $3,000 and $9,000 payments). Any installments received afterward are a return of capital and are tax-free.

If the second disposition is a disposition other than by a sale or exchange, gain is computed on it to the original seller by taking into account the fair market value of the property, instead of the amount realized on the second disposition.[163]

If the second disposition occurs after two years from the first disposition, the related party rule does not apply. However, if the property consists of marketable securities, the two-year period limitation rule does not apply and the second disposition is subject to the related party sale rule.[164]

[C] Exceptions

A second disposition will not be treated as a second disposition in the following instances:

- Reacquisitions of stock by the issuing corporation;[165]
- Involuntary conversions not treated as second dispositions;[166] and

---

161 *See* IRC § 453(g).
162 IRC § 453(e)(5).
163 IRC § 453(e)(4).
164 IRC § 453(e)(2).
165 IRC § 453(e)(6)(A).
166 IRC § 453(e)(6)(B).

- Dispositions after death. Any transfer after the earlier of:
  - — the death of the person making the first disposition; or
  - — the death of the person acquiring the property in the first disposition;[167]

and any transfer thereafter shall not be treated as a second disposition.[168] Additionally, the second disposition will not be treated as a second disposition if it is established to the satisfaction of the Secretary that neither the first disposition nor the second disposition had as one of its principal purposes the avoidance of federal income tax.[169]

§ 10.10 Non-Dealer Rule

[A] Generally

Installment sales by non-dealers may be reported under the installment method. However, two special rules apply to limit the benefits of installment reporting:

- The interest rule; and
- The pledge rule.

[B] The Interest Rule

"The interest rule" requires that interest be paid on the deferred tax liability attributable to obligations arising from certain installment sales.[170] IRC § 453A(e) provides that regulations be issued providing that the sale of an interest in a partnership or other pass-through entity will be treated as a sale of the proportionate share of the assets of the partnership or other entity.[171] In addition, regulations will be issued which partially or wholly disallow the use of the installment method for transactions in which the interest and pledge rules are avoided through the use of related persons, pass-through entities, or intermediaries.[172]

The interest rule applies to any obligations arising from a non-dealer installment sale only if the sales price exceeds $150,000.[173] In determining whether the $150,000 threshold has been exceeded, all sales that are parts of the same transaction (or in a series of related transactions) are aggregated and treated as one sale.[174] The interest rule does not apply to:

---

[167] IRC § 453(e)(6)(C).
[168] IRC § 453(e)(6).
[169] IRC § 453(e)(7).
[170] IRC § 453A(a)(1).
[171] IRC § 453A(e)(2).
[172] IRC § 453A(e)(1).
[173] IRC § 453A(b)(1).
[174] IRC § 453A(b)(5).

- Personal use property defined in IRC § 1275(b)(3);[175]
- Property used or produced in a trade or in the business of farming;[176] and
- Residential lots and timeshares, which are subject to separate interest payment rules.[177]

[C] Application of Rule

Interest must be paid on the deferred tax from a non-dealer installment obligation arising during the year and outstanding at the end of that year if the aggregate *face amount* of all such obligations held by the taxpayer that arose in and are outstanding as of the close of the taxable year exceeds $5 million.[178] Note that TAM 9853002 makes it clear that each spouse has a separate $5 million threshold under IRC § 453A if each sells his or her own interest in an asset or a business. However, if a transfer of an interest in the property to be sold is made to a spouse contemporaneously with or just before the sale, this could be challenged as not being a bona fide transaction.

In determining whether this $5 million threshold is exceeded in any tax year, the face amount of the installment obligation arising in and outstanding at the end of that year is reduced by the amount treated as paid on the obligation in that year under "the pledge rule."[179] In applying the threshold, and in determining the applicable percentage for the interest charge, all persons treated as a single employer under IRC § 52 are treated as one person.

In the case of partnerships and S corporations, the $5 million threshold is applied (and any interest charge computed) at the individual partner or shareholder level, rather than at the entity level.[180]

If interest is required to be paid on an obligation arising in any tax year, it must also be paid for any subsequent tax year in which the obligation is outstanding at year-end.

[D] Interest Computation

The interest payable on an installment obligation to which the interest rule applies is an amount equal to the "applicable percentage" of the "deferred tax liability" multiplied by the underpayment rate (under IRC § 6621(a)(2)) in effect for the month in which the taxable year ends.[181]

---

175 IRC § 453A(b)(3)(A).

176 *Id.*

177 *See* § 10.08, *infra.*

178 IRC § 453A(b)(2). Note that the threshold amount of $5,000,000 was part of the Installment sale Revision Act of 1980 which in not indexed for inflation.

179 *See* § 10.10 below.

180 Notice 88-81, 1988-2 CB 397.

181 IRC § 453A(c)(2).

The applicable percentage for all obligations arising during a taxable year can be obtained by dividing the portion of the aggregate face amount of the obligations outstanding as of the close of the taxable year in excess of $5 million by the aggregate face amount of the obligations arising in and outstanding at the close of the taxable year.

Example 10-31

Sam, a non-dealer, sells an apartment building for $20 million in 2020. Sam receives a down payment of $5 million and an installment note for $15 million. At the close of 2020, $15 million of the installment note remains outstanding (buyer made no further payments in 2020). The *applicable percentage* is 66.66% ($10 million, the amount of the $15 million note that exceeds $5 million, divided by $15 million, the amount remaining outstanding at the close of the year).

The applicable percentage will not change as payments are made (or deemed made under the pledge rule) in later years.[182]

The deferred tax liability for any taxable year with respect to an installment obligation is the amount of the still unrecognized gain in the obligation at the close of the taxable year multiplied by the applicable maximum income tax rate for the taxpayer in effect for that year.[183] For purposes of applying this definition, with respect to the amount of gain that will be treated as long-term capital gain when recognized, the maximum rate on net capital gain under IRC § 1(h) applies.

Example 10-32

Assume the same facts as in the example above, and further assume that the amount of gain that has not been recognized at the close of 2020 is $10 million. If the maximum tax rate in effect at the close of 2020 is 20%, Sam's interest payable on the unrecognized gain is computed as follows:

Gain Unrecognized		$10,000,000
applicable percentage	66.66%	
Portion of unrecognized gain		6,666,000
deferred tax liability ($6,666,000 × .20)		1,333,200
AFR underpayment rate	4%	
Interest charge		$53,328

[182] H.R. Rep. No. 100-495, at 930 (1987) (Conf. Rep.).
[183] IRC § 453A(c)(3).

Example 10-33

Assume that the outstanding balance of the note at the close 2021 is $5 million. Also, assume that the applicable underpayment rate is 5% and the capital gains rate is 20%. The amount of the interest charge payable is as follows:

Gain Unrecognized		$5,000,000
applicable percentage	66.66%	
Portion of unrecognized gain		3,333,000
deferred tax liability ($3,333,000 × .20)		666,600
AFR underpayment rate	5%	
Interest charge		$33,330

This computation is continued until the note is paid off.

Note: It is the IRS's position that IRC § 453A applies to contingent payment sales.[184]

[E] *The Pledge Rule*

The pledge rule requires that the proceeds from a pledge of an installment obligation used to secure any indebtedness be treated as payment on that obligation.[185] An arrangement that gives a taxpayer the right to satisfy an obligation with an installment note will be treated in the same manner as the direct pledge of the installment note.[186] When loan proceeds are treated as a payment received on an installment obligation, the taxpayer recognizes gain in an amount equal to the net loan proceeds multiplied by the gross profit ratio applicable to that installment obligation.[187]

The pledge rule applies to any obligations arising from a non-dealer installment sale if, and only if, the sales price exceeds $150,000.[188] The pledge rule does not apply to:

- Personal use property defined in IRC § 1275(b)(3);[189]
- Property used or produced in a trade or in the business of farming;[190] and
- Residential lots and timeshares, which are subject to separate interest payment rules.[191]

---

184 *See* FSA 199941001.

185 IRC § 453A(d)(1).

186 IRC § 453A(d)(4).

187 H.R. Rep. No. 100-495, at 930 (1987) (Conf. Rep.)

188 IRC § 453A(b)(1).

189 IRC § 453A(b)(3)(A).

190 *Id.*

191 *See* § 10.08, *infra.*

If a non-dealer property installment obligation is pledged as debt security, the net loan proceeds are treated as payment received on that obligation on the later of the date the debt is secured or the date the net proceeds are received. "Net loan proceeds" are the gross proceeds less any direct expenses of obtaining the loan. Gain on the obligation is recognized by applying the applicable gross profit ratio to the net loan proceeds received.[192]

Debt is secured by an installment obligation to the extent that interest or principal on the debt is directly secured, under the debt's terms, or otherwise, by an interest in the obligation.[193]

Example 10-34

In 2020, Sam sells rental property with a basis of $250,000 to P for $500,000. Sam receives a cash down payment of $50,000 and an installment note of $450,000. Sam's gross profit percentage is 50% ($500,000 contract price divided by $250,000 gross profit). In 2021, Sam obtains a loan from X and receives the net proceeds of $200,000. Sam uses the installment note received from the prior sale as security for the loan. Under the pledge rule, Sam must treat the $200,000 net loan proceeds as an installment payment on the note. Gain must be recognized in the amount of $100,000 ($200,000 × 50%).

Under IRC § 453A(d)(3), if any amount is treated as payment received under the pledge rule, subsequent payments on the installment obligation actually received are not taken into account until the total payments actually received exceed the amount of the deemed payment under the pledge rule.

As an alternative to electing out, the pledge rule can afford the taxpayer the ability to "terminate" installment reporting if the need should arise, *i.e.*, tax rates increase or the taxpayer suffers a capital loss. Indeed, the taxpayer has the ability to pledge some or all of the installment obligation and therefore control his tax consequences.

Example 10-35

A calendar year taxpayer sells privately held stock in 2020 for a $3 million installment note, bearing adequate interest. The property sold has an adjusted basis of $1 million; consequently, the gross profit ratio is 67%. The note calls for three annual $1 million payments. In the second year after the sale, the taxpayer pledges installment note as collateral on a $1 million loan.

---

192 IRC § 453A(d)(2).
193 IRC § 453A(d).

The $1 million of loan proceeds are treated as a deemed payment on the installment note; as a result, the taxpayer must recognize $667,000 of gain in 2021. The principal payments received in 2022 will not trigger any gain recognition until the total payments actually received exceed the amount of the deemed payment.

§ 10.11 Mortgages and Other Liabilities

[A] Generally

If a buyer assumes or takes property subject to any *qualifying indebtedness*, the indebtedness is *not* treated as payment received in the year of sale, except to the extent that the debt exceeds the seller's basis in the property sold.[194] Qualifying debt includes:

- Debt that constitutes an encumbrance on the property, such as a mortgage or lien; and
- Debt that is not secured by the property but is incurred or assumed by the buyer in connection with the purchase, holding or operation in the ordinary course of business, or investment of the property.[195]

[B] Assumption of Mortgage

If a buyer assumes a mortgage or takes property subject to a mortgage, the amount of the mortgage is not considered a payment received in the year of sale, so long as the mortgage is less than the seller's basis in the property.[196] The amount of the mortgage is treated as a return of basis and is subtracted from the selling price to determine the contract price for purposes of computing gross profit percentage.

Example 10-36

Chris sells property to Dave for a selling price of $160,000. The property is encumbered by a mortgage with a principal amount of $60,000. Dave will assume or take subject to the mortgage and pay the remaining $100,000 in ten equal annual installments along with adequate stated interest. Chris's basis in the property is $90,000. There are no selling expenses. The contract price is $100,000 ($160,000 selling price reduced by the assumed mortgage of $60,000). The gross profit is $70,000 ($160,000 selling price less Chris's basis of $90,000). Chris's gross profit ratio is 7/10ths (gross

---

194 Reg. § 15A.453-1(b)(3)(i).
195 Reg. § 15A.453-1(b)(2)(iv).
196 Reg. § 15A.453-1(b)(3)(i).

profit of $70,000 divided by $100,000 contract price). Thus, $7,000 (7/10ths of $10,000) of each $10,000 annual payment is gain attributable to the sale, and $3,000 ($10,000 less $7,000) is recovery of basis.

If the amount of the assumed mortgage exceeds the seller's basis, the seller recovers the entire basis in the year of sale and the excess is treated as payment in the year of sale.[197] Thereafter, the gross profit percentage will always be 100% for sales in which the buyer assumes a mortgage in an amount greater than seller's basis in the property.

Example 10-37

Assume the same facts as in the example above, except that Chris's basis is $40,000. In the year of the sale, Chris is deemed to have received payment of $20,000 ($60,000 - $40,000, the amount by which the mortgage Dave assumed exceeds Chris's basis). Since basis is fully recovered in the year of sale, the gross profit percentage is 100% ($120,000 divided by $120,000). Chris will report $20,000 of deemed payment in the year of sale, and each $10,000 annual payment as gain attributable to the sale.

If a purchaser of property also holds the mortgage and agrees to cancel the mortgage as part of the consideration in purchasing the property, the mortgage is considered cancelled, rather than assumed, and the amount of the cancelled debt is treated as payment received by seller in the year of sale.[198]

[C] Purchaser Assumes Other Debt

If the purchaser assumes any other debts, such as a loan or back taxes, it may be considered a payment in the year of sale.[199]

If the purchaser assumes the debt instead of paying it off, only part of it may have to be treated as a payment. Compare the debt to the installment sale basis in the property being sold. If the debt is less than the installment sale basis, none of it is treated as a payment. If it is more, only the difference is treated as a payment. If the purchaser assumes more than one debt, any part of the total that is more than the installment sale basis is considered a payment. This rule applies to the following types of debt the purchaser assumes:

- Those acquired from ownership of the property being sold, such as a mortgage, lien, overdue interest, or back taxes; and
- Those acquired in the ordinary course of business, such as a balance due for inventory purchased.

---

197 *Id.*

198 Temp. Reg. § 15A.453-1(b)(3).

199 *See* Rev. Rul. 76-269, 1976-2 CB 129.

If the purchaser assumes any other type of debt, such as a personal loan or legal fees relating to the sale, the assumption is treated as if the purchaser had paid off the debt at the time of the sale. The value of the assumed debt is considered a payment in the year of sale.[200]

[D] *Wrap-Around Mortgages*

A wrap-around mortgage is a mortgage on the property sold that the buyer does not assume or take "subject to." The buyer makes installment payments large enough to cover all of the payments on the underlying mortgage that continue to become due.

The Temporary Regulations dealing with the treatment of wrap-around mortgages take the position that a wrap-around mortgage should be treated as though the buyer had assumed or taken "subject to" the seller's mortgage, even though there has been no passage of title and the seller still remains liable for the payments on the underlying mortgage. Consequently, if the underlying liability exceeds basis, the excess is treated as payment in the year of the sale.

Example 10-38

In 1982, G sells Blackacre to H. Blackacre is encumbered by a first mortgage with a principal amount of $500,000 and a second mortgage with a principal amount of $400,000 for a selling price of $2 million. G's basis in Blackacre is $700,000. Under the agreement between G and H, passage of title is deferred and H does not assume and purportedly does not take subject to either mortgage in the year of sale. H pays G $200,000 in cash and issues a wrap-around mortgage note with a principal amount of $1,800,000 bearing adequate stated interest. H is deemed to have acquired Blackacre subject to the first and second mortgages (wrapped indebtedness) totalling $900,000. The contract price is $1,300,000 (selling price of $2 million less $700,000 mortgages within the seller's basis assumed or taken subject to). Gross profit is also $1,300,000 (selling price of $2 million less $700,000 basis). Accordingly, in the year of sale, the gross profit ratio is 1 ($1,300,000/$1,300,000). Payment in the year of sale is $400,000 ($200,000 cash received plus $200,000 mortgage in excess of basis ($900,000 – $700,000)). Therefore, G recognizes $400,000 gain in the year of sale ($400,000 × 1). In the hands of G, the wrap-around installment obligation has a basis of $900,000, equal to G's basis in Blackacre ($700,000) increased by the gain recognized by G in the year of sale

[200] Temp. Reg. § 15A.453-1(b)(2)(iv).

($400,000) reduced by the cash received by G in the year of sale ($200,000). G's gross profit with respect to the note is $900,000 ($1,800,000 face amount less $900,000 basis in the note) and G's contract price with respect to the note is its face amount of $1,800,000. Therefore, the gross profit ratio with respect to the note is 1/2 ($900,000/$1,800,000).[201]

In *Professional Equities, Inc. v. Commissioner*,[202] the taxpayer's business consisted of buying and selling undeveloped parcels of land and taking wrap-around and installment obligations as part of the sales price. In the process of determining the reportable proportion of installment gain, a disagreement arose as to the computation of the total contract price.

The IRS argued that the selling price was reduced by the outstanding mortgage liabilities under Temp. Reg. § 15A.453-1(b)(3)(ii). The taxpayer contended that the contract price was simply the sales price used in computing gross profit and that the Temporary Regulations were erroneous.

The taxpayer relied on *Stonecrest Corp. v. Commissioner*.[203] In *Stonecrest*, the seller retained title to the property, agreeing to apply the installment payments to the mortgage and convey the property on the expiration of a stipulated period of time. The court in *Stonecrest* refused to find an assumption of a mortgage or a conveyance subject to a mortgage.

The Tax Court in *Professional Equities* invalidated the wrap-around mortgage regulations, stating that the regulations must comply with the purpose of the installment method to be valid, *i.e.*, they must allow for the recognition of gain to be spread over the period during which payments are to be received. The wrap-around mortgage regulations relied on by the IRS required gain to be accelerated artificially into the first year of the wrap-around sale regardless of the payment rate. The rationale behind the *Professional Equities* decision was affirmed in *Webb v. Commissioner*.[204]

The IRS has since acquiesced in the Tax Court's decision in *Professional Equities*.[205]

§ 10.12 Disposition of Installment Obligations

[A] Generally

In general, the sale or other disposition of an installment obligation results in the recognition of gain or loss to the seller.[206]

---

[201] Temp. Reg. § 15a.453-1(b)(5), Example 5.

[202] 89 T.C. 165 (1987), *acq.* 1988-2 CB 1.

[203] 24 T.C. 659 (1955), *non acq.*, 1956-1 CB 6.

[204] T.C. Memo. 1987-451.

[205] *See* AOD, 1988-2 CB 1.

[206] IRC § 453B.

If an installment obligation is sold or exchanged, or the seller accepts less than face value, the gain or loss is the difference between the seller's basis and the amount realized.[207]

If the installment obligation is distributed, transmitted, or disposed of other than by way of sale or exchange, the gain or loss recognized is the difference between the seller's basis and the fair market value of the obligation at the time of the distribution, etc.[208] Accordingly, if a seller were to cancel a note owed to the seller by an obligor or make a gift of the obligation to another, the gain or loss would be determined by the difference between the value of the obligation at the time of the distribution and the seller's basis in the obligation.

The seller's basis is determined by the excess of the face value of the obligation over the amount equal to the income that would be returnable were the obligation satisfied in full.[209] The unrecognized profit from the sale remaining in the unpaid balance of the obligation is determined by multiplying the unpaid balance by the gross profit percentage on the sale; the remainder of the unpaid balance is the seller's basis in the obligation.[210]

Example 10-39

In 2020, the Marlin Corporation sold a piece of unimproved real estate to Ben for $200,000. Marlin Corporation acquired the property in 2010 at a cost of $100,000. From the sale, the Marlin Corporation received $50,000 in cash and $150,000 in an installment obligation for the remainder of the selling price payable in five equal annual payments of $30,000. In 2021, before the buyer made any further payments, Marlin Corporation sold the installment obligation for $130,000. The income to be reported for the year 2021 is $55,000, computed as follows:

Proceeds of sale of notes		$130,000
Selling price of property	$200,000	
Cost of property	100,000	
Total profit	$100,000	
Total contract price	$200,000	

207 IRC § 453B(a)(1).
208 IRC § 453B(a)(2).
209 IRC § 453B(b).
210 Reg. § 1.453-9(b).

Percentage of profit returnable as income ($100,000/$200,000)	50%	
Face value of notes	$150,000	
Amount of income returnable if notes are satisfied in full	75,000	
Basis of obligation		75,000
Taxable income in 2021		$55,000

Example 10-40

Assume in the example above that Marlin Corporation, instead of selling the installment obligation, distributed it in 2021 to its shareholders as a dividend, and at the time of the distribution, the fair market value of the obligation was $140,000.

The income to be reported for 2021 is $65,000, computed as follows:

Fair market value of notes	$140,000
Basis of obligation (excess of face value of notes over amount of income returnable if the notes are satisfied in full)	$75,000
Taxable income to be reported for 2021	$65,000

The gain or loss recognized from the disposition of the installment obligation is derived from the property for which the obligation was received by the seller. Accordingly, the character of the property sold that gave rise to the obligation determines the character of gain or loss on the disposition of the installment obligation. If the original sale of the property resulted in ordinary gain, disposition of the installment would result in ordinary gain.[211]

The following type of dispositions trigger gain or loss to the seller:

- A sale or exchange of the obligation;[212]
- A pledge of the obligation;[213]
- A gift of the obligation;[214]
- A sale, exchange, or gift of an interest in the partnership holding the installment obligation;[215]

---

[211] Reg. § 1.453-9(c)(3).

[212] IRC § 453B(a).

[213] Rev. Rul. 55-292, 1955-1 CB 331.

[214] Rev. Rul. 79-371, 1979-2 CB 294.

[215] Rev. Rul. 60-352, 1960-2 CB 208.

- A substantial change in or modification of the terms of the installment obligation where the rights of the seller are materially changed;[216]
- A cancellation of the installment obligation;[217]
- Where the installment obligation becomes unenforceable;[218]
- Where the parties are related, the obligation's fair market value is deemed to be not less than the face amount;[219]
- A distribution of an installment obligation by a C corporation as a dividend or in liquidation;[220]
- The conversion of an installment obligation into a stock or a security;[221]
- The transfer of an installment obligation to a trust other than a grantor trust;[222]
- A distribution of an installment obligation by a trust where the obligation arose from the sale of the property by the trust; and
- A distribution of an installment obligation by a trust other than a grantor trust in satisfaction of a specific dollar amount or at the termination of the trust.[223]

§10.13 Modification of Installment Obligations

[A] Generally

Often, installment obligations held by sellers of property are modified. Most of the time, minor modifications do not constitute a taxable disposition, and therefore do not accelerate the reporting of income. On the other hand, when substantial changes or modifications are made to an installment obligation, and the rights of the seller are materially changed, a taxable disposition may result.

[B] Minor Modifications/Non-taxable Dispositions

Minor modifications of installment obligations do not constitute a taxable disposition, and therefore do not accelerate the reporting of income.

Examples of minor modifications include:

---

[216] Rev. Rul. 82-188, 1982-2 CB 90.

[217] IRC §453B(f)(1).

[218] IRC §453B(f)(1). *See also Estate of Frane v. Comm'r*, 98 T.C. 341 (1992), *aff'd in part, rev'd in part*, 998 F.2d 567 (8th Cir. 1993) (installment obligations held by decedent at his death were cancelled, thereby treating each installment obligation as if it were disposed of in a transaction other than a sale or exchange; moreover, because obligor and obligee were related, gain reported on decedent's final return is excess of face amount over obligation's basis).

[219] IRC §453B(f)(2).

[220] IRC §§311 and 336. *See also* Reg. §1.453-9(c).

[221] Rev. Rul. 72-264, 1972-1 CB 131.

[222] Rev. Rul. 76-530, 1976-2 CB 132.

[223] Rev. Rul. 55-159, 1955-1 CB 391.

- A modification of the term of an installment obligation to defer a date of payment or to raise an interest rate;[224]
- The re-issuance of a bond with a new interest rate, a temporary deferral of principal payments, and an addition of a prepayment penalty;[225] and
- The substitution of two promissory notes on two parcels of land for a single note securing the two parcels, even though some acreage of the underlying property was released and some principal payments were made.[226]

Likewise, modifications of installment obligations were not considered substantial modifications when:

- Payment of the principal and interest on the unpaid balance was reduced retroactively;
- Simple interest was increased from 9% to 10%;
- A new quarterly payment was added based on a percentage of cash flow from the property;
- A clause was added recognizing the seller's right to use part of the property sold;[227] and
- Changes were made in debentures in exchange under reorganization.[228]

In general, the transactions listed below will not be considered taxable dispositions:

- Renegotiation of the sale price;[229]
- Substitution of the obligor;[230]
- Non-recognition transfers to control corporations;[231]
- Non-recognition transfers to corporate reorganizations;[232]
- Complete liquidation of a subsidiary;[233]
- Capital contributions to partnerships;[234]
- Distributions of an installment obligation by a partnership to a partner;[235]
- Transfer of installment obligations at death;[236]
- Transfers between spouses incident to a divorce;[237] and
- Liquidation and distribution by an S corporation.[238]

---

224 *See* Rev. Rul. 68-419, 1968-2 CB 196.

225 Priv. Ltr. Rul. 8649046.

226 Rev. Rul. 74-157, 1974-1 CB 115.

227 *See* Priv. Ltr. Rul. 8932011.

228 Priv. Ltr. Rul. 9412013.

229 Rev. Rul. 72-570, 1972-2 CB 241.

230 Rev. Rul. 75-457, 1975-2 CB 196.

231 Prop. Reg. § 1.453B-1(c)(1).

232 *Id.*

233 IRC § 453B(d).

234 Prop. Reg. § 1.453B-1(c)(1).

235 Reg. § § 1.453-9(c)(2), 1.721-1(a).

236 IRC § 453B(c).

237 IRC § 453B(g)(1).

238 *See* IRC § 453B(h).

In Rev. Rul. 72-570,[239] a taxpayer sold shares of stock in 1969 on the installment method. In 1971, the parties agreed to reduce the purchase price of that stock because of a decline in its market value. The IRS held that the modification of the terms of the Note by a reduction of the purchase price was *not a disposition or satisfaction* of the installment obligation, citing *JP Jerpe v. Commissioner*.[240] By reducing the purchase price of the original transaction and modifying the Note, the taxpayer was able to recompute his gross profit and report the transaction based on this reduction.

In Priv. Ltr. Rul. 201144005, a similar transaction took place. In this ruling, the taxpayer sold stock and received a Promissory Note payable over a ten-year period with a down payment and nine consecutive, equal annual payments of principal and interest on the outstanding balance. The parties at the time intended that the note would be paid by distributions from the company. It turned out that there was an economic downturn and the company experienced financial difficulties. Only the initial payment was made. The taxpayer wanted to reduce the interest rate to the lowest applicable federal rate from the time of the amendment going forward and to amend the Promissory Note to reflect the reduction in purchase price.

The IRS ruled that the modification of an installment obligation by changing payment terms, reducing the purchase price and interest rate was not a disposition or satisfaction of the installment obligation.

Example 10-41

In 2010, Frank sold his stock in Small Town Pharmacy, Inc. for $2,500,000 to Philip. Philip gave Frank $300,000 in cash and a promissory note fully amortizable over ten years with interest at 8% for $2,200,000. In 2014, Philip fell behind in his payments due to a downturn in the economy. By 2019, Phillip only paid $200,000 in principal. Frank does not want to repossess the pharmacy and is agreeable to a renegotiation. Because of economic conditions, Frank agrees to extend the payment to 2029, have the value of the note redetermined based on market conditions and agrees to an interest rate tied to the long-term applicable federal rate redetermined annually. Based on Priv. Ltr. Rul. 201144005, Frank and Phillip may have a basis for the modification of the promissory note.[241]

[C] Substantial Modifications/Taxable Dispositions

When substantial changes or modifications are made to an installment obligation, and the rights of the parties are materially changed, a taxable disposition may result.

---

[239] 1972-2 CB 241.

[240] 45 BTA 1999 (1941).

[241] It is recommended however that the parties obtain a private letter ruling.

In Rev. Rul. 82-188,[242] the IRS held that a taxable disposition occurred when the obligor substantially increased the face amount of its outstanding installment obligation in consideration of the taxpayer's waiver of his right to convert the obligation into common stock of the corporation. The IRS concluded that the substantial increase in the face amount of the note was a material change in the seller's rights. As a result, the original obligation was cancelled and held to be a taxable disposition.

Other transactions that result in taxable dispositions include the following:

- A sale, exchange, or gift of an installment obligation;[243]
- A cancellation of an installment obligation;[244]
- A distribution of an installment obligation by a corporation to its shareholders as a dividend, or in a liquidation;[245]
- A conversion of a convertible installment obligation;[246] and
- A transfer to a trust.[247]

[D] Transfers of Installment Obligations at Death

The transfer of an installment obligation resulting from the death of the holder is not a taxable disposition and does not accelerate the reporting of income on the decedent's return.[248]

The remaining unreported gain from the obligation, however, is an item of income in respect of a decedent under IRC § 691. The income is reported as payments under the obligations received by the estate or beneficiaries.[249]

If the installment obligation is transferred by a bequest, devise, or inheritance to the obligor, the transfer constitutes a taxable disposition, and any remaining gain must be recognized and reported by the decedent's estate.[250]

---

242 1982-2 CB 90.

243 IRC § 453B(a) and Rev. Rul. 76-530, 1976-2 CB 132. A sale or exchange of an installment obligation, including a fractional interest, is a taxable disposition. Even if the seller is required to pledge a portion of the sale proceeds as additional collateral, a disposition may occur.

244 IRC § 453B(f)(1). If an installment obligation is canceled or it becomes unenforceable (*e.g.*, because the statute of limitations has expired), it is treated as a transaction other than a sale or exchange.

245 IRC §§ 311 and 336. IRC § 453(h)(1)(A), however, allows a shareholder who receives an installment note in a corporate liquidation (to which IRC § 331 applies) to use the installment method to report the shareholder level gain allocable to the installment note.

246 Rev. Rul. 72-264, 1972-1 CB 131. If the seller has the right to convert the installment obligation into stock, the exercise of the conversion privilege results in a taxable disposition.

247 Rev. Rul. 74-613, 1974-2 CB 153. The transfer will result in a taxable disposition unless the seller is considered the owner of the trust under the grantor trust rules.

248 IRC § 453B(c). *See* IRC § 691(a)(4); Reg. § 1.691(a)-5(a).

249 *Id.*

250 IRC § 691(a)(5).

[E] Debt Instrument Modifications under IRC §1001

Under IRC §1001 and Reg. §1.1001-1(a), a significant modification of a debt instrument results in an exchange of the original debt instrument for a modified instrument that differs materially either in kind or in extent. A modification that is not a significant modification is not an exchange for purposes of Reg. §1.1001-1. The fact that an alteration is not a modification or a significant modification does not preclude other tax consequences.

As noted in the preamble to the proposed regulations under IRC §1001, a modification of a debt instrument that results in an exchange under IRC §1001 does not determine if there has been an exchange or other disposition of an installment obligation under IRC §453B. Whether or not there has been an exchange or other disposition of an installment obligation is determined under the cases and rulings applicable to IRC §453B. Similarly, the fact that an alteration does not constitute a modification or a significant modification does not preclude other tax consequences.

§10.14 Default and Repossession of Real Property

If, after an installment sale of real property, the buyer defaults and the seller repossesses the property, a substantial gain may result upon the repossession of the property. Repossession may be by purchase in a foreclosure sale, as well as by any other means.

IRC §1038 provides special relief to lessen the impact. Under IRC §1038, a seller's repossession of real property sold on the installment basis does not give rise to the recognition of loss by the seller or to a bad debt deduction for the worthlessness of the purchaser's obligation.[251] IRC §1038 governs the amount of gain recognized; however, it has no effect on its character. If the original sale was reported on the installment basis, the regulations provide that the repossession gain have the same character as the original gain, that is, capital or ordinary, etc.

In the case of a personal residence, the gain on the sale previously reported does not include any IRC §121 personal exclusion amount, since that amount was excluded from income and therefore could not have been returned as income in prior years.[252] If the personal residence is resold within one year, IRC §1038(e) provides a special rule for retaining the IRC §121 personal exclusion.[253]

[A] Gain Recognition

Where IRC §1038 is applicable, the amounts of gain recognized by the seller on the repossession is limited to the lesser of:

---

[251] Reg. §1.1038-1(a)(1).
[252] IRC §1038(a).
[253] IRC §1038(b)(1).

- The amount of cash and the fair market value of other property (other than the obligation of the purchaser) received before the repossession, minus the amount of gain on the sale reported as income in periods prior to the repossession;[254] or
- The amount of gain realized on the original sale, minus (i) the gain previously recognized for periods before the reacquisition and (ii) the amount of cash and the fair market value of the other property (other than the obligation of the purchaser) transferred by the taxpayer in connection with the reacquisition.[255]

Payments of interest are not taken into account in performing the above calculations

Example 10-42

Sandy sold real estate in 2020 for $250,000 as follows: $50,000 down payment in cash and a purchase money mortgage for $200,000, which is payable $50,000 per year commencing in 2020.

The adjusted basis was $200,000. The potential gain is $50,000. In 2020, the cash down payment results in $10,000 of reportable gain.

The purchaser made payments in 2021, 2022, and 2023, and the seller recognized a gain of $10,000 in each of those years. Total gain reportable at the end of 2022 is $40,000.

The buyer defaults on January 1, 2024. Repossession costs are $5,000. Under IRC § 1038, Sandy's repossession gain is limited to $5,000 ($50,000 gain on the original sale less $40,000 already reported on prior payments, and less the $5,000 repossession costs).

The effect of the rule for determining taxable gain in these situations is that all the payments received by the seller before the repossession are treated as income, but total taxable gain is limited to the original gross profit expected from the sale. Any gain in excess of that expected from the sale adjusts the seller's basis downward in the repossessed property resulting in the postponement of gain until the property is resold.

[B] Bad-Debt Basis

Under IRC § 1038(a), the seller may not claim a bad debt deduction as a result of the repossession. In addition, the seller must restore any previously claimed bad debt deduction to income under the tax benefit rule. In such event, the adjusted basis of the indebtedness is increased by the amount included in income.[256]

---

254 IRC § 1038(b)(2).

255 Reg. § 1.1038-1(b)(2)(ii) and (c)(3).

256 IRC § 111. *See* IRC § 1038(d)(1) and Reg. § 1.1038-1(f)(2).

Under IRC § 1038(c), the basis of the reacquired property in the hands of the taxpayer is equal to the sum of the following amounts:

- The adjusted basis of the installment note (as increased by any bad debt recovery under IRC § 1038(d));
- Any amount paid or transferred by the taxpayer at the time of the of the transfer; and
- The amount of any gain recognized by the taxpayer under IRC § 1038.

[C] Holding Period

The holding period for the repossessed property includes the taxpayer's original holding period for the property, but does not include the period of time that the property was held by the purchaser.

Example 10-43

In 2020, seller sold land to a buyer for $20,000 in cash and the buyer's $80,000 promissory note providing for eight annual payments of $10,000 plus adequate interest, secured by a lien on the property sold. The seller's adjusted basis is $40,000 and the gross profit ratio is 60%. In the year of sale, the seller reports a gain of $12,000. Before the purchaser makes any payments on the installment note he defaults and the seller repossesses the property on July 1, 2021. On the date of the repossession, the property is worth $70,000. The seller incurs $3,000 of legal and other expenses in connection with the repossession. The tentative amount of gain to be recognized under IRC § 1038 is calculated as follows:[257]

Cash received prior to repossession	$20,000
Gain reported prior to repossession	$12,000
Tentative gain under IRC § 1038	$8,000

The limitation on the amount the reportable gain is calculated as follows:

Sale price of land	$100,000
Adjusted basis of land	$40,000
Gain reported prior to repossession	$12,000
Cash paid in connection with repossession	$3,000
Limitation on gain	$45,000

[257] *See also* examples in Reg. § 1.1038-1(h).

Since the tentative gain is less than the limitation amount, the taxpayer recognizes an $8,000 gain upon the repossession. Assuming the land was a capital asset; such gain would be capital gain. The sellers basis in the repossessed land is computed follows;

Adjusted basis of indebtedness ($80,000 times 40%)	$32,000
Cash paid in connection with repossession	+ $3,000
Gain recognized on repossession	+ $8,000
Basis	$43,000

§ 10.15 Like-Kind Exchange

[A] *Generally*

If you exchange business or investment real property solely for the same kind of property to be held as business or investment property, you can postpone reporting the gain. These trades are known as like-kind exchanges. The property you receive in a like-kind exchange is treated as if it were a continuation of the property you gave up.

You do not have to report any part of your gain if you receive only like-kind property. However, if you also receive money or other property (boot) in the exchange, you must report your gain to the extent of the money and the FMV of the other property received.

[B] *Installment Payments*

If, in addition to like-kind property, you receive an installment obligation in the exchange, the following rules apply to determine the installment sale income each year.

- The contract price is reduced by the FMV of the like-kind property received in the trade;
- The gross profit is reduced by any gain on the trade that can be postponed; and
- Like-kind property received in the trade is not considered payment on the installment obligation.

Example 10-44

In 2020, Renata Brown trades real property with an installment sale basis of $400,000 for like-kind property having an FMV of $200,000. She also receives an installment note for $800,000 in the trade. Under the terms of the note, she is to receive $100,000 (plus interest) in 2021 and the balance of $700,000 (plus interest) in 2022.

Renata's selling price is $1,000,000 ($800,000 installment note + $200,000 FMV of like-kind property received). Her gross profit is $600,000 ($1,000,000 − $400,000 installment sale basis). The contract price is $800,000 ($1,000,000 − $200,000). The gross profit percentage is 75% ($600,000 ÷ $800,000).

She reports no gain in 2020 because the like-kind property she receives is not treated as a payment for determining gain. She reports $75,000 gain for 2021 (75% of $100,000 payment received) and $525,000 gain for 2022 (75% of $700,000 payment received).

§10.16 Reporting an Installment Sale

[A] Form 6252

Use Form 6252 to report a sale of property on the installment method. The form is used to report the sale in the year it takes place and to report payments received in later years. Also, if you sold property to a related person, you may have to file the form each year until the installment debt is paid off, whether or not you receive a payment in that year.

[B] Which Parts to Complete

Which part to complete depends on whether you are filing the form for the year of sale or a later year.

[C] Year of Sale

Complete lines 1 through 4, Part I, and Part II. If you sold property to a related party during the year. Also complete Part III.

[D] Later Years

Complete lines 1 through 4 and Part II for any year in which you receive a payment from an installment sale.

[E] Related Person

If you sold property to a related person during the year, complete lines 1 through 4 and Parts I, II, and III of Form 6252.

[F] Other Forms

The gain from Form 6252 is entered on Schedule D (Form 1040) or Form 4797, or both.

[G] Schedule D (Form 1040)

Enter the gain figured on Form 6252 (line 26) for personal-use property (capital assets) on Schedule D (Form 1040) as a short-term gain (line 4) or long-term gain (line 11). If your gain from the installment sale qualifies for long-term capital gain treatment in the year of sale, it will continue to qualify in later tax years. Your gain is long term if you owned the property for more than one year when you sold it.

[H] Form 4797

An installment sale of property used in your business or that earns rent or royalty income may result in a capital gain, an ordinary gain, or both. All or part of any gain from the disposition of the property may be ordinary gain from depreciation recapture. For trade or business property held for more than one year, enter the amount from line 26 of Form 6252 on Form 4797, line 4. If the property was held for one year or less or you have an ordinary gain from the sale of a noncapital asset (even if the holding period is more than one year); enter this amount on Form 4797, line 10, and write "From Form 6252."

[I] Sale of Your Home

If you sell your home, you may be able to exclude all or part of the gain on the sale. See IRS Pub. 523 for information about excluding the gain. If the sale is an installment sale, any gain you exclude is not included in gross profit when figuring your gross profit percentage.

[J] Seller-Financed Mortgage

If you finance the sale of your home to an individual, both you and the buyer may have to follow special reporting procedures.

When you report interest income received from a buyer who uses the property as a personal residence, write the buyer's name, address, and Social Security Number (SSN) on line 1 of Schedule B (Form 1040A or 1040).

When deducting the mortgage interest, the buyer must write your name, address, and SSN on line 11 of Schedule A (Form 1040).

If either person fails to include the other person's SSN, a penalty will be assessed.

Appendix 10-1 Form 6252

Form **6252**
Department of the Treasury
Internal Revenue Service

Installment Sale Income

► Attach to your tax return.
► Use a separate form for each sale or other disposition of property on the installment method.
► Go to *www.irs.gov/Form6252* for the latest information.

OMB No. 1545-0228
2019
Attachment Sequence No. 67

Name(s) shown on return | Identifying number

1 Description of property ►
2a Date acquired (mm/dd/yyyy) ► b Date sold (mm/dd/yyyy) ►
3 Was the property sold to a related party (see instructions) after May 14, 1980? If "No," skip line 4 . . . . . ☐ Yes ☐ No
4 Was the property you sold to a related party a marketable security? If "Yes," complete Part III. If "No," complete Part III for the year of sale and the 2 years after the year of sale . . . ☐ Yes ☐ No

Part I Gross Profit and Contract Price. Complete this part for all years of the installment agreement.

5	Selling price including mortgages and other debts. **Don't** include interest, whether stated or unstated		5
6	Mortgages, debts, and other liabilities the buyer assumed or took the property subject to (see instructions)	6	
7	Subtract line 6 from line 5	7	
8	Cost or other basis of property sold	8	
9	Depreciation allowed or allowable	9	
10	Adjusted basis. Subtract line 9 from line 8	10	
11	Commissions and other expenses of sale	11	
12	Income recapture from Form 4797, Part III (see instructions)	12	
13	Add lines 10, 11, and 12		13
14	Subtract line 13 from line 5. If zero or less, **don't** complete the rest of this form (see instructions)		14
15	If the property described on line 1 above was your main home, enter the amount of your excluded gain (see instructions). Otherwise, enter -0-		15
16	**Gross profit.** Subtract line 15 from line 14		16
17	Subtract line 13 from line 6. If zero or less, enter -0-		17
18	**Contract price.** Add line 7 and line 17		18

Part II Installment Sale Income. Complete this part for all years of the installment agreement.

19	Gross profit percentage (expressed as a decimal amount). Divide line 16 by line 18. (For years after the year of sale, see instructions)		19
20	If this is the year of sale, enter the amount from line 17. Otherwise, enter -0-		20
21	Payments received during year (see instructions). **Don't** include interest, whether stated or unstated		21
22	Add lines 20 and 21		22
23	Payments received in prior years (see instructions). **Don't** include interest, whether stated or unstated	23	
24	**Installment sale income.** Multiply line 22 by line 19		24
25	Enter the part of line 24 that is ordinary income under the recapture rules (see instructions)		25
26	Subtract line 25 from line 24. Enter here and on Schedule D or Form 4797 (see instructions)		26

Part III Related Party Installment Sale Income. Don't complete if you received the final payment this tax year.

27 Name, address, and taxpayer identifying number of related party

28 Did the related party resell or dispose of the property ("second disposition") during this tax year? . . . ☐ Yes ☐ No

29 **If the answer to question 28 is "Yes," complete lines 30 through 37 below unless one of the following conditions is met. Check the box that applies.**

a ☐ The second disposition was more than 2 years after the first disposition (other than dispositions of marketable securities). If this box is checked, enter the date of disposition (mm/dd/yyyy) . . . ►

b ☐ The first disposition was a sale or exchange of stock to the issuing corporation.

c ☐ The second disposition was an involuntary conversion and the threat of conversion occurred after the first disposition.

d ☐ The second disposition occurred after the death of the original seller or buyer.

e ☐ It can be established to the satisfaction of the IRS that tax avoidance wasn't a principal purpose for either of the dispositions. If this box is checked, attach an explanation (see instructions).

30	Selling price of property sold by related party (see instructions)	30
31	Enter contract price from line 18 for year of first sale	31
32	Enter the **smaller** of line 30 or line 31	32
33	Total payments received by the end of your 2019 tax year (see instructions)	33
34	Subtract line 33 from line 32. If zero or less, enter -0-	34
35	Multiply line 34 by the gross profit percentage on line 19 for year of first sale	35
36	Enter the part of line 35 that is ordinary income under the recapture rules (see instructions)	36
37	Subtract line 36 from line 35. Enter here and on Schedule D or Form 4797 (see instructions)	37

For Paperwork Reduction Act Notice, see page 4. Cat. No. 13601R Form **6252** (2019)

General Instructions

Section references are to the Internal Revenue Code unless otherwise noted.

Future Developments

For the latest information about developments related to Form 6252 and its instructions, such as legislation enacted after they were published, go to *www.irs.gov/Form6252*.

What's New

Installment sale reporting. In 2019 and later, if you have an outstanding installment sale balance after the initial year, complete lines 1 through 4, Part I, and Part II for each year of the installment agreement. If you sold property to a related party during the year, also complete Part III.

Purpose of Form

Use Form 6252 to report income from an installment sale on the installment method. Generally, an installment sale is a disposition of property where at least one payment is received after the end of the tax year in which the disposition occurs. Ordinarily, an installment sale doesn't include a disposition of personal property by a person who regularly sells or otherwise disposes of personal property of the same type, or a disposition of real property which is held by the taxpayer for sale to customers in the ordinary course of the taxpayer's trade or business. However, gain on some dispositions by dealers in real property or farmers who dispose of any property used or produced in the trade or business of farming may be reported on the installment method.

Don't file Form 6252 for sales that don't result in a gain, even if you will receive a payment in a tax year after the year of sale. Instead, report the entire sale on Form 4797, Sales of Business Property, Form 8949, Sales and Other Dispositions of Capital Assets, or the Schedule D for your tax return, whichever applies.

Don't file Form 6252 to report sales during the tax year of stock or securities traded on an established securities market. Instead, treat all payments as received during the year of sale.

Don't file Form 6252 if you elect not to report the sale on the installment method. To elect out, report the full amount of the gain on a timely filed return (including extensions) on Form 4797, Form 8949, or the Schedule D for your tax return, whichever applies. If you filed your original return on time without making the election, you can make the election on an amended return filed no later than 6 months after the due date of your tax return, excluding extensions. Write "Filed pursuant to section 301.9100-2" at the top of the amended return.

Which Parts To Complete

For All Years

Complete lines 1 through 4, Part I, and Part II. If you sold property to a related party during the year, also complete Part III. Complete Form 6252 for each year of the installment agreement, including the year of final payment, even if a payment wasn't received during the year.

If you sold a marketable security to a related party after May 14, 1980, and before 1987, complete Form 6252 for each year of the installment agreement, even if you didn't receive a payment. Complete lines 1 through 4. Complete Part III unless you received the final payment during the tax year.

After 1986, the installment method isn't available for the sale of marketable securities.

Note: If you sold property other than a marketable security to a related party after May 14, 1980, complete Form 6252 for the year of sale and for 2 years after the year of sale, even if you didn't receive a payment. Complete lines 1 through 4. Complete Part II for any year during this 2-year period in which you receive a payment from the sale. Complete Part III for the 2 years after the year of sale unless you received the final payment during the tax year.

Special Rules

Interest

If any part of an installment payment you received is for interest or original issue discount, report that income on the appropriate form or schedule. Don't report interest received, carrying charges received, or unstated interest on Form 6252. See Pub. 537, Installment Sales, for details on unstated interest.

Installment Sales to Related Party

A special rule applies to a first disposition (sale or exchange) of property under the installment method to a related party who then makes a second disposition (sale, exchange, gift, or cancellation of installment note) before making all payments on the first disposition. For this purpose, a related party includes your spouse, child, grandchild, parent, brother, sister; or a related corporation, S corporation, partnership, estate, or trust. See section 453(f)(1) for more details.

Under this rule, treat part or all of the amount the related party realized (or the fair market value (FMV) if the disposed property isn't sold or exchanged) from the second disposition as if you received it from the first disposition at the time of the second disposition. Figure the gain, if any, on lines 30 through 37. This rule doesn't apply if any of the conditions listed on line 29 are met.

Sale of Depreciable Property to Related Person

Generally, if you sell depreciable property to a related person (as defined in section 453(g)(3)), you can't report the sale using the installment method. For this purpose, depreciable property is any property that (in the hands of the person or entity to whom you transfer it) is subject to the allowance for depreciation. However, you can use the installment method if you can show to the satisfaction of the IRS that avoidance of federal income taxes wasn't one of the principal purposes of the sale (for example, no significant tax deferral benefits will result from the sale). If the installment method doesn't apply, report the sale on Form 4797, Form 8949, or Schedule D, whichever applies. Treat all payments you will receive as if they were received in the year of sale. Use FMV for any payment that is contingent as to amount. If the FMV can't be readily determined, basis is recovered ratably.

Pledge Rule

For certain dispositions under the installment method, if an installment obligation is pledged as security on a debt, the net proceeds of the secured debt are treated as payment on the installment obligation. However, the amount treated as payment can't be more than the excess of the total installment contract price over any payments received under the contract before the secured debt was obtained.

An installment obligation is pledged as security on a debt to the extent that payment of principal and interest on the debt is directly secured by an interest in the installment obligation. For sales after December 16, 1999, payment on a debt is treated as directly secured by an interest in an installment obligation to the extent an arrangement allows you to satisfy all or part of the debt with the installment obligation.

The pledge rule applies to any installment sale after 1988 with a sales price of over $150,000 except:

- Personal use property disposed of by an individual,
- Farm property, and
- Timeshares and residential lots.

However, the pledge rule doesn't apply to pledges made after December 17, 1987, if the debt is incurred to refinance the principal amount of a debt that was outstanding on December 17, 1987, and was secured by nondealer installment obligations on that date and at all times after that date until the refinancing. This exception doesn't apply to the extent that the principal amount of the debt resulting from the refinancing exceeds the principal amount of the refinanced debt immediately before the refinancing. Also, the pledge rule doesn't affect refinancing due to the calling of a debt by the creditor if the debt is then refinanced by a person other than this creditor or someone related to the creditor.

Interest on Deferred Tax

Generally, you must pay interest on the deferred tax related to any obligation that arises during a tax year from the disposition of property under the installment method if:

- The property had a sales price over $150,000; and
- The aggregate balance of all nondealer installment obligations arising during, and outstanding at the close of, the tax year is more than $5 million.

You must pay interest in subsequent years if installment obligations that originally required interest to be paid are still outstanding at the close of a tax year.

The interest rules don't apply to dispositions of:

- Farm property,
- Personal use property by an individual,
- Real property before 1988, or
- Personal property before 1989.

See section 453(l) for more information on the sale of timeshares and residential lots under the installment method.

How to report the interest. The interest isn't figured on Form 6252. See Pub. 537 for details and an example on how to report the interest under section 453A.

Capital Gains

If you have a capital gain, you can invest that gain into a Qualified Opportunity Fund (QO Fund) and elect to defer part or all of the gain that you would otherwise include in income. The gain is deferred until you sell or exchange the investment or December 31, 2026, whichever is earlier. You may also be able to permanently exclude gain from the sale or exchange of an investment in a QO Fund if the investment is held for at least 10 years. For information about what types of gains entitle you to elect these special rules, see the Instructions for Schedule D. Report the eligible gain on the form and in the manner otherwise instructed. See the Form 8949 instructions on how to report your election to defer eligible gains invested in a QO Fund.

Additional Information

See Pub. 537 for additional information, including details about reductions in selling price, the single sale of several assets, like-kind exchanges, dispositions of installment obligations, and repossessions.

Specific Instructions

Part I—Gross Profit and Contract Price

Line 1

Enter a code from the list below and describe the installment sale property.

Code:

1. Sale property is timeshare or residential lot.
2. Sale by an individual of personal use property (within the meaning of section 1275(b)(3)).
3. Sale of any property used or produced in the trade or business of farming (within the meaning of section 2032A(e)(4) or (5)).
4. All other installment sales not listed.

Line 5

Enter the total of any money, face amount of the installment obligation, and the FMV of other property or services that you received or will receive in exchange for the property sold. Include on line 5 any existing mortgage or other debt the buyer assumed or took the property subject to. Don't include stated interest, unstated interest, any amount recomputed or recharacterized as interest, or original issue discount.

If there is no stated maximum selling price, such as in a contingent payment sale, attach a schedule showing the computation of gain. Enter the taxable part of the payment on line 24 and also on line 35 if Part III applies. See Temporary Regulations section 15A.453-1.

Line 6

Enter only mortgages, debts, or other liabilities the buyer assumed from the seller or took the property subject to. Don't include new mortgages the buyer gets from a bank, the seller, or other sources.

Line 8

Enter the original cost and other expenses you incurred in buying the property. Add the cost of improvements, etc., and subtract any casualty losses and any of the following credits previously allowed with respect to the property.

- Nonbusiness energy property credit.
- Residential energy efficient property credit.
- Adoption credit.
- District of Columbia first-time homebuyer credit.
- Disabled access credit.
- New markets credit.
- Credit for employer-provided childcare facilities and services.
- Energy efficient home credit.
- Alternative motor vehicle credit.
- Alternative fuel vehicle refueling property credit.
- Qualified railroad track maintenance credit.
- Enhanced oil recovery credit.
- Qualified plug-in electric drive motor vehicle credit.
- Qualified plug-in electric vehicle credit.
- Qualified electric vehicle credit.

For additional information, see Pub. 551, Basis of Assets.

Line 9

Enter all depreciation or amortization you deducted or were allowed to deduct from the date of purchase until the date of sale. Adjust the depreciation or amortization amount by adding any of the following deductions previously taken with respect to the property.

- Commercial revitalization deduction.
- Section 179 expense.
- Deduction for clean-fuel vehicles and refueling property.
- Deductions claimed under sections 190 and 193.
- Deductions claimed under section 1253(d)(2) and (3) (as in effect before enactment of P.L. 103-66).
- Basis reduction to investment credit property.

Subtract the following recapture amounts and credits previously allowed with respect to the property.

- Section 179 or 280F.
- Clean-fuel vehicles and refueling property.
- Investment credit amount.
- Credit for employer-provided childcare facilities and services.
- Alternative motor vehicle credit.
- Alternative fuel vehicle refueling property credit.
- Qualified plug-in electric drive motor vehicle credit.
- Qualified plug-in electric vehicle credit.
- Qualified electric vehicle credit.

Line 11

Enter sales commissions, advertising expenses, attorney and legal fees, and other selling expenses incurred to sell the property.

Line 12

Any ordinary income recapture under section 1245 or 1250 (including sections 179 and 291) is fully taxable in the year of sale even if no payments were received. To figure the recapture amount, complete Form 4797, Part III. The ordinary income recapture is the amount on line 31 of Form 4797. Enter it on line 12 of Form 6252 and also on line 13 of Form 4797. Don't enter any gain for this property on line 32 of Form 4797. If you used Form 4797 only to figure the recapture amount on line 12 of Form 6252, enter "N/A" on line 32 of Form 4797. Partnerships and S corporations and their partners and shareholders, see the Instructions for Form 4797.

Line 14

Don't file Form 6252 if line 14 is zero or less. Instead, report the entire sale on Form 4797, Form 8949, or the Schedule D for your tax return.

Line 15

If the property described on line 1 was your main home, you may be able to exclude part or all of your gain. See Pub. 523, Selling Your Home, for details.

Part II—Installment Sale Income

Line 19

Enter the gross profit percentage determined for the year of sale even if you didn't file Form 6252 for that year. Enter it as a decimal rounded to at least 4 digits, and include all zeros (for example, 25% = 0.2500, 35.25% = 0.3525, or 100% = 1.0000).

Line 21

Enter all money and the FMV of any property or services you received in 2019. Include as payments any amount withheld to pay off a mortgage or other debt or to pay broker and legal fees. Generally, don't include as a payment the buyer's note, a mortgage, or other debt assumed by the buyer. However, a note or other debt that is payable on demand or readily tradable in an established securities market is considered a payment. For sales occurring before October 22, 2004, a note or other debt is considered a payment only if it was issued by a corporation or governmental entity. If you didn't receive any payments in 2019, enter zero. If in prior years an amount was entered on the equivalent of line 34 of the 2019 form, don't include it on this line. Instead, enter it on line 23. See *Pledge Rule*, earlier, for details about proceeds of debt secured by installment obligations that must be treated as payments on installment obligations.

Line 23

Enter all money and the FMV of property or services you received before 2019 from the sale. Include allocable installment income and any other deemed payments from prior years.

Deemed payments include amounts deemed received because of:

- A second disposition by a related party, or
- The pledge rule of section 453A(d).

Line 25

Enter here and on Form 4797, line 15, any ordinary income recapture on section 1252, 1254, or 1255 property for the year of sale or all remaining recapture from a prior year sale. Don't enter ordinary income from a section 179 expense deduction. If this is the year of sale, complete Form 4797, Part III. The amount from line 27c, 28b, or 29b of Form 4797 is the ordinary income recapture. Don't enter any gain for this property on line 31 or 32 of Form 4797. If you used Form 4797 only to figure the recapture on line 25 or 36 of Form 6252, enter "N/A" on lines 31 and 32 of Form 4797.

Also report on this line any ordinary income recapture remaining from prior years on section 1245 or 1250 property sold before June 7, 1984.

Don't enter on line 25 more than the amount shown on line 24. Any excess must be reported in future years on Form 6252 up to the taxable part of the installment sale until all of the recapture has been reported.

Line 26

For trade or business property held more than 1 year, enter this amount on Form 4797, line 4. If the property was held 1 year or less or you have an ordinary gain from the sale of a noncapital asset (even if the holding period is more than 1 year), enter this amount on Form 4797, line 10, and write "From Form 6252." If the property was section 1250 property (generally, real property that you depreciated) held more than 1 year, figure the total amount of unrecaptured section 1250 gain included on line 26 using the Unrecaptured Section 1250 Gain Worksheet in the Instructions for Schedule D (Form 1040 or 1040-SR).

For capital assets, enter this amount on Schedule D as a short- or long-term gain on the lines identified as from Form 6252.

Part III—Related Party Installment Sale Income

Line 29

If one of the conditions is met, check the appropriate box and skip lines 30 through 37. If you checked box 29e, attach an explanation. Generally, the nontax avoidance exception will apply to the second disposition if:

- The disposition was involuntary (for example, a creditor of the related party foreclosed on the property or the related party declared bankruptcy), or
- The disposition was an installment sale under which the terms of payment were substantially equal to or longer than those for the first sale. However, the resale terms must not permit significant deferral of recognition of gain from the first sale (for example, amounts from the resale are being collected sooner).

Line 30

If the related party sold all or part of the property from the original sale in 2019, enter the amount realized from the part resold. If part was sold in an earlier year and part was sold this year, enter the cumulative amount realized from the resale.

Amount realized. The amount realized from a sale or exchange is the total of all money received plus the FMV of all property or services received. The amount realized also includes any liabilities that were assumed by the buyer and any liabilities to which the property transferred is subject, such as real estate taxes or a mortgage. For details, see Pub. 544, Sales and Other Dispositions of Assets.

Line 33

If you completed Part II, enter the sum of lines 22 and 23. Otherwise, enter all money and the FMV of property you received before 2019 from the sale. Include allocable installment income and any other deemed payments from prior years. Don't include interest, whether stated or unstated.

Line 36

See the instructions for line 25. Don't enter on line 36 more than the amount shown on line 35. Any excess must be reported in future years on Form 6252 up to the taxable part of the installment sale until all of the recapture has been reported.

Line 37

See the instructions for line 26.

Paperwork Reduction Act Notice. We ask for the information on this form to carry out the Internal Revenue laws of the United States. You are required to give us the information. We need it to ensure that you are complying with these laws and to allow us to figure and collect the right amount of tax.

You are not required to provide the information requested on a form that is subject to the Paperwork Reduction Act unless the form displays a valid OMB control number. Books or records relating to a form or its instructions must be retained as long as their contents may become material in the administration of any Internal Revenue law. Generally, tax returns and return information are confidential, as required by section 6103.

The time needed to complete and file this form will vary depending on individual circumstances. The estimated burden for individual taxpayers filing this form is approved under OMB control number 1545-0074 and is included in the estimates shown in the instructions for their individual income tax return. The estimated burden for all other taxpayers who file this form is shown below.

Recordkeeping	1 hr., 18 min.
Learning about the law or the form	24 min.
Preparing the form	1 hr.
Copying, assembling, and sending the form to the IRS	20 min.

If you have comments concerning the accuracy of these time estimates or suggestions for making this form simpler, we would be happy to hear from you. See the instructions for the tax return with which this form is filed.

11

Long-Term Contracts

§11.01 Long-Term Contracts

[A] Generally

In the case of a long-term contract, the tax accounting rules under IRC §§451 and 461 are superseded by IRC §460. A "long-term contract" is any contract for the manufacture, building, installation, or construction of property that is not completed in the taxable year in which it was entered into.[1] A long-term contract can be less than one year so long as the completion of the contract spans from one tax year to another. For example, a builder with a December 31 year-end starts building a structure in November 2020 and completes the structure in July 2021. The contract is a long-term contract even if it did not take more than 12 months to complete.

The key difference between the otherwise applicable tax accounting rules and the long-term contract rules is that part of the profit is taxed during construction under the percentage of completion method (PCM), rather than upon a sale, as is the case when a completed property is sold (*i.e.*, where there is no contract for sale before the construction is finished).[2] Under PCM, income is based upon estimates rather than physical completion.

At one time, a taxpayer had the option of selecting the rules under IRC §451 or IRC §461 and several permissible methods to account for long-term contracts. Along with many other changes made by the Tax Reform Act of 1986 came changes made to long-term contracts and other exceptions described in §11.02. Subsequent legislation made further changes so that taxpayers in most cases must use the percentage of completion method to account for long-term contracts. Certain construction contracts are exempt from the use of the PCM while others are partially exempt.[3]

The TCJA amended IRC §460(e)(1)(B) to simplify certain accounting rules by increasing the gross receipts ceiling amount for a taxpayer to be exempt from the requirement to use the percentage of completion method for long-term construction contracts. The exception for small construction contracts which prior to the TCJA

---

[1] IRC §460(f)(1). Reg. §1.460-1(b)(1). The IRS website has a Construction Industry Audit Technique Guide (ATG) intended for use by examiners conducting audits in the construction industry. The guide can also be helpful to taxpayers and practitioners in understanding the terms and methods of accounting used in the construction industry. This guide can be found on the IRS website at: https://www.irs.gov/businesses/cost-segregation-audit-techniques-guide-table-of-contents.

[2] Reg. §1.460-1(b)(2)(i) provides that "A contract is a contract for the manufacture, building, installation, or construction of property if the manufacture, building, installation, or construction of property is necessary for the taxpayer's contractual obligations to be fulfilled and if the manufacture, building, installation, or construction of that property has not been completed when the parties enter into the contract. If a taxpayer has to manufacture or construct an item to fulfill its obligations under the contract, the fact that the taxpayer is not required to deliver that item to the customer is not relevant. Whether the customer has title to, control over, or bears the risk of loss from, the property manufactured or constructed by the taxpayer also is not relevant. Furthermore, how the parties characterize their agreement (*e.g.*, as a contract for the sale of property) is not relevant."

[3] *See* §11.02[C], *infra*.

applied to contractors with $10 million or less in average annual gross receipts in the preceding three taxable years, was expanded to apply to contracts entered into by taxpayers with average annual gross receipts of $25[4] million or less (indexed for inflation) for the prior three taxable years. Taxpayers that meet such exception would be permitted to use the completed contract method (or any other permissible exempt contract method).[5]

In general, taxable income from "long-term contracts" must be determined under the PCM.[6] Under this method, income is reported proportionally over the life of the contract as contract costs are incurred.[7] Additionally, the taxpayer must apply the "look back" method based on actual contract price and costs when the contract is completed.[8] If a taxpayer reports income under the PCM, then the taxpayer is required to pay, or is entitled to receive, interest[9] on the amount of the tax liability that is either deferred or accelerated. This is because the use of an estimate can result in underestimating the total contract or overestimating the contract.

Long-term contracts refer to building, installing or construction of "property." For long-term construction contract purposes, the property must be real property or inherently permanent structures.[10]

If a taxpayer "sells" property that is not complete at the time of sale, the IRS takes the position that the long-term contract rules apply if they would otherwise apply to a contract to manufacture or construct the property being sold. In this context, the percentage of completion method would be applied from the point the contract is entered into.

One must first determine whether the contract is a long-term contract within the meaning of IRC § 460. If it is, the next inquiry is what type of a long-term contract it is.

The principal methods subject IRC § 460 include:

- The Percentage of Completion Method;
- Exempt Contract Percentage of Completion Method;
- The 10% Method;
- Percentage of Completion Method Look-back Rule;
- Completed Contract Method;
- Exceptions to the Percentage of Completion Method which include:
  - Small Construction Contracts; and
  - Home Construction Contracts.

---

[4] $26 million for tax years 2019 and 2020.

[5] IRC § 460(e)(1)(B) as amended by § 13102(d)(2) of Pub. L. No. 115-97.

[6] IRC § 460.

[7] IRC § 460(b)(1); Reg. § 1.460-4(a)(1).

[8] *See* § 11.06[A], *infra*.

[9] IRC § 460(b).

[10] Reg. § 1.460-3(a).

Proposed reliance regulations on small business tax accounting rules. The IRS has issued proposed reliance regulations[11] that implement legislative changes to IRC § 460 that simplify the application of those tax accounting provisions for certain businesses having average annual gross receipts that do not exceed $25,000,000, adjusted for inflation. These regulations contain special accounting rules for long-term contracts under IRC § 460 to implement legislative changes applicable to corporate taxpayers.

The TCJA made additional amendments to the IRC § 460 rules for long-term contracts to reflect the fact that the TCJA repealed the corporate alternative minimum tax (AMT) imposed by IRC § 55 and added the base erosion anti-abuse tax IRC § 59A.[12]

The proposed regulations, generally. The proposed regulations make numerous changes to existing regulations to reflect the above changes made by the TCJA.

IRC § 460(a) provides that income from a long-term contract must be determined using the percentage-of-completion method (PCM). A long-term contract is defined in IRC § 460(f) as generally any contract for the manufacture, building, installation, or construction of property if such contract is not completed within the tax year in which such contract is entered into.

IRC § 460(b) provides that, upon the completion of any long-term contract, the look-back method is applied to amounts reported under the contract using the PCM, whether for regular income tax purposes or for AMT purposes. Under the look-back method, taxpayers are required to pay interest if the taxpayer's federal income tax liability is deferred as a result of underestimating the total contract price or overestimating total contract costs. Alternatively, a taxpayer is entitled to receive interest if the taxpayer's federal income tax liability has been accelerated as a result of overestimating the total contract price or underestimating total contract costs.

Any interest to be paid is based on a comparison of the difference between the federal income tax liability actually reported by the taxpayer with the federal income tax liability that would have been reported if the taxpayer had used actual contract prices and costs instead of estimated contract prices and costs in computing income under the PCM.[13]

Look-back rules and the AMT. Section 12001 of the TCJA amended IRC § 55(a) so that the AMT is no longer imposed on corporations for tax years beginning after December 31, 2017.

Consistent with § 12001 of the TCJA, the proposed regulations reflect the changes to IRC § 55(a) by providing that in applying the look-back method, alternative minimum taxable income is redetermined only for tax years in which the AMT is applicable. Similarly, the recomputed tax liability for prior contract years includes the AMT only for the tax years in which the AMT is applicable.[14]

---

[11] Preamble to Prop. Reg. REG-132766-18; Prop. Reg. § § 1.460-1, 1.460-3, 1.460-4, 1.460-5, 1.460-6.
[12] TCJA § § 12001 and 14401.
[13] Reg. § 1.460-6(c)(1)(i).
[14] Prop. Reg. § 1.460-6(c).

Consequently, for tax years beginning after December 31, 2017, for purposes of the look-back method, a corporation will not redetermine alternative minimum taxable income or recompute AMT liability. However, a corporation that has a contract that spans a period beginning before the TCJA (tax years beginning before January 1, 2018) and ending after the TCJA (tax years beginning after December 31, 2017), is required to redetermine alternative minimum taxable income and recompute AMT for those tax years beginning before January 1, 2018.[15]

De minimis exception to look-back rules. IRC § 460(b)(3) provides an exception to the requirement to apply the look-back method. Under the exception, the look-back method need not be applied if the contract price does not exceed the lesser of $1,000,000 or 1% of the taxpayer's average annual gross receipts for the prior three-taxable-year period ending with the year preceding the tax year in which the contract is completed, and if the contract is completed within two years of the commencement of the contract.

Prop. Reg. § 1.460-3(b)(3) provides that, for purposes of this *de minimis* exception, gross receipts are determined in accordance with the regulations under IRC § 448(c).

Look-back rules and the BEAT. For any tax year, the base erosion anti-abuse tax (BEAT) imposed by IRC § 59A is a tax on each applicable taxpayer equal to the base erosion minimum tax amount (BEMTA) for that year. Generally, the taxpayer's BEMTA equals the excess of (1) the applicable tax rate for the tax year (BEAT rate) multiplied by the taxpayer's modified taxable income under Reg. § 1.59A-3(b) for the tax year over (2) the taxpayer's adjusted regular federal income tax liability for that year.

Prop. Reg. § 1.460-6 applies the look-back method to redetermine the taxpayer's modified taxable income under Reg. § 1.59-3(b) and the taxpayer's BEMTA for the tax year. Specifically, the taxpayer must determine its modified taxable income and BEMTA for each year prior to the filing year that is affected by contracts completed or adjusted in the filing year as if the actual total contract price and costs had been used in applying the percentage of completion method.[16]

The IRS has proposed this rule because the income from long-term contracts determined using the PCM may be overestimated or underestimated, which may change the taxpayer's modified taxable income or BETMA, or whether or not a taxpayer is an applicable taxpayer in a particular tax year. Clarifying in the regulations under IRC § 460 that the look-back method must take into account any application of the BEAT makes clear that IRC § 460 provides that taxpayers will pay or receive interest (whichever is the case) if their federal income tax liability, including any BEAT liability, is deferred, eliminated, understated, or overstated as a result of the taxpayer's estimation of the total contract price or total contract costs.[17]

---

[15] Preamble to Prop. Reg. REG-132766-18.

[16] Prop. Reg. § 1.460-6(c).

[17] Preamble to Prop. Reg. REG-132766-18.

[B] Manufacturing Contracts

A contract for the manufacture of personal property is a manufacturing contract. A manufacturing contract is a long-term contract if and only if the contract involves the manufacture of:

- Any unique item of a type that is not normally carried in the finished goods inventory of the taxpayer; or
- Any item that normally requires more than 12 calendar months to complete (without regard to the period of the contract).[18]

A contract that meets one or both of these criteria is subject to long-term contract rules.

[C] More Than 12 Months to Complete

To qualify as a long-term manufacturing contract, a manufactured item normally requires more than 12 calendar months to complete.[19] A manufactured item normally requires more than 12 months to complete if its production period is reasonably expected to exceed 12 months. An item's production period begins when a taxpayer incurs at least 5% of the estimated total allocable costs to that item, and the period ends when the item is ready for shipment to the purchaser and all reasonably expected production activities are completed.[20]

[D] General Definition of "Unique Item"

The IRS has issued regulations that contain general guidance on the definition of "unique" and provide three safe harbors. If a taxpayer meets the requirements of any of these safe harbors, the taxpayer is assured that the contract is not for the manufacture of a unique item; however, it may still be a long-term contract if it requires more than 12 months to complete.

The regulations state that "unique" means designed for the needs of a specific customer. The extent to which research, development, design, engineering, retooling, and other customizing activities are required in the performance of the contract is relevant in determining whether the item is designed for the needs of a particular customer, and thus unique. Also, an important determining factor is whether the item could be sold to other customers with little or no modification.[21]

A contract may require the taxpayer to manufacture more than one unit of a unique item. If a contract requires a taxpayer to manufacture more than one unit of the same item, then the taxpayer must determine whether that item is unique by

---

[18] IRC § 460(f)(2).
[19] IRC § 460(f)(2)(B).
[20] Reg. § 1.460-2(c)(1).
[21] Reg. § 1.460-2(b)(1).

considering the customizing activities that would be needed to produce only the first unit.[22]

[E] Safe Harbors

An item is not unique if it satisfies one or more of the safe harbors below. If an item does not satisfy one or more safe harbors, the determination of uniqueness will depend on the facts and circumstances. The safe harbors are:

- *Short Production Period.* An item is not unique if it normally requires 90 days or less to complete. In the case of a contract for multiple units of an item, the item is not unique only if it normally requires 90 days or less to complete each unit of the item in the contract.[23]
- *Customized Item.* An item is not unique if the total allocable contract costs attributable to customizing activities that are incident to or necessary for the manufacture of the item do not exceed 10% of the estimated total allocable contract costs allocable to the item. In the case of a contract for multiple units of an item, this comparison must be performed on the first unit of the item and the total allocable contract costs attributable to customizing activities that are incident to or necessary for the manufacture of the first unit of the item must be allocated to that first unit.[24]
- *Inventoried Item.* A unique item ceases to be unique no later than when the taxpayer normally includes similar items in its finished goods inventory.[25]

[F] Normal Time to Complete

The amount of time normally required to complete an item is the item's reasonably expected production period, determined at the end of the contracting year.[26] Thus, in general, the expected production period for an item begins when a taxpayer incurs at least 5% of the costs that would be allocable to the item and ends when the item is ready to be held for sale and all reasonably expected production activities are complete.[27] In the case of components that are assembled or reassembled into an item or unit at the customer's facility by the taxpayer's employees or agents, the production period ends when the components are assembled or reassembled into an operable item or unit. To the extent that several distinct activities related to the production of the item are expected to occur simultaneously, the period during which these distinct activities occur is not counted more than once. Furthermore, when determining the normal time to complete an item, a taxpayer is not required to

[22] Reg. § 1.460-2(b)(2)(ii).
[23] Reg. § 1.460-2(b)(2)(i).
[24] Reg. § 1.460-2(b)(2)(ii).
[25] Reg. § 1.460-2(b)(2)(iii).
[26] Reg. § 1.460-2(c).
[27] *Id.*

consider activities performed or costs incurred that would not be allocable contract costs under IRC § 460 (*e.g.*, independent research and development expenses and marketing expenses).[28] Moreover, the time normally required to design and manufacture the first unit of an item of which the taxpayer intends to produce multiple units generally does not indicate the normal time to complete the item.

[G] Production by Related Parties

To determine the time normally required to complete an item, a taxpayer must consider all relevant production activities performed and costs incurred by itself and by related parties. For example, if a taxpayer's item requires a component or subassembly manufactured by a related party, the taxpayer must consider the time the related party[29] takes to complete the component or subassembly, and, for purposes of determining the beginning of an item's production period, the costs incurred by the related party that are allocable to the component or subassembly. However, if more than 50% of the average annual gross receipts attributable to the sale of an item for the three-taxable-year-period ending with the contracting year comes from unrelated parties, a taxpayer does not consider the activities performed or the costs incurred by a related party when determining the normal time to complete an item.[30]

Example 11-1

Unique Item and Classification. In December 2001, C enters into a contract with B to design and manufacture a new type of industrial equipment. C reasonably expects the normal production period for this type of equipment to be eight months. Because the new type of industrial equipment requires a substantial amount of research, design, and engineering to produce, C determines that the equipment is a unique item and its contract with B is a long-term contract. After delivering the equipment to B in September 2002, C contracts with B to produce five additional units of that industrial equipment with certain different specifications. These additional units, which also are expected to take eight months to produce, will be delivered to B in 2003. C determines that the research, design, engineering, retooling, and similar customizing costs necessary to produce the five additional units of equipment does not exceed 10% of the first unit's share of estimated total allocable contract costs. Consequently, the additional units of equipment satisfy the customized item safe harbor and are not unique items. Although C's contract with B to produce the five additional units is not completed within the contracting year, the contract is not a long-term contract since the additional units of equip-

---

[28] Reg. § 1.460-2(c)(1).

[29] Reg. § 1.460-1(b)(4); Reg. § 1.460-1(g)(3).

[30] Reg. §§ 1.460-2(c)(2) and 1.460-1(g)(1)(ii), Exception For Components And Subassemblies.

ment are not unique items and do not normally require more than 12 months to produce. C must classify its second contract with B as a non-long term contract, notwithstanding that it classified the previous contract with B for a similar item as a long-term contract, because the determination of whether a contract is a long-term contract is made on a contract-by-contract basis. A change in classification is not a change in method of accounting because the change in classification results from a change in underlying facts.[31]

Example 11-2

12-Month Rule—Related Party. C manufactures cranes. C purchases one of the crane's components from R, a related party under. Less than 50% of R's gross receipts attributable to the sale of this component comes from sales to unrelated parties; thus, the exception for components and subassemblies is not satisfied. Consequently, C must consider the activities of R as R incurs costs and performs the activities rather than as C incurs a liability to R. The normal time period between the time that both C and R incur 5% of the costs allocable to the crane and the time that R completes the component is five months. C normally requires an additional eight months to complete production of the crane after receiving the integral component from R. C's crane is an item of a type that normally requires more than 12 months to complete because the production period from the time that both C and R incur 5% of the costs allocable to the crane until the time that production of the crane is complete is normally 13 months.[32]

Example 11-3

12-Month Rule—Duration of Contract. The facts are the same as in Example 11-2, except that C enters into a sales contract with B on December 31, 2001 (the last day of C's taxable year), and delivers a completed crane to B on February 1, 2002. C's contract with B is a long-term contract under paragraph (a)(2) of this section because the contract is not completed in the contracting year, 2001, and the crane is an item that normally requires more than 12 calendar months to complete (regardless of the duration of the contract).[33]

---

[31] Reg. § 1.460-2(e), Example 1.

[32] Reg. § 1.460-2(e), Example 2.

[33] Reg. § 1.460-2(e), Example 3.

Example 11-4

12-Month Rule—Normal Time to Complete. The facts are the same as in Example 11-2, except that C (and R) actually complete B's crane in only ten calendar months. The contract is a long-term contract because the normal time to complete a crane, not the actual time to complete a crane, is the relevant criterion for determining whether an item is a unique item.[34]

Example 11-5

Normal Time to Complete. C enters into a multi-unit contract to produce four units of an item. C does not anticipate producing any additional units of the item. C expects to perform the research, design, and development that are directly allocable to the particular item and to produce the first unit in the first 24 months. C reasonably expects the production period for each of the three remaining units will be three months. This contract is not a contract that involves the manufacture of an item that normally requires more than 12 months to complete because the normal time to complete the item is three months. However, the contract does not satisfy the 90-day safe harbor for unique items because the normal time to complete the first unit of this item exceeds 90 days. Thus, the contract might involve the manufacture of a unique item depending on the facts and circumstances.[35]

§ 11.02 Construction Contracts

[A] Generally

A contract for the production or installation of real property or any improvements to real property is considered to be a contract for building, installation, or construction and is subject to the long-term contract rules of IRC § 460. Also included are contracts for the rehabilitation of real property, installation of integral components to real property, and improvement of real property.[36]

Real property means land, buildings, and inherently permanent structures[37] such as roadways, dams, and bridges, but does not include vessels, offshore drilling platforms, or unsevered natural products of land. An "integral component to real

---

[34] Reg. § 1.460-2(e), Example 4.

[35] Reg. § 1.460-2(e), Example 5.

[36] Reg. § 1.460-3(a).

[37] Reg. § 1.263A-8(c)(3).

property" includes property not produced at the site of the real property, but which is intended to be permanently affixed to the real property (*e.g.*, elevators, central heating and cooling systems). Thus, for example, a contract to install an elevator in a building is a construction contract, because a building is real property; a contract to install an elevator in a ship is not a construction contract, because a ship is not real property.[38]

On the other hand, a contract for the provision of personal services such as architectural services, engineering, or construction management is not a long-term contract when the sole subject matter is the service itself.[39]

[B] De Minimis Construction Activities

A contract is not a construction contract if it includes the provision of land by the taxpayer and the estimated total allocable contract costs attributable to the taxpayer's construction activities are less than 10% of the contract's total contract price.[40]

Example 11-6

C, a master developer whose taxable year ends December 31, owns 5,000 acres of undeveloped land with a cost basis of $5,000,000 and a fair market value of $50,000,000. To obtain permission from the local county government to improve this land, a service road must be constructed on this land to benefit all 5,000 acres. In 2001, C enters into a contract to sell a 1,000-acre parcel of undeveloped land to B, a residential developer, for its fair market value, $10,000,000. In this contract, C agrees to construct a service road running through the land that C is selling to B and through the 4,000 adjacent acres of undeveloped land that C has sold or will sell to other residential developers for its fair market value, $40,000,000. C reasonably estimates that it will incur allocable contract costs of $50,000 (excluding the cost of the land) to construct this service road, which will be owned and maintained by the county. C must reasonably allocate the cost of the service road among the benefitted parcels. The portion of the estimated total allocable contract costs that C allocates to the 1,000-acre parcel being sold to B (based upon its fair market value) is $10,000 ($50,000 × ($10,000,000 ÷ $50,000,000)). Construction of the service road is finished in 2002. Because the estimated total allocable contract costs attributable to C's construction activities, $10,000, are less than 10% of the contract's total contract price, $10,000,000, C's contract with B is not a

[38] Reg. § 1.460-3(a).

[39] *See* Rev. Rul. 70-67, 1970-1 CB 117; Rev. Rul. 80-18, 1980-1 CB 103; and Rev. Rul. 82-134, 1982-2 CB 88.

[40] Reg. § 1.460-1(b)(2)(ii).

construction contract. Thus, C's contract with B is not a long-term contract notwithstanding that construction of the service road is not completed in 2001.[41]

[C] Exempt Construction Contracts

Home Construction Contracts. The general requirement to use the percentage completion method and the cost allocation rules does not apply to any exempt construction contract,[42] which include home construction contracts and small construction contracts. The exception for small construction contracts, which prior to the TCJA applied to contractors with $10 million or less in average annual gross receipts in the preceding three taxable years, was expanded to apply to contracts entered into by taxpayers with average annual gross receipts of $25[43] million or less (indexed for inflation) for the prior three taxable years. To apply the gross receipts test, a taxpayer is not required to aggregate the gross receipts of persons treated as a single employer solely under IRC § 414(m) and any regulations prescribed under IRC § 414.[44] Taxpayers that meet such exception are permitted to use the completed contract method (or any other permissible exempt contract method).[45]

Taxpayers that meet the IRC § 448(c) threshold and elect to change methods of accounting for long-term contracts from the PCM method to the CCM will do so on the cut-off basis. As a result, there will not be an IRC § 481(a) adjustment resulting from this change in method of accounting.[46]

A "home construction" contract is an exempt construction contract in which 80% or more of the estimated total costs (as of the close of the year the contract was entered into) are reasonably expected to be attributable to building, construction, reconstruction, or rehabilitation of, or the installation of any integral component to, or improvements of, real property with respect to:

- dwelling units contained in buildings with four or fewer dwelling units (if the dwelling unit is a townhouse or rowhouse, each townhouse or rowhouse is considered a separate building);[47] and
- improvements to real property directly related to the dwelling units and located on the site of the dwelling units.[48]

---

[41] Reg. § 1.460-1(j), Example 2.

[42] IRC § 460(e).

[43] $26 million for tax years 2019 and 2020.

[44] Reg. § 1.460-3(b)(3)(ii).

[45] IRC § 460(e)(1)(B) as amended by § 13102(d)(2) of Pub. L. No. 115-97.

[46] IRC § 460(e)(2)(B).

[47] Reg. § 1.460-3(b)(2)(ii).

[48] IRC § 460(e)(6)(A).

A "dwelling unit" is a house or apartment used to provide living accommodations in a building or structure, but not a unit in a hotel, motel, or other establishment in which more than half of the units are used on a transient basis.[49]

Common improvements. A taxpayer includes in the cost of the dwelling units his or her allocable share of the cost that the taxpayer reasonably expects to incur for any common improvements (e.g., sewers, roads, clubhouses) that benefit the dwelling units and that the taxpayer is contractually obligated, or required by law, to construct within the tract or tracts of land that contain the dwelling units.[50]

Mixed use costs. If a contract involves the construction of both commercial units and dwelling units within the same building, a taxpayer must allocate the costs among the commercial units and dwelling units using a reasonable method or combination of reasonable methods, such as specific identification, square footage, or fair market value.[51]

Attribution of gross receipts. A taxpayer must aggregate a proportionate share of the construction-related gross receipts of any person that has a five percent or greater interest in the taxpayer. In addition, a taxpayer must aggregate a proportionate share of the construction-related gross receipts of any person in which the taxpayer has a five percent or greater interest. For this purpose, a taxpayer must determine ownership interests as of the first day of the taxpayer's contracting year and must include indirect interests in any corporation, partnership, estate, trust, or sole proprietorship according to principles similar to the constructive ownership rules under IRC §§1563(e), (f)(2), and (f)(3)(A). However, a taxpayer is not required to aggregate under Reg. §1.460-3(b)(3)(iii) any construction-related gross receipts required to be aggregated under Reg. §1.460-3(b)(3)(i).[52]

Residential construction contracts. A taxpayer may determine the income from a long-term construction contract that is a residential construction contract using either the PCM or the percentage of completion/capitalized-cost method (PCCM) of accounting described in Reg. §1.460-4(e). A residential construction contract is a home construction contract, as defined in Reg. §1.460-4(b)(2), except that the building or buildings being constructed contain more than four dwelling units.[53]

Small Construction Exemption. The use of the PCM is not required for regular tax purposes for most construction contracts entered into by small contractors. This exception for small contractors applies if three criteria are met:

---

[49] IRC §168(e)(2)(A)(ii)(I).

[50] Reg. §1.460-3(b)(2)(iii).

[51] Reg. §1.460-3(b)(2)(iv).

[52] Reg. §1.460-3(b)(3)(iii).

[53] Reg. §1.460-3(c).

- The contract must be a construction contract. A "construction contract" is a contract for the building, construction, reconstruction, or rehabilitation of, or the installation of any integral component to, or improvements of, real property.[54]
- It must be estimated, at the time the contract is entered into, that the contract will be completed within a two-year period beginning on the contract commencement date. The estimate must be a reasonable estimate and must include anticipated time for delay, rework, change orders, technology or design problems, or other problems that reasonably can be anticipated based on the nature of the contract and the taxpayer's prior experience with this type of contract. If the contract prescribes an anticipated delivery date or completion date, this constitutes evidence of the estimated time of completion, especially if the contract calls for penalties for failure to meet such date. Note that the taxpayer need not take into account unforeseeable factors beyond the taxpayer's control, such as third-party litigation, extreme weather conditions, strikes, or delays in securing permits or licenses.[55]
- The contractor's (or its predecessor's) average annual gross receipts for the three tax years preceding the tax year in which the contract is entered into must be $25 million or less for contracts entered into after December 31, 2017 ($10 million or less for contracts entered into prior to January 1, 2018).[56]

For purposes of IRC § 460(e)(1)(B)(ii), in the case of any taxpayer which is not a corporation or a partnership (*e.g.*, an individual), the gross receipts test of IRC § 448(c) is applied in the same manner as if each trade or business of the taxpayer were a corporation or a partnership.[57] The TCJA redesignated pre-TCJA IRC § 460(e)(4) through IRC § 460(e)(6) as IRC § 460(e)(3) through IRC § 460(e)(5), respectively.

To apply the gross receipts test, a taxpayer is not required to aggregate the gross receipts of persons treated as a single employer solely under IRC § 414(m) and any regulations prescribed.[58]

Attribution of gross receipts. A taxpayer must aggregate a proportionate share of the construction-related gross receipts of any person that has a 5% or greater interest in the taxpayer. In addition, a taxpayer must aggregate a proportionate share of the construction-related gross receipts of any person in which the taxpayer has a 5% or greater interest. For this purpose, a taxpayer must determine ownership interests as of the first day of the taxpayer's contracting year and must include indirect interests in any corporation, partnership, estate, trust, or sole proprietorship according to principles similar to the constructive ownership rules under IRC § 1563(e), (f)(2), and (f)(3)(A).[59]

---

[54] IRC § 460(e)(3); Reg. § 1.460-3(a). The term "residential construction contract" is defined in the same way as the term "home construction contract," except there is no limit on the number of dwelling units in the building. IRC § 460(e)(5)(B).

[55] *Id.*

[56] IRC § 460(e)(1)(B). The threshold has been increased to $26 million for tax years 2019 and 2020.

[57] IRC § 460(e)(2)(A).

[58] Reg. § 1.460-3(b)(3)(ii).

[59] Reg. § 1.460-3(b)(3)(iii).

§11.03 Completed Contracts Method (CCM)

[A] Generally

Prior to the Revenue Reconciliation Act of 1989, the completed contract method of accounting was the method used by contractors to account for long-term contracts. The Revenue Reconciliation Act of 1989 limited the application of the completed contract method. Now it can be used only by small construction companies and for home and other residential construction contracts. The completed contract method can be used only for construction expected to be completed within two years by taxpayers and by contractors with average annual gross receipts of $26 million or less ("small contractor exception") and for "home construction" contracts. The completed contract method is an exception to the annual accounting concept.[60] This exception allows for the deferral of tax on profitable contracts until the completion of the contracts. When there are loss contracts, however, or when the use of the completed contract method creates wide swings in taxable income, and therefore in tax rates applicable to the contract profits, this method may not be advantageous.

Under the completed contract method, gross income derived from long-term contracts must be reported by including the gross contract price of each contract in gross income for the taxable year in which that contract is completed. Costs properly allocable to a long-term contract must be deducted from gross income for that taxable year in which the contract is completed. Account must be taken of any material and supplies charged to the contract but remaining on hand at the time of completion.

Gross contract price includes all amounts (including holdbacks, retainages, and reimbursements) that a taxpayer is entitled by law or contract to receive, whether or not the amounts are due or have been paid. In addition, gross contract price includes all bonuses, awards, and incentive payments, such as a bonus for meeting an early completion date, to the extent the all-events test is satisfied. If a taxpayer performs a non-long-term contract activity, as defined in Reg. §1460-1(d)(2), that is incident to or necessary for the manufacture, building, installation, or construction of the subject matter of one or more of the taxpayer's long-term contracts, the taxpayer must include an allocable share of the gross receipts attributable to that activity in the gross contract price of the contract(s) benefitted by that activity. Gross contract price also includes amounts reimbursed for independent research and development expenses (as defined in Reg. §1.460-1(b)(9)), or bidding and proposal costs under a federal or cost-plus long-term contract (as defined in IRC §460(d)), regardless of whether the research and development or bidding and proposal activities are incident to or necessary for the performance of that long-term contract.

---

[60] Reg. §1.460-3(b)(3).

[B] Contract Costing Rules for Contracts Using the Completed Contract Method

Taxpayers that perform construction contracts that are exempt from the mandatory use of the percentage completion method because these contracts meet the small contractor exception and for which the completed contract method (CCM) is used have two different sets of costing rules to choose from.[61]

A taxpayer using the CCM to account for a long-term contract must take into account in the contract's completion year, as defined in Reg. § 1.460-1(b)(6), the gross contract price and all allocable contract costs incurred by the completion year. A taxpayer may not treat the cost of any materials and supplies that are allocated to a contract, but actually remain on hand when the contract is completed, as an allocable contract cost.[62]

The first option is to use the uniform capitalization rules as they are used under the standard IRC § 460 costing rules. Use of these rules generally requires the taxpayer to treat more costs as contract costs than the second option discussed below. However, to the extent that the taxpayer is otherwise subject to the uniform capitalization rules, the taxpayer might find it administratively more convenient to use the uniform capitalization rules for its exempt contracts.[63]

The other option is to use the costing rules prescribed in the current IRC § 460 regulations. This set of rules is essentially the rules applicable to pre-1982 (and some pre-1986) long-term contracts.[64]

The second option generally does not require as many costs to be treated as contract costs as under the uniform capitalization rules or the standard IRC § 460 costing rules. The list of costs required to be treated as contract costs is generally closer to the list of costs associated with contracts under GAAP. For example, the amount of depreciation claimed for financial statement purposes is treated as a contract cost; the excess of tax depreciation over book depreciation is not treated as a contract cost.

---

[61] These are contracts that are expected to be completed within two years, where the taxpayer's average annual gross receipts do not exceed $26 million. *See* IRC § 460(e)(1)(B) and Reg. § 1.460-3(b)(1).

[62] Reg. § 1.460-4(d).

[63] Reg. § 1.460-5(d)(1), which provides that direct costs, as defined in Reg. § 1.263A-1(e)(2)(i) and indirect costs, as defined in Reg. § 1.263A-1(e)(3), must be treated as contract costs.

[64] *See* Reg. §§ 1.460-5(d)(1) and 1.460-5(d)(2). Pursuant to these regulations, direct costs, as defined in Reg. § 1.263A-1(e)(2)(i), and indirect costs, as defined in Reg. § 1.460-5(d)(2), are treated as contract costs of exempt contracts accounted for using the CCM.

§ 11.04 Percentage of Completion Method (PCM)

[A] Application of Method

In general, taxable income from "long-term contracts" must be determined under the percentage of completion method (PCM).[65] Under this method, income is reported proportionally over the life of the contract as contract costs are incurred.[66] Contract-related expenses are deducted in the year they are incurred.[67] Under the percentage of completion method, all income from a long-term contract must be reported by the end of the taxable year following the year that the contract is completed.[68] A taxpayer may elect not to recognize income from or the costs of the contract if less than 10% of the estimated total contract costs are incurred by the end of the taxable year.[69] After a contract subject to the PCM is completed, a taxpayer must, in general, apply the "look-back method"[70] to determine the amount of interest owed on any hypothetical underpayment of tax, or earned on any hypothetical overpayment of tax.

A PCM taxpayer must, in general, include in income the portion of the total contract price that corresponds to the percentage of the entire contract that the taxpayer has completed during the taxable year. The percentage of completion must be determined by comparing allocable contract costs incurred with estimated total allocable contract costs. The taxpayer includes a portion of the total contract price in gross income as the taxpayer incurs allocable contract costs.[71]

The long-term contract rules are generally unfavorable to manufacturers because the rules require them to include income as the item is produced as opposed to when they ship or when title passes.[72]

For contracts which are expected to produce a loss, the percentage of completion method can be advantageous because it allows taxpayers to recognize the loss as items are produced, rather than delaying reporting of the loss until shipment, delivery and acceptance, or title passage.

Of particular note is that the percentage of completion method can result in deferring advance payments which could not otherwise be deferred under the rules

---

65 IRC § 460.

66 IRC § 460(b)(1); Reg. § 1.460-4(b)(1).

67 Reg. §§ 1.460-4(b)(2)(iv) and 1.460-1(b)(8).

68 IRC § 460(b)(1).

69 IRC § 460(b)(5). *See* § 11.05, *below* (Ten-Percent Method).

70 *See* § 11.06, *below*.

71 Reg. § 1.460-4(b)(1).

72 Reg. § 1.446-1(c)(1)(ii)(C).

of former Reg. § 1.451-5.[73] This is because under the percentage of completion method, the timing of receipt of cash has no relevance.[74]

[B] Percentage-of-Completion/Capitalized-Cost Method

Under the PCCM, a taxpayer must determine the income from a long-term contract using the PCM for the applicable percentage of the contract and its exempt contract method for the remaining percentage of the contract. For residential construction contracts described in Reg. § 1.460-3(c), the applicable percentage is 70%, and the remaining percentage is 30%. For qualified ship contracts described in Reg. § 1.460-2(d), the applicable percentage is 40%, and the remaining percentage is 60%.

[C] Computation of Long-term Contract Income

To determine the income from a long-term contract, a taxpayer must follow four steps.

Step 1
First, the taxpayer computes the completion factor for the contract, which is the ratio of the

(1) Cumulative allocable contract costs that the taxpayer has incurred through the end of the taxable year to the
(2) Estimated total allocable contract costs that the taxpayer reasonably expects to incur under the contract.[75]

Step 2
Second, the taxpayer computes the amount of cumulative gross receipts from the contract by multiplying the completion factor by the total contract price.[76]

Step 3
Third, the taxpayer computes the amount of current-year gross receipts, which is the difference between

(1) The amount of cumulative gross receipts for the current taxable year, and
(2) The amount of cumulative gross receipts for the immediately preceding taxable year.

The difference can be a positive or negative number.[77]

---

[73] Reg. § 1.460-4(h).

[74] Reg. § 1.460-4(h). Example 4 demonstrates a situation where progress payments are received, but are not includible in income upon receipt. Rather, while the fact that C receives progress payments is specifically stated, this fact plays no role in the computation of gross income for each year.

[75] Reg. § 1.460-4(b)(2)(i).

[76] Reg. § 1.460-4(b)(2)(ii).

[77] Reg. § 1.460-4(b)(2)(iii).

Step 4

Fourth, and finally, the taxpayer takes both the current-year gross receipts and the allocable contract costs incurred during the current year into account in computing taxable income.[78]

The current year's contract income can therefore be expressed by the following formula:

$$\frac{\text{Cumulative allocable contract costs}}{\text{Estimated total allocable costs}} \times \text{Total contract price} - \text{Gross receipts reported in prior years} = \text{Current year gross receipts}$$

Example 11-7

C, whose taxable year ends on December 31st, determines income from long-term contracts using the percentage of completion method. During the year 2020, C agrees to manufacture for customer B a unique item for a total contract price of $1,000,000. Under C's contract, B is entitled to retain 10% of the total contract price until it accepts the item. By the end of 2020, C has incurred $200,000 of allocable contract costs and estimates that the total allocable contract costs will be $800,000. By the end of 2021, C has incurred $600,000 of allocable contract costs and estimates that the total allocable contract costs will be $900,000. In 2022, after completing the contract, C determines that the actual cost to manufacture the item was $750,000.

For each of the taxable years, C's income from the contract is computed as follows:

	2020	2021	2022
(A) Cumulative incurred costs	$200,000	$600,000	$750,000
(B) Estimated total costs	800,000	900,000	750,000
(C) Completion factor: (A) / (B)	25.00%	66.67%	100.00%
(D) Total contract price	1,000,000	1,000,000	1,000,000

[78] Reg. § 1.460-4(b)(2)(iv).

	2020	2021	2022
(E) Cumulative gross receipts: (C) × (D)	250,000	666,667	1,000,000
(F) Cumulative gross receipts (prior year)	(0)	(250,000)	(667,000)
(G) Current-year gross receipts	250,000	416,667	333,333
(H) Cumulative incurred costs	200,000	600,000	750,000
(I) Cumulative incurred costs (prior year)	(0)	(200,000)	(600,000)
(J) Current-year costs	200,000	400,000	150,000
(K) Gross income: (G) – (J)	$50,000	$16,667	$183,333

§ 11.05 Ten-Percent Method

Instead of determining the income from a long-term contract beginning with the contracting year, a taxpayer may elect to use the ten-percent method under IRC § 460(b)(5). Under the ten-percent method, a taxpayer does not include in gross income any amount related to allocable contract costs until the taxable year in which the taxpayer has incurred at least 10% of the estimated total allocable contract costs (the "ten-percent year").[79] Costs incurred before the ten-percent year are treated as pre-contracting year costs and are capitalized in a later year, when they are taken into account in computing taxable income.[80]

The election applies to all contracts entered into during the year of the election and subsequent years.[81] The ten-percent method is a method of accounting, which, once elected, cannot be changed without the consent of the Commissioner. The election is made by using this method for all contracts entered into for the year of election. The election is made on the original return for the year of the election.[82]

Example 11-8

C, whose taxable year ends December 31st, determines the income from long-term contracts using the percentage of completion method. In November 2020, C agrees to manufacture a unique item for $1,000,000. C reasonably estimates that the total allocable contract costs will be $600,000. By December 31, 2020, C has received $50,000 in progress

---

[79] *Id.*

[80] A taxpayer using this method makes an election under Reg. § 1.460-4(b)(6)(ii) and must use it for all long-term contracts entered into during the taxable year of the election.

[81] IRC § 460(b)(5)(C).

[82] Reg. § 1.460-4(b)(6)(ii).

payments and incurred $40,000 of costs. C elects to use the ten-percent method effective for 2020 and all subsequent taxable years. During 2021, C receives $500,000 in progress payments and incurs $260,000 of costs. In 2022, C incurs an additional $300,000 of costs, finishes manufacturing the item, and receives the final $450,000 payment.

For each of the taxable years, C's income from the contract is computed as follows:

	2020	2021	2022
(A) Cumulative incurred costs	$40,000	$300,000	$600,000
(B) Estimated total costs	600,000	600,000	600,000
(C) Completion factor: (A) / (B)	6.67%	50.00%	100.00%
(D) Total contract price	1,000,000	1,000,000	1,000,000
(E) Cumulative gross receipts: (C) × (D)*	0	500,000	1,000,000
(F) Cumulative gross receipts (prior year)	(0)	(0)	(500,000)
(G) Current-year gross receipts	0	500,000	500,000
(H) Cumulative incurred costs	0	300,000	600,000
(I) Cumulative incurred costs (prior year)	(0)	(0)	(300,000)
(J) Current-year costs	0	300,000	300,000
(K) Gross income: (G) – (J)	0	$200,000	$200,000

* Unless (C) is less than 10%.

§ 11.06 Look-Back Method

[A] Generally

The look-back rule was enacted as a means of truing up the estimates made in computing the percentage of completion formula for long-term contracts.[83] When a contract reported under the percentage of completion method is completed, a taxpayer is required to pay or is entitled to receive interest on the amount of the tax deferred or accelerated as a result of overestimating or underestimating the total

[83] IRC § 460(b)(1), IRC § 460(b)(2), IRC § 460(b)(5)(D)(ii); Reg. § 1.460-6(b)(1).

contract price or contract costs. The look-back method applies to any income from a long-term contract required to be reported under the percentage of completion method.

Under the look-back method, a taxpayer must pay interest for any deferral of tax resulting from the underestimation of the total contract price or overestimation of total contract costs.[84]

Conversely, if the total contract price is overestimated or total contract costs are underestimated, a taxpayer is entitled to receive interest for any resulting acceleration of tax.[85] The look-back recomputations are hypothetical and are used only for purposes of determining the amount of interest owed by or due the contractor; prior years' returns are not amended.[86] Once a contract is completed, a separate look-back computation must be done for each prior year of the contract. A taxpayer's tax liability is not adjusted for the amounts of deferred or accelerated tax computed under the look-back method, which are used solely for the computation of interest that may be payable by or due to the taxpayer. The year that the contract is completed is known as the "filing year," and the prior years, for which estimated income and expenses are adjusted to actual income and expenses, are known as "redetermination years."[87] Once a contract is completed, a separate look-back computation must be made for each prior year of the contract. Because a taxpayer must recalculate all prior year's estimates, a level of complexity is added to this already complex method.

Example 11-9

Z elected to use the 10% method of IRC §460(b)(5) for reporting income under the percentage of completion method. Z entered into a contract in 1990 for a fixed price of $1,000x. During 1990, Z incurred allocable contract costs of $80x and estimated that it would incur a total of $900x for the entire contract. Since $80x is less than 10% of total estimated contract costs, Z reported no revenue from the contract in 1990 and deferred the $80x of costs incurred. In 1991, Z incurred an additional $620x of contract costs, and completed the contract. Accordingly, in its 1991 return, Z reported the entire contract price of $1,000x, and deducted the $620x of costs incurred in 1991 and the $80x of costs incurred in 1990.

Under IRC §460(b)(5), the 10% method applies both for reporting contract income and the look-back method. Under the look-back method, since the costs incurred in 1990 ($80x) exceed 10% of the actual total contract costs ($700x), Z is required to allocate $114x of contract revenue ($80x/$700x x $1,000x) and the $80x of costs incurred to 1990. Thus,

---

[84] IRC §460(b)(2).
[85] IRC §460(b)(7).
[86] Reg. §1.460-6(a)(1).
[87] Reg. §1.460-6(c).

application of the look-back method results in a net increase in taxable income for 1990 of $34x, solely for purposes of the look-back method.[88]

[B] Exceptions

In general, the look-back method does not apply to the regular taxable income from any long-term construction contract that:

- Is a home construction contract within the meaning of IRC § 460(e)(1)(A), or
- Is *not* a home construction contract but is estimated to be completed within a two-year period by a taxpayer whose average annual gross receipts for the three tax years preceding the tax year in which the contract was formed do not exceed $25 million.[89]

Another exception allows an electing taxpayer not to apply the look-back method in the completion year of a contract if, for each prior contract year, the cumulative taxable income (or loss) actually reported under the contract is within 10% of the cumulative look-back income (or loss).[90]

Under another exception—the *de minimis* exception—the look-back method does not apply to any long-term contract that:

- Is completed within two years of the contract commencement date, and
- Has a gross contract price (as of the completion of the contract) that does not exceed the lesser of $1 million or 1% of the average annual gross receipts of the taxpayer for the three tax years preceding the tax year in which the contract is completed.[91]

[C] Operation of Method of Computing Interest

A standard method of computing interest to be charged or credited to the taxpayer under the look-back method involves three steps.

---

[88] Reg. § 1.460-6(c)(2)(v)(B).

[89] IRC § 460(e)(1)(B). These contracts are not subject to the look-back method for regular tax purposes, even if the taxpayer uses a version of the percentage of completion method permitted under Reg. § 1.451-3, unless the taxpayer has properly changed its method of accounting for these contracts to the percentage of completion method as modified by IRC § 460(b). The look-back method, however, applies to the alternative minimum taxable income from a contract of this type, unless it is exempt from the required use of the percentage of completion method under IRC § 56(a)(3).

[90] IRC § 460(b)(6)(B).

[91] IRC § 460(b)(6)(B). This *de minimis* exception is mandatory and, therefore, precludes application of the look-back method to any contract that meets the requirements of the exception. The *de minimis* exception applies for purposes of computing both regular taxable income and alternative minimum taxable income. For this purpose, the determination of whether a long-term contract meets the gross receipts test for both alternative minimum tax and regular tax purposes is based only on the taxpayer's regular taxable income.

Step 1

The first step in the operation of the look-back method is to reapply, hypothetically, the percentage of completion method to all long-term contracts that are completed or adjusted in the current year (the "filing year"), using the actual, rather than the estimated, total contract price and contract costs. Based on this reapplication, the taxpayer determines the amount of taxable income (and alternative minimum taxable income) that would have been reported for each year prior to the filing year that is affected by contracts completed or adjusted in the filing year if the actual, rather than estimated, total contract price and costs had been used in applying the percentage of completion method to these contracts, and to any other contracts completed or adjusted in a year preceding the filing year.

For taxpayers using the ten-percent method, application of the look-back method could change the year in which the ten-percent threshold is met.[92]

Step 2

The second step in the operation of the look-back method is to compare what the tax liability would have been under the percentage of completion method (as reapplied in the first step) for each tax year for which the tax liability is affected by income from contracts completed or adjusted in the filing year (a "redetermination year") with the most recent determination of tax liability for that year to produce a hypothetical underpayment or overpayment of tax.[93]

Step 3

The third step in the operation of the look-back method is to apply the rate of interest on overpayments designated under IRC § 6621, compounded daily, to the hypothetical underpayment or overpayment of tax for each redetermination year to compute interest that runs, generally, from the due date (determined without regard to extensions) of the return for the redetermination year to the due date (determined without regard to extensions) of the return for the filing year. The net amount of interest computed under the third step is paid by or credited to the taxpayer for the filing year.[94]

[D] Reporting Interest

Interest due or to be refunded is computed and reported on Form 8697, which is attached to the taxpayer's return if interest is due, but filed separately if interest is to be refunded.

---

[92] Reg. § 1.460-6(c)(1).

[93] Reg. § 1.460-6(c)(3).

[94] Reg. § 1.460-6(d) provides a simplified marginal impact method that simplifies the second step—the computation of hypothetical underpayments or overpayments of tax liability for redetermination years—and, in some cases, the third step—the determination of the time period for computing interest.

[E] *Tax Treatment of Interest*

Interest paid is treated as income tax only for the purposes of penalties, such as for the failure to file Form 8697 or the failure to pay the interest due. This interest paid is treated as an interest expense in computing taxable income. Interest received is taxable interest income for all purposes.

Interest received is includible in gross income, and interest paid is deductible in the year properly taken into account under the taxpayer's method of accounting.[95]

§ 11.07 Special Rules

[A] *Terminated Contracts*

The IRC § 460 regulations provide special rules for contracts terminated before completion.[96] If a contract is terminated before completion and the property is retained by the taxpayer, the taxpayer must reverse the income or loss previously recognized under the PCM. Hence, a taxpayer who has reported cumulative losses will have gain in the year of termination and a taxpayer who has reported income will have a loss.[97]

In addition, the regulations say that the look-back method does not apply to terminated contracts.[98]

[B] *Mid-Contract Change in Taxpayer*

Special rules apply to transactions involving the transfer of a contract prior to its completion to a different taxpayer.[99] The rules depend on whether the transaction is a constructive completion transaction or a "step-in-the-shoes" transaction.

[C] *Step-in-the-Shoes Transaction*

The step-in-the-shoes rules generally apply to the following transactions:[100]

- Transfers to which IRC § 361 applies if the transfer is in connection with a reorganization described in IRC § 368(a)(1)(A), (C), or (F);
- Transfers to which IRC § 361 applies if the transfer is in connection with a reorganization described in IRC § 368(a)(1)(D) or (G), provided that the requirements of IRC § 354(b)(1)(A) and (B) are met;

---

[95] Reg. § 1.460-6(f)(2).
[96] Reg. § 1.460-4(b)(7).
[97] Reg. § 1.460-4(b)(7)(i).
[98] Reg. § 1.460-4(b)(7)(iii).
[99] Reg. § 1.460-4(k).
[100] Reg. § 1.460-4(k)(3).

- Distributions to which IRC § 332 applies, provided that the contract is transferred to an 80-percent distributee;
- Transfers described in IRC § 351;
- Transfers to which IRC § 361 applies if the transfer is in connection with a reorganization described in IRC § 368(a)(1)(D) with respect to which the requirements of IRC § 355 (or so much of IRC § 356 as relates to IRC § 355) are met;
- Transfers (*e.g.*, sales) of S corporation stock;
- Conversion to or from an S corporation;
- Members joining or leaving a consolidated group;
- Contributions of contracts accounted for under a long-term contract method of accounting to which IRC § 721(a) applies;
- Contributions of property (other than contracts accounted for under a long-term contract method of accounting) to a partnership that holds a contract accounted for under a long-term contract method of accounting;
- Transfers of partnership interests (other than transfers that cause the partnership to terminate under IRC § 708(b)(1)(A));
- Distributions to which IRC § 731 applies (other than the distribution of the contract); and
- Any other transaction designated in the Internal Revenue Bulletin by the Internal Revenue Service.

[D] Constructive Completion Transaction

The constructive completion rules apply to transactions (constructive completion transactions) that result in a change in the taxpayer responsible for reporting income from a contract and that are not included in the list of step-in-the-shoes transactions.[101] Hence, constructive completion transactions generally apply to taxable sales under IRC § 1001 and deemed asset sales under IRC § 338.

[E] Method of Accounting—Change of Accounting

A taxpayer's method of classifying contracts is a method of accounting under IRC § 446 and, thus may not be changed without the Commissioner's consent. If a taxpayer's method of classifying contracts is unreasonable, that classification method is an impermissible accounting method.[102]

A taxpayer using one or more of the long-term contract methods of accounting set forth below must apply that method consistently for all similarly classified contracts, until the IRS consents to the taxpayer's change to another method of accounting:[103]

---

[101] Reg. § 1.460-4(k)(2)(i).

[102] Reg. § 1.460-1(h)(2).

[103] Reg. § 1.460-4(g).

- the percentage of completion method (PCM);
- the exempt percentage of completion method;
- the percentage of completion/capitalized-cost method;
- the completed contract method;
- the 10% method;
- the elective alternative minimum taxable income method; or
- a method changed to with IRS consent.

Similarly, a taxpayer must consistently use the same cost allocation method for all similarly classified long-term contracts, unless the taxpayer obtains IRS consent under IRC § 446(e) to change to another cost allocation method.[104]

Any change in a taxpayer's method of accounting necessary to comply with the long-term contract rules is a change in method of accounting to which the provisions of IRC § 446 and the regulations thereunder apply. A taxpayer that wants to change its method of accounting under must follow the automatic consent procedures in Rev. Proc. 2018-40[105] and Rev. Proc. 2018-31.[106] Because a change is made on a cut-off basis, an IRC § 481 adjustment is not permitted or required.[107] Moreover, the taxpayer does not receive audit protection.[108]

Any change in method of accounting made under IRC § 460(e)(1)(B)(ii) (the gross receipts test which must be satisfied to qualify for the exception from the requirement to use the percentage of completion method) will be treated as initiated by the taxpayer and made with the consent of the IRS. The change will be effective on a cut-off basis for all similarly classified contracts entered into on or after the year of change.[109]

---

[104] Reg. § 1.460-5(g).

[105] 2018-34 IRB 320.

[106] 2018-22 IRB 637.

[107] Reg. § 1.460-4(g).

[108] Rev. Proc. 2015-14, 2015-5 IRB 450.

[109] IRC § 460(e)(2)(B).

Appendix 11-1 Form 8697

Form **8697**
(Rev. November 2018)
Department of the Treasury
Internal Revenue Service

Interest Computation Under the Look-Back Method for Completed Long-Term Contracts

▶ Go to *www.irs.gov/Form8697* for instructions and latest information.

OMB No. 1545-1031
Attachment Sequence No. **97**

For the filing year beginning , and ending . See instructions.

Type or Print	
Name	**A** Identifying number
Number, street, and apt., room, or suite no. If a P.O. box, see instructions.	**B** Check applicable box to show type of taxpayer: ☐ Corporation ☐ S corporation ☐ Individual ☐ Partnership ☐ Estate or trust
City or town, state, and ZIP code	

C If you were an owner of an interest in a pass-through entity (such as a partnership or an S corporation) that holds one or more long-term contracts to which this interest computation relates, enter the name and employer identification number of the entity. Attach a schedule if there is more than one such entity.

Name of entity	**Employer identification number**

Part I **Regular Method** (see instructions)

	Filing Year	Redetermination Years		(c) Totals (Add columns (a) and (b).)
	Year ended mo. yr.	(a) Year ended mo. yr.	(b) Year ended mo. yr.	
1 Taxable income or loss for the prior years shown on tax return (or as previously adjusted) before net operating loss or capital loss carrybacks (other than carrybacks that must be taken into account to properly compute interest under section 460) (see instructions). If you were required to file Form 8697 for an earlier year, enter adjusted taxable income for the prior years from line 3, Form 8697, for the most recent filing year that affects the prior years . . .				
2 Adjustment to income to reflect the difference between: **(a)** the amount of income required to be allocated for post-February 1986 contracts completed or adjusted during the tax year based on the **actual** contract price and costs, and **(b)** the amount of income reported for such contracts based on **estimated** contract price and costs. See instructions and attach a schedule listing each separate contract, unless you were an owner of an interest in a pass-through entity reporting this amount from Schedule K-1 or a similar statement				
3 Adjusted taxable income for look-back purposes. Combine lines 1 and 2. If line 3 is a negative amount, see instructions				
4 Income tax liability on line 3 amount using tax rates in effect for the prior years (see instructions)				
5 Income tax liability shown on return (or as previously adjusted) for the prior years (see instructions). If you were required to file Form 8697 for an earlier year, enter the amount required to be reported on line 4, Form 8697, for the most recent filing year that affects the prior years .				
6 Increase or decrease in tax for the prior years on which interest is due (or is to be refunded). Subtract line 5 from line 4				
7 Interest due on increase, if any, shown on line 6 (see instructions)				
8 Interest to be refunded on decrease, if any, shown on line 6 (see instructions)				
9 Net amount of **interest to be refunded to you.** If line 8, column (c), exceeds line 7, column (c), enter the excess. File Form 8697 separately; **do not** attach it to your tax return (see instructions)				
10 Net amount of **interest you owe.** If line 7, column (c), exceeds line 8, column (c), enter the excess. Attach Form 8697 to your tax return. See instructions for where to include this amount on your return				

For Privacy Act and Paperwork Reduction Act Notice, see instructions. Cat. No. 64598V Form **8697** (Rev. 11-2018)

Form 8697 (Rev. 11-2018) Page **2**

Part II **Simplified Marginal Impact Method** (see instructions)

		Date of each prior year to which interest computation relates:			(d) Totals (Add columns (a), (b), and (c).)
		(a) Year ended mo. yr.	(b) Year ended mo. yr.	(c) Year ended mo. yr.	
1	Adjustment to regular taxable income to reflect the difference between: **(a)** the amount of such income required to be allocated for post-February 1986 contracts completed or adjusted during the tax year based on **actual** contract price and costs, and **(b)** the amount of such income reported for such contracts based on **estimated** contract price and costs. See instructions and attach a schedule listing each separate contract, unless you were an owner of an interest in a pass-through entity reporting this amount from Schedule K-1 or a similar statement				
2	Increase or decrease in regular tax for prior years. Multiply line 1 in each column by the applicable regular tax rate (see instructions)				
	Note: For prior years beginning before 1987, skip lines 3 and 4 and enter on line 5 the amount from line 2.				
3	Adjustment to alternative minimum taxable income to reflect the difference between: **(a)** the amount of such income required to be allocated for post-February 1986 contracts completed or adjusted during the tax year based on **actual** contract price and costs, and **(b)** the amount of such income reported for such contracts based on **estimated** contract price and costs. See instructions and attach a schedule listing each separate contract, unless you were an owner of an interest in a pass-through entity reporting this amount from Schedule K-1 or a similar statement **Note:** For tax years beginning after 2017, the alternative minimum tax for corporations has been repealed.				
4	Increase or decrease in alternative minimum tax (AMT) for prior years. Multiply line 3 in each column by the applicable AMT rate (see instructions)				
5	Enter the **larger** of line 2 or line 4. See instructions if either amount is negative				
	Pass-through entities: *Skip line 6 and enter on line 7 the amount from line 5.*				
6	Overpayment ceiling. For each column in which line 5 is a negative number, enter your total tax liability for the prior year, as adjusted for past applications of the look-back method and after net operating loss, capital loss, net section 1256 contracts loss, and credit carryovers and carrybacks to that year. For each column in which line 5 is a positive number, leave line 6 blank and enter on line 7 the amount from line 5				
7	Increase or decrease in tax for the prior years on which interest is due (or is to be refunded). Enter the amount from line 5 or line 6, whichever is smaller. Treat both numbers as positive when making this comparison, but enter the amount as a negative number				
8	Interest due on increase, if any, shown on line 7 (see instructions)				
9	Interest to be refunded on decrease, if any, shown on line 7 (see instructions)				
10	Net amount of **interest to be refunded to you.** If line 9, column (d), exceeds line 8, column (d), enter the excess. File Form 8697 separately; **do not** attach it to your tax return (see instructions)				
11	Net amount of **interest you owe.** If line 8, column (d), exceeds line 9, column (d), enter the excess. Attach Form 8697 to your tax return. See instructions for where to include this amount on your return				

Signature(s) Complete this section **only** if this form is being filed separately.

Sign Here

Under penalties of perjury, I declare that I have examined this form, including accompanying schedules and statements, and to the best of my knowledge and belief, it is true, correct, and complete. Declaration of preparer (other than taxpayer) is based on all information of which preparer has any knowledge.

Your signature	Date
Spouse's signature. If a joint return, both must sign	Date

Paid Preparer Use Only

Print/Type preparer's name	Preparer's signature	Date	Check ☐ if self-employed	PTIN
Firm's name ▶			Firm's EIN ▶	
Firm's address ▶			Phone no.	

Form **8697** (Rev. 11-2018)

Appendix 11-2 Instructions for Form 8697

Instructions for Form 8697

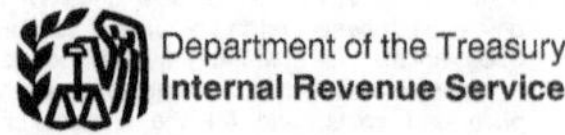

Department of the Treasury
Internal Revenue Service

(Rev. November 2018)

Interest Computation Under the Look-Back Method for Completed Long-Term Contracts

Section references are to the Internal Revenue Code unless otherwise noted.

General Instructions

Future Developments

For the latest information about developments related to Form 8697 and its instructions, such as legislation enacted after they were published, go to *IRS.gov/Form8697*.

What's New

- The tax rate used for the interest computation for individuals, corporations, and certain pass-through entities has changed. See the instructions for Part II, line 2, later.
- The 2-year carryback rule will generally not apply to net operating losses (NOLs) arising in tax years ending after 2017. Exceptions apply to NOLs for farmers and non-life insurance companies. See section 172(b) as amended by P.L. 115-97, section 13302.
- For tax years beginning after 2017, the alternative minimum tax for corporations has been repealed.

Purpose of Form

Use Form 8697 to figure the interest due or to be refunded under the look-back method of section 460(b)(2) on certain long-term contracts that are accounted for under either the percentage of completion method or the percentage of completion-capitalized cost method. For guidance concerning these methods, see Regulations section 1.460-4. For details and computational examples illustrating the use of the look-back method, see Regulations section 1.460-6.

Who Must File

General Rule

You must file Form 8697 for each tax year in which you completed a long-term contract entered into after February 28, 1986, that you accounted for using either the percentage of completion method or the percentage of completion-capitalized cost method for federal income tax purposes. You also must file Form 8697 for any tax year, subsequent to the year of completion, in which the contract price or contract costs are adjusted for one or more of these long-term contracts from a prior year.

Pass-Through Entities

A pass-through entity (partnership, S corporation, or trust) that is not closely held must apply the look-back method at the entity level to any contract for which at least 95% of the gross income is from U.S. sources. A pass-through entity is considered closely held if, at any time during any tax year for which there is income under the contract, 50% or more (by value) of the beneficial interests in the entity is held (directly or indirectly) by or for five or fewer persons. For this purpose, rules similar to the constructive ownership rules of section 1563(e) apply. For a mid-contract change in taxpayer resulting in the conversion of a C corporation into an S corporation, the look-back method is applied at the entity level with respect to contracts entered into prior to the conversion regardless of whether the S corporation is considered closely held. See the section discussing *Mid-Contract Change in Taxpayer.*

If you are an owner of an interest in a pass-through entity in which a long-term contract was being accounted for under the percentage of completion method or the percentage of completion capitalized cost method and the pass-through entity is not subject to the look-back method at the entity level, you must file this form for your tax year that ends with or includes the end of the entity's tax year in which the contract was completed or adjusted in a post-completion tax year. The pass-through entity will provide on Schedule K-1 the information you need to complete this form.

Mid-Contract Change in Taxpayer

If prior to the completion of a long-term contract accounted for using the percentage of completion method or the percentage of completion capitalized cost method, there is a transaction that makes another taxpayer responsible for accounting for income from the same contract, the taxpayer responsible for computing look-back interest depends on whether the ownership change is due to a constructive completion transaction or a step-in-the shoes transaction. For guidance regarding these transactions, see Regulations section 1.460-4(g). In the case of constructive completion transactions, the old taxpayer treats the contract as completed in the transaction year and applies the look-back method to the pre-transaction years. The new taxpayer is treated as entering into a new contract and applies the look-back method to the post-transaction years upon the contract's completion. In the case of step-in-the-shoes transactions, the new taxpayer applies the look-back method to both the pre- and post-transaction years. See Regulations section 1.460-6(g) for additional guidance.

Exception for Certain Construction Contracts

The look-back method does not apply to the regular taxable income from:

- Any home construction contract (as defined in section 460(e)(5)(A)) or
- Any other construction contract entered into by a taxpayer: (a) who estimates the contract will be completed within 2 years from the date the contract begins and (b) whose average annual gross receipts for the 3 tax years preceding the tax year in which the contract is entered into do not exceed $10 million. The annual gross receipts is increased to $25 million (adjusted for inflation) for contracts entered into after 2017. See section 460(e).

However, the look-back method does apply to the alternative minimum taxable income from any such contract that is not a home construction contract and, therefore, must be accounted for using the percentage of completion method for alternative minimum tax purposes. See section 56(a)(3) for details.

Small Contract Exception

The look-back method does not apply to any contract completed within 2 years of the contract start date if the gross price of the contract (as of contract completion) does not exceed the smaller of:

Oct 22, 2018 Cat. No. 10703K

- $1 million or
- 1% of the taxpayer's average annual gross receipts for the 3 tax years before the tax year of contract completion.

See section 460(b)(3)(B) for details.

De Minimis Exception

You may elect not to apply the look-back method in certain de minimis cases for completed contracts. The look-back method does not apply in the following cases if the election is made.

1. In the completion year if, for each prior contract year, the cumulative taxable income (or loss) actually reported under the contract is within 10% of the cumulative look-back income (or loss). Cumulative look-back income (or loss) is the amount of taxable income (or loss) that you would have reported if you had used actual contract price and costs instead of estimated contract price and costs.

2. In a post-completion year if, as of the close of the post-completion year, the cumulative taxable income (or loss) under the contract is within 10% of the cumulative look-back income (or loss) under the contract as of the close of the most recent year in which the look-back method was applied to the contract (or would have been applied if the election had not been made).

For purposes of item 2, discounting under section 460(b)(2) does not apply.

To make the election, attach a statement to your timely filed income tax return (determined with extensions) for the first tax year of the election. Write at the top of the statement "NOTIFICATION OF ELECTION UNDER SECTION 460(b)(6)." Include on the statement your name, identifying number, and the effective date of the election. Also identify the trades or businesses that involve long-term contracts. Once made, the election applies to all contracts completed during the election year and all later tax years, and may not be revoked without IRS consent. See Regulations section 1.460-6(j) for more details. If you timely filed your return without making the election, you may make the election on an amended return filed no later than 6 months after the due date of your tax return (excluding extensions). Write "Filed pursuant to section 301.9100" at the top of the amended return.

Filing Instructions

If You Owe Interest (or No Interest Is To Be Refunded to You)

Attach Form 8697 to your income tax return. The signature section of Form 8697 does not have to be completed by you or the paid preparer.

For individuals, include any interest due in the amount to be entered for total tax (after credits and other taxes) on your return (for example, 2018 Form 1040, line 15). Write on the dotted line to the left of the entry space "From Form 8697" and the amount of interest due.

For partnerships (that are not closely held), write "From Form 8697" and include any interest due in the bottom margin of the tax return. Attach a check or money order for the full amount made payable to "United States Treasury." Write the partnership's employer identification number (EIN), daytime phone number, and "Form 8697 Interest" on the check or money order.

For S corporations that are not closely held, include any interest due in the amount to be entered for additional taxes (for example, 2018 Form 1120S, line 22c). Write on the dotted line to the left of the entry space "From Form 8697" and the amount of interest due. A closely held S corporation would also follow these procedures following a conversion from a C corporation for the contracts entered into prior to the conversion. See the rules related to *Mid-Contract Change in Taxpayer*, earlier.

For closely held pass-through entities, look-back interest is applied at the owner level and not the entity level.

For corporations, include the amount of interest due on the appropriate line of Form 1120, Schedule J, Part I (for example, 2018 Form 1120, Schedule J, line 9c).

Look-back interest owed is not subject to the estimated tax penalty. See Regulations section 1.460-6(f)(2).

If Interest Is To Be Refunded to You

Do not attach Form 8697 to your income tax return. Instead, file Form 8697 separately with the IRS at the applicable address listed below.

- Individuals:

  Department of Treasury
  Internal Revenue Service
  Philadelphia, PA 19255-0001

- All others:

  Department of Treasury
  Internal Revenue Service
  Cincinnati, OH 45999-0001

Complete the signature section of Form 8697 following the instructions for the signature section of your income tax return. If you file a joint return, the signature of both spouses is required on Form 8697. If additional Forms 8697 are needed to show more than 2 redetermination years, sign only the first Form 8697.

File Form 8697 by the date you are required to file your income tax return (including extensions). Keep a copy of Form 8697 and any attached schedules for your records.

Filing a Corrected Form 8697

You must file a corrected Form 8697 only if the amount shown on Part I, line 6, or Part II, line 7, for any prior year changes as a result of an error you made, an income tax examination, or the filing of an amended tax return.

When completing Part I, line 1, of the corrected Form 8697, follow the instructions on the form but do not enter the adjusted taxable income from Part I, line 3, of the original Form 8697. When completing Part I, line 5 (or Part II, line 6), of the corrected Form 8697, do not include the interest due, if any, from Part I, line 10 (or Part II, line 11), of the original Form 8697 that was included in your total tax when Form 8697 was filed with your tax return.

- If both the original and corrected Forms 8697 show an amount on the line for interest you owe, file an amended income tax return.
- If both the original and corrected Forms 8697 show an amount on the line for interest to be refunded to you, write "Amended" in the top margin of the corrected Form 8697, and file it separately.
- If your original Form 8697 shows an amount on the line for interest you owe and the corrected Form 8697 shows an amount on the line for interest to be refunded to you, you must:

  1. File an amended income tax return showing $0 interest from Form 8697 and

  2. File the corrected Form 8697 separately (but do not write "Amended" at the top of the form because this is the first Form 8697 that you will file separately).

- If the original Form 8697 shows an amount on the line for interest to be refunded to you and the corrected Form 8697 shows an amount on the line for interest you owe, you must:

1. File the corrected Form 8697 separately (with "Amended" written at the top) showing $0 interest to be refunded and

2. File an amended income tax return and attach a copy of the corrected Form 8697.

Attachments

If you need more space, attach separate sheets to the back of Form 8697. Put your name and identifying number on each sheet.

Applying the Look-Back Method Under Special Situations

10% Method

For purposes of the percentage of completion method, a taxpayer may elect to postpone recognition of income and expense under a long-term contract entered into after July 10, 1989, until the first tax year as of the end of which at least 10% of the estimated total contract costs have been incurred. For purposes of the look-back method, the recognition of income and expense must be postponed for such contracts until the first tax year as of the end of which at least 10% of the actual total contract costs have been incurred. Therefore, income and expense will be allocated to a different tax year if the first tax year that the 10% threshold is exceeded based on actual costs differs from the first tax year that the 10% threshold is exceeded based on estimated costs. The election to use the 10% method applies to all long-term contracts entered into during the tax year for which the election is made and all later years. See section 460(b)(5) for more details.

Change Orders

A change order for a contract is not treated as a separate contract for purposes of applying the look-back method unless the change order would be treated as a separate contract under the rules for severing and aggregating contracts provided in Regulations section 1.460-1(e). Therefore, if a change order is not treated as a separate contract, that portion of the actual contract price and contract costs attributable to the change order must be taken into account in allocating contract income to all tax years of the contract, including tax years before the change order was agreed to.

Post-Completion Adjustments

General Rule

If the contract price or costs are revised to reflect amounts properly taken into account after the contract completion date for any reason, you must apply the look-back method in the year such amounts are properly taken into account, even if no other contract is completed in that year. Generally, the amount of each such post-completion adjustment to total contract price or contract costs is discounted, solely for look-back purposes, from its value at the time the amount is taken into account in computing taxable income to its value at the time the contract was completed. The discount rate for this purpose is the federal midterm rate under section 1274(d) in effect at the time the amount is properly taken into account.

However, you may elect not to discount post-completion adjustments for any contract. The election not to discount is made on a contract-by-contract basis and is binding with respect to all post-completion adjustments that arise with respect to that contract. To make this election, attach a statement to your timely filed income tax return (determined with extensions) for the first tax year after completion in which you take into account any adjustment to the contract price or contract costs. Indicate on the statement that you are making an election not to discount post-completion adjustments under Regulations section 1.460-6(c)(1)(ii)(C)(2) and identify the contracts to which the election applies.

Delayed Reapplication Method

For purposes of reapplying the look-back method after the year of contract completion, you may elect the delayed reapplication method to minimize the number of required reapplications of the look-back method. Under this method, the look-back method is reapplied after the contract completion year (or after a later reapplication of the look-back method) only when one of the following conditions is met for that contract:

1. The net undiscounted value of increases or decreases in the contract price occurring from the time of the last application of the look-back method exceeds the smaller of $1 million or 10% of the total contract price at that time,

2. The net undiscounted value of increases or decreases in contract costs occurring from the time of the last application of the look-back method exceeds the smaller of $1 million or 10% of the total actual contract costs at that time,

3. The taxpayer goes out of existence,

4. The taxpayer reasonably believes the contract is finally settled and closed, or

5. None of the above conditions (1–4) are met by the end of the 5th tax year that begins after the last previous application of the look-back method.

To elect the delayed reapplication method, attach a statement to your timely filed income tax return (determined with extensions) for the first tax year of the election. Indicate on the statement that you are making an election under Regulations section 1.460-6(e) to use the delayed reapplication method. Once made, the election is binding for all long-term contracts for which you would reapply the look-back method in the absence of the election in the year of the election and all later years, unless the IRS consents to a revocation of the election. See Regulations section 1.460-6(e) for more details.

Specific Instructions

All filers must complete the information at the top of the form above Part I according to the following instructions. Then, complete either Part I or Part II as appropriate. Also sign the form at the bottom of page 2 if interest is to be refunded to you. A signature is not required if you are filing the form with your tax return.

Filing Year

Fill in the filing year line at the top of the form to show the tax year in which the contracts for which this form is being filed were completed or adjusted in a post-completion year. If you were an owner of an interest in a pass-through entity that has completed or adjusted one or more contracts, enter your tax year that ends with or includes the end of the entity's tax year in which the contracts were completed or adjusted.

Name

Enter the name shown on your federal income tax return for the filing year. If you are an individual filing a joint return, also enter your spouse's name as shown on Form 1040.

Address

Enter your address only if you are filing this form separately. Include the apartment, suite, room, or other unit number after the street address. If the Post Office does not deliver mail to the street address and you have a P.O. box, show the box number instead.

Item A—Identifying Number

If you are an individual, enter your social security number. Other filers must use their EIN.

Part I—Regular Method

Use Part I only if you are not electing, do not have an election in effect, or are not required to use the simplified marginal impact method as described in the instructions for Part II, later.

Filing year column

Enter the filing year listed at the top of this form.

Columns (a) and (b)

Enter at the top of each column the ending month and year for:

- Each prior tax year in which you were required to report income from the completed long-term contract(s) and
- Any other tax year affected by such years.

Note. If there were more than 2 prior years, attach additional Forms 8697 as needed. On the additional Forms 8697, enter your name, identifying number, and tax year. Complete lines 1 through 8 (as applicable), but do not enter totals in column (c). Enter totals only in column (c) of the first Form 8697.

Line 1

Do not reduce taxable income or increase a loss on line 1 by any carryback of a net operating loss, capital loss, or net section 1256 contracts loss, except to the extent that carrybacks must be taken into account to properly compute interest under section 460.

Note. The 2-year carryback rule does not apply to net operating losses arising in tax years ending after 2017. An exception applies to farmers and non-life insurance companies. See section 172(b) as amended by P.L. 115-97, section 13302.

Line 2

In each column, show a net increase to income as a positive amount and a net decrease to income as a negative amount.

In figuring the net adjustment to be entered in each column on line 2, be sure to take into account any other income and expense adjustments that may result from the increase (or decrease) to income from long-term contracts (for example, a change to adjusted gross income affecting medical expenses under section 213). If there are no adjustments besides the look-back adjustments, the sum of all line 2 amounts should be zero and reflected in column 2(c). If there are additional adjustments that result from the application of the look-back, leave column 2(c) blank and reflect the amounts in the schedule below as described in item 3.

Include the following on an attached schedule.

1. Identify each completed long-term contract by contract number, job name, or any other reasonable method used in your records to identify each contract.
2. For each contract, report in columns for each prior year: (a) the amount of income previously reported based on estimated contract price and costs and (b) the amount of income allocable to each prior year based on actual contract price and costs. Total the columns for each prior year and show the net adjustment to income from long-term contracts.
3. Identify any other adjustments that result from a change in income from long-term contracts and show the amounts in the columns for the affected years so that the net adjustment shown in each column on the attached schedule agrees with the amounts shown on line 2.

An owner of an interest in a pass-through entity is not required to provide the detail listed in 1 and 2 above with respect to prior years. The entity should provide the line 2 amounts with Schedule K-1 or on a separate statement for its tax year in which the contracts are completed or adjusted.

Note. Taxpayers reporting line 2 amounts from more than one Schedule K-1 (or a similar statement) must attach a schedule detailing by entity the net change to income from long-term contracts.

Line 3

If line 3 results in a negative amount, it represents a look-back net operating loss (NOL). The adjustment in line 2 either created, increased, or decreased the net operating loss. The change in the amount of the net operating loss would be carried back or forward to the appropriate tax year and the hypothetical tax would be recomputed in the carryback/forward year. See Regulations section 1.460-6(c)(3)(v). However, the computation period for computing interest on NOLs is different. See the exceptions listed on lines 7 and 8 below.

Note. The 2-year carryback rule does not apply to net operating losses arising in tax years ending after 2017. An exception applies to farmers and non-life insurance companies. See section 172(b) as amended by P.L. 115-97, section 13302.

Lines 4 and 5

Reduce the tax liability to be entered on lines 4 and 5 by allowable credits (other than refundable credits, for example, the credit for taxes withheld on wages, the earned income credit, the credit for federal tax on fuels, etc.), but do not take into account any credit carrybacks to the prior year in computing the amount to enter on lines 4 and 5 (other than carrybacks that resulted from or were adjusted by the redetermination of your income from a long-term contract for look-back purposes). Include on lines 4 and 5 any taxes (such as alternative minimum tax for individuals) required to be taken into account in the computation of your tax liability (as originally reported or as redetermined).

Lines 7 and 8

For the increase or decrease in tax for each prior year, interest due or to be refunded must be computed at the applicable interest rate and compounded on a daily basis, generally from the due date (not including extensions) of the return for the prior year until the earlier of:

- The due date (not including extensions) of the return for the filing year or
- The date the return for the filing year is filed and any income tax due for that year has been fully paid.

Exceptions:

- The time period for determining interest may be different in cases involving loss or credit carrybacks or carryovers in order to properly reflect the time period during which the taxpayer or IRS had use of the hypothetical underpayment or overpayment. See Regulations section 1.460-6(c)(4)(ii) and (iii) for additional information.

- If a net operating loss, capital loss, net section 1256 contracts loss, or credit carryback is being increased or decreased as a result of the adjustment made to net income from long-term contracts, the interest due or to be refunded must be computed on the increase or decrease in tax attributable to the change to the carryback only from the due date (not including extensions) of the return for the prior year that generated the carryback and not from the due date of the return for the year in which the carryback was absorbed. See section 6611(f).
- In the case of a decrease in tax on line 6, if a refund has been allowed for any part of the income tax liability shown on line 5 for any year as a result of a net operating loss, capital loss, net section 1256 contracts loss, or credit carryback to such year, and the amount of the refund exceeds the amount on line 4, interest is allowed on the amount of such excess only until the due date (not including extensions) of the return for the year in which the carryback arose.

Note. If a different method of interest computation must be used to produce the correct result in your case, use that method and attach an explanation of how the interest was computed.

Applicable Interest Rates

The overpayment rate designated under section 6621 is used to calculate the interest for both hypothetical overpayments and underpayments. The applicable interest rates are published quarterly in revenue rulings in the Internal Revenue Bulletin available at *IRS.gov*.

However, for contracts completed in tax years ending after August 5, 1997, an interest rate is determined for each interest accrual period. The interest accrual period starts on the day after the return due date (not including extensions) for each prior tax year and ends on the return due date for the following tax year. The interest rate in effect for the entire interest accrual period is the overpayment rate determined under section 6621(a)(1) applicable on the first day of the interest accrual period.

Even though the interest rates change quarterly, for look-back purposes the interest rate stays the same for the accrual period which is generally one year. The applicable interest rates for non-corporate taxpayers are shown in Table 1 (for interest accrual periods beginning after Jan. 1, 2008).

The applicable interest rates for corporate taxpayers for the first $10,000 are shown in Table 2. The applicable interest rates for corporate taxpayers for amounts in excess of $10,000 are shown in Table 3.

Following the conversion of a C corporation into an S corporation, the look-back method is applied at the entity level (1120S) with respect to contracts entered into prior to the conversion. See Regulations section 1.460-6(g)(3)(iv). For the C corporation years, the taxpayer would apply the rates reflected in Table 2 for the first $10,000 and apply the rates in Table 3 for the amounts in excess of $10,000.

Line 9

See *If Interest Is To Be Refunded to You*, earlier, for where to file Form 8697. Additional interest to be refunded for periods after the filing date of Form 8697, if any, will be computed by the IRS and included in your refund. Report the amount on line 9 (or the amount refunded by the IRS if different) as interest income on your income tax return for the tax year in which it is received or accrued.

Line 10

See *If You Owe Interest* under *Filing Instructions*, earlier, for how to report this amount on your tax return. Corporations (other than S corporations) may deduct this amount (or the amount computed by the IRS if different) as interest expense for the tax year in which it is paid or incurred. For individuals and other taxpayers, this interest is not deductible.

Estimated Tax Penalty

Look-back interest owed is not subject to the estimated tax penalty. See Regulations section 1.460-6(f)(2)(i). See the instructions for the 2018 Form 2210, line 2, for individuals and 2018 Form 2220, line 2(b), for corporations.

Part II—Simplified Marginal Impact Method

Part II is used only by pass-through entities required to apply the look-back method at the entity level (see *Who Must File*, earlier) and taxpayers electing (or with an election in effect) to use the simplified marginal impact method. Under the simplified method, prior year hypothetical underpayments or overpayments in tax are figured using an assumed marginal tax rate, which is generally the highest statutory rate in effect for the prior year under section 1 (for an individual) or section 11 (for a corporation). This method eliminates the need to refigure your tax liability based on actual contract price and actual contract costs each time the look-back method is applied.

To elect the simplified marginal impact method, attach a statement to your timely filed income tax return (determined with extensions) for the first tax year of the election. Indicate on the statement that you are making an election under Regulations section 1.460-6(d) to use the simplified marginal impact method. Once made, the election applies to all applications of the look-back method in the year of the election and all later years, unless the IRS consents to a revocation of the election.

Columns (a), (b), and (c)

Enter at the top of each column the ending month and year for each prior tax year in which you were required to report income from the completed long-term contract.

Note. If there were more than 3 prior tax years, attach additional Forms 8697 as needed. On the additional Forms 8697, enter your name, identifying number, and tax year. Complete lines 1 through 9 (as applicable), but do not enter totals in column (d). Enter totals only in column (d) of the first Form 8697.

Line 1

In each column, show a net increase to income as a positive amount and a net decrease to income as a negative amount.

On an attached schedule:

- Identify each completed long-term contract by contract number, job name, or any other reasonable method used in your records to identify each contract; and
- For each contract, report in columns for each prior year: (a) the amount of income previously reported based on estimated contract price and costs and (b) the amount of income allocable to each prior year based on actual contract price and costs. Total the columns for each prior year and show the net adjustment to income from long-term contracts.

An owner of an interest in a pass-through entity is not required to provide the detailed schedule listed above for prior years. The entity should provide the line 1 amounts with Schedule K-1 or on a separate statement for its tax year in which the contracts are completed or adjusted.

Note. Taxpayers reporting line 1 amounts from more than one Schedule K-1 (or a similar statement) must attach a schedule detailing by entity the net change to income from long-term contracts.

Line 2

Multiply the amount on line 1 by the applicable regular tax rate for each prior year shown in column (a), (b), or (c). The applicable regular tax rate is as follows:

1. Individuals and pass-through entities in which, at all times during the year, more than 50% of the interests in the entity are held by individuals directly or through other pass-through entities:

a. Tax years beginning before 1987 .... 50%
b. Tax years beginning in 1987 .... 38.5%
c. Tax years beginning in 1988, 1989, or 1990 ... 28%
d. Tax years beginning in 1991 or 1992 .... 31%
e. Tax years beginning in 1993 through 2000 .... 39.6%
f. Tax years beginning in 2001 .... 39.1%
g. Tax years beginning in 2002 .... 38.6%
h. Tax years beginning in 2003 through 2012 .... 35%
i. Tax years beginning in 2013 through 2017 .... 39.6%
j. Tax years beginning in 2018 or later 37%

2. Corporations (other than S corporations) and pass-through entities not included in 1 above:

a. Tax years ending before July 1, 1987 .... 46%
b. For tax years beginning before July 1, 1987, that include July 1, 1987, the rate is 34% plus the following:

$$\frac{\text{Number of days in tax year before 7/1/87}}{\text{Number of days in tax year}} \times 12\%$$

c. Tax years beginning after June 30, 1987, and ending before 1993 .... 34%
d. For tax years beginning before 1993 that include January 1, 1993, the rate is 34% plus the following:

$$\frac{\text{Number of days in tax year after 12/31/92}}{\text{Number of days in tax year}} \times 1\%$$

e. Tax years beginning after 1992, and ending before 2018 .... 35%
f. Tax years beginning after 2017 .... 21%

Line 3

See the instructions for Part II, line 1, earlier, and complete line 3 in the same manner, using only income and deductions allowed for alternative minimum tax (AMT) purposes.

Note. For tax years beginning after 2017, the alternative minimum tax for corporations has been repealed.

Line 4

Multiply the amount on line 3 by the applicable AMT rate, which is as follows:

1. Individuals and pass-through entities in which, at all times during the year, more than 50% of the interests in the entity are held by individuals directly or through other pass-through entities:

a. Tax years beginning in 1987 through 1990 .... 21%
b. Tax years beginning in 1991 or 1992 .... 24%
c. Tax years beginning in 1993 or later 28%

2. Corporations (other than S corporations) and pass-through entities not included in 1 above:

a. Tax years ending before 2018 .... 20%
b. Tax years beginning after 2017 .... 0%

Line 5

If both lines 2 and 4 are negative, enter whichever amount is greater. Treat both numbers as positive when making this comparison, but enter the amount as a negative number. (If the amount on one line is negative, but the amount on the other line is positive, enter the positive amount.)

Lines 8 and 9

For the increase (or decrease) in tax for each prior year, interest due or to be refunded must be computed at the applicable interest rate and compounded on a daily basis from the due date (not including extensions) of the return for the prior year until the earlier of:

- The due date (not including extensions) of the return for the filing year or
- The date the return for the filing year is filed and any income tax due for that year has been fully paid.

See *Applicable Interest Rates* in the instructions for Part I, lines 7 and 8, earlier.

Line 10

See the instructions for Part I, line 9, earlier.

Line 11

See the instructions for Part I, line 10, earlier.

Table 1
Interest Rates for Non-corporate Taxpayers

From	Through	Rate	Table	Page
1/1/08	3/31/08	7%	67	621
4/1/08	6/30/08	6%	65	619
7/1/08	9/30/08	5%	63	617
10/1/08	12/31/08	6%	65	619
1/1/09	3/31/09	5%	15	569
4/1/09	12/31/10	4%	13	567
1/1/11	3/31/11	3%	11	565
4/1/11	9/30/11	4%	13	567
10/1/11	12/31/11	3%	11	565
1/1/12	12/31/12	3%	59	613
1/1/13	12/31/15	3%	11	565
1/1/16	3/31/16	3%	59	613
4/1/16	12/31/16	4%	61	615
1/1/17	3/31/18	4%	13	567
4/1/18	9/30/18	5%	15	569

Table 2
Interest Rates for Corporate Increases or Decreases in Tax of $10,000 or Less

From	Through	Rate	Table	Page
1/1/08	3/31/08	6%	65	619
4/1/08	6/30/08	5%	63	617
7/1/08	9/30/08	4%	61	615
10/1/08	12/31/08	5%	63	617
1/1/09	3/31/09	4%	13	567
4/1/09	12/31/10	3%	11	565
1/1/11	3/31/11	2%	9	563
4/1/11	9/30/11	3%	11	565
10/1/11	12/31/11	2%	9	563
1/1/12	12/31/12	2%	57	611
1/1/13	12/31/15	2%	9	563
1/1/16	3/31/16	2%	57	611
4/1/16	12/31/16	3%	59	613
1/1/17	3/31/18	3%	11	565
4/1/18	9/30/18	4%	13	567

Table 3
Interest Rates for Corporate Increases or Decreases in Tax Exceeding $10,000

From	Through	Rate	Table	Page
1/1/08	3/31/08	4.5%	62	616
4/1/08	6/30/08	3.5%	60	614
7/1/08	9/30/08	2.5%	58	612
10/1/08	12/31/08	3.5%	60	614
1/1/09	3/31/09	2.5%	10	564
4/1/09	12/31/10	1.5%	8	562
1/1/11	3/31/11	.5%	–	–
4/1/11	9/30/11	1.5%	8	562
10/1/11	3/31/16	.5%	–	–
4/1/16	12/31/16	1.5%	56	610
1/1/17	3/31/18	1.5%	8	562
4/1/18	9/30/18	2.5%	10	564

Example of Applicable Interest Rates for Look-back Interest. A C corporation taxpayer completed contracts subject to look-back interest during the 2017 calendar year. The contracts were started in 2015, so 2015 and 2016 are redetermination years. The corporate tax return due date, without extensions, for all years is April 15.

For computing look-back interest, the interest rates and accrual period for the 2015 redetermination year would be:

- 4/16/2016 – 4/15/2017: 3% for the 1st $10,000 (1.5% for any amount exceeding $10,000).
- 4/16/2017 – 4/15/2018: 3% for the 1st $10,000 (1.5% for any amount exceeding $10,000).

The interest rate and accrual period for the 2016 redetermination year would be:

- 4/16/2017 – 4/15/2018: 3% for the 1st $10,000 (1.5% for any amount exceeding $10,000).

Privacy Act and Paperwork Reduction Act Notice. We ask for the information on this form to carry out the Internal Revenue laws of the United States. We need this information to ensure that you are complying with these laws and to figure and collect or refund the correct amount of interest.

Section 460 provides special rules for computing interest under the look-back method for completed long-term contracts. Section 6001 and its regulations require you to file a return or statement with us for any tax you are liable for. Section 6109 and its regulations require you to put your identifying number on what you file. If you do not provide the information we ask for, or provide fraudulent information, you may forfeit any refund of interest otherwise owed to you and/or be subject to penalties.

You are not required to provide the information requested on a form that is subject to the Paperwork Reduction Act unless the form displays a valid OMB control number. Books or records relating to a form or its instructions must be retained as long as their contents may become material in the administration of any Internal Revenue law. Generally, tax returns and return information are confidential, as required by section 6103.

We may give this information to the Department of Justice for civil or criminal litigation, and to other federal agencies as authorized by law. We may give it to cities, states, the District of Columbia, and U.S. commonwealths or possessions to carry out their tax laws. We may give it to foreign governments because of tax treaties they have with the United States. We also may disclose this information to federal and state agencies to enforce federal nontax criminal laws and to combat terrorism.

The time needed to complete and file this form will vary depending on individual circumstances. The estimated burden for individual taxpayers filing this form is approved under OMB control number 1545-0074 and is included in the estimates shown in the instructions for their individual income tax return. The estimated burden for all other taxpayers who file this form is shown below.

Recordkeeping	
Part I	8 hr., 36 min.
Part II	9 hr., 19 min.
Learning about the law or the form	
Part I	2 hr., 22 min.
Part II	2 hr., 5 min.
Preparing, copying, assembling, and sending the form to the IRS	
Part I	2 hr., 37 min.
Part II	2 hr., 19 min.

If you have comments concerning the accuracy of these time estimates or suggestions for making this form simpler, we would be happy to hear from you. You can send us comments from *IRS.gov/FormComments*. Or you can send your comments to Internal Revenue Service, Tax Forms and Publications Division, 1111 Constitution Ave. NW, IR-6526, Washington, DC 20224. Don't send the tax form to this office. Instead, see *Filing Instructions*, earlier.

12

Accounting for Income Taxes by Marty D. Van Wagoner, CPA

§12.01 Accounting for Income Taxes

[A] An Overview

As this text is primarily based on the Federal Income Tax Code, this chapter will provide an abbreviated "plain English" overview of the principles addressed in Accounting for Income Taxes. Guidance for these principles are in the FASB ASC, the single body of authoritative literature for U.S. GAAP. Specifically, the guidance for Accounting for Income Taxes found in FASB ASC Topic 740.

The acronyms above will be used throughout the book and have the following meaning:

FASB	Financial Accounting Standards Board
ASC	Accounting Standards Codification
ASU	Accounting Standards Update
GAAP	Generally Accepted Accounting Principles
U.S. GAAP	Accounting Principles Generally Accepted in the United States of America
Topic 740	References to FASB ASC Topic 740 may be shortened to just Topic 740

Keep in mind that these materials primarily address the U.S. GAAP rules, not the Internal Revenue Code. In commonly used jargon, U.S. GAAP addresses "book" accounting, not "tax" accounting. However, the very reason this topic is even an accounting issue is because there are differences in the way we account for things in accordance with U.S. GAAP and the way we account for income and deduction items under tax laws. It is precisely those differences that give rise to the need for deferred tax assets and liabilities and the other issues that comprise this topic. Therefore, some understanding of tax law is required to properly understand and apply the material. It is usually best to have those with tax expertise to work closely with those who have U.S. GAAP expertise in order to properly account for these items.

The basic steps we follow in accounting for income taxes are:

1. Calculate current taxes payable or receivable.
2. Identify differences between the book basis and tax basis of assets and liabilities.
3. Determine, for each difference, whether it will result in taxes paid in the future; that is, a future tax obligation; or a future tax benefit.
4. Apply an appropriate tax rate to the difference to calculate a deferred tax.
5. Classify differences that result in a future tax obligation as deferred tax liabilities and those that result in a future tax benefit as deferred tax assets.
6. Determine if a valuation allowance is required for any or all deferred tax assets.

After we address a few more basic concepts, we will address each of the steps above in more detail. We will also address items related to these steps, such as a net operating loss, which has a tax rate applied to it in order to calculate a deferred tax asset; and tax credits, carryforwards and carrybacks.

More detailed topics to be addressed include uncertainty in income taxes, intraperiod tax allocations, and disclosure requirements.

[B] Asset and Liability Method

We use the asset and liability approach to account for income taxes. This concept can be perceived in three different ways. First, we focus on the balance sheet and let changes run through the income statement. That is, we calculate the proper current and deferred assets and/or liabilities and adjust them by recording income tax expense or benefit on the income statement.

Second, we use the difference between the book basis and the tax basis of assets and liabilities for our calculations, not the difference between book revenue/expenses and taxable income/deductions.

Third, we use the definition of an asset and a liability to guide us in proper recognition. This can best be shown with an example. The most commonly identified difference between books and taxes is depreciation. Generally, books use a straight-line approach and taxes use MACRS (Modified Accelerated Cost Recovery System), which is, as the name implies, an accelerated method. The following diagram shows how the depreciation expense is recorded over time:

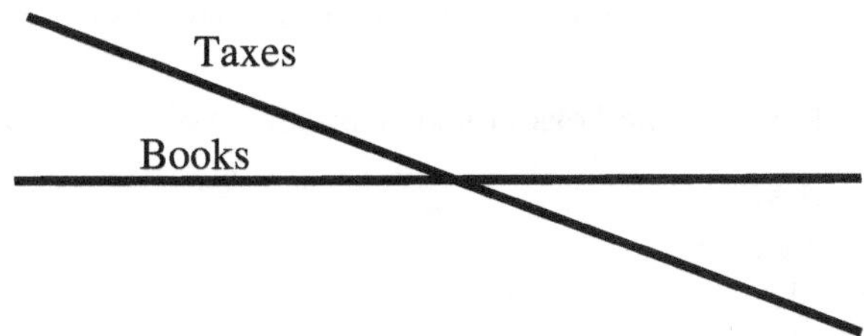

Think about it this way – because MACRS is used for taxes, the earlier years will provide a company a greater deduction, or benefit, for tax purposes than the book expense would give. In later years, less depreciation will be taken for taxes than for books. We refer to that as the book-tax difference reversing. When it reverses, the company will have to pay more taxes than its books would indicate. Because it has to pay more in the future than would be expected from its net income, that is a future obligation. It meets the definition of a liability. A difference that goes the other way would provide a future economic benefit to the company, which is the definition of an asset. As noted above, we do not calculate deferred assets and liabilities on the differences in depreciation expense. Rather, the calculations are based on the differences in net fixed assets. This allows the differences to be identified based on accumulated information rather than just for one year, resulting in more proper measurement of the differences and their eventual reversals.

[C] Current Tax Assets and Liabilities

The first step in the process of accounting for income taxes is the calculation of a current tax asset or liability. This is simply the amount of tax refund or tax payable calculated on the tax return.

This concept is simple but there is a bit of a challenge in its implementation. The challenge is that a tax return is generally completed *after* the financial statements are prepared and, if those financial statements are audited, the tax return uses the completed, audited financial statements as a starting point for the income tax return. Therefore, an estimate is generally used in the preparation of the financial statements and the accuracy of that estimate is assessed by the auditors. A very common way of calculating that estimate is by preparing a tax provision.

[D] Tax Provision

The primary purpose of a tax provision is to provide an estimate of current tax expense or benefit in the financial statements. Depending on tax amounts paid during the year, that calculation also provides an estimate of the current tax refund receivable or the amount payable.

The tax provision is calculated by following the steps to prepare a tax return in order to calculate an estimate of taxable income. However, the tax provision is also calculated by beginning with net income according to U.S. GAAP and making adjustments to arrive at a taxable income from which a current tax expense or benefit may be calculated.

The following is a simplified example of a tax provision:

Net income (U.S. GAAP)	$726,453
Adjustments to net income	
50% of meals	16,274
Key man life insurance premiums	12,000
Interest income from non-taxable municipal bonds	(23,478)
Tax depreciation in excess of books	(63,552)
Bad debt expense in excess of write-offs	24,663
Non-deductible expenses recorded for reserves	48,559
Taxable income	$740,919
Multiplied by tax rate	21 %
Estimated tax expense	$155,593
Less amounts paid during the year	144,000
Taxes payable (refund receivable)	$11,593

Note that this provision is simplified. There may be more adjustments to bring net income for U.S. GAAP to a taxable income. In addition, the tax rate shown does not take into consideration any graduated tax rates, should they exist. In a period when graduated rates are applicable, they should be considered. Any applicable state or local tax rate should be considered, as well.

Although a tax provision is primarily used to estimate current amounts, it is also helpful in identifying deferred amounts, which will be discussed in detail later. The reason this is the case is that most differences have an impact on current and deferred taxes. Again using depreciation as an example, the difference between book depreciation expense for a year and tax depreciation expense for a year should be one of the adjustment items in the tax provision in order to calculate an estimate of taxable income. The difference between the tax basis and book basis of net fixed assets is used in calculating deferred tax amounts. The difference in the expense for the current year is a portion of the difference in the net asset due to the impact of accumulated depreciation. Therefore, the provision helps in the identification of temporary differences for deferred taxes, as well as in the calculation of current taxes.

§ 12.02 Identifying Tax Differences

The best way to identify tax differences is to have experience in this area and to know where to look. Of course, that is not very helpful for those who do not yet have that kind of experience.

A company may prepare a tax basis balance sheet and roll it forward from year to year. This can be a very helpful tool in identifying differences between books and tax. It is also helpful in ensuring accuracy in a company's tax return preparation. However, this seems to be seldom done—particularly in small companies.

In the absence of a tax balance sheet, one may look at the tax returns in previous years and compare them to the financial statements for those years. In particular, it is helpful to examine Schedule M-1,[1] which shows a reconciliation of income or loss per books with income per the return. If done appropriately, this will identify items with differences. In case such things are not available or if their accuracy may be uncertain, we will provide examples of the primary types of differences in a later section.

§ 12.03 Differences Without Future Tax Consequences

A reference was made earlier to the "reversing" of book-tax differences. The example given was depreciation, where a larger amount is deducted for taxes than books in an asset's early years, but the book expense is higher than the tax deduction in later years. However, some differences do not reverse. Traditionally, those differences are called permanent differences. While Topic 740 still uses the term temporary differences, it no longer uses the term permanent differences. It simply refers to such items as differences without future tax consequences, or basis differences that are not temporary differences. Notwithstanding, many practitioners still use the term permanent differences for such items.

Differences without future tax consequences do not result in deferred tax assets or liabilities because there is no future obligation or benefit arising from such differences. They will never reverse.

Examples of differences without future tax consequences are:

- tax penalties and fines;
- the 50% limitation on deductibility of meals;
- key man life insurance premiums;
- proceeds from key man life insurance policies;
- interest income from investments in non-taxable municipal bonds;
- nondeductible goodwill amortization under the purchase method for acquisitions;
- certain start-up costs, such as the cost of raising capital for a new business;
- special dividends received deduction;
- book depreciation expense in excess of the amount allowed by tax law;
- percentage depletion of natural resources in excess of their cost; and
- certain compensation related to some forms of stock option plans.

---

[1] *See* Appendix 12-1.

In addition, there are certain items specified in Topic 740 that may reverse in the foreseeable future, in which case they would result in deferred taxes, but generally do not. These items are rare and some apply to older transactions. Examples provided for these items are:

- basis of an investment in a foreign subsidiary or a foreign corporate joint venture that is essentially permanent in duration;
- undistributed earnings of a domestic subsidiary or a domestic corporate joint venture that is essentially permanent in duration that arose in fiscal years beginning on or before December 15, 1992 using a last-in, first-out (LIFO) pattern;
- bad debt reserves for tax purposes of U.S. Savings and loan associations (and other qualified thrift lenders) that arose in tax years beginning before December 31, 1987; and
- policyholders' surplus of stock life insurance entities that arose in fiscal years beginning on or before December 15, 1992.

Finally, there are certain other items identified as exceptions from the basic requirements of calculating deferred tax assets or liabilities from temporary differences:

- after-tax income for leveraged leases or allocation of purchase price in a purchase business combination to acquired leveraged leases;
- intra-entity transfers of inventory from one tax-paying component to another of the same consolidated group; and
- items remeasured from the local currency into the functional currency under certain conditions.

§ 12.04 Temporary Differences

In opposition to the section above, temporary differences are those which do reverse over time and will result in deferred tax assets or liabilities. These can be categorized into four basic areas, with a few additional items outside of those areas.

The four basic areas are:

1. revenues or gains that are taxable *after* they are recognized in financial income;
2. revenues or gains that are taxable *before* they are recognized in financial income;
3. expenses or losses that are deductible *after* they are expensed in financial income; and
4. expenses or losses that are deductible *before* they are expensed in financial income.

The additional items are:

1. reduction in the tax basis of depreciable assets because of tax credits;
2. investment tax credits accounted for by the deferral method;
3. increase in tax basis of assets because of indexing whenever the local currency is the functional currency; and
4. business combinations and combinations of not-for-profit entities.

Common examples of temporary differences in the four basic areas identified above are:

1. revenues or gains that are taxable *after* they are recognized in financial income:
   a. installment sales;
   b. construction revenue when completed contract method is used for taxes and percentage-of-completion is used for books;
   c. unremitted earnings of foreign subsidiaries; and
   d. unrealized gains on marketable securities.
2. revenues or gains that are taxable *before* they are recognized in financial income:
   a. subscriptions received in advance; and
   b. rent received in advance, or any other similar revenue item when payment is received before the revenue is earned in accordance with financial accounting rules—generally titled deferred revenues or unearned revenues.
3. expenses or losses that are deductible *after* they are expensed in financial income:
   a. product warranty liability;
   b. allowance for doubtful accounts;
   c. inventory obsolescence reserves and other similar liabilities;
   d. many accruals;
   e. liabilities for contingencies;
   f. amortization of goodwill and other intangible assets when the private company council option is used and the asset is amortized more quickly for books than for taxes;
   g. unrealized losses from marketable securities; and
   h. impairment losses.
4. expenses or losses that are deductible *before* they are expensed in financial income:
   a. accelerated depreciation;
   b. amortization of goodwill and other intangible assets unless the private company council option is used;
   c. capitalized interest; and
   d. certain software development costs.

Keep in mind, although the categories above are related to differences in revenues and expenses, temporary differences result from differences in assets and liabilities. For example, the first example listed is installment sales. The difference used to calculate deferred tax assets or liabilities would actually be the difference in accounts receivable. Book basis accounts receivable would include the entire amount of revenue for the items that were sold, less any payments already received, while tax basis accounts receivable would be zero because revenue is only recognized when the installment payment is received. The difference in revenue during the year is used in the calculation of the tax provision but the difference in accounts receivable is used to arrive at a deferred tax liability after following the additional steps in the process.

§ 12.05 Are Differences Taxable or Deductible

Once we are able to identify book-tax differences and the amount of those differences, we then need to determine if those differences result in payment of higher taxes in the future or a reduction in the payment of future taxes.

Determining if a difference is taxable or deductible refers to what will happen in the future as a result of that difference. If more taxes will be paid in the future, it is a taxable difference. If less taxes will be paid in the future, it is a deductible difference. Returning to our depreciation example, an accelerated depreciation method for tax purposes means a higher deduction is taken in early years for tax purposes than the expense recorded for books. Net fixed assets are reported at a higher amount for books than for taxes in those early years. In the future, the difference will reverse between the book basis of those fixed assets and their tax basis. When that happens, more expense will be taken for books than the deduction taken for tax. So taxes will be paid on a higher taxable net income than book net income in those future years. In other words, more tax will be paid in the future than would have been paid using book net income. Therefore, it is a taxable difference because of that higher tax that will be paid in the future.

In contrast to the above example, consider accounts receivable, net of an allowance for doubtful accounts. Bad debt expense is recorded to establish or increase the allowance for doubtful accounts. That results in a decrease of net income. However, a deduction for tax purposes cannot be taken until the account receivable is actually written off. Therefore, a current book expense is recorded but the tax deduction will be taken in the future. Therefore, the difference between book and tax net accounts receivable would be a deductible difference.

§ 12.06 Applicable Tax Rate

After identifying whether temporary differences are taxable or deductible, an applicable tax rate is applied to each difference in order to calculate a deferred tax asset or liability.

The applicable tax rate to be used in the U.S. federal tax jurisdiction is the regular tax rate. In jurisdictions where an alternative minimum tax (AMT), or something similar, is used, no alternative minimum tax rate should be used. The only consideration of alternative minimum tax is any credit carryforward that results. Such a credit carryforward will be reflected as a deferred tax asset like other credit carryforwards, which are addressed in a later section. The Tax Cuts and Jobs Act of 2017 (TCJA) eliminated the corporate AMT in the United States of America so AMT credit carryforwards, after those already existing are used up, will only be applicable to other jurisdictions where such a tax may exist.

Ideally, the tax rate to be used would be the rate that will be applicable when the difference reverses. That would result in an accurate asset or liability. Since we may not be certain of the rate that will then be in place because of possible changes in tax law that could occur, we use existing law to determine the rate to be used. We must use rates identified by currently enacted tax law. If a law has been passed that identifies 25% as the tax rate for the current year and 27% in the next year, and the difference is expected to reverse in the next year, 27% would be the properly applicable tax rate to use. Estimates or expectations may not be used; only tax rates that have been enacted into law. A discounted basis may not be used so there are no time-value of money calculations used to calculate deferred assets or liabilities. In the United States, the tax rate set by the TCJA is 21%. Because that is the currently enacted tax rate, it will be used for U.S. federal income taxes.

Additionally, graduated tax rates should be considered when applicable. If, during a period in which a difference is expected to reverse, an entity's taxable income falls in a range that would require the use of graduated tax rates, the rate to be used will be an average graduated tax rate expected to be applicable in the year of reversal.

§12.07 Deferred Tax Assets and Liabilities

After following each of the preceding steps, it is easy to arrive at deferred tax assets and liabilities. Applying the applicable tax rate to a taxable difference results in a deferred tax liability. Doing the same to a deductible difference results in a deferred tax asset.

§12.08 Net Operating Losses, Tax Credits, Carryforwards and Carrybacks

Temporary differences are not the only things that result in a deferred tax asset. Net operating losses (NOLs) and credits also result in deferred tax assets.

Net operating losses can be carried forward to offset net taxable income in a different year. A taxable loss may be carried forward for the next 20 years.[2]

When the net operating loss is carried forward, it results in a deferred tax asset because there would be a future benefit from the use of that NOL. In that case, the NOL would be multiplied by an applicable tax rate to calculate the resulting deferred tax asset.

Certain tax credits may also be carried back and/or forward. A loss reduces taxable income, which then has a tax rate applied to calculate the amount of tax. A credit reduces taxes directly, with no rate applied. Therefore, a credit carryback will result in a tax refund receivable in the amount of the credit. A credit carryforward results in a deferred tax asset of the same amount as the credit carryforward.

---

[2] Under the TCJA, net operating losses (NOLs) may no longer be carried back but may be carried forward indefinitely. However, the five-year carryback period for farming losses is reduced to two years and a two-year carryback and 20-year carryforward period is retained for insurance companies other than life insurance companies. A net operating loss may only reduce 80% of taxable income in a carryback or carryforward tax year.

§ 12.09 Valuation Allowance

Any asset recorded assumes the asset will provide future benefit. If the future benefit of a deferred tax asset is questionable, a valuation allowance should be recorded to reduce the amount of the asset.

A valuation allowance is similar to an allowance for doubtful accounts related to accounts receivable or an inventory obsolescence reserve. It is a contra-asset used so the net book value of the asset reflects the amount at which the asset will be realized.

A valuation allowance is recorded for all or a portion of any deferred tax asset which is more likely than not to not be realized.

In assessing the need for a valuation allowance, an entity must consider positive and negative evidence that the asset will be realized. Information about an entity's financial position and results of operations are considered. When a deferred tax asset arises from an NOL or tax credit carryforward, additional items that may be considered are future settlement of deferred tax liabilities against which the deferred tax asset may be offset, future taxable income exclusive of reversing temporary differences and carryforwards, taxable income in prior carryback periods when carryback is permitted by law, and tax-planning strategies. Examples of tax planning strategies are the acceleration of taxable amounts, a change in the character of certain items from ordinary income to capital gain, or a change of certain items such as investments from tax-exempt to taxable. Tax-planning strategies must be prudent and feasible, an action the entity normally might not take but would do so in order to not lose the NOL or tax credit carryforward, and would result in realization of deferred tax assets.

Examples of negative evidence are a history of NOL or tax credit carryforwards expiring unused; losses expected in early future years; unsettled circumstances that could adversely affect future operations; and a carryback or carryforward period so brief that its use is doubtful.

Examples of positive evidence are existing contracts or firm sales backlog; excess of appreciated asset value over the tax basis of net assets; or a strong earnings history exclusive of the specific loss that caused the NOL, along with evidence such earnings are likely to return in the near future.

After consideration of positive and negative evidence, professional judgment must be used to assess the need for a valuation allowance and, if needed, the amount that should be recorded.

§ 12.10 Classification as Long-term or Short-term

There is a recent change in the guidance for classification of deferred tax assets and liabilities as current or noncurrent. Because of FASB ASU 2015-17, all deferred tax assets and liabilities are to be classified as noncurrent after the effective date. For public companies, the amendments in the update are effective for years beginning after December 15, 2016 and, for all other entities, they are effective for years beginning after December 15, 2017.

Although those effective dates are now past, some financial statements may yet be prepared for previous periods so we will present the guidance that was previously applicable.

Under previous guidance, there were two approaches to classifying deferred tax assets and liabilities as current or noncurrent. If the deferred tax asset or liability arose from an asset or liability, it was classified the same as the asset or liability from which it arose. For example, a deferred tax liability related to depreciation differences was classified as noncurrent because it arose from the book-tax difference in fixed assets, which are noncurrent. A deferred tax asset related to bad debt expense would have been current because it arose from the book-tax difference in accounts receivable, which are current.

If a deferred tax asset or liability arose from something other than an asset or liability, such as a deferred tax asset based on an NOL, it would be classified based on when it was expected to reverse. If the NOL would entirely be used up in the next year because of expected net income in that year, the associated deferred tax asset would be current. If the NOL would not be used until after a year, the deferred tax asset would be noncurrent. If some would be used within a year and the rest after a year, the related deferred tax asset would be partially current and partially noncurrent.

Any valuation allowance would be allocated to current and noncurrent on a pro rata basis.

§12.11 Putting it All Together

To review the basic steps we follow in accounting for income taxes:

1. Calculate current taxes payable or receivable.
2. Identify differences between the book basis and tax basis of assets and liabilities.
3. Determine, for each difference, whether it will result in taxes paid in the future; that is, a future tax obligation; or a future tax benefit.
4. Apply an appropriate tax rate to the difference to calculate a deferred tax.
5. Classify differences that result in a future tax obligation as deferred tax liabilities and those that result in a future tax benefit as deferred tax assets.
6. Determine if a valuation allowance is needed for any or all deferred tax assets.

Each of these steps are addressed in more detail in the preceding sections. Now let us put them all together in a spreadsheet.

There are a variety of different models to follow in a variety of spreadsheets that have been developed. The following is just one example of such a spreadsheet. It lists the book basis and tax basis of each of the assets and liabilities that are different for books and taxes. The difference between those bases is calculated and classified as deductible or taxable. A tax rate is then applied to calculate deferred tax assets for those that are deductible and deferred tax liabilities for those that are taxable. If there is an NOL, it is then multiplied by the applicable tax rate to arrive at a deferred tax asset. Any tax credit carryforwards do not have a tax rate applied; they are simply recorded as deferred tax assets. After all amounts are totaled, it is determined whether or not a valuation allowance is needed. If so, it is calculated and deducted from the deferred tax asset, arriving at a net total of deferred tax assets and deferred tax liabilities.

Assets & liabilities	Book Basis	Tax Basis	Differences Deductible	Taxable	Tax Rate	Def Tax Assets	Def Tax Liab
Accounts Receivable	xxx	xxx	xxx		xx%	xxx	
Inventory	xxx	xxx	xxx		xx%	xxx	
Fixed assets	xxx	xxx		xxx	xx%		xxx
Accruals and reserves etc . . .	xxx	xxx	xxx		xx%	xxx	
Net Operating Loss			xxx		xx%	xxx	
Tax credit carryforwards					—	xxx	—
Totals						xxxx	xxxx
Valuation Allowance						(xxx)	
Net						xxxx	xxxx

Presentation of this information on the face of the financial statements and in the footnotes is further discussed in a later section.

§ 12.12 Uncertainty in Income Taxes

Whenever an income tax return is prepared, certain tax positions are taken. Sometimes those positions may be questioned. A tax position is taken when a preparer decides how to identify, recognize and measure taxable revenues and deductible expenses or other tax-related matters. Some tax positions are easily taken, with clear, strong support in tax law or cases. Other positions may be in more of a gray area and are more easily questioned.

ASC 740 requires the application of a more-likely-than-not criterion to recognize tax positions. That is, the likelihood of the tax position to be sustained upon examination is greater than 50%. In making such an assessment, the following presumptions are required:

- the tax position will be examined by the relevant taxing authority and that taxing authority has full knowledge of all relevant information (Whether or not the position is actually examined is irrelevant. Application of the more-likely-than-not criterion requires us to *presume* it will be examined.);
- technical merits of the tax position are derived from tax law, including legislation and statutes, legislative intent, regulations, rulings and case law, and their applicability to the tax position; and
- tax positions are evaluated individually, with no offset or aggregation with other positions.

When the more-likely-than-not criteria is not met in a particular period, it should be monitored to see if it is met in a later period. This could result from a change in law, a change in facts and circumstances, passing of a statute of limitations, or the tax position may be effectively settled through examination, negotiation or litigation.

With certain positions, there may be an incremental probability of the position being sustained. In such cases, we should look at the position in increments, not in total. For example, say a company claims a $100 deduction on its tax return. Instead of the possible amounts to be recognized being either the full $100 or zero, it might be more appropriate to recognize a portion of the total amount. Management may determine that only a portion will be disallowed, not the entire $100. It may decide there is only a 25% likelihood of the entire $100 being sustained. But it may also determine there is a 20% likelihood of $80 being sustained and a 20% likelihood that $60 will be sustained. We must look at the cumulative likelihood in order to determine when the more-likely-than-not threshold is passed. It's certainly not passed for the full $100, which is only 25%. There is a cumulative probability of 45% that at least $80 will be sustained. There is a cumulative probability of 65% that at least $60 will be sustained, which has now passed the 50% mark. So $60 would be the amount that should be recognized as a deduction for this item.

Now let's look at the proper accounting for the situation described in the previous paragraph. Assume management is aggressive and claims the entire $100 deduction on the company's tax return. Are they being dishonest or unethical? Perhaps, but not necessarily. Being more aggressive does not always equate to being dishonest. Some people would rather not deal with an IRS investigation or have their positions questioned, so they may be more conservative. Others may believe they have a supportable position, even though it may be questioned, and are willing to negotiate, and maybe even litigate, with the IRS in support of their position. Given the example we have been using, some might claim $100 on a tax return, some $80, some $60 and some even less than that. The point is that there is a wide range of positions taken. We must know how to account for whatever position is taken.

For purposes of this discussion, we can identify positions that meet the more-likely-than-not criterion to be relatively certain positions. If an entity takes a position that does not meet that criterion, it would be deemed an uncertain tax position. As explained above, the entire position might not be an uncertain tax position—only the portion that does not meet the criterion. In the example above, if an entity claimed the entire $100 as a deduction on its tax return, $40 would be an uncertain tax position. Because it is more-likely-than-not an examination would overturn or disallow that portion of the position, we must assume the taxes related to that portion of the deduction will later have to be paid, probably with interest and penalties, so we record a liability for the tax effect of that amount.

Traditionally, the diagram used to reflect deferred tax assets and liabilities has been as follows:

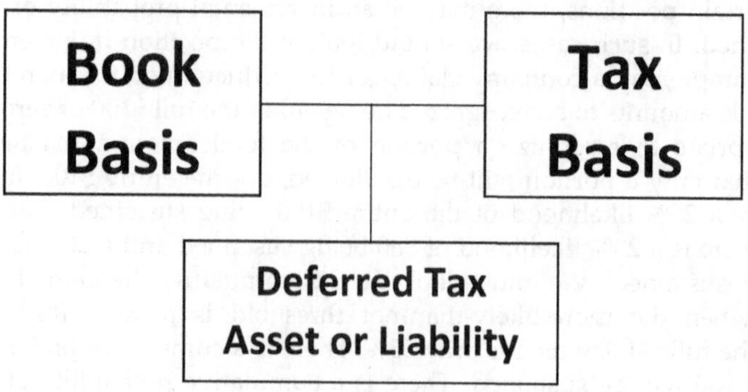

When considering uncertainty in income taxes, we add another box to the diagram:

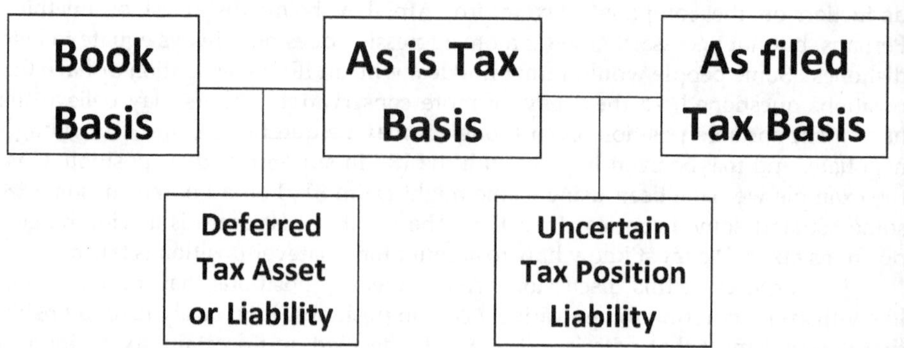

As described above, a liability arises from the difference between what is actually filed on the tax return and what meets the more-likely-than-not criterion and, therefore, what should be recorded. This amount is interchangeably called an Uncertain Tax Position (UTP) Liability or an Unrecognized Tax Benefit (UTB) because it is benefit claimed on the return that should not be recognized. We will generally refer to it as a UTP.

The UTP cannot be netted against or appended to the deferred tax asset or liability except in one situation. When the deferred tax asset arises from an NOL, the UTP is netted against that deferred tax asset. Presumably, the deduction claimed on the tax return increases any tax loss taken and has thus increased the NOL. A reduction in that deduction would cause a reduction in the NOL so it can be used to offset, or reduce, the amount of the deferred tax asset arising from the NOL.

It may also be important to note that any uncertain tax position recorded in the financial statements requires a Schedule UTP[3] to be filed with an entity's tax return.

---

[3] *See* Appendix 12-2.

§12.13 Intraperiod Tax Allocations

This topic is more complex than can reasonably be addressed in this brief overview. It is an area that does not impact many entities; but, unfortunately, there are some it does impact, or *should* impact, and sometimes they do not properly implement it.

Intraperiod tax allocations become an issue when an entity has other taxable categories besides operating income. For example, an entity may have discontinued operations, which require gains and losses to be shown net of tax, after net income. Another example are items that go directly to equity, such as other comprehensive income items. When such items exist, an entity should follow the guidance in ASC 740 to calculate the amount of income tax expense or benefit to properly apply to each of the items.

§12.14 When an Entity Is Part of a Consolidated Tax Return

Occasionally, a reporting entity is part of a consolidated entity for tax purposes and does not file a stand-alone tax return. That fact does not excuse such an entity from following the guidance in ASC 740. Some reasonable allocation must be made of tax expenses and benefits, tax payables and receivables, and deferred tax assets and liabilities.

Assume an entity has a consolidated loss and, therefore, no income tax expense. It is not reasonable to assume that all subsidiaries are able to individually report no tax expense. It may be the case that some entities in the group have losses and others have gains. Those with losses would likely report income tax benefits while those with gains would report income tax expense. The preferred method for making a proper allocation is to follow the guidance in ASC 740 for each entity and allocate the consolidated information pro rata, based on the separate calculations.

§12.15 Presentation and Disclosure

A key point about presentation is that deferred items are combined and presented differently on the balance sheet from the way they are presented in the footnotes; but we will first address current items.

On the income statement, there is generally one-line item for income taxes or benefits related to ongoing operations. It includes current tax expenses and benefits, as well as deferred tax expenses and benefits. Those items are then broken out in more detail in the footnotes.

Current taxes payable or refunds receivable are reflected as such on the balance sheet. If an entity pays taxes in more than one tax jurisdiction, it may show both a refund receivable and a tax payable. Amounts due to or from separate tax jurisdictions are broken out separately. This is true of deferred taxes, as well.

Deferred taxes are combined and shown net on the balance sheet. If deferred tax assets exceed deferred tax liabilities, the net amount will be shown as a deferred tax asset, and vice-versa. The only way there would ever be both a deferred tax asset and a deferred tax liability reported is if there is more than one tax jurisdiction. As with current taxes, deferred taxes are not netted together across separate tax jurisdictions.

Under the now-superseded guidance, when there were current and noncurrent deferred tax assets and liabilities, all current items were netted together and reflected as either a current deferred tax asset or a current deferred tax liability, depending on which amount was greater. Noncurrent items were also netted together and reflected as a noncurrent deferred tax asset or liability.

In contrast to balance sheet presentation, the footnote disclosure requires deferred tax assets to be combined and reported net of the valuation allowance. Deferred tax liabilities must also be combined.

Generally, it is expected that three tables are included in the income tax footnote. One is generally referred to as an expected-to-actual reconciliation. It begins with an expected tax, which is calculated by multiplying net income on the income statement by an expected tax rate. The subsequent lines adjust for all items that bring it to the actual amount of income tax expense or benefit shown on the income statement. Adjusting items may include things like state taxes, deferred tax expense or benefit, the effect of differences with no future tax consequence, etc.

The second table is a breakout of income tax expense or benefit between state and federal, as well as current and deferred.

The third table discloses deferred tax assets and the valuation allowance, as well as deferred tax liabilities.

Additional detailed disclosure requirements are presented in ASC 740.

Appendix 12-1 Filled-in Form 1120-F and Attachment

Filled in Form 1120-F.

SCHEDULES M-1 and M-2 (Form 1120-F)

Department of the Treasury Internal Revenue Service

Reconciliation of Income (Loss) and Analysis of Unappropriated Retained Earnings per Books

▶ Go to *www.irs.gov/Form1120F* for the latest information.
▶ Attach to Form 1120-F.

OMB No. 1545-0123

2018

Name of corporation	Employer identification number
ACME Corporation	12-3456789

Schedule M-1 **Reconciliation of Income (Loss) per Books With Income per Return**
Note: The corporation may be required to file Schedule M-3 (see instructions).

1	Net income (loss) per books	92,400	7	Income recorded on books this year not included on this return (itemize):	
2	Federal income tax per books	7,500			
3	Excess of capital losses over capital gains	2,000	a	Tax-exempt interest $ 5,000	
4	Income subject to tax not recorded on books this year (itemize):		b	Other (itemize): life insurance on key man employee - $50,000	55,000
			8	Deductions on this return not charged against book income this year (itemize):	
5	Expenses recorded on books this year not deducted on this return (itemize):		a	Depreciation $	
a	Depreciation $		b	Charitable contributions $	
b	Charitable contributions $		c	Other (itemize):	
c	Travel and entertainment $				
d	Other (itemize): life ins prem - $2,600; tax exempt bond - $500	3,000	9	Add lines 7 and 8	55,000
6	Add lines 1 through 5	104,900	10	Income—line 6 less line 9	50,000

Schedule M-2 **Analysis of Unappropriated Retained Earnings per Books**

1	Balance at beginning of year		5	Distributions: a Cash	
2	Net income (loss) per books			b Stock	
3	Other increases (itemize):			c Property	
			6	Other decreases (itemize):	
			7	Add lines 5 and 6	
4	Add lines 1, 2, and 3		8	Balance at end of year (line 4 less line 7)	

Who Must File

Generally, any foreign corporation that is required to complete Form 1120-F, Section II must complete Schedules M-1 and M-2 (Form 1120-F). However, the following rules apply.

Do not complete Schedules M-1, M-2, and M-3 if total assets at the end of the tax year (Schedule L, line 17, column (d)) are less than $25,000.

Complete Schedule M-3 in lieu of Schedule M-1 if total assets at the end of the tax year that are reportable on Schedule L are $10 million or more.

A corporation filing Form 1120-F that is not required to file Schedule M-3 may voluntarily file Schedule M-3 instead of Schedule M-1. See the Instructions for Schedule M-3 (Form 1120-F) for more information.

Foreign corporations that **(a)** are required to file a Schedule M-3 (Form 1120-F) and have less than $50 million in total assets at the end of the tax year, or **(b)** are not required to file a Schedule M-3 (Form 1120-F) and voluntarily file a Schedule M-3 (Form 1120-F) must either **(1)** complete Schedule M-3 (Form 1120-F) entirely, or **(2)** complete Schedule M-3 (Form 1120-F) through Part I and complete Schedule M-1 instead of completing Parts II and III of Schedule M-3 (Form 1120-F). If the foreign corporation chooses **(2)**, then Schedule M-1, line 1 must equal Schedule M-3 (Form 1120-F), Part I, line 11. See the Instructions for Schedule M-3 (Form 1120-F) for more information.

Note: If Schedule M-3 is completed in lieu of Schedule M-1, the corporation is still required to complete Schedule M-2.

Specific Instructions

Schedule M-1

Line 1. Net income (loss) per books. The foreign corporation must report on line 1 of Schedule M-1 the net income (loss) per the set(s) of books taken into account on Schedule L.

Line 5c. Travel and entertainment expenses. Include any of the following.

- Entertainment expenses not deductible under section 274(a).
- Meal expenses not deductible under section 274(n).
- Expenses for the use of an entertainment facility.
- The part of business gifts over $25.
- Expenses of an individual over $2,000 that are allocable to conventions on cruise ships.
- Employee achievement awards of nontangible property or of tangible property if the value is over $400 ($1,600 if part of a qualified plan).
- The part of luxury water travel expenses not deductible under section 274(m).
- Expenses for travel as a form of education.
- Other nondeductible travel and entertainment expenses.

Line 7a. Tax-exempt interest. Report any tax-exempt interest received or accrued, including any exempt-interest dividends received as a shareholder in a mutual fund or other regulated investment company. Also report this same amount in item P at the top of page 2 of Form 1120-F.

Schedule M-2

Line 1. Beginning balance of unappropriated retained earnings. Enter the beginning balance of unappropriated retained earnings per the set(s) of books taken into account on Schedule L.

Note: For additional information for Schedule M-2 reporting, see the Instructions for Schedule M-3 (Form 1120-F).

For Paperwork Reduction Act Notice, see the Instructions for Form 1120-F. Cat. No. 49678K **Schedules M-1 and M-2 (Form 1120-F) 2018**

ATTACHMENT TO FORM 1120-F
ACME CORPORATION

During the current year, ACME Corporation had the following transactions:

Net income per books (after tax)	$92,400
Taxable income	50,000
Federal income tax expense per books	7,500
Interest income from tax-exempt bonds	5,000
Interest paid on a loan, the proceeds of which were used to purchase the tax-exempt bonds	500
Life insurance proceeds received as a result of the death of a key employee	50,000
Premiums paid on the key employee life insurance policy	2,600
Excess of capital losses over capital gains	2,000

For book and tax purposes, ACME determines depreciation under the straight-line method. ACME's Schedule M-1 for the current year follows.

Appendix 12-2 Form UTP

Filled in Form 1120.

SCHEDULE UTP (Form 1120) Department of the Treasury Internal Revenue Service	**Uncertain Tax Position Statement** ▶ File with Form 1120, 1120-F, 1120-L, or 1120-PC. ▶ Go to *www.irs.gov/ScheduleUTP* for instructions and the latest information.	OMB No. 1545-0123 **2018**

Name of entity as shown on page 1 of tax return	EIN of entity
ABCDEFG HIJKLMN Corporation	13-1234567

This Part I, Schedule UTP (Form 1120) is page 1 of 1 Part I pages.

Part I **Uncertain Tax Positions for the Current Tax Year.** See instructions for how to complete columns (a) through (g). Enter, in Part III, a description for each uncertain tax position (UTP).

Check this box if the corporation was unable to obtain information from related parties sufficient to determine whether a tax position is a UTP. See instructions. ▶ ☐

(a) UTP No.	(b) Primary IRC Sections (for example, "61","108", "263A") / Primary IRC Subsections (for example, (f)(2)(A)(ii))			(c) Timing Codes (check if Permanent, Temporary, or both)		(d) Pass-Through Entity EIN	(e) Major Tax Position	(f) Ranking of Tax Position	(g) Reserved for Future Use
C	165 ( )( )( )( )	280G ( )( )( )( )	( )( )( )( )	☑ P	☐ T	-	☐	G1	
C	( )( )( )( )	( )( )( )( )	( )( )( )( )	☐ P	☐ T	-	☐		
C	( )( )( )( )	( )( )( )( )	( )( )( )( )	☐ P	☐ T	-	☐		
C	( )( )( )( )	( )( )( )( )	( )( )( )( )	☐ P	☐ T	-	☐		
C	( )( )( )( )	( )( )( )( )	( )( )( )( )	☐ P	☐ T	-	☐		
C	( )( )( )( )	( )( )( )( )	( )( )( )( )	☐ P	☐ T	-	☐		
C	( )( )( )( )	( )( )( )( )	( )( )( )( )	☐ P	☐ T	-	☐		
C	( )( )( )( )	( )( )( )( )	( )( )( )( )	☐ P	☐ T	-	☐		
C	( )( )( )( )	( )( )( )( )	( )( )( )( )	☐ P	☐ T	-	☐		
C	( )( )( )( )	( )( )( )( )	( )( )( )( )	☐ P	☐ T	-	☐		
C	( )( )( )( )	( )( )( )( )	( )( )( )( )	☐ P	☐ T	-	☐		
C	( )( )( )( )	( )( )( )( )	( )( )( )( )	☐ P	☐ T	-	☐		
C	( )( )( )( )	( )( )( )( )	( )( )( )( )	☐ P	☐ T	-	☐		
C	( )( )( )( )	( )( )( )( )	( )( )( )( )	☐ P	☐ T	-	☐		
C	( )( )( )( )	( )( )( )( )	( )( )( )( )	☐ P	☐ T	-	☐		
C	( )( )( )( )	( )( )( )( )	( )( )( )( )	☐ P	☐ T	-	☐		
C	( )( )( )( )	( )( )( )( )	( )( )( )( )	☐ P	☐ T	-	☐		
C	( )( )( )( )	( )( )( )( )	( )( )( )( )	☐ P	☐ T	-	☐		
C	( )( )( )( )	( )( )( )( )	( )( )( )( )	☐ P	☐ T	-	☐		
C	( )( )( )( )	( )( )( )( )	( )( )( )( )	☐ P	☐ T	-	☐		
C	( )( )( )( )	( )( )( )( )	( )( )( )( )	☐ P	☐ T	-	☐		

For Paperwork Reduction Act Notice, see the Instructions for Form 1120. Cat. No. 54658Q Schedule UTP (Form 1120) 2018

Schedule UTP (Form 1120) 2018 Page **2**

Name of entity as shown on page 1 of tax return	EIN of entity
ABCDEFG HIJKLMN Corporation	13-1234567

This Part II, Schedule UTP (Form 1120) is page 1 of 1 Part II pages.

Part II **Uncertain Tax Positions for Prior Tax Years.**

See instructions for how to complete columns (a) through (h). Enter, in Part III, a description for each uncertain tax position (UTP).

Check this box if the corporation was unable to obtain information from related parties sufficient to determine whether a tax position is a UTP. See instructions. ▶ ☐

(a) UTP No.	(b) Primary IRC Sections (for example, "61", "108", "263A") / Primary IRC Subsections (for example, (f)(2)(A)(ii))			(c) Timing Codes (check if Permanent, Temporary, or both)		(d) Pass-Through Entity EIN	(e) Major Tax Position	(f) Ranking of Tax Position	(g) Reserved for Future Use	(h) Year of Tax Position
P	832			P ☑	T ☐	-	☑	G1		2017-12
P	812	166		P ☑	T ☐	-	☐	G2		2017-12
P				P ☐	T ☐	-	☐			
P				P ☐	T ☐	-	☐			
P				P ☐	T ☐	-	☐			
P				P ☐	T ☐	-	☐			
P				P ☐	T ☐	-	☐			
P				P ☐	T ☐	-	☐			
P				P ☐	T ☐	-	☐			
P				P ☐	T ☐	-	☐			
P				P ☐	T ☐	-	☐			
P				P ☐	T ☐	-	☐			
P				P ☐	T ☐	-	☐			
P				P ☐	T ☐	-	☐			
P				P ☐	T ☐	-	☐			
P				P ☐	T ☐	-	☐			
P				P ☐	T ☐	-	☐			
P				P ☐	T ☐	-	☐			
P				P ☐	T ☐	-	☐			
P				P ☐	T ☐	-	☐			
P				P ☐	T ☐	-	☐			

Schedule UTP (Form 1120) 2018

Schedule UTP (Form 1120) 2018 Page 3

Name of entity as shown on page 1 of tax return	EIN of entity
ABCDEFG HIJKLMN Corporation	13-1234567

This Part III, Schedule UTP (Form 1120) is page 1 of 1 Part III pages.

Part III **Concise Descriptions of UTPs.** Indicate the corresponding UTP number from Part I, column (a) (for example, C1) or Part II, column (a) (for example, P2). Use as many Part III pages as necessary. See instructions.

UTP No.	Concise Description of Uncertain Tax Position
C 1	In 2001, XXXXXX entered into an agreement (XXX Agreement) to acquire YYYYYY (YYY), now known as YYY Holdings. The XXX Agreement required YYY to pay XXX a break-up fee of $XXX million if YYY breached the XXX Agreement by failing to close on the agreement. Before YYY closed on the agreement, it entered into an agreement to be acquired by XXX (XXX Agreement) in a sale in which XXX made a Section 338(h)(10) election. As part of the XXX Agreement, YYY received a fairness opinion from J Bank which valued the various business assets of YYY. The valuation, as published in the 2001 proxy agreement filed with the U.S. Securities and Exchange Commission, determined that YYYs consumer lending unit, ZZZZZ (ZZZ), was valued as 0.0083105% of the total value of YYY. As a result of YYY breaching the XXX Agreement, it was required to pay to XXX the $XXX million break-up fee. YYY subsequently claimed a $XXX million deduction related to the break-up fee on its 2001 federal tax return. The IRS disallowed the deduction; however, the parties subsequently entered into a closing agreement which allowed YYY to deduct $YYY million of the break-up fee, but required YYY to capitalized the remaining $ZZZ million. Under case law, a capitalized expense may be deducted in the year in which an enterprise which generated the capitalized expense is dissolved. In 2017, ZZZZZ; therefore, XXX is entitled to claim a Section 165 deductible loss of $OOO (0.0083105% of $ZZZ million) for the portion of YYY that was dissolved.
P 1	Internal Revenue Code Section 832(b)(1)(A) requires that XXX type of business entities report investment and underwriting income as computed on the basis of the underwriting and investment exhibit of the annual statement approved by the regulator. XXX No. 3 establishes statutory accounting principles for corrections of errors in previously issued financial statements. Corrections of errors in previously issued financial statements are reported as adjustments to the unassigned funds (surplus) of the period in which an error is detected. As a result of ongoing reconciliation efforts, XXX was required, per XXX No. 3, to correct certain errors related to temporary pretax surplus adjustments in its 2015 financial statements. As a consequence of Section 832(b)(1)(A), XXX was required to report such adjustments to its 2017 financial statements in its 2015 federal tax return. Due to the number of items in the adjustment, their temporary nature, and the fact that the items span many years, clear guidance related to the most appropriate year for reporting such items does not exist. Companies impacted by such adjustments include XYZ, YZX, ZXY, ABD and GHJ.
P 2	XYZ, ZXY and GHJ calculated its dividends received deduction for its XXX type of company separate accounts by excluding short-term capital gain income from the computation of gross investment income under Section 812. The issue is whether short-term capital gains should be included in gross investment income for purposes of Section 812.

Schedule UTP (Form 1120) 2018

Appendix 12-3 Instructions for Form UTP

Instructions for Form 1120

2018 Instructions for Schedule UTP (Form 1120)

Department of the Treasury
Internal Revenue Service

Uncertain Tax Position Statement

Section references are to the Internal Revenue Code unless otherwise noted.

Future Developments

For the latest information about developments related to Schedule UTP (Form 1120) and its instructions, such as legislation enacted after they were published, go to *IRS.gov/ScheduleUTP*.

General Instructions

Purpose of Schedule

Schedule UTP asks for information about tax positions that affect the U.S. federal income tax liabilities of certain corporations that issue or are included in audited financial statements and have assets that equal or exceed $10 million.

Reporting Uncertain Tax Positions on Schedule UTP

Tax positions to be reported. Schedule UTP requires the reporting of each U.S. federal income tax position taken by an applicable corporation on its U.S. federal income tax return for which two conditions are satisfied.

1. The corporation has taken a tax position on its U.S. federal income tax return for the current tax year or for a prior tax year.

2. Either the corporation or a related party has recorded a reserve with respect to that tax position for U.S. federal income tax in audited financial statements, or the corporation or related party did not record a reserve for that tax position because the corporation expects to litigate the position.

A tax position for which a reserve was recorded (or for which no reserve was recorded because of an expectation to litigate) must be reported regardless of whether the audited financial statements are prepared based on U.S. generally accepted accounting principles (GAAP), International Financial Reporting Standards (IFRS), or other country-specific accounting standards, including a modified version of any of the above (for example, modified GAAP).

If the corporation reconsiders whether a reserve is required for a tax position and eliminates the reserve in an interim audited financial statement issued before the tax position is taken in a return, the corporation need not report the tax position to which the reserve relates on Schedule UTP.

A tax position is based on the unit of account used to prepare the audited financial statements in which the reserve is recorded (or in which no reserve was recorded because of an expectation to litigate). A tax position taken on a tax return is a tax position that would result in an adjustment to a line item on that tax return if the position is not sustained. If multiple tax positions affect a single line item on a tax return, report each tax position separately on Schedule UTP. See *Tax position taken on a tax return,* later.

Reporting current year and prior year tax positions. Tax positions taken by the corporation on the current year's tax return are reported in Part I. Tax positions taken by the corporation on a prior year's tax return are reported on Part II. A corporation is not required to report a tax position it has taken in a prior tax year if the corporation reported that tax position on a Schedule UTP filed with a prior year tax return. If a transaction results in tax positions taken on more than one tax return, the tax positions must be reported in Part I of the Schedule UTP attached to each tax return in which a tax position is taken regardless of whether the transaction or a tax position resulting from the transaction was disclosed in a Schedule UTP filed with a prior year's tax return. See Example 7 and Example 8. Do not report a tax position on Schedule UTP before the tax year in which the tax position is taken on a tax return by the corporation.

If, after a subsidiary member leaves a consolidated group, the subsidiary, or a related party of the subsidiary, records a reserve in an audited financial statement with respect to one of the subsidiary's tax positions in its former group's prior return, the subsidiary should report the tax position on Part II of the Schedule UTP filed with its current tax return, if it files a separate return. If the subsidiary is included in the return of another consolidated group that is required to file Schedule UTP, the common parent of that consolidated group should report the tax position on Part II of the Schedule UTP filed with its current tax return.

Concise description of tax position. A corporation that reports a tax position in either Part I or Part II is required to provide a concise description of each tax position in Part III. See Examples 12 and 13.

Consistency with financial statement reporting. The analysis of whether a reserve has been recorded for the purpose of completing Schedule UTP is determined by reference to those reserve decisions made by the corporation or a related party for audited financial statement purposes. If the corporation or a related party determined that, under applicable accounting standards, either no reserve was required for a tax position taken on a tax return because the amount was immaterial for audited financial statement purposes, or that a tax position was sufficiently certain so that no reserve was required, then the corporation need not report the tax position on Schedule UTP. For a corporation subject to FASB Interpretation No. (FIN) 48, a tax position is considered "sufficiently certain so that no reserve was required," and therefore need not be reported on Schedule UTP, if the position is "highly certain" within the meaning of FIN 48.

Transition rule. A corporation is not required to report on Schedule UTP a tax position taken in a tax year beginning before January 1, 2010, even if a reserve is recorded with respect to that tax position in audited financial statements issued in 2010 or later. See Example 9. In addition, a corporation is not required to report accruals of interest on a tax reserve recorded with

Aug 09, 2018 Cat. No. 55028G

respect to a tax position taken on a pre-2010 tax return.

Periods covered. File a 2018 Schedule UTP with the corporation's 2018 income tax return for the calendar year 2018 and for a fiscal year that begins in 2018.

Who Must File

A corporation must file Schedule UTP for 2018 if:

1. The corporation files Form 1120, U.S. Corporation Income Tax Return; Form 1120-F, U.S. Income Tax Return of a Foreign Corporation; Form 1120-L, U.S. Life Insurance Company Income Tax Return; or Form 1120-PC, U.S. Property and Casualty Insurance Company Income Tax Return;
2. The corporation has assets that equal or exceed $10 million;
3. The corporation or a related party issued audited financial statements reporting all or a portion of the corporation's operations for all or a portion of the corporation's tax year; and
4. The corporation has one or more tax positions that must be reported on Schedule UTP.

Do not file a blank Schedule UTP if there are no tax positions to be reported.

Attach Schedule UTP to the corporation's income tax return. Do not file it separately. A taxpayer that files a protective Form 1120, 1120-F, 1120-L, or 1120-PC must also file Schedule UTP if it satisfies the four requirements set forth above.

A corporation required to file Schedule UTP also must check "Yes" to Form 1120, Schedule K, Question 14; Form 1120-F, Additional Information, Question AA; Form 1120-L, Schedule M, Question 15; or Form 1120-PC, Schedule I, Question 13.

Computation of assets that equal or exceed $10 million. For the following corporate income tax returns:

Forms 1120, 1120-L, and 1120-PC. A corporation's assets equal or exceed $10 million if the amount reported on page 1, item D of Form 1120, or the higher of the beginning or end of year total assets reported on Schedule L of Form 1120-L or Form 1120-PC, is at least $10 million.

Form 1120-F. The assets of a corporation filing a Form 1120-F equal or exceed $10 million if the higher of the beginning or end of year total worldwide assets of the corporation reported on Form 1120-F, Schedule L, line 17, would be at least $10 million if the corporation were to prepare a Schedule L on a worldwide basis.

Affiliated groups. An affiliated group of corporations filing a consolidated return will file one Schedule UTP for the affiliated group. The affiliated group need not identify the member of the group to which the tax position relates or which member recorded the reserve for the tax position. Any affiliate that files its U.S. federal income tax return separately and satisfies the requirements set forth above must file a Schedule UTP with its return setting forth its own tax positions.

Definitions and Special Rules

Note. All examples in these instructions assume the calendar year is the reporting year both for U.S. federal income tax and financial statement purposes and the independent auditor's opinion on the audited financial statements is issued before the filing of the tax return.

Audited financial statements. Audited financial statements mean financial statements on which an independent auditor has expressed an opinion, whether qualified, unqualified, disclaimed, or adverse, under GAAP, IFRS, or another country-specific accounting standard, including a modified version of any of the above (for example, modified GAAP). Compiled or reviewed financial statements are not audited financial statements.

Record a reserve. A corporation or a related party records a reserve for a U.S. federal income tax position when a reserve for U.S. federal income tax, interest, or penalties with respect to that position is recorded in audited financial statements of the corporation or a related party. A reserve is recorded when an uncertain tax position or a FIN 48 liability is stated anywhere in a corporation's or related party's financial statements, including footnotes and any other disclosures, and may be indicated by any of several types of accounting journal entries. Some of the types of entries that, entered alone or in tandem, indicate the recording of a reserve are: (1) an increase in a current or non-current liability for income taxes, interest or penalties payable, or a reduction of a current or non-current receivable for income taxes and/or interest with respect to the tax position; or (2) a reduction in a deferred tax asset or an increase in a deferred tax liability with respect to the tax position.

The initial recording of a reserve will trigger reporting of a tax position taken on a return. However, subsequent reserve increases or decreases with respect to the tax position will not.

If a corporation is included in multiple audited financial statements, the corporation must report a tax position on Schedule UTP if a reserve for that position was recorded in any of those audited financial statements.

Example 1. General rule regarding recording a reserve. A corporation recorded a reserve in its 2016 audited financial statements relating to a tax position taken on its tax return for the 2016 tax year. The corporation filed its 2016 tax return on September 15, 2017. The corporation reported the 2016 tax position on Part I of Schedule UTP and filed Schedule UTP with its 2016 tax return. If the corporation increases its reserve with respect to the tax position taken on its 2016 tax return in its 2018 audited financial statements, the corporation is not required to report the 2016 tax position again on its 2018 tax return as a result of the reserve increase in 2018.

Example 2. Reporting reserves in subsequent years. A corporation claimed a deduction in 2016 and determined under applicable accounting standards that it could recognize the full benefit of the position. In 2018 the IRS began an examination of the 2016 tax return and decided to examine whether the deduction was proper. The corporation subsequently reevaluated the tax position and recorded a reserve for that position in 2018. The corporation has taken a tax position in its 2016 tax return and recorded a reserve with respect to that tax position. The corporation must report the tax position on Schedule UTP filed with its 2018 tax return even if the IRS identifies the tax position for examination prior to the recording of the reserve.

Related party. A related party is any entity that has a relationship to the corporation that is described in sections 267(b), 318(a), or 707(b), or any entity that is included in consolidated audited financial statements in which the corporation is also included.

Example 3. Related party general rule. Corporation A is a corporation filing Form 1120 that has $160 million of assets. Corporation B is a foreign corporation not doing business in the United States and is a related party to Corporation A. Corporations A and B issue their own audited financial

-2-

statements. Corporation A takes a tax position on its tax return. If Corporation B records a reserve with respect to that tax position in its own audited financial statements, even though Corporation A does not, then that tax position must be reported by Corporation A on its Schedule UTP.

Example 4. Reserve recorded in consolidated financial statements. Corporation C files a tax return and has assets of $160 million. Corporations C and D issue consolidated audited financial statements, but they do not file a consolidated tax return. Corporation C takes a tax position for which a reserve was recorded in the consolidated financial statements of Corporations C and D. The tax position taken by Corporation C on its tax return must be reported on its Schedule UTP because a reserve was recorded for its tax position in consolidated financial statements in which Corporation C was included.

Reserve not recorded based on expectation to litigate. A corporation must report on Schedule UTP a tax position taken on its return for which no reserve for income tax was recorded if the tax position is one which the corporation or a related party determines the probability of settling with the IRS to be less than 50% and, under applicable accounting standards, no reserve was recorded in the audited financial statements because the corporation intends to litigate the tax position and has determined that it is more likely than not to prevail on the merits in the litigation.

Example 5. Reserve not recorded after a change in circumstances based on expectation to litigate. A corporation takes a tax position on its 2016 tax return for which no reserve is recorded because the corporation determines the tax position is correct. Circumstances change, and in 2018 the corporation determines that the tax position is uncertain, but does not record a reserve because of its expectation to litigate the position. That is, the corporation or a related party determines the probability of settling with the IRS to be less than 50% and, under applicable accounting standards, no reserve was recorded because the corporation intends to litigate the tax position and has determined that it is more likely than not to prevail on the merits in the litigation. The corporation must report that position on Part II of the Schedule UTP filed with the 2018 tax return either if it records a reserve or if it does not record a reserve because it expects to litigate, even if that decision to record or not record occurs because of a change in circumstances in a later year.

Tax position taken on a tax return. A tax position taken on a tax return means a tax position that would result in an adjustment to a line item on any schedule or form attached to the tax return (or would be included in a section 481(a) adjustment) if the position is not sustained. If multiple tax positions affect a single line item on a tax return, each tax position is a separate tax position taken on a tax return. For example, a tax position that is reported on a line item on Form 5471 is a tax position taken on a return, even though an adjustment to that line item might not result in the payment of any additional tax.

A single decision about how to report an item of income, gain, loss, deduction, or credit may affect line items in multiple years' returns. If so, that decision can result in a tax position taken on each affected year's return. For example, a decision to amortize an expense rather than currently deduct that expense, or a decision to currently deduct rather than amortize an expense, affects line items on each year's return in which the tax position is taken during the period of amortization. Whether these tax positions taken on a return are reported on Schedule UTP for a particular tax year, and when they are reported, depends on whether and when a reserve is recorded. See Example 7 and Example 8.

Note. Although the use of a net operating loss (NOL) or a credit carryforward is a tax position taken on a tax return, do not report the use of the NOL or credit carryforward if the corporation has previously reported the tax position that created or added to the NOL or credit carryforward on Schedule UTP. See Example 10.

Unit of account. A unit of account is the level of detail used in analyzing a tax position, taking into account both the level at which the taxpayer prepares and supports the tax return and the level at which the taxpayer anticipates addressing the issue with the IRS. The unit of account used by a GAAP or modified GAAP taxpayer for reporting a tax position on Schedule UTP must be the same unit of account used by the taxpayer for GAAP or modified GAAP.

In the case of audited financial statements prepared under accounting standards other than GAAP or modified GAAP, a corporation that issues audite financial statements with a unit of account that is based upon the entire tax year may not use that unit of accour for Schedule UTP. The corporation mus instead identify a unit of account based on similar principles applicable to GAAI or modified GAAP taxpayers, or use an other level of detail that is consistently applied if that identification is reasonably expected to apprise the IRS of the identity and nature of the issue underlying the tax position taken on the tax return.

Example 6. Unit of account. Corporation A and Corporation B each have two individual research projects and each anticipates claiming a research and development credit arisin out of their projects. Corporation A chooses each individual research project as the unit of account for GAAP financial reporting purposes, since the corporation accumulates information fo the tax return about the projects at the project level and expects the IRS to address the issues during an examination of each project separately. Corporation B determines that the appropriate unit of account for GAAP financial reporting purposes is the functional expenditures, based on the amount of its expenditures, the anticipated credits to be claimed, its previous experience, and the advice of its tax advisors. Based on the unit of account used for financial reporting purposes, Corporation A must use each project as its unit of account for Schedule UTP reporting, and Corporation B must use functional expenditures as its unit of account for Schedule UTP reporting, regarding the research and development credit.

Ranking Tax Positions by Size

The corporation must rank by size each tax position listed in Part I. The size of a tax position, however, need not be reported anywhere on Schedule UTP. See the instructions for Part I, column (f), regarding coding to be used to rank the corporation's tax positions.

Size. The size of each tax position is determined on an annual basis and is the amount of U.S. federal income tax reserve recorded for that position. If a reserve is recorded for multiple tax positions, then a reasonable allocation of that reserve among the tax positions to which it relates must be made in determining the size of each tax position.

If an amount of interest or penalties relating to a tax position is not

-3-

separately identified in the books and records as associated with that position, then that amount of interest and penalties is not included in the size of a tax position used to rank that position or compute whether the position is a major tax position.

Expectation to litigate. Do not determine a size for positions listed because of an expectation to litigate. See the instructions for Parts I and II, column (f), regarding ranking of these positions.

Affiliated groups. The determination of the size of a tax position taken in a tax return by an affiliated group filing a consolidated return is to be determined at the affiliated group level for all members of the affiliated group.

Coordination with Other Reporting Requirements

A complete and accurate disclosure of a tax position on the appropriate year's Schedule UTP will be treated as if the corporation filed a Form 8275, Disclosure Statement, or Form 8275-R, Regulation Disclosure Statement, regarding the tax position. A separate Form 8275 or Form 8275-R need not be filed to avoid certain accuracy-related penalties with respect to that tax position.

Comprehensive Examples

Example 7. Multiple year positions. A corporation incurred an expenditure in 2015 and claimed the entire amount as a deduction on its 2015 return. During the course of reviewing its tax positions for purposes of establishing reserves for U.S. federal income taxes for its 2015 audited financial statements, the corporation determines it is uncertain whether the expenditure should instead be amortized over 5 years and records a reserve with respect to the position taken in 2015. The corporation did not record a reserve for any of the positions taken in tax years 2016 through 2019. The corporation has taken a tax position in each of the 5 tax years because, on each year's tax return, there would be an adjustment to a line item on that return if the position taken in that year's return is not sustained. The tax position taken in the 2015 tax year must be reported on Part I of Schedule UTP filed with the 2015 tax return. None of the 2016 to 2019 tax positions must be reported on Schedule UTP because the corporation did not record a reserve with respect to any of those tax positions.

Example 8. Multiple year positions. A corporation incurred an expenditure in 2013 and takes the position that the expenditure may be amortized over 15 years beginning on its 2013 tax return. During the course of reviewing its tax positions for purposes of establishing reserves for U.S. federal income taxes for its 2013 audited financial statements, the corporation determines it is uncertain whether any deduction or amortization of this expenditure is allowable. In the 2013 audited financial statements, the corporation recorded a reserve with respect to the amortization deduction to be claimed in each tax year. The corporation has taken a tax position in each of the 15 tax years because on each year's tax return there would be an adjustment to a line item on that return if the position taken in that year is not sustained. The corporation must report the 2013 tax position on Part I of Schedule UTP for the 2013 tax year. In addition, the tax position to be taken in each of the 2014 to 2027 tax years must be reported on Part I of the Schedule UTP filed with the tax return for the respective tax year in which the tax position was taken. The result would be the same if, instead of recording the reserve in 2013 for all of the tax positions taken in each of the 15 years, the corporation records a reserve in each year that specifically relates to the tax position taken on the return for that year.

Example 9. Transition rule. The facts are the same as in Example 8, except that the corporation incurred the expenditure and recorded the reserve in 2009. The corporation has taken a tax position in each of the 15 tax years (2009 through 2023) because on each year's tax return there would be an adjustment to a line item on that return if the position taken in that year is not sustained. However, the corporation was not required to report the tax position taken in the 2009 tax year because it was taken in a tax year beginning before January 1, 2010. The corporation reports the tax position taken in each of the 2010 to 2023 tax years on Part I of the Schedule UTP filed with its tax return for the respective tax year in which the position was taken.

Example 10. Creation and use of net operating loss (NOL). A corporation incurred a $50 expenditure in 2017 and claimed the entire amount as a deduction on its 2017 tax return. The deduction increases the corporation's NOL carryforward from $100 to $150. The corporation uses the entire $150 NOL carryforward on its 2018 tax return. Claiming the $50 deduction in 2017 is a tax position taken in the 2017 tax year because the position would result in an adjustment to a line item on the 2017 tax return if the position is not sustained. The deduction in 2018 of the NOL carried forward from 2017 is a tax position taken on the 2018 tax return, because the position would result in an adjustment to a line item on the 2018 tax return if the position is not sustained. The corporation recorded a reserve with respect to its 2017 tax position in its 2017 audited financial statements. Because the corporation recorded a reserve with respect to the tax position taken in 2017, it reported the 2017 tax position on the Schedule UTP filed with its 2017 tax return. Because it reported the tax position in its 2017 tax return, the corporation should not report the 2018 tax position on the Schedule UTP filed with its tax return for the 2018 tax year.

Example 11. Corporate merger. On June 30, 2018, MergerCo merges into AcquiringCo, in a transaction in which AcquiringCo survives. MergerCo's tax year ends on that date. After the merger, AcquiringCo records a reserve with respect to a tax position that is taken on MergerCo's final return in its audited financial statements. That tax position must be reported on Part I of the Schedule UTP filed with MergerCo's 2018 tax return even though the reserve was recorded by AcquiringCo. AcquiringCo should not report the tax position on the Schedule UTP filed with its 2018 tax return because MergerCo's final return is a prior year tax return on which the tax position was reported.

Specific Instructions

Part I. Uncertain Tax Positions For the Current Tax Year

When to Complete Part I

Complete Part I to report tax positions taken by the corporation on its 2018 tax return.

Information From Related Parties

Check the box at the top of Part I if the corporation was unable to obtain sufficient information from one or more related parties and was therefore unable to determine whether a tax position taken on its current year's tax return is

-4-

required to be reported in Part I of this schedule.

Column (a). UTP No.

Enter a number in column (a) for each tax position reported. The UTP numbers on Part I, column (a), include a preprinted "C" prefix to indicate that they are positions for the current tax year. A corresponding UTP number with the letter "C" prefix will be used on Part III for reporting the concise description of the tax position. Begin with the number 1, do not skip any whole numbers, do not enter extraneous characters, and do not duplicate any numbers (for example, C1, C2, C3, where the letters "C" are preprinted on the schedule and the numbers are entered).

Column (b). Primary IRC Sections

Provide the primary IRC sections (up to three) relating to the tax position. Enter one primary IRC section in each box (for example, "61," "108," "263A," etc.). Do not include descriptive references or any other text such as "IRC," "Section," or "IRC Sec.". Beneath each primary IRC section, you may enter the applicable IRC subsections (for example, (f)(2)(A)(ii)), using the preprinted parentheses. If there are more than four subsection components, list only the first four.

Column (c). Timing Codes

Check "T" for temporary differences,"P" for permanent differences, or check both "T" and "P" for a tax position that creates both a temporary and permanent difference. Categorization as a temporary difference, permanent difference, or both must be consistent with the accounting standards used to prepare the audited financial statements.

Column (d). Pass-Through Entity EIN

If the tax position taken by the corporation relates to a tax position of a pass-through entity, enter the EIN of the pass-through entity to which the tax position relates. For example, if the corporation is a partner in a partnership and the tax position involves the partner's distributive share of an item of income, gain, loss, deduction, or credit of the partnership, enter the EIN of the partnership. A pass-through entity is any entity listed in section 1(h)(10). If the tax position is not related to a tax position of a pass-through entity, leave this blank.

Enter "F" if the pass-through entity is a foreign entity that does not have an EIN.

Column (e). Major Tax Position

Check this box if the relative size of the tax position is greater than or equal to 0.10 (10%). The relative size of a tax position is the amount computed by dividing the size of that position by the sum of all of the sizes for all of the tax positions listed on Parts I and II. Disregard expectation to litigate positions for column (e) purposes. Round amounts using rules similar to the rules in the Instructions for Form 1120 (or the instructions for the applicable tax return) for rounding dollar amounts.

Column (f). Ranking of Tax Position

Enter a letter and a ranking number for each tax position. Use the letter T for transfer pricing positions and the letter G for all other tax positions.

Rank all tax positions in Parts I and II together, regardless of type. Starting with the largest size, assign the number 1 to the largest, the number 2 to the next largest, and so on, in order. This number is the ranking number for the tax position. Expectation to litigate positions may be assigned any ranking number.

For example, the corporation has 1 transfer pricing tax position and 2 other tax positions. The transfer pricing position is the largest and one of the other tax positions is the expectation to litigate position. The expectation to litigate position is assigned a rank of 2. Enter T1 for the transfer pricing position, G2 for the expectation to litigate position, and G3 for the second other tax position.

Part II. Uncertain Tax Positions For Prior Tax Years

When to Complete Part II

Complete Part II to report tax positions taken by the corporation in a prior tax year that have not been reported on a Schedule UTP filed with a prior year's tax return. Do not report a tax position taken in a tax year beginning before January 1, 2010. See *Transition rule* under *Reporting Uncertain Tax Positions on Schedule UTP*, earlier.

Information From Related Parties

Check the box at the top of Part II if the corporation was unable to obtain sufficient information from one or more related parties and was therefore unable to determine whether a tax position taken on its prior year's tax return is required to be reported in Part II of this schedule.

Column (a). UTP No.

Continue the numeric sequence based on the last UTP number entered on Part I. For example, if the last UTP listed on Part I is 3, enter 4 for the first UTP listed on Part II. The UTP numbers on Part II, column (a), include a preprinted "P" prefix to indicate that they are positions for prior tax years. A corresponding UTP number with a letter "P" prefix will be used on Part III for reporting the concise description of the tax position. Do not skip any whole numbers, do not enter extraneous characters, and do not duplicate any numbers (for example, P4, P5, P6, where the letters "P" are preprinted on the schedule and the numbers are entered).

Column (b). Primary IRC Sections

See the instructions for Part I, column (b).

Column (c). Timing Codes

See the instructions for Part I, column (c).

Column (d). Pass-Through Entity EIN

See the instructions for Part I, column (d).

Column (e). Major Tax Position

See the instructions for Part I, column (e).

Column (f). Ranking of Tax Position

See the instructions for Part I, column (f).

Column (h). Year of Tax Position

List the prior tax year in which the tax position was taken and the last month of that tax year, using a six-digit number. For example, enter 201512 for tax years ending December 31, 2015, and 201608 for tax years ending August 2016.

Part III. Concise Description of UTPs

When to Complete Part III

Part III must be completed for every tax position listed in Part I or Part II. Enter the corresponding UTP number from Part I, column (a) (for example, C1, C2, C3) or Part II, column (a) (for example, P4, P5, P6), related to the description.

Concise description. Provide a concise description of the tax position, including a description of the relevant facts affecting the tax treatment of the position and information that reasonably can be expected to apprise the IRS of the identity of the tax position and the nature of the issue. In most cases, the description should not exceed a few sentences. Stating that a concise description is "Available upon request" is not an adequate description.

A concise description should not include an assessment of the hazards of a tax position or an analysis of the support for or against the tax position.

Examples of Concise Descriptions for Hypothetical Fact Patterns

The following examples set out a description of hypothetical facts and the uncertainties about a tax position that would be reportable on Schedule UTP. Following each set of hypothetical facts, which would not be disclosed on the schedule, is an example of a sufficient concise description that would be reported in Part III to disclose that hypothetical case.

Example 12. Allocation of costs between uncompleted and completed acquisitions.

Facts. The corporation investigated and negotiated several potential business acquisitions during the tax year. One of the transactions was completed during the tax year, but all other negotiations failed and the other potential transactions were abandoned during the tax year. The corporation deducted costs of investigating and partially negotiating potential business acquisitions that were not completed and capitalized costs allocable to one business acquisition that was completed. The corporation established a reserve for financial accounting purposes in recognition of the possibility that the amount of costs allocated to the uncompleted acquisition attempts was excessive.

Sample concise description. The corporation incurred costs of completing one business acquisition and also incurred costs investigating and partially negotiating potential business acquisitions that were not completed. The costs were allocated between the completed and uncompleted acquisitions. The issue is whether the allocation of costs between uncompleted acquisitions and the completed acquisition is appropriate.

Example 13. Recharacterization of distribution as a sale.

Facts. The corporation is a member of Venture LLC, which is treated as a U.S. partnership for tax purposes. During the tax year, Venture LLC raised funds through (i) admitting a new member for a cash contribution and (ii) borrowing funds from a financial institution, using a loan partially guaranteed by the corporation. Also during the tax year, Venture LLC made a cash distribution to the corporation that caused its membership interest in Venture LLC to be reduced from 25% to 2%. The corporation has taken the position that the cash distribution is properly characterized as a nontaxable distribution that does not exceed its basis in its Venture LLC interest, but has established a reserve for financial accounting purposes, recognizing that the transaction might be recharacterized as a taxable sale of a portion of its Venture LLC interest under section 707(a)(2).

Sample concise description. The corporation is a member of Venture LLC, which is treated as a U.S. partnership for tax purposes. The corporation received a cash distribution during the year from Venture LLC. The issue is the potential application of section 707(a)(2) to recharacterize the distribution as a sale of a portion of the corporation's Venture LLC interest.

13

Distinguishing between Capital Expenditures and Repairs

§13.01 Introduction

IRC §263(a) generally requires taxpayers to capitalize an amount paid to acquire, produce, or improve tangible property. Over the years, the standards for applying IRC §263(a) proved to be difficult to discern and apply in practice and led to considerable uncertainty and controversy. To address this discord, the IRS and Treasury, through a series of proposed regulations, notices and announcements, sought to provide definitive rules for when costs are required to be capitalized. The final regulations provide a general framework for distinguishing capital expenditures from supplies, repairs, maintenance, and other deductible business expenses. The final regulations are collectively known as the "Tangible Property Regulations."

- Reg. §1.263(a)-1 provides general rules for capital expenditures, including an election to utilize a *de minimis* safe harbor;
- Reg. §1.263(a)-2 provides rules for amounts paid for the acquisition or production of tangible property; and
- Reg. §1.263(a)-3 provides rules for amounts paid for the improvement of tangible property.

Changes were made to related regulations to correspond with changes made in the final regulations. For example, the final regulations revise the definition and treatment of materials and supplies under Reg. §1.162-3, and permit taxpayers to elect to capitalize and depreciate amounts paid for certain materials and supplies. If the *de minimis* safe harbor is elected, it applies to most eligible materials and supplies property. The rules for repairs contained in Reg. §1.162-4 are amended to be consistent with the capitalization rules. Reg. §1.162-4 provides that a taxpayer is permitted to deduct amounts paid to repair and maintain tangible property, provided that such amounts are not required to be capitalized under IRC §263(a). These final regulations also amend the general rules for rental and leased property (Reg. §1.162-11 and §1.167(a)-4) and provide for coordination with IRC §263A. Revisions for dispositions of property subject to IRC §168 are also included with changes to Reg. §1.168(i)-8 to include the retirement of a structural component of a building. These final regulations also contain changes to Reg. §1.167(a)-7 (accounting for depreciable property), Reg. §1.167(a)-8 (concerning retirements) and Reg. §1.168(i) (accounting for general asset accounts).

Capitalization under IRC §263(a) does not change the treatment of any amount that is specifically provided for under any provision of the Code or Regulations other han IRC § 162(a) or IRC § 212. This has always been true and continues to be so under the final regulations.

The implementation of the final regulations may impact the adjusted basis of each asset.

[A] Capital Expenditures

Capital expenditures are distinguishable from deductible expenditures, such as repairs and maintenance. Determining whether an expenditure is a currently deductible expense or a capital expenditure often depends upon the circumstances of the particular expense.

Applying the *Encyclopedia Britannica* test, the IRS ruled that if an expense is of a recurring nature and produces short-term benefits, the costs are not capital expenditures.[1] On September 19, 2013, the IRS released final regulations under IRC § § 162(a) and 263(a) on the deduction and capitalization of expenditures for tangible property—the so-called repair regulations.[2] In response to taxpayer comments, the final regulations contain several safe harbors and *de minimis* rules that benefit small businesses. The final regulations are effective for tax years beginning on or after January 1, 2014.[3]

[1] Basic Steps

Consider the following steps regarding capitalization of amounts paid:

- Understand what the regulations require to be capitalized and currently expensed;
- Apply regulations to the client's fact situation;
- Determine potential IRC § 481(a) adjustments;
- Consider if the client qualifies for Rev. Proc. 2015-20[4] relief and what such guidance should consist of;
- If necessary/advisable, file Form 3115; and
- Develop procedures for dealing with annual elections.

The regulations provide deductibility (or required capitalization) of amounts paid (or incurred) to acquire, produce, or improve tangible property.

The IRS acknowledges the difficulty of applying the rules in practice, but has offered these general distinctions: Repairs can be deducted, but renovations, betterments and adaptions should be capitalized.

---

[1] *Encyclopedia Britannica, Inc. v. Comm'r*, 685 F.2d 212, 82-2 USTC ¶9530 (7th Cir. 1982), *rev'g* T.C. Memo. 1981-255, 41 TCM 1573.

[2] T.D. 9636, 2013-43 IRB 331; 78 F.R. 57686.

[3] *See* Reg. § § 1.263(a)-3(r)(3), 1.263(a)-2(j)(3), 1.263(a)-1(h)(3), and 1.263(a)-3(j)(3). *See also* Rev. Proc. 2014-16, 2014-16 IRB 606. This revenue procedure has been modified in part by Rev. Proc. 2014-54, 2014-41 IRB 675 and Rev. Proc. 2015-14, 2015-5 IRB 450.

[4] 2015-9 IRB 694.

The overriding purpose of these regulations is to change the approach to deductibility. Under prior regulations, taxpayers were to look first to IRC § 162 to see if such an expenditure were deductible. Now, a taxpayer should first look to IRC § 263 to see if such an expenditure is to be capitalized.

[B] *What Constitutes a Repair*

In general. A taxpayer may deduct amounts paid for repairs and maintenance to tangible property if the amounts paid are not otherwise required to be capitalized. Reg. § 1.263(a)-3(h)(1) provides the taxpayer with an optional election to capitalize amounts paid for repair and maintenance consistent with the taxpayer's books and records.[6] Before the final regulations were promulgated, it was common to think of maintenance to tangible property as a repair; however, under the final regulations the analysis is one of whether the amount paid for an improvement is for a betterment to a UOP.[7]

In *Illinois Merchants Trust Co. v. Commissioner*,[8] the court explained that repair and maintenance expenses are incurred for the purpose of keeping property in an ordinarily efficient operating condition over its probable useful life for the uses for which the property was acquired. Capital expenditures, in contrast, are for replacements, alterations, improvements, or additions that appreciably prolong the life of the property, materially increase its value, or make it adaptable to a different use.

In *Plainfield-Union Water Co. v. Commissioner*,[9] the Tax Court stated that if the expenditure merely restores the property to the state it was in before the situation prompting the expenditure arose and does not make the property more valuable, more useful, or longer-lived, then such an expenditure is usually considered a deductible repair. In contrast, a capital expenditure is generally considered to be a more permanent increment in the longevity, utility, or worth of the property.

Accounting method changes. A change in the treatment of repairs is a change in a method of accounting to which the provisions of IRC §§ 446 and 481 and the accompanying regulations apply. A taxpayer seeking to change a method of accounting must obtain the consent of the Commissioner[10] and follow the administrative procedures[11] for obtaining the Commissioner's consent to change its accounting method.

---

[5] Reg. § 1.162-4.

[6] *Id.*

[7] *See* § 13.01[D].

[8] 4 BTA 103, 106 (1926).

[9] 39 T.C. 333, 338 (1962).

[10] Reg. § 1.446-1(e).

[11] Reg. § 1.446-1(e)(3)(ii). *See* Rev. Rul. 2015-20, 2015-9 IRB 694 for consent procedures.

[C] *Improvement Rules–Betterment*

IRC § 263(a)(1) provides that no deduction shall be allowed for any amounts paid out for new buildings or for permanent improvements or betterments made to increase the value of any property or estate.

The final regulations contain a "betterment" standard, which reflects the manner in which IRC § 263(a) has been interpreted and applied under current law. The betterment tests do not measure an increase in value in terms of a monetary worth. A material increase in fair market value, insured value, residual value, property value, business enterprise value or going concern value, is not a pre-requisite to any of the betterment tests. Instead, the measure of betterment depends entirely on the nature of the expenditure and the effect the expenditure has on the UOP. For example, if an amount is paid to materially increase the strength of a building structure or to materially increase the efficiency of any one of the building systems, the expenditure would generally result in a betterment and an improvement to the building UOP.

Under Reg. § 1.263(a)-3(j)(1), a taxpayer must capitalize as an improvement an amount paid for a betterment to a UOP. An amount is paid for a betterment if it:

- Ameliorates a material condition or defect that either existed prior to the taxpayer's acquisition of the UOP or arose during its production, whether or not the taxpayer was aware of the condition or defect at the time of acquisition or production;
- Is for a material addition to the UOP, including a physical enlargement, expansion, extension, or addition of a major component or a material increase in its capacity, including additional cubic or linear space; and
- Is reasonably expected to materially increase the productivity, efficiency, strength, quality or output of the UOP.

Ameliorates a Material Condition or Defect. Under the final regulations, the taxpayer is required to capitalize an amount paid to *ameliorate a material condition or defect* existing prior to the acquisition of a UOP or arising during the production of the UOP. In *Stoeltzing v. Commissioner*,[12] the Appeals Court affirmed that, in substance, the work performed by the taxpayer was to put its recently purchased building into a tenantable condition, and the costs were required to be capitalized.

A Material Addition to the UOP. Capitalization is required when a *material addition* is made to a UOP, including a physical enlargement, an expansion, an extension, or an addition of a major component. See *Hotel Sulgrave, Inc. v. Commissioner*,[13] where the court found that an expenditure for a new fire sprinkler system to comply with a city order was a betterment because it was a permanent addition that gave an apartment building additional protection from fire.

Material Increase in Productivity, Efficiency, Strength, Quality or Output Test. Under Reg. §§ 1.263(a)-3(e)(2)(ii) and (j)(2)(ii), an amount is paid to improve a building unit of property if it is paid for a betterment to the building structure or any

---

[12] 266 F.2d 374 (3d Cir. 1959).

[13] 21 T.C. 619 (1954).

building system. For example, N owns a factory building with a storage area on the second floor. N pays an amount to reinforce the columns and girders supporting the second floor to permit storage of supplies with a gross weight 50% greater than the previous load-carrying capacity of the storage area. The columns and girders are part of the building structure defined under Reg. § 1.263(a)-3(e)(2)(ii)(A). N must treat the amount paid to reinforce the columns and girders as a betterment under Reg. §§ 1.263(a)-3(j)(1)(ii) and (j)(1)(iii) because it materially increases the load-carrying capacity and the strength of the building structure. Therefore, N must capitalize this amount as an improvement to the building under Reg. §§ 1.263(a)-3(d)(1) and (j).

[D] Units of Property–UOP

The final tangible property regulations ("final regulations") define the UOP for most types of property and provide improvement rules. Determining whether there is an improvement to property is a two-step process. First, the UOP is established. Second, the facts and circumstances are considered to determine whether the work constitutes an improvement to that UOP. The definition of the UOP depends on an analysis of the machinery and equipment in the plant. However, neither the size of the equipment nor the cost of the equipment is a determining factor in defining the UOP.

[E] Functional Interdependence

Generally, the functional interdependence standard is used to determine the UOP. This standard provides that all the components that are "functionally interdependent" comprise a single UOP. Components are functionally interdependent if the placing in service of one component is dependent on the placing in service of the other component. For example, a locomotive is comprised of functionally interdependent components. The engine, generators, batteries and trucks in combination make up the locomotive. These parts are functionally interdependent on each other and comprise a single UOP.

The regulations require that a taxpayer capitalize amounts paid to improve a unit of property.[14] A unit of property is improved if the amount paid is for betterment of the unit,[15] restoration of the unit it to its original condition,[16] or the unit is adapted to a new or different use.[17]

For real and personal property, a unit comprises all components that are functionally interdependent. Components of property are functionally interdependent if placing one component in service by the taxpayer is dependent on the placing of another component in service by the taxpayer.[18]

---

[14] Reg. § 1.263(a)-3(d).

[15] Reg. § 1.263(a)-3(j).

[16] Reg. § 1.263(a)-3(k).

[17] Reg. § 1.263(a)-3(l).

[18] Reg. § 1.263(a)-3(e)(3)(i).

Example 13-1

Personal property. H owns locomotives that it uses in its railroad business. Each locomotive consists of various components, such as an engine, generators, batteries, and trucks. H acquired a locomotive with all its components. Because H's locomotive is property other than a building, the initial unit is comprised of the components that are functionally interdependent; the locomotive is a single unit of property because it consists entirely of components that are functionally interdependent.[19]

Example 13-2

Personal property. J provides legal services to its clients. J purchased a laptop computer and a printer for its employees to use in providing legal services. The computer and the printer are separate units of property because the computer and the printer are not components that are functionally interdependent (that is, the placing in service of the computer is not dependent on the placing in service of the printer).[20]

Example 13-3

Building systems. A owns an office building that contains a HVAC system. The HVAC system incorporates ten roof-mounted units that service different parts of the building. The roof-mounted units are not connected and have separate controls and duct work that distribute the heated or cooled air to different spaces in the building's interior. A pays an amount for labor and materials for work performed on the roof-mounted units. A must treat the building and its structural components as a single unit of property. An amount is paid to improve a building if it is for an improvement to the building structure or any designated building system. In this example, the entire HVAC system, including all of the roof-mounted units and their components, comprises a building system. Therefore, an amount paid by A for work on the roof-mounted units is an improvement (for example, a betterment) to the HVAC system, and A must treat this amount as an improvement to the building.

---

[19] Reg. § 1.263(a)-3(e)(6), Example 8.
[20] Reg. § 1.263(a)-3(e)(6), Example 9.

Example 13-4

Building structure and systems; leased building. K is a retailer of consumer products. K conducts its retail sales in a building that it leases from L. The leased building consists of the building structure (including the floor, walls, and roof) and various building systems, including a plumbing system, an electrical system, an HVAC system, a security system, and a fire protection and prevention system. K pays an amount for labor and materials to perform work on the HVAC system of the leased building. Because K leases the entire building, K must treat the leased building and its structural components as a single unit of property. An amount is paid to improve a leased building property if it is for an improvement (for example, a betterment) to the leased building structure or to any building system within the leased building. Therefore, if an amount paid by K for work on the HVAC system is for an improvement to the HVAC system in the leased building, K must treat this amount as an improvement to the entire leased building property.

While the functional interdependence rule works well for determining the UOI for many types of personal and real property, it provides illogical results wher applied to certain types of property, such as buildings, plant and network assets. As a result, the UOP rules apply differently for these assets. In addition, the UOP rules provide special rules when a component of functionally interdependent UOP is depreciated using a different MACRS class or using a different depreciation methoc than the depreciation method of the UOP of which the component is a part.

As a result, the final regulations provide specific rules for determining the UOF for the following types of property:

1. Buildings under Reg. § 1.263(a)-3(e)(2):
   a. Condominiums under Reg. § 1.263(a)-3(e)(2)(iii);
   b. Cooperatives under Reg. § 1.263(a)-3(e)(2)(iv); and
   c. Leased buildings or portions of buildings under Reg. § 1.263(a)-3(e)(2)(v),
2. Property other than buildings under Reg. § 1.263(a)-3(e)(3)(i):
   a. Plant property under Reg. § 1.263(a)-3(e)(3)(ii);
   b. Network assets under Reg. § 1.263(a)-3(e)(3)(iii); and
   c. Leased non-building property under Reg. § 1.263(a)-3(e)(3)(iv); and
3. Improvements to property under Reg. § 1.263(a)-3(e)(4).

[F] Capital Expenditure

General rule for capital expenditures.[21] Amounts required to be capitalized under Reg. § 1.263(a)-2 are capital expenditures and must be taken into account through a

[21] Coordination with other provisions of the Internal Revenue Code. Unless otherwise stated in IRC § 162(a) or IRC § 212 and the regulations under those sections nothing changes the treatment of any amount that is specifically provided for under any provision of the Code. For example, see IRC

charge to a capital account or basis, or in the case of property that is inventory in the hands of a taxpayer, through inclusion in inventory costs. Amounts that are capitalized are recovered through depreciation, cost of goods sold, or by an adjustment to basis at the time the property is placed in service, sold, used or otherwise disposed of by the taxpayer.[22]

A taxpayer also must capitalize amounts paid to acquire real or personal property for resale and to produce real or personal property. See IRC § 263A for the direct and allocable indirect costs that must be capitalized to property produced by the taxpayer or to property acquired for resale.

In the case of an accrual method taxpayer, the terms amount paid and payment mean a liability is incurred. A liability may not be taken into account under this section prior to the taxable year during which the liability is incurred.[23]

Examples of capital expenditures. The following amounts paid are examples of capital expenditures:

- An amount paid to acquire or produce a unit of real or personal tangible property;[24]
- An amount paid to improve a unit of real or personal tangible property;[25]
- An amount paid to acquire or create intangibles;[26]
- An amount paid or incurred to facilitate an acquisition of a trade or business, a change in capital structure of a business entity, and certain other transactions;[27]
- An amount paid to acquire or create interests in land, such as easements, life estates, mineral interests, timber rights, zoning variances, or other interests in land;
- An amount assessed and paid under an agreement between bondholders or shareholders of a corporation to be used in a reorganization of the corporation or voluntary contributions by shareholders to the capital of the corporation for any corporate purpose;[28] and
- An amount paid by a holding company to carry out a guaranty of dividends at a specified rate on the stock of a subsidiary corporation for the purpose of securing new capital for the subsidiary and increasing the value of its stockholdings in the subsidiary. This amount must be added to the cost of the stock in the subsidiary.

(Footnote Continued)

§ 263A, which requires taxpayers to capitalize the direct and allocable indirect costs to property produced by the taxpayer and property acquired for resale. *See also* IRC § 195 requiring taxpayers to capitalize certain costs as start-up expenditures. *See* Reg. § 1.263(a)-1 which provides general rules for capital expenditures, including an election to utilize a de minimis safe harbor.

[22] Reg. § 1.263(a)-2(g) and (h).

[23] Reg. § 1.263(a)-2(b).

[24] *See* Reg. § 1.263(a)-2.

[25] *See* Reg. § 1.263(a)-3

[26] *See* Reg. § 1.263(a)-4

[27] *See* Reg. § 1.263(a)-5.

[28] *See* IRC § 118 and Reg. § 1.118-1.

In *Difco Laboratories, Inc. v. Commissioner*,[29] the court held that expenditures fo lowering one basement room to the level of another basement room, along with othe alterations connected therewith, to facilitate the wheeling of trucks from one room t the other, adapted the basement for a different use and were therefore capita expenditures.

[G] Amounts Paid to Sell Property

Commissions and other transaction costs paid to facilitate the sale of propert are not currently deductible under IRC §§162 or 212. Instead, the amounts ar capitalized costs that reduce the amount realized in the taxable year in which the sal occurs or are accounted for in the taxable year in which the sale is abandoned if deduction is permissible.[30]

Dealer in property. In the case of a dealer in property, amounts paid to facilitat the sale of such property are considered ordinary and necessary business expenses.[31]

Example 13-5

Sales costs of real property. A owns a parcel of real estate. A sells the real estate and pays legal fees, recording fees, and sales commissions to facilitate the sale. A must capitalize the fees and commissions and, in the taxable year of the sale, must reduce the amount realized from the sale of the real estate by the fees and commissions.[32]

Example 13-6

Sales costs of dealers. Assume the same facts as in the prior example, except that A is a dealer in real estate. The commissions and fees paid to facilitate the sale of the real estate may be deducted as ordinary and necessary business expenses under IRC §162.[33]

---

[29] 10 T.C. 660, 668 (1948).
[30] Reg. §1.263(a)-1(e)(1).
[31] Reg. §1.263(a)-3(d)(3)(ii).
[32] Reg. §1.263-1(e)(3), Example 1.
[33] Reg. §1.263-1(e)(3), Example 2. Additional examples can be found in Reg. §1.263-1(e)(3).

[H] *De Minimis Safe Harbor Election*

While the final regulations generally require a taxpayer to capitalize amounts paid to acquire, produce, or improve a unit of property, they also provide a *de minimis* safe harbor that allows small businesses to deduct those amounts, subject to an annual per item dollar limitation.

The *de minimis* safe harbor ("safe harbor") election eliminates the burden of determining whether every small dollar expenditure for the acquisition of property is properly deductible or capitalizable under the more detailed acquisition and improvement rules. This election allows taxpayers to follow financial accounting treatment of these expenditures for tax purposes, provided the amounts deducted under their financial accounting policies adhere to specific dollar limitations.[34]

The final regulations provide a safe harbor limit for taxpayers that have an Applicable Financial Statement ("AFS") and a different safe harbor limit for taxpayers that do not have an AFS. In both cases, a taxpayer must properly make the election to use the safe harbor for each taxable year.

The safe harbor is not a limitation on the amounts taxpayers are permitted to deduct under IRC § 162. An otherwise deductible amount is still deductible, even if the amount exceeds the safe harbor ceilings. For example, a taxpayer can deduct amounts paid for incidental or non-incidental materials and supplies under Reg. § 1.162-3, repairs and maintenance under Reg. § 1.162-4 or amounts that they can prove clearly reflect income under IRC § 446.

This election is not an accounting method change. A taxpayer elects to apply the safe harbor by attaching a statement to its timely filed original return.[35]

The safe harbor is an annual election. A taxpayer may choose to apply the safe harbor in one year, but not in the next. A taxpayer must consistently apply the safe harbor to all amounts paid during an election year for the acquisition or improvement of tangible property, including the acquisition of materials and supplies that also meet the safe harbor requirements. A taxpayer cannot choose to apply the safe harbor to some items and not to others.

[I] *Applicable Financial Statements*

The final regulations permit taxpayers who have an AFS to treat property the same way for tax as they would for book provided the cost does not exceed $5,000. For taxpayers without an AFS, the cost cannot exceed $2,500. Applicable financial statements in descending priority order include:

1. A financial statement required to be filed with the Securities and Exchange Commission (SEC) which includes a Form 10-K or Annual Statement to Shareholders;

---

[34] Reg. § 1.263(a)-1(f).

[35] Reg. § 1.263(a)-1(f)(5).

2. A certified audited financial statement that is accompanied by the report of an independent certified public accountant (or a similar foreign professional) that is used for:
   a. Credit purposes;
   b. Reporting to shareholders; or
   c. Any other substantial non-tax purpose; or
3. A financial statement, other than a tax return that is required to be provided to the federal or state government or any federal or state agency, other than to the IRS or the SEC.[36]

A larger safe harbor limitation is reasonable for a taxpayer with an AFS because an AFS provides independent assurance that the taxpayer's *de minimis* policies are consistent with the requirement of generally accepted accounting principles and do not materially distort the taxpayer's financial statement income. Financial statements other than those included in the final regulations, such as reviewed financial statements, do not qualify as AFS.

Taxpayer with applicable financial statement. A taxpayer electing to apply the de minimis safe harbor may not capitalize under Reg. § 1.263(a)-2(d)(1) or Reg. § 1.263(a)-3(d) nor treat as a material or supply under Reg. § 1.162-3(a) any amount paid in the taxable year for property described in paragraph (f)(1) of this section if—

(A) The taxpayer has an applicable financial statement;

(B) The taxpayer has at the beginning of the taxable year written accounting procedures treating as an expense for non-tax purposes—

   (1) Amounts paid for property costing less than a specified dollar amount or

   (2) Amounts paid for property with an economic useful life;

(C) The taxpayer treats the amount paid for the property as an expense on its applicable financial statement in accordance with its written accounting procedures; and

(D) The amount paid for the property does not exceed $5,000 per invoice (or per item as substantiated by the invoice) or other amount as identified in published guidance in the Federal Register or in the Internal Revenue Bulletin.[37]

Taxpayer without applicable financial statement. A taxpayer electing to apply the de minimis safe harbor may not capitalize under Reg. § 1.263(a)-2(d)(1) or Reg. § 1.263(a)-3(d) nor treat as a material or supply under Reg. § 1.162-3(a) any amount paid in the taxable year for property described in paragraph (f)(1) of this section if—

(A) The taxpayer does not have an applicable financial statement;

(B) The taxpayer has at the beginning of the taxable year accounting procedures treating as an expense for non-tax purposes—

---

[36] Reg. § 1.263(a)-1(f)(4).

[37] Reg. § 1.263(a)-1(f)(1)(i).

(1) Amounts paid for property costing less than a specified dollar amount; or

(2) Amounts paid for property with an economic useful life of 12 months or less;

(C) The taxpayer treats the amount paid for the property as an expense on its books and records in accordance with these accounting procedures; and

(D) The amount paid for the property does not exceed $2,500 per invoice (or per item as substantiated by the invoice) or other amount as identified in published guidance in the Federal Register or in the Internal Revenue Bulletin.[38]

In measuring the cost per item or invoice limitation, installation charges and transaction costs listed on an invoice as well as other amounts paid to facilitate the acquisition or production of the property are to be included in the cost of the item.[39]

If the additional costs on an invoice are related to several items, they should be allocated to each property under a reasonable method, a pro rata allocation, or a weighted average based on each property's relative cost.[40]

A taxpayer who has both an applicable financial statement and a non-qualifying financial statement must meet the requirements of an AFS to qualify to elect the *de minimis* safe harbor.[41]

A taxpayer can generally rely on its financial accounting procedures in place at the beginning of a taxable year that provide a *de minimis* expense policy for financial or book accounting. A taxpayer is required to follow its limitations for book purposes in accordance with its accounting procedures. In addition, taxpayers that have AFS are required to put their accounting procedures in writing and to follow the procedures of their AFS.

[J] *Time and Manner of Election*

A taxpayer that makes the *de minimis* election must make the election for all amounts paid during the taxable year for all applicable property. A taxpayer makes the election by attaching a statement to its timely filed original federal tax return (including extensions) for the taxable year in which these amounts are paid.[42] The statement must be titled "*Section 1.263(a)-1(f) de minimis safe harbor election*" and include the taxpayer's name, address, taxpayer identification number, and a statement that the taxpayer is making the *de minimis* safe harbor election under Reg. § 1.263(a)-1(f).

---

[38] Reg. § 1.263(a)-1(f)(1)(ii).

[39] Reg. § 1.263(a)-1(f)(3)(i).

[40] *Id.*

[41] Reg. § 1.263(a)-1(f)(1)(iii).

[42] Reg. § 1.263(a)-1(f)(5).

[K] Treatment of De Minimis Amounts

An amount paid for property to which a taxpayer properly applies the *de minimis* safe harbor is treated as a capital expenditure under Reg. §§1.263(a)-2(d)(1) or 1.263(a)-3(d) or as a material and supply under Reg. §1.162-3, and may be deducted under Reg. §1.162-1 in the taxable year the amount is paid provided the amount otherwise constitutes an ordinary and necessary expense incurred in carrying on a trade or business.

[L] Coordination with IRC §263A

Amounts paid for tangible property may be subject to capitalization under IRC §263A if the amounts paid for tangible property comprise the direct or allocable indirect costs of other property produced by the taxpayer or property acquired for resale.[43]

The following examples illustrate the *de minimis* safe harbor. Unless otherwise provided, assume that IRC §263A does not apply to the amounts described.

Example 13-7

De minimis safe harbor; a taxpayer without AFS. In Year 1, A purchases ten printers at $250 each for a total cost of $2,500 as indicated by the invoice. Assume that each printer is a unit of property. A does not have an AFS. A has accounting procedures in place at the beginning of Year 1 to expense amounts paid for property costing less than $2,500, and A treats the amounts paid for the printers as an expense on its books and records. The amounts paid for the printers meet the requirements for the *de minimis* safe harbor. If A elects to apply the *de minimis* safe harbor in Year 1, A may not capitalize the amounts paid for the ten printers or any other amounts meeting the criteria for the *de minimis* safe harbor. Instead, A may deduct these amounts under Reg. §1.162-1 in the taxable year the amounts are paid provided the amounts otherwise constitute deductible ordinary and necessary expenses incurred in carrying on a trade or business.[44]

---

[43] *See, for example,* Reg. §1.263A-1(e)(3)(ii)(R) requiring taxpayers to capitalize the cost of tools and equipment allocable to property produced or property acquired for resale.

[44] Reg. §1.263(a)-1(f)(7), Example 1.

Example 13-8

De minimis safe harbor; a taxpayer without AFS. In Year 1, B purchases ten computers at $2,600 each for a total cost of $26,000 as indicated by the invoice. Assume that each computer is a unit of property. B does not have an AFS. B has accounting procedures in place at the beginning of Year 1 to expense amounts paid for property costing less than $2,500 and B treats the amounts paid for the computers as an expense on its books and records. The amounts paid for the printers do not meet the requirements for the *de minimis* safe harbor because the amount paid for the property exceeds $2,500 per invoice (or per item as substantiated by the invoice). B may not apply the *de minimis* safe harbor election to the amounts paid for the ten computers.[45]

Example 13-9

De minimis safe harbor; taxpayer with AFS. C is a member of a consolidated group for Federal income tax purposes. C's financial results are reported on the consolidated applicable financial statements for the affiliated group. C's affiliated group has a written accounting policy at the beginning of Year 1, which is followed by C, to expense amounts paid for property costing $5,000 or less. In Year 1, C pays $6,250,000 to purchase 1,250 computers at $5,000 each. C receives an invoice from its supplier indicating the total amount due ($6,250,000) and the price per item ($5,000). Assume that each computer is a unit of property under Reg. § 1.263(a)-3(e). The amounts paid for the computers meet the requirements for the *de minimis* safe harbor rule. If C elects to apply the *de minimis* safe harbor rule for Year 1, C may not capitalize the amounts paid for the 1,250 computers or any other amounts meeting the criteria for the *de minimis* safe harbor. Instead, C may deduct these amounts under Reg. § 1.162-1 in the taxable year the amounts are paid provided the amounts otherwise constitute deductible ordinary and necessary expenses incurred in carrying on a trade or business.[46]

Example 13-10

De minimis safe harbor; taxpayer with AFS. D is a member of a consolidated group for federal income tax purposes. D's financial results are reported

---

[45] *Id.*, Example 2.
[46] *Id.*, Example 3.

on the consolidated applicable financial statements for the affiliated group. D's affiliated group has a written accounting policy at the beginning of Year 1, which is followed by D, to expense amounts paid for property costing less than $5,000. In Year 1, D pays $4,800,000 to purchase 800 elliptical machines at $6,000 each. D receives an invoice from its supplier indicating the total amount due ($4,800,000) and the price per item ($6,000). Assume that each elliptical machine is a unit of property under Reg. § 1.263(a)-3(e). D may not apply the de minimis safe harbor election to the amounts paid for the 800 elliptical machines because the amount paid for the property exceeds $5,000 per invoice (or per item as substantiated by the invoice).[47]

Example 13-11

De minimis safe harbor; additional invoice costs. E is a member of a consolidated group for Federal income tax purposes. E's financial results are reported on the consolidated applicable financial statements for the affiliated group. E's affiliated group has a written accounting policy at the beginning of Year 1, which is followed by E, to expense amounts paid for property costing less than $5,000. In Year 1, E pays $45,000 for the purchase and installation of wireless routers in each of its ten office locations. Assume that each wireless router is a unit of property under Reg. § 1.263(a)-3(e). E receives an invoice from its supplier indicating the total amount due ($45,000), including the material price per item ($2,500), and total delivery and installation ($20,000). E allocates the additional invoice costs to the materials on a pro rata basis, bringing the cost of each router to $4,500 ($2,500 materials + $2,000 labor and overhead). The amounts paid for each router, including the allocable additional invoice costs, meet the requirements for the *de minimis* safe harbor. If E elects to apply the *de minimis* safe harbor for Year 1, E may not capitalize the amounts paid for the ten routers (including the additional invoice costs) or any other amounts meeting the criteria for the *de minimis* safe harbor under Reg. § 1.263(a)-1(f)(1). Instead, E may deduct these amounts under Reg. § 1.162-1 in the taxable year the amounts are paid provided the amounts otherwise constitute deductible ordinary and necessary expenses incurred in carrying on a trade or business.[48]

---

[47] *Id.*, Example 4.
[48] *Id.*, Example 5.

Example 13-12

De minimis safe harbor; coordination with IRC §263A. J is a member of a consolidated group for federal income tax purposes. J's financial results are reported on the consolidated AFS for the affiliated group. J's affiliated group has a written accounting policy at the beginning of Year 1, which is followed by J, to expense amounts paid for property costing less than $1,000 or that has an economic useful life of 12 months or less. In Year 1, J acquires jigs, dies, molds, and patterns for use in the manufacture of J's products. Assume each jig, die, mold, and pattern is a unit of property under Reg. §1.263(a)-3(e) and costs less than $1,000. In Year 1, J begins using the jigs, dies, molds and patterns to manufacture its products. Assume these items are materials and supplies under Reg. §1.162-3(c)(1)(iii), and J elects to apply the *de minimis* safe harbor rule to amounts qualifying under the safe harbor in Year 1. The amounts paid for the jigs, dies, molds, and patterns may be subject to capitalization under IRC §263A if the amounts paid for these tangible properties comprise the direct or allocable indirect costs of other property produced by the taxpayer or property acquired for resale.[49]

Example 13-13

De minimis safe harbor; anti-abuse rule. K is a corporation that provides hauling services to its customers. In Year 1, K decides to purchase a truck to use in its business. K does not have an AFS. K has accounting procedures in place at the beginning of Year 1 to expense amounts paid for property costing less than $2,500. K arranges to purchase a used truck for a total of $3,500. Prior to the acquisition, K requests the seller to provide multiple invoices for different parts of the truck. Accordingly, the seller provides K with four invoices during Year: one invoice of $1,500 for the cab, a second invoice of $1,500 for the engine, a third invoice of $300 for the trailer, and a fourth invoice of $200 for the tires. K treats the amounts paid under each invoice as an expense on its books and records. K elects to apply the *de minimis* safe harbor in Year 1 and does not capitalize the amounts paid for each invoice pursuant to the safe harbor. K has applied the *de minimis* rule to amounts substantiated with invoices created to componentize property that is generally acquired as a single unit of tangible property in the taxpayer's type of business, and this property, if treated as single unit, would exceed the limitations provided under the *de minimis* rule. Accordingly, K is deemed to manipulate the transaction to acquire the truck with the intent to avoid the purposes safe harbor rule.

---

[49] *Id.*, Example 10.

As a result, K may not apply the *de minimis* rule to these amounts and is subject to appropriate adjustments.[50]

[M] Making Election

Reg. § 1.263(a)-1(f)(5) requires that a statement be filed making the *de minimis* safe harbor election under Reg. § 1.263(a)-1(f). The election should be titled "Section 1.263(a)-1(f) *de minimis* safe harbor election" and should include the name and EIN of the taxpayer making the election as well as statement indicating that an election is being made under Reg. § 1.263(a)-1(f) A partnership or S corporation must elect at the entity level and not the equity holder level.

Example 13-14

Reg. § 1.263(a)-1(f) *de minimis* safe harbor election.

Taxpayer Information: XYZ Bluebird 4000 East 1st Street Anywhere, USA 00000. EIN: 90-1111111.

Required Statement: The taxpayer is making the *de minimis* safe harbor election under Reg. § 1.263(a)-1(f).

[N] Materials and Supplies

[1] In General

The final regulations clarify the treatment of materials and supplies under Reg § 1.162-3. Prior regulations provided rules for the deduction of the cost of materials and supplies, but they did not specifically define what type of property qualified as materials and supplies. For that, taxpayers and examiners had to rely on a variety of court cases and administrative guidance.

The final regulations retain the general rules for the deduction of materials and supplies and incorporate the pre-existing case law and administrative guidance to clarify the definition of materials and supplies. These regulations also address the interaction of the materials and supplies rules and the *de minimis* safe harbor under Reg. § 1.263(a)-1(f).[51]

Non-incidental materials and supplies. Under the general rules for materials and supplies, the timing of the deduction for the acquisition or production of materials and supplies depends, in part, on the method the taxpayer uses to account for the

[50] *Id.*, Example 11.

[51] Reg. § 1.263(a)-1(f)(1)(ii) is amended by Notice 2015-82, 2015-50 IRB 859.

particular materials or supplies in its books and records. The timing of the deduction will depend on whether the materials and supplies are "incidental" or "non-incidental."

Non-incidental materials and supplies are generally tracked on the taxpayer's books and records, either through records of consumption or by periodic physical inventory. The amounts paid to acquire or produce non-incidental materials and supplies are generally deductible in the taxable year in which the materials and supplies are first used in the taxpayer's operations or are consumed in the taxpayer's operations.[52]

Certain exceptions from these timing rules apply to rotable, temporary, and standby emergency spare parts. The definitions, treatment, and alternative methods for rotable, temporary, and standby emergency spare parts are found in the tangible property regulations.

Incidental materials and supplies. Amounts paid to acquire or produce incidental materials and supplies that are carried on hand and for which no record of consumption is kept or of which physical inventories at the beginning and end of the taxable year are not taken, are deductible in the taxable year in which these amounts are paid, provided taxable income is clearly reflected.[53]

Use or consumption of rotable and temporary spare parts. Generally, for purposes of non-incidental materials and supplies, rotable and temporary spare parts are first used in the taxpayer's operations or are consumed in the taxpayer's operations in the taxable year in which the taxpayer disposes of the parts.[54]

[2] Coordination with Other Provisions of the Internal Revenue Code

The requirements of the repair regulations do not change the treatment provided for under any provision of the Internal Revenue Code or regulations other than IRC §§162(a) or 212 and the regulations under those sections.[55]

[O] Definitions

Materials and supplies. Under the general rules for materials and supplies, the timing of the deduction for the acquisition or production of materials and supplies depends, in part, on the method the taxpayer uses to account for the particular materials or supplies in its books and records. The timing of the deduction will depend on whether the materials and supplies are "incidental" or "non-incidental."

---

[52] Reg. §1.162-3(a)(1).

[53] Reg. §1.162-3(a)(2).

[54] Reg. §1.162-3(a)(3).

[55] Reg. §1.263(a)-3(b). For example, *see* Reg. §1.263(a)-3, which requires taxpayers to capitalize amounts paid to improve tangible property and IRC §263A and the regulations under IRC §263A, which require taxpayers to capitalize the direct and allocable indirect costs, including the cost of materials and supplies, of property produced by the taxpayer and property acquired for resale. *See also* Reg. §1.471-1, which requires taxpayers to include in inventory certain materials and supplies.

Materials and supplies are defined as tangible property that is not inventory and that are used or consumed in the taxpayer's operations and meet at least one of the following characteristics—that they:

(i) Are a component acquired to maintain, repair, or improve a unit of tangible property (as determined under Reg. § 1.263(a)-3(e)) that is owned, leased, or serviced by the taxpayer and that is not acquired as part of any single unit of tangible property;
(ii) Consist of fuel, lubricants, water, and similar items, reasonably expected to be consumed in 12 months or less, beginning when used in the taxpayer's operations;
(iii) Are a unit of property as determined under Reg. § 1.263(a)-3(e) that has an economic useful life of 12 months or less, beginning when the property is used or consumed in the taxpayer's operations;
(iv) Are a unit of property as determined under Reg. § 1.263(a)-3(e) that has an acquisition cost or production cost (as determined under IRC § 263A) of $200 or less (or other amount as identified in published guidance in the Federal Register or in the Internal Revenue Bulletin); or
(v) Are identified in published guidance in the Federal Register or in the Internal Revenue Bulletin[56] as materials and supplies for which treatment is permitted.[57]

Rotable and temporary spare parts. Rotable spare parts are materials and supplies that are acquired for installation on a unit of property, removable from that unit of property, generally repaired or improved, and either reinstalled on the same or other property or stored for later installation.[58] Temporary spare parts are materials and supplies that are used temporarily until a new or repaired part can be installed and then are removed and stored for later installation.[59]

Standby emergency spare parts. Standby emergency spare parts are materials and supplies that are—

(i) Acquired when particular machinery or equipment is acquired (or later acquired and set aside for use in particular machinery or equipment);
(ii) Set aside for use as replacements to avoid substantial operational time loss caused by emergencies due to particular machinery or equipment failure;
(iii) Located at or near the site of the installed related machinery or equipment so as to be readily available when needed;
(iv) Directly related to the particular machinery or piece of equipment they serve;
(v) Normally expensive;
(vi) Only available on special order and not readily available from a vendor or manufacturer;

---

[56] *See* Reg. § 601.601(d)(2)(ii)(b).
[57] Reg. § 1.162-3(c)(1).
[58] Reg. § 1.162-3(c)(2).
[59] *Id.*

(vii) Not subject to normal periodic replacement;

(viii) Not interchangeable in other machines or equipment;

(ix) Not acquired in quantity (generally only one is on hand for each piece of machinery or equipment); and

(x) Not repaired and reused.[60]

Economic useful life. *General rule.* The economic useful life of a unit of property is not necessarily the useful life inherent in the property but is the period over which the property may reasonably be expected to be useful to the taxpayer or, if the taxpayer is engaged in a trade or business or an activity for the production of income, the period over which the property may reasonably be expected to be useful to the taxpayer in its trade or business or for the production of income, as applicable.[61]

For taxpayers with an applicable financial statement, the economic useful life of a unit of property is the useful life initially used by the taxpayer for purposes of determining depreciation in its applicable financial statement, regardless of any salvage value of the property. If a taxpayer does not have an applicable financial statement for the taxable year in which a unit of property was originally acquired or produced, the economic useful life of the unit of property must be determined under Reg. §1.263(a)-3(c)(4)(i). Further, if a taxpayer treats amounts paid for a unit of property as an expense in its AFS on a basis other than the useful life of the property or if a taxpayer does not depreciate the unit of property on its AFS, the economic useful life of the unit of property must be determined under Reg. §1.263(a)-3(c)(4)(i). For example, if a taxpayer has a policy of treating amounts paid for a unit of property costing less than a certain dollar amount as an expense on its AFS, notwithstanding that the unit of property has a useful life of more than one year, the economic useful life of the unit of property must be determined under Reg. §1.263(a)-3(c)(4)(i).[62]

Definition of applicable financial statement (AFS). The taxpayer's AFS is the taxpayer's financial statement listed in §13.01[I], *supra*, that has the highest priority. The financial statements are, in descending priority:

(A) A financial statement required to be filed with the Securities and Exchange Commission (SEC) (the 10-K or the Annual Statement to Shareholders);

(B) A certified audited financial statement that is accompanied by the report of an independent certified public accountant (or in the case of a foreign entity, by the report of a similarly qualified independent professional), that is used for—

(1) Credit purposes;

(2) Reporting to shareholders, partners, or similar persons; or

(3) Any other substantial non-tax purpose; or

---

[60] Reg. §1.162-3(c)(3).

[61] The factors that must be considered in determining this period are provided under Reg. §1.167(a)-1(b).

[62] Reg. §1.162-3(c)(4).

(C) A financial statement (other than a tax return) required to be provided to the federal or a state government or any federal or state agency (other than the SEC or the Internal Revenue Service).[63]

Amount paid. In the case of a taxpayer using an accrual method of accounting, the terms amount paid and payment mean a liability incurred. A liability may not be taken into account under Reg. § 1.162-3 prior to the taxable year during which the liability is incurred.[64]

§ 13.02 Election to Capitalize and Depreciate Certain Materials and Supplies

[A] In General

A taxpayer may elect to treat as a capital expenditure, and to treat as an asset subject to the allowance for depreciation, the cost of any rotable spare part, temporary spare part, or standby emergency spare parts. Except as otherwise specified, an election made applies to amounts paid during the taxable year to acquire or produce any rotable, temporary, or standby emergency spare parts. Any property for which this election is made shall not be treated as a material or a supply.[65]

[B] Exceptions

A taxpayer may not elect to capitalize and depreciate any amount paid to acquire or produce a rotable, temporary, or standby emergency spare part if:

(i) The rotable, temporary, or standby emergency spare part is intended to be used as a component of a unit of property;

(ii) The rotable, temporary, or standby emergency spare part is intended to be used as a component of a property and the taxpayer cannot or has not elected to capitalize and depreciate that property; or

(iii) The amount is paid to acquire or produce a rotable or temporary spare part and the taxpayer uses the optional method of accounting for rotable and temporary spare parts under Reg. § 1.162-3(e).[66]

[C] Manner of Electing

A taxpayer makes the election by capitalizing the amounts paid to acquire or produce a rotable, temporary, or standby emergency spare part in the taxable year the amounts are paid and by beginning to depreciate the costs when the asset is

---

63 Reg. § 1.162-3(c)(4)(iii).
64 Reg. § 1.162-3(c)(5).
65 Reg. § 1.162-3(d)(1).
66 Reg. § 1.162-3(d)(2).

placed in service by the taxpayer for purposes of determining depreciation under the applicable provisions of the Internal Revenue Code and the Treasury Regulations.[67]

A taxpayer must make the election under Reg. § 1.162-3(d) in its timely filed original federal tax return (including extensions) for the taxable year the asset is placed in service by the taxpayer for purposes of determining depreciation.[68]

In the case of an S corporation or a partnership, the election is made by the S corporation or partnership, and not by the shareholders or partners. A taxpayer may make an election for each rotable, temporary, or standby emergency spare part that qualifies. This election does not apply to an asset or a portion thereof placed in service and disposed of in the same taxable year. A taxpayer may revoke an election made only by filing a request for a private letter ruling and obtaining the Commissioner's consent to revoke the election. The Commissioner may grant a request to revoke this election if the taxpayer acted reasonably and in good faith and the revocation will not prejudice the interests of the government. An election may not be made or revoked through the filing of an application for change in accounting method or, before obtaining the Commissioner's consent to make the late election or to revoke the election, by filing an amended federal tax return.[69]

A taxpayer can revoke the election or make a late election, only by filing a request for a private letter ruling and obtaining the Commissioner's consent to revoke the election or make a late election. An election may not be made or revoked through the filing of an application for change in accounting method (Form 3115) or, before obtaining the Commissioner's consent to make the late election or to revoke the election, by filing an amended federal income tax return.

§ 13.03 Optional Method of Accounting for Rotable and Temporary Spare Parts

The optional method for rotable parts is a method of accounting under IRC § 446(a). A taxpayer may use the optional method for rotable parts to account for its rotable and temporary spare parts. A taxpayer that uses the optional method for rotable parts must use this method for all of its pools of rotable and temporary spare parts used in the same trade or business and for which it uses this method for its books and records. If a taxpayer uses the optional method for rotable parts for pools of rotable and temporary spare parts for which the taxpayer does not use the optional method for its books and records, then the taxpayer must use the optional method for all its pools in the same trade or business, whether rotable or temporary. Under the optional method for rotable parts, the taxpayer must apply the rules in Reg. § 1.162-3(e) to each rotable or temporary spare part upon the taxpayer's initial

---

[67] Reg. § 1.263(a)-2 provides for the treatment of amounts paid to acquire or produce real or personal tangible property.

[68] Reg. § 1.162-3(d)(3).

[69] Reg. § 1.162-3(d)(3).

installation, removal, repair, maintenance or improvement, reinstallation, and disposal of each part.[70]

Description of optional method for rotable parts.

(i) Initial installation. The taxpayer must deduct the amount paid to acquire or produce the part in the taxable year that the part is first installed on a unit of property for use in the taxpayer's operations.

(ii) Removal from unit of property. In each taxable year in which the part is removed from a unit of property to which it was initially or subsequently installed, the taxpayer must—

(A) Include in gross income the fair market value of the part; and

(B) Include in the basis of the part the fair market value of the part included in income under Reg. § 1.162-3 and the amount paid to remove the part from the unit of property.

(iii) Repair, maintenance, or improvement of part. The taxpayer may not currently deduct and must include in the basis of the part any amounts paid to maintain, repair, or improve the part in the taxable year these amounts are paid.

(iv) Reinstallation of part. The taxpayer must deduct the amounts paid to reinstall the part and those amounts included in the basis of the part under Reg. § 1.162-3(e)(2)(ii)(B) and (e)(2)(iii), to the extent that those amounts have not been previously deducted in the taxable year that the part is reinstalled on a unit of property.

(v) *Disposal of the part.* The taxpayer must deduct the amounts included in the basis of the part to the extent that those amounts have not been previously deducted in the taxable year in which the part is disposed of by the taxpayer.[71]

Application of de minimis safe harbor. If a taxpayer elects to apply the *de minimis* safe harbor to amounts paid for the production or acquisition of tangible property, then the taxpayer must apply the *de minimis* safe harbor to amounts paid for all materials and supplies that meet the requirements of Reg. § 1.263(a)-1(f), except for those materials and supplies that the taxpayer elects to capitalize and depreciate under Reg. § 1.162-3(d) or for which the taxpayer properly uses the optional method of accounting for rotable and temporary spare parts under Reg. § 1.162-3(e). If the taxpayer properly applies the *de minimis* safe harbor under Reg. § 1.263(a)-1(f) to amounts paid for materials and supplies, then these amounts are not treated as amounts paid for materials and supplies under Reg. § 1.162-3.[72]

---

[70] Reg. § 1.162-3(e)(1). To change to this method, taxpayers must file Form 3115 and follow the procedures contained in § 10.11 of Rev. Proc. 2015-14, 2015-5 IRB 450, or if applicable, § 11.08 of Rev. Proc. 2016-29, 2016-21 IRB 880.

[71] Reg. § 1.162-3(g)(2).

[72] *See* Reg. § 1.263(a)-1(f)(5) for the time and manner of electing the *de minimis* safe harbor and Reg. § 1.263(a)-1(f)(3)(iv) for the treatment of safe harbor amounts.[60]

Materials and Supplies Summary

	Deductible	When:
General Rule	Incidental	Paid
General Rule	Non-incidental	First Used or Consumed
General Rule	Rotable/Temporary Spare Parts	Disposed of
	Or	**Capitalized when:**
Election to Capitalize	Rotable, Temporary and Standby Emergency Spare Parts	Elect on a timely filed federal tax return by capitalizing the costs in the taxable year the amounts are paid and by beginning to depreciate the costs when the asset is placed in service by the taxpayer.
	Or	**Capitalized when:**
Optional Method of Accounting	Rotable/Temporary Spare Parts	First Installed and then must include The FMV of the removed part in income; and the new basis of this part will include: 1. The FMV of the part included in income; 2. The removal cost; 3. The reinstallation cost; and Any amount paid to maintain, repair or improve the part.

§ 13.04 Sale or Disposition of Materials and Supplies

Upon sale or other disposition, materials and supplies as defined in Reg. § 1.162-3(g) are not treated as a capital asset under IRC § 1221 or as property used in the trade or business under IRC § 1231. Any asset for which the taxpayer makes the election to capitalize and depreciate under Reg. § 1.162-3(d) shall not be treated as a material or supply, and the recognition and character of the gain or loss for such depreciable asset are determined under other applicable provisions of the Code.

The rules for materials and supplies are illustrated by the following examples, in which it is assumed, unless otherwise stated, that the property is not an incidental material or supply, that the taxpayer computes its income on a calendar year basis, that the taxpayer does not make the election to apply Reg. § 1.162-3(d), or use the method of accounting described in Reg. § 1.162-3(e), and that the taxpayer has not elected to apply the *de minimis* safe harbor under Reg. § 1.263(a)-1(f). The following examples illustrate only the application of Reg. § 1.162-3 and, unless otherwise stated, do not address the treatment under other provisions of the Code (for example, IRC § 263A).

Example 13-15

Non-rotable components. A owns a fleet of aircraft that it operates in its business. In Year 1, A purchases a stock of spare parts, which it uses to maintain and repair its aircraft. A keeps a record of consumption of these spare parts. In Year 2, A uses the spare parts for the repair and maintenance of one of its aircraft. Assume each aircraft is a unit of property under Reg. § 1.263(a)-3(e) and that spare parts are not rotable or temporary spare parts. Assume these repair and maintenance activities do not improve the aircraft. These parts are materials and supplies because they are components acquired and used to maintain and repair A's aircraft. The amounts that A paid for the spare parts in Year 1 are deductible in Year 2, the taxable year in which the spare parts are first used to repair and maintain the aircraft.[73]

Example 13-16

Rotable spare parts; disposal method. B operates a fleet of specialized vehicles that it uses in its service business. Assume that each vehicle is a unit of property under Reg. § 1.263(a)-3(e). At the time that it acquires a new type of vehicle, B also acquires a substantial number of rotable spare parts that it will keep on hand to quickly replace similar parts in B's vehicles as those parts break down or wear out. These rotable parts are removable from the vehicles and are repaired so that they can be reinstalled on the same or similar vehicles. In Year 1, B acquires several vehicles and a number of rotable spare parts to be used as replacement parts in these vehicles. In Year 2, B repairs several vehicles by using these rotable spare parts to replace worn or damaged parts. In Year 3, B removes these rotable spare parts from its vehicles, repairs the parts, and reinstalls them on other similar vehicles. In Year 5, B can no longer use the rotable parts it acquired in Year 1 and disposes of them as scrap. Assume that B does not improve any of the rotable spare parts under Reg. § 1.263(a)-3. Under Reg. § 1.263(a)-3(a)(1)(a)(3), the rotable spare parts acquired in Year 1 are materials and supplies. Under Reg. § 1.162-3, rotable spare parts are generally used or consumed in the taxable year in which the taxpayer disposes of the parts. Therefore, under Reg. § 1.162-3(a)(1), the amounts that B paid for the rotable spare parts in Year 1 are deductible in Year 5, the taxable year in which B disposes of the parts.[74]

---

[73] Reg. § 1.162-3(h), Example 1.

[74] *Id.*, Example 2.

Example 13-17

Rotable spare parts; application of optional method of accounting. C operates a fleet of specialized vehicles that it uses in its service business. Assume that each vehicle is a unit of property under Reg. § 1.263(a)-3(e). At the time that it acquires a new type of vehicle, C also acquires a substantial number of rotable spare parts that it will keep on hand to replace similar parts in C's vehicles as those parts break down or wear out. These rotable parts are removable from the vehicles and are repaired so that they can be reinstalled on the same or similar vehicles. C uses the optional method of accounting for all its rotable and temporary spare parts under Reg. § 1.162-3(e). In Year 1, C acquires several vehicles and a number of rotable spare parts (the "Year 1 rotable parts") to be used as replacement parts in these vehicles. In Year 2, C repairs several vehicles and uses the Year 1 rotable parts to replace worn or damaged parts. In Year 3, C pays amounts to remove these Year 1 rotable parts from its vehicles. In Year 4, C pays amounts to maintain, repair, or improve the Year 1 rotable parts. In Year 5, C pays amounts to reinstall the Year 1 rotable parts on other similar vehicles. In Year 8, C removes the Year 1 rotable parts from these vehicles and stores these parts for possible later use. In Year 9, C disposes of the Year 1 rotable parts; C must deduct the amounts paid to acquire and install the Year 1 rotable parts in Year 2, the taxable year in which the rotable parts are first installed by C in C's vehicles. In Year 3, when C removes the Year 1 rotable parts from its vehicles, C must include in its gross income the fair market value of each part. Also, in Year 3, C must include in the basis of each Year 1 rotable part the fair market value of the rotable part and the amount paid to remove the rotable part from the vehicle. In Year 4, C must include in the basis of each Year 1 rotable part the amounts paid to maintain, repair, or improve each rotable part. In Year 5, the year that C reinstalls the Year 1 rotable parts (as repaired or improved) in other vehicles, C must deduct the reinstallation costs and the amounts previously included in the basis of each part. In Year 8, the year that C removes the Year 1 rotable parts from the vehicles, C must include in income the fair market value of each rotable part removed. In addition, in Year 8, C must include in the basis of each part the fair market value of that part and the amount paid to remove each rotable part from the vehicle. In Year 9, the year that C disposes of the Year 1 rotable parts, C may deduct the amounts remaining in the basis of each rotable part.[75]

[75] *Id.*, Example 3.

Example 13-18

Rotable part acquired as part of a single unit of property; not material or supply. D operates a fleet of aircraft. In Year 1, D acquires a new aircraft, which includes two new aircraft engines. The aircraft costs $500,000 and has an economic useful life of more than 12 months, beginning when it is placed in service. In Year 5, after the aircraft is operated for several years in D's business, D removes the engines from the aircraft, repairs or improves the engines, and either reinstalls the engines on a similar aircraft or stores the engines for later reinstallation. Assume the aircraft purchased in Year 1, including its two engines, is a unit of property under Reg. § 1.263(a)-3(e). Because the engines were acquired as part of the aircraft, a single unit of property, the engines are not materials or supplies nor rotable or temporary spare parts. Accordingly, D may not apply the rules of Reg. § 1.162-3 to the aircraft engines upon the original acquisition of the aircraft nor after the removal of the engines from the aircraft for use in the same or similar aircraft. Rather, D must apply the rules under Reg. §§ 1.263(a)-2 and 1.263(a)-3 to the aircraft, including its engines, to determine the treatment of amounts paid to acquire, produce, or improve the unit of property.[76]

Example 13-19

Consumable property. E operates a fleet of aircraft that carries freight for its customers. E has several storage tanks on its premises, which hold jet fuel for its aircraft. Assume that once the jet fuel is placed in E's aircraft, the jet fuel is reasonably expected to be consumed within 12 months or less. On December 31, Year 1, E purchases a two-year supply of jet fuel. In Year 2, E uses a portion of the jet fuel purchased on December 31, Year 1, to fuel the aircraft used in its business. The jet fuel that E purchased in Year 1 is a material or supply because it is reasonably expected to be consumed within 12 months or less from the time it is placed in E's aircraft. Under Reg. § 1.162-3(a)(1), E may deduct in Year 2 the amounts paid for the portion of jet fuel used in the operation of E's aircraft in Year 2.[77]

Example 13-20

Unit of property that costs $200 or less. F operates a business that rents out a variety of small individual items to customers (rental items). F maintains a supply of rental items on hand. In Year 1, F purchases a large quantity of

[76] *Id.*, Example 4.
[77] *Id.*, Example 5.

rental items to use in its rental business. Assume that each rental item is a unit of property under Reg. § 1.263(a)-3(e) and costs $200 or less. In Year 2, F begins using all the rental items purchased in Year 1 by providing them to customers of its rental business. F does not sell or exchange these items on established retail markets at any time after the items are used in the rental business. The rental items are materials and supplies under Reg. § 1.162-3(a)(1). The amounts that F paid for the rental items in Year 1 are deductible in Year 2, the taxable year in which the rental items are first used in F's business.[78]

Example 13-21

Materials and supplies that cost less than $200; de minimis safe harbor. Assume the same facts as above except that G's scanners qualify for the *de minimis* safe harbor under Reg. § 1.263(a)-1(f), and G properly elects to apply the *de minimis* safe harbor under Reg. § 1.263(a)-1(f) to amounts paid in Year 1. G must apply the *de minimis* safe harbor under Reg. § 1.263(a)-1(f) to amounts paid for the scanners, rather than treat these amounts as costs of materials and supplies under Reg. § 1.162-3. In accordance with Reg. § 1.263(a)-1(f)(3)(iv), G may deduct the amounts paid for all 50 scanners under Reg. § 1.162-1 in the taxable year the amounts are paid.[79]

Example 13-22

Materials and supplies used in improvements; coordination with Reg. § 1.263(a)-3. J owns various machines that are used in its business. Assume that each machine is a unit of property under Reg. § 1.263(a)-3(e). In Year 1, J purchases a supply of spare parts for its machines. J acquired the parts to use in the repair or maintenance of the machines under Reg. § 1.162-4 or in the improvement of the machines under Reg. § 1.263(a)-3. The spare parts are not rotable or temporary spare parts. In Year 2, J uses all of these spare parts in an activity that improves a machine under Reg. § 1.263(a)-3. Under Reg. § 1.263(a)-3(c)(1)(i), the spare parts purchased by J in Year 1 are materials and supplies. Under Reg. § 1.263(a)-3(a)(1), the amounts paid for the spare parts are otherwise deductible as materials and supplies in Year 2, the taxable year in which J uses those parts. However, because these materials and supplies are used to improve J's

---

[78] *Id.*, Example 6.

[79] *Id.*, Example 8.

machine, J is required to capitalize the amounts paid for those spare parts under Reg. § 1.263(a)-3.[80]

Example 13-23

Election to capitalize and depreciate. M is in the mining business. M acquires certain temporary spare parts, which it keeps on hand to avoid operational time loss in the event it must make temporary repairs to a unit of property that is subject to depreciation. These parts are not used to improve property under Reg. § 1.263(a)-3(d). These temporary spare parts are used until a new or repaired part can be installed and then are removed and stored for later temporary installation. M does not use the optional method of accounting for rotable and temporary spare parts for any of its rotable or temporary spare parts. The temporary spare parts are materials and supplies. Under Reg. § 1.162-3(a)(1) and (a)(3), the amounts paid for the temporary spare parts are deductible in the taxable year in which they are disposed of by M. However, because it is unlikely that the temporary spare parts will be disposed of in the near future, M would prefer to treat the amounts paid for the spare parts as capital expenditures subject to depreciation. M may elect to treat the cost of each temporary spare part as a capital expenditure and as an asset subject to an allowance for depreciation. M makes this election by capitalizing the amounts paid for each spare part in the taxable year that M acquires the spare parts and by beginning to recover the costs of each part on its timely filed Federal tax return for the taxable year in which the part is placed in service for purposes of determining depreciation under the applicable provisions of the Internal Revenue Code and the Treasury Regulations.[81]

Example 13-24

Election to apply de minimis safe harbor. (i) N provides consulting services to its customers. In Year 1, N pays amounts to purchase 50 laptop computers. Each laptop computer is a unit of property under Reg. § 1.263(a)-3(e), costs $400, and has an economic useful life of more than 12 months. Also in Year 1, N purchases 50 office chairs to be used by its employees. Each office chair is a unit of property that costs $100. N has an AFS and N has a written accounting policy at the beginning Year 1 to expense amounts paid for units of property costing $500 or less. N treats

---

[80] *Id.*, Example 10.

[81] *Id.*, Example 13.

amounts paid for property costing $500 or less as an expense on its AFS in Year 1.

(ii) The laptop computers are not materials or supplies. Therefore, the amounts N pays for the computers must generally be capitalized as amounts paid for the acquisition of tangible property. The office chairs are materials and supplies. Thus, under Reg. § 1.162-3(a)(1), the amounts paid for the office chairs are deductible in the taxable year in which they are first used in N's business. However, if N properly elects to apply the *de minimis* safe harbor to amounts paid in Year 1, then N must apply the *de minimis* safe harbor to amounts paid for the computers and the office chairs, rather than treat the office chairs as the costs of materials and supplies under Reg. § 1.162-3. Under the *de minimis* safe harbor, N may not capitalize the amounts paid for the computers under Reg. § 1.263(a)-2 nor treat the office chairs as materials and supplies under Reg. § 1.162-3. Instead, in accordance with Reg. § 1.263(a)-1(f)(3)(iv), under Reg. § 1.162-1, N may deduct the amounts paid for the computers and the office chairs in the taxable year paid.[82]

Accounting method changes. Changes described above is a change in method of accounting to which the provisions of IRC §§ 446 and 481 and the accompanying regulations apply. A taxpayer seeking to change to a method of accounting permitted in Reg. § 1.162-3 must obtain the consent of the Commissioner in accordance with Reg. § 1.446-1(e) and follow the administrative procedures issued under Reg. § 1.446-1(e)(3)(ii) for obtaining the Commissioner's consent to change its accounting method.[83]

§ 13.05 Amounts Paid to Acquire or Produce Tangible Property

Definitions. For purposes of determining amounts paid to acquire or produce tangible property, the following definitions apply:[84]

(1) *Amount paid.* In the case of a taxpayer using an accrual method of accounting, the terms amount paid and payment mean a liability incurred (within the meaning of Reg. § 1.446-1(c)(1)(ii)). A liability may not be taken into account under Reg. § 1.263(a)-2 prior to the taxable year during which the liability is incurred.
(2) Personal property means tangible personal property as defined in Reg. § 1.48-1(c).
(3) Real property means land and improvements thereto, such as buildings or other inherently permanent structures (including items that are structural components of the buildings or structures) that are not personal property.

---

[82] *Id.*, Example 14.
[83] Reg. § 1.162-3(i).
[84] Reg. § 1.263(a)-2(b).

Any property that constitutes other tangible property under Reg. § 1.48-1(d) is treated as real property for purposes of Reg. § 1.263(a)-2. Local law is not controlling in determining whether property is real property for purposes of Reg. § 1.263(a)-2.

(4) Produce means construct, build, install, manufacture, develop, create, raise, or grow. This definition is intended to have the same meaning as the definition used for purposes of IRC § 263A(g)(1) and Reg. § 1.263A-2(a)(1)(i), except that improvements are excluded from the definition in Reg. § 1.263(a)-2(b)(4) and are separately defined and addressed in Reg. § 1.263(a)-3.

Coordination with other provisions of the Code. Nothing in determining amounts paid to acquire or produce tangible property changes the treatment of any amount that is specifically provided for under any provision of the Code or the Treasury Regulations other than IRC § § 162(a) or 212 and the regulations under those sections. For example, see IRC § 263A requiring taxpayers to capitalize the direct and allocable indirect costs of property produced by the taxpayer and property acquired for resale. See also IRC § 195 requiring taxpayers to capitalize certain costs as start-up expenditures.

[A] Defense or Perfection of Title to Property

Amounts paid to defend or perfect title to real or personal property are amounts paid to acquire or produce property within the meaning of Reg. § 1.263(a)-2 and must be capitalized.[85] For example, if a county files an eminent domain complaint condemning a portion of a taxpayer's real property to use as a roadway, amounts paid to an attorney to contest the condemnation must be capitalized because the costs were incurred to defend title to the property. In contrast, amounts paid to preserve business activities, such as attorney fees to contest an ordinance that prohibits the taxpayer's business, are not required to be capitalized.

Example 13-25

Amounts paid to contest condemnation. X owns real property located in County. County files an eminent domain complaint condemning a portion of X's property to use as a roadway. X hires an attorney to contest the condemnation. The amounts that X paid to the attorney must be capitalized because they were to defend X's title to the property.[86]

---

[85] Reg. § 1.263(a)-2(e).

[86] Reg. § 1.263(a)-2(e)(2), Example 1.

Example 13-26

Amounts paid to invalidate ordinance. Y is in the business of quarrying and supplying for sale sand and stone in a certain municipality. Several years after Y establishes its business, the municipality in which it is located passes an ordinance that prohibits the operation of Y's business. Y incurs attorney's fees in a successful prosecution of a suit to invalidate the municipal ordinance. Y prosecutes the suit to preserve its business activities and not to defend Y's title in the property. Therefore, the attorney's fees that Y paid are not required to be capitalized.[87]

Example 13-27

Amounts paid to challenge building line. The board of public works of a municipality establishes a building line across Z's business property, adversely affecting the value of the property. Z incurs legal fees in unsuccessfully litigating the establishment of the building line. The amounts Z paid to the attorney must be capitalized because they were to defend Z's title to the property.[88]

[B] *Transaction Costs*

In general. Except as provided in Reg. § 1.263(a)-1(f)(3)(i) (for purposes of the *de minimis* safe harbor), a taxpayer must capitalize amounts paid to facilitate the acquisition of real or personal property. See Reg. § 1.263(a)-5 for the treatment of amounts paid to facilitate the acquisition of assets that constitute a trade or business. See Reg. § 1.167(a)-5 for allocations of facilitative costs between depreciable and non-depreciable property.[89]

Scope of facilitate.

(i) *In general.* An amount is paid to facilitate the acquisition of real or personal property if the amount is paid in the process of investigating or otherwise pursuing the acquisition. Whether an amount is paid in the process of investigating or otherwise pursuing the acquisition is determined based on all of the facts and circumstances. In determining whether an amount is paid to facilitate an acquisition, the fact that the amount would (or would not) have been paid but for the acquisition is relevant

[87] *Id.*, Example 2.
[88] *Id.*, Example 3.
[89] Reg. § 1.263(a)-2(f).

but is not determinative. Amounts paid to facilitate an acquisition include, but are not limited to, inherently facilitative amounts.

(ii) *Inherently facilitative amounts.* An amount is paid in the process of investigating or otherwise pursuing the acquisition of real or personal property if the amount is inherently facilitative. An amount is inherently facilitative if the amount is paid for—

(A) Transporting the property (for example, shipping fees and moving costs);

(B) Securing an appraisal or determining the value or price of property;

(C) Negotiating the terms or structure of the acquisition and obtaining tax advice on the acquisition;

(D) Application fees, bidding costs, or similar expenses;

(E) Preparing and reviewing the documents that effectuate the acquisition of the property (for example, preparing the bid, offer, sales contract, or purchase agreement);

(F) Examining and evaluating the title of property;

(G) Obtaining regulatory approval of the acquisition or securing permits related to the acquisition, including application fees;

(H) Conveying property between the parties, including sales and transfer taxes, and title registration costs;

(I) Finders' fees or brokers' commissions, including contingency fees (defined in Reg. § 1.263(a)-2(f)(3)(iii));

(J) Architectural, geological, survey, engineering, environmental, or other inspection services pertaining to particular properties; or

(K) Services provided by a qualified intermediary or other facilitator of an exchange under IRC § 1031.

(iii) *Special rule for acquisitions of real property—*

(A) *In general.* An amount paid by the taxpayer in the process of investigating or otherwise pursuing the acquisition of real property does not facilitate the acquisition if it relates to activities performed in the process of determining whether to acquire real property and which real property to acquire.

(B) *Acquisitions of real and personal property in a single transaction.* An amount paid by the taxpayer in the process of investigating or otherwise pursuing the acquisition of personal property facilitates the acquisition of such personal property, even if such property is acquired in a single transaction that also includes the acquisition of real property subject to the special rule set out in Reg.

§ 1.263(a)-4(f)(2)(iii)(A). A taxpayer may use a reasonable allocation method to determine which costs facilitate the acquisition of personal property and which costs relate to the acquisition of real property and are subject to the special rule.[90]

(iv) *Employee compensation and overhead costs—*

(A) *In general.* For purposes of Reg. § 1.263(a)-4(f), amounts paid for employee compensation (within the meaning of Reg. § 1.263(a)-4(e)(4)(ii)) and overhead are treated as amounts that do not facilitate the acquisition of real or personal property. However, IRC § 263A provides rules for employee compensation and overhead costs required to be capitalized to property produced by the taxpayer or to property acquired for resale.

(B) A taxpayer may elect to treat amounts paid for employee compensation or overhead as amounts that facilitate the acquisition of property. The election is made separately for each acquisition and applies to employee compensation or overhead, or both. For example, a taxpayer may elect to treat overhead, but not employee compensation, as amounts that facilitate the acquisition of property. A taxpayer makes the election by treating the amounts to which the election applies as amounts that facilitate the acquisition in the taxpayer's timely filed original federal tax return (including extensions) for the taxable year during which the amounts are paid.

In the case of an S corporation or a partnership, the election is made by the S corporation or by the partnership, and not by the shareholders or partners. A taxpayer may revoke an election made under Reg. § 1.263(a)-4(f)(2)(iv)(B) with respect to each acquisition only by filing a request for a private letter ruling and obtaining the Commissioner's consent to revoke the election. The Commissioner may grant a request to revoke this election if the taxpayer acted reasonably and in good faith and the revocation will not prejudice the interests of Government. See generally Reg. § 301.9100-3. The manner of electing and revoking the election to capitalize under Reg. § 1.263(a)-4(f)(2)(iv)(B) may be modified through guidance of general applicability. An election may

[90] Reg. § 1.263(a)-2(f)(2)(iii).

not be made or revoked through the filing of an application for change in accounting method or, before obtaining the Commissioner's consent to make the late election or to revoke the election, by filing an amended federal tax return.[91]

Treatment of transaction costs.

(i) *In general.* Except as provided under Reg. § 1.263(a)-1(f)(3)(i) (for purposes of the *de minimis* safe harbor), all amounts paid to facilitate the acquisition of real or personal property are capital expenditures. Facilitative amounts allocable to real or personal property must be included in the basis of the property acquired.

(ii) *Treatment of inherently facilitative amounts allocable to property not acquired.* Inherently facilitative amounts allocable to real or personal property are capital expenditures related to such property, even if the property is not eventually acquired. Except for contingency fees as defined in Reg. § 1.263(a)-1(f)(3)(iii), inherently facilitative amounts allocable to real or personal property not acquired may be allocated to those properties and recovered as appropriate in accordance with the applicable provisions of the Code and the Treasury Regulations (for example, IRC § § 165, 167, or 168).

(iii) *Contingency Fees.* For purposes of Reg. § 1.263(a)-2, a contingency fee is an amount paid that is contingent on the successful closing of the acquisition of real or personal property. Contingency fees must be included in the basis of the property acquired and may not be allocated to the property not acquired.[92]

Example 13-28

Broker's fees to facilitate an acquisition. A decides to purchase a building in which to relocate its offices and hires a real estate broker to find a suitable building. A pays fees to the broker to find property for A to acquire. Under Reg. § 1.263(a)-1(f)(2)(ii)(I), A must capitalize the amounts paid to

[91] Reg. § 1.263(a)-2(f)(2)(iv).

[92] Reg. § 1.263(a)-2(f)(3).

the broker because these costs are inherently facilitative of the acquisition of real property.[93]

Example 13-29

A taxpayer pays for separate appraisals on two potential building sites. Even though it intends to construct only one building, the costs of both appraisals (inherently facilitative costs) must be capitalized. The appraisal costs for the property the taxpayer acquires are capitalized and added to basis. The appraisal costs for the real property that the taxpayer never acquires are deductible as a loss under IRC § 165 only when the taxpayer abandons that transaction (assuming all the requirements for deducting a loss under IRC § 165 are met).

Example 13-30

Moving costs to facilitate an acquisition. C purchases all the assets of D and, in connection with the purchase, hires a transportation company to move storage tanks from D's plant to C's plant. Under Reg. § 1.263(a)-1(f)(2)(ii)(A), C must capitalize the amount paid to move the storage tanks from D's plant to C's plant because this cost is inherently facilitative to the acquisition of personal property.[94]

Example 13-31

Geological and geophysical costs; coordination with other provisions. E is in the business of exploring, purchasing, and developing properties in the United States for the production of oil and gas. E considers acquiring a particular property but first incurs costs for the services of an engineering firm to perform geological and geophysical studies to determine if the property is suitable for oil or gas production. Assume that the amounts that E paid to the engineering firm constitute geological and geophysical expenditures under IRC § 167(h). Although the amounts that E paid for the geological and geophysical services are inherently facilitative to the acquisition of real property under Reg. § 1.263(a)-1(f)(2)(ii)(J), E is not required to include those amounts in the basis of the real property acquired. Rather, under Reg. § 1.263(a)-2(c), E must capitalize these costs

---

[93] Reg. § 1.263-2(f)(4), Example 1.
[94] *Id.*, Example 3.

separately and amortize such costs as required under IRC § 167(h) (addressing the amortization of geological and geophysical expenditures).[95]

Example 13-32

Scope of facilitate. F is in the business of providing legal services to clients. F is interested in acquiring a new conference table for its office. F hires and incurs fees for an interior designer to shop for, evaluate, and make recommendations to F regarding which new table to acquire. Under Reg. § 1.263(a)-1(f)(1) and (2), F must capitalize the amounts paid to the interior designer to provide these services because they are paid in the process of investigating or otherwise pursuing the acquisition of personal property.[96]

Example 13-33

Transaction costs allocable to multiple properties. G, a retailer, wants to acquire land for the purpose of building a new distribution facility for its products. G considers various properties on Highway X in State Y. G incurs fees for the services of an architect to advise and evaluate the suitability of the sites for the type of facility that G intends to construct on the selected site. G must capitalize the architect fees as amounts paid to acquire land because these amounts are inherently facilitative to the acquisition of land under Reg. § 1.263(a)-1(f)(2)(ii)(J).[97]

Example 13-34

Transaction costs; coordination with IRC § 263A. H, a retailer, wants to acquire land for the purpose of building a new distribution facility for its products. H considers various properties on Highway X in State Y. H incurs fees for the services of an architect to prepare preliminary floor plans for a building that H could construct at any of the sites. Under these facts, the architect's fees are not facilitative to the acquisition of land. Therefore, H is not required to capitalize the architect fees as amounts paid to acquire land. However, the amounts paid for the architect's fees may be subject to capitalization under IRC § 263A if these amounts

---

[95] *Id.*, Example 4.

[96] *Id.*, Example 5.

[97] *Id.*, Example 6.

comprise the direct or allocable indirect cost of property produced by H, such as the building.[98]

Example 13-35

Contingency fee. K owns several restaurant properties. K decides to open a new restaurant in City X. In October, Year 1, K hires a real estate consultant to identify potential property upon which K may locate its restaurant, and is obligated to compensate the consultant upon the acquisition of property. The real estate consultant identifies three properties, and K decides to acquire one of those properties. Upon closing of the acquisition of that property, K pays the consultant its fee. The amount paid to the consultant constitutes a contingency fee under Reg. § 1.263(a)-1(f)(3)(iii) because the payment is contingent on the successful closing of the acquisition of property. Accordingly, K must include the amount paid to the consultant in the basis of the property acquired. K is not permitted to allocate the amount paid between the properties acquired and not acquired.[99]

Example 13-36

Employee compensation and overhead. L, a freight carrier, maintains an acquisition department whose sole function is to arrange for the purchase of vehicles and aircraft from manufacturers or other parties to be used in its freight carrying business. As provided in Reg. § 1.263(a)-1(f)(2)(iv)(A), L is not required to capitalize any portion of the compensation paid to employees in its acquisition department or any portion of its overhead allocable to its acquisition department. However, under Reg. § 1.263(a)-1(f)(2)(iv)(B), L may elect to capitalize the compensation and/or overhead costs allocable to the acquisition of a vehicle or aircraft by treating these amounts as costs that facilitate the acquisition of that property in its timely filed original Federal tax return for the year the amounts are paid.[100]

---

98 *Id.*, Example 7.
99 *Id.*, Example 9.
100 *Id.*, Example 10.

[C] *Treatment of Capital Expenditures*

Recovery of capitalized amounts. *In general.* Amounts capitalized under the regulations are recovered through depreciation, cost of goods sold, or by an adjustment to basis at the time the property is placed in service, sold, used, or otherwise disposed of by the taxpayer. Cost recovery is determined by the applicable provisions of the Code and regulations relating to the use, sale, or disposition of property.[101]

The following examples illustrate the treatment of capitalized amounts. For purposes of these examples, assume that the taxpayer does not elect the *de minimis* safe harbor under Reg. § 1.263(a)-1(f).

Example 13-37

Recovery when property placed in service. X owns a ten-unit apartment building. The refrigerator in one of the apartments stops functioning, and X purchases a new refrigerator to replace the old one. X pays for the acquisition, delivery, and installation of the new refrigerator. Assume that the refrigerator is the unit of property, as determined under Reg. § 1.263(a)-3(e), and is not a material or supply under Reg. § 1.162-3. Under Reg. § 1.263(a)-1(d)(1), X is required to capitalize the amounts paid for the acquisition, delivery, and installation of the refrigerator. Under Reg. § 1.263(a)-2(h), the capitalized amounts are recovered through depreciation, which begins when the refrigerator is placed in service by X.[102]

Example 13-38

Recovery when property used in the production of property. Y operates a plant where it manufactures widgets. Y purchases a tractor loader to move raw materials into and around the plant for use in the manufacturing process. Assume that the tractor loader is a unit of property, as determined under Reg. § 1.263(a)-3(e), and is not a material or supply under Reg. § 1.162-3. Under Reg. § 1.263(a)-2(d)(1), Y is required to capitalize the amounts paid to acquire the tractor loader. Under Reg. § 1.263(a)-2(h), the capitalized amounts are recovered through depreciation, which begins when Y places the tractor loader in service. However, because the tractor loader is used in the production of property, under IRC § 263A the cost recovery (that is, the depreciation) may also be capitalized to Y's property produced, and, consequently, recovered through cost of goods sold.[103]

---

[101] Reg. § 1.263(a)-2(g).

[102] Reg. § 1.263(a)-2(h)(2), Example 1.

[103] *Id.*, Example 2

[D] *Accounting Method Changes*

Unless otherwise provided under Reg. § 1.263(a)-2, a change to comply with Reg. § 1.263(a)-2 is a change in method of accounting to which the provisions of IRC §§ 446 and 481 and the accompanying regulations apply. A taxpayer seeking to change to a method of accounting permitted in Reg. § 1.263(a)-2 must obtain the consent of the Commissioner in accordance with Reg. § 1.446-1(e) and follow the administrative procedures issued under Reg. § 1.446-1(e)(3)(ii).

§ 13.06 Procedural Rules

The IRS has issued a new updated list of automatic method changes. See Chapter 7 for details on the latest automatic change rules.

[A] *Small Business Taxpayer*

In 2015, the IRS issued Rev. Proc. 2015-20,[104] which provides an exception from the requirements of Rev. Proc. 2014-16 (discussed below) for certain small business taxpayers with total *assets* of $10 million or less for the prior three years, to make certain tangible property changes in methods of accounting. Rev. Proc. 2015-20 permits a small business taxpayer to adopt the final regulations prospectively (*i.e.*, without computing an IRC § 481(a) adjustment) and without filing a Form 3115 for its first tax year that begins on or after Jan. 1, 2014. Instead, the taxpayer simply adopts the final regulations on its federal tax return. No disclosure is required to apply the exception.[105] In addition, the taxpayer would not receive audit protection for amounts paid or incurred in taxable years beginning before January 1, 2014. Thus, if a taxpayer uses this Revenue Procedure, and then decides to make a change by calculating an IRC § 481(a) adjustment and by filing a Form 3115 to use the final regulations in a later taxable year, it must calculate its IRC § 481(a) adjustment by taking into account only amounts paid or incurred, and dispositions, in taxable years beginning on or after January 1, 2014.

A taxpayer is eligible for the small taxpayer exception if it has one or more separate and distinct trades or businesses[106] that has:

- Total *assets* of less than $10 million as of the first day of the tax year for which a change in method of accounting under the final regulations (and related procedural guidance) is effective; or

---

[104] 2015-9 IRB 694.
[105] Rev. Proc. 2015-20, 2015-9 IRB 694, Sec. 5.01.
[106] Reg. § 1.446-1(d).

- Each separate and distinct trade or business has average annual gross receipts of $25 (formerly $10 million) million or less for the prior three tax years.[107]

Note

A taxpayer that elects to apply the small business exception does not have audit protection for prior years with respect to the item. Additionally, a taxpayer using the small business exception cannot choose to implement a portion of the method by filing a Form 3115 and with an IRC § 481(a) adjustment computed taking into account amounts paid or incurred (or dispositions) prior to a tax year beginning on or after January 1, 2014.[108]

Rev. Proc. 2015-20 does not affect the taxpayer's ability to make the following elections, provided the taxpayer wants to make the elections:[109]

- *De minimis* safe harbor;
- Small taxpayer small building safe harbor; or
- Capitalize repair and maintenance costs.

In the event the taxpayer elects to use Rev. Proc. 2015-20, it must be aware of the following consequences:

- Must still file Form 3115 for other changes if need/wish to make;
- No audit protection for prior years;
- Cannot take into account dispositions occurring in years beginning before January 1, 2014; and
- There are two sets of regulations that will apply to depreciation schedules going forward.

[B] Methods of Accounting—Automatic Consent Procedures

A taxpayer seeking to change to a method of accounting permitted by the tangible property regulations[110] must secure IRS consent in accordance with Reg. § 1.466-1(e) and the administrative procedures issued thereunder for obtaining IRS consent to change its accounting method.

---

[107] Rev. Proc. 2015-20, 2015-9 IRB 694, Sec. 501. It would appear that, because of the TCJA, the gross receipts requirement should be increased to $25 million.

[108] *Id.*

[109] Covers most changes (Designated Change Numbers (DCNs) 184, 185, 186, 187, 188, 189, 190, 191, 192, 193, 200, 205 and 206).

[110] *See* Reg. § 1.162-3(i) (materials and supplies), Reg. § 1.162-4(b) (repairs), Reg. § 1.167(a)-4(b)(4) (leased property), Reg. § 1.168(i)-7(e)(5) (accounting for MACRS property), Reg. § 1.263(a)-1(g) (capital expenditures in general), Reg. § 1.263(a)-2(i) (transaction costs) and Reg. § 1.263(a)-3(q) (improvements).

In Rev. Proc. 2019-43,[111] the IRS has provided automatic consent and procedural guidance for taxpayers to change their accounting methods to comply with the tangible property regulations with respect to:

- materials and supplies;[112]
- capital expenditures generally;[113] and
- acquisition or production costs.[114]

The IRS has provided automatic consent and procedural guidance for taxpayers to change their accounting methods to comply with the tangible property regulations with respect to:

- deducting incidental materials and supplies when purchased;[115]
- deducting non-incidental materials and supplies when used or consumed;[116]
- deducting non-incidental rotables when used or consumed (*i.e.*, when disposed of);[117]
- using the optional method for rotables;[118] and
- complying with Reg. § 1.263(a)-3.

Rev. Proc. 2019-43[119] updated the list of automatic method changes and modified and amplified prior Revenue Procedures and now contains the primary list of automatic accounting method changes for taxpayers.

Rev. Proc. 2019-43[120] adopted the changes described in Rev. Proc. 2014-54[121] that apply to taxpayers that want to make a change in method of accounting for depreciation of an asset:

- to which IRC § 168 applies (MACRS property);
- for which the present and proposed methods of accounting are permissible methods of accounting under Reg. §§ 1.168(i)-1, 1.168(i)-7, or 1.168(i)-8, as applicable; and
- that is owned by the taxpayer at the beginning of the year of change.

---

111 2019-48 IRB 1107.

112 Rev. Proc. 2019-43, 2019-48 IRB 1107, § 11.08.

113 Rev. Proc. 2019-43, 2019-48 IRB 1107, § 11.08.

114 Reg. § 1.263(a)-2.

115 Regs. § 1.162-3(a)(2), (c)(1).

116 Regs. § 1.162-3(a)(1), (c)(1).

117 Regs. § 1.162-3(a)(3), (c)(2)

118 Reg. § 1.162-3(e).

119 2019-48 IRB 1107.

120 2019-48 IRB 1107.

121 2014-41 IRB 675.

§ 13.07 Designated Automatic Accounting Method Change Numbers for Tangible Property

See the following table for the designated automatic accounting method change numbers (DCN) for the changes in method of accounting under Rev. Proc. 2019-43,[122] § 11.08.

[A] *Changes under the Final Tangible Property Regulations*

Description of Change	Designated Change Number (DCN)	Citation
A change in deducting amounts paid or incurred for repair and maintenance or a change in capitalizing amounts paid or incurred for improvements to tangible property and, if depreciable, to depreciating such property under 167 or 168. Includes a change, if any, in the method of identifying the unit of property, or in the case of a building, identifying the building structure or building systems for the purpose of making this change	184	§ § 1.162-4, 1.263(a)-3
Change to the regulatory accounting method	185	§ 1.263(a)-3(m)
Change in deducting non-incidental materials and supplies when used or consumed	186	§ 1.162-3(a)(1), (c)(1)
Change in deducting incidental materials and supplies when paid or incurred	187	§ 1.162-3(a)(2), (c)(1)
Change in deducting non-incidental rotable and temporary spare parts when disposed of	188	§ 1.162-3(a)(3), (c)(2)
Change in the optional method for rotable and temporary spare parts	189	§ 1.162-3(e)
Change by a dealer in property in deducting commissions and other costs that facilitate the sale of property	190	§ 1.263(a)-1(e)(2)
Change by a non-dealer in property in capitalizing commissions and other costs that facilitate the sale of property	191	§ 1.263(a)-1(e)(1)

[122] 2019-48 IRB 1107.

Description of Change	Designated Change Number (DCN)	Citation
Change in capitalizing acquisition or production costs and, if depreciable, in depreciating such property under § 167 or § 168	192	§ 1.263(a)-2
Change in deducting certain costs for investigating or pursuing the acquisition of real property (whether and which)	193	§ 1.263(a)-2(f)(2)(iii)

[B] Final Regulations under 2019-43

Summary of certain changes in methods of accounting related to dispositions of MACRS property. The following chart summarizes the changes in methods of accounting under Reg. § § 1.167(a)-4, 1.168(i)-1, 1.168(i)-7, and 1.168(i)-8 that a taxpayer may make under Rev. Proc. 2019-43.

	Final Regulation Section	Section # in Rev. Proc. 2019-43	Designated Change Number (DCN)
	Reg. § 1.167(a)-4, Depreciation of leasehold improvements	6.11	199
General Asset Accounts:			
a.	Reg. § 1.168(i)-1(c), Change in grouping assets	6.12	200
b.	Reg. § 1.168(i)-1(e)(2)(viii), Change in determining asset disposed of	6.15	207
c.	Reg. § 1.168(i)-1(j)(2), Change in method of identifying which assets or portions of assets have been disposed of from one method to another method specified in Reg. § 1.168(i)-1(j)(2)	6.12	200
d.	Reg. § 1.168(i)-1(j)(2), Change in method of identifying which assets or portions of assets have been disposed of from a method not specified in Reg. § 1.168(i)-1(j)(2) to a method specified in Reg. § 1.168(i)-1(j)(2)	6.15	207
e.	Reg. § 1.168(i)-1(j)(3), Change in determining unadjusted depreciable basis of disposed asset or disposed portion of an asset from one reasonable method to another reasonable method when it is impracticable from the taxpayer's records to determine the unadjusted depreciable basis of the disposed asset or the disposed portion of the asset.	6.12	200

	Final Regulation Section	Section # in Rev. Proc. 2019-43	Designated Change Number (DCN)
f.	Reg. § 1.168(i)-1(j)(3), Change in determining unadjusted depreciable basis of the disposed asset or the disposed portion of an asset from not using to using the taxpayer's records when it is practicable from the taxpayer's records to determine the unadjusted depreciable basis of the disposed asset or the disposed portion of the asset.	6.15	207
g.	Reg. § § 1.168(i)-1(j)(3), Change in determining unadjusted depreciable basis of the disposed asset or the disposed portion of an asset from an unreasonable method to a reasonable method when it is impracticable from the taxpayer's records to determine the unadjusted depreciable basis of the disposed asset or the disposed portion of the asset.	6.15	207
Single Asset Accounts or Multiple Asset Accounts for MACRS Property:			
a.	Reg. § 1.168(i)-7, Change from single asset accounts to multiple asset accounts, or vice versa.	6.12	200
b.	Reg. § 1.168(i)-7(c), Change in grouping assets in multiple asset accounts.	6.12	200
Dispositions of MACRS Property (not in a general asset account):			
a.	Reg. § 1.168(i)-8(c)(4), Change in determining asset disposed of.	6.13 (Building or structural component).	205
		6.14 (Property other than a building or structural component)	206

	Final Regulation Section	Section # in Rev. Proc. 2019-43	Designated Change Number (DCN)
b.	Reg. § 1.168(i)-8(f)(2) or (3), Change in determining unadjusted depreciable basis of the disposed asset in a multiple asset account or the disposed portion of an asset from one reasonable method to another reasonable method when it is impracticable from the taxpayer's records to determine the unadjusted depreciable basis of thye disposed asset or the disposed portion of asset.	6.12	200
c.	Reg. § 1.168(i)-8(f)(2) or (3), Change in determining unadjusted depreciable basis of the disposed asset in a multiple asset account or the disposed portion of an asset from not using to using the taxpayer's records when it is practicable from the taxpayer's records to determine the unadjusted depreciable basis of the disposed asset or the disposed portion of the asset.	6.13 (Building or structural component)	205
		6.14 (Property other than a building or structural component)	206
d.	Reg. § 1.168(i)-8(f)(2) or (3), Change in determining the unadjusted depreciable basis of the disposed asset in a multiple asset account or thr disposed portion of an asset from an unreasonable method to a reasonable method when it is impracticable from the taxpayer's records to determine the unadjusted depreciable basis of thr disposed asset or the disposed portion of the asset.	6.13 (Building or structural component)	205
		6.14 (Property other than a building or structural component)	206

	Final Regulation Section	Section # in Rev. Proc. 2019-43	Designated Change Number (DCN)
e.	Reg. § 1.168(i)-8(g), Change in method of identifying which assets in a multiple asset account or portions of assets have been disposed of from one method to another method specified in Reg. § 1.168(i)-8(g)(1) or (2).	6.12	200
f.	Reg. § 1.168(i)-8(g), Change in method of identifying which assets in a multiple asset account or portions of assets have been disposed of from a method not specified in Reg. § 1.168(i)-8(g)(1) or (2) to a method specified in Reg. § 1.168(i)-8(g)(1) or (2).	6.13 (Building or structural component)	205
		6.14 (Property other than a building or structural component)	206
g.	Reg. § 1.168(i)-8(h)(1), Change from depreciating a disposed asset or disposed portion of an asset to recognizing gain or loss upon disposition when a taxpayer continues to depreciate the asset or portion that the taxpayer disposed of prior to the year of change.	6.13 (Building or structural component)	205
		6.14 (Property other than a building or structural component)	206
h.	Reg. § 1.168(i)-8(d)(2)(iii), Partial disposition election for the disposition of a portion of an asset to which the IRS's adjustment pertains.	6.10	198

[C] *Filing Requirements*

Notwithstanding § 6.03(1)(a) of Rev. Proc. 2015-13,[123] a taxpayer making a change in accordance with section 6.07(3)(b) of Rev. Proc. 2019-43[124] must attach the original Form 3115 to the taxpayer's timely-filed amended federal tax return for the year of change and must file the required copy (with signature) of the Form 3115 with the IRS in Ogden, UT, no later than when the original Form 3115 is filed with the amended federal tax return for the year of change. If a taxpayer is making this change in accordance with section 6.07(3)(a) of Rev. Proc. 2019-43, the filing requirements in § 6.03(1)(a) of Rev. Proc. 2015-13 apply.

Reduced filing requirement for qualified small taxpayers. A qualified small taxpayer, as defined in § 6.01(4)(b) of Rev. Proc. 2019-43, is required to complete only the following information on Form 3115 to make this change:

- The identification section of page 1 (found above Part I);
- The signature section at the bottom of page 1;
- Part I;
- Part II, all lines except lines 13, 15b, 16, 17, and 19;
- Part IV, all lines except line 25; and
- Schedule E.
    - *Section 481(a) adjustment period.* A taxpayer must take the entire IRC § 481(a) adjustment into account in computing taxable income for the year of change.
    - *Concurrent automatic change.* A taxpayer making this change for more than one asset for the same year of change should file a single Form 3115 for all such assets.

---

[123] 2015-5 IRB 419.

[124] 2019-48 IRB 1107.

Appendix 13-1 Repair Regs. Flowchart

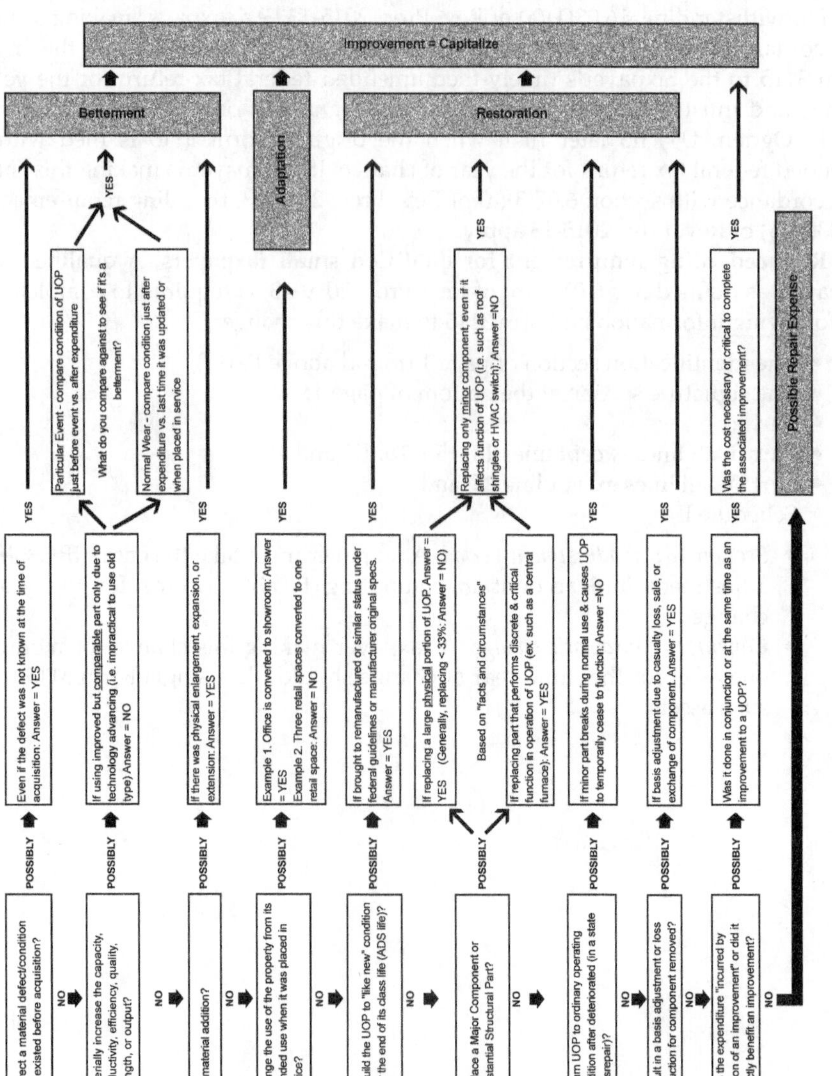

Illustration provided by Kenneth Bagner, CPA

Appendix 13-2 Filled-in Form 3115 and Statement

Form **3115** (Rev. December 2018) Department of the Treasury Internal Revenue Service

Application for Change in Accounting Method

▶ Go to *www.irs.gov/Form3115* for instructions and the latest information.

OMB No. 1545-2070

Name of filer (name of parent corporation if a consolidated group) (see instructions) ABC Corporation, Inc.	Identification number (see instructions) 55-1234567 Principal business activity code number (see instructions) 448900
Number, street, and room or suite no. If a P.O. box, see the instructions. 555 Johnson Road	Tax year of change begins (MM/DD/YYYY) 01/01/2013 Tax year of change ends (MM/DD/YYYY) 12/31/2013
City or town, state, and ZIP code Orlando, FL 12345	Name of contact person (see instructions)
Name of applicant(s) (if different than filer) and identification number(s) (see instructions)	Contact person's telephone number (555) 555-5555

If the applicant is a member of a consolidated group, check this box . . . ▶ ☐

If **Form 2848,** Power of Attorney and Declaration of Representative, is attached (see instructions for when Form 2848 is required), check this box . . . ▶ ☑

Check the box to indicate the type of applicant.

- ☐ Individual
- ☑ Corporation
- ☐ Controlled foreign corporation (Sec. 957)
- ☐ 10/50 corporation (Sec. 904(d)(2)(E))
- ☐ Qualified personal service corporation (Sec. 448(d)(2))
- ☐ Exempt organization. Enter Code section ▶
- ☐ Cooperative (Sec. 1381)
- ☐ Partnership
- ☐ S corporation
- ☐ Insurance co. (Sec. 816(a))
- ☐ Insurance co. (Sec. 831)
- ☐ Other (specify) ▶

Check the appropriate box to indicate the type of accounting method change being requested. See instructions.

- ☐ Depreciation or Amortization
- ☐ Financial Products and/or Financial Activities of Financial Institutions
- ☐ Other (specify) ▶

Caution: To be eligible for approval of the requested change in method of accounting, the taxpayer must provide all information that is relevant to the taxpayer or to the taxpayer's requested change in method of accounting. This includes **(1)** all relevant information requested on this Form 3115 (including its instructions), and **(2)** any other relevant information, even if not specifically requested on Form 3115.
The taxpayer must attach all applicable statements requested throughout this form.

Part I Information for Automatic Change Request

		Yes	No
1	Enter the applicable designated automatic accounting method change number ("DCN") for the requested automatic change. Enter only one DCN, except as provided for in guidance published by the IRS. If the requested change has no DCN, check "Other," and provide both a description of the change and a citation of the IRS guidance providing the automatic change. See instructions.		
a	(1) DCN: 184 (2) DCN: 186 (3) DCN: 187 (4) DCN: (5) DCN: (6) DCN: (7) DCN: (8) DCN: (9) DCN: (10) DCN: (11) DCN: (12) DCN:		
b	Other ☐ Description ▶		
2	Do any of the eligibility rules restrict the applicant from filing the requested change using the automatic change procedures (see instructions)? If "Yes," attach an explanation.		✓
3	Has the filer provided all the information and statements required **(a)** on this form and **(b)** by the List of Automatic Changes under which the applicant is requesting a change? See instructions. **Note:** Complete Part II and Part IV of this form, and, Schedules A through E, if applicable.	✓	

Part II Information for All Requests

		Yes	No
4	During the tax year of change, did or will the applicant **(a)** cease to engage in the trade or business to which the requested change relates, or **(b)** terminate its existence? See instructions.		✓
5	Is the applicant requesting to change to the principal method in the tax year of change under Regulations section 1.381(c)(4)-1(d)(1) or 1.381(c)(5)-1(d)(1)? If "No," go to line 6a. If "Yes," the applicant cannot file a Form 3115 for this change. See instructions.		✓

Sign Here Under penalties of perjury, I declare that I have examined this application, including accompanying schedules and statements, and to the best of my knowledge and belief, the application contains all the relevant facts relating to the application, and it is true, correct, and complete. Declaration of preparer (other than applicant) is based on all information of which preparer has any knowledge.

Signature of filer (and spouse, if joint return)	Date	Name and title (print or type)

Preparer (other than filer/applicant)

Print/Type preparer's name	Preparer's signature	Date
Firm's name ▶		

For Privacy Act and Paperwork Reduction Act Notice, see the instructions. Cat. No. 19280E Form **3115** (Rev. 12-2018)

Form 3115 (Rev. 12-2018) Page 2

Part II Information for All Requests *(continued)*

		Yes	No
6a	Does the applicant (or any present or former consolidated group in which the applicant was a member during the applicable tax year(s)) have any federal income tax return(s) under examination (see instructions)? If "No," go to line 7a.		✓
b	Is the method of accounting the applicant is requesting to change an issue under consideration (with respect to either the applicant or any present or former consolidated group in which the applicant was a member during the applicable tax year(s))? See instructions.		✓
c	Enter the name and telephone number of the examining agent and the tax year(s) under examination. Name ▶ ____ Telephone number ▶ ____ Tax year(s) ▶ ____		
d	Has a copy of this Form 3115 been provided to the examining agent identified on line 6c?	✓	
7a	Does audit protection apply to the applicant's requested change in method of accounting? See instructions. If "No," attach an explanation.	✓	
b	If "Yes," check the applicable box and attach the required statement. ☐ Not under exam ☐ 3-month window ☐ 120 day: Date examination ended ▶ ____ ☐ Method not before director ☐ Negative adjustment ☐ CAP: Date member joined group ▶ ____ ☐ Audit protection at end of exam ☐ Other		
8a	Does the applicant (or any present or former consolidated group in which the applicant was a member during the applicable tax year(s)) have any federal income tax return(s) before Appeals and/or a federal court? If "No," go to line 9.		✓
b	Is the method of accounting the applicant is requesting to change an issue under consideration by Appeals and/or a federal court (for either the applicant or any present or former consolidated group in which the applicant was a member for the tax year(s) the applicant was a member)? See instructions. If "Yes," attach an explanation.		✓
c	If "Yes," enter the name of the (check the box) ☐ Appeals officer and/or ☐ counsel for the government, telephone number, and the tax year(s) before Appeals and/or a federal court. Name ▶ ____ Telephone number ▶ ____ Tax year(s) ▶ ____		
d	Has a copy of this Form 3115 been provided to the Appeals officer and/or counsel for the government identified on line 8c?		
9	If the applicant answered "Yes" to line 6a and/or 8a with respect to any present or former consolidated group, attach a statement that provides each parent corporation's **(a)** name, **(b)** identification number, **(c)** address, and **(d)** tax year(s) during which the applicant was a member that is under examination, before an Appeals office, and/or before a federal court.		
10	If for federal income tax purposes, the applicant is either an entity (including a limited liability company) treated as a partnership or an S corporation, is it requesting a change from a method of accounting that is an issue under consideration in an examination, before Appeals, or before a federal court, with respect to a federal income tax return of a partner, member, or shareholder of that entity?		✓
11a	Has the applicant, its predecessor, or a related party requested or made (under either an automatic or non-automatic change procedure) a change in method of accounting within any of the five tax years ending with the tax year of change? If "No," go to line 12.		✓
b	If "Yes," for each trade or business, attach a description of each requested change in method of accounting (including the tax year of change) and state whether the applicant received consent.		
c	If any application was withdrawn, not perfected, or denied, or if a Consent Agreement granting a change was not signed and returned to the IRS, or the change was not made or not made in the requested year of change, attach an explanation.		
12	Does the applicant, its predecessor, or a related party currently have pending any request (including any concurrently filed request) for a private letter ruling, change in method of accounting, or technical advice?		✓
	If "Yes," for each request attach a statement providing **(a)** the name(s) of the taxpayer, **(b)** identification number(s), **(c)** the type of request (private letter ruling, change in method of accounting, or technical advice), and **(d)** the specific issue(s) in the request(s).		
13	Is the applicant requesting to change its **overall** method of accounting? If "Yes," complete Schedule A on page 4 of the form.		✓

Form **3115** (Rev. 12-2018)

Form 3115 (Rev. 12-2018) Page 3

Part II Information for All Requests *(continued)* | Yes | No

14 If the applicant is either **(i) not** changing its overall method of accounting, or **(ii)** changing its overall method of accounting **and** changing to a special method of accounting for one or more items, attach a detailed and complete description for each of the following (see instructions):

a The item(s) being changed.

b The applicant's present method for the item(s) being changed.

c The applicant's proposed method for the item(s) being changed.

d The applicant's present overall method of accounting (cash, accrual, or hybrid).

15a Attach a detailed and complete description of the applicant's trade(s) or business(es). See section 446(d).

b If the applicant has more than one trade or business, as defined in Regulations section 1.446-1(d), describe **(i)** whether each trade or business is accounted for separately; **(ii)** the goods and services provided by each trade or business and any other types of activities engaged in that generate gross income; **(iii)** the overall method of accounting for each trade or business; and **(iv)** which trade or business is requesting to change its accounting method as part of this application or a separate application.

Note: If you are requesting an automatic method change, see the instructions to see if you are required to complete lines 16a–16c.

16a Attach a full explanation of the legal basis supporting the proposed method for the item being changed. Include a detailed and complete description of the facts that explains how the law specifically applies to the applicant's situation and that demonstrates that the applicant is authorized to use the proposed method.

b Include all authority (statutes, regulations, published rulings, court cases, etc.) supporting the proposed method.

c Include either a discussion of the contrary authorities or a statement that no contrary authority exists.

17 Will the proposed method of accounting be used for the applicant's books and records and financial statements? For insurance companies, see the instructions. . . . . [Yes:] [No: ✓]

If "No," attach an explanation.

18 Does the applicant request a conference with the IRS National Office if the IRS National Office proposes an adverse response? [Yes: ✓] [No:]

19a If the applicant is changing to either the overall cash method, an overall accrual method, or is changing its method of accounting for any property subject to section 263A, any long-term contract subject to section 460 (see 19b), or inventories subject to section 474, enter the applicant's gross receipts for the 3 tax years preceding the tax year of change.

1st preceding year ended: mo. yr.	2nd preceding year ended: mo. yr.	3rd preceding year ended: mo. yr.
$	$	$

b If the applicant is changing its method of accounting for any long-term contract subject to section 460, in addition to completing 19a, enter the applicant's gross receipts for the 4th tax year preceding the tax year of change:

4th preceding year ended: mo. __________ yr. _____ $ ______________________________

Part III Information for Non-Automatic Change Request | Yes | No

20 Is the applicant's requested change described in any revenue procedure, revenue ruling, notice, regulation, or other published guidance as an automatic change request? . . . .

If "Yes," attach an explanation describing why the applicant is submitting its request under the non-automatic change procedures.

21 Attach a copy of all documents related to the proposed change (see instructions).

22 Attach a statement of the applicant's reasons for the proposed change.

23 If the applicant is a member of a consolidated group for the year of change, do all other members of the consolidated group use the proposed method of accounting for the item being changed? . . . .

If "No," attach an explanation.

24a Enter the amount of **user fee** attached to this application (see instructions). ▶ $ ______________________________

b If the applicant qualifies for a reduced user fee, attach the required information or certification (see instructions).

Form **3115** (Rev. 12-2018)

Form 3115 (Rev. 12-2018) Page 4

Part IV Section 481(a) Adjustment

		Yes	No
25	Does published guidance require the applicant (or permit the applicant and the applicant is electing) to implement the requested change in method of accounting on a cut-off basis? . . . . If "Yes," attach an explanation and do not complete lines 26, 27, and 28 below.		
26	Enter the section 481(a) adjustment. Indicate whether the adjustment is an increase (+) or a decrease (-) in income. ▶ $ -1,555,063 Attach a summary of the computation and an explanation of the methodology used to determine the section 481(a) adjustment. If it is based on more than one component, show the computation for each component. If more than one applicant is applying for the method change on the application, attach a list of the **(a)** name, **(b)** identification number, and **(c)** the amount of the section 481(a) adjustment attributable to each applicant.		
27	Is the applicant making an election to take the entire amount of the adjustment into account in the tax year of change? If "Yes," check the box for the applicable elective provision used to make the election (see instructions). ☐ $50,000 de minimis election ☐ Eligible acquisition transaction election		
28	Is any part of the section 481(a) adjustment attributable to transactions between members of an affiliated group, a consolidated group, a controlled group, or other related parties? . . . . If "Yes," attach an explanation.		✓

Schedule A—Change in Overall Method of Accounting (If Schedule A applies, Part I below must be completed.)

Part I Change in Overall Method (see instructions)

1 Check the appropriate boxes below to indicate the applicant's present and proposed methods of accounting.

Present method: ☐ Cash ☐ Accrual ☐ Hybrid (attach description)

Proposed method: ☐ Cash ☐ Accrual ☐ Hybrid (attach description)

2 Enter the following amounts as of the close of the tax year preceding the year of change. If none, state "None." Also, attach a statement providing a breakdown of the amounts entered on lines 2a through 2g.

		Amount
a	Income accrued but not received (such as accounts receivable)	$
b	Income received or reported before it was earned (such as advanced payments). Attach a description of the income and the legal basis for the proposed method.	
c	Expenses accrued but not paid (such as accounts payable).	
d	Prepaid expenses previously deducted	
e	Supplies on hand previously deducted and/or not previously reported	
f	Inventory on hand previously deducted and/or not previously reported. Complete Schedule D, Part II. .	
g	Other amounts (specify). Attach a description of the item and the legal basis for its inclusion in the calculation of the section 481(a) adjustment. ▶	
h	**Net section 481(a) adjustment** (Combine lines 2a–2g.) Indicate whether the adjustment is an increase (+) or decrease (-) in income. Also enter the net amount of this section 481(a) adjustment amount on Part IV, line 26.	$

3 Is the applicant also requesting the recurring item exception under section 461(h)(3)? . . . . ☐ Yes ☐ No

4 Attach copies of the profit and loss statement (Schedule F (Form 1040) for farmers) and the balance sheet, if applicable, as of the close of the tax year preceding the year of change. Also attach a statement specifying the accounting method used when preparing the balance sheet. If books of account are not kept, attach a copy of the business schedules submitted with the federal income tax return or other return (such as, tax-exempt organization returns) for that period. If the amounts in Part I, lines 2a through 2g, do not agree with the amounts shown on both the profit and loss statement and the balance sheet, attach a statement explaining the differences.

5 Is the applicant making a change to the overall cash method as a small business taxpayer (see instructions)? ☐ Yes ☐ No

Part II Change to the Cash Method for Non-Automatic Change Request (see instructions)

Applicants requesting a change to the cash method must attach the following information:

1 A description of inventory items (items whose production, purchase, or sale is an income-producing factor) and materials and supplies used in carrying out the business.

2 An explanation as to whether the applicant is required to use the accrual method under any section of the Code or regulations.

Form **3115** (Rev. 12-2018)

Schedule B—Change to the Deferral Method for Advance Payments (see instructions)

1 If the applicant is requesting to change to the deferral method for advance payments, as described in the instructions, attach the following information:

a Explain how the advance payments meet the definition of advance payment, as described in the instructions.

b Does the taxpayer use an applicable financial statement as described in the instructions and, if so, identify it.

c Describe the taxpayer's allocation method, if there is more than one performance obligation, as defined in the instructions.

d Describe the taxpayer's legal basis for deferral. See instructions.

e If the applicant is filing under the non-automatic change procedures, see the instructions for the information required.

Schedule C—Changes Within the LIFO Inventory Method (see instructions)

Part I General LIFO Information

Complete this section if the requested change involves changes within the LIFO inventory method. Also, attach a copy of all **Forms 970,** Application To Use LIFO Inventory Method, filed to adopt or expand the use of the LIFO method.

1 Attach a description of the applicant's present and proposed LIFO methods and submethods for each of the following items:

a Valuing inventory (for example, unit method or dollar-value method).

b Pooling (for example, by line or type or class of goods, natural business unit, multiple pools, raw material content, simplified dollar-value method, inventory price index computation (IPIC) pools, vehicle-pool method, etc.).

c Pricing dollar-value pools (for example, double-extension, index, link-chain, link-chain index, IPIC method, etc.).

d Determining the current-year cost of goods in the ending inventory (such as, most recent acquisitions, earliest acquisitions during the current year, average cost of current-year acquisitions, rolling-average cost, or other permitted method).

2 If any present method or submethod used by the applicant is not the same as indicated on Form(s) 970 filed to adopt or expand the use of the method, attach an explanation.

3 If the proposed change is not requested for all the LIFO inventory, attach a statement specifying the inventory to which the change is and is not applicable.

4 If the proposed change is not requested for all of the LIFO pools, attach a statement specifying the LIFO pool(s) to which the change is applicable.

5 Attach a statement addressing whether the applicant values any of its LIFO inventory on a method other than cost. For example, if the applicant values some of its LIFO inventory at retail and the remainder at cost, identify which inventory items are valued under each method.

6 If changing to the IPIC method, attach a completed Form 970.

Part II Change in Pooling Inventories

1 If the applicant is proposing to change its pooling method or the number of pools, attach a description of the contents of, and state the base year for, each dollar-value pool the applicant presently uses and proposes to use.

2 If the applicant is proposing to use natural business unit (NBU) pools or requesting to change the number of NBU pools, attach the following information (to the extent not already provided) in sufficient detail to show that each proposed NBU was determined under Regulations sections 1.472-8(b)(1) and (2):

a A description of the types of products produced by the applicant. If possible, attach a brochure.

b A description of the types of processes and raw materials used to produce the products in each proposed pool.

c If all of the products to be included in the proposed NBU pool(s) are not produced at one facility, state the reasons for the separate facilities, the location of each facility, and a description of the products each facility produces.

d A description of the natural business divisions adopted by the taxpayer. State whether separate cost centers are maintained and if separate profit and loss statements are prepared.

e A statement addressing whether the applicant has inventories of items purchased and held for resale that are not further processed by the applicant, including whether such items, if any, will be included in any proposed NBU pool.

f A statement addressing whether all items including raw materials, goods-in-process, and finished goods entering into the entire inventory investment for each proposed NBU pool are presently valued under the LIFO method. Describe any items that are not presently valued under the LIFO method that are to be included in each proposed pool.

g A statement addressing whether, within the proposed NBU pool(s), there are items both sold to unrelated parties and transferred to a different unit of the applicant to be used as a component part of another product prior to final processing.

3 If the applicant is engaged in manufacturing and is proposing to use the multiple pooling method or raw material content pools, attach information to show that each proposed pool will consist of a group of items that are substantially similar. See Regulations section 1.472-8(b)(3).

4 If the applicant is engaged in the wholesaling or retailing of goods and is requesting to change the number of pools used, attach information to show that each of the proposed pools is based on customary business classifications of the applicant's trade or business. See Regulations section 1.472-8(c).

Form 3115 (Rev. 12-2018) Page 6

Schedule D—Change in the Treatment of Long-Term Contracts Under Section 460, Inventories, or Other Section 263A Assets (see instructions)

Part I Change in Reporting Income From Long-Term Contracts (Also complete Part III on pages 7 and 8.)

1 To the extent not already provided, attach a description of the applicant's present and proposed methods for reporting income and expenses from long-term contracts. Also, attach a representative actual contract (without any deletion) for the requested change. If the applicant is a construction contractor, attach a detailed description of its construction activities.

2a Are the applicant's contracts long-term contracts as defined in section 460(f)(1) (see instructions)? . . . ☐ Yes ☐ No

b If "Yes," do all the contracts qualify for the exception under section 460(e) (see instructions)? . . . . . ☐ Yes ☐ No
If line 2b is "No," attach an explanation.

c Is the applicant requesting to use the percentage-of-completion method using cost-to-cost under Regulations section 1.460-4(b)? . . . . . ☐ Yes ☐ No

d If line 2c is "Yes," in computing the completion factor of a contract, will the applicant use the simplified cost-to-cost method described in Regulations section 1.460-5(c)? . . . . . ☐ Yes ☐ No

e If line 2c is "No," is the applicant requesting to use the exempt-contract percentage-of-completion method under Regulations section 1.460-4(c)(2)? . . . . . ☐ Yes ☐ No
If line 2e is "Yes," attach an explanation of what method the applicant will use to determine a contract's completion factor.
If line 2e is "No," attach an explanation of what method the applicant is using and the authority for its use.

3a Does the applicant have long-term manufacturing contracts as defined in section 460(f)(2)? . . . . . ☐ Yes ☐ No

b If "Yes," attach a description of the applicant's manufacturing activities, including any required installation of manufactured goods.

4a Does the applicant enter into cost-plus long-term contracts? . . . . . ☐ Yes ☐ No

b Does the applicant enter into federal long-term contracts? . . . . . ☐ Yes ☐ No

Part II Change in Valuing Inventories Including Cost Allocation Changes (Also complete Part III on pages 7 and 8.)

1 Attach a description of the inventory goods being changed.

2 Attach a description of the inventory goods (if any) NOT being changed.

3a Is the applicant subject to section 263A? If "No," go to line 4a. . . . . . ☐ Yes ☐ No

b Is the applicant's present inventory valuation method in compliance with section 263A (see instructions)? If "No," attach a detailed explanation. . . . . . ☐ Yes ☐ No

4a Check the appropriate boxes in the chart.

	Inventory Method Being Changed		Inventory Method Not Being Changed
	Present method	Proposed method	Present method
Identification methods:			
Specific identification			
FIFO			
LIFO			
Other (attach explanation)			
Valuation methods:			
Cost			
Cost or market, whichever is lower			
Retail cost			
Retail, lower of cost or market			
Other (attach explanation)			
b Enter the value at the end of the tax year preceding the year of change.	$	$	

5 If the applicant is changing from the LIFO inventory method to a non-LIFO method, attach the following information (see instructions).

a Copies of Form(s) 970 filed to adopt or expand the use of the method.

b **Only for applicants requesting a non-automatic change.** A statement describing whether the applicant is changing to the method required by Regulations section 1.472-6(a) or (b), or whether the applicant is proposing a different method.

c **Only for applicants requesting an automatic change.** The statement required by section 23.01(5) of Rev. Proc. 2018-31 (or its successor).

Form **3115** (Rev. 12-2018)

Form 3115 (Rev. 12-2018) Page 7

Part III **Method of Cost Allocation** (Complete this part if the requested change involves either property subject to section 263A or long-term contracts as described in section 460.) See instructions.

Section A—Allocation and Capitalization Methods

Attach a description (including sample computations) of the present and proposed method(s) the applicant uses to capitalize direct and indirect costs properly allocable to real or tangible personal property produced and property acquired for resale, or to allocate direct and indirect costs required to be allocated to long-term contracts. Include a description of the method(s) used for allocating indirect costs to intermediate cost objectives such as departments or activities prior to the allocation of such costs to long-term contracts, real or tangible personal property produced, and property acquired for resale. The description must include the following:

1 The method of allocating direct and indirect costs (for example, specific identification, burden rate, standard cost, or other reasonable allocation method).

2 The method of allocating mixed service costs (for example, direct reallocation, step-allocation, simplified service cost using the labor-based allocation ratio, simplified service cost using the production cost allocation ratio, or other reasonable allocation method).

3 Except for long-term contract accounting methods, the method of capitalizing additional section 263A costs (for example, simplified production with or without the historic absorption ratio election, simplified resale with or without the historic absorption ratio election including permissible variations, the U.S. ratio, or other reasonable allocation method).

Section B—Direct and Indirect Costs Required to be Allocated

Check the appropriate boxes showing the costs that are or will be fully included, to the extent required, in the cost of real or tangible personal property produced or property acquired for resale under section 263A or allocated to long-term contracts under section 460. Mark "N/A" in a box if those costs are not incurred by the applicant. If a box is not checked, it is assumed that those costs are not fully included to the extent required. Attach an explanation for boxes that are not checked.

		Present method	Proposed method
1	Direct material		
2	Direct labor		
3	Indirect labor		
4	Officers' compensation (not including selling activities)		
5	Pension and other related costs		
6	Employee benefits		
7	Indirect materials and supplies		
8	Purchasing costs		
9	Handling, processing, assembly, and repackaging costs		
10	Offsite storage and warehousing costs		
11	Depreciation, amortization, and cost recovery allowance for equipment and facilities placed in service and not temporarily idle		
12	Depletion		
13	Rent		
14	Taxes other than state, local, and foreign income taxes		
15	Insurance		
16	Utilities		
17	Maintenance and repairs that relate to a production, resale, or long-term contract activity		
18	Engineering and design costs (not including section 174 research and experimental expenses)		
19	Rework labor, scrap, and spoilage		
20	Tools and equipment		
21	Quality control and inspection		
22	Bidding expenses incurred in the solicitation of contracts awarded to the applicant		
23	Licensing and franchise costs		
24	Capitalizable service costs (including mixed service costs)		
25	Administrative costs (not including any costs of selling or any return on capital)		
26	Research and experimental expenses attributable to long-term contracts		
27	Interest		
28	Other costs (Attach a list of these costs.)		

Form **3115** (Rev. 12-2018)

Form 3115 (Rev. 12-2018) Page **8**

Part III **Method of Cost Allocation** *(continued)* See instructions.

Section C—Other Costs Not Required To Be Allocated (Complete Section C only if the applicant is requesting to change its method for these costs.)

		Present method	Proposed method
1	Marketing, selling, advertising, and distribution expenses		
2	Research and experimental expenses not included in Section B, line 26		
3	Bidding expenses not included in Section B, line 22		
4	General and administrative costs not included in Section B		
5	Income taxes		
6	Cost of strikes		
7	Warranty and product liability costs		
8	Section 179 costs		
9	On-site storage		
10	Depreciation, amortization, and cost recovery allowance not included in Section B, line 11		
11	Other costs (Attach a list of these costs.)		

Schedule E—Change in Depreciation or Amortization. See instructions.

Applicants requesting approval to change their method of accounting for depreciation or amortization complete this section. Applicants ***must*** provide this information for each item or class of property for which a change is requested.

Note: See the ***Summary of the List of Automatic Accounting Method Changes*** in the instructions for information regarding automatic changes under sections 56, 167, 168, 197, 1400I, 1400L, or former section 168. **Do not** file Form 3115 with respect to certain late elections and election revocations. See instructions.

1 Is depreciation for the property determined under Regulations section 1.167(a)-11 (CLADR)? ☐ **Yes** ☐ **No**
If "Yes," the only changes permitted are under Regulations section 1.167(a)-11(c)(1)(iii).

2 Is any of the depreciation or amortization required to be capitalized under any Code section, such as section 263A? ☐ **Yes** ☐ **No**
If "Yes," enter the applicable section ▶ ____________

3 Has a depreciation, amortization, expense, or disposition election been made for the property, such as the election under sections 168(f)(1), 168(i)(4), 179, 179C, or Regulations section 1.168(i)-8(d)? ☐ **Yes** ☐ **No**
If "Yes," state the election made ▶ ____________

4a To the extent not already provided, attach a statement describing the property subject to the change. Include in the description the type of property, the year the property was placed in service, and the property's use in the applicant's trade or business or income-producing activity.

b If the property is residential rental property, did the applicant live in the property before renting it? ☐ **Yes** ☐ **No**

c Is the property public utility property? ☐ **Yes** ☐ **No**

5 To the extent not already provided in the applicant's description of its present method, attach a statement explaining how the property is treated under the applicant's present method (for example, depreciable property, inventory property, supplies under Regulations section 1.162-3, nondepreciable section 263(a) property, property deductible as a current expense, etc.).

6 If the property is not currently treated as depreciable or amortizable property, attach a statement of the facts supporting the proposed change to depreciate or amortize the property.

7 If the property is currently treated and/or will be treated as depreciable or amortizable property, provide the following information for both the present (if applicable) and proposed methods:

a The Code section under which the property is or will be depreciated or amortized (for example, section 168(g)).

b The applicable asset class from Rev. Proc. 87-56, 1987-2 C.B. 674, for each asset depreciated under section 168 (MACRS) or under section 1400L; the applicable asset class from Rev. Proc. 83-35, 1983-1 C.B. 745, for each asset depreciated under former section 168 (ACRS); an explanation why no asset class is identified for each asset for which an asset class has not been identified by the applicant.

c The facts to support the asset class for the proposed method.

d The depreciation or amortization method of the property, including the applicable Code section (for example, 200% declining balance method under section 168(b)(1)).

e The useful life, recovery period, or amortization period of the property.

f The applicable convention of the property.

g Whether the additional first-year special depreciation allowance (for example, as provided by section 168(k), 168(l), 168(m), 168(n), 1400L(b), or 1400N(d)) was or will be claimed for the property. If not, also provide an explanation as to why no special depreciation allowance was or will be claimed.

h Whether the property was or will be in a single asset account, a multiple asset account, or a general asset account.

Form **3115** (Rev. 12-2018)

Client Name
EIN: 99-99999
Tax Year Ended 12/31/2014

Automatic Change #184, #186 & #187
Reg. § § 1.162-4 and 1.263(a)-3; 1.162-3(a)(1), (c)(1); and 1.162-3(a)(2), (c)(1)
Filed Pursuant to Appendix Section 10.11 of Rev. Proc. 2011-14,
As Modified by Rev. Proc. 2012-39 and Rev. Proc. 2014-16

Page 1, Name of Applicants

Unless otherwise specified, a reference to the "Taxpayer" in this document refers to the following applicant:

Client Name.
EIN: 99-99999
Principal business activity code: 423700

Request for Faxed Documents

In accordance with the procedures set forth in section 9.04(3) of Rev. Proc. 2014-1, the Taxpayer requests that a copy of any document related to this request (e.g., a request for additional information) be provided to the Taxpayer and the Taxpayer's authorized representatives via fax at the numbers below.

Taxpayer's Fax Number:

This person is authorized to file this Form 3115.

Page 2, Part II, Questions 9b & 10b

The following change(s) in accounting method were requested by the Taxpayer or a related party within the past 5 years (including the year of change):

Year	Filer/Applicant	EIN	Method Change	Consent
12/31/2014			184-186-187	Automatic
12/31/2014			184-186-187-196	Automatic

Statement 1

Client Name
EIN: 99-99999
Tax Year Ended 12/31/2014

Automatic Change #184, #186 & #187
Reg. § § 1.162-4 and 1.263(a)-3; 1.162-3(a)(1), (c)(1); and 1.162-3(a)(2), (c)(1)
Filed Pursuant to Appendix Section 10.11 of Rev. Proc. 2011-14,
As Modified by Rev. Proc. 2012-39 and Rev. Proc. 2014-16

Page 3, Part II, Question 14

a) Item being changed

Unit of Property:
The taxpayer is changing its method of accounting for the following Items under this automatic method #184:

Determining and expensing of repairs and maintenance costs for its expenditures paid or incurred for tangible property to the rules outlined in Reg. § 1.162-4. Taxpayer's prior accounting method followed superseded Treasury guidance that generally concluded that those amounts paid or incurred for tangible property required capitalization under IRC § 263(a).

- The costing criteria of § 1.263(a)-3(g) for improvement related to direct and indirect costs.
- The betterment criteria of § 1.263(a)-3(j) for improvements to tangible property.
- The restoration criteria of § 1.263(a)-3(k) for improvements to tangible property.
- The adaption criteria of § 1.263(a)-3(l) for improvements to tangible property.
- Routine maintenance safe harbor of § 1.263(a)-3(i). The taxpayer has not been employing this method.
- Unit of property criteria for its building(s) and land improvements under § 1.263(a)-3(e) and/or leased property under § 1.263(a)-3(f). For further details on the unit of property issues, see more detailed descriptions and answers below.

Non-incidental and Incidental Materials and Supplies:
The taxpayer is changing its method of accounting for the following items under these automatic methods #186 & #187:

The Taxpayer is seeking to change Its method of accounting for non-incidental materials and supplies, as defined in § 1.162-3(a)(1) and (c)(1), to comply with the definition therein and to deduct such amounts in the taxable year in which they are actually used or consumed, consistent with § 1.162-3(a).

Statement 2

- -

Client Name
EIN: 99-99999
Tax Year Ended 12/31/2014

Automatic Change #184, #186 & #187
Reg. §§1.162-4 and 1.263(a)-3; 1.162-3(a)(1), (c)(1); and 1.162-3(a)(2), (c)(1)
Filed Pursuant to Appendix Section 10.11 of Rev. Proc. 2011-14,
As Modified by Rev. Proc. 2012-39 and Rev. Proc. 2014-16

Additionally, the Taxpayer is seeking to change its method of accounting for incidental materials and supplies, as defined in §1.162-3(a)(2) and (c)(1), to comply with the definition therein and to deduct such amounts in the taxable year in which they are paid, consistent with §1.162-3(a).

These changes do not apply to any materials and supplies for which the Taxpayer has elected to apply the de minimis safe harbor under §1.263(a)-1(f).

b) & c) The applicant's present and proposed methods for the item being changed

Unit of Property

Present and Proposed Methods for Identifying the Unit of Property:

Under the Taxpayer's present method of accounting, the Taxpayer has not been employing any defined unit of property criteria. The taxpayer currently accounts for amounts paid for tangible property either as items requiring capitalization under 263(a) or as amounts paid as repairs and maintenance costs.

The taxpayer proposes to use the guidance of §1.162-4 and other sections of the tangible property regulations to determine whether an expenditure should be written off as a repair and maintenance cost under §1.263(a)-1, -2, and/or -3, or be capitalized. The taxpayer will employ the routine maintenance safe harbor of §1.263(a)-3(i).

The taxpayer will account for each of its buildings as the building, its building structures and building systems as one unit of property for each building. Additionally, the taxpayer will account for its land improvements consisting of parking lots, landscaping, signage and side lighting site utilities as one unit of property, separate from the building unit of property for each building. The taxpayer will also account for each Sec. 1245 asset, such as furniture & fixtures, automobiles & trucks, and machinery & equipment, as separate units of property.

Statement 3

Client Name
EIN: 99-99999
Tax Year Ended 12/31/2014

Automatic Change #184, #186 & #187
Reg. § § 1.162-4 and 1.263(a)-3; 1.162-3(a)(1), (c)(1); and 1.162-3(a)(2), (c)(1)
Filed Pursuant to Appendix Section 10.11 of Rev. Proc. 2011-14,
As Modified by Rev. Proc. 2012-39 and Rev. Proc. 2014-16

The taxpayer will account for its leasehold improvements made by a lessee, including improvements to leasehold improvements, so as to treat the unit of property to be based on the general definitions of the unit of property, but with respect to the portion of the property that is subject to the lease, and not just with reference to the leasehold improvements.

Incidental and Non-incidental Materials and Supplies:
Present and Proposed Methods for Incidental and Non-incidental Materials and Supplies:

Under the Taxpayer's present method of accounting, Taxpayer currently does not hold incidental material, supplies, expenses non-incidental material, and supplies when paid. They taxpayer is filing the method changes to adopt the guidance under § 1.162-3.

Under the Taxpayer's proposed method of accounting, the Taxpayer will deduct amounts paid for non-incidental materials and supplies, as defined in § 1.162-3(a)(1) and (c)(1), in the taxable year in which the material or supply is first used or consumed, consistent with § 1.162-3.

Under the Taxpayer's proposed method of accounting, the Taxpayer will deduct amounts paid for incidental materials and supplies, as defined in § 1.162-3(a)(2) and (c)(1), in the taxable year in which such amounts are paid, consistent with Reg. § 1.162-3(a).

The applicant's present overall method of accounting
The Taxpayer's overall method of accounting is the accrual method.

Page 3. Part II. Line 15(a)
Taxpayer's Trade or Business: Wholesale trade – building & plumbing products
Principal Business Activity Code: 423700
The Taxpayer has only one trade or business as defined in § 1.446-1(d).

Statement 4

- -

Client Name
EIN: 99-99999
Tax Year Ended 12/31/2014

Automatic Change #184, #186 & #187
Reg. § § 1.162-4 and 1.263(a)-3; 1.162-3(a)(1), (c)(1); and 1.162-3(a)(2), (c)(1)
Filed Pursuant to Appendix Section 10.11 of Rev. Proc. 2011-14,
As Modified by Rev. Proc. 2012-39 and Rev. Proc. 2014-16

Page 3. Part II. Line 18

If it is tentatively determined that the Taxpayer has changed its method of accounting without complying with all the applicable provisions of Rev. Proc. 2011-14, as modified by Rev. Proc. 2012-39 and Rev. Proc. 2014-16 (e.g., the Taxpayer changed to a method of accounting that varies from the applicable accounting method described in Rev. Proc. 2011-14, as modified by Rev. Proc. 2012-39 and Rev. Proc. 2014-16, or the Taxpayer is outside the scope of Rev. Proc. 2011-14, as modified by Rev. Proc. 2012·39 and Rev. Proc. 2014-16), the privilege of a conference is hereby requested. To arrange the time and place of such a conference, please contact the Taxpayer's representative(s):

Partner
DEF, LLP
973-867 ·5309
973-867-5310 (fax)
Partner@DEF.com

Page 3, Part IV, Line 2.6

The method change revenue procedures being applied for results in a -0- Sec. 481(a) adjustment for this taxpayer.

Statement 5

14

The Time Value of Money

§14.01 Interest, Original Issue Discount and Time Value of Money

Tax accounting concerns itself with the timing of income and deductions. Because money is fungible, tax accounting must take into account items such as interest, original issue discount, and the time value of money.

With the passing of successive tax legislation, the IRS has imposed limitations on interest deductions and the accounting for interest income. Distortions result, particularly for cash method taxpayers, when an interest payment is deferred or prepaid.

Further distortions are created when interest is unstated and one has to determine the true economic effect of a transaction.

§14.02 Interest

[A] Stated Interest

Most loan transactions state interest in terms of an annual percentage rate that is paid annually or more frequently. Stated interest is taxed according to the taxpayer's method of accounting.

Cash method taxpayers recognize income when cash or its equivalent is actually or constructively received and claim deductions upon the payment of cash.[1]

Accrual method taxpayers recognize income when all events that fix the right to income have occurred and when the amount can be determined. All the events that fix the right to receive income occur when (1) the required performance occurs, (2) payment therefor is due, or (3) payment therefor is made, whichever happens earliest.[2] In applying this rule to the accrual of interest income, performance occurs when the lender allows the borrower to use his money. Interest accrues with the passage of time.[3] When the lender allows the borrower to use the money for one day, one day's performance has occurred and one day's interest accrues (assuming the payment has not already been made or come due). Thus, unless interest is paid or such payment is due earlier, interest accrues ratably over the term of the loan.[4] Because interest reflects the time value of money, economic performance occurs as time passes, creating issues of timing and character for the accrual method taxpayer for interest that is prepaid or deferred.[5]

Surprisingly there is no definition of interest in the code or regulations. However, the Supreme Court, in *Old Colony Railroad Co. v. Commissioner*, described interest as "the amount one has contracted to pay for the use of borrowed money."[6]

In *Deputy v. du Pont*, the Supreme Court said interest is "compensation for the use or forbearance of money."[7]

IRC §446 and Reg. §1.446-2(a)(1) provide the general rules on deductibility of interest and for determining the portion of a payment that consists of accrued interest. Under the regulations, interest includes original issue discount and amounts treated as interest (whether stated or unstated) in any lending or deferred payment

---

[1] *See* Chapter 5. *See also* Reg. §1.451-1(a).

[2] *Id.*

[3] Rev. Rul. 74-607, 1974-2 CB 149. *See also* Reg. §1.451-1(a).

[4] *Id.*

[5] *See* Chapter 6. *See also* Reg. §1.461-1(a)(1), (2).

[6] 284 U.S. 552, 560 (1932).

[7] 308 U.S. 488, 498 (1940). *See, e.g.,* Rev. Rul. 69-188, 1969-1 CB 54.

transaction. In *Gunderson Brothers Engineering Corp. v. Commissioner*,[8] the taxpayer, an accrual method dealer, sold trucks and trailers under a deferred payment plan that required a purchaser to sign a non-interest-bearing note for the total price of the vehicle, plus the total amount of finance charges that would be due over the period between the date of the sale and final payment. Each purchaser opting to make deferred payments signed a retail installment contract and a non-interest-bearing note. The note included the principal balance plus finance charges. The dealer accrued the finance charges as each installment payment became due using the sum-of-the-digits method.

In holding that the dealer did not have to accrue the full amount of the balance of the note (including the finance charge) in the year of sale, the court said: "we feel the finance charge under the circumstances of this case is in the nature of interest . . . Interest has been defined as 'the compensation allowed by law or fixed by the parties for the use, or forbearance, or detention of money.'"[9] The court went on to approve the taxpayer's treatment of the installment payment by use of the sum-of-the-digits method and deferring the remaining portion of the finance charge until the note became due. In Rev. Rul. 67-316,[10] the IRS announced that it would follow *Gunderson* and similar cases. The principle that interest accrues over time was reinforced in the *Estate of Ratliff v. Commissioner*.[11]

Example 14-1

Bob loaned Dale $10,000 for five years at 10% simple interest, with equal annual payments of $2,500. The term of the note provided that all payments are to be applied first to principal then to the $2,500 of interest. Dale agreed to report on the same basis. Accordingly, both Bob and Dale treated the entire $2,500 annual payments for the first four years as principal, which is non-taxable to Bob and non-deductible by Dale, and the entire $2,500 payment in the fifth year as interest, which is taxable to Bob and deductible, within applicable limits, by Dale.

Are Bob and Dale allowed to report the interest and principal as described above? If not what is the correct reporting procedure?

In *Estate of Ratliff v. Commissioner*,[12] the court said payments allocated first to principal and then to interest are not respected because interest is earned over the term of a note.

---

[8] 42 T.C. 419 (1964).

[9] *Id.* at 430.

[10] 1967-2 CB 171.

[11] 70 TCM 600 (1995).

[12] *Id.*

[B] Requirements for Interest Deduction

IRC § 163(a) provides that "There shall be allowed as a deduction all interest paid or accrued within the taxable year on indebtedness." To be deductible under IRC § 163(a), amounts paid as interest must be paid on genuine indebtedness.[13] "Indebtedness" is defined as "an existing, unconditional, and legally enforceable obligation for the payment of a principal sum."[14] There are four general requirements for deducting interest:

- The payment made must actually constitute "interest";[15]
- The payment must be paid or incurred within the tax year at issue;[16]
- The payment at issue must be made on a valid, existing "indebtedness";[17] and
- The indebtedness at issue must belong to the taxpayer seeking the deduction.[18]

[C] Rule of 78's

The rule of 78's is a method of allocating interest that determines when interest is to be allocated to each time period by multiplying the total interest payable over the loan term by a fraction (i) the numerator of which is the number of periods remaining on the loan at the time the calculation is made and (ii) the denominator of which is the sum of all time periods during the loan term. It is a method that was used by banks in calculating interest on short-term loans. For example, under the rule of 78's, the first month's interest is 12÷78's of a year's interest, the second is 11÷78's. The processes continue down to 1÷78's for the last month. This results in interest being overstated in the early months and understated in the later months. The rule of 78's is an artificial way of accruing interest. The IRS does not recognize the rule of 78's because it is not economically sound.[19]

The rule of 78's represents a mechanical formula for allocating interest among periods. Previously there was an administrative exception to the application of the rule in Rev. Proc. 83-40 for short-term consumer loans.[20]

---

[13] *Knetsch v. United States*, 364 U.S. 361, 365 (1960).

[14] *Midkiff v. Comm'r*, 96 T.C. 724, 734-35 (1991).

[15] IRC § 163(a).

[16] *Id., Heyman v. Comm'r*, 70 T.C. 482 (1978), *aff'd*, 652 F.2d 598 (6th Cir. 1980).

[17] *See First Nat'l Co. v. Comm'r*, 289 F.2d 861 (6th Cir. 1961). The existence of a valid indebtedness is determined under state law. *Gilman v. Comm'r*, 53 F.2d 47 (8th Cir. 1931).

[18] *Little v. Comm'r*, 21 BTA 911 (1930).

[19] *See* Rev. Rul. 83-84, 1983-1 CB 97. *See also* § 5.04[B].

[20] 1983-1 CB 774. This ruling has been obsoleted by Rev. Proc. 97-37, 1997-2 CB 455.

[D] Prepaid Interest

Because interest accrues over time, there can be no such thing as prepaid interest. Any payment of interest at the time of borrowing or significantly in advance of its due date is in reality a reduction in principal. IRC § 461(g) provides that a deduction of prepaid interest shall be charged to the capital account and shall be treated as paid in the period to which it is allocable.[21] There is no similar provision for income. In essence, prepaid interest is merely a reduction in a loan properly taxed under original issue discount ("OID"). Prepaid interest must be included in income by a lender when received, regardless of the lender's method of accounting, but cannot be deducted by the payor until the interest accrues.[22]

[E] Personal Interest

Temp Reg. § 1.163-9T defines personal expenditures and, therefore, personal interest as any interest expense other than:

- Interest paid or accrued on indebtedness properly allocable (within the meaning of Reg. § 1.163-8T) to the conduct of trade or business (other than the trade or business of performing services as an employee);
- Any investment interest (within the meaning of IRC § 163(d)(3));
- Any interest that is taken into account under IRC § 469 in computing income or loss from a passive activity of the taxpayer;
- Any qualified residence interest (within the meaning of IRC § 163(h)(3) and Reg. § 1.163-10T); and
- Any interest payable under IRC § 6601 with respect to the unpaid portion of the tax imposed by IRC § 2001 for the period during which an extension of time for payment of such tax is in effect under IRC § 6163, 6166, or 6166A (as in effect before its repeal by the Economic Recovery Tax Act of 1981).

Therefore, unless the interest payment falls within the aforesaid categories, the interest is not deductible. Note that Temp. Reg. § 1.163-9T(b)(2) provides that individual interest on income tax deficiencies attributable to business income is personal interest. This prohibition includes interest paid by a trust, S corporation, or other pass-through entity on underpayments of State or local income taxes and on indebtedness used to pay such taxes.

Example 14-2

A, an individual, owns stock of an S corporation. On its return for 1987, the corporation underreports its taxable income. Consequently, A under-

---

[21] The exception being for "points" on residential mortgages that is based on consideration other than tax principles, IRC § 461(g)(2).

[22] Prop. Reg. § 1.446-2(e)(3)(iii).

reports A's share of that income on A's tax return. In 1989, A pays the resulting deficiency plus interest to the IRS. The interest paid by A in 1989 on the tax deficiency is personal interest, notwithstanding the fact that the additional tax liability may have arisen out of income from a trade or business. The result would be the same if A's business had been operated as a sole proprietorship.[23]

In several Tax Court decisions, the court has emphasized that in many other tax contexts expenditures contesting tax deficiencies and interest on such potential deficiencies were considered business, not personal.[24] On the other hand, in *True v. United States*,[25] interest on tax deficiencies attributable to pass-through entities was determined to be an itemized deduction, not deductible in determining adjusted gross income.

Similarly, in *Seymour v. Commissioner*,[26] the court held that interest indebtedness incurred to purchase assets from the taxpayer's ex-wife as part of a divorce was not necessarily personal interest because the sale was part of the divorce, but was characterized by the nature of the asset acquired under the tracing rules.[27]

[F] Investment Interest

IRC § 163(d) limits the deductibility of investment interest. A noncorporate taxpayer's deduction for investment interest[28] is limited to the taxpayer's net investment income for the tax year. The deduction for investment interest allowed during the tax year is limited to the lesser of the investment interest paid or net investment income. IRC § 163(d)(2) permits an unlimited carryforward of any amounts disallowed under the general limitation. Thus, the disallowed amounts may be carried over and deducted as investment interest paid or accrued in the succeeding tax year to the extent the taxpayer has investment income in that year. The language of IRC § 163(d)(2) provides a carryover only for interest not allowed as a deduction by reason of the limitation on investment interest. Read literally, the provision would disallow a carryover for investment interest in excess of taxable income because the excess could not be deducted, even apart from the investment interest limitation. However, investment interest paid in excess of the IRC § 163(d)(1) limit may be carried over as a deduction in a later year regardless of taxable income in the loss

---

[23] Temp. Reg. § 1.163-9T(b)(2)(ii). *See, e.g., Redlark v. Comm'r*, 141 F.3d 936 (1998).

[24] *See Standing v. Comm'r*, 28 T.C. 789 (1957), *aff'd*, 259 F.2d 450 (4th 1958) (deficiency interest on taxes on business income and expenditures and settling the deficiencies were held to be deductible in determining adjusted gross income). In AOD 1992-14, the IRS acquiesced in *Standing*. *See also* Rev. Rul. 70-40, 1970-1 CB 50, where state income taxes on business income are business expenses to determine net operating losses.

[25] 93-2 USTC ¶ 50,461 (D. Wyo. 1993).

[26] 109 T.C. 279 (1997).

[27] Temp. Reg. § 1.163-8T(a)(3) *See also* Priv. Ltr. Rul. 9031022.

[28] *See* IRC § 163(d)(4).

year, according to the Federal Circuit decision in *Sharp v. United States*.[29] After a series of court losses, the IRS accepted the broader reading, in which all interest in excess of the limitation is available for carryover, regardless of the level of taxable income.[30]

Net investment income, which serves as the ceiling on the deductibility of investment interest, is the excess of investment income over investment expenses.[31] Investment income includes gross income from interest, annuities, and royalties not derived in the ordinary course of business.[32] However, investment income does not include any income taken into account when calculating income or loss from a passive activity.[33] Under IRC § 163(d)(4)(B), net investment income also generally includes net capital gain that a taxpayer elects to take into account as net investment income and "qualified dividend income"[34] to the extent the taxpayer elects to treat such income as investment income.[35]

Thus, a taxpayer who recognizes long-term capital gain, which is taxed at favorable rates, is prevented from being able to use that gain to deduct otherwise nondeductible investment interest against ordinary income.[36] The provision for taking ordinary gain into account is rather intricate and does not always result in considering ordinary gain as investment income.

Investment expenses are those deductible expenses directly connected with the production of investment income, such as brokerage and investment counsel fees. Investment expenses do not include interest expenses.

IRC § 267(a)(2) outlines the related party rules regarding the matching of deductions and income. Generally, an accrual-basis taxpayer is placed on the cash basis regarding the deductibility of items accrued, but not yet paid, to related cash-basis taxpayers. IRC § 267(a)(2) provides that the deduction is allowed on the day the amount is included in the recipient's income.

There is, however, no direct matching of indebtedness with specific investments. The limitation is based on net investment income, which, in effect, includes income on investment property and gain on the sale of investment property that is not taxed at special capital gains rates net of investment expenses. The determination of interest subject to the limitation is based on tracing the proceeds of any borrowing, regardless of security, into the next expenditures.[37] When the borrowing is to acquire an interest in an entity, the assets of the entity determine the allocation of the funds.[38]

---

[29] 14 F.3d 583 (Fed. Cir. 1993).

[30] Rev. Rul. 95-16, 1995-1 CB 9.

[31] IRC § 163(d)(4)(A).

[32] IRC § 163(d)(4)(B).

[33] IRC § 469(e)(1)(A)(ii); Temp. Reg. § 1.469-2T(c)(2)(A).

[34] *See* IRC § 1(h)(11)(B).

[35] IRC § 163(d)(4)(B).

[36] TAM 9549002.

[37] Temp. Reg. § § 1.163-8T, 1.163-9T(b)(2).

[38] Notice 89-35, 1989-1 CB 675.

Unlike, for example, IRC § 265(a)(2) (expenses and interest related to tax-exempt bonds), IRC § 163(d) does not disallow the excess interest, but postpones the deduction until there is sufficient investment income to absorb the deduction.

Because IRC § 163(d) is intended as a deferral provision, it provides a carryover of investment interest that is not deductible in one year to future years, where it is added to any investment interest incurred in the carryover year to determine the investment interest deduction in that year, and, to the extent not used, carried forward indefinitely to future years. Because the carryover is unlimited, there is no need to provide any tracing of the source of the interest. By definition, investment interest is nonbusiness interest, and it would not be a part of any net operating loss carryover to the extent that nonbusiness expenses exceed nonbusiness income in the year incurred.[39]

Example 14-3

Dan, a lawyer, used borrowed funds to purchase undeveloped property with the intent to develop it as residential condominiums. He had previously realized ordinary income when he purchased a similar parcel jointly with Sam, a real estate broker, and sold it a little over a year later without developing it.

This time Dan has decided to go it alone. However, shortly after he acquired property, the local government changed the Master Plan to make it more difficult to develop the property. During this time, he leased the property to a tenant farmer to qualify for lower real estate taxes. This required a long-term commitment to the farmer. After three years, he abandoned the property to the lender.

Is the interest subject to the investment interest rule limit rules?

In *Morley v. Commissioner*,[40] the court found that a failed real estate transaction was a business; however, in *Polakis v. Commissioner*,[41] the court found a similar transaction to be an investment.

For tax years beginning after 2017, the deduction for business interest expense cannot exceed the sum of the taxpayer's:

1. Business interest income for the tax year;
2. 2.30% of adjusted taxable income (ATI) for the year, or zero, if the taxpayer's ATI is less than zero; and
3. Floor plan financing interest expense.

The prior Section 163(j) rules, which covered so-called earnings stripping and denied a corporation's interest deduction for disqualified interest to the extent it had

---

[39] *See Beyer v. Comm'r*, 916 F.2d 153 (4th Cir. 1990). In Rev. Rul. 95-16, 1995-1 CB 9, the IRS said it would follow *Beyer*.

[40] 87 T.C. 1206 (1987).

[41] 91 T.C. 660 (1988).

excess interest expense in a year that its debt-to-equity ratio was greater than 1.5 to 1, have been repealed.[42]

[G] Qualified Residence Interest

The general personal interest deduction was eliminated many years ago. However, there still remains a deduction for "qualified residential interest."[43] Unfortunately, because of the alternative minimum tax not everyone is able to obtain a deduction for their qualified residential interest.[44]

Prior to the TCJA, as a general matter, personal interest was not deductible. Qualified residence interest was not treated as personal interest and was allowed as an itemized deduction, subject to limitations. Qualified residence interest is interest paid or accrued during the taxable year on either acquisition indebtedness or home equity indebtedness. A qualified residence means the taxpayer's principal residence and one other residence of the taxpayer selected to be a qualified residence.[45] A qualified residence can be a house, condominium, cooperative, mobile home, house trailer, or boat.[46] For purposes of IRC § 121 (and by incorporation IRC § 163(h)(4)), a taxpayer's principal residence is determined based upon a review of all relevant facts and circumstances.[47] Notwithstanding the foregoing, "property used by the taxpayer as the taxpayer's residence does not include personal property that is not a fixture under local law."[48] Further, if a taxpayer alternates between two properties, using each as a residence for successive periods of time, the property that the taxpayer uses a majority of the time during the year ordinarily is considered the taxpayer's principal residence.[49]

Factors that would be taken into account when attempting to determine a taxpayer's principal residence include, but is not limited to:

- The taxpayer's place of employment;[50]
- The principal place of abode of the taxpayer's family members;[51]
- The address listed on the taxpayer's federal and state tax returns, driver's license, automobile registration, and voter registration card;[52]
- The taxpayer's mailing address for bills and correspondence;[53]

---

[42] IRC § 163(j)(1); Prop. Reg. § 1.163(j)-2(b).
[43] IRC § 163(h)(3); Temp. Reg. § 1.163-10T(b).
[44] IRC § 56(c)(1) and (e).
[45] IRC § 163(h)(4).
[46] Reg. § 1.121-1(b)(1).
[47] Reg. § 1.121-1(b)(2).
[48] Reg. § 1.121-1(b)(1).
[49] Reg. § 1.121-1(b)(2).
[50] Reg. § 1.121-1(b)(2)(i).
[51] Reg. § 1.121-1(b)(2)(ii).
[52] Reg. § 1.121-1(b)(2)(iii).
[53] Reg. § 1.21-1(b)(2)(iv).

- The location of the taxpayer's banks;[54] and
- The location of religious organizations and recreational clubs with which the taxpayer is affiliated.[55]

Note that vacant land does not constitute the taxpayer's principal residence unless:

- The vacant land is adjacent to land containing the dwelling unit of the taxpayer's principal residence;[56] or
- The taxpayer owned and used the vacant land as part of the taxpayer's principal residence.[57]

Qualified residence interest" includes interest on a mortgage for both a first and second residence.[58] Specifically, interest is qualified residence interest if: (1) it is secured by a house or other dwelling unit owned by the taxpayer;[59] (2) the dwelling unit is a "qualified residence" of the taxpayer;[60] and (3) the indebtedness is either "acquisition indebtedness" or, for tax years beginning before 2018,[61] "home equity indebtedness."[62] Accordingly, for tax years beginning in 2018 through 2025, "home equity indebtedness" is not deductible.[63] Notwithstanding the foregoing, the IRS has issued guidance stating that interest on home equity loans may nevertheless be deductible for tax years beginning in 2018 through 2025, so long as the indebtedness otherwise qualifies as acquisition indebtedness and is otherwise within the deductibility limitations. Reg. § 1.163-10T(o)(1) clarifies what constitutes "secured debt." In general, debt is "secured" by a qualified residence when the residence can be used to settle the debt should the borrower default on his repayment commitment. It is expected that the security interest be recorded or otherwise perfected as legally required.

Under Reg. § 1.163-10T(o), the term "security" appears to be limited to the pledging of the residence itself, and an attempt to substitute property that does not constitute the interest of the debtor in the qualified residence as specific security for the repayment of the debt is not permitted. Thus, where the interest on the debt incurred to purchase a principal residence is secured by commercial property rather than by the residence itself, there is no "security" and no deduction for qualified residence interest is permissible, even though the loan proceeds can be traced to the purchase of the residence.[64]

---

54 Reg. § 1.121-1(b)(2)(v).
55 Reg. § 1.121-1(b)(2)(vi).
56 Reg. § 1.121-1(b)(3)(i)(A).
57 Reg. § 1.121-1(b)(3)(i)(B).
58 IRC § 163(h)(3)(A), IRC § 163(h)(4)(A)(i)(II).
59 IRC § 163(h)(3)(B)(i)(II).
60 IRC § 163(h)(3)(A)(i), IRC § 163(h)(3)(A)(ii). *See also* IRC § 163(h)(4)(A)(i).
61 IRC § 163(h)(3)(F)(i)(I).
62 IRC § 163(h)(3)(C).
63 IRC § 163(h)(3)(F)(i)(I).
64 *See* TAM 9418001.

Acquisition indebtedness is indebtedness that is incurred in acquiring, constructing, or substantially improving a qualified residence of the taxpayer and which secures the residence. The maximum amount treated as acquisition indebtedness prior to December 15, 2017, was $1 million ($500,000 in the case of a married person filing a separate return). Acquisition indebtedness[65] also includes indebtedness from the refinancing of other acquisition indebtedness but only to the extent of the amount (and term) of the refinanced indebtedness.

Example 14-4

If the taxpayer incurs $200,000 of acquisition indebtedness to acquire a principal residence and pays down the debt to $150,000, the taxpayer's acquisition indebtedness with respect to the residence cannot thereafter be increased above $150,000 (except by indebtedness incurred to substantially improve the residence).

Interest on acquisition indebtedness is allowable in computing alternative minimum taxable income. However, in the case of a second residence, the acquisition indebtedness may only be incurred with respect to a house, apartment, condominium, or a mobile home that is not used on a transient basis.

The itemized deduction for home mortgage interest is limited for tax years 2018 through 2025. A taxpayer is limited to claiming the home mortgage interest deduction only for interest paid or accrued on acquisition debt during those years; moreover, the deduction of interest on home equity debt is suspended. The maximum amount that may be treated as acquisition debt is also reduced to $750,000 ($375,000 if married filing separately) for any acquisition debt incurred after December 15, 2017.[66]

Acquisition indebtedness also includes indebtedness from the refinancing of other acquisition indebtedness but only to the extent of the amount (and term) of the refinanced indebtedness. In the case of debt refinancings prior to January 1, 2026, for acquisition indebtedness that was originally incurred on or before December 15, 2017, or treated has having been so under the so-called "binding contract exception,"[67] the limitation on the aggregate amount of acquisition indebtedness remains $1,000,000 ($500,000 for a married taxpayer filing separately) upon its refinancing.[68] The new loan shall be deemed to be incurred on the date of the original loan it refinances to the extent the new loan does not exceed the amount of the original acquisition indebtedness.[69]

---

[65] IRS News Release IR-2018-32 (Feb. 21, 2018).
[66] IRC § 163(h)(3)(F)(i)(I)
[67] IRC § 163(h)(3)(F)(i)(IV).
[68] IRC § 163(h)(3)(F)(iii)(I).
[69] IRC § 163(h)(3)(F)(iii)(I).

Interest Deduction for Second Home Still Allowed. The deduction for second homes is still allowed. The House version would have eliminated the deduction for mortgage acquisition debt for a second home. The conference agreement preserves the mortgage interest deduction for a second home. Despite the new lower limit on mortgage loans for a newly acquired home, interest remains deductible for loans that are used to buy, build, or substantially improve a taxpayer's principal residence and one other residence of the taxpayer, which is selected for the tax year. If a taxpayer owns more than two residences, the taxpayer must continue to select only one second home each year for the purpose of the mortgage interest deduction.

Qualified Principal Residence Debt. The $2 million ($1 million if married filing separately) limit on the exclusion of discharged qualified principal residence debt[70] is not affected by the temporary reduction of the limit of acquisition debt for the home mortgage interest deduction.[71] For indebtedness incurred prior to December 15, 2017, qualified residential interest is interest on indebtedness of up to $1,000,000 (not adjusted for inflation) incurred to acquire or to substantially improve (or refinance the acquisition or improvement of) a principal or second residence (including a mobile home or recreational vehicle or boat that has sleeping, toilet, and cooking facilities).[72] However, pursuant to the TCJA, qualified residential interest is generally limited to indebtedness of up to $750,000 for purchases after December 14, 2017.[73]

The limitations in IRC § 163(h)(2) and (3) apply on a per-taxpayer basis, rather than a per-residence basis, which allow each taxpayer to deduct mortgage interest on indebtedness of up to either $1,000,000 or $750,000, depending on when the indebtedness was incurred, and $100,000, respectively on a qualified residence.

Prior to December 31, 2017, Qualified Residence Indebtedness also included home-equity indebtedness on the borrowing of up to $100,000 secured by a principal or second residence, even if the proceeds were used for personal expenditures that were not acquisition indebtedness.[74] In Rev. Rul. 2010-25,[75] the IRS ruled that interest on indebtedness paid to acquire a principal residence that exceeded the $1 million limitation could qualify as home equity indebtedness up to the $100,000 limitation, which effectively increases the limitation to $1,100,000 for indebtedness incurred prior to December 15, 2017. If the sum of the average balances for the taxable year of

---

[70] IRC § 108(h)(2).

[71] IRC § 163(h)(3)(F)(iv).

[72] IRC § 163(h)(3)(B); Temp. Reg. § 1.163-10T(e) and (p). Qualified residence interest is not subject to limitation or otherwise taken into account under IRC § 163(d) (limitation on investment interest), IRC § 163(h)(1) (disallowance of deduction for personal interest), IRC § 263A (capitalization and inclusion in inventory costs of certain expenses) or IRC § 469 (limitations on losses from passive activities). Qualified residence interest is subject to the limitation imposed by IRC § 263(g) (certain interest in the case of straddles), IRC § 264(a)(2) and (4) (interest paid in connection with certain insurance), IRC § 265(a)(2) (interest relating to tax-exempt income), IRC § 266 (carrying charges), IRC § 267(a)(2) (interest with respect to transactions between related taxpayers), IRC § 465 (deductions limited to amount at risk), IRC § 1277 (deferral of interest deduction allocable to accrued market discount), and IRC § 1282 (deferral of interest deduction allocable to accrued discount).

[73] IRC § 163(h)(3)(F). This limitation is scheduled to increase back to $1,000,000 after December 31, 2025.

[74] IRC § 163(h)(3)(e).

[75] 2010-2 CB 571.

all secured debts exceeds the adjusted purchase price of the qualified residences (determined as of the end of the taxable year), the taxpayer must use either the simplified method or the exact method to determine the amount of interest that is qualified residence interest.

Example 14-5

T purchases a qualified residence in 1987 for $65,000. T pays $6,500 in cash and finances the remainder of the purchase with a mortgage of $58,500. In 1988, the average balance of the mortgage is $58,000. Because the average balance of the mortgage is less than the adjusted purchase price of the residence ($65,000), all of the interest paid or accrued during 1988 on the mortgage is qualified residence interest.

Example 14-6

The facts are the same as in Example 14-5, except that T incurs a second mortgage on January 1, 1988, with an initial principal balance of $2,000. The average balance of the second mortgage in 1988 is $1,900. Because the sum of the average balance of the first and second mortgages ($59,900) is less than the adjusted purchase price of the residence ($65,000), all of the interest paid or accrued during 1988 on both the first and second mortgages is qualified residence interest.

Example 14-7

P borrows $50,000 on January 1, 1988, and secures the debt by a qualified residence. P pays the interest on the debt monthly, but makes no principal payments in 1988. There are no other debts secured by the residence during 1988. On December 31, 1988, the adjusted purchase price of the residence is $40,000. The average balance of the debt in 1988 is $50,000. Because the average balance of the debt exceeds the adjusted purchase price by $10,000, some of the interest on the debt is not qualified residence interest. The portion of the total interest that is qualified residence interest must be determined using either the simplified method or the exact method to determine the amount of interest that is qualified residence interest.

Deduction for home equity interest is suspended for 2018–2025. The deduction for qualified residence interest paid on home equity indebtedness doesn't apply. Thus, for tax years beginning after Dec. 31, 2017 and before Jan. 1, 2026, taxpayers may not claim a deduction for interest on home equity indebtedness.[76]

[H] *Determination of Qualified Residence Interest when Secured Debt Exceeds Adjusted Purchase Price—Simplified Method*

Under the simplified method, the amount of qualified residence interest for the taxable year is equal to the total interest paid or accrued during the taxable year with respect to all secured debts multiplied by a fraction (not in excess of one), the numerator of which is the adjusted purchase price (determined as of the end of the taxable year) of the qualified residence and the denominator of which is the sum of the average balances of all secured debts.

Under the simplified method, the excess of the total interest paid or accrued during the taxable year with respect to all secured debts over the amount of qualified residence interest is personal interest.

Example 14-8

R's principal residence has an adjusted purchase price on December 31, 1988, of $105,000. R has two debts secured by the residence, with the following average balances and interest payments:

Debt	Date secured	Average balance	Interest
Debt 1	June 1983	$80,000	$8,000
Debt 2	May 1987	40,000	4,800
Total		120,000	12,800

The amount of qualified residence interest is determined under the simplified method by multiplying the total interest ($12,800) by a fraction (expressed as a decimal amount) equal to the adjusted purchase price ($105,000) of the residence divided by the combined average balances ($120,000). For 1988, this fraction is equal to 0.875 ($105,000/$120,000). Therefore, $11,200 ($12,800 × 0.875) of the total interest is qualified residence interest. The remaining $1,600 in interest ($12,800 – $11,200) is personal interest, even if such remaining interest would be allocated to some other category of interest.[77]

---

[76] *See* IRC § 163(h)(3)(F)(i)(I).

[77] Under the rules of Temp. Reg. § 1.163-8T.

[I] Determination of Qualified Residence Interest when Secured Debt Exceeds Adjusted Purchase Price—Exact Method

Under the exact method, the amount of qualified residence interest for the taxable year is determined on a debt-by-debt basis by computing the applicable debt limit for each secured debt and comparing each such applicable debt limit to the average balance of the corresponding debt. If, for the taxable year, the average balance of a secured debt does not exceed the applicable debt limit for that debt, all of the interest paid or accrued during the taxable year with respect to the debt is qualified residence interest. If the average balance of the secured debt exceeds the applicable debt limit for that debt, the amount of qualified residence interest with respect to the debt is determined by multiplying the interest paid or accrued with respect to the debt by a fraction, the numerator of which is the applicable debt limit for that debt and the denominator of which is the average balance of the debt.

For each secured debt, the applicable debt limit for the taxable year is equal to:

(i) The lesser of—

(A) The fair market value of the qualified residence as of the date the debt is first secured, and

(B) The adjusted purchase price of the qualified residence as of the end of the taxable year;

(ii) Reduced by the average balance of each debt previously secured by the qualified residence.[78]

Example 14-9

R's principal residence has an adjusted purchase price on December 31, 1988, of $105,000. R has two debts secured by the residence. The average balances and interest payments on each debt during 1988 and fair market value of the residence on the date each debt was secured are as follows:

Debt	Date secured	Fair market value	Average balance	Interest
Debt 1	June 1983	$100,000	$80,000	$8,000
Debt 2	May 1987	140,000	40,000	4,800
Total			120,000	12,800

The amount of qualified residence interest for 1988 under the exact method is determined as follows. Because there are no debts previously secured by the residence, the applicable debt limit for Debt 1 is $100,000 (the lesser of the adjusted purchase price as of the end of the taxable year and the fair market value of the residence at the time the debt was secured). Because the average balance of Debt 1 ($80,000) does not exceed

[78] For purposes of (ii) the average balance of a debt shall be treated as not exceeding the applicable debt limit of such debt.

its applicable debt limit ($100,000), all of the interest paid on the debt during 1988 ($8,000) is qualified residence interest.

The applicable debt limit for Debt 2 is $25,000 ($105,000 (the lesser of $140,000 fair market value and $105,000 adjusted purchase price) reduced by $80,000 (the average balance of Debt 1)). Because the average balance of Debt 2 ($40,000) exceeds its applicable debt limit, the amount of qualified residence interest on Debt 2 is determined by multiplying the amount of interest paid on the debt during the year ($4,800) by a fraction equal to its applicable debt limit divided by its average balance ($25,000/$40,000 = 0.625). Accordingly, $3,000 ($4,800 × 0.625) of the interest paid in 1988 on Debt 2 is qualified residence interest.[79]

[J] Selection of Method

For any taxable year, a taxpayer may use the simplified method or the exact method by completing the appropriate portion of Form 8598. A taxpayer with two qualified residences may use the simplified method for one residence and the exact method for the other residence.

[K] Prepaid Points

IRC § 461(g) creates an exception for points paid on mortgages financing the acquisition or improvements of a principal residence (but not a secondary residence). Points are a form of discount interest customarily charged by lending institutions in addition to stated interest. One point amounts to 1% of the amount borrowed. Points appear to be charged and paid at the time the loan is made. In reality, points involve discount interest, which is paid over the life of the loan. Because of the issue discussed in Chapter 5 dealing with payment with borrowed funds,[80] points must be paid to be deductible. In *Schubel v. Commissioner*,[81] a homebuyer who had the points deducted from the mortgage principal was not entitled to a deduction. In Rev. Rul. 87-22,[82] the IRS denied a deduction for points on a refinancing of a home loan except to the extent attributable to the improvement of the home even if paid from separate funds. In *Huntsman v. Commissioner*,[83] points paid in connection with refinancing a

---

[79] The character of the remaining $1,800 of interest paid on Debt 2 is determined under Reg. § 1.163-8T which generally allocates debt (and the associated interest expense) by tracing disbursements of the debt proceeds to specific expenditures. Notice 88-74, 1988-2 CB 385, sets out additional rules for determining the application of the tracing rules in determining qualified residential interest rules, including a provision that debt must be treated as qualified residents interest if incurred within 90 days before or after the acquisition of the residence, and a 24-month rule for construction or improvements of a residence.

[80] *See* § 5.03[E], *supra*.

[81] 77 T.C. 701 (1981).

[82] 1987-1 CB 146.

[83] 905 F.2d 1182 (8th Cir. 1990).

three-year balloon note for acquisition purposes was considered sufficiently related to the acquisition to qualify for a deduction.

Example 14-10

R purchases a principal residence on June 17, Year 1. As part of the purchase price, R gets a conventional 30-year mortgage secured by the residence. At closing, R pays 1 point on the mortgage and interest on the mortgage for the period June 17-30 of Year 1. The points are actually paid by R and are not merely withheld from the loan proceeds. R incurs no additional secured debt during Year 1. Assuming the points satisfy the requirements of IRC § 461(g)(2), the entire amount of points and the interest paid at closing is Qualified Residential Interest.

Rev. Proc. 94-27[84] provides the IRS's guidelines for deducting points. Under the Revenue Procedure, the IRS will, as a matter of administrative practice, treat as deductible any amounts paid by a cash-basis taxpayer during the tax year if *all* of the following requirements are satisfied:

- The Uniform Settlement Statement (Form HUD-1) must clearly designate the amounts as points payable in connection with the loan (for example, as "loan origination fees" (including amounts so designated on VA and FHA loans), "loan discount," "discount points," or "points.") The amounts designated as points on the Form HUD-1 may be shown as paid from either the borrower's or the seller's funds at settlement;
- The amounts must be computed as a percentage of the stated principal amount of the indebtedness incurred by the taxpayer;
- The amounts paid must conform to an established business practice of charging points for loans for the acquisition of principal residences in the area in which the residence is located, and the amount of points paid must not exceed the amount generally charged in that area. If amounts designated as points are paid in lieu of amounts that are ordinarily stated separately on the settlement statement (such as appraisal fees, inspection fees, title fees, attorney fees, and property taxes), those amounts are not deductible as points under Rev. Proc. 94-27;
- The amounts must be paid in connection with the acquisition of the taxpayer's principal residence, and the loan must be secured by that residence. Rev. Proc. 94-27 does not apply to points allocable to an amount of principal in excess of the aggregate amount that may be treated as acquisition indebtedness under IRC § 163(h)(3)(B)(ii); and
- The amounts must be paid directly by the taxpayer. An amount is so paid if the taxpayer provides, from funds that have not been borrowed for this purpose as part of the overall transaction, an amount at least equal to the

---

[84] 1994-1 CB 613.

amount required to be applied as points at the closing. The amount provided may include down payments, escrow deposits, earnest money applied at the closing, and other funds actually paid over by the taxpayer at the closing. In addition, for these purposes, points paid by the seller (including points charged to the seller) in connection with the loan to the taxpayer will be treated as paid directly by the taxpayer from funds that have not been borrowed for this purpose, provided the taxpayer subtracts the amount of any seller-paid points from the purchase price in computing the residence's basis.

If the points are not deductible because they do not meet the requirements of IRC § 461(g)(2), they should be amortized under compound interest principles as original issue discount.

Protecting the Interest Deduction

Although the deductibility of prepaid interest by a cash basis taxpayer has been severely restricted, one exception allows a deduction for points paid by the buyer to obtain financing for the purchase or improvement of a principal residence in the year of payment. However, these points must actually be paid by the taxpayer obtaining the loan and must represent a charge for the use of money. Taxpayers financing home purchases or improvements should direct their planning deciding on immediate deductibility.

In some cases, a taxpayer may find it desirable to forgo the immediate expensing of points in the year paid. Instead, it could prove beneficial to capitalize the points and write them off as interest expense over the life of the mortgage.

Example 14-11

Victor, a single filer, purchases a home on December 15, 2020, for $380,000 with $120,000 cash and a 15-year mortgage of $260,000 financed by the Large National Bank. Victor pays two points in addition to interest allocated to the period from December 15 until December 31, 2020, at an annual rate of 4%.

If Victor does not have enough itemized deductions to exceed the standard deduction for 2018, he should elect to capitalize the points and amortize them over 15 years. In this instance, Victor would deduct $346.67 for 2020, as part of his qualified residence interest expense [$5,200 (two points) divided by 15 years], if he elects to itemize that year.

§ 14.03 Original Issue Discount

[A] *Original Issue Discount Generally*

The basic principle underlying the original issue discount (OID) rules can be illustrated as follows: If a lender lends money to a borrower, then interest is *taxed as it accrues economically*. If all interest is paid annually, the borrower deducts it, and the lender includes it in income annually. If some or all interest is not paid annually as it accrues but instead is deferred to be paid later, the OID rules put both the borrower and the lender on the accrual method for tax purposes with respect to the deferred interest. The OID rules require that the parties determine the interest rate actually being charged by comparing the amount loaned with the amount and times of the payments to be made. Once that rate is determined, the parties treat interest as accruing at that rate. Any interest not paid when it accrues is nonetheless *taxed* to the lender and is deductible by the borrower (subject to the limits of IRC § 163) as it accrues.

An OID obligation generally arises if a borrower receives a sum of money and executes a note under the terms of which he or she undertakes to repay a principal amount greater than the amount received by him or her. The obligation may or may not also provide for current payments of interest or of interest and principal.

IRC §§ 1271 through 1275 and the regulations thereunder provide the basis for original issue discount ("OID"). Under IRC § 1272, there is included in the gross income of the holder of any debt instrument having original issue discount an amount equal to the sum of the daily portions of the original issue discount for each day during the taxable year on which such holder held such debt instrument.[85]

The exceptions are:

- Tax-exempt obligations;
- United States savings bonds;
- Short-term obligations (any debt instrument which has a fixed maturity date not more than one year from the date of issue);
- Obligations issued by natural persons before March 2, 1984; and
- Loans between natural persons. In general, any loan is made by a natural person to another natural person if:
  - — such loan is not made in the course of a trade or business of the lender, and
  - — the amount of such loan (when increased by the outstanding amount of prior loans by such natural person to such other natural person) does not exceed $10,000.[86]

The above exceptions do not apply to a loan where tax avoidance is a principal purpose.

[B] Defining OID

OID is the difference between the issue price of an obligation and its stated redemption price at maturity.[87] A debt instrument's "stated redemption price at maturity is the sum of all payments provided by the debt instrument other than qualified stated interest." If the payment schedule of a debt instrument is determined

---

[85] IRC § 1272(a)(1).
[86] IRC § 1272(a)(2).
[87] IRC § 1273(a).

under Reg. § 1.1272-1(c) (relating to certain debt instruments subject to contingencies), that payment schedule is used to determine the instrument's stated redemption price at maturity.[88]

The OID rules focus on discount obligations; their main concern is to achieve an appropriate matching of deductions by the debtor and income by the creditor. An accrual basis debtor can accrue interest deductions on a discount obligation, but absent IRC § 1272, a cash basis creditor does not take the interest into income until it is actually paid. IRC § 1272 generally requires taxpayers to include OID in income on a current basis as it accrues, regardless of the method of accounting used. As a matter of symmetry, IRC § 163(e) allows taxpayers to deduct OID as it accrues; in the absence of a statute, a cash basis taxpayer could not deduct OID until it was paid.[89]

Example 14-12

If a 7%, 20-year bond is issued for $745 when the market rate of interest is 10%, the OID is $255, calculated as follows: $1,000 redemption price less $745 issue price, because the 7% interest payment payments are qualified stated interest that is not taken into account in determining OID. The difference between the stated interest and the OID interest however is not allocated ratably but instead begins at a lower amount, $4.50 for the first year, reflecting the difference between the interest on $745 at 10% of $74.50 and the stated interest paid of $70. Since only the $70 stated interest was paid, the $4.50 amortized OID increases the adjusted issue price of the obligation to $740.50 in the second year with amortized OID of $4.95, increasing at an accelerating rate each year until it is approximately $25 in the last year.

The obligations covered by the OID amortization rules and the method of amortization are presented in IRC §§ 1272-1275. Similar rules for other obligations can be found in IRC §§ 1276-1288.

[C] Determining Issue Price

The statutory provisions for determining the issue price of a debt instrument are contained in IRC § 1273(b)(1) through (5). Special rules are provided in IRC § 1273(c). IRC § 1273(b) divides all debt instruments into four categories. Categories (1) and (2) include debt instruments not issued for "property." Category (3) includes debt instruments issued for "property" which is "publicly traded debt," and Category (4) includes all other debt instruments except those to which IRC § 1274 applies.

IRC § 1274 applies to certain non-publicly traded debt instruments issued as consideration for non-publicly traded property. "Property" is defined for purposes of

---

[88] Reg. § 1.1273-1(b).

[89] Rev. Rul. 59-260, 1959-2 CB 137; *Foster v. Comm'r*, T.C. Memo. 1973-53, 32 TCM 243.

these rules (and only for such purposes), as including debt services and the right to use property but not money. Hence, a debt instrument that is not issued for property is, by definition, issued for money. The regulations divide debt instruments into the following categories:

- debt instruments issued for money;
- publicly traded debt instruments issued for property;
- debt instruments issued for publicly traded property; and
- other debt instruments.[90]

Reg. § 1.1273-2(g) also provides rules relating to:

- the effect on the issue price of a debt instrument of certain cash payments made incident to lending transactions;
- the determination of the issue price of a debt instrument which is issued as part of an investment unit;
- the issue price of convertible debt instruments;
- the issue price of certain below-market loans; and
- the treatment of amounts representing pre-issuance accrued interest.

The issue price of a debt instrument issued for services or rent is determined by the value of the services or the use of the property. When a debt obligation is retired for more (or less) than its stated redemption price or its issue price as adjusted for accrued OID, the difference, if more, is generally treated as additional interest by the issuer and capital gain by the holder. If the difference is less, then such difference is discharge of indebtedness income by the issuer and a capital loss by the holder. The issuer is responsible for determining the OID and is required to report it to the holder and the IRS on Form 1099-OID.[91]

No portion of the issue price of a convertible debt obligation is allocated to conversion rights, thus the interest rate on the debt obligation determines the yield.[92] This means that if a $1,000 convertible debt obligation is issued for an amount equal to its stated principal, there is no OID, even if it is proved that an identical non-convertible obligation will sell for only 90% of its stated principal or $900. On the other hand, if a debt obligation and warrant or option are sold as a package, the price is allocated between the two, resulting in OID when, for example, the price of the package equals the $1,000 redemption price of the debt obligation. Thus, if a debt obligation is worth 90% of the value of the package or $900, and the warrant is worth 10% of the value or $100, the issue price of the debt obligation is $900, so there is $100 of OID. The basis of the warrant is $100.

---

[90] Reg. § 1.1273-2(g).

[91] Reg. § § 1.1275-2(e), 1.6049-1(a)(1)(ii)(a).

[92] Reg. § 1.1273-2(j).

[D] Short Term Obligations

IRC § 1272(a)(2)(C) provides an exception to the OID rules for short term obligations. Short term obligations are those with an original maturity of one year or less on a theory equivalent to the one year rule for prepayments.[93] The distortion of a shift in deduction or income is not sufficient to justify the administrative difficulties for accurate reporting. On the other hand, IRC § 1281(b)(1) provides for ratable daily accrual of "acquisition discount" on short term obligations that are similarly defined.

§ 14.04 Imputed Interest on Below-Market Loans

[A] Generally

Prior to 1984, loans made to family members or to employees or even shareholders were not required to bear interest. That changed when the Supreme Court decided *Dickman v. Commissioner*.[94] Because of the *Dickman* decision, an interest-free or below-market interest rate loan without consideration, such as a loan to a family member, results in a gift from the lender to the borrower for federal gift tax purposes. On the other hand, the IRS took the position that, in the case of an interest-free or below-market interest rate loan to an employee or shareholder (other than a loan to which IRC § 482 applies), the borrower derived an economic benefit that should be included in income for federal income tax purposes. Notwithstanding the IRS's position, the Tax Court consistently held that these non-family interest-free or below-market interest rate loans do not result in taxable income.[95]

The Tax Reform Act of 1984 changed the treatment of below-market loans by enacting the below-market loan rules. A below-market loan is one in which the stated interest rate is lower than the rate required for tax purposes. With such a loan, IRC § 7872 requires recognition of a deemed transfer of money from the lender to the borrower equal to the amount of forgone interest (imputed interest) and a corresponding retransfer of that interest by the borrower back to the lender. The characterization of the deemed transfer and the timing of reporting the forgone interest depend on the nature of the transaction and the type of loan.

The imputed interest rules apply to the following *types* of below-market loans:

- Gift loans (made out of love, affection, or generosity);
- Compensation-related loans (employer loans to employees); and
- Corporation-shareholder loans (a corporation's loans to its shareholders).

The type of loan determines the tax consequences to the lender and the borrower. For example, a gift loan as described above results in interest income to the

---

[93] *See* § 5.03[G].

[94] 465 U.S 330 (1984).

[95] *Dean v. Comm'r*, 35 T.C. 1083 (1961); *Greenspun v. Comm'r*, 72 T.C. 931, *aff'd*, 670 F.2d 123 (9th Cir. 1982).

lender and an interest expense to the borrower. It also results in a gift made by the lender and a gift received by the borrower.

A compensation related loan results in interest income to the lender and interest expense to the borrower. It also results in compensation expense to the lender and compensation income to the borrower.

In the case of a corporate shareholder loan, it results in interest income to the lender and interest expense to the borrower and a dividend paid by the lender and dividend income by the borrower.

[B] Exceptions to the Imputed Interest Rules for Below-Market Loans

Note the following regarding imputed interest rules for below-market loans:

- Exceptions include a *de minimis* exception for aggregate loans of up to $10,000 or less for gift loans where the proceeds are used to purchase income producing assets;
- The same *de minimis* exception applies to employer and employee loans so long as such loan is not for tax avoidance purposes; and
- The same *de minimis* exception also applies for corporation shareholder loans as well.

For loans in the aggregate of $100,000 or less between individuals, such loans are excepted unless the principal purpose is tax avoidance. Assuming there is no tax avoidance; interest is imputed to the extent of the borrower's net investment income (gross income from all investments less the related expenses). On loans of $100,000 or less between individuals, the imputed interest cannot exceed the borrower's net investment income for the year (gross income from all investments less the related expenses).[96]

[C] Computation of Forgone Interest

The term "forgone interest" means, with respect to any period during which the loan is outstanding, the excess of:

> the amount of interest which would have been payable on the loan for the period if interest accrued on the loan at the applicable federal rate were payable annually on the last day of the taxable year, over any interest payable on the loan properly allocable to such period.[97]

In the case of any term loan, the applicable federal rate shall be the applicable federal rate in effect under IRC § 1274(d) as of the day on which the loan was made, compounded semi-annually.

---

[96] If the borrower's net investment income for the year does not exceed $1,000, no interest is imputed on loans of $100,000 or less.

[97] IRC § 7872(e)(2).

In the case of a demand loan, the applicable federal rate shall be the federal short-term rate in effect under IRC § 1274(d) for the period for which the amount of forgone interest is being determined, compounded semi-annually.

Example 14-13

Assume that tax avoidance is not a principal purpose of the following loans. Betty made interest-free loans as follows:

To Sandra—$8,000 for her education. Sandra has no net investment income.

To David—$9,000 to purchase stock. David has $500 of net investment income.

To Nancy—$25,000 to purchase a business. Nancy has no net investment income.

To Mary—$90,000 to purchase a residence. Mary has $15,000 of net investment income.

To Arnold—$120,000 to purchase a new residence. Arnold does not have net investment income

Analysis:

The loan to Sandra is not subject to the imputed interest rules because the $10,000 exception applies.

The $10,000 exception does not apply to the loan to David because the proceeds were used to purchase income producing assets. However, under the $100,000 exception, imputed interest is limited to David's investment income, which is $500. Because the $1,000 exception also applies to this loan, no interest is imputed.[98]

No interest is imputed to Nancy because the $100,000 exception applies.

Interest is imputed on the loan to Mary based on the smaller of (a) the borrower's $15,000 net investment income or (b) the interest is calculated by applying the federal rate to the outstanding loan.

None of the exceptions apply to the loan to Arnold because the loan was for more than $100,000.

Assume that the relevant federal rate is 5% and the loans were outstanding for the entire year, Betty would recognize interest income, compounded semi-annually, as follows:

Loan to Mary

For first six months (5% × $90,000 × 1/2 year)	$2,250
For second six months (5% × $92,250 × 1/2 year)	$2,363
	$4,613

[98] IRC § 7872(d)(1)(E).

Loan to Arnold	
For first six months (5% × $120,000 × 1/2 year)	$3,000
For second six months (5% × $123,000 × 1/2 year)	$3,150
	$6,150

§ 14.05 IRC § 483 Interest on Certain Deferred Payments

[A] *Generally*

If IRC § 483 applies to a contract, unstated interest under the contract is treated as interest for tax purposes. Thus, for example, unstated interest is not treated as part of the amount realized from the sale or exchange of property (in the case of the seller), and is not included in the purchaser's basis in the property acquired in the sale or exchange.

IRC § 483 applies to a contract for the sale or exchange of property if the contract provides for one or more payments to be made more than one year after the date of the sale or exchange, and the contract does not provide for adequate stated interest.[99] In general, a contract has adequate stated interest if the contract provides for a stated rate of interest that is at least equal to the test rate[100] and the interest is paid or compounded at least annually. IRC § 483 may apply to a contract whether the contract is express (written or oral) or implied. For purposes of IRC § 483, a sale or exchange is any transaction treated as a sale or exchange for tax purposes. In addition, for purposes of IRC § 483, property includes debt instruments and investment units, but does not include money, services, or the right to use property.

Any stated or unstated interest on a contract subject to IRC § 483 is taken into account by a taxpayer under the taxpayer's regular method of accounting (*e.g.*, an accrual method or the cash receipts and disbursements method).

[B] *Exceptions to and Limitations on the Application of IRC § 483*

Note the following exceptions to and limitations on the application of IRC § 483:

- Sales price of $3,000 or less;
- Certain transfers subject to IRC § 1041 relating to transfers of property between spouses or incident to divorce;
- Any debt instrument for which an issue price is determined under IRC § 1273(b) other than paragraph four of that section and IRC § 1274;
- Amounts that are deemed to include interest under IRC § 163(b);

---

[99] IRC § 483(c).

[100] Determined under Reg. § 1.483-3.

- Transfers described in IRC § 1235(a) which relates to a sale or exchange of patents;
- Sale of personal use property;
- Certain below-market loans described in IRC § 7872;
- Annuity contracts; and
- Payments under an option to buy or sell property.[101]

[101] Reg. § 1.483-1(c).

Table of Cases

References are to section (§) numbers.

E

F

G

H

R

S

T

Table of Internal Revenue Code Sections

References are to section (§) numbers.

Table of Treasury Regulations

References are to section (§) numbers.

Final Regulations

Temporary Regulations

Table of IRS Releases

References are to section (§) numbers.

Announcements

Chief Counsel Advice

Field Service Advice

General Counsel's Memoranda

Private Letter Rulings

Notices

Revenue Rulings

Technical Advice Memoranda

Treasury Decisions

Index

References are to chapter and section (§) numbers.

References are to chapter and section (§) numbers.

References are to chapter and section (§) numbers.

References are to chapter and section (§) numbers.

References are to chapter and section (§) numbers.

References are to chapter and section (§) numbers.

References are to chapter and section (§) numbers.

References are to chapter and section (§) numbers.

References are to chapter and section (§) numbers.

References are to chapter and section (§) numbers.

References are to chapter and section (§) numbers.

References are to chapter and section (§) numbers.

References are to chapter and section (§) numbers.

References are to chapter and section (§) numbers.

M

References are to chapter and section (§) numbers.

References are to chapter and section (§) numbers.

References are to chapter and section (§) numbers.

References are to chapter and section (§) numbers.

References are to chapter and section (§) numbers.

References are to chapter and section (§) numbers.

References are to chapter and section (§) numbers.

References are to chapter and section (§) numbers.

V

W

Y